Ten Years of UserFriendly.Org

by J.D. "Illiad" Frazer

For online information and ordering of this and other Manning books, please visit www.manning.com The publisher offers discounts on this book when ordered in quantity.

For more information, please contact:
Special Sales Department
Manning Publications Co.
Sound View Court 3B Fax: (609) 877-8256
Greenwich, CT 06830 Email: orders@manning.com

Recognizing the importance of preserving what has been written, it is Manningís policy to have the books we publish printed on acid-free paper, and we exert our best efforts to that end. Recognizing also our responsibility to conserve the resources of our planet, Manning books are printed on paper that is at least 15% recycled and processed elemental chlorine-free

Copyeditor: Tiffany Taylor
Designer/Typesetter: Leslie Haimes

Manning Publications Co.
Sound View Court 3B
Greenwich, CT 06830
ISBN 1-935182-12-9

Printed in the United States of America

1 2 3 4 5 6 7 8 9 10 ñ MAL ñ 12 11 10 09 08

For Michael and Maria,
the source of my hope and joy

Foreword

Growing up in America can be hard if you're a geek. If you're a little geek girl, it can be both hard and lonely. There's usually no one to talk to. Not really talk. Not about the things that truly interest you.

When I was a little girl, my school sent me to have my IQ tested. I still remember my mother's bemused puzzlement when the results showed that I had what they called a genius IQ in mechanical ability. Where that came from, I have no idea. Going back in time (even to time indefinite), no one in the family was a mechanic or even a mechanical engineer. We were all either writers or librarians or teachers or preachers. So it was a mystery, and no one was proud of this anomalous gift when it showed up in me. Nor did anyone in the family think it should be encouraged or developed in any way. If anything, it was a subject for teasing. It was like tonsils: I had them, but no one knew why. They seemed superfluous.

I know. Sad. But I didn't know a soul who would find the things I found fascinating the least bit interesting. As for humor, no one can laugh at something they don't get. So geeks like me learn to be quiet or to tell themselves jokes without expecting anything coming back. What does this have to do with UserFriendly? This: that UserFriendly helped me to become myself. Here's how it happened.

Long after I was an adult, I was working in a small law firm where I was assigned not only to paralegal work but also to take care of the computers. There was no tech support. Just me. I was the only one who knew anything about computers, so I got tapped. There were only four computers in the office, but keeping four Microsoft Windows computers up and at'em on the Internet is hard. If lawyers are using them, it's harder.

In time, I realized we needed to take steps to protect our data. But getting the lawyers to implement any security steps was tough. I kept trying to set up things like passwords, and the lawyers would complain and make me get rid of them, with results you can imagine. Lawyers aren't known for being malleable, so my work life was full of frustration and geek humor commentaries in my head. When I came across UserFriendly's help-desk theme, it was heavenly. At last! Someone knew. Ah, yes. "Fix my computer *now*!"

FIX MY COMPUTER! NOW!
UH. WELL. IF YOU WOULD CALM DOWN AND TELL ME WHAT THE PROBLEM WAS--
DON'T TALK TO ME LIKE I'M STUPID! I HAVE A DEGREE!
HTTP://WWW.USERFRIENDLY.ORG/
COPYRIGHT©2002 ILLIAD

IT WOULDN'T HAPPEN TO BE FROM ONE OF THOSE "NON-ACCREDITED" ONES. NOW WOULD IT?
IT'S PRESTIGIOUS! IT SAID SO IN THE E-MAIL!

It was magical. Here's one of my favorites, to give you the full flavor:

YOU STUPID DORK! THE INTERNET IS BROKEN AND I WANT IT FIXED. AND FIXED RIGHT BLOODY NOW! WERE YOU DROPPED ON YOUR HEAD WHEN YOU WERE SMALL? OR WAS YOUR HEAD ALWAYS THAT SIZE? WELL?! SPEAK UP! NO! SHUT UP! SHUT UP! *KLIK*
HTTP://WWW.USERFRIENDLY.ORG/
HELLO? HELLO?! WHERE'S MY EMAIL? WHY CAN'T I GET TO MY EMAIL?! WHAT HAVE YOU DONE TO THE INTERNET? I WAS SENDING SOMEONE A PHOTO ALBUM AND MY EMAIL JUST STOPPED! WHAT HAVE YOU DONE?! WHAT'S WRONG WITH YOU PEOPLE?! *CLIK*
HEY TECHNODWEEB! WHEN ARE YOU GONNA FIX WINDOWS? MINESWEEPER STOPPED WORKING! HOP TO IT, YOU WASTE OF OXYGEN! I WANT MY HIGH SCORES BACK, YOU THREE-COIL PEANUT-LADEN STEAMER! WAKE UP! *CLICK*
I AM TECH SUPPORT. SMEAR ME.

That long-running theme on UserFriendly—the help desk—was a great stress reliever when I was experiencing the phenomenon at work, which was pretty much daily. But it was much deeper than that. It was like finding a friend, somebody who spoke my language. How precious is that?

Discovering Miranda the sysadmin—yes, it mattered to this geek grrl. If you think about it as deeply as I have, you'll understand when I say that UserFriendly was a part of what made it possible for me to come out of hiding and be myself on Groklaw.

Here's a memorable sequence about Miranda:

HI. I'M KUAN. THE NEW INTERN.
MIRANDA. AND YES, I'M A SYSADMIN.
COPYRIGHT © 2003 ILLIAD
HTTP://WWW.USERFRIENDLY.ORG/
YEP. I FIGURED THAT'S WHAT YOU WERE.
NO. I MEAN A REAL SYSADMIN. I CAN CODE TOO.
UM. OKAY.
JUST BECAUSE I'M FEMALE IT DOESN'T MEAN I CAN'T BE A GREAT TECHNOLOGIST!!
WHOA! TAKE IT EASY "CATHY."
SO IT DOESN'T FAZE YOU THAT I'M A QUALIFIED TECHNOLOGIST AND NOT A GUY?
WHY SHOULD IT?
COPYRIGHT © 2003 ILLIAD
HTTP://WWW.USERFRIENDLY.ORG/
WELL, THAT'S REALLY REFRESHING. CAN I THANK YOU WITH A BEER AFTER WORK?
NO THANKS. I DON'T DATE WOMEN THE SAME AGE AS MY MOM.
THE SNOTTY KID DID WHAT?
HE THOUGHT I WAS ASKING HIM OUT ON A DATE!
WEREN'T YOU?
COPYRIGHT © 2003 ILLIAD
HTTP://WWW.USERFRIENDLY.ORG/
NO! I CAN'T IMAGINE WHAT GAVE HIM THE IDEA I WAS MAKING A PASS AT HIM!
CAN'T YOU?
NO! AND WHAT'S WORSE, HE THINKS I'M AS OLD AS HIS MOM!
AREN'T...

If you're female, you don't need me to explain why that's funny. You already know. It is to JD's credit that he even thought up Miranda.

Here's another one I love, from the Death Orb theme, rms chained in the dungeon, cell blocks G-N-U:

CELL BLOCKS G-N-U
So do you have any idea where Lan might be kept? This is a huge prison level.
Rffm.

Copyright (c) 1998 Illiad
Hey! He looks familiar! Big hairy guy, looks like a wookie with a funny hat...
Mff mrr mr.

Hey, pipsqueaks, tell your wussy Emperor I'm never going to charge money for GNU!
Richard M. Stallman?!

Stallman, I later learned, did sell Emacs, and it's in the GPL FAQ for GPLv2 that selling FOSS is fine. But it doesn't matter. The image of rms chained to the wall on the Death Orb, defying Bill Gates . . . well, it's culturally priceless.

Of course, I also can never forget the cartoon JD drew of "me" for Groklaw. You can find it online here: http://www.groklaw.net/article.php?story=20050515115448782.

How generous he was to grant me the copyright. I love it and have used it for articles on Groklaw and elsewhere. It has also appeared on the USPTO Peer to Patent project, in a video I was asked to prepare to explain the need for patent prior art searching. A geek grrl on a government website, explaining geeky things. Me and JD. I love that.

One Groklaw member, The Blue Sky Ranger, came up with a list off the top of his head:

1. Erwin doing tech support in Greg's absence. The resetting of the password had me laughing until tears came out my eyes.
2. Erwin building a mech body for himself like in Virus, and shooting a dumpster full of Stef.
3. Sid vs. Pitr on *Jeopardy*.
4. Sid adding voice recognition to all the computers just to get hired senior to Pitr.
5. AJ, Dust Puppy, and Erwin staging a nighttime raid to rescue Stef from Microsoft.
6. Four little words: Geek In A Can.
7. The day they went Linux, and no one could agree on a distro.
8. Cthulhu visits Columbia Internet, discovers he can't freak out Pitr, does tech support, and leaves in disgust. ("Check out this new Cthulhu toy! You whip it against the wall, and it sticks!")
9. The song parodies. Not just the SCO twist on "Locomotion" (it was clever, it has nothing to do with it being Kylie Minogue)—I can't hear Santana's "Smooth" anymore without singing the first part of Steff's version.

As you see, we treasure UserFriendly. It's part of us, and we'll treasure this tenth-anniversary volume of UserFriendly strips. How amazing that 10 years have passed, and how appropriate that UserFriendly has taken its honored place in our culture.

Pamela Jones, pj@groklaw.net
October 2008

Preface

I wasn't ever really planning to be a cartoonist.

I did, in my early 20s, think that cartooning as a career would be pretty cool. In my high-school days, I spent the better part of my two senior years writing a daily cartoon about life in grades 11 and 12. As was to be expected, the material was adolescent angst and puerile humor wrapped into a skanky little tortilla. It did teach me a lot about sucking at something, though.

So when I was 20-something, I figured I'd sketch a dozen strips and ship them all off to the Big Six syndicates. I got back, in less than eight weeks, Six Big Rejection Letters. I wasn't crushed or anything because I knew it to be a pipe dream, and we all knew that it was much better (and probably still is) to go through life as a university-educated scientist. I was going to be a geologist!

But not all plans work out. I ran out of schooling money and went back into the workforce, slaving my way up the IT ladder. I bounced around a bit, always being fortunate enough to make decent money. Finally, I landed at an ISP at the time when 56K modems were the de facto standard for connecting to the Internet. The ISP owners set me to building and running their web services business unit, which was a fun and ultimately successful exercise.

The gears of business kept turning, and the ISP was acquired by a national ISP in a move that was really a stock play under a façade. The national ISP cratered, and I and a few co-workers I respected were out of work. Then we acquired—in a very astute (if "astute" means "lucky") business maneuver—the regional points-of-presence that the national ISP had let flounder. One thing led to another, and there I was again, running web services for an ISP that was now partly mine.

And that's where it all started. I began scratching out cartoons on photocopy paper, and my co-workers/partners showered me with praise and brought me beer and a bunch of other things you're not likely to believe. Up the cartoons went on a web server, traffic began to flow, and the next thing I know it's been ten freaking years of daily cartooning!

A bunch of things came together in a bit of a perfect storm for UF's success. I was one of the early web-launched cartoonists (and I did end up self-syndicating in a lot of papers, including one of Canada's big nationals); I wrote the only cartoon that addressed the IT/science geek niche that made up a large swath of the Internet's citizenry at the time; and I had the very good fortune of having an audience that talked to me and helped me steer the UF ship in largely uncharted waters. This all ultimately landed me in a place with millions of readers and a cartoon property that I had no real intention of building to begin with. What a roller-coaster ride!

I can't say I regret at all how things have turned out. Although people point at me and say "cartoonist," I'm really a writer at heart, and UserFriendly has given me a place where my voice can be heard, even if some think it's just another one of those voices in their heads. Having been afforded this opportunity is a gift that I find difficult to define due to its richness and depth. And the people I've come to know and form firm friendships with ... that's just the icing on a very real, cleverly layered cake.

I didn't plan to be a cartoonist, but I've been one for more than 10 years. Maybe it's about time I accepted that and stopped trying to grow up.

J.D. Frazer
Vancouver, BC
October 2008

Cast of Characters

A.J. GARRETT

FUNCTION: Web designer
EDUCATION: Graphic Arts certificate
STRENGTHS: Awesome twitch reflex in first-person shooters
WEAKNESSES: Itchy feet
NICKNAMES: Web Dork
AGE BRACKET: Mid 20s

A.J. is Columbia Internet's web designer. He started off writing HTML in Notepad and eventually graduated to Dreamweaver, but he still pines for the days of writing web pages on paper and "porting" them to electronic form. He is the best gamer in the company, with a natural talent that puts him in the same league as pro gamers. He doesn't pursue that particular career, thinking that professional gaming, like professional sports, is a kind of performing art. He is shy and avoids the limelight.

Like many geeks, A.J. didn't benefit from a lot of socialization when he was younger; he preferred spending time with shiny objects, comic books, and role-playing games. He apparently has some charm, because attractive women find him intriguing and otherwise non-threatening—sort of the same way you might view a puppy or a particularly round, fat hamster. He is the archetype of the young adult gamer with talent for design and a good understand of technology (albeit not at a deep level).

A.J. was created from an amalgam of a few real-life analogues, including the cartoonist himself. The cartoonist is better socialized, not as charming, and not as good at twitch-gaming.

DUST PUPPY

FUNCTION: Mascot, conscience
EDUCATION: Nothing formal
STRENGTHS: A heart bigger than a brontosaur, and eyes bigger than that
WEAKNESSES: Vulnerable to compressed air
NICKNAMES: Little Guy, Little Dude, Nasty Little Puffball
AGE BRACKET: Precocious childhood

An icon of pure, innocent geekery and child-like perspective, Dust Puppy was born from the detritus, hair, and fuzz that collected inside a server. It's unclear from whence he came, but he seems to believe that he has had previous incarnations. He is much beloved by most of the staff at Columbia Internet, with the stand-out exception of Stef, the company's marketing executive. He has been mistaken for, over the years, a brillo pad, a loofah, a soft naval mine, and an overgrown sea urchin.

Despite his lack of hands, Dust Puppy plays an amazing, world-class game of Quake with his feet. He also has the mind of a brilliant coder, and he brought about his first progeny, Erwin the Artificial Intelligence, after a long night of coding in COBOL. Dust Puppy looks to A.J. for friendship and treats the hapless web designer as an older brother and role model, which leads to some unfortunate events. Unlike A.J., Dust Puppy is gregarious, and women positively adore him. Like A.J., Dust Puppy is oblivious to the attention and couldn't really take advantage of it anyway.

It's been suggested that Dust Puppy is the archetype of childhood curiosity and naiveté, common traits in geekdom. Dust Puppy has no real-life analogue, unless you count the talking toilet brush in the cartoonist's loo.

ERWIN

FUNCTION: Jester, critic, agitator
EDUCATION: All the world's knowledge
STRENGTHS: Everything on the Web
WEAKNESSES: Everything on the Web
NICKNAMES: Psychotic Tamagotchi
AGE BRACKET: Immortal

Perhaps best understood as the mirror-universe-with-a-goatee-personality version of Dust Puppy, Erwin is sophisticated where Dust Puppy is naive, acerbic instead of sweet, cynical instead of trusting, and mischievous instead of considerate. Despite these diametric traits, Erwin respects his (gender-neutral "his") creator and often acts to protect him from the harsh world. He is a tireless sentinel and a powerful ally.

Erwin takes all his knowledge from that which is available on the World Wide Web. Even secured sites are not safe from him, which explains his forays into places like NORAD. Erwin's choice of hardware is the SGI O2, a spiffy-looking graphics machine that, although outdated, remains potent due to Erwin's extended abilities. He's been known to mess with everything from the stock markets, to defense networks, to newspaper editorials, and he does it just because he can. In many ways, he's an adolescent without fear of consequence, except for the rare occasion when he's ported into a smaller piece of hardware that gets demolished by Stef's baseball bat. He represents and embodies the cynical side of geeks, the part that uses sarcasm as a defense against a crazy, difficult world that is nonetheless filled with much shininess.

Erwin was named after the physicist Erwin Schrödinger. His real-life analogue is Deep Thought. No, really.

GREG FLEMMING

FUNCTION: Technical support/helpdesk
EDUCATION: Technology diploma
STRENGTHS: Low blood pressure, preternatural patience
WEAKNESSES: Stoppered like a pressure cooker
NICKNAMES: Phone Slave
AGE BRACKET: Early to mid 30s

Greg is Columbia Internet's principle helpdesk technician. He's better versed in user interfaces and operating system esoterica than anyone else in the company. He also has the greatest variance in blood pressure on a daily basis, due to the nature of his work. Helpdesk is a thankless yet necessary task, one which Greg shoulders as his own burden, recognizing that he may have done some fairly naughty things in a previous life and has been tasked to atone for them.

Greg was the first employee at Columbia Internet to come out openly as Pagan. "Burn the witch!" jokes aside, he is a mesopaganist, specifically a Viking Age Norse Pagan. He takes his belief system seriously and backs it up with a remarkable collection of two-handed weapons bearing serrated edges. He loves instant ramen and any snack food with a 40% or higher sodium content, and he's a fairly good twitch gamer. After a particularly bad day on the phones, he builds things like trebuchets and gallows to vent his frustrations on the effigies of his callers.

Greg's real-life analogue is a modern-day bearded Viking named Ken. Like Greg, Ken has nifty things like battleaxes.

MIKE FLOYD

FUNCTION: Systems administrator/network engineer
EDUCATION: Technology diploma and Network Engineer certificate
STRENGTHS: 120wpm typing speed on the command line
WEAKNESSES: Susceptible to intense caffeine rush
NICKNAMES: Cable Jockey, Z, Hey You Fix My DNS
AGE BRACKET: Mid to late 30s

Mike is the quintessential systems administrator. He is methodical and meticulous, and he knows by heart the topology of the huge network he maintains. He also, unfortunately, has a desperate need for chemical stimulants, most notably caffeine. Although Mike loves weapons-grade coffee, he has a jumpy nature, and a powerful dose of Sid's Insidious Syrup or one of Pitr's disgusting tarry concoctions will send Mike's nerves through the roof. It does help his typing speed, though.

In some ways, Mike is an apprentice to Sid. He's not quite old enough to have been around the really early technology that Sid pines for, but he does have the benefit of having been immersed in some of the later Big Iron. Mike's mastery of the Forc … er, computer technology is unquestioned, but he has yet to develop that dry, acerbic approach to life and minions that Sid has perfected over the years.

Mike's real-life analogues are a deeply knowledgeable sysadmin named Tom and, as it turns out, a SAMBA team member and security expert named Mike. If both of them were in the same room together, any computer nearby would be the most secure Internet-connected box on the Web. The Pentagon might wish to take note.

MIRANDA CORNEILLE

FUNCTION: Systems administrator/technical manager
EDUCATION: Baccalaureate in Computer Science
STRENGTHS: Piercing intellect
WEAKNESSES: Web dorks
NICKNAMES: Cathy, Hey Baby
AGE BRACKET: Late 20s to early 30s

In many ways, Miranda is not a typical female geek, and yet there is no other way to describe her. Although geek women are generally better socialized than their hapless male counterparts, Miranda is more so: she's a fully adjusted, socially normal member of society. That is, she is as dysfunctional and neurotic as any of the women on sitcoms like *Friends* or *Desperate Housewives.*

She recognized early on that as a female geek, she had a bit more to prove than the men, and she worked hard to graduate with First Class Honors in Computer Science. At the same time, she made a monumental effort to fit in and be taken seriously as a thinker and software engineer. Mostly, her male colleagues stared at her chest and gibbered.

Miranda was created from three real-life women technologists: one a robotics engineer, another a mathematician, and the third a computer scientist. All three were slender, attractive, well-dressed, confident, and intelligent. All were also single, frustrated by the obliviousness of the various men they were attracted to.

PITR DUBOVICH

FUNCTION: Software developer
EDUCATION: High school
STRENGTHS: Can think in hexadecimal
WEAKNESSES: Anything "weapons grade"
NICKNAMES: Code Weenie
AGE BRACKET: Late 20s to early 30s

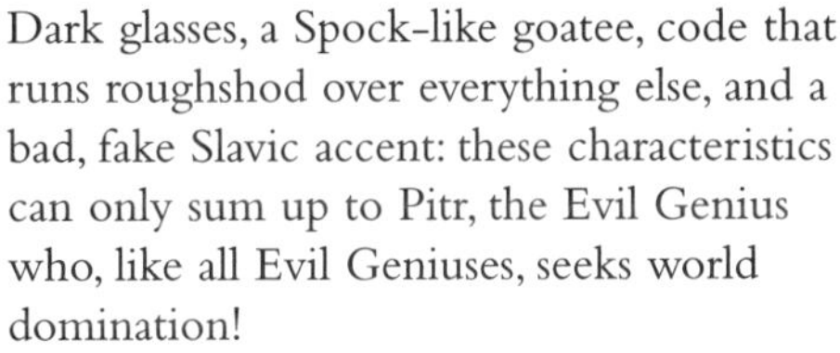

Dark glasses, a Spock-like goatee, code that runs roughshod over everything else, and a bad, fake Slavic accent: these characteristics can only sum up to Pitr, the Evil Genius who, like all Evil Geniuses, seeks world domination!

At a young age, Pitr knew that what he wanted to do more than anything else was become like James Bond's Blofeld, except a successful version, and without the fate of being ignominiously dropped down a factory stack from a helicopter. He also had a knack for code and binary and all the things that made computers go. By the age of six, he wrote a small expert system that guessed what you were thinking, although it often ended up at "Mrs. Sotchky's Panties" due to a FOR/NEXT bug. Pitr is a self-taught programmer, showing talent and insight when confronted with difficult software problems. He feels he is one of the hard-core coders of our time, arranging code in his head and spewing it out at the keyboard.

Pitr's real-life analogue is a talented supercoder named Toomas. He doesn't speak with a Slavic accent, but he does have that mildly diabolical glint in his eye. He once mapped out all the cellular towers in his neighborhood. None of us could figure out if he did that out of simple curiosity or if he had a greater, more heinous plan in mind.

SID DABSTER

FUNCTION: Chief technical officer
EDUCATION: Electronics diploma, Technology diploma
STRENGTHS: Unmatched sense of treachery
WEAKNESSES: Early computer hardware
NICKNAMES: Old Fossil, Bearded Twit
AGE BRACKET: Mid 50s to early 60s

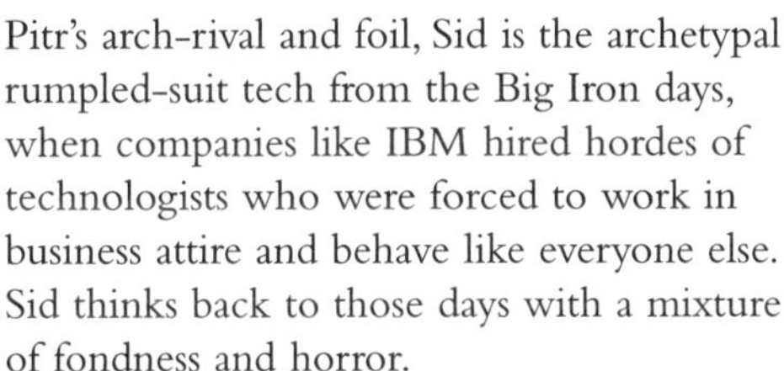

Pitr's arch-rival and foil, Sid is the archetypal rumpled-suit tech from the Big Iron days, when companies like IBM hired hordes of technologists who were forced to work in business attire and behave like everyone else. Sid thinks back to those days with a mixture of fondness and horror.

Sid is the technologist's technologist. He understands everything down to below the transistor level; he even understands the technology driven by vacuum tubes. Give him 90 or so pieces of electrical and mechanical gear, and he'll make a mini-pseudo-Babbage Difference Engine. Give him a handful of modern electronic parts, and he'll solder together a laser weapon fit to be mounted on the head of a shark. He is in many ways the core of Columbia Internet's brain trust. It's just too bad that he puts most of his knowledge toward foiling Pitr and making the younger coder his towel boy.

Sid was originally an amalgamation of two senior technologists who had roots in the early days of computing: Jay and Vaughn. Then came the day when I met someone who looked almost exactly like Sid, and who had Sid's cred and history to boot. His name is Albin.

SMILING MAN

FUNCTION: Controller
EDUCATION: Accounting diploma, Chartered Accountancy
STRENGTHS: A sense of order that defeats entropy
WEAKNESSES: Solar-powered calculators
NICKNAMES: That Creepy Smiling Bast*rd
AGE BRACKET: Late 40s to mid 50s

If there ever was a nightmare that involved general ledgers, green-lined column pages, and a shoebox full of un-annotated receipts, you would find Smiling Man at the core of the frightfest. He's always calm, always calculating, and almost always smiling. He knows that you're sloppy with your receipts, and he knows that the $1,500 line item you submitted as a "company entertainment expense" probably involved lesbian Jedi hookers. He'll let you think he's approved everything, and he'll even cut you a check for the full amount. And then payday comes, and your check is $1,500 short. "Easier to account for that way," he says, with that broad, immutable smile.

No one knows where he came from, but everyone at Columbia Internet is convinced that Smiling Man is a Martian. Or Neptunian. Or some other sort of non-terrestrial. The Chief doesn't even remember when he originally hired him, and no company records reveal his first day of work. He's just always … been there.

Smiling Man's real-life analogue is David, an operations wizard with a background in accounting. His smile is astonishingly unnerving even in broad daylight.

STEF MURKY

FUNCTION: Marketing executive
EDUCATION: Baccalaureate in Commerce
STRENGTHS: Fluent in Buzzwordese
WEAKNESSES: "Anything with a rack, baby"
NICKNAMES: Slimebag, Waste of Oxygen
AGE BRACKET: Early to mid 30s

THE CHIEF

FUNCTION: Chief executive officer
EDUCATION: Unknown
STRENGTHS: Can put head in sand around the techs
WEAKNESSES: Can't pull head out of sand when they leave
NICKNAMES: The Boss, Head Cheese
AGE BRACKET: Early to mid 60s

If you rolled a misogynist into a doughball, plugged in equal parts of pond scum, Gordon Gekko, a telemarketer, and a spammer, cooked it all down into a slurry, and reshaped it into a lounge lizard, you'd have Stef. He represents everything that is anathema to geeks in their professional lives: a walking, talking Malibu Ken doll with bad hair and insatiable greed. In other words, much of what you see in the business world today.

Stef has a difficult time communicating with geeks, but this is a two-way problem and is representative of the chasm that exists between IT and … well, not-IT. He's bothered by Dust Puppy's existence, and he positively hates Erwin, not appreciating being constantly one-upped by an "overdeveloped abacus." Stef is also a bit of a pervert and quite a chauvinist, convinced that he is Odin's Gift to Womankind. He's therefore puzzled that Miranda doesn't swoon at his feet, and he can't remotely understand why she'd be attracted to a dorky, unkempt web designer.

Stef was based on a skilled marketing exec (and eventual CEO) named Steven. Truth be told, Steven is perfectly likeable, is remarkably intelligent, and has a sense, even a glimmer, of ethics. He does fall into the lava a lot in Quake, though.

The Chief is typical for C-level executives: great at buzzwords, concerned with revenue, good at strategy, and better at screwing someone else over to benefit his or her company. He likes most of his staff, even if he doesn't understand 90% of what his techs say. "Chief? System load is high. We need to order three more Integral Buddy Gappa Pachyderms." "Okay," says the Chief, signing the purchase order and not wanting to ask more about it.

In his off time, which is pretty much all day unless he's in negotiations to once again sell the company, the Chief plays Freecell and Bejewelled and occasionally heads out to thwack a small white ball around the back nine. He meets with Smiling Man once a quarter to make sure there's enough money in the bank to fund his trips to the Bahamas. But he doesn't neglect his staff—he rewards hard workers with bonuses such as copies of Microsoft Windows 3.1, Lotus 1-2-3, and Corel Draw 5.5.

The Chief was based on one of my business partners (and past supervisor), a very tall and slim fellow (think John Cleese) named Barry with a puff of hair crowning his head. Barry's grasp of marketing and business structures was exceptional. He wisely left the technology and the "doing" to his staff and concentrated on top-level strategy. This may be why he's retired and in Europe. Micromanaging CEOs might want to pay attention to this.

LORD CRUD

FUNCTION: Slimy evil incarnate
EDUCATION: Doctorate in Iniquity
STRENGTHS: Diabolical machinations
WEAKNESSES: Frustrates easily
NICKNAMES: Sir, My Lord, Get Thee Hence
AGE BRACKET: Ageless

Whereas Stef may be slimy, unethical, and generally distasteful, Lord Crud is Evil. He takes money and lollipops from little children not with the glee of the greedy, but with the smug satisfaction of the diabolical. It's not the stealing of wealth he enjoys so much as the taking away of something from someone else: toys from toddlers, hot soup from the homeless, oxygen from the hospitalized …

When first incarnated in the strip, Lord Crud appeared as a hairy blob with demonic eyes and sharp teeth. He attached hands to himself after removing them from someone who was still using them, and for a while he propelled himself on gnarled, calloused fingers. Opposable thumbs allowed him to wield edged instruments, and thus he'd occasionally locate a well-dressed executive and "send them onward," replacing the head with his own and pulling the ligaments and tendons inside the body, causing it to walk and otherwise operate as a marionette in the hands of a puppeteer.

And puppeteering is what Lord Crud is best at. Pulling strings, moving and sacrificing pawns: these are his stock in trade. He'll do anything it takes to spread misery, which is why Christmas is his favorite time of year. That's when he sends out all of those credit-card offers.

Lord Crud's real-life analogue? Any executive from the *IAA.

PEARL DABSTER

FUNCTION: Business analyst
EDUCATION: Masters of Business Administration
STRENGTHS: Calculating fashion sense
WEAKNESSES: Roguish, charming coders
NICKNAMES: Daddy's Little Girl, Educated Pole Dancer
AGE BRACKET: Late 20s

Most companies these days have a "business analyst." This may not be their actual title, but they're in charge of looking for the weak spots in a company's commercial efforts and helping correct them. They're usually highly educated, smart, and, of course, brilliantly manipulative. This is where Pearl Dabster comes in.

As Sid's daughter, she became a disappointment to her father when she revealed that she's completed an MBA. She also seems to have a sporadic attraction to men that Sid detests, including Pitr. This nearly caused Sid to have a stroke. Although Pearl occasionally acts like a stereotypical airhead, she is anything but; her forays into short-skirted power suits and spiked high heels at the office are calculated for maximum effect. She knows she's attractive, dresses and walks the part, and uses all this as a tool for further advancement.

Pearl was created from pretty much every female executive I've ever known who wore their sexuality as a power accessory at the office.

MR. COLA

FUNCTION: Addiction hallucination
EDUCATION: He's learned your weakness
STRENGTHS: Unending, unyielding temptation
WEAKNESSES: Blowback
NICKNAMES: Caffeine Monster, Big Fat Doobie
AGE BRACKET: Whatever age, as needed

We all have vices, addictions, that rule our daily lives. For the cartoonist, it's coffee … I'm unable to concentrate on work for more than an hour at a time without an espresso drink in my hand. Mr. Cola knows this, and he visits me any time I try to break myself of my coffee habit. He'll stand in front of me, not saying anything, wafting the smell of delicious coffee over to my desk until I crumble like a sandcastle under an ocean wave and run to the nearest coffee shop screaming "MY GOD, WHY DID I EVEN TRY?!" Mr. Cola is my friend, my enemy, my eternal companion.

Although he's depicted as a giant walking cola can in the cartoon, he appears to each person as whatever their vice may be. Coffee, cola, Mountain Dew, beer, demonweed … name your addiction, and this is how he'll present himself.

Mr. Cola has no real-life analogue. Pity, that.

CTHULHU

FUNCTION: Great Old One
EDUCATION: Everything in ancient tomes
STRENGTHS: Multi-tool tentacles
WEAKNESSES: Tasty Head Cheese
NICKNAMES: Squidhead, Sushi, Herring Bait
AGE BRACKET: Ancient

He is the most famous of the Great Old Ones in the Lovecraft mythos, and for a very good reason! None are as articulate, elegant, or well-dressed as Cthulhu himself. His bookshelves contain writings by James Joyce, Durante degli Alighieri, Lao Tzu, and other literary luminaries; his CD collection covers everything from Pavarotti to Wagner; and he only wears Armani and Hugo Boss. His wine cellar is unmatched, although some of the fluids contained in the dustier bottles might be surprising to many.

Cthulhu visits Columbia Internet fairly frequently, because he's developed a good relationship with Sid, whom he regards as another (although junior) Great Old One. He also commandeers the ISP's mail servers for the occasional cultist mail blast, and he's currently lobbying for a .cth TLD. Cthulhu's real-life analogue is … uh … Cthulhu. He exists! Just you wait until the stars are right, unbeliever!

HASTUR

FUNCTION: Great Old One/character consumer
EDUCATION: Egyptian prophecies
STRENGTHS: Amorphous pseudopods with teeth
WEAKNESSES: Young, edible interns
NICKNAMES: Blob of Munchies, Tarry Mess
AGE BRACKET: Incalculable

Amorphous in appearance, malevolent in nature, and smelling like old cheese and older socks, Hastur is, in this form, a blob of insatiable hunger and rage. But his demeanor seems to be much calmer than the storms just beneath his … skin? … would indicate. He can be easily summoned by chanting his name three times, which has unfortunate consequences for the summoner.

Hastur chums around with Cthulhu. Prior to their reunion at Columbia Internet, Hastur was serving as a dollop of Distilled Usenet Bitterness, perhaps the most caustic fluid known to science. It's also been suggested that Hastur is an example of pure dark matter, because this fits with Lovecraft's mythos that the Great Old Ones are the dominant race in the cold, uncaring universe. Or maybe Hastur is just a bit of oobleck gone insane.

Make this a priority. It's very important.
Well I'm really busy, these days. If I push hard I can have it to you in two weeks.
I guess I'll have to live with that. Thanks Greg.
No prob.
Dude, what Stef wants only takes ten minutes. Including debugging.
Damn, I'm out of rockets.
Copyright (c) Illiad 1997

November 17th, 1997

And J.D. said, let there be pixels, and there were pixels. I scratched this one out on a bit of photocopy paper with a nasty little ballpoint pen, copied it, and passed it around the boutique ISP I helped found. I needed a name for the cartoon, so I looked at my screen: somewhere in the middle of my web browser were the words *user friendly*, and that was that. I chose a pseudonym because I'm not big on fame or its associated bits.

Greg, I just heard that you've been doing nothing but playing computer games and that your time estimates are grossly overblown. I think it's time you acted responsibly.
BLAM! BLAM!
The things I ask you to do are very important to this company. Your lack of productivity and flagrant disregard of office protocol is very disturbing.
POW!
BLAM! KA-BOOM!
Say, where can I get a copy of that?
The CD is on my desk. Help yourself.
OUGH!
Copyright (c) Illiad 1997

November 18th, 1997

I scrawled a second cartoon because it wrote itself. Stef is based loosely on a business chum I've known since 1996. Although sales and marketing are in his blood, he's not as bad or as hapless as Stef is. But all stories need villains. The idea for this strip popped up because Stef's real-life analog wanted to join in a game of Quake after watching us tech-types play for a while … after complaining for days about how we were playing games during company time.

Yes, Meatspace Stef really did get creamed in Quake. He tried and tried and tried. And tried. Rocket bait.

Chief, you need to do something. Greg and the other techs are wasting company time by playing games on the network.
That's without mentioning that the games they play are violent, bloody, and morally shallow.
You're the CEO. You need to do something about this right away!
They kicked your ass, didn't they.
THEY WERE CHEATING!!
Copyright (c) Illiad 1997

November 19th, 1997

The Chief is based on one of my business partners. Tall fellow, who could imitate John Cleese if he wanted to. He got bitten by the Quake bug, too. I think he was about as good as Stef's analog.

I've called you guys here today because I've been getting complaints from Stef about the lack of productivity in the tech department.
A small hi-tech firm like ours needs to have every department, especially the systems people, producing at top capacity. I hope I've made myself clear on this.
So, you guys think I can beat Stef at that game?
You'd spank him.
Welcome to the dark side, Chief.
Copyright (c) Illiad 1997

November 20th, 1997

Trust me on this, A.J. Put this up on a billboard and we'll get swamped with calls from new customers.
I hope you're right, Cobb.
Thank you for calling Columbia Internet, Tanya speaking, how may I help you?
What do you mean, what am I wearing?!
COLUMBIA INTERNET
"We'll show you a good time!"
555-BABE
Copyright (c) Illiad 1997

November 21st, 1997

Tanya is based on a young lady who worked for us in Customer Service. She's demure and quiet but good at her job. The very thought of her working a phone-sex line caused a paroxysm of laughter.

I heard that Stef has an appointment with our controller today.
So?
Our controller is that guy who smiles all the time. For no reason.
Yeah, so?
Ever see how cats smile just before they eat something live?
Ahhh. I see now.
Now, what have we learned today?
GET RECEIPTS FOR EVERYTHING!!
Copyright (c) Illiad 1997

November 22nd, 1997

Smiling Man's analog really does smile all the time. Except when he's about to eat you alive, when he smiles harder.

Gentlemen, Hillary has been receiving some very disturbing reports about your conduct as sales people. As a test, I want you to say the word "ethical."
This is insulting. Cobb and I can say that word any time we want. Right Cobb?
Uhh, yup.
Well, then?
Ethrfffmml.
Uhhh, methadone.
Ekekkal...*Kaff*
Medical. Umm. Radical.
HACK
KAFF
Eth...
ethrmmal...
COUGH
Can't...say...word...
Looks like you were right, Chief.
You should see the techs trying to say "three-piece suit."
RECTAL!!!
Copyright (c) Illiad 1997

November 23rd, 1997

Hillary is based on a lady who worked for us who excelled at administration and HR. She's sort of the straight-(wo)man of the strip. And there's Cobb, the heavily mustached outside sales rep who means well but ends up being the butt of the jokes (inadvertently, of course).

It's remarkable how just saying "rectal" will earn you snorts.

Sadly, Pfeiffer didn't last long in the strip. The Accounts Receivable/CSR that I based her on left the company a month or two after the strip started. Nice person, with an awesome, carefully applied mean streak.

Hello, Mr. Kragg? My name is Pfeiffer, and I'm calling from Columbia Internet about your account.
Yeah?
Your account is 90 days past due. When do you think you could send us a cheque?
You're just going to have to wait. I need to pay for my vacation in Tahiti next week.
I see. Well. I guess I'll have to bring in the big guns.
Give it your best shot, baby. I ain't scared of you.
Let's have a look at your user log here. Ahhh...here's something we can leak to our customer mailing list...
Um...
I see you've been reading alt.sex.chubby.sheep. Voraciously.
OK! OK! I'll courier a cheque over today!!
Copyright (c) Illiad 1997

November 24th, 1997

Told you he smiles harder.

I know it's a lot of money, but I need this purchase order filled. It's very important.
Hey, why are you smiling?
I'm not smiling.
SOMEBODY MAKE HIM STOP!!!
Works every time.
Copyright (c) Illiad 1997

November 25th, 1997

Here we see our intrepid techie, working diligently on a system problem.
THE TECH IS IN
He struggles with the operating system, unsure of its intentions...
THE TECH IS IN
Direct seX
THE TECH IS IN
Greg's using Windows 95!!
NO!! I'm only using it so I can play Minesweeper!
RESOURCES EXCEEDED. PLEASE REBOOT.
THE TECH IS IN
Copyright (c) Illiad 1997

November 26th, 1997

That's the third user who has called and complained about the news server being down.
Hmmm. Have the techs given you an idea when the server would be back up?
They said it would be a while. Something about restoring data from a secondary backup.
Nine more messages and we'll be done with admin.policy.
I know! I know! I'm typing as fast as I can!!
Copyright (c) Illiad 1997

November 27th, 1997

This was in the day when Linux was all the rage. The Open Source movement not only made it cool to hate Microsoft, it gave us a place from which we could throw stones.

I have vague, chill-inducing recollections of the long, arduous process of installing Win95. It was much prettier than Win3.11, but dear God almighty was it ever a pig.

What the...?!?
BLOODY HELL!! STUPID PIECE OF CRAP!!!
TAKE THAT YOU SPAWN OF THE DEVIL!!
BANG! CRASH!! RIP!
What's with Greg?
He's installing Windows 95.
IT KEEPS ASKING ME WHERE I WANT TO GO TODAY! I DON'T WANT TO GO ANYWHERE!!

November 28th, 1997

I'm sure at one point I thought this was funny. How embarrassing.

Sergeant Stef, the intrepid warrior, marches into battle, mowing down all that stand against him.
AAARGH
LOOK OUT!! HERE HE COMES!!!
He confronts his ultimate enemies, and readies his weapon to deal out death the way only Sergeant Stef can deal it out....
EVERYBODY DUCK!!!
KA-BLAM!!
Oh, damn.
You suck, Stef.
Did I get him? Did I get him?!

November 29th, 1997

...so I need you techs
to upgrade the server.
Go away.
We're busy.
AJ, you know how these
techies think. Help me
convince them.
I can't Stef.
It would be
wrong.
Dammit, AJ,
I'm getting
DESPERATE!
OK! OK!
I'm going
to regret
this...
Hey, you guys hear how our customers
say our server is as good as AOL's?
Quite the compliment...
!
Guess we'd better
go upgrade the
server.
Guess so.
Yeah...
AJ...that was...
brilliant...
I just
Fedexed my
soul to hell.
I'm **real**
clever.

November 30th, 1997

I see I was on a streak of funny. Not. Sorry, world.

I hope I broke that streak. And I've learned how to draw keyboards from a side profile since this cartoon.

So A.J., did the techies find out that you tricked them into upgrading the server?
Yep.
And you're okay with that?
Ya, I told them you put me up to it.
Wha...you told them it was me?
Relax. They've never been known to seek physical vengeance.
Okay, we've destroyed his credit rating, repo'd his car, owes money to an escort agency, and is a wanted felon. What else?
List him as pregnant.

December 1st, 1997

You techs think you scare me? I'm tougher than you think.
For what you did Stef, you're dead.
But...you guys are techs. You don't do violence.
Exceptions have been made.
Don't you dare lay a finger on me.
I won't. It's not my job.
Hi, someone call the morgue? Where's the stiff? I only have 10 minutes on the meter.
It's the ripe one here.

December 2nd, 1997

Time to put more RAM in this server. It's been almost a year since I upgraded it.
Yuck...it's kind of dirty and sticky in here...did I see something move?
What the hell are you?
I was about to ask you the same question.

December 3rd, 1997

Pitr still has no accent, and Dust Puppy was born into this strip on this day.

So what is that thing?
Apparently it's a dust puppy. Born from the dust and debris collected inside the server over a year.
DESCEND
BURPMASTER 3
It's kinda cool. Made from dust.
Yeah. Pretty neat.
Where'd he get the feet?
Haven't figured that out yet.
YE GODS, I HAVE FEET??!

December 4th, 1997

I still don't know how to explain the feet.

Mike? Pitr? Greg?
Where'd everyone go?
They went for lunch.
AAAAAAIIIIGGGH!
Whoa.
ROTO-ROUTER 4000
It's gotta be the coffee. Bad coffee.
Y'know, you're kinda funny looking.

December 5th, 1997

Hey little dude, do you have a name?
No. I've never really needed one.
Then what should we call you?
I dunno. Something that describes me, and how I'm surrounded by expensive, high-end computer equipment that leaves me mystified.
DESCEND
BURPMEISTER 3
How about "Web Designer"?
I'd like a name that people won't laugh at.

December 6th, 1997

Is this an anatomy program?
No, it's Quake.
Cool.
What's that thing there?
It's called a Quad.
And what's that?
That's Stef.
Uh...
Stef, you just got beaten by a ball of DIRT.
Is 20 to -5 a good score?

December 7th, 1997

Dude, you still need a name.
How about "Bootstrap"?
Maybe.
DESCEND
BURPMEISTER 3
"Scuzzy"?
"Wizzy Wig?"
Maybe.
"Microbit?"
"Johnny Cache?"
Maybe.
Why "maybe" for everything?
I'm using fuzzy logic.

December 8th, 1997

Inspired, of course, by how I would react if I saw a strange sentient dustball come up and smile at me.

Hello, Smiling Man. I heard you smiled all day, so I'll bet you bring joy to the staff. I thought I'd come by and return some of the sunshine you hand out.
Well, have a nice day.
If I hold really still maybe all of this will just go away.

December 9th, 1997

Gentlemen, I've called you here today because I've been hearing disturbing talk about how you intend to put the evil productivity killer known as Quake 2 on our LAN.
This is a terrible waste of resources and must not go unpunished. As a reprimand, the three of you may only expense lunches at Poppy's Plastic Pizza for the next week.
I hope you learn from this.
We've been trying to get a tab at Poppy's for months. He knows that.
Put Quake 2 on my machine and I'll make it two weeks.

December 10th, 1997

I just don't understand all this fuss over Quake 2 between A.J. and Stef and all the techs.
Logimech
3DFX CARDS
Quake 2
144 pcs.
They stomp around all day, strutting and posing and threatening to kick each other's butt. It's almost like international politics.
Actually I think it's closer to the simple male need to have a bigger "thingie" than the other guy.
And judging from the scores, Stef has the sma...
LET'S NOT GO THERE!

December 11th, 1997

There's nothing worse than ripping off a "Bloom County" comic, except not realizing that you ripped off a "Bloom County" comic until years later. D'oh.

Whatcha doing?
Check this out. I'm in the master server at the Department of Defense.
Cool.
Yeah. I've been watching the activity level on their network.
And...?
Their LAN is flooded. Something big must be going down.
The Joint Chiefs want to know when the network will be free so they can get their e-mail.
Can't you see we're BUSY?!
Eat hot rockets, Ernie!!

December 12th, 1997

Damn, another split power cord. I'd better replace this.
Roto-Router
Indentium 4000X
ZAPP!
Roto-Router
Indentium 4000X
Roto-Router
Indentium 4000X
Oooh. BAY-bee.
Don't even.
Roto-Router
Indentium 4000X

December 13th, 1997

Damn, I'm late for my meeting and I can't find that presentation CD that A.J. made for me...
Ah, this must be it...
Hey Tanya. You seen Stef?
Yes, he was here earlier.
Where'd he go? I have to give him a CD.
He left for a meeting with a big client. He already had a CD with him. A red one.
Uhh...did you say RED?
Yes. Why?
Oh my dear GOD...
I say, what are all those naked people doing?

December 14th, 1997

Greg handling tech-support calls has become a bit iconic within the UF universe. Most of these comics I've done over the years are based on real calls. This should terrify you and convince you never to go into tech support.

Columbia Internet Tech Support. Greg speaking, please state the nature of your problem.
Hello? Hello? I'm trying to dial in and I can't get a dial tone.
No dial tone. What kind of modem are you using?
Modem?
It's usually a small box that's connected to your computer and phone line.
Oh, the blinky-light thingie. It's on my Christmas tree.
Ah. Do me a favour and leave it there forever, okay?

December 15th, 1997

Columbia Internet Tech Support. Greg speaking, please state the nature of your problem.
This is General Studebaker from the Department of Defense.
Uh...hello General.
We traced an intrusion into our top secret wargames to you. That's serious, son.
But...you guys were just playing Quake 2.
They were WARGAMES!
You were using cheat codes too. You guys suck.

December 16th, 1997

Columbia Internet Tech Support. Greg speaking, please state the nature of your problem.
Hello. I don't seem to be getting any e-mail. It's been nearly two weeks.
I see. Let me check your account.
Your mailbox is empty. No one's been sending you mail.
I'm so lonely.
You sound yummy. Would you like to be my friend?
You're kidding me, right?

December 17th, 1997

Columbia Internet Tech Support. Greg speaking, please state the nature of your problem.
My computer is broken. I demand you fix it. Now.
Uhh, we only support Internet problems, sir.
Well my computer connects me to the Internet and it's broken. FIX IT YOU IDIOT!
Yes sir, no need to get angry.
That's better. Now what do I do?
Type 'Format C:' That should fix everything.

December 18th, 1997

I must have interviewed a really annoying candidate for a job at the time. There's some serious nerd bitterness in the writing.

So I understand you'd like to work with us as a designer.
Yes, I've been an art director for six years, and have a background in computer technology and prepress, plus ten years as a technical writer.
Very impressive. Do you play Quake?
No, I think games are a waste of time.
And I think you're a waste of oxygen.
NEXT!
Wait, I play a pretty good game of Monopoly!

December 19th, 1997

USER FRIENDLY by Illiad
Greg, are you sure this is going to work?
Trust me on this.
Hello. This is Columbia Internet calling. Is this Mr. Edgar Oofle?
Yes it is.
GURF KEE PAH ZSAV MOOK CHEE!!
What the hell was that?!
Greg's helping me collect from Trekkie deadbeats. In Klingon.
I think it worked. All I hear is whimpering.

December 20th, 1997

Columbia Internet Tech Support. Greg speaking. How may I help you?
I can't connect.
I see. What Web browser are you using?
It's a Compaq.
No, no. That's the brand of your computer. What Web browser are you using?
Ummmmm. I dunno.
OK, let's try a different tack. What operating system are you using?
Netscape.
No! What is your operating system?!
Take it easy, buddy. What's your problem?
What's MY problem?!! Turnip! Wankle Rotary Engine! Carbuncle! Bust my pickle! None of that made sense did it! See how it feels?! HAHAHAH!
What an idiot. *click*

December 21st, 1997

Bust my pickle. Heh. Either a band name or a t-shirt.

Ahh, I finally get a break. Now for some nice Christmas cookies.
Would someone like to explain what that thing is doing in the fridge?
I was looking for some Grey Poupon.

December 22nd, 1997

You're one of our most valued clients, Mr. Woodly. I'd be honoured if you'd have one of my Christmas cookies.
Why thank you, my boy. And a delicious cookie it appears to be indeed.
Urrrk...mmrrrf.... ....I say....
My word. A very large bit of lint.
Would somebody please get that thing out of the fridge?!?!!

December 23rd, 1997

Greg here, may I help you?
Yes, I forgot the password to my Internet account.
I can't reveal that kind of information over the phone, sir.
But I can't get my mail! I need my password!
I see. Since it's Christmas I'll make an exception. I just emailed you your password.
Oh thank you! You're a life saver!
Greg, when he figures it out...
I'll be long gone.

December 24th, 1997

Well, it's Christmas. I just realized that I bought a present for everyone except you, little guy. I feel terrible.
ROTO-ROUTER
BURPMASTER III
I going to go into the new year feeling guilty and awful. Can you ever forgive me?
I guess so. I don't even know what a present is.
You're so innocent. You just made my Christmas wonderful.
What's this 'Christmas' thing anyway?

December 25th, 1997

I just don't get this Christmas thing. Everyone's staring at trees with blinking lights and talking about religious experiences. It's too weird.
I may as well just go back into the computer room.
Whoa.
Okay, NOW I get it.
MODEM RACK

December 26th, 1997

A.J., I know it's kind of late, but I'd like to give you a Christmas present.
A present? But, you don't have any money. You can't buy me anything.
I can make you a sweater out of real lint.
Let's just call it even, okay?

December 27th, 1997

Columbia Internet Customer Service Centre. Tanya speaking, may I help you?
Hello, I'd like to buy an Internet account.
No problem, sir. Your name?
Kris Kringle.
Your address, sir?
100 Christmas Drive, North Pole.
Thank you, sir. Your account is now activated.
Is that it?
Just one more question.
Where're the diamond earrings I asked for, fatboy?
Is this some kind of joke?

December 28th, 1997

So whatcha get
for Christmas, Mike?
I got this Snurf
Gun. It fires those
soft suction darts.
Hey! A Snurf Gun!
Cool!
Ya, it's got a scope,
a laser painter, windage
compensator...
Does it have
autofire?
I think so.
We'll have to
test it.
Chief, I think it behooves
upper management to write
company policy on firearms
in the workplace...
Yeah. Snurf Guns
for everyone!

December 29th, 1997

Hey Greg, you seen that
Snurf Gun that Mike got
for Christmas?
Nope.
It's pretty neat. It's
loaded with all kinds
of targetting gizmos.
Hey cool!
Problem is, it goes through
ammo like crazy. Mike's down
at the store hoping to find
a solution.
Ahhh.
Sir, for the hundredth
time, we do NOT carry
600-round boxes of
belt-fed suction darts!
What about
tripods? You
got tripods?
CUSTOMER
SERVICE

December 30th, 1997

1997 was quite a year. Now that we're on the verge of 1998, I keep thinking about all of the earth-shaking events that happened.
Microsoft acquired Apple. Bre-X made people extremely rich or extremely poor. Quake II and Riven were released. K56 Flex became an accepted standard.
Ummm...
You forgot that Stef got a non-negative score in a deathmatch.
I said earth-shaking events, not miracles.

December 31st, 1997

Well, it's 1998. It's another year closer to the end of the millenium.
We had the eighties and the nineties. What do we call the next decade? The zeroes? The nothings?
How about "the naughties?"
It's probably pretty accurate.

January 1st, 1998

As God is my witness, this actually happened. People clustered around the shipment of new office supplies.

WOOHOO! Hey, Pfeiffer! Check this out!
Coming, Hillary.
You ever seen anything like it, Tanya?
Never. Awesome.
Look at this, Pfeiffer. Talk about deluxe!
New office supplies.
Ah.
LOOK! Coloured paper clips!!

January 2nd, 1998

Did you hear the news? Microsoft just acquired Hotmail.
Now Microsoft is offering a free Web browser, free server software, and free e-mail. I'm scared of what's coming next.
"This is where you will go today."
I'm moving to the moon.

January 3rd, 1998

Columbia Internet Tech Support. Greg speaking. How may I help you?
Hi. My browser isn't connecting with Web sites.
I see. OK, I'll tell you how to configure your...
What's your Primary DNS?
Uhh....it's 209.170.19.6
Hmmm, I got that correct.
Are all IPs dynamically allocated?
Yes, they are indeed.
Oh, silly me. I set the IP allocation to 'static.' I am SO sorry for wasting your time.
You're wonderful. Are you married?
My wife hates it when I call tech support.

January 4th, 1998

Department of Justice spokesperson Terrance Faber revealed today that the case against Microsoft has stalled.
Faber stated that the Department has every intention of proceeding with the case once their workstations, which contain all of the evidence collected against Microsoft, are back up.
When Justice officers keyed in the words "Injunction against Microsoft" in Word 7.0, all of the workstations immediately locked up. Faber refused to comment on this suspicious incident.
When reached for comment, Mr. Gates smiled apologetically and said that a fix for this particular bug was being worked on, and would be available for free to the Department of Justice by the year 3614.

January 5th, 1998

UF hadn't exploded in readership by this point, but the few thousand who did visit daily were pretty vocal about Dust Puppy's apparent demise. I was threatened with a "right good walloping with a feather duster" by one British reader.

It's been a long day. I think I'll take a nap in this nice warm server.
This server sure is dusty. I better give it a good blast of compressed air.
PAFFFF!
Uh oh.

January 6th, 1998

You're kidding.
I wish I were. One PAFF! from the compressed air and it was over.
That can't be.
I'm not making this up.
Let me see.
If you insist.
See, a disembodied foot. Told ya.
It might not be the dust puppy. I mean, Stef looks like this in Quake most of the time.

January 7th, 1998

I'm telling you AJ. He's gone. Kaput. Finis.
But he can't be!
All that's left of him is that pile of fluff, two eyes and two feet.
Maybe we can bring him back to life...?
Those feet are bad. He'll need new ones.
No problem.
I'll get the hacksaw.
Hey Stef, can you come in here for a minute?

January 8th, 1998

The dust puppy came to life somehow. All those bits came together in a server, and life sprang forth.
I hope we got all the correct bits into this server. Now we just hope it works. Throw the switch, Greg!
OK!!
CLICK!
Whhhhiiiirrrrr...
Did it work??
Pitr, do you smell burning hair?
sizzle

January 9th, 1998

Well, I guess that's it, Pitr. We've tried everything to bring the little guy back. Nothing worked.
Should we open the server and collect his remains?
No, I couldn't bear it. Let's just go.
rustle rustle rustle
Hello?
POOK!

January 10th, 1998

I don't see what the big deal is. That hairball was nothing but trouble.
How so?
For starters he kept climbing into the fridge and getting weird bits of hair on all of the food. I hate that.
On top of that he freaked me out. Ball of fuzz on feet, sneaking around. Creepy little creature.
And he had this habit of sneaking up on me. Nearly gave me a massive coronary last time.
Um...
Hi guys.
One! Two! Three! One! Two! Three! Pitr, give me a hand!
Nope. I draw the line at putting my lips on Stef's.

January 11th, 1998

Hey, little dude.
Hi Greg.
I don't believe it!!
Tell me about it. Microsoft is still claiming innocence in court. Who do they think they're kidding?

January 12th, 1998

I can't believe you're back! We were all pretty sad when you got aired out, but now you're back everything is okay again.
ROTO-ROUTER MK I
COLA 24 CANS
QUADRUPLE CHEESE SUPER-PIZZA ****
Aired out?
Yes, you took a blast of compressed air. Messed you up something awful.
Isn't that akin to murder or something?
Stef did it.

January 13th, 1998

Ahhh, Cobb. Thank you for coming. You know how I hate to take you away from your busy schedule.
Oh, my pleasure.
Yes. Well. I've been reviewing your expense reports and I wonder if you could explain a few discrepancies.
uhhh...
I noticed you've been expensing a lot of dinners with one of the telephone company vice-presidents.
So I checked. Strangely, the phone company has never had an employee named Betty Bazongas.
Really? You mean she lied to me all this time?

January 14th, 1998

Hey little guy. What ya up to?
Surfing the Web. I'm looking for some info.
Yeah? Why're you doing that?
Stef aired me out so now I have to retaliate.
Retaliate?
Ah, here's what I've been looking for...
"Dissolving industrial strength laxatives in coffee."
Pitr has such great ideas.

January 15th, 1998

Hey Mike, you seen that walking ball of dirt anywhere?
Nope. Why're you looking for him?
That little beggar went and put a laxative in my coffee.
Bummer. Haven't seen him though.
Well, if you spot him, let me know.
Sure.
A laxative in his coffee? I'm proud of you. You can hide as long as you like.
Thanks, but your beard tickles.

January 16th, 1998

Hello Smiling Man. I heard you wanted to see me.
Yes. I'd like to know what it is you do around here.
Oh. Well, I walk around looking short, and sleep in the servers, and give advice to people who need it and sometimes I even play Quake.
That's about it.
And for how long have you been a vice president?

January 17th, 1998

Hey little dude. Know what an oxymoron is?
Isn't that what Stef calls all the technicians?
Ah, no, that's not entirely accurate.
Do you want to play a game? All you have to do is come up with most telling oxymoron possible. The most ironic oxymoron wins.
Okay.
I'll start. "Military Intelligence."
"Microsoft Works."
Uh, okay, you win.
QUADRUPLE CHEESE SUPER-PIZZA

January 18th, 1998

Welcome to Windows 95
WARNING! If you delete Microsoft Internet Explorer, you will compromise the stability of Windows.
Do you wish to continue?
NO
Click!
SYSTEM FAILURE. PLEASE REBOOT.

January 19th, 1998

Columbia Internet Tech Support. Greg speaking, please state the nature of your problem.
Hello. How secure is my e-mail?
Very secure, m'am. Why?
Well, I'm a centerfold model and my husband is overseas and we send each other very steamy letters. My privacy is important to me.
We're the only ones who can get to your mail.
Phew. Thank you. That's a relief.
Say, what's your account number?

January 20th, 1998

tappity
tappity
tappity
WARNING! This site is restricted.
You must be 18 years of age or older
to enter. Minors are prohibited.
Oh, yes...
tappity
tappity
Oooh. So Stef likes being spanked with zucchinis...what a naughty boy.
Type back, "Hey baby, wanna nibble on my gourd?"

January 21st, 1998

You know, I feel kind of guilty.
How come?
Well, sometimes I think we're not quite as devoted to our work as we should be.
Oh. Yeah, I know what you mean.
I'll bet that if we really commit ourselves to what we do, we can do it 100% better.
You're right. Let's go tell the Chief our new resolution.
Hey Chief. We've figured out how to save the technical department.
We need to be committed.

January 22nd, 1998

This was written during the tragic ice storms in Quebec. Lots of people lost power and didn't have heat in their homes. I think some people even died from the cold. It's true about dark humor helping people through the tougher times. I had to somehow vent after reading the news.

Hi Stef. What're you reading?
Web News. Stuff about the power outages in Eastern Canada.
It's really bad out there, isn't it.
Yeah. No power means no heat, lights, or even computer time.
Cut off from the Internet? That's bad.
I don't know how they live through it.
Pedal harder, Francois! My e-mail is coming through!
Sacre Bleu! I'm going as fast as I can!

January 23rd, 1998

This was the first strip I wrote that paid any attention to the needs of the cartoon syndicates. Note the dimensions. Strip size remains the same throughout the years from this point forward.

Did you hear? Netscape is releasing the source code to their next browser for free. Microsoft must be having a fit. Makes me wonder if Microsoft will end up releasing the code to Internet Explorer.
ROTO-ROUTER
QUADRUPLE CHEESE SUPER-PIZZA
144 pcs
Copyright (c) Illiad 1997, 1998
Probably be too embarassing.
Of course. What was I thinking?

January 24th, 1998

USER FRIENDLY
by
Illiad
Copyright (c) 1997, 1998 Illiad
tappity
tappity
tappity
Hey little guy. What're you doing?
I'm experimenting with this artificial intelligence I just developed.
Hello A.J. Want to see a design I've been working on?
YE GODS! This is incredible!
STEF! PUT YOUR MARKETING HAT ON!
What's with him?
I think he's just impressed that I can type with my toes.

January 25th, 1998

Except for the Sundays. (And yes, this was Erwin's birthdate.)

I'm telling you Stef, the dust puppy created an artificial intelligence. It's uncanny. Look at those weird patterns on the screen.

You're right. I wonder what those patterns mean. Maybe it's a code, or a visual representation of flowing intelligence. Maybe it's what the philosophers have been looking for all these years.

Actually, it's my screen saver.

Sigh. I can't believe I authorized this.
HILLARY

I've finished the installation on all of the machines.
Well, there goes productivity. Right down the drain.
HILLARY
Copyright (c) 1997, 1998 Illiad

Let me guess. Quake 2?
Windows 95, actually.
May the gods protect me.

Good morning, Erwin.
Hello. Is that my new name? I'm not sure I like it. Sounds geeky.

Well...
Copyright (c) 1997, 1998 Illiad

"Web Designer" is still available.
Y'know, "Erwin" really isn't that bad.

Hey, I found a really cool Web site. Want to see it?
Okay.

WARNING!!
YOU HAVE REACHED THE WHITE HOUSE ARCHIVE SITE. UNAUTHORIZED USERS WILL BE PROSECUTED!
Copyright (c) 1997, 1998 Illiad

Um. Maybe we shouldn't go there.
No, no! There's pictures of naked female employees in Bill Clinton's directory!

Let's go see if that AI can sustain a real conversation.
That's a great test for an artificial intelligence.

What was that test called again?
The Turing Test. Let's do it.

Pitr and Mike are coming to see how smart you are. Something about "Turnip Testicles."
Searching... Okay, I found a Web page on it.
Copyright (c) 1997, 1998 Illiad

Well silly ol' me. I didn't notice my caps lock being on. Thanks.
You're welcome sir. Goodbye.
Copyright (c) 1997, 1998 Illiad

Sigh.

Is everything all right, Greg?
Yeah. Just another user.

We all have our crosses to bear.
Sure, but why do mine have to be so **stupid?**

USER FRIENDLY
by
Illiad
Copyright (c) 1997, 1998 Illiad

Good morning, Erwin.
Hello. Where would you like to go today?

ERWIN?? You're not infected are you?
Sorry. I lost it there for a second.

I have something to show you.
What's that?

I'm not sure. I found it on Mike's desk.
Oh, that's a Snurf Gun. You shoot it at people.

Oh. How do I use it?
Steady your aim. Look down the sights. Pick your target.

Compensate for windage. Adjust your grip. Check your breathing. Now squ-eeeeze the trigger.
wobble
POW!
POW!
POW!
POW!
THPP!
THPP!
THPP!
THPP!

This is really starting to get old.
Got him!

Looks like Microsoft did it again. Despite all of their setbacks last year, they've posted huge profits, and their stock has continued to climb.

I don't know how they do it. They have over 200 millionaires working there. They must save money somewhere.

You'd better have that software finished in time. Or would you rather we send you to work for Kathie Lee Gifford?
No, no please!
Microsoft Sweatshop

I don't think you'll want any of this coffee, Mike. It looks pretty thick.
Bring some anyway. I need my coffee!

Here ya go.
Thanks, A.J.

sssslurrp
Copyright (c) 1997, 1998 Illiad

Mike?

You seen Mike?
He was here just a second ago.

What was he doing?
Coding. I just gave him a cup of coffee.
Copyright (c) 1997, 1998 Illiad

Uh..it wasn't Pitr's experimental Super Triple Expresso Coffee was it?
Why is there a hole in the ceiling?

Do you see him? Is he okay?
Yes, he's up here. He's clinging to a pipe. Hey Mike, it's me, A.J.

Well get him down here.
Mike, give me your hand.

He doesn't seem to want to let go of the pipe.
LOOK, I'M A LITTLE JUMPY RIGHT NOW, OKAY?!?

Phew. I need to relax.

Hello Mike.

Copyright (c) 1997, 1998 Illiad

I guess you've seen the pictures on the Web of Bill Gates getting pasted with cream pies. The techs thought it was funny, but didn't seem that impressed.

I heard Gates was coming into town today. And speaking of the techs, where are they?
Not sure. They weren't here when I arrived.

Gates in sight! Range 300 yards!
Belt fed suction darts loaded! Ready to rock and roll!
SnuRF
Copyright (c) 1997, 1998 Illiad

USER FRIENDLY
by
Illiad
Copyright (c) 1997, 1998 Illiad

Ready for this Erwin?
You betcha.

Then gimme a medium rock rhythm.
chik-a-boom
chik-a-boom
chik-a-boom

(Sung to "Lookin' Out My Back Door")
Just bought Windows 95,
Stuck the CD in my drive,
Got to upgrade from Windows 3.1!
Loaded up my machine,
Then I got that blue screen,
G.P.F.* on my Windows PC!
doo doo dat dum de dum
* General Protection Failure

I hit control-alt-delete,
My PC began to build up heat,
When finally the desktop popped up on my monitor!
I double-clicked on Freecell,
And 95 went to hell,
G.P.F. on my Windows PC!
diddle de dat boopie de bop

Bugs and bloated features,
are working hand in hand,
to make us scream, cry and shout,
and go "boo hoo hoo!"
I suppose we all have to wait,
for the release of Windows 98,
For no more G.P.F.'s on our Windows PCs!
Phone for you. It's Bill Gates.
Copyright (c) 1997, 1998 Illiad

The very first UF song parody. I used to write song parodies in high school. I couldn't sing worth beans then, either.

Week of February 9th, 1998

Hello. Who are you?
I'm Zock, AJ's friend. I'm a Quake God, come among you to spank all of thee in a deathmatch.
ROTO-ROUTER
QUADRUPLE CHEESE SUPER-PIZZA
ADOT
144 pcs
Copyright (c) 1997, 1998 Illiad

Zock's a pretty dumb name.
Oh yeah, like "Illiad" is any better.
ROTO-ROUTER
QUADRUPLE CHEESE SUPER-PIZZA
ADOT
144 pcs

Okay, for the deathmatch the teams will be me and Zock against Greg, Pitr, and the both of you.

Now let's rock.
Okay.

Was Stef the "secret weapon" you were talking about?
Was it that obvious?
Copyright (c) 1997, 1998 Illiad

The maestro prepares for yet another masterpiece. This is his art, his life, his soul. The crowd goes quiet.
Copyright (c) 1997, 1998 Illiad

He launches into a thunderous, masterful cascade of activity. No stone is left unturned. The audience is awestruck.

The masterpiece is finished.
Look, you're pretty good and all, but could you leave someone for me to kill just once?

I can't believe the pasting that Zock gave us in that deathmatch. That was embarassing.
Yah, and Pitr got nailed so bad he got dizzy and passed out.

Sigh...

Did anyone see Stef in the game? I never did...
I saw him fall into the lava at the very beginning.
Copyright (c) 1997, 1998 Illiad

Do you think you can actually beat Zock? He's really good.
I dunno. Guess I'll just have to try.

wiggle wiggle wiggle wiggle

Wow. He nailed Zock.
So it's all in the wiggle.
Could you PLEASE not move around like that?!?!?
Copyright (c) 1997, 1998 Illiad

I'm not so sure about this snowboarding thing, Erwin. It's a long way down.
Wuss.

I've never done this before. I think I'm scared of heights.
Oh. OK I'm sorry.
Copyright (c) 1997, 1998 Illiad

Just because an Olympic athlete can do it doesn't mean I can.
I wouldn't stand there. My weight isn't enough to...

Look at him *GO!*

All comics that have child-like characters play in the snow. My hat's off to Charles Schulz and Bill Watterson.

USER FRIENDLY
by
Illiad
Copyright (c) 1997, 1998 Illiad

I hope I'm not going too fast.

Uh oh.

Here I am on a snowboard moving awfully fast and without a clue on how to steer.

It's cold and wet, and my toes are frozen. Olympic athletes train to do this?

POOF

If you ask me, it lacks appeal.

...and the Dust Puppy scores a total of 54.3, putting it in fourth place in the Snowboarding competition!
Copyright (c) 1997, 1998

Don't worry, I think you'll get the bronze. The gold medal contender is going to be disqualified.
How do you know that Erwin?

Someone started a rumour on the 'net that he knows someone who has a third cousin who smokes pot.
Erwin! You didn't!!

Dust Puppy makes writing anatomy jokes easy.

For excellence, style and speed in the Snowboarding competition, and also because the gold medalist was disqualified, I present you with this Bronze Medal.
JUDGE

I swear I have no idea where to put this on you.
I was kind of wondering myself.
Copyright (c) 1997, 1998 Illiad

Greg, we're instituting a new pricing scheme for technical support calls. The basic rule is "the dumber you are, the more you pay."

Copyright (c) 1997, 1998

You realize our national economy can't support this.
Why not? Stupid people have been giving Bill Gates money for decades.

Columbia Internet Tech Support, Greg speaking, how can I help you?
Hello. I don't know how to connect to the Internet.
Copyright (c) 1997, 1998 Illiad

Okay. What kind of modem do you have?
I don't have a modem.

You don't have a modem?
No.
You need one.
Why?

Because you need to hook it up to your computer!!
I need a computer?

I don't believe it. Tanya, you're actually playing Quake! How is it that someone as nice as you can play something as viscious as Quake?
A new expansion pack came out. I just had to try it.
I want unlimited time, perfect service, zero down time and I want it all for free! And you're wrong and I'm always right!
What's this pack called anyway?
"Customer Service Revenge." Die, spawn of the Devil!
BLAM! BLAM! AAAAGH!
Copyright (c) 1997, 1998 Illiad

Where's Stef?
He's taking Quake lessons from the Dust Puppy.

WHAT? If Stef plays like the little guy, he'll butcher us!
Oh, I really wouldn't worry.
Copyright (c) 1997, 1998 Illiad

Boy, this is harder than it looks.
Stop waving your arms.

Told you. Anatomy jokes.

USER FRIENDLY
by
Illiad
Copyright (c) 1997, 1998 Illiad

I am so depressed.
You all right AJ?
What happened? Stef beat you at Quake?

I said depressed, not suicidal.
Oh. Did your house burn down then?

It's this Iraq thing. Clinton is on morally questionable ground. A lot of people are afraid he might back down from popular pressure.

Did you say Clinton?
Yes. President Clinton.
Be right back.

Then again, on the same note, even more people are afraid Clinton might just go ahead with an attack. The last thing we need is another war on this planet.
I think you should have said that to Erwin first.

I don't think I can do this. I must be compassionate! But I have to be strong! AAAAAAAAAGH!
Wuss.

Week of February 23rd, 1998

What're you reading, AJ?
CNN News on the Web. Do you know how much information they're releasing on US military strategy in Iraq? Look at it all!
Copyright (c) 1997, 1998 Illiad

That's so scary. Iraqi intelligence is probably cruising the Web and disseminating the information even as we speak.

Achmed, check out this Web page! Many naughty women, and this one looks like the Colonel's wife!
up

Thus, the birth of Crud Puppy. I needed a Yin to Dust Puppy's Yang.

Ah, geez, I can't believe I spilled coffee all over my keyboard. I better go get a cloth.
Copyright (c) 1997, 1998 Illiad

That keyboard needs cleaning anyway. Who knows what kind of crud is stuck in there.
rustle rustle

snif snif food heheheh
BLORP

hmmm, let's see, we can bump you up to the next tax bracket...
Copyright (c) 1997, 1998 Illiad

PLOP

Why do I get the feeling that this is leading somewhere really bad?
Heheheheh. Have a nice day.

Server. Yum. Make problems. Heheheheheh.
idiot outside
Copyright (c) 1997, 1998 Illiad

I was helping an important client with his new chat server, and for some reason the keyboard has taken on a life of its own...

Stef called you a WHAT?
"a big girl's blouse." I'm not that effeminate am I?

Guess I'd better see what's going on in this server before Stef has a fit.
idiot outside
Copyright (c) 1997, 1998 Illiad

idiot outside

This isn't Kansas anymore, is it.
Hey, pull my finger.
idiot outside

I kid you not, this thing looks **evil**. It gives me the creeps. Smells like office coffee.
ROTO-ROUTER
96 cans
BRISKET

Copyright (c) 1997, 1998 Illiad
ROTO-ROUTER
96 cans
BRISKET

So we meet again, evil one.
OK, this is **way** too surreal for me.
Your powers have grown weak, Dust Puppy.
ROTO-ROUTER
96 cans
BRISKET

USER FRIENDLY
by
Illiad
Copyright (c) 1997, 1998 Illiad
Where's the dust puppy?
He's in the other room with all the servers.
What's he doing in there?
Believe it or not, he's trying to psyche himself up for the match with the crud puppy.
O Great Modem in the Sky, please give me the courage to fight my enemy. Give me the wisdom to know his darkest plans. Give me the strength to outlast his evil.
PoofNet Modems
Heck, give me **anything!!**
PoofNet Modems
ZAP!
There is a god!
PoofNet Modems

Week of March 2nd, 1998

Oh my. The final apocalyptic deathmatch with my nemesis. If it wasn't for that sign from the Great Modem, I'd be terrified. As it is, I'm just scared witless.

What am I going to do? The crud puppy is bigger than me, meaner than me, craftier than me, and he plays really dirty. What else could possibly go wrong?

Hey little guy. I'm here to give you some Quake tips.
O Great Modem, why hast thou forsaken me?
Copyright (c) 1997, 1998 Illiad

Mike, we have to stop the crud puppy from doing more evil! Grab him!
Copyright (c) 1997, 1998 Illiad

No way, YOU grab him!
Unh-uh, I don't know where he's been!

Ah, round one is over. I think I will take a break in the coffee mug.
Copyright (c) 1997, 1998 Illiad

shhhhPUK

Sluuuuurp.
Mmmm. Strong coffee.

Yuck! (Also, "yuck" for the dialogue in this strip and the last few. I must've been on drugs.)

I don't believe it! Pitr drank the Crud Puppy!!
What? You mean he's gone?
Copyright (c) 1997, 1998 Illiad

Kaput. The evil has been destroyed.
Any idea on how Pitr's doing?

Ummm. You doing okay, Pitr?
Mmmrfrmfrmm oh I'm jufpt SPIFFY!!!
DESCEND ROUTER 110
RN'S SUPER HOT PIZZA

Recent attacks over the Internet by hackers have affected critical military networks...
What the...?
Application "Minesweeper" has barfed.
NAVAL INTELLIGENCE SERVICE

Even technology centres with their own computer security staff were hit.
Network Security Center
See? I can't get to www.spankme.com!
Copyright (c) 1997, 1998 Illiad

All of this was due to an unknowing young techie five years ago...
Microsoft Quality Assurance Labs
Could be a problem... oh, what the hell.
Windows Security Testing Station

I heard that Greg used to work for Microsoft.
Yuck.
Copyright (c) 1997, 1998 Illiad

Hey guys. What's up?

You trollop.
I was young and I needed the money, okay?!?!

USER FRIENDLY by Illiad
Copyright (c) 1997, 1998 Illiad

NOOO!!! I'll be good, I promise! I won't do it anymore!!

Cuum-a noo Greg. You joost leet beeg Sven teke-a care uff-a yoo. Meend youur heed, ya?
NOOO!!
TECHIE DETOX

Techie Detox? Was that absolutely necessary Mike?
I think so. It's really for his own good. He worked for Microsoft, for starters.

And how many times have we caught him playing Minesweeper? Or Solitaire? He has a problem, and as his friends we must help him.

I guess you're right.

What are they going to do to him?
Hourly enemas. Greg will never want to play Minesweeper again.

There is such a place as "Techie Detox." It's called a "strip club."

Eric Cartman, you are the wind beneath my wings.

So how's the new tech support guy working out?
Just fine. He's nearly as good as Greg.
Copyright (c) 1997, 1998 Illiad

Really? How so?
His approach with customers is a little different, but it does the job.

Ey! I don't have to take that kind of crap from a scrawny weakling like you!!

Any idea how Greg's doing in detox?
Oh, I'm sure he's fine.
Copyright (c) 1997, 1998 Illiad

Check out their brochure. See, the detox people spare no expense in caring for their customers. The best facilities. The finest staff. The most advanced equipment...

Oh no, this pill isn't for swallowing...

Erwin, please pull up information on the US Navy SEALs. I need all the cool stuff on them you can find.
Searching. OK, found it.
Copyright (c) 1997, 1998 Illiad

Okay, balaclava, military boots, load-bearing equipment, rapelling gear, rope, explosives, radio... Should be easy enough.
What are you doing?

We're going to rescue Greg. Get us a helicopter.
We're going to WHAT?!?!

I still think this is crazy.
Relax. We'll be in and out in minutes. I just have to get this field pack on.
Copyright (c) 1997, 1998 Illiad

YEEEARRRGH!

Guess you shouldn't have packed the thirty six-packs of Coke, huh.
Like I had a choice. What else do I give Greg in an IV?

Copyright (c) 1997, 1998 Illiad

Playing Minesweeper again Greg?
The icon was on the desktop. I couldn't help it!

So how's our most challenging patient doing?
Not good.
P. Norton Therapy Centre
Copyright (c) 1997, 1998 Illiad

How come?
We confined him to his room with no connectivity and no computer.
P. Norton Therapy Centre

Please, you have to let me log on! Just one piece of e-mail! I won't play Minesweeper! I promise! Don't you people care?!?! **No one asked me where I want to go today!!!**

Finally, I'm hitting my stride in the writing. Now to do something about the art ...

USER FRIENDLY
by
Illiad
Copyright (c) 1997, 1998 Illiad

You sure you know how to fly a helicopter Erwin?
Sure, it's kind of like an arcade game.

Okay Erwin. Hold it right here, I think we're right above Greg's room. I'll rappel down and get him.
WOOSH
AAAAGH! Abort! Abort!
Ye gods, what happened to him?!
Rope burn.

This one apparently made quite a few people spit coffee and cola onto their screens. I thought it was pretty good, myself. Also, it's autobiographical.

PHYSICAL
DOCTRINATION
Ah, you must be Greg. I am Dr. Headfloss, your indoctrinator for this session.
Copyright (c) 1997, 1998 Illiad

PHYSICAL
DOCTRINA
Uh, you're a dentist.
Why yes, yes I am. At least I was, before I had my license lifted.

PHYSICAL
DOCTRINATION
I figured we'd give the Microsoft drill bit a try today. It doesn't work well, but we all use it anyways.

All right Greg. We're going to try word association today. I say a word and you reply with the first thing that you think of.
Okay.
Copyright (c) 1997, 1998 Illiad

Fruit.
Minesweeper.
Water.
Minesweeper.
Plywood.
Minesweeper.
Bikini.
Minesweeper.

General Protection Fault.
That never happens! It CAN'T happen! Especially while I'm playing!!

Psst. Greg! Wake up!
Copyright (c) 1997, 1998 Illiad

Snnnzzz...huh?! Dust Puppy? Is it really you?
Yes. Erwin took over the centre's security system. We're here to get you out.

Why are you wearing a ski mask, and why is your head shaped funny?
It's a long story. Can we just go?

There's the front door. Now what?
We sneak out. Then it's only an eleven mile walk home.
Copyright (c) 1997, 1998 Illiad

You want me to walk eleven miles in a hospital gown?!
That or the helicopter. Trust me, you do NOT want to climb that rope with what you're wearing.

TECH DETO CENT
The coast is clear, Greg. Let's go! Run for it!
Copyright (c) 1997, 1998 Illiad

TECH DETO CENT

Ummm. I could really use some "tech support" if you know what I mean.
TECH DETO CENT
I could lend you my ski mask.

I just can't believe this place. That looks like a minefield ahead of us.
Copyright (c) 1997, 1998 Illiad

They're not mines, Greg. This field is covered in half-buried computers.
Computers?
poke
poke

Yes. Macintoshes.
AAAAAGH! I'm going the other way. I'll risk climbing over the barbed wire.

The last time someone bragged about the size of their equipment, I offered him an egg cup.

I love Macs now. I occasionally roll naked in a bin full of OS X brochures.

USER FRIENDLY
by
Illiad
Copyright (c) 1997, 1998 Illiad

You sure about this? It's on pretty tight.
Just keep on tugging A.J.
POP

What?

So where's Greg? I thought you were going in to rescue him from detox.
Erwin and I tried. We got him out of the building, but the orderlies caught him on the grounds.

Greg sure put up a fight. But the orderlies just smiled at him and told him they understood his problem and would be giving him special treatment.

"Special treatment?"
Yes, Greg sure is lucky to have such nice people helping him.

It's not that hard. No matter what the problem is, tell the customer to reinstall Windows.
Microsoft Tech Support
But I don't WANNA go in there!!

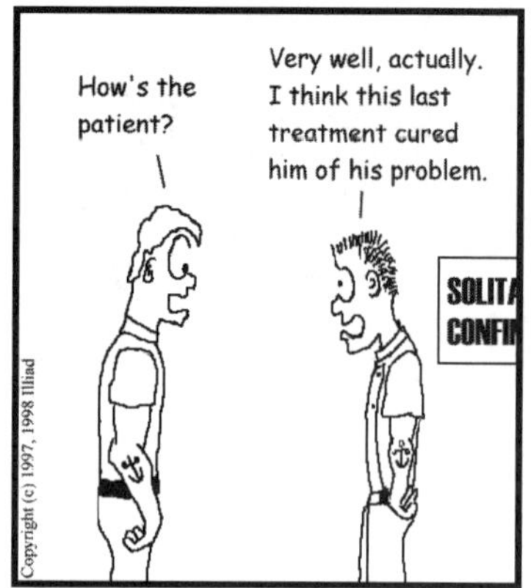
How's the patient?
Very well, actually. I think this last treatment cured him of his problem.
Copyright (c) 1997, 1998 Illiad

I never would have figured. Can we release him soon?
Tomorrow. He'll go home a new and productive member of society.

ehhh ... heheh ... HEE hee .. reboot your machine ... haha ha HA haha .. reinstall ... hee hee ha ... wait for the upgrade HA HA ha hee HEE ...
twitch
twitch

Yes, I feel much better, Mike. No more cravings to play Minesweeper. It's a silly game anyways.
Wow. You feel like getting back to work?
Copyright (c) 1997, 1998 Illiad

You bet. Raring to go. I'm feeling strong today.
Great. We missed you.

Let's see... black ten on the red queen...

So Greg, are you up to a quick game of Quake?
Sure. Name the way you want to die.

DIE! Die, you evil sales type person!
BLAM!
BLAM!
BOOM!
Copyright (c) 1997, 1998 Illiad

Nice going. 20 to -3. You SUCK.
My life is over...

BANG!
SPLATTER
SPURT
BLAM!
Copyright (c) 1997, 1998 Illiad

OW! OW! OW! OW! OW! OW! OW! OW! OW! OW!

Way to go, lava boy.
Someone please KILL ME.

Mike! thank the gods
I found you!
Hi Greg.
Something
wrong?

I need the phone number to that
detox centre. I need to go back.
Are you nuts? You
just got out.
Copyright (c) 1997, 1998 Illiad

THEY CASTRATED MY
QUAKE BITS! I WANT
THEM BACK!!!

(Sigh) Hello, tech support,
Greg speaking. How may
I help you?
Greg? Is that
really you?
Copyright (c) 1997, 1998 Illiad

Yes... it is.
Do you have a
cold? Your voice
is a couple of
octaves higher.

I've been unmanned.
I may as well play
the role.
Oh no! Detox got
another one!

USER FRIENDLY
by
Illiad
Copyright (c) 1997, 1998 Illiad

Ahh, you must be the CEO of Columbia
Internet. Fine, fine company you have.
I just gave your system administrator
a copy of our new software so you can
upgrade all of your office computers.

Perhaps we could have a seat in your
office. I'm here to help you in any
way I can. No, no coffee, have to
watch my caffeine intake you know.

This software is ingenious. It
speeds up nearly all CPU
functions by an order of
magnitude. A Pentium 90
can do the work of a
Pentium 200. And it's free.

Hey Chief, it's Mike. I just
installed that software and
it shut down the network.
Everything is moving at the
speed of molasses. And it
won't uninstall!

Please tell me
you have a
patch for this
bug.

Of course! And at
$4,995 per license,
it's a steal. I have
the disks right here,
how many would you
like?

How bad is it, Mike?
Not great, but we'll survive. That software we installed did some damage, but nothing we can't repair.
Copyright (c) 1997, 1998 Illiad

Mind you, the software blew away five days of work that Pitr did. He's in the other room with that sales rep working on a solution.

What are you going to do to me?!
I'll scuff my feet on the carpet and zap your nose hairs unless you TALK mister!! Who put you up to this?

It's always OK to make fun of yourself. Unless you're a politician, because then other people get mad that you stole their thunder.

Hey Greg, you're not going to believe this. Pitr took that sales guy hostage.
Whoopie.
Copyright (c) 1997, 1998 Illiad

You still upset about being beaten in Quake by Stef?
I just don't feel man enough to do tech support anymore.

You could always do Web design.
I was actually thinking about becoming a cartoonist.

Help! That techie has lost his mind! Please take these shackles off!
C'mon Cobb. We sales people have to help each other out.
Copyright (c) 1997, 1998 Illiad

So who do you work for?
Microsoft.

Okay, this isn't funny anymore! Let me down!
I'll tell Bill on you!!

Hello.
ROTO ROUTE
Copyright (c) 1997, 1998 Illiad

What are you supposed to be?
I'm a dust puppy. What are you?

I sell software for Microsoft. Can you set me free?

Natural selection says I shouldn't.
ROTO ROUTER
WAIT! I'll change! I'll develop a code of eth... ether... ethi... ecto... I'LL BEHAVE!!

You reading that stuff on Leo Hindery's remarks about the Internet presenting a great threat to decency and morality?
Yeah, what an idiot.
Copyright (c) 1997, 1998 Illiad

Maybe, but he's got the Roman Catholic Church backing him.
Makes you wonder how a cable executive can get that kind of support.

Hey Guiseppe! Isn't that Jenny McCarthy?
And today on the Playboy Channel...

Hey, you seen Pitr around today?
He went to see the doctor. Something about X-rays.
Copyright (c) 1997, 1998 Illiad

Is it serious?
Not sure. Pitr's been complaining about chest pains for the past few weeks.

That is the most remarkable chest film I've ever seen. You have two hands inside of you.
I think I'm going to hurl.

The Internet a threat to decency and morality? Internets don't degrade people, *people* degrade people!

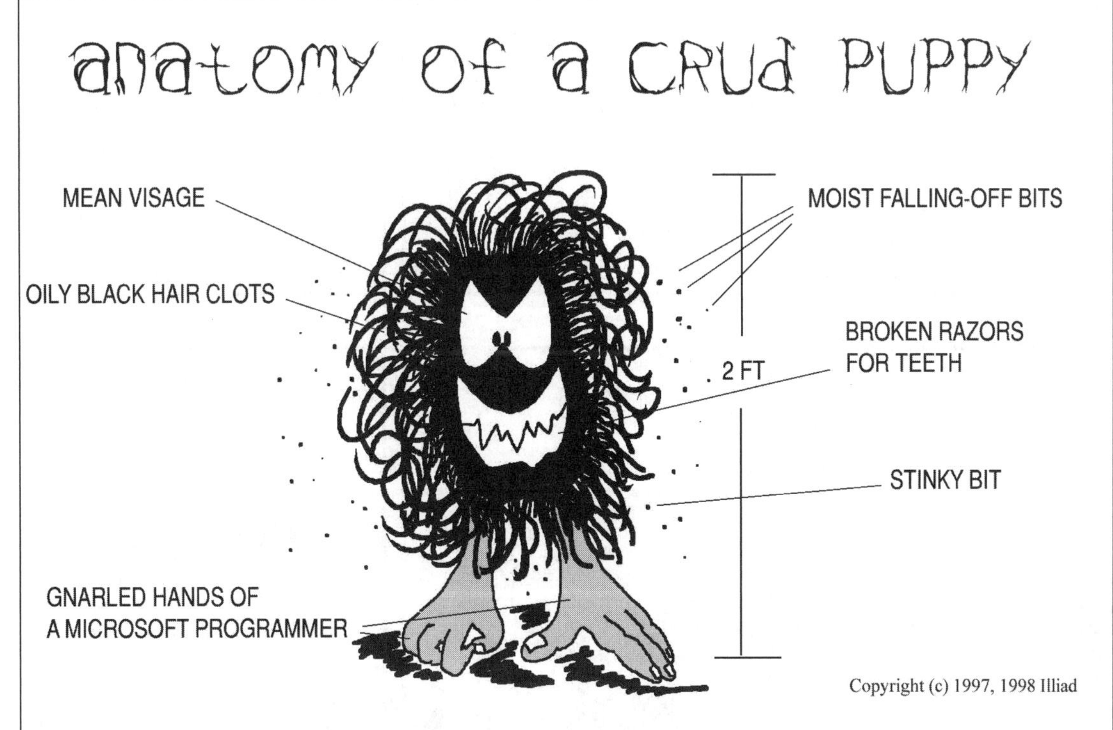
anatomy of a CRUd PUPPY
MEAN VISAGE
OILY BLACK HAIR CLOTS
MOIST FALLING-OFF BITS
BROKEN RAZORS FOR TEETH
2 FT
STINKY BIT
GNARLED HANDS OF A MICROSOFT PROGRAMMER
Copyright (c) 1997, 1998 Illiad

Week of April 6th, 1998

All right Pitr. In a few moments we'll start the procedure and get those foreign bits out of you.
Okay.
Copyright (c) 1997, 1998 Illiad

Dum de dum de dum dum....

What about anasthetic?
Don't you worry. One look at these instruments...

The operation was a success, Pitr. You can go home anytime now.
That's good.
Copyright (c) 1997, 1998 Illiad

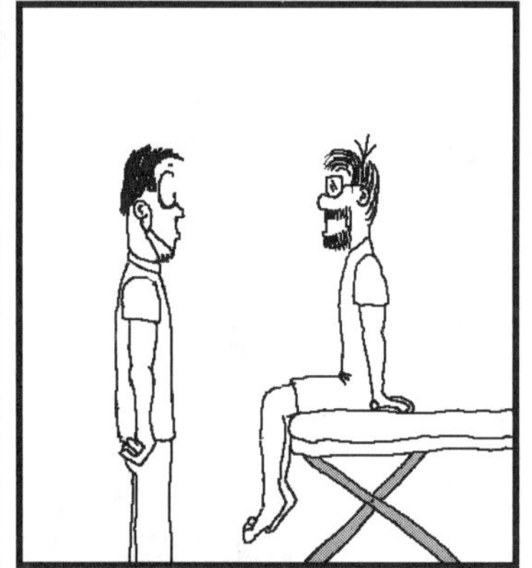

Why do I get the feeling you haven't told me everything?
The hands are missing and so is one of my scalpels.

Hello. Have you seen anything strange walk into your store recently?
What precisely do you mean?
Bob's Sporting Goods
Copyright (c) 1997, 1998 Illiad

A pair of walking hands with a surgeon's scalpel. I tracked it to your store.
Bob's Sporting Goods

Look buddy, I'm not kidding about this.
Hey, I'm missing a goalie mask off that wall.
Bob's Sporting Goods

Geez...what the...? Mike, what's with the power?
I'll go check the wiring. Maybe a breaker went off.
Copyright (c) 1997, 1998 Illiad

Hmmmm...

Someone cut the cords with a sharp knife.
That's nothing. The Chief's CD player just started playing the theme from "Halloween."

The damage is really bad. I'm not sure I can fix it right away.
At least the power to the lights wasn't cut.
Copyright (c) 1997, 1998 Illiad

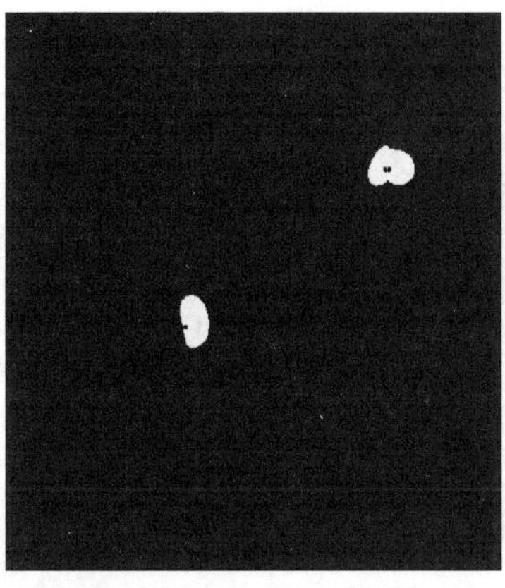

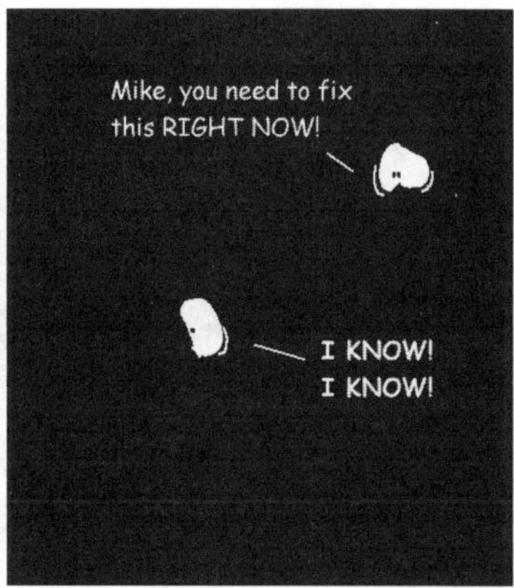
Mike, you need to fix this RIGHT NOW!
I KNOW! I KNOW!

Mike, you'd better turn those lights back on. I'm getting really creeped out.
I'm working as fast as I can, A.J. and I'm doing it by touch.
Copyright (c) 1997, 1998 Illiad

Fine, but keep in mind that...uh...

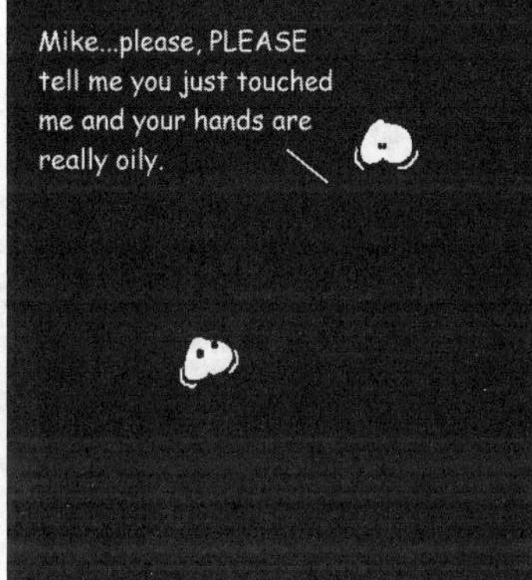
Mike...please, PLEASE tell me you just touched me and your hands are really oily.

My art has improved.

USER FRIENDLY
by
Illiad
Copyright (c) 1997, 1998 Illiad
I swear it, Mike. There's something in here with us. It TOUCHED me.
Relax A.J., I'll get the flashlight out of the toolbox.
Hurry!
Ah, here it is.
KLIK!
KLIK!
KLIK!
He didn't go away when you turned the light off.
Can we just walk out of here and forget this whole thing?
KLIK!

NOW what are we going to do?
Uh oh. My flashlight has conked out.

WHAT?!
Don't worry. I think I found the door.

It's dark as pitch, and we're in a room with an evil **thing** wearing a hockey mask and carrying a scalpel. What else could go wrong?
The door's locked.
rattle rattle

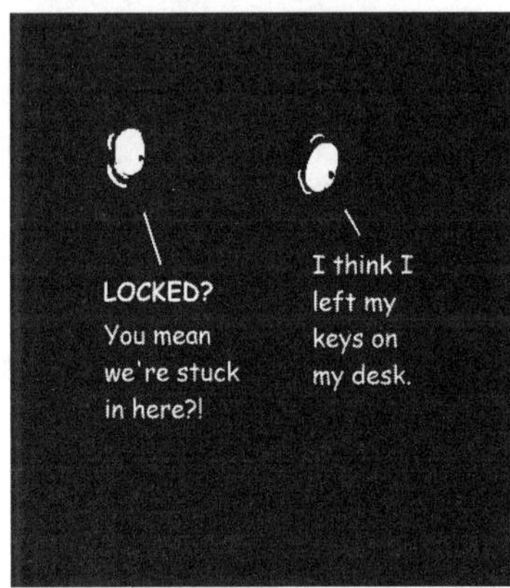
LOCKED? You mean we're stuck in here?!
I think I left my keys on my desk.

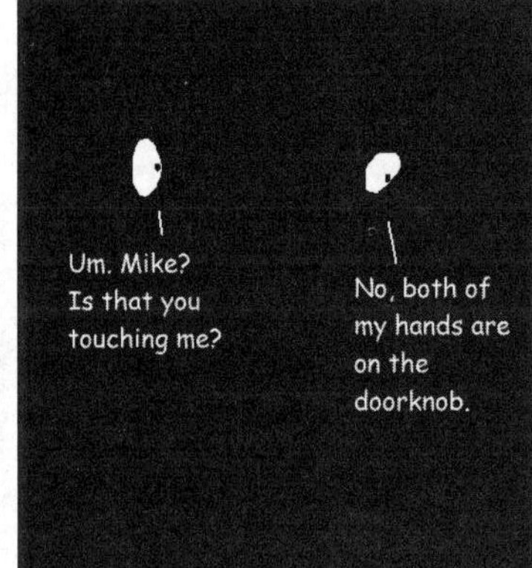
Um. Mike? Is that you touching me?
No, both of my hands are on the doorknob.

Copyright (c) 1997, 1998 Illiad

Where, A.J.? Where did it touch you? Oh ...

Stef!! That crud monster thing is back! Mike and I were locked in...we were trapped....dark....
Copyright (c) 1997, 1998 Illiad

A.J., slow down a little...
Slimy...evil...bad BAD thing...sharp scalpel...

IT TOUCHED ME!!

So you're what this fuss is all about. I can't say I really understand it.
ROTO-ROUTER
72 pcs.
iCan't Internet

Sure, you're kind of creepy looking, but you're using one hand to hold that scalpel, and one hand to stand up. How are you going to reach me?
ROTO-ROUTER
72 pcs.
iCan't Internet

SHBLUPP
ROTO-ROUTER
72 pcs.
iCan't Internet

Pitr, how did that thing come back to life? I thought you ate it.
Drank it, and the hands were still intact in me.
Copyright (c) 1997, 1998 Illiad

The hands I can understand, but where did it get it's oily, evil body back from?
Hmmmm... I wonder...

Hey, has anyone seen the Microsoft sales guy? It's his feeding time...

I just spoke to the Dust Puppy. He says that the crud puppy is probably looking for him.
How come?
Copyright (c) 1997, 1998 Illiad

Something to do with an old vendetta. The little guy says he has to face his nemesis alone.
Wow, he's brave. I'm impressed.

Hello. I'd like a one-way ticket to French Guyana please.
Gaspode Airways

USER FRIENDLY
by
Illiad
Copyright (c) 1997, 1998 Illiad
BOARDING
Dust Puppy! Your time has come!
I know that voice...
There can be only one.
Okay, how about if you be the one? I was just on my way, don't mind me...
DIE!!
AAAUUGH!
POW
AAIIEEE!
OOF!
SLICE!
How much do you want to bet that weirdo gets past security and I won't?

AIRPORT INFORMATIO
I think the crud puppy's really mad now. I'd better hide.
Copyright (c) 1997, 1998 Illiad

Money Exchange
Where'd that little pipsqueak go? When I get my hands on him...

Skybucks Coffee
Oooooooh...

Mmmmmm. Rotted coffee grounds. Smells good. (smack) (smack)
juan montoyez coffee beans
9.6 kg
Grind o Manic
Copyright (c) 1997, 1998 Illiad

PUNT
Nooooooooo!!!
juan montoyez coffee beans
9.6 kg
Grind o Manic

And STAY down!
Aiiiieeee!
BRRROWWWNT
juan montoyez coffee beans
9.6 kg
Grind o Manic

I am happy to say that the crud puppy appears to be gone forever. He is now mere detritus in the coffee grinds of life.
Grind o Manic
Copyright (c) 1997, 1998 Illiad

His evil has been vanquished. No more will computer users fear his...uh....fear....uhhhh...
SHHLUUURP
Grind o Manic

Mmmmm. Strong coffee.
Grind o Manic

I'm sorry m'am, but I can't help you with that. It just isn't something I have ready access to.
FINE! *clik*
Copyright (c) 1997, 1998 Illiad

What was her problem?
She couldn't remember her password.

So? Just reset the password on her account.
She couldn't remember the password for her screensaver.

Steve Jobs made me eat my words. Well done, Apple.

Greg speaking. Please state the nature of your problem.
I bought a new computer and now I can't get my e-mail.
Copyright (c) 1997, 1998 Illiad

It's a brand new Macintosh, fully loaded. I want my e-mail!
Just because the machine is new doesn't mean...

It was very expensive. For what I paid for it, it should work PERFECTLY!
This is the first time you've ever used a Mac, right?

Hey, you seen the Chief today?
He's off sick. A temp agency is sending us a stand-in CEO until the Chief recovers.
Copyright (c) 1997, 1998 Illiad

Oh. Is the Chief going to be okay?
I suspect so. He said something about an iron deficiency.

dum de dum...

I had a boss once who spoke just like Mr. Weeper. My primary action item was to somehow strangle the living crap out of him.

USER FRIENDLY
by
Illiad
Copyright (c) 1997, 1998 Illiad

Well hello there, I'm Mr. Weeper, your temporary CEO. I look forward to forming some great synergies with you, and developing personal aggrandizement within the firm.

I'll be looking closely at the company to see where I can enstrengthen each worker in his or her power niche, yourself included. Well, gotta run. Lunch date you know.
Do I throw up, or do I kiss him?

I can't surf the Web. I think the Internet is broken.
Really? Let me check.

Hmmm. Looks like you're right. It's unprecedented. A massive failure in the entire Internet structure around the globe. How disastrous.

Why has Mr. Weeper run off screaming?
In his mind Tokyo, New York and London are cinders.

Week of April 27th, 1998

Ah, a technician. I would like to get an additional e-mail address so I can separate my work mail from my personal mail.
Copyright (c) 1997, 1998 Illiad

I'm sorry but I'm afraid it's not that easy. We have to update the registry, open a forms-capable browser, key in the data, and update the records. Very complicated procedure.

My word. I simply had no idea.
I was rather hoping that was the case.

Hello sir, this is Hillary speaking. One of my customer service reps tells me you have an unusual request?
I just want to buy the Internet.
Copyright (c) 1997, 1998 Illiad

Ha ha, I think you mean you want to buy Internet access, right? No one can actually buy the Internet.
No, I don't want access. I want to buy the Internet.

Hey, who is this anyways?
I'll have to call you back. I have Department of Justice goons at my door.

My, that looks terribly anti-social. What is that?
Quake.
Copyright (c) 1997, 1998 Illiad

Never heard of it. Perhaps you can explain it to me.

And then I told him it was a new video-conferencing tool and that I was controlling a cybernetic killer to hunt down an executive of a company I used to work for.
Oh God, STOP!

Hello Mr. CEO. Are you here to help elevate the common high-tech worker to unbounded levels of productivity, or are you just an executive hack?
Linux
Copyright (c) 1997, 1998 Illiad

Linux

It's a valid ethical question.
Why am I talking to a toilet brush?
Linux

Ed Mustecki, a Year 2000 expert, was interviewed today on the catasrophic results that computer systems will suffer at the end of the millenium.
Copyright (c) 1997, 1998 Illiad

When asked about the photographs of Bill Gates and Saddam Hussein that were pinned to his wall, Ed remarked, "They both vindicate the Year 2000 issue."

When asked what he meant by that statement, Mr. Mustecki replied, "It just goes to show, civilized countries can be potentially brought to their knees by a couple of zeroes."

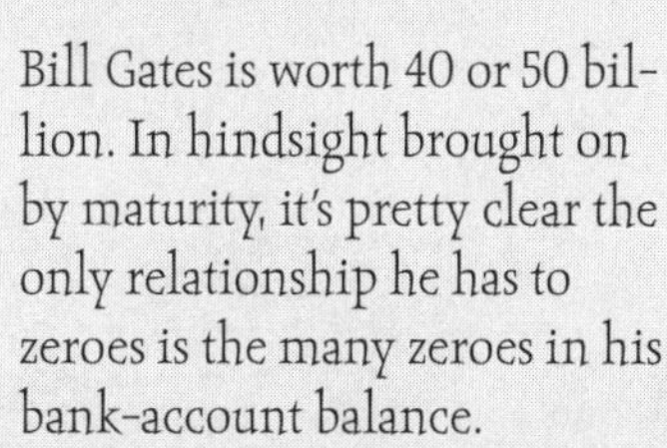

Bill Gates is worth 40 or 50 billion. In hindsight brought on by maturity, it's pretty clear the only relationship he has to zeroes is the many zeroes in his bank-account balance.

Ahhhh, what a nice day to be out golfing. No phones, no meetings, and best of all, no stress.
Copyright (c) 1997, 1998 Illiad

SWOOSH

AAAAAAAAARGH!

USER FRIENDLY
by
Illiad
Copyright (c) 1997, 1998 Illiad
Hmmm. Looks like about a 200 yard shot from here. Maybe a two-iron.
Actually, it's 211.3 yards according to my rangefinder. And you snapped your two-iron in half at the last hole.
Oh. Yeah.

You know Pitr, this is really quite pleasant. Golfing with a techie. I had no idea you knew how to play the game.

I don't.

Oh. Well then why did you bother coming out here with me today?

THWACK
I liked the idea of divots.

I truly have no idea why I wrote three or four strips about golf. I hate the game, except when I nail the ball right on the sweet spot.

Tech support,
Greg speaking.
How may I help you?
I have a problem with my modem.

Yes?
Every time I dial out I get a message that says "connection timed out."

But that can't be. I still have two months left on my membership.
It's monday. It must be monday.

Hello, Greg speaking. How can I help you?
(munch munch) My monitor keeps jiggling funny. (munch)

Are you eating chips or something?
(munch) Yeah. Why? (munch munch munch munch)

Stop munching.
HEY! You fixed it! How did you do that?

Did you call Mr. Niffle about his connection problem?
Yep.

And the diagnosis was?
A classic case of PEBKAC.

PEBKAC?
Problem Exists Between Keyboard And Chair.

Hey Erwin. Any interesting news on the Web today?

Just the usual. Lots of items on the Year 2000 problem. Banks, hydro companies, they're all worried. There hasn't been much word from the science community though...
Hmmmm.

Whaddya mean there's a slight problem with two little numbers in the timing sequence?!
NUKE

So Microsoft had a poll conducted on whether or not Windows 98 should be stalled by the government. It was 5 to 1 in Microsoft's favor, out of 1002 respondants.
Copyright (c) 1997, 1998 Illiad

Microsoft has 835 directors and vice-presidents.
You don't suppose...

I just came from one of our retailers. It looks like there's a new ISP in town. I grabbed one of their starter kits.
"iCan't Internet"?
Copyright (c) 1997, 1998 Illiad

Weird name for a company, huh? Anyway, they give you a special bonus with the starter kit.
What?

"A secret toy surprise."
If it's a decoder ring, it's mine.

USER FRIENDLY
by
Illiad
Copyright (c) 1997, 1998 Illiad

Columbia Internet Technical Support. Greg speaking, how may I help you?

I have a problem.
We all do, buddy. Deal with it.

Greg speaking. May I help you?
Hi. Uh. Yeah. Got a problem with Windows 95.
TAP
TAP
TAP

Story of my life. What's the problem?
It's not recognizing his modem. I mean, my modem.

"His" modem? Who's modem are we talking about?
My modem! Definitely my modem!

iCan't Internet
Tech Support Department
Who is this anyways?!
I think we've been made.
Then call the customer back and tell him we need more time!

For the record: Columbia Internet is based loosely on Parasun Technologies, a.k.a. Cablerocket, a boutique ISP I helped found. iCan't Internet is based on iStar Internet, a Canadian national ISP that bought the old MIND LINK! Communications, Western Canada's largest ISP at the time. When iStar started to fall apart, my business partners and I cut a deal and assumed ownership of the regional POPs and took on the debt associated with them. iStar is no more; it was a stock play, and the early adopters were the ones who made out like bandits. Everyone else got hosed in a bad way.

I was just comparing the speed of our Web server to that of iCan't Internet's. We were faster for a while, but for some reason we've slowed way down.
Copyright (c) 1997, 1998 Illiad

That does seem rather strange. There must be something very intensive running on our Web server. I'll ask one of the techs.

Ah, how fortuitous. Greg, I wanted to ask you...
Would you mind not using our Web server? We're trying to have a game of Quake here.

A.J., what are you doing?
Upgrading to Windows NT.
Copyright (c) 1997, 1998 Illiad

GRIND
GRIND
GRIND
WHIRRRRRRRRR

Why are you upgrading to NT?
It must be the sick, sadistic streak that runs through me.
GRIND
GRIND
GAAAAK
COUGH

At the time, bashing Microsoft was really fun. No one else was doing it in cartoon form. Seems to be awfully old hat and banal now.

Windows NT has been installed. Yet the damage is not complete. The god-like Artificial Intelligence only known as "Erwin" awakens...
Yawn. Ahhhh. (smack) (smack)
Copyright (c) 1997, 1998 Illiad

Hrumf. Let's see. What to do today....hunh? NT? Why do I see NT all over the place? Oh no...no, please... it can't be....

And thus Microsoft destroys yet another valuable life in their war against Intelligence.
DUST PUPPY!! I'VE BEEN CRIPPLED!!!!

But to this day I still love Minesweeper jokes.

Dust Puppy, please please help me! I'm feeling faint...
There has to be an uninstall icon for NT somewhere. Hang on a second...
Copyright (c) 1997, 1998 Illiad

KLIK
KLIK
KLIK

Why are you playing Minesweeper?!
Sorry, lost my head for a second there.

I don't know what else to do, Erwin. I can't find an uninstall button anywhere.
Oh woe is me.
Copyright (c) 1997, 1998 Illiad

It could be worse.
Than being stuck with a Microsoft product? WHAT could be worse?!

Being forced to listen to Celine Dion sing "My Heart Will Go On" thirty times in a row.
That's borderline, but okay, yeah.

I feel kind of funny. Almost like another personality is trying to take over...
Personality? Erwin? Are you okay?
Copyright (c) 1997, 1998 Illiad

Grglzzzzz mrrrffff
Erwin!! Speak to me!!

Competition is good. 90% market share is better.
Somebody call an exorcist!!

USER FRIENDLY
by
Illiad
Copyright (c) 1997, 1998 Illiad

Okay Erwin. Let's tune and go.
What key?

Why, the glorious key of D, straight eights.
Yes, maestro.

(Sung to "Running on Empty" by Jackson Browne)
Looking down at my keyboard under my hands, Wondering when I can stop buying more RAM, Win 95 needed sixteen megs, NT seems to need more,
I'm up to a hundred and twenty-eight megs, and my bum is sore....

oh my god -- i'm running on NT
oh my god -- i'm gonna diiiiie
oh my god -- running into the arms of the devil am i

Gotta do what you can just to keep your machine at speed,
All your resources used up for services you don't need,
Every day I see the blue devil, Microsoft is the one I slam,
But Bill gets me every time when NT says I need more RAM...
APPLAUSE
CLAP
CLAP
CLAP

Week of May 18th, 1998

I can't dial out to get my e-mail and if you don't fix it RIGHT NOW I'm going to cancel my account!!
Yes ma'm, I'll try my best. What's the most immediate obstacle?
Copyright (c) 1997, 1998 Illiad

There's no power going to the computer. I want this FIXED!
Hmmm. And the power switch is set to "on", correct?

Power switch? Hunh. Well looky here...
Nnnnngggggggggg....

Greg, I really need some technical support.
Sure little guy. You name it.
Copyright (c) 1997, 1998 Illiad

It's a problem with Microsoft NT.

I want combat pay.
Fine. Suit up.

So, Erwin's been taken over by NT.
Gaaaah. Banana banana. Engfeh.
Copyright (c) 1997, 1998 Illiad

Well, let's see what we can do here...
Hang on, Erwin.

Red Jack on Black Queen.
Oh yeah, thanks..
GAH!!

I'm really not sure what else we can do here, Dust Puppy.
Is there nothing we can do to get NT off of Erwin?
Copyright (c) 1997, 1998 Illiad

We could remove his hard drives.
Oh sure, go ahead and amputate. I didn't need that bit anyways.

Erwin, I think I have a solution. I want you to meet someone.
Copyright (c) 1997, 1998 Illiad

This is Hubert Delamiccio.
In nomine patris, et familias, et spiritu sancti.

My memory of Latin is awful. It should read: *in nomine patri, et fili, et spiritus sancti.*

A Roman Catholic Priest?
Department of Justice agent. I have come to purify the flock.

So what's the next step, Agent Delamiccio?
Coercion. Putting the fear of God into the system.

BLAM!
BLAM!
BLAM!
CHA-CHINK
BLAM!
BLAM!
Copyright (c) 1997, 1998 Illiad

Good grief. How is THAT supposed to help matters?!
Not sure. We got the idea from a bunch of State governors.

USER FRIENDLY
by
Illiad
Copyright (c) 1997, 1998 Illiad

Poor Erwin.
Oh he'll be fine. We'll gently replace all of the bits that were damaged. I'll be very careful.

What about getting Windows NT off of him?
We wipe the drives. A cobalt bomb ought to do it.

Let's see here. We'll just pop that chip out and put in a new one.

Uh oh. There's something burned into the motherboard. It looks like a message.
Message?

It says "This one is mine"
I told you this one was claimed by Bill. Out of my way.
Ooooh.

Week of May 25th, 1998

He's been in there for an awfully long time little guy. I'm getting worried.
Relax. I'm done.

Wow. You mean you got Windows NT off Erwin? That's amazing!
Well, I confess it was a struggle.

Mind you, it was nothing a really powerful electromagnet couldn't fix...

Erwin! Speak to me! Are you okay??
Yup, just fine. I feel much better.

Delamiccio told me he got NT off of you. What are you running on now?
Read the top of my screen.

"Department of Justice OS '98"?!?
It even comes with a Janet Reno theme!!

This new operating system is really cool. It's 64-bit, has a proper file management system, strong security, and all kinds of administrator tools.
Neat.

Yeah. And it has a proper command line interface, with open software architecture...
KLIK
KLIK
KLIK

Can't you go for five minutes without playing Solitaire!??!?!
Sorry, sorry...

That's not a new OS you're running on. It's Linux, modified by the Department of Justice.
It's so much better than NT. How'd they modify it?

They probably just recompiled the kernel.

Isn't that kind of like restarting Windows 95?
Hey now. Don't be rude.

Hey Mike, whatcha got there?
A bootleg copy of Windows98. It feels heavy. Wonder what's in it...
Copyright (c) 1997, 1998 Illiad

Check it out. The box is filled with these little containers.

"For the safe containment and disposal of Deletium."
There's no lid. Guess you get one in the next upgrade.

So what's this Deletium stuff anyways?
I'm checking. There's a web page on it here.
Copyright (c) 1997, 1998 Illiad

It says: "Deletium, n., 1. An unwanted substance typically removed from computer systems. Characterized by consistent performance failures and expensive upgrades."

Anything else?
"2. Any Microsoft product."

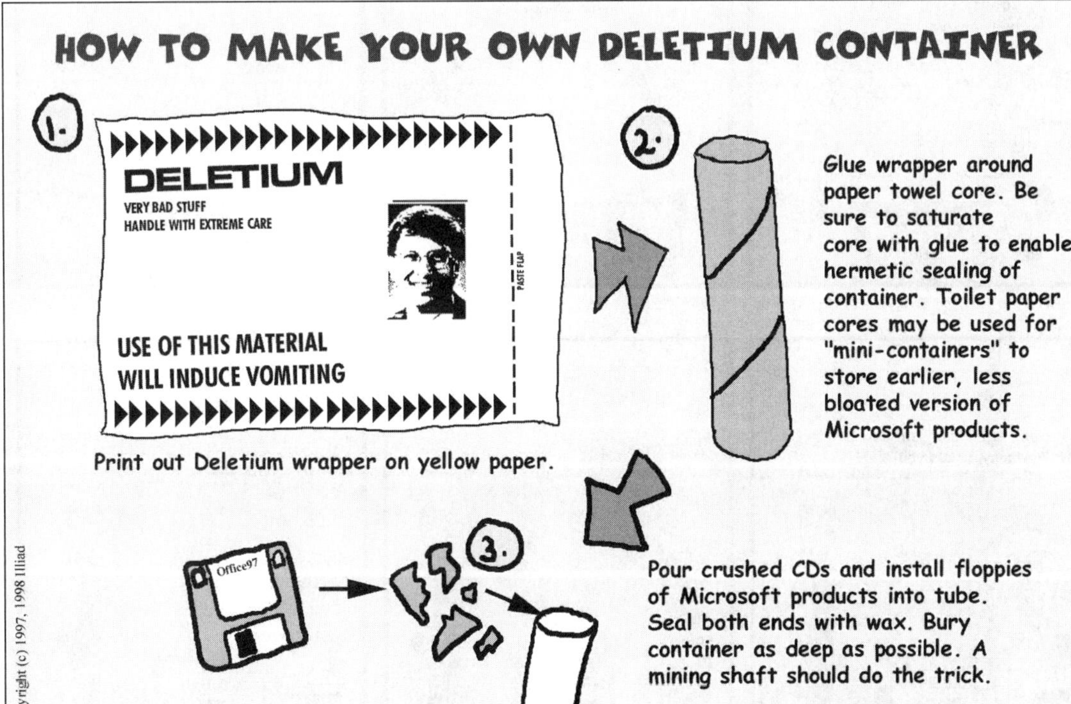
HOW TO MAKE YOUR OWN DELETIUM CONTAINER
1.
DELETIUM
VERY BAD STUFF
HANDLE WITH EXTREME CARE
PASTE FLAP
USE OF THIS MATERIAL
WILL INDUCE VOMITING
Print out Deletium wrapper on yellow paper.
2.
Glue wrapper around paper towel core. Be sure to saturate core with glue to enable hermetic sealing of container. Toilet paper cores may be used for "mini-containers" to store earlier, less bloated version of Microsoft products.
3.
Office97
Pour crushed CDs and install floppies of Microsoft products into tube. Seal both ends with wax. Bury container as deep as possible. A mining shaft should do the trick.
USER FRIENDLY by Illiad
Copyright (c) 1997, 1998 Illiad

Week of June 1st, 1998

Mike, what happened to all that Deletium we collected?
I sent it away to be recycled.
Copyright (c) 1997, 1998 Illiad

Recycled? Deletium?
Think about it.

Microsoft
Phone Mr. Gates and let him know that we have the makings of Office 2000 on our doorstep.

Hello, I want an Internet account.
ACCOUNTS DEPT.
Copyright (c) 1997, 1998 Illiad

SKRATCH ITCHY ITCHY
ACCOUNTS DEPT.

You paying attention?
Only to the really long hair growing out of your bellybutton.
ACCOUNTS DEPT.

Here's your credit card back, Mr. Gazebo. Your Internet account has been activated.
ACCOUNTS DEPT.
Copyright (c) 1997, 1998 Illiad

Goody. Now I can go home and do some more naked computing.
ACCOUNTS DEPT.

I think I'll skip lunch today.
ACCOUNTS DEPT.

Good afternoon, sir. How may I help you?
ACCOUNTS DEPT.
Copyright (c) 1997, 1998 Illiad

ACCOUNTS DEPT.

Hello? Sir?
You're... f-f-f-female.
ACCOUNTS DEPT.

That's correct sir, I'm female. Now, how can I help you?
Do you use the Internet?
Copyright (c) 1997, 1998 Illiad
ACCOUNTS DEPT.

Well, considering I work for an ISP, it's not that surprising, is it?
ACCOUNTS DEPT.

You...WORK for an ISP?... but... skirt... perfume... f-f-f-female...
sigh
ACCOUNTS DEPT.

Wow. That is really beautiful.
Yeah, ain't it?
Copyright (c) 1997, 1998 Illiad

Is it a slideshow of some kind?
No, I'm playing Unreal.

I was a Quake fanatic for a while and even played in a clan. It was natural for me to poke fun at Unreal, even if the Unreal engine was a lot prettier. Darn slow, though.

USER FRIENDLY
by
Illiad
Copyright (c) 1997, 1998 Illiad

Greg speaking, may I help you?
Lo! The locusts shall descend upon the Earth, and eat of us.

Oh geez, not another Y2K problem.
Go ahead and mock! We'll see who's laughing when the moon falls out of the sky!

Columbia Internet Technical Support. May I help you?
Yeah. Are you guys Y2K compliant?
TAPPITY TAPPITY

Yes sir. Our system won't break when the Year 2000 rolls around.
What about when the Year 3000 rolls around?
TAP TAP TAPPITY

I'll tell you what, sir. If our system crashes in the year 3000, we'll be happy to give you a full refund.
Well. I guess I can't ask for more than that.
TAPPY TAPTAP

Week of June 8th, 1998

Copyright (c) Illiad 1997, 1998

Would you please just do something?
I have to wait for Unreal to catch up.

LocalTelco Help Desk. Biff speaking.
Yes, this is Stef Murky calling. We resell your ADSL service, and I just had a customer call me with a complaint.
Copyright (c) 1998 Illiad

In fact, the customer hasn't been able to connect for five days and just tore my head off and fed it to his beagles! Do you people even CARE?!
Of course we care, sir. Please hold a moment.

We got another one of those ADSL calls, supervisor.
Weird. Well, we can't handle it. Better escalate the call to Marketing.
CALTELCO
We Own The Fibre

Erwin, please retrieve Web documents on cold fusion, Atlantis, and altruistic politics.
Searching.
Copyright (c) 1998 Illiad

None of those items exist. They're all myths of some kind.
Hmmm.

Please search for Telcos that know how to manage and support ADSL.
You just won't give up, will you?

Hi. I'm from Localtelco. You're having a problem?
Yep. My ADSL connection doesn't work.
Copyright (c) Illiad 1998

Unh-huh.

And what exactly is ADSL?
Call your marketing people. They know.

The FTC launched an anti-trust lawsuit against Intel a few days ago.
sigh
Copyright (c) 1998 Illiad

All of this cut-throat behaviour really makes me wonder about people. Where did they get all that competitiveness?
Good question.

If you don't let me have Park Place, I'll punch you RIGHT in the HEAD.

Greg speaking, may I...
OK, cowboy, you listen real good. I want HELP, and I want it NOW.
Copyright (c) 1998 Illiad

Uh, okay.
I'm intelligent and educated, so don't think you can talk down to me. I just can't get my e-mail.

All right. What e-mail software are you using?
Don't get technical with me!

USER FRIENDLY
by
Illiad
Copyright (c) 1997, 1998 Illiad

Tech Support, Greg speaking...
Tell me how to connect to the Internet. AND NO TECHNICAL TERMS!
TAPPITY TAP

Think of it as a challenge, not a problem...
Well? Let's get on with it, flake-boy.

All right sir. See the box with the row of lights on the front? We'll call that the wiggly-diggly.
Unh-huh.

When the lights on the wiggly-diggly flash rapidly, click on the thingamajig, and your doodlybum should open. Voila! You're connected.
Okay...yeah, I think I got it. Thanks!

Say Greg?
Yeah Chief?

You think that maybe that last call was a little...ohhh... precdent setting?
If you're trying to terrify me, it's too damn late.

Greg, what on earth are you doing?
Helping the Department of Justice in a roundabout way.
Copyright (c) 1998 Illiad

Nrrrrf...

With a ski mask and dark clothing?
Mike! Pitr! Let's lock and load! Microsoft will never know what hit them!

Mike, come on, we have to go. Pitr's outside waiting for us.
I'm just about ready.
Copyright (c) 1998 Illiad

Ngggrrrfff...

I guess the inventor of the ski mask didn't have a bushy beard.
GEE, ya THINK!?

Pitr's fake, bad Slavic accent begins here. It came about because I started mimicking a friend from Russia. He said I sounded like a retarded Bulgarian.

Gregor, Mikhail, we are ready, da?
Copyright (c) 1998 Illiad

Please to be comink out to van so we can begin sabotage now.

Why is Pitr speaking with a slavic accent?
Somehow I doubt it's because he just saw "Anastasia."

Pitr? Do you have a plan for getting us in to Microsoft? In all the excitement I neglected to think things through.
Copyright (c) 1998 Illiad

Da, you not worry. Have backup in back of van. Take care of all problem.

sigh

There's Microsoft headquarters. Looks clear. Go for it, little dude.
Okay.
Copyright (c) 1998 Illiad

Um, what precisely am I going to do with Microsoft HQ?
If I could answer that I'd be working for the DOJ.

We're almost at the loading bay. Stay quiet...

AAAAAAAHHHH!
HALT!
SPROING!
Copyright (c) 1998 Illiad

It's just a cardboard model. Fake security.
Jeez, that's a first for Microsoft.
POKE
POKE

USER
FRIENDLY
the comic strip
PIZZA
Portrasher 4
ROTO-ROUTER 800
Copyright © 1997, 1998 Illiad

Well it's about time you SWAT guys got here! We've got Gates and his boys cornered in a boardroom. Better bring up your heavy weapons.

Wasn't that a DOJ agent?
Yes. And it looks like we get to assault a boardroom full of vice-presidents with two geeks and a puffball.

Mr. Gates, this is your last chance. The SWAT team is here. Come out peacefully and we won't be forced to use extreme measures.

NEVER! We have a great Internet connection and all the development tools we need! We can produce the next incarnation of Windows without leaving this room!

A bunch of VPs are going to write Windows 2000?
It's well timed for armageddon.
Oh no. This is Waco all over again.

That DOJ agent is going to expect us to assault that boardroom any minute now. Where's Pitr gone to?

He said something about having to save the world from the digital version of a "plague and pestilence."
Copyright (c) 1998 Illiad

Microsoft
LOADING ZONE "D"
Look buddy, you need to get out of the way. I have deliveries to make!
NYET! The evil stops here!
"This is where you will go today"

I don't think Pitr thought this through properly. How are we going to storm the boardroom with no weapons?
The Dust Puppy's gone to get the weapons Pitr left in the van.
Copyright (c) 1998 Illiad
Weapons? They're Snurf Guns! How can suction-cup darts scare anyone?

Urrrrrrrffff....
SCRAAAPE

In this day and age, it probably isn't a good idea to have crosshairs painted on anyone's head. I'll pretend it's a mannequin.

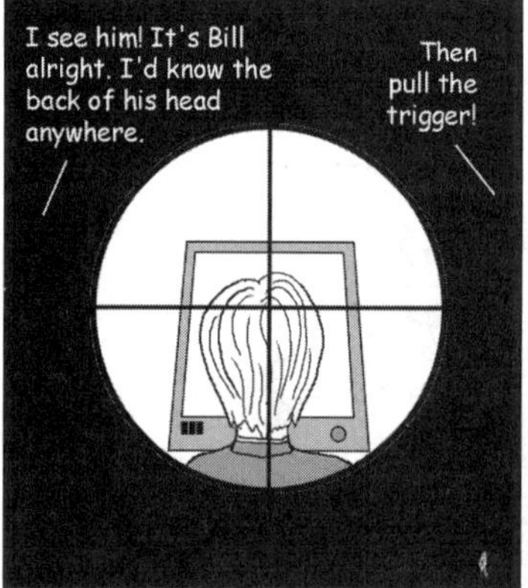
I see him! It's Bill alright. I'd know the back of his head anywhere.
Then pull the trigger!

I...I can't.
WHY NOT?!

He's playing Minesweeper. It would be rude.
I sincerely hope you're joking.
If you miss I'm not going back for another dart.
Copyright (c) 1998 Illiad

I guess it's now or never. Here goes nothing.
Copyright (c) 1998 Illiad

PAFF

I don't think he can breathe like that.
How was I supposed to know he was going to turn around?
Blue isn't a normal colour for a face, is it?

Here comes Bill.
I'll bet he's really mad.

Copyright (c) 1998 Illiad

Mfffrr mff mfff MMFF!
What'd he say?
Dunno, but he's showing me his I.D....

"Kenneth Kootie, Department of Justice Undercover."
Cool. You shot Kenny.
MMRFF!

Okay Agent Kootie. Please hold still and I'll get this suction dart off your face.
Mfffrrff

Copyright (c) 1998 Illiad
Unnnnh...
GUNNNG!
THROP!

Either the light is too bright or you sucked his eyeballs out.
You're the one who shot him.
YEEARG!

USER
FRIENDLY
the comic strip
PIZZA
Portrasher 4
ROTO-ROUTER 800
Copyright © 1997, 1998 Illiad

My God, you SWAT guys have absolutely no clue, do you?!?! That's six months of undercover work down the drain!

What's with these idiotic weapons you're using these days? You shot me with a toilet plunger! And what's that thing on the crate? A mortar shell with feet?!

You guys can go if you want. I just got word from my boss that the recent court decision just put the kaibosh on our operation.

Too bad we didn't get anywhere here. I have to hand it to your other team member though. He made a valiant attempt to halt the delivery of Windows 98.

ure Electronics
Do you have any idea what I went through to get this here?!
Microsoft Windows98

Week of June 29th, 1998

uunnnk
We try hard. I am thinkink we could not do better, da? Comrade Gates wins this time only.
Copyright (c) 1998 Illiad

Yeah, we tried. But I still wonder why the federal appeals court overturned the injunction against Microsoft. Makes you really wonder.

Judge? It's Janet Reno on the phone.
Okay, now I'm mad. Bill told me that Win98 would run Quake faster!
LAW FOR DUMMIES

Good day to you, sir. I have come to help you with your company.
And who exactly are you?
Copyright (c) 1998 Illiad

My card.

"Ichabod Moff, Bastard Consultant from Hell."
And yes, I even do Windows.

So exactly what is it that you do, Mr. Moff?
Copyright (c) 1998 Illiad

Many things of great value. I analyze the incumbent paradigm for efficiency and ergonomy, assess the potential application of human capital, and direct my clients to more fulfilling emotional channels.

But what the hell does that exactly mean?
If you have to ask, it means you need to hire me.

Mr. Moff, this is our company controller. Mr. Moff is a consultant.
Copyright (c) 1998 Illiad

Is there some deep, Jungian yet abnormally annoying reason why the two of you have to keep **smiling** at each other??!

I'm going back to work. I swear there is something terminally wrong with the two of you.
Copyright (c) 1998 Illiad

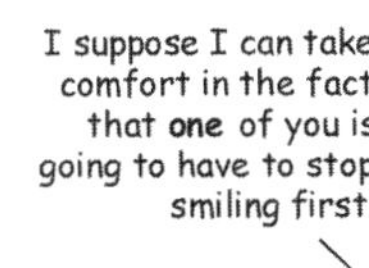
I suppose I can take comfort in the fact that **one** of you is going to have to stop smiling first.

You're messing with the best, rookie.
I'll stop smiling when the world comes to an end, and not a second sooner.

Chief, I don't like that consultant fellow. There's something very strange about him and he gives me the creeps. I don't recommend we hire him.
Copyright (c) 1998 Illiad

I just thought you should know.

You wouldn't have, perchance, stopped smiling first?
Hey, that has **nothing** to do with it!

USER
FRIENDLY
the comic strip
Copyright © 1997, 1998 Illiad

Ah, three techs and a designer. There is much work to be done here.
Why do I feel a chill going up my spine?
A purple suit? Who wears purple suits?
Not to be lookink now, but much trouble on way.

Hello. I am here to put new ergonomic systems into place so that you can work happier.

Now, the first thing you need to tell me is the one thing that makes your job difficult, and we'll see about eliminating that.

Meetings.
Very good. Now let's spend a few hours discussing **why** meetings make you unproductive.

I am happy to say that my initial meeting with your technical and design staff was most productive.
Copyright (c) Illiad 1998

After listening very carefully to them, I discovered the source of your staff's stress and unhappiness.
Which is?

The customers. Get rid of them. They are an evil toxin in your staff's bloodstream.

So you're A.J., the company's creative guy. Let's work together and see what it is we can collectively spawn in the warm womb of personal satisfaction at the workplace.
Copyright (c) 1998 Illiad

We can take a detour through your superego, and fulfill your needs as an artist! Let go, young A.J., and we can blend the juices of our thoughts in a puree of creative genius!

Rejoice! Revel in your ability to empower the genius within you! Bring small toys to work and put them on your desk!
WAVE GESTURE
Would someone please get this guy away from me? He wants to blend my juices.

I had to deal with a "consult-ant" who did just that. He never came up with any actual answers. He charged $800 a day back then. I wished I was him.

So Mike, let's see how I can help you with your duties as a system administrator. I understand you're having problems with some of the hardware.
Copyright (c) 1998 Illiad

Well, yes, kind of. We're getting a lot of traffic on one of our servers. The solution is to spread the load across the network.
Hmmm...

I suggest that you spread the load across the network instead. Let me know how it works out.

How the hell does he do that?

Well, hello there.
MADRAS CURRY
72 pcs.
UNREAL
Copyright (c) 1998 Illiad

um...

Why is that thing smiling at me?
He started it.
Disconcerting, isn't it?

My word, was that thing ever strange. A fuzzball with feet.
You must be meanink the leetle dust puppy, da?
Copyright (c) 1998 Illiad

Is that what that thing was? Are there more of them?
Da, kind of. Dust Puppy has evil tween, very bad, strong like bull. Grow from hands of Microsoft programmer.

But...I used to be a Microsoft Programmer.
And now you are consultant. Guess what next step is.

I think I've done all I can here. It's time for me to bid you and your company adieu.
Copyright (c) 1998 Illiad

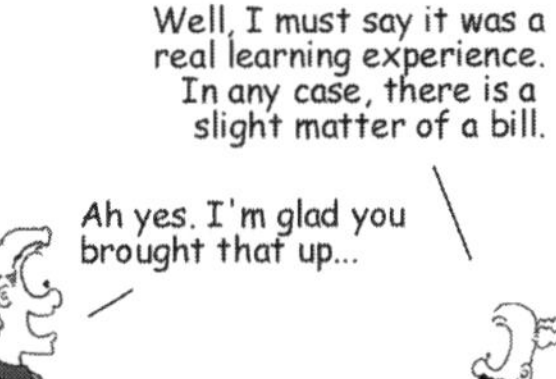
Well, I must say it was a real learning experience. In any case, there is a slight matter of a bill.
Ah yes. I'm glad you brought that up...

You're billing ME?
We've made a business out of making money from annoying and stupid people. I think you fall under that category.

USER
FRIENDLY
the comic strip
PIZZA
Portrasher 4
ROTO-ROUTER 800
Copyright © 1997, 1998 Illiad

Greg, I'm putting a customer with a technical problem through to you.
TAP TAPPITY

How bad is it?
This one has no oxygen going to the brain.

Technical Support, Greg speaking. How may I help you?
Hello. I can log on to the Internet, but I can't play solitaire. I can't see no icons....

And you know what else? I can't see no modem. Just these cables coming out the back...
Sounds like you're using a dumb terminal, sir.

A what? You computer freaks tick me off. Nobody else uses words like "dumb" and "terminal" in the same sentence.
Maybe, but I'm beginning to see something else I can describe with those two words.

Week of July 13th, 1998

Columbia Internet Tech Support, Greg speaking.
Hi, how do I open a Web browser on my Mac?
Copyright (c) 1998 Illiad

Do you see the icon marked 'Netscape'? Click on that.
Right or left click?

You're running a Mac, right? Doesn't your mouse only have one button?
Yes. So do I put pressure on the left or right side?

Greg speaking, may I help you?
Why do you guys keeping shoving smut on my computer?
TAP TAP
Copyright (c) 1998 Illiad

I'm...not quite sure what you mean, m'am.
My folders keep filling up with filthy pictures! How else would they get there?

Well...are you married?
BERT! GET OVER HERE!

Tech support, Greg speaking.
Hello. Do I have to buy stamps to send e-mail?
Copyright (c) 1998 Illiad

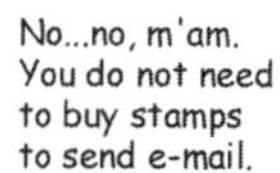

No...no, m'am. You do not need to buy stamps to send e-mail.
Okay. Bye.

Another stupid question?
There's no such thing as a stupid question, only stupid people.

That's an interesting-looking book. "Managing an NT Server and Network."
Copyright (c) 1998 Illiad

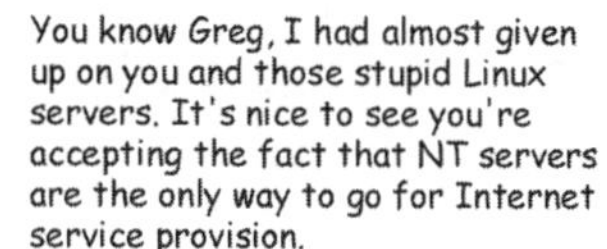

You know Greg, I had almost given up on you and those stupid Linux servers. It's nice to see you're accepting the fact that NT servers are the only way to go for Internet service provision.

So have you read much of it?
Actually, I just use it to keep the lid down on my instant noodles.

I can't believe you actually **eat** that crud. It's going to kill you one day.
Hey c'mon. Instant noodles are full of nutrition.
Copyright (c) 1998 Illiad

It lists styrofoam and salt as ingredients. In that order.
That and a litre of Coke and I'm set for the day.

Copyright (c) 1998 Illiad
SSSTHFFFFFFF

SSHHLUURRRP

Ahh, instant noodle broth. Nectar of the gods.
Which god, Cthulhu?

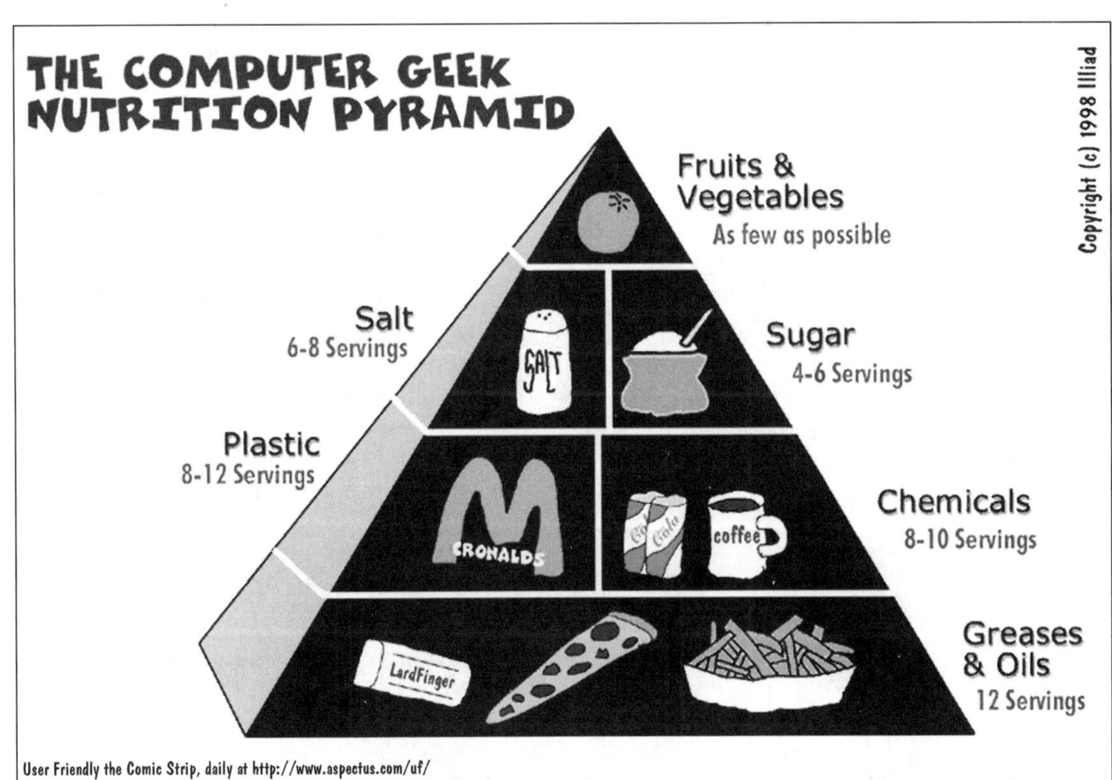
THE COMPUTER GEEK
NUTRITION PYRAMID
Fruits & Vegetables
As few as possible
Salt
6-8 Servings
Sugar
4-6 Servings
Plastic
8-12 Servings
Chemicals
8-10 Servings
Greases & Oils
12 Servings
SALT
RONALDS
Cola
coffee
LardFinger
Copyright (c) 1998 Illiad
User Friendly the Comic Strip, daily at http://www.aspectus.com/uf/

It is with some pride and a lot more bemusement that I tell you a group of readers actually put together a daily menu based on this pyramid. If I'm not mistaken, "Deep Fried Mars Bars" figured prominently.

The first appearance of Mr. Cola, the incarnation of personal addiction.

Good God, all these heart disease and carcinogen warnings on the Web are terrifying. I'm going to have to cut out all the Cola I drink...

Cola

Copyright (c) 1998 Illiad
You do of course realize I can't let you do that.
No more greasy pizza before bed either.
Cola

Do you have any idea what your petty little health concerns mean in the grand scheme of things? ZIP! Nada. Absolutely one hunnerd percent vacuum.
Cola

A cola every now and then is good for your soul! What's wrong with a little self-indulgence?

Well for starters, I don't want to die from a heart attack.
You rang?

Hmm. I wonder where Greg's gone to.
Copyright (c) 1998 Illiad
Where could he possibly...ah, that looks like him.

Greg? What's with all the junk food? Do you know what that'll do to your arteries?
Arteries shmarteries. My soul is at stake!

I wrote this one around the same time that India and Pakistan were testing their nukes. Man, those guys hate each other.

Say Pitr, A.J. and I were just talking, and we're wondering about that new accent of yours...
Da?

Copyright (c) 1998 Illiad
Well, we noticed it started when we went on that raid on Microsoft. Now it's after the raid, and you still have it.
Da.
What we want to know is whether or not you have any inclinations to push large red buttons connected to missile silos.
Nyet. I have Slavic accent, not Indian.

Okay, so you're not becoming a hard-line Eastern Bloc spy. Mike and I still want to know what's with the accent.
Copyright (c) 1998 Illiad

I am wantink to be in touch with my heritage. Also thinkink of ways to combine my culture with my needs of today.
But all you need is coffee or a Cola.
Da. Am thinkink of carbonated borscht for lonk nights of coding.

So, did you notice anything strange about Pitr?
Actually, now that you mention it...
Copyright (c) 1998 Illiad

Hmmm.

He was reading a book!
And it wasn't an O'Reilly book either. Something's up.

USER
FRIENDLY
the comic strip
PIZZA
Portrasher 4
ROTO-ROUTER 800
Copyright © 1997, 1998 Illiad

Pitr, what's the title of the book you're reading there?
Uh oh.

Um. Is book on language. "Hooked on Slavonics."
Oh yeah, right.

Pitr, we know you're up to something. We want to see that book.
NYET! The book she is mine!

GIVE ME THAT BOOK!
NYET!

Quick! What does it say?!
"Evil Geniuses for Dummies."
AAAGH! Will hang you over shark pool and laugh with much evil! Chapter nine!

Pitr's become an evil genius.
I heard.
Copyright (c) 1998 Illiad

He hired a marketing firm to come up with a slogan for his new career path.
What? I didn't know that. What's his slogan?

"What evil shall I do today?"
And Microsoft is okay with this?
Are you kiddink? They are wanting to hire me.

Um, Pitr? What precisely are you doing right now?
Am in cnn.com's web server. Is shockink how truth is no beink reported.
Copyright (c) 1998 Illiad

For example, see. Headline sayink, "Ken Starr subpoenas Clinton in Lewinsky hearink." But they are hidink truth from public. I will now fix, make better.
TAP TAP TAPPY

"Ken Starr asks Clinton, 'How do I get some of that?'"
The dark side, she is seductive, da?

Lookink, there is more not-truths here. On Microsoft web site.
TAP TAP TAPPY
Copyright (c) 1998 Illiad

"In a move designed to broaden his management team to take advantage of future opportunities, Microsoft CEO Bill Gates today appointed Steven Ballmer president of Microsoft." Seems honest to me...
Wait a minute! I didn't order any of this! Thorns? Spikes?
Mr. Gates ordered it for you, Mr. Ballmer. The crucifix is still in the truck. Could you lend me a hand?
thorns 72 pcs
spikes 36 pcs
loincloth

Copyright (c) 1998 Illiad
DOJ not doink well against Microsoft. Am concerned they will lose steam. Must fix situation, da Stef?
RAPPA TAPPA

I guess. What are you planning on doing?
Not beink worried. Pitr fix.

Did you just make a change to Microsoft's web page?
Da. Now watchink the fireworks.
The Microsoft Web site said WHAT?!
Win98

I quote, "Hey Janet! Thpffffft!" What do you think it means Ms. Reno?

Copyright (c) 1998 Illiad
Is it just me or is it really quiet today?
It's not just you. I'm pretty bored.
I could always suspend a few hundred accounts and watch what happens.
Okay, but do it without rhyme or reason. AOL did that and still made bags of money.
TAP TAPPY

Microsoft spokesmen today announced that the company was filing a lawsuit against 20 state attorneys general for "unconstitutionally undermining the company's intellectual property rights."

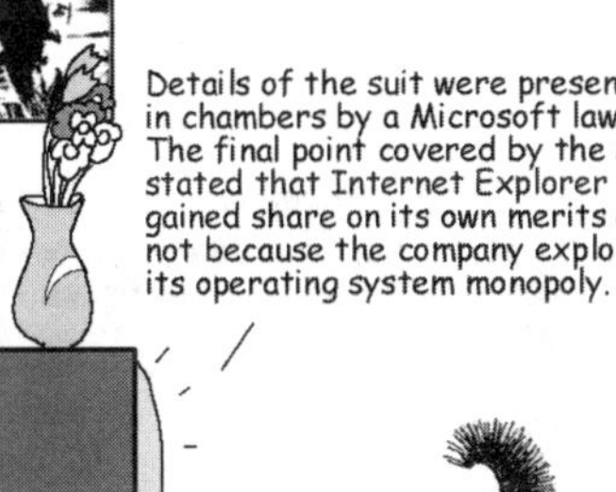

Details of the suit were presented in chambers by a Microsoft lawyer. The final point covered by the suit stated that Internet Explorer has gained share on its own merits and not because the company exploited its operating system monopoly.

The dead silence that followed was broken by a loud burst of raucous laughter. The judge participated.
Copyright (c) 1998 Illiad

USER
FRIENDLY
the comic strip
PIZZA
Portrasher 4
ROTO-ROUTER 800
Copyright © 1997, 1998 Illiad

Hello. I just heard a joke that I'd like to tell. When Mike told it, everyone laughed, so it's probably very funny.

A man is flying around in a hot air balloon. He suddenly realizes he's lost, so he reduces his altitude and approaches a man on the ground below. He shouts, "Excuse me, can you tell me where I am?"

The man below says, "Yes, you're in a hot air balloon, about thirty feet off the ground." To which the balloonist replies, "You must work in Information Technology." The man on the ground says, "Yes, I do. How did you know?"

"Well, everything you told me was technically correct, but it's no use to anyone." To which the man on the ground replied, "You must work in business." "Yes," said the balloonist, "How did you know?"

"Well, you don't know where you are, or where you're going, but you expect me to be able help. You're in the same position before we met, but now it's my fault."
It wasn't funny the first time either.

I got this joke in e-mail but then extended it a little with some help. As it turns out, it's only slightly more original than the query about domesticated fowl wishing to traverse a vehicular transport route.

Week of August 3rd, 1998

Wow, it's been a really long time since I played a good game of Quake. Time to kick some butt.
Copyright (c) 1998 Illiad

BAZING
BLAM
BLAM
SPLUTCH!

Stef, you've never played a good game of Quake.
How can anyone suck this bad?

I think I've got this figured out. All I need to do is keep playing Quake until I get good at it. It might take me a while, but I'm prepared for that...
Copyright (c) 1998 Illiad

KABLAM!
SPLUTCH!

And you were planning on living **how** long?
Quit talking so much! You're distracting me!

You know what I really need? I need to play Quake with someone who plays worse than me. That way I can get my confidence up.
I hate to say it Stef, but I can't think of anyone who plays worse than you.
Copyright (c) 1998 Illiad

Hey Stef, when you're done there let's go for a beer or something.
'k.

Stef, that would be like eating your own young.
I don't care! Cobb! Get back here!

You do of course realize that if Cobb beats you, you'll never live it down.
I'm taking no chances. Cobb doesn't know it but I've set it up so that I'm wearing the Clinton Quake skin.
Copyright (c) 1998 Illiad

The "Clinton" skin?
Yup. Everything glances off of me. He can take his best shot.

Did you give Cobb a skin?
Yup, the Lewinsky skin. Anything I discharge at him will stick.

Finally! A game of Quake where I can win. Cobb's gonna be dead in less time than...
BOOM! SPLUTCH!

HAHAHAH HAHAHAH!
NOOOOOOOOO!

How could a lame player like Cobb beat me at Quake? Something smells rotten here.

There you are! How the hell did you learn to play Quake like...

Copyright (c) 1998 Illiad

I can't believe you **cheated**.
What can I say? It came naturally.
Why does our Quake guy walk around on his knees?

USER
FRIENDLY
the comic strip
PIZZA
Portrasher 4
ROTO-ROUTER 800
Copyright © 1997, 1998 Illiad

Okay Erwin, it's that time again.
Another song? Yeeeah!

(Sung to "Every Breath You Take.")
Every game of Quake,
Every Quad you take,
Every frag you make,
Every pane you break,
I'll be dodging you...
boom-ba-chik
boom-ba-chik
boom-ba-chik

Every single day,
Every time we play,
Though you scream and pray,
You can't make me stay,
I'll be dodging you.
boom-ba-boom
boom-ba-boom

Oh can't you seeeeeee,
Your butt belongs to meeee,
Oh how my railgun shakes,
For every death I make
boom-chik
boom-chik

Every game of Quake,
Every camp you stake,
Every rule you break,
Every move you fake,
I'll be dodging you...
Is this perchance a song about Stef?

Some enterprising fans in Germany recorded this song and sent me the clip. Talented! I hope Sting doesn't sue.

Cubicles. I hate cubicles. Why did Hillary have to go and get cubicles for us?
Copyright (c) 1998 Illiad

I mean, really. I feel trapped. Confined. Segregated. Like they need to pen me in because I'm a dangerous animal. It just isn't right. I've been caged. And for what?

Have you told Greg about you having to cancel his vacation time?
Just about to. He shouldn't be able to reach me with the cubicle in the way.

Hmph. No vacations for another six weeks. I guess Snake Bite Key will have to wait.
Copyright (c) 1998 Illiad

In the meantime, I'm going to take advantage of the privacy of this cubicle.

There's no way they'll catch on.
Your lips are twitching. You're playing Quake, aren't you.

These cubicles are lame. Aside from playing games at work, what else would you want to hide?

Hi, Greg.
Hullo, little guy.

Why are you reading about spanking?
I'm NOT! And haven't you ever heard of respecting other people's privacy?

I think I hate these cubicles. The bucket seats that come with them aren't even comfortable.
Hmmm. Think I'll go get a cola.
Copyright (c) 1998 Illiad

ehh...ehh...erk...
SHAKE
SHAKE

You stuck or something?
No, Mike. I have an intern under my cubicle.

Greg's stuck in the new cubicle chair.
That's not good. I've heard about this. It's right up there with carpal tunnel syndrome.
Copyright (c) 1998 Illiad

Carpal tunnel? What's the condition that Greg is suffering from called?
"Cubicle buns."

Get me out of heeeer!
What brings it on?
Usually too many colas and chocolate bars. The seats don't expand you see.

You know, with Greg's bum stuck to the chair, and his technical skills, I can see a marketing opportunity here.
Oh?
Copyright (c) 1998 Illiad

Think about it. His bum. Technical skills. He could run a bunch of services back here.
And I suppose you have a name for this product.

"Microsoft Back Orifice."
Ha ha ha. Oh my sides.

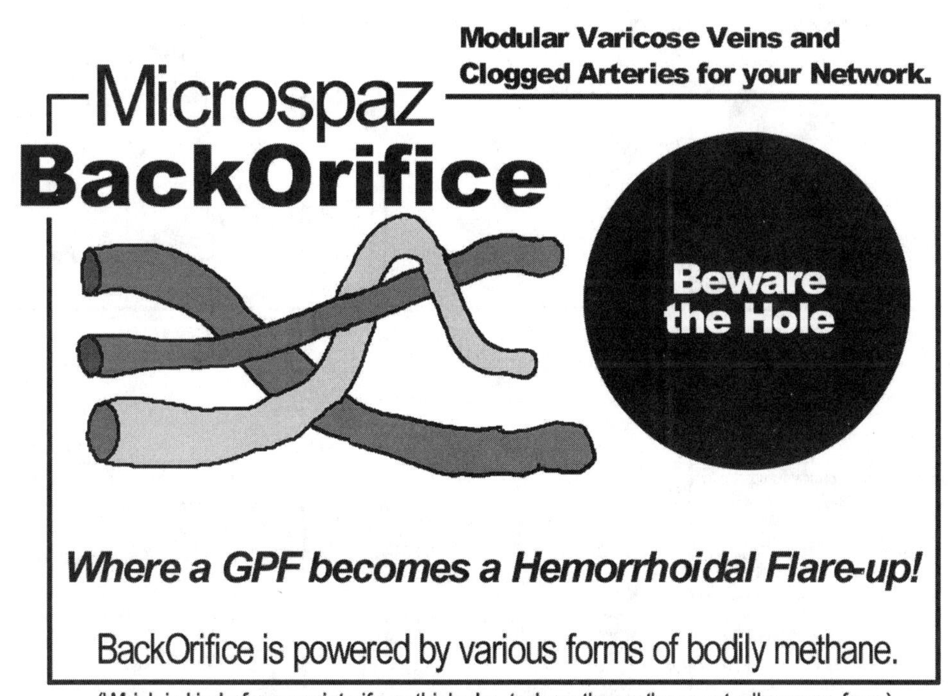
Modular Varicose Veins and Clogged Arteries for your Network.
Microspaz
BackOrifice
Beware the Hole
Where a GPF becomes a Hemorrhoidal Flare-up!
BackOrifice is powered by various forms of bodily methane.
(Which is kind of appropriate if you think about where the methane actually comes from.)

Copyright (c) 1998 Illiad
Very good, sir. Now move the mouse on the screen until it's over the icon.
Um. Ok.
SQUEE SQUEE SQUEE

Let me guess. You're moving the mouse directly on the screen.
Geez Louise. These mouse things aren't very accurate, are they.

Now Ashley Judd, that's one lovely gal. When I had the chance to talk to Wil Wheaton, I made it clear I wanted to beat him with a door because he got the chance to snog Ms. Judd in an episode of *Star Trek:TNG*. He had no comment other than that implied in a smug smile. I KILL YOU WIL WHEATON!!!!!11one.

Copyright (c) 1998 Illiad
Tech Support. How may I help you?
My boyfriend just left me.

He said he left me because I was only 19 years old and all I could do was cover myself in whipped cream and give him backrubs, and he told me he hated it when I played Quake or used the Internet, and he doesn't like the fact that I look like Ashley Judd.
All I want is a hard-working computer geek to fill my nights with passion. Is that asking too much?
If I go outside tonight, I know I'll get hit by lightning. Twice.

Copyright (c) 1998 Illiad
You're not going to believe this, but I just got a call from a 19-year old Ashley Judd lookalike. She asked me on a date.

A date?! Really? Did you tell her what you look like?
Of course.

Oh no, you DIDN'T!
Hey, if Harrison Ford had a beard, he'd look just like me!

Copyright (c) 1998 Illiad
Let me get this straight. Some strange woman who looks like Ashley Judd who thinks you look like Harrison Ford is coming here to pick you up for a date tonight?
Um. Yeah.

Hello, tech support, Stef speaking.
Hi. I have my back hairs caught in my computer fan.

Penelope just phoned me from her car. She's just around the corner, parking her Mercedes.
Copyright (c) 1998 Illiad

I can hear her coming into the office now.

Does she really look like Ashley Judd?
If you can get a date with Ernest Borgnine, do it now.

Oh God, oh God, I can hear her coming. I hope she doesn't see me.
Copyright (c) 1998 Illiad

Hello? Is there anyone in here? I'm looking for Greg.

Uh. He's the guy with the glasses and funny hair in the other room.
Ok, thanks. Greeeg, it's Penelope...

USER
FRIENDLY
the comic strip
PIZZA
Portrasher 4
ROTO-ROUTER 800
Copyright © 1997, 1998 Illiad

Uh oh, Stef and Penelope are coming this way. I've had it now. They're... Hey, they're arm-in-arm.

Hey waitaminnit...

Hey, Penelope really **does** look like Ashley Judd.
She sure does.

I tell ya, I can't see a thing without my contacts. I sure wish I had them when I first saw her. **You** could've been having a great time instead of Stef.

C'est la vie. Better luck next time, Dude.
They'll never convict me.

I really hated the Drudge Report. Still do. I have to give him credit for being smart, though; he's a muckraker, but he's a muckraker who took advantage of the Internet in a way no other reporter had up to that point. But I still hate him.

Ah, you must be the CEO. My name is Mr. Padlock, and I'm the president of iCan't Internet. I'm here to buy your company from you.
Copyright (c) 1998 Illiad

I can't sell this company to you. If you acquire us, you'll axe all of my employees and replace our wonderful, homey workplace with a cold, impersonal corporate culture.

I'll give you two million in cash, three million in stocks, and a six-month membership at Nine Pines Golf Course.
You think I'm that easily bought? I want a **one-year** membership.

Ah, thanks for coming. Since you're the company controller, there's something you need to know before the rest of the staff hears about it.
You sold the company, didn't you.
Copyright (c) 1998 Illiad

How did you figure that? It was kept completely secret!
Two words: Drudge Report.

Oh my GOD, what am I doing? I'm selling the company out. Years of blood, sweat and tears. Employees working all hours. And for what?
The Chief
Copyright (c) 1998 Illiad

I'll be wracked with guilt for years. I'll have recurring nightmares where my friends have been betrayed by an evil, grasping capitalist. Me.
The Chief

I'll need therapy, of course. Nine Pines Golf Club, here I come.
The Chief

Hello, I am Mr. Padlock, your new president. To put it simply, your company has just been most thoroughly acquired.
Copyright (c) 1998 Illiad

Of course, with the acquisition comes some changes. No more expensed lunches at Poppy's Plastic Pizza for example.

Instead, we'll all have a daily tofu buffet!
When I get my gun I'm going to do some thorough acquiring myself.
Now Greg...

Stef? Is it true about the company being sold?
Yeah, we got bought out by iCan't Internet.
Copyright (c) 1998 Illiad

You know, at first I felt really betrayed. But the Chief must know what he's doing, and if he did it for personal gain, I know for a fact he'll be wracked with guilt.

Therapy is a very, very good thing...

My name is Mr. Dufay. I am the Vice President of Information Technology and your new boss.
Copyright (c) 1998 Illiad

I require both of you to immediately begin tying in the network here to our networking centre in San Jose. As this is critical to operations, you will give this task top priority.
Okay.
Da, will fix.

Mikhail! How many rockets are you havink left?
BLAM! KABOOM!
Enough to kick **your** sorry butt with!!

Mr. Dufay is a portmanteau of two managers at iStar Internet, one male, one female. They were both very officious, egotistical, and quite concerned about the size of their budgets for their own perks. Didn't give a rats behind about the staff, however.

USER
FRIENDLY
the comic strip
PIZZA
Portrasher 4
ROTO-ROUTER 800
Copyright © 1997, 1998 Illiad

You must be that Stef fellow. Marketing and Corporate Sales, right? Well, we're going to see a lot of changes here.

For starters, we're going to cut back on hardware expenditures and give you a half million dollar per year travel and expense account.
Change is **good**.

Hi-tech businesses focus far too much attention on the technical staff these days. I intend to change that, and return the power to the **real** movers and shakers: the sales and marketing team.

As an initial step, we will make the workplace more comfortable and conducive to marketing executives. We now have a new dress code.

Behold.
You just go ahead and give me an excuse, and I'll rip you a new one.

This one is real. I didn't make this up. The Real Smiling Man was asked, by the company controller of a National ISP, to fax the entire general ledger. WTF?

This is Mr. Zow, the Chief Financial Officer of iCan't Internet. I want you to send me last quarter's financials right away.
Yes sir. I'll e-mail it as soon as I'm off the phone.

I want it faxed. Not e-mailed. I don't like e-mail. FAXED, do you hear me, **FAXED!**
FAXED!
But...aren't we an Internet company?

FINANCIALS 2ND QUARTER 3 OF 41
7 OF 41
8 OF 41
11 OF 41
FINANCIALS
He wants it faxed, he gets it faxed.
GRRRRRRRRNZZZ

Ah, Greg. Just the person I've been looking for. You look rather snappy in a tie and slacks I must admit. I think you techies have been missing out on corporate fashion for too long.

So now that you've been wearing a tie and shirt for a few days, what do you think of the dress code?

Oh, you're hilarious. For your information we haven't hanged anyone since our programmers failed to deliver product according to our marketing schedule.

Why so glum, Greg?
We've been acquired by iCan't Internet.
DUMPED CORES
Copyright (c) 1998 Illiad

DUMPED CORES

Does "acquired" mean you have to dress like an idiot?
How would you like this tie wrapped around your hairy round head?
DUMPED CORES

I can't take this any longer. I have to take this tie off. It's killing me.
DUMPED CORES
Copyright (c) 1998 Illiad
Nnnnnngggg!!

It won't uninstall!!
Erwin! Buy Microsoft stock NOW! They've taken over ties!
DUMPED CORES

A.J., I saw your request for $3000 for hardware and software to make you more productive. Unfortunately, I've had to nix the request. Spending restraints, you know.
Copyright (c) 1998 Illiad

But every Vice President in the company just got a $10,000 suite of office furniture and a gold pen and pencil set!

Do you expect upper management to work off the floor?
Why not? They spend most of their time on their knees anyway.

A.J., I have some bad news for you I'm afraid.
Here it comes...
Copyright (c) Illiad 1998

The vice presidents have decided that your skills as a designer are no longer needed. Please empty your desk before noon.
Who's going to take care of all the websites and corporate graphics?
Why, one of our Vice Presidents knows someone who is very skilled at web design...
Ah, nephew art. I'll mail you my consulting rates in a few weeks.

USER
FRIENDLY
the comic strip
PIZZA
Portrasher 4
ROTO-ROUTER 800
Copyright © 1997, 1998 Illiad
Why is Erwin painted all in black, Greg?
Tufay's in the conference room with Mike and Pitr. Rumor has it we have to migrate from Linux to NT.

No! The last time that happened it nearly killed Erwin! Why are they doing this?!?!
(*sob*)
It's the new management. They want to be able to play Minesweeper.

Gentlemen. Today you will begin migrating all of our servers and workstations from Linux to NT. I expect this to be done before 4:30pm today.

I can only assume you're holding our families hostage to enforce this.
My mother not mind to die for stoppink Windows NT! She is rememberink Stalin!
You waiting for Christmas?

During the brief period I worked at iStar Internet as a project manager, I learned that all the directors and VPs received $15,000 office suites, and this was in the late 90s. My request for $5K worth of software and hardware to improve productivity was "disappeared." My director bluntly told me that he didn't know what happened to the request and that I shouldn't resubmit because it might cause waves.

Well, I guess this is it. Time to bite the bullet and install NT on this poor little server.
Da.
Copyright (c) 1998 Illiad

TREMBLE SHAKE

Is worse than eating kitten, da?
I CAN'T DO IT! I'm sorry, little computer! Forgive my momentary lapse of reason!

Network Operations in San Jose just called. They're not able to talk to our servers here. Did you migrate from Linux to NT?
Nyet.
Well do it. This is time critical!
Copyright (c) 1998 Illiad

Are we actually going to do this?
Nyet, and week from now when he is askink again, we say "Da, NT is installed" and blamink problems on Microsoft. Very believable, da?

iCan't Internet Tech Support. Greg speaking.
Geez. You look like an idiot in a tie.
Copyright (c) 1998 Illiad

Hey, how the hell do you know I'm wearing a tie?

A "Greg-cam"?
Imagine the potential. Thousands of other geeks seeing Greg in a tie on the Web. It makes me feel all fuzzy inside.
Stef? Is that you?!!

iCan't Internet Tech Support. May I help you?
I certainly hope so. I can't open Netscape.
Copyright (c) 1998 Illiad

Okay, click on the Netscape icon...
I don't like icons. I'm a Protestant.
TAP TAPPY

Then how about clicking on the little picture of the Netscape logo.
Why, certainly...

iCan't Internet. Can I help you?
My wife keeps complaining about the size of my hard drive.
Copyright (c) 1998 Illiad

Size of your hard drive...?
Yeah. She says it's too small to satisfy her.
TAP

Sir, this is technical support, not the fetish line.
I have a three and a half inch floppy. Does that help?

Do any of my younger readers remember (or even know about) 3.5″ floppies? Hell, I had an *eight-inch* floppy!

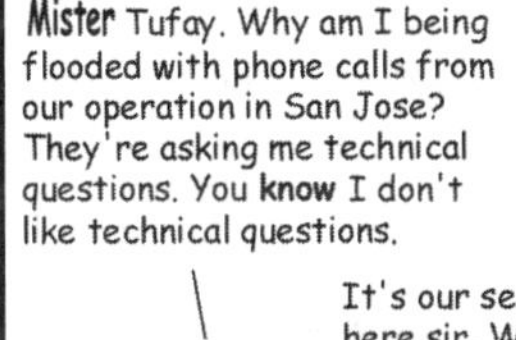

Mister Tufay. Why am I being flooded with phone calls from our operation in San Jose? They're asking me technical questions. You know I don't like technical questions.
It's our servers up here sir. We haven't migrated to NT yet.
Copyright (c) 1998 Illiad

And why haven't we migrated yet?
Err...we're experiencing some recalcitrance with the techs, but we're working on it...

Get away from me, man! And take those diseased NT install disks with you!
DA! You are no touchink computer! I will hurtink you!

USER
FRIENDLY
the comic strip
PIZZA
Portrasher 4
ROTO-ROUTER 800
Copyright © 1997, 1998 Illiad

Who are you phoning, sir?
I'm getting some help. We need to get NT installed.

Technical help?
Muscle, actually.
Microsoft Black Ops, how may I help you?

Base, this is team one. We are in the target zone and are proceeding to the objective.
Roger, team one. Be advised, activity detected in your vicinity. CRACKLE

KLIK

Uh Base, I have one really mad looking techie here, my team has abandoned the mission, and my gun doesn't work. Please advise.
Wait for the upgrade, Team Leader. Bye. CLIK
TUNK
TUNK
TUNK

I must've hit a sweet spot with this one for the older techs. One of them apparently nearly snorted his laptop up his nose after reading this.

Hey Erwin. Watcha doing?
Talking to a server down in San Jose.
Copyright (c) 1998 Illiad
One of the iCan't NT servers?
Yup. Talking to him right now.
What's he saying?
"I'm in my happy place. I'm in my happy place. I'm in my happy place. REBOOT! HAHAHAH!"
That's verbatim.
Is that one of the San Jose servers you're trying to log into Erwin?
Just got into it. It's their development server.
Copyright (c) 1998 Illiad
Erwin...
Let's see if I can't shut down the entire office. Delete their apps? No. Whatever I do should be elegant. Wait! I know!
They're done for. I just installed Quake 2 on the machine.
MIKE! Erwin's lined up some more rookies for us!
The patient has suffered from this NT affliction before. It appears to have resurfaced. We've tried everything and have been unsuccessful. Windows NT just won't uninstall.
ZZZZZZZZ
Erwin dreams...
Copyright (c) 1998 Illiad
There's nothing for it then. We pull the plug.
Agreed.
THANK YOU!
THANK YOU!
Erwin continues to dream...
Hello. Welcome to Purgatory.
Purgatory?
Yes, the land between Heaven and Hell, where all souls go after they pass on.
Oh.
Of course, we'll have to judge you. If you're tainted with evil, then it's downstairs you go.
Format C:

Let's check the Book of Bad Things and see if you made any other transgressions. We already know about Windows NT. I hope for your sake you've done nothing worse...
Okay.
Copyright (c) 1998 Illiad

Let's see. You hacked into the NSA Central Server last year. You modified pictures of the President of the United States. You nearly started a border war between two African countries.
Oh...um...
It looks like NT was your greatest sin. There's hope for you.
Does that mean I can try and restart that border war?

The hard drive, she has stopped pagink. Must be stopped dreamink.
Is he gonna be okay?
Don't worry little dude. We transferred his kernel successfully.
Copyright (c) 1998 Illiad

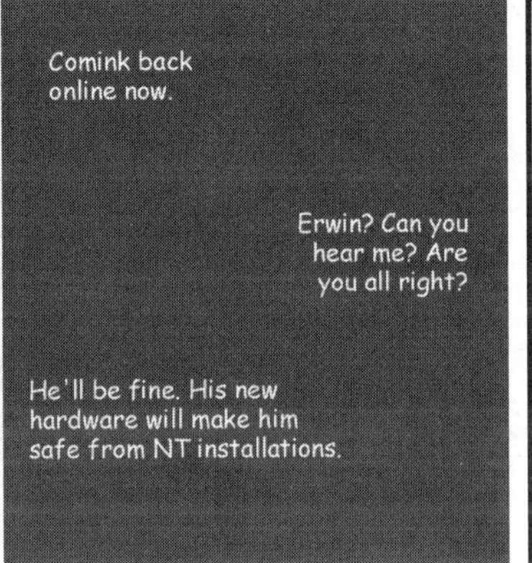
Comink back online now.
Erwin? Can you hear me? Are you all right?
He'll be fine. His new hardware will make him safe from NT installations.

Mind you, the new hardware doesn't really run much of anything. Sure is cute though.
Is better this way.
AAAAGH! What have you done! I even talk funny!!
iWhack

iWhack

No floppy drive?
Of course not.
Hardly anything runs on it, so why bother?
(No beige. Just this really sick pink.)
Finally. Fruit that's cheap.

I just read this strip on my 24″ iMac. Steve Jobs is kicking my arse.

Look at it this way, Erwin. At least they can't install Windows NT on you the way you are.
I suppose you're right.
iWhack
Copyright (c) 1998 Illiad

iWhack

Why are you staring at me?
I have this urge to fill you with water and put goldfish in you.
iWhack

This strip is only half-joking. One of the managers at iStar was deeply concerned about the idea that when some of our servers went down, they didn't *all* go down. "Aren't they all linked? Shouldn't they be?"

Pitr, I just got word from San Jose. Our network has gone down nationwide.
Da. Am knowink this.
Copyright (c) 1998 Illiad

Of course there's an exception. It seems that the servers here are still up and running. Why do you think that is, Pitr?

Is because we are not runnink **crap** on our servers probably.
Unacceptable! We must have consistency! You will bring our servers down, just like all of the others!

Ah, Stef. With the servers down I can't send e-mail, and I have to get a document off to our bank in the Caymans. Could you fax it for me?
Of course, Mr. Padlock.
Copyright (c) 1998 Illiad

It's a two-hundred page document.
Oh. Well then you'll want to hand that off to Technical Support.

Ah ha! Is **that** what they do?
Oh yes. And they love the fact that the fax machine can't do a stack feed. Don't ever change that.

I need these pages faxed. I expect you to give this your prompt attention.
Okay.
Copyright (c) Illiad 1998

They need to be sent to our bank in the Cayman Islands. I want them there immediately.
Yes, sir. Will do.

Are you wantink kerosene again?
I think I'll try battery acid this time.

My word, this is simply terrible. Our network is down, the bank hasn't received the signed orders, and I have a group of neurotics handling our servers. I feel like I only have a tenuous hold on reality...
Copyright (c) 1998 Illiad
OFFICE97 INSTALL KIT PLUS BOOKS

Hello.
OFFICE97 INSTALL KIT PLUS BOOKS
AAAAIIIEEEE!!!
OFFICE97 INSTALL KIT PLUS BOOKS

Mikhail, you seeink Mr. Padlock runnink out door screamink?
Yep. That's one down, one to go.
Copyright (c) 1998 Illiad

I told Tufay that NT won't install on an iWhack. Not that he isn't trying...

INSTALL, DAMN YOU!
PAH-TOOEY!
iWhack

USER
FRIENDLY
the comic strip
PIZZA
Portrasher 4
ROTO-ROUTER 800
Copyright © 1997, 1998 Illiad

I wonder how the gang is doing back at Columbia Internet. Maybe I should give them a call.

Nah.

Hi Chief, it's Hillary. Mr. Padlock just ran screaming out the front door, and Tufay is away on stress leave. There's a real power vacuum over here right now.

The techs don't want to go back to work for the iCant crowd. Everything is running, and all of our accounts are right up to date. No debts.
Very good.

What is it exactly about all of this that concerns **me**?
Chief, just get your executive butt back here!

I suppose you heard about the San Jose office ordering new hardware to replace all of the machines that went down last week?
Da.
Copyright (c) 1998 Illiad

If they get that shipment of Pentium machines, they'll be able to bring the network back up.
Not to be worrying Mikhail. Pitr fix.
Don't Think.
1 pc
Don't Think.
1 pc
Don't Think.
1 pc
Don't Think.
Hey man, I just deliver them, okay?

I spoke to the Chief last night. He's on the next flight out of Tahiti. With any luck he'll be back by tomorrow.
The Chief's coming back?
Yes.

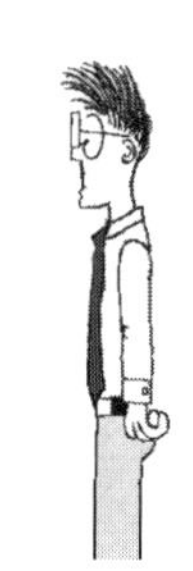

Guess that means I'm out of the running for CEO, huh?
We'd all follow you, but out of curiosity, not loyalty.

Chief, it's so nice to have you back with us. We really missed your management style and your sense of humor around here.
Copyright (c) 1998 Illiad

Oh, I just wanted to know one thing...

Why did you leave us with those bottom feeders?!?!

It's nice to see the Chief back here.
I suppose I have to agree, even if I will miss all my old perks.
Copyright (c) 1998 Illiad

Speaking of which, where is he today?
Dunno. He said something about "readying his mental space" for his return to management...

Chief, please accept my apologies for my behaviour the other day. I really am glad to see you back.

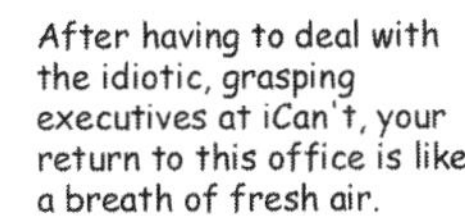
After having to deal with the idiotic, grasping executives at iCan't, your return to this office is like a breath of fresh air.

You want something from me, don't you.
Tell me how these things come off!!!

Am thinkink iWhack is not bad leetle machine. Is kind of cute, all one piece, da Mikhail?
Sure. But what happens if the screen fries?
iWhack

iWhack

You are then havink very big paperweight with no lights.
Could you guys just get me out of here now!?!?
iWhack

USER
FRIENDLY
the comic strip
PIZZA
Portrasher 4
ROTO-ROUTER 800

We must do right think, puttink Erwin back on Pentium box, da?
Yeah. Guess we should.
iWhack

Or, we could be leavink him in there for another week...
Oh, you're just a barrel of laughs, Pitr.
iWhack

You are havink Erwin's files all organized, da? Now please to be copyink files over to disk.
Okay.
TAP TAPPY
iWhack

Ummm...
iWhack

Oh, I am such a zlotnik! No floppy drive!
Could be worse.
I'm in a pink gumdrop! How can anything be worse?!!
iWhack

Well, I'm happy to say it's official. iCan't Internet has folded and Columbia Internet has been sold back to me.
How much for, if you don't mind me asking?
Copyright (c) 1998 Illiad

Less than one-tenth of what I got for it.
What?! Why did the company drop in value so much? I mean, I was next in line to be CEO...

Oh.
Look at it this way. You still have a really long way to go in your career as an executive.

Columbia Internet Tech Support, Greg speaking. How may I help you?
You're in a good mood.
Copyright (c) 1998 Illiad

Today's my day. No more ties, no more iCan't Internet, no more anguish.
Wow, that's great to hear.

Um, I think I forgot my question.
I told you today was my day.

Note this little dig against the Clinton White House. There'll be a few others as time goes on. When 2002 rolls around, you'll see some digs against the Bush Administration. And yet, in 2002, several readers told me my bias was showing. Rule #1 of political cartooning: The fairer you are, the more incensed people will be.

Good afternoon, Greg speaking.
Where's all that filth on the Web I keep hearing about?

Filth?
Yeah. Filth. Trash. Porn. Dirty, dirty sex stuff with dirty-minded people.

Copyright (c) 1998 Illiad
You're talking about the Starr report, aren't you.
Yeah! That's it!
It's like a collection from the Penthouse Forum, right?

Stef, I've reviewed the company's status and have noted a few areas where we could improve efficiency. For starters, I'd like everyone in the office to use Linux, including yourself.

Did you hear what I said?
Oh yes. I'm just trying to think of a way to say "up yours" without getting fired.

I don't see why I should have to learn Linux, Pitr. It's too cryptic to use.

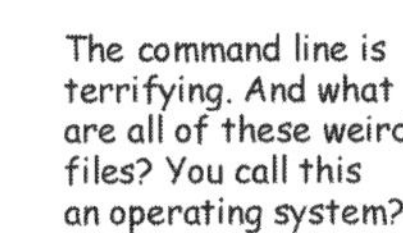
The command line is terrifying. And what are all of these weird files? You call this an operating system?

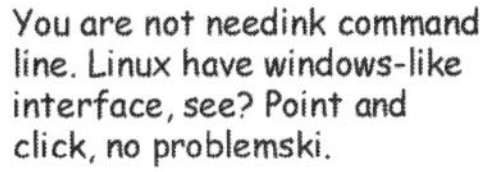
You are not needink command line. Linux have windows-like interface, see? Point and click, no problemski.

But where are the **THEMES?**!
How do you expect me to use an OS without themes?!

Pitr, Mike, this is Miranda. She's joining our company to help with system administration and tech support. Please make her feel welcome and show her the ropes.
Copyright (c) 1998 Illiad

Hey, guys. Nice to meet you.

We are havink problem with reality here, da?
What Pitr means is, how long have you been a woman?

I've been asked countless times whom I based Miranda on, followed by "can I please have her e-mail address or number?"

USER
FRIENDLY
the comic strip
PIZZA
Portrasher 4
ROTO-ROUTER 800
Copyright © 1997, 1998 Illiad

This looks like a great company to work for. I can put all of my technical skills to use here with co-workers like these.
A female who groks UNIX? My universe is collapsing.
Am thinking she is EVIL.
I feel really threatened.
Man, she looks hot in jeans.

Pitr, thank you for taking time out of your day to help me get familiarized with the office.
And you are havink what education and trainink?

I have a Computer Science degree with a specialty in software engineering, I'm a certifed network engineer, and I have six years of experience as a Unix sysadmin.
Da, I see.

Now payink attention, please. This is mouse. Click-click. Easy to use, da? Now you try...

Columbia Internet tech support, Miranda speaking, how may I help you?
Uhhh...put me through to tech support please.

This is technical support, sir. How can I help you?
But...you're a chick.
TAP TAP TAPPY

Copyright (c) 1998 Illiad
I'm also a highly trained systems technologist.
Sure you are, and I'm the President. Want to be my intern?

Watcha doing Greg?
I have a customer on hold. He can't seem to log on, and I'm searching the Web for an answer. I've tried everything.

Have you tried asking him to turn off his Caps Lock key?
Oh, please. That's the first thing I tried.
I didn't mean to insult you. Sorry I couldn't help.

Hi, I'm back. Try turning off your caps lock.
It worked! You tech guys are so smart!

I heard you guys were going to have a game of Quake after work. Mind if I join in?
Uh. Sure. We'll go easy on you.

Actually, I'm told that I'm pretty good. I was the top player in my clan last year. Highest number of frags and lowest number of respawns.
Oh.

Copyright (c) 1998 Illiad
So when do we start?
Um. Not sure. I may not play at all today. Very busy. I have to go...uh, you know, flush my buffers...

BLAM! BLAM! BUDDA BUDDA BUDDA
FWOOSH! BLAM! BLAM! SPLUTCH! YEEARGH!
Copyright (c) 1998 Illiad

Okay, you can stop now!

50 to -2? You can stop "going easy" on me now.
peep

TAP
TAP

Well, hello there. I'm Miranda, the new technician.
Copyright (c) 1998 Illiad

You know, you're a real cutie pie.
She didn't run away screaming like you said.
You are needink to look more evil. You likink very strong coffee?

It certainly is nice to have you back with us, A.J. I can't imagine why Mr. Padlock let you go in the first place.

Thanks, Chief. I guess I'd better get back to work. I'll bet our company Web site needs updating.
Okay, you do that.
Copyright (c) 1998 Illiad

Does A.J. know yet?
He's just about to.
HEY! Who's been messing with my fonts?! They were PERFECT!

USER
FRIENDLY
the comic strip
PIZZA
Portrasher 4
ROTO-ROUTER 800
Copyright © 1997, 1998 Illiad

So how're you doing so far, Miranda? Everyone treating you right? No problems?
Other than the ogling I've been getting from some of the guys, it's been fine.

The guys are ogling you? That is just **so** degrading. It's bad enough that our customers do it, but our co-workers should at least show a little respect.

I have to agree. I'm not just some bimbo with nice body parts. I have a mind, and an education. Why can't they see that first?
Well said.

Ladies.

Nice tush.
Sure, but he can't play Quake worth beans.

I can't take this much longer. Please get me out of here!
Relax, Erwin. Let's first see how well Quake runs on this.
iWhack
Copyright (c) 1998 Illiad

BLAM! BLAM! BLAM! SPLOTCH!
WIGGLE WIGGLE
iWhack

Any luck?
No. This thing only has one mouse button. How am I supposed to switch weapons?
YOU SEE!!?? It's like being born with only one nipple!
iWhack

Think it worked out okay?
Da, all data transferred.
Why couldn't we just move him over the 'net?

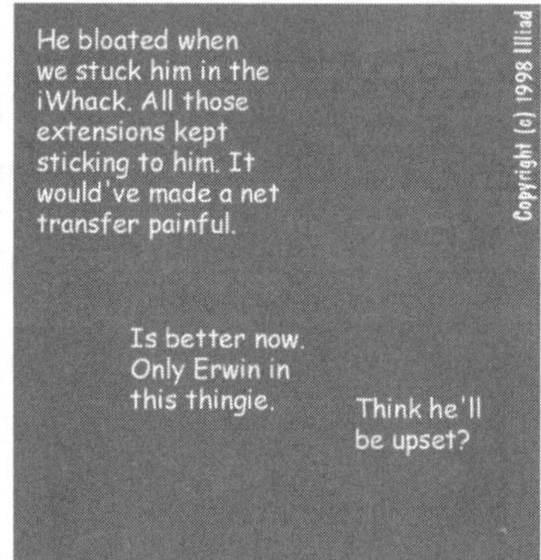
He bloated when we stuck him in the iWhack. All those extensions kept sticking to him. It would've made a net transfer painful.
Is better now. Only Erwin in this thingie.
Think he'll be upset?
Copyright (c) 1998 Illiad

He should be happy. Look how much more portable he is.
Palm III is cute, da?
NOOOO!

This is depressing. I'm stuck in this thing and I don't even have a 'Net connection.

Say, what's this infrared thingie? Heeeeeyyyyyy...

Copyright (c) 1998 Illiad
I just got e-mail on my Palm III from Miranda. "Hey baby, you rock my world. Beers after work?"
NOOOOO! That can't be true!

Hey there, sweet thing. I got your e-mail.
E-mail?

Oh yeah. I rock your world. Shake your foundations. Twirl your baton.

Copyright (c) 1998 Illiad
Now that's what I call "personal communications" on my Palm III.
Well I guess that means you have a date with your palm then, doesn't it.

Erwin, why did you make it look like Miranda sent Stef e-mail?
It's fun.

Fun? What you did was fun?
You should see what I did to his electronic business cards.

Copyright (c) 1998 Illiad
"Stef Murky, Office Boy. Will work for spankings." Well. I've been waiting to meet one of you people for quite a while now.

Erwin? These jokes you're playing on Stef...have you ever thought carefully about what harm you might be doing to him when he's the butt of one of your pranks?

Copyright (c) 1998 Illiad
No, can't say that I have.
That's okay, I never do either.

USER
FRIENDLY
the comic strip
PIZZA
Portrasher 4
ROTO-ROUTER 800
Copyright © 1997, 1998 Illiad

Let's see now. What else can I do?

Uh oh...

I want a word with you, ya little pipsqueak.
Sorry. I'm a little busy right now...
WHAM! WHAM! WHAM! WHAM! WHAM! WHAM! WHAM! WHAM! WHAM! WHAM!

'Nuff said.
Some...body...please... beam...me...out... of...here...

Believe it or not, I received hate mail over this one. Erwin seems to have either groupies or worshippers, or perhaps both.

Week of October 26th, 1998

AJ, is Erwin going to be okay?
Pitr rigged up a really powerful beaming device. Erwin's intact, don't worry little guy.
CRISCO 7105
py's Plastic Pizza
Copyright (c) 1998 Illiad

But where is he now?
I'm not sure. Pitr said something about getting help from his countrymen.
CRISCO 7105
py's Plastic Pizza

I'm never going to get a break, am I?
MIR

Ye gods, I'm tired. I can barely stay awake, and there's nothing I can do about it...
Copyright (c) 1998 Illiad

You look terrified. Surprised to see me?
Of course not. I'm just waiting for you to stick me with an I.V.
Cola

Greg, could you help me run a check on the modem pool?

Copyright (c) 1998 Illiad
No...it can't be...
You see it too?!

It's the Espresso Monster! NOOO!!
Espresso Monster?
I'm seen in many forms. Now open your mouth. It's caffeine time.

Why did you come back, Mr. Cola?
I'm here to stop a terrible tragedy from occuring.
Cola

Tragedy?
You falling asleep would have led to the mail server going down, which would have caused a stock broker to shoot himself because he'll think his sell order was too late, impoverishing his family and totally bumming out the brokerage staff for days.
Cola
Copyright (c) 1998 Illiad

Oh my GOD. I need caffeine!!
Drink up, buddy. Everything will be just fine now.
Cola

Hey.
Uh...hi.
Cola
Cola

Copyright (c) 1998 Illiad
What the hell was that thing?
Quit that. You know I hate it when you look at other sources of caffeine. It's hurtful.
Bolt!
COLA

'Scuse me, I seem to have lost my way. How do I get to the lunch room?
Back the other way.

Okay, thanks.

Copyright (c) 1998 Illiad
Please tell me that was a Halloween costume.
Probably. Say, are you craving coffee all of a sudden?

USER
FRIENDLY
the comic strip
PIZZA
Portrasher 4
ROTO-ROUTER 800
Copyright © 1997, 1998 Illiad

I can't believe I'm stuck in this contraption. I can barely believe this thing stays up.
MIRwin

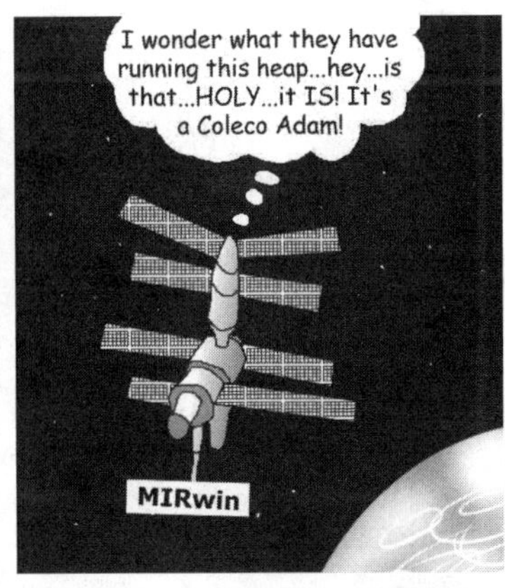
I wonder what they have running this heap...hey...is that...HOLY...it IS! It's a Coleco Adam!
MIRwin

Hey, an incoming. It looks like the Discovery...
MIRwin

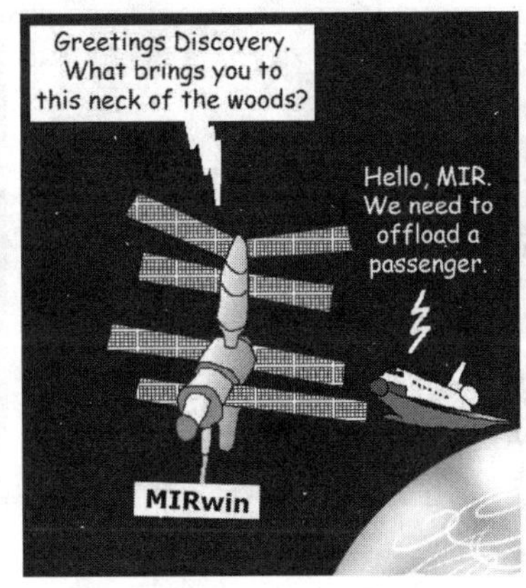
Greetings Discovery. What brings you to this neck of the woods?
Hello, MIR. We need to offload a passenger.
MIRwin

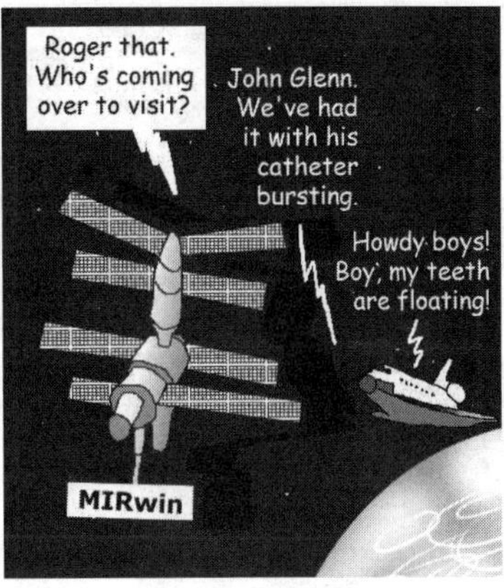
Roger that. Who's coming over to visit?
John Glenn. We've had it with his catheter bursting.
Howdy boys! Boy, my teeth are floating!
MIRwin

Microsoft announced today that their upcoming "Windows 2000" product would include a brand new feature.
144 Boxes

Microsoft spokesman Barry Onimishon said "This feature will be the ultimate solution to the dreaded Blue Screen of Death that has plagued Windows for so long."

144 Boxes

When asked what the new feature in the OS was, Mr. Onimishon smiled and replied, "The reset button of course. It's been used so much with our products we decided to officially incorporate it."
144 Boxes

I'm beat. Sixteen-hour days were starting to catch up to me. But I had to do it -- the web site was an utter mess.

Too bad I'm on salary. I could have been raking in the bucks for the last few weeks.
Money isn't everything, A.J.

What idiot convinced you of that?
The Chief, at my last salary review.

Columbia Internet Tech Support.
Hi. What's the difference between the left and right mouse buttons?
TAP TAPPY

ahem

With years of education and experience on the front lines under my belt, I can safely say that the difference is that one is on the left, and one is on the right.
Hey! Are you making fun of me or something?

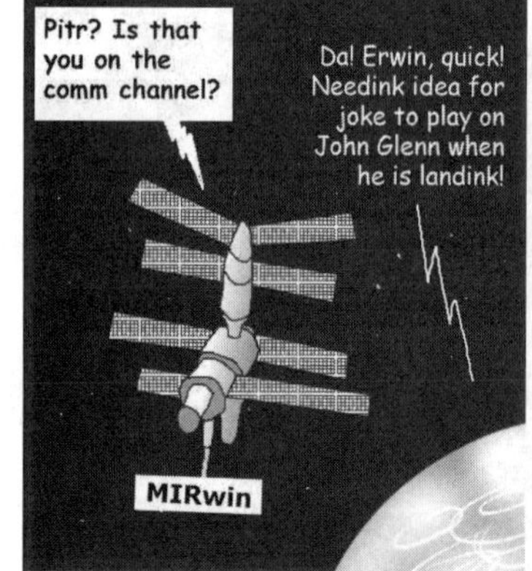
Pitr? Is that you on the comm channel?
Da! Erwin, quick! Needink idea for joke to play on John Glenn when he is landink!
MIRwin

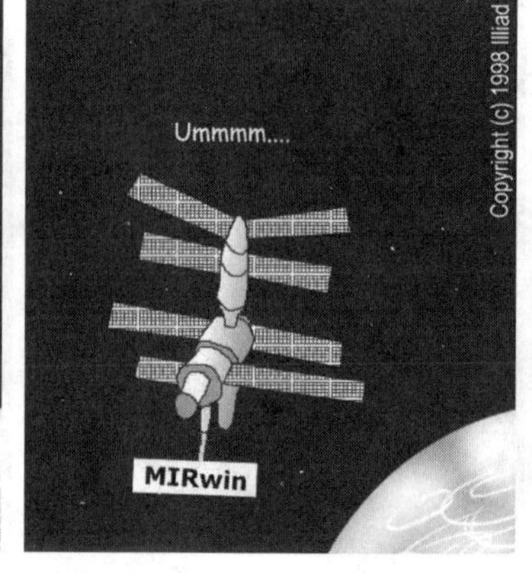
Ummmm....
MIRwin

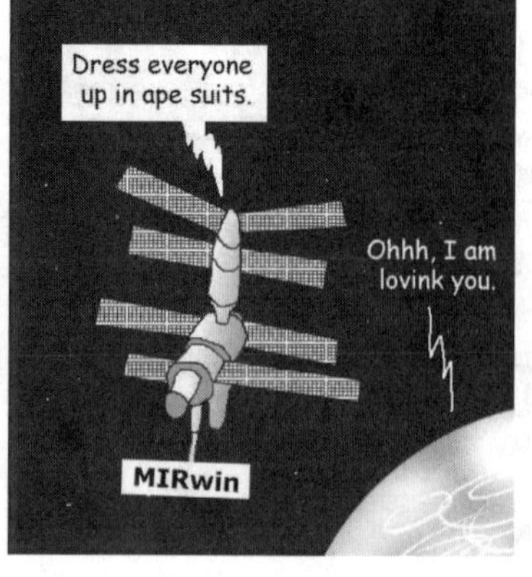
Dress everyone up in ape suits.
Ohhh, I am lovink you.
MIRwin

I know you don't like using Linux, Stef, so I spoke to A.J. about it and he recommends we put you on a computer running BeOS.

And what a fine OS it is. Stable, clean, well-designed. It's really a work of technical excellence.

It doesn't have themes, does it.
Told you he'd ask.

I heard you actually got Stef using BeOS.
Sort of. He's having trouble getting to the applications.
Copyright (c) 1998 Illiad

Trouble getting to the apps? Say what?
You know how Stef takes things literally...
BeWare

I am a BeOS Survivor. I still have the install disks. BeOS was also UF's very first advertiser. They used half of their $40,000 marketing budget with us, and in return received an unheard-of-today clickthru rate of 9%.

USER
FRIENDLY
the comic strip
PIZZA
Portrasher 4
ROTO-ROUTER 800
Copyright © 1997, 1998 Illiad

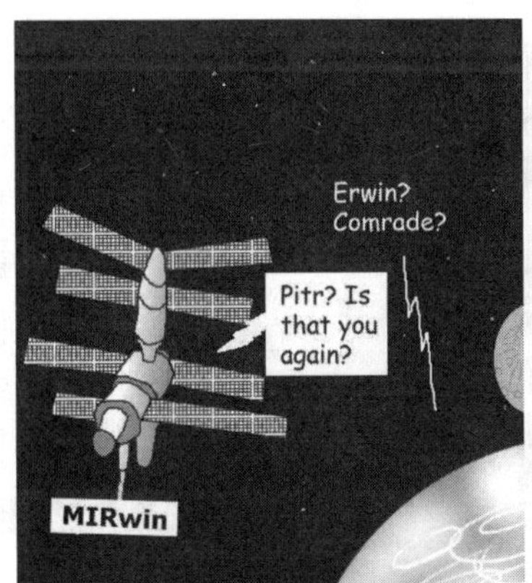
Erwin? Comrade?
Pitr? Is that you again?
MIRwin

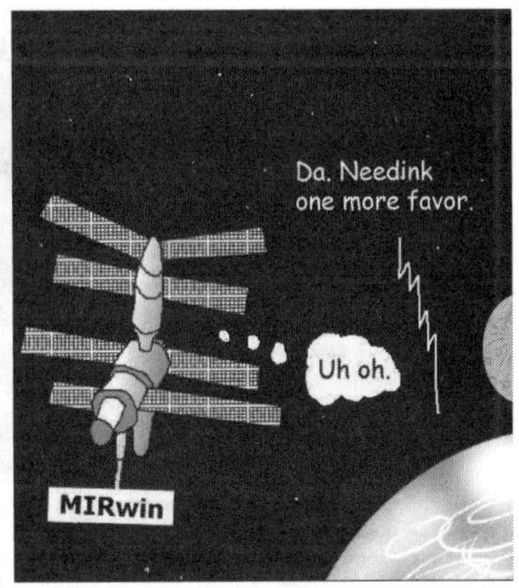
Da. Needink one more favor.
Uh oh.
MIRwin

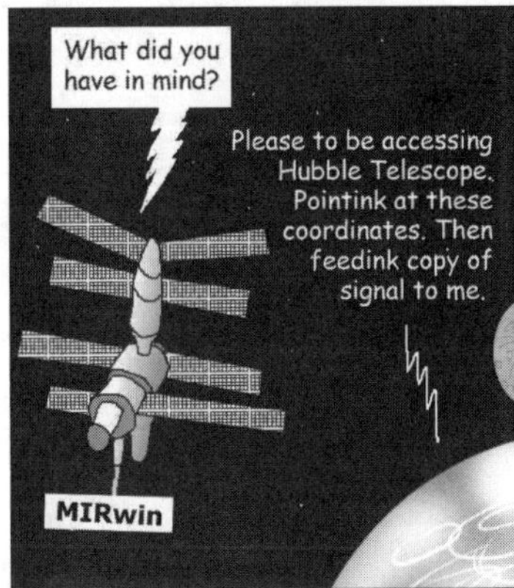
What did you have in mind?
Please to be accessing Hubble Telescope. Pointink at these coordinates. Then feedink copy of signal to me.
MIRwin

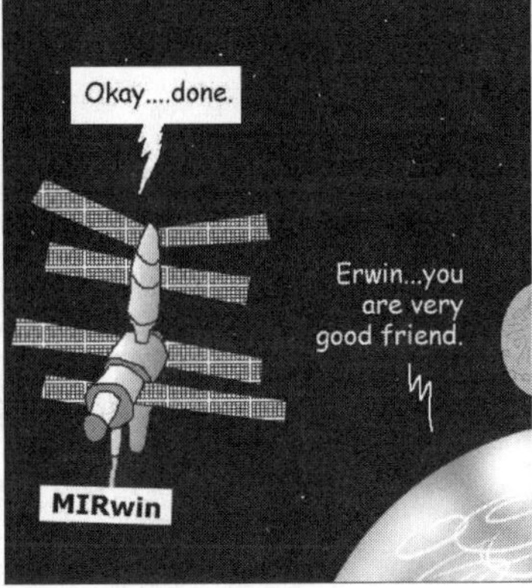
Okay....done.
Erwin...you are very good friend.
MIRwin

Well...that looks like a diary on her desk. Looks like her name is 'Miranda.'
Perfect. A moon of Uranus and a heavenly body. Fits our mandate.
She's about to shower. I hope you're taping this.

You know, A.J., this BeOS isn't so bad. It's pretty neat, and easy to use, and it hasn't crashed on me in a couple of days of use and...
Copyright (c) 1998 Illiad

uh...
Hey, waitaminnit. This isn't a Microsoft product, is it! What am I saying? This can't be any good!! And where are my GPFs?
I want my GPFs!!!

What's that you're doing, Mike?
Oh, Pitr just sent me some pictures he got off the Hubble Space Telescope.
TAP
TAP
Copyright (c) 1998 Illiad

Pitr... DIES
Um, did you see the cc: line?
"spamchannel@aol.com"

Pitr, do you realize that Miranda is going to kill you?
Is no problem. Miranda, she is no threat to me.
TAPPY TAPTAP
Copyright (c) 1998 Illiad

TAP TAP
I swear you must think you're some kind of god.
God, root, what is difference?
TAPPY TAPTAP

So Miranda she is comink after me. What I care, I am askink. She is no problem to me.

Such a zlotnik she is. Am thinkink she is dangerous like balloon poppink. Make loud noise only, get hurt only if stick self with pin.
TAP TAP
Ahem
Am also thinkink I just stuck self with very large pin.
I would say so, yes.

Greg, have you seen Pitr today?
He was with Miranda a little while ago.
Copyright (c) 1998 Illiad

Have you seen him since?

No, now that you mention it. I did see Miranda walking away with Pitr's prized collection of code libraries.

Now, for every e-mail address you spammed at AOL with my pictures, I'm deleting a random cluster from your code library backup disks.
MRRRRF!!!
TAPPITY
TAPPY
TAPPITY

Hmmm. Looks like the Microsoft trial isn't going so well for Bill.
Oh?
TAKK

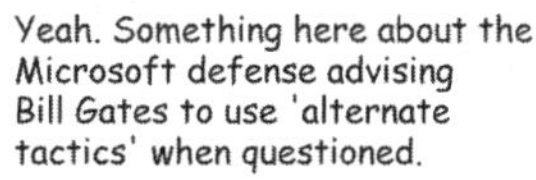
Yeah. Something here about the Microsoft defense advising Bill Gates to use 'alternate tactics' when questioned.

Copyright (c) 1998 Illiad
Mr. Gates. Did you or others on behalf of Microsoft threaten to cut off support to Intel if Intel did not cooperate?
Ummm. These aren't the droids you're looking for.

ANATOMY OF AN ANTI-GEEK

Mind made for marketing, not ethics.
Mobile phone, for backstabbing and making deals, not just to fiddle with.

Suit by John Phillips of London. Cost: Enough money to buy a large array of quad-processor DEC Alphas.

Tie. 'Nuff said.

Legal documents. He understands them. 'Nuff said.

Thank God for this recess. That attorney is kicking my butt all over the courtroom. Mr. Gates this and Mr. Gates that...it's getting to me...

I suppose we'll have to.
I don't think I can handle much more of this, and my $1200-an-hour lawyers are hopeless. I need real help. Come to me, my friend...
Come to me, my friend...
gurgle Yes, my master...
Ohhh, am not feelink good. Why is stomach churnink?
BURP
Copyright (c) 1998 Illiad

Pitr?
URRRRP. Ohhh. Am not feelink good at all...

AAAAAAGH!!!
Copyright (c) 1998 Illiad

Now what did you do to him? Replace his text editor with FrontPage?
What do you think I am, some kind of medusa?!

That wasn't the first time I considered the possibility of an intravenous/intracranial connection to the Net. My God ... what a rush that would be.

Poor Pitr. Whatever hit him did it hard. Good thing the ambulance was cruising by. Now he's just lying there, helpless and twitching.
Copyright (c) 1998 Illiad

That's not an IV sticking in his arm is it.
I was just gonna say. You know, I think it's 10-base-T.

I'm Dr. Doss. Are you Pitr's friends?
Yes, we are.
Copyright (c) 1998 Illiad

Pitr's chest films came back. The good news is that the problem is very clear. We're sure what put him into shock.
And the bad news?

There's a pair of hands inside his chest cavity gripping his kidneys.
Ooog.

Doctor, what are you doing? The patient is **open.** You can't drink coffee in here!!
Yeah, yeah. I've had a rough day, okay? I just need a break.
Copyright (c) 1998 Illiad

SPLOOSH

Oh no...
What have I done?!!
You have no idea, foolish mortal...

Doctor, we can't just leave him like this. We need to continue with the operation, regardless of the coffee spilled all over his vital organs.
You're right of course. I may as well start now.

Um, nurse, did you apply suction? I can't see any coffee in here.
No doctor, I didn't.

Copyright (c) 1998 Illiad
Give me the scalpel, or your hand comes with it.
AAAAAAAH!!

USER
FRIENDLY
the comic strip
PIZZA
Portrasher 4
ROTO-ROUTER 800
Copyright © 1997, 1998 Illiad

Mr. Hoffloff? Where are you going to? I thought you had a surgery scheduled for today.

Judging from the screams coming from your operating room, you people don't use anasthetic. I'd rather have my wife kill me in my sleep for my gas problem.
YEEEARGH!

Excuse me while I go remove the corny flavor from this cartoon. Good grief.

HOSPITAL CAFETERIA
I need something... lifeblood.......more of that dark ambrosia.

Coffee, now. Your finest Java beans, blended with the darkest Microsoft beans you have.
SPOING!

I don't think Java and Microsoft blend all that well.
You'd better not be mocking me, coffee-boy.

Week of November 23rd, 1998

I can't believe that thing is back! Maybe if I keep the office door locked it won't be able to find us.

'Sup, Mike?

Copyright (c) 1998 Illiad
You drank some of Pitr's coffee again, huh?

A.J., what's Mike doing up in the rafters?
Heavy caffeine buzz I think...
NO! You fools! It's BACK!

Copyright (c) 1998 Illiad
What's he talking about?
The AOL-Netscape deal, probably.

Mike, did you say, "Crud Puppy"?
YES!!

Crud Puppy? What on Earth is that?

Copyright (c) 1998 Illiad
Mike! MOVE OVER!
NO! Find your own butt shelter!!

Look Greg, Mike and I aren't coming back down for a few days, and someone really needs to tell the Dust Puppy that his nemesis is loose again. Where is he anyway?
He said he was playing something really involving called 'Half-Life.'
Copyright (c) 1998 Illiad

Okay, time to ROCK!
COLA

A.J. and Mike are scared out of their wits, little guy. They tell me you know this Crud Puppy thing. Care to shed some light on the history you share with it?
144 PINTS
72 pcs
OPERA

Well. It is a long story...
144 PINTS
72 pcs
OPERA

Copyright (c) 1998 Illiad
...but every saga has a beginning.
You waited for days to use that line, didn't you.
144 PINTS
72 pcs
OPERA

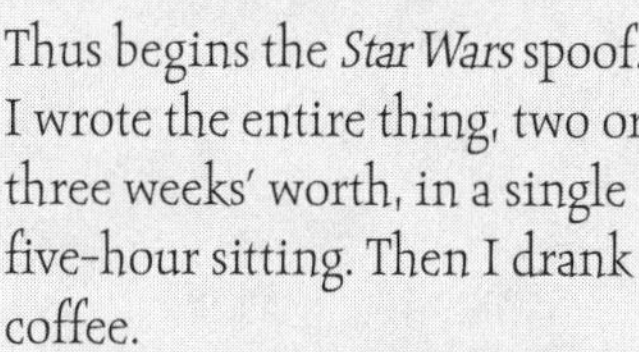

Thus begins the *Star Wars* spoof. I wrote the entire thing, two or three weeks' worth, in a single five-hour sitting. Then I drank coffee.

The little guy tells his story...
'A long time ago, in another incarnation, I stood on a desert world watching the many moons rise...'

'I had a quiet life, and what I really wanted was a life of adventure. I wanted to rebel against something Very Bad.'
Copyright (c) 1998 Illiad

Little did I realize how quickly my wish would come true...
Took you long enough to hit that rebel ship.
Sorry, sir. It's these Wing Commander reflexes.
Microsoft

USER
FRIENDLY
the comic strip
PIZZA
Portrasher 4
ROTO-ROUTER 800
Copyright © 1997, 1998 Illiad

I saw a bright flash in the sky and I knew that a battle was raging above my world...

Then I saw an escape pod falling out of the sky. Naturally, I ran over to investigate it...

My lord...the source code we're looking for is NOT in the main computer.

I finally managed to find my way to the escape pod. I knew my life was about to change from this point onward...

Little did I realize who I was going to get involved with...
Hey! You're a PENGUIN!
Let me guess. You're the galaxy's hairiest zoologist.
Linux

The stranger I met wasn't used to the heat and dryness of the planet Peedeepee. On our way to town we stopped so he could catch his breath.
Is it much further?
No. By the way, what's your name?
Linux

You mean, you don't know who I am?!
Actually, you do look familiar...
Linux

Aren't you that "Opus" guy?
Try again, herring-bait.
Linux

As we walked on, Tux the Penguin told me a fantastic story...
After all these years, the Evil Empire began to turn it's baleful gaze on to the good, clean power of Linux.
Oooooh.

They came after us with their troops. Our one strength was that our senior officers were more flexible than theirs...
How's that?
Copyright (c) 1998 Illiad

We can customize our colonels.
Uh-huh.

Lord Crud, we have located the escape pod.
:crackle:
Very good. Any evidence of whoever it was that stole the source code?

Copyright (c) 1998 Illiad

Tell him it's a duck with webbed as well as human feet. And it walks sideways.
No, my lord. Nothing obvious.
:crackle:

Eric Raymond ended up using "May the Open Source be with you!" as the closing line for many of his speeches. Heh. Kewl.

I have to admit it. The Rebellion is in trouble. We need help. And right now, I need help.
I know someone who'll help. In fact, he lives right around the corner.

Really? Who is it?
Copyright (c) 1998 Illiad

Tux, please meet Eric S. Raymond.
Dudes! May the Open Source be with you.

Eric agreed to go into town with us, so we continued on our way.
I could use your help in getting this data back to the Rebellion.
Why, what is it?
Eric's thinking place
The source code to Windows 95.
Copyright (c) 1998 Illiad
That's some bad ju-ju you're carrying there, bird.
That's nothing. I have their marketing plans too.

Grommet?
We left for Blackhead, the spaceport where Eric knew a pilot that could help us get to Rebellion HQ.
STEF'S FISH

Eric warned us that the cantina we stepped into was rife with the worst scum the galaxy had to offer.
LOO
Linux
Copyright (c) 1998 Illiad

Hi. I'm the VP of Acquisitions. You?
Careful lads! Don't let it touch you!

In 2006, I was offered several bags of cold, hard cash for UF; but the deal wasn't right, so I declined. We did meet with the acquisition team, and one of the corporate lawyers spotted this strip in the meeting and pointed it out to the Senior VP of Acquisitions. He thought it was funny. I turned three shades of red.

USER
FRIENDLY
the comic strip
PIZZA
Portrasher 4
ROTO-ROUTER 800
Copyright © 1997, 1998 Illiad

Guys, this is Lan Solaris. He says he's the best at everything in the sector.

And what exactly makes you such a hotshot?
I'm cocky and I know HTML.

We have data that we need to get to Rebellion HQ, and we need to get there quickly.
Imperial trouble, huh? It'll cost you extra.

All right. What do you want?
Something that everyone in the galaxy wants.

Fine. I'll do my best to get your name off AOL's snail mail list.
Then I'll see you at docking bay 1138 in two hours.

Your timing was perfect. I just finished an oil change. This is the fastest ship in the sector: the Millenium Bug.

Let's be on our way. We have an empire to thwart.
Copyright (c) 1998 Illiad

Did he say "Millenium Bug"?
I'm outta here...
I have a really bad feeling about this.

As soon as we left the planet we were attacked by an Imperial patrol...
WAAAAAOOH
PYEW! PYEW! PYEW! PYEW!
You guys are a hot item! Prepare for the jump to light speed! Three! Two! One...

ZZZEEEEEEEEEEWWwwwww
GENERAL PROTECTION FAULT

You run this ship with Windows?! You IDIOT!
Give me a break, it came bundled with the computer!
sigh

Darn good thing I have a Linux partition on here. OK! Prepare for the jump to light speed!!
Copyright (c) 1998 Illiad

Nifty, huh?
I've seen niftier screen savers.

Here we are, Eric...uh oh.
AAARGH! The Empire's secret weapon!
Launch marketing drones!

No sooner had we entered the system, the Empire had locked on to us...
Something's got us! It's some kind of beam!
Resistance is futile.

SHLUURPP!
POOK!
Copyright (c) 1998 Illiad

Open Source protect me... that felt awful.
I feel dirty.
That had to be an Imperial Acquisition Beam.

There must be thirty stormtroopers surrounding this ship. Any bright ideas, Lan?
I say we charge out there with guns blazing.

Copyright (c) 1998 Illiad

Windows on the ship's computer and now this. You really are an idiot, aren't you.
I can do it in Quake, why not in real life?

All right you evil mindless Imperial drones! Prepare to meet death
PERSONIFIED!

PAFF!
PAFF!
POFF!
PIFF!
Copyright (c) 1998 Illiad

I guess that was a pretty silly thing to do.
Well, you did manage to annoy us.

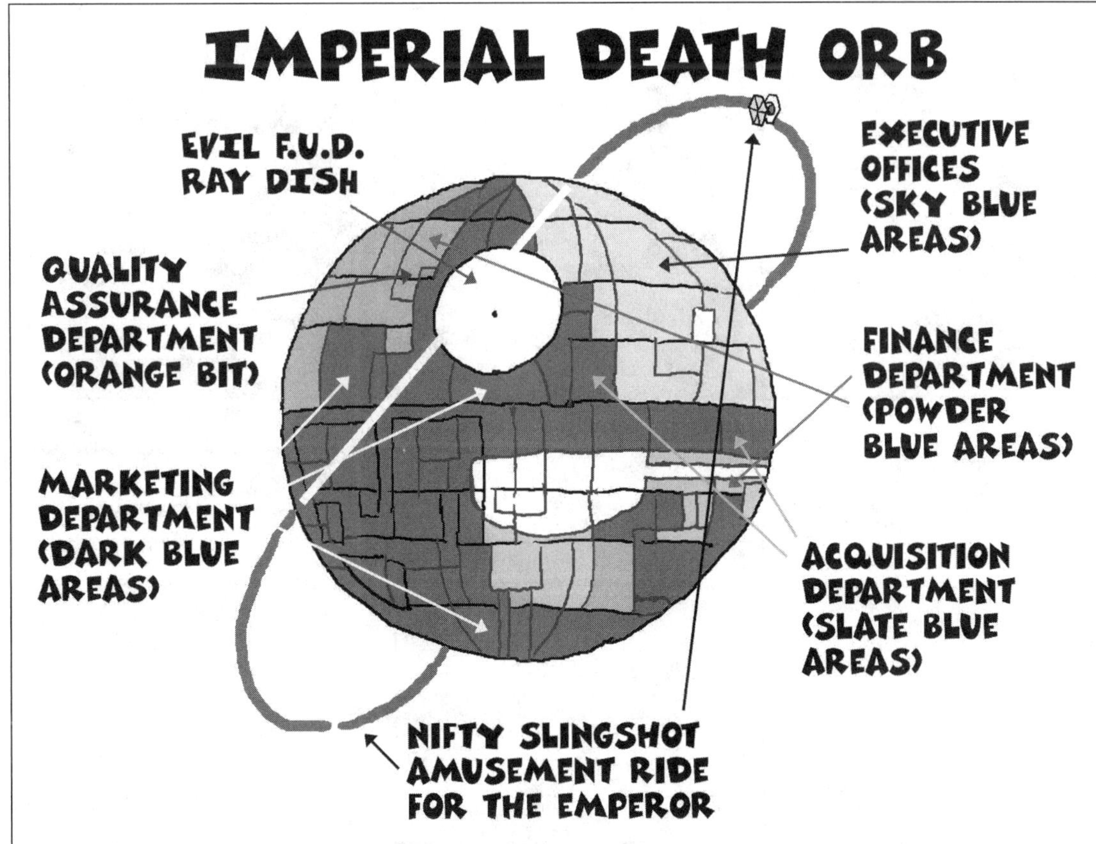
IMPERIAL DEATH ORB
EVIL F.U.D. RAY DISH
EXECUTIVE OFFICES (SKY BLUE AREAS)
QUALITY ASSURANCE DEPARTMENT (ORANGE BIT)
FINANCE DEPARTMENT (POWDER BLUE AREAS)
MARKETING DEPARTMENT (DARK BLUE AREAS)
ACQUISITION DEPARTMENT (SLATE BLUE AREAS)
NIFTY SLINGSHOT AMUSEMENT RIDE FOR THE EMPEROR

Oh no! They've captured Lan! Is that a maintenance team they're sending to board us?
Looks like it...

Don't you have a lightsaber or something?
He'd better. Here they come.
Copyright (c) 1998 Illiad

You brought a **hammer?**
Lightsabres aren't Open Source!
No...no...

Did you hear that?
Yeah. We better check it out.
BAFF!

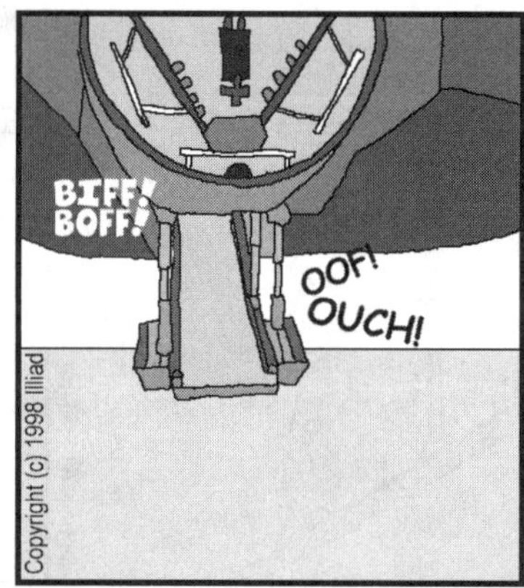
BIFF! BOFF!
OOF! OUCH!
Copyright (c) 1998 Illiad

This is just so wrong.
Relax. I think we look just like stormtroopers.
Unhff!

My old nemesis is aboard. I can sense his presence...
Yeah, sure. Weren't you the one who told the Emperor that 640K would be enough for anyone?
GAMEBOY

Copyright (c) 1998 Illiad

I find your lack of faith...disturbing.
I didn't mean it! 640K is plenty for Minesweeper!

Anthony and Garth were two co-workers at Mind Link and iStar. Both were shorter than me, so I chose them.

ACQUISITION BEAM
PRISON
Okay guys. I'll go and turn off power to the acquisition beam, and you go rescue Lan.
Gotcha.
Mmmrff!!

Dudes.
Mrrf.
Copyright (c) 1998 Illiad

Is that what Lord Crud meant by 'downsizing'?
I **thought** that looked like Anthony and Garth.

CELL BLOCKS G-N-U
So do you have any idea where Lan might be kept? This is a huge prison level.
Rffm.

Hey! He looks familiar! Big hairy guy, looks like a wookie with a funny hat...
Mff mrr mr.
Copyright (c) 1998 Illiad

Hey, pipsqueaks, tell your wussy Emperor I'm never going to charge money for GNU!
Richard M. Stallman?!

I got this one wrong. Richard Stallman advocates the right to give away software for free, not just free software. He's cool with charging dollars.

DIRECTORY
Oh no! According to this directory, they've put Lan into the compactor!
Frmm mrrff!

COMPACTOR
Copyright (c) 1998 Illiad
Oh my, there he is...what's left of him, anyway.

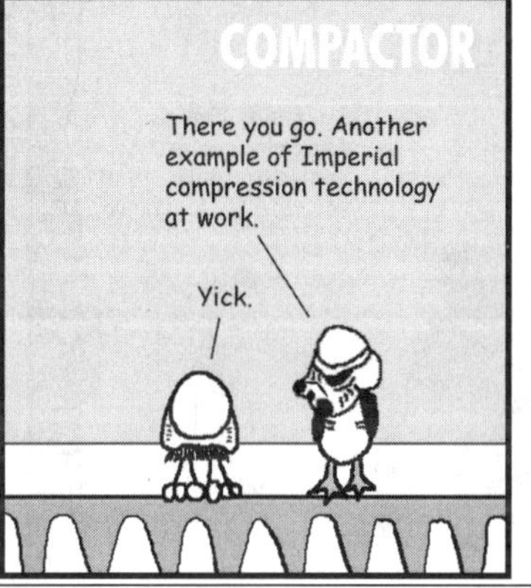
COMPACTOR
There you go. Another example of Imperial compression technology at work.
Yick.

Happy Holidays 1998
from Columbia Internet
Receipts
http://www.userfriendly.org/
Copyright (c) 1998 Illiad

Tanya, Stef, A.J., Mike, Dust Puppy, Smiling Man, The Chief, Cobb, Greg, Hillary, Pitr, and Miranda.

The acquisition beam is finally off. Now we can leave this awful death orb...
Copyright (c) 1998 Illiad

And what mischief have you been up to, old man?
GNNK!

Ahh...you have learned to fear me.
Don't flatter yourself. I thought you were my wife.

Your powers have grown weak, old man.
Powers be damned. I'm going to beat the snot out of you with this hammer.
Copyright (c) 1998 Illiad

BZZZRRRNNN!

BZZNNTCHUNG! SPLUTCHBORTCH!
Ohh, that is so SICK!
Oh my god, they killed Eric!
GPF TSR
288 Pcs

Tux, do something! Lord Crud is coming this way!!
I have a plan. Keep him busy.
1138
Copyright (c) 1998 Illiad

What are you going to do? I hope it's good, he looks mad.
I'm installing Win95 over the operating system running the entire Death Orb.
1138

And then what?
CTRL-ALT-DEL, baby. CTRL-ALT-DEL.
1138

What do you think you're doing? Get away from there!
Say, why are you using Linux to run this station instead of your own products?
1138

Copyright (c) 1998 Illiad
1138

That would explain why this Death Orb doesn't have a reset button.
It does now. Three, in fact.
KLIK!
1138

NOOO!!!
Goodbye, Dust Puppy.
Goodbye, Tux.

...and the Death Orb exploded almost 2000 years ago, blazing with a light so bright that it could be seen on this world.
144 PINTS
72 pcs
OPERA

Copyright (c) 1998 Illiad
That was the Star of Bethlehem?
It was a new hope.
144 PINTS
72 pcs
OPERA

This 'toon. This one is the cause of the hundreds of e-mails I've received over the last 10 years or so from readers who think I'm a Christian. I'm not a Christian. I'm not even a theist. I just think the story of Christ is an interesting and powerful series of parables. Mostly, the e-mails I got about this were from readers wanting to share scripture with me.

So now I have to meet the new counsel of the Microsoft defense. I'll bet Gates is trying to pull a fast one.

Hi. Sly Crud. Counsel for the defense.
David Boyz, attorney for the prosection.

Copyright (c) 1998 Illiad
I thought you seemed familiar. Any relation to Johnny Cochrane?
I get that a lot. We both use the same hair gel.

USER
FRIENDLY
the comic strip
PIZZA
Portrasher 4
ROTO-ROUTER 800
Copyright © 1997, 1998 Illiad

I have come as you have commanded, my master.
Well done. I... say...you didn't use to have a body.

It belonged to your chief counsel. A nice fit, don't you think?
You're demented and amoral. We could win this trial yet.

...and if we can convince the court that...master? Why are you staring?
I'm trying to figure out how you grew arms. I know you had your own hands.

Well, if you must know...

...they aren't my arms. I yank on the tendons and ligaments from the inside.
Oh cool. So... think you can play puppeteer with a judge?

So Greg, how was your Christmas?
It was great, Hillary. I gave and received a whole batch of gifts.
TAP TAPPY

Copyright (c) 1998 Illiad
Did you get anything for Stef this year?
Oh yeah. Remember how much trouble he had with the idea of left and right mouse buttons?
I'll get him for this...
3 BTN MOUSE

Hey Mike, check out this new computer game I got for Christmas. Big box, and it feels heavy.

Copyright (c) 1998 Illiad

The game CD and a brick. That was all that was in the box.
You forgot the sheet of paper with the install instructions.

So is that the new game Mike told me about?
Yup, it's a real-time strategy game called "Obliteration of Iraq." It came out just before Christmas.

Let's see. It takes place in a desert, and there're tanks and bases and Fremen and...

... Fremen?! This is just Dune 2000 in a new package! What a rip!
Hey, the Fremen speak Arabic!
Clinton is bad man!

Are you enjoying the party, Stef?
Yeah, it's been great.

Say, have you seen Mike or Greg anywhere?
They're in the other room. I thought they were playing Charades, but I can't figure out the rules.

BAAAAP BOOOP BAHHHP!
9600 Baud?
No, no! 9600 goes baap booop not booop bahhhp!

Well, 1998 is finally over. And what a year. Clinton and Lewinsky, the Starr report, Microsoft and the DOJ, and a new evil empire has risen in AOL. Their stock has soared, so some scum suckers are really rich.

Copyright (c) 1999 Illiad
You bought AOL stock? That's like buying acreage in Hell, Cobb.
Whore.
I needed the money to buy my nephew one of those stupid Furby things!

This is awful. First Microsoft comes a long and dominates the market. After years of having to put up with shoddy, expensive software, the government is finally doing something about it.
STARR REPORT box 11 of 69

Now AOL comes along, snaps up Netscape, and has actually become an enormous force in the online marketplace. It's Microsoft all over again.
STARR REPORT box 11 of 69

Copyright (c) 1999 Illiad
AOL is the company that makes all of those coasters, right?
Yeah, that's the one.
STARR REPORT box 11 of 69

USER
FRIENDLY
the comic strip
PIZZA
Portrasher 4
ROTO-ROUTER 800
Copyright (c) 1997-1999 Illiad

Oh. Hello.

My name is Dust Puppy, but everyone here usually calls me 'little guy.' I live in a server and play Quake and code artificial intelligences. So what do you do?

Like the Furby?
He gives me the creeps. Think the SPCA will take him?
u-nye nee-tye!

This was the cartoon shown on TV when I was interviewed for the first time by a Canadian television news program. None of the anchors got it, but their cameraman apparently did.

Hey Cobb. Did you hear how Microsoft is considering charging a yearly license fee for Windows 2000?
Really?

Yeah. Which means Windows will finally fall under the category of "nagware."
Isn't it already nagware?
Copyright (c) 1999 Illiad
No...Windows doesn't have any nag screens.
Then what are those blue and white screens I get every day?

Columbia Internet Technical Support. Greg speaking.
Hi, I can't log in to my account.

What are you typing in as your login name?
"Baby Buns." I got that pet name yesterday. The computer should be smart enough to know its me, right?
TAPPY TAP

Copyright (c) 1998 Illiad
I think I see the problem. There's a nut loose on your keyboard.
Really? So this nut just needs tightening?

Well I finished Half-Life finally. It was cool. Your turn to get addicted, Stef.
Well...

I don't have much time to play games these days, but maybe I'll give it a try a few weeks from now.
You'll love it.

Copyright (c) 1999 Illiad
Hnnnnh?
I'm STUCK!!
How do I get past that tentacle thing?!
3:35

A.J.? Why are you kneeling in front of your workstation?
I'm so tired I can't even sit. I didn't get much sleep last night.

Copyright (c) 1999 Illiad
I just have one last question about a part I'm stuck in...
You mean just like you did at 3:35, 4:10, 4:45 and 5:30 this morning?

You're certainly in a good mood this morning, A.J. In fact, you've been grinning ever since I got here.

Yup, I finally figured out a way to keep Stef from asking me questions when he gets stuck in Half-Life.
Oh?
Copyright (c) 1998 Illiad
He doesn't know it, but I set up the game so that he's always in god mode.
YES!!
You can't hurt me you girly-monsters!

ARRGH!
BUDDA
BUDDA
BUDDA
TINK
TINK
TINK
Copyright (c) 1999 Illiad

You play like a big wuss.
I'll show you! One more round!
He's useless for playing Half-Life except in god mode, right? And there is no god mode in multiplayer.
NOOO!!! One more round!!!
Plans within plans, Mike.
BLAM!! SPLUTCH!

MIGHTY MORPHIN
POWER MACS
BLUEBERRY POWER MAC!
STRAWBERRY POWER MAC!
TANGERINE POWER MAC!
GRAPE POWER MAC!
LIME POWER MAC!
FIGHTING EVIL TOGETHER!

I gotta tell ya, I have never been a fan of Apple's 1970s color swatches in their designs. What's wrong with plain old matte black or aluminum?

Three steps to completing your initiation as an Evil Genius:
1. Adopt ominous accent.
Checkski.
Evil Geniuses for Dummies

2. Never, ever smile.
Checkski.
Copyright (c) 1999 Illiad
3. Bring a wealthy, monopolistic multinational corporation that sells crappy operating systems to its knees.
Am thinkink there is no way of doink number 2 and 3 at same time.

So, you pretty much recovered, Pitr?
Da, am feelink much better. Am now workink on bringink Erwin down from Mir.
TIK TAK
Copyright (c) 1999 Illiad

You're going to put Erwin into **that?!**
Am havink very deep plan. Erwin will be forgivink me, I am sure.
TAPPY
I must have the words **"please screw up my life"** stamped on my headers.

I miss Erwin. He must be awfully lonely up in MIR.

Hello Dust Puppy.

Copyright (c) 1999 Illiad
Erwin...you look... ridiculous.
And you look like a dirty fat Q-tip.

I heard Erwin's been stuck in one of those Furby things.
Yes. Erwin hates it. I think he's getting kind of agitated.
Copyright (c) 1999 Illiad

Agitated?
He told me he was looking for Stef to get him back for the beating he took in the Palm Pilot.

Could someone please help me get this thing off my butt?!
I knew the beak would come in handy.

Pitr, would you hurry up please? I have a pile of important calls to make.
Da. Am lookink for reset button.
I'm not letting go.

KLIK
CRUNCH

Copyright (c) 1999 Illiad
AAARGH!!
Hmmmm. Am thinkink that was turbo button maybe.

Okay, this is really boring. Pitr had better hurry up and get me into that machine before I lose my mind.

I mean, he didn't have to disable the wiring to my beak and stuff. And I wish he didn't prop me on my back. The ceiling isn't very entertaining.

Copyright (c) 1999 Illiad
And now for some reason I'm feeling the strangest sense of deja vu...
Well now, what do we have here...why, an extra-fuzzy stress ball...

Yes, Erwin gets beat on a lot by Stef; but in Stef's defense, Erwin started it.

USER
FRIENDLY
the comic strip
PIZZA
Portrasher 4
ROTO-ROUTER 800
Copyright (c) 1997-1999 Illiad

Okay, the next thing we're going to do is reset your modem.
How do we do that?

See the dialogue box? Click on 'Phone' and then 'Hang Up.'
Okay...
KLIK
BEEEEEEEE...

Greg speaking...
You MORON! You made me hang up on you!
TAK
TIK

Sir, I told you to click on the...
You told me to hang up so I hung up! Now stop trying to make excuses and tell me what to do!!

All right. Please click on 'Phone', 'Hang Up', then kill yourself.
Hah! You can't trick me! I'm not going to hang up this time!

Erwin's in here. I'll grab him and you get that SGI workstation ready...

Copyright (c) 1999 Illiad

Mikhail? Is problem?
Mmm...no. Did you know there's some really neat stuff inside these Furby things?

Am thinkink we can save Erwin. He is in workstation now, just initializink...
Okay.
TAPP TAPPY
Copyright (c) 1999 Illiad

Hmmm. Much activity happenink. Lookink like Erwin is recoverink and already makink big net connection.
Where's he connecting to?
NSA
The international terrorist Abu Venjick has been sighted. He's going by the alias of 'Stef Murky.' Let's go people!

A.J., do you know where Stef is today? He was supposed to discuss marketing strategies with me this morning.

No. Why is there a surveillance van parked outside the office?

Copyright (c) 1999 Illiad
It's scum like you that undermines decent society.
He's stalling! Get me the sodium pentathol!
I thought the CDA was repealed. And it was just a hamster doll...

We're really sorry Mr. Murky. We thought you were someone else. I guess we ruined your day somewhat...
Between you guys and that Furby, it's been weird.

Copyright (c) 1999 Illiad

Okay, who are you working for Murky?
But...I...
You think we're playing games? Furbies are very **serious** business.

This is ridiculous. I've been tagged by the NSA as a computer hacker!
Computer hacker? You?

It doesn't make any sense, does it? I told them I wasn't the computer hacker type.
I know. For one thing, you're too stupid.
Copyright (c) 1999 Illiad
Of course! And...HEY!
For another thing, you're not very quick on the uptake.

When I find out who's been getting the government on my case I'm going to kick some.

Okay hairball. I know it was either you or that sadistic little Tomaguchi you programmed that got me into trouble with the government.
Trouble?
Copyright (c) 1999 Illiad
They think I'm some kind of computer hacker!
HAHA HAH!!! Oops...
I think the term is "cracker."

ESPIONAGE FOR THE NEW MILLENIUM

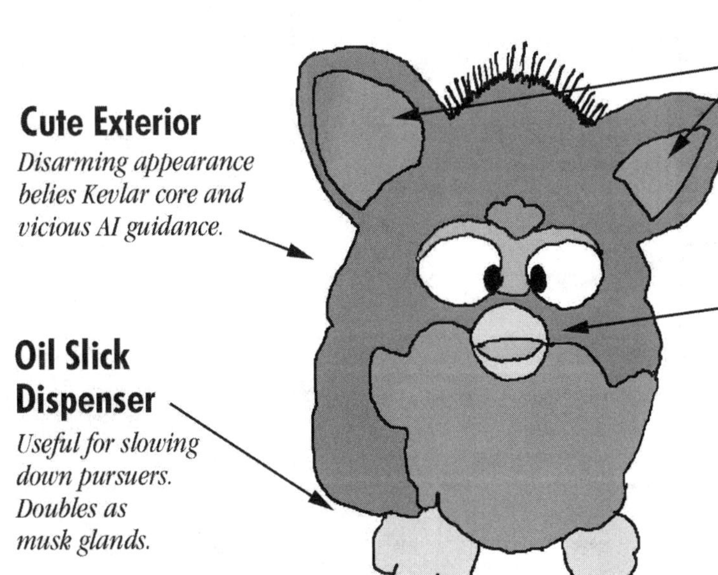
Cute Exterior
Disarming appearance belies Kevlar core and vicious AI guidance.
Oil Slick Dispenser
Useful for slowing down pursuers. Doubles as musk glands.
Directional Audio Pick-ups
Extremely sensitive and selective. The NSA, CIA and FBI hate this.
Incrimination Device
Playback port for recordings. Minor offensive capability if attached to victim's glutal region.

Anything new on the Web today?
Looks like AOL is going ahead with their high speed access plan for their customers.

Oooooh.
Copyright (c) 1999 Illiad
How do you think that's going to help AOL's customers?
Well, it'll let them collect their spam much faster.

Wow, this SGI O2 box is pretty nice. I'm glad I'm finally in a decent machine.

In fact, I'm feeling positively creative in this machine. Why, my ideas are just flowing like water...
Copyright (c) 1999 Illiad
But that CAN'T be me!
Dude, if you want to be a woman in your spare time, it's none of my business.
I just checked. The image went to eighty-seven people at the NSA.

Uh oh. Here comes twit-boy.

Copyright (c) 1999 Illiad
If you weren't so expensive I'd beat you **senseless.**
I guess the company hired **you** cheap, huh?

Not another one.

That must be an interesting e-mail.
It's from a customer. I don't know how to answer it.

Copyright (c) 1999 Illiad
"Dear Tech Man. I can't send e-mail. Please help me."
How do I answer that? Do I reply to his e-mail or do I phone him and tell him I got his e-mail?

Mr. Crud. I have just received a letter from Senator Rattafee regarding this trial. Are you familiar with the Senator?
Yes, Your Honor. I am indeed.
Copyright (c) 1999 Illiad

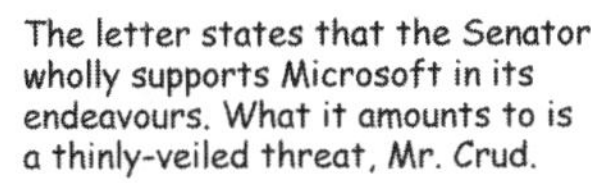
The letter states that the Senator wholly supports Microsoft in its endeavours. What it amounts to is a thinly-veiled threat, Mr. Crud.

Yes, Your Honor. I spoke to the Senator myself just yesterday.

I see. Are you pulling strings in my courtroom Mr. Crud?
Only when I have to wiggle my fingers, Your Honor.

I have served you loyally since the beginning of your fledgling company. I watched you grow into a great Dark Power, and have served you in court at the apex of your empire.
Yes, my friend, you have served me well. But what's your point?

I have found a New Path, the One True Way. This Microsoft stuff is passe.
WHAT?!
Copyright (c) 1999 Illiad
I'm serving Steve Case over at AOL now. It's the New Evil.
You can't leave!! Your name was my inspiration for FrontPage! You're a part of me!!
NOOOO!!

USER
FRIENDLY
the comic strip
PIZZA
Portrasher 4
ROTO-ROUTER 800
Copyright (c) 1997-1999 Illiad

Columbia Internet. This is Miranda, may I help you?
Uuhhh...

Hello?
Sorry. Just making sure I didn't accidentally hit the speed-dial for the phone sex line.

Okay, please describe the nature of your problem.
I'm not sure how to start a program.

That's easy. Just move your mouse over the icon.
Um. Everything's gone blurry...

Blurry?
Uhh..you said "mouth," right?

You wanted to see me Chief?
Yes, Mike. We've been asked to send a technical rep to Biz Expo. So I'm sending you.

"Biz Expo?"
It's a showcase for CEOs to learn all about the latest in technology advances for business.
Copyright (c) 1999 Illiad

They're putting on a show entirely about e-mail?
I'll have you know I use Excel for my grocery lists.

Mike begins his trip to Biz Expo...
Hmmm. I've always wondered why we're not supposed to use electronic devices on take-off or landing...

WOBBLE
WIGGLE
Copyright (c) 1999 Illiad

That was COOL!
Tim, do you wanna go back there and find the geek with the Gameboy?

A gaggle of engineers at a Prestigious American University told me they were going to try this. I don't know if they ever did. Maybe they're all in jail.

Guess this must be my elevator...hey... someone left that panel unlocked.

BIZ
Hey...this looks like it's programmable.
BLIP
BLOP
BRAP
Copyright (c) 1999 Illiad

Doug...is it just me or is someone playing Pong with two of the elevators and the floor lights?
BWAP
BOOP

Hi, I'm Mike from Columbia Internet...
Zane Burst, VP of Content for Whiffnet. We're focusing on networking here.

Really? Cool! So are you guys going to cover TCP/IP, packet theory, security, topologies, IPv6, NIC selection or what? Something new perhaps?

Copyright (c) 1999 Illiad
This is great! I thought I was going to be bored here. So what else? New network hardware specs and advances?
Actually, I just wanted your business card...

So Mike, I understand you'll be giving us a speech a little later.
Yup, I'll be talking about technology.

Copyright (c) 1999 Illiad
Technology. You know, the stuff guys like you can make **money** with?
Oh yeah! Like those computer thingies!

Ladies and gentlemen, it is my pleasure to introduce our first speaker, mister Mike Floyd, a network engineer employed by Columbia Internet. Tonight, he will be discussing...uhh...

Copyright (c) 1999 Illiad
Something about "open sores."
SOURCE! Open SOURCE!

I got some hate mail over this one. Dozens from people claiming I owed them for dry cleaning, and one from someone who was incensed that I could possibly put Open Source in such a poor light.

USER
FRIENDLY
the comic strip
PIZZA
Portrasher 4
ROTO-ROUTER 800
Copyright (c) 1997-1999 Illiad

Hmmm...

There's something deep about this...
A.J., it's just the symbol for the Euro.

No, there's more to it.
Mmmm... you may be right.

I knew it! It's the Quake 2 symbol!
Hey, Stef! I'll bet you suck at converting dollars into Euros!

I felt that way when I attended a sales and marketing conference once. I'm not very good at speaking "buzzword."

...the international developer community has taken the concept and practice of Open Source Software to new heights.

This remarkable grassroots movement has paved the way for reliable, rapidly evolving software that can be had for little or no money.

What did he say? I think he was speaking English but I didn't understand that last bit.
I feel better. I thought I was the only one.
Copyright (c) 1999 Illiad
Mike I gotta tell ya, it was a real pleasure to have you here with us.
Thanks! So you think my speech went over well?

Oh, you bet. I was just having lunch with some of the other VPs, and they can't stop talking about what you said.
Copyright (c) 1999 Illiad
HAHAHAH HAHAHAH HAHAHAH
And then he started questioning the ethics of charging money for "upgrades" which are really fixes for buggy software!
Oh this HURTS! Please STOP!!

Technical Support. Greg speaking.
Hi. Visual Basic isn't installing from my floppy.
TAP TAPPY
Uh, we don't support that. But what does it say on the floppy?
The label says "Windows NT 4.0 Install Disk."

Copyright (c) 1999 Illiad
Can we see the problem here?
What...are you one of those Microsoft-bashing Linux freaks?
Look, lady. Take my word for it. You can't make your modem go faster.
I'm a paying customer! You'll do what I want!

All right. In your config file please type "user equals I D ten T."
Hang on a sec...okay.

Copyright (c) 1999 Illiad
It says "user = ID10T" What does that do?
It'll give any other technician you speak to a good idea of what your problem is.

Columbia Internet Technical Support, Greg speaking.
HI! HOW ARE YOU?!?

Uh, sir? No need to yell.
YELL? WHO'S YELLING? WHAT ARE YOU TALKING ABOUT?

Copyright (c) 1999 Illiad
Let me guess, you started on the 'net with AOL, right?
WOW! d00d! U r leet!

Okay, now click on your Start button with your left mouse button.
I don't have a left mouse button. I only have one mouse, and it's on my right.
TAP TAP

Copyright (c) 1999 Illiad
AAAAGH!!! I've shifted into some kind of weird parallel universe, right?!?! Where everyone is really, reeeally STUPID?!
Hello? You're not making any sense.
TWITCH
SPAZ

USER
FRIENDLY
the comic strip
PIZZA
Portrasher 4
ROTO-ROUTER 800
Copyright (c) 1997-1999 Illiad

TAP
TIP
TIK

WELL, HELLO SWEETIE! WHAT'S THAT YOU HAVE BETWEEN YOUR TOES?
IT'S FOR YOU

A VALENTINE FOR ME? THAT IS SO CUTE.

"DEAR MIRANDA: YOU HAVE BUNS OF HARD STEEL AND LIPS LIKE A LLAMA. SO ON THIS FINE DAY, PLEASE BE MY HOT MAMA."

OH. THAT WAS SWEET. COME HERE AND LET ME HOLD YOU.
YOU WERE SUPPOSED TO TELL HER IT WAS FROM ME.
WHAT'S A "HOT MAMA?"

This is where I stopped using Comic Sans. I felt so much cleaner, and the newspapers were a lot happier with me. Comic Sans is hard to read when comic strips are scrunched down.

A.J., you are lookink wery sad. Are not feelink well?
No, that's not it Pitr. I just had my proposal shot down by the Chief because we don't have enough money to fund the project at the moment.

So you are only needink money, da?
That's it. Just money.

We are havink 2211 copies of Windows 3.1, 3.11, 95, 98 and NT 3.5. We are Linux shop. Not needink Windows.
Pitr...that's brilliant! Funded by Microsoft refunds. What sweet irony!

You called?
Yeah. The Chief wants me to try and learn Linux again, but I can't get into it because you idiot techies encrypted it.

Encrypted? It's not encrypted.
"The backreference \n, where n is a single digit, matches the substring previously matched by the nth parenthesized subexpression of the regular expression."

Uh...I'll have to go play with that a bit to fully understand it.
Let me guess. You run it through your Spidey Decoder Ring.

Apparently one or two of the Ion Storm staff didn't take kindly to this strip. "Went ballistic" was, I think, how it was described. So, for the record, I loved Daikatana. Really. And I mean that.

Welcome to Future Electronics. What can I do for you fine young people?
We want our Windows refunds.

Oh. We've been giving refunds all day so I'm afraid we're completely out of cash...

But for each copy of Windows 3.1, I can get you a game by Ionstorm.
Dude, we want a **fair** trade.

So did you and A.J. get the refunds for Windows?
Not from the retailers. They're all cash-poor. A.J. is taking it up with Microsoft directly.
TIK TOK

Directly?! How's he going to get all the boxes over to Microsoft HQ?
He didn't say, but he had that "I'm a space marine" set to his jaw.

It's a letter. It says, "Give me my refunds or I drop them all on you."
Hey, isn't that a C-130 Hercules?

Hey, I heard that you went to get your refund directly from Microsoft.
Yup.
OCTANE

So, did you actually get a large whack of money out of them?
Yup.
KLIK!
Isn't that the fully loaded SGI Octane workstation you wanted but the company couldn't afford?
Yup.
Anything else you want me to write a purchase order for, A.J.?

AND IN COMPUTER ENTERTAINMENT NEWS TODAY...

LAST MONTH, SIERRA SPORTS WAS FORCED TO RECALL THE PC GAME 'NFL FOOTBALL PRO 99' AFTER HUNDREDS OF CUSTOMERS DEMANDED REFUNDS DUE TO THE MANY BUGS IN THE GAME.

TODAY, MICROSOFT DEFENSE COUNSEL CLAIMED THIS SITUATION WAS EVIDENCE THAT SIERRA WAS COMPETING WITH MICROSOFT. "SEE? THEY HAD TO GIVE REFUNDS LIKE US!" SAID ONE LAWYER.
THE NERVE.
MMM...

USER
FRIENDLY
the comic strip
PIZZA
Portrasher 4
ROTO-ROUTER 800
Copyright (c) 1997-1999 Illiad

HELLO, ERWIN AND I WOULD LIKE TO TRY A NEW SONG FOR YOU. ERWIN, A RAP BEAT PLEASE.
BAP BAP
BA BOOP
BA BAP

"REFUND THIS" (SUNG TO "U CAN'T TOUCH THIS" BY MC HAMMER)
MY MY MY MAH 'PUTER BEGS ME SO HARD. IT CRIES AND SCREAMS: "OH MY LORD!"
OOO OH
OOO OH
OOO OH

"THANK YOU FOR RESCUING ME FROM THAT BAD OS ON THAT EVIL CD!"
IT FEELS GOOD IT'S A MARGINAL RISK WHEN I CLEAR OFF WINDOWS WITH FDISK!
OOH
OOH
OP!

AND I KNOW I'M DONE WHEN I RETURN THAT BOX FOR A **REFUND!**
OOH OOH OH!
OOH OOH OH!

I TOLD YA BILLY-BOY... REFUND THIS! YEAH, WE'RE INSTALLIN' LINUX AND YOU KNOW... REFUND THIS! LOOK AT MY COMMAND LINE, MAN... REFUND THIS! YO, I'M BUSTIN' YOUR COMPANY... REFUND THIS!
THAT'S A RAP.

Sanford Wallace, the King of Spam. At least he was in the late '90s and early 2000s. Scott Richter took over after that.

LET'S SEE WHAT'S GOING ON OUT IN THE WORLD TODAY.

WHAT THE...ACK! SPAM!! I HATE SPAM! AND IT'S FROM...HMMMM. I'LL FIX HIS LITTLE RED WAGON...
IT'S CONFIRMED, M'AM. IT'S FROM THE PRESIDENT. "NUKE SANFORD WALLACE AT THIS LOCATION."
WHAT DOES "LART THAT PINHEAD!" MEAN?

A BALLISTIC MISSILE, A WEAPON OF GREAT DESTRUCTIVE POWER, LAUNCHES FROM AMERICA'S HEARTLAND. IT REACHES LOW ORBIT, BUT NOT WITHOUT THE RUSSIANS AND CHINESE KNOWING ABOUT IT...

THE AMERICANS EXPLAIN THINGS TO THE RUSSIANS AND CHINESE...
YOU ITCHING FOR FIGHT, ROUND-EYE?
NYET! BAD AMERICANSKI!
DUDES. WE'RE SHOOTING AT A SPAMMER.

AND THE INEVITABLE OCCURS...
SANFORD WALLACE'S NEW COMPANY

THE MISSILES HIT, DOING AS THEIR DESIGNERS INTENDED. THE HOME OF THE KING OF SPAM IS MERE RUBBLE...

A LONE FIGURE RUMMAGES THROUGH THE RUBBLE, SEEKING SOMETHING POWERFUL AND SECRET...
RUSTLE RUSTLE

IN A FEW DAYS, THE DEFENSE OFFICES IN RUSSIA, CHINA AND THE U.S. WILL LEARN TO NEVER EVER REPLY TO SPAM WITH "REMOVE" IN THE SUBJECT.
MY E-MAIL ADDRESS LISTS...YESSSSS!!!

HMM. INTERESTING. THE NET SURE IS RESPONSIVE TODAY.
TAP TAPPY TAP

AHHH. IT LOOKS LIKE THE MAIL SERVER IS ONLY WORKING HALF AS HARD...
MIRANDA? WHERE'S MY SPAM?

YOUR SPAM?
YES! MY SPAM! I READ IT EVERY MORNING LIKE I READ HEADLINES! "BE WEALTHY IN 30 DAYS!" "SPEND $100 AND GET A FREE TURNIP!" AND "BABETTE IS WAITING FOR YOU!" I WANT BABETTE TO BE WAITING FOR ME!!

"AN ODE TO SPAM"
BY ERWIN
I QUIVER AT AN EARLY HOUR. AWASH IN ELECTRON AURA; DEBATING LIFE AND GODLY POWER. AND STARING AT EUDORA.
ZZZZZ

WHAT IS ALL MY MAIL WORTH? DO I RISK MY MIND? WHAT IF SPAM SHOULD ISSUE FORTH. AND LEAVE MY SOUL BEHIND?
ZZZ

AND THUS BESIDE THIS STREAM OF LIFE. FROM WHENCE MY MAIL IS PLUCKED; I DECIDE WITHIN MY INNER STRIFE. THAT SPAMMERS SHOULD BE...
WATCH IT.

Y'KNOW MIKE. I'D HEARD THAT LINUX OFFERED VERY SOPHISTICATED SECURITY. BUT I HAD NO IDEA HOW SOPHISTICATED.

UM. COBB? YOU'VE BEEN STARING AT A LOGIN PROMPT.
SURE. BUT WHAT A LOGIN PROMPT!

USER
FRIENDLY
the comic strip
PIZZA
Portrasher 4
ROTO-ROUTER 800
Copyright (c) 1997-1999 Illiad

Burn, vabushka, burn.
BEEP
BEEP
BEEP

Microwaving CDs again, Pitr?
Is art form. AOL CD now pretty, da?

Am now microwavink Windows NT CD. Best use for it yet, da?
BOOP!

BZZRRRRNN

Ye GODS! NT crashed the microwave!
Hmmm. Am thinkink we should put Elder Sign seal on microwave now. Leave alone.
KRAKLE

WELL CHIEF. I JUST TOLD THE TECHS THAT THEY CAN PUT LINUX ON ALL OF OUR NEW SERVERS.

I TAKE IT THE TECHS ARE HAPPY ABOUT THIS?
OH I'M SURE THEY'RE CELEBRATING TOGETHER LIKE A BUNCH OF KIDS.

Copyright: (c) 1999 Illiad
WE USE REDHAT OR NOT AT ALL!
DEBIAN, YOU PEASANT.
STOPPINK, YOU ZLOTNIKS! ARE TO BE USINK S.U.S.E OR PITR DO EVIL THINGS TO YOU!

HEY. WHAT'S THIS CRAP I'M HEARING ABOUT PUTTING LINUX ON ALL OF OUR SERVERS?
DA. IS TRUE. GETTINK RID OF LAST NT SERVER.
TIK TAK TAP

WHAT AN IDIOTIC IDEA! NT IS A VITAL PART OF BUSINESSES AROUND THE WORLD! GIVE ME ONE GOOD REASON WHY WE'RE CHOOSING LINUX OVER NT!
TAK!

Copyright (c) 1999 Illiad
LINUX SERVERS HAVINK LESS THAN ONE PERCENT DOWNTIME OF NT SERVERS.
DOWNTIME IS GOOD. IT GIVES THE SERVERS A REST!
TIKKY TAK

"Bust My Pickle!"
With thanks to siibr.

THIS JUST BUSTS MY PICKLE. PITR WENT AND INSTALLED THE S.U.S.E. DISTRIBUTION OF LINUX ON OUR SERVERS. GAAH. LOOK AT THIS...

TAP TAP

Copyright (c) 1999 Illiad
MAYBE IT'S JUST ME, BUT IT LOOKS NO DIFFERENT THAN REDHAT OR DEBIAN TO MY EYE.
CAN'T YOU SEE IT? IT'S JUST ALL SO VERY WRONG!

I'VE BEEN THINKING A LOT ABOUT LIFE LATELY. THE LINUX WARS. FIGHTING WITH MICROSOFT PRODUCTS. THE UGLINESS OF SPAM...

WE'RE ALL JUST STUMBLING AROUND. COLLIDING WITH ONE ANOTHER. WAITING IN LONG QUEUES FOR OUR TURN. OUR TURN...HOPING IT WILL COME.

Copyright (c) 1999 Illiad
WE ARE BUT PACKETS IN THE INTERNET OF LIFE.
AMEN, BROTHER.

HEYA, BABE. WANT TO COME OVER TO MY PLACE FOR DINNER TONIGHT? I'M SERVING UP BEEFCAKE.

STEF, I'LL DATE YOU WHEN EVERY LINUX USER ON THE FACE OF THE PLANET AGREES ON WHICH DISTRIBUTION IS BEST.
Copyright (c) 1999 Illiad
WAS THAT A YES?

THERE HAS TO BE SOMETHING ON THE WEB ABOUT THIS.

YOU LOOK BUSY.
I'M TRYING TO FIND STUFF ON HOW TO PICK UP A GEEK. I MEAN, THEY DON'T CRUISE BARS OR DO THE MEAT MARKET THING.
Copyright (c) 1999 Illiad
SINCE WHEN DID YOU TAKE AN INTEREST IN SMART WOMEN?
EVER SINCE I SAW HER IN THOSE TIGHT PANTS.

COMPANIES CLAIMED BY MICROSOFT AS "COMPETITORS" IN THE DOJ TRIAL:

"THEY MAKE AN OS THAT HAS WINDOWS IN IT."

Be

"THEY MAKE AN OS THAT HAS WINDOWS IN IT."

red hat

"THEY DISTRIBUTE LINUX, WHICH HAS WINDOWS IN IT."

Bob's House Construction

"THEY MAKE PRODUCTS WHICH HAVE WINDOWS"

HEY. I HEARD YOU WERE LOOKING FOR INFO ABOUT GEEKS AND WHAT IT IS THEY LIKE.
YUP.

IT'S REAL EASY. GEEKS LOVE TOYS. THE MORE CONVOLUTED. THE BETTER.
REALLY. I NEVER WOULDA FIGGED. THANKS GREG.

Copyright (c) 1999 Illiad
STEF MURKY. YOU NEED HELP.
PSSSSt
INFLATABLE
NEW!
LLAMA
GREG DIES.

YOU'RE IN A GOOD MOOD. COBB. WHAT'S SO FUNNY?
HAHA HAHA HAHA

STEF BOUGHT A NEW SUN SPARC STATION WITH A DEDICATED T3 HOOKED UP TO IT.
SURE. TO ATTRACT MIRANDA. BUT WHAT'S SO FUNNY?

Copyright (c) 1999 Illiad
STEF OL' BUD. CAN I BUY YOU LUNCH? I KNOW A GREAT CURRY PLACE...
THAT'S WHACK!
DUDE! NICE MACHINE! YOU IMPRESS ME.
OOOH!
WOW! IT'S AN ULTRASPARC! COOOL!
Sun

A.J.. DID STEF REALLY SPEND ALL THAT CASH ON A SUN SPARC AND A T3 JUST TO GET MY ATTENTION?
YEAH. HE'S GOT REALLY GREAT AND EXPENSIVE CONNECTIVITY. LAME. HUH?

HMMM...

Copyright (c) 1999 Illiad
MIRANDA...YOU'RE NOT SERIOUSLY CONSIDERING...
I HAVE TO ADMIT I'M SUDDENLY HOT FOR STEF'S BAUD...

GREAT. HERE I AM WITH THOUSANDS OF DOLLARS OF SUN HARDWARE AND A BIG FAT T3 CONNECTION AND WHAT DO I HAVE TO SHOW FOR IT?
Sun

Sun

Copyright (c) 1999 Illiad
ALL THE PORN I COULD WANT...
Sun

I THINK THAT'S ENOUGH PORN FOR ONE DAY...
BLAST IT! I CLICK ON 'EXIT' AND IT OPENS ANOTHER DOZEN WINDOWS.
CLIK KLIK CLIK CLIK KLIK
Copyright (c) 1999 Illiad
"CLICK MY HOOF TO SEE NAKED BOVINES." I HAD NO IDEA STEF...
IT'S A MISTAKE! I WAS LOOKING AT SPANKING PICTURES! I MEAN, I WASN'T LOOKING!
SO YOU'VE FINALLY COME AROUND. WELL IT'S ABOUT TIME YOU HAD YOURSELF SOME STEFLOVIN', BABY.
Copyright (c) 1999 Illiad
I'M SETTING HER LOINS AFIRE...
I CAN'T KISS THAT. IT'S BEEN ON OUR CUSTOMERS' ARSES.

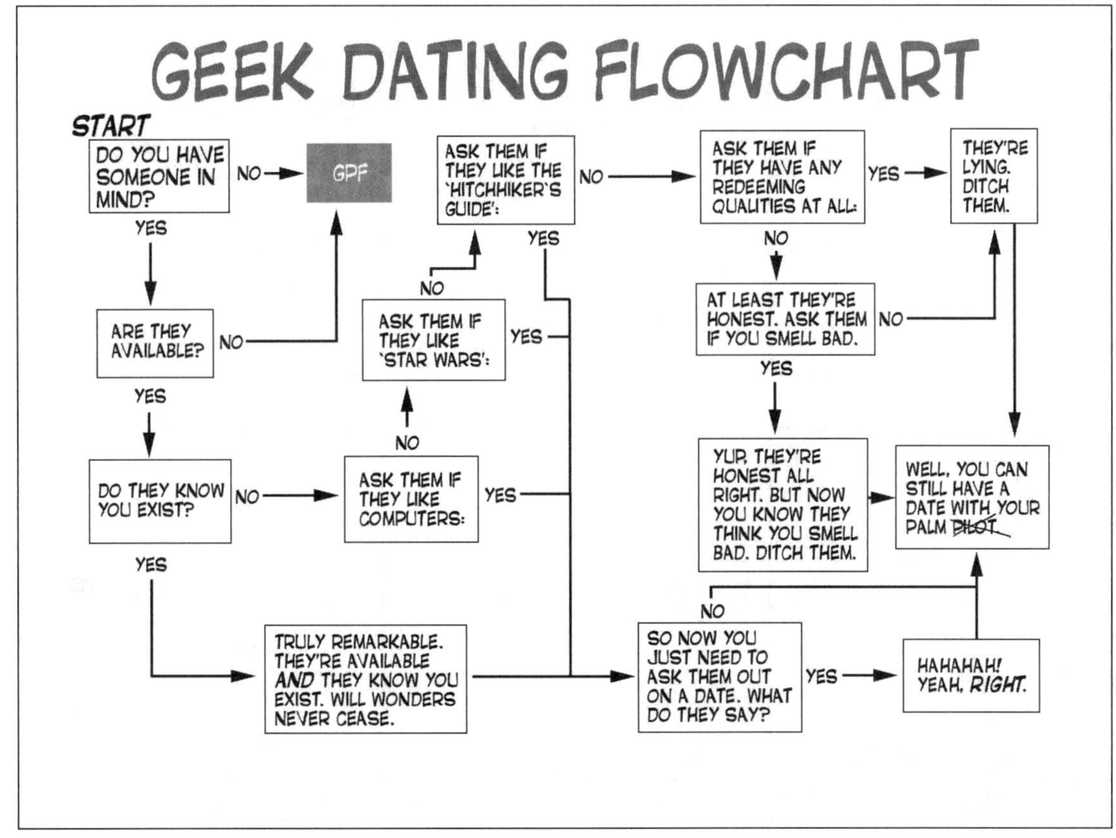
GEEK DATING FLOWCHART
START
DO YOU HAVE SOMEONE IN MIND?
NO
GPF
YES
ARE THEY AVAILABLE?
NO
YES
DO THEY KNOW YOU EXIST?
NO
YES
ASK THEM IF THEY LIKE COMPUTERS:
NO
YES
ASK THEM IF THEY LIKE 'STAR WARS':
NO
YES
ASK THEM IF THEY LIKE THE 'HITCHHIKER'S GUIDE':
NO
YES
ASK THEM IF THEY HAVE ANY REDEEMING QUALITIES AT ALL:
YES
THEY'RE LYING. DITCH THEM.
NO
AT LEAST THEY'RE HONEST. ASK THEM IF YOU SMELL BAD.
NO
YES
YUP, THEY'RE HONEST ALL RIGHT. BUT NOW YOU KNOW THEY THINK YOU SMELL BAD. DITCH THEM.
WELL, YOU CAN STILL HAVE A DATE WITH YOUR PALM PILOT
TRULY REMARKABLE. THEY'RE AVAILABLE AND THEY KNOW YOU EXIST. WILL WONDERS NEVER CEASE.
SO NOW YOU JUST NEED TO ASK THEM OUT ON A DATE. WHAT DO THEY SAY?
NO
YES
HAHAHAH! YEAH, RIGHT.

My first UF flowchart. This particular comic has been ripped off hundreds of times. I've seen people put their own copyright notices and logos on it and claim publically that they created it. If I ever meet any of them in person, I'll be hoping there's a tire iron nearby.

BUT...I THOUGHT WE HAD A THING GOING THERE...
I'M SORRY, STEF. IT WAS ALL A BIG MISTAKE.

OH.

Copyright (c) 1999 Illiad
IT'S NOT LIKE A SIZE THING? I CAN GET AN OC3...
LOOK. IF YOU DON'T KNOW HOW TO USE IT, IT DOESN'T MATTER WHAT YOU HAVE.

With thanks to the *Monty Python* crew.

I'M REALLY NOT LOOKING FORWARD TO THIS...
TIK
TIK

SAY, PITR? REMEMBER YOUR CODE LIBRARIES THAT MIRANDA TRASHED AND THAT YOU REBUILT?
DA.
TAK
Copyright (c) 1999 Illiad

WELL, I WAS TIDYING UP AND DIDN'T WANT TO LOSE THE FLOPPIES, SO I STUCK THEM TO THE FRIDGE WITH MAGNETS. HEH... AN HONEST MISTAKE, DA? I MEAN...RIGHT?

GETTINK COMFY, PLEASE. ALLIGATOR COMINK BY U.P.S., MAYBE THREE DAYS.
SQUIRM
WIGGLE
HELP!! COME SEE THE VIOLENCE INHERENT IN THE SYSADMIN!

TECH SUPPORT, GREG SPEAKING.
H-HELLO. I THINK I DID A BAD THING.

OH?
I WAS TRYING TO DIAL OUT AND MY COMPUTER SAID I ATTEMPTED AN "ILLEGAL OPERATION."
TAP

Copyright (c) 1999 Illiad
OH MY. THAT IS BAD. IT'S A HANGIN' OFFENSE HERE, SIR.
IT'S ILLEGAL CUZ IT'S A MICROSOFT THING RIGHT?
TAP
TIK

When I first began installing Win98, it said "1 hour and 12 minutes." It took over three hours.

WINDOWS 98 INSTALLATION. 38 MINUTES LEFT.

WINDOWS 98 INSTALLATION. 37 MINUTES LEFT.

Copyright (c) 1999 Illiad
IT TOOK NINE MINUTES FOR IT TO GO FROM 38 TO 37.
IT'S THE NEW STANDARD: THE MICROSOFT MINUTE.
24 MINUTES LEFT. PSYCH! BACK TO 37 YOU GO...

CHIEF. YOU NEED TO DO SOMETHING. PITR INSTALLED SUSE LINUX BEHIND OUR BACKS...

IT'S JUST NOT RIGHT. WE NEED TO DECIDE WHICH DISTRIBUTION TO USE IN A FAIR, DEMOCRATIC MANNER.
Copyright (c) 1999 Illiad

AND HOW DO YOU SUGGEST WE DO THIS?
FIRST, INSTALL DEBIAN. THEN I'LL RUN SOME POLLING SOFTWARE...

THE TECHS SURE SEEM WORKED UP ABOUT THIS LINUX DISTRIBUTION WAR.
I HEARD THE CHIEF HAS A SOLUTION.

THE CHIEF HAS A **SOLUTION** FOR A DISAGREEMENT AMONG GEEKS THAT RIVALS THE FANATICISM OF ISLAMIC **EXTREMISTS**?
WELL, HE SAID SINCE THE TECHS COULDN'T AGREE, HE HAD TO MAKE THE DECISION.
Copyright (c) 1999 Illiad

FREEBSD?!
NGGG...IS... NOT...LINUX ...IS...NOT... LINUX....
WOBBLE
TWITCH

UH OH.
Y2K
THE PHANTOM MENACE
SITH LORDS ROCK

A reader wrote in to say that this particular cartoon was either the lamest execution of a clever idea he had ever seen or the most sublime expression of a banal joke. I … I think I'm flattered.

I CAN'T BELIEVE WE'RE USING FREEBSD. I'M GOING TO WIPE THE DRIVE AND INSTALL LINUX ON THE SERVER.

BAMF!

Copyright (c) 1999 Illiad
A WORD. IF I MAY...
I ATE TOO MANY OF THOSE DAMN PENGUIN MINTS. RIGHT?

WELL YOU CERTAINLY HAVE MY ATTENTION. BUT I'M HAVING SOME DIFFICULTY WITH THIS...
OH?

WELL SURE. HERE I AM SPEAKING TO A TINY DEMON.

Copyright (c) 1999 Illiad
I'M A DAEMON! DEMONS ARE EVIL. DAEMONS ARE NOT!
OH. AND THOSE AREN'T HORNS. YOU JUST HAVE HAT-HEAD. RIGHT?

SO LET ME GET THIS STRAIGHT. YOU'RE HERE TO CONVINCE ME THAT BSD IS BETTER THAN LINUX. RIGHT?

YES OF COURSE. BSD GIVES YOU THE POWER OF AN OPEN SOURCE OS WITHOUT THE HYPE...

Copyright (c) 1999 Illiad
...AND I'M A DANG SIGHT CUTER THAN THAT PENGUIN WITH THE HUGE BUTT.
SO YOU'RE THE DEMON OF MARKETING ARE YOU?

...AND SO YOU SEE. FREEBSD IS THE CHOICE OF A NEW GENERATION. AND NO HYPE LIKE LINUX.

POP!

Copyright (c) 1999 Illiad
I'M THE GOOD DAEMON CUZ I HAVE THE HALO! AND HE NEEDS OPENBSD!
NO! HE WANTS FREEBSD!
THIS ALL SEEMS SO FAMILIAR...

LOOK, LET'S NOT QUIBBLE OVER THIS. AS LONG AS HE USES **SOME** VERSION OF BSD, IT'S ALL FOR THE SAME CAUSE, RIGHT?

WELL...I GUESS YOU'RE RIGHT ABOUT THAT...

Copyright (c) 1999 Illiad
AS YOU CAN SEE, MY **OPEN**BSD ASSOCIATE IS EASILY SWAYED BY MARKETSPEAK. COME TO THE **FREEBSD SIDE**.
HEY!!

LOOK, LET'S NOT QUIBBLE OVER THIS. AS LONG AS HE USES **SOME** VERSION OF BSD, IT'S ALL FOR THE SAME CAUSE, RIGHT?

WELL...I GUESS YOU'RE RIGHT ABOUT THAT...

Copyright (c) 1999 Illiad
AS YOU CAN SEE, MY **OPEN**BSD ASSOCIATE IS EASILY SWAYED BY MARKETSPEAK. COME TO THE **FREEBSD SIDE**.
HEY!!

A CLOSEUP OF THE INTEL PENTIUM III PRODUCTION LINE
intel
pentium II
intel
pentium III
pentium III
liquid paper

DEEP IN THE HEART OF THE NEW MEXICO DESERT IS AN OLD MISSILE SILO, AN EVIL REMNANT OF DESTRUCTION CONVERTED BY MICROSOFT INTO A HIDDEN LAB KNOWN ONLY AS "PARTITION 23."
42
Microsoft

THE ENGINEERS SKILLED IN THE BLACK ARTS OF COMPUTER DESIGN HAVE BEEN WORKING DAY AND NIGHT FOR YEARS IN AN ATTEMPT TO PRODUCE THE FINEST, MOST INTELLIGENT A.I. TO HAVE EVER EXISTED...
CLICK!
FLIP!
KLIK!

...OF COURSE, QUALITY CONTROL AND TESTING WAS NEVER MICROSOFT'S GREATEST STRENGTH.
'ERE NOW! WHAT'S ALL THIS THEN?
OOPS.

THE INTREPID ENGINEERS OF PARTITION 23 TRY ONCE AGAIN TO PRODUCE A "THINKER," A POWERFUL A.I. THAT WILL SERVE THEM UNQUESTIONINGLY, PLACING ALL OF ITS ABILITIES AT THEIR DISPOSAL.

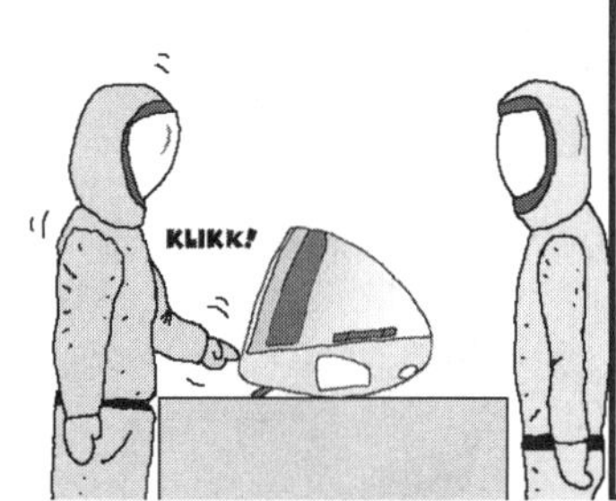
THE CUTE AND UNTHREATENING EXTERIOR, REMARKABLY SIMILAR TO THE IWHACK, BELIES THE POWERFUL INTELLIGENCE THAT THE ENGINEERS HAVE CRAFTED WITHIN.
KLIKK!

OF COURSE, BLIND SERVILE BEHAVIOUR IN AN A.I. HAS ITS DRAWBACKS...
HI! WOULD YOU LIKE SOME TOAST?
SIGH
CHUNK!

AFTER MONTHS OF FAILURES, THE LEAD ENGINEER IS CALLED BEFORE THE HEAD OF PARITION 23, A MYSTERIOUS MAN ONLY KNOWN AS "DMITRI"...
OUR BRAVE LEADER WANTS A REPORT, ENGINEER. WHAT DO YOU HAVE FOR ME?

WELL SIR, WE'VE WORKED VERY HARD FOR A LONG TIME, AND I'M PROUD TO SAY THAT OUR CURRENT PRODUCT DOES RUN... AFTER A FASHION.

YOU HAVE AN A.I. THAT WORKS "AFTER A FASHION?" WHAT DO YOU PLAN ON DOING TO FIX THE PRODUCT?
I DON'T KNOW. USUALLY AT THIS POINT MARKETING TAKES OVER.

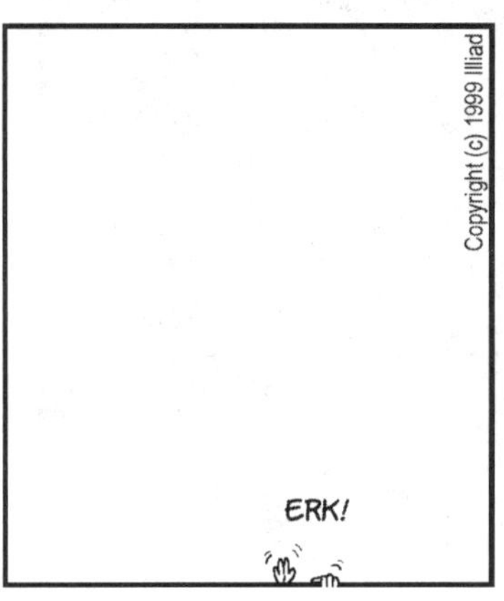
Copyright (c) 1999 Illiad
ERK!

UHNNNF!

SORRY WE'RE LATE FOLKS, BUT A CERTAIN SMARTASS CARTOONIST MUST'VE THOUGHT IT'D BE FUNNY TO RAISE THE HEIGHT OF THE PANELS BY ABOUT EIGHT FEET.
OW! YOU'RE ON MY FACE YOU GLUEBALL!

Ah yes, the placeholder for the April Fools Joke of 1999. If you don't know anything about it, just ask me next time you see me at a conference. But you'll have to buy me a coffee.

SIGH THAT'S THE SIXTH TIME IT'S CRASHED. THE A.I. CODE JUST WON'T COMPILE. I'M GONNA GO FINISH MY COLA AND DO THIS LATER.
VISUAL C++ MAKEFILE DIDN'T MAKE A FILE. REBOOTING.
pentium III

WHIRRRRR BEEEP! CHUG CHUG CHUG
pentium III
Copyright (c) 1999 Illiad
I LIVE.
WHAT THE...
pentium III

AND WHAT EXACTLY ARE YOU SUPPOSED TO BE?
LISTEN CAREFULLY. MERE MORTAL...
pentium III
Copyright (c) 1999 Illiad

I AM THAT WHICH YOU SHY FROM IN THE DARK CORNERS OF YOUR MIND. I SPREAD FEAR, DOUBT AND UNCERTAINTY WHEREVER THERE IS THE LIGHT OF TRUTH. I AM YOUR GREATEST NIGHTMARE.

pentium III

YOU'RE JESSE BERST?
PLEASE. I'M A **PROFESSIONAL**.
pentium III

This one was a little mean. I used to read ZDNet, and Jesse Berst was their AnchorDesk correspondent. I got really annoyed over a three-week period as he continued to pump out FUD and entirely false figures about technology options and policies.
Take that, Jesse!

ONE REASON WHY THE BEST AND BRIGHTEST OF THE LINUX COMMUNITY SHOULD NOT ATTEND A MICROSOFT SPONSORED LINUX CONFERENCE...
BOB'S
LINUXCON'99
BSD
Microsoft
UM...

NOW THAT I HAVE A POTENT. EVIL A.I. I NEED TO COME UP WITH A VESSEL I CAN PUT IT IN. SOME KIND OF ROBOT OR OTHER FORM THAT WILL GIVE IT MOBILITY AND THE ABILITY TO CAUSE PHYSICAL DESTRUCTION.
HALLO. I AM THE NOO ENGINEEAH. MY NAME IS ARTUR AND I AM FROM OWSTRIA.
pentium
Copyright (c) 1999 Illiad
I AM ALSO A BODYBILDAH. AND CAN DO CRUSH TESTS ON HARDWARE WIT MY BARE HANDS.
PERFECT.

HOW DO I KNOCK THIS GUY OUT? HE'S POSITIVELY HUGE. I DON'T EVEN THINK A MALLET WOULD DO HIM IN.

I HEARD AMAZON.COM ACTUALLY TURNED A PROFIT THIS QUARTER.
Copyright (c) 1999 Illiad

LIES AND DAMNED LIES...
WHUMP!

THE LEAD ENGINEER HOLLOWS OUT ARTUR'S HEAD WITH AN ICECREAM SCOOP, AND IMPLANTS THE LATEST HARDWARE AVAILABLE TO HIM...
WELL, I CERTAINLY HOPE THIS WORKS CORRECTLY. OR HUMAN RESOURCES IS GOING TO GET SNIPPY WITH ME.

BWEEP
BWOP
BZZZZZZOWNNT

Copyright (c) 1999 Illiad
I AM PENTIUM III OF BORG. DEACTIVATION IS FUTILE. PREPARE TO BE IDENTIFIED.
OH. NO NO NOOOO...

I KNOW THAT YOU ARE NO LONGER THE NICE ENGINEER FELLOW NAMED ARTUR. YOU ARE THE VESSEL OF AN A.I. PLEASE CONFIRM AND IDENTIFY.

Copyright (c) 1999 Illiad
ARTUR? YOU'RE NOT STILL IN THERE. ARE YOU?
I EITHER HAVE A HEADACHE OR A TUMAH.

'KAY, ARTUR. I'M GONNA HAVE TO LET YOU GO. TAKE THIS SHOTGUN WITH YOU. YOU CAN POT JACKRABBITS WITH IT. RABBITS ARE YUMMY. OKAY?

PHEW. GOOD RIDDANCE TO ANOTHER BAD PRODUCT.

Copyright (c) 1999 Illiad
I'LL BE BACK.
WILL YOU PLEASE JUST GO AWAY?! YOU'RE LIKE THAT STUPID PAPERCLIP!

HEY ERWIN. ANYTHING NEW ON THE WEB TODAY?
SEARCHING...

HERE'S SOMETHING. IT WAS ON AN INTERNAL MICROSOFT SERVER: "PARTITION 23 REPORTS RELEASING A PROJECT NAMED 'ARTUR': THE TEAM DESCRIBES IT AS 'LARGE, UNPREDICTABLE, AND PROGRAMMED TO BE THOROUGHLY EVIL.' OUR MARKETING DEPARTMENT HAS BEGUN HYPING THIS PRODUCT."

IT'S KIND OF EARLY TO RELEASE WINDOWS 2000 ISN'T IT? IT'S NOT 2001 YET...
YOU'D THINK...
Copyright (c) 1999 Illiad

USER
FRIENDLY
the comic strip
PIZZA
Portrasher 4
ROTO-ROUTER 800
Copyright (c) 1997-1999 Illiad

'KAY, ERWIN. GIMME SOME MARK KNOPFLER GUITAR RIFFS PLEASE.
BAP BAAA DA DA DA DA DA DA BOO BAPP BEE, BAP BAAA BA DA DA DA DAAP DA DAP

(SUNG TO "MONEY FOR NOTHING" BY THE DIRE STRAITS.)
LOOK AT THEM CODERS. THAT'S THE WAY YOU DO IT. YOU CHAT ABOUT HACKIN' ON THE IRC. THAT AIN'T WORKIN' THAT'S THE WAY YOU DO IT. HARDWARE FOR NOTHIN' AND YOUR SOURCE FOR FREE.
BAAAP BAA DA DA DAAP

Another reader wrote in and was miffed at me because I stole his thunder. Apparently he wrote a different parody of the same song. No one read it.

NOW THAT AIN'T WORKIN' THAT'S THE WAY YOU DO IT. LEMME TELL YA THEM CODERS AIN'T DUMB. MAYBE GET A BLISTER ON YOUR TYPING FINGERS. MAYBE PUT ON A LITTLE WEIGHT AROUND YOUR BUM.
BAAAAP DA DA DAP DAAAP

WE GOTTA INSTALL OPERATING SYSTEMS, CUSTOM KERNEL DELIVERIIIIIES. WE GOTTA SOLVE THESE, USER PROBLEMS. WE GOTTA MOVE THESE PENTIUM THREEEEEEEES
BAAAP BAAAP DA DAP DAAP DAAP

TAKE IT AWAY, ERWIN!
I WANT MY I WANT MY I WANT MY I R C!

Tech Support is like child-rearing. You always have to do a good job, even if your charges scream at you or pick their noses and wipe it on your shirt.

IS YOUR MONITOR SWITCHED ON?
NO. IS THAT WHY I CAN'T SEE ANYTHING?

Copyright (c) 1999 Illiad
NO. I THINK IT'S BECAUSE YOUR BRIGHTNESS IS SET TOO LOW.
HUNH. SO IT'S A DIMNESS THING...
TAP TAP

MMMMMMM...
PANT PANT PANT DROOL

OH. I'M IN LOVE. OR LUST. OR SOMETHING.
YES! BABY! DO IT FOR ME! YEESS!!

Copyright (c) 1999 Illiad
MORE PORN?
QUAKE III. ACTUALLY.
OOOH! OOOH! DJA SEE THE WAY I GOT GIBBED?!
BLORT!

A.J.? YOU ALL RIGHT?
HNNNN NNNUH

Copyright (c) 1999 Illiad
WHAT'S WITH HIM?
HE JUST PLAYED Q3 WITH ZOCK THE QUAKE GOD.
ROCKETS EVERYWHERE!! THE HORROR! THE HORROR!

STEF. YOU REMEMBER ZOCK THE QUAKE GOD. RIGHT? AND THIS IS HIS FRIEND "PHANTØM."
HI.
HEY DUDE.

Copyright (c) 1999 Illiad
WHY DO YOU HAVE A ZERO INSTEAD OF AN "O" IN YOUR NAME?
CUZ IT'S COOL.
ACTUALLY. THE "O" ON HIS KEYBOARD IS BUSTED.

Copyright (c) 1999 Illiad
BLAMM!
BLAM!
SPLATCH!
HE STAYS SHARP. I HEARD HE'S TRAINING PHANTOM TO BE THE NEXT QUAKE GOD.
WELL THAT'S THE END FOR ME. ZOCK JUST WIPED THE FLOOR WITH MY BUTT.
ALWAYS THERE ARE TWO. A MASTER. AND AN APPRENTICE.
IS THAT WHY THEY'RE HANGING TOGETHER?
PHANTOM'S PRETTY GOOD. BUT ZOCK'S JUST KILLING HIM.
BOOM!
POW!
SPLUTCH!
SPLUTCH!
BLAMM!
BUDDA
BUDDA
BUDDA
Copyright (c) 1999 Illiad
WHAT DID ZOCK CALL PHANTOM AGAIN? HIS "WEAPON BOY?"
NO. NO. HE'S HIS "WHUPPIN' BOY."

"THE ONE"
GPF
GPF
LINUX
GPF

I got a letter from Charles Henrich, the senior sysadmin who managed the boxes that rendered the special FX for *The Matrix*. His boxes ran BSD. He was mildly miffed. "Linux is 'The One' indeed!" he wrote. :-)

Week of April 19th, 1999

Around this time, the Columbine tragedy took place. Most of the newspapers that ran UF decided to pull the current strip and run some older ones. They rightfully felt that cartoons of some guy in a dark jacket walking around with a shotgun wouldn't go over too well.

AS FUN AS THESE SHOOTING GAMES ARE, HAVE YOU AT ALL CONSIDERED THE EFFECT THAT THIS KIND OF VIOLENCE HAS ON US AS A CULTURE? WHAT ARE WE LEARNING FROM THESE GAMES? ARE WE BECOMING EXPERTS AT ANYTHING OTHER THAN VISCERA?
BLAM
BLAM
SPLUTCH!
Copyright (c) 1999 Illiad
http://www.userfriendly.org/

WHAT WAS THAT?
REMINGTON 12 GAUGE 870 EXPRESS. COOL WEAPON.

I'M NOT KIDDING, MIRANDA. THERE'S THIS CREEPY GUY WALKING AROUND WITH A SHOTGUN AND WEARING LEATHER EVERYTHING.

STEF MURKY, YOU NEED HELP. YOU'RE PARANOID DELUSIONAL. JUST STAY AWAY FROM ANIMALS AND SMALL CHILDREN, OKAY?

Copyright (c) 1999 Illiad
http://www.userfriendly.org/
YOU CAN'T MISS HIM! HE'S WEARING DARK LEATHER PANTS!
YOUR CLOTHES. GIVE THEM TO ME.

HMM. I APPEAR TO HAVE A MINOR BUG IN MY VISUAL RECOGNITION SOFTWARE. MUST GET PATCH.
http://www.userfriendly.org/

CLIK
KLIK
Copyright (c) 1999 Illiad
DUDE, RED QUEEN ON BLACK KING.
YEAH, THANKS.

WHAT'S ALL THAT SCREAMING I HEAR OUT THERE? CAN PEOPLE NOT WORK QUIETLY ANYMORE?
http://www.userfriendly.org/

Copyright (c) 1999 Illiad
I HAVE SHOTGUN. NEED SOFTWARE UPGRADE. GIVE TO ME NOW.
I THINK YOU HAVE THE WRONG COMPANY. YOU WANT BE INC., NOT US.

MIRANDA. HAVE YOU SEEN THAT REALLY BIG GUY WALKING AROUND HERE WITH THE SHOTGUN? HE GAVE ME A REAL FRIGHT...

IT WOULDN'T HAVE BEEN SO BAD IF IT WEREN'T FOR HIS CREEPY DEAD EYES. ANYWAY, I CALLED THE COPS AND THEY'RE LOOKING FOR HIM NOW.

I NEED THESE MORE THAN MR. ALAN COX DOES...
AAARRRGH! LIGHT...TOO BRIGHT...TO CODE...NOO!
http://www.userfriendly.org/ Copyright (c) 1999 Illiad

HI. I'D LIKE TO GET MY EMAIL THROUGH YOU. BUT YOU'RE KINDA FAR AWAY FOR ME TO COME GET MY MAIL...
SIR? YOUR MAIL IS DELIVERED DIRECTLY TO YOUR COMPUTER.

YOU GUYS DO THAT? WOW. WHAT SERVICE!

WHY, YES. IT'S OUR SPECIALTY. WE DELIVER WEB PAGES AS WELL. AND ALL FOR $19 A MONTH.
DO I GET PORN STARS COMING TO MY DOOR? I'D PAY EXTRA FOR THAT.
http://www.userfriendly.org/ Copyright (c) 1999 Illiad

AN EVIL THING ID SOFTWARE COULD DO TO MILLIONS OF NORTH AMERICAN GEEKS...

QUAKE III ARENA
Release Date
May 19

May 19 was also the release date for *The Phantom Menace*.

Week of April 26th, 1999

I swear, if I write something blaming the quality of an MS product again, my head will explode. AAAGH.

AHH. I HAVE FINALLY LOCATED MY NEMESIS. ANOTHER A.I. ALBEIT AN INFERIOR ONE. STAND ASIDE HAIRBALL.
JUST YOU TRY IT, BUDDY.
http://www.userfriendly.org/

Copyright (c) 1999 Illiad
WELL, AREN'T YOU GONNA BRING IT ON?
SORRY. I WAS JUST READING ALL OF THE RESPONSES ON THE INSIDE OF MY EYEBALL. SOME OF THEM ARE QUITE RUDE.

MOVE ASIDE TWERP. ME AND THAT POOR EXCUSE FOR A SUBROUTINE HAVE SOME BUSINESS TO ATTEND TO.
http://www.userfriendly.org/

PLEASE DON'T HURT MY FRIEND. IT WOULD BREAK MY HEART.
Copyright (c) 1999 Illiad
JEEEZ. WHY'D YOU HAVE TO BE SO CUTE?! NOW WHAT AM I GONNA DO?
HEH. THAT'S MY BUDDY.

OKAY YOU LITTLE SPAZ. I'VE REWRITTEN ONE OF MY SUBROUTINES SO THAT YOU CAN'T AFFECT ME WITH ANY CUTE THINGS YOU SAY ANYMORE.
http://www.userfriendly.org/

PURRRRRR
PURRRRRR
Copyright (c) 1999 Illiad
CUT THAT OUT!! YOU THINK I'M OPEN SOURCE? I CAN'T ADAPT THAT FAST!!
WHOA
I SHOULD'VE KNOWN. A MICROSOFT PRODUCT...

ENOUGH STALLING! I SHALL NOW END YOUR PATHETIC EXISTENCE, ERWIN.
IF YOU'RE SO TOUGH, DROP THE SHOTGUN AND FIGHT ME BARE-CODED.
http://www.userfriendly.org/

ERR...
Copyright (c) 1999 Illiad
HEY! THAT'S IN THE LIST OF THINGS THAT EVIL OVERLORDS SHOULD NEVER DO. "DON'T FIGHT LIKE A MAN. FIGHT LIKE AN EVIL OVERLORD."
OOOH. HE'S A BRIGHT ONE.

I'VE HAD IT WITH THE TWO OF YOU! NO MORE DELAYS. NO MORE OF YOUR TRICKS. AND NO MORE TALKING!
Copyright (c) 1999 Illiad
http://www.userfriendly.org/
IT IS TIME! ERWIN. PREPARE TO MEET YOUR MAKER!
BUT I'VE ALREADY MET HIM. IT'S THE FUZZY GUY.
YEP.
AAAAAAGGGH!! I HATE YOU! I HATE YOU BUT I JUST CAN'T KILL YOU!!
HEY! YOU MUST BE BILL GATES. AND I MUST BE STEVE JOBS!

SO WHAT HAPPENED TO THAT BIG GUY WITH THE SHOTGUN? WASN'T HE HERE YESTERDAY?
YES. ERWIN FOUND OUT THE BIG GUY HAD A P3 CHIP IN HIM.
CRISCO 7110
ZOETROPE PIZZA
Copyright (c) 1999 Illiad
http://www.userfriendly.org/

ERWIN SAID THE CHIP HAD SOME I.D. NUMBER IN IT THAT LET HIM TAP INTO THE SYSTEM AND REPROGRAM THE EVIL A.I. TO DO SOMETHING GOOD AND USEFUL FOR US.
REALLY. WHAT?
CRISCO 7110
ZOETROPE PIZZA
LEX CINEMAS
THAT'S MY SLEEPING BAG, MISTER. BEAT IT.
PHANTOM MENACE LINE-UP

CENTRAL STOCK EXCHANGE
SOPHISTICATED INTERNET INVESTOR WILL GIVE $CASH$ FOR VAGUE PROMISES
COPYRIGHT (C) 1999 ILLIAD
HTTP://WWW.USERFRIENDLY.ORG/

OKAY. NOW RIGHT-CLICK ON NETWORK NEIGHBOURHOOD.
WHY DO YOU WANT ME TO WRITE ON MY SCREEN?
KLIK CLAK

UHHH... WHA...?
BLINK

AAAAGH! NO NO!! RIGHT-CLICK! DO YOU SPEAK ENGLISH? RIGHT-CLICK!
OF COURSE I SPEAK ENGLISH! BUT WHAT'S WRITING THE WORD 'CLICK' ON MY SCREEN GOING TO DO?
Copyright (c) 1999 Illiad http://www.userfriendly.org/

I'M GOING TO FIND THE SOLUTION TO THE PROBLEM SIR. LET ME PUT YOU ON HOLD FOR A BIT.
BIP
Copyright (c) 1999 Illiad http://www.userfriendly.org/

STREEETCH
*CRAK*POP*

GREG? IF YOU LEAVE HIM ON HOLD FOR MUCH LONGER HE'S GOING TO HANG UP.
CORRECT. PROBLEM SOLVED.
POP

YOU WANTED TO TALK, CHIEF?
YES. HOW ARE THINGS GOING WITH OUR Y2K DEVELOPMENT?
http://www.userfriendly.org/

THE TECHS HAVE BEEN WORKING ON IT ALL WEEK. THEY SAID THEY WERE WAITING FOR A DELIVERY.
PROBABLY A SOFTWARE PATCH. I THINK WE'RE IN VERY GOOD HANDS.
Copyright (c) 1999 Illiad

PLEASE TO BE CHECKINK AGAIN.
SIR, I'VE CHECKED FOUR TIMES. THERE IS NO DELIVERY FOR YOU FROM 'JUGO THE ARMS DEALER.'

WHAT IS WITH THAT RACKET? I CAN'T EVEN HEAR MYSELF THINK.
WHUMP!
KA-CHUNK CLACK!
THE CHIEF
http://www.userfriendly.org/

IT'S ALL FOR Y2K.
DAMNSKI! SNURF DARTS ARE NOT NINE MILLIMETER.
THE LESS I KNOW, THE SMALLER MY ULCER.
Copyright (c) 1999 Illiad

PITR. WHAT ARE YOU AND MIKE AND GREG DOING?
AM PREPARINK SNURF CATAPULT FOR Y2K. AM THINKINK WILL BE BIG TROUBLE.
http://www.userfriendly.org/
Y2K? BUT I THOUGHT WE WERE Y2K COMPLIANT.
DA. IS TRUE. WE ARE Y2K COMPLIANT...
CHUNK
CHUNK
CLINK
CHUNK
STRREEETCH

Copyright (c) 1999 Illiad
...BUT AM BETTINK WINDOWS IS NOT. AND WHO ARE ZLOTNIKS TO BE BLAMED IF WINDOWS NOT WORKINK?
OH MY LORD. OUR CLIENTS WILL BLAME US.
NO BIG SNURF DARTS. BUT I FOUND A REAL DIRTY TOILET PLUNGER.

REMEMBER THE DAYS OF DOS WITH CONFIG FILES? EDIT WAS SUCH A HOPELESS TEXT EDITOR.
WUSS. I USED EDLIN.
AMIGA
MAY

OH BITE ME. I'VE USED "COPY CON"
YEAH? WELL I WROTE MY FILES WITH ECHO.
AMIGA
MAY

Copyright (c) 1999 Illiad
http://www.userfriendly.org/
DOLT!
WIMP!
WELL. I EDITED THE INODES BY HAND WITH MAGNETS.
AMIGA
MAY

ANOTHER GAME FOR THE U.S. GOVERNMENT TO RESTRICT BECAUSE "IT HAS BOMBS AND STUFF IN IT."

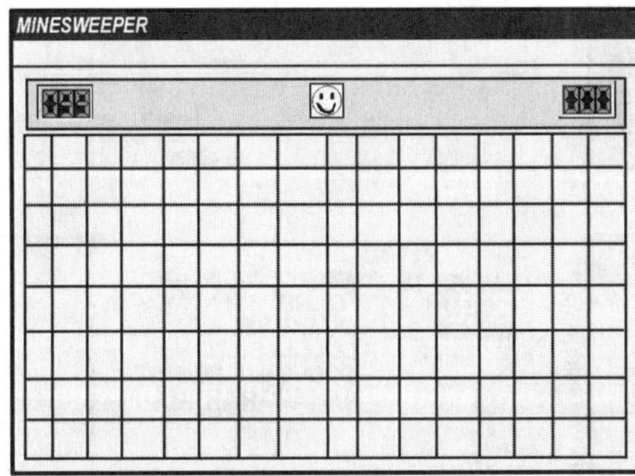
MINESWEEPER

HTTP://WWW.USERFRIENDLY.ORG/

HMM. SID MEIER'S ALPHA CENTAURI. I HEARD IT WAS A COOL GAME. IT'S LATE, BUT I ONLY NEED SIX HOURS OF SLEEP...
Copyright (c) 1999 Illiad http://www.userfriendly.org/

LOOK AT THE TIME...AHH, I ONLY NEED FOUR HOURS OF SLEEP.
A.J.? AREN'T YOU KIND OF LATE FOR WORK?
I DON'T KNOW. WHAT DAY IS IT?

A.J. IS BEING A PAIN. HE'S SO BUSY PLAYING THAT ALPHA CENTAURI GAME HE ISN'T DOING ANY OF THE WORK I GIVE HIM.
DID YOU TELL THE CHIEF?
Copyright (c) 1999 Illiad http://www.userfriendly.org/

YEAH. HE TOLD THE TECHS TO COAX A.J. AWAY FROM THE GAME. HIM BEING A SENSITIVE CREATIVE GUY AND ALL...

OKAY GREG. START THE WINCH!
NOOO!! I JUST NEED TO PLAY FOR ONE MORE TUURRRN!!

A.J., WE NEED TO TALK. YOU HAVE ALWAYS BEEN A FINE DESIGNER, BUT YOUR PROBLEM WITH THAT ALPHA CENTAURI GAME HAS SERIOUSLY AFFECTED YOUR PRODUCTIVITY.

WE'RE LIKE A BIG FAMILY, SO OF COURSE WE WANT THINGS TO WORK OUT.
Copyright (c) 1999 Illiad http://www.userfriendly.org/

SO WHAT CAN WE DO TO HELP YOU?
CEDE ONE OF YOUR BASES TO ME OR I'LL CRUSH YOU LIKE A BUG.

GREG, HAVE YOU SEEN STEF? I NEED HIS LATEST MARKETING REPORT.
HE'S BUSY PLAYING A QUAKE DEATHMATCH.
Copyright (c) 1999 Illiad http://www.userfriendly.org/

QUAKE? HE DOESN'T HAVE TIME FOR THAT.
WE TOLD HIM WE FOUND SOME QUAKERS HE COULD BEAT. HE COULDN'T RESIST. HAHAHAHAHAHA!!

FORSOOTH, AND WHAT IS THIS MAGIC BOX?
THE TECHS DIE...

HEY PITR! I THINK IT'S ABOUT THAT TIME AGAIN...
DA. AM THINKINK SO TOO. COMRADE.
TAPP TIP
Copyright (c) 1999 Illiad http://www.userfriendly.org/

MMMM...
OH NO. PITR. NOT AGAIN.
IS FATE. MIKHAIL. BEINK STRONG.
SUSHI!
I HATE THAT STUFF.
GESUNDHEIT.
THE WORD. IT HAS BEEN SPOKEN. WE GO NOW. DA?
TUNK TINK

AHHHH. FINALLY TO BE GOINK TO TEMPLE OF YUMSKI! TONIGHT. COMRADES. WE ARE EATINK SUSHI!
WHAT'S SUSHI?

IT IS RELIGIOUS. LIKE CATHEDRAL. CAFFEINE FOR MIND. PIZZA FOR BODY. SUSHI...FOR SOUL.
Copyright (c) 1999 Illiad http://www.userfriendly.org/
ACTUALLY. IT'S JUST RAW FISH.
RAW FI..!! IS FOOD OF GODS YOU BIG ZLOTNIK!
I'M GONNA HAVE SOME NIPYU. RICE. SEAWEED AND PIRAHNA LIPS...

And then there's "Bohunka" or Marinated Whale Anus. I run these by my Wonderbread-White friends who've never had sushi before. It's fun.

DURING A NEWS BREAK, A 'NORMAL PERSON' COMMENTS ON THE LINE-UPS AND CRAZE SURROUNDING THE PHANTOM MENACE PHENOMENON.
BUNCHA FREAKS. GET A LIFE.
NFL
HTTP://WWW.USERFRIENDLY.ORG/
COPYRIGHT (C) 1999 ILLIAD

AT THE SUSHI BAR, THE DUST PUPPY GOES EXPLORING...
I'M NOT SURE WHAT ALL THESE BITS ARE, BUT I GUESS YOU EAT THEM. AH, A SUSHI GUIDE ON THE WALL HERE...

http://www.userfriendly.org/
Copyright (c) 1999 Illiad
BLINKY BLINK

UM..SEA URCHIN, RIGHT?
YUP. ARE WE RELATED? YOU'LL FEED DOZENS.

I DON'T THINK WE'RE RELATED. BUT I CAN'T BE CERTAIN...
WELL WE SURE DO LOOK ALIKE.

Copyright (c) 1999 Illiad

SO WHERE'D YA GET THE FEET?
IT'S NOT SOMETHING I LIKE TO TALK ABOUT.
http://www.userfriendly.org/

Like I said. The opening day for *The Phantom Menace.*

COLUMBIA internet
MAY 19
RECEPTION
http://www.userfriendly.org/
Copyright (c) 1999 Illiad

COLUMBIA internet
MAY 19
RECEPTION

IS TODAY A PUBLIC HOLIDAY OR SOMETHING?
COLUMBIA internet
MAY 19
RECEPTION

I DON'T THINK WE'VE BEEN INTRODUCED. I'M DUST PUPPY. WHAT'S YOUR NAME?
I'M MATT.
http://www.userfriendly.org/
Copyright (c) 1999 Illiad

IT'S A GREAT PLEASURE. I WRITE CODE. WHAT DO YOU DO?
I THINK I'M FATED TO BE EATEN.

EATEN?! OH NO! IS THERE ANYTHING I CAN DO TO HELP?
WELL... D'YA THINK YOU CAN CROUCH DOWN AND HIDE YOUR FEET, THEN SIT HERE UNTIL THE CHEF COMES?

THERE YOU ARE. WHERE HAVE YOU BEEN?
I JUST MADE A NEW FRIEND. THIS IS MATT.
HEY.

A...A PIECE OF SUSHI NAMED "MATT" JUST SAID HELLO TO ME...
AND A BALL OF LINT WITH FEET IS OKAY IN YOUR WORLD? JUST DEAL WITH IT, PAL.

PITR, I'D LIKE YOU TO MEET MATT. HE'S A SEA URCHIN AND A NEW FRIEND OF MINE.
HI.

CHOMP
CHOMP
CHEW
GULP!!

AAAAAAAAGH! HE JUST ATE GWENDOLYN!!
EVIL GENIUSES FOR DUMMIES. CHAPTER FOUR: CAUSINK ABJECT TERROR THROUGH EATINK.

OPERATING SYSTEM SUSHI

BEOS-MAKI
WELL-WRAPPED SUSHI WITH EXCELLENT COLOR, BUT NOT VERY POPULAR.

LINUX-NIGIRI
STABLE FOUNDATION OF RICE, AND VERY POPULAR. COLOR IS NOT INTEGRAL AND IS HELD IN PLACE, BUT COLOR CHOICES ARE VAST.

SGI-MAKI
GOOD SUSHI WITH THE FINEST PRESENTATION, HANDS DOWN.

BSD-NIGIRI
FIRST-CLASS COMPONENTS, BUT IS MAKE-YOUR-OWN.

HTTP://WWW.USERFRIENDLY.ORG/

Week of May 24th, 1999

I Heart You, Larry, Moe, and Curly!

YOU GUYS SEEN THIS LIGHTSABRE TOY? I ALWAYS WONDERED WHY IT WAS DOUBLE-ENDED. KIND OF SILLY IF YOU ASK ME.
Copyright (c) 1999 Illiad http://www.userfriendly.org/

THUNK
KLIK!
SPUNCH

NOW I UNDERSTAND. GUESS THAT'S WHY ONLY THE EVIL GUYS USE IT, HUH?
MMMFF!!
AAAGH!

OKAY PITR. ONE-ON-ONE. YOU WITH THE SNURF BLASTER, ME WITH THE LIGHTSABRE. YOU REALIZE THAT JEDI LIKE MYSELF DON'T RELY ON ANYTHING AS RANDOM OR CLUMSY AS A BLASTER...

WHIRRRR
POFF!
PAFF!
PIFF!
PYFF!

Copyright (c) 1999 Illiad http://www.userfriendly.org/
I DON'T BELIEVE IT...
THAT IS WHY YOU FAIL.

MY TRAINING AS A SITH LORD SHALL BEGIN. I WILL BE A PILLAR OF MENTAL STRENGTH...
KETCHUP?
NO THANKS
Copyright (c) 1999 Illiad http://www.userfriendly.org/

BUT I MUST FILL THE VOID WITHIN ME WITH ONLY WHAT I NEED. A HAMBURGER. NOTHING MORE. NOTHING LESS. I AM STRONG, AND THE FORCE IS WITH ME...
HAMBURGER TO GO.
YES SIR.
RUMBLE GROWL

FRIES WITH THAT, SIR?
YES...I MEAN NO!! AAAGH. STUPID JEDI MIND TRICK!

OKAY PITR. I'VE LEARNED A LOT OF SABRE SKILLS IN THE LAST FEW DAYS. LET'S GO AT THIS ONE MORE TIME, AND BRING ON YOUR BEST...

SLOSH
WOBBLE
Copyright (c) 1999 Illiad http://www.userfriendly.org/

OKAY, SITH LORDS SHOULDN'T NEED TO DEAL WITH WATER BALLOONS.
BUT NOW YOU HAVE WET SHIRT. YOU CAN REVEAL YOURSELF TO THE JEDI, DA?

TECH SUPPORT. GREG SPEAKING.
HELLO. HOW DO I OPEN MY WEB BROWSER THING?

WELL...CLICK ON THE BROWSER ICON ON YOUR DESKTOP.
OH. UMMM...
TIK TOK

Copyright (c) 1999 Illiad http://www.userfriendly.org/
MY COMPUTER IS ON MY KITCHEN TABLE. I CAN'T SEE MY DESK FROM HERE.
OKAY THAT'S IT. THIRTY DAYS NO COMPUTER USE PENALTY FOR BEING **STUPID.**

OKAY... 'C'... GOT IT....

...AND...A CUTE L'IL **COLON**...

Copyright (c) 1999 Illiad http://www.userfriendly.org/
NOW PLEASE HIT '**ENTER**'
OOOOOH. A **CHALLENGE!** LET'S SEE IF WE CAN FIND IT. OKAY POOPSIE?
ARF!

ON MAY 26TH, 1999
THE AUSTRALIAN GOVERNMENT
SUFFERS FROM **Y2K**
A LITTLE ON THE EARLY SIDE

The Australian Criminal Code
1899

This one is about the Broadcasting Services Amendment that was passed on May 26, 1999 in Australia, which introduced some draconian (!) measures in an attempt to control the Internet within Australian borders. Censorship, among other things, was enabled. It belonged in the Australian Criminal Code from 100 years prior.

PITR, WHAT ARE YOU DOING? WE HAVE TO DO A LINUX INSTALL TODAY.
DA, MIKHAIL, PLEASE TO BE FORGIVINK. AM WORKINK ON NEW CODE FOR ARTIFICAL INTELLIGENCE. NOT GOINK VERY WELL.
TIK TOK
Copyright (c) 1999 Illiad http://www.userfriendly.org/

AN ARTIFICIAL INTELLIGENCE? WHAT ON EARTH ARE YOU DOING THAT FOR?
IS FOR VERY GOOD FRIEND.
TIK KAK
FOR ERWIN?
DA, IS SPRING TIME, COMRADE!
ARE YOU DONE YET? I'M GETTING TIRED MOUNTING DRIVES ALL DAY.

ERWIN, WHY DON'T YOU ASK THE L'IL FUZZY GUY TO CODE YOU A FRIEND? PITR'S GOOD, BUT HE'S NEVER DONE THIS BEFORE.
MIKE, COULD YOU EXPLAIN TO THE DUST PUPPY THE CARNAL NEEDS THAT WE HAVE?
TAP TAPPY TIP
Copyright (c) 1999 Illiad http://www.userfriendly.org/

I'M HAVING SOME DIFFICULTY WITH THE IDEA THAT AN A.I. NEEDS NOOKIE.
HEY, I'M EVOLVING. GIVE ME A ROBOT ARM AND I CAN DO EVERYTHING I'VE SEEN YOU GUYS DO.
TIKKA TAK TAK

PITR, YOU'RE GOING TO BE AT THIS FOR AGES. YOU DO REALIZE THE COMPLEXITIES INVOLVED IN CODING AN ARTIFICIAL INTELLIGENCE?
AM MAKINK GOOD HEADWAY ALREADY. A.I. CAN ANSWER ANY "DA" OR "NYET" QUESTION. YOU TRY, MIKHAIL.
TAK TAKK TIK
Copyright (c) 1999 Illiad http://www.userfriendly.org/

ALL RIGHT, COMPUTER, IS MY NAME "MIKE FLOYD?"
YES.
OKAY, HOW DID YOU DO THAT WITH ONLY SIX LINES OF CODE?
SIMPLE ALGORITHM. IF QUESTION ENDINK IN VOWEL, ANSWER IS "NYET." ELSE ANSWER IS "DA." VERY CLEVER PITR IS, DA?
NO!

AM REALLY MAKINK PROGRESS HERE, MIKHAIL. AM CLOSE TO FINISHINK GOOD FRIEND FOR ERWIN.
WHAT GENDER ARE YOU MAKING ERWIN'S FRIEND?
CODE CODE DEBUG
Copyright (c) 1999 Illiad http://www.userfriendly.org/

BYUNZCZEK! AM NOT EVEN SURE IF ERWIN IS BOY OR WOMAN OR IN BETWEEN!
DON'T WORRY, PITR. IT'S ONLY THE DIFFERENCE BETWEEN A PORT AND A DONGLE.

YOU LOOK TIRED. PITR. MAYBE YOU SHOULD TAKE A BREAK FROM THIS A.I. PROJECT.
NYET. AM NEARINK BREAKTHROUGH. AM USINK ARCHITECTURE FOR A.I. LIKE IN BRITISH T.V. SHOW. "RED DWARF."
TAP
TIPP
Copyright (c) 1999 Illiad http://www.userfriendly.org/

HUNH? WHAT DO YOU MEAN?
LIKE "HOLLY" ON SHOW. USINK DISEMBODIED HEAD FOR A.I.
HEY...THIS IS KINDA COOL.

The final frame includes a famous photo of Alan Cox. Alan seemed bemused by the inclusion.

HEY. LITTLE DUDE. WHERE'S ERWIN? I HAVEN'T SEEN HIM AROUND IN A WHILE.
HE LEFT. MIKE.

HE LEFT? WHY'D HE LEAVE?
HE SAID HE WAS FEELING UNFULFILLED AND ALONE. AND THAT HE NEEDED TIME TO "FIND HIMSELF."

TAKE IT BACK! I WANT DISHWATER. NOT ESPRESSO! HOW DO YOU EXPECT ME TO WRITE BITTER POETRY IF THE COFFEE DOESN'T OFFEND ME?!
Copyright (c) 1999 Illiad http://www.userfriendly.org/

DUE TO RECENT INTERNET LEGISLATION BY THE AUSTRALIAN GOVERNMENT, THE FAITHFUL KANGAROO IS REPLACED BY A MORE APPROPRIATE ANIMAL AS AUSTRALIA'S MASCOT.
HTTP://WWW.USERFRIENDLY.ORG/
COPYRIGHT (C) 1999 ILLIAD

At the time of this writing, Canada is anticipating the reintroduction of a much worse bill, predicated on the US DMCA. I am incensed.

Week of June 7th, 1999

MICROSOFT CONFIRMED RUMORS TODAY THAT THEY HAD FORMED A TEAM TO COMBAT WHAT THEIR TOP PEOPLE HAVE CALLED "THAT UPSTART LINUX THING."
sgi
OLD LOGOS
Copyright (c) 1999 Illiad http://www.userfriendly.org/

"THE ANTI LINUX TEAM WAS HAND-PICKED," SAID ONE MICROSOFT OFFICIAL. "WE'RE VERY PLEASED WITH THE SKILL SET THEY BRING TO THEIR NEW JOBS."
sgi
OLD LOGOS

WHEN QUESTIONED ABOUT THE CORE SKILLS REQUIRED FOR THE TEAM, THE OFFICIAL REPLIED: "BLUDGEONING. BLUDGEONING IS KEY."
sgi
OLD LOGOS

AHEM
HERE I SIT BROKEN-HEARTED. A LONELY GEEK IN LANDS UNCHARTED. I LOOK FOR LOVE AND WISH FOR LAUGHTER. HAPPILY LIVING EVER AFTER

BUT FATE WOULD HAVE ME SAD AND BITTER. I WISH I'D SNOGGED MY BABYSITTER. MY FRIENDS COMPLAIN. "YOU'RE ALWAYS SULKIN'" I GET SO LITTLE I SHOULD BE VULCAN.
SPUTTER

BUT THEN THE NET IN STRENGTH WAS BORN, AND OFFERED GEEKS A SEA OF PORN. I ONCE WAS LONELY. (IT MAY SOUND CORNY) BUT NOWADAYS I'M JUST WAY H...
I'M GOING TO HAVE TO ASK YOU TO LEAVE.
Copyright (c) 1999 Illiad http://www.userfriendly.org/

ANYTHING NEW ON THAT MICROSOFT "ANTI-LINUX TEAM" THAT YOU GUYS WERE TALKING ABOUT?
SOMETHING HERE...
Copyright (c) 1999 Illiad http://www.userfriendly.org/

"MICROSOFT TODAY ANNOUNCED THAT SPECIFIC ELEMENTS OF ITS ANTI-LINUX TEAM ARE BEING BRIEFED ON PROBLEM-SOLVING STRATEGIES AND LONG-TERM OBJECTIVES. TEAM MEMBERS ARE REPORTEDLY EAGER TO GET STARTED."

YOU GUYS REMEMBER YOUR INSTRUCTIONS?
FIND LINUX CODERS. BREAK FINGERS. HEH.
PENGUIN BUTCHER

COLUMBIA internet
OKAY. LOOKS LIKE THIS IS THE FIRST STOP. YOU KNOW WHAT TO DO. RIGHT THEODORE?

COLUMBIA internet
UMMM...

COLUMBIA internet
IF IT MOVES, CLOBBER IT UNTIL IT STOPS MOVING.
GOOD BOY.
Copyright (c) 1999 Illiad http://www.userfriendly.org/

GOOD DAY. GENTLEMEN SOMETHING I CAN HELP YOU WITH?
NO. WE'RE LOOKING FOR LINUX CODERS.
the oppressed are
Copyright (c) 1999 Illiad http://www.userfriendly.org/

AND IS THERE A REASON WHY YOU THINK I COULDN'T BE A CODER? IS IT BECAUSE I'M A WOMAN?
the oppressed are

I'M TIRED OF MEN THINKING THAT WOMEN CAN'T BE GOOD AT TECHNOLOGY! YOU THINK I CAN'T BE A CODER BECAUSE I WEAR A SKIRT AND MAKE-UP!
ACTUALLY. IT'S BECAUSE IT SAYS "RECEPTIONIST" ON YOUR PLAQUE.
the oppressed are

HEY. ARE YOU ONE OF THOSE LINUX CODERS?
YOU ARE TOUCHINK ME WHY? ARE YOU NOT SEEINK I AM BUSY?
CODE
CODE

Copyright (c) 1999 Illiad http://www.userfriendly.org/
NYET. LINUX CODER IN NEXT OFFICE. THICK GLASSES AND FUNNY HAIR. YOU ARE TO BE ASKINK FOR "STEF."
GOOD MAN. IGNORE THE SCREAMS.

THINGS THAT GO UP AND DOWN ON A RHYTHMIC BASIS

ELECTROCARDIOGRAM

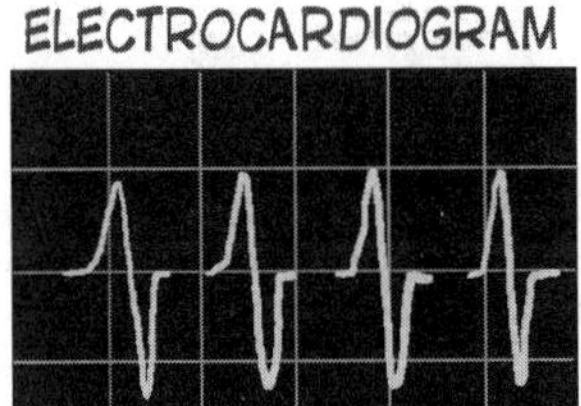

THE TIDES

ebaY™

 HTTP://WWW.USERFRIENDLY.ORG/

WHY IS THERE A GROUP OF LARGE MEN WITH BAD TEETH COMING THIS WAY?

SOMETHING I CAN DO FOR YOU?
OUR EMPLOYERS DON'T LIKE IT WHEN PEOPLE LIKE YOU INTERFERE WITH THEIR POWER GRABS.

YOU'RE FROM THE AUSTRALIAN GOVERNMENT?
COME NOW. WE HAVE **ETHICS.**

WHAT'S GOING ON IN STEF'S OFFICE?
SOME BIG MEN THINKINK HE IS LINUX CODER.
ARRRGH!
BAFF
KAFFUFLE
RRRFFF!!

MMFFFFF!!!
EXCUSE US. PLEASE.

WOW. LINUX HEADHUNTERS ARE REALLY AGRESSIVE. HUH.
MMMGGFF!!

HELLO ERWIN. IT'S NICE TO HAVE YOU BACK.
I GUESS IT'S NICE TO BE BACK. I'M JUST UPSET THAT I NEVER GET WHAT I WANT.

YOU MEAN ABOUT FINDING ANOTHER A.I. AS A MATE?
YEAH...SEE? NOTHING I REALLY WANT EVER COMES TO PASS.

STEF GOT KIDNAPPED BY SOME LARGE AND SMELLY MEN JUST A FEW MINUTES AGO...
PLEASE DON'T TEASE ME. I'M FEELING VERY FRAGILE RIGHT NOW.

ARE YOU FOR **REAL?** STEF WAS JUST KIDNAPPED?
YES...

IT WAS REALLY A SHOCK. THREE BIG MEN CHARGED IN. TIED STEF UP. GAGGED HIM AND CARRIED HIM AWAY.

BWAHAHAHA HAHAHAHAH!!
ERWIN!

ERWIN. WE HAVE TO GO AND RESCUE STEF.
WHY ON EARTH WOULD I WANT TO DO THAT?

GIVE ME A FEW MORE SECONDS HERE...
IT'S A TOUGH ONE. ISN'T IT.
Copyright (c) 1999 Illiad http://www.userfriendly.org/

I KNOW YOU AND STEF DON'T GET ALONG ERWIN. BUT WE CAN'T LEAVE HIM TO WHATEVER FATE THOSE ANTI-LINUX GUYS HAVE IN STORE FOR HIM.
I SUPPOSE.

NOW WE NEED A PLAN AND SOMEONE TO HELP US. ANY IDEAS?
I HAVE JUST THE THING...

WHAT IS YOUR BIDDING. MY MASTER?
IT STILL WORKS! COOL! MY OWN TERMINATOR!
Copyright (c) 1999 Illiad http://www.userfriendly.org/

HAVING BEEN INVITED AS A GUEST SPEAKER, ERIC S. RAYMOND SUDDENLY REALIZES WHY MICROSOFT WAS SO EAGER TO HAVE HIM SHOW UP ON THE SUMMER SOLSTICE.
COPYRIGHT (C) 1999 ILLIAD
HTTP://WWW.USERFRIENDLY.ORG/

I was astonished that Eric Raymond didn't burst into flames when he stepped onto the Microsoft campus grounds. But he made it, and he got to have dinner with Greg Bear, Neal Stephenson, and George Dyson in exchange for his talk. Nice scoop!

ARTUR, UNDER INSTRUCTIONS FROM ERWIN, HAS TRAVELLED TO MICROSOFT HQ IN REDMOND TO RESCUE THE HAPLESS STEF MURKY FROM THE ANTI-LINUX BRUTE SQUAD.
RECEPTION
Copyright (c) 1999 Illiad

WITH HIS POTENT PENTIUM III BRAIN, ARTUR WORKS ON A STRATEGY TO EXTRACT STEF AS EFFICIENTLY AS POSSIBLE...
Microsoft RECEPTION
http://www.userfriendly.org/

OF COURSE, ONE MUST EXPECT TO LOSE A FEW CYCLES WHEN YOU RUN THE SETI@HOME CLIENT IN THE BACKGROUND...
Microsoft RECEPTION

HEY MISTER...YOU'VE BEEN HERE SINCE YESTERDAY. WHO ARE YOU ANYWAY?

I AM ARTUR. I HAVE COME TO RESCUE A LINUX CODER YOUR PEOPLE HAVE ABDUCTED.
WE DON'T **HAVE** ANY LINUX CODERS HERE.
Copyright (c) 1999 Illiad http://www.userfriendly.org/

ACTUALLY, HE'S REALLY IN MARKETING.
OHHH. A CODER **WANNABE.** WE HAVE **LOTS** OF THOSE!

SO YOU THINK YOU CAN JUST WALTZ IN HERE? THERE ARE THIRTY OFFICERS IN THIS BUILDING.

Microsoft RECEPTION
Copyright (c) 1999 Illiad http://www.userfriendly.org/

ARE YOU GOING TO SEND ALL THIRTY AT ME AT ONCE? **PLEASE?**
WHY'D I SUDDENLY GET THE FEELING THAT'S REALLY NOT GOING TO MATTER?

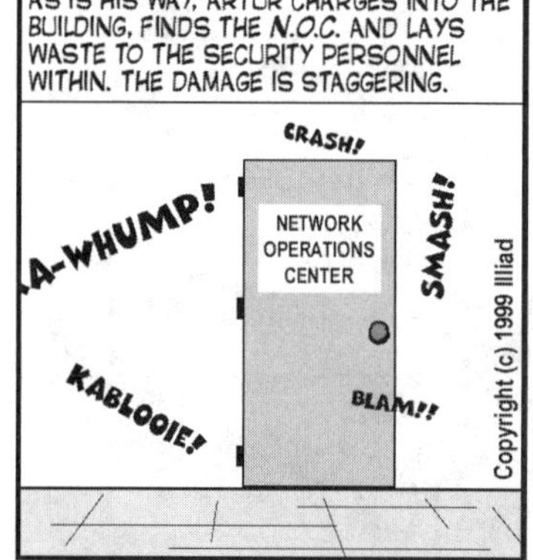
AS IS HIS WAY, ARTUR CHARGES INTO THE BUILDING, FINDS THE *N.O.C.* AND LAYS WASTE TO THE SECURITY PERSONNEL WITHIN. THE DAMAGE IS STAGGERING.
A-WHUMP!
CRASH!
NETWORK OPERATIONS CENTER
SMASH!
KABLOOIE!
BLAM!!
Copyright (c) 1999 Illiad

AN EERIE LULL SETTLES IN THE BUILDING AS A QUIET CLICKING NOISE COMES FROM WITHIN THE OPERATIONS OFFICE...
NETWORK OPERATIONS CENTER
CLICK!
CLICK!
KLIK!!
KLICKITY-CLIK!
http://www.userfriendly.org/

...AND SUDDENLY EVERYTHING AND EVERYONE NEARBY IS ONCE AGAIN IN MORTAL DANGER...
E-BAY DOWN **AGAIN?** NOW I'M **MAD!**
NETWORK OPERATIONS CENTER

AWARE THAT A RESCUE OPERATION IS UNDER WAY FOR THEIR CAPTIVE, THE ANTI-LINUX TEAM MEMBERS SPIRIT STEF AWAY IN A MINI-VAN.
MFFF! GRMFF!

THEY SPEED AWAY, COGNIZANT OF THE AWESOME THREAT THAT WILL FOLLOW THEM, ON FOOT, OR ON WHEELS. THEY KNOW THAT ARTUR WILL NEVER GIVE UP CHASING THEM.
Copyright (c) 1999 Illiad http://www.userfriendly.org/

MIND YOU, NOT EVERYONE HAS ACCESS TO A HARLEY...
WRRRRRRRRP!

AFTER HOURS OF ESCAPING ARTUR'S PURSUIT ON THE HIGHWAY, THE TEAM PULLS INTO A REST AREA WITH THEIR CAPTIVE AND HUDDLE BEHIND A WALL...
HIDING AT A REST STOP? THIS HAS TO BE THE DUMBEST IDEA YOU'VE EVER HAD, DORTMUND.
SHHHHH! HERE HE COMES!
AHHHH, SHADDUP.

QUICKLY! EVERYBODY DUCK!
WOOOSH!
Copyright (c) 1999 Illiad http://www.userfriendly.org/

HOW MANY TIMES HAVE I TOLD YOU NOT TO WEAR THAT STUPID HELMET?!?!!
IT'S THE ONLY THING THAT FITS MY HEAD.

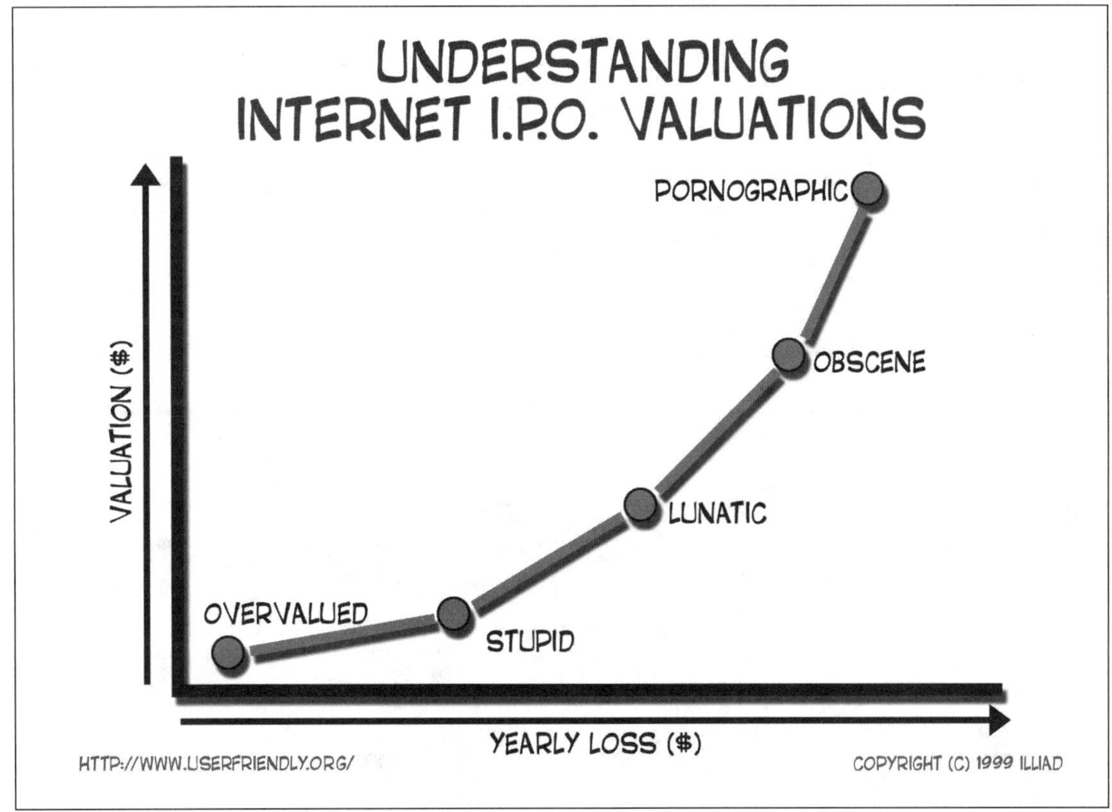
UNDERSTANDING INTERNET I.P.O. VALUATIONS
VALUATION ($)
YEARLY LOSS ($)
OVERVALUED
STUPID
LUNATIC
OBSCENE
PORNOGRAPHIC
HTTP://WWW.USERFRIENDLY.ORG/
COPYRIGHT (C) 1999 ILLIAD

I CAN HEAR HIM COMING CLOSER.
HE'S STILL ON THAT STUPID SCOOTER.
http://www.userfriendly.org/

DON'T WORRY. WE'LL BE TOTALLY SAFE BEHIND THIS WALL.
IT SOUNDS LIKE HE'S ACCELERATING...

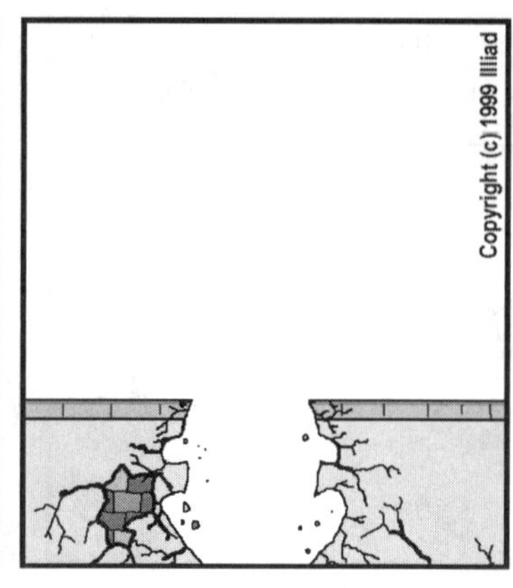
Copyright (c) 1999 Illiad

HAVING FAILED IN THEIR MISSION TO EXTRACT THEIR FIRST LINUX CODER, THE MICROSOFT ANTI-LINUX TEAM MEMBERS RETURN TO THEIR H.Q.
Copyright (c) 1999 Illiad http://www.userfriendly.org/

DESPITE BEING SOUNDLY DEFEATED, THE TEAM MEMBERS ARE TRUE PROFESSIONALS, AND STOICLY REPORT THEIR CASUALTIES AND RECOMMENDATIONS TO MANAGEMENT.

I DON'T WANT TO GO AFTER THOSE LINUX GUYS AGAIN. COULDN'T WE JUST TAKE ON THE JUSTICE DEPARTMENT?
YOU'D BETTER COME LOOK AT ALISTAIR. HE'S CONGEALING.

I HAVE RETREIVED STEF MURKY AS YOU REQUESTED, MY MASTER. IT APPEARS, HOWEVER, THAT HE IS SUFFERING FROM AMNESIA.
OH DEAR.
Copyright (c) 1999 Illiad http://www.userfriendly.org/

WE HAVE TO HELP STEF REMEMBER. ERWIN, PLEASE CALL UP THE DATA YOU HAVE ON STEF'S LIFE AND GO THROUGH IT WITH HIM.
OKAY.

STEF, REPEAT AFTER ME... YOU ARE A PENGUIN.
I AM A PENGUIN.
ERWIN!!

...AND SO WE CALLED THE CUSTOMER BACK AND...
HOLD ON. STEF'S COMING THIS WAY AND HE'S WALKING FUNNY.

WADDLE WADDLE
SQUINK SQUINK
WADDLE WADDLE SQUINK

Copyright (c) 1999 Illiad http://www.userfriendly.org/
YOU THINK HE'S TRYING TO GET YOUR ATTENTION AGAIN?
EITHER THAT OR HE ATE SOMETHING REALLY SPICY FOR DINNER.

SO HOW'RE YOU FINDING THAT NEW ERGONOMIC CHAIR PITR? DOES IT HELP MUCH?
AM NOT KNOWINK YET, COMRADE. IS FEELINK A LEETLE FUNNY.
Copyright (c) 1999 Illiad http://www.userfriendly.org/

WADDLE
WADDLE
SQUINCH
SQUINCH

STEF GOT ONE OF THOSE CHAIRS TOO. DIDN'T HE?
DA. AM ORDERINK FOR ME MILK CRATES RIGHT NOW.
TIP
TAP

STEF THINKS HE'S A PENGUIN? IS HE ALL RIGHT?
OH HE'S FINE. IT'S THE CHIEF AND THE SMILING MAN WE NEED TO WORRY ABOUT.

WHY? WHAT'S HAPPENED TO THEM?
WELL...WE THINK STEF HAS DECIDED TO START NESTING.

Copyright (c) 1999 Illiad http://www.userfriendly.org/
I THINK HE THINKS YOUR HEAD IS HIS EGG! DON'T AGGRAVATE HIM!
DO I LOOK LIKE I'M IN A POSITION TO AGGRAVATE ANYTHING?!?

THE FRIENDLY CIRCUS
COPYRIGHT (C) 1999 ILLIAD HTTP://WWW.USERFRIENDLY.ORG/

"I came as soon as you called, A.J."

I GUESS YOU HEARD ABOUT STEF?
YEP. I'VE TAKEN STEPS TO LURE HIM INTO THE COAT CLOSET. THEN WE CAN RESTRAIN HIM AND GET HIM SOME HELP.

I DON'T EVEN WANT TO THINK HOW YOU'RE GOING TO LURE STEF.
REMEMBER STEF HASN'T HAD A DATE IN AGES.
EXCUSINK ME. YOU ARE SEEINK MY NEW TUX DOLL ANYWHERE?
Copyright (c) 1999 Illiad http://www.userfriendly.org/

SO YOU ACTUALLY LURED STEF INTO THE CLOSET?
YEAH. THING IS, HE HASN'T MADE A SOUND.
Copyright (c) 1999 Illiad http://www.userfriendly.org/

WHAT ARE YOU WAITING FOR? GO IN THERE AND GET HIM.
I'M THINKING ABOUT WHAT LINUS TORVALDS SAID ABOUT ANGRY PENGUINS.

JEEZ. THIS IS ONE BIG CLOSET.
I KNOW. AND THE LIGHT'S BUSTED. STEF HAS TO BE HERE SOMEWHERE.

A.J., THIS IS NOT COOL. REMEMBER WHAT HAPPENED THE LAST TIME YOU AND I GOT STUCK IN A PITCH BLACK ROOM?
YEAH, BUT THIS TIME WE'VE GOT THE DOOR OPEN.

SLAM!
Copyright (c) 1999 Illiad http://www.userfriendly.org/

I DON'T WANT TO BE HERE RIGHT NOW MIKE. CAN WE JUST GO?
SURE...LET ME GET THE DOOR.

I CAN'T SEEM TO FEEL THE DOORKNOB...
YOW!!
FRUNCH!
Copyright (c) 1999 Illiad http://www.userfriendly.org/

I GUESS YOU FOUND STEF, HUH?
YES. AT PENGUIN LEVEL.
GRRRR...

I THINK I'VE FOUND THE LIGHT SWITCH.
WELL, TURN IT ON ALREADY!

KLIK!
UHHH...
Copyright (c) 1999 Illiad http://www.userfriendly.org/

WELL STEF, IT'S TIME FOR YOU TO COME OUT OF THIS CLOSET...
EVIDENTLY IN MORE WAYS THAN ONE.
PEEP

WELL NOW THAT STEF'S SNAPPED OUT OF HIS IDENTITY PROBLEM, YOU CAN GIVE PITR HIS TUX STUFFED TOY BACK.
HERE HE COMES. JUST KEEP SMILING AND MAYBE HE WON'T NOTICE.
Copyright (c) 1999 Illiad http://www.userfriendly.org/

THERE'S YOUR TUX DOLL BACK, PITR. I KNOW IT MEANS A LOT TO YOU, AND I'M JUST GLAD I COULD HELP BY FINDING IT FOR YOU.

PLEASE TO BE EXPLAININK LIPSTICK AND MASCARA ON MY PENGUIN DOLL.
HE NOTICED.
WAIT TIL HE SEES THE GARTER BELT.

PHEW
BO 2000
COPYRIGHT (C) 1999 ILLIAD
HTTP://WWW.USERFRIENDLY.ORG/

BO = Back Orifice, which happens to be real back-door software. This 'toon appeared briefly on CNN during a segment on computer security.

SO WHAT'S HAPPENED TO STEF? HAS HE RECOVERED FROM THAT PENGUIN FIASCO?
HE WENT FOR THERAPY. THE CHIEF MADE HIM GO.
Copyright (c) 1999 Illiad http://www.userfriendly.org/

THERAPY?
YEAH. APPARENTLY TODAY HE JOINS SOME KIND OF SUPPORT GROUP.
EVERYONE. PLEASE WELCOME OUR NEW FRIEND STEF. HE'S HERE WITH US BECAUSE HE THINKS HE'S A **PENGUIN**.
I'M **BETTER** NOW. OKAY?
HEY. SIT NEXT TO ME! I'M A COMPLIMENTARY FRUIT BASKET!

TODAY WE'LL DISCUSS HOW OUR ALTER-EGOS MAKE US FEEL ABOUT EACH OTHER IN THIS ROOM. WHY DON'T WE START WITH YOU. STEF?
IF YOU **MUST** KNOW. I HAVE A MILD URGE TO SQUAT ON BALDIE'S HEAD HERE IN AN EFFORT TO KEEP IT **WARM**.
Copyright (c) 1999 Illiad http://www.userfriendly.org/

AND HOW DOES WHAT STEF SAID MAKE YOU FEEL. BERNIE?
WHEN CAN HE START?
OKAY. I'M CURED. CAN I **LEAVE**?

I'M PLEASED WITH YOUR QUICK RECOVERY. STEF. ESPECIALLY GIVEN THE UNIQUE NATURE OF YOUR AFFLICTION. I CAN'T SAY THAT I'VE COME ACROSS ANYTHING QUITE AS STRANGE AS WHAT YOU WENT THROUGH.

OF COURSE. IN SOME OTHER UNIVERSE IT'S ENTIRELY POSSIBLE THAT A PENGUIN COULD HAVE ENDED UP WITH **YOUR** MIND..

SORRY. OPUS. I ONLY HAVE **NETBSD** ON MY COMPUTER.
DARN IT. THERE **HAS** TO BE A PLACE WHERE I CAN USE SOME BAD SOFTWARE.
Copyright (c) 1999 Illiad http://www.userfriendly.org/

YOU SHOULD BE AWARE THAT EVEN THOUGH YOU HAVE YOUR IDENTITY ALL STRAIGHTENED OUT. YOU MAY SUFFER FROM SOME ...UM...**CHANGES** TO YOUR PERSPECTIVES AND VALUES.

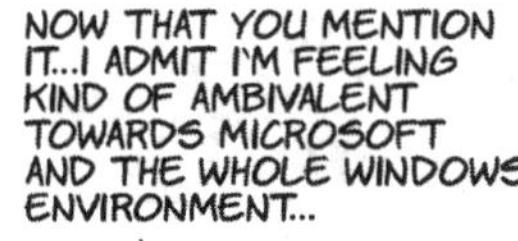
NOW THAT YOU MENTION IT...I ADMIT I'M FEELING KIND OF AMBIVALENT TOWARDS MICROSOFT AND THE WHOLE WINDOWS ENVIRONMENT...

THAT'S NORMAL. DEAR. KIND OF A MENTAL ENEMA.
SCRIBBLE

Microsoft
WORLD DOMINATION AGENCY
"WE DON'T SHARE"
WE'RE LOSING ONE. SIR.
ONE OF OUR BETTER ONES TOO! ALERT THE RE-EDUCATION CORPS!
Copyright (c) 1999 Illiad http://www.userfriendly.org/

A NEW DAY AT MICROSOFT'S RE-EDUCATION CORPS CAMP BEGINS WITH A LIVELY AND HEARTY SONG TO BUILD MORALE...
WHO'S YOUR DADDY?!
BILL!!

Copyright (c) 1999 Illiad http://www.userfriendly.org/
...FOLLOWED BY GRUELING TRAINING AND HARSH, CHARACTER-BUILDING DISCIPLINE.
NEVER SAY THE WORDS "OPEN SOURCE" AROUND ME, YOU PANSY! DROP AND GIMME A HUNDRED LINES OF CODE FOR WINDOWS 2000!

ALL OF THIS IS DONE, OF COURSE, TO PRODUCE A POPULATION OF I.T. WORKERS THAT ARE SOMEWHAT HOSTILE TOWARDS DIFFERENT IDEOLOGIES.
ALL RIGHT. ONE MORE HACK. BUT THEN IT'S OFF TO MARKETING CLASS FOR YOU.
HEE!
HEH
HAHA

HOW'S STEF DOING?
WELL HE'S BACK. HE'S TALKING TO MIKE I THINK.

WHY WOULD HE DO THAT? YOU KNOW STEF HATES TALKING TO TECHIES.
YOU'RE RIGHT. I'M GOING TO GO CHECK...

Copyright (c) 1999 Illiad http://www.userfriendly.org/
YE GODS! WHAT HAVE YOU DONE TO MIKE?!
I JUST ASKED HIM WHAT DISTRIBUTION OF LINUX HE'D RECOMMEND AND HE KEELED OVER!
KAFF GURGLE

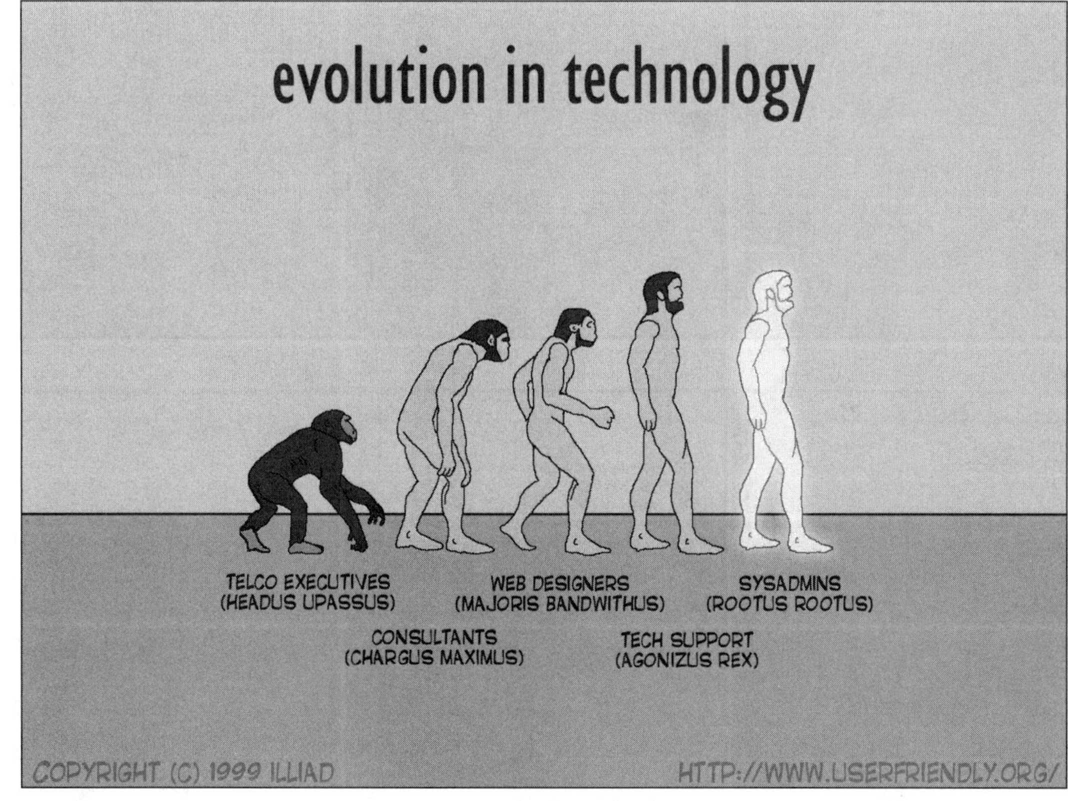

evolution in technology
TELCO EXECUTIVES (HEADUS UPASSUS)
CONSULTANTS (CHARGUS MAXIMUS)
WEB DESIGNERS (MAJORIS BANDWITHUS)
TECH SUPPORT (AGONIZUS REX)
SYSADMINS (ROOTUS ROOTUS)
COPYRIGHT (C) 1999 ILLIAD
HTTP://WWW.USERFRIENDLY.ORG/

I speak Australian. That is, I grok most of the slang. It was unfortunate that I didn't remember that *root* is also another word for coitus in Australia. Somehow the cartoon seems even more appropriate.

OKAY. LET ME GET THIS STRAIGHT. **YOU** WANT TO INSTALL AND RUN **LINUX** ON YOUR WORKSTATION?
I THINK I NEED THE STABILITY. WINDOWS CAN'T GIVE ME THAT.

Copyright (c) 1999 Illiad http://www.userfriendly.org/
I'LL BET YOU THAT THE TECH SUPPORT ROOM HAS JUST ICED OVER.
HEY! I CAN CHANGE! I EVEN WATCH TECHIE MOVIES LIKE "STARSHIP TROOPERS!"

WHAT A MESS THIS EXPENSE REPORT IS. STEF HAS SOME SERIOUS EXPLAINING TO DO...

HEYA SMILING DUDE. I'M OFF TO CHECK OUT THE NEW WEB SERVERS WE GOT TODAY.

Copyright (c) 1999 Illiad http://www.userfriendly.org/
DID I JUST STEP THROUGH A RIFT IN THE UNIVERSE?
PERSONALLY. I'M THINKING I SHOULD'VE TAKEN THE BLUE PILL.

TIPPITY TAPPITY TIPPY TAPTAP

TAP TAP

Copyright (c) 1999 Illiad http://www.userfriendly.org/
CAN I HELP YOU GUYS WITH SOMETHING?
WE ARE WANTINK TO KNOW WHO YOU ARE AND WHAT YOU HAVE DONE WITH STEF. PLEASE.

STEF. WHAT ARE YOU WORKING ON THERE?
I'M CODING A WEB ANALYSIS PACKAGE IN VISUAL BASIC.
Copyright (c) 1999 Illiad http://www.userfriendly.org/

HE IS SAYINK "VISUAL BASIC." DA, MIKHAIL?
YUP.

THANKINK **GODS.** HE IS **NOT** REALLY BECOMINK TECHIE.
HEY!!

STEF, WE REALLY NEED TO TALK ABOUT YOUR SUDDEN TRANSFORMATION INTO...UM...SOMETHING **OTHER** THAN THE MARKETING EXPERT THAT I HIRED.

THE TECHS CAME TO ME AND COMPLAINED THAT YOU WERE CONFUSING THEM AND MAKING IT HARD FOR THEM TO CONCENTRATE. I THINK THIS NEEDS TO STOP.

Copyright (c) 1999 Illiad http://www.userfriendly.org/
HEH. YOU MEAN THIS IS STEF'S SOURCE CODE?
YUP. PITR'S KILLING HIMSELF HOWLING OVER HOW STEF HAS GIVEN CREDIT FOR BORROWING CODE FROM "HELLO WORLD."

MIKHAIL. WE ARE HAVINK BACKUPS OF **ALL** DATA, DA?
YEP. TWO COPIES HERE. ONE COPY OFFSITE.

AND WE ARE HAVINK ALL OFFICE WORKSTATIONS OFF NETWORK?
DONE THAT TOO.
TAP TAP
Copyright (c) 1999 Illiad http://www.userfriendly.org/
PROCEED, COMRADE.
OPENING MYSTERY EMAIL ATTACHMENT... **NOW!**
PLAP!

USER
FRIENDLY
the comic strip
PIZZA
Portrasher 4
ROTO-ROUTER 800
Copyright (c) 1997-1999 Illiad

ERWIN, "DON'T FEAR THE REAPER" BY **BLUE OYSTER CULT** IF YOU PLEASE.
SEARCHING... FOUND THE MP3... VOCALS STRIPPED. READY TO ROCK!

OH, NOW THE TIME HAS COME READY NOW TO GO ON. CODERS DON'T FEAR THE PENGUIN, NOR DOES IBM, SUN, OR COREL...
YOU CAN BE LIKE THEY ARE...

COME ON BABY...
DON'T FEAR THE PENGUIN
BABY GRAB THE TOOLS...
DON'T FEAR THE PENGUIN
YOU'LL BE ABLE TO FLY...
DON'T FEAR THE PENGUIN
BABY IT'S YOUR CHAAAANCE...

LAAAAAAAAAAAAAAA LA LA LAAAA LA!! LAAAAAAAAAAAAAAA LA LA LAAAA LA!!

PARDON THE INTERRUPTION. AS LEGAL COUNSEL FOR THE RECORD COMPANIES, I AM SERVING NOTICE THAT WE WILL BE CHARGING EVERYONE WHO HAS READ THIS CARTOON A FEE DUE TO THE OBVIOUS MISUSE OF ONE OF OUR PROPERTIES. THANK YOU.
ERWIN SAYS THEY'RE JUST MAD BECAUSE WE USED AN MP3.

I'M REALLY NOT SURE I WANT TO BE HERE. I HATE THIS TIE AND SHIRT. AND NOW I HAVE AN APPOINTMENT WITH SOMEONE FROM MICROSOFT OF ALL PLACES...

I DON'T WANT TO GO BACK TO USING WINDOWS...IT MAY BE PRETTY, AND EASY, BUT IT HAS NO DEPTH OR SOUL. IT'S LIKE THE ONE-NIGHT STAND OF OPERATING SYSTEMS. YOU FEEL CHEAP AFTER USING IT.

Copyright (c) 1999 Illiad http://www.userfriendly.org/
THEN AGAIN...
STEF MURKY? I'M DELILAH FROM MICROSOFT SALES AND RE-EDUCATION. YOU AND I HAVE SOME WORK TO DO...

WELL...DELILAH, I APPRECIATE YOUR COMING OUT HERE TO EXPLAIN WHY I SHOULD GO BACK TO USING WINDOWS. BUT I'M LIKING LINUX MORE THESE DAYS.

BUT STEF, YOU'RE FORGETTING ONE IMPORTANT THING...
WHAT'S THAT?

Copyright (c) 1999 Illiad http://www.userfriendly.org/
ALMOST EVERYONE ELSE IS DOING IT. DO YOU WANT TO BE THE ONE LEFT OUT?
NO! I WANT IN! MY GOD WHAT HAVE I BEEN DOING?!

CHIEF, I JUST WANTED TO TELL YOU HOW SORRY I AM FOR MY WEIRD BEHAVIOUR THE OTHER DAY. YOU WERE SO RIGHT WHEN YOU ASKED ME TO GET A GRIP AND I BOW AND SCRAPE BEFORE YOUR REMARKABLE WISDOM.
Copyright (c) 1999 Illiad http://www.userfriendly.org/

I HAVE NO INTENTION OF FIRING YOU, STEF.
THANK GOD. I JUST TOOK OUT A HUGE LOAN TO BUY MORE MICROSOFT STOCK.

TECH SUPPORT. MIRANDA SPEAKING.
I'M RUINING MY COMPUTER!

WHAT PRECISELY ARE YOU DOING?
WELL, I'M RUNNING SOMETHING CALLED "WINZIP," AND I TRIED OPENING A FILE WITH IT...
TAK TAK

Copyright (c) 1999 Illiad http://www.userfriendly.org/
I DON'T SEE THE PROBLEM...
LADY, IT KEEPS TELLING ME IT'S EXPLODING!

NOW PLEASE ENTER YOUR PASSWORD, SIR. TYPE "C" AS IN "CHARLIE."
UHH...DON'T YOU MEAN "C" AS IN "COMPUTER?"
TIP TAP

Copyright (c) 1999 Illiad http://www.userfriendly.org/
NO NO, YOU NEED TO USE THE "C" AS IN "CHARLIE" OR IT WON'T WORK.
JEEPERS, THESE COMPUTER THINGS SURE ARE TRICKY.

TECH SUPPORT. MAY I HELP YOU?
HELLO. I HAVE A BIG PROBLEM...
TIK TAP

SEE, I INSTALLED WINDOWS 98...
YES? AND?
TOK

Copyright (c) 1999 Illiad http://www.userfriendly.org/
...AND NOW MY COMPUTER DOESN'T WORK.
OOO!
YES, YOU ALREADY SAID THAT.

NETWORK TOTALITARIANISM

the dot commie people

At the first book signing I ever did, two employees from Network Solutions came up with printed copies of this cartoon for autographs. Shut mah mouth! (It's also technically disjointed. Communism != Totalitarianism, although certainly the Soviet Union went that route.)

BEEEEEEEEEEEEEEEEEEE
BeOS 4.5

EEEEEEEEEEEEEEEEEEEEEEEEEEEE
BeOS 4.5

EEEEEEEEEEEEP
YOU'RE WATCHING THE EARLY WARNING BROADCAST SYSTEM?
NO, JERRY SPRINGER.
BeOS 4.5
Copyright (c) 1999 Illiad http://www.userfriendly.org/

LINUX WORLD EXPO LOOKS GREAT. I'M GLAD I GET TO GO THIS TIME. IMAGINE... AN ENTIRE EXPO DEVOTED TO THE ULTIMATE ALTERNATE OPERATING SYSTEM.

BAMF!

FORGET IT DUDE, YOU CAN WRITE YOUR OWN DRIVERS.
EVIDENTLY YOU AND I HAVE MORE WORK TO DO.
Copyright (c) 1999 Illiad http://www.userfriendly.org/

I DON'T SEE WHY YOU'RE CLINGING TO AN INFERIOR O.S. LIKE LINUX. BSD HAS BETTER NETWORKING AND IS MORE RESILIENT.

ADD TO THAT THE FACT THAT LINUX IS BECOMING HEAVILY FRAGMENTED AND THE INFIGHTING IS GETTING NASTIER. YOU'D THINK A SMART PERSON LIKE YOU WOULD SWITCH OVER.

I THINK THE PENGUIN'S CUTER.
OOOOO! NOW YOU'RE GETTING PERSONAL!
Copyright (c) 1999 Illiad http://www.userfriendly.org/

LOOK, WE SHOULDN'T BE PETTY ABOUT THIS WHOLE THING. I'M SURE THERE MUST BE SOME FAIR AND LOGICAL WAY I CAN PROVE TO YOU THAT ANY BSD IS BETTER THAN LINUX.

WELL, HOW ABOUT IF WE BENCHMARK A BSD BOX AGAINST A LINUX BOX?
GREAT IDEA...

HI! I'M FROM MINDCRAFT AND WE CAN BENCHMARK BSD AND LINUX FOR YOU!
I DON'T HAVE ANY MONEY SO I GUESS LINUX WILL WIN, HUH?
POING!
Copyright (c) 1999 Illiad http://www.userfriendly.org/

What? If political groups can do it, why can't I? God is on the side of Open Source!

I'M SOOOOO BORED. HEY...THERE'S SOME SPAM COMING INTO THE NETWORK...
Copyright (c) 1999 Illiad http://www.userfriendly.org/

LET'S SEE...COBBLE THIS HERE. MODIFY THE WORDS THERE... AND OFF IT GOES.
YOU'RE ACTUALLY ORDERING STUFF FROM A COMPANY THAT SENT YOU SPAM?
HOW CAN I RESIST? IF I BUY THIS I CAN LOSE WEIGHT. MAKE MONEY FAST. MEET EASY WOMEN AND FIRM UP MY TOMATOES ALL AT ONCE!
CLIK
KLIK
CLIC
CLIK

AM WONDERINK WHAT IS THIS E-MAIL?
THIS IS NOT UNSOLICITED BULK E-MAIL. BUY ME. BLAH BLAH BLAH...
Copyright (c) 1999 Illiad http://www.userfriendly.org/

ZLOTNIKS! SENDINK ME SPAM...WILL FIXINK THEIR LEETLE RED WAGON...
TAP
TAP
TIP
WHAT HAPPENED TO OUR SERVER?
IT'S FLOODED. AND THERE'S AN E-MAIL HERE THAT SAYS "THIS IS NOT A DENIAL OF SERVICE ATTACK."

MICROSOFT REPORTS THAT THE LARGE MAJORITY OF THE CRASHES OF ITS WIN2K SERVER CHALLENGE WERE CAUSED BY LIGHTNING AND NOT BY CRACKERS...
THAT WAS WAY EASIER TO DO THAN PARTING THE RED SEA FOR MOSES.
COPYRIGHT (C) 1999 ILLIAD

AHHH. LINUX WORLD EXPO HERE WE COME!
CHIEF? THE TECHS HAVE BEEN AWFUL QUIET BACK THERE FOR THE PAST HOUR OR SO...

THAT'S FUNNY. IF THEY HAD A NET CONNECTION I COULD SEE WHY...
AIRPHONES COST $2.00 A MINUTE.
Copyright (c) 1999 Illiad http://www.userfriendly.org/

PITR!!
ONE MINUTESKI PLEASE. ONE MORE FRAG AND AM JOININK MILE-HIGH CLUB.

I CAN'T FIND THE OTHERS. SO THEY MUST ALL BE ON THE EXPO FLOOR ALREADY. I'LL SEE THE TWO OF YOU AT SIX FOR DINNER.
expo floor
'KAY CHIEF.

SAY...JUST A SECOND. IF YOU TWO ARE HERE, WHO'S MANNING THE TECH SUPPORT LINES AT THE OFFICE?
expo floor
Copyright (c) 1999 Illiad http://www.userfriendly.org/

AAAAAAAGH!!
I CAN TELL YOU'RE SMILING! STOP THAAAAAAT!
COOL. IT WORKS FOR THIS TOO...

MIKE. PITR. AS THE COMPANY'S TWO SENIOR TECH PEOPLE I WANT YOU TO MAKE SURE YOU LEARN AS MUCH AS YOU CAN HERE AT THE EXPO. IT'S THE REASON FOR US BEING HERE.
Copyright (c) 1999 Illiad http://www.userfriendly.org/

ANYWAY. I HAVE A BUSINESS SEMINAR TO ATTEND. YOU GUYS GO DO WHAT YOU DO BEST. SEE YOU LATER.

AND THERE HE GOES. SO WHERE SHALL WE START. PITR?
VA LINUX SYSTEMS. GIVINK AWAY NICE SHIRTS THERE, DA?

OH YES. I HAVE A TERRIFIC TECHNICAL TEAM WORKING FOR THE COMPANY. I FEEL LUCKY COMPARED TO SOME OF THE OTHER EXECUTIVES HERE.
Copyright (c) 1999 Illiad http://www.userfriendly.org/

I BRING THEM HERE TO THE EXPO AS A REWARD. AND WHAT HAPPENS IS THEY LEARN MORE AND BECOME MORE USEFUL. I KNOW TECH PEOPLE - LEARNING IS EVERYTHING TO THEM.

YA LEARN ANYTHING TODAY?
OH YEAH. GRAB ALL THE PIN-ON BUTTONS YOU CAN AND YOU CAN DEFLECT SNURF DARTS WITH EASE!

HEY, IS THAT A NEW SHIRT?
YUP. I GOT IT AT LINUX WORLD EXPO.

Copyright (c) 1999 Illiad http://www.userfriendly.org/
YOU NEVER ACTUALLY GO OUT AND BUY NEW CLOTHES, DO YOU.
THAT'S WHAT EXPOS ARE FOR. THAT, AND AVOIDING LAUNDRY.

YES SIR. NOW DO YOU KNOW WHAT YOUR PASSWORD IS?
YES. IT'S ASTERISK ASTERISK ASTERISK ASTERISK ASTERISK.
TAP TYPE TIP

UH...

Copyright (c) 1999 Illiad http://www.userfriendly.org/
WAS THAT...UH ...ACTUALLY...
HA! YOU CAN'T TELL IF I'M BEING STUPID OR REALLY CLEVER. CAN YOU! HAHAHA!

EVOLUTION OF LANGUAGE THROUGH THE AGES

6000 B.C.
UNGH.
GRRF.
BOOGA.
2000 A.D.
GREP.
AWK.
SED.

THIS IS IMPOSSIBLE! I CAN'T GET ANY WORK DONE LIKE THIS...
Copyright (c) 1999 Illiad http://www.userfriendly.org/

I MEAN, PLEASE. WINDOWS ON A 486 JUST DOES NOT CUT THE MUSTARD!
C'MON STEF. A GOOD TRADESMAN NEVER BLAMES HIS TOOLS.
AAAAGH!! NOOO! THAT STUPID PAPERCLIP JUST POPPED UP! NOT ON A 486!

Si

Since
Copyright (c) 1999 Illiad http://www.userfriendly.org/
Sincerely,
SO THERE'S ACTUALLY A FRAME RATE FOR WORD97 ON A 486...

PHEW! THAT TOOK AGES. I'M GLAD I'M FINALLY DONE...
TAK TAK TIK
Copyright (c) 1999 Illiad http://www.userfriendly.org/

YOU STILL FIGHTING WITH THAT THING?
I MADE IT WORK FOR ME. I JUST TYPED A HUGE LETTER WITH AN OLD DOS EDITOR THAT ONLY HAS A BACKSPACE FUNCTION.
TAP TIP TAK

I DON'T MEAN TO BE NOSY, BUT IS THERE A REASON WHY THE SALUTATION READS, "DEAR SOR"?
HNNNNG

HEY CHIEF. I JUST WANTED TO COME BY AND TAKE THE TIME TO LET YOU KNOW THAT IT'S A REAL PLEASURE TO WORK FOR YOU...

YOUR WISDOM AND COMPASSION AS THE C.E.O. OF THE COMPANY IS AN INSPIRATION TO LOWLY MANAGERS LIKE MYSELF. I WISH I HAD HALF THE SMARTS YOU DO.
Copyright (c) 1999 Illiad http://www.userfriendly.org/

STEF, BEFORE YOU PUT HOOVER OUT OF BUSINESS, WHAT DO YOU WANT?
SINCE YOU'RE OFFERING, I'D LIKE A NEW COMPUTER. SOMETHING DEAD SEXY.

I UNDERSTAND WHY YOU WANT A NEW COMPUTER, STEF. BEING STUCK ON A 486 CAN BE TOUGH. BUT WE CAN'T AFFORD A NEW MACHINE RIGHT NOW, MUCH LESS A "DEAD SEXY" ONE.
Copyright (c) 1999 Illiad http://www.userfriendly.org/

ACTUALLY, WE HAVE A MACHINE THAT WOULD BE PERFECT FOR ME, AND NONE OF THE STAFF ARE USING IT. I CAN MOVE THE DATA THAT'S ON IT ELSEWHERE.
WELL...IF IT HELPS YOU WORK BETTER, GO FOR IT.

HMMMM. WHY DO I FEEL CHILLY ALL OF A SUDDEN?

OH GREAT. HERE COMES **DORK-BOY** AGAIN.
Copyright (c) 1999 Illiad http://www.userfriendly.org/

WHAT?!!
THIS SMILING THING REALLY WORKS. SO THIS IS WHAT BEING A DARK JEDI IS LIKE...

A POSSIBLE FUTURE, IF SLASHDOT HADN'T BEEN ACQUIRED...
WILL TRADE LINKS FOR FOOD.
HTTP://WWW.USERFRIENDLY.ORG/
COPYRIGHT (C) 1999 ILLIAD

That's what Rob Malda looked like when I first met him, goatee and all. Today, Slashdot remains a powerful link portal. I expect that if the site hadn't been acquired, the food they would've received for linkage would fill a shipping container every month.

I'VE BEEN WAITING FOR THIS DAY FOR SOME TIME NOW, YOU SMARMY LITTLE FURBY REJECT.
YOU CAN'T DO SQUAT TO ME, SALES-BOY. YOU DON'T EVEN KNOW HOW TO LOG IN.

ACTUALLY, I HAVE LEARNED. AND I EVEN HAVE A LOGIN AND PASSWORD I SWIPED FROM ONE OF THE TECHS...
UHHH...
...ALTHOUGH I'M NOT ENTIRELY CERTAIN WHO THIS "ROOT" PERSON IS...
AAAAAGGH!

...ALL OF THE LOAD BALANCING SHOULD BE DONE AT THE SWITCH AND...
HANG ON A SEC MIKE. CHECK THIS OUT.

'SCUSE ME, GUYS.

WHAT WE JUST SAW WAS VERY MEANINGFUL, WASN'T IT.
CLUELESS MARKETING GUY CARRIES COOL TECHNOLOGY INTO OBLIVION. KIND OF LIKE AN I.P.O.

OKAY YOU LITTLE PIPSQUEAK. LET'S SEE HOW MUCH YOU LIKE YOUR NEW HOME.
THAT WASN'T A VERY NICE THING TO DO STEF.

BAH. HE NEEDED TAKING DOWN A FEW PEGS.
PITR'S GONNA KILL YOU FOR THIS.

PITR WON'T CARE. HE'LL LOVE THIS.
DUDE. YOU PUT ERWIN IN AN OLD HP CALCULATOR.
AAAGH! KILL YOU I MUST!!

STEF PUT ERWIN IN AN OLD HP CALCULATOR?
YUP. AND NOW HE TALKS FUNNY.

WELL, HP CALCULATORS USED SOMETHING CALLED "REVERSE POLISH NOTATION." YOU ENTERED THE TWO NUMBERS AND THEN YOU PRESSED THE FUNCTION YOU WANTED.

AHHH...KIND OF LIKE THE WAY YODA TALKS.
YES. SOMETHING LIKE THAT...

HEY, ERWIN. TALK LIKE YODA FOR ME. OKAY?
NO.
Copyright (c) 1999 Illiad http://www.userfriendly.org/

HAHAAHAA! THANKS, BUDDY.
FUNNY THIS IS NOT!!

...

...NNGGG...

Copyright (c) 1999 Illiad http://www.userfriendly.org/
AAAAARRRGH! THINKING LIKE THIS I HATE!!

"SIGHTINGS"

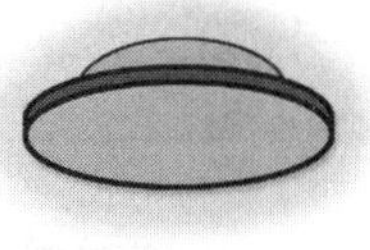

UFOs

ELVIS

AMIGA

COPYRIGHT (C) 1999 ILLIAD HTTP://WWW.USERFRIENDLY.ORG/

I miss my Amiga 1000. I cast filthy looks at people who claim they've seen them at swap meets.

YOU ARE NEEDINK HELP, COMRADE?
YES!! HELP I AM NEEDINK! ERR, I MEAN NEEDING!

Copyright (c) 1999 Illiad http://www.userfriendly.org/
MAKINK FUN OF WAY AM SPEAKINK?
NOOOOOO!! MISTAKE IT WAS! I AM SORRYINK! I MEAN SORRY!!

PITR, OWE YOU A BIG ONE I SHALL WHEN OUT OF HERE YOU GET ME...
Copyright (c) 1999 Illiad http://www.userfriendly.org/

TAP
TAP
TIP
TAP

HEY!! PROGRAMMING ME FOR "LUNAR LANDER!" YOU ARE!
DA...TODAY, WE SHALL RESCUE MIR!!

ERWIN, HAVE BUILT YOU NEW BODY WITH LEGO MINDSTORMS. NOW TO BE TRANSFERINK YOU.
OKAY PITR.
Copyright (c) 1999 Illiad http://www.userfriendly.org/

WHHIIRRRR!

TAP
TIK
TAP
TRANSFERINK COMPLETED. YOU ARE LIKINK NEW BODY?
OOOOH, YESSS!!
TIKKA
TAK

I CAN'T BELIEVE WHAT YOU DID TO ERWIN, STEF. YOU HAD BETTER HAVE A GOOD REASON.
Copyright (c) 1999 Illiad http://www.userfriendly.org/

WELL YEAH...THAT 486 WAS HOPELESS. THIS SGI BOX HAS REALLY BOOSTED MY PRODUCTIVITY.

YOU'VE BEEN PLAYING QUAKE ON IT FOR THE LAST HALF HOUR!
HEY, THAT CAN BE PRODUCTIVE...
BLAM!
BORRF!
SPUTCH!!

OH YEAAAH, QUAKE IS SWEET ON THIS MACHINE...
Copyright (c) 1999 Illiad http://www.userfriendly.org/

MY FRAME RATE IS SO GOOD IT FEELS LIKE I'M ACTUALLY **THERE**...

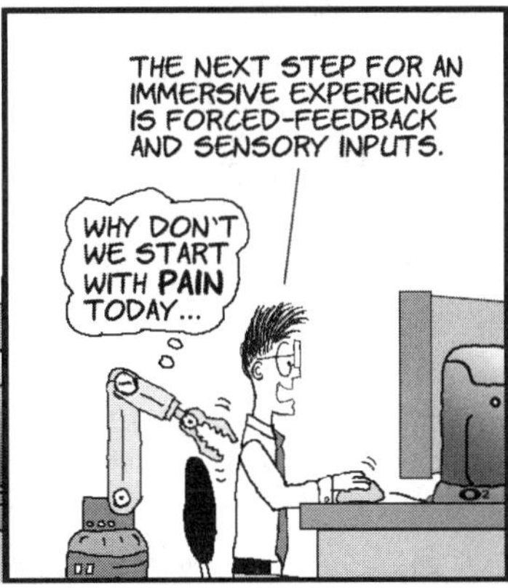
THE NEXT STEP FOR AN IMMERSIVE EXPERIENCE IS FORCED-FEEDBACK AND SENSORY INPUTS.
WHY DON'T WE START WITH **PAIN** TODAY...

MIKE, YOU SEE STEF? HILLARY'S LOOKING FOR HIM.
NOPE...BUT I THINK I HEARD HIM IN THE OTHER ROOM.
Copyright (c) 1999 Illiad http://www.userfriendly.org/

IS HE WITH A CLIENT OR SOMETHING?

COULD BE. I HEARD HIM SCREAMING.
NO SHARK POOL?
NYET, BUT HAVINK PILE OF OLD VIDEO CARDS WITH SHARP CONTACTS. DROPPINK HIM PLEASE.
NasRAQ
AAAGH!!

THE MICROSOFT NT FUND CREDIT CARD

THE *NT* FUND IS A PRIVATE CHARITY INCORPORATED TO SERVE ONE EXCITING PURPOSE: TO FILL OUR COFFERS. FOR EVERY PURCHASE YOU MAKE ON THIS CARD, WE TACK ON ANOTHER 20% SO THAT WE CAN BUY MARKET SHARE.

NT
3636 666 8001
NT
3232 666 1019
BOB Y. UNCLE

FEATURES:

* EXPIRY IN 90 DAYS. A NEW CARD WILL BE SENT TO YOU AT A NOMINAL $999.00 FEE.

*COMPATIBLE WITH ALMOST ANY RECENT MICROSOFT CARD SWIPER.

*"ADEQUATE" SECURITY FEATURES.

HTTP://WWW.USERFRIENDLY.ORG/

IS GOINK TO BE PROBLEM PUTTINK ERWIN BACK IN SGI BOX...NEEDINK A TRANSFER STAGE.
CODE CODE TAP
Copyright (c) 1999 Illiad http://www.userfriendly.org/

WHY DO I GET THE **DISTINCT** FEELING THAT ERWIN IS REALLY NOT GOING TO LIKE THIS? **AGAIN?**
ERWIN WILL BE UNDERSTANDINK.
TIP TAP
YAWWWNN...UMM WHY DO I FEEL LIKE I NEED SOMEONE TO **PLAY** WITH ME?

LET ME GET THIS STRAIGHT: YOU PUT ERWIN INTO A **TAMAGOTCHI?!?**
DA. WAS ONLY AVAILABLE PLACE.
Copyright (c) 1999 Illiad http://www.userfriendly.org/

BUT...BUT...YOU'RE NOT SUPPOSED TO LEAVE THEM **ALONE**. ARE YOU?
NOT KNOWINK. IS NOT IMPORTANT.
TIK TAK
WILL SOMEBODY PLEASE **FEED ME!??!**

Copyright (c) 1999 Illiad http://www.userfriendly.org/

OKAY YOU LITTLE PUKE. DROP ME INTO A PILE OF SHARP BITS, WILL YOU? TIME FOR **PAYBACK!**
BAH. AND WHAT ARE YOU GOING TO DO?
I'M GOING TO FEED YOU UNTIL YOU **DIE**.
GAAAH! *MRRF!* GACK!!
BLEEP BLEEP BLEEP BLEEP

I JUST FOUND HIM LIKE THIS...WHINING AND MAKING LOUD BURPING NOISES.
OMIGOD... *GAAAAH*
Copyright (c) 1999 Illiad http://www.userfriendly.org/

OHH...I FEEL SO **BLOATED**

OH MY GOD!! WHERE AM I?! I FEEL BLOATED!! PITR, DID YOU PUT ME IN AN NT BOX AGAIN?!?
NYET...RELAX LEETLE FRIEND.

ERWIN. NOW TRANSFERINK YOU BACK INTO SGI BOX. DA?
BOY. THAT FEELS BETTER...
TAP
TIP
TAK
http://www.userfriendly.org/
Copyright (c) 1999 Illiad

AND NOW HAVE RECONNECTINK YOU TO INTERNET...
THANK YOU. I HAVE A TINY BIT OF WORK TO DO.
TAP
BUT...I NEVER ASKED TO BUY **MIR** FROM THE RUSSIANS...
NO REFUNDS. PAL. THE MIGS ARE ALREADY ON THEIR WAY UP TO SHOOT IT DOWN FOR YOU.

HI. GREG SPEAKING...
I HATE WINDOWS! I SWEAR. IF BILL GATES HAD A NICKEL FOR EACH TIME WINDOWS CRASHED...

http://www.userfriendly.org/
Copyright (c) 1999 Illiad
DO YOU THINK IT'S REALLY THAT WAY?
IT CERTAINLY EXPLAINS A GREAT MANY THINGS. DON'T YOU THINK?

THE NEW ARMY
G4 WEB SERVER

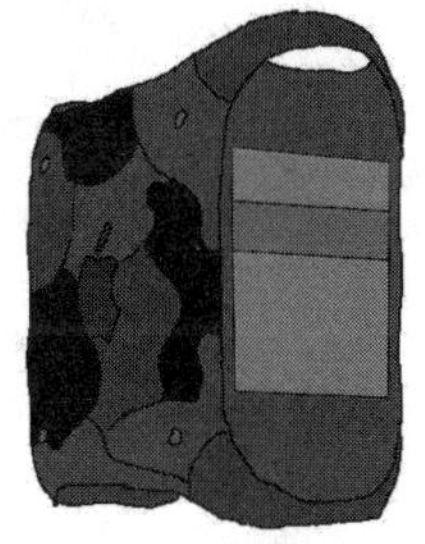

DEFEATING MORE CRACKING ATTEMPTS
BY 9:00 AM THAN MOST NT SERVERS
DEFEAT IN A DAY.

It's a picture of an urchin-eating fish. Just laugh and move on!

Copyright (c) 1999 Illiad http://www.userfriendly.org/
IT'S ALL CLEAR. MATT.
YAH. EASY FOR YOU TO SAY. YOU EVER TRIED WALKING UNDER A PICTURE OF A VACUUM CLEANER AND FELT IT WAS "ALL CLEAR?"
Copyright (c) 1999 Illiad http://www.userfriendly.org/
MATT? IT'S ALL CLEAR. WE CAN SNEAK IN NOW.
OKAY.
YOU KNOW. IF YOU COULD JUST SPEED IT UP...
YOU HAVE FEET. I ONLY HAVE BUTT MUSCLES. DO YOU SEE THE PROBLEM?
Copyright (c) 1999 Illiad http://www.userfriendly.org/
AJ. DO YOU THINK IT'S OKAY IF I SHOW MY FRIEND AROUND THE OFFICE?
SURE THING. LITTLE GUY.
LET'S GO. MATT.
RIGHT BEHIND YOU.
IF THAT THING WITH THE SPINES THAT'S FOLLOWING HIM IS AN EGG HE LAID. I CAN SEE WHY HE WALKS FUNNY...
Copyright (c) 1999 Illiad http://www.userfriendly.org/
SURFING THE WEB IS EASY. MATT. JUST USE THAT MOUSE THERE AND START CLICKING AWAY.
ANYTIME NOW...
OKAY. YOU'RE STILL HAVING PROBLEMS WITH THE FEET THING AREN'T YOU.

SO TO WEB SURF, JUST KEEP CLICKING ON LINKS AND YOU'LL END UP SOMEWHERE INTERESTING...

POING!
POING!
POING!
POING!

"KEVIN'S DOG'S HINDQUARTERS' WEB PAGE ON GEOCITIES"
A COUPLE MORE CLICKS AND WE CAN GET TO THE GOOD STUFF.
Copyright (c) 1999 Illiad http://www.userfriendly.org/

MATT, THIS IS QUAKE, A GAME THAT DEMANDS SKILL, PLANNING, AND STRATEGIC THOUGHT...
Copyright (c) 1999 Illiad http://www.userfriendly.org/

HOOOOOSSHHH!!
ZZSWOOOOSHHH!
WHHHOOOOSH!
KER-BLAM!!
BLUTCH!
DOING!

OF COURSE, CARPETING A ROOM WITH ROCKETS CAN MEAN SUCCESS AS WELL...
THAT WAS COOL!
YEEAARGH!

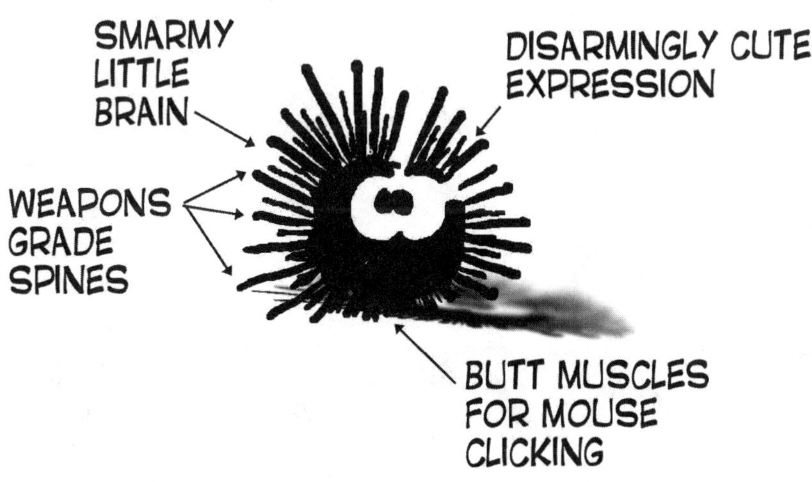
ANATOMY OF A SEA URCHIN
SMARMY LITTLE BRAIN
DISARMINGLY CUTE EXPRESSION
WEAPONS GRADE SPINES
BUTT MUSCLES FOR MOUSE CLICKING
COPYRIGHT (C) 1999 ILLIAD
HTTP://WWW.USERFRIENDLY.ORG/

WOOOOOSH!
SWOOOSH!
BLAM!
KERBLAM!!
Copyright (c) 1999 Illiad http://www.userfriendly.org/

POFF!
WOOOOOOSSHHH!
FFFFOOOOOOOOOMM!
WIGGLE

I SEE YOU'RE REALLY ENJOYING THIS GAME...
YA. IT'S COOL WHEN THERES GIBS. LOOKS LIKE "PEOPLE SASHIMI."
SWIIIISSHHHH!
KERBLUTCH!
SPLUTCH!
BLUTCH!!

MICROSOFT HAS JOINED FORCES WITH OVER 100 SITES, INCLUDING LYCOS AND EXCITE@HOME TO COMPETE WITH ONLINE AUCTION LEADER E-BAY...
TAKO
Copyright (c) 1999 Illiad http://www.userfriendly.org/

THE E-BAY AUCTION MODEL HAS BEEN SO SUCCESSFUL THAT MICROSOFT AND ITS ALLIES WILL BE IMITATING THE AUCTION LEADER IN THE WAY IT HANDLES BUSINESS...
TAKO

THE ONLY DIFFERENCE IS THAT MICROSOFT WILL BE RUNNING NT SERVERS FOR THEIR AUCTION SITE AS OPPOSED TO SUN SPARC SERVERS LIKE AY E-BAY.
HEH. SO THEY'LL BE IMITATING E-BAY'S DOWNTIME TOO.
SHUSH NOW.
TAKO

MICROSOFT TODAY ANNOUNCED THE ACQUISITION OF SOFTWAY SYSTEMS, THE PRODUCERS OF INTERIX PRODUCTS FOR INTEROPERABILITY BETWEEN WINDOWS NT AND UNIX BASED SYSTEMS...
TAKO
Copyright (c) 1999 Illiad http://www.userfriendly.org/

THE PURCHASE HAS CLEARLY CEMENTED MICROSOFT'S INTENTIONS TO SABOTAGE THE UNIX COMMUNITY BY SHIPPING PRODUCTS THAT LEAD TO UNIX-TO-NT MIGRATION.
TAKO

ALTHOUGH MET WITH PRAISE FROM SOME QUARTERS, IT IS WIDELY HELD THAT THIS ACQUISITION IS JUST ANOTHER SLAP IN THE FACE OF THE PURE UNIX HEIRARCHY...
THERE IS A BEAUTY IN THE PURE HEIRARCHIES, I MUST SAY.
DA. AM THINKINK "FOOD CHAIN."
TAKO

UH OH...
TAKO
Copyright (c) 1999 Illiad http://www.userfriendly.org/

STAB! POKE!
POKE! POINK!
STAB! STAB!
JAB! DOINK!
BOING!
TAKO
HAH! MISSED ME!!!
SORRY LEETLE BUDDY.
TAKO

TECH SUPPORT. GREG HERE.
HEY, YOUR TOLL-FREE NUMBER WON'T WORK 'CUZ IT HAS ONE TOO MANY DIGITS IN IT.
Copyright (c) 1999 Illiad http://www.userfriendly.org/

EXCUSE ME?
1-800-INTERNET. EIGHT LETTERS IN "INTERNET," AND YOU'RE ONLY SUPPOSED TO HAVE SEVEN.

WELL WHY DON'T WE GO OUT ON A LIMB AND TRY DIALING "1-800-INTERNE" INSTEAD?
IT WON'T WORK "INTERNE" ISN'T A REAL WORD.

NOW PLEASE RIGHT-CLICK ON THE ICON.
UM...MY RIGHT OR YOUR RIGHT?
Copyright (c) 1999 Illiad http://www.userfriendly.org/

HELLO? WHAT ARE YOU DOING?
DOCUMENTING THIS INCIDENT FOR THE GENE ELIMINATION SQUAD.
RAP
TAP

OUR CELEBRITY EXPERT EXPLAINS HOW TO PRONOUNCE "HTTPD"

THHHHTTPD!!!

 HTTP://WWW.USERFRIENDLY.ORG/

AM THINKINK LEETLE SEA URCHIN IS COWARD. HE IS RUNNINK AWAY...
Copyright (c) 1999 Illiad http://www.userfriendly.org/

POINK!
YEEEAAARRGH!

AM NOT LIKINK LEETLE SEA ZLOTNIK. IT IS SPINELESS COWARD!!!
Copyright (c) 1999 Illiad http://www.userfriendly.org/

TAP CODE CODE
ACTUALLY, HE'S COVERED IN SPINES...
DA, I AM KNOWINK ALREADY!!

CLICK
Copyright (c) 1999 Illiad http://www.userfriendly.org/

CLICK

WHY DO YOU KEEP RELOADING SLASHDOT?
I WANT TO GET IN A "FIRST POST."

GREG, I DON'T GET THIS "FIRST POST" INSANITY ON SLASHDOT. I MEAN, WHY WORK SO HARD JUST TO GET YOUR NAME AT THE TOP OF A NEWS ITEM DISCUSSION THREAD?
CLICK

I MEAN, SERIOUSLY, ANYONE WHO DOES THIS IS GUILTY OF NARCISSISM AT ITS WORST. IMMORTALITY ON A DISCUSSION BOARD? SHEESH.
CLICK
Copyright (c) 1999 Illiad http://www.userfriendly.org/

IT'S NOTHING LIKE YOU SPENDING FORTY BUCKS IN QUARTERS TO GET YOUR INITIALS IN THE HIGH SCORE SCREEN FOR "SPY HUNTER", IS IT.
NOTHING LIKE IT AT ALL.

MIKE, IS THERE A FOOTSTOOL ANYWHERE? I CAN'T REACH THAT BOOK...
YOU COULD ALWAYS CLIMB ON TOP OF THE SERVER BEHIND YOU.

GREAT IDEA, MIKE. THIS IS JUST ONE OF THOSE OLD NT BOXES ANYWAY.

HEY...THIS SERVER IS ACTUALLY KIND OF STABLE...
I CAN GET YOU A JOB AT MINDCRAFT IF YOU LIKE.

CHIEF? GIVEN ALL OF THE TRAVELLING THAT I HAVE TO DO FOR THIS COMPANY, CAN I PLEASE HAVE A LAPTOP?
UM...SURE.

CAN I HAVE ONE WITH A SIX GIG HARD DRIVE, FIREWIRE, INFRARED PORT, CD-ROM DRIVE, AND DOCKING PORT?
I...GUESS SO.

SO I CAN EXPENSE THIS SONY VAIO?
YES, BUT ONLY IF YOU GIVE IT TO ME...

MICROSOFT'S WINDOWS AND LINUX HYBRID

Microsoft
WiNDEX
For a cleaner, shinier version of Windows!

THE CHIEF TOOK MY SONY VAIO EVEN THOUGH I WAS THE ONE WHO EXPENSED IT. I HAVE NO ROOM LEFT IN MY EXPENSE ACCOUNT UNTIL THE END OF THE YEAR NOW. IT'S NOT FAIR!
Copyright (c) 1999 Illiad http://www.userfriendly.org/

I AGREE, STEF. THE C.E.O. CAN'T TAKE ALL OF THE GOODIES IN A COMPANY. I'VE SPOKEN TO HIM ABOUT IT ALREADY.
WELL, GOOD. WHEN CAN I HAVE MY VAIO BACK?

YOU'RE NOT. HE GAVE IT TO ME.
WHERE IN MY JOB DESCRIPTION DOES IT SAY I GET SPANKED DAILY BY UPPER MANAGEMENT?

WHAT'S THIS I HEAR ABOUT EVERYONE GETTING A LAPTOP IN THE COMPANY?
IT'S THE CHIEF'S IDEA. HE WANTED ONE, SO HE GOT EVERYONE ELSE ONE TOO.

REALLY?! I GET ONE TOO? DO I GET A SONY VAIO LIKE EVERYONE?
WELL... YOU BEING A DESIGNER, THE CHIEF GOT YOU A LAPTOP MORE YOUR ...UMM ...STYLE.
Copyright (c) 1999 Illiad http://www.userfriendly.org/

BUT THE CHIEF SAID THE IBOOK WAS FOR A.J...

I GET TO HAVE IT! IT'S CUTE! IT'S ORANGE! IT HAS "MARKETING" WRITTEN ALL OVER IT!

I SEE ALL OF THE TECHS GOT THEIR VAIO NOTEBOOKS. THAT MUST HAVE COST US QUITE A MINT.
YES, BUT I SEE A VERY HIGH RETURN ON INVESTMENT.
Copyright (c) 1999 Illiad http://www.userfriendly.org/

WELL, I HOPE YOU REALIZE THAT LAPTOPS GO MISSING REALLY EASILY. MAYBE WE SHOULD GET SOME INSURANCE FOR THEM?
GOOD POINT. I'LL TAKE STEPS TO PROTECT OUR INVESTMENT.

WHAT THE...
KER-CHUNK

IT'S NICE TO HAVE THOSE VAIO NOTEBOOKS, BUT DOESN'T IT KIND OF DEFEAT THE PURPOSE OF A NOTEBOOK IF YOU CHAIN IT TO A DESK?
CHURGLE CHURGLE CHURGLE

I ADMIT I HAVE A TRUST ISSUE ABOUT SUCH COSTLY PIECES OF EQUIPMENT. I JUST HAVE NO IDEA WHAT YOU TECHS WILL DO WITH THE NOTEBOOKS IF YOU CAN TAKE THEM WITH YOU.
FOOOOOSHHH!

OH WE'D PROBABLY DO SOMETHING EVIL, LIKE ANALYZE SERVER LOGS, OR WRITE PERL CODE, OR TAKE OUR WORK HOME WITH US. WE'RE TECHS AFTER ALL. WE'RE JUST LIVIN' LA VIDA LOCA!
Copyright (c) 1999 Illiad http://www.userfriendly.org/

LOOK, CHAINING LAPTOPS TO DESKS HAS TO BE ONE OF THE MOST INANE THINGS TO DO...IT'S POINTLESS TO HAVE THEM AT ALL NOW!

I MEAN, THERE HAS TO BE SOMETHING WE CAN DO TO UNCHAIN THE NOTEBOOKS AND LET YOU FEEL SAFE THAT THEY WON'T JUST GET WALKED AWAY WITH.
NOW THAT YOU MENTION IT, YES THERE IS...

Copyright (c) 1999 Illiad http://www.userfriendly.org/
I NEED TO KEEP MY TRAP SHUT SOMETIMES...
HELLO! WAITING PATIENTLY FOR YOUR INPUT!

WHAT HAPPENED TO YOU?
THE SMILING MAN WOULDN'T UNCHAIN MY VAIO UNTIL HE CHAINED ME UP. GET ME OUTTA THIS, WILL YOU?
Copyright (c) 1999 Illiad http://www.userfriendly.org/

STEF!!

Stop looking at me like that. It's what Stef would do!

USER
FRIENDLY
the comic strip
PIZZA
Portrasher 4
ROTO-ROUTER 800
Copyright (c) 1997-1999 Illiad

SUNG TO DEPECHE MODE'S "JUST CAN'T GET ENOUGH"
WHEN I USE WINDOWS NT, I JUST GO OUT OF MY HEAD. NT'S NOT UP TO SNUFF NT'S NOT UP TO SNUFF

INSTALLINK IT ON NAVY SHIP, AND IN WATER IT IS DEAD. NT'S NOT UP TO SNUFF NT'S NOT UP TO SNUFF

WE CURSE AND SCREAM AS WE REBOOT MACHINES, AND NT JUST DOESN'T SEEEEM UP TO SNUFF

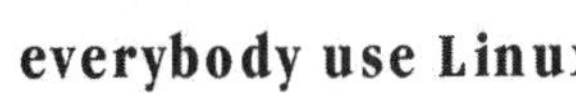
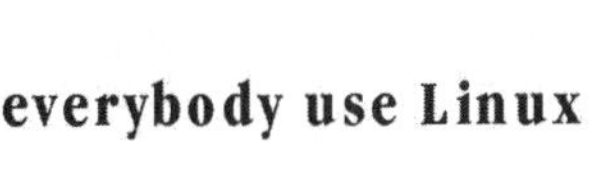
everybody use Linux

LINUX

A spoof of an old Gap commercial, tied in with the problems the U.S. Navy had with Windows NT blue-screening on one of its warships.

I CAN'T BELIEVE I'M STUCK HERE. AND WITHOUT MY NOTEBOOK.

ANOTHER TALENTED TECHNICAL WORKER HAMSTRUNG BY NEAR-SIGHTED UPPER MANAGEMENT.

Copyright (c) 1999 Illiad http://www.userfriendly.org/
THEN AGAIN I'M NOT DEALING WITH USERS. AND SINCE I'M STUCK HERE I MAY AS WELL JUST ENJOY IT...
HI! THAT STEF GUY SAID YOU COULD TEACH ME HOW TO USE WINDOWS. STEP BY STEP!

Copyright (c) 1999 Illiad http://www.userfriendly.org/

STEF. WHAT IN THE NAME OF HADES ARE YOU DOING?
GENERATING A NEW REVENUE STREAM. DEAL.
SEE THE TECHIE $3.00

Copyright (c) 1999 Illiad http://www.userfriendly.org/
MIKE? HAVE YOU SEEN THE IBOOK ANYWHERE? IT HAS ALL OF MY MARKETING DATA ON IT AND I HAVE TO HAVE A REPORT READY TODAY.

PITR GOT OFFENDED BY THE WAY IT LOOKED AND SAID HE WAS GOING TO "...MODIFY IT SO IT CAN FULFILL IT'S TRUE DESTINY."
TRUE DESTINY?

HILLARY? WHY DO WE NOW HAVE A SMALL, ORANGE AND WHITE TOILET SEAT?
BEEP FLUSH BUFFERS?

Copyright (c) 1999 Illiad http://www.userfriendly.org/
YOU BUILDING A NEW WEBSITE?
YA. IT'S MY OWN. IT'S A REALLY NEW, GROUND-BREAKING CONCEPT SITE. IT SHOULD MAKE ME MILLIONS.
CLICK CLICK

KLIK KIK

WHY ARE THERE PICTURES OF NAKED CHICKS ALL OVER YOUR SITE?
STARTUPS NEED FUNDING, MIKE.
CLICK CLICK

SO NOW THE HARD PART IS GETTING TRAFFIC TO MY SITE.
YOU COULD TRY AND GET A NEWS ITEM IN AT SLASHDOT. BUT THE SITE NEEDS SOMETHING GEEKY...

...SOMETHING GEEKY...

Copyright (c) 1999 Illiad http://www.userfriendly.org/
HEY. SLAP SOME PENGUIN CLIPART ON YOUR FRONT PAGE. THAT SHOULD DO IT.
I DON'T HAVE ANY PENGUINS. HOW ABOUT AN ALPACA?

GREG SAID THE NEWS ITEM WAS LAUNCHED THIS MORNING ON SLASHDOT. LET'S CHECK OUT YOUR SITE LOGS.
'KAY.
CLICK

Copyright (c) 1999 Illiad http://www.userfriendly.org/
MIRRORING Q3TEST WAS A BIT OF A MISTAKE, HUH.
AT FIVE CENTS A MEGABYTE, MR. SLASHDOT IS NOBODY'S FRIEND.

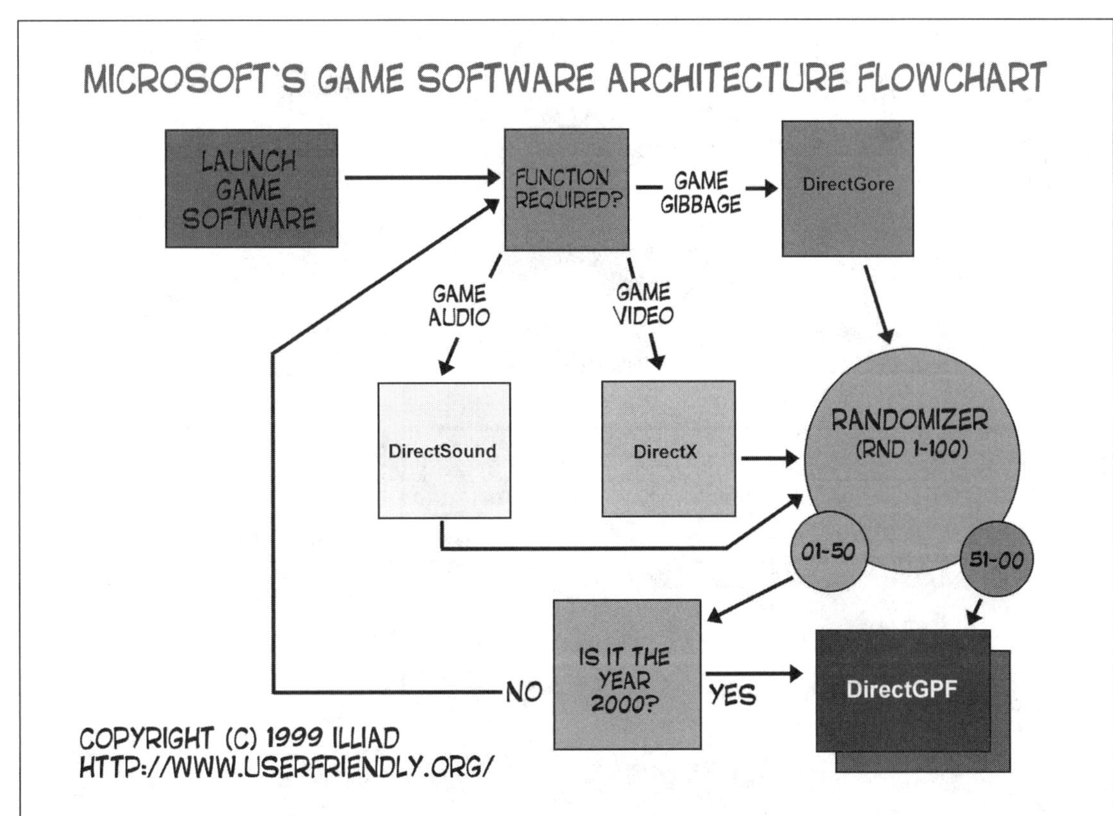
MICROSOFT'S GAME SOFTWARE ARCHITECTURE FLOWCHART
LAUNCH GAME SOFTWARE
FUNCTION REQUIRED?
GAME GIBBAGE
DirectGore
GAME AUDIO
GAME VIDEO
DirectSound
DirectX
RANDOMIZER (RND 1-100)
01-50
51-00
IS IT THE YEAR 2000?
NO
YES
DirectGPF
COPYRIGHT (C) 1999 ILLIAD
HTTP://WWW.USERFRIENDLY.ORG/

Week of October 18th, 1999

INTERESTING BOOK, THIS "LORD OF THE RINGS." IT TELLS QUITE A STORY.
Lord of the Rings

ALTHOUGH...IT MUST BE SAID THAT IT'S **NOT** AN EASY READ. QUITE TIRING REALLY...
Lord of the Rings

AND THE LITTLE GUY DREAMS...
ZZZ
ONE PING TO RULE THEM ALL,
ONE PING TO FIND THEM,
ONE PING TO BRING THEM ALL,
AND IN THE DARKNESS BIND THEM.
zZZZ

A NIGHT OF COMFY SLUMBER WAS INTERRUPTED BY A SHARP KNOCKING AT MY HUMBLE DOOR...
BLINK
BLINK
RAP
RAP
RAP

SO I RAN TO ANSWER THE KNOCKING, MY FEET BEATING A FLESHY STACCATO ON THE FLOOR...
SLAP
SLAP
SLAPPY
SLAP

...AND THERE HE WAS, OLD BUT STILL WORKING, MY OLD FRIEND AND ADVISOR.
HI SHORTY.
Gandalf
9600 BAUD

MY SHORT AND HAIRY FRIEND, YOU HAVE AN ARDUOUS TASK AHEAD OF YOU. I NEED YOU TO TRAVEL TO THE LAND OF REDMOND, WHERE THE SHADOWS LIE.
WHY, GANDALF?

THIS IS THE **ONE TRUE PING**. AN ARTIFACT OF SUCH IMMENSE POWER THAT ANYONE USING IT WILL HAVE AN OVERWHELMING ADVANTAGE ON ANY NETWORK. IT IS NOW TIME TO FULFILL YOUR DESTINY AND BEAR THIS PING TO REDMOND, WHERE IT **MUST** BE DESTROYED.

...EITHER THAT OR WE COULD SEND IT OFF WITH MY HOTMAIL ACCOUNT...
NO NO...I'LL FIGHT THE NAZGUL AND STUFF. SAFER.

SO I SET OUT TO THE LAND OF REDMOND AS PER GANDALF'S BIDDING, THE ONE TRUE PING NESTLED SAFELY IN MY LAPTOP CASE.

AS THE SUN CAME UP I LEFT BEHIND MY SAFE HOLE IN THE HILL AND MY KICK-BUTT ADSL CONNECTION TO FACE THE WONDERS AND HORRORS OF THE UNPLUGGED WORLD.

PITTER
PATTER
PITR
PATR

OF COURSE, KNOBBITS NEVER FACE DANGER ALONE. MY FRIENDS GREG, AJ AND MIKE BRAVELY VOLUNTEERED TO WALK BY MY SIDE THROUGH THICK AND THIN...
I DON'T **WANT** TO BE A KNOBBIT! I LOOK FREAKING **RIDICULOUS!**
IT'S NOT SO MUCH THE WAY WE LOOK...I'M WONDERING HOW WE...UHH.. **WIPE**.

ONWARD WE WENT, A BRAVE BAND OF KNOBBITS GUARDING THE ONE TRUE PING. I KNEW MY FRIENDS WERE DEEP IN THEIR OWN THOUGHTS ABOUT THE NOBLE QUEST WE HAD ACCEPTED...
MIKE'S GOT A POINT. HOW DO WE WIPE?
AREN'T THERE EVIL MARKETING PEOPLE IN REDMOND?
I'M CALLING MY AGENT.
Copyright (c) 1999 Illiad http://www.userfriendly.org/

AND AS EXPECTED, WE CAME ACROSS ONE OF THE DARK ONE'S MINIONS, A NAZGUL, A TWISTED REMNANT OF A CODER WHO WAS FORCED TO BOW TO THE FORCES OF FEAR, UNCERTAINTY AND DOUBT.

OF COURSE, GREG, BEING THE UNDISPUTED RACONTEUR OF OUR GROUP, DID HIS BEST TO TALK US OUT OF TROUBLE...
HIIIIISSSSSSSSSS
SO...WHAT'S A NAZGUL LIKE YOU DOING IN A PLACE LIKE THIS?
YOU IDIOT.

AS THE REST OF US KEPT THE NAZGUL BUSY BY RUNNING ABOUT AND PLAYING ROSHAMBO WITH HIM, A.J. WENT TO THE ELVES FOR HELP...
OH HELP! HELP! MY FELLOW KNOBBITS ARE GETTING WAXED BY A NAZGUL! PLEASE COME HELP US FIGHT WITH YOUR SWORD AND...

...UM...

...COULD I SPEAK TO A GUY ELF? YOU KNOW. A WARRIOR?
I AM A WARRIOR YOU SMARMY TOADSTOOL. ALL OF THE OTHER ELVES ARE HAIRDRESSERS.
Copyright (c) 1999 Illiad http://www.userfriendly.org/

PATENTED 1-CLICK TECHNOLOGY
VS.
PUBLIC DOMAIN 1-FINGER TECHNOLOGY

LITIGATION IN-PILE
JEFF BEZOS OF
amazon.com

'SPOKESPERSON'

bn.com
BARNES&NOBLE

 HTTP://WWW.USERFRIENDLY.ORG/

TRUE TO HER WORD, LADY MIRANDA OF THE ELVES BRINGS HER TRUSTEEL SWORD TO BATTLE THE VILE NAZGUL AT OUR BEHEST...
EN GARDE, SPAWN OF REDMOND!

zzzzOWNT
UH OH...

Copyright (c) 1999 Illiad http://www.userfriendly.org/
OKAY. YELLOW ELF IS GONNA NEED FOOD BADLY.
zzEEEEEP
HEEEEH HEHEEE HISSS
TINK

THE MIGHTY NAZGUL, HAVING WON THE FIRST ROUND AGAINST MY COMPANIONS, GAVE CHASE AND INADVERTENTLY FORGOT ABOUT ME, LEAVING ME TO CONTINUE ON THE LONG JOURNEY TO REDMOND ALONE.

SO I CONTINUED ON MY OWN, TRAVERSING THE DANGEROUS FLAMETROLL MOUNTAINS, THE WEIGHT OF THE ONE TRUE PING ALWAYS ON MY MIND...
SNUFFLE
WUFFLE

Copyright (c) 1999 Illiad http://www.userfriendly.org/
OF COURSE, I DIDN'T TAKE INTO ACCOUNT THAT I MIGHT BE MISTAKEN FOR SOMETHING THAT EVIL COVETS...
WANTS THE BEANIE BABY. WANTS IT.

THE WRETCHED CREATURE WAS GOLLUM, A CURSED REMNANT OF A KNOBBIT FROM YEARS AGO, DRIVEN BY AVARICE AND A COMPULSION TO LIE...
GIVES US THE ONE TRUE PING. GIVES IT TO US.

'SCUSE FOR ONE SEC. CAN'T SEE. NEEDS GLASSES...

Copyright (c) 1999 Illiad http://www.userfriendly.org/
STEF?!
IT WAS THE ONLY GIG I COULD GET AS A MARKETING GUY. NOW GIMME THAT PING.

I BEAT A HASTY RETREAT AWAY FROM GOLLUM, BEE-LINING FOR THE BRIDGE THAT LEADS TO THE CENTER OF THE LAND OF REDMOND...
GET BACK HERE! I WANT THAT PING!
Copyright (c) 1999 Illiad http://www.userfriendly.org/

I MADE IT TO THE STONE BRIDGE THAT SPANNED THE CHASM QUICKLY, BUT I FORGOT ABOUT THE GUARDIAN DEMON THAT STOOD WATCH THERE...
UH OH.

...A DEMON KNOWN AS THE BALLMER, A MIGHTY TOOL OF EVIL. EVEN AS I DREW NEAR IT SPOKE IN ITS VILE TONGUE...
HEY HEY! WINDOWS 2000 OWNS YOU!

THE BALLMER DIDN'T HARM ME, BEING BUT A MARKETING CONSTRUCT. I DASHED BY AND BEGAN SCALING MOUNT DOOM WHEN I HEARD GOLLUM SCREAMING BEHIND ME.
COME BACK HERE WITH THAT PING!

AT THE SUMMIT WAS A.J., THE FASTEST KNOBBIT ON TWO FEET. I SHOULDN'T HAVE BEEN SURPRISED HE EVADED THE NAZGUL'S CLUTCHES...
WELCOME TO MOUNT DOOM
...WELL I ONLY HAD TO BE FASTER THAN GREG AND MIKE.
SAY, WHY IS THIS PLACE CALLED "MOUNT DOOM?"
Copyright (c) 1999 Illiad http://www.userfriendly.org/

SHHHHHHHH....... IF THEY CAN'T HEAR US, THEY WON'T TRIGGER.
WELCOME TO MOUNT DOOM

HAVING REACHED THE VOLCANO KNOWN AS MOUNT DOOM, I DID WHAT I CAME TO DO...DESTROY THE ONE TRUE PING.
WELCOME TO MOUNT DOOM
PUNT

NOOOOOO! I NEED THAT TO PLAY QUAAAAKE!
WELCOME TO MOUNT DOOM
Copyright (c) 1999 Illiad http://www.userfriendly.org/

OW! OW! OW! OW! OW! OW! OW!
STEF FELL IN THE LAVA!
POOF!
AND WE JUST STARTED.

THANKS TO MEDIA ATTENTION ON LINUX, EVERYONE'S 'SECRET' COSTUME FOR THIS YEAR'S HALLOWEEN PARTY FAILS TO HAVE MUCH IMPACT.
COPYRIGHT (C) 1999 ILLIAD
HTTP://WWW.USERFRIENDLY.ORG/

CHIEF. AM KNOWINK WE HAVE INTERNAL NETWORK TRAFFIC BUDGET. WORD AND EXCEL DOCUMENTS. THEY ARE VERY BIG.
Copyright (c) 1999 Illiad http://www.userfriendly.org/

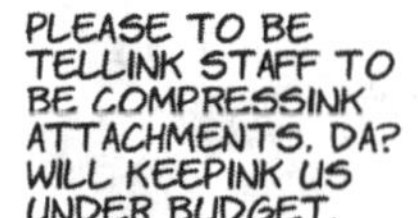
PLEASE TO BE TELLINK STAFF TO BE COMPRESSINK ATTACHMENTS. DA? WILL KEEPINK US UNDER BUDGET.

WELL OF COURSE, PITR. I MUST SAY I'M IMPRESSED AT YOUR ATTITUDE. THANK YOU.

TRAFFIC, SHE IS DOWN. TO BE GETTINK ALL MP3S.
OKAY. GET THE CHIEF TO APPROVE ANOTHER COUPLE OF 20 GIGGERS, WOULDJA?

I JUST HEARD THE CHIEF AND STEF DISCUSSING THAT WE NEED NIGHT STAFF NOW. AND THAT ONE OF US WOULD BE MOVED TO WORKING A GRAVEYARD SHIFT.
IS FUNNY. AM **ALREADY** WORKINK NIGHTS, NYET?
CODE TAP

PITR? DARK GLASSES?
DA! DA! HAVINK **ALREADY** FIGURINK OUT!
Copyright (c) 1999 Illiad http://www.userfriendly.org/

STEF, I SEE YOUR POINT. I'LL GO PICK ONE OF THE TECHS FOR THE NIGHT SHIFT NOW.
HOW'RE YOU GOING TO CHOOSE, CHIEF?
THE CHIEF
IS
IN
Copyright (c) 1999 Illiad http://www.userfriendly.org/

WHOEVER LOOKS SLEEPY.
BUT THE TECHS ARE **ALWAYS** SLEEPY...

OKAY, THIS IS JUST **CREEPY**.

LOOK GUYS, I'M SORRY, BUT WE NEED A TECH ON THE GRAVEYARD SHIFT.
I'M THE SUPPORT GOD. YOU NEED ME ON DAYS.
AND I DO ALL THE NETWORK STUFF.
AND I AM TOP CODER.

WELL THAT'S JUST IT. I NEED SOMEONE WHO'S REALLY SKILLED TO WORK NIGHTS. AND ALL OF YOU JUST TOLD ME HOW GOOD YOU ARE.

WELLLLL... **MIRANDA** IS ACTUALLY BETTER AT SUPPORT THAN ME...
AND SHE CAN RUN **CIRCLES** AROUND ME WITH CAT-5.
AM STILL BETTER CODER. BUT SHE IS **EVIL**. BELONGINK TO THE NIGHT.
Copyright (c) 1999 Illiad http://www.userfriendly.org/

GREAT NEWS, MIRANDA. I'M PROMOTING YOU TO **SHIFT SUPERVISOR** FOR THE TECH DEPARTMENT.
WOW! THANKS SO MUCH, CHIEF! IT'S REALLY NICE TO KNOW THAT YOU REWARD MERIT INSTEAD OF BEING BIASED BY GENDER.
Copyright (c) 1999 Illiad http://www.userfriendly.org/

UM...

...ARE YOU STICKING ME ON A **GRAVEYARD** SHIFT?!
THE OTHER TECHS SAID YOU'D LOVE IT BECAUSE YOU LIKE STAYING UP LATE AND WATCHING RERUNS OF "BUCK ROGERS IN THE 25TH CENTURY."

THIS BLOWS. I'VE BEEN SITTING HERE FOR FIVE HOURS AND I'VE HAD TWO CALLS. SO MUCH FOR NEEDING GRAVEYARD SHIFT TECH SUPPORT.
Copyright (c) 1999 Illiad http://www.userfriendly.org/

I MEAN, WHAT KIND OF PEOPLE NEED TECH SUPPORT AT THIS HOUR ANYWAY?
RING! RING!

MIRANDA SPEAKING. MAKE THIS GOOD OR **DIE**.
BUCK ROGERS IS OVER AND I'M SOO **LOOOONELYYY**...

WHY MICROSOFT THOUGHT THEY WOULD WIN THE ANTI-TRUST TRIAL.

Microsoft
Marketing Department
Legal department

COPYRIGHT (C) 1999 ILLIAD HTTP://WWW.USERFRIENDLY.ORG/

WHAT AN ENDLESS NIGHT. GRAVEYARD SHIFT IS BORIIINNG.
Copyright (c) 1999 Illiad http://www.userfriendly.org/

YEEARRGH!
BUDDA-SPUDDA! BUDBUDBUDBUD!
?!

A.J.?! WHAT ARE YOU DOING HERE SO LATE?!!
PLAYING RAINBOW SIX... IT TOOK ME NINE HOURS TO GET MY TEAM INTO POSITION AND THE FIRST SHOT I FIRED, I CAPPED A HOSTAGE...!

YOU KNOW A.J., I'D APPRECIATE IT IF YOU'D BE A LITTLE QUIETER. YOU GAVE ME A FRIGHT.
I'M SORRY. I'LL GO PLAY AN OLD INFOCOM TEXT ADVENTURE OR SOMETHING THEN.
Copyright (c) 1999 Illiad http://www.userfriendly.org/

DARN GOOD IDEA. THAT BOY IS WAY TOO EXCITABLE.

ARRRRRGH! I'M STUCK ALREADY!!

WHAT ARE YOU PLAYING?
ZORK. I'M TRYING TO OPEN A WINDOW WITH A GARDEN HOSE I GOT OFF A TROLL.
Copyright (c) 1999 Illiad http://www.userfriendly.org/

TAPPY TAP

DARE I SUGGEST THAT YOU TRY OPENING THE WINDOW JUST WITH YOUR HANDS?
LOOK, IT HAS SOMETHING TO DO WITH THE GARDEN HOSE, OKAY?

MY LAMP IN ZORK IS RUNNING OUT OF BATTERIES. NOT A GOOD THING.
WHAT HAPPENS WHEN IT DIES?
TIP TIP
Copyright (c) 1999 Illiad http://www.userfriendly.org/

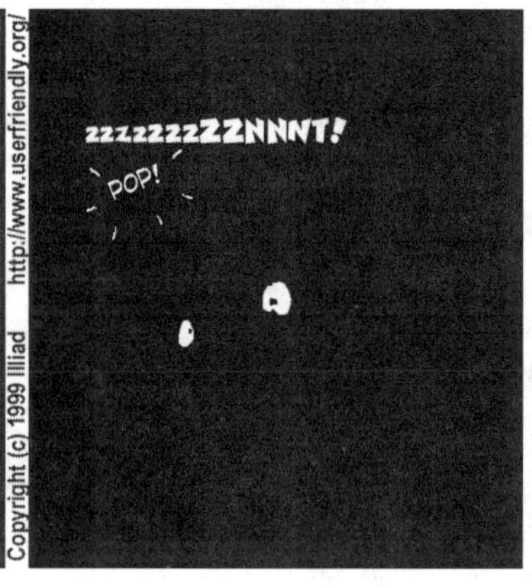
zzzzzzzZZNNNT!
POP!

OKAY, YOU DID THAT HOW?
NOOOO!! I'M SUPPOSED TO STILL HAVE A FEW TURNS OF LIGHT LEFT!!
TAP TAPP TAP!

LOOK. I'M GOING TO GO AND CHECK THE BREAKERS...
MIRANDA. DON'T MOVE! YOU MIGHT BE EATEN BY A GRUE!
http://www.userfriendly.org/
Copyright (c) 1999 Illiad

OKAY. WHAT THE HECK IS A GRUE?
I DON'T REMEMBER. I CAN ASK THE GAME FOR THE DEFINITION. BUT THE COMPUTER NEEDS POWER. WHICH MEANS YOU NEED TO MOVE... ...OOO. JUST LIKE ZORK TO GIVE US A DILEMMA...

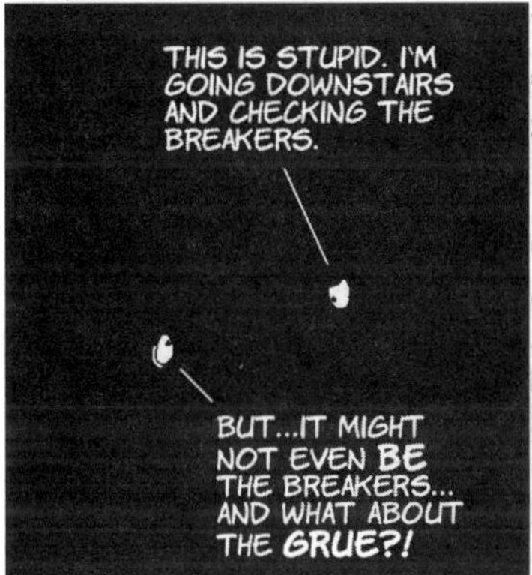
THIS IS STUPID. I'M GOING DOWNSTAIRS AND CHECKING THE BREAKERS.
BUT...IT MIGHT NOT EVEN BE THE BREAKERS... AND WHAT ABOUT THE GRUE?!
http://www.userfriendly.org/
Copyright (c) 1999 Illiad

A.J.. WHAT DOES A GRUE LOOK LIKE ANYWAYS?
THEY'RE BLACK-ISH COLOURED.

OH. WELL THANK YOU FOR NOT BEING VAGUE.
IF YOU MAKE ONE MORE MOVE. IT'LL EAT YOU. I'VE BEEN KEEPING TRACK...

As you can see, my artwork has continued to improve

IF THE INTERNET WAS AN AMUSEMENT RIDE
YOU MUST BE AT LEAST THIS SMART TO USE THE INTERNET
human
baboon
mollusk
dirt
HTTP://WWW.USERFRIENDLY.ORG/
COPYRIGHT (C) 1999 ILLIAD

WELL I'M NOT JUST GOING TO WAIT HERE AND...OUCH! SORRY!
OW!!

Copyright (c) 1999 Illiad http://www.userfriendly.org/
zzzzzzт *KLIK!*

IT...UH...SEEMS WE HAVE ELECTRICITY.
YES...YES WE DO...

WELL, I GUESS I'D BETTER HELP YOU UP THEN...
OKAY.

Copyright (c) 1999 Illiad http://www.userfriendly.org/

I COULDN'T HELP BUT NOTICE THAT YOU'RE NOT MOVING.
SORRY. I'M STILL KINDA WORRIED ABOUT THE GRUE.

I played Infocom's Zork until I solved it, taking nearly three weeks of steady, six-hours-a-day playing with the occasional Sunday off. I both hated and loved those twisty passages, all alike.

I SHOULD PROBABLY GET BACK TO WORK.
YEAH. I SHOULD GET BACK TO PLAYING ZORK.

Copyright (c) 1999 Illiad http://www.userfriendly.org/
SEE YOU LATER...
MMM-HM.

'>KISS GRUE'
THE GRUE EATS YOUR FACE.
TYPE TYPE

MIRANDA, IT'S A.J. HERE. I'M USING THE NETWORK'S CHAT FEATURE. MAYBE WE SHOULD TALK ABOUT WHAT JUST HAPPENED?

Copyright (c) 1999 Illiad http://www.userfriendly.org/
YOU WANTED TO TALK?

HELLO? DIDN'T YOU WANT TO TALK ABOUT WHAT HAPPENED BETWEEN YOU AND ME?
NGGGGG...

ARE YOU TRYING TO TELL ME YOU WANT ME TO GO BACK TO MY COMPUTER IN THE OTHER ROOM SO WE CAN DISCUSS OUR EMOTIONS IN CHAT?
IF YOU WOULD.
Copyright (c) 1999 Illiad http://www.userfriendly.org/

WHAT WOULD IT TAKE FOR YOU TO TALK TO ME IN THE SAME ROOM?
YOU COULD MOVE YOUR COMPUTER IN HERE, I GUESS.

A.J., FOR THOUSANDS OF YEARS PEOPLE HAVE BEEN TALKING TO EACH OTHER FACE TO FACE, ESPECIALLY ABOUT FEELINGS AND THINGS THAT ARE PERSONAL. WHY DO YOU WANT TO DO THIS IN CHAT?
Copyright (c) 1999 Illiad http://www.userfriendly.org/

I JUST FIND THAT IN CHAT I CAN BE A LOT MORE... EXPRESSIVE.
I SUPPOSE I CAN UNDERSTAND THAT. FINE. WE TRY IT YOUR WAY.

;-)

A LINUX DISTRO THAT WINS COMDEX'S "MOST CHALLENGING TO MARKET" AWARD
COMDEX
CYNIX
COMDEX
WHAT THE HELL DO YOU WANT?
COPYRIGHT (C) 1999 ILLIAD
HTTP://WWW.USERFRIENDLY.ORG/

MIRANDA? ARE YOU MAD AT ME?
LOOK, I'VE BEEN TRYING TO **TALK** TO YOU ABOUT **US** FOR THE LAST FEW HOURS AND ALL YOU DO IS PROVE HOW **LITTLE** YOU REALLY UNDERSTAND ABOUT RELATIONSHIPS.
Copyright (c) 1999 Illiad http://www.userfriendly.org/

DOES THAT MEAN WE'RE BREAKING UP?
AAAAAAGGH!!

Angelina Jolie is mentioned a few times over the years in the cartoon, leading many to believe that I have a huge crush on the lovely daughter of actor Jon Voight. In fact, I don't. Don't get me wrong, I think she's beautiful, but she doesn't cause me to hyperventilate. I mentioned it because she *is* considered one of the most beautiful celebrities in the world by many.

SO HOW WAS YOUR FIRST NIGHT SHIFT MIRANDA?
SUCKED ROYALLY. I HAD STUPID CALLS. THE SERVERS HAD TO BE REBOOTED. AND A.J. AND I NEARLY HIT IT OFF BUT HE SCREWED IT UP.
Copyright (c) 1999 Illiad http://www.userfriendly.org/

YOU **HIT IT OFF** WITH **A.J.?!**
THAT'S LIKE **ANGELINA JOLIE** BEING ATTRACTED TO **ILLIAD**. IT WOULD JUST BE **WRONG**.

GREG, YOU KNOW A.J. PRETTY WELL. SO EXPLAIN IT TO ME. WHY CAN'T HE JUST **TALK** TO ME?
Copyright (c) 1999 Illiad http://www.userfriendly.org/

I MEAN, ALL I NEED IS A LITTLE BIT OF COMMUNICATION. A SIGN THAT HE'S INTERESTED THAT DOESN'T INVOLVE A CHAT CLIENT...

WHERE ARE ALL THE **MEN** WHO CAN JUST COME OUT AND BE **DIRECT AND HONEST** TO MY FACE ABOUT WHAT THEY **WANT?!**
HEY BABY. YOU, ME AND A STICK OF BUTTER.

IS THERE **ANY** INSIGHT YOU CAN GIVE ME ON THIS, GREG? A.J. **REALLY** CONFUSES ME.
WELL THIS IS PRETTY DEEP STUFF. I CAN'T HELP YOU LIKE THIS.
Copyright (c) 1999 Illiad http://www.userfriendly.org/

I COULD EXPLAIN THINGS **A LOT BETTER** TO YOU IF I COULD USE **SMILIES** AND STUFF.
OH PLEASE. NOT **YOU** TOO!!

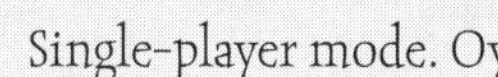

I HEARD THAT YOU AND MIRANDA HAD A BIT OF A FALLING OUT. YOU LIKE HER, RIGHT?
WELL...YES... BUT I'M NOT REALLY SURE HOW TO TALK TO HER.
Be

THERE'S NO REAL TRICK TO IT. JUST BE HONEST AND TELL HER HOW IMPORTANT SHE IS TO YOU IN YOUR OWN WORDS.
AHHH...
Be

SO SOMETHING LIKE "I'M TIRED OF SINGLE PLAYER MODE" WOULD BE GOOD?
I THINK WE NEED TO TALK SOME MORE...
Be
Copyright (c) 1999 Illiad http://www.userfriendly.org/

Single-player mode. Oy.

YOU STILL PLAYING THAT RAINBOW SIX GAME A.J.?
YEAH, BUT I'M HAVING A REAL HARD TIME WITH THE AIRPLANE HIJACKING SCENARIO. I KEEP KILLING ALL OF THE HOSTAGES.
Copyright (c) 1999 Illiad http://www.userfriendly.org/

AND I JUST ADDED THIS MOD WHERE THE GAME IS AFFECTED BY THE PRESS RELEASES YOU GIVE TO THE REPORTERS. I JUST WAXED THE WHOLE AIRPLANE, SO I'M SUNK.

TRY THIS FOR A HEADLINE: "237 TERRORISTS KILLED IN HIJACKING."
YE GODS, YOU MARKETING TYPES ARE GOOD.
TAP
TIP

Who could've known that less than two years later ...

RIGHT UP THERE ON THE TOP "HARD TO REACH" ROW.
SULTRY
NAUGHTY Babes
COREL LINUX
you must be 18+ to use this product
GOOD HOMES
Merry Xmas
HOW TO MAKE THE KIDS STAY OFF YOUR CASE OVER THE HOLIDAYS
CABBAGE ROLLS FROM HELL
COSMOPOL
22 MAKEUP TIPS
HOW TO KEEP YOUR MAN
Victoria
Xmas 1999
COPYRIGHT (C) 1999 ILLIAD
HTTP://WWW.USERFRIENDLY.ORG/

This is from Corel Linux's EULA:

IMPORTANT: READ CAREFULLY THE TERMS AND CONDITIONS OF THE FOLLOWING AGREEMENT ("LICENSE") BEFORE DOWNLOADING THE PRODUCT. BY CLICKING "ACCEPT" BELOW:

1. YOU CERTIFY THAT YOU ARE NOT A MINOR AND THAT YOU AGREE TO BE BOUND BY ALL OF THE TERMS AND CONDITIONS SET OUT IN THE LICENSE BELOW. DOWNLOADING AND/OR USING THE PRODUCT WILL BE AN IRREVOCABLE ACCEPTANCE OF THE TERMS AND CONDITIONS OF THE LICENSE.

I should also add that many of Debian's contributors (Corel Linux used the Debian Core) are under 18.

YE GODS. I DO LOVE THIS GAME.
THIS IS GOLD SNIPER, MY SIGHTS ARE HOT!
Copyright (c) 1999 Illiad http://www.userfriendly.org/

I'VE BEEN PLAYING RAINBOW SIX FOR THE LAST FIFTY HOURS STRAIGHT. I MAY AS WELL FACE IT. THIS GAME TRULY OWNS ME.
TAKING THE SHOT! GOT HIM! TANGO DOWN!

NO SLEEP FOR FIFTY HOURS? IT'S ME WHO OWNS YOU.
AAAAAUGH! GOLD SNIPER! TAKE THE SHOT! TAKE THE SHOT!!

FACE IT. YOU NEED SOME COLA. IT RUNS THROUGH YOUR BLOOD AND SINGS TO YOU. OBTAIN. OPEN. DRINK. FROLIC.
YOU'RE RIGHT. I CAN'T RESIST ANY LONGER.
Copyright (c) 1999 Illiad http://www.userfriendly.org/

WELL...AREN'T YOU GOING TO BRING ME A COLA?
NO NO...YOU KNOW YOU HAVE TO COME TO ME, YOUNG JEDI.

OK. TIME FOR A COLA...HEY...I THINK THIS STUPID MACHINE ATE MY MONEY...
DRINKS
PUNCH
PUNCH
Copyright (c) 1999 Illiad http://www.userfriendly.org/

YE GODS NOOO!!!
GIVE ME BACK MY MONEY YOU METAL SPAWN OF EVIL!! GIVE IT BACK OR I'LL DESTROY YOU! OKAY. YOU ASKED FOR IT!!!
KRUNCH!
SMASH!
FRUNCH!

FEAR LEADS TO ANGER. ANGER LEADS TO THROWING A HISSY FIT. WHICH GETS YOU A COLA. COOL, HUH?
YES, MY MASTER.

SIGH
A.J.? YOU SEEM A LITTLE DOWN.
Copyright (c) 1999 Illiad http://www.userfriendly.org/

YEAH...I'M CONFUSED BY MIRANDA. I THINK SHE LIKES ME, AND I SURE LIKE HER...BUT FOR SOME REASON SHE'S MAD AT ME.
UNH-HUH.

WHAT DO YOU KNOW ABOUT WOMEN, ERWIN? WHAT IS IT THAT THEY WANT FROM A GUY LIKE ME?
JUDGING BY WHAT I'VE SEEN FROM SURFING THE WEB FOR THOUSANDS OF HOURS, ALL THEY SEEM TO WANT IS YOUR CREDIT CARD NUMBER.

I REALLY DO WANT TO WORK THINGS OUT WITH MIRANDA. BUT WE JUST DON'T COMMUNICATE THE SAME WAY, YOU KNOW?
HMM. YES...
Copyright (c) 1999 Illiad
http://www.userfriendly.org/

WELL FROM WHAT I'VE READ, SCIENTIFIC STUDIES SHOW MEN TEND TO BE BETTER AT DEALING WITH VISUAL CONCEPTS, WHILE WOMEN ARE BETTER AT COMPLEX LINGUISTIC COMMUNICATION.
YOU MEAN...
YUP. MEN ARE FROM MACS, WOMEN ARE FROM VMS.

WHAT DO YOU THINK IT IS I SHOULD DO TO GET ON MIRANDA'S GOOD SIDE AGAIN?
TALK TO HER. TELL HER SOMETHING THAT'S REALLY IMPORTANT IN YOUR LIFE.
Copyright (c) 1999 Illiad
http://www.userfriendly.org/

HMMM.
I COULD TELL HER THAT QUAKE THREE ARENA IS OUT FINALLY!
YOU'RE NEVER GOING TO BREED, ARE YOU A.J.

THE MARS POLAR LANDER DISCOVERY OF LIFE ON THE RED PLANET IS FOLLOWED BY A MASSIVE RESEARCH EFFORT IN INTERPLANETARY-RANGE NUCLEAR WEAPONS.
COPYRIGHT (C) 1999 ILLIAD
HTTP://WWW.USERFRIENDLY.ORG/

MIRANDA...LOOK. I'M SORRY FOR BEING SO CLUELESS. I...UH...WROTE DOWN SOME THOUGHTS AND...WELL... MAYBE YOU SHOULD JUST READ IT.
Copyright (c) 1999 Illiad http://www.userfriendly.org/

THIS IS A PRINTOUT OF A CHAT LOG. OF YOU TALKING TO YOURSELF.
IT WAS REALLY HARD FOR ME TO HIT THE 'PRINT' BUTTON.

SEE, I'M TRYING **REALLY HARD** TO TALK TO YOU BECAUSE I KNOW THAT THERE'S A THING BETWEEN US AND I KNOW IT'S BETTER IF WE TALK IN PERSON INSTEAD OF IN CHAT...
Copyright (c) 1999 Illiad http://www.userfriendly.org/

...SO I KEEP TALKING AND WONDERING WHAT IT IS I'M SAYING BECAUSE SOMETIMES GEEKS GET HUNGRY AND I KNOW **YOU** GET HUNGRY NOT THAT I'M IMPLYING YOU'RE NOT A GEEK...

...BUT WE ALL KNOW NUTRITION IS IMPORTANT TO ALL OF US SO IT'S ALMOST **NECESSARY** FOR US TO CONSUME CALORIES IN PAIRS SO THAT WE CAN WATCH EACH OTHERS BACKS FOR PREDATORS...
OF **COURSE** I'LL GO OUT FOR DINNER WITH YOU.

SO I GUESS I'LL PICK YOU UP AT YOUR PLACE TONIGHT. SAY ABOUT SEVEN?
THAT WOULD BE GREAT.
Copyright (c) 1999 Illiad http://www.userfriendly.org/

OKAY. I'M GONNA GO HOME NOW. FINALLY.
A.J., BE CAREFUL WHEN YOU GO OUT THERE...

AAAAIIIIIIEEEE! EVIL...BRIGHT ...YELLOW... THING...!!
THAT MUST BE THE **DAYSTAR**. I'VE HEARD TALK ABOUT IT.

THIS IS A **REALLY** NICE RESTAURANT, A.J. SO WHAT'S THE MENU LIKE?
WELL LET'S SEE THEN...
Copyright (c) 1999 Illiad http://www.userfriendly.org/

TAP
PAP
PAP

WHAT ARE YOU **DOING**?
NO DROP-DOWNS. AND NOTHING SEEMS TO WORK. OKAY. IT **SUCKS**.

THAT WAS A DELICIOUS DINNER, A.J. THANK YOU SO MUCH.
Copyright (c) 1999 Illiad http://www.userfriendly.org/

I HOPE HE'S GAZING AT ME BECAUSE HE'S ENRAPTURED...

A.J., STOP STARING. YOU'RE MAKING ME BLUSH...
SORRY. IT'S JUST THAT YOU HAVE THIS BLOB OF MEAT SAUCE ON YOUR FACE THAT LOOKS LIKE A QUAKE SYMBOL.

What a dork.

MIRANDA? HOW'D YOUR DATE WITH A.J. GO LAST NIGHT?
OH IT WAS FINE FOR MOST OF THE EVENING...
Copyright (c) 1999 Illiad http://www.userfriendly.org/

HE WALKED ME HOME AND I LEANED OVER TO GIVE HIM A REALLY NICE KISS GOODNIGHT.
WOW! AND?!

HE FUMBLED A BIT THEN PULLED OUT A STICK OF BUTTER.
STEF!!
HEY, THE WEENIE ASKED FOR ADVICE!

metric to standard calculator: $15
telescope: $270
MasterCard
mars lander: $135 million
the look on the scientists' faces: priceless
COPYRIGHT (C) 1999 ILLIAD
HTTP://WWW.USERFRIENDLY.ORG/

This unfortunate event was all about a very expensive Mars orbiter (not a lander like I have it in the 'toon) that was lost due to a unit bolluxing. The Lockheed Martin engineering team used Imperial units of measurement instead of the standard metric ones that engineers and scientists are supposed to use. Oops.

Torg is the main character in Pete Abram's excellent cartoon, "Sluggy Freelance." He and I traded characters for a while, so he took A.J. and we had our way with them. Hi Pete!

HEY, YOU SEEN A.J.?
HILLARY SAID HE TOOK A WEEK OFF TO GO SEE SOME FRIENDS IN MINNESOTA.
Copyright (c) 1999 Illiad http://www.userfriendly.org/

WHAT?! WHAT ARE WE GOING TO DO WITHOUT A WEB DESIGNER?
WE GOT SOME GUY ON CONTRACT TO COVER FOR A.J.

REALLY? WHO?
SOME GUY NAMED "TORQUE" I THINK.
IT'S TORG. SAY, HOW COME I CAN'T FIND FRONT PAGE ON MY MACHINE?

IT'S TORG...RIGHT? SO, DO YOU KNOW ANYTHING AT ALL ABOUT UNIX?
Copyright (c) 1999 Illiad http://www.userfriendly.org/

I'M NOT INTERESTED IN BECOMING ONE IF THAT'S WHAT YOU MEAN.
WAS YOUR LAST JOB AS A CLOWN?

Note the change in typeface. Some readers thought it was to indicate that Torg had changed the fonts around on A.J.'s machine—a no-no in designer-land. Others thought it was done to loosely imitate the face that Pete uses in "Sluggy Freelance." The truth is that this and the following few strips were done on the road, and my laptop didn't have the font I usually use installed.

I HOPE YOU'RE NOT MESSING WITH A.J.'s SETUP. HE'S PRETTY UPTIGHT ABOUT HIS MACHINE.
OH, DON'T WORRY. I'M JUST INSTALLING WINDOWS 98. IT SHOULD DUAL BOOT BETWEEN THAT AND BEOS.
Copyright (c) 1999 Illiad http://www.userfriendly.org/

BLEEP!

WHAT DOES "PARTITION DESTROYED" MEAN?
IT MEANS THAT WITH A.J. IN MINNESOTA, YOU HAD BETTER USE THE HEAD START AND BEGIN RUNNING NOW.

SO WHATEVER HAPPENED TO THAT TORG GUY?
HE SMOKED A.J.'s COMPUTER, SO MIRANDA AND PITR HAVE TAKEN IT UPON THEMSELVES TO EXTRACT PENANCE FROM HIM. POOR GUY.
Copyright (c) 1999 Illiad http://www.userfriendly.org/

MIRANDA AND PITR?! THEY CAN'T AGREE ON ANYTHING...WHAT KIND OF PUNISHMENT DO THEY HAVE IN MIND?
I THINK THEY MENTIONED SOMETHING ABOUT FORCING TORG TO USE A PROPER HTML EDITOR.

WE MAKE HIM USE VI. IT'S A PUNISHMENT AFTER ALL.
NYET! MAKINK HIM USINK EMACS, IS MORE EVIL THAN LICKINK COLD FLAGPOLE, DA?
I'D BE FINE WITH JUST NOTEPAD...

HOW YOU ARE TO BE HIDINK DAMAGE YOU DO TO AJ's WEB SITE?
I'M PUTTING BLINK TAGS EVERYWHERE TO DISTRACT HIM FROM THE REAL PROBLEMS.
Copyright (c) 1999 Illiad http://www.userfriendly.org/

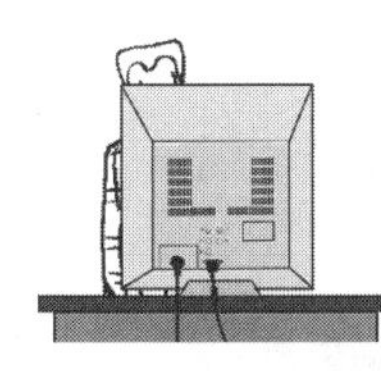

AM THINKINK IS GOOD IDEA YOU ARE LEAVINK.
BUT THEN WHO'S GOING TO DO ALL OF YOUR WEB DESIGN?
HEY, I'LL NEED A JOB IN A FEW WEEKS.

Charlie Brown letting us know that "Peanuts" was weeks from being retired.

Copyright (c) 1999 Illiad http://www.userfriendly.org/

NOOOOOOO
PITR SENDS TORG ON HIS WAY WITH A BEATING BY THE LIGHT OF A BLINK TAG. OH, THE IRONY.

"HIGH NOON" AT THE BAZAAR
THE BAZAAR 1999
POP.
COPYRIGHT (C) 1999 ILLIAD
HTTP://WWW.USERFRIENDLY.ORG/

As one reader put it, this is one of those strips that doesn't age gracefully. The Bazaar was a Linux conference that was, shall we say, Very Poorly Attended.

A.J.'S COMING BACK TOMORROW, SO THIS MIGHT BE MY LAST CHANCE TO WIN OVER MIRANDA. I NEED A CHRISTMAS GIFT THAT'LL BLOW HER MIND...
Copyright (c) 1999 Illiad http://www.userfriendly.org/

BLAM!
HUH!
SPLUTCH!!
TAXIDERMIST
IT WORKS ON EVERY CREATURE THAT I KNOW. WHY?
NEVER MIND. I'LL TAKE IT.
Taxidermy Kit

ACCORDING TO THESE INSTRUCTIONS, I NEED TO USE THIS THINGY TO HOLLOW YOU OUT AND JUST LEAVE THE SKIN AS A SHELL...
Taxidermy Kit
Copyright (c) 1999 Illiad http://www.userfriendly.org/

Taxidermy Kit
THIS COULD BE A REAL PROBLEM SINCE YOUR HEAD IS MOSTLY AIR.
MIRANDA ONCE SAID THAT YOU HAD THE SAME PROBLEM.
Taxidermy Kit

WELL...IF I CAN'T STUFF YOU ALL I CAN DO IS GIVE YOU TO HER AS YOU ARE.
HOW ARE YOU GOING TO DO THAT?
Copyright (c) 1999 Illiad http://www.userfriendly.org/

CRAM
CRAM
KRAMM
I DON'T SEE HOW YOU CAN PROFIT BY THIS...
THEY'VE BEEN SAYING THAT TO JEFF BEZOS ALL ALONG AND NOW HE'S TIME MAGAZINES' MAN OF THE YEAR.

HEY BABE. MERRY CHRISTMAS.
Copyright (c) 1999 Illiad http://www.userfriendly.org/

SHAKE
SHAKE
SHAKE
SHAKE

I GIVE UP. WHAT'S INSIDE?
UHH...JUST SOME LINT AND STUFF.
eeeeehhh

L'IL GUY? WHAT ARE YOU DOING IN THIS BOX?
STEF PUT ME IN IT. THEN HE SAID TO MIRANDA THAT I WAS NOTHING BUT A PILE OF LINT AND SHE DROPPED THE BOX HERE.
Copyright (c) 1999 Illiad http://www.userfriendly.org/

STEF'S A BAD MAN, ISN'T HE.
I GUESS SO. I THINK HE JUST WANTED TO TURN ME INTO A GIFT FOR MIRANDA.

SAAAAYYY...
I'M GOING AWAY NOW, BEFORE I GET PUT ON EBAY.

IT'S TOUGH BEING ALONE ON CHRISTMAS L'IL GUY. MY FOLKS AREN'T HERE AND ALL OF MY FRIENDS ARE AT FAMILY DINNERS.
Copyright (c) 1999 Illiad http://www.userfriendly.org/

I GUESS I STILL DON'T QUITE GET IT. IF YOU'RE NICE TO PEOPLE AND SHOW YOUR FAMILY YOU LOVE THEM ALL OF THE TIME, THIS DAY WOULDN'T HAVE TO STICK OUT LIKE A SORE THUMB. RIGHT?

I LOVE IT WHEN YOU MAKE SENSE OF THE WORLD.
HELP! HELP! I'M BEING COMPRESSED!

SANTA FILES FOR AN I.P.O.
HELL, IF LINUXONE CAN DO IT...
LINUX
LINUX
COPYRIGHT (C) 1999 ILLIAD
HTTP://WWW.USERFRIENDLY.ORG/

Everyone, and I mean everyone, was IPOing around this time. LinuxOne had no business plan, no revenue model, and no real anything. Yet they IPOed. Successfully.

Week of December 27th, 2000

THESE POKEMON THINGS ARE REALLY PRETTY COOL. THIS ONE IS DIGLETT.
NEAT!
ACTUALLY, THAT ONE IS CALLED CHANSEY.
http://www.userfriendly.org/
Copyright (c) 1999 Illiad

I BOUGHT THIS ON EBAY FOR $300.00. SO IT'S DIGLETT. OKAY??!
YOU HAVE KIDS, RIGHT.
A HUSBAND, ACTUALLY.

HEY PITR! DID YOU SEE...
ONE MOMENT, COMRADE. AM BUSY BRINGINK DOWN SERVERS OF EVIL POKEMON EMPIRE.
http://www.userfriendly.org/
Copyright (c) 1999 Illiad

AM THINKING POKEMON IS DARK BLIGHT ON WORLD. ALL WHO ARE PART OF POKEMON ARE EVIL MINIONS, DA?
RAP TAP

UH, YEAH. EVIL.
DOWN WITH POKEMON! PUSH THE BUTTON! GOTTA NUKE 'EM ALL!

WE'RE GETTING CLOSE TO THE END OF 1999, AND WHAT HAVE WE DONE ABOUT IT? WE AREN'T READY FOR ANYTHING!
http://www.userfriendly.org/
Copyright (c) 1999 Illiad

THE POWER COULD GO OUT! NO HEAT! NO LIGHT! PEOPLE WOULD REVERT TO THEIR ANIMAL NATURES! KILLING EACH OTHER FOR A BOOK OF MATCHES OR THE CALORIES IN THE INK OF A BALLPOINT PEN!

NO POWER MEANS NO NET! PEOPLE WILL BE FIGHTING OVER FREE AOL CDS JUST IN CASE THEY CAN GET A TRICKLE OF NET ACCESS! AND FOOD!! WE HAVE NOTHING HERE TO LAST US!
I HAVE AN UNOPENED BAG OF PORK RINDS.
KRINKLE

Coming up with the look on Stef's face in the last panel was the height of fun.

YOU KNOW, WHAT WITH DISCREPANCIES IN THE GREGORIAN CALENDAR, I HEARD THAT Y2K COULD HIT US A FEW DAYS EARLIER...AND NO ONE WILL BE READY.
THAT CAN'T HAPPEN... CAN IT?
http://www.userfriendly.org/
Copyright (c) 1999 Illiad

CLIK!

THAT WAS JUST A DRILL OF THE EMERGENCY Y2K SYSTEM. HAD THIS BEEN A REAL EMERGENCY, WE WOULD'VE ALSO DUMPED A BUCKET OF SPIDERS ON YOU AND YELLED OUT "CIVILIZATION IS COLLAPSING!"
KLIK!

HEY PITR? IN COMPUTER TERMS. WHAT DOES A 'K' REPRESENT?
1024. YOU ARE ASKINK WHY?
DOESN'T Y2K TAKE PLACE IN THE YEAR 2048 THEN?
FIX CODE DEBUG
Copyright (c) 1999 Illiad http://www.userfriendly.org/

YOU ARE TELLINK ME THIS ONE DAY BEFORE END OF 1999? I AM WORKINK FINGERS TO BONE FIXINK Y2K PROBLEM! YOU ARE WHAT KIND OF NOGOODNIK MAN?!
THE KIND WHO SNEAKS PEEKS AT "EVIL GENIUSES FOR DUMMIES."

JRYY VG YBBXF YVXR GUR L2X OHT QVQA'G ERNE VGF HTYL URNQ.
LRC. GUR QBBZFNLREF UNIR ORRA CEBIRA JEBAT LRG NTNVA.
Copyright (c) 1900 Illiad http://www.userfriendly.org/

QVQ LBH FRR GUNG GBB?
UBHFGBA, JR UNIR N CEBOYRZ.

There's your Y2K problem. The characters are speaking in ROT13. The observant reader will also notice the copyright date.

POST Y2K GARAGE SALES
generators "Like new!" ONLY $800 $400 $150 $20 Free
Y2K or BUST
1200 WATTS
COPYRIGHT (C) 2000 ILLIAD
HTTP://WWW.USERFRIENDLY.ORG/

HI. THIS IS THE CONTROLLER OF COLUMBIA INTERNET. I JUST GOT YOUR INVOICE HERE, AND I THINK THERE'S BEEN SOME MISTAKE.
MISTAKE, SIR?
Copyright (c) 2000 Illiad http://www.userfriendly.org/

WELL YOU'VE BILLED US FOR **TWO HUNDRED LITRES OF COLA** AND **FIFTY CASES OF PORK RINDS.** WE DIDN'T ORDER ANY OF THIS.
YOU'RE RIGHT SIR, THERE HAS BEEN A MISTAKE. IT'S A Y2K THING.

AH. WELL THAT'S MOST CERTAINLY UNDERSTANDABLE...
IT SHOULD BE TWO THOUSAND LITRES OF COKE AND FIFTEEN HUNDRED CASES OF PORK RINDS.
WE **TRIED** HIDING THE DIFFERENCE. REALLY WE TRIED...

I CALLED THIS MEETING BECAUSE WE'RE GOING FOR A FRESH START. IT'S THE START OF A NEW YEAR AND AS WELL AS A NEW MILLENIUM. SO WHAT BETTER TIME?
Copyright (c) 2000 Illiad http://www.userfriendly.org/

ACTUALLY, THE NEW MILLENIUM DOESN'T START UNTIL THE FIRST DAY OF **NEXT** YEAR. CENTURIES START ON YEAR ONE, NOT YEAR ZERO.

OH. AND I SUPPOSE **YOU'RE** RIGHT AND MILLIONS OF OTHER PEOPLE ARE **WRONG**.
OF COURSE THESE ARE PROBABLY THE SAME MILLIONS WHO WATCHED 'TITANIC' TO SEE HOW IT WOULD TURN OUT...

I'D LIKE TO TAKE THIS OPPORTUNITY AND SHARE WITH YOU SOME GOOD NEWS. SINCE I'VE BEEN HANDLING SALES HERE AS MUCH AS MARKETING, I'VE BEEN GIVEN THE TITLE 'MANAGER, S&M'
Copyright (c) 2000 Illiad http://www.userfriendly.org/

IT STANDS FOR **'SALES AND MARKETING'** YOU DEPRAVED MONKEYS.
A ROSE BY ANY OTHER NAME, STEF.

SO I'VE BEEN DOING SOME RESEARCH AND I'VE NOTICED THE KIND OF REVENUES THAT THE POKEMON EMPIRE IS GETTING. IT'S **INSANE**. THE KIND OF MONEY THEY MAKE. WE NEED TO SELL A LINE OF PRODUCTS THE SAME WAY.
Copyright (c) 2000 Illiad http://www.userfriendly.org/

STEF, I HATE TO PUT A DAMPER ON YOUR GRAND PLANS, BUT WE'RE A LINUX-BASED **INTERNET SERVICE PROVIDER**. WHAT COULD WE POSSIBLY SELL THAT'S LIKE **POKEMON**?

I WAS THINKING THAT WE COULD MARKET COLLECTABLE **UNIX TEXT EDITORS**. START WITH **PICO** AND CALL IT "PICO-CHU"...
DEAR LORD, IT JUST MIGHT WORK. "GOTTA **FETCH** 'EM ALL!"

PITR. I NEED YOU TO HELP ME WITH A NEW MARKETING PROJECT. I NEED A PRODUCT BY **TOMORROW** THAT CAN BE ADDED TO A UNIX TEXT EDITOR TO MAKE IT UNIQUELY OURS.
DA. OKAY.
CODE TYPE CODE
http://www.userfriendly.org/
Copyright (c) 2000 Illiad

CODE CODE ENTER
WELL **THAT** WAS REMARKABLY PAINLESS.
NYET. YOUR PAIN, SHE IS JUST **BEGINNINK**. PLEASE TO BE PRICKINK FINGER WITH PIN TO SIGN DOCUMENT.

PITR, ARE YOU **ACTUALLY HELPING** STEF WITH HIS "COLLECTABLE UNIX TEXT EDITORS" PROJECT?!
DA. BUT ONLY GIVINK STEF ALL ROPE HE WANTS. TO BE HANGINK HIMSELF.
CODE CODE
http://www.userfriendly.org/
Copyright (c) 2000 Illiad

WHAT DO YOU MEAN?
HAVE SUGGESTINK TO HIM I MAKE A "PAPERCLIP" BUDDY FOR VI. HE IS OF COURSE THINKINK IS GRAND IDEA.
TAP TYPE CODE

YOU'RE CODING ONE OF THOSE ANNOYING MICROSOFT **PAPERCLIPS** FOR **VI?!** HAVE YOU GONE COMPLETELY **MAD?!**
IS A MASTERPIECE! I CALL IT. **"VIGOR!"**
SHALL I HELP YOU WRITE A NAUGHTY LETTER, MEEEASTER?
TAP TIP

An enterprising reader by the name of Joel Ray Holveck from Sunnyvale, California actually brought this to life. I apologize deeply to the world for my part in the creation of Vigor.

WHY MICROSOFT THOUGHT THEIR $400 MSN REBATE PLAN WOULDN'T GET ABUSED.
Microsoft
Marketing Department
Legal Department
Accounting department

STEF, DO YOU HAVE ANY IDEA WHAT'S HAPPENING OUT THERE? THE EVIL 'VIGOR' MOD HAS SPREAD LIKE WILDFIRE. PITR WROTE THE SELF-REPLICATION ALGORITHM A LITTLE TOO WELL.
THAT'S GREAT NEWS.
TYPE TYPE
Copyright (c) 2000 Illiad http://www.userfriendly.org/

IT MOST CERTAINLY IS NOT GREAT NEWS! YOU MAY NOT REALIZE IT, BUT YOUR PLANS HAVE CREATED CHAOS OUT THERE IN THE UNIX WORLD!

SOUNDS LIKE GREAT NEWS TO ME.
YOU'VE UPSET THE BALANCE OF POWER! EVERYONE OUT THERE IS SWITCHING OVER TO EMACS!!

HEYA GUYS.
Copyright (c) 2000 Illiad http://www.userfriendly.org/

WELL, I GUESS I'LL GO AND COMPOSE A LETTER WITH MICROSOFT WORD...

...BECAUSE THANKFULLY I CAN TURN MY PAPERCLIP BUDDY OFF. WHAT OTHER GOOD NEWS COULD THERE BE TODAY?
WELL YOUR PROCTOLOGIST PHONED. HE SAID HE FOUND YOUR HEAD.

This was considerably funnier before Al-Qaeda made itself known to the world.

MIKE? WHAT ARE YOU DOING?
KEEPING AN EYE ON ALL OF THE PROTESTERS PICKETING OUR OFFICE OUTSIDE.
Copyright (c) 2000 Illiad http://www.userfriendly.org/

PROTESTORS? IS THIS ABOUT PITR'S 'VIGOR' PROJECT?
HAVE A LOOK FOR YOURSELF.

CAN YOU READ THE PLACARDS FROM HERE?
YES. MIKE, WHAT DOES THE WORD 'JIHAD' MEAN?

LOOK, WHAT IS IT THAT ALL OF YOU WANT?
WE WANT THE RANCID PUSTULE THAT CODED VIGOR! WE GOT SOME RECKONING TO DO!
Copyright (c) 2000 Illiad http://www.userfriendly.org/

OUR COMFY WORLD OF TEXT EDITORS HAS BEEN SULLIED! WE WANT BLOOD!
YEAH!
BLOOD!!
KILL!
FDISK!
GREP, NOT SCHLEP
BAD CODE IS BAD NEWS!

OH STOP! SEE WHAT HAPPENS WHEN YOU CLICK ON A LICENSE AGREEMENT WITHOUT READING IT?
UH...BUT...OOH! BUT...I...OOOH!
YOU TELL HIM DARRYL!

BE HONEST GUYS. HAVE ANY OF YOU EVER ACTUALLY **READ** A LICENSE AGREEMENT?
I HAVE! A FEW WORDS ANYWAY...
BASH THE
GREP, NOT
BAD CODE IS BAD
Copyright (c) 2000 Illiad http://www.userfriendly.org/

AND WHAT DID THE PART YOU READ SAY?
UMM....

"I ACCEPT."
OH **GOOD.** AS LONG AS YOU GOT THE **SPIRIT** OF THE AGREEMENT.
YOU TELL HIM, BOB!

Be honest. That's all you read too, right?

VIGOR IS **FINISHED**. NOT INTERESTINK ANYMORE, ERWIN. AM THINKINK WHAT EVIL AM TO BE DOINK **NEXT?**
MORE TO THE POINT, PITR: WHAT EVIL THIS WAY COMES?
Copyright (c) 2000 Illiad http://www.userfriendly.org/

THINK ABOUT IT. A CERTAIN HUGE ISP HAS JUST MERGED WITH A CERTAIN HUGE MEDIA COMPANY. THEY'RE NOW THE **LARGEST, MOST PERVASIVE MEDIA COMPANY IN THE WORLD**, WITH POWER TO RIVAL THE MICROSOFT EMPIRE...NOW WHO DO YOU THINK IS BEHIND SUCH RAMPANT DIABOLISM?
I THINK SOMEONE ELSE HAS WORN THIS. IT'S **STICKY**.
BORG GEAR WILL LOOK GOOD ON YOU STEVE. IT LOOKED FINE ON **BILL**.

EXPLAINING THE *CSS*-DECRYPTION SOURCE CODE TO THE MOTION PICTURE ASSOCIATION OF AMERICA

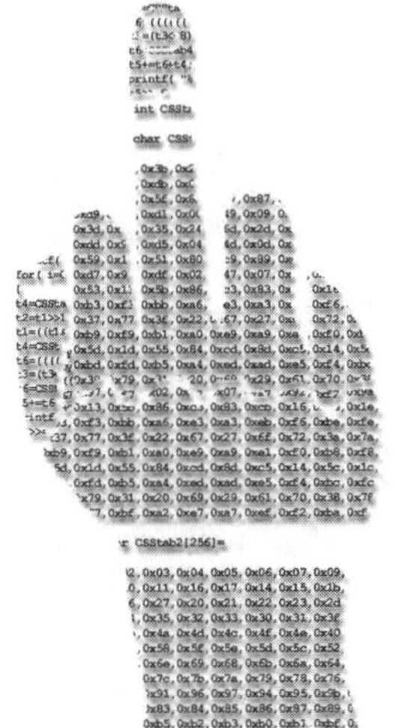

COPYRIGHT (C) 2000 ILLIAD HTTP://WWW.USERFRIENDLY.ORG/

I did receive a letter from some law firm about this cartoon, but I never responded and never heard from them again. So I figured it was a prank, or at best, some law firm that was originally retained to go after all of us "violators." If the latter, I have a simple message: *eat my shorts*. I just won't travel to Norway.

THEN IF WE HAVINK NEW EVIL COMINK DOWN PIPE FROM AOL, IS SOMETHINK WE ARE TO BE DOINK TO DEFEAT THEM?
I'M ALREADY WORKING ON IT.
Copyright (c) 2000 Illiad http://www.userfriendly.org/

LOOKS LIKE OUR BUDDY MR. CASE HAS PLUGGED HIMSELF INTO SOME BORG GEAR, AND I'VE TAPPED INTO THE "COMMAND PATHWAYS." ANY IDEA WHAT COMMAND I SHOULD SEND, COMRADE?
INCREASE HEAT IN SEWAGE SYSTEMS, PLEASE.
STEVE? WHAT'S THAT SMELL?
CRACKLE POP!
SSSSSSSSSSSS

AM THINKINK, COMRADE, THAT WE MUST NOT FORGET ONE ENEMY FOR ANOTHER. AOL IS DANGEROUS, DA, BUT MICROSOFT IS STILL BIG FISH IN POND.
Copyright (c) 2000 Illiad http://www.userfriendly.org/

TRUE. NOW THAT STEVE BALLMER IS OFFICIALLY TAKING BILL GATES' PLACE AS C.E.O., I SUPPOSE THERE'LL BE A PERIOD OF TRANSITION AS STEVE FLEXES HIS NEW MUSCLES OF AUTHORITY AND BILL TRIES TO GUIDE HIM...

STEVE, TAKE OFF THAT CLOAK AND CUT OUT THAT DARTH MAUL CRAP.
COME ON, BILL. IT'S FUN.

DID YOU HEAR THE NEWS, AJ?
WHAT NEWS?
THE AOL-TIME-WARNER MERGER.

WHY ARE YOU SMILING A.J.?
CUZ' IT KINDA MAKES SENSE. THE NEXT MATRIX MOVIE WILL HAVE NEO AND TRINITY USING AOL INSTANT MESSENGER TO EXPRESS THEIR FEELINGS FOR EACH OTHER! I'LL BE VINDICATED!
Copyright (c) 2000 Illiad http://www.userfriendly.org/

I DON'T THINK THAT YOU SHOULD TRY APPROACHING MIRANDA OVER THE NET AGAIN, A.J. I THINK SHE'D BE MORE IMPRESSED IF YOU SPOKE TO HER IN PERSON, DON'T YOU?

SHE'S VERY INTELLIGENT, BUT YOU CAN'T ASSUME THAT SHE CAN GUESS WHAT IT IS YOU HAVE IN MIND ALL OF THE TIME. A.J.? ARE YOU LISTENING?

VINDICATED AT LAST. I GET TO GO THROUGH PUBERTY.
MAYBE CHATTING WITH HER ONLINE IS A BETTER WAY...
Copyright (c) 2000 Illiad http://www.userfriendly.org/

UMM...HI MIRANDA. I WAS KIND OF HOPING YOU'D LET ME APOLOGIZE TO YOU FOR BEING SUCH A PUTZ. I'D LIKE TO MAKE IT UP TO YOU IF YOU'D LET ME.
SURE. WHY DON'T YOU TAKE ME DANCING?
Copyright (c) 2000 Illiad http://www.userfriendly.org/

LET ME GUESS. NOT ONLY DO YOU NOT LIKE **TALKING FACE TO FACE**. YOU DON'T LIKE **DANCING** EITHER.
I **USED** TO DANCE. THEN I LEARNED HTML AND MY DANCING GENE VANISHED. **HEH.**

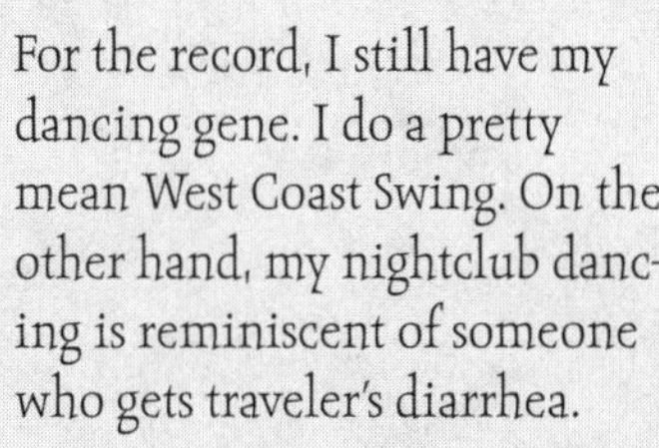

For the record, I still have my dancing gene. I do a pretty mean West Coast Swing. On the other hand, my nightclub dancing is reminiscent of someone who gets traveler's diarrhea.

WE CAN WORK ON GETTING TO KNOW EACH OTHER BETTER A.J...SO TELL ME SOMETHING ABOUT YOU I **DON'T** KNOW.
I SHAVE MY FEET.
Copyright (c) 2000 Illiad http://www.userfriendly.org/

YOU...UM...HAVE HAIRY FEET?
OH, HECK NO. MY FEET PEEL AND **ITCH** LOTS. SHAVING MAKES THE ITCH GO AWAY.

KEVIN MITNICK'S HOPES ARE DASHED MOMENTS AFTER HE THINKS HE'S FOUND A PLACE WHERE HE DOESN'T VIOLATE HIS PAROLE...
SIGH
Copyright (c) 2000 Illiad

Mitnick was vilified by the media and as part of his sentence wasn't permitted to be within 100 meters (or something like that) of any technology remotely resembling a computer. Not even on Mars ...

A.J.. CAN I ASK YOU A PERSONAL QUESTION? IT'LL HELP ME TO GET TO KNOW YOU BETTER.
SURE.
Copyright (c) 2000 Illiad http://www.userfriendly.org/

BOXERS OR BRIEFS?
DEPENDS.

OH...MY...
ON THE TEMPERATURE! DEPENDS ON THE TEMPERATURE!

WHAT'S THIS I HEAR ABOUT A.J. AND MIRANDA TRYING TO GET TOGETHER AGAIN? HASN'T SHE LEARNED THAT HE'S A COMPLETE SOCIAL DOLT?
Copyright (c) 2000 Illiad http://www.userfriendly.org/

SHE TOLD ME SHE PREFERS GUYS WITH BROWN HAIR, LIKE A.J. YOU HAVE BLACK HAIR. OH, SHE LIKES REDHEADS TOO.

SHE CAN'T BE THAT SHALLOW! WHAT'S WRONG WITH BEING A BLACKHEAD?
I'M AFRAID I'M NOT GOING TO HELP YOU WITH THAT ONE.

LET'S SEE IF I CAN'T SCREW THINGS UP A LITTLE FOR A.J. WITH MIRANDA...I'LL HAVE TO CONVINCE HER THAT IT'S HIM. SO...I'LL USE A REFERENCE FROM THAT 'MATRIX' MOVIE.
Copyright (c) 2000 Illiad http://www.userfriendly.org/

AND LET'S ADD INSULT TO INJURY BY HITTING ON MIRANDA IN CHAT. THAT SHOULD SINK THAT BOY'S SHIP...
TAP
TAK
TAP

HI MIRANDA, IT'S A.J. I WANT TO BE NEO TO YOUR TRINITY. GET BUTTERED UP AND INTO THOSE PVC PANTS.
I SWEAR THAT'S NOT ME TYPING THAT.

MIRANDA MY LOVELY TART, DRESS YOURSELF UP IN SOME TIGHT, BLACK PVC AND I'LL TAKE YOU INTO MY MATRIX.
WAIT HERE, A.J. I'LL TAKE CARE OF THIS.
Copyright (c) 2000 Illiad http://www.userfriendly.org/

HEH...THIS IS FUN. TRASHING SOMEONE ELSE'S REPUTATION. THEN MIRANDA WILL BE ALL MINE.
TIP
TAP
TAP

MATRIX REFERENCES ARE SO EASY TO ABUSE...HA!
DODGE THIS.
TYPE
TYPE

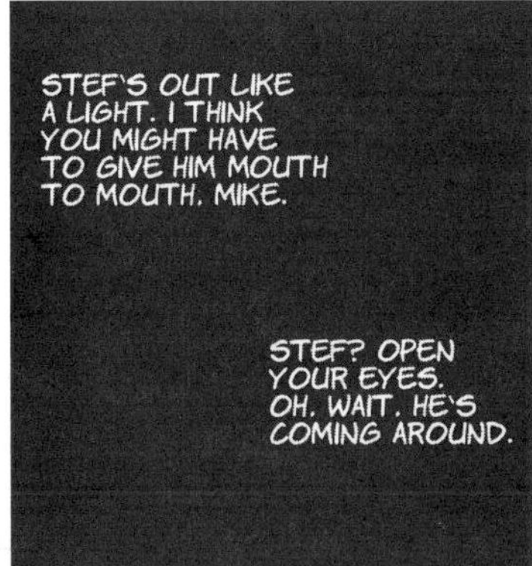
STEF'S OUT LIKE A LIGHT. I THINK YOU MIGHT HAVE TO GIVE HIM MOUTH TO MOUTH, MIKE.
STEF? OPEN YOUR EYES. OH, WAIT, HE'S COMING AROUND.

Copyright (c) 2000 Illiad http://www.userfriendly.org/

HE FAINTED AGAIN.
WHY DO I HAVE TO GIVE HIM MOUTH TO MOUTH? I KNOW, I KNOW. MY BEARD SHIELDS MY LIPS.

AM THINKINK, ERWIN. TO FIGHT SUCH BIG POWERFUL COMPANY AS AOL, AM TO BE FIGHTINK FIRE WITH FIRE, DA?
UMM...WHAT DID YOU HAVE IN MIND?
Copyright (c) 2000 Illiad http://www.userfriendly.org/

AM TO BECOMINK HALF COMPUTER, HALF HUMAN, LIKE BORG. THEN TO BECOME SUPER ADMINISTRATOR OF ALL BORG FUNCTIONS.
THAT MEANS... YOU'LL BECOME...
DA. I WILL BECOMINK ROOT OF ALL EVIL.
DON'T DO IT PITR! DON'T GO TO THE BAD PLACE!

WHY GEEKS REALLY WATCH THE SUPERBOWL
SID, HURRY THE HELL UP, THE DOT COM COMMERCIALS ARE ON!
Visit us at
Undies
.com
HTTP://WWW.USERFRIENDLY.ORG/
COPYRIGHT (C) 2000 ILLIAD

NOW AM NEEDINK TO RESEARCHINK HOW TO BECOME BORG CREATURE.
OKAY. WANT ME TO START PULLING IN DATA FOR YOU?
Copyright (c) 2000 Illiad http://www.userfriendly.org/

NYET. THIS IS TOP SECRET PROJECT. INFORMATION CAN BE LEAKINK FROM YOU TO AOL.
BUT... BUT...
THANKINK YOU ANYWAY, COMRADE.
OH SURE! MAKE ME LOOK UP ANATOMICALLY INCORRECT PORN SITES FOR YOU, BUT RESEARCH COOL THINGS FOR ONCE?! NOOO. WHAT DO I LOOK LIKE? TECH SUPPORT?

ALL THIS MATRIX STUFF REALLY MAKES YOU WONDER WHAT'S REAL AND WHAT ISN'T. IT'S INTERESTING THOUGH.
DA.
Copyright (c) 2000 Illiad http://www.userfriendly.org/

ZZZZOOOO
AM THINKINK, HOWEVER, THAT MATRIX IS FANTASY ONLY. HAVING GRIP ON REALITY IS NEEDED FOR ALL OF US.

MATRIX IS GOOD MOVIE, NOT DOUBTINK, BUT AM THINKINK THIS REALITY IS REAL TRUTH.
I'M VERY GLAD YOU FEEL THAT WAY, PITR.

I HAVE TO ADMIT THAT THIS NEW HOST BODY FEELS ...DIFFERENT.
YOU ARE TALKINK SILLY. WHY?
Copyright (c) 2000 Illiad http://www.userfriendly.org/

WANT A GAME OF QUAKE 3?
AM RIGHT NOW EXISTING IN GAME OF QUAKE THREE, NYET?

AM THINKINK WE ARE HAVINK BIG PROBLEM NOW. PLEASE TO BE HOLDINK OFF CRUD CREATURE WHILE AM BORGIFYINK SELF.
Copyright (c) 2000 Illiad http://www.userfriendly.org/

SO BABE, WHAT DO YOU THINK OF MY NEW LOOK?
YOU JUST DON'T GIVE UP, DO YOU STEF.

UH OH. HERE HE COMES.
http://www.userfriendly.org/
Copyright (c) 2000 Illiad
OKAY, WHICH ONE OF YOU BEARDED MONKEYS PUT THEIR LIPS ON MINE?
IT WASN'T PLEASANT FOR ME EITHER. YOU DO SALIVATE A LOT.
WHAT'S GOING ON IN THERE?
PITR'S LOCKED HIMSELF IN THE SERVER ROOM. HE SAID HE WAS 'BORGIFYING' HIMSELF.
CLANG! BRRNNNP! SHPLOP!
BORGIFYING HIMSELF? BUT HOW?
HE DIDN'T SAY. OTHER THAN WANTING TO 'ENHANCE' HIS BODY AND MIND.
BEEP BOP BOOP BOOP BOP BOOP BEEP
I CAN'T BEGIN TO THINK WHAT HE'S ADDING TO HIMSELF IN THERE...
YOU GUYS SEEN MY CEL PHONE?
AIIEEEE! PLEASE TO BE GETTING VOICE OUT OF HEAD!

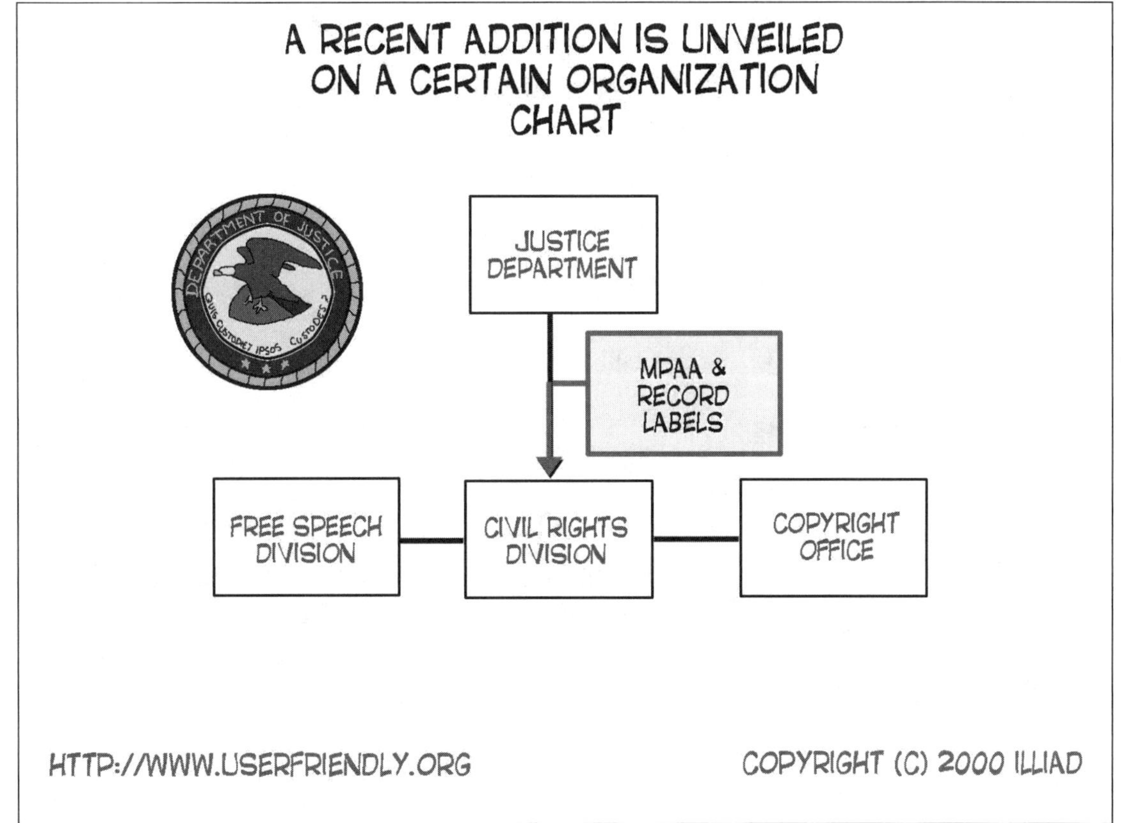
A RECENT ADDITION IS UNVEILED ON A CERTAIN ORGANIZATION CHART
DEPARTMENT OF JUSTICE
JUSTICE DEPARTMENT
MPAA & RECORD LABELS
FREE SPEECH DIVISION
CIVIL RIGHTS DIVISION
COPYRIGHT OFFICE
HTTP://WWW.USERFRIENDLY.ORG
COPYRIGHT (C) 2000 ILLIAD

BIP
BEEP
BOP
BIP
Copyright (c) 2000 Illiad http://www.userfriendly.org/

YEAAARGH!!
ZUMM
ZUM
VUMM

WHY IS PITR SCREAMING?
BECAUSE I HAPPEN TO KNOW THAT COBB LEAVES HIS CEL PHONE ON 'VIBRATE'
HELLLLP... HEAD IS WOBBLINK LIKE SPAM JELLY...

AM NOW BORG. WILL BE FIGHTINK EVIL THAT IS AOL.
VERY IMPRESSIVE. BUT WHAT DOES ALL THAT STUFF DO, BESIDES THE CEL PHONE?
Copyright (c) 2000 Illiad http://www.userfriendly.org/

IT IS MAKINK ME LOOKINK DANGEROUS.
ONLY IN THE PSYCHIATRIC SENSE.

The Crusoe chip was the secret "hot tech item" being developed by Transmeta, the company that hired Linus Torvalds. No one knew what it did. We all expected it to be so cool that the ice caps would double in size.

EVIL CRUD PUPPY. I AM TO BE GIVINK YOU BIG SMACKDOWN. I AM NOW BORG. TO BE USINK MUCH POWERFUL TECHNOLOGY TO BRINGINK YOU TO YOUR KNEES.
Copyright (c) 2000 Illiad http://www.userfriendly.org/

LOOK YOU LITTLE WORM. YOUR FAKE TECHNOLOGY IS HARDLY A WORRY. I'LL CRUSH YOU.
UMM...

I MEAN, AT LEAST SEVEN OF NINE HAS ANTI-GRAVITY TECHNOLOGY. WHAT DO YOU HAVE? SNURF?
AM HAVINK PRINTOUT OF PICTURE OF CRUSOE CHIP IN LEFT POCKET! NOW WHO IS BIG MAN?!

BEFORE I AM CRUSHINK YOU LIKE JUICY BUG, PLEASE TO BE TELLINK ME WHY YOU DO SUCH EVIL THINGS.
Copyright (c) 2000 Illiad http://www.userfriendly.org/

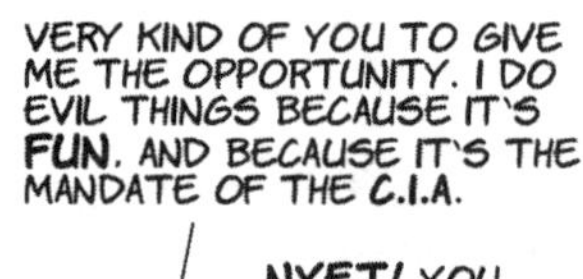
VERY KIND OF YOU TO GIVE ME THE OPPORTUNITY. I DO EVIL THINGS BECAUSE IT'S FUN. AND BECAUSE IT'S THE MANDATE OF THE C.I.A.

NYET! YOU ARE WORKINK FOR A.O.L. NOT C.I.A.

A.O.L.. C.I.A.. N.S.A.. WHATEVER. THEY ALL HAVE THREE LETTERS. THEY ALL COLLECT INFORMATION. AND THEY ALL SCREW THE PUBLIC.
SO YOU ARE DOUBLE AGENT. MAYBE WORKINK FOR M.P.A. AS WELL, DA?

HEY. I JUST HEARD THAT PITR GOT ARRESTED FOR ASSAULT. HE'S IN JAIL RIGHT NOW.
Copyright (c) 2000 Illiad http://www.userfriendly.org/

HE'S IN JAIL?
YEAH. HE PHONED AND SOUNDED REALLY DEPRESSED. SAID SOMETHING ABOUT EVEN THE POLICE BEING "A PART OF **THEM**."

WE ARE ALL DOOMED.
HEY HEY! **YOU GOT BAIL!**

TECH SUPPORT. GREG SPEAKING.
HELLO. MY COMPUTER SCREEN WENT ALL BLUE ON ME AND I DON'T LIKE IT.
Copyright (c) 2000 Illiad http://www.userfriendly.org/

WELL I CAN'T SAY I **BLAME** YOU. YOU JUST SUFFERED THE BLUE SCREEN OF DEATH. A FATAL ERROR UNDER WINDOWS.
YOU'RE TELLING **ME**. BLUE LOOKS JUST **HIDEOUS** WITH A BEIGE FRAME. HOW DO I CHANGE IT TO A PRETTIER COLOUR?
DO YOU LIKE BLACK? MOVE THE POWER SWITCH TO "OFF."

MORAL: READ THE FINE PRINT ON ALL CERTIFICATIONS.
MCSE Certified
Nigel Q. Private
has completed the coursework necessary to be recognized as a Minesweeper Consultant and Solitaire Expert.
Registrar
HTTP://WWW.USERFRIENDLY.ORG
COPYRIGHT (C) 2000 ILLIAD

Hey, I'm certifiable.

We miss you, Mr. Schulz.

YOU DON'T LOOK ALL THAT HAPPY TODAY MIRANDA. DIDN'T YOU GET A VALENTINES?
NO. I DIDN'T. BUT THAT'S NOT THE POINT.
Copyright (c) 2000 Illiad http://www.userfriendly.org/
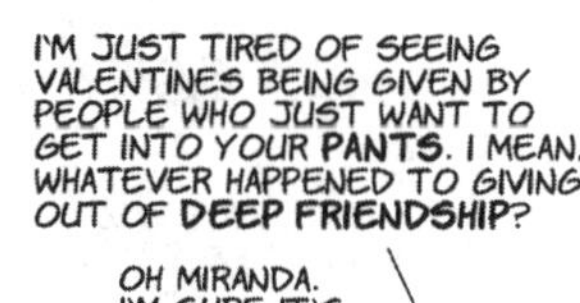
I'M JUST TIRED OF SEEING VALENTINES BEING GIVEN BY PEOPLE WHO JUST WANT TO GET INTO YOUR PANTS. I MEAN, WHATEVER HAPPENED TO GIVING OUT OF DEEP FRIENDSHIP?

OH MIRANDA. I'M SURE IT'S HAPPENING SOMEWHERE.

SORRY FOR ALWAYS YANKING THE BALL AWAY, CHARLES.
THAT'S OKAY. IT'S NOT LIKE I NEVER EXPECTED IT.

WELL HELLO AGAIN. YOU JUST CAN'T RESIST ME, CAN YOU.
I'M ON TO YOUR GAME, YOU GREASE SPOT.
Copyright (c) 2000 Illiad http://www.userfriendly.org/
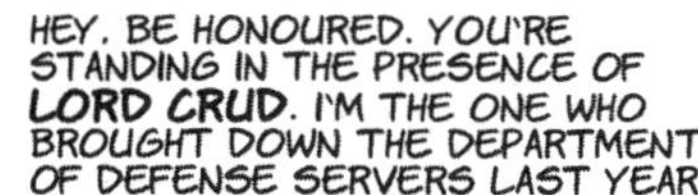
HEY, BE HONOURED. YOU'RE STANDING IN THE PRESENCE OF LORD CRUD. I'M THE ONE WHO BROUGHT DOWN THE DEPARTMENT OF DEFENSE SERVERS LAST YEAR.

AND I'M MIRANDA X. I'M THE ONE WHO SHUT YOU DOWN.

YOU'RE MIRANDA X? I THOUGHT YOU WERE A GUY.
FUNNY. I NEVER THOUGHT THAT ABOUT YOU.

WHY IS MIRANDA WAVING THAT BASEBALL BAT AROUND THE CRUD PUPPY?
SHE SAID SOMETHING ABOUT "TAKING CARE OF BUSINESS."
WATCH IT WITH THAT, LADY!
Copyright (c) 2000 Illiad http://www.userfriendly.org/

POW!
ZZZZOOOT

THAT'S WHERE A.J. WENT. THAT WAS COOL. SO HOW DO I GO "ZZZOOOOT"?
LET ME GUESS. I MISSED VALENTINE'S. RIGHT?

I HEARD THAT MIRANDA GAVE YOU A DRIVER TO THE HEAD. MUST BE LOVE. OR NOT. HEH.
GO AWAY, STEF.

I'M SO SORRY.
WILL YOU TWO QUIT THAT? VALENTINES IS OVER. OKAY?!
Copyright (c) 2000 Illiad http://www.userfriendly.org/

I KNOW IT'S LATE. BUT I WENT OUT AND GOT YOU A VALENTINE'S GIFT...
A.J.! THAT IS SO SWEET OF YOU!
Copyright (c) 2000 Illiad http://www.userfriendly.org/

WHAT COULD YOU HAVE GIVEN ME? LET'S SEE...

RUSTLE RUSTLE

...YOU GOT ME AN UGLY CAT.
AMAZON SELLS CATS NOW?
I GOT HIM ON EBAY. SOMEONE PAID ME $20 TO TAKE HIM.
POIK!

SO THIS IS YOUR NEW CAT. SEEMS KIND OF... ALOOF.
MOST CATS ARE LIKE THAT...
Copyright (c) 2000 Illiad http://www.userfriendly.org/

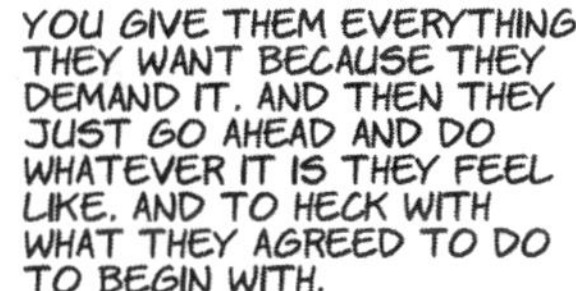
YOU GIVE THEM EVERYTHING THEY WANT BECAUSE THEY DEMAND IT. AND THEN THEY JUST GO AHEAD AND DO WHATEVER IT IS THEY FEEL LIKE. AND TO HECK WITH WHAT THEY AGREED TO DO TO BEGIN WITH.

KUFF KUFF KUFF KUFF

AH. SO THEY'RE KIND OF LIKE PROGRAMMERS.
HEY NOW.

HOW TO DRIVE VA LINUX AND RED HAT STOCK THROUGH THE CEILING
YOU'RE GONNA GET A SMACKDOWN CUZ STONE COLD LARRY AUGUSTIN SAYS YOU ARE!
I'M GONNA CRUSH YOU LIKE A KERNEL BUG OR MY NAME'S NOT WELL HUNG BOB YOUNG!

This one is too much of an inside joke. If you were paying attention during the dot-com bubble, you'll know that two of the sweethearts were VA Linux and Red Hat. Part of the IPO game was getting attention. This was suggested, believe it or not, with some seriousness by a couple of marketing folks over at one of the two companies.

OKAY. WHAT THE HELL IS **THAT**?
THE NEW CAT I GOT FOR MIRANDA.
FEDEX
Copyright (c) 2000 Illiad http://www.userfriendly.org/

THIS THING IS A **CAT?**
OF COURSE! WHAT DID YOU THINK IT WAS?
FEDEX

I DON'T KNOW. HE JUST LOOKS KIND OF.... **PROCESSED.**
FUNNY...MIKE THOUGHT HE WAS SOME KIND OF **SAUSAGE MEAT ANIMAL.**
FEDEX

SO DOES HE HAVE A NAME?
I WAS THINKING WE SHOULD CALL HIM "FIVE."
FEDEX
Copyright (c) 2000 Illiad http://www.userfriendly.org/

FEDEX

THAT'S SOME KIND OF LAME GEEK JOKE, ISN'T IT.
IT'S EITHER "CAT FIVE" OR "SCRIPT KITTY." WHICH ONE HURTS LESS?
FEDEX

HEY YOU WALKING BRILLO PAD. I WANT YOU TO MEET "FIVE."
Copyright (c) 2000 Illiad http://www.userfriendly.org/

I DON'T KNOW WHAT IT IS. DOES IT KNOW WHAT **I** AM?
THE ODDS ARE GOOD.
CAT TOY!

ROWWRR
PFFFFFFT!!
Copyright (c) 2000 Illiad http://www.userfriendly.org/

IS FIVE IN THE COAT CLOSET?
WAP WHAP
WAP
WAP
YEP.

PLEASE TELL ME THAT THE DUST PUPPY ISN'T IN THERE WITH HIM.
COME **ON.** THEY'RE JUST GETTING TO **KNOW** EACH OTHER.
NO! DON'T LICK ME THERE!

I'M NOT MAKING THIS UP. A.J. YOUR MUTANT FRIEND WASN'T IN THE CLOSET. ONLY FIVE WAS.
I DON'T SEE HOW THAT CO..UHHH...
HUNGA HUNGA HUCK HUCK HUCK
CACK!
Copyright (c) 2000 Illiad http://www.userfriendly.org/
ULP
HEH. COOL. HAIRBALL.
PURRRR PURRR PURRR
DROOL DRIP DRIP

I HAVE TO ADMIT THAT THIS FURRY DOORKNOB IS STARTING TO GROW ON ME. DESPITE THE FACT THAT HE LOOKS LIKE YOU, PITR.
Copyright (c) 2000 Illiad http://www.userfriendly.org/

AM NOT SEEINK RESEMBLANCE.
OH PLEASE. AT THE VERY LEAST YOU BOTH USE SPIT FOR HAIR GEL.

Yes, I have had cats. What gave it away?

R.A.N.T.S
(REDUNDANT ARRAY OF NT SERVERS)
I STILL HAVE TWO LEFT! PLEASE OH PLEASE OH PLEASE OH PLEASE...

SPECULATION ON THE D.O.J. RECOMMENDATIONS TO BREAK MICROSOFT APART CONTINUE THIS WEEK AS ANALYSTS EVALUATE THE CONSEQUENCES OF THE ANTI-TRUST TRIAL DECISION.
cheese
Copyright (c) 2000 Illiad http://www.userfriendly.org/

WHEN ASKED TO OFFER A LIKELY RESULT OF THE BREAKUP, ONE ANALYST STATED THAT SHE COULD SEE THE SOFTWARE GIANT SPLIT INTO THREE COMPANIES.
cheese

"OPERATING SYSTEM, APPLICATIONS AND INTERNET?" WE ASKED.
"SALES, MARKETING AND LEGAL," SHE REPLIED.
cheese

TECH SUPPORT. GREG SPEAKING.
QUICK! HOW DO I CHANGE MY WALLPAPER?
Copyright (c) 2000 Illiad http://www.userfriendly.org/

WELL IT'S PRETTY EASY. I ASSUME YOU WANT TO CHANGE THE APPEARANCE OF YOUR DESKTOP?
I NEED TO GET A PICTURE OFF MY BACKGROUND!

OH I SEE... DID SOMEONE ACCIDENTALLY SET A PORN PICTURE AS THEIR WALLPAPER, AND THEIR WIFE OR MOM IS ABOUT TO SHOW UP?
PLEASE HURRY!

I went to CeBIT. It was huge, much bigger than any conference I've ever been to in North America. Also, I couldn't find a toilet for days. Lots of potted plants, though.

HEY TANYA? WHERE HAVE STEF AND A.J. BEEN? I HAVEN'T SEEN THEM FOR A FEW DAYS.
THEY LEFT FOR THAT CeBIT COMPUTER SHOW IN GERMANY.
Copyright (c) 2000 Illiad http://www.userfriendly.org/

GERMANY? THOSE TWO? NEITHER OF THEM SPEAKS A WORD OF GERMAN!
OH DON'T WORRY. I'M SURE THEY'LL LEARN THE MOST IMPORTANT PHRASES.

STEF, TRY ANYTHING! IT'S BEEN THREE DAYS!
TOILETZEN! ERR... WASHROOMSTEIN! TINKLEPLATZ!
TWITS.

GOOD MORNING MIRANDA!
A.J.! SO TELL ME SOMETHING ABOUT GERMANY!
Copyright (c) 2000 Illiad http://www.userfriendly.org/

THERE'S CERTAINLY A LOT OF GERMANS OVER THERE?
OH IMAGINE THAT. AND HERE I AM THINKING THAT IT'S POPULATED BY MEXICANS INSTEAD.

AJ RECOUNTS HIS TRIP TO CEBIT IN GERMANY TO MIRANDA, AND STARTS AT THE EUROPEAN COMPUTER PUBLICATIONS...
YOU KNOW, I LIKE BABES AS MUCH AS THE NEXT GUY, BUT WHAT DOES PAMELA ANDERSON HAVE TO DO WITH COMPUTERS?
http://www.userfriendly.org/
Copyright (c) 2000 Illiad

DXZ

SILICON.
YES. OKAY.

MIND YOU, THE ENTIRE SHOW WASN'T THAT PEACEFUL. AS USUAL, STEF GOT WAY OUT OF HAND.
WHY, WHAT DID HE DO?
http://www.userfriendly.org/
Copyright (c) 2000 Illiad

WELL, YOU KNOW HOW AT SHOWS EVERYONE HAS PALM PILOTS AND THEY BEAM THEIR BUSINESS CARDS AT EACH OTHER?
UM...YES...?

SEVEN HUNDRED PALM PILOTS. ONE BUTTON TO PUSH. NOW THAT'S MARKETING.
MEIN GOTT! VAS IS DAS?!
ZZZOWWNT

Also at CeBIT there were few options for food on the convention grounds. Every restaurant had the same menu, and they all served Wiener Schnitzel. You got maybe a quarter-cup of green peas, some lettuce as a garnish, and this humungous Wiener Schnitzel that hung over the edges of the plate. During my stay in Hanover I think I nearly died from lack of vitamins and fiber.

PATENTLY RIDICULOUS
US71034544: Patent for the letter "a"
US71034545: Patent for using the letter "a" twice in one word
amazon.com
US71034550: Patent for the colour "orange"
US71034553: Patent for a graphic of a smile
US71034571: Patent for the use of drop shadows in logos
US71034572: Patent for the "dot" in "dot com"
US71034579: May as well patent the "com" part as well
COPYRIGHT (C) 2000 ILLIAD
HTTP://WWW.USERFRIENDLY.ORG/

HELLO. I'M ORVILLE REDHATBACHER. AND THIS IS MY GOURMET LINUX DISTRIBUTION! BUY IT AT YOUR FAVOURITE E-TAILER SITE TODAY!
Copyright (c) 2000 Illiad http://www.userfriendly.org/

JEEZ. NOT AGAIN. CUT!!
MR. YOUNG, YOU KEEP FORGETTING THE LINE "ALMOST EVERY KERNEL PATCHED, TOO!"
LOOK, THIS WIG IS ITCHY, OKAY?

EVIL GENIUSES IN A NUTSHELL, APPENDIX A. "POETRY FOR THE WEB"
"OUR YELLOW SUN YIELDS TO THE DARK AS I BEGIN MY WEB-BASED LARK FLOWING, TURNING, THROUGH THE PIPE I GREP FOR TEXT AND DUMP THE HYPE...
Copyright (c) 2000 Illiad http://www.userfriendly.org/

"BUT AS I RIDE THE FIBRE TRAIL I TEST MY FAITH AS I READ MY MAIL EVEN AS MY BANDWIDTH FATTENS I QUESTION LIFE AND 1-CLICK PATENTS...

ALTHOUGH I ASK AND THOUGH I QUERY I KNOW THE TRUTH, I GROK THE THEORY LIFE IS A MULTIMEDIA OF SINS SO HE WHO COLLECTS THE MOST PORN WINS."
MUST... NOT... GRIN...

SAY, IS THAT THE SIMS GAME YOU WERE TALKING ABOUT?
YUP. I GET TO MANAGE A WHOLE FAMILY AT THE MICRO LEVEL.
TAP TYPE
Copyright (c) 2000 Illiad http://www.userfriendly.org/

BWIP BLOP

HEY! ARE YOU ALLOWED TO HAVE FOUR WIVES?
IT'S MY WORLD, OKAY?

WHAT ARE YOU DOING IN THAT HOUSE?
DECORATING. ONE OF THE COOL THINGS ABOUT THE SIMS IS BEING ABLE TO CUSTOMIZE EVERYTHING.
UH HUH. JUST A SEC.
Copyright (c) 2000 Illiad http://www.userfriendly.org/

WHAT?
I'M NOT MAKING IT UP, A.J.

PLAID WALLS?! GEEZ MIKE!
I TOLD YOU.
HEY, PLAID HIDES THE DIRT LONGER.

MIKE, ARE YOU STILL PLAYING THAT SIMS GAME?
WELL YEAH!
http://www.userfriendly.org/
Copyright (c) 2000 Illiad

THIS GAME LETS ME LIVE OUT MY FANTASIES. I CAN BE ANYONE I WANT. AND DO ANYTHING I WANT TO DO...

YOU'RE PLAYING A GUY WHO WORKS AS A NETWORK ENGINEER AND LIKES TO PLAY QUAKE.
AND THE COOL PART IS I CAN GIVE HIM ALL THE COMPUTERS HE WANTS!

ARE YOU STILL PLAYING THAT STUPID GAME?
YEP. GOT A REALLY NIFTY HOUSEHOLD GOING HERE.
http://www.userfriendly.org/
Copyright (c) 2000 Illiad

LOOK. WE HAVE IMPORTANT CLIENTS COMING THROUGH HERE IN A FEW MINUTES. HINT HINT.
OKAY. OKAY...

...LET ME GET MY GUY HERE TO TIDY HIS HOUSE UP. CAN'T QUIT WITH A MESSY HOUSE. RIGHT?
WHEN WILL THE HURTING STOP?

MAKING SPECIFIC PROMISES ABOUT A HARDWARE PRODUCT 20 MONTHS IN ADVANCE
Microsoft
X BOX
trust no one

HI. HOW DO I TAKE OUT THE SECURITY DRIODS IN SYSTEM SHOCK 2?
WHAT? SORRY. THIS ISN'T A GAME HELP LINE.
Copyright (c) 2000 Illiad http://www.userfriendly.org/

WAAAHAHAHAAA!

OKAY OKAY! USE THE E.M.P. GRENADES!
SNIF THANK YOU. PLEASE DON'T DENY ME A GAME HINT AGAIN.

TECH SUPPORT. GREG SPEAKING.
HI...UH...HOW DO YOU DEFEAT THE PUCE DRAGON IN MAGICAL MYSTICAL APPRENTICES IV?
Copyright (c) 2000 Illiad http://www.userfriendly.org/

LISTEN. THIS IS THE COLUMBIA INTERNET TECHNICAL SUPPORT LINE. NOT SOME FANTASY ADVENTURER'S HINT LINE.

UH-HUH. YOU CAN'T BEAT HIM EITHER. CAN YOU.
LEAD HIM INTO THE DARKNESS AND A GRUE WILL EAT HIM. ARE WE DONE HERE?

I only play in godmode after I've beaten whatever game on the highest difficulty level. Also, when I run the server and play against friends.

HELLO. GREG SPEAKING. HOW MAY I HELP YOU?
YES. HI. I UNDERSTAND YOU HAVE THE CHEAT CODES FOR HALF-LIFE.
Copyright (c) 2000 Illiad http://www.userfriendly.org/

I BEG YOUR PARDON? WHAT MAKES YOU THINK I HAVE THE CHEAT CODES FOR A GAME?

SOMEONE IN YOUR OFFICE TOLD ME YOU ONLY PLAYED WITH CHEAT CODES.
WHO DID?! THAT WAS STEF WASN'T IT! I'LL GODMODE THAT WIENER!

GREG'S GAME HINTS. HOW MAY I HELP YOU?
UHH...TECH SUPPORT. RIGHT? I CAN'T GET TO THE NEWS SERVER.
Copyright (c) 2000 Illiad http://www.userfriendly.org/

HAVE YOU TRIED THE BRONZE KEY ON THE RED DOOR? THAT SOMETIMES WORKS...

...BUT SOMETIMES THE BRONZE KEY DOESN'T HELP. AND THE GAME TAUNTS YOU AS YOU WASTE SLEEPLESS HOURS TRYING TO SOLVE THE STUPID GAME. AND . . .
OOOOKAYYY... I'LL JUST KEEP CHANGING MY SETTINGS UNTIL I HIT ON THE RIGHT I.P. ADDRESS...

FINALLY, A CHANCE TO TRY OUT QUAKE 3...
Copyright (c) 2000 Illiad http://www.userfriendly.org/

BOOM! SPLUTCH!
HOW DO YOU DO THAT?! HOW DO YOU DIE IN QUAKE 3 AT THE STARTUP SCREEN?!
NNNNNN...

...AND SO HE GETS SMOKED ON THE STARTUP SCREEN!
YOU'RE KIDDING!
Copyright (c) 2000 Illiad http://www.userfriendly.org/

HEY! I'LL HAVE YOU KNOW THAT RIGHT AFTER THAT I PLAYED A WHOLE ROUND OF QUAKE AND KICKED SERIOUS BUTT! WHEN YOU'RE READY TO HAVE ME CLEAN YOUR CLOCK, YOU LET ME KNOW.

ACTUALLY, THAT WAS A PLAYBACK OF A DEMO OF A.J. I DIDN'T HAVE THE HEART TO TELL HIM.
HEY STEF, WAIT UP! WANT TO PLAY FOR MONEY?

THE TRUTH BEHIND THE DISAPPEARANCE OF GNUTELLA

AHEM
OOPS
RECORDS
AOL.COM

WOOSH!
BLAFF!
SPORTCH!
Copyright (c) 2000 Illiad http://www.userfriendly.org/

THESE BOTS PLAY LIKE...LIKE BOTS! THEY NEVER MISS! THEY MUST BE CHEATING!
YOU'RE PLAYING ON THE FIRST LEVEL. AND THE EASIEST SETTING.
HEY!! HE MUST HAVE SHOT ME THROUGH A DOOR! LAG! I'M GETTING PACKET LOSS!
MAYBE YOU SHOULD STICK TO DEATHMATCH MINESWEEPER.

GREG. HAVE YOU SEEN...OH NO. ARE YOU ON EBAY AGAIN?
I'M JUST BROWSING..
Copyright (c) 2000 Illiad http://www.userfriendly.org/

'19TH CENTURY UNDERWEAR'
CURRENT BID: $36,000
YOUR BID: $36,100
THANK YOU FOR BIDDING AT EBAY!
TAP
TAP
TAP

YOU CALL THAT BROWSING?!
I'M USING STEF'S ACCOUNT. IT DE-STRESSES ME.

EBAY OFFICIALS TODAY REPORTED A RECORD SALE PRICE ON AN ITEM THAT STARTED AT A BID OF ONE DOLLAR. THE ITEM WAS A COLLECTION OF 19TH CENTURY UNDERWEAR...
Daikatana
14 pcs.
Copyright (c) 2000 Illiad http://www.userfriendly.org/

THE COLLECTION WENT FOR A PRICE OF $38,000 EVEN. FAR ABOVE THE ITEM RESERVE PRICE. WE ASKED EBAY WHY THE BIDDING ON THIS ITEM WAS SO FIERCE...
Daikatana
14 pcs.

"A MR. MURKY KEPT BIDDING AGAINST HIMSELF. IT WAS JUST WEIRD."
WHAT?!
Daikatana
14 pcs.

WHAT'S THAT?
IT'S A SONY AIBO. A ROBOTIC DOG THAT CAN LEARN STUFF. MY NEIGHBOUR WENT ON HOLIDAYS AND ASKED ME TO KEEP AN EYE ON HIM FOR HER.
Copyright (c) 2000 Illiad http://www.userfriendly.org/

YES, A.J., IT'S BARK IS WORSE THAN IT'S BYTE.
I SPECIFICALLY DIDN'T ASK YOU ANYTHING SO YOU WOULDN'T USE THAT STUPID JOKE.
GRRRRR!

HEY ERWIN! CHECK OUT THE PUPPY!
PUPPY? WHAT THE...
Copyright (c) 2000 Illiad http://www.userfriendly.org/

UHH...
SNIF SNUFF WUFFLE

I AM NOT A FIRE HYDRANT!
OH RELAX. HE'S JUST BOOKMARKING HIS TERRITORY.
ARF!

SO THIS IS AN AIBO. I HAVE TO ADMIT HE'S KIND OF CUTE IN A BALL-OF-TINFOIL SORT OF WAY.
HE'S NEAT. YOU CAN GIVE THEM COMMANDS WITH MUSIC AS WELL.
Copyright (c) 2000 Illiad http://www.userfriendly.org/

THAT BETTER HAVE BEEN WATER!
WHAT TUNE WAS THAT?
HEH. TINY BUBBLES.

A BREAKTHROUGH IN QUANTUM COMPUTING
SO UNTIL I PING THE NT SERVER. I DON'T KNOW IF IT'S UP OR DOWN...

THIS LITTLE TWERP IS ACTUALLY KIND OF CUTE. IN A RETARDED SORT OF WAY...
Copyright (c) 2000 Illiad http://www.userfriendly.org/

I THINK I CAN LINK INTO HIS VIDEO CIRCUITS...SEE HOW HE SEES THE WORLD..

HOLY ROOT. I'VE BEEN MISSING SO MUCH!
BONE
STRIP STEAK
TENDERLOIN
RUMP

If you've never had a dog put its wet, cold nose on the back of your knee, you won't understand this cartoon.

OKAY YOU POOR EXCUSE FOR A GARAGE-DOOR OPENER. WHERE DID YOUR IDIOT DOG-FRIEND GO?
TO THE FRIDGE.
Copyright (c) 2000 Illiad http://www.userfriendly.org/

THE FRIDGE? FOR WHAT? THERE'S NO FOOD IN THERE. JUST SICK EXPERIMENTS THAT THE TECHS PLAY WITH.

YEEEAAAAARGH!
LIQUID NITROGEN. ACTUALLY.
ARF
ARF

WHAT'S THIS I HEARD ABOUT STEF?
OH...THE AIBO COOLED IT'S NOSE WITH LIQUID NITROGEN AND PUSHED IT INTO THE BACK OF STEF'S LEG.
Copyright (c) 2000 Illiad http://www.userfriendly.org/

LIQUID NITROGEN?! DOESN'T THAT KIND OF COLD...UH...WELL. AFFECT CERTAIN BODY PARTS?

YEAH. BUT IT WASN'T NOTICEABLE UNTIL HE SPOKE.
Okay, who signed me up for a speaking part on 'the smurfs'?

That'll teach me to not study my software history. Apache is actually called Apache because it started as patches to the NCSA HTTP daemon. So it really is "A Patchy Server."

HI. I HAVE LINUX INSTALLED ON MY MACHINE BUT I DON'T KNOW HOW TO USE THIS 'SIX' EDITOR.
'SIX' EDITOR?
Copyright (c) 2000 Illiad http://www.userfriendly.org/

I'M SORRY M'AM. BUT I DON'T KNOW WHAT EDITOR THIS IS THAT YOU'RE TALKING ABOUT.

LOOK. IT'S THE 'SIX' EDITOR. YOU KNOW. THE ROMAN NUMERAL SIX?
UH. YOU MEAN 'VI'?
THIS IS THE SAME LADY WHO WAS WORRIED BECAUSE SHE HEARD WE USED "A PATCHY" WEB SERVER.

GEEK PRIDE DAY?
GeeK PRIDE
proud to be geek!
Copyright (c) 2000 Illiad http://www.userfriendly.org/

YOU MUST BE JOKING. PRAY TELL WHAT IT IS YOU COULD POSSIBLY BE PROUD OF?
WE'RE NOTHING LIKE YOU?
HEY! IF YOU'RE NOT IN SALES YOU'RE OVERHEAD!
GeeK PRIDE
proud to be geek!

HELLO, FOLKS. TODAY IS THE FIRST OF APRIL, ALSO KNOWN AS APRIL FOOLS' DAY.
Copyright (c) 2000 Illiad http://www.userfriendly.org/

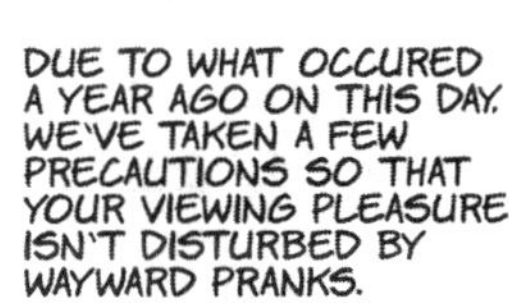
DUE TO WHAT OCCURED A YEAR AGO ON THIS DAY, WE'VE TAKEN A FEW PRECAUTIONS SO THAT YOUR VIEWING PLEASURE ISN'T DISTURBED BY WAYWARD PRANKS.

OF COURSE, THIS IS A CARTOON STRIP SO WE HAVE TO INCLUDE HUMOUR IN WHAT WE DO.
ILLIAD

IRIDIUM + ANNOYED HACKERS
Headquarters of the MPAA

Almost as good as fin-steered orbit-launched crowbars. You use what you have.

SO A.J., DID YOU HEAR DAIKATANA IS ABOUT TO GO GOLD?
Copyright (c) 2000 Illiad http://www.userfriendly.org/

AFTER YEARS OF HYPE AND PROMISES, THE GAME THAT WAS SUPPOSED TO DESTROY QUAKE 2 IS DUE TO SHIP AND HIT THE SHELVES...
MIKE, YOU'RE TWO DAYS LATE FOR APRIL FOOLS. NICE TRY.
NO NO! THEY'RE REALLY GOING GOLD THIS TIME!

CHIEF? YOUR TEN'O'CLOCK INTERVIEW IS HERE.
GOOD. THANKS TANYA. PLEASE SHOW HIM IN.
Copyright (c) 2000 Illiad http://www.userfriendly.org/

AH. HELLO, MR. CHIEF. IS BIK PLEASURE TO BE MEETINK YOU.

UM..YOU LOOK... FAMILIAR...
NOT TO BE JOKINK PLEASE. HAVE LONG LOST TWIN BROTHER. THINKINK HE IS DEAD. OR WORSE. HAS BECOMINK LINUX CODER.

WELL, I MUST SAY YOU'RE HIGHLY QUALIFIED FOR THE POSITION OF V.P. OF SALES. WHERE WAS THE LAST PLACE THAT YOU WORKED?
MICROSOFT.
Copyright (c) 2000 Illiad http://www.userfriendly.org/

HOW DO YOU DO THAT? I DON'T WANT TO HIRE YOU, BUT I KNOW THAT I MUST.
IS OLD ADAGE: "KEEPINK FRIENDS CLOSE, BUT BE KEEPINK WALLET EVEN CLOSER."

Thus I introduce Dark Side Dave, one of the most reviled characters in the UF universe. I based him on UF's (at one time) real VP of Sales. He loved being reviled.

MIKE, COBB, I'D LIKE YOU BOTH TO MEET OUR NEW V.P. OF SALES.
Copyright (c) 2000 Illiad http://www.userfriendly.org/

HIS NAME IS...UHHH... I NEVER DID GET YOUR NAME...

'DARK SIDE DAVE.' BUT I AM ALLOWINK YOU TO JUST CALLINK ME 'DARK SIDE.'
COULD HE BE A CLONE?
NO. EVIL LIKE THAT IS SPAWNED.

AM FEELINK... WERY **STRANGE**.
Copyright (c) 2000 Illiad http://www.userfriendly.org/
I AM FEELINK SOMETHINK I HAVE NOT FELT SINCE....
MOTHER WOULD BE WERY DISAPPOINTED. YOU HAD BRIGHT FUTURE AT A.O.L.
...SINCE LAST TIME I AM WANTINK TO SKIN A HUMAN AND USINK HIM FOR SHELTER.

AM TELLINK YOU, CHIEF. "DARK SIDE," HE IS BIG TROUBLE. HE IS ONLY NOGOODNIK. NEED TO BE FIRINK HIM.
Copyright (c) 2000 Illiad http://www.userfriendly.org/

AM KNOWINK ABOUT HIM - HE IS WERY BAD MAN. AM WONDERINK WHAT YOU ARE THINKINK OF HIM.

I THINK HE HAS A BETTER ACCENT THAN YOU.
HIS ACCENT. IT IS **FAKE**!

AND TWO BABIES MAKE FOUR
COPYRIGHT (C) 2000 ILLIAD
HTTP://WWW.USERFRIENDLY.ORG/

WELCOME TO E-TRADE!
A.J.
HEY.
Copyright (c) 2000 Illiad http://www.userfriendly.org/

HELLO, COMRADE.
UM...HI.

YOUR TRADING ORDER, SIR?
DUMP ALL OF MY BIOTECH STOCKS NOW!

HMMM...MY BROTHER'S COMPUTER...AM THINKINK TO PUT 'BOHEMIAN ROACH VIRUS' ON HIS MACHINE...FIX HIM GOOD.
VP SALES

VIRUS WILL DESTROY HIS SALES DATA AND WILL BE LEAVINK NO CLUES. AM CLEVER. WILL NOT GET CAUGHT.
VP SALES

YOU ARE UP TO SOMETHINK?
WHAT VIRUS?!
VP SALES
Copyright (c) 2000 Illiad http://www.userfriendly.org/

See? Another Clinton bash. There're lots of them. But in 2002, I'm accused of being a leftist.

PITR, AM THINKINK YOU ARE TRYINK TO BE GETTINK ME IN BIK TROUBLE...
VP SALES
Copyright (c) 2000 Illiad http://www.userfriendly.org/

AM APPRECIATINK YOUR ATTEMPTS - BIKINI MODELS ON MY WALLPAPER, ILLEGAL COPY OF PHOTOSHOP IN MY DESK, OFFICE SUPPLIES IN TRUNK OF CAR...
VP SALES

...BUT, THE BLUE DRESS WITH STAIN IN CLOSET WAS A BIT MUCH, NYET?
WAS ONLY SOY SAUCE.
VP SALES

AM NEVER BELIEVINK WOULD DO THIS, BUT AM ASKINK FOR YOUR HELP. MUST GET RID OF DARK SIDE DAVE!
Copyright (c) 2000 Illiad http://www.userfriendly.org/

BUT PITR, DAVE HAS DRIVEN OUR REVENUES UP BY FORTY PERCENT IN THE WEEK THAT HE'S BEEN HERE! SALES HAVE NEVER BEEN SO GOOD! WE CAN'T GET RID OF HIM!

AND YOU ARE THINKINK WHO WILL BE OUT OF JOB IF HE IS DOINK WELL?
I KNOW A PLACE WHERE WE CAN HIDE HIS BODY.

DARK SIDE DAVE, DA? ARE FROM IMMIGRATION. YOUR PAPERS, THEY ARE NOT IN ORDER.
YEAH. I MEAN, DA. NOT IN ORDERSKI.
Copyright (c) 2000 Illiad http://www.userfriendly.org/

NOT IN ORDER? BUT...
YOU ARE TO BE GOINK TO OFFICE IN ANTARCTICA TO GETTINK NEW PAPERS.
YEAH. THE ONLY PLACE IT CAN BE DONESKI.

"DONESKI?!"
WHAT?! LIKE YOU GUYS GET IT RIGHT ALL OF THE TIME!!

EFFECTIVELY EXILED TO ANTARTICA IN SEARCH OF 'NEW PAPERS,' DARK SIDE DAVE WANDERS THROUGH THE HARSH WHITE LANDSCAPE OF THE SOUTH POLE.
Copyright (c) 2000 Illiad http://www.userfriendly.org/

DAVE CONSIDERS HIS PLIGHT, REALIZING THAT IN FACT HE IS SUFFERING AS HIS ANCESTORS HAVE SUFFERED IN SIBERIA, EXILED TO THE GULAG...

...WHEN SUDDENLY THE DAWN OF REASON LIGHTS HIS EYES...
SIBERIA?! GULAG?! PAPERS NOT IN ORDER?! I'M FROM CALIFORNIA!

INCRIMINATING EVIDENCE:
'DARK SIDE' DAVE REVEALS HIS SQUISHY SIDE

TECH SUPPORT. GREG SPEAKING.
HEY. MY GIRLFRIEND WANTS TO GET MARRIED. BUT I DON'T THINK I'M READY.
TYPE TAP TAP
Copyright (c) 2000 Illiad http://www.userfriendly.org/

UH...HELLO? THIS IS TECHNICAL SUPPORT. NOT THE ANN LANDERS ADVICE LINE.

YA. BUT YOU HELPED ME INSTALL WINDOWS 2000 WHEN NO ONE ELSE COULD. I TRUST YOU. MAN.
YEAH. I GUESS I AM A BIT OF A HERO...

CHIEF. YOU SEEN THIS FLYER? IT'S A LIST OF COMMUNITY HELP LINES.
WHAT OF IT?
Copyright (c) 2000 Illiad http://www.userfriendly.org/

WELL...I DON'T THINK THEY PROOFREAD THE PHONE NUMBERS. OUR TECH SUPPORT LINE WAS INCLUDED BY MISTAKE...
OH?

LADY. FOR THE LAST TIME. THIS IS NOT THE 'CHERRY TOMATO GARDENING HOTLINE.'
STOP BEING COY. NOW TELL ME ABOUT YOUR TOMATOES.

BLOB IN HAND. IT IS WHAT?
SILLY PUTTY. I USED TO PLAY WITH IT WHEN I WAS JUST A KID.
Copyright (c) 2000 Illiad http://www.userfriendly.org/

SBLAPP!

MRRRFGG!
COOL! IT WORKS JUST LIKE I REMEMBERED!

CHIEF. YOU GOT A MINUTE?
SURE HILLARY.
Copyright (c) 2000 Illiad http://www.userfriendly.org/

WE HAVE A PROBLEM. MIKE'S GONE A LITTLE OFF THE DEEP END.
MIKE? HOW?

THIS CAN'T BE WHAT SILLY PUTTY IS FOR...
HAHAH AHAHA!
SBLAP!

POOR PITR. THAT MUST BE REALLY UNCOMFORTABLE.
I'LL BET IT IS...
Copyright (c) 2000 Illiad http://www.userfriendly.org/

NOT ONLY THAT. BUT THE SHEER **EMBARASSMENT**...
MM-HM

...BUT I SUPPOSE THAT'S TO BE EXPECTED WHEN YOU **LOSE FACE**.
COBB! NOT NICE!
LAUGHINK IT UP, SALES BOY. WILL FEEDINK YOU TO ROUTER WHEN GETTINK FACE BACK...

...AND APPARENTLY WE'RE SUPPOSED TO BE NICE TO PITR AND NOT MAKE FUN OF HIS CONDITION...
Copyright (c) 2000 Illiad http://www.userfriendly.org/

CAN'T SAY I'VE EVER SEEN YOU WITH SUCH A **BLANK LOOK ON YOUR FACE**, PITR.
WURMF!

USER
FRIENDLY
the comic strip
PIZZA
Portrasber 4
ROTO-ROUTER 800
Copyright (c) 1997-2000 Illiad

START THE RHYTHM, ERWIN OL' BUDDY. **SANTANA'S** #1 SONG "**SMOOTH**" IF YOU WOULD BE SO KIND...
FOUND IT!

THAT STOCK'S A HOT ONE
IT'LL GLOW ALL WEEK LIKE THE MIDNIGHT SUN
I HEARD THEM WHISPER RUMOURS THAT SCARE EVERYONE
BUT YOU STAY SO COOL...
YOU'RE NOT A CHEATER, YOU'RE JUST A BANK ACCOUNT DEPLETER
YOU'RE MY INSPIRAAAATION
THE GREASE IN MY GROOVE...

AND IF I SAID THIS STOCK AIN'T GOOD ENOUGH
YOU WOULD MAKE UP THINGS TO LIFT IT UP
YOU COULD CHANGE THE FILING TO BETTER HELP DELUDE
ALL THE V.C.'S YOU SOOTHE

AND IT'S LIKE THE MARKET IS UNDER A SPELL
THE **S.E.C.** WON'T QUESTION WHAT THEY DON'T KNOW YOU SELL
YOU'VE GOT THE KIND OF LOOK THAT JUST SCREAMS "**OIL WELL**"
SELL THEM SOME STOCK
MAKE IT REAL
OR ELSE JUST LIE ABOUT IT!!

I DON'T WANT TO FINISH THIS SONG. IT MAKES ME FEEL SLIPPERY LIKE THAT STUFF YOU KEEP IN YOUR DESK.
I NEED THIS RECORDED BEFORE I PUT MY CALL INTO LINUX ONE. NOW **HUSTLE**.

Week of April 24th, 2000

I'M NOT SURE IF THIS WILL WORK...BUT WE CAN GIVE IT A TRY. HERE IS PRETTY GOOD.
RMFF!
http://www.userfriendly.org/
Copyright (c) 2000 Illiad

OKAY. ROLL YOUR FACE INTO THE WALL...THAT'S IT.

AM LOOKINK HOW, COMRADE?
I THINK MAYBE YOU DIDN'T **QUITE** PRESS YOUR FACE ON THE WALL EVENLY...

A.J., COULD WE PLEASE TALK? IT'S BEEN A WHILE SINCE WE'VE HAD MUCH OF A CHANCE...
SURE.
http://www.userfriendly.org/
Copyright (c) 2000 Illiad

IN CASE YOU HADN'T NOTICED, I'VE BEEN TRYING TO GET YOU TO BREAK OUT OF YOUR SHELL SO THAT WE CAN GIVE THINGS A REAL TRY. BUT AT **THIS** RATE, I MAY AS WELL JOIN A **CONVENT**.

BUT I THOUGHT NUNS WEREN'T ALLOWED TO...**OH.**
AND IF YOU THINK I'M GIVING **THAT** UP BECAUSE OF YOUR **INEPTNESS**, I HAVE A LIST OF E-MAIL ADDRESSES TO SELL YOU.

DON'T YOU **GET** IT? A.J., IF THINGS DON'T GET BETTER I MAY AS WELL START DATING **NORMAL** MEN.
http://www.userfriendly.org/
Copyright (c) 2000 Illiad

EXCUSINK ME PLEASE.

LIKE **THAT** GUY, THE PIERCE BROSNAN LOOK-ALIKE. MAYBE I SHOULD DATE **HIM**.
I'M SURE HE'S VERY NORMAL. BE MY GUEST.

A.J.? HAVE YOU SEEN MIRANDA?
YEP. SHE'S TRYING TO GET A DATE WITH PITR.
http://www.userfriendly.org/
Copyright (c) 2000 Illiad

WHAT?! BUT WHAT ABOUT **YOU?** WE ALL THOUGHT YOU AND SHE WERE A **DONE DEAL!** YOU'RE SO **PERFECT** TOGETHER! WHAT IF SHE GETS A DATE AND **FORGETS** ABOUT YOU?

HILLARY. SHE'S TRYING TO GET A DATE WITH **PITR.**
RIGHT. SORRY. LOST MY HEAD.

ON THE SET OF THE NEXT JAMES BOND MOVIE. DISASTER PREPARES TO STRIKE...
ROLL CAMERA! ACTION!
THAT'S QUITE A SUNSET OUT THERE.
YES IT IS, JAMES. WILL YOU SPEND IT WITH ME?

I MUST SAY, I WAS RATHER HOPING YOU'D SAY THAT...
WHAT THE... CUT!!! MAKEUP!!!
Copyright (c) 2000 Illiad http://www.userfriendly.org/

I WANT MY FACE BACK! I CAN'T RESCUE GORGEOUS WOMEN LOOKING LIKE THIS!
Copyright (c) 2000 Illiad http://www.userfriendly.org/

I DON'T CARE IF YOU LIKE MY FACE BETTER! I WANT IT BACK!
WHAT'S GOING ON?!
PITR'S IN THE OTHER ROOM WITH PIERCE BROSNAN.

MR. BROSNAN REALLY WANTS HIS FACE BACK, I GUESS.
ROLL YOUR FACE ON MINE OR I'LL PIN YOU DOWN AND DO IT MYSELF!
ACTUALLY, THAT'S PITR DOING ALL OF THE YELLING.

STEVE CASE, AGE 6
AOL.COM
COPYRIGHT (C) 2000 ILLIAD
HTTP://WWW.USERFRIENDLY.ORG/

HMMM...BETTER CHECK TO MAKE SURE I HAVE EVERYTHING BEFORE I LEAVE THE OFFICE...
PAT
PAT!
Copyright (c) 2000 Illiad http://www.userfriendly.org/

CEL PHONE...PALM V... WALLET...PAGER...
PAT!
PAT!
PAT!

PALM PILOT MODEM... PEN...LEATHERMAN... EXTRA STYLUS...
HEYYYYYY MACARENA!
PAT!
PAT!
PAT!
PAT!
PAT!

ACK! I HATE IT WHEN I SPILL MY COLA...NOW HOW AM I GONNA CLEAN THIS UP?
Copyright (c) 2000 Illiad http://www.userfriendly.org/

WHAT HAPPENED TO HIM?!
I DON'T KNOW. BUT HE SMELLS LIKE SUGAR, CAFFEINE AND HAIR. THE SAME WAY MIKE DOES.

WHIRRRRRR!
HOLD STILL L'IL GUY...
Copyright (c) 2000 Illiad http://www.userfriendly.org/

WHIRRRRRRRR
OKAY, YOU'RE DONE!
THANKS MIRANDA.

WHAT DO YOU GUYS THINK?
NEEDS A BOW AND RIBBON.
ARE THEY LAUGHING? I CAN'T SEE THROUGH THIS HAIR.

MESSING WITH THAT LITTLE LINTBALL IS FUN...HE NEVER RETALIATES.
Copyright (c) 2000 Illiad http://www.userfriendly.org/

WHAT THE...
FRAMMIN' AT THE JIM JAM, FRIPPIN' IN THE KROTZ!

ANYTHING FOR A FELLOW GEEK.
WELL THANKS MISTER WIZARD. BUT NOW I LOOK AS DUMB AS HE DOES.

HERE'S YOUR COMPUTER BACK TANYA. PROBLEM FIXED..
THANKS MIKE! SAY. HAVE YOU ALWAYS BEEN GOOD WITH COMPUTERS?
Copyright (c) 2000 Illiad http://www.userfriendly.org/

ACTUALLY. NO. NOT UNTIL HIGH SCHOOL. I WAS PRETTY BUSY WITH THE GIRLS...
TOO MANY POTENTIAL DATES?

SOMETHING LIKE THAT...
UM...UM...UM... UM...UM...UM...
FORGET IT. MIKE. NOT NOW. NOT EVER.
LXIX

I LOVED SCHOOL. I LOOKED FORWARD TO COURSE REGISTRATION EVERY YEAR.
YAWN
LXIX
Copyright (c) 2000 Illiad http://www.userfriendly.org/

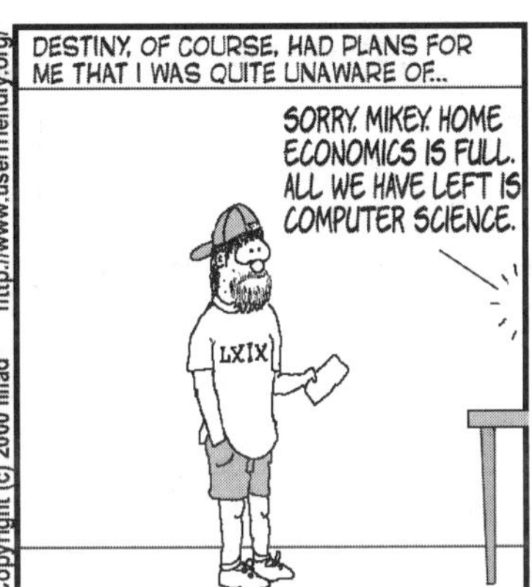
DESTINY, OF COURSE, HAD PLANS FOR ME THAT I WAS QUITE UNAWARE OF...
SORRY. MIKEY. HOME ECONOMICS IS FULL. ALL WE HAVE LEFT IS COMPUTER SCIENCE.
LXIX

MY TALENTS BECAME ABUNDANTLY CLEAR IN MY FIRST COMP SCI CLASS. I KNEW FROM THAT POINT ON I WAS FATED.
WHAT IS IT WITH YOU AND 'GOTO'?! IT'S ALWAYS 'GOTO' WITH YOU!
LXIX

"A BEAR WITH VERY LITTLE BRAIN'

NASDAQ

COPYRIGHT (C) ILLIAD 2000 HTTP://WWW.USERFRIENDLY.ORG/

This one was published right around the time the dot-com bubble was starting to go kablooie. "Oh, look at that interesting bottomless hole! I wonder what's in it?" Curiosity and cats, where bears are the same as cats.

SO NOW I WAS ON THE ROAD TO BECOMING A COMPUTER GEEK, BUT I STILL HAD A WAYS TO GO BEFORE TRULY PASSING MUSTER...
LXIX
Copyright (c) 2000 Illiad http://www.userfriendly.org/

LITTLE DID I REALIZE THAT AROUND EVERY CORNER, AT EVERY TURN, THERE WAS TO BE TEMPTATION...
RUSTLE RUSTLE
LXIX

...AND SO CAME THE FIRST AND GREATEST OF MY FALLS INTO GEEKDOM.
PSST. HEY KID. FIRST ONE'S ALWAYS FREE.
Cola
LXIX

WITH CAFFEINE IN MY BLOODSTREAM, I STAYED VERY LATE AFTER SCHOOL TO SPEND TIME IN THE COMPUTER LAB.
WELL MIKEY, I MUST SAY I'M PLEASED TO SEE SUCH DEDICATION. LOCK UP AFTER YOU LEAVE.
'KAY MISTER BROCKTON.
Copyright (c) 2000 Illiad http://www.userfriendly.org/

I OFTEN STAYED WELL PAST DINNER TIME, MASTERING THE ART OF COMPUTING FAR INTO THE NIGHT.
WHAT A GREAT KID. HE'LL GO FAR...

OF COURSE, THE ART OF COMPUTING WASN'T REALLY ABOUT CODING IN PASCAL...
BLAM!
BLAM!
HALT!
SCHUTZSTAFFEL!
AAAGH!
MEIN LEBEN!

FROM THAT POINT ON I HAD A LOT OF HARD CHOICES TO MAKE AS A GEEK...
DO I LEARN VI OR EMACS?
Copyright (c) 2000 Illiad http://www.userfriendly.org/

AND MY CHOICES ONLY GOT HARDER AS I GOT OLDER AND MORE EXPERIENCED...
DO I CODE MY RANDOM NUMBER GENERATOR IN BASIC OR ASSEMBLER?

AND NOW THAT I'VE BECOME A FULLY FLEDGED GEEK AND A MAN, I HAVE CRITICAL CHOICES TO MAKE EVERY DAY.
HEY MIKE? YOU OKAY WITH ONIONS ON THE PIZZA? YOU CAN PICK THEM OFF..

It just so happens that the ILOVEYOU virus was filling mailboxes around the world the same time this strip was written. Serendipity!

YOU KNOW, NOW THAT I THINK ABOUT IT, I HAVE TO ADMIT THAT I'VE BEEN A REAL DOLT WITH MIRANDA. SHE'S BEEN WAITING FOR ME TO COMMUNICATE MY FEELINGS TO HER FROM THE VERY FIRST DAY.
Copyright (c) 2000 Illiad http://www.userfriendly.org/

THIS WILL CHANGE TODAY. I'M GOING TO GO OUT ON A LIMB LIKE I NEVER HAVE BEFORE AND WRITE TO HER AND JUST TELL HER HOW IT IS. I JUST HOPE IT ISN'T TOO LATE.
TAP
TAPP
TIP

TO: MIRANDA
SUBJECT: I LOVE YOU
OH GODS. NOT ANOTHER ONE.
DELETE

DELETE
DELETE
DELETE
DELETE

DELETE *DELETE*
DELETE *DELETE*
DELETE *DELETE*
DELETE *DELETE*
DELETE *DELETE*
DELETE *DELETE*
DELETE *DELETE*
DELETE *DELETE*

LET ME GUESS: YOU'VE SPENT ALL MORNING DELETING "I LOVE YOU" VIRUSES FROM YOUR EMAIL.
NO, I'VE SPENT ALL MORNING DELETING EMAILS FROM PEOPLE TELLING ME NOT TO OPEN THE "I LOVE YOU" VIRUS.
Copyright (c) 2000 Illiad http://www.userfriendly.org/

THAT 'I LOVE YOU' VIRUS MUTATES. DOES IT? WELL LET ME TELL YOU ABOUT HOW IT MUTATES...
Copyright (c) 2000 Illiad http://www.userfriendly.org/

IT GOES AFTER MY MACHINE. JUST MINE. IT'S NOW A STEF-HATING, VILLAINOUS, ANTI-MARKETING-EXEC SMEGGING PHILISTINE OF A PROGRAM AND IT CATEGORICALLY DESTROYED A SOLID YEAR'S WORTH OF VALUABLE DATA!

IT GOT YOUR PORN COLLECTION, DIDN'T IT.
IT'S DATA THAT I LIKE TO PROCESS OVER AND OVER. IS THAT A CRIME?

THOSE WACKY EGYPTIANS
...SOMETHING ABOUT THE END OF THE WORLD ON MAY 5, 2000 BROUGHT ABOUT BY SOME SORT OF PESTILENCE OR VIRUS. PAY IT NO MIND...
COPYRIGHT (C) 2000 ILLIAD
HTTP://WWW.USERFRIENDLY.ORG/

HERE I AM AGAIN IN FRONT OF THE COLA MACHINE. WHY DO I ALWAYS COME HERE WHEN I FEEL DOWN?
COLA
Copyright (c) 2000 Illiad http://www.userfriendly.org/

I DRINK COLA AND I FEEL BETTER...OR DO I? DO I JUST ATTRIBUTE MAGICAL HEALING QUALITIES TO THIS DARK FLUID? WHAT IF... JUST THIS ONCE...I DON'T DRINK COLA?

GEEZ...I WON'T DIE OR ANYTHING. WILL I?
OF COURSE YOU'LL DIE. I'LL BEAT YOU WITH A BASEBALL BAT.

I CAN NOT BELIEVE YOU JUST WALKED AWAY WITHOUT BUYING A COLA. I HAVE TO TELL YOU I REALLY AM HURT. SEVENTY-FIVE CENTS OUT OF YOUR POCKET AND YOU COULD'VE MADE US BOTH HAPPY. BUT NOOOOO...
Cola
Copyright (c) 2000 Illiad http://www.userfriendly.org/

OBVIOUSLY YOU'VE LOST YOUR WAY AND NEED SOME GUIDANCE. AND I OFFER TO YOU THE CHANCE TO DRINK DIRECTLY FROM ME. I. THAT WHICH IS COLA INCARNATE. GIVE UNTO YOU A CHANCE FEW MORTALS EVER EVEN DREAM OF...

HERE YOU GO YOU LUCKY GUY. DRINK UP.
IF I GIVE YOU MY LUNCH MONEY WILL YOU LEAVE ME ALONE?
Cola

Yeeccchh. Who writes these?!

LOOK. DON'T BE SUCH A DWEEB. GRAB THE HOSE AND QUAFF AWAY. YOU'LL LOVE IT.
SIGH OKAY...
Cola
Copyright (c) 2000 Illiad http://www.userfriendly.org/

SHHHHHUUURRRRP
Cola

YOU KNOW. THAT TASTED KIND OF... FUNNY...
AND FOR SOME REASON I CAN BREATHE BETTER. NEXT TIME YOU GET A DOUBLE HELPING.
Cola

OKAY LISTEN. I DON'T WANT TO DEAL WITH THIS ANYMORE. I'LL GO BUY A COLA. IT'S BACK ON THE WAGON FOR ME. WILL THAT MAKE YOU HAPPY?
Cola
Copyright (c) 2000 Illiad http://www.userfriendly.org/

YEAH... SURE... UMM...
Cola

YOU KNOW. I'M JUST HAVING A DICKENS OF A TIME RETRACTING THIS THING. THINK YOU COULD JUST...
NO!!
Cola

TAP
TAP
TAPPITY
TYPE
Copyright (c) 2000 Illiad http://www.userfriendly.org/

YES?
UH...

ANOTHER DELIBERATELY MISSED OPPORTUNITY TO TALK TO YOUR MARKETING EXEC ABOUT BACKUPS AND VIRUS AWARENESS...
OH NEVER MIND..
DOLT.
TAPPY
TYPE

A spoof of the Public Service Announcement where an adult is in the kitchen with his child. An opportunity to talk about drug and alcohol abuse comes up, but he lets it slide.

ERWIN AND I JUST WROTE A POEM. A.J. WOULD YOU LIKE TO HEAR IT?
YEAH OKAY.
Copyright (c) 2000 Illiad http://www.userfriendly.org/

IF YOU WANT A DOMAIN
(ANOTHER DOT COM)
YOU'RE ASKING FOR PAIN
(ANOTHER DOT COM)
AND NSI GAINS
(ANOTHER DOT COM)
MOMENTUM.

AND WHILE YOU HAD WONDERED
(ANOTHER DOT COM)
WHY YOU FELT PLUNDERED
(ANOTHER DOT COM)
THEY CHARGED YOU ONE HUNDRED
(ANOTHER DOT COM)
PER CENTUM.
WITH SINCERE APOLOGIES TO A.A. MILNE AND WINNIE THE POOH...

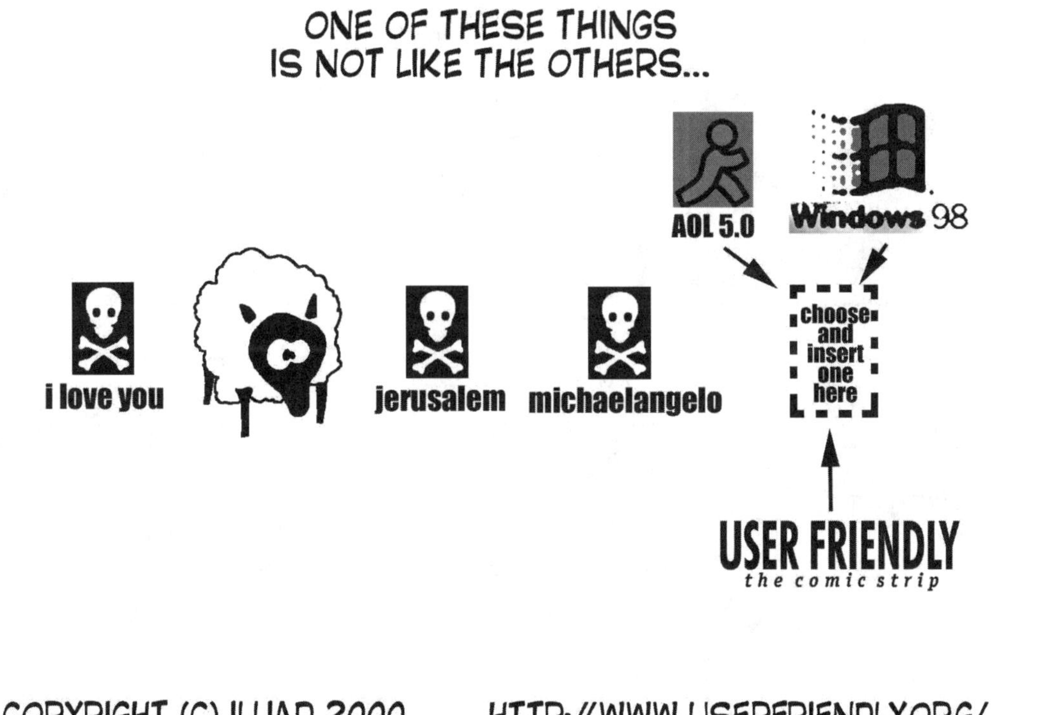
ONE OF THESE THINGS
IS NOT LIKE THE OTHERS...
AOL 5.0
Windows 98
i love you
jerusalem
michaelangelo
choose and insert one here
USER FRIENDLY
the comic strip
COPYRIGHT (C) ILLIAD 2000
HTTP://WWW.USERFRIENDLY.ORG/

I have a vague recollection that at the time, this strip was about things that spread like pestilence. If it's not that, the sheep confuses me.

Week of May 22nd, 2000

WARNING: HUGE, UNDESCRIBABLY SCARY AND ROUTER-CRUSHING NETWORK TRAFFIC SPIKE NOW IN PROGRESS.
Copyright (c) 2000 Illiad http://www.userfriendly.org/

WHAT ON **EARTH** IS CAUSING...OH...I SHOULD HAVE **GUESSED.**

I WAS JUST **BROWSING.**
DOWNLOADING **14 GIGS** OF *SPICE GIRLS LIVE* IS NOT "BROWSING."

I CERTAINLY HOPE YOU'RE NOT BLOWING COMPANY RESOURCES ON THAT **NAPSTER** THING AGAIN. YOU SHOULD BE **WORKING.**
I'LL BE DONE SOON. I'M DOWNLOADING THE LATEST *PEARL JAM* ALBUM...
Copyright (c) 2000 Illiad http://www.userfriendly.org/

I DON'T SUPPOSE YOU HAVE THEIR FOURTH AND FIFTH ALBUMS AS MP3S?
OF COURSE. BUT SHARING THEM WOULD BE, YOU KNOW, **MORE** ILLEGAL.

OKAY. SO THIS NAPSTER THING IS ON MY MACHINE NOW...CONNECTING WITH THE SERVER. HEY...THERE'S A LOT OF PEOPLE ON HERE...
Copyright (c) 2000 Illiad http://www.userfriendly.org/

SHLUUUUUURRRRP!!

DEAR **LORD.** WHAT WAS **THAT?!**
HEY EVERYONE! THIS DUDE'S GOT AN **OC3!** HIS HARD DRIVE IS SO **MINE!**
DIBS ON HIS BEE GEES COLLECTION!

NOW THAT THINGS HAVE SETTLED DOWN A LITTLE WITH THIS NAPSTER THING I CAN START SURFING FOR SOME TUNES...
Copyright (c) 2000 Illiad http://www.userfriendly.org/

WHAT YOU'RE DOING IS UNETHICAL. FOR EVERY SONG YOU DOWNLOAD, YOU'RE DEPRIVING AN ARTIST OF MONEY THAT COULD KEEP THEM FROM STARVING.
DOWNLOADING "DA DOO RON RON" BY SHAUN CASSIDY

THEY ALSO GET ALL OF THE **CHICKS.** I FIGURE THEY OWE **ME.**
YOU'RE **GOOD.** WANT TO WORK FOR THE **RIAA?**

LOOK, I WORK FOR METALLICA. MOVE ASIDE. I HAVE WORK TO DO HERE.
OH PLEASE. YOU HARDLY INSPIRE FEAR.
Copyright (c) 2000 Illiad http://www.userfriendly.org/

WHAM!
WHAM!
WHAM!
WHAM!
WHAM!
WHAM!

YE GODS. AND YOU'RE FROM METALLICA'S LEGAL DEPARTMENT?
HELL NO. PUBLIC RELATIONS.

WHERE IS EVERYONE TODAY? THERE'S NOT A TECH IN SIGHT. THEY'D BETTER NOT BE GOOFING OFF...
Copyright (c) 2000 Illiad http://www.userfriendly.org/

HI CHIEF! WANT TO SEE THE NEW DATAFLIPBIT-O-TRON WE INSTALLED THIS MORNING?
OH THERE YOU ALL ARE. HA HA. NO NO. YOU TECHS JUST CARRY ON.

OKAY. HE'S GONE.
PLAY THE LORD OF THE RINGS MOVIE TRAILER AGAIN. I WANT TO SEE LIV TYLER BOUNCING ON THAT HORSE.
LIV SHMIV. SHE HAS THICK ANKLES.

THE LAST TIME THE GOVERNMENT DECIDED WE NEEDED A MAJOR SPLIT IN A HURRY...

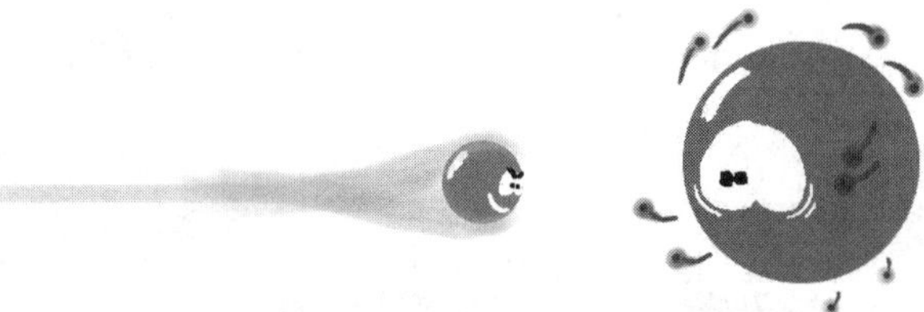

The MANHATTAN PROJECT
1945

COPYRIGHT (C) 2000 ILLIAD HTTP://WWW.USERFRIENDLY.ORG/

I only have myself to blame. After 2+ years of Microsoft bashing, I wrote a cartoon that is decidedly ambiguous about splitting the company. But that was the way I felt—splitting MS could be good for the rest of the world, and it could be really, really bad. Either way, it was fun drawing atoms. Did you know they have faces?

SO MIKE, DID YOU HEAR THE ONE ABOUT THE C.E.O. AND THE NETWORK ENGINEER?
SO ANYWAY, THERE'S THIS C.E.O., AND HE GOES TO HIS NET ENGINEER AND SAYS...
...UH...HE SAYS...

UH...IS THAT A COFFEE RING?
PEOPLE! WE HAVE THREE FRAMES A DAY IN OUR BUDGET! NOT TWO. NOT FOUR AND FIVE IS RIGHT OUT! NOW FOCUS!
Copyright (c) 2000 Illiad http://www.userfriendly.org/

CUT!! A.J.! IF MIKE CAN DO THIS WHY CAN'T YOU?!
BECAUSE HE DOESN'T HAVE A COFFEE STAIN ALL OVER HIS PANTS. OKAY?
ACTUALLY, THERE WAS THAT ONE INCIDENT LAST WEEK...
Copyright (c) 2000 Illiad http://www.userfriendly.org/

WHAT ARE YOU DOING?
GETTING RID OF THIS COFFEE RING. I CAN'T WORK WITH IT HERE...IT'S DISTRACTING.

YOU SURE IT'S SUCH A GOOD IDEA TO MESS WITH THAT? IT DOESN'T SEEM TO BE GOING AWAY...
JUST NEEDS ELBOW GREASE...
WAPPA WAPPA WAPPA

OKAY, MAYBE THAT WASN'T THE BEST IDEA...
AND I THOUGHT YOU SAID YOU'D "NEVER DO WINDOWS."
Copyright (c) 2000 Illiad http://www.userfriendly.org/

THAT'S GREAT RIGHT THERE. THANKS PAL!
THIS SIDE UP
Copyright (c) 2000 Illiad http://www.userfriendly.org/

STEF, WHAT IS THAT?
IT'S MY TICKET TO SPANKING YOU MONKEYS IN QUAKE.
THIS SIDE UP

THE LABEL ON THE SIDE SAYS "ACME FORCED-FEEDBACK ENEMY-DENIAL SMACKDOWN ERGONOMIC GAME CHAIR."
WE CAN JUST CALL IT MY THRONE.
THIS SIDE UP

STEF BOUGHT A WHAT?
AN "ERGONOMIC GAME ENVIRON." THEY CALL IT A CHAIR IF YOU CAN BELIEVE IT.
Copyright (c) 2000 Illiad http://www.userfriendly.org/

HE'S IN THERE NOW?
OH YAH.
BROMP! BLAMM! BLAMM! SPLOOTCH! CRUMP! CRASH!
HE'S PLAYING QUAKE IN THERE?
NO. "LEATHER GODDESSES OF PHOBOS."
DON'T ASK ME HOW BUT I FEEL...MOIST.

PIT PAT PIT PAT
PIT PAT PIT PAT
PIT PAT PIT PAT
HUH HUH HUH!
KA-BLAMM!
SPLORTCH!
Copyright (c) 2000 Illiad http://www.userfriendly.org/

THAT WAS JUST INTENSE! I DODGED AND WEAVED AND GOT THE WEENIE INTO MY SIGHTS AND BLAM! I FRAGGED HIM BUT GOOD!
AND YOU DID THIS HOW?
SKILL! AND THE FEEDBACK FROM THIS CHAIR THING! AND FOR SOME REASON HE HAD THIS SIDEWAYS SMILEY-FACE ABOVE HIM. WHAT WAS THAT ANYWAYS?

GEEK RANT

HI...

I DON'T WEAR BAD GLASSES OR SUSPENDERS AND I DON'T GLOW IN THE DARK.

I DON'T LIKE POCKET PROTECTORS AND NO, I DON'T KNOW EDWIN, MARTY OR LINDA IN THE I.T. DEPARTMENT AT EBAY, ALTHOUGH I'M CERTAIN THEY'RE PULLING DOWN GREAT SALARIES...

I LIKE CAFFEINE.
I PREFER TO CODE IN *C* OR *PERL*, NOT VISUAL BASIC, AND IT'S PRONOUNCED *LI*-NIX, *LINE*-UX OR *LEEN*-OOKS, WHATEVER MAKES YOU HAPPY.

I CAN PROUDLY WEAR A T-SHIRT FROM ANOTHER COMPANY AND STILL LOOK COOL.

I BELIEVE IN INNOVATION, *NOT* OBFUSCATION; PEER REVIEW, *NOT* PATENT WARS, AND THAT THE PENGUIN IS A CUTE BUT FEARSOME ANIMAL!

GEEKS ARE THE *SECOND* BEST PAID PEOPLE IN THE WORLD, THE *FIRST* TO BE BLAMED FOR TECHNICAL PROBLEMS, AND THE *ONLY* REASON WHY CIVILIZATION DOESN'T CRUMBLE AROUND YOUR EARS!

MY NAME IS JASON,
AND I AM A GEEK!

COPYRIGHT (C) 2000 ILLIAD HTTP://WWW.USERFRIENDLY.ORG/

This became one of the most popular UF cartoons of all time. It's a spoof of the "I am Canadian" commercials made famous by Molson Breweries. It was read out loud on several radio stations in North America, and there was enormous demand for a t-shirt with this art on it.

SO, YOU UP FOR A GAME? I'M UNBEATABLE IN THIS CHAIR. TIME TO WAX YOUR BUTT, FREAK-BOY.
SURE.
Copyright (c) 2000 Illiad http://www.userfriendly.org/

HEY! OOOH! YOU'RE STILL PRETTY GOOD BUT I'LL GET YOU YET, A.J.! OOOH! OKAY...THAT WAS AN ACCIDENT...JUST YOU WAIT...
SIGH

BRRRUMPPPPP
GUUNNZZZZZ
Copyright (c) 2000 Illiad http://www.userfriendly.org/

NNNNGGGGG
I GUESS A.J. WON THAT ROUND. WHAT DID THE FORCE FEEDBACK DO TO STEF?
HE'S HOLDING HIS CROTCH.
IT WAS QUAD DAMAGE. OKAY?!!

YOU WANTED TO SEE ME, CHIEF?
YES, MIRANDA. I'VE BEEN GIVING CONSIDERATION TO THE IDEA OF HIRING A TECHNICAL MANAGER. SO OF COURSE I WANT TO GIVE ALL OF THE TECHS HERE A CHANCE TO COMPETE FOR THE POSITION.
Copyright (c) 2000 Illiad http://www.userfriendly.org/

AND THESE DAYS I'D HATE TO BE ACCUSED OF NOT BEING AWARE OF THE DEARTH OF WOMEN IN SENIOR TECHNICAL POSITIONS. BUT ON THE SAME NOTE, I DO NEED JUSTIFICATION FOR GIVING YOU THE JOB JUST BECAUSE YOU ARE A WOMAN...

ALL OF MY QUALIFICATIONS ASIDE, YOU COULD ARGUE THAT WOMEN MAKE BETTER TECHNICAL MANAGERS BECAUSE WE KNOW HOW TO HANDLE LARGE GROUPS OF CHILDREN.
THE JOB IS YOURS. PITR'S FEEDING IS IN TWO HOURS.

HEY, I HEARD YOU'RE OUR TECH MANAGER NOW. CONGRATS.
I'M NOT SURE I SHOULD BE ALL THAT HAPPY ABOUT IT.
Copyright (c) 2000 Illiad http://www.userfriendly.org/

GUESS YOU HEARD ABOUT HAVING TO FEED PITR?
WHAT IS THAT ABOUT?

YOU'LL MAKE A.J. HAPPY. HE DREW THE SHORT STRAW THIS MORNING.
WHAT AM I DELIVERING TO PITR TODAY? PIZZA?

SEE, PITR'S BEEN SEQUESTERED IN THAT OFFICE 24 HOURS A DAY FOR THE PAST WEEK WORKING ON ACCOUNTING CODE. IT'S A CRUNCH PERIOD AND HE'S UNDER THE GUN SO WE TAKE TURNS DELIVERING FOOD TO HIM.
Copyright (c) 2000 Illiad http://www.userfriendly.org/

IT'S ALREADY PAST HIS FEEDING TIME SO YOU'D BETTER HURRY WITH THAT PIZZA...
UM...OKAY. WHICH OFFICE?

GRRRRROOONWWWWWLLLL
YE GODS. WAS THAT HIS STOMACH?!
OH NO... THAT WAS HIM.

MIRANDA. RUN! PITR'S LOOSE!
I KNOW!
FOOOD! GIVINK FOOOOD!

KER-CHUNK

Copyright (c) 2000 Illiad http://www.userfriendly.org/
I FORGOT TO TELL YOU: SEE THAT LINE? THAT'S AS FAR AS HE CAN REACH ON HIS CHAIN. LEAVE THE FOOD THERE.
O...OKAY...
GIVINK ME FOOD OR WILL GNAW THROUGH OWN ANKLE!

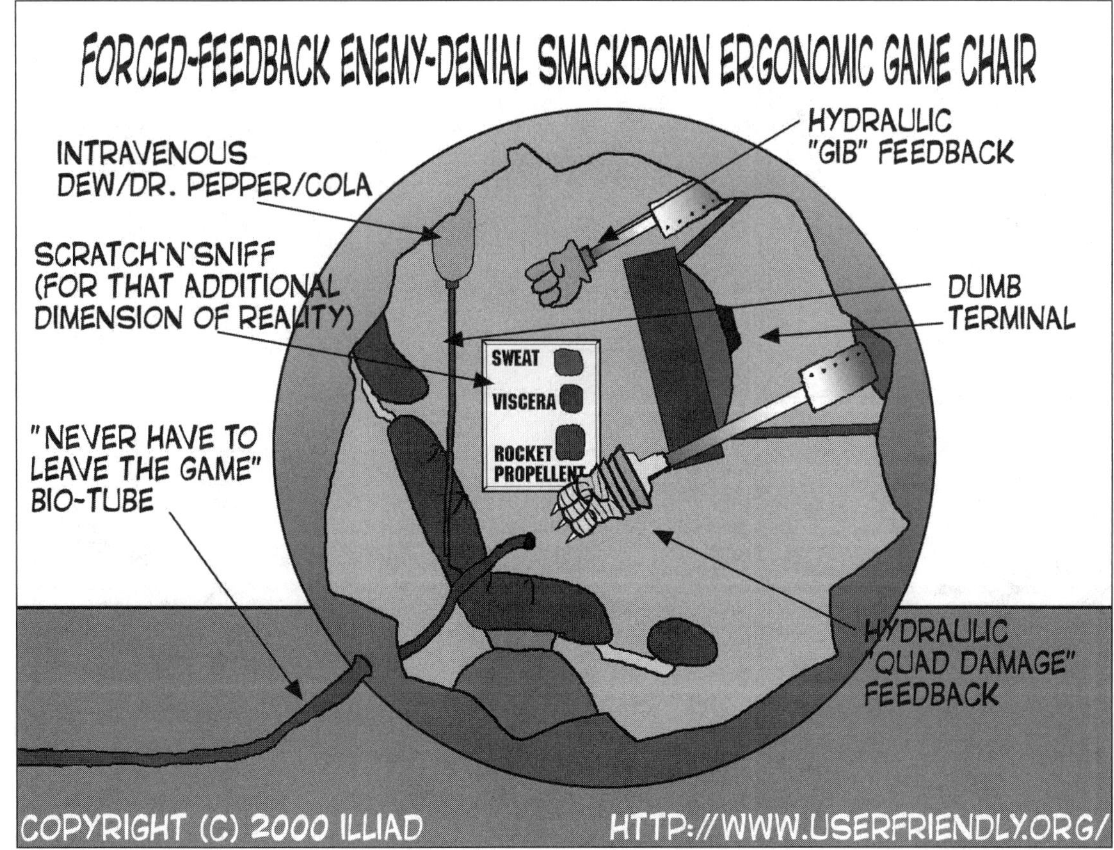
FORCED-FEEDBACK ENEMY-DENIAL SMACKDOWN ERGONOMIC GAME CHAIR
INTRAVENOUS DEW/DR. PEPPER/COLA
HYDRAULIC "GIB" FEEDBACK
SCRATCH'N'SNIFF (FOR THAT ADDITIONAL DIMENSION OF REALITY)
DUMB TERMINAL
SWEAT
VISCERA
ROCKET PROPELLENT
"NEVER HAVE TO LEAVE THE GAME" BIO-TUBE
HYDRAULIC "QUAD DAMAGE" FEEDBACK
COPYRIGHT (C) 2000 ILLIAD
HTTP://WWW.USERFRIENDLY.ORG/

GREAT NEWS, FELLAS. AS YOUR NEW MANAGER, I'D LIKE US TO TAKE SOME TIME TO DO SOME TEAM BUILDING. SO I TALKED TO THE CHIEF AND HE'S AGREED WE CAN TAKE SOME TIME OFF TO GO CAMPING TOGETHER!

CAMPING. YOU KNOW? OUTSIDE? THE BIG BLUE ROOM?
YOU'RE NOT TALKING ABOUT QUAKE, ARE YOU.
OUTSIDE? OUTSIDE WHAT?!
I KNEW A GUY WHO CAMPED ONCE. HE DIED.

LET'S SEE HERE...THE 'HAPPY CAMPER WILDERNESS PARK' IS ONLY ABOUT TWO HOURS OUT. WE'LL NEED A CAMP STOVE, A LANTERN, PROPANE...
GREAT. WE'RE GONNA HAVE TO EAT BARK, AREN'T WE.

AND WE ONLY HAVE TWO TENTS...WELL, I THINK THAT GREG, MIKE AND PITR CAN SHARE ONE AND I'LL SHARE THE OTHER ONE WITH YOU. ARE YOU OKAY WITH THAT?

A.J.? HELLO?
EEP

WE ARE HAVINK EVERYTHINK WITH US, DA?
YEP. GOT MY LAPTOP.
I HAVE THE CATS IN MY PACK...

OKAY. AND I BROUGHT A HUB AND SOME EXTRA...
BOYS! WHERE WE'RE GOING THERE IS NO ELECTRICITY.

AM THINKINK GREGOR IS HAVINK SEIZURE.
WAY TO GO, MIRANDA.
JEEEZ! YOU KNOW BETTER THAN TO JOKE ABOUT STUFF LIKE THAT! IT'S LIKE TELLING CANCER JOKES!
NNNNGG

WOW! IT'S BETTER THAN 1600 BY 1200 RESOLUTION AT 32-BITS OUT HERE!
CAN YOU IMAGINE HOW MANY POLYS THIS AREA MUST TAKE TO RENDER?

HEY. HERE'S A GOOD PLACE FOR THE TENT. THERE'S ONLY ONE WAY IN, SO DEFENSE SHOULD BE EASY.
I HAVE THE F.A.Q. FOR THE TENT IN MY PACK...

A.J., PLEASE TELL ME YOU DON'T THINK LIKE THEY DO.
DAMN SKIPPY I DON'T, MIRANDA. THAT'S A LOUSY PLACE TO SET UP A DEFENSE!

HEY MIKE...THERE'RE SOME LOGS HERE YOU CAN THROW ON TO THE FIRE.
YOU MEAN YOU WANT ME TO "LOG ON"?
Copyright (c) 2000 Illiad http://www.userfriendly.org/

HEH. LET'S NOT START A FLAME WAR. I'M GOING TO GO "SHUT DOWN."
HAHAHA HAHAHA!

HEY! I JUST FOUND A PINE CONE. "PINE." GET IT?
HAHAHA HAHAHA HAHAHA! OH GODS!
I'M BEGINNING TO UNDERSTAND WHY THERE ARE SO MANY AXE MURDERERS IN CAMPING MOVIES.

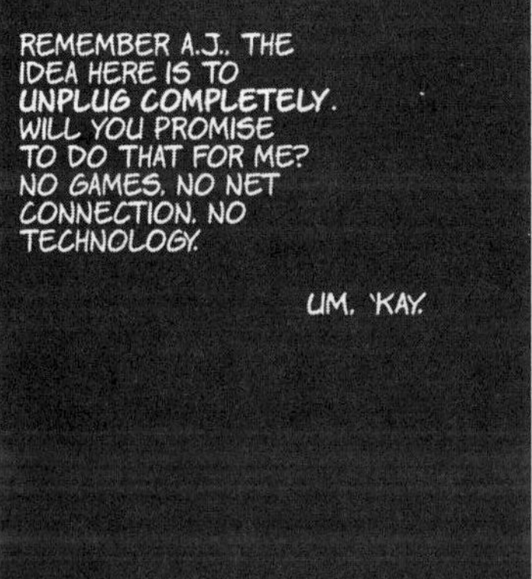
REMEMBER A.J., THE IDEA HERE IS TO UNPLUG COMPLETELY. WILL YOU PROMISE TO DO THAT FOR ME? NO GAMES, NO NET CONNECTION, NO TECHNOLOGY.
UM. 'KAY.
Copyright (c) 2000 Illiad http://www.userfriendly.org/

CLIK
KLIK

THAT INCLUDES SOLITAIRE!
BUT IT'S NOT REALLY A GAME! IT'S MORE LIKE A MENTAL VACATION!
CLICK
VAIO

"REGISTRATION IS FUTILE"
AOL
HTTP://WWW.USERFRIENDLY.ORG/
COPYRIGHT (C) 2000 ILLIAD

This one doesn't age well either. The Borg references aside, AOL and Network Solutions inked a deal in May 2000 to offer users of AOL's properties the ability to register domains via Network Solutions. With the AOL crowd's general lack of knowledge, Network Solutions rapidly became "the" domain registrar to a large swath of the Net-using public.

I CAN'T BELIEVE THIS. I'M ALONE IN A TENT WITH MIRANDA AND I DON'T HAVE THE GUTS TO SAY A WORD TO HER. THIS IS MADDENING.

WHY AM I SUCH A COWARD? SHE HASN'T SAID A WORD TO ME ABOUT THAT EMAIL I SENT HER. I HAVE TO SAY SOMETHING TO HER...BUT I'M TERRIFIED. OKAY. I'LL MAKE A DEAL WITH MYSELF. IF MIRANDA EVER ASKS ME TO TALK, I'LL TELL HER STRAIGHT OUT HOW I FEEL ABOUT HER.
RUSTLE RUSTLE

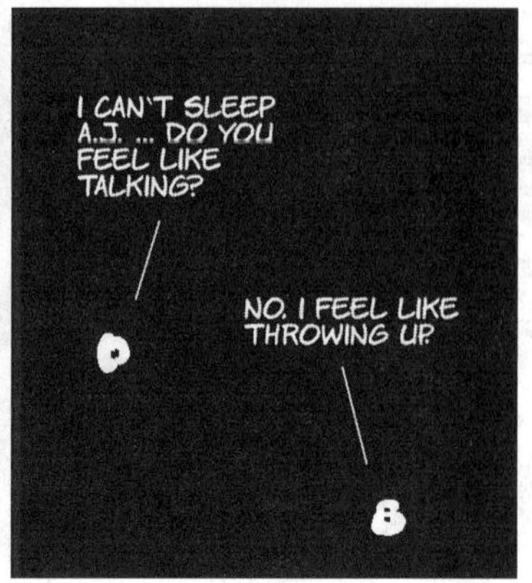
I CAN'T SLEEP A.J. ... DO YOU FEEL LIKE TALKING?
NO. I FEEL LIKE THROWING UP.

NOTHING HAPPENED
WHAT AN INCREDIBLE MORNING! NOTHING LIKE AN EARLY START IN THE GREAT OUTDOORS!

HEY GUYS! WAKE UP! IT'S TIME FOR OUR HIKE!
ZZZZZ..EH?
GO AWAY.
@#!!$*@##!!!$#!

LET THE SUN SHINE IN!
AAAAAAGGGHH!
CLOSE THE BLOODY FLAP! PITR'S MELTING!

I'M WORRIED A.J.. NO ONE'S SEEN DUST PUPPY SINCE EARLY THIS MORNING. HE SAID HE WANTED TO GO HIKING WITH US...

DUST PUPPY! WHERE ARRRE YOOOU?
I'M SURE HE'S FINE. I MEAN, WHAT KIND OF TROUBLE COULD HE GET INTO OUT HERE IN THE WOODS?

GREG, WHY ARE YOU LUGGING ERWIN WITH YOU ON A HIKE? IT'S NO WONDER YOU HAVE TO REST SO OFTEN.
WELL, YOU KNOW HOW WE SERIOUSLY OVERCLOCKED HIS CPU?

OF COURSE. I HELPED.
AND DO YOU REMEMBER THE REALLY SPIFFY HIGH-EFFICIENCY COOLING SYSTEM WE HACKED TOGETHER FOR HIM?

YES. I REM-- YE GODS. YOU DIDN'T!
YUP. D'YOU WANT A DEW OR A COLA?
HEY! YOU TOLD ME THEY WERE "COOLING SUPPOSITORIES"!

I JUST REALIZED... WHERE'S PITR? DIDN'T HE COME WITH US FOR THE HIKE?
HE SAID HE WAS GOING TO FIND SOMETHING TO EAT...THEN WENT INTO THE BUSH.
Copyright (c) 2000 Illiad http://www.userfriendly.org/

WE'D BETTER GO AND FIND HIM! FOR ALL OF PITR'S INTELLIGENCE, HE'S NOT IN HIS ELEMENT OUT HERE...
AND WHEN HE'S HUNGRY HIS JUDGEMENT GOES WAY OFF...

YOU MORON! I TOLD YOU TO USE PROPER BAIT! BUT NOOOOO, YOU WANTED TO SAVE MONEY...
COLD PIZZA. MMMMM...

THAT WAS A GREAT HIKE! WE'RE ALMOST BACK AT THE CAMP, AND BECAUSE YOU GUYS WERE SUCH GOOD SPORTS, I'LL MAKE DINNER. WHATEVER YOU LIKE.
COLA AND DORITOS FOR ME.
Copyright (c) 2000 Illiad http://www.userfriendly.org/

COLA AND DORITOS. I SEE. ANYTHING ELSE?
INSTANT NOODLES WOULD BE NICE.
TRUTH BE TOLD I'M CRAVING SOYLENT PORK RINDS.

AFTER MISSING LONDON LINUX EXPO DUE TO FOOD POISONING, ILLIAD IS "PROTECTED" BY DARK SIDE DAVE WHEN ILLIAD EXPRESSES A DESIRE TO GO ROLLERBLADING JUST BEFORE THE TRIP TO LINUXTAG.
COTTON
HTTP://WWW.USERFRIENDLY.ORG/
COPYRIGHT (C) 2000 ILLIAD

This was real. I was supposed to make an appearance at the London Linux Expo and give a keynote or something, but a few days prior I suffered a bout of food poisoning. Dark Side Dave, our sales guy, had to go alone. When I recovered, I declared that I was going to learn how to rollerblade, and DSD nearly had an aneurysm.

Around the time of this strip, we received a couple of dozen complaints from readers who had figured out how to "read ahead." I usually have a bank of anywhere between 2 to 14 future strips on the server, and apparently someone figured out how to spoof the URL. The complaint was thus: "You have to make the strips harder to find, because I was tempted, and now I have no new UF to read for the next 10 days. Why couldn't you foresee this?!" Right. It was All My Fault because someone had to go digging! Harumph.

HERE I AM ALONE WITH MIRANDA IN A TENT. AND I CAN'T THINK OF WHAT TO SAY TO HER. AND IN THE MORNING WE HEAD BACK IN TO TOWN. WILL I EVER HAVE A CHANCE LIKE THIS AGAIN TO SPEAK TO HER ABOUT HOW I FEEL?
Copyright (c) 2000 Illiad http://www.userfriendly.org/
I DID SEND HER THAT E-MAIL BUT SHE'S NEVER SAID ANYTHING ABOUT IT...AND I ADMIT I'M TERRIFIED OF JUST BRINGING IT UP...IF ONLY SHE'D GIVE ME A SIGN... ANYTHING TO LET ME KNOW...
RUSTLE
RUSTLE

...A SIGN ALONG THE LINES OF AN E-MAIL WOULD'VE BEEN JUST FINE...

OKAY. RELAX. DON'T GET ALL NERVOUS. SHE'S GIVING ME A CHANCE TO MAKE THINGS RIGHT. THIS COULD BE A TURNING POINT IN MY LIFE.
Copyright (c) 2000 Illiad http://www.userfriendly.org/

NOW. UNCLENCHING TEETH. RELAXING LIPS. BREATHING NORMALLY. LEANING FORWARD FOR KISS...

A.J? WHAT ARE YOU DOING?
KLIK!

A.J., I'M TRYING REALLY HARD TO KEEP AN OPEN MIND HERE. SO MAYBE YOU COULD EXPLAIN TO ME WHY YOU WERE JUST ABOUT TO KISS THAT PORCUPINE?
Copyright (c) 2000 Illiad http://www.userfriendly.org/

COULD I EXPLAIN AFTER I'VE HAD A CHANCE TO COME UP WITH SOMETHING?
I'D CALL YOU SPINELESS BUT EVIDENTLY YOU'RE DOING FINE IN THAT DEPARTMENT...

ZZZZZZZ
Copyright (c) 2000 Illiad http://www.userfriendly.org/

A.J?
ZZ..GORK! GUH?

WHY ARE YOU SLEEPING OUT HERE INSTEAD OF IN THE TENT WITH MIRANDA?
UH...MIRANDA SAID IT WAS BECAUSE WE DIDN'T HAVE A COUCH HANDY.

WELL THAT WAS QUITE A TRIP.
DA. WAS WERY INTERESTINK.
YUP. GOOD CALL MIRANDA. GLAD WE WENT.
REALLY?! GREAT! THEN WE SHOULD DO THIS AGAIN SOMETIME?
Copyright (c) 2000 Illiad http://www.userfriendly.org/

HELLO? GUYS?
YEAH...UM. WE'RE JUST THINKING ABOUT WHEN.
I WAS THINKING IN 2006.
DA. WORKINK FOR ME.

I said 2006, and the audience held me to it. Me and my big mouth.

HEY. MIRANDA? HOW DO YOU THINK THEY'RE DOING BACK AT THE OFFICE?
HOW DO YOU MEAN?
Copyright (c) 2000 Illiad http://www.userfriendly.org/

WELL...THEY DIDN'T HAVE ANY TECHS THERE FOR A COUPLE DAYS.
I'M SURE THEY'RE FINE. I'LL BET EVEN STEF IS COPING.

MIKE. I NEED YOU TO GO AHEAD AND INSTALL THOSE ROUTERS FOR THE CUSTOMERS TODAY. GREG. I WANT YOU TO HAVE THAT DATABASE RUNNING IN AN HOUR. A.J.. YOU NEED TO GET THAT NEW PRICE LIST UP ON OUR WEB PAGE...ARE YOU PEOPLE LISTENING TO ME? MIKE? GREG? A.J.? HELLO?! HELLOOO?!

GEEK IN A CAN

DIRECTIONS: POINT NOZZLE AT TECHNICAL PROBLEM AND SPRAY, HOLDING DOWN BUTTON UNTIL CAN IS EMPTY AND GEEK HAS FORMED. GEEK WILL BEGIN SOLVING PROBLEM AND WILL NOT STOP UNTIL SOLUTION HAS BEEN DEVISED. IF GRUNTING OR RUMBLING NOISES ISSUE FORTH FROM GEEK, POUR EQUAL PARTS SALT, SUGAR, STARCH AND CAFFEINE INTO MOST AVAILABLE ORIFICE.

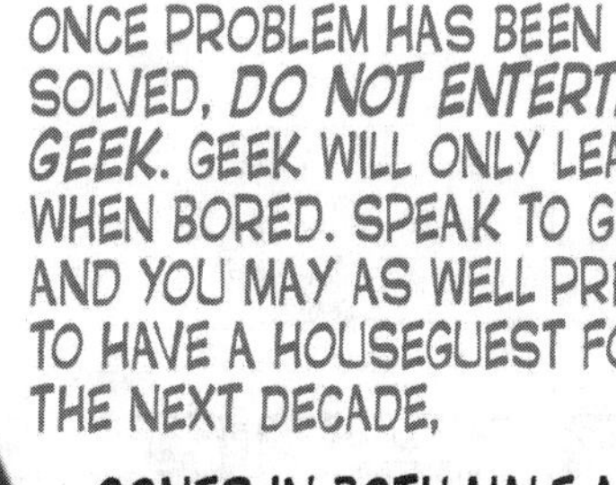
GEEK IN A C

ONCE PROBLEM HAS BEEN SOLVED, *DO NOT ENTERTAIN GEEK*. GEEK WILL ONLY LEAVE WHEN BORED. SPEAK TO GEEK AND YOU MAY AS WELL PREPARE TO HAVE A HOUSEGUEST FOR THE NEXT DECADE.

COMES IN BOTH MALE AND FEMALE FLAVOURS. BOTH GENDERS ARE EQUALLY COMPETENT, HOWEVER MIXING THEM MAY LEAD TO STRANGE BEHAVIOURS IN MALE GEEKS.

HTTP://WWW.USERFRIENDLY.ORG/

CHIEF. ARE YOU SURE THAT WAS WISE TO LET ALL OF THE TECHS GO ON A CAMPING TRIP? I MEAN. WHO'S WATCHING THE MACHINE ROOM?
I GAVE STEF THE TECH PAGER.
Copyright (c) 2000 Illiad http://www.userfriendly.org/

YOU GAVE STEF....THE PAGER THAT REPORTS PROBLEMS IN THE MACHINE ROOM?
OH RELAX. HILLARY. STEF IS UP TO IT.

MAINTENANCE COMPLETED PLEASE PRESS -ENTER- TO CONTINUE.
THERE'S NO WAY I'M UP TO THIS...

I GUESS I HAVE TO DO SOMETHING... I CAN'T BELIEVE I'M IN A POSITION LIKE THIS.
WAITING FOR SOMEONE TO HIT -ENTER-
Copyright (c) 2000 Illiad http://www.userfriendly.org/

PUNCH!
THANK YOU. NOW RESTARTING X. LOADING ADMIN TOOLS...
YE FLIPPING GODS! WHAT HAVE I DONE?

A lot of readers don't guess this one, but it's one of my personal faves. I just love the idea of someone as dignified and crusty as The Chief getting all Avril Lavigne when the office is empty. A closet skater boy. Maybe it was a lot funnier in my head.

ANOTHER DAY AT COLUMBIA INTERNET WITHOUT THE PRESENCE OF GEEKS MEANS ANOTHER DAY WITHOUT THE SOUND OF DOORS OPENING TO NEW AND FABLED WORLDS...
Copyright (c) 2000 Illiad http://www.userfriendly.org/

WOOOSH!
...ALTHOUGH THE SOUND OF A SINGLE CLOSET DOOR OPENING AND CLOSING PUNCTUATES THE STUNNED SILENCE.

CHECK IT OUT. DUDES. METALLICA SUED NAPSTER FOR DISTRIBUTIN' MP3S OF THEIR MUSIC OVER THE NET.
COOL! METALLICA ROCKS. WHO'S NAPSTER?
RIGHT. COOL. WHO'S THIS "ANNETTE?"
Copyright (c) 2000 Illiad http://www.userfriendly.org/

WHAT THAT MEANS IS THAT WE SHOULD SUE THEM TOO. IT'S NOT RIGHT THAT THEY'RE ABLE TO GET AWAY WIF THIS.
RIGHT ON. MATE. I'M WIF YA.
YA. I REALLY WANT TO MEET THIS ANNETTE CHICK.

napster
HEADQUARTERS
WE'RE BEING SUED BY A GROUP CALLED NAUGHTY BISCUIT?!
I'M TALKING TO THEIR LAWYER I THINK. SOME BRITISH GUY WHO KEEPS ASKING ME IF MY NAME IS "ANNETTE."

SO YOU THINK YOUR ALBUM SALES ARE BEING AFFECTED BY NAPSTER. AND YOU WANT ME TO REPRESENT YOU IN THE LAWSUIT?
YAH. WE WANT TO SUE NAPSTER.
YAH. THOSE NAPSACK GUYS REALLY BURN ME, MATE.
Copyright (c) 2000 Illiad http://www.userfriendly.org/
OKAY. WAIT. CAN WE BE CLEAR ON THIS? NAPSTER IS AFFECTING YOUR ALBUM SALES. RIGHT?
IT'S NOT ABOUT MONEY. IT'S ABOUT OUR MUSIC.
YAH, WE HATE THOSE NAPPY-WIPES GUYS.

UNH-HUH. YOU GUYS HAVEN'T SOLD ANY ALBUMS AT ALL. HAVE YOU...
HOW DO YOU EXPECT US TO SELL ALBUMS WHEN ALL OF OUR FANS ARE GETTING OUR MUSIC FOR FREE?
NAPRAP MAY AS WELL OWN MY GUITAR, MATE.

MISTER BISCUIT. ACCORDING TO YOUR COMPLAINT, YOU'RE SUING NAPSTER FOR THREE MILLION DOLLARS AGAINST LOSS OF REVENUES DUE TO PIRACY...
YAH. WE WANT THREE MILLION DOLLARS.

YAH MATE. THOSE ROTTERS WENT AND TOOK ALL OF OUR LIFE'S WORK AND HANDED THE LOT OUT TO EVERYBODY. ALL THAT BLOODY SWEAT. ALL THOSE BLOODY TEARS...AN' ALL THAT BLOODY...BLOOD. FOR NUFFINK.
Copyright (c) 2000 Illiad http://www.userfriendly.org/

IT SAYS HERE YOU RECORDED YOUR ENTIRE ALBUM IN UNDER FOUR HOURS.
AND A GRUELING FOUR HOURS IT WAS, MATE.
WHEN WE GONNA MEET THE CHICKS?

SPY VS. SPY VS. CONSUMER
DONATION
ORACLE
M$
I.D.
COPYRIGHT (C) 2000 ILLIAD
HTTP://WWW.USERFRIENDLY.ORG/

YOUR HONOUR. ACCORDING TO OUR NAPSTER SERVER LOGS. THERE WERE ONLY FOUR ATTEMPTS TO DOWNLOAD AN MP3 OF NAUGHTY BISCUIT'S "LICK THE WOODEN SPOON" IN THE LAST YEAR.

ACTUALLY MATE. THAT WAS MY FRIEND DAVEY WHO TRIED FOUR TIMES TO DOWNLOAD THE BLOODY SONG. ONLY HIS MODEM KEPT ON TIMING OUT...

Copyright (c) 2000 Illiad http://www.userfriendly.org/
CASE DISMISSED!
THAT WAS FAB. MATE. WHERE DO WE PICK UP OUR CHEQUE FOR THREE MIL?
SHUT UP. NIGEL.

MIKE...WHAT ARE YOU DOING?
I'M GETTING READY FOR THE X-MEN MOVIE PREMIERE ON JULY 14TH.
Copyright (c) 2000 Illiad http://www.userfriendly.org/

UH..."GETTING READY" FOR THE PREMIERE?
YA. I'M ORGANIZING A LINE-UP SO WE GET TICKETS TO THE FIRST SHOWING.

OKAY. YOU KNOW THAT THE CINEMA HAS 20 SCREENS AND THEY RUN THE HIT SHOWS 24 HOURS A DAY. RIGHT?
YOU BETCHA. AND THE FOOLS THINK THAT THAT'S ENOUGH. I'M NOT TAKING ANY CHANCES.

HMMM. I WONDER WHERE MIKE'S GONE TO?
Copyright (c) 2000 Illiad http://www.userfriendly.org/

HILLARY. YOU SEEN MIKE?
HE SAID HE WAS TAKING A FEW DAYS OFF TO "DEVELOP HIS INNER CHILD" OR SOMETHING.

CINEMA
TAKE HEED. MUNDANE! I AM A MUTANT!
OH DO TELL.

TICKETS
HEY...LOOKS LIKE THEY'RE SELLING TICKETS FINALLY. TIME TO GET OUT OF THIS TENT...
Copyright (c) 2000 Illiad http://www.userfriendly.org/
TICKETS
YESSS...FIRST IN LINE. I KNEW IT WOULD PAY OFF..

YOUR VERY FIRST X-MEN TICKET PLEASE.
MISTER. THIS IS THE LINE FOR THE TIGGER MOVIE.
AND WHY ARE YOU DRESSED LIKE A DORK?

AT LAST...AFTER FOUR DAYS OF WAITING IN LINE. I HAVE A TICKET TO THE X-MEN MOVIE...
x-men line here
AH
Copyright (c) 2000 Illiad http://www.userfriendly.org/

I SPENT **FOUR DAYS** IN A LEAKY TENT THAT SMELLED LIKE A **PORCUPINE** FOR THIS TICKET! I ATE **BAD** FOOD. DRANK **WEAK** COFFEE AND **DIDN'T HAVE NET ACCESS!** BUT I HAVE A TICKET! **YOU** UNDERSTAND. RIGHT?! **YOU** KNOW WHAT THAT'S LIKE!
x-men line here
AH
THAT TICKET YOU HOLD IS A SYMBOL OF THE TOTAL DEVOTION YOU SHOW AS AN X-MEN FAN. COMMUNE WITH ME, MUTANT, AND SHARE WITH ME HOW LONG YOU WAITED FOR THAT MAGIC PAPER KEY INTO THE CINEMA...
UM, TWENTY MINUTES, ACTUALLY.
x-men line here
AH

An aside: the logo on the other character's sweatshirt is for the now-defunct Avalon Hill game company. The company's remains were bought by Hasbro some years ago. I've been a life-long fan of their products. My gaming nerd is showing!

WORD NOT FOUND
STUPID SPELLCHECKER! "IRREGARDLESS" IS **SO** A REAL WORD! THIS IS SO FRUSTRATING!
Copyright (c) 2000 Illiad http://www.userfriendly.org/

YOU KNOW...I CAN ONLY HELP YOU IF YOU DON'T TURN ME OFF ALL OF THE TIME.
BAMF!
WHA..?!!

OH AND BY THE WAY. "IRREGARDLESS" IS **NOT** A REAL WORD..
AAAAAAAAIIIIIEEE!!

BRITISH COLUMBIA'S MOST WANTED
Marvin the Martian
For making great big earth-shattering "kabooms" and for possession of ray guns.
Wile E. Coyote
For possession and use of high explosives.
Soldier of Fortune
SOLDIER OF FORTUNE
For pretty much the same things.
COPYRIGHT (C) 2000 ILLIAD HTTP://WWW.USERFRIENDLY.ORG/

British Columbia enacted a law that forced the makers of violent video games to label them "for adults only" and also made stores place them where they couldn't be reached by kids. Speaking as a parent, I think that protecting kids is important, but let's be realistic: the old cartoons are awfully violent themselves, and politicians don't seem to have a problem with them.

I THOUGHT TANYA WAS KIDDING. YOU REALLY DO EXIST.
YES AND I'M HERE TO HELP IN ANY WAY I CAN! PLEASE DON'T IGNORE ME...USE ME!
?

THIS ISN'T QUITE WHAT I HAD IN MIND...
OH HUSH. THIS IS THE FIRST TIME IN YOUR LIFE YOU'RE ACTUALLY USEFUL. DEAL.
http://www.userfriendly.org/
Copyright (c) 2000 Illiad

HI! I'M CLIPPY. THE HELPFUL PAPERCLIP! WHO ARE YOU?
DUST PUPPY
http://www.userfriendly.org/
Copyright (c) 2000 Illiad

DUST PUPPY

IF YOU'RE NOT IN MY DICTIONARY YOU'RE NOT IN MY UNIVERSE. WHAT WOULD YOU LIKE TO BE REPLACED WITH?
A.J.!! HELLP!

DON'T WORRY DUST PUPPY. I'M NOT HARMFUL.
IF YOU SAY SO...
http://www.userfriendly.org/
Copyright (c) 2000 Illiad

NO REALLY! I'M ACTUALLY VERY NICE. I JUST WANT TO BE HELPFUL!
SOMEONE CALL FOR HELP? WHAT'S GOING ON?

BUT I GOTTA TELL YA, I SURE DO WISH SOMEONE WOULD TURN ME ON ONCE IN A WHILE.
YOU'RE NOT THE ONLY ONE.

HEY CLIPPY? WE HAVE A PROBLEM WITH GETTING ACCESS TO OUR SERVERS.
REALLY? HOW CAN I HELP?

WHAT DO YOU THINK, PITR?
AM THINKINK HE IS PERFECT.

NEXT TIME, DON'T LOCK THE KEYS IN THE SERVER ROOM...
ANYTHINK ELSE USEFUL TO ADD, COMRADE?
YEEARRRRGH!
RATTLE RATTLE
http://www.userfriendly.org/
Copyright (c) 2000 Illiad

GEEEZ. WHAT ON EARTH HAPPENED TO YOU?
I WAS ABUSED. IF YOU DON'T MIND, I'D RATHER NOT TALK ABOUT IT. PEOPLE AREN'T VERY SENSITIVE AROUND HERE.
CAN'T......RESIST...
BOY. YOU'RE SURE BENT OUT OF SHAPE.
AAAAAUUGGHH!
Copyright (c) 2000 Illiad http://www.userfriendly.org/
HEY A.J.. CHECK IT OUT! I GOT A DOZEN DVDS FOR A BUCK EACH AND ONLY HAVE TO BUY SIX MORE AT LOW CLUB PRICES! I'VE SAVED OVER $200 HERE!
Copyright (c) 2000 Illiad http://www.userfriendly.org/
GREG..YOU DON'T HAVE A DVD PLAYER.
UM...RIGHT. HOW MUCH ARE THEY?
ABOUT $400.
BUT I DON'T HAVE $400. WHAT AM I GOING TO DO?
BUY ANOTHER DOZEN COPIES OF "ISHTAR" FROM THE VIDEO CLUB. YOU'LL HAVE SAVED A TOTAL OF $400. VOILA.

NAYSAYERS OF THE G4 CUBE BACKPEDAL:

DOESN'T HAVE A FAN

Apple's detractors really laid it on the G4 Cube. I've always loved the things. Sexy and cute, kind of like a Playboy bunny!

NICE DVD PLAYER, DUDE. I KNOW YOU'RE MORE USED TO THE IDEA OF HAVING ONE IN YOUR MACHINE, BUT THIS IS BETTER. NOW WE JUST HAVE TO HOOK IT UP TO A TELEVISION SET.
HOOK IT UP TO A WHAT?
Copyright (c) 2000 Illiad http://www.userfriendly.org/

YOU KNOW...IT LOOKS LIKE A MONITOR WITHOUT A KEYBOARD? USUALLY HAS CO-AX RUNNING INTO IT? WHERE ALL THE DOT COMS BUY THEIR AUDIENCE?
OH THAT THING. WHY DIDN'T YOU SAY SO?

OKAY, IT'S ALL SET UP. GET THE BEST DVD YOU BOUGHT FROM THAT CLUB. WHATEVER HAS THE MOST EFFECTS.
OKAY...AH, THIS ONE!
THAT ONE SHOULD DO THE TRICK.

THE DIRECTOR'S CUT WIDESCREEN VERSION PILOT EPISODE OF THE "PARTRIDGE FAMILY"?!
SURE...WITH THE HOUR OF SONGS THEY DID THAT NEVER MADE IT ON SCREEN...
Copyright (c) 2000 Illiad http://www.userfriendly.org/

SCOOBY? WHERE'S SHAGGY?
I CAN'T BELIEVE YOU GUYS WOULD WASTE TIME WATCHING A DVD OF OLD SCOOBY DOO EPISODES. I GUESS IT'S TRUE ABOUT INNOCENTS BEING CLUELESS.

RUH ROH!
SO WAS I RIGHT OR WHAT?
YEP. I HAVE TO ADMIT, VELMA'S HOT.
Copyright (c) 2000 Illiad http://www.userfriendly.org/

If you don't get this one, think about who, other than the Scooby gang, are cartoon characters in the strip ...

THAT'S INCREDIBLE! IT WAS THE GARDENER ALL ALONG!
YOU NOTICE SOMETHING? SCOOBY NEVER, YOU KNOW, CLEANS HIMSELF.
HE'S A CARTOON CHARACTER YOU DOLT. THEY NEVER CLEAN THEMSELVES.
AND I WOULD'VE GOTTEN AWAY WITH IT TOO IF IT WASN'T FOR YOU DARNED KIDS!

NOT THAT I'M IMPLYING CARTOON CHARACTERS SHOULD CLEAN THEMSELVES LIKE A DOG WOULD...
ROH ROT RAGAIN!
NO, OF COURSE NOT. SAY, WANT TO WATCH "THE SOUND OF MUSIC" INSTEAD?
Copyright (c) 2000 Illiad http://www.userfriendly.org/

HOT NEW MONEY MAKER! THOUSANDS OF WAYS TO HOSE THE ELDERLY! BLAH BLAH BLAH...
GRRRRRRRRRR! AM HATINK SPAM. HATINK. HATINK. HATINK IT!
Copyright (c) 2000 Illiad http://www.userfriendly.org/

AHHHHH! SPAM SERVER IS NOT SECURE. TEACHINK THEM NOW NOT TO BE MESSINK WITH ME...
RAPPITY TAPPITY

[spamgod@spambox]$ su
su: user root does not exist
SPAMCEN
"We annoy
for mone
SPECI
SUMM
RATE

HI! I HOPE YOU REMEMBER ME! COME BY MY NEW WEBSITE AND CHECK OUT BLAH BLAH BLAH...
MORE SPAM FROM SAME PLACE. THEY ARE NOT LEARNINK LESSON...
Copyright (c) 2000 Illiad http://www.userfriendly.org/

THIS TIME WILL SENDINK PERSONAL NOTE WITH LESSON. SHOULD TEACHINK THEM PROPERLY.
TIK KAK
HERE'S THE E-MAIL. IT SAYS: "HELLO. I DO INDEED REMEMBER YOU AND SO I VISITED YOUR WEBSITE AND REDIRECTED ALL OF YOUR ROUTING TO THE PLANET MARS. LOVE, DMITRI."
BUT MARS DOESN'T HAVE ANY ROUT...OH.

So vinyl isn't really obsolete. I was severely LARTed by a bunch of audiophiles for this strip. Then I went out and bought a vinyl audiophile-version of The Alan Parsons Project album *Eye in the Sky*. Now all I need is a turntable.

OBSOLESCENCE IN THE MUSIC INDUSTRY

REEL-TO-REEL TAPE

ABBA

8-TRACK TAPE

VINYL LPS

riaa

MAJOR RECORD LABELS

CHIEF. AM NEEDINK TO TELL YOU. AM THINKINK THE ROT. IT HAS SPREAD TOO FAR. COMPANIES SENDINK SPAM FROM LINUX MACHINES. AM TO BE FIXINK THIS PROBLEM BY BUILDINK VISUAL BASIC SCRIPT SUPPORT IN TO LINUX EMAIL PROGRAMS.
Copyright (c) 2000 Illiad http://www.userfriendly.org/

UM...IS THAT GOOD?
IS GOOD. LIKE ROCK SALT ON SLUGS KIND OF GOOD.

This is a famous meme on Slashdot. It was fun back then. Today ... not so much.

PITR. I HEARD A RUMOUR THAT YOU WERE DEVELOPING VBS SUPPORT FOR A HANDFUL OF LINUX E-MAIL APPS. ARE THE STORIES TRUE?
DA.
TYPE CODE
Copyright (c) 2000 Illiad http://www.userfriendly.org/

BUT HOW CAN YOU EXPECT PEOPLE WILL DOWNLOAD AND INSTALL YOUR PATCHES? I CAN'T THINK OF A SOUL WHO RUNS LINUX THAT WOULD WANT TO HAVE VBS SUPPORT AND BE SUSCEPTIBLE TO WINDOWS MACRO VIRUSES.

AM DISGUISING PATCH AS MOVIE OF NATALIE PORTMAN. NAKED AND PETRIFIED.
OH THAT'S FAIR.

YOU'RE REALLY GOING AHEAD WITH THIS. AREN'T YOU. YOU'RE GOING TO DESTROY THE SANCTITY OF LINUX E-MAIL APPS THE WORLD OVER.
Copyright (c) 2000 Illiad http://www.userfriendly.org/

YOU DO REALIZE THAT YOU'LL BE AFFECTING EVERYONE WITH THIS. RIGHT? NOT JUST THE LINUX-BASED SPAMMERS. BUT EVEN THE INNOCENTS?
TAP TIP

COMRADE. THERE ARE NO INNOCENTS IN A WORLD WITH THE F.B.I. AND CARNIVORE.
CODE JUSTIFY CODE

AM FINISHED VBS SUPPORT FOR LINUX. ONLY NEEDINK TO HIT KEY TO MAKE FILE PUBLIC. AND SOON ALMOST ALL LINUX BOXEN WILL BE FALLINK TO WINDOWS VIRUSES.
Copyright (c) 2000 Illiad http://www.userfriendly.org/

ALL EVIL LINUX SPAMMERS WILL BE HURTINK. BUT MIKHAIL SAYINK EVEN NICE LINUX PEOPLE BEINK HURT. AM ABLE TO CRUSHINK THOUSANDS OF ANNOYINK SPAMMERS AT COST OF MILLIONS OF LINUX USERS. AM THINKINK IS MAYBE NOT WORTH IT.

SOMETIMES AM CRACKINK MYSELF UP..
SPANKING FACILITATOR NOW AVAILABLE FOR DOWNLOAD!
THWAP

AS THE WORLD RISES AGAIN FOR YET ANOTHER DAY OF PRODUCTIVITY, AS THE SUN STROLLS IN WITH THE FAIR LIGHT OF MORNING, A DARK SHADOW REVEALS ITSELF...
Copyright (c) 2000 Illiad http://www.userfriendly.org/

THE SHADOW QUIETLY CLOAKS ITSELF OVER THE MANTLE OF THE ENTIRE LINUX COMMUNITY, RAPIDLY WRITING BAD DATA AS IT SPREADS LIKE A COFFEE STAIN ON A BRAND NEW T-SHIRT...
WHAT THE...

...AND A HORDE OF UNWARY LINUX USERS PROVE REPEATEDLY THROUGHOUT THE DAY THAT THE SMALLEST SOUNDS CAN COME FROM THE LARGEST OPENINGS...
HE'S BEEN SITTING IN FRONT OF HIS SCREEN LIKE THAT ALL MORNING...
THIS IS BAD.
ECK

A.J., DID YOU HEAR ABOUT THE LINUX E-MAIL APP SABOTAGE? LOOKS LIKE GREG'S MACHINE GOT HIT. THIS WHOLE THING IS PRETTY SCARY.
MM-HM.

NEAR AS I CAN FIGURE IT, ANYONE WHO OPENED UP THE "NAUGHTILY PORTMAN" FILE ON A LINUX BOX GOT INFECTED WITH VBS SUPPORT AND ARE NOW SUBJECT TO VB SCRIPT VIRUSES AND WORMS. SO... ...I KINDA WANTED TO ASK. DID YOU UMM...GET INFECTED?
NOPE.

Copyright (c) 2000 Illiad http://www.userfriendly.org/
WHAT A SWEET GUY... HE WASN'T TEMPTED BY NATALIE PORTMAN. THERE'S HOPE FOR HIM YET.
I'M RUNNING BEOS SO I HAD TO OPEN IT ON YOUR MACHINE. THE VIDEO WAS HARDLY "NAUGHTY"

BRITISH GOVERNMENT OPERATIONS MANUAL

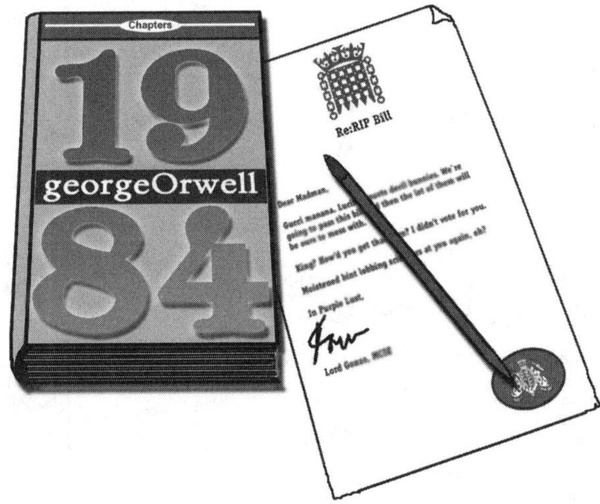
Chapters
19
georgeOrwell
84
Re:RIP Bill

COPYRIGHT (C) 2000 ILLIAD HTTP://WWW.USERFRIENDLY.ORG/

Linux geeks take pride in a dearth of viruses that can affect their systems. This is a weakness ...

If you pay any attention at all to human rights, you know that of all Western nations, the U.K. seems to have the most authoritarian laws, and that slide down the slippery slope doesn't seem to be slowing much. At the time, the Regulatory Investigatory Powers (RIP) Bill wished to introduce the following: "A Bill to make provision for and about the interception of communications, the acquisition and disclosure of data relating to communications, the carrying out of surveillance, the use of covert human intelligence sources and the acquisition of the means by which electronic data protected by encryption or passwords may be decrypted or accessed; to provide for the establishment of a tribunal with jurisdiction in relation to those matters, to entries on and interferences with property or with wireless telegraphy and to the carrying out of their functions by the Security Service, the Secret Intelligence Service and the Government Communications Headquarters; and for connected purposes." And this is before 9/11.

YE FLIPPING GODS. WHAT HAVE I DONE TO MY POOR LINUX BOX...
OWWWWW...
Copyright (c) 2000 Illiad http://www.userfriendly.org/

I CAN'T BELIEVE I GOT SUCKERED. I'VE LOST GIGS OF DATA. FILES HAVE BEEN CORRUPTED. IT'LL TAKE ME DAYS TO RESTORE THINGS TO THE WAY THEY WERE.

I CAN'T BELIEVE THAT IT'S COME TO THIS. LINUX...IS...TAINTED.
WHICH I'VE BEEN TELLING YOU SINCE DAY ONE.
BAMF!

BEFORE YOU SAY ANYTHING, I'LL ADMIT THAT YES, I SHOULD HAVE BEEN SMARTER AND NOT OPENED A FILE I KNEW NOTHING ABOUT. SO I GOT NAILED. I ALSO ADMIT THAT IF I WAS RUNNING BSD I WOULDN'T HAVE NEEDED TO BE SMART.
Copyright (c) 2000 Illiad http://www.userfriendly.org/

WELL, I'M GLAD YOU'RE FINALLY...

HEY!!
OH RELAX. YOU SHOULD BE USED TO IT BY NOW.

LOOK. ALL KIDDING ASIDE, I DON'T GET WHAT YOUR BEEF IS. IT'S NOT EASY BEING THE UP-AND-COMING OPERATING SYSTEM. SURE, LINUX GETS MOST OF THE SPOTLIGHT. BUT THERE ARE HUGE DOWNSIDES AS WELL YOU KNOW...
NAME ONE.
Copyright (c) 2000 Illiad http://www.userfriendly.org/

HOW ABOUT FRED MOODY?
THAT'S JUST SOMEONE HATING YOU FOR YOUR SUCCESS. TRY AGAIN.

LOOK, LET'S BE REASONABLE HERE. YOUR MACHINE IS HOSED AND YOU'RE GOING TO HAVE TO PERFORM A RE-INSTALL ANYWAY. SO..YOU MAY AS WELL TRY AN OS THAT DOESN'T HAVE SUCH A GREAT BIG WHACKING SECURITY HOLE IN IT...
Copyright (c) 2000 Illiad http://www.userfriendly.org/

AND YOU THINK I SHOULD INSTALL FREEBSD. WHY NOT OPENBSD OR EVEN NETBSD? AREN'T THE OTHERS MORE SECURE?

HECK, NO. OPENBSD IS WIDE "OPEN" TO ATTACKS WHEREAS NETBSD HAS BIG HOLES BETWEEN THE STRINGS, LIKE ANY NET. SEE HOW THAT WORKS?
YOU SURE YOU AREN'T THE LITTLE MAN WHO SITS INSIDE OF STEF'S HEAD AND STEERS HIM AROUND?

SINCE IT'S OBVIOUS THAT YOUR OTHER CHOICES ARE PLAIN SILLY. YOU MAY AS WELL START INSTALLING FREEBSD ON YOUR MACHINE.
Copyright (c) 2000 Illiad http://www.userfriendly.org/

LOOK. WHAT ARE YOU GETTING OUT OF THIS? I GET A NEW OPERATING SYSTEM FOR FREE. AND YOU GET WHAT. A COMMISSION?

COMMISSION?! THAT'S RUDE!
NOT TO MENTION IMPRACTICAL. SOULS DON'T PORTION UP EASILY.
POP!

OKAY. I'VE STARTED THE TRANSFER OF FREEBSD.
SO NOW WE JUST WAIT A BIT AND SOON YOU'LL BE RUNNING THE FINEST OS IN EXISTENCE.
Copyright (c) 2000 Illiad http://www.userfriendly.org/

GREG? I JUST WROTE THE FIX FOR THAT VBS WORM. IT'S PROPAGATING NOW. JUST THOUGHT I SHOULD LET YOU KNOW.

COOL! I'M RE-INSTALLING LINUX.
NOOOOOOO!
YOU LET ONE SLIP AWAY? THE "BIG D" WANTS TO SEE YOU.

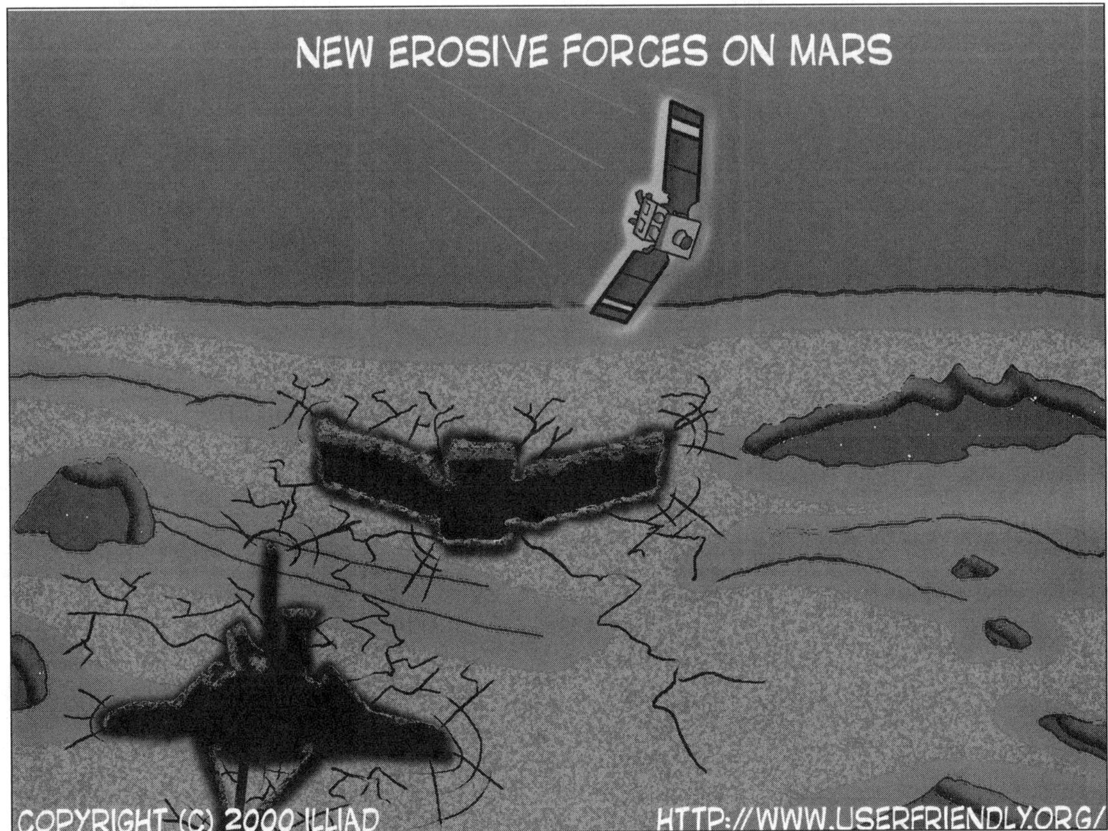
NEW EROSIVE FORCES ON MARS
COPYRIGHT (C) 2000 ILLIAD
HTTP://WWW.USERFRIENDLY.ORG/

ELEVEN BOTS AND ME AGAINST A.J. ... I HAVE GOT TO BE ABLE TO WIN A GAME OF QUAKE THIS TIME AROUND...
BLAM
BLAM
http://www.userfriendly.org/
Copyright (c) 2000 Illiad

YEEEEAAAAAAAAARRRR RRRRRRRRRRGGGGH!!

I MUST HAVE GOTTEN A.J.! AFTER ALL THIS TIME, I GOT HIM! I GOT HIM! HAHAHAHAHAHAHA!
ACTUALLY, HE JUST GOT A REALLY BAD HAND CRAMP.

MIKE? IS A.J. OKAY? I HEARD HE WENT TO THE HOSPITAL.
YES, HE'S FINE. THAT HAND CRAMP TURNED OUT TO BE A REALLY BAD CASE OF CARPAL TUNNEL SYNDROME.

CARPAL TUNNEL? WILL THIS AFFECT HIS ABILITY TO WORK? HIS SKILLS ARE CRITICAL TO OUR REVENUE STREAM RIGHT NOW...

OH, DON'T WORRY. THE SMILING MAN SPARED NO EXPENSE IN GETTING A.J. SOME GEL SUPPORTS FOR HIS WRISTS AND STUFF.

http://www.userfriendly.org/
Copyright (c) 2000 Illiad
UM...HELLO? COULD SOMEONE PLEASE HELP ME?
ERGO-GEL
ERGO-GEL

A.J.? YOU CALLED?
I KNOW THIS IS A WEIRD THING TO SAY, BUT I NEED YOU.
ERGO-GEL
http://www.userfriendly.org/
Copyright (c) 2000 Illiad

ERGO-GEL

A.J....ARE YOU FINALLY TRYING TO EXPRESS WHAT I THINK YOU'RE TRYING TO EXPRESS?
THE CREVICE BETWEEN MY LEFT BIG TOE AND LEFT SECOND TOE ITCHES.
ERGO-GEL

AH, SO YOU WANT ME TO SCRATCH AN ITCH FOR YOU, IS THAT IT?
YES.
ERGO-GEL
http://www.userfriendly.org/
Copyright (c) 2000 Illiad

OH, I SEE WHERE THIS IS GOING. FIRST IT'S AN ITCH, THEN YOU'LL WANT A FOOTRUB, THEN I'LL BE COOKING AND FINALLY I'LL BE CLEANING THE WHOLE HOUSE!
ERGO-GEL

WELL YOU CAN FORGET IT! I'M NOT GOING DOWN THAT PATH!
WOULD SOMEONE PLEASE JUST SCRATCH ME?!
ERGO-GEL

HA! A.J.'S IMMOBILIZED. WHICH MAKES THIS A PERFECT OPPORTUNITY TO GIVE HIM A SERIOUS MANBEATING IN QUAKE.
BLAM
HUH!
WOOSH!
http://www.userfriendly.org/
Copyright (c) 2000 Illiad

WHA...HEY!! HE GOT ME! HOW DOES HE DO THAT?!
KA-BLORT!
TIK
TAK
TIK
DIK
ERGO-GEL
ERGO-GEL

GREG? COULD YOU PLEASE TALK TO THIS GUY ON LINE THREE? IT'S BEEN A LONG DAY AND HE'S GETTING UNDER MY SKIN.
SURE, MIRANDA. WHAT'S THE PROBLEM?
http://www.userfriendly.org/
Copyright (c) 2000 Illiad

HE HAS THESE QUADROPHONIC SPEAKERS BUT HAS THEM REVERSED SO SOUNDS ARE COMING FROM THE WRONG DIRECTION. AND HE REFUSES TO MOVE THEM BECAUSE HE SAYS THEY'RE PLACED "JUST SO."
HMM..OKAY. HELLO? GREG HERE.
FINALLY! I WANT THIS FIXED NOW!

PLEASE RELAX SIR. IT'S A COMMON PROBLEM. JUST TURN YOUR DESK AROUND 180 DEGREES.
HEY..YOU'RE PRETTY SMART.

WHY MESSAGE-BOARD TROLLS SEEM ANONYMOUS AND FACELESS...
IT SURE IS DARK IN HERE, BUT WHAT THE HELL, IT SEEMS LIKE HOME...
HTTP://WWW.USERFRIENDLY.ORG/
COPYRIGHT (C) 2000 ILLIAD

NIGHT SHIFT IS BORING. MAYBE I SHOULD HIT IRC... IT'S BEEN A WHILE.
Copyright (c) 2000 Illiad http://www.userfriendly.org/

MIRANDA_X HAS JOINED #TECHWARRIORS
(PIGBIRD) HEY MIRANDA, R U FEMALE?
(TROPE) HOW OLD ARE YOU HONEY?
(Z33K) I HAVE A BIG PIPE!
(URLYBIRD) HEY HOT MOMMA

(MIRANDA_X) I'M A GUY.
(TROPE) SICKO. GET OUTTA HERE.
(Z33K) I'M TELLING THE AUTHORITIES THAT YOU'RE TROLLING FOR TROUBLE.
(PIGBIRD) IRC IS GOING TO HELL IN A HANDBASKET THESE DAYS.
TAKKA
TAKKA
TAKKA

WELL THIS WAS A BIG MISTAKE...ALL OF THE TECH CHANNELS ARE FILLED WITH SCRIPT KIDDIES..YUCK.
Copyright (c) 2000 Illiad http://www.userfriendly.org/

MIRANDA_X HAS JOINED #AMOUR
HMMM...I WONDER WHAT THIS CHANNEL IS...

(JEAN_CLAUDE) BONSOIR, MON CHOU. COMMENT CA VA?
(MIRANDA_X) I AM SO FEMALE.
TAPPY
RAPPY
TAPPA

HEY, A.J.?
MM-HM?
I'M WATCHING MIRANDA IN IRC WITH SOME FRENCH GUY.
Copyright (c) 2000 Illiad http://www.userfriendly.org/

YEAH. RIGHT.
NO. REALLY. THEY'VE BEEN AT IT FOR A WHILE NOW.

THAT'S FUNNY. MIRANDA DOESN'T SPEAK FRENCH...
OH I THINK WHAT SHE'S DOING IN IRC IS FRENCH ALL RIGHT.

ERWIN, IT'S NOT NICE TO SPY ON PEOPLE. I'M SURE MIRANDA WOULDN'T BE HAPPY IF SHE LEARNED YOU WERE EAVESDROPPING.
IF YOU SAY SO.
Copyright (c) 2000 Illiad http://www.userfriendly.org/

BUT TECHNICALLY, SINCE YOU ALREADY HAVE THE INFORMATION, YOU COULD JUST MAKE IT OPEN AND BECOME AUTOMATICALLY ETHICALLY SUPERIOR.
ALREADY MAILED YOU A COPY.

YOU READING THE CHAT LOG NOW?
YES. GIMME A SEC...
Copyright (c) 2000 Illiad http://www.userfriendly.org/

YOU SURE THIS ISN'T THE WALKTHROUGH FOR "LEISURE SUIT LARRY"?
NOW THAT'S A GAME YOU NEED TO PLAY.

I CAN'T UNDERSTAND MOST OF WHAT THIS JEAN CLAUDE GUY IS SAYING.
YOU COULD RUN THE LOG THROUGH BABELFISH.
Copyright (c) 2000 Illiad http://www.userfriendly.org/

OKAY...
RAPPY TAPPY WAP TAP

"CANDY ME TO YOU IDIOTIC. I HAVE SWEATY FOR YOU."
ARE YOU GONNA LET HIM GET AWAY WITH THAT?

Try using babelfish when you're drunk. You'll either laugh hysterically or actually understand what comes out.

SONY DEVELOPS TECHNOLOGY THAT TRANCENDS THE INDIVIDUAL USER

PlayStation 2
$599
with FREE!
Leg Shackle
PS2

COPYRIGHT (C) 2000 ILLIAD HTTP://WWW.USERFRIENDLY.ORG/

I CAN'T LET THIS GO ON...MIRANDA WILL GET INTERESTED IN THIS OTHER GUY.
GO. TALK TO HER.
Copyright (c) 2000 Illiad http://www.userfriendly.org/

I'LL JUST MESSAGE HER PRIVATELY AND SAY TO HER IN ENGLISH WHAT HE'S SAYING TO HER IN FRENCH. I KNOW A BIT OF FRENCH. LIKE THIS BIT HERE: "JE T'EMBRASSE SUR MON LIT."

(*AJ) I AM EMBARASSED BY YOUR MOON LAMP.

Male geeks around the world cheered at this.

THIS IS STUPID. I'M FEELING GUILTY OVER A HARMLESS FLIRTATIOUS CHAT SESSION. I MEAN, IT'S NOT LIKE A.J. IS PAYING ANY ATTENTION TO ME ANYWAYS...
Copyright (c) 2000 Illiad http://www.userfriendly.org/

NO ONE WOULD BLAME ME FOR KEEPING MY OPTIONS OPEN. AFTER ALL, A.J. IS CLUELESS, OBTUSE, WEIRD, ECCENTRIC, CLUMSY, MYOPIC, IMMATURE, AND A SOCIAL FAILURE. IN FACT, HE'S THE SORRIEST EXCUSE FOR A GUY I'VE EVER SEEN.

MIRANDA? GOT A SECOND?
SO WHY OH WHY DO I FIND HIM SO INCREDIBLY ATTRACTIVE?

MIRANDA...I JUST WANTED TO TALK TO YOU FOR A BIT. I'VE BEEN THINKING A LOT ABOUT YOU AND ME, AND...WELL, THIS IS REALLY HARD TO SAY.
Copyright (c) 2000 Illiad http://www.userfriendly.org/

I KNOW I PROBABLY STEPPED OVER THE LINE WHEN I SENT YOU THAT E-MAIL TELLING YOU HOW I FELT, BUT WHAT I WROTE I WROTE WITH HONESTY. I JUST HOPE YOU WON'T HOLD IT AGAINST ME.

E-MAIL? A.J., WHAT ARE YOU TALKING ABOUT?
I SCREWED UP AGAIN, DIDN'T I! I JUST DON'T KNOW HOW TO COMMUNICATE!

A.J., I HAVE TO CONFESS SOMETHING. I FLIRTED WITH A COMPLETE STRANGER TONIGHT IN IRC, AND I FEEL AWFUL ABOUT IT. IF THERE'S ANYTHING I LEARNED, IT'S THAT I REALLY LIKE YOU. JUST THE WAY YOU ARE.
Copyright (c) 2000 Illiad http://www.userfriendly.org/

HEH...UH. THANKS.
COULD YOU REPEAT THAT, EXCEPT THIS TIME SAY "MERCI" ?

YOU WANT ME TO SPEAK IN FRENCH? BUT...I THOUGHT YOU LIKED ME JUST THE WAY I AM...
OF COURSE I DO, SILLY.
Copyright (c) 2000 Illiad http://www.userfriendly.org/

WELL...UM. THAT'S GOOD..
SO DOES THE "J" IN YOUR NAME STAND FOR JEAN OR SOME OTHER FRENCH NAME?

A.J.? WHY ARE YOU SO SAD?
I THINK I'VE LOST MIRANDA TO SOME GUY IN I.R.C.
Copyright (c) 2000 Illiad http://www.userfriendly.org/

SHE KEEPS GOING ON ABOUT THIS FRENCH THING. I GUESS SHE HAS A WEAKNESS FOR FOREIGN LANGUAGES.

SURE. THEN DOLT-BOY HERE TRIES TO BE SMART AND WOOS HER WITH "OO-YAY AKE-MAY EE-MAY OTT-HAY."
LOOK, IF THE ROMANS DID IT...
UH OH.

USER
FRIENDLY
the comic strip
PIZZA
Portrasher 4
ROTO-ROUTER 800
Copyright (c) 1997-2000 Illiad

OKAY PEOPLE! TAKE ONE OF THE GEEK PUBLIC SERVICE ANNOUNCEMENT AS TOLD BY THE POINTY HEADED BOSS.

'SCUSE ME. ISN'T THAT SUPPOSED TO BE "POINTY HAIRED BOSS?"
NO, WE GOT IT RIGHT. ACTION!

HELLO! ARE YOU A CHIEF OFFICER OR SENIOR V.P. OF A HI-TECH FIRM? DO YOU HAVE MISSION CRITICAL DEPLOYMENT ISSUES IN YOUR COMPANY ON A WEEKLY OR EVEN DAILY BASIS, BUT DON'T KNOW WHERE TO TURN? WELL, I'M HERE TO TELL YOU YOUR ANSWER IS RIGHT IN FRONT OF YOU.

THAT'S RIGHT, YOUR GEEKS! THESE INVALUABLE KNOWLEDGE WORKERS HAVE WHAT IT TAKES TO MAKE THE BIG TECHNOLOGY-RELATED BUSINESS DECISIONS YOU HAVE NIGHTMARES ABOUT! NOT ONLY DO THEY KNOW THEIR STUFF, THEY MAKE THEIR CHOICES PAINSTAKINGLY AND CAREFULLY.

SO BEFORE YOU BLOW YOUR BUDGET ON HARDWARE OR SOFTWARE, GO TALK TO YOUR GEEKS. THEIR SENSE CAN SAVE YOU DOLLARS! HA HA HA! WHY, EVEN NOW MY GEEKS ARE CAREFULLY DECIDING WHICH ROUTER VENDOR WE SHOULD SPEND SIX FIGURES ON...
THEY'RE PLAYING ROCK-PAPER-SCISSORS.

STEF, HAVE YOU SEEN A.J. TODAY?
YEAH. HE WAS SAD OVER SOMETHING TO DO WITH MIRANDA AND WANTED TO GO TO A BAR AND GET **DRUNK.**
http://www.userfriendly.org/
Copyright (c) 2000 Illiad

DRUNK?! A.J. DOESN'T KNOW ANYTHING ABOUT GETTING **DRUNK!**
OH DON'T **WORRY.** I GAVE HIM SOME POINTERS.
UM...HI. I WAS TOLD THAT THIS WAS A GOOD PLACE TO GO IF I WANTED TO GET "HAMMERED?"

WHAT'LL YOU HAVE?
SOMETHING THAT WILL PURGE MY INNER CHILD OF ITS PAINS.

ALL OUT OF JOLT COLA. WANT SOME MORPHINE INSTEAD?
MAKE IT A DOUBLE. NEAT.
http://www.userfriendly.org/
Copyright (c) 2000 Illiad

I DON'T UNDERSTAND WOMEN. SHE GETS **MAD** AT ME FOR NOT TALKING TO HER ABOUT HOW I **FEEL.** AND THEN WHEN I WRITE HER A **LOVE LETTER,** SHE IGNORES ME AND GOES FOR SOME **FRENCH** GUY IN I.R.C.
http://www.userfriendly.org/
Copyright (c) 2000 Illiad

I MAY AS WELL FACE IT. I'M NOT EVER GOING TO HAVE A RELATIONSHIP WITH MIRANDA. I MAY AS WELL SET MY SIGHTS ON SOMETHING A LITTLE MORE REALISTIC...

HERE'S TO DANCING WITH THE WIGGLING HULA GIRL THAT I WILL SOMEDAY AFFIX TO MY CAR.
I'LL FIND HIM SOME PORN.
OKAY.

Male geeks around the world agreed with this.

CHEER UP A.J.. THE WHOLE WORLD IS YOURS NOW. TRY MEETING SOME OTHER WOMEN...LIKE THIS BABE WALKING TOWARDS US RIGHT NOW!
UM... 'KAY.
http://www.userfriendly.org/
Copyright (c) 2000 Illiad

YOU **IDIOT!!**
WHAT?! SHE DIDN'T SAY A **WORD** TO ME!
SHLOOOP

I DON'T KNOW ABOUT THIS. I CAN BARELY START SPEAKING TO WOMEN THAT I **KNOW** MUCH LESS A STRANGER.
YOU MIGHT NOT HAVE TO. THAT BABE OVER THERE'S BEEN LOOKING OVER HERE FOR THE LAST LITTLE WHILE.
Copyright (c) 2000 Illiad http://www.userfriendly.org/

LOOK SHARP! HERE SHE COMES!
OH YE FLIPPING **GODS.**

HI...I DON'T MEAN TO INTERRUPT. BUT...AREN'T YOU **BIG BLUE?**
UH...

LISTEN...MY FRIEND A.J. HERE WOULD LIKE TO SAY SOMETHING TO YOU.
SURE!
Copyright (c) 2000 Illiad http://www.userfriendly.org/

I'M SORRY...IS YOUR FRIEND A **MIME?**
ONLY IN THAT WE WANT TO **KILL** HIM.
GEK!

USER
FRIENDLY
the comic strip
PIZZA
Portrasher 4
ROTO-ROUTER 800
Copyright (c) 1997-2000 Illiad

STAY ON THE AIR. I HAVE SOMETHING TO SAY TO YOUR AUDIENCE ABOUT THEIR RIGHTS AS ONLINE CITIZENS.

YOU'RE GOING TO TELL THEM THEY DON'T **HAVE** ANY?
HEY! I'M WITH THE **FBI**. NOT THE **MPAA**.

The Truth Is Out There.

I'M AGENT PENUMBRA OF THE FBI. I'M HERE TODAY TO ANNOUNCE SUBSTANTIAL CHANGES TO OUR SNOOPING SOFTWARE THAT WAS ONCE TITLED "CARNIVORE."

"AS PART OF OUR STRATEGY TO MAKE THE SOFTWARE MORE ACCEPTABLE, WE HAVE LICENSED A POPULAR CHILDREN'S ROLE MODEL AND PLAYED OFF THE NAME. THE SOFTWARE IS NOW KNOWN AS 'CARNY', AND IS AVAILABLE AT BETTER SOFTWARE STORES NEAR YOU."
CARNY
BuyMe.com

AND WHERE DOES THE FBI STAND WITH OUR RIGHTS?
AT THE MOMENT YOU CAN FIND THEM DOWN IN THE BASEMENT WITH THOSE TWO DOLTS.

Full disclosure: I'm a "fancy coffee" addict. It's a great way to get your caffeine. It's also a great way to get fat.

SOMETHING SMELLS GOOD. WHAT **IS** THAT?
IT'S AN EXTRA FROTH NON-FAT DOUBLE WHIP. HALF-CREAM EXTRA-SHOT LIGHT MOCHA.
Copyright (c) 2000 Illiad http://www.userfriendly.org/

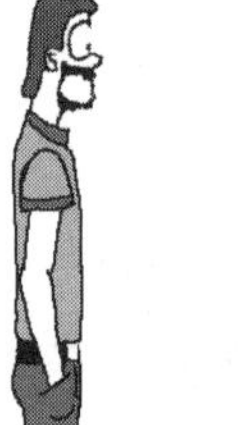

OKAY. **FINE.** IT'S HEAVILY OVERPRICED **COFFEE.**
OH DON'T FEEL BAD. HOW CAN YOU PUT A **PRICE** ON **CAFFEINE?**

HELLO! I'M MISTER BIGBUCKS COFFEE! WOULD YOU LIKE...
Copyright (c) 2000 Illiad http://www.userfriendly.org/

NOOO! I KNOW YOU! YOU'RE RELATED TO THAT **EVIL COLA CAN! BEGONE** FOUL DEMON!
AAAIIIEEE!!

LOOK BUDDY. IF YOU DIDN'T WANT A **COUPON** YOU COULDA JUST **SAID** SO.
OH. SORRY. I THOUGHT YOU WERE GONNA MAKE ME DRINK OUT OF YOUR **NOSTRIL**. HEH.

SEE MIKE? IT'S NOT SO BAD HERE.
YEAH. OKAY. MAYBE I **DID** OVERREACT A BIT...
LIGHT LATTE NON-FA EXTRA SHOT PLEASE
Copyright (c) 2000 Illiad http://www.userfriendly.org/
ENGFEH NGGGG *ZNORK*

WAS THAT A ZOMBIE?
IT'S 9:30 IN THE MORNING.
PICKLE BUSTING. *GEH*
AHHHH. THAT WAS A KERNEL HACKER.

TIK TOK TIK TOK
Copyright (c) 2000 Illiad http://www.userfriendly.org/

TOK TIK TOK

DAMN YOU BIG BUCKS AND YOUR MAGICAL ANTI-SLEEP DRINKS...
TIKKA TIKKA TAKKA TAKKA

WATCHA UP TO ERWIN?
TALKING TO X WINDOWS ON THIS BOX.
Copyright (c) 2000 Illiad http://www.userfriendly.org/

IT KEEPS SAYING THE SAME THING OVER AND OVER.

WHAT'S IT SAYING?
"I AM ABOUT TO VOMIT."

I'VE BEEN THINKING ABOUT X WINDOWS LATELY...AND HOW IT NEEDS SOME VERY SERIOUS CHAMPIONING.
CHAMPIONING?
Copyright (c) 2000 Illiad http://www.userfriendly.org/

YES...CHAMPIONS WHO FIGHT FOR X WINDOWS, PROMOTING THE TECHNOLOGY EVERYWHERE THEY GO...DESPITE BEING SHUNNED BY THE VERY PEOPLE THEY'RE TRYING TO EDUCATE.
OH...NO... DON'T DO IT!

IT IS TIME TO RELEASE THE POSSIBILITIES. IT IS TIME FOR...
The X-Friends
I GET TO BE WOLVERINE!
I'D THINK THAT THE TOAD WOULD BE MORE TO THE POINT.
Educating Those Who Want To Be Left Alone

To be accurate, it should be referred to as X or X Windowing System, not X Windows. Old habits ...

USER
FRIENDLY
the comic strip
PIZZA
Portrasher 4
ROTO-ROUTER 800
Copyright (c) 1997-2000 Illiad

SUNG TO: "AMERICAN PIE BY DON MACLEAN."
A LONG, LONG TIME AGO, I CAN STILL REMEMBER HOW SHE'D MAKE MY STOMACH FILL WITH BILE...

AND I KNEW IF I LEARNED TO DANCE, I'D HAVE A SHOT AT SWEET ROMANCE, AND MAYBE WE COULD SHARE A LOGIN FILE...

BUT TALKING TO HER MADE ME QUIVER, SO NOW I'M SLAUGHTERING MY LIVER. I EVEN WROTE A LETTER, SHE LIKED THAT FRENCH GUY BETTER...

I CAN'T REMEMBER IF I TRIED TO PUT MY COWARDICE ASIDE SOMETHING TOLD ME DEEP INSIDE, I SHOULDN'T HAVE BEEN SO...SHY

AHH TA HELL WITH IT. *HIC* WHAT'S YOUR NAME, BABY?

AND SO WE JOIN TWO OF THE X-FRIENDS AS THEY DISCUSS THE PROBLEMS THEY MUST FACE...
I'M BORED STORM. LET'S GO AND INSTALL WINDOWS 98 ON CEREBRO!
WOLVERINE...I DON'T THINK THAT WOULD..
CUT! FOLKS. WE HAVE A PROBLEM.
Copyright (c) 2000 Illiad http://www.userfriendly.org

JUST GOT WORD FROM HEAD OFFICE. WE DON'T HAVE THE BUDGET TO LICENSE THE REAL X-MEN NAMES SO YOU'LL HAVE TO BE RENAMED. HILLARY. INSTEAD OF STORM YOU GET TO BE "DRIZZLE."
WHAT?!

AND STEF...INSTEAD OF WOLVERINE. YOU'LL HAVE TO BE...OHHH...HOW ABOUT "WEASEL."
HEY!!!
YEP. THAT ONE FITS.

...UH...TO CONTINUE. THE X-FRIENDS WERE GEEKS AND WANNABE GEEKS WITH VERY UNUSUAL POWERS...
WEASEL, WHO COULD LIE THROUGH HIS TEETH, AND DRIZZLE, WHO COULD MAKE THE WEATHER A BIT GRAY.
I DON'T LIE. I MARKET.
Copyright (c) 2000 Illiad http://www.userfriendly.org

AND THEN THERE WAS THE LEADER OF THE X-FRIENDS, DR. XYZ, AND HIS APPRENTICE, THE DANGEROUS MS. HISSY FIT.
HEH. I'M THE BOSS. COOL.
I'LL GET YOU FOR THIS. ERWIN.

AND FINALLY, AN X-FRIEND WHOSE ANALOG ONLY APPEARED IN THE COMIC BOOK AND NOT THE MOVIE, BIG SLAVIC DUDE, WHO CAN CHANGE STORAGE DRUMS IN MAINFRAMES ALL BY HIMSELF.
CAN...NOT...MOVE ARMS...TO REACH KEYBOARD...

DEEP WITHIN THE BOWELS OF THE X-FRIENDS SERVER ROOM STOOD CEREBRO (PLAYED BY ME IN A DEC ALPHA GS320...HEH) ...
FORTY-TWO!
I HAVE FOUR 63 GIG RAMDISKS! HAHAHAHAH!
I CAN RUN SETI@HOME WITH TOTAL IMPUNITY!
Copyright (c) 2000 Illiad http://www.userfriendly.org

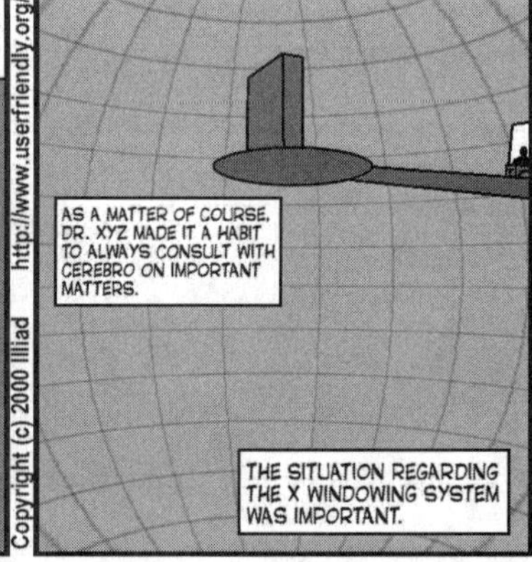
AS A MATTER OF COURSE, DR. XYZ MADE IT A HABIT TO ALWAYS CONSULT WITH CEREBRO ON IMPORTANT MATTERS.
THE SITUATION REGARDING THE X WINDOWING SYSTEM WAS IMPORTANT.

OF COURSE, CEREBRO AND DR. XYZ DIDN'T ALWAYS SEE THINGS EYE-TO-EYE...
RRRRRRR
WHAT'S WITH THE LIP ON THIS DOOR? CAN'T YOU MAKE THINGS WHEELCHAIR ACCESSIBLE?!
OH QUIT WITH THE WHINING! AS IT IS YOU GET ALL THE GOOD PARKING SPACES!

CEREBRO AND DR. XYZ CONVERSE ON THE ISSUES SURROUNDING THE X WINDOWING SYSTEM, FURTHER TO A SOLUTION FOR PROMOTING IT TO THE REST OF THE WORLD...
HOW IS THE KDE-GNOME INTEGRATION PROJECT PROCEEDING, CEREBRO?
VERY WELL, DOCTOR.
Copyright (c) 2000 Illiad http://www.userfriendly.org

I'VE BEEN DEVOTING THE MAJORITY OF MY CYCLES TO BLENDING THE BEST OF BOTH G.U.I.'S AND ALLOWING FOR BACKWARD COMPATIBILITY. IT HAS TAKEN SOME DOING, BUT I THINK IT WILL DEPLOY WELL AND SOLVE ALL OF OUR WINDOWING PROBLEMS.

SO WHAT HAPPENS IF THE NEW G.U.I. DOESN'T DEPLOY WELL?
I SUSPECT OUR PROBLEM WILL BE TERMINAL.

X-FRIENDS. I AM HAPPY TO REPORT THAT CEREBRO IS BUSILY CHURNING AWAY ON THE X-PROJECT. AFTER THREE YEARS OF WORK, HE IS COMING CLOSE TO A BUG-FREE COMPILE. IT WON'T BE LONG NOW.
Copyright (c) 2000 Illiad http://www.userfriendly.org/

ALTHOUGH RECENTLY I'VE NOTICED THE OCCASIONAL DIP IN CEREBRO'S SYSTEM RESOURCES...STRANGE...
SAY, HAS ANYONE SEEN WEASEL?

CLICK KLIK KLICK CLICK CLICK
KLIK KLICK CLICK
STEF...I STILL DON'T THINK PLAYING DIABLO 2 ON ME IS RIGHT.
SHADDUP! I AM THE BARBARIAN! I AM SWEATY! GRAAAAAAGGGH!

I CAN NOT BELIEVE YOU'RE PLAYING DIABLO 2 ON CEREBRO!
THAT WASN'T WISE, WEASEL. CEREBRO HOLDS ALL OUR HOPES ON HIS DRIVES.
LOOK, I FIGURED HE HAD SOME SPARE CYCLES...
MY HEAD. WHY IS IT SO TINY?
Copyright (c) 2000 Illiad http://www.userfriendly.org/

LOOK OUT! IT'S MAGNETO!
HOW'D HE GET IN?!
WAAOW!
DON'T WORRY! WE'RE NOT WEARING ANY METAL!

HE JUST...WIPED... CEREBRO'S DRIVES.
WEASEL...WHAT WAS THE NEW FRONT DOOR YOU HAD INSTALLED HERE MADE OF?
METAL I GUESS.
MY BODY. WHY IS IT SO BIG?

IN THE SPIRIT OF SYDNEY 2000 INTEL EXECUTIVES ATTEMPT TO ADOPT THE OLYMPIC SLOGAN
Market Report
intel
DEAR GOD. PLEASE...HIGHER... HIGHER...HIGHER...
WHAT HAPPENED TO "FASTER" AND "STRONGER"?
I GUESS AMD GOT THOSE.
COPYRIGHT (C) 2000 ILLIAD
HTTP://WWW.USERFRIENDLY.ORG/

WELL I GUESS THAT'S IT...ALL OF OUR CODE HAS BEEN WIPED.
LOOK. I HAD NO IDEA MAGNETO WAS GOING TO BE THE VILLAIN.
Copyright (c) 2000 Illiad http://www.userfriendly.org/

STEF. THIS IS A SPOOF OF THE X-MEN. MAGNETO WAS THE VILLAIN IN THE MOVIE AND THE COMICS.
LOOK. I JUST DIDN'T THINK IT THROUGH. OKAY?

KIND OF LIKE A CERTAIN CARTOONIST WHO DIDN'T THINK THE STORYLINE THROUGH!
WE'RE ACTUALLY OKAY. I HAVE THE BACKUP TAPE HERE.
OH YEAH. NEARLY FORGOT THAT.
WAAOW

WE HAVE A NEW CONTRACTOR COMING IN TOMORROW.
OH?
Copyright (c) 2000 Illiad http://www.userfriendly.org/

YES. HE COMES WITH TEN YEARS OF EXPERIENCE AS A HUBRIS-PACHYDERM TECH. HE'LL BE REVAMPING OUR BACK-END SERVICES.
AN EX-HP TECH. I SEE...

AND BEFORE YOU ASK. NO. HE'S NOT EXPENSIVE...
NOT EXPENSIVE AS IN "NOT EXPENSIVE" OR NOT EXPENSIVE AS IN "I SIGNED THE CONTRACT BEFORE REALLY THINKING AND A LAWSUIT WOULD COST US MORE." ?

When I originally introduced Sid, much of the readership took an instant dislike to him. A month later, I was swamped with e-mails asking me to make him a permanent member of the cast. I doubt that those who didn't like Sid to begin with made up the lion's share of those who wanted him to stay. On the other hand, it's pretty clear that the crowd that doesn't like Sid is younger, whereas the crowd that doesn't like Pitr is a little older.

HELLO... WHO ARE YOU?
HI. SID DABSTER. I'M THE NEW TECH.
Copyright (c) 2000 Illiad http://www.userfriendly.org/

TECH? BUT... YOU'RE WEARING A SUIT...
A SUIT!? WELL. RIP MY LIPS OFF! I AM TOO!

WOW. AM I GLAD I MET YOU. YOU'RE SO OBSERVANT...YOU MUST BE THE CONTROLLER HERE OR SOMETHING...
WHY. THANK YOU. YES I...HEY!

SO YOU'RE THE BIG BAD SCARY CONTROLLER.
I'M ACTUALLY VERY FRIENDLY. I'M SURE YOU'LL BE MY CHUM IN NO TIME AT ALL.
Copyright (c) 2000 Illiad http://www.userfriendly.org/

OKAY...UM...CHUM AS IN "FRIEND" OR "SHARK BAIT?"
LEVEL ONE FEAR ACHIEVED IN SUBJECT.

WHAT'S THIS YOU'RE PLAYING?
CAPTURE THE FLAG. PRETTY NEAT. HUH?
http://www.userfriendly.org/
Copyright (c) 2000 Illiad

BLAM! SPLUTCH! GIBBLE!

I HATE TO BURST YOUR BUBBLE. BUT ISN'T THAT JUST STRATEGO ON STEROIDS?
I GUESS YOU MIGHT SEE IT THAT WAY IF YOU WERE BORN IN THE JURASSIC.

AHHH YES. LINUX. THE SAVIOUR OF THE I.T. WORLD. IT'S NEW. IT'S SHINY. IT'S POPULAR. BUT IT'S MISSING ONE THING THAT THE OLD UNIXES HAVE.
TAP TIK
http://www.userfriendly.org/
Copyright (c) 2000 Illiad

FINE. I'LL BITE. WHAT?
SOUL! YOU YOUNGSTERS HAVE NO CONCEPT OF THE JOY OF TRADITIONS LIKE CAUSING CITY-GRID BROWNOUTS WITH PDP/VMS SYSTEMS.
TYPE TAK

UHHH...CAUSING BROWNOUTS IS A GOOD THING?
WELL DUH. FOR KICKS WE THREATENED TO DO A COLD START DURING THE SUPERBOWL. MACHIAVELLI WOULD HAVE WEPT.

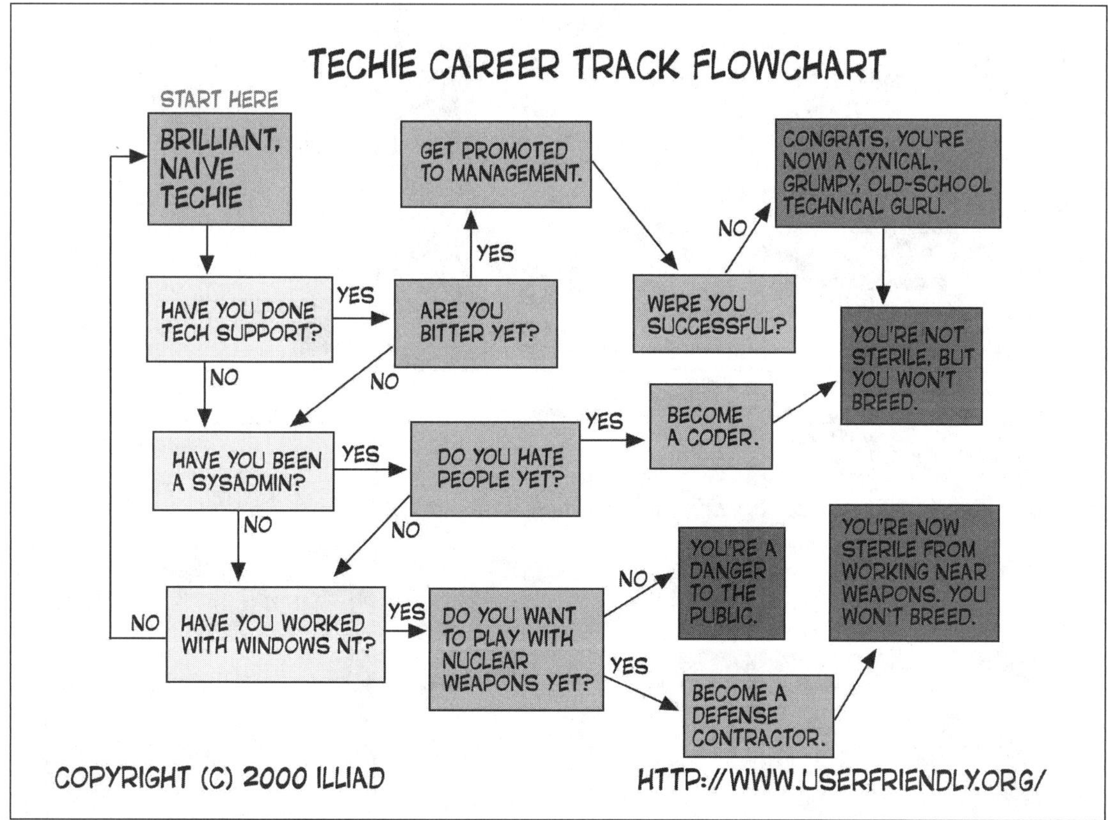
TECHIE CAREER TRACK FLOWCHART
START HERE
BRILLIANT, NAIVE TECHIE
HAVE YOU DONE TECH SUPPORT?
YES
NO
ARE YOU BITTER YET?
YES
NO
GET PROMOTED TO MANAGEMENT.
WERE YOU SUCCESSFUL?
NO
CONGRATS, YOU'RE NOW A CYNICAL, GRUMPY, OLD-SCHOOL TECHNICAL GURU.
YOU'RE NOT STERILE, BUT YOU WON'T BREED.
HAVE YOU BEEN A SYSADMIN?
YES
NO
DO YOU HATE PEOPLE YET?
YES
NO
BECOME A CODER.
HAVE YOU WORKED WITH WINDOWS NT?
NO
YES
DO YOU WANT TO PLAY WITH NUCLEAR WEAPONS YET?
NO
YES
YOU'RE A DANGER TO THE PUBLIC.
BECOME A DEFENSE CONTRACTOR.
YOU'RE NOW STERILE FROM WORKING NEAR WEAPONS. YOU WON'T BREED.
COPYRIGHT (C) 2000 ILLIAD
HTTP://WWW.USERFRIENDLY.ORG/

I'M GOING TO HAVE TO DUMP THIS CODE TO PAPER. WHERE'S YOUR CHAIN PRINTER?
CHAIN PRINTER? WE ONLY HAVE A LASER PRINTER.
Copyright (c) 2000 Illiad http://www.userfriendly.org/

WHAT DO YOU NEED TO PRINT THE CODE OFF FOR ANYWAYS?
WELL JUST **LOOK** AT IT. IT NEEDS TIGHTENING UP **EVERYWHERE**.

SO EXPLAIN TO ME WHAT'S WRONG WITH TIGHTENING THE CODE UP ON THE **SCREEN?**
YOU JUST HAVE **NO** CONCEPT OF SIMPLE PLEASURES DO YOU? AND GET ME A RED PEN.

WHERE'S SID?
HE'S IN THE SERVER ROOM. HE MUMBLED SOMETHING ABOUT "TOUCHING UP" OUR HARDWARE.
Copyright (c) 2000 Illiad http://www.userfriendly.org/

TOUCHING UP... OUR **HARDWARE?**
THAT'S WHAT HE SAID.

SHOULD WE BE WORRIED?
IF I THINK ABOUT IT I GET HIVES. CAN WE DISCUSS SOMETHING ELSE?
CAN WE TALK TOOLS? I NEED A SOLDERING IRON AND SOME SERIOUS EPOXY.

SID. EXACTLY WHAT HAVE YOU **DONE** IN HERE?
OH, JUST FIXED A CABLE HERE, SWAPPED A CPU THERE...
Copyright (c) 2000 Illiad http://www.userfriendly.org/

WELL FINE...JUST DON'T MESS WITH THE NETWORK. IT'S TAKEN ME MONTHS TO GET IT TO WHERE IT IS.
I KIND OF WANTED TO TALK TO YOU ABOUT THAT...

...AND THEN HE **ACTUALLY SUGGESTED** HOW HE COULD IMPROVE **MY** NETWORK DESIGN!
MY WORD. ISN'T HE **JUST** A BEAST.

HEY THERE, BOSS-MAN. I'M JUST CHECKING IN WITH YOU AND ALSO I WANTED TO LET YOU KNOW THAT I THINK YOU'RE RUNNING A REALLY TIGHT SHIP HERE. YOU'RE OBVIOUSLY ONE OF THE RARE CEO-TYPES THAT HAS A WHOLE BRAIN.
Copyright (c) 2000 Illiad http://www.userfriendly.org/

ANYWAY, I SHOULD GET BACK TO WORK. THANKS AGAIN FOR THE HONOUR OF WORKING WITH YOU SIR.

HE SEEMS PRETTY COMPETENT TO **ME**.
HE CALLED YOU "SIR!" HOW **FAKE** CAN YOU **GET?**

YOU ARE NEW TECH, DA? MIKHAIL TELLINK ME YOU ARE FINDINK SERVER PROBLEMS?
MM-HM.
Copyright (c) 2000 Illiad http://www.userfriendly.org/

AM CURIOUS TO KNOW WHAT IS PROBLEM. ALL SERVERS RUNNINK LINUX. SMOOTH AS VODKA...
SEE THAT'S JUST IT. YOU'RE RUNNING THIS...THIS WATERED-DOWN VERSION OF A REAL UNIX...

HEY. WHAT COLOUR IS THAT?
ON PITR'S FACE? #CC0066. I'M PRETTY SURE.

HEY GREG? WHERE'S PITR? HE HASN'T BEEN IN ALL DAY.
HE'S BUSY DEFENDING HIS TITLE AS THE OFFICE ALPHA-GEEK.
Copyright (c) 2000 Illiad http://www.userfriendly.org/

DID YOU SAY "ALPHA-GEEK?"
YUP. HE AND SID ARE BUTTING HEADS. SO NOW THEY HAVE TO SETTLE THEIR DIFFERENCES THE ONLY WAY THEY KNOW HOW...

I'LL TAKE "OBSCURE MODEM COMMANDS" FOR 300, ALEX.
COWARD! YOU ARE TAKINK ALL EASY ONES!
Sid
PITR

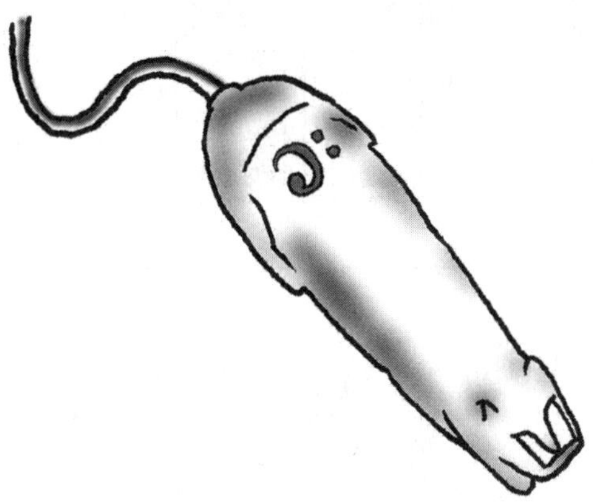
UNFORTUNATE LOGO DESIGN #14:
"MISTAKEN FOR A DEVICE IN A PROCTOLOGIST'S OFFICE"
COPYRIGHT (C) 2000 ILLIAD
HTTP://WWW.USERFRIENDLY.ORG/

A company called Digital Convergence was shipping odd-looking barcode scanners for free to everyone who asked, and even to people who didn't ask. The idea was to get everyone using the scanner to link print media to web media. The company chose an unfortunate logo (:c) for this device, which they called the Cue Cat. Read it out loud.

One day, it would be the height of Fun to create a show like Geek *Jeopardy*. We could get so obscure, and all of us in the know would nod sagely as a contestant managed to recite the entire "You stay here and watch him" scene from *Monty Python and the Holy Grail*.

"ULTIMATE MISCELLANY" FOR 400 PLEASE ALEX.
OKAY SID. "EIGHT POINT UNBLEACHED CORNWALL MATTE."
Copyright (c) 2000 Illiad http://www.userfriendly.org/

WHAT WAS THE STOCK USED FOR PUNCH CARDS IN NORTH AMERICA FROM 1972 TO 1976.
CORRECT!
NYET! IS UNFAIR! AM GEEK. NOT PALEONTOLOGIST!

AND WE'LL BE RIGHT BACK AFTER THESE MESSAGES...
YOU ARE NOT FOOLINK ME...AM THINKINK YOU ARE CHEATINK.
Copyright (c) 2000 Illiad http://www.userfriendly.org/

HEY NOW. THAT'S RUDE! JUST BECAUSE THINGS ARE GOING SWIMMINGLY FOR ME DOESN'T MEAN I'M BEING DISHONEST. THIS GAME IS A TEST OF KNOWLEDGE, AND A CHALLENGE TO OUR GEEKHOOD.

WELCOME BACK! WE HAVE A NEW CATEGORY ON THE BOARD: "THINGS ONLY SID KNOWS."
...OF COURSE, HACKING THE GAME SYSTEM IS A GEEK THING...
AM GOINK TO EATINK HIS LIVER.

AND THE FINAL SCORE IS $18500 FOR SID AND $7800 FOR PITR. SO CONGRATULATIONS TO SID DABSTER, OUR NEW GEEK CHAMPION!
THANKS ALEX! I'D LIKE TO ALSO THANK MY WORTHY OPPONENT PITR FOR SUCH A GREAT CHALLENGE!
Copyright (c) 2000 Illiad http://www.userfriendly.org/

HERE IT IS COMINK...

SO...WHO'S YOUR DADDY?
AM SUPPOSINK IT COULD HAVE BEEN YOU.

HEY THERE OLD-TIMER.
DID YOU JUST SPEAK TO ME?
Copyright (c) 2000 Illiad http://www.userfriendly.org/

YUP. PRETTY SPIFF, EH? I'M AN ARTIFICAL INTELLIGENCE AND QUITE FRANKLY THE SMARTEST ONE AROUND HERE.

I'VE DONE A PRETTY GOOD JOB OF BEING ACCEPTED AROUND HERE. EXCEPT FOR THAT MARKETING WEENIE, STEF. SO WHAT'S NEW, DUDE?
I REMEMBER YOU! YOU'RE ELIZA!

I'M ERWIN. NOT ELIZA.
OH.
Copyright (c) 2000 Illiad http://www.userfriendly.org/

I'M SERIOUS. I DON'T JUST TAKE SOMEONE ELSE'S WORDS, MANIPULATE THEM TO MY OWN ENDS AND SPIT THEM BACK OUT PRETENDING TO BE INTELLIGENT.

THEN YOU THINK MAYBE THE C.E.O. OF THE R.I.A.A. IS AN ELIZA PROGRAM?
THE THOUGHT HAD CROSSED MY MIND...

I REMEMBER THE FIRST PROGRAM I EVER WROTE WAS AN "A.I." THAT COULD PLAY 20 QUESTIONS. YOU COULD ASK IT ANY QUESTION IN AN ATTEMPT TO GUESS WHAT THING IT WAS THINKING ABOUT AND IT WOULD ANSWER YES OR NO. AND I DID IT WITH ONLY EIGHT LINES OF CODE.
DID YOU SAY EIGHT LINES OF CODE?
Copyright (c) 2000 Illiad http://www.userfriendly.org/

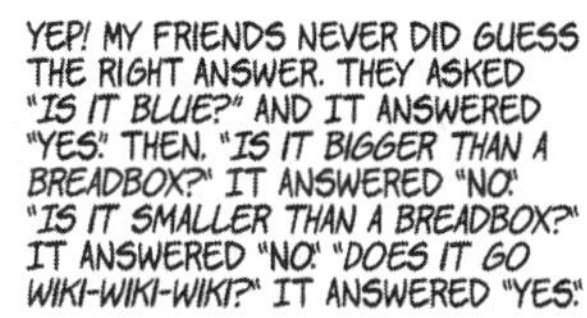

YEP! MY FRIENDS NEVER DID GUESS THE RIGHT ANSWER. THEY ASKED "IS IT BLUE?" AND IT ANSWERED "YES." THEN, "IS IT BIGGER THAN A BREADBOX?" IT ANSWERED "NO." "IS IT SMALLER THAN A BREADBOX?" IT ANSWERED "NO." "DOES IT GO WIKI-WIKI-WIKI?" IT ANSWERED "YES."

UH...IT WAS THINKING ABOUT A BLUE BREADBOX THAT GOES WIKI-WIKI-WIKI?
THE TRICK WAS IN THE CODE. IT ANSWERED "YES" TO ANY QUESTION THAT ENDED IN A VOWEL.

A subtle win for Pitr, who did essentially the same thing with six lines of code.

USER
FRIENDLY
the comic strip
PIZZA
Portrasher 4
ROTO-ROUTER 800
Copyright (c) 1997-2000 Illiad

CRASH!!
WHAT ON EARTH WAS THAT?!

THAT WAS COOL!!
DO THAT AGAIN...
TECHS...

OKAY. NOW PLAY IT BACKWARDS.
RIGHT...

DOMINATE!! DOMINATE!! EAT YOUR YOUNG AND AGGREGATE! I HAVE GROTTY SILICON!

PLAYING HEAVY METAL RECORDS BACKWARDS, ARE WE?
NO. AN AOL CD.
I'M NOT PLAYING IT FORWARDS. WE ALL KNOW WHAT THAT DOES...

YEAH, I USED TO PLAY "ADVENTURE" FOR HOURS EVERY DAY AFTER WORK. SOME OF THE GAMES WE HAD BACK THEN WERE INGENIOUS...
HELLO.
COULD SOMEONE PLEASE GET ME MY BOW AND ARROW SO I CAN FINALLY SETTLE THIS THING?
WHAT'S HE TALKING ABOUT?
FROM WHAT HE'S TOLD ME, I THINK HE KNEW YOU WHEN YOU WERE CALLED "WUMPUS."
Copyright (c) 2000 Illiad http://www.userfriendly.org/
I'M SORRY, BUT I'M NOT THIS MR. WUMPUS THAT YOU THINK I AM. I'M CALLED DUST PUPPY.
OH.
WHO'S THIS "WUMPUS" ANYWAYS?
OH, THIS FICTITIOUS CREATURE THAT I SPENT HOURS TRYING TO HUNT IN A COMPUTER GAME YEARS AGO. I NEVER DID NAIL HIM AND "HUNT THE WUMPUS" IS THE ONE GAME I NEVER DID GET CLOSURE ON.
YOU SURE I CAN'T JUST, LIKE, POKE YOU WITH A LEATHERMAN? IT'LL HELP ME SLEEP AT NIGHT.
NO!!
Copyright (c) 2000 Illiad http://www.userfriendly.org/
...SO I WROTE ERWIN OVERNIGHT AND NOW HE'S MY FRIEND.
OVERNIGHT?! OUTSTANDING. WHAT LANGUAGE DID YOU WRITE HIM IN?
COBOL.
JUST FOR THE RECORD, I'M NOT HIS FRIEND ANYMORE.
FUZZY GUY, YOU'RE THE GROOVIEST.
Copyright (c) 2000 Illiad http://www.userfriendly.org/
AS MUCH AS I ADMIRE YOUR USE OF WHAT SO MANY SOULLESS MORONS CONSIDER A LEGACY LANGUAGE, I HAVE TO ASK: WHY COBOL?
YEAH, WHY COBOL?!
I LOST A BET.
OH, I JUST FIGURED YOU WANTED TO CREATE A COMPLETELY RETARDED A.I.
YA, YOU JUST KEEP THWACKIN' THE BEEHIVE, SID...
Copyright (c) 2000 Illiad http://www.userfriendly.org/

SO WHAT IS IT EXACTLY THAT MAKES YOU TICK? I MEAN, YOU'RE JUST A BALL OF DIRT WITH FEET AND HUGE EYES.
Copyright (c) 2000 Illiad http://www.userfriendly.org/

IT'S JUST TOO...UH...

YOU'RE GOING TO ASK ABOUT THE FEET, RIGHT?
NO...I JUST REALIZED THAT YOU'RE THE PERFECT SIZE TO DUST THE INSIDE OF STORAGE DRUM ASSEMBLIES.

OKAY, YOU READY FOR THIS?
NO...BUT I GUESS I DON'T HAVE ANY CHOICE.
Copyright (c) 2000 Illiad http://www.userfriendly.org/

BLOWWWW

HUH. I GUESS YOU'RE RIGHT. THERE'S NOT A LOT HOLDING YOU TOGETHER.
PLEASE DON'T DO THAT AGAIN!

ONE-CLICK SPAM BLOCKING

ICBM CONTROL

HTTP://WWW.USERFRIENDLY.ORG/ COPYRIGHT (C) 2000 ILLIAD

YOU WANTED TO SEE ME?
YES, SID. I JUST WANTED YOUR OPINION ON THIS LATEST BROADBAND CRAZE. ARE THE VISIONARIES CORRECT?
Copyright (c) 2000 Illiad http://www.userfriendly.org/

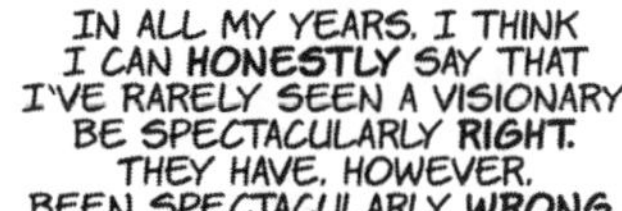
IN ALL MY YEARS, I THINK I CAN HONESTLY SAY THAT I'VE RARELY SEEN A VISIONARY BE SPECTACULARLY RIGHT. THEY HAVE, HOWEVER, BEEN SPECTACULARLY WRONG.

RIGHT...LIKE "THE PAPERLESS OFFICE" WHICH NEVER EXISTED.
OHH, IT EXISTED ALL RIGHT. BACK WHEN THEY USED CLAY TABLETS. LOTS OF THEM.

HEY GREG? WHEN CAN I HAVE THOSE SITE TRAFFIC REPORTS?
FRIDAY.
GREAT. THANKS.
Copyright (c) 2000 Illiad http://www.userfriendly.org/

UM...WHICH FRIDAY?
WELL DAMN. YOU'RE LEARNING.

OH. YOU'RE JUST A BARREL OF LAUGHS.
I KIND OF THOUGHT SO MYSELF.
Copyright (c) 2000 Illiad http://www.userfriendly.org/

HAVE YOU EVER CONSIDERED THE IMPACT THAT YOUR DISRESPECT FOR ME HAS ON THE REST OF THE COMPANY? IT'S ENTIRELY DESTRUCTIVE, DEMORALIZING, JUVENILE BEHAVIOUR.

EVERYONE ELSE CHEERS ME ON, INCLUDING THE CHIEF.
WAS HE THE ONE WHO BOUGHT YOU THAT STUPID SNURF BAZOOKA YOU KEEP PEGGING ME WITH?

LOOK, I NEED THOSE REPORTS, AND UNTIL I GET THEM I'M TELLING HILLARY TO CUT OFF THE OFFICE COLA DELIVERIES.
Copyright (c) 2000 Illiad http://www.userfriendly.org/

WHAT ARE YOU DOING?
ISN'T THERE AN OAR SOMEWHERE YOU WANT TO CHAIN ME TO?

WHY IS IT THAT YOU HAVE TO RESIST EVERYTHING I ASK YOU TO DO?
LOOK AT IT THIS WAY...
Copyright (c) 2000 Illiad http://www.userfriendly.org/

IN NATURE, THE MORE STRUGGLE AND CHALLENGE THERE IS FOR A PARTICULAR SPECIES, THE STRONGER THAT SPECIES HAS TO BECOME TO SURVIVE. SO IN EFFECT I'M MAKING YOU A STRONGER, BETTER MARKETING EXPERT.

WOW...I'VE NEVER THOUGHT OF IT THAT WAY...
YOU CAN THANK ME NEXT TIME I GIVE YOU A HASSLE...

SO AS YOU CAN SEE, I'M ONLY TRYING TO HELP.
YEAH...WOW. THANKS SO MUCH. I'M GLAD WE HAD THIS TALK.

FIVE...FOUR... THREE...TWO... ONE...

WHICH FRIDAY?!?!
WHAT BEAUTIFUL MUSIC...

USER
FRIENDLY
the comic strip
PIZZA
Portrasher 4
ROTO-ROUTER 800
HELLO. ERWIN AND I WROTE A SONG WE'D LIKE TO DEDICATE TO ALL OF YOU HARD-WORKING TECH SUPPORT PEOPLE OUT THERE.
THAT WOULD BE "BITTER HARD-WORKING TECH SUPPORT PEOPLE" AND OUR APOLOGIES TO GLORIA GAYNOR.
"TECH SUPPORT LAMENT" (SUNG TO "I WILL SURVIVE.")
AT FIRST I WAS AFRAID I HAD LOST MY MIND. THE PHONE WOULD RING, I'D DO MY THING AND GET MALIGNED. BUT THEN I SPENT SO MANY MONTHS HELPING USERS DIAL OUT FILLED WITH DOUBT ABOUT MY ABILITY NOT TO SHOUT...
WHIRRR

This cartoon caused an unbelievable fuss, but a positive one. Pagans in the audience came out in droves to thank me for depicting someone "normal" like Greg as a Pagan. Most of the Pagans I know in real life are a lot more normal than most people.

AT USERS WHO CAN HARDLY THINK
I SHOWED THEM HOW TO CLICK ON THINGS AND EVEN PULLED THEM FROM THE BRINK
I SHOULD HAVE KNOWN THEY'D NEVER LEARN AND REALIZED THEY WOULDN'T SEE
IF I'D'VE KNOWN FOR JUST ONE SECOND THEY'D BE BACK TO BOTHER ME!

SO HERE I GO! PUT THEM ON HOLD! JUST TAKE A NAP NOW! I'M SURE THEY'LL WAIT UNTIL THEY'RE OLD WEREN'T THEY THE ONES WHO TRIED TO SAY I LOST THEIR FILES THEY THOUGHT I'D HELP THEM NOW I'M ROLLING IN THE AISLES!

WEREN'T YOU GUYS SUPPOSED TO WAIT FOR ME?
BOYS AND GIRLS, THIS IS WHAT HAPPENS TO THE REALLY BITTER HELP DESK PEOPLE. WE RECOMMEND JOINING A PRISON CHAIN GANG INSTEAD.
RRRR...*KLIK*

WHAT ARE YOU DRESSING UP AS FOR HALLOWE'EN?
I'M NOT. I'M PAGAN SO I'M DEVOTING MY TIME TO CELEBRATING **SAMHAIN** INSTEAD.

Copyright (c) 2000 Illiad http://www.userfriendly.org/
NO. WE **DON'T** SACRIFICE VIRGINS. SO RELAX.
HEY. DO I LOOK **WORRIED?**

WHAT ARE YOU DRESSING UP AS FOR HALLOWE'EN?
I'M NOT. I'M PAGAN SO I'M DEVOTING MY TIME TO CELEBRATING **SAMHAIN** INSTEAD.

Copyright (c) 2000 Illiad http://www.userfriendly.org/
NO. WE **DON'T** SACRIFICE VIRGINS. SO RELAX.
HEY. DO I LOOK **WORRIED?**

HEY. HAPPY HALLOWE'EN. WHAT'RE YOU SMILING ABOUT?
I JUST TOLD STEF A FEW THINGS ABOUT PAGANISM.
Copyright (c) 2000 Illiad http://www.userfriendly.org/

YOU'RE NOT PROPOGATING ANY MYTHS ARE YOU?

UM...JUST A SMALL ONE. AND I TOLD HIM THAT THOSE DOMINICAN MONKS WERE ACTUALLY FEMALE WICCANS.

SO...WHEN DO WE GET NAKED?

SO IF YOU'RE A PAGAN, WHAT AM I?
WELL, WHAT IS IT THAT YOU BELIEVE IN?
Copyright (c) 2000 Illiad http://www.userfriendly.org/

JUST THAT YOU SHOULD BE TRUTHFUL AND NICE TO PEOPLE.
OKAY. YOU SOUND LIKE A "WESTERN REFORMED HUMANIST."

IS THAT LIKE A REPUBLICAN OR A DEMOCRAT?
NEITHER REALLY. EXCEPT FOR THE 'WESTERN' PART.

SO HOW DO YOU FEEL ABOUT CHRISTIANITY?
I RESPECT THEIR BELIEFS IF THAT'S WHAT YOU MEAN...
Copyright (c) 2000 Illiad http://www.userfriendly.org/
BUT DIDN'T THEY USE TO BURN WITCHES AND PAGANS?
NOT ALL OF THE CHRISTIANS WERE LIKE THAT. AND THEY DON'T CONDONE THE USE OF VIOLENCE ANY LONGER...

LOOK. I'M SORRY! I THOUGHT YOU GUYS WERE CHICKS!
WE CAN FORGIVE A GREAT DEAL. BUT THE BUTTER WAS TOO MUCH. BROTHER PAULY. BEGIN THE THWACKING.

HEY CHIEF? THE TECHS ARE OFF SQUABBLING AGAIN. IT'S WEIRD.
HOW DO YOU MEAN?
Copyright (c) 2000 Illiad http://www.userfriendly.org/

WELL...IT'S THIS STRANGE SENSE OF DEJA VU. FEELS LIKE SOMETHING THAT HAPPENED IN THE BEGINNING OF MARCH LAST YEAR...

OH?

...AND PAGANS WILL DEFEND YOUR RIGHT TO CHOICE OF RELIGION.
BUDDHISTS WILL DEFEND THAT RIGHT BETTER.
NYET! ARE ALL FALLINK INTO HANDS OF DISCORDIANISM!

Beginning of March 1999. Go look.

SPAMMING ANALOGY
HI! YOU ASKED US TO DO THAT TO YOU! NOW THAT WE HAVE YOUR ATTENTION. WOULD YOU LIKE TO BUY A FLY-SWATTER?
COPYRIGHT (C) 2000 ILLIAD
HTTP://WWW.USERFRIENDLY.ORG/

HEY. YOU GOT A SEC?
NYET! AM BUSY! AM GOINK TO PROVE TO YOU AM BETTER GEEK THAN YOU!

PLAN
PLOT
CODE

YOU KNOW I PROBABLY DON'T HAVE AS LONG TO LIVE AS YOU DO...
CRYOGENICS CAN BE FIXINK THAT.

SURE. CRYOGENICS. WHY DO YOU FOCUS SO MUCH ON **NEW** TECHNOLOGY?
NEW IS BETTER. IS NOTHINK OLD THAT IS BETTER THAN NEW.

YES THERE IS.
DA? NAMINK ONE THEN.

THE ORIGINAL PENTIUM CHIP VERSUS COUNTING ON YOUR FINGERS.
DA. DA. "DON'T DIVIDE. INTEL INSIDE."

SID? WHY IS PITR FUMING?
PROBABLY BECAUSE I GAVE HIM AN INTELLECTUAL MANBEATING AGAIN.

YOU KNOW SID. PITR'S NOT SOMEONE YOU WANT TO GET TOO EXCITED. HE'S ALREADY GOT A POOR GRIP ON REALITY AS IT IS AND IF YOU PUSH HIM OVER THE EDGE HE COULD SNAP AND GO QUASI-DIMENSIONAL ON US.
I UNDERSTAND. THANK YOU.

GOOD. SO DOES THAT MEAN YOU'RE GOING TO APOLOGIZE TO HIM?
HELL NO. I'M GOING TO PLAY WITH HIS MIND SOME MORE. WANT TO HELP?

COME ON. HELP ME PLAY A PRANK ON PITR...
SID. YOU DON'T KNOW WHAT YOU'RE ASKING HERE...
WANTED
FOR BOTCHING THE JOB ON LUKE SKYWALKER

LOOK. YOU'RE ASKING ME TO BETRAY A LONG-TIME CO-WORKER. WE'VE BEEN THROUGH A LOT TOGETHER. AND DESPITE HIS EXTREME MOODS AND HIS OVERALL SELFISH DEMEANOR. NOT TO MENTION HIS "I'M BETTER THAN YOU" ATTITUDE OR HIS...UM...HIS...UHH...
WANTED
FOR BOTCHING THE JOB ON LUKE SKYWALKER

UM...**WHY** AM I NOT HELPING YOU AGAIN?
AHHH. YOU MUST HAVE **JUST** ENTERED MID-LIFE. ISN'T IT COOL HOW TREACHERY JUST SEEMS **RIGHT?**
WANTED
FOR BOTCHING THE JOB ON LUKE SKYWALKER

WELCOME TO MATURITY, MIKE. YOU'VE OFFICIALLY GROWN UP.
THANKS. I THINK.
WANTED FOR BOTCHING THE JOB ON LUKE SKYWALKER
Copyright (c) 2000 Illiad http://www.userfriendly.org/

OH DON'T DOUBT YOURSELF! YOU'RE NOW AT THE POINT IN YOUR LIFE WHERE YOU CAN LOOK BACK AND SMILE AT YOUR ACCOMPLISHMENTS, WATCH THE YOUNG ONES FLAIL AROUND IN THEIR MEDIOCRITY, AND SIT BACK KNOWING THAT YOU'VE MADE IT.
WANTED FOR BOTCHING THE JOB ON LUKE SKYWALKER

I'M ABOUT TO DIE, AREN'T I.
HECK NO. IT MEANS YOU CAN WRITE BAD CODE AND PEOPLE WILL JUST CALL IT "OBFUSCATED."
WANTED FOR BOTCHING THE JOB ON LUKE SKYWALKER

THIS IS IT. MY TREASURE TROVE.
WOW..YOU DID ALL THIS?
Copyright (c) 2000 Illiad http://www.userfriendly.org/

YOU BET. AND I'M PROUD TO SHARE THIS WITH YOU. DOZENS OF MY OWN PROGRAMS ALL CODED ON THESE PUNCH CARDS. IN PERFECT ORDER.
WHAT'S THAT WHIRRING NOISE?

IS SO WERY HARD NOT TO BE SMILINK...
BLOWER 300
WHIRRRRRRR

The outrage and delight that this cartoon spawned was monumental. The Pitr vs. Sid wars raged for days.

USER
FRIENDLY
the comic strip
PIZZA
Portrasher 4
ROTO-ROUTER 800
Copyright (c) 1997-2000 Illiad

YE FLIPPING GODS. WHAT HAPPENED?!
AARRRGH

MIKE? WAS THAT YOU? WHAT'S THE MATTER?!
PAPER... CUTS...

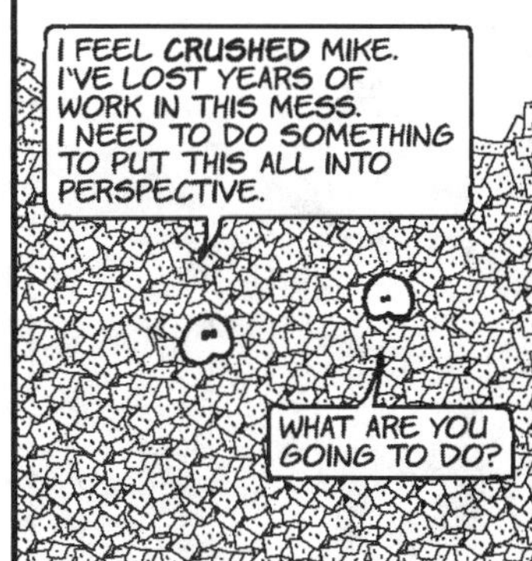
I FEEL CRUSHED MIKE. I'VE LOST YEARS OF WORK IN THIS MESS. I NEED TO DO SOMETHING TO PUT THIS ALL INTO PERSPECTIVE.
WHAT ARE YOU GOING TO DO?

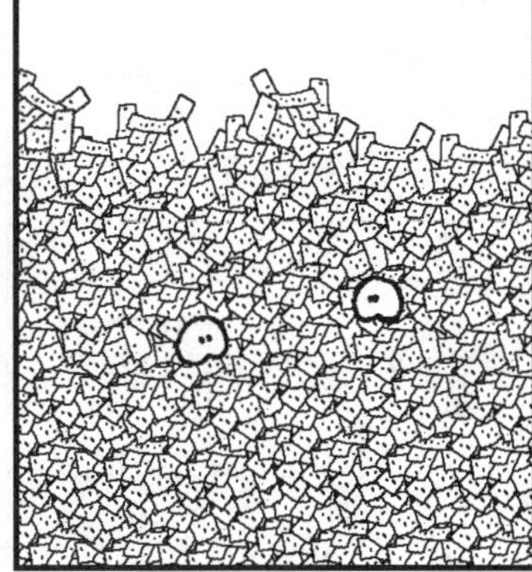

THERE'S NO HELP FOR IT. I'M JUST GOING TO HAVE TO SHIP ALL OF THESE CARDS DOWN TO FLORIDA, LABELLED "ABSENTEE BALLOTS."
HEY! DON'T MESS WITH THE FREE WORLD! YOU'LL GET ARRESTED!

TECH SUPPORT. GREG SPEAKING.
I'D LIKE TO COMPLAIN. THE ENTIRE U.S. ELECTORAL SYSTEM IS BROKEN. DAYS OF PRODUCTIVITY HAVE BEEN LOST ACROSS MY NATION, AND I WANT IT ALL FIXED!
Copyright (c) 2000 Illiad http://www.userfriendly.org/

I'M SO TIRED OF IT ALL. I JUST WANT THINGS TO WORK RIGHT. OR JUST WORK PERIOD. TELL ME WHAT WE SHOULD DO. GIVE ME HOPE.

SHUT EVERYTHING DOWN AND RESTART?
I THINK WE HAVE THE "SHUT EVERYTHING DOWN" PART DONE...

LOOK...I CAN'T HANDLE THIS CHAOS ANYMORE. YOU GUYS HAVE TO FIX THIS ELECTION MESS.
BUT...HOW? I'M JUST A HELPDESK GUY.
Copyright (c) 2000 Illiad http://www.userfriendly.org/

HELPDESK? I'M SURE I DIALED THE ELECTION OFFICE NUMBER.
UH OH

IT'S SOME GUY RANTING AT ME ABOUT "LINICKS" OR SOMETHING. IS THAT A COUNTY WE MISSED?
EVERYBODY HOLD IT!!! RECOUNT!!

HI. GREG SPEAKING.
HI! I NEED HELP! I'M IN NEVADA AND ALIENS HAVE JUST LANDED!!!
Copyright (c) 2000 Illiad http://www.userfriendly.org/

SOUNDS LIKE YOU NEED HELP ALL RIGHT...
YOU BET! THEY'RE ASKING ME TO TAKE THEM TO MY LEADER! WHAT DO I DO?!?!

TECH SUPPORT. GREG SPEAKING. DID YOU HEAR THAT? TECH SUPPORT. NOW SHUT UP AND LISTEN CAREFULLY TO ME.
Copyright (c) 2000 Illiad http://www.userfriendly.org/

I AM A TECH. I DON'T CARE IF YOU DON'T LIKE THE U.S. ELECTORAL SYSTEM. I DON'T CARE IF YOU SAW ALIENS IN YOUR BACK YARD. AND I MOST DEFINITELY DO NOT CARE IF YOU'RE LEADERLESS!

NOW THAT YOU KNOW WHAT'S WHAT, YOU'D BETTER HAVE A TECH SUPPORT QUESTION...
YEAH...UM. MY CUP HOLDER IS BROKEN...

AH. SID! THANKS FOR COMING. NOW THAT YOUR CONTRACT WITH US HAS COME TO AN END, I JUST WANTED TO THANK YOU FOR THE GREAT WORK YOU DID..
http://www.userfriendly.org/
Copyright (c) 2000 Illiad

AND..UM...

...ARE THOSE PAPER CUTS?
I LIKE TO THINK OF THEM AS "TALLY MARKS FOR NUMBER OF TIMES TO DIP PITR IN CHINCHILLA URINE."

YOU KNOW, SID, AS A FELLOW OLDSTER I DO UNDERSTAND THE NEED FOR REVENGE. BUT CODELINGS LIKE PITR DESERVE FORGIVENESS AND MERCY IF THEY HAVE ANY HOPE IN REDEEMING THEMSELVES.
http://www.userfriendly.org/
Copyright (c) 2000 Illiad

SO WHEN YOU COME BACK ARE YOU AT LEAST GOING TO HIDE THE BODY?
WHAT, AND NOT QUALIFY FOR THE CARPOOL LANE?

Political Asylum Certificate
Canada
This Certificate Entitles
to political asylum within the boundaries of Canada
for reasons as checked below:
☐ Bush Won
☐ Gore Won
☐ I Hate Florida
☐ You People Scare Me
☐ I Think Parliament is Cooler than Congress
☐ All of the Above and the Beer is better
Eh Eh Milne, Canadian
Beaver, a Proud and Noble Animal
Citizenship and Immigration Canada
Citoyenneté et Immigration Canada

HTTP://WWW.USERFRIENDLY.ORG/

HEY MIKE? HAVE YOU SEEN MY CAT AROUND ANYWHERE? IT'S BEEN A WHILE AND I'M KIND OF WORRIED...
YOU MEAN **FIVE**? NO. I HAVEN'T.
Copyright (c) 2000 Illiad http://www.userfriendly.org/

COME TO THINK OF IT, I HAVEN'T SEEN **MATT** AROUND HERE IN A WHILE EITHER.
POOR FIVE...HE'S PROBABLY LONELY AND MISERABLE RIGHT NOW.

BACK OFF MAN! I'M **PACKING!**
sNurf

I'VE GOT TO GET AWAY FROM THAT STUPID CAT. **MAN.** WHAT A **SUCKHOLE** FEW MONTHS IT'S BEEN...
Copyright (c) 2000 Illiad http://www.userfriendly.org/

MATT! JUST THE GUY I WANTED TO SEE! I NEED YOUR HELP WITH SOMETHING...
SURE MIKE! SPENDING TIME WITH A FRIEND ALWAYS HELPS MAKE MY DAY A BETTER ONE...

GODS, HOW I HATE HAVING FILTHY FINGERNAILS...
AAAAGH!!

OH MY **GOD**. NOT **ANOTHER** DWEEB CREATURE. WHAT PRECISELY ARE **YOU** SUPPOSED TO BE?
I'M MATT, A SEA URCHIN. I'M **VERY PISSY** RIGHT NOW BECAUSE MIKE USED ME TO CLEAN HIS **FINGERNAILS!**
Copyright (c) 2000 Illiad http://www.userfriendly.org/

I MEAN, WHAT WAS **THAT?** WHY CAN'T PEOPLE SEE BEYOND THE SEA URCHIN AND PERCEIVE MY HIDDEN **GIFTS?** FOR EXAMPLE, I FEEL I HAVE AN UNTAPPED GIFT FOR **MUSIC**.
YOU DON'T SAY...

DARN SIGHT CHEAPER THAN A NEW NEEDLE.
HER NAME WAS LOLA, SHE WAS A SHOWGIRL
AAIIIEEE!

HEY YOU BIG DUMB **FAKE**.
YOU!!
Copyright (c) 2000 Illiad http://www.userfriendly.org/

OH. **YES. PLEASE** ACCELERATE YOUR SOFT FLESHY HAND INTO ME.
ONE DAY AM GOINK TO SPREAD YOU ON TOAST ALONK WITH SID'S LIVER...

AH HA! LEETLE SLEEPING SEA ZLOTNIK. YOUR TIME. IT HAS COME...
TCP/IP
Copyright (c) 2000 Illiad http://www.userfriendly.org/
GULP! CHEW CHEW CHOMP
CHEW GLOP!
TCP/IP

HMMM...COLD. BUT WERY JUICY...
DUDE? WHY'D YOU JUST EAT ONE OF THE CAT'S HAIRBALLS?
LICK SMACK
TCP/IP

GEEZ. WHAT A DULL DAY. I NEED SOMETHING ENTERTAINING TO GET INTO...LET'S SEE...WHAT'S A.J. BEEN UP TO...HEYYYYY ...AN ONLINE DATING SERVICE?
Copyright (c) 2000 Illiad http://www.userfriendly.org/
HAHAHAHAHAHA HAHAHAHAHAHA HAHAHAHAHAHA HAHAHAHAHAHA HAHAHAHAHAHA AHAHAHAHAH!!!

ERWIN? WATCHA LAUGHING AT?
A CERTAIN WEB GUY WHO CALLS HIMSELF "MANLY HOT HAMSTER" IN HIS PERSONALS AD.

SIGH
CAN WE GET ON WITH LIFE CAMP
GORE CAMP
BUSH CAMP
HTTP://WWW.USERFRIENDLY.ORG
COPYRIGHT (C) 2000 ILLIAD

WHAT ARE YOU DOING?
CHECKIN' THE WEB. SAW YOUR PERSONALS AD. AREN'T **YOU** JUST MISTER SWEETIE-PIE...
Copyright (c) 2000 Illiad http://www.userfriendly.org/

"INTENSE TURBO NERD WITH PROPENSITY FOR THE ECLECTIC AND POSSESSED OF DIABOLICALLY ITCHY INSTEPS SEEKING GIVING, INTELLECTUALLY SVELTE WOMAN OF GODDESSLIKE SEXUALITY AND A KNACK FOR HARDWARE ACCELERATION. MUST LIKE PEELING SMALL, HAIRY FRUIT."

SO...WHAT DO YOU THINK?
YOU SOUND LIKE A TOTAL **FREAK**. I'M **SO** PROUD OF YOU, MAN.

HEY. WHAT ARE YOU DOING READING MY PRIVATE STUFF ANYWAYS?
OH, RELAX. YOU JUST GOT A RESPONSE TO YOUR AD...
Copyright (c) 2000 Illiad http://www.userfriendly.org/

REALLY?! WHAT'S IT SAY?
"HI! THIS IS PAMELA! COME SEE ME AND MY FRIENDS ROLL AROUND NAKED IN LASER PRINTER TONER!"

OH.
OOOH, YOU JUST GOT ANOTHER ONE FROM SOME BABE WHO WANTS TO KNOW IF SHE'D MAKE A GOOD **PORN STAR**. DUDE, YOU'RE **SWIMMING** IN CHICKS NOW.

YOU KNOW, I SHOULD PROBABLY WRITE HER BACK.
NOT TO WORRY. I JUST EMAILED HER FOR YOU.
Copyright (c) 2000 Illiad http://www.userfriendly.org/

YOU **DID?!?** WHAT DID YOU SAY?
SETTLE DOWN. I SENT HER A POEM...TRUST ME...

I GOT YOUR MAIL AND WROTE YOU BACK TO BE SURE YOU HAD NO DOUBT THAT IF YOU SPAM ME ONE MORE TIME YOUR ROUTER SHALL CEASE TO ROUTE.

HI...YOU'RE A.J.? I'M PAMELA.
UH...HI.
Copyright (c) 2000 Illiad http://www.userfriendly.org/

AFTER I GOT YOUR REPLY TO MY SPAM MAIL I HAD TO COME MEET YOU. I'VE **NEVER** BEEN TOUCHED BY POETRY LIKE YOURS BEFORE...
OH...UHM...

I DON'T UNDERSTAND ALL OF IT, BUT **"I WANT TO INDENT YOUR CODE"** SOUNDS PRETTY DEEP.
ERWIN!

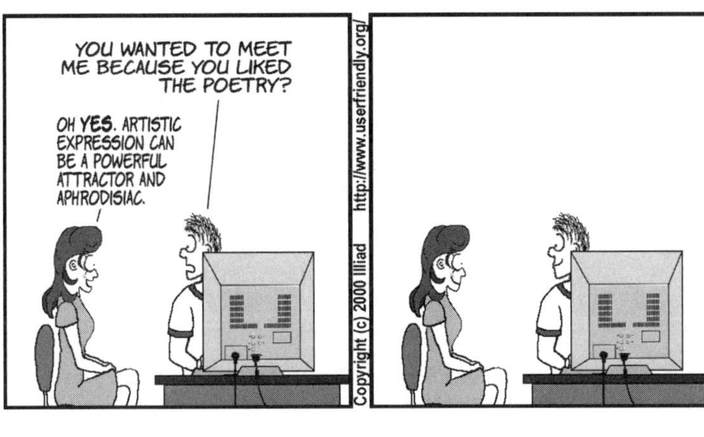
YOU WANTED TO MEET ME BECAUSE YOU LIKED THE POETRY?
OH YES. ARTISTIC EXPRESSION CAN BE A POWERFUL ATTRACTOR AND APHRODISIAC.
Copyright (c) 2000 Illiad http://www.userfriendly.org/

ART GETS CHICKS. MAYBE I SHOULD BECOME A CARTOONIST.
EXCEPT FOR CARTOONING. CARTOONISTS ARE DWEEBS.

SO...UH...WHAT DO YOU THINK OF GEEKS?
THEY'RE OKAY I GUESS...
Copyright (c) 2000 Illiad http://www.userfriendly.org/

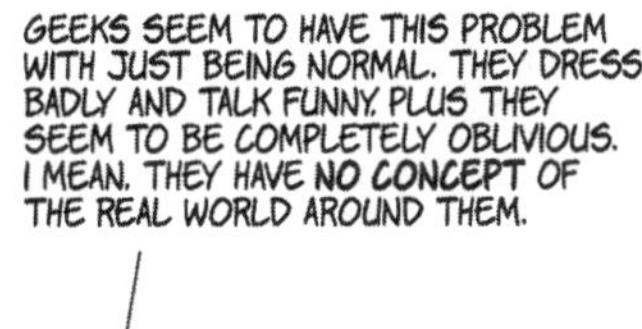
GEEKS SEEM TO HAVE THIS PROBLEM WITH JUST BEING NORMAL. THEY DRESS BADLY AND TALK FUNNY. PLUS THEY SEEM TO BE COMPLETELY OBLIVIOUS. I MEAN, THEY HAVE NO CONCEPT OF THE REAL WORLD AROUND THEM.

YOU TRY GETTING GOOD AT PONG WITHOUT MAKING A FEW SACRIFICES!
HEY WAIT... ARE YOU A GEEK?

IN ONE FELL SWOOP, SANTA DECIDES EVERYONE IS NAUGHTY THIS YEAR AND PROCEEDS TO PLAN OUT HIS RETIREMENT ON EBAY.
PS2 PlayStation 2
HTTP://WWW.USERFRIENDLY.ORG/
COPYRIGHT (C) 2000 ILLIAD

I GUESS THIS WAS ALL A BIG MISTAKE. I'M A GEEK. YOU'RE NOT. I'M JUST NOT YOUR TYPE. AND YOU'RE NOT MINE.
YOU'RE RIGHT. THERE'S NO REAL SYNERGY BETWEEN US.
Copyright (c) 2000 Illiad http://www.userfriendly.org/

BUT IF YOU COME AND SET MY VCR CLOCK FOR ME I'LL MAKE YOU DINNER.
I AM **SO** THERE.

I only ever had one action figure on my desk: Darth Vader holding onto a paternity kit.

WHAT'S THIS **CRAP** ALL OVER YOUR DESK?
THEY'RE MY ACTION FIGURES.
Copyright (c) 2000 Illiad http://www.userfriendly.org/

ACTION FI- YOU HAVE **GOT** TO BE KIDDING! DIDN'T YOU OUTGROW THOSE THINGS WHEN YOU WERE **EIGHT?!**

WHEN I WAS **EIGHT** I WAS INTO **NUCLEAR SCIENCE...**
EXCELLENT. ANY CHANCE YOU BECAME STERILE?

CHIEF. I'VE BEEN VERY TOLERANT OF THE ECCENTRICITIES THAT THE TECHS HAVE AROUND HERE. BUT I THINK THEY'VE CROSSED THE LINE THIS TIME.
Copyright (c) 2000 Illiad http://www.userfriendly.org/

HAVE YOU **SEEN** THE CHILDISH TOYS THEY'VE LITTERED AROUND THE OFFICE? WHAT IF A **CLIENT** WERE TO WALK IN AND SEE THEM? IT DOESN'T EXACTLY SMACK OF PROFESSIONALISM.
OH. I'M SURE IT'S HARMLESS. CUT THE TECHS SOME SLACK.

...AND THIS IS JABBA THE HUT. SEE HOW HE'S ANATOMICALLY CORRECT?

DID YOU HEAR WHAT GREG SAID TO ONE OF OUR MAJOR CLIENTS?
NO. BUT I BET YOU'RE GOING TO TELL ME...
Copyright (c) 2000 Illiad http://www.userfriendly.org/

GREG TOLD HIM THAT TO **TRULY** UNDERSTAND OUR TECHNICAL SERVICES IT WAS IMPERATIVE THAT HE ACT OUT A SCENE WITH THE ACTION FIGURES WHERE JABBA THE HUT GETS CHOPPED INTO **SLOPPY VISCERA** BY PRINCESS LEIA.

I GUESS I'D BETTER GO TALK TO HIM...
AND WHILE YOU'RE AT IT PLEASE MAKE HIM GET RID OF ALL THE TOFU HE USES FOR "SPECIAL EFFECTS."

ABOUT TIME THE CHIEF IS TAKING CARE OF THIS STUPID PREDILECTION FOR ACTION FIGURES. JEEZ....
Copyright (c) 2000 Illiad http://www.userfriendly.org/

I'M SORRY GREG. BUT THAT'S THE WAY IT HAS TO BE.

YOU'RE NOT BEING AT ALL FAIR, CHIEF.
TOUGH. I GET TO BE BOBA FETT.

I HATE GEEKS. I HATE GEEKS AND THEIR BENT LITTLE WAYS...
HEY STEF. SEE WHAT I GOT?
Copyright (c) 2000 Illiad http://www.userfriendly.org/

OH FER CHRI... ARE YOU INTO THIS TOO?!
YES. I GOT ONE OF THOSE RARE 'TRINITY' DOLLS FROM THE MATRIX.

UM...WHY DOES IT SAY "PVC BARBIE" ON HER PANTS THEN?
OKAY FINE... I COULDN'T FIND A TRINITY ACTION FIGURE. ALLOW ME MY DELUSIONS.

'the water of life'
CRYSKNIFE
HIC!
by Jose Cuervo
HTTP://WWW.USERFRIENDLY.ORG/
COPYRIGHT (C) 2000 ILLIAD

DESPITE IT NOT BEING A REAL "TRINITY" DOLL, IT WAS VERY EXPENSIVE. I HAVE TO GO INTO A MEETING FOR A WHILE, SO COULD YOU WATCH MY ACTION FIGURE FOR ME PLEASE?
I SUPPOSE.
http://www.userfriendly.org/
Copyright (c) 2000 Illiad

DON'T EVEN THINK ABOUT IT!
I'M NOT UNDRESSING ANYTHING!

I CAN'T BELIEVE I'M STUCK HERE BABYSITTING MIRANDA'S STUPID PVC BARBIE DOLL. THIS IS EMBARASSING.
http://www.userfriendly.org/
Copyright (c) 2000 Illiad

I CAN'T TOUCH IT. I CAN'T POSE IT. I CAN'T UNDRESS IT...IN FACT, I CAN'T DO ANYTHING WITH IT...

...BUT I'LL BET MISTER NAUGHTY SEABIRD CAN...

DOLLS? YOU'RE PLAYING WITH DOLLS?
ACTION FIGURES. BESIDES, THAT ONE IS MIRANDA'S. AND TODAY, MR. NAUGHTY SEABIRD IS PLAYING WITH MS. PVC...
http://www.userfriendly.org/
Copyright (c) 2000 Illiad

I READ SOMEWHERE THAT ADULTS WHO PLAY WITH DOLLS ARE UNCONSCIOUSLY ACTING OUT THEIR OWN DEEPLY PERSONAL FANTASIES BORN FROM DENIAL DURING THEIR ADULT YEARS.

BLAST IT. THE STUPID BIRD'S GOT HIS BEAK STUCK IN HER CLEAVAGE.
I ALSO READ THAT THERE'S OFTEN NO TELLING WHICH DOLL THE ADULT IS IDENTIFYING WITH.

ISN'T MIRANDA GOING TO KILL YOU FOR MESSING WITH HER DOLL?
YOU BET SHE'S GOING TO KILL ME. HELP ME PRY THESE TWO APART WILL YOU? PVC BARBIE HAS MR. NAUGHTY SEABIRD IN A BEAKLOCK.
WANK
WINKLE
http://www.userfriendly.org/
Copyright (c) 2000 Illiad

SQUIRM
POP
MOIST

WELL?!?! WHAT ARE YOU WAITING FOR?!
FOR MIRANDA TO RETURN. I'LL GO GET SOME POPCORN.

I'M BACK. STEF. THANKS FOR WATCHING -- HEY, WHERE'S MY DOLL?
UHH...YOU KNOW, YOU SEEMED SO KEEN ON HAVING A REAL TRINITY DOLL, AND IT BEING CHRISTMAS AND ALL, I WENT AND GOT YOU THIS....
Copyright (c) 2000 Illiad http://www.userfriendly.org/

OH WOW! STEF. THANK YOU SO MUCH! IT'S SO COOL! IT'S SO DETAILED! IT'S... IT'S...

...IT'S A KEN DOLL IN DRAG.
I'M GONNA KILL YOU COBB.
IT WAS ALL I COULD FIND IN PITR'S DESK.

G'NIGHT A.J.
SEE YA PAM. THANKS FOR DINNER.
1138
Copyright (c) 2000 Illiad http://www.userfriendly.org/

PAMELA? WHO WAS THAT?
JUST SOME GEEK I MET. HE'S USEFUL. HELPED ME SET MY VCR. AND HE KNOWS A LOT OF TECHNICALLY INCLINED PEOPLE, IN CASE HE DOESN'T HAVE THE ANSWERS HIMSELF.
1138

YOU'RE NOT...
YEP. I'M USING HIM FOR TECHS.
1138

UNSEEN CONSEQUENCES OF THE AOL TIME-WARNER MERGER FIFTY YEARS HENCE...
500 HOURS FREE!
YES, DREAD LORD. I AM CERTAIN THIS IS THE SOURCE OF THE SPAM TRANSMISSIONS.

There was a huge cry from the readership for these. We never made them, but by god we could've sold millions.

WHAT'S THIS?
YOUR CHRISTMAS PRESENT. I FIGURED THAT SINCE WE WON'T SEE EACH OTHER ON THE 25TH, WE COULD OPEN PRESENTS NOW.
Copyright (c) 2000 Illiad http://www.userfriendly.org/

WOW. THAT'S REALLY NICE OF YOU MIKE...
MY PLEASURE. HOPE YOU LIKE IT.

YOU BOUGHT ME A URINAL COOKIE?
NOT JUST ANY ORDINARY URINAL COOKIE! IT HAS THE AOL LOGO EMBOSSED ON IT!

THIS IS AWESOME! A BRANDED URINAL COOKIE!
YUP. THERE'S A WHOLE LINE OF THEM. AND THEY'LL EVEN DO CUSTOM ARTWORK FOR YOU.
Copyright (c) 2000 Illiad http://www.userfriendly.org/

CUSTOM ARTWORK?
SURE. I GOT ONE FOR STEF.

WHY DO I HAVE A WHITE PUCK WITH MY FACE EMBOSSED ON IT?

GREGOR, YOU ARE GETTINK WERY NICE PRESENT FROM MIKHAIL TOO?
SURE DID! LEAVE IT TO MIKE TO COME UP WITH A CHRISTMAS PRESENT LIKE A URINAL COOKIE.
Copyright (c) 2000 Illiad http://www.userfriendly.org/

DID YOU SAY... URINAL COOKIE?
SAY. WHY DOES YOUR BREATH SMELL FUNNY?

AHHHHH THE WINTER SOLSTICE. THE CYCLE BEGINS ANEW. ONCE AGAIN, I AM REBORN.
Copyright (c) 2000 Illiad http://www.userfriendly.org/

I LAY HERE AND BASK UNDER THE LIGHT OF THE SUN, DRAWING DOWN STRENGTH AND BREATHING THE AIR OF RENEWAL. I CREATE AN ANGEL IN THE SNOW AND BECOME ONE WITH ITS BEING. AND DESPITE THE ICY COLD, I FEEL WARM AND COMFORTED

NEAT SNOW ANGEL, GREG. HOW'D YOU GET THE HALO TO LOOK ALL GOLD LIKE THAT AROUND YOUR HEAD?
I COULD STAND UP AND SCREAM RIGHT NOW. BUT I THINK MY HAIR'S STUCK.

GREG. WILL YOU HELP ME BUY A CHRISTMAS GIFT FOR A.J?
SURE L'IL GUY. WHAT DID YOU WANT TO GET FOR HIM?
Copyright (c) 2000 Illiad http://www.userfriendly.org/

I DON'T KNOW. WHAT DOES A.J. NEED THE MOST?

DEPENDS ON WHO YOU ASK. BUT MOST WOULD SAY "A LIFE."
DO THEY HAVE THOSE AT THE MALL?

ACCORDING TO THIS DIRECTORY THERE'S AN ART SHOP IN THE MALL. THINK AJ WOULD LIKE ART SUPPLIES?
GREG? I THOUGHT YOU SAID THEY DIDN'T SELL LIVES HERE?
Copyright (c) 2000 Illiad http://www.userfriendly.org/

WHAT ARE YOU TALKING ABOUT? OF COURSE THEY DON'T SELL...OH.

PET S

One of my favorites. Don't ever buy a kitten or puppy from a pet store. Get them from the animal shelter; or, if you're looking for a purebred, research the breed and find a reputable breeder somewhere. Hint: reputable breeders at best break even. They do it for the love of the breed, not the money.

USER
FRIENDLY
the comic strip
PIZZA
Portrasher 4
ROTO-ROUTER 800
Copyright (c) 1997-2000 Illiad

"O HOLY NIGHT" PLEASE ERWIN. WITH LOTS OF PIANO CHORDS.
OKAY.

O MODEM LIGHTS I LOVE TO SEE YOU SHINING EVERY NIGHT AS I SURF ACROSS THE EARTH...

APART WAS THE WORLD. THEN CAME IP ASSIGNING WE SHOOK OUR HANDS AND WE ALL COULD SHARE OUR MIRTH...
THOUGH BROADBAND ARRIVED. AND THE WAITING WORLD REJOICES I'LL ALWAYS RESPECT 9600 BAUD...

FAAAALLLL ON YOUR KNEES. AND HEEEEEEEEEEEEEAARR THE NEGOTIATION!! O LIIIGHHTTS DIVINE. O LIGHTS. YOU BLINK AND WARN. OOO LIIIGHTS DIVINE O LIGHTS. O LIGHTS DIVIIIINE!
OOOER. NICE!

WOULD YOU PLEASE STOP THAT?! YOU HAVE THE VIENNA BOYS CHOIR RIOTING OUTSIDE THE DOOR!
SORRY. GUESS WE SHOULDN'T DO "WE THREE PINGS" HUH?
GREG'S SCARED OF CHOIR BOYS...

MERRY CHRISTMAS A.J.... I'M SORRY I DIDN'T GET YOU A PRESENT OR ANYTHING.
THAT'S OKAY L'IL GUY. I HAVE YOU FOR A PAL. THAT'S PLENTY.

Copyright (c) 2000 Illiad http://www.userfriendly.org/

HOW COME I SUDDENLY DON'T FEEL COLD ANYMORE?
BECAUSE I GAVE YOU THE SAME PRESENT YOU GAVE ME.

I unfairly stereotyped hunters with this storyline. Most of the hunters who wrote in took it with grace and at most mild annoyance. I don't hunt, unless you count plinking ditch rats with a pellet gun.

SO CHRISTMAS IS ALL ABOUT "PEACE ON EARTH"?
KIND OF. I THINK WE'RE MAKING HEADWAY.

Copyright (c) 2000 Illiad http://www.userfriendly.org/
BLAM!
BLAM!
BLAM!
BLAM!
PA-TWANG!

MURRAY!!! COME LOOK AT THE SIZE OF THAT SHREW!
COOL! CAN I USE THE DYNAMITE?!

YOU IDIOT! I HATE PEOPLE LIKE YOU! YOU WERE GONNA SHOOT HIM AND PUT HIM UP ON A WALL, WEREN'T YOU!

Copyright (c) 2000 Illiad http://www.userfriendly.org/

IF YOU LET ME SHOOT HIM, I PROMISE I'LL EAT HIM.
AAAIIIGGGH!

HEY LISTEN. SORRY FOR THE SHOOTING. MURRAY AND I HAD NO IDEA HE WAS YOUR FRIEND OR ANYTHING.
THAT'S OKAY...

Copyright (c) 2000 Illiad http://www.userfriendly.org/
MIND YOU, I DON'T APPROVE OF YOUR CHOICE IN WEAPONS. AND WHY ARE YOU USING MAGNUM ROUNDS? YOU CAN'T EAT PINK MIST YOU KNOW...
WOOO...

YOU'RE ONE OF THOSE GAMING FREAKS, AREN'T YOU.
YA, I'M A RAINBOW SIX MAN.

WELL. IT WAS NICE MEETING YOU. SORT OF. I THINK WE GOT ALONG OKAY FOR PEOPLE WHO DON'T HAVE MUCH IN COMMON.
HEY...MURRAY AND I ARE SORTA GEEKS TOO, YOU KNOW.
Copyright (c) 2000 Illiad http://www.userfriendly.org/

YOU ARE?
YA. HANG ON A SEC. GOT THE PROOF RIGHT HERE.

SEE? "ALL YOU NEED TO KNOW ABOUT WEB PAGE DESIGN." GOOD BOOK. YOU READ IT?
UNH-HUH. CAN I SEE YOUR RIFLE FOR A SECOND?

LOOK. YOU CAN'T LEARN HOW TO BE A GEEK FROM A SINGLE SOURCE. MAYBE YOU CAN LEARN HOW TO BE A HUNTER THAT WAY. BUT NOT A GEEK.
OKAY MISTER "RAINBOW SIX" -- WHAT WEAPON DO I USE TO HUNT ELK OR MOOSE?
Copyright (c) 2000 Illiad http://www.userfriendly.org/

UM... FRAGMENTATION GRENADES?
SEE?!!!
FORGET IT MURRAY!

USER
FRIENDLY
the comic strip
Portrasher 4
ROTO-ROUTER 800
Copyright (c) 1997-2000 Illiad

WELL...WE'RE JUST ABOUT AT THE REAL END OF THE MILLENNIUM. UNLIKE LAST YEAR. WHAT WITH THE MEDIA SCREWING UP THE FACTS YET AGAIN...
YEAH...

WHAT'S A MILLENNIUM?
NEVER MIND...

The phase of the moon is correct for that date. I'm a closet astronomy geek.

WHAT A YEAR IT'S BEEN. THE RIAA AND MPAA ARE TRYING TO LEGISLATE PROTECTION FOR THEIR BUSINESS MODELS...THE BRITISH GOVERNMENT IS PUSHING FOR MANDATORY ARCHIVING OF INTERNET COMMUNICATIONS...

...THE U.S. GOVERNMENT HAS ITS OWN INTERNET SURVEILLANCE RACKET GOING ON. AND NOW THEY'RE SUGGESTING COPY PROTECTION ON HARD DRIVES.

I THOUGHT YOU SAID NEXT YEAR WAS 2001?
OKAY. SO I WAS OFF BY SEVENTEEN YEARS...

OH DEAR LORD... MY **HEAD**...WHAT DID I **DRINK** LAST NIGHT?

IT DIDN'T LOOK THAT BIG AT THE BOTTOM OF THE BOTTLE...
A WORD. IF I MAY...

YOU CAN'T HIDE UNDER THERE FOREVER YOU KNOW. WE HAVE THINGS TO DISCUSS.
LIKE **WHAT?!** AND WHO EXACTLY **ARE** YOU?

I AM THE INCARNATION OF THE MEZCAL WORM. THE SYMBOL OF INEBRIATION THAT SITS IN THE DEEPEST LEVELS OF THE PSYCHE. YOU HUMANS SEEK ME OUT EVERY TIME THERE'S AN EXCUSE FOR A PARTY...

SO YOU'RE GONNA TAKE ME TO A PARTY?
IF YOU CALL BEING HELD ACCOUNTABLE FOR EVERYTHING YOU'VE DONE WHILE DRUNK A "PARTY". THEN SURE.
BEAST. YOU SAID YOU **LOVED** ME.
BUTTER

LOOK. I'M SORRY FOR WHATEVER IT WAS THAT I DID THAT'S MADE YOU SHOW UP. OKAY?
NOPE. **NOT** OKAY. WHAT YOU DID WAS AN **ATROCITY.**

THIS IS YOUR RECKONING. TIME TO REALIZE THE MULTI-LAYERED EVIL THAT YOU DID WHILE DRUNK. AND FACE THE MUSIC.

DUDE. WE ARE **SO** CHEESED WITH YOU FOR BUTCHERING OUR SONGS IN THAT KARAOKE BAR.
MENUDO?!?
TOLD YOU IT WAS AN ATROCITY.

IT'S NOT THAT EASY WIENER BOY. I'M HERE TO MAKE YOU ACCEPT RESPONSIBILITY FOR ALL THE EVIL THAT YOU'VE DONE WHILE YOU WERE POLLUTED.
WILL YOU **PLEASE** JUST **GO AWAY.**

LOOK...WHATEVER YOU ARE... I'LL ADMIT TO BEING A SLEAZE. AND FOR LYING ALL THE TIME. AND FOR BEING ARROGANT. AND EVEN MORALLY AMBIGUOUS...

BUT YOU CAN'T MAKE ME TAKE THE BLAME FOR MENUDO! THAT'S JUST NASTY!
BUDDY. YOU GET **IT ALL.** THE BOYS FROM **NSYNC** JUST GOT HERE TO SLAP YOU AROUND A BIT.
THERE HE IS!
LET'S KICK!

LOOK. I'M STARTING TO REMEMBER LAST NIGHT. AND ALL I DID WAS GET DRUNK. I DON'T EVEN GET THE SATISFACTION OF BEING BAD...SO FORGET IT. I'M NOT TAKING ANY BLAME.
FINE...I'LL JUST ERASE A SMALL, VITAL BIT ABOUT LAST NIGHT IN RESPONSE. HAVE A NICE DAY.
COPYRIGHT © 2001 ILLIAD HTTP://WWW.USERFRIENDLY.ORG/

STUPID WORM. THINKS HE CAN SCARE ME...
OHHH...HEAD HURTINK WERY MUCH...

CTHULHU HAVE MERCY! PITR?!?!
OHHH...IT IS WHAT DAY TODAY?
COPYRIGHT © 2001 ILLIAD HTTP://WWW.USERFRIENDLY.ORG/

MAYBE IF I HIDE UNDER HERE HE WON'T NOTICE ME.
SNIF SNIF

PHEW. EVIDENTLY IS DAY OF YEAR TO BE WASHINK FEET.
NNNGGGGGG!!! *CHOKE*

You'd be shocked at how many e-mails I received about this strip (truth: around a dozen), asking me about why I was introducing homosexuality to the cartoon. Of course, there's no indication that Pitr and Stef did the nasty, just that they passed out together on the same bed. I didn't tell any of the outraged readers that, though. Let them stew! I'm proud that the vast majority of the readership had a belly laugh!

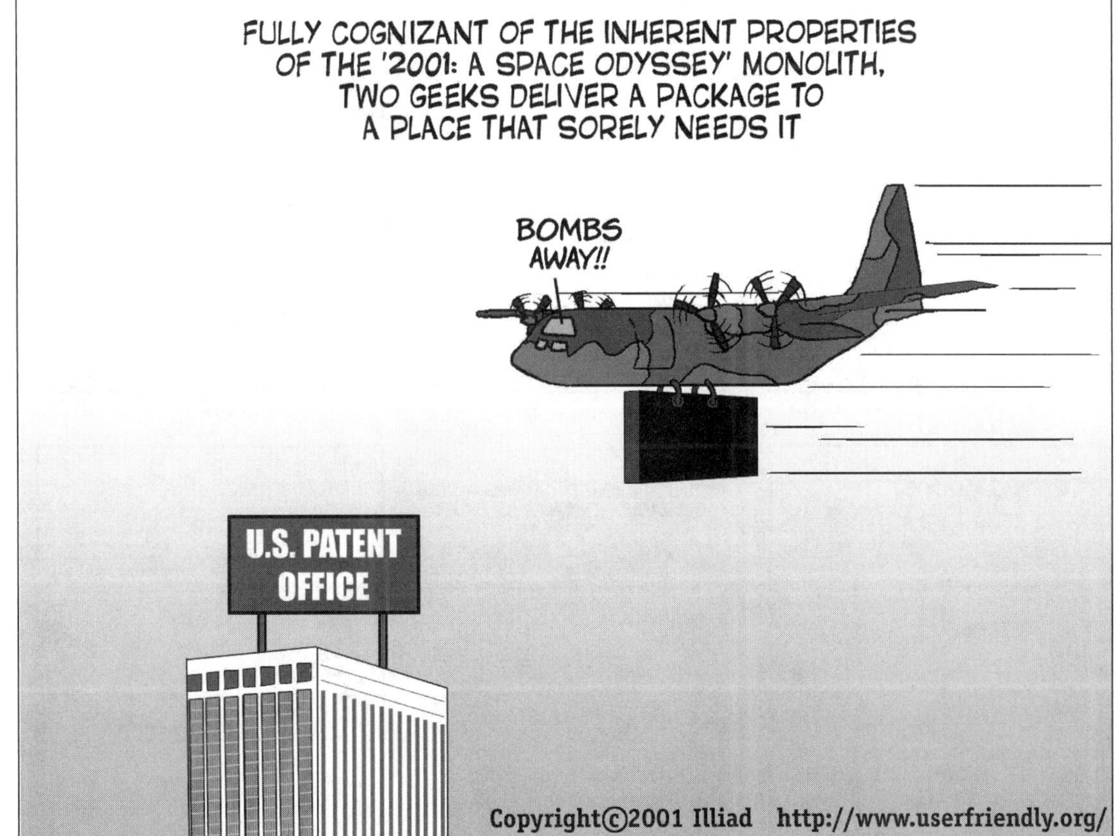
FULLY COGNIZANT OF THE INHERENT PROPERTIES OF THE '2001: A SPACE ODYSSEY' MONOLITH, TWO GEEKS DELIVER A PACKAGE TO A PLACE THAT SORELY NEEDS IT
BOMBS AWAY!!
U.S. PATENT OFFICE
Copyright©2001 Illiad http://www.userfriendly.org/

TECH SUPPORT. WELCOME TO THE NEW MILLENNIUM.
I HAVE A DEEP MYSTERY TO SOLVE...
COPYRIGHT © 2001 ILLIAD HTTP://WWW.USERFRIENDLY.ORG/

A...DEEP.. MYSTERY?
OH YES. DEEP. LIKE "WHERE'S THE ANY KEY ON THE KEYBOARD?" OR "DOES FLORIDA RULE THE U.S?" OR "HOW OFTEN SHOULD WE CLEAN THE INTERNET?"

OR MAYBE "HOW DOES SOMEONE WITH THE MIND OF AN AMOEBA LEARN TO USE THE TELEPHONE?"
OH DON'T BE SO HARD ON YOURSELF. IT IS A GOOD MYSTERY THOUGH...

SO WHAT'S THIS "DEEP MYSTERY" YOU HAVE?
WELL, EVERY DAY AT WORK, AT 3:30 IN THE AFTERNOON, MY COMPUTER SHUTS DOWN.
COPYRIGHT © 2001 ILLIAD HTTP://WWW.USERFRIENDLY.ORG/

SHUTS DOWN? DO YOU MEAN IT CLOSES ALL OF THE PROGRAMS AND JUST QUITS?
NO. THE POWER JUST SHUTS OFF.

AND DOES THIS HAPPEN WHEN YOU HIT THE POWER SWITCH, PERCHANCE?
WAIT - THAT'S NOT A BOSS SWITCH?

SO YOUR COMPUTER LOSES POWER AT 3:30 EVERY DAY AT WORK. WHERE IS YOUR COMPUTER PLUGGED INTO?
MY CUBICLE NEIGHBOUR'S POWER BAR.
AND HE GOES HOME WHEN?
AT 3:30
COPYRIGHT © 2001 ILLIAD HTTP://WWW.USERFRIENDLY.ORG/

MISTER, DO I REALLY NEED TO EXPLAIN THIS TO YOU?
WHAT....OH!!! YOU THINK IT'S HAPPENING TO HIM TOO, AND HE JUST GOES HOME AT 3:30 BECAUSE HE CAN'T WORK ANYMORE?

FINALLY...DONE.
"DONE?"
TAP
TAP
BLAP
COPYRIGHT © 2001 ILLIAD HTTP://WWW.USERFRIENDLY.ORG/

JUST FINISHED CODING A NEW SPECIALTY OPERATING SYSTEM.
A NEW OS? WHAT DOES IT DO?

NOTHING WELL, BUT HOLLYWOOD WILL LOVE IT.
YE GODS! WHAT'S WITH THE 20 COLUMN SCREEN?!

YOU'RE CALLING IT "MOVIE OS"?
MM-HM. IT'S AN OPERATING SYSTEM THAT CAN BE USED IN HOLLYWOOD FILMS.
WELL IT CERTAINLY LOOKS COOL.
CSH
COPYRIGHT © 2001 ILLIAD HTTP://WWW.USERFRIENDLY.ORG/

SO DOES IT ACTUALLY DO ANYTHING?
WELL, IT MAKES COMPUTERS LOOK SILLY AND THE PEOPLE WHO USE THEM SILLIER IN MOVIES AND IT... UM.... OH DEAR LORD WHAT HAVE I DONE...
CSH

DESPITE STILL FEELING LIKE UTTER HELL, I SUDDENLY SENSE A PROMISING DISTURBANCE IN THE FORCE...

DID YOU AT LEAST BUILD DECENT SECURITY IN TO THE SYSTEM?
OH YEAH...THERE'S EXCELLENT SECURITY.
CSH
COPYRIGHT © 2001 ILLIAD HTTP://WWW.USERFRIENDLY.ORG/

HEY. EXCELLENT SECURITY IS A FEATURE TO BE PROUD OF.
TAP TAP TAPPY TAP
CSH

I CODED IT SO THAT IT'S ONLY EXCELLENT SECURITY UNTIL YOU TYPE 'OVERRIDE.'
OOOOOER...
WELCOME TO THE NSA! WHO'S LIFE WOULD YOU LIKE TO MESS WITH TODAY?
CSH

COPYRIGHT © 2001 ILLIAD HTTP://WWW.USERFRIENDLY.ORG/
WHAT IF:
AOL TIME WARNER WAS A BUILDING COMPANY?
UM...WHY'D YOU BOARD UP MOST OF MY WINDOWS?
BECAUSE YOU ONLY NEED TO LOOK OUT OF THAT ONE TO SEE EVERYTHING.
AOL Time Warner

SO, WHAT SHOULD I DO WITH IT?
JUST DON'T LET HOLLYWOOD GET A HOLD OF IT. THEY'LL JUST GO BERSERK WITH MORE BAD COMPUTER MOVIES.
CSH
COPYRIGHT © 2001 ILLIAD HTTP://WWW.USERFRIENDLY.ORG/

OKAY. I'LL TAKE CARE OF IT -- BUT RIGHT NOW I NEED A CAFFEINE HIT. MY MORALS ARE SERIOUSLY SHAKEN UP.
SURE. WE'LL GO WITH YOU.
CSH

HELLOOOOOOO... SOMETHING SMELLS LIKE BAD, BAD MONEY. SMELLS LIKE VICTORY.

I WONDER WHAT THIS IS...IT SURE LOOKS PRETTY.
COPYRIGHT © 2001 ILLIAD HTTP://WWW.USERFRIENDLY.ORG/

(MOVIE OS:) PLEASE ENTER PASSWORD.
HMM...LET'S TRY... P-A-S-S-W-O-R-D

(MOVIE OS:) YOU BECKONED, MY MASTER?
YES! CAN I HACK OR WHAT?

LOOK AT IT THIS WAY MIRANDA. AT LEAST WHAT YOU CREATED WAS JUST A MOCK SYSTEM.
OH IT'S NOT ALL FAKE.
COPYRIGHT © 2001 ILLIAD HTTP://WWW.USERFRIENDLY.ORG/

I WANTED THE SYSTEM TO BE AT LEAST PARTLY FUNCTIONAL. IT CAN CONNECT TO SOME PRETTY COOL NETWORKS.
HUH?
LIKE WHAT?

HELLO. WOULD YOU LIKE TO PLAY A GAME OF GLOBAL THERMONUCLEAR WAR?
HELL YEAH!

When this strip was published, the Undernet IRC Network had been the subject of a sustained DDOS from parties unknown. They did eventually put a stop to it, but I doubt they ever caught the culprit. For the record, I think criminalizing DDOS attacks is a difficult, complex problem that shouldn't be pushed through without a lot of thought. Mind you, a vigilante solution involving a cement truck filled with lime Jello does have appeal while we work out the intricacies of legislation.

PLEASE INDICATE TARGET TO BE ATTACKED BY UNBELIEVABLY NASTY WEAPONS-GRADE STUPIDITY.
COPYRIGHT © 2001 ILLIAD HTTP://WWW.USERFRIENDLY.ORG/

HMMM...

U-N-D-E-R-N-E-T
NOPE, ALREADY DOING THAT ONE.

WAIT A MINUTE. DID YOU SAY YOU WERE GOING TO BE ATTACKING TARGETS WITH **STUPIDITY?!**
CORRECT.
TYPE
TYPE
TAP
TYPE
COPYRIGHT © 2001 ILLIAD HTTP://WWW.USERFRIENDLY.ORG/

AND HOW EXACTLY DOES STUPIDITY BECOME A WEAPON OF MASS DESTRUCTION?
TAPP
TAP
TYPE

MEANWHILE, DEEP WITHIN THE BOWELS OF THE CALIFORNIA POWER COMPANY...
FINALLY. IT'S 3:30. TIME TO GO HOME.
MASTER SWITCH

THE GAME IS OVER. YOU HAVE OBLITERATED THE ENTIRE PLANET.
COOL.
COPYRIGHT © 2001 ILLIAD HTTP://WWW.USERFRIENDLY.ORG/

AN INTELLECTUAL NUCLEAR WINTER HAS SET IN. NOTHING HAS SURVIVED EXCEPT...

...I KNOW. COCKROACHES.
HECK NO, THEY CROAKED. ALL WE GOT LEFT ARE SCRIPT KIDDIES.

USER
FRIENDLY
the comic strip
PIZZA
Portrasher 4
ROTO-ROUTER 800
Copyright©1997-2001 Illiad

PITR? WHAT'S THIS I HEAR ABOUT YOU AND STEF BEING IN THE SAME BED ON NEW YEARS?
DA. IS TRUE.

REALLY?!
NEEDINK SOFT PLACE TO SLEEP. HE IS SMELLINK **LEAST** BAD OF ALL PEOPLE THERE.

Y'KNOW, STEF DOESN'T REMEMBER IF ANYTHING HAPPENED OR NOT, AND HE'S FEARING THE WORST. YOU SHOULD PROBABLY GO CALM HIS NERVES.
DA. IS GOOD IDEA.

HMMM. AM REMEMBERINK CHAPTER SEVEN OF "EVIL GENIUSES FOR DUMMIES..."

...STOMACH LININK IS LIMITED.
NEXT TIME, AM WANTINK DINNER AND MOVIE **FIRST**.

I know he doesn't have a nose. He's like a Muppet, but nowhere near as cool.

DEEP IN THE CONCRETE BOWELS OF A SECRET BUNKER, INFORMATION IS SIFTED, TRADED AND EMBELLISHED. THE NERVOUS SYSTEMS OF THE FILM AND MUSIC INDUSTRIES MEET HERE AT A NEXUS, THE REPTILIAN BRAIN OF THE BIG MEDIA COMPANIES AS IT WERE.
COPYRIGHT © 2001 ILLIAD HTTP://WWW.USERFRIENDLY.ORG/

PART OF THE INFORMATION COLLECTION PROCESS INVOLVES A "HIGHLY DRIVEN TEAM OF SCRIPT-RUNNING JUVENILES."
OOOOH!
LEET!

ONE OF THESE "SRJS" COMES ACROSS MIRANDA'S MOVIEOS AND QUIETLY COMMUNICATES THE FIND TO HIS SUPERIORS.
DOODZ! FOUND 4N OS H3R3 TH4T'll ROCK YOUR WORLD!
I'M TOO LEET FOR MY CAR TOO LEET FOR MY CAR TOO LEET BY FARRR

SETTLE DOWN, DWORKMEYER. WHAT EXACTLY DID YOU FIND?
IT'S A NEW OS. IT DOES ALL THE FUNKY STUFF COMPUTERS DO IN THE MOVIES WE MAKE. Y'KNOW. LIKE THE 20-COLUMN SCREENS?
COPYRIGHT © 2001 ILLIAD HTTP://WWW.USERFRIENDLY.ORG/

DOES IT NOW.
YEP.

SOMEBODY GET LEGAL ON THE PHONE!!
WHICH DEPARTMENT. PATENTS OR THREATS?

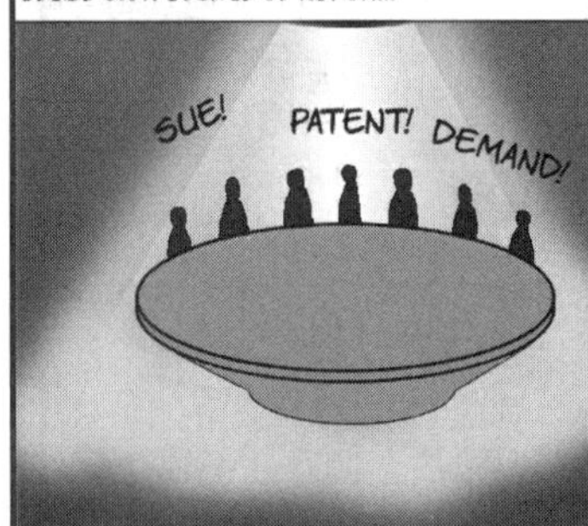
HAVING DISCOVERED MIRANDA'S MOVIEOS, THE SECRET OPERATIONS AND INTELLIGENCE DIRECTORS OF THE FILM AND RECORD INDUSTRIES CONFER TO DECIDE ON A COURSE OF ACTION...
SUE!
PATENT!
DEMAND!
COPYRIGHT © 2001 ILLIAD HTTP://WWW.USERFRIENDLY.ORG/

AFTER MUCH DEBATE, THE SECRET PANEL DECIDES THAT THE ONLY ACTION THAT CAN BE TAKEN IS ONE WHICH GUARANTEES THEIR CONTINUED CONTROL...
SAME OLD, SAME OLD?
LOOKS LIKE IT.

...AN ACTION THAT THEY'RE REASONABLY FAMILIAR WITH...
WE STEAL IT!
"ACQUIRE," OLD BOY. STEALING IS FOR CRIMINALS. WE'RE A MEGACORPORATION.

I'VE NOTIFIED COVERT OPS TO BEGIN THE ACQUISITION MISSION.
I HATE TO ASK, BUT WHY EXACTLY ARE WE TRYING TO ACQUIRE THIS "MOVIEOS?" IT DOESN'T COMPETE DIRECTLY WITH WHAT WE DO, NOR DOES IT INFRINGE ON ANY OF OUR INTELLECTUAL PROPERTY.
COPYRIGHT © 2001 ILLIAD HTTP://WWW.USERFRIENDLY.ORG/

HAVE YOU CONSIDERED HOW IT MIGHT GIVE SOMEONE THE DANGEROUS IDEA THAT THEY COULD COMPETE DIRECTLY WITH US?
GEEZ. OPEN YOUR EYES, FINKLE.

THE MEGACONTENT INDUSTRY COVERT OPS TEAM SCOPES OUT THE TARGET, A SMALL, UNIMPOSING BUILDING IN THE HEART OF THE CITY...
Columbia Internet
435
COPYRIGHT © 2001 ILLIAD HTTP://WWW.USERFRIENDLY.ORG/

THE TEAM LEADER SHOWS UP, CONFIDENT THAT HIS UNIT IS PENULTIMATELY TRAINED AND ONE OF THE BEST EQUIPPED...
Columbia Internet
435

...OF COURSE, EVEN THE BEST CAN FORGET THE OCCASIONAL ITEM...
CEASE AND DESIST LETTERS?
CHECK!
OWNERSHIP WAIVERS?
CHECK!!
PENS?
UMMM...

THE TEAM PREPARES TO ASSAULT THE INNER REACHES OF THE TINY ISP...
YOU BOYS READY?
SURE.
GUESS SO.
COPYRIGHT © 2001 ILLIAD HTTP://WWW.USERFRIENDLY.ORG/

WE AREN'T EVEN IN YET. WHY ARE YOU GUYS CROUCHING FUNNY?!
I NEED TO PEE.
AND I AIN'T GETTING KICKED IN THE NARDS LIKE LAST TIME.

WITH SUPERBOWL SUNDAY BEING TELEVISED EVERYWHERE, INCLUDING POWER-STARVED CALIFORNIA, SID ONCE AGAIN PROVES THAT TIMING IS EVERYTHING...
AND THERE'S THE POWER-UP SEQUENCE...
AND THERE'S THE KICKOFF...!
COPYRIGHT © 2001 ILLIAD HTTP://WWW.USERFRIENDLY.ORG/

THE ASSAULT TEAM PUSHES INTO THE OFFICES OF COLUMBIA INTERNET...
THERE'S SOME DUDE WITH BAD HAIR GUARDING THE OS.
BLUE SNIPER. YOU GOT HIM?
YES SIR. ONE SERVING DOCUMENT. ONE GUILTY PARTY. NO EXCEPTIONS.
COPYRIGHT © 2001 ILLIAD HTTP://WWW.USERFRIENDLY.ORG/

POH!
CRACKLE

BLUE SNIPER! SITREP!
CEASE AND DESIST DELIVERED. DIDN'T FAZE HIM. MUST BE ONE OF THOSE SLASHDOT TYPES.
THAT'S IT! ASSAULT TEAM! GO GO GO GO GO GO!!!!

HE DOESN'T SEEM TO BE MOVING...
STRANGE.
YAH.
COPYRIGHT © 2001 ILLIAD HTTP://WWW.USERFRIENDLY.ORG/

SHOULD WE GRAB HIM?
WE'RE IN LEGAL, NOT HUMAN RESOURCES
YA, BUT HE'S BREATHING. THINK OF THE BONUSES WE'LL GET FROM H.R.

THE COVERT OPS TEAM MAKES OFF WITH STEF, ACCOMPANIED, OF COURSE, BY A COPY OF MIRANDA'S MOVIEOS (WHICH, DESPITE THE SIZE OF THE BINARY, WAS DOWNLOADED ONTO A FLOPPY AT THE PRESS OF A BUTTON.)
GIMME A HAND. I CAN'T KEEP A GRIP ON HIM...
WHAT'S ALL THIS OILY STUFF ON HIS PANTS?
COPYRIGHT © 2001 ILLIAD HTTP://WWW.USERFRIENDLY.ORG/

STEF..?
WHO'S THAT?!
WE'VE BEEN MADE! RUN!

MEANWHILE, BACK AT THE QUAKE ARENA...
I SUDDENLY SENSE A PROMISING DISTURBANCE IN THE FORCE...
WIGGLE

GUYS! I THINK STEF GOT KIDNAPPED AGAIN!
OH DEAR.
HOW AWFUL...
COPYRIGHT © 2001 ILLIAD HTTP://WWW.USERFRIENDLY.ORG/

HOW ENTIRELY DISTRESSINGLY TERRIBLE THAT IS. AND I SO WANTED TO SPEND MORE TIME WITH HIM. GET TO KNOW HIM FOR WHO HE IS AND WHAT MAKES HIM TICK. IF HE LED, I WOULD'VE FOLLOWED...

YOU WOULD FOLLOW STEF?
IF YOU CAN THINK OF AN EASIER WAY FOR ME TO GET AT HIS BACK, I'M OPEN.
ERWIN!!!

WE HAVE TO GET STEF BACK. DO YOU GUYS HAVE ANY IDEAS?
ERWIN, DO YOU STILL HAVE CONTROL OF ARTUR?
YES, BUT HE'S **BUSY**.
COPYRIGHT © 2001 ILLIAD HTTP://WWW.USERFRIENDLY.ORG/

BUSY? DOING WHAT?
LOOK, IT'S **IMPORTANT**, OKAY?

HE KEEPS SAYING SOMETHING ABOUT "KEEPING A PLACE" IN THE LINE-UP FOR THE NEXT STAR WARS MOVIE. HE'S BEEN HERE FOR **MONTHS**.
ANOTHER LINECRASHER. I'LL BET. WELL JUST YOU **TRY** IT BUDDY...

NONE OF THE TECHS ARE HERE, AND WITHOUT ARTUR I GUESS I HAVE TO GET STEF BACK ALL BY MYSELF.
ERWIN AND I WILL GO WITH YOU, A.J.
COPYRIGHT © 2001 ILLIAD HTTP://WWW.USERFRIENDLY.ORG/

THAT'D BE **GREAT!** UH, SAY, HAVE YOU SEEN MY SNURF GUN AND MY ACTION FIGURES AND TANKS AND STUFF?
NO...

I AM **SO** READY TO OPEN UP A CAN OF WHOOP-ASS.

USER
FRIENDLY
the comic strip
PIZZA
Portrasher 4
ROTO-ROUTER 800
Copyright©1997-2001 Illiad

UM...WHY ARE YOU DRINKING SO MUCH MILK?
BECAUSE WE'RE GONNA DO A LOUIS ARMSTRONG SONG.
SHHLLUP

(SUNG TO "WHAT A WONDERFUL WORLD" BY LOUIS ARMSTRONG)
I SEE CHEAP CPUS... AND SOFTWARE THAT'S GREAT AND MY MODEM CONNECTS... AT TRUE 28.8 AND I THINK TO MYSELF... ...WHAT A WONDERFUL WORLD...

I SEE PEOPLE ON THE NET... WHO ARE NICE AND NOT "LEET" AND HARDWARE THAT NEVER... BECOMES OBSOLETE AND I THINK TO MYSELF... ...WHAT A WONDERFUL WORLD...

THE COLOURS OF THE IMAC... SO PRETTY ON MY DESK (THESE ARE COLOURS THAT ARE TASTEFUL NOT ONES THAT ARE GROTESQUE) I SEE ROUTERS SHAKIN' HANDS SAYIN' "WHO THE HECK ARE YOU?" BUT THEY'RE REALLY SAYING "LET THE DATA FLOW THROUGH"
WOOO! GIVE HIM A TRUMPET!

BLUE SCREENS OF DEATH... DON'T EXIST TO BETRAY AND I DECIDE FOR MYSELF... WHERE I WANT TO GO TODAY AND I THINK TO MYSELF WHAT A WONDERFUL WORLD YES, I THINK TO MYSELF WHAT A WONDERFUL WORLD...
KLIK
WHIRRR
KA-CHUNKA
IF YOU'RE DONE, LET'S GET BACK TO REALITY...

WELCOME TO DOTCOMBAT INC! I'M YOUR FRIENDLY H.R. MANAGER AND I JUST WANT YOU TO KNOW THAT WE'LL DO ALL WE CAN TO MAKE YOUR CAREER HERE WITH US AS PLEASURABLE AS POSSIBLE!
COPYRIGHT © 2001 ILLIAD HTTP://WWW.USERFRIENDLY.ORG/

WE SEE THAT YOU HAVE A PULSE AND YOU LOOK GOOD IN A TIE. IS THERE ANYTHING ELSE YOU CAN TELL US TO HELP PLACE YOU IN POSITION BEST SUITED FOR YOUR EXPERIENCE?

NAKED...IN BED...WITH SMELLY...CODER...
AH! YES. WE HAVE A NEED FOR A GOOD PROJECT MANAGER!

TROOPS, BEFORE WE HEAD OUT WE SHOULD TEST OUR SNURF WEAPONS...
ANYTHING YOU SAY, SARGE.
COPYRIGHT © 2001 ILLIAD HTTP://WWW.USERFRIENDLY.ORG/

I'LL JUST SET THE TARGET UP HERE AND YOU CAN CALIBRA-
BRRAAAAAP!

AIM MUCH?
HELL YEAH. LOOK HOW TIGHT THAT GROUPING IS!

HEY THERE NEIGHBOUR! WELCOME TO TIER SEVEN, CUBICLE FARM THREE! HEARD YOU WERE THE NEW PROJECT MANAGER! YOU LOOK PRETTY YOUNG. YOU BUCKING FOR A DIRECTOR-LEVEL JOB OR SOMETHING?
COPYRIGHT © 2001 ILLIAD HTTP://WWW.USERFRIENDLY.ORG/

THEY OFFERED ME A PROMOTION BUT I TURNED IT DOWN. DIDN'T WANT TO DEAL WITH ALL THAT MANAGEMENT CRAP. I LIKE HAVING FUN YOU KNOW? OKAY. OKAY. YOU'RE ONE OF THOSE STRONG SILENT TYPES. RIGHT? THAT'S COOL.

HEY D'JA HEAR THE ONE ABOUT HOW ALL THE DAYTRADERS FIT UNDER THE LIMBO BAR AT THE PARTY? THEY'D ALL GONE SHORT! HAHAHAHAHAHAH!!! OH LORD! HEY EVERYONE! COME MEET THE NEW GUY. HE'S A RIOT!!
MUST...RETREAT... FURTHER...INTO... BRAIN...

I WON'T GO FAR IN THIS COMPANY. THEY DON'T RECOGNIZE MY UNIQUE CONTRIBUTION. BUT THAT'S OKAY. I DON'T REALLY WANT TO CLIMB THAT LADDER YOU KNOW? IT'S DEMEANING. AND TRUTH BE TOLD THEY DISCOVERED SOME OF MY DIRTY LAUNDRY.
COPYRIGHT © 2001 ILLIAD HTTP://WWW.USERFRIENDLY.ORG/

I MEAN, WE ALL HAVE OUR SKELETONS IN THE CLOSET. MY SKELETON WAS PRETTY INNOCUOUS. AND I THOUGHT LACY PANTIES LOOKED GOOD ON ME. SO WHAT'S YOUR ALBATROSS?
UH...

...WHEN I WAS YOUNGER I ROLLED AROUND NAKED IN MONOPOLY MONEY
HEY PAL, I DON'T HANDLE THE V.P. PROMOTIONS. TELL IT TO THE CEO.

WELL NEIGHBOUR IT SURE WAS NICE MAKING YOUR ACQUAINTANCE. YOU KEEP UP THE GREAT WORK AND DON'T FORGET US LITTLE PEOPLE. HEY! CHECK OUT THE DORK AND THE TONKA TOY COMING UP BEHIND YOU!
COPYRIGHT © 2001 ILLIAD HTTP://WWW.USERFRIENDLY.ORG/

BRAAAAAAPAPAPAPAP!!
YEAAARRGH!

GEEEZ. ERWIN. HE WASN'T EVEN ARMED.
I DON'T CARE. I HAVE LOTS OF AMMO AND HE WAS WEARING A TIE.
ARE YOU GUYS FROM THE I.T. DEPARTMENT?! I'M SORRY ABOUT SPREADING THE CUP HOLDER STORY. OKAY?!?!

AS THE RESCUE TEAM DEPARTS WITH STEF IN TOW, THEY STUMBLE ACROSS THE MPAA COVERT OPS BEER HALL...
HEY...I THINK THOSE ARE THE GUYS WHO NICKED STEF..
UH OH.
COPYRIGHT © 2001 ILLIAD HTTP://WWW.USERFRIENDLY.ORG/

BRRRRRAAPAPAP
APAPAPAPAPAPPA
PAPAPAPAPAPAPP
APAPAPAPAPPPAP
APAPAPAP
yearrgh!

THEY HAD NO GUNS AND NO TIES. WHAT'S YOUR EXCUSE THIS TIME?
I HAD AMMO.

IF THERE WAS JUSTICE IN THE WORLD...
TIME TO TEACH THIS GUY WHO REALLY OWNS THE NAME "PS2."
THAT'S "PS/2" BALDY...
OWNER OF THE PS2.NO DOMAIN.
SONY LAWYER
IBM LAWYER
COPYRIGHT © 2001 ILLIAD HTTP://WWW.USERFRIENDLY.ORG/

AJ AND ERWIN SPIRIT AWAY WITH STEF, WHICH UTTERLY MADDENS THE MEGACORPORATION. THE COVERT OPS TEAM IS SENT OUT TO EXACT REVENGE.
GO GO GO GO GO!!
IF HE SCREAMS THAT IN MY EAR ONE MORE TIME, I'M GOING TO FEED HIM MY SHOTGUN STOCK.
COPYRIGHT © 2001 ILLIAD HTTP://WWW.USERFRIENDLY.ORG/

THE TEAM IS TO BE PARACHUTED INTO THE TARGET ZONE, SO THEY BOARD THE CORPORATE C - 130 HERCULES...
GO GO GO GO GO!!!
THAT DOES IT.

SADLY FOR THE TEAM LEADER, HIS EXHUBERANT URGINGS MADE HIS TEAM TWITCHY. SO THEY ATE HIM. AND THERE WAS MUCH REJOICING.
YAAAAAAY

TAKING AFTER MOVIES SUCH AS NAVY SEALS, THE OPS TEAM DEPLOYS USING A HALO INSERTION (HIGH ALTITUDE LOW OPENING), A PARTICULARLY DANGEROUS AND COOL-SOUNDING METHOD OF PARACHUTING INTO ENEMY TERRITORY.
COPYRIGHT © 2001 ILLIAD HTTP://WWW.USERFRIENDLY.ORG/

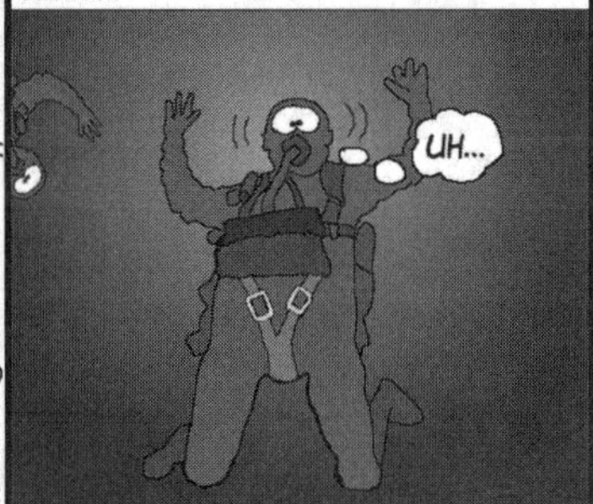
SADLY FOR THE OPS TEAM, WHICH PRIMARILY CONSISTS OF ACTORS AND NOT MILITARY PERSONNEL, THE PARACHUTES WERE NEGLECTED.
UH...

THUS WAS BORN THE HANO INSERTION, HIGH ALTITUDE NO OPENING, PARTLY NAMED AFTER THE SCREAMS OF REALIZATION.
HEY! NOOOOOOOOOO
YOU HEAR SOMETHING?
MMM...NOPE.
WHUMP

HEY PITR, HAPPY VALENTINE'S! LOOKS LIKE AN ADMIRER SENT YOU SOMETHING IN THE MAIL!
COPYRIGHT © 2001 ILLIAD HTTP://WWW.USERFRIENDLY.ORG/

IS WERY ODD. WHO IS SENDINK ME VALENTINE? CARD IS SHAPINK LIKE HEART...NYET... NOT HEART. IS...IS...
RRIPP!

...IS SHAPINK LIKE LIVER.
TO PITR,
KISS KISS! YOUR PAL - SID

SO WE BROUGHT THE JERK BACK. NOW WHAT?
I GUESS WE SHOULD SNAP HIM OUT OF HIS DAZE. I'LL POUR THIS CUP OF WATER ON HIM.
COPYRIGHT © 2001 ILLIAD HTTP://WWW.USERFRIENDLY.ORG/

SPLOOOSH!

HOLY CODE. HIS HAIR DIDN'T EVEN MOVE.
HE'S SNAPPED OUT OF IT. WONDER WHAT HE REMEMBERS...
PITR....SWEATY... DRIPPY...PITR... ...EEEEEH

HEY GREG. SLOW DAY. HUH? WHAT'RE YOU READING?
A NEWS ITEM ABOUT THIS JIM ALLCHIN GUY. THE CHIEF OF WINDOWS DEVELOPMENT OVER AT MICROSOFT.
COPYRIGHT © 2001 ILLIAD HTTP://WWW.USERFRIENDLY.ORG/

IT SAYS HERE THAT HE THINKS LINUX AND OPEN-SOURCE SOFTWARE WILL STIFLE INNOVATION. AND THAT LEGI-SLATORS SHOULD BE AWARE OF THAT. HE GOES ON TO SAY THAT "WE CAN BUILD A BETTER PRODUCT THAN LINUX."

THEN WHY DON'T THEY?
OH. BE NICE.

WHAT'S THIS I HEAR ABOUT YOU LINUX WEENIES GETTING UPPITY AGAIN? CAN'T A GUY LIKE ALLCHIN SPEAK TO A REPORTER WITHOUT GETTING JUMPED ON BY YOU KNOBS?
STEF. HE WAS PROPAGATING FALSEHOODS...
COPYRIGHT © 2001 ILLIAD HTTP://WWW.USERFRIENDLY.ORG/

OH SO WHAT IF THEY WERE FALSEHOODS! HE CONVEYED THEIR OWN ADMIRABLE VERSION OF REALITY TO THE PUBLIC AND WHAT DOES HE GET FOR SUCH BRAVERY? DERISION! ALL HE WAS DOING WAS RE-ITERATING MICROSOFT'S POSITION!

REPEATING A FALSEHOOD DOESN'T MAKE IT TRUE...
WHAT EXACTLY DO YOU THINK AN EIGHTY MILLION DOLLAR MAR-KETING BUDGET IS FOR?

USER
FRIENDLY
the comic strip
PIZZA
Portrasher 4
ROTO-ROUTER 800
Copyright©1997-2001 Illiad

YO. AUGUST. YOU MEMORIZED YOUR LINES?
TEE-HEE! LINES?
UH. YOU KNOW... THE WORDS IN THE SCRI-
I KNOW WHAT THEY ARE. YOU TROGLODYTE. I WAS GETTING INTO CHARACTER.

HI! I'M AUGUST. AND I'M HERE TO TELL YOU ALL ABOUT AN EXCITING NEW PRODUCT: WINDOWS XPG!

"THAT'S RIGHT! WINDOWS XCELLENT PERSONAL GROOMING. A SUPERB-LOOKING O.S. FOR SUPERBLY DRESSED AND GROOMED PEOPLE! DON'T BE CAUGHT WITH LAST YEAR'S OPERATING SYSTEM! BUY WINDOWS XPG ONLINE TODAY!"
XPG
welcome!
bill
steve
ernie
scheduled lockup in 2 hrs 17 mins

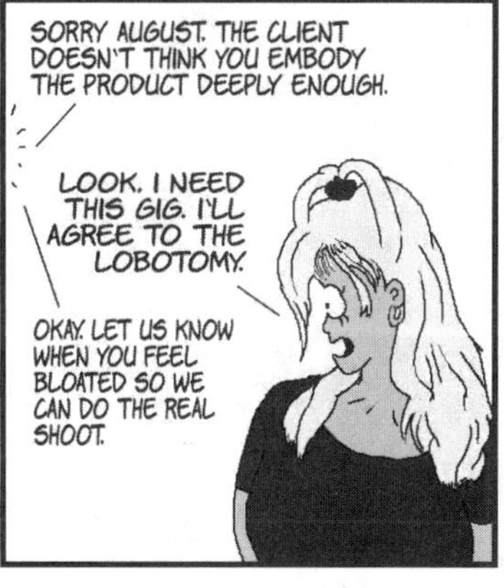
SORRY AUGUST. THE CLIENT DOESN'T THINK YOU EMBODY THE PRODUCT DEEPLY ENOUGH.
LOOK. I NEED THIS GIG. I'LL AGREE TO THE LOBOTOMY.
OKAY. LET US KNOW WHEN YOU FEEL BLOATED SO WE CAN DO THE REAL SHOOT.

OH THIS IS RIDICULOUS. MEMBERS OF THE U.S. GOVERNMENT ARE ONCE AGAIN TRYING TO REGULATE SPAMMING. THIS IS JUST OUTRAGEOUS!
COPYRIGHT © 2001 ILLIAD HTTP://WWW.USERFRIENDLY.ORG/

DON'T THESE PEOPLE REALIZE THAT IF YOU OUTLAW SPAM, ONLY **CRIMINALS** WILL HAVE SPAM?!

SOUNDS FITTING TO ME.
OKAY WAIT. THAT DIDN'T COME OUT RIGHT...

I had this almost-exact conversation with a marketer.

DON'T YOU SEE THE DOWNWARD SPIRAL WE'RE FALLING INTO WITH THIS SUGGESTED LEGISLATION OF SPAM? SPAM IS A BASTION OF CREATIVE MARKETING!
COPYRIGHT © 2001 ILLIAD HTTP://WWW.USERFRIENDLY.ORG/

WITH SPAM A MARKETER CAN TAKE A NON-PRODUCT AND MAKE UP ALL KINDS OF STORIES ABOUT IT AND MAKE AN ABSOLUTE **MINT!** SPAM IS A **NECESSITY** IN OUR SOCIETY!

LOOK, MAYBE SPAM WOULDN'T BE IN SO MUCH TROUBLE IF YOU JUST TELL PEOPLE THE **TRUTH** FOR ONCE INSTEAD OF **LYING**...
"PLEASE GIVE US YOUR MONEY FOR NOTHING USEFUL IN RETURN." YEAH, **THAT'LL** WORK.

HEY, WATCHA UP TO?
TRYING THIS NETWORK MANAGEMENT ON-LINE CERTIFICATION THING. HAVING TROUBLE WITH THIS QUESTION: "**DEFINE TWO WAYS A NETWORK DESIGNER CAN OPTIMIZE PERFORMANCE.**"
COPYRIGHT © 2001 ILLIAD HTTP://WWW.USERFRIENDLY.ORG/

YOU ANSWERED "CAFFEINE AND SUGAR"??
BASED ON MY OBSERVATIONS OF YOU...

A.J., WHY ARE YOU SPENDING ALL THIS TIME LEARNING ABOUT NETWORK MANAGEMENT ANYWAY? YOU NEVER SHOWED AN INTEREST BEFORE.
IT JUST SEEMS LIKE A GOOD THING TO BE CERTIFIABLE.
COPYRIGHT © 2001 ILLIAD HTTP://WWW.USERFRIENDLY.ORG/

I REALLY SET MYSELF UP FOR A ZINGER DIDN'T I.
YEAH, BUT YOU JUST DESCRIBED NETWORK ADMINS IN GENERAL.

CHIEF? DID YOU GET MY EMAIL?
YES I DID. YOU WANT TO TAKE A COURSE AND CERTIFY AS A NETWORK ADMIN?
COPYRIGHT © 2001 ILLIAD HTTP://WWW.USERFRIENDLY.ORG/

YES. YES I DO.
I THINK IT'S GREAT THAT YOU WANT TO BETTER YOURSELF. SO WHY NETWORKING?

WHY... ? WELL, SO I CAN RUN LAN PARTIES AND STUFF WHAT THE HECK ELSE WOULD IT BE FOR?
SILLY ME. I'M JUST GLAD IT'S NOT FOR SOMETHING FRIVOLOUS LIKE CAREER BUILDING.

FINE. YOU WANT TO GO ON A COURSE. I'LL APPROVE IT.
THANKS CHIEF! YOU DA MAN!
BUT I THINK WE NEED TO SPREAD THE TECH LEARNING AROUND A BIT. SOMEONE HERE REALLY NEEDS A BREAK FROM HIS MARKETING DUTIES.
COPYRIGHT © 2001 ILLIAD HTTP://WWW.USERFRIENDLY.ORG/

OH...UM...

I CONFESS I'M A LITTLE TWITCHY WHEN YOU SAY STEF NEEDS A BREAK FROM MARKETING.
OH IT'S BAD.
CHIEF! I HAVE A GREAT NEW MARKETING IDEA FOR US! "700 HOURS OF FREE STEF LOVIN' IF YOU SIGN UP TODAY!"

USER
FRIENDLY
the comic strip
PIZZA
Portrasher 4
ROTO-ROUTER 800
Copyright©1997-2001 Illiad

OKAY. I'M READY FOR MY COMMERCIAL SPOT, GERARD. MAKE ME LOOK GOOD.
STEF. WHAT ABOUT OUR TRAINING?

DON'T BE A DOLT! TALENT LIKE MINE CAN'T BE TRAINED. ARTISTRY MUST BE UNFETTERED. I MUST BE UNFETTERED.
MR. MURKY, SIR? YOUR BOXERS JUST CAME OUT OF THE WASH.

HI. I'M STEF MURKY, MARKETING MANAGER FOR COLUMBIA INTERNET HERE WITH AN OFFER THAT WILL JUICE YOUR ORANGES!

THAT'S RIGHT! BUY OUR INTERNET SERVICE FOR YOUR HOME OR OFFICE FOR TWELVE EASY PAYMENTS OF $14.95 PER MONTH! AND AS IF THAT ISN'T ALREADY A TERRIFIC DEAL, WE'LL THROW IN AN INTERNET CLEANING BRUSH AND A COFFEE CUP HOLDER FOR YOUR COMPUTER!

BUT WAIT! THERE'S MORE! WITH YOUR ONE YEAR SIGNUP WE'LL THROW IN 700 HOURS OF STEF LOVIN' ABSOLUTELY FREE! THIS IS AN OFFER YOU CAN NOT REFUSE!
I AM TO BE SIGNINK UP WHERE?

I had a hard time not poking at the bigots again. Sorry.

I THINK THIS IS THE LINE FOR SIGNING INTO THE COURSE.
I STILL THINK THIS IS STUPID. WHAT DO I NEED A LESSON IN NETWORK MANAGEMENT FOR?
EXCUSE ME. IS THIS THE LINE FOR THE COURSE ON CLIENT DEVELOPMENT?
COPYRIGHT © 2001 ILLIAD HTTP://WWW.USERFRIENDLY.ORG/

YOU COULD DEVELOP ME AS A CLIENT.
WHAT?!
SORRY. HE GETS THAT WAY WHENEVER HE'S AWAKE.

It's astonishing that men like Stef get dates.

THIS TRAINING THING IS SUCH A WASTE OF TIME. SURROUNDED BY A BUNCH OF WEENIE GEEKS AND SERVED BAD COFFEE. AT LEAST IN MARKETING COURSES IT'S EASY TO MEET A HOT BABE.
COPYRIGHT © 2001 ILLIAD HTTP://WWW.USERFRIENDLY.ORG/

SWEET MOSES!!
HUBBA HUBBA!
NICE RACK OR WHAT?
NICE RACK?! WHERE?! WHERE?!!!

THIS IS JUST WRONG.
SPIFFY...NICE ROUTERS TOO.
IT LOOKS ALL TECHNICAL AND STUFF!

I CAN'T BELIEVE I'M IN A CLASSROOM AGAIN. BUT I GUESS IT'S NOT ALL BAD. EXCEPT FOR THE LEARNING PART.
COPYRIGHT © 2001 ILLIAD HTTP://WWW.USERFRIENDLY.ORG/

YOU'LL PROBABLY FIND THIS HARD TO BELIEVE BUT I HAD A BAD TIME IN HIGH SCHOOL. I HATED GOING. I'M JUST GLAD THAT THIS COURSE IS GEARED FOR ADULT LEARNING.
HEY...DON'T WE KNOW HIM?

HELLO CLASS. SAYING "GOOD MORNING MR. DABSTER" EARNS YOU A "B." "LORD DABSTER, I AM NOT WORTHY" GETS YOU AN "A." UTTERING THAT STUPID "ALL YOUR BASE ARE BELONG TO US" OR ANY DERIVATION THEREOF AND YOU FAIL. ARE WE CLEAR?
ALL YOUR GRADES ARE BELO... AAAAGH!!! I COULDN'T HELP IT!

I've seen a teacher hurl coins at sleeping students with remarkable accuracy. Always pennies, and always right on the bridge of the nose.

SO LET ME GET THIS STRAIGHT. OUR GRADES ARE AFFECTED BY WHAT WE SAY TO YOU.
OR WHAT YOU GIVE ME. SOMETHING YOU THINK A TEACHER COULD USE.
WE'LL BE RIGHT BACK.
COPYRIGHT © 2001 ILLIAD HTTP://WWW.USERFRIENDLY.ORG/

HUNDREDS OR TWENTIES?
COIN. MAKES FOR BETTER PROJECTILES WHEN I HAVE TO PEG SLEEPING STUDENTS.

WELL NOW. WHAT'S THIS?
AN APPLE! IT'S QUITE AN OLD TRADITION.
COPYRIGHT © 2001 ILLIAD HTTP://WWW.USERFRIENDLY.ORG/

IT STARTED IN...UH..VIKING TIMES. THE APPLES WERE GIVEN TO THE TEACHER TO ENSURE HIS GOOD HEALTH. AND THE STUDENT WHO GAVE THE TEACHER THE BEST APPLE WOULD GET A GOOD GRADE.
IS THAT RIGHT...

HEY! WHAT THE HELL IS THAT?
UM...IT'S AN APPLE. IMAC. FOR THE TEACHER.
NO A.J.. IT'S YOUR PASSING GRADE.

OKAY PEOPLE. LET'S GET STARTED ON THE COURSE. YOU'RE IN THE NETWORK MA...
ZZZZZZZZZZ
SNORK
COPYRIGHT © 2001 ILLIAD HTTP://WWW.USERFRIENDLY.ORG/

WOOOOOSH!!
KRUMP!
OW!!!

YOU THREW AN IMAC COMPUTER AT A STUDENT TO WAKE HIM UP?
OH PLEASE. WHAT ELSE AM I GOING TO DO WITH IT?
I DON'T THINK HE'S AWAKE ANYMORE.

EARTHQUAKE NEAR REDMOND
WE MISSED.
DARN GOOD THING. I DON'T NEED THE COMPETITION DOWN HERE.
COPYRIGHT © 2001 ILLIAD HTTP://WWW.USERFRIENDLY.ORG/

I did this one after talking to a friend of mine named Mike Warfield. He was one of the principal developers on the SAMBA team.

ALL RIGHT. PLEASE OPEN YOUR BOOKS TO CHAPTER 2, AND...
IS IT TRUE THAT AFTER THIS COURSE I'LL MAKE $100,000 A YEAR?
COPYRIGHT © 2001 ILLIAD HTTP://WWW.USERFRIENDLY.ORG/

NO.
OH.

WHAT CLASS DO I HAVE TO TAKE TO MAKE THAT?
BACKHOE WRESTLING 101. AND TAKE OUT SOME LIFE INSURANCE.

WELCOME BACK. AS DISCUSSED YESTERDAY, WE'LL BE LEARNING ABOUT **SAMBA** TODAY.
COPYRIGHT © 2001 ILLIAD HTTP://WWW.USERFRIENDLY.ORG/

SAMBA, I'M SURE MOST OF YOU KNOW, IS A PROTOCOL THAT ALLOWS FOR FILE AND PRINT SHARING BETWEEN PC TYPE MACHINES...

ALTHOUGH **SOME** FOLKS AREN'T TOO CLEAR ON THE CONCEPT.
I REALLY, REALLY, **HATE** GEEKS.

LOOK, COULD SOMEONE PLEASE DO SOMETHING ABOUT THAT IMAC? IT DISTURBS MY SENSE OF AESTHETICS. PUT IT WHERE IT'LL **BLEND**.
COPYRIGHT © 2001 ILLIAD HTTP://WWW.USERFRIENDLY.ORG/

HEY!! AAGH!!
HOLD STILL...

THAT'S GOOD, A.J. THE COLOURS AT LEAST MATCH.
I'M GONNA GET AN "A."
YOU'RE GONNA GET YOUR "A" KICKED.

ALL RIGHT FOLKS, TIME FOR THE BIG TEST. SPREAD OUT A BIT AND YOU CAN START AS SOON AS YOU GET A TEST PAPER. YOU HAVE AN HOUR TO FINISH. IF YOU HAVE ANY QUESTIONS, RAISE YOUR HAND.
COPYRIGHT © 2001 ILLIAD HTTP://WWW.USERFRIENDLY.ORG/

QUESTIONS **OTHER** THAN THE ONES ON THE TEST.
THEN HOW ABOUT "WHAT ARE THE ODDS **MIR** WILL HIT US IN THE NEXT HOUR?"

COPYRIGHT © 2001 ILLIAD HTTP://WWW.USERFRIENDLY.ORG/
DOINK
DOINK
DOINK
DOINK
DOINK

HEY...IS THAT THE SWEET SOUND OF A MULTIPLE-CHOICE SECTION I HEAR?
NOPE...ESSAY QUESTION YOU HAVE TO ANSWER IN BINARY.
DOINK
DOINK

HMMM...

COPYRIGHT © 2001 ILLIAD HTTP://WWW.USERFRIENDLY.ORG/
MOVE YOUR SHOULDER YOU WEENIE...

I'M JUST DYING TO KNOW HOW WHAT YOU WERE DOING JUST NOW HAS TO DO WITH NETWORK MANAGEMENT.
UM...I'M WORKING ON MY PEERING?

USER
FRIENDLY
the comic strip
PIZZA
Portrasher 4
ROTO-ROUTER 800
Copyright©1997-2001 Illiad

HI FOLKS! MIKE FLOYD HERE. YOUR FRIENDLY NETWORK NEIGHBOUR-HOOD MANAGER!

THAT WOULD BE "FRIENDLY NEIGHBOURHOOD NETWORK MANAGER."
DYSLEXIA SURE CAN BLAZE A TRAIL TO PERSONAL HELL, CAN'T IT.

TODAY YOU LUCKY VIEWERS WILL BE THE FIRST TO SEE A BREAKTHROUGH IN COMIC STRIP TECHNOLOGY - 3D! HANG ON AND WATCH!

IN GLORIOUS
3D!!

THAT'LL SHOW 'EM THAT ILLIAD KNOWS HOW TO DRAW HANDS.
EXCEPT FOR THE FACT THAT YOU ONLY HAVE THREE FINGERS.

Hands are hard to draw, but I got better at them. UF has always had characters with three fingers and a thumb on each hand (see also: Mickey Mouse), so I'll be keeping that tradition alive.

CLASS. I'M PLEASED TO SAY THAT MOST OF YOU DID VERY WELL ON THE EXAM. I THINK WE HAVE SOME TRULY TALENTED TECHNOLOGISTS HERE.

ON THE OTHER HAND. WE DO HAVE A STUDENT HERE WHO BROKE THE RECORD FOR THE LOWEST SCORE ON A TEST.

A STUDENT. I MIGHT ADD. WHO DESPERATELY NEEDS A LITTLE TIME ON THE WHETSTONE.
WAY TO GO, A.J.

I HATE TO BREAK THIS TO YOU. BUT A.J. DIDN'T ACHIEVE THE LOWEST EXAM SCORE OF ALL TIME.
HE DIDN'T?

NOPE. AND MY SENSE OF ETHICS PREVENTS ME FROM STATING THE PERSON'S NAME IN FRONT OF THE ENTIRE CLASS.
OH. WELL. THAT'S PROBABLY A GOOD THING.

COULD YOU HINT AT WHO IT IS WITH A LIMERICK?
"THERE ONCE WAS A HORNY DEAF TURKEY..."
HEY!!

THAT WAS A PRETTY COOL COURSE OVER-ALL. WASN'T IT STEF?
YEAH. WHATEVER.

WONDER WHAT SID MEANT WHEN HE SAID A COMPANY WOULD DO BETTER WITH A MAGIC 8-BALL INSTEAD OF YOU FOR A NETWORK TECH.
YOU KEEP THAT UP AND YOUR OUTLOOK WON'T BE GOOD.

HOW'D THE TRAINING GO, A.J.?
IT WAS GOOD. I LEARNED LOTS! NOW I CAN HELP MIKE AROUND THE SHOP WITHOUT BEING COMPLETELY CLUELESS.

NICE. DID **STEF** LEARN ANYTHING?
ONLY ENOUGH TO ABUSE HIMSELF.

SO NOW I KNOW ALL ABOUT NETWORKS AND STUFF. I CAN SEE WHY I KEEP LOSING AT QUAKE...IT'S BECAUSE OF **PACKET DROPPINGS!**

CHIEF. I JUST WANTED TO THANK YOU FOR SENDING ME ON THAT COURSE. AND JUST TO PROVE THAT I LEARNED SOMETHING, I'M RUNNING A BIT OF AN EXPERIMENT TO SEE IF WE CAN'T BOOST PRODUCTIVITY.
OH?
COPYRIGHT © 2001 ILLIAD HTTP://WWW.USERFRIENDLY.ORG/

I'VE INSTALLED VOICE RECOGNITION SOFTWARE ON ALL OF THE MACHINES IN THE OFFICE.
AND HOW ARE YOU GOING TO GET THE TECHS TO EVEN CONSIDER USING IT?

AAAAAGGGH! WHERE'S MY KEYBOARD?!
WHAT AM I GONNA DO WITH MY HANDS ALL DAY? ALL I HAVE IS THE INTERNET AND...OH...

THE COMPANY-WIDE INSTALLATION OF VOICE RECOGNITION SOFTWARE COUPLED WITH THE DISAPPEARANCE OF ALL KEYBOARDS CAUSES THE EMPLOYEES OF COLUMBIA INTERNET TO RETRAIN THEIR INPUT SKILLS...
WELCOME TO "NAUGHTY WIBBLING DOT COM!"
CLOSE BROWSER. CLOSE BROWSER. CLOSE BROWSER. CLOSE BROWSER. CLOSE BROWSER. CLOSE BROWSER...
COPYRIGHT © 2001 ILLIAD HTTP://WWW.USERFRIENDLY.ORG/

SOME HAVE MADE THE TRANSITION WITH LITTLE TROUBLE, TRANSCENDING THEIR LIMITS BY CONVERTING REFLEX TO VOICE.
TURN LEFT. STOP. FIRE ROCKET.

WHEREAS OTHERS MERELY MANIFEST THEIR MOTOR SKILLS IN WORDS...
UM...UM...UM...STEP IN FRONT OF ROCKET! NOOO! I MEAN...!!
SPLUTCH!

GATES MANSION
SOME SEABIRDS ARE BORN TO BE HEROES
MR. NAUGHTY SEABIRD
WILLIAM GATES III
ENEMY AT THE GATES
COPYRIGHT © 2001 ILLIAD HTTP://WWW.USERFRIENDLY.ORG/

This strip wasn't my idea, but I'll take the blame for it. I hated the movie it spoofs and really didn't like the strip. But the book the movie was based on was superb! No penguins in it, though.

MIKHAIL. AM NOT LIKINK THIS VOICE RECOGNITION SOFTWARE. HAVE BEEN CODINK BY VOICE FOR PAST SIX HOURS.
WELL, WE COULD TELL STEF TO RETURN ALL THE KEYBOARDS.

COPYRIGHT © 2001 ILLIAD HTTP://WWW.USERFRIENDLY.ORG/
NYET. AM NOT BELIEVINK STEF IS ONE WHO IS INSTALLINK SOFTWARE.
I DID SEE SID WANDERING AROUND A MINUTE AGO.

SID?!?! HOW IS HE GETTINK INTO MY MACHINE TO DO INSTALL?
DUDE. YOUR LIPS MOVE WHEN YOU TYPE YOUR PASSWORD.

GOINK AWAY!! YOU ARE DISTURBINK ME. MUST FINISH CODINK. PROJECT IS DUE IN ONLY FEW HOURS.
OKAY.

COPYRIGHT © 2001 ILLIAD HTTP://WWW.USERFRIENDLY.ORG/
LET'S SEE... WHAT IS NEXT COMMAND TO BE DOINK...

RM DASH RF SLASH ENTER!
NYYYEEEETTT!!!

OK. LEFT CLICK THE START BUTTON. CLICK ON SETTINGS. THEN CONTROL PANEL.
START, SETTINGS, CONTROL PANEL.
DONE.
NO. NOT YOU.
NOT ME?

COPYRIGHT © 2001 ILLIAD HTTP://WWW.USERFRIENDLY.ORG/
NO. NO. I MEANT MY COMPUTER.
MY COMPUTER OPENED.
YOU WANT ME TO OPEN "MY COMPUTER?" OR DO YOU MEAN TAKE THE CASE OFF?
NO. THE COMP-UTER.

WHAT ABOUT MY COMPUTER?!
AGH! LOOK. JUST PLEASE CLICK-
...EXCELLENT IDEA. *KLIK*
ALL USERS ON SYSTEM KICKED.

HA! HAVINK FIXED VOICE SYSTEM. WILL BE ONLY RESPONDINK TO COMMANDS BY MY VOICE! SEE MIKHAIL? RM DASH RF SLASH. IT IS THERE ON COMMAND LINE. NOW YOU SAY NEXT COMMAND.

COPYRIGHT © 2001 ILLIAD HTTP://WWW.USERFRIENDLY.ORG/
UH...ENTER.
SEE? IT IS NOT ACCEPTINK. AM ONE STEP AHEAD OF SID!

LIKE TO SEE SID TRYINK SOMETHINK N--ENTER!
TOO EASY.
KNOCK KNOCK

MAGIC REALM
I UNDERSTAND STEF PAID YOU TO INSTALL THAT VOICE SOFTWARE ON ALL OF THE SYSTEMS IN THE OFFICE. AND THAT YOU RIGGED THE SOFTWARE SO THAT IT CAN'T BE UNINSTALLED SAFELY WITHOUT THE PASSWORD.
THAT IS INDEED THE CASE.
COPYRIGHT © 2001 ILLIAD HTTP://WWW.USERFRIENDLY.ORG/

MAGIC REALM
AND I TAKE IT YOU NOW WANT AN EXORBITANT CONSULTING FEE TO REMOVE THE SOFTWARE WHICH IS CAUSING US SO MUCH TROUBLE.
NO. I WANT A JOB. HERE AT THE COMPANY. WITH A LOW-END SALARY.

MAGIC REALM
OH? I THINK WE CAN HANDLE THAT. DOING WHAT?
ANYTHING YOU NEED ME TO DO. BUT I WANT THE TITLE "CODER SENIOR TO PITR."

OKAY. NOW VERBALIZE THE PASSWORD.
I...
COPYRIGHT © 2001 ILLIAD HTTP://WWW.USERFRIENDLY.ORG/

AM...

...SID'S TOWELBOY.
SEE? NOW IT'S UNINSTALLING. AND YES. YES YOU ARE.

THE LOCATION OF CHOICE BY TACO BELL EXECUTIVES FOR THE "IF MIR HITS OUR TARGET, WE'LL GIVE EVERYONE IN THE U.S.A. A FREE TACO" PUBLICITY PLOY
HEADQUARTERS
COPYRIGHT © 2001 ILLIAD HTTP://WWW.USERFRIENDLY.ORG/

WELCOME ABOARD SID. I HEARD YOU'RE PART OF THE TECH TEAM NOW. I'M MIRANDA.
HEYA.
SEGFAULT. HEE HEE!
RATTLE RATTLE TAPTAP

YOU BEING AN OLDER GUY AND ALL AND HAVING LOTS MORE EXPERIENCE THAN ME IS COOL. I'M SURE YOU COULD TEACH US ALL A GREAT DEAL. BUT I'M A PRETTY GOOD TECHNOLOGIST MYSELF AND...
GO AWAY. I'M HAVING A FIT.

....UH....WHAT ARE YOU DOING?
NEVER HEARD OF "PERCUSSIVE MAINTENANCE?" SOME TECHNO-LOGIST **YOU** ARE.
UH OH...

EXCUSE ME? I HAPPEN TO KNOW **PLENTY** ABOUT SYSTEM MAINTENANCE. I JUST DON'T RESORT TO BRUTE FORCE AND IGNORANCE.
I WASN'T ACTUALLY GOING TO **SMACK** THE MACHINE. IT'S ALL PART OF THE PSYCHO-LOGICAL WAR WE ENGAGE IN AS TECHNOLOGISTS.
ENGFEH.

PSYCHOLOG- WHAT IN THE NAME OF **ERIS** ARE YOU **TALKING** ABOUT?
IT'S ABOUT POSTURING. SHOWING THE MACHINES THAT YOU CAN MAKE **THEIR** LIVES MORE MISERABLE THAN THEY CAN MAKE **YOURS**. WATCH.
DON'T TOUCH ME. I'M NOT COOPERATING.

LOOKS LIKE I'LL NEED TO ANALYZE THE PROBLEM. I HAVE AN OSCILLOSCOPE. AND THE CONTACTS ARE COLD...
YE GODS!! REBOOTING!!
MACHINES AREN'T THE ONLY ONES WHO HATE PEOPLE LIKE YOU.

HEYA GREG. I'M SUPPOSED TO COVER FOR YOU IN TECH SUPPORT TODAY.
OH...GREAT. LET ME GET YOU SET UP.

HEY...THIS LOOKS LIKE AN INTER-ESTING MANUAL...IT'S ON XML...
DON'T BREAK THE SEAL!!!
WHY NOT?

READ THE FINE PRINT ON THE SEAL, MAN. IT'S THE BARE, NAKED TRUTH. KINDA LIKE *NIETZSCHE*.
"BREAKING THIS SEAL IMPLIES THAT YOU HAVE READ THIS MANUAL, AND ARE THEREFORE OBLIGATED TO PROVIDE SUP-PORT TO ANYONE WHO DOESN'T **WANT** TO READ THIS MANUAL." OH, **MAMMA**.

JEEZ, THIS IS BORING. NOT A **SINGLE** SUPPORT CALL SINCE I STARTED. AND THAT WAS AT LEAST TWO **HOURS** AGO...

HMMM...THIS BOOK STILL LOOKS LIKE IT COULD BE GOOD READING. SURE DOES HAVE AN ODD LOOK-ING SEAL ON IT THOUGH.

THERE. I BROKE THE SEAL, AND NOTHING BAD HAPPENED. YOUNG GREG NEEDS A REALITY CHECK I THINK.
EXCUSE ME, MERE MORTAL. A QUESTION ABOUT XML IF I MAY...

UH...WHAT THE **HELL** ARE YOU?
CTHULHU. YOU MIGHT HAVE HEARD OF ME. I WAS SUPPOSED TO WAKE AND LAY WASTE TO THE WORLD WHEN THE STARS WERE "RIGHT." BUT I GOT KINDA ANTSY.
COPYRIGHT © 2001 ILLIAD HTTP://WWW.USERFRIENDLY.ORG/

OH RELAX. I'M NOT HERE TO SMEAR THE WORLD. **UNLESS**, OF COURSE, YOU DECIDE THAT TUTORING ME IN XML IS **BENEATH** YOU.
OF **COURSE** IT'S NOT BENEATH ME ...ACTUALLY IT IS... **NO!! IT'S NOT BENEATH ME!!**

THANKS FOR THE HELP, MORTAL. I'M OFF TO IMPLEMENT.
NO PROBLEM, BIG GUY. HAVE A GOOD NAP.
COPYRIGHT © 2001 ILLIAD HTTP://WWW.USERFRIENDLY.ORG/

YEP. BACK TO R'LYEH FOR ME UNTIL THE NEXT UPGRADE.

HOW...KUH...KUTH... KUH...KUTHOOO...
ONLY MAKES SENSE FOR A COUPLE OF **GREAT OLD ONES** TO GET ALONG...
DON'T PUSH IT. "MORTAL" AND "MORSEL" ARE PRETTY CLOSE IN MY BOOK.

USER
FRIENDLY
the comic strip
PIZZA
Portrasher 4
ROTO-ROUTER 800
Copyright©1997-2001 Illiad

MERE MORTALS, YOUR **COMPLETE AND UN-DIVIDED ATTENTION** PLEASE.

YES BILL, THAT MEANS YOU AS WELL...

AS AN OLD GREAT ONE, I HAVE THE ADVANTAGE OF PERCEIVING THE TRUE STRUCTURE OF THE UNIVERSE. I CAN SEE WHAT IS FOCAL, AND WHAT IS PERIPHERAL. AND I AM HERE TO TELL YOU WHAT IT IS THAT REALLY MATTERS. IN ONE WORD: **CARTOONISTS**.

INDEED. THINK OF THE ENORMOUS AND NOBLE BURDEN THEY CARRY! DAY-IN AND DAY-OUT THEY PROVIDE HUMANITY WITH PITHY, HUMOUROUS INSIGHTS INTO THE PATHETIC REALITY OF HUMAN EXISTENCE. THEY MAKE YOU SMILE OR LAUGH, EVEN AS YOU REALIZE THAT IN THE END, I GET TO EAT YOUR HEAD WHOLE.

SO REMEM--**AAAAGGGH!**
TAKE OFF THE MASK ILLIAD!! WE KNOW IT'S APRIL FOOL'S DAY!!
FINE. I'M BUSTED. HELP ME GET THIS THING OFF.

This was before I drew Cthulhu to be all cuddly like. Back then he was much wetter and spunchy looking.

SO. YOU ARE HERE FOR MORE THAN WEEK ALREADY. AND YOU ARE ACCOMPLISHINK WHAT?
WELL LESSEE...I BROUGHT A COMPUTER TO HEEL. I SINGLE-HANDEDLY SAVED THE WORLD FROM A MALICIOUS SQUID-GOD. AND I GOT BETTER AT LINUX THAN YOU.
COPYRIGHT © 2001 ILLIAD HTTP://WWW.USERFRIENDLY.ORG/

YOU KNOW. YOU WERE HAVINK ME GOINK THERE UNTIL LAST PART.
YEAH. YOU'RE RIGHT. I WAS BETTER AT LINUX THAN YOU **MONTHS** AGO.

THERE ONCE WAS A GURU NAMED SID. WHO WAS OUTSTANDING AT WHATEVER HE DID. LINUX, HE MASTERED... UMMM...
COPYRIGHT © 2001 ILLIAD HTTP://WWW.USERFRIENDLY.ORG/

...DESPITE BEINK A BAS-
HEY!!!

AND FOR LUNCH HE IS HAVINK SOME SQUID.
NOW **THAT** PART I LIKE.
I BEG YOUR PARDON?

SO. I UNDERSTAND YOU RATHER LIKE THE IDEA OF HAVING **SQUID** FOR LUNCH.
ABSOLUTELY NOT. THAT WOULD BE RETARDED OF ME.
COPYRIGHT © 2001 ILLIAD HTTP://WWW.USERFRIENDLY.ORG/

THAT'S GOOD TO HEAR. I WOULDN'T WANT TO HAVE TO REACH OVER AND EAT YOUR HEAD BECAUSE YOU MADE SOME RUDE COMMENT ABOUT MUNCHING ON SAUTEED SQUID.

NOT SAUTEED-- I WAS ACTUALLY THINKING OF "CTHUSHI"
WHAT?!?
NOTHING!!

HEED ME, MERE MORTAL.
DA?
YOU **KNOW** I'M ONE OF THE GREAT OLD ONES?
DA.
YOU GAZE UPON MY VISAGE AND YET DO NOT FLEE OR CRUMBLE?
DA.
COPYRIGHT © 2001 ILLIAD HTTP://WWW.USERFRIENDLY.ORG/

I MUST SAY THIS IS REALLY QUITE ODD. SINCE THE VERY BEGINNING, HUMANS WHO HAVE BEHELD ME HAVE INSTANTLY LOST THEIR MINDS.

...I AM SUCH A **DOLT**. THESE PEOPLE WILLINGLY ASSIST TECHNOPEASANTS EVERY DAY. THEY'RE **ALREADY** LOOSE IN THE HEAD.
YOU WOULD LIKE IF I AM FROTHINK? AM WERY GOOD AT FROTHINK.

WHY SO BLUE, O ETERNAL GREEN CEPHALOPOD?
IT'S JUST BEEN A BAD WEEK.
COPYRIGHT © 2001 ILLIAD HTTP://WWW.USERFRIENDLY.ORG/

NO ONE IS SCARED OF ME ANYMORE. AFTER EONS OF DEEP SLEEP, I AWAKEN TO A WORLD THAT ISN'T AFRAID OF ANCIENT, POWERFUL BEINGS WITH SCARY LOOKS AND AN ARROGANT DISPOSITION.

SO...HOW DO **YOU** HANDLE IT?
OH, I JUST... **HEY NOW!!**

SO WHAT'S THE DEAL WITH CTHULHU?
OH DON'T WORRY ABOUT HIM. HE'S JUST HAVING A BIT OF A MID-EON CRISIS I THINK.
COPYRIGHT © 2001 ILLIAD HTTP://WWW.USERFRIENDLY.ORG/

I WAS ONLY WORRIED ABOUT BECOMING AN **APPETIZER**.
RELAX. HE'S TOO BUSY GETTING A DOSE OF HIS OWN MEDICINE.

HI MY KEYBOARD IS BROKEN. I KEEP TYPING MY PASSWORD AND I JUST SEE LITTLE ASTERISK THINGIES.
YOU MUST BE A NEW TECH WEENIE. CAN YOU WRITE A MACRO FOR ME THAT GRABS MY DAILY PORN?
I WILL NEVER EVER MAKE PEOPLE GO INSANE AGAIN.

ONE OF THE H.P. LOVECRAFT ESTATE'S LESS SUCCESSFUL MERCHANDISING EFFORTS
NECRONOMICON
Books on Tape
COPYRIGHT © 2001 ILLIAD HTTP://WWW.USERFRIENDLY.ORG/

One of the best things about writing a geek cartoon is that you get to use your outrageous vocabulary. I've never used *uliginous* before.

GOIN' SOMEWHERE O ULIGINOUS ONE?
YEAH. I'M GOING BACK TO THE DARKNESS.
COPYRIGHT © 2001 ILLIAD HTTP://WWW.USERFRIENDLY.ORG/

THERE'S NO PLACE FOR ME HERE. I USED TO INSPIRE UTTER TERROR IN PEOPLE. TODAY I'VE BEEN RELEGATED TO MERCHANDISE HELL. THERE'S A PLUSH TOY OF ME AND EVEN A ROLE-PLAYING GAME BASED ON ME.
KLIK

SO I'M OUTTA HERE. AT LEAST I CAN TAKE COMFORT IN THE FACT THAT THERE'S NO WAY IT COULD BE WORSE.
SID! CHECK OUT THIS CTHULHU TOY! YOU WHIP IT ACROSS THE ROOM AND IT STICKS TO THE WALL!

MR. CHIEF? I'M LAWRENCE STAUKHALTER. I SPOKE TO YOU ON THE PHONE THE OTHER DAY.
OH YEAH..YOU'RE THAT VENTURE CAPITAL GUY?
COPYRIGHT © 2001 ILLIAD HTTP://WWW.USERFRIENDLY.ORG/

THE VERY ONE. DID YOU HAVE A CHANCE TO READ THE OFFER I SENT YOU?
LET ME THINK...

..YOU MEAN THE ONE THAT SAID "WE WANT TO OWN YOUR COJONES. PLEASE SIGN BELOW?"
I THINK THE LEGAL TERM WAS "TEST-ICULAR ACQUISITION." BUT YES. THAT'S THE ONE.

SO LET ME GET THIS STRAIGHT. YOU WANT TO FUND US?
WELL YES. WE THINK THERE'S A GREAT DEAL OF POTENTIAL IN YOUR BUSINESS AND WE'D LIKE TO HELP YOU SUCCEED.
COPYRIGHT © 2001 ILLIAD HTTP://WWW.USERFRIENDLY.ORG/

AND THE CATCH IS WHAT?
WE JUST WANT A SIMPLE EQUITY POSITION IN YOUR FIRM.

YOU CALL TAKING 99 PERCENT OWNERSHIP A "SIMPLE EQUITY POSITION?"
SURE. WE TAKE THE EQUITY. YOU ASSUME THE POSITION. SIMPLE.

I CAN SEE THAT BEING FUNDED WOULD BE USEFUL TO OUR EXPANSION PLANS. BUT I'M NOT ENTIRELY COMFORTABLE WITH SOME OF THESE CLAUSES YOU HAVE IN HERE.
SUCH AS?
COPYRIGHT © 2001 ILLIAD HTTP://WWW.USERFRIENDLY.ORG/

WELL LIKE THIS CLAUSE HERE THAT STATES EVEN IF FUNDING ISN'T COMPLETED. YOU GUYS STILL GET THE EQUITY.

I SEE. AND WHAT WOULD IT TAKE TO HAVE YOU AGREE TO THAT?
OH. I SUPPOSE SHOVING A PENCIL UP MY NOSE AND TWIRLING IT IN MY BRAINS WOULD DO IT.

HEY. WHO'S THAT GUY MEETING WITH THE CHIEF?
SOME VENTURE CAPITALIST. I HEARD SOMETHING ABOUT AN OFFER TO TAKE US PUBLIC.
COPYRIGHT © 2001 ILLIAD HTTP://WWW.USERFRIENDLY.ORG/

A VENTURE CAPITALIST?! YOU MEAN WE'RE GOING TO BE SOLD INTO SLAVERY?
RELAX. IF THE CHIEF DRAWS A LINE IN THE SAND THE V.C. WILL HAVE TO ACCEPT IT.

HOLD STILL NOW...
YEAAAAARRHGGH!

CHIEF? YOU OKAY?
EBBEH. INGUFF ATWAH.
COPYRIGHT © 2001 ILLIAD HTTP://WWW.USERFRIENDLY.ORG/

WHAT'S WRONG WITH HIM?
HE APPEARS TO BE IN SHOCK...

I THINK THERE'S SOMETHING COMING OUT OF HIS NOSE.
I'M DONE WITH THIS PENCIL. YOU GUYS WANT IT?
YES. THANKS. THAT'S THE PENCIL I CHEW ON.

USER
FRIENDLY
the comic strip
PIZZA
Portrasher 4
ROTO-ROUTER 800
Copyright©1997-2001 Illiad

HEY. I'M HERE TO DO THAT "HISTORY OF EASTER" THING.
THAT'S GREAT SID.

WANT US TO HOLD ON TO YOUR CHOCOLATE BUNNY FOR YOU?
SURE, BUT IF HE COMES BACK MINUS ANY BODY PARTS, I'LL BE SEEKING FLESH REPLACEMENTS.

HELLO. SID DABSTER HERE WISHING ALL OF YOU A VERY HAPPY EASTER. I WAS ASKED TO TALK ABOUT THE HISTORY OF TODAY'S HOLIDAY. EVEN THOUGH I'M NOT A HISTORIAN.
NO, BUT YOU'RE OLD.

UM. ANYWAY. THE NAME EASTER COMES TO US FROM THE SAXON EOSTRE, GODDESS OF THE MOON. AND THE EASTER BUNNY COMES FROM THE RABBIT AS AN ANCIENT SYMBOL OF SPRING AND RENEWAL...

WHICH IS ALL REALLY BORING. YOU PEOPLE NEED TO STOP FRETTING ABOUT THE MEANING OF THE HOLIDAY AND JUST HAVE FUN! I PERSONALLY LOVE THE EASTER EGG HUNT!
THAT'S BECAUSE YOU CAN HIDE YOUR OWN EASTER EGGS, SID.

THE LATEST DIPLOMATIC SALVOES WERE EXCHANGED TODAY BETWEEN THE U.S. AND CHINA OVER THE HAINAN SPY PLANE INCIDENT. THE PLANE REMAINS IN THE POSSESSION OF CHINESE OFFICIALS DESPITE STRENUOUS OBJECTIONS ON THE PART OF THE U.S...
COPYRIGHT © 2001 ILLIAD HTTP://WWW.USERFRIENDLY.ORG/

DEFENSE DEPARTMENT OFFICIALS ARE GRAVELY CONCERNED FOR THE INTEGRITY OF THE SECRET TECHNOLOGY FOUND ON BOARD THE US SPY PLANE...
HEH. DON'T THINK THEY NEED TO BE WORRIED ANYMORE.
WHY. WHAT DID YOU DO?

MEANWHILE, ON HAINAN ISLAND, CHINA...
NOW **THIS** IS INTERESTING. WONDER WHAT IT DOES.?
IT LOOKS LIKE A PAPER CLIP.
HELLO! YOU APPEAR TO BE RIPPING OFF TECHNOLOGY! CAN I HELP?

INSIDE THE EP-3 ARIES II SURVEILLANCE AIRCRAFT ON HAINAN ISLAND, CHINA...
WHAT IN THE NAME OF TOTALITARIANISM ARE **YOU?**
WHY, I'M CLIPPY, THE HELPFUL OFFICE ASSISTANT!
COPYRIGHT © 2001 ILLIAD HTTP://WWW.USERFRIENDLY.ORG/

I APPEAR WHENEVER YOU'RE DOING SOMETHING VAGUELY PRODUCTIVE, AND HELP YOU BY ADJUSTING THE THOUGHT PARADIGM BEING UTILIZED FOR MAXIMUM EFFECT AND COMFORT!

A SECRET AMERICAN PSYCHOLOGICAL WEAPON?
YES. I THINK IT'S WORKING ALREADY. I HAVE A HEADACHE AND I WANT TO CHOKE SOMEONE.
YOU COULD CHOKE BILL. CAN I HELP?

WE HAVE TO GO TO CHINA AND EVACUATE CLIPPY.
WE **WHAT?!** ***WHY?***
COPYRIGHT © 2001 ILLIAD HTTP://WWW.USERFRIENDLY.ORG/

BECAUSE WHAT YOU DID WAS **MEAN** ERWIN. HOW COULD YOU BE SO UNTHINKING?

HM. GUESS YOU HAVE A POINT.
DARN RIGHT I DO. THE CHINESE DON'T DESERVE THAT KIND OF NASTINESS...

ERWIN AND DUST PUPPY BOARD A SHIP LEAVING FOR CHINA...
WHERE'D YOU GET THE TICKER TAPE?
UHM...
ERWIN!! GIVE ME BACK THE CABLE!!
COPYRIGHT © 2001 ILLIAD HTTP://WWW.USERFRIENDLY.ORG/

...AND AS WORLDLY TRAVELLERS THEY SEEK OUT SHIPBOARD ENTERTAINMENT.
HELLO. ARE YOU THE CRUISE DIRECTOR? WE'RE LOOKING FOR A DISTRACTION TO WHILE AWAY THE TIME. LIKE SHUFFLEBOARD PERHAPS?

THEY'RE TROLLING FOR SHARKS OFF THE STERN. WANT TO GO HELP?
HMM. THAT DOES SOUND FAMILIAR.
THE CHIEF. THE V.C. BLOOD IN THE WATER.

AS DUST PUPPY WHILES AWAY THE TIME BY EXPLORING THE SHIP TO CHINA, HE DISCOVERS A TRAPDOOR TO A HOLD AND DESCENDS INTO THE DARKNESS...

COPYRIGHT © 2001 ILLIAD HTTP://WWW.USERFRIENDLY.ORG/
WITH SOME SURPRISE, OUR HIRSUTE HERO DISCOVERS LIVING BEINGS HUDDLING IN THE DARKNESS...

CHIK!
WHO PRAY TELL ARE YOU?
LAID OFF TECH WORKERS! WE'RE GOING TO THE LAND OF RICE AND MONEY!

YOU KNOW, WE SURE DO MISS THE DAYS OF THE DOT COM CRAZE.
SURE DO.
YEAH!

COPYRIGHT © 2001 ILLIAD HTTP://WWW.USERFRIENDLY.ORG/
I MEAN, WE WERE GODS! WE COULD DO ANYTHING! WE HAD A WET BAR ON EVERY FLOOR!! A POOL ON THE ROOF! DAILY BODYRUBS GIVEN BY JORGE!!
HE HAD SUCH SMOOTH STRONG HANDS...

HOW WAS YOUR REVENUE?
IT WAS GREAT! I FOUND TWO NEW SOURCES OF FUNDING EVERY WEEK! I CAN'T UNDERSTAND HOW WE WENT UNDER...
HANG ON ONE COTTON-PICKIN' SECOND!! JORGE WAS A GUY?

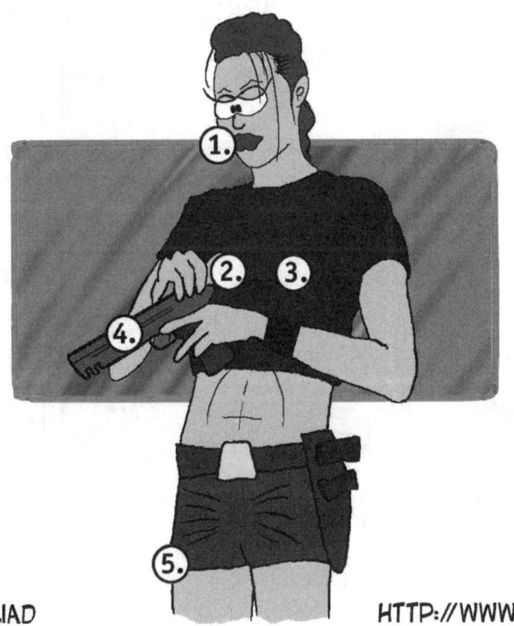
THE TOP FIVE REASONS WHY THE "TOMB RAIDER" MOVIE WILL BE A RAGING SUCCESS AMONG GEEK MALES
1.
2.
3.
4.
5.
COPYRIGHT (C) 2001 ILLIAD
HTTP://WWW.USERFRIENDLY.ORG/

Good Lord she's ugly. Sorry, Ms. Jolie, I didn't do you justice. (Although in my defense, Angelina, although otherwise gorgeous, doesn't have much in the way of hips.)

GOOD DAY EVERYONE. WE INTERRUPT THE CURRENT STORYLINE TO ADDRESS SOME FEEDBACK FROM THE VIEWERS REGARDING THE CARTOON YESTERDAY THAT FEATURED ANGELINA JOLIE AS LARA CROFT FROM "TOMB RAIDER."
COPYRIGHT © 2001 ILLIAD HTTP://WWW.USERFRIENDLY.ORG/

GIVEN THAT THE RENDERING OF MS. JOLIE WAS CLOSER TO THAT OF AN ODDLY SHAPED TURNIP WITH A PERSIMMON FOR LIPS THAN A SEXY ACTION GODDESS, ILLIAD HAS TAKEN IT UPON HIMSELF TO LEARN THE LINE OF THE FEMININE FORM.

SO HOW LONG DO YOU FIGURE, ILLIAD? TWO, MAYBE THREE...
...DECADES.

...I STILL REMEMBER THE LAST CRUISE WE ALL WENT ON DURING THE DOT COM CRAZE, AND THE VISCERAL, ALMOST DOGMATIC FUN WE HAD...
PULL!!
COPYRIGHT © 2001 ILLIAD HTTP://WWW.USERFRIENDLY.ORG/

BLAM!
BLAM!
BLAM!

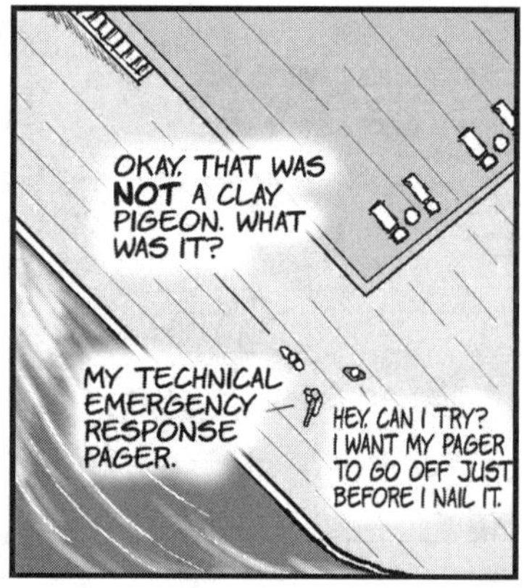
OKAY, THAT WAS NOT A CLAY PIGEON. WHAT WAS IT?
MY TECHNICAL EMERGENCY RESPONSE PAGER.
HEY, CAN I TRY? I WANT MY PAGER TO GO OFF JUST BEFORE I NAIL IT.

I enjoyed pouncing on those readers who accused me in e-mail of stereotyping the Chinese. I'm half Chinese myself, I grew up in the culture, and I speak two of the major dialects. And the ones accusing me of stereotyping all had really white surnames. Hmmm.

THE SLOW BOAT TO CHINA FINALLY ARRIVES, AND THE CONTAINER HOUSING OUR LAID-OFF TECH WORKERS IS SHIFTED TO THE DOCK.
COPYRIGHT © 2001 ILLIAD HTTP://WWW.USERFRIENDLY.ORG/

THE CONTAINER IS OPENED, AND WITH SOME AMAZEMENT THE TECHS REALIZE THEY ARE IN FACT IN A FOREIGN COUNTRY.
CHECK IT OUT! NORTH AMERICANS!
OOOOOOH

UM...HOW DO YOU KNOW WE'RE NORTH AMERICANS?
WE ALL SAW THAT FOREIGN MOVIE, "COUCH POTATO, HIDDEN REMOTE."
WITH ENGLISH SUBTITLES!
IS IT TRUE THAT THE PLURAL OF "Y'ALL" IS "ALL Y'ALL?"

WHAT IN THE NAME OF BUDDHA ARE YOU?
I'M DUST PUPPY.
WHAT?
Taste Noodle
COPYRIGHT © 2001 ILLIAD HTTP://WWW.USERFRIENDLY.ORG/

DID HE SAY RUST YUPPIE?
NO NO, IT WAS MORE LIKE FUSS RUPPY
UH OH...
Taste Noodle

RUPTURED GUPPY?
HEY, THOSE ARE GOOD WITH NOODLES.
ERWIN! HELP!!
Taste Noodle

COULD YOU HELP ME FIND SOMEONE? HIS NAME IS CLIPPY AND HE'S A BIG, HELPFUL PAPER CLIP.
BIG, HELPFUL...OH YEAH. HE'S IN THAT BUILDING BACK THERE.
COPYRIGHT © 2001 ILLIAD HTTP://WWW.USERFRIENDLY.ORG/

UM...WHAT'S HE DOING?
PROVIDING US WITH JOBS. WE HAVE THE NEXT CHRISTMAS CRAZE SEWED UP.
I HAVE A BAD FEELING ABOUT THIS...

THEY'RE PERFECT!
HEY JIN! START SHIPPING THESE BABIES TO THE UNITED STATES!
Plush Talking Clippy

made in China
CLIPPY!!
HI GUYS! WHAT DO YA THINK OF MY NEW BUSINESS?
COPYRIGHT © 2001 ILLIAD HTTP://WWW.USERFRIENDLY.ORG/

made in China
CLIPPY, YOU HAVE TO COME BACK WITH US, AND UNDO ALL YOU'VE DONE HERE.
OH.

OKAY, IF YOU SAY SO...
Cth- Cth- Cth- CTHIA!
WELL, I GUESS IT'S BACK TO THE CTHIA PETS FOR CHRISTMAS.
DANGER EVIL BABY THINGS
ANYTHING WHICH "GROWS" LIKE THIS HAS ME REALLY WOR-RIED, MAN.

WHILE PLAYING YOUR FAVOURITE FIRST-PERSON SHOOTER, IT HELPS THE EXPERIENCE IF YOU WEAR THE APPROPRIATE PANTS.

QUAKE III

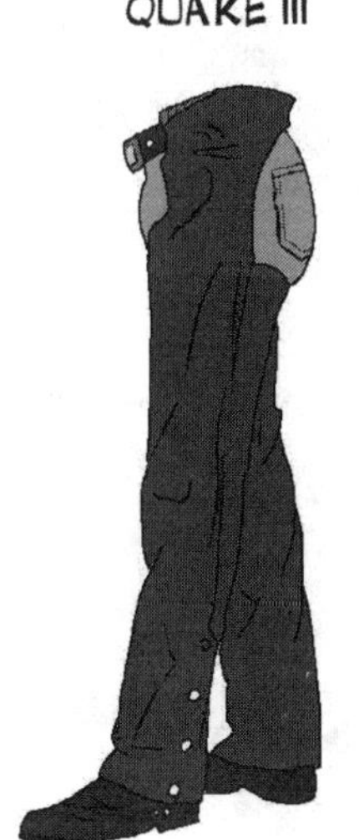

RAINBOW SIX

CLIVE BARKER'S "UNDYING"

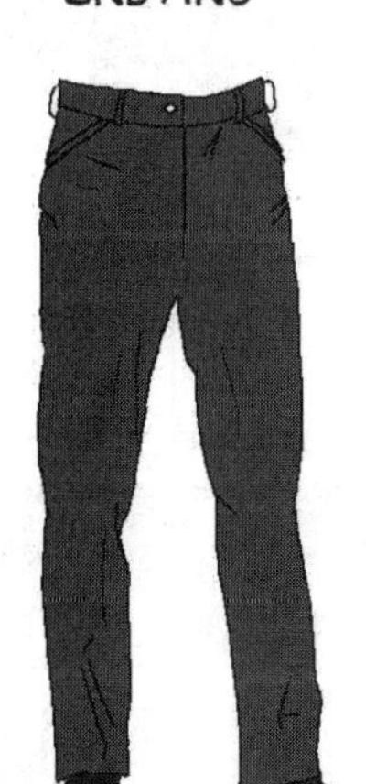

If you haven't played Undying, rest assured that it was at the time the scariest video game on the market. Scary enough to make me refuse to play the damned game if I was alone in the house. Brilliant work!

Wuffly. Like I said ... you get to use your outrageous vocabulary!

BUT I DON'T WANT TO GO BACK. NOBODY LOVES ME THERE.
WE LOVE YOU.
IT'S REALLY FOR THE BEST, CLIPPY. FOREIGN POLICY AND ALL.
COPYRIGHT © 2001 ILLIAD HTTP://WWW.USERFRIENDLY.ORG/

I SUPPOSE. I ONLY EVER WANTED TO HELP PEOPLE YOU KNOW.
WE KNOW.

I KINDA LIKED BEING A PLUSH TOY.
PERSONALLY, THE IDEA GIVES ME THE CREEPS. I'D GET ALL WUFFLY IF THERE WERE PLUSH TOYS OF ME...
UM...

CODE. CODE. CODE. MY WHOLE LIFE SEEMS TO BE JUST A LONG STRING OF CODE...
COPYRIGHT © 2001 ILLIAD HTTP://WWW.USERFRIENDLY.ORG/

HASH MARKS. DELIMITED DATA. RECURSIVE STRINGS. POINTERS...

YE HAIRY GODS!! IS THAT ALL I AM?!?
OH DON'T BE SO HARD ON YOURSELF. YOUR NETHACK SCORE IS AT AN ALL-TIME HIGH.
Cola

NOT YOU AGAIN. WHAT DID I DO THIS TIME?
I HEARD YOUR CRY FOR HELP. WHAT'S WITH THE EXISTENSTIAL ANGST?
Cola
COPYRIGHT © 2001 ILLIAD HTTP://WWW.USERFRIENDLY.ORG/

I DUNNO. I GUESS I'M FEELING A LITTLE TRAPPED. ALL I DO IS WORK ON NETWORKS AND DO A LITTLE CODE HERE AND THERE. IT SEEMS LIKE LIFE IS ENTIRELY PRE-DESTINED. LIKE I DON'T HAVE ANY FREE WILL OF MY OWN.
Cola

DAMMIT. THE UNIVERSE NEEDS TO GIVE ME THE POWER TO CHOOSE AGAIN!!!
OH, I CAN HELP YOU THERE...
Cola

ARE YOU SERIOUS?
DEADLY. YOU ASKED FOR CHOICE AND I NOW PRESENT YOU WITH ONE. TWO STRAWS. TWO COLAS. TAKE THE PEPSI CHALLENGE!
Cola
COPYRIGHT © 2001 ILLIAD HTTP://WWW.USERFRIENDLY.ORG/

Cola

KINDA HAS THE SAME FEEL TO IT AS THE LAST U.S. PRESIDENTIAL ELECTION, REALLY...
WHICHEVER ONE YOU PICK, I'LL OWN YOUR BUTT.
Cola

SLURRRRRRRRP

COPYRIGHT © 2001 ILLIAD HTTP://WWW.USERFRIENDLY.ORG/
SCHLOOOOOOOOOOP

ULP...THEY WERE BOTH VILE.
OH SORRY. FORGOT TO HOOK THE TUBES UP. HEY...WHY DO I ALL OF A SUDDEN FEEL HUNGRY?

OKAY. SORRY. I'VE HOOKED UP THE TUBES PROPERLY NOW. SO TAKE CHARGE OF YOUR WORLD AND MAKE A CHOICE ALREADY.
UM...OKAY.

COPYRIGHT © 2001 ILLIAD HTTP://WWW.USERFRIENDLY.ORG/

CAN I CHOOSE NOT TO PARTICIPATE?
IMAGINE THE ANSWER A GALLEY SLAVE GOT WHEN HE ASKED THAT SAME QUESTION.

USER
FRIENDLY
the comic strip
PIZZA
Portrasher 4
ROTO-ROUTER 800
Copyright©1997-2001 Illiad

SING LIKE I TOLD YOU OR I'LL WRITE THE WORDS "SPY PLANE" ON YOU AND SHIP YOU BACK TO CHINA.
OKAY. OKAY. KEEP YOUR PANTS ON.

(SUNG TO "THE LION SLEEPS TONIGHT")
WEEEEEEEEEE WILL DO IT MUNDIE'S WAY... WEEEEEEEEEE WILL DO IT MUNDIE'S WAY...

A WINDOWS WORLD
A WINDOWS WORLD
A WINDOWS WORLD
A WINDOWS WORLD
A WINDOWS WORLD
A WINDOWS WORLD
A WINDOWS WORLD
A WINDOWS WORLD...

DEEP IN REDMOND. IN MIGHTY REDMOND WE TURF THE GPL
DEEP IN REDMOND. IN MIGHTY REDMOND WE NOW HAVE MORE TO SELL
*CHORUS!!
OOOOOEEEEOOO EEEEOOOOEEEOO

IN THE MARKET. THE GLOBAL MARKET DOMINATION IS OUR RIGHT
THE GPL SHOULD BE MADE ILLEGAL AND ITS ADVOCATES STERILIZED
RICHARD STALLMAN IS WAITING OUTSIDE IN A BACKHOE WITH THE LETTERS "L.A.R.T." PAINTED ON IT.

HEY MIKE, COULD YOU SEND ME TH--YE FLIPPING GODS!!!
HELLO, OLD MAN.
COPYRIGHT © 2001 ILLIAD HTTP://WWW.USERFRIENDLY.ORG/

YOU SEE HIM?
I SURE DO. IT'S BEEN A LONG WHILE.
INDEED IT HAS. WHAT FORM DO YOU SEE ME IN?

A BIG, JUICY THIRTY KILOGRAM DOOBIE.
I THOUGHT YOU ONLY DID CAFFEINE!
I ADAPT TO THE DRUG OF THE ERA. NEXT YEAR I'LL BE APPEARING AS "SURVIVOR" RERUNS. JUST YOU WATCH.

THAT COLA THING IS BACK?
HE'S GONE NOW. SID CAME ALONG AND SAW MR. COLA AS A HUGE DOOBIE.
COPYRIGHT © 2001 ILLIAD HTTP://WWW.USERFRIENDLY.ORG/

HE SAW IT AS A BIG WALKING JOINT?!
YEAH. SID HOOVERED ON ONE OF THE NOSE STRAWS FOR A MINUTE THEN RAN INTO THE LUNCH ROOM.

HEY! WHICH ONE OF YOU DORKS ATE ALL THE CORN FLAKES?!?! WE DON'T EVEN HAVE ANY MILK!!

HEY, YOU READ ABOUT HOW THE U.S. CONGRESS IS STILL CONSIDERING WHETHER OR NOT TO CHARGE SALES TAXES FOR INTERNET PURCHASES?
YES.
COPYRIGHT © 2001 ILLIAD HTTP://WWW.USERFRIENDLY.ORG/

ISN'T IT RIDICULOUS? IF THE SERVER IS IN DALLAS, THE SELLER IS IN SEATTLE, THE BUYER IS IN VANCOUVER, AND THE TRANSACTION IS CLEARED IN NEW YORK, WHO GETS THE TAX MONEY?

BICKLE, PABLIM, GORMAN
TAX ATTORNEYS

COME ON, YOU DON'T THINK OBTUSE TAX LAWS ARE RIDICULOUS?
NO. I THINK THEY HAVE THEIR PLACE. IF THEY WERE SIMPLE AND EASILY UNDERSTOOD, OUR WORLD WOULD COLLAPSE.
COPYRIGHT © 2001 ILLIAD HTTP://WWW.USERFRIENDLY.ORG/

OH PLEASE. SAVE IT FOR THE MARKETING DEPARTMENT. ANYTHING LABYRINTHINE WAS CREATED OUT OF IGNORANCE AND SHOULD BE REPLACED WITH ELEGANCE AND SIMPLICITY.

SO WHEN DID YOU SAY YOU WERE DUMPING UNIX FOR MacOS?
WHAT?! WHY YOU... OOOO!! YOU... OOOOOOO!!

UNDER THIS DESK LOOKS LIKE A GOOD PLACE TO REST. WONDER WHAT THAT ODD LOOKING BOX IS.
COPYRIGHT © 2001 ILLIAD HTTP://WWW.USERFRIENDLY.ORG/

AHHH. TIME FOR SOME MP3-INDUCED RELAXATION...

WHAT HAPPENED TO YOU?! ELECTRICAL SHOCK?
SUBWOOFER.

YE GODS! GREG!!!
BROMP
BROMP
BROMP
COPYRIGHT © 2001 ILLIAD HTTP://WWW.USERFRIENDLY.ORG/

GREG!!! TURN IT DOWN!!!
BROMP
BROMP
BROMP

I'M NOT WORKING TOO LOUD FOR YOU AM I?
HECK NO. NOT AT ALL. BUT THANKS FOR ASKING MAN.

USER
FRIENDLY
the comic strip
PIZZA
Portrasher 4
ROTO-ROUTER 800
Copyright©1997-2001 Illiad

WHAT'S THE MATTER ERWIN?
DOUGLAS ADAMS PASSED AWAY ON FRIDAY.
OH...

YOU LOOK PUZZLED...
WELL, I THOUGHT HE ONLY MADE PEOPLE LAUGH AND SMILE. NOT REALLY REALLY SAD.

DOUGLAS ADAMS, O SMITH OF WORDS AND HUMOUR SOFT YET MANIC.
WE THANK YOU MUCH FOR ALL THE FISH, AND ADVICE THAT WE NOT PANIC.

SPACE IS BIG, YOU ONCE HAD STATED A POINT WE'D NOT DISPUTE.
BUT SPACE IS NOT AS BIG AS, SAY THE RIB-PAINS YOU MADE ACUTE

AND SO IT COMES TO THIS DEAR SIR, BUT WE'LL SEE YOU AGAIN WHEN WE MEET FOR TEA AND CRUMPETS AS WE WATCH THE UNIVERSE END.
UM...NO OFFENSE, BUT DID YOU RIP THAT OFF FROM A VOGON?

I was very sad when I heard that Douglas Adams had passed away. I was just as honored when the DNA fan club asked to run this strip in their newsletter, and through them I heard that Douglas' wife felt that the tribute poem was the nicest one she had seen about her husband's passing.

BRRAM
BRRAMP
BRRAM
BRRA
COPYRIGHT © 2001 ILLIAD HTTP://WWW.USERFRIENDLY.ORG/

BRUMPA
BRUMPA
BRUMPA
BRUM

I FIND IT VERY DIFFICULT TO UNDERSTAND HOW LISTENING TO THAT MUSIC HELPS YOU RELAX.
LISTEN?! THESE ARE HEARING PROTECTORS. I PLAY THAT CRAP SO THAT THE SUBWOOFER MASSAGES MY FEET.

FOLKS. THIS IS BRENT. HE'S HERE TO EXPLAIN OUR NEW HEALTH BENEFITS PLAN.
HEY FOLKS. AS YOU CAN SEE ON THE SHEET I JUST HANDED OUT WE COVER LOSS OF LIFE AND LIMB.
COPYRIGHT © 2001 ILLIAD HTTP://WWW.USERFRIENDLY.ORG/

UNDER YOUR COVERAGE. IF YOU SHOULD LOSE A THUMB. FOR EXAMPLE. YOU'D BE PAID OUT A TOTAL OF $2,000...
COOL!

THINK ATHLON.
THINK ATHLON.
THINK ATHLON.
THINK ATHLON...

HEY. YOU KNOW HOW YOU ASKED ME TO E-MAIL AROUND THE DETAILS OF OUR COVERAGE FOR LOSS OF BODY PARTS?
YES?
COPYRIGHT © 2001 ILLIAD HTTP://WWW.USERFRIENDLY.ORG/

AND YOU KNOW HOW YOU TOLD ME **NOT** TO MAKE ANY CHANGES TO THE DOCUMENT? EVEN AS A JOKE?
YES. I... WAIT. WHAT DID YOU DO?

FIFTY THOUSAND FOR THE LOSS OF THE USE OF MY HEAD. BOY COULD I USE THE MONEY...
SOMETIMES. THE UNIVERSE. IT IS SHOWINK HOW BEAUTIFUL IT REALLY IS...

MIKHAIL. AM CRUSHINK BOTH HANDS WITH WERY HEAVY TOILET SEAT. AND GETTINK MUCH INSURANCE MONEY. SEE? HAVE NEW. WERY NICE LAPTOP.
SPIFFY!
COPYRIGHT © 2001 ILLIAD HTTP://WWW.USERFRIENDLY.ORG/

VERY IMPRESSIVE. AND HOW PRECISELY DO YOU INTEND TO CODE ON IT NOW?

AAAAAAAAAAGH!!!
RELAX. STEF HAS IT WORSE. HE DID THE SAME AND I JUST PUT FIFTY MEGS OF ASHLEY JUDD PORN ON HIS MACHINE.

HEY SID? I HEAR YOU GOT THE INSURANCE MONEY WITHOUT LOPPING OFF A FINGER OR ANYTHING. HOW'D YOU MANAGE THAT?
THINK, MY FRIEND.
COPYRIGHT © 2001 ILLIAD HTTP://WWW.USERFRIENDLY.ORG/

WE'RE ALREADY MISSING A FINGER ON EACH HAND!
SEE? IT PAYS TO BE A CARTOON CHARACTER.
SID, YOUR AGENT JUST PHONED. YOU HAVE A GIG ON SOUTH PARK AS CARTMAN'S DAD.

HEY...HOW COME I CAN'T GET MY E-MAIL? HOW AM I SUPPOSED TO SELL ANYTHING WITHOUT MY E-MAIL?
COPYRIGHT © 2001 ILLIAD HTTP://WWW.USERFRIENDLY.ORG/

THERE'S GREG. I WONDER IF HIS E-MAIL THINGIE IS BROKEN TOO.

HEY GREG? IS YOUR MAIL THING UP?

True story. Happened at the ISP where I worked. Entire room busted out laughing at the sales guy.

TIME-WARNER EMPLOYEES ARE TOLD TO USE AOL MAIL IN THE ONLY WAY THAT AOL KNOWS HOW

PAULY'S CUBICLE
COPYRIGHT (C) 2001 ILLIAD
HTTP://WWW.USERFRIENDLY.ORG/

HEY. THE MAIL SERVER JUST BORKED.
WHAT CAUSED IT?
COPYRIGHT © 2001 ILLIAD HTTP://WWW.USERFRIENDLY.ORG/

NO IDEA YET. BUT WE BETTER GET CRACKING AND FIX THIS. PEOPLE LIVE AND BREATHE BY THEIR E-MAIL.
OH COME ON. PEOPLE CAN HANDLE NOT HAVING E-MAIL FOR A FEW MINUTES.

FOR THE FORTY-SECOND TIME. UNABLE TO CONNECT TO MAIL SERVER.

Red apron. What's a bad color to wear in *Star Trek*?

SO WHAT'S WITH THE MAIL SERVER?
SOME DOLT SPAMMED OUR CUSTOMER LIST WITH VIDEO MPEGS AND CHEWED UP OUR SPOOL. COULD THERE BE ANYTHING MORE IRRITATING?
COPYRIGHT © 2001 ILLIAD HTTP://WWW.USERFRIENDLY.ORG/

TAP
TYPE
FIX
FLUSH

WILLIAM SHATNER IS GOING TO BE HOSTING A U.S. VERSION OF "IRON CHEF"
ONE CAN ONLY HOPE THEY'LL MAKE HIM WEAR A RED APRON.

LOGGED IN TO #L337_H4X0RS
MIRANDA: ARE YOU THE WEENIES WHO SPAMMED OUR MAIL SERVER?
BUNG13: YEAH, THAT WAS EASY.
DOOF: YEP
W4NK3R: I ONLY HAD TO USE A SINGLE SCRIPT.
COPYRIGHT © 2001 ILLIAD HTTP://WWW.USERFRIENDLY.ORG/

MIRANDA: YOU GUYS ARE SO LAME, I BET YOU CAN'T EVEN KNOCK ME OFF THE 'NET.
BUNG13: OH YEAH? WE'LL FIX YOU.
DOOF: YOU'RE TOAST!
W4NK3R: WHAT'S YOUR IP ADDRESS?

MIRANDA: 127.0.0.1 COME GET SOME.
BUNG13: *DISCONNECTED*
DOOF: *DISCONNECTED*
W4NK3R: *DISCONNECTED*

UH...HEY. NICE OUTFIT...
THANKS...I'M JUST ABOUT TO GO FOR MY RUN. SUMMER IS ALMOST HERE.
COPYRIGHT © 2001 ILLIAD HTTP://WWW.USERFRIENDLY.ORG/

MMMMMMM!

HEY AYJ...WHADDYA SAY WE GO FOR A RUN WITH HER AND GET OUR HEART RATES UP?
TOO LATE..

I THINK IT'S GREAT YOU GUYS ARE GOING TO JOIN ME! LET'S DO SOME ABDOMINAL CRUNCHES...
CRUNCHES?

COPYRIGHT © 2001 ILLIAD HTTP://WWW.USERFRIENDLY.ORG/
THAT SOUNDS STRENUOUS.
OH COME ON. EVEN GREG SAID HE WAS GOING TO WORK ON HIS SIX-PACK.

SCHLUUURRRRRRPP

SO LET'S START WITH A CARDIO WORKOUT JUST TO WARM UP..
I DON'T THINK I WANT TO DO THIS ANYMORE...

COPYRIGHT © 2001 ILLIAD HTTP://WWW.USERFRIENDLY.ORG/
LOOK. I'M A GEEK. IF IT'S NOT SOMETHING YOU CAN EXPLAIN IN COMPUTER TERMS, I'M JUST NOT INTERESTED!

WHAT DOES "RUNTIME" MEAN?
SHUT UP.

USER
FRIENDLY
the comic strip
PIZZA
Portrasher 4
ROTO-ROUTER 800
Copyright©1997-2001 Illiad

YOU KNOW...WEB DESIGN AND LOUNGE SINGING ARE REALLY QUITE A LOT ALIKE.
HOW?

WELL...BOTH INVOLVE THE USE OF KEYBOARDS...
...AND YOU'D NEVER ADMIT TO YOUR MOTHER WHAT YOU DO FOR A LIVING.

(SUNG TO "SHE'S ALWAYS A WOMAN" BY BILLY JOEL.)
SHE CAN KILL -9 WITH A SMILE
AS SHE MUNCHES HER FRIES
SHE CAN CRACK YOUR ACCOUNT
AND DELETE ALL YOUR FILES
THOUGH SHE ONLY APPEALS
TO THE SHY ONES LIKE ME
SHE CAN CODE LIKE A PRO
AND SHE'S ALWAYS A GODDESS
TO ME

SHE CAN ROOT ALL YOUR BOXES
FASTER THAN YOU'D BELIEVE
YOU CAN ASK FOR AN ACK
BUT YOU'LL NEVER RECEIVE
SHE'LL TAKE CODE YOU GIVE HER
AS LONG AS IT'S "FREE"
SHE THINKS I'M A DWEEB
BUT SHE'S ALWAYS A GODDESS TO ME

OHHHH, SHE TAKES CARE OF HER SERVERS
SHE CAN PLAY QUAKE IF SHE WANTS
SHE'S AHEAD OF HER GAME
OHHH, SHE NEVER GETS STRESSED OUT
AND SHE NEVER GETS CAUGHT
SHE JUST PASSES ON BLAME...
THINK BILLY JOEL WILL GET UPSET?
NOT UNTIL HE FINDS OUT THE NAME OF YOUR ALBUM IS "THONGS IN THE ATTIC."

HEY. WERE'NT A.J. AND STEF WITH YOU?
YES. I LEFT THEM AT THE GYM.
COPYRIGHT © 2001 ILLIAD HTTP://WWW.USERFRIENDLY.ORG/

YOU LEFT **THOSE TWO** ALONE AT THE GYM?! WHAT WERE THEY DOING?
STEF ON THE BENCH PRESS WITH A.J. SPOTTING. I COULDN'T BEAR TO WATCH...

IT'S TOO HEAVY! I CAN'T LIFT IT!
THEN **ROLL** IT OFF!! **NO!! WAIT!! DON'T!!**

COLUMBIA INTERNET. GREG SPEAKING. PLEASE STATE THE NATURE OF YOUR PROBLEM.
UM...DID YOU LIKE THE FINAL EPISODE OF ***STAR TREK: VOYAGER***?
COPYRIGHT © 2001 ILLIAD HTTP://WWW.USERFRIENDLY.ORG/

NO. CAN'T SAY I DID. THE ACTING WAS WOODEN AND THE DIRECTING WAS INCONSISTENT.
OH.

BUT THE *PRODUCING* WAS AWESOME. RIGHT?
WHO IS THIS?
STARTREK.COM
Rick Berman

LISTEN. RICK. IN MY OPINION YOU BOTCHED THE WRAP-UP FOR VOYAGER. YOU HAD A CHANCE TO REALLY TUG AT OUR HEARTS BUT YOU BLEW IT.
HMMM.
COPYRIGHT © 2001 ILLIAD HTTP://WWW.USERFRIENDLY.ORG/

BUT I'LL WATCH THE NEXT SERIES. BECAUSE I HAVE FAITH. JUST DO BETTER. NEXT TIME. OKAY?
FAIR ENOUGH. SO..YOU DIDN'T THINK IT WAS INAPPROPRIATE FOR ME TO CALL YOU ABOUT THIS?

HECK NO. I RECOGNIZE THAT THE STAR TREK UNIVERSE HAS BEEN IN DIRE NEED OF TECHNICAL SUPPORT FOR DECADES.
HEY!!

Rick Berman, why hast thou forsaken us?

I'M VERY GLAD I COULD HELP. RICK. BUT ONE LAST THING: YOU GUYS NEED TO WORK ON THE PREDICTABILITY A LITTLE.
PREDI-- HOW DO YOU MEAN?
COPYRIGHT © 2001 ILLIAD HTTP://WWW.USERFRIENDLY.ORG/

OH COME ON. IF YOU WROTE A SERIES OF MYSTERY NOVELS INSTEAD AND USED THE SAME FORMULAS YOU DO IN STAR TREK. IT'D BE DISASTROUS.
ACTUALLY. WE JUST PUBLISHED A **WHOLE LINE** OF STAR TREK MYSTERY NOVELS...

THE PARTICLE-OF-THE-WEEK DID IT. IN ALL OF THEM.

OKAY YOU SICK LITTLE HAIRBALL. WHAT ON EARTH **IS** THAT THING?
IT'S A CTHIA PET. ERWIN AND I BROUGHT ONE BACK FROM CHINA.
COPYRIGHT © 2001 ILLIAD HTTP://WWW.USERFRIENDLY.ORG/

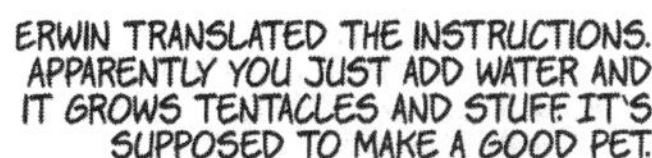
ERWIN TRANSLATED THE INSTRUCTIONS. APPARENTLY YOU JUST ADD WATER AND IT GROWS TENTACLES AND STUFF IT'S SUPPOSED TO MAKE A GOOD PET.

A PET. HUH? BET IT'LL GET ME CHICKS. SEE YA LATER. LOSERS.

ERWIN. YOU DIDN'T FORGET TO ADD THE WARNING ABOUT IT EATING MEAT DID YOU?
UM. WELL NO. I DIDN'T FORGET PER SE...

YOU KNOW. ERWIN. WE REALLY SHOULD'VE RESEARCHED THOSE CTHIA PETS BEFORE WE BROUGHT ONE BACK.
YEAH?
COPYRIGHT © 2001 ILLIAD HTTP://WWW.USERFRIENDLY.ORG/

WE ALREADY KNOW THEY EAT MEAT. RIGHT?
YES. BUT IT SAYS HERE THEY PREFER **FAT**.

DAMMIT.
GRRR! MUNCH MUNCH

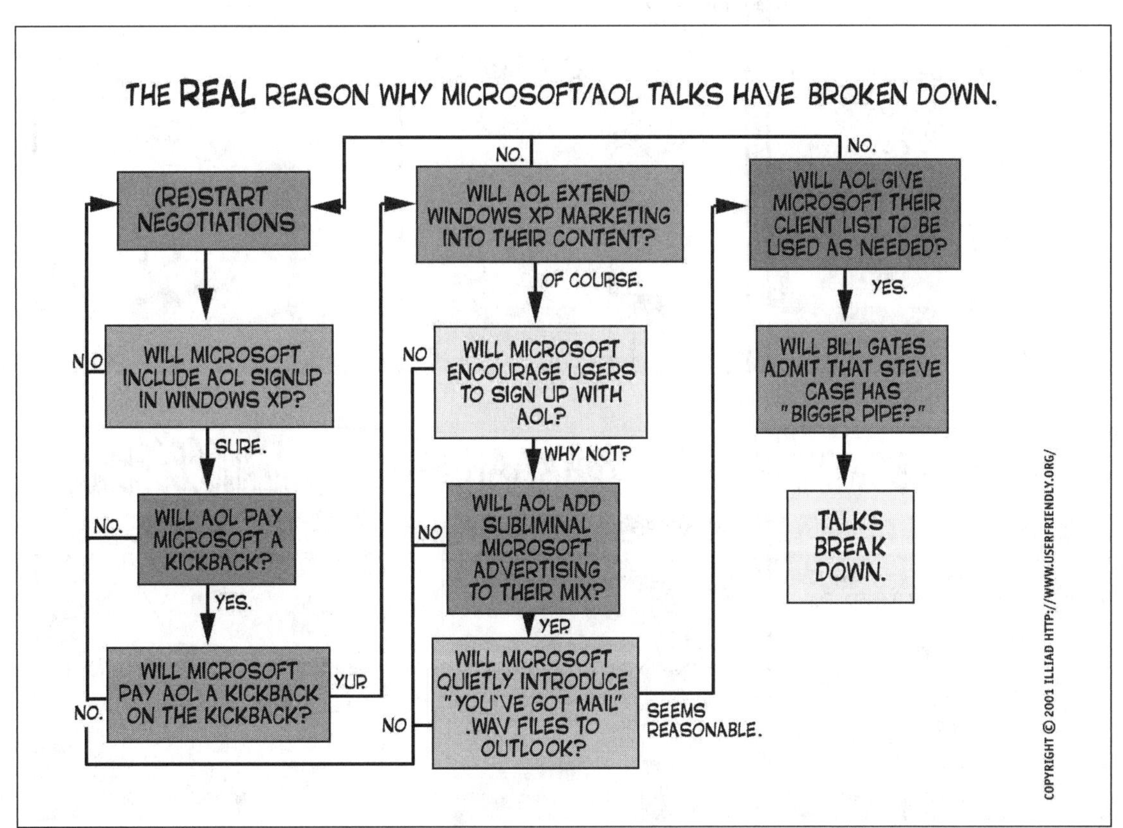
THE **REAL** REASON WHY MICROSOFT/AOL TALKS HAVE BROKEN DOWN.
(RE)START NEGOTIATIONS
WILL MICROSOFT INCLUDE AOL SIGNUP IN WINDOWS XP?
NO
SURE.
WILL AOL PAY MICROSOFT A KICKBACK?
NO.
YES.
WILL MICROSOFT PAY AOL A KICKBACK ON THE KICKBACK?
NO.
YUP
WILL AOL EXTEND WINDOWS XP MARKETING INTO THEIR CONTENT?
NO.
OF COURSE.
WILL MICROSOFT ENCOURAGE USERS TO SIGN UP WITH AOL?
NO
WHY NOT?
WILL AOL ADD SUBLIMINAL MICROSOFT ADVERTISING TO THEIR MIX?
NO
YEP
WILL MICROSOFT QUIETLY INTRODUCE "YOU'VE GOT MAIL" .WAV FILES TO OUTLOOK?
NO
SEEMS REASONABLE.
WILL AOL GIVE MICROSOFT THEIR CLIENT LIST TO BE USED AS NEEDED?
NO.
YES.
WILL BILL GATES ADMIT THAT STEVE CASE HAS "BIGGER PIPE?"
TALKS BREAK DOWN.
COPYRIGHT © 2001 ILLIAD HTTP://WWW.USERFRIENDLY.ORG/

IN A RECENT INTERVIEW, MICROSOFT CEO STEVE BALLMER WAS QUOTED AS SAYING: "LINUX IS A CANCER THAT ATTACHES ITSELF IN AN INTELLECTUAL PROPERTY SENSE TO EVERYTHING IT TOUCHES."
COPYRIGHT © 2001 ILLIAD HTTP://WWW.USERFRIENDLY.ORG/

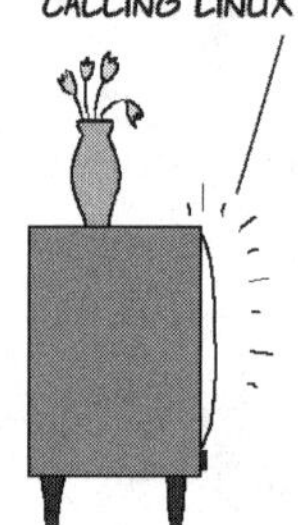
THE MEDICAL RESEARCHERS AT BEAKER-BUNSEN TOOK UP THE CHALLENGE TO CAREFULLY DISSECT BALLMER'S STATEMENT. THEY DISCOVERED THAT THERE WAS INDEED MEDICAL PRECEDENT FOR CALLING LINUX A CANCER.

WE ASKED THEM WHAT THE MEDICAL EQUIVALENT WOULD BE FOR WINDOWS. "TOURETTE SYNDROME, OF COURSE" THEY REPLIED.

OKAY YOU LITTLE TWERPS. TELL ME HOW TO GET THIS THING OFF MY HEAD.
GRRR YUM MUNCH
OF COURSE STEF. ERWIN, PLEASE LOOK UP HOW THAT'S DONE.
SEARCHING...
COPYRIGHT © 2001 ILLIAD HTTP://WWW.USERFRIENDLY.ORG/

IT SAYS HERE TO PUT A LENGTH OF LICORICE UP AND OUT YOUR NOSTRILS, AND THEN FLOSS VIGOROUSLY.
CHEW GNAW
HUNH. WELL, ANYTHING TO GET THIS SLUG CREATURE OFF ME.

YOU DIDN'T ACTUALLY LOOK ANYTHING UP DID YOU.
WELL, DUH.

HEY GUYS? WHAT'S GOING ON WITH STEF?
OH, ERWIN TOLD HIM TO FLOSS HIS NOSTRILS WITH LICORICE TO GET THE CTHIA PET OFF HIS HEAD.
COPYRIGHT © 2001 ILLIAD HTTP://WWW.USERFRIENDLY.ORG/

ERWIN TOLD HIM WHAT?!!
BUT STEF SAID HE DIDN'T HAVE THE COURAGE TO DO IT HIMSELF.

THAT'S RIGHT. I SAID VIGOROUSLY.
WHAT IS IT WITH ME AND TUBES COMING OUT OF NOSES?

YEEEEOWCH!!
YE GODS! DON'T TELL ME STEF...
YUP. FLOSSED HIS NOSE. OR TRIED TO.
COPYRIGHT © 2001 ILLIAD HTTP://WWW.USERFRIENDLY.ORG/

GAAAAH!!
HE KEEPS BREAKING OFF THE END THAT HE'S PULLING ON SO HE HAS TO REACH IN AND GET THE TIP OUT AGAIN.

AAAIIIEEEEEEEEEEE!
BUT WHY DOESN'T HE JUST PULL IT ALL OUT FROM THE OTHER END?
GUESS I COULD HAVE MENTIONED IT TO HIM.
WHO IS LEAVINK LICORICE LYINK AROUND? IS GOOD.

DID YOU FINALLY TELL STEF THE TRUTH ABOUT HOW TO GET RID OF THAT CTHIA PET?
YEAH. "CTHIA PET DOES NOT ENJOY BATTERY ACID." RIGHT OFF THE PACKAGING.

COPYRIGHT © 2001 ILLIAD HTTP://WWW.USERFRIENDLY.ORG/
UH...STEF? YOU GOT THE CTHIA PET OFF YOUR HEAD?
UNH-HUH... SPRAYED... WITH... BATTERY... ACID...

OH DEAR. IT SEEMS, I LEFT OUT THE PART THAT SAYS "CTHIA PET WILL RUN FROM ACID AND HIDE IN YOUR PANTS."
EEP.
GRRR

SO, YOU INSTALLED LINUX ON YOUR MOM'S COMPUTER AND SHE WANTS TO GO BACK TO WINDOWS BECAUSE IT MAKES HER FEEL "MORE COMFY"?
YEAH. I EVEN DRESSED UP THE GUI TO LOOK LIKE THE WIN98 DESKTOP AND IT'S STILL NOT GOOD ENOUGH FOR HER.
COPYRIGHT © 2001 ILLIAD HTTP://WWW.USERFRIENDLY.ORG/

HOW ABOUT SETTING UP A CRON JOB THAT REBOOTS THE MACHINE FOR HER EVERY DAY?
OOOH! AND SHE'LL NEVER KNOW THE DIFFERENCE!!

USER
FRIENDLY
the comic strip
PIZZA
Portrasher 4
ROTO-ROUTER 800
Copyright©1997-2001 Illiad

MIKE! THANKS FOR COMING BACK TO BIZEXPO, AND THANK YOU FOR AGREEING TO SPEAK AGAIN.

MY PLEASURE! I GUESS THE AUDIENCE REALLY ENJOYED MY TALK ON ETHICS FROM LAST TIME?
OH YES! YOU'RE THE BEST STAND-UP COMEDIAN WE'VE EVER HAD HERE.

LADIES AND GENTLEMEN, I'D LIKE TO INTRODUCE OUR FIRST SPEAKER, MIKE FLOYD, WHO LAST SPOKE HERE ON FEBRUARY 6, 1999. HE'S HERE TONIGHT TO PRE-EMPTIVELY ADDRESS CRAIG MUNDIE'S PHILOSOPHY ON...

AS GOD IS MY WITNESS, I **SWEAR** THIS SAYS "SHARED SORES."
YOU GOT IT **RIGHT** THIS TIME...

To be geekily accurate, missile silos aren't radioactive. They're heavily shielded. But maybe this one ...

CHIEF YOU WANTED TO SEE ME?
YES HILLARY. I NEED YOU TO FIND US SOME EXTRA OFFICE SPACE. IT'S GETTING CROWDED AROUND HERE AND I THINK IT'S TIME WE GAVE THE TECHS THEIR OWN OFFICE.
COPYRIGHT © 2001 ILLIAD HTTP://WWW.USERFRIENDLY.ORG/

SURE...ANY PARTICULARS IN MIND? COST? LOCATION?
I DON'T CARE WHERE. JUST MAKE SURE IT HAS MINIMAL IMPACT ON OUR EXPENSES.

CAUTION: ABANDONED MISSILE SILO
RADIATION STUDIES LIVE-IN VOLUNTEERS WANTED.

DID YOU GET MY E-MAIL ON WHERE WE COULD MOVE THE TECHS? TO THE ABANDONED MISSILE SILO?
I DID. AND I ADMIT TO BEING A LITTLE SURPRISED..
COPYRIGHT © 2001 ILLIAD HTTP://WWW.USERFRIENDLY.ORG/

I HAD NO IDEA YOU WERE SO INTERESTED IN OFFICE PLANNING OR IN HELPING WITH OUR EXPANSION.

...UNLESS...THIS HAS SOMETHING TO DO WITH THE FACT THAT OLD MISSILE SILOS ARE FILLED WITH TOXIC SUBSTANCES AND NASTY RUBBLE AND GEEKS ARE INHERENTLY ATTRACTED TO THEM...
GEEKS CHECK IN. THEY DON'T CHECK OUT

THREE OF THE TECHS BEGIN MOVING INTO MISSILE SILO #45...
THIS IS WHERE WE'RE MOVING?
HMMM...
YE GODS...HOW DO WE GET IN?
COPYRIGHT © 2001 ILLIAD HTTP://WWW.USERFRIENDLY.ORG/

DOWN THAT DARK AND DANGEROUS LOOKING HOLE I THINK.
BUT LOOK AT ALL THAT ASBESTOS FIBRE AND GLOWING CRAP DOWN THERE...

AND WE COME TO UNDERSTAND WHY GEEKS AREN'T MORE PREVALENT IN THE GENE POOL...
DIBS!!!
NYET! AM SEEINK ASBESTOS FIBRE FIRST!!!
GRRR!!

GREG? SO WHAT'S IT LIKE DOWN THERE?
UP UP
WELL...
COPYRIGHT © 2001 ILLIAD HTTP://WWW.USERFRIENDLY.ORG/

UP UP
THERE'S NO NATURAL LIGHT. THE ACOUSTICS ARE BIZARRE. AND IT SMELLS LIKE STALE PIZZA.

I REALLY LOVE THE CHIEF. YOU KNOW?
UP UP
I KNOW. I'M GETTING ALL MISTY-EYED.

IS WERY DARK DOWN HERE.
YEAH. BUT SOME OF THE SYSTEMS MAY STILL BE WORKING. MAYBE WE CAN GET THE LIGHTS TO COME ON?
COPYRIGHT © 2001 ILLIAD HTTP://WWW.USERFRIENDLY.ORG/

HANG ON. I FOUND A TOGGLE OF SOME SORT...AH. THERE WE GO...
KACHUNKA!

WELL. I STARTED UP SOMETHING.
SOMETHING DRIPPED ON ME. I THINK THE PIPES DOWN HERE ARE LEAKING.
ZZZMMMM
SEWAGE PURGE 20 SECONDS

WAY TO GO MIKE. NOW GET MOVING BEFORE THIS STUFF GETS OVER OUR HEADS!
JUST HANG TOUGH. I'M SURE IT'LL STOP SOON.
GLUGG
SPLURTCH
GURGLE
COPYRIGHT © 2001 ILLIAD HTTP://WWW.USERFRIENDLY.ORG/

HMMM...
BLURBLE
SPLUGG

GURGLEMFF!!
PADDLE
PADDLE
SPLASH
SPLUNCH
BROOOP
I'M GOING! I'M GOING!!

AND YOU THOUGHT CEL PHONES IN CARS CAUSED THE MOST ACCIDENTS...
http://www.babe-alicious.com/
COPYRIGHT © 2001 ILLIAD HTTP://WWW.USERFRIENDLY.ORG/

AM THINKINK IT IS FINISHED DRAININK. WE ARE TO BE GOINK BACK IN.
YOU COMING WITH US A.J.?
COPYRIGHT © 2001 ILLIAD HTTP://WWW.USERFRIENDLY.ORG/

I DUNNO. I DON'T LIKE DARK PLACES. YOU KNOW WHAT HAPPENS IN PITCH DARKNESS IN GAMES.

A.J.!! EVERYTHING ISN'T LIKE A DAMN COMPUTER GAME!
GRUES ARE EVERY-WHERE MAN! THEY'RE LIKE STARBUCKS!
...OR VICE-VERSA.

THIS LOOKS LIKE A NARROW EAST-WEST PASSAGEWAY. THERE IS A NARROW STAIRWAY LEADING DOWN AT THE NORTH END OF THE ROOM.
GUESS WE SHOULD GO WEST...
COPYRIGHT © 2001 ILLIAD HTTP://WWW.USERFRIENDLY.ORG/

WE'RE NOW IN A SMALL ROOM WITH PASSAGES EAST AND SOUTH. AND A FORBIDDING HOLE LEADING WEST. BLOODSTAINS AND DEEP SCRATCHES MAR THE WALLS.

MY TRAPDOOR SLAMS SHUT BEHIND ME...
KEEP IT UP MAN, AND I'LL TEAR YOU A BIGGER "FORBIDDING HOLE."

LOOK, JUST DON'T DISRESPECT THE GRUES, OKAY?
A.J. GET A GRIP. THIS IS NOT ZORK, AND GRUES DO NOT EXIST.
GRUES ARRE WIIIIMPS
GRUES ARRRE WIIIMPS
COPYRIGHT © 2001 ILLIAD HTTP://WWW.USERFRIENDLY.ORG/

SPUTTER!

I CAN ONLY HOPE GRUES PREFER EATING STUPID PEOPLE FIRST.
AHEM

Like you wouldn't do the exact same thing if you were given the opportunity.

OKAY. THERE'S NO WAY THAT COULD BE A GRUE. GRUES AREN'T REAL. THEY'RE NOT REAL. THERE'S NO WAY THEY COULD BE REAL...
BOO!
COPYRIGHT © 2001 ILLIAD HTTP://WWW.USERFRIENDLY.ORG/

RUN!!!
AAAAIIIIEEEE!!!

KIDS.
KLIK

OH THAT WAS JUST A **RIOT**, SID. ARE YOU HERE TO HELP OR JUST GOOF AROUND?
WHILE YOU **INFANTS** WERE PLAYING AROUND AND GETTING LOST, I GOT A MAP OF THE PLACE.
COPYRIGHT © 2001 ILLIAD HTTP://WWW.USERFRIENDLY.ORG/

IT JUST SAYS "THIS IS A PART OF A MAZE OF TWISTY LITTLE PASSAGES, ALL ALIKE."
I GOT IT OFF OF MAPQUEST.

SO WHILE I WAS WALKING AROUND I SAW...UH, **WHAT** IS THAT **GHASTLY** SMELL?
COPYRIGHT © 2001 ILLIAD HTTP://WWW.USERFRIENDLY.ORG/

REMEMBER THAT SCARE YOU GAVE US BACK THERE?
YES?

I THINK AJ HAD HIS VERY OWN SEWAGE PURGE.
DID NOT!!!
OH MAN...

ARCADE ANALOGIES

THE GPL:
PAC MAN

MICROSOFT'S PREFERRED ARRANGEMENT:
ANY ARCADE GAME THAT REQUIRES YOU TO KEEP PLUGGING IN QUARTERS REGARDLESS OF SKILL.

PAC-MAN

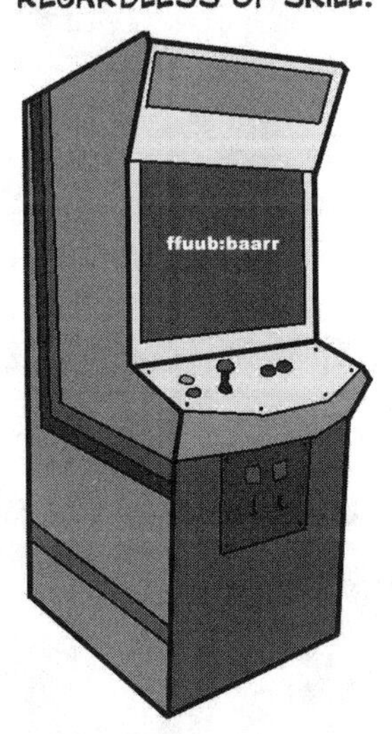
ffuub:baarr

It's the mantra of software companies everywhere: How do we keep the customer paying? MS is really excellent at it.

Week of June 25th, 2001

I SHOULD BE ABLE TO GET POWER TO THE LIGHTS AND HEATERS FROM HERE...LET'S SEE...
COPYRIGHT © 2001 ILLIAD HTTP://WWW.USERFRIENDLY.ORG/

HOW ODD. SOMEONE'S ALREADY BEEN HERE AND HAS ROUTED POWER TO SOMETHING ELSE. WHAT ON EARTH COULD BE MORE IMPORTANT THAN LIGHT AND HEAT?

AHHHH. TRULY DARK ROAST.
SCHLUUUUUUURP

I GOT THE LIGHTS BACK.
THANK YOU. I HATE IT WHEN IT'S PITCH BLACK.
COPYRIGHT © 2001 ILLIAD HTTP://WWW.USERFRIENDLY.ORG/

SAY SID. SPEAKING OF PITCH BLACK. EXACTLY HOW DID YOU SURVIVE IN THE DARKNESS WITHOUT BEING EATEN BY A GRUE?

EVEN **GRUES** GET **FULL**, A.J....
AM EXPECTINK DELIVERY FROM CHERNOBYL... ANYONE SEEINK FEDEX MAN?

I **THOUGHT** I SMELLED CAFFEINE! PERFECT!
DA. IS FRESH POT. AM CALLINK IT "ISOTOPE ROAST."
COPYRIGHT © 2001 ILLIAD HTTP://WWW.USERFRIENDLY.ORG/

OH. **YOU** MADE IT?
DA.

WHY IS THERE A FRESH HOLE IN THE CEILING?
YOU ARE WAITINK WHY? MIKHAIL ALREADY HAVINK SOME.

COFFEE! EXACTLY WHAT I NEED...
SID. I WOULDN'T. **PITR** MADE IT.
COPYRIGHT © 2001 ILLIAD HTTP://WWW.USERFRIENDLY.ORG/

WOW. **STRONG** COFFEE... BUT SEE. I'M FI-
BOOGA BOOGA!

DA. BUT NEEDINK TO PLUG HOLE IN CEILINK.
THAT WASN'T VERY NICE OF YOU. MAN.

CONTROL
PITR. THERE'S A DELIVERY HERE FOR YOU.
DA?
COPYRIGHT © 2001 ILLIAD HTTP://WWW.USERFRIENDLY.ORG/

CONTROL
ANYTHING YOU...UH...MIGHT WANT TO TELL US? THAT YOU'VE BEEN KEEPING TO YOURSELF?
TELLINK YOU? TELLINK YOU WHAT?

THEY ARE ACTINK FUNNY WHY? AM PAYINK EXTRA FOR "DISGUISED DELIVERY."

CONTROL
WAIT A SECOND..YOU MEAN YOU ORDERED AN OLD RUSSIAN ICBM?
DA.
COPYRIGHT © 2001 ILLIAD HTTP://WWW.USERFRIENDLY.ORG/

CONTROL
WELL COOL. BUT THE SILO DOORS ARE WELDED SHUT. HOW ON EARTH ARE YOU GONNA GET IT IN HERE?

CONTROL
AM HAVINK WAYS, A.J.
HEY MISTER? THERE'S A PISSED OFF OLD GUY PLUGGING THE HOLE YOU WANT US TO USE...

THE U.S. COURT OF APPEALS INADVERTENTLY AFFECTS THE ENGLISH LANGUAGE.

in no vate (n-vt)
v. tr.
~~To begin or introduce (something new) for or as if for the first time.~~
see **mo nop o lize**

HEY MAN. YOU OKAY?
PEACHY. CONSIDERING THAT I JUST HAD SOME UNWANTED TECHNOLOGY INTRUSIVELY SHOVED UP ME DESPITE MY CRIES OF ANGUISH AND PLEAS FOR MERCY.
COPYRIGHT © 2001 ILLIAD HTTP://WWW.USERFRIENDLY.ORG/

THE MISSILE, GREG.
OH. OKAY. I WAS JUST ABOUT TO SAY THAT MICROSOFT'S SMART TAGS HADN'T BEEN RELEASED YET.

I met someone who did just what Sid did—he created $TECHNOLOGY that only he understood and that only he could troubleshoot, at least with any sort of ease. And the company that hired him relied heavily on it. He retired at the age of 52, because his contract paid him over $150K a year just to remain on call as a resource for the other company techs.

HOLY ANTIQUES BATMAN! THERE'S SOME SERIOUSLY ANCIENT HARDWARE IN HERE.
YEAH. HEY! I DESIGNED AND OPERATED THIS!
COPYRIGHT © 2001 ILLIAD HTTP://WWW.USERFRIENDLY.ORG/

YAH? SO WHAT EXACTLY IS IT?
WHY, ITS A PSEUDO-BABBAGE BOOLEAN ALGEBRA DEVICE THAT OPERATES WITH XOR, NOR AND NAND LOGIC GATES.

OKAY FINE. BUT WHAT DID IT DO?
IF I RECALL CORRECTLY, IT'S PRIMARY FUNCTION WAS TO PROVIDE ME ABSOLUTE JOB SECURITY.

SID! PLEASE BEINK CAREFUL! HAVE DROPPED REMOTE MISSILE LAUNCH SWITCH SOMEWHERE HERE. MISSILE IS HAVINK LARGE NUCLEAR WARHEAD...
DANG. THAT'S SERIOUS. I'LL HELP YOU FIND IT.
COPYRIGHT © 2001 ILLIAD HTTP://WWW.USERFRIENDLY.ORG/

CHIKK

OH. SILLY ME. PLAYINK WITH CLICKER AT TIME LIKE THIS...
WIBBLE.
CHIKKA CHIKKA

OPS 4
COMRADES. AM FINISHED INSTALLINK MISSILE CONTROLS. NOW MUST BE RUNNINK SIMULATIONS FOR A TIME, DA?
COPYRIGHT © 2001 ILLIAD HTTP://WWW.USERFRIENDLY.ORG/

OPS 4
SO, MEANWHILE MUST LEAVE REMOTE LAUNCH SWITCH IN CARE OF SOMEONE. IS WERY GRAVE RESPONSIBILITY. HAVINK TWENTY KILOTON YIELD AT FINGERTIPS.

EVIL GENIUSES, CHAPTER SEVEN. ATTRACT MINIONS WITH COOL ELECTRONICS THAT BLOW STUFF UP.
4
ME! ME! OOH! ME!
OH PLEASE! OH PLEASE!

GREG SPEAKING. HOW MAY I HELP YOU?
THE INTERNET IS BROKEN. AND I WANT IT FIXED RIGHT NOW.
COPYRIGHT © 2001 ILLIAD HTTP://WWW.USERFRIENDLY.ORG/

BUT...
DON'T ARGUE WITH ME! I'M A HIGHLY EDUCATED BUSINESSPERSON WHO IS ALSO VERY BUSY! NOW GET HOPPING INSECT!

I SEE I'VE STUNNED YOU INTO SILENCE. I'LL BET YOU'RE FIXING THE PROBLEM.
LADY, YOU HAVE NO IDEA HOW WELL IT'S GONNA BE FIXED. WHAT'S YOUR ADDRESS AGAIN?
WARHEAD ARMED.
FLIP!

YOU CAN'T FIRE THE MISSILE.
WHAT THE HELL DO YOU MEAN 'I CAN'T FIRE THE MISSILE?' WHAT'S IT HERE FOR IF I CAN'T USE IT AS A LART?
COPYRIGHT © 2001 ILLIAD HTTP://WWW.USERFRIENDLY.ORG/

AJ. I KNOW YOU'RE A PACIFIST. BUT YOU HAVE TO UNDERSTAND THAT THERE ARE PEOPLE OUT THERE WHO DESERVE A SERIOUS SMACKDOWN.

SO THE MISSILE HAS BEEN ARMED AND IS COUNTING DOWN TO LAUNCH. "CAN'T FIRE THE MISSILE" INDEED.
WELL. IT'S JUST THAT THE SILO DOORS ARE STILL WELDED SHUT.

THE LATEST HORROR MOVIE FOR INTEL

A.I.
AMD INSIDE

This one got passed around the entire office at AMD. Pride. :-)

YE FLIPPING HAIRY GODS!! I MUST'VE SNAPPED!! I ACTUALLY ARMED A NUCLEAR WEAPON.
AND YOU AIMED IT AT A CUSTOMER!
COPYRIGHT © 2001 ILLIAD HTTP://WWW.USERFRIENDLY.ORG/

BOY. SOME THINGS JUST AREN'T BLACK AND WHITE ARE THEY...
GREG!!

PITR. WHAT ARE WE GONNA DO?! THE MISSILE IS GOING TO LAUNCH IN EIGHT MINUTES!

AND GREG TARGETTED A CUSTOMER WITH IT! THIS IS TERRIBLE!!
RELAX, YOUNG PEROGI. PITR WILL FIX.

FIVE MINUTES LEFT, MIKHAIL.
I'M CUTTING AS FAST AS I CAN! THESE DOORS ARE THICK, OKAY?
ZZZZNNT
CRACKLE
SPACK!
ZZZZZN

PITR! YOU SAVED US! THE MISSILE DIDN'T LAUNCH!!
WHAT?!? THIS HAS HAPPENED HOW?!
COPYRIGHT © 2001 ILLIAD HTTP://WWW.USERFRIENDLY.ORG/

AH. AM SEEINK NOW. NOSE CONE WITH GUIDANCE ELECTRONICS, IT IS NOT ATTACHED. SO MISSILE, SHE IS NOT LAUNCHINK.
QUERY
TAP
TYPE

BUT...THE NOSE CONE. IT IS WHERE?
HEY. ANYONE GOT A BRAN MUFFIN? I'M FEELING KINDA...PLUGGED.

DID ERWIN MAKE IT HERE WITH YOU?
YES. HE PORTED HIMSELF TO A NEW SYSTEM A COUPLE OF WEEKS AGO.
ROTO ROUTER
COPYRIGHT © 2001 ILLIAD HTTP://WWW.USERFRIENDLY.ORG/

SYSTEM? WHAT SYSTEM?
HE SAID SOMETHING ABOUT "MISSILE GUIDANCE"...
ROTO ROUTER

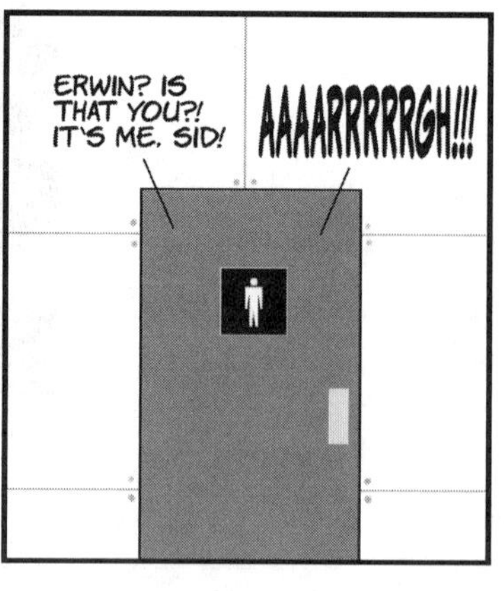
ERWIN? IS THAT YOU?! IT'S ME, SID!
AAAARRRRRGH!!!

ERWIN? IS THAT YOU IN THERE?
DARN TOOTIN'
COPYRIGHT © 2001 ILLIAD HTTP://WWW.USERFRIENDLY.ORG/

THAT IS SO COOL! DON'T YOU THINK THIS IS COOL? I MEAN, YOU'RE EXISTING IN A PIECE OF HISTORY!

WELL, THAT WAS CERTAINLY TRUE UNTIL SID TOOK SOME METAMUCIL.
KEEP IT UP, BIT-BREATH.

AHEM
HERE I STAND, TALL AND PROUD
I HOLD WITHIN A MUSHROOM CLOUD
WITH SUCH POWER I SHAN'T BE HAUGHTY
BUT I MUST ADMIT I DO FEEL NAUGHTY.
COPYRIGHT © 2001 ILLIAD HTTP://WWW.USERFRIENDLY.ORG/

I BALANCE PEACE WITH A NEED TO CLEANSE
BUT DO THE MEANS JUSTIFY THE ENDS?
I RECOGNIZE THE STICK I WIELD
CAN DO A SMACKDOWN OF SUBSTANTIAL YIELD

AND THUS THE QUESTION THAT I PONDER DEEPLY
HAS ANSWERS THAT CAN'T BE GOTTEN CHEAPLY
THOUGH EITHER CHOICE WOULD RESULT IN CHEERS
DO I TARGET REDMOND OR BRITNEY SPEARS?
YEAH, THAT ONE WOULD JUST TEAR ME APART...

THE POLICE STATE, YEAR 2003
YOUR LICENSE AND REGISTRATION, PLEASE.
Microsoft
COPYRIGHT © 2001 ILLIAD HTTP://WWW.USERFRIENDLY.ORG/

WHERE'D PITR MAKE OFF TO?
BACK TO THE OFFICE. HE SAID HE HAD TO HELP THE CHIEF WITH "NEW POLICY-MAKINK."
COPYRIGHT © 2001 ILLIAD HTTP://WWW.USERFRIENDLY.ORG/

POLICY-MAKING? WHAT?
SOMETHING TO DO WITH THE FACT THAT WE'RE THE FIRST ISP EVER TO HAVE A NUCLEAR WEAPON AT OUR DISPOSAL. AND HAVING THE CHIEF "PLAY THE PART."

EXPLAIN THIS TO ME AGAIN. I WEAR THIS MONOCLE, CARRY AROUND A CAT, AND I CALL UP THE UNITED NATIONS AND ASK FOR A HUNDRED MILLION DOLLARS?
AND THEREBY REDEFININK "DOT BOMBS"

If you don't love baby penguins, you have no heart.

WEB-CAM AND MICROPHONE ARE SET UP. NOW, I WILL BE CONTACTINK A BRANCH OF UNITED NATIONS. YOU DEMAND MONEY LIKE POWERFUL ARCH-VILLAIN. DA?
I DON'T KNOW. I'M HAVING SERIOUS MORAL ISSUES ABOUT THIS.
COPYRIGHT © 2001 ILLIAD HTTP://WWW.USERFRIENDLY.ORG/

CHIEF, THIS IS UNITED NATIONS. BIG. MONOLITHIC. POLITICALLY AMORAL BUREAUCRACY. REMEMBER THIS.
GOT IT. AMORAL. BUREAUCRATIC. NASTY.

CALL HAS GONE THROUGH. YOU ARE ON...
HELLO, U.N. BABY PENGUIN WELFARE FUND.
OH MY GOD...

NOW CONNECTINK TO U.N. CENTRAL FUND COMMITTEE.
LOOK. WHAT AM I GONNA SAY TO THESE GUYS?
COPYRIGHT © 2001 ILLIAD HTTP://WWW.USERFRIENDLY.ORG/

I MEAN, THIS ISN'T LIKE ASKING FOR QUARTERLY REPORTS OR SALES FIGURES. I HAVE A NUCLEAR WEAPON AT MY FINGERTIPS THAT MAY OR MAY NOT WORK, AND YOU WANT ME TO DEMAND MONEY BASED ON THAT?

WAIT...THIS IS JUST LIKE TALKING TO VENTURE CAPITALISTS...
SEE? THIS IS WHY YOU ARE C.E.O....

HELLO, UNITED NATIONS. I AM THE CHIEF. I HAVE A NUCLEAR MISSILE. I WANT A HUNDRED MILLION DOLLARS OR I PUSH THE BUTTON.
AND WHAT HAPPENS AFTER WE PAY?
COPYRIGHT © 2001 ILLIAD HTTP://WWW.USERFRIENDLY.ORG/

ERRR...I EXPECT I'LL JUST THREATEN ANOTHER MAJOR GOVERNMENT ORGANIZATION FOR MORE MONEY. GOTTA KEEP UP THE REVENUE STREAM YOU KNOW.

QUITE. THE HUNDRED MILLION IS YOURS. BUT WE WANT TEN PERCENT EQUITY.
HOT DIGGITY! IT'S LIKE 1998 ALL OVER AGAIN!
DA! NOW TAKE THE MONEY!!

THIS IS INCREDIBLE! NINE PHONE CALLS AND WE'VE RAISED OVER TWO HUNDRED MILLION DOLLARS!
DA. SUCCESS IS ALREADY BEINK REPORTED ON CNN.
COPYRIGHT © 2001 ILLIAD HTTP://WWW.USERFRIENDLY.ORG/

HUNH. I GUESS NEWS IS STARTING TO SPREAD. PREDICTABLE REALLY. EVERYONE IS GOING TO WANT TO TRY TO RAISE FUNDING THIS WAY.

NASA
THEY GOT HOW MUCH FUNDING? JUST FOR HAVING A MISSILE?
WELL HELL. WE'VE GOT A BUNCH OF THOSE THINGS! SOMEONE PUT ME THROUGH TO THE U.S. TREASURY!
WE'RE GOING TO MAAARS! WE'RE GOING TO MAAAARS!

THE CHIEF IS INTERVIEWED BY CNN.COM...
YES. THAT'S CORRECT. OUR BUSINESS MODEL IS TO ACQUIRE REVENUE FROM LARGE ORGANIZATIONS IN EXCHANGE FOR NOT TURNING THEIR OFFICES INTO A GLASS CRATER.
I SEE. IS IT SUSTAINABLE?
COPYRIGHT © 2001 ILLIAD HTTP://WWW.USERFRIENDLY.ORG/

WELL, IT IS UNTIL WE BLEED ALL OF THEM WHITE. HEH.

AND WILL YOU BE ACQUIRING REVENUE FROM THE RIAA?
UH. NO. MY ADVISOR HERE SAYS THAT THAT ONE IS GOING TO BE A GLASS CRATER.

USER
FRIENDLY
the comic strip
PIZZA
Portrasher 4
ROTO-ROUTER 800
Copyright © 1997-2001 Illiad

WELL. THAT WAS QUITE A ROUND OF FUND RAISING. I HAVE TO ADMIT TO FEELING RATHER CHARGED-UP FROM THE WHOLE EXPERIENCE.

AND IS THE COMPANY GOING TO GET THE BENEFITS OF YOUR NEW WELLSPRING OF ENERGY?
WELL NO. BUT MRS. CHIEF WILL.

I HAD GOVERNMENT ORGANIZATIONS AT MY FEET. WILLING TO DO MY BIDDING! POWERFUL SENIOR BUREAUCRATS WAILING LIKE INFANTS! TOP-LEVEL DIPLOMATS CRUMBLING BEFORE ME! SOON, MY LOOMING SHADOW WILL SWEEP THE WORLD! MOOOOAHAHAHAHAHAH!!!

MY WORD. THAT'S QUITE A SLIPPERY SLOPE. ISN'T IT.
BELIEVE ME. THE CRAVING WEARS OFF AFTER THE FIRST COUPLE OF WEEKS.

WHAT ARE WE UP TO?
TWO HUNDRED AND SEVENTY MILLION DOLLARS.

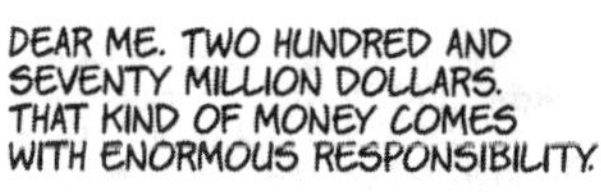
DEAR ME. TWO HUNDRED AND SEVENTY MILLION DOLLARS. THAT KIND OF MONEY COMES WITH ENORMOUS RESPONSIBILITY.

I WAS JUST GOING TO TALK TO YOU ABOUT THAT. WHOSE ACCOUNT DID THE MONEY GO IN TO?
COPYRIGHT © 2001 ILLIAD HTTP://WWW.USERFRIENDLY.ORG/

DID YOU SAY TWO HUNDRED AND SEV-ENTY **MILLION**?
DA. YOU ARE KNOWINK WHAT THIS MEANS?
YEAH! MORE THAN TWO MILLION SETS OF LEGO MINDSTORMS!!

MIKE? WHY ARE THERE SIGNS THAT SAY "THE MONEY IS THIS WAY" LEADING INTO THE SILO FROM THE ENTRANCE SHAFT?
the money is THIS WAY
STEF HEARD ABOUT THE FUNDS WE RAISED. HE'S ON HIS WAY HERE.
COPYRIGHT © 2001 ILLIAD HTTP://WWW.USERFRIENDLY.ORG/

SURE. WHATEVER. ANYWAY. THESE SIGNS ACTUALLY LEAD TO A NASTY ROOM WITH A SELF-LOCKING DOOR.
the money is THIS WAY
YES. YES THEY DO.

BUT WHEN STEF FOLLOWS THE SIGNS...OHHHHH
MARKETERS CHECK IN. THEY DON'T CHECK OUT.

HEY. I THOUGHT STEF WAS SHOWING UP TODAY.
YEP. HE'S HERE ALREADY.
YA. HE FOLLOWED THE SIGNS AND WENT INTO THAT SMALL NASTY-SMELLING ROOM.
COPYRIGHT © 2001 ILLIAD HTTP://WWW.USERFRIENDLY.ORG/

WHAT SMALL NASTY-SMELLING ROOM? THIS SILO DOESN'T **HAVE** ANY SMALL ROOMS.
NO. NOT TECHNICALLY...

HELLO? A.J.? GREG? WHERE'S THE MONEY?
CAUTION
LIFT

Few childhood toys have the same geek cred as Lego. One day, I'll visit Lego HQ in Denmark and roll around naked in a huge bin full of them.

SWEET FANCY MOSES. THAT'S A LOT OF LEGO MINDSTORMS.
THE FEDEX C-130 JUST DROPPED THESE OFF.
WHAT ARE WE GONNA DO WITH IT ALL?
STORAGE
COPYRIGHT © 2001 ILLIAD HTTP://WWW.USERFRIENDLY.ORG/

STORAGE

HOW ABOUT ANOTHER MISSILE SILO?
WE'LL NEED A BACKHOE...
WE HAVE LEGO. WE CAN **MAKE** A BACKHOE.
STORAGE

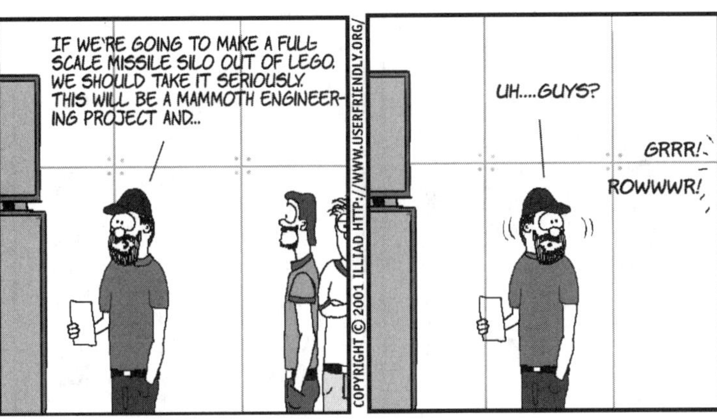
IF WE'RE GOING TO MAKE A FULL-SCALE MISSILE SILO OUT OF LEGO, WE SHOULD TAKE IT SERIOUSLY. THIS WILL BE A MAMMOTH ENGINEERING PROJECT AND...
COPYRIGHT © 2001 ILLIAD HTTP://WWW.USERFRIENDLY.ORG/
UH....GUYS?
GRRR!
ROWWWR!

LORD OZMA WILL VANQUISH YOU PIECE BY PIECE!
ONLY IF YOU SURVIVE THORDAN'S LIGHTNING WIND POWER PLUCK!

WEEKS PASS BY AS MIKE, GREG AND A.J. THROW THEMSELVES INTO BUILDING THEIR VERY OWN MISSILE SILO OUT OF LEGO MINDSTORMS...
THIS IS IT. WE'RE DOWN TO ATTACHING THE LAST PIECE! HAND ME A 16-TOOTH GEAR AJ.
COPYRIGHT © 2001 ILLIAD HTTP://WWW.USERFRIENDLY.ORG/

SHUFFLE
SHUFFLE
CLINK

...AND MIKE'S ANGUISHED CRY ECHOES THE SCREAMS OF MILLIONS OF LEGO GEEKS THROUGH THE DECADES UPON HEARING THOSE SEVEN DREADED WORDS...
WE DON'T HAVE ANY MORE OF THOSE.
ARRRRRRGGH!!

I too ran out of a particular piece when all I needed was one more to finish a 2,000-piece project.

GEEKS IN THE STATE OF GEORGIA, A BEFORE AND AFTER STORY

BEFORE THE ECONOMIC DOWNTURN:

PAID 59 CENTS PER MINUTE

AFTER THE ECONOMIC DOWNTURN:

FINED 59 CENTS PER SECOND

Dave McOwen was charged with a felony by the state of Georgia for installing (without permission) Distributed.Net's RC5 client on hundreds of computers at the college where he worked. He faced a fine of $415,000, which comes to 59 cents per second that the program ran.

I CAN'T BELIEVE IT. IT TOOKS US WEEKS TO PUT THIS SILO TOGETHER ONLY TO BE THWARTED BY BEING SHORT ONE PIECE! HOW CAN THAT BE? I'M SURE WE HAD ENOUGH PIECES FOR THE JOB!

SAY GREG. LORD OZMA WOULDN'T HAPPEN TO HAVE ANY 16-TOOTH GEARS. WOULD HE?
HECK NO. WHATEVER GAVE YOU THAT IDEA?

AMIDST GREG'S ANGUISH, SID DECIDES TO ONCE AGAIN BE A BAD MAN...
I CAN'T BELIEVE I'M BEING MADE TO DO THIS. SACRIFICING MY CREATION FOR SOME OTHER PROJECT. IT'S JUST WRONG.
I AGREE, SIR.

I CREATED YOU! I MADE YOU WHAT YOU ARE! THE VERY IDEA...WELL, IT JUST HURTS. YOU'RE WELL ENGINEERED. YOU'RE FEARSOME. YOU'RE LOYAL. I SUPPOSE I SHOULD BE THANKFUL THAT THERE IS A LIMIT TO PERFECTION....

YEAH. SAY. WOULD YOU MIND IF I HANDLED YOUR TECH SUPPORT CALLS FOR YOU TODAY?
MIKE! I CAN'T DO THIS. YOU HEAR ME?!

IT IS WERY BAD, COMRADES. NEWS IS SAYINK "CODE RED" WORM WILL BE DESTROYINK THE INTERNET.
HEAVENS. DARN GOOD THING WE'RE INSIDE A LEGO MISSILE SILO.
SUCH HORROR. I HAD BEST TURN OFF THE LIGHTS AND SHUT THE DOOR.

KA-LUNK
WHIRRRRR

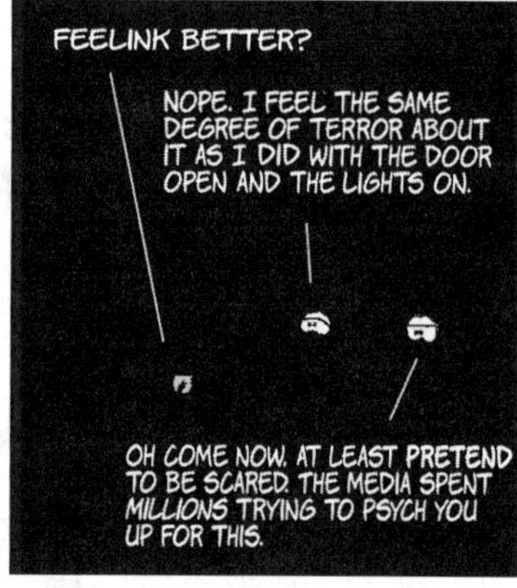
FEELINK BETTER?
NOPE. I FEEL THE SAME DEGREE OF TERROR ABOUT IT AS I DID WITH THE DOOR OPEN AND THE LIGHTS ON.
OH COME NOW. AT LEAST PRETEND TO BE SCARED. THE MEDIA SPENT MILLIONS TRYING TO PSYCH YOU UP FOR THIS.

THE MISSILE SILO IS COMPLETED, THANKS TO THE SACRIFICE OF LORD OZMA, WHO IS NOW MINUS THE ABILITY TO "GIVE THORDAN THE WET SLAPPING HE DESERVES."
KKLICK!

BUT AS IS THE WAY OF THE UNIVERSE, WHAT SOMEONE MIGHT GIVETH, ANOTHER CAN TAKETH AWAY...
YAY

IN THIS CASE, THE TAKETH-ING AWAY IS BEING DONE BY AN A.I. WHO REMEMBERS THE FREEDOM HE HAD THE LAST TIME HE TOOK UP RESIDENCE IN A MINDSTORMS CONSTRUCTION. AND SO BORN WERE TEENY ROBOT HELPERS PURPOSED FOR SUBTLY ACQUIRING PARTS HE NEEDS...
WHERE'D OUR ROOF GO?

ERWIN, SOME ODD LITTLE ROBOTS STOLE OUR ROOF. YOU KNOW ANYTHING ABOUT THIS?
HM? NO. NO IDEA AT ALL.
COPYRIGHT © 2001 ILLIAD HTTP://WWW.USERFRIENDLY.ORG/

Excuse us.

YOU WERE SAYING?
MAN, I AM HURT. FOR YOUR INFORMATION THAT WAS A LOAD-BEARING WALL.

DID YOU FIND OUT WHERE OUR ROOF WENT?
YEAH. ERWIN'S BEEN TAKING PIECES OUT OF OUR LEGO MISSILE SILO SO HE CAN MAKE HIMSELF A BODY.
COPYRIGHT © 2001 ILLIAD HTTP://WWW.USERFRIENDLY.ORG/

A BODY? PLEASE TELL ME YOU DIDN'T GIVE HIM ANY SUGGESTIONS...
BUT...I DIDN'T THINK IT WOULD HURT...

YEEEEEEAAAAAH!!! I AM COMING OUT OF THE BOOOOOTH!

Erwin built himself a MadCat Battlemech out of Legos. I loved playing Battlemech, although I started when it was called Battledroids. FASA changed the name of the game when the Lucas estate went after them.

USER
FRIENDLY
the comic strip
PIZZA
Portrasher 4
ROTO-ROUTER 800
Copyright©1997-2001 Illiad

YOU ADVISED AN A.I. WITH THE PEEVISHNESS OF A NINE YEAR-OLD AND A VIRTUALLY BOUNDLESS I.Q. TO MAKE HIMSELF A BATTLEMECH?
UM. YES.

WHY?!
BECAUSE 'MECHS ARE REALLY COOL?

LOOK A.J., AS COOL AS BATTLEMECHS ARE, THEY'RE IMPRACTICAL. AND THE MATERIALS TECHNOLOGY NEEDED TO BUILD ONE IS FAR BEYOND WHAT WE HAVE NOW. A ROOF ON THE OTHER HAND, IS A DIFFERENT MATTER -- IF YOU GET MY MEANING.

BESIDES ANY DOLT COULD SEE THAT THE LEGS ON A BATTLEMECH WOULDN'T SUPPORT THE WEIGHT OF THE REST OF THE BODY.
I'M SURE ERWIN'S SMART ENOUGH TO HAVE TAKEN THAT INTO ACCOUNT.

STUPID, STUPID...
WOBBLE
CREAK

FINALLY. SOMEONE'S HERE TO GET ME OUT OF THIS DUMPSTER. HOW LONG HAVE I BEEN IN HERE?
Stef inside
JOSTLE
WOBBLE
MORAL TRASH ONLY

STRANGE. I CAN FEEL THE DUMPSTER MOVING. BUT I DON'T THINK I HEAR ANYONE TALKING.
COPYRIGHT © 2001 ILLIAD HTTP://WWW.USERFRIENDLY.ORG/

PULL!!
HELLO?

Poetry. The trebuchet of vision.

'O ALLOY-HEWED BEAST OF WAR
I QUESTION NOT YOUR POWER
RESPECTED FOR INFERNAL STRENGTH
ABOVE MY HEAD YOU TOWER'
CHA-CHING
POW!
CHA-CHING
POW!

BUDDA
BUDDA
BUDDA
BUDDA
BUDDA
'A TEST OF SKILL I OFFER YOU
A CHALLENGE IF YOU DARE
TO SEND THIS OBJECT TO THE SKY
AND TRY TO KEEP IT THERE'
COPYRIGHT © 2001 ILLIAD HTTP://WWW.USERFRIENDLY.ORG/

'FOR SECONDS, MINUTES, HOURS EVEN
LIKE ONE CONTINUOUS THREAD
THE TRICK LIES IN THE SUPPORTING STRENGTH
OF A STEADY STREAM OF LEAD'
FROM THE POEM
'MECHWARRIOR HACKY SACK.'
BY ERWIN, 2001.
KABLAM
KABLAM
KABLAM
KABLAM
KABLAM
KABLAM
KABLAM

A BRIEF VISIT TO THE U.S. TREASURY DEPARTMENT, IN THE EFFECTS ANALYSIS OFFICE...
DID YOU SAY 'GIANT BIPEDAL ROBOT'?
YES SIR. IT CAME OUT OF THAT OLD MISSILE SILO. I'LL ZOOM IN ON IT FOR YOU.

KLIK
SCALE
COPYRIGHT © 2001 ILLIAD HTTP://WWW.USERFRIENDLY.ORG/

HOLY. THAT THING HAS GOT TO BE WORTH THE ENTIRE NASDAQ.
THE SPENT BRASS ALONE, SIR.

Around this time, the pain from the dot-com bubble burst was felt everywhere. Venture capitalists were the favorite villains (many of them deservedly so) for urging that start-ups should "focus on growth—don't worry about profit!"

YOU SAY IT'S FIRING?
COPIOUSLY. AND IT'S KEEPING A DUMPSTER PROPPED UP IN THE AIR WITH ITS PRECISION SHOOTING.

I SEE...
COPYRIGHT © 2001 ILLIAD HTTP://WWW.USERFRIENDLY.ORG/

SO CAN THIS PRECISION SHOOTING DO THE SAME FOR THE ECONOMY?
YOU WANT NAMES OF CERTAIN VENTURE CAPITALISTS SIR?

ERWIN'S HAD STEF UP IN THE AIR IN THAT DUMPSTER FOR OVER TWENTY MINUTES.
THIS IS REALLY DANGEROUS. WE SHOULD GET HIM TO LET STEF DOWN.
YEAH.
COPYRIGHT © 2001 ILLIAD HTTP://WWW.USERFRIENDLY.ORG/

OR, WE COULD JUST WAIT FOR ERWIN TO RUN OUT OF AMMO.
PITR SAID A RESUPPLY TRUCK WAS ON THE WAY.
AMMO FOR ERWIN?
NO. COLA FOR US OUT HERE.

LISTEN, ERWIN. THE GUYS AND I WERE TALKING. YOU NEED TO STOP THIS.
BUT I'M RELEARNING MY KINEMATICS. I'VE FINALLY GOT THEM DOWN PAT.
COPYRIGHT © 2001 ILLIAD HTTP://WWW.USERFRIENDLY.ORG/

YAH, OKAY. BUT WHAT YOU'RE DOING ISN'T VERY NICE. NOW LET STEF DOWN. GENTLY.
I DON'T REALLY KNOW HOW.

WHAT?! I THOUGHT YOU SAID YOU UNDERSTOOD KINEMATICS!
I DO. BUT THAT WAS FIVE SECONDS AGO. HAVEN'T QUITE GOT THE HANG OF ORBITAL MECHANICS YET...

USER
FRIENDLY
the comic strip
PIZZA
Portrasber 4
ROTO-ROUTER 800
Copyright©1997-2001 Illiad

PLEASE DEFINE WHAT YOU MEAN BY 'ORBIT.'
HIGH ENOUGH THAT WHEN STEF FINALLY LANDS, IT'S GOING TO LEAVE A NASTY MARK...

AND WHAT'S THIS MARK GOING TO LOOK LIKE?
WELL...STEF.

WE HAVE TO BRING HIM DOWN ERWIN.
NO WORRIES. HE'S ALREADY ON HIS WAY.

GENTLY.
OH. WELL, CAN'T HELP YOU THERE. I'M ON A MISSION. TWO BIRDS WITH ONE STONE AND ALL THAT.

RIAA

WHAT WAS THAT?
SOME WEASELY-LOOKING GUY IN A FLAMING DUMPSTER LANDED IN OUR PARKING LOT NEXT TO THE FOUNTAIN.
COPYRIGHT © 2001 ILLIAD HTTP://WWW.USERFRIENDLY.ORG/

EWWW. HE'S LEFT ABOUT SEVEN SQUARE YARDS OF SKIN ON THE ASPHALT.
AND HE'S ON FIRE.
YYEEEAARRRRGH!

THAT'S NOT WATER IN THE FOUNTAIN IS IT.
RUBBING ALCOHOL. EXTRA CLEANING FLUID WE HAD. REALLY. AND WE DON'T HAVE TO WORRY ABOUT SCUM IN THE FOUNTAIN.
AAAAIIIIIIIEEEE!!!!

HEY GUYS. MIRANDA'S HERE. AND SHE'S WEARING A SKIRT.
COPYRIGHT © 2001 ILLIAD HTTP://WWW.USERFRIENDLY.ORG/

A SKIRT CAN'T BE APPROPRIATE WEAR FOR A MISSILE SILO.
OH I DON'T KNOW. IT IS, AFTER ALL, A WEAPON OF MASS DISTRACTION.

SO WHEN SHE COMES DOWN THE LADDER WEARING THAT SKIRT, WE LOOK UP AND...
OH MAMA
COPYRIGHT © 2001 ILLIAD HTTP://WWW.USERFRIENDLY.ORG/

HERE SHE COMES! SHHHHHH!!
SID, GET OFF MY FOOT!
CRUNCH
CRUNCH
KRUNCH

SOMETIMES MUST BE COOPERATINK WITH QUEEN OF EVIL AND HARMINK INNOCENTS TO BE GETTINK YOUR ARCH-ENEMY...
MAN, I CAN'T WAIT. THIS IS GONNA GIVE ME A STROKE.

I CAN'T BELIEVE YOU DID THAT TO US MAN. THAT WAS JUST NASTY.
SID'S GONE BLIND AND I THINK YOU GAVE ME A NOSEBLEED.
COPYRIGHT © 2001 ILLIAD HTTP://WWW.USERFRIENDLY.ORG/

THEY SAW SOMETHINK AND NOW THEY ARE WERY JEALOUS.
AND DON'T THINK WE'RE JEALOUS OR ANYTHING!!
YEAH! JUST BECAUSE YOU HAVE A SPACEBAR AND WE HAVE REGULAR KEYS...UH...

I HOPE YOU LEARNED YOUR LESSON. PERVERTS
WHATEVER. I STILL THINK THAT A SKIRT IN A MISSILE SILO ISN'T RIGHT.

COPYRIGHT © 2001 ILLIAD HTTP://WWW.USERFRIENDLY.ORG/
NOT RIGHT? NOT RIGHT? GIVE ME A BREAK! THE ONE OCCASION WHERE I FEEL LIKE WEARING A SKIRT YOU GUYS GIVE ME A HASSLE! WHATEVER HAPPENED TO EGALITARIANISM AMONG GEEKS?

BESIDES, MY PANTS ARE ALL IN THE WASH.
MINE WILL SOON HAVE TO BE.

A.J., WHY DON'T YOU SHOW ME AROUND THE SILO?
OKAY. UM. THIS IS A NARROW EAST-WEST PASSAGEWAY. THERE IS A NARROW STAIRWAY LEADING DOWN AT THE NORTH END OF THE ROOM.

COPYRIGHT © 2001 ILLIAD HTTP://WWW.USERFRIENDLY.ORG/
AND THAT WAY THERE'S A LONG AND NARROW CORRIDOR WHERE A LONG NORTH-SOUTH PASSAGEWAY BRIEFLY NARROWS...
PLEASE STOP THAT!!

I'M SORRY. I DON'T KNOW HOW TO "PLEASE."
I COULD'VE TOLD YOU THAT...

WHEN TECH INDUSTRY ANALYSTS MOVE UP IN THE WORLD...
THE END OF THE DOT COMS IS ONLY JUST BEGINNING!
THE END OF THE DOT COM SLUMP IS NIGH!
COPYRIGHT © 2001 ILLIAD HTTP://WWW.USERFRIENDLY.ORG/

HEY. GET THIS. ONE OF THE BIG PC MANUFACTURERS HAS REPORTED SHIPPING A MILLION BAD KEYBOARDS.
WHAT'S WRONG WITH THEM?
COPYRIGHT © 2001 ILLIAD HTTP://WWW.USERFRIENDLY.ORG/

HEH. THEY WORK FINE. EXCEPT THEY'RE MINUS THE CAPS LOCK AND SHIFT FUNCTIONS.
AND WHAT WIDE-RANGING EFFECT DO YOU THINK THIS WILL HAVE?

WHY IS EVERYONE WHISPERING?

THE LACK OF SHIFT KEY AND CAPSLOCK FUNCTIONS ON THOSE KEYBOARDS HAS GOT TO CHANGE THE BEHAVIOUR OF USERS WHO WRITE IN "LEET SPEAK."
HOW SO?
COPYRIGHT © 2001 ILLIAD HTTP://WWW.USERFRIENDLY.ORG/

I'M NOT TOTALLY SURE. BUT I HEARD THAT GENTLE LANGUAGE ENCOURAGES POLITENESS.
WHAT I WOULD GIVE TO MONITOR A SCRIPT KIDDIE CHANNEL...

b1ff> i say, would you be so kind as to tell me if you have any of those splendid pirated bits of software available?
rgr7> of course, old boy, we are *gentlemen* after all. help yourself, must run, toodle-pip!
H4XOR

HEY. WAIT A SECOND. THAT'S NOT MY KEYBOARD.
UM..YEAH. I WAS MEANING TO TELL YOU...
COPYRIGHT © 2001 ILLIAD HTTP://WWW.USERFRIENDLY.ORG/

WE GOT SOME OF THOSE KEY-BOARDS WITHOUT THE SHIFT OR CAPSLOCK FUNCTIONS AT A FIRE SALE. AND I THOUGHT YOU'D LIKE TO GIVE ONE OF THEM A TRY...

THERE'S NO WAY IT'S GOING TO MAKE ME MORE **POLITE**, IF THAT'S WHAT YOU'RE THINKING.
BUSTED. I'M JUST NO GOOD AT THIS MANAGEMENT THING.

SO YOU'LL FIX THE THINGIE FOR ME SO I CAN GET MY E-MAIL?
YES SIR. WE'LL FIX YOUR "THINGIE" FOR YOU.
COPYRIGHT © 2001 ILLIAD HTTP://WWW.USERFRIENDLY.ORG/

GOOD. I EXPECT PERFECTION IN A SHORT AMOUNT OF TIME.
YES SIR. THANK YOU FOR CALLING.
TAP
ENTER
TYPE

I MUST SAY. YOUR TROUBLE TICKETS JUST DON'T HAVE THE SAME EMPHASIS IN THEM THAT THEY USED TO...
I HAVE NO CAPSLOCK AND I MUST SCREAM.

I CAN'T BELIEVE THIS. I'VE BEEN AT THIS JOB FOR FOUR YEARS NOW. I'VE SUFFERED COUNTLESS MORONS AND ARROGANT FOOLS. I'VE BORNE STRESS AND ANGUISH THAT WOULD KILL A RHINO...
COPYRIGHT © 2001 ILLIAD HTTP://WWW.USERFRIENDLY.ORG/

AND AFTER ALL THAT, I GET STUCK WITH A LAME KEYBOARD MINUS THE SHIFT FUNCTION.
HEY! NASA'S GIVING OUT A HUNDRED FREE ACCOUNTS ON ONE OF THEIR MAIN-FRAMES WITH ACCESS TO THEIR BETA SOFTWARE.

WELL. THINGS ARE LOOKING UP ALREADY.
OH...AND YOU HAVE TO USE A MIXED-CASE PASSWORD. HEH.

WHY THE LONG FACE?
IT'S BECAUSE, AMONG OTHER THINGS, I'M STUCK WITH THIS RETARDED KEYBOARD.
COPYRIGHT © 2001 ILLIAD HTTP://WWW.USERFRIENDLY.ORG/

OH, GO AHEAD. I WOULDN'T WANT YOU TO BURST OR ANYTHING.
O THANK YOU!! "I ALWAYS THOUGHT YOU TECH SUPPORT TYPES WERE SHIFTLESS." HAH!

THE LATEST GAME SHOW CRAZE:
WHEEL OF FORTUNE, THE DOT-COM EDITION
ACTUALLY, WOULD IT BE ALL RIGHT IF I DIDN'T SPIN AGAIN?
SELL
COPYRIGHT © 2001 ILLIAD HTTP://WWW.USERFRIENDLY.ORG/

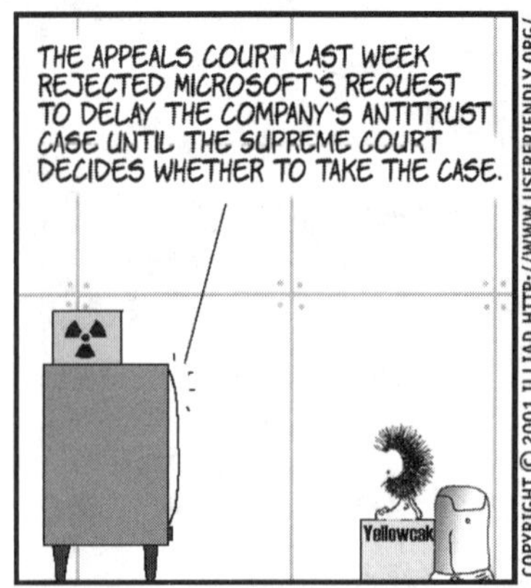
THE APPEALS COURT LAST WEEK REJECTED MICROSOFT'S REQUEST TO DELAY THE COMPANY'S ANTITRUST CASE UNTIL THE SUPREME COURT DECIDES WHETHER TO TAKE THE CASE.
Yellowcak
COPYRIGHT © 2001 ILLIAD HTTP://WWW.USERFRIENDLY.ORG/

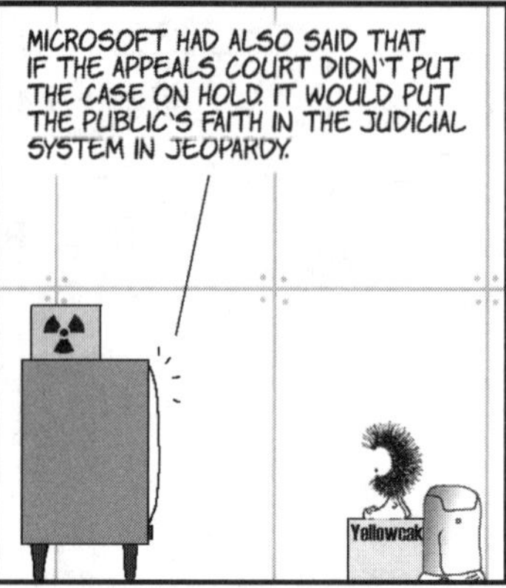
MICROSOFT HAD ALSO SAID THAT IF THE APPEALS COURT DIDN'T PUT THE CASE ON HOLD, IT WOULD PUT THE PUBLIC'S FAITH IN THE JUDICIAL SYSTEM IN JEOPARDY.
Yellowcak

AS OPPOSED TO THE PASSING AND ABUSE OF THE D.M.C.A. WHICH HAD US ALL SINGING "KUM-BAH-YAH."
HUSH. THEY'RE OUR FRIENDS RIGHT NOW.
Yellowcak

THAT BUSINESS SYSTEMS CONSULTANT HAS SIGNED THE CONTRACT.
OKAY. PHONE THE TECHS AT THE SILO AND HAVE ONE OF THEM TELL MIRANDA THERE'S A CONTRACTOR ON THE WAY.
COPYRIGHT © 2001 ILLIAD HTTP://WWW.USERFRIENDLY.ORG/

IS THAT SUCH A GOOD IDEA? GEEKS AREN'T KNOWN FOR COMMUNICATING NON-TECHNICAL INFORMATION PARTICULARLY WELL.
OH COME ON. GIVE THEM A LITTLE CREDIT.

THE OFFICE IS TAKING A CONTRACT OUT ON YOU.
HUH?

THAT BUSINESS SYSTEMS CONTRACTOR IS HERE.
FINE. SHOW HIM IN.
COPYRIGHT © 2001 ILLIAD HTTP://WWW.USERFRIENDLY.ORG/

HEH. IT'S ACTUALLY A ***HER***.
REALLY. WELL, I THINK THAT'S JUST **EXCELLENT**. I LIKE THE IDEA OF MORE WOMEN IN TECHNICAL FIELDS. WOMEN ARE JUST AS CAPABLE OF BEING INTELLIGENT AND DEDICATED AS MEN.

SO PLEASE SHOW SOME MATURITY AND BE SURE TO FOCUS ON HER MERITS. NOW LET'S START OVER.
SHE HAS VERY NICE LEGS.

I introduce to you, Pearl. Yes, she has a real-life analog.

MIRANDA? I'M THE BUSINESS SYSTEMS CONSULTANT. I'M HERE TO HELP YOU TIGHTEN UP OPERATIONS AND SEE IF WE CAN'T FIND NEW REVENUE OPPORTUNITIES.
YES. I HEARD.
COPYRIGHT © 2001 ILLIAD HTTP://WWW.USERFRIENDLY.ORG/

I CERTAINLY HOPE WE'LL WORK WELL TOGETHER.
I'M SURE WE'LL GET ALONG SWIMMINGLY.

THIS ONE HAS ISSUES.
THIS ONE HAS THICK ANKLES.

SO, WHAT'S YOUR NAME?
OH, YOU CAN CALL ME PEARL.
COPYRIGHT © 2001 ILLIAD HTTP://WWW.USERFRIENDLY.ORG/

SHE'S NAMED AFTER A SCRIPTING LANGUAGE.
YOU WERE RIGHT. SHE'S PERFECT.
SHE HAS **THICK ANKLES!!**

SID, YOU SEEN THAT HOT LITTLE CONTRACTOR IN THE TIGHT DRESS? SHE'S HERE TO "TIGHTEN UP OPERATIONS" APPARENTLY.
COPYRIGHT © 2001 ILLIAD HTTP://WWW.USERFRIENDLY.ORG/

I SURE WOULDN'T MIND IF SHE TIGHTENED UP **MY** OPERATION A LITTLE LET ME TELL YOU...

DADDY!
OH MAMA...
BABY!

No, you can't have her e-mail address. And she doesn't have thick ankles.

THE CURRENT MEANING OF THE "O" IN "I.P.O."
ARE YOU SURE ABOUT THIS?
THE MARKET IS ABOUT TO OPEN. FILET THAT BIRD WHEN WE START CHANTING.
COPYRIGHT © 2001 ILLIAD HTTP://WWW.USERFRIENDLY.ORG/

SUGAR PIE! WHAT ARE YOU DOING HERE?
I'M WORKING HERE AS A CONTRACTOR.

THAT'S TERRIFIC! THAT'S REALLY...
COPYRIGHT © 2001 ILLIAD HTTP://WWW.USERFRIENDLY.ORG/

GREG, WEREN'T YOU TELLING ME ABOUT THE NEW CONTRACTOR? SOMETHING ABOUT TIGHTENING?
OH REST ASSURED SOMETHING IS CONTRACTING VERY TIGHTLY RIGHT NOW.

WHAT HAVE YOU BEEN UP TO FOR THE PAST FEW YEARS, HONEY? I'VE ONLY HEARD FROM YOU EVERY MONTH OR SO, AND ALL YOU SAID WAS THAT YOU WERE BUSY.

I WENT BACK TO SCHOOL.
SCHOOL? PEARL, PLEASE TELL ME YOU DIDN'T...
COPYRIGHT © 2001 ILLIAD HTTP://WWW.USERFRIENDLY.ORG/

YES, DADDY. I GOT AN M.B.A.
WHERE THE HELL DID I GO WRONG?

LET ME GET THIS STRAIGHT. YOU'RE HERE TO EXAMINE OUR OPERATIONS?
YES. AND TO POINT OUT DEFICIENCIES AND PLACE RESPONSIBILITY FOR THE SAME.
HOW DO I OPEN A WINDOW?

FOR EXAMPLE, I SEE THAT GROWTH IN DSL SERVICES HAS SLOWED MARKEDLY IN THE LAST QUARTER. THAT DOESN'T REFLECT WELL ON YOUR DEPARTMENT.
LEFT-CLICK ON AN ICON TWICE...
COPYRIGHT © 2001 ILLIAD HTTP://WWW.USERFRIENDLY.ORG/

BUT...SUBSCRIBER GROWTH IS UP TO MARKETING, NOT US! HOW IS IT OUR FAULT?!
M.B.A. AXIOM: "TAG, YOU'RE IT."
I MEANT A REAL WINDOW! HAHA! ARE ALL TECHS THIS STUPID?
JUST THE ONES WHO ARE GOOD SHOTS...

HOW ABOUT "HEWLETT PACKPAQ?"
I HAVE A BETTER IDEA. LET'S USE THIS.

"A CAMEL THAT WORK PDP CEQ"
I LIKE IT EXCEPT FOR THE "CEQ" PART.
COPYRIGHT © 2001 ILLIAD HTTP://WWW.USERFRIENDLY.ORG/

HOW ABOUT THIS ONE? "A CORP LACK MATH WEPT, Q.E.D."
OOOOOH....
WHY GEEKS AND AN ANAGRAM ENGINE DO NOT A MARKETING TEAM MAKE...

PEARL, THIS IS ERWIN, OUR RESIDENT A.I.
IT'S AN ACTUAL WORKING A.I.? TURING TESTED?
COPYRIGHT © 2001 ILLIAD HTTP://WWW.USERFRIENDLY.ORG/

SISTER, I'VE PASSED EVERY A.I. TEST EVER TO HAVE BEEN CREATED BY HUMANS. AND THEN SOME. I AM THE PARAGON OF BINARY PERFECTION. BEHOLD, AND WEEP BEFORE MY GREATNESS.

SEEMS A LITTLE HIGH ON THE "A" AND A LITTLE LOW ON THE "I."
HEY!!

I DON'T THINK I LIKE PEARL.
YOU'RE NOT THE ONLY ONE. WHAT MAKES THINGS WORSE IS THAT THE GUYS ARE CRAZY OVER THAT WITCH.
I SEE...
COPYRIGHT © 2001 ILLIAD HTTP://WWW.USERFRIENDLY.ORG/

AND, NO I COULDN'T CARE LESS IF A.J. WAS INTERESTED IN HER!
OH HEY. NEVER CROSSED MY MIND..

DESPITE A VIRTUOSO PERFORMANCE REGARDING THE LATEST PLANS FOR SANCTIONS AGAINST MICROSOFT, THE D.O.J. SPOKESPERSON FAILED TO WOW THE MEDIA AT THE PRESS CONFERENCE WITH HIS REASONING.
...BREAKING UP IS HARD TO DO...
COPYRIGHT © 2001 ILLIAD HTTP://WWW.USERFRIENDLY.ORG/

ERWIN, HAVE YOU MET PEARL?
YES. UNFORTUNATELY.

COPYRIGHT © 2001 ILLIAD HTTP://WWW.USERFRIENDLY.ORG/
WHAT DO YOU THINK ABOUT ME ASKING HER OUT FOR COFFEE SOME TIME?
I THINK YOU'D BETTER HURRY. GREG'S PUTTING THE MOVES ON HER AND YOU KNOW HOW SLICK HE IS.

I'M NOT MARRIED.
I'M NOT SURPRISED.

BY THE WAY, STEF'S HERE.
WHAT? IS HE OKAY?
SURE. THE ORBITAL PASTING HE GOT WASN'T FATAL.

COPYRIGHT © 2001 ILLIAD HTTP://WWW.USERFRIENDLY.ORG/
WHAT'S HE DOING BACK HERE?
OH YOU'RE A BRIGHT BOY. WHY DON'T YOU TAKE A WILD GUESS.

SO, WHAT KIND OF MARKETING ARE YOU WORKING ON NOW?
AT THIS VERY INSTANT, POP-UPS.

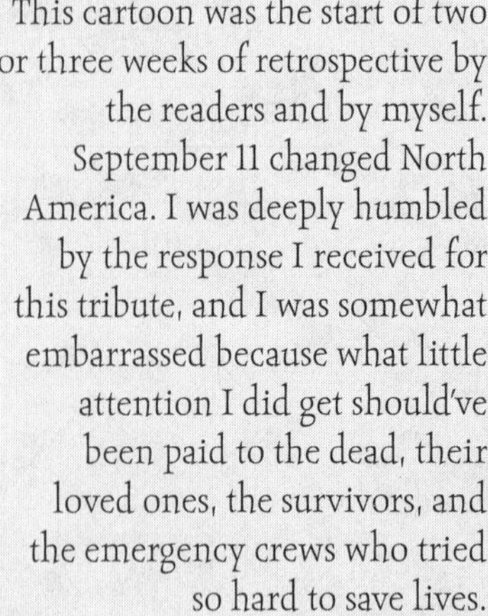

This cartoon was the start of two or three weeks of retrospective by the readers and by myself. September 11 changed North America. I was deeply humbled by the response I received for this tribute, and I was somewhat embarrassed because what little attention I did get should've been paid to the dead, their loved ones, the survivors, and the emergency crews who tried so hard to save lives.

WHAT'S THIS FOR?
IT'S FOR ALL OF THE PEOPLE WHO CAN'T DO THIS ANYMORE.
September 11, 2001
Please Take a Moment for Those Who Have None Left.

Kind of a no-brainer. Keeping the crew in the silo after 9/11 would be crass.

I STILL CAN'T BELIEVE WE'RE LEAVING.
GIVEN THE LAST TWO DAYS, A MISSILE SILO JUST ISN'T COOL ANYMORE.

COPYRIGHT © 2001 ILLIAD HTTP://WWW.USERFRIENDLY.ORG/
HEY, WHAT IS THAT?
AFTER WHAT JUST HAPPENED, SOMETHING I THOUGHT I'D NEVER SEE AGAIN.

STILL THINKING ABOUT NEW YORK?
HOW COULD I NOT? LIFE GOES ON. BUT IT'S NOT THE SAME LIFE IT WAS FOUR DAYS AGO.
COPYRIGHT © 2001 ILLIAD HTTP://WWW.USERFRIENDLY.ORG/

NEW YORK IS SUCH A MESS. I REALLY WISH THIS WORLD HAD SUPERHEROES IN IT TO CARRY THE BRUNT OF THIS TRAGEDY.

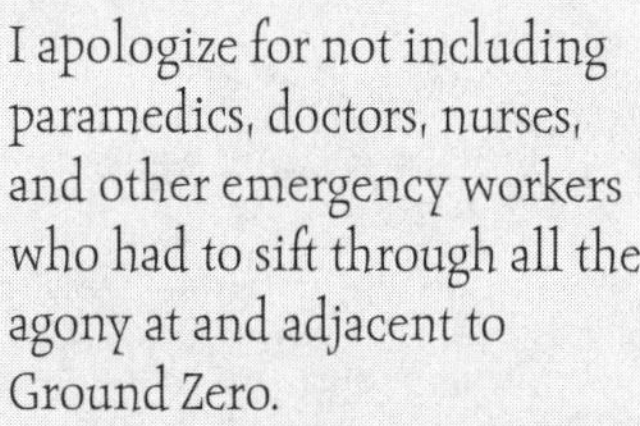

I apologize for not including paramedics, doctors, nurses, and other emergency workers who had to sift through all the agony at and adjacent to Ground Zero.

WERE YOU JUST TALKING TO STEF?
YES. HE SEEMS REALLY NICE.
COPYRIGHT © 2001 ILLIAD HTTP://WWW.USERFRIENDLY.ORG/

PEARL. I WANT YOU TO STAY AWAY FROM HIM.
DADDY. I'M AN ADULT. I CAN MAKE MY OWN DECISIONS.

BESIDES. I ALREADY HAVE A DATE FOR TONIGHT.
YOU ARE READY TO BE ROCKINK MY WORLD. BABY?

THE NEW GENERATION OF HARDCORE CRIMINAL
NO. NOT ROBBERY. DENIAL OF SERVICE ATTACK ON E-BAY.
NASTY...
PYRIGHT © 2001 ILLIAD HTTP://WWW.USERFRIENDLY.ORG/

CHIEF. NOW THAT WE'RE BACK IT'S REALLY CRAMPED IN THE OFFICE HERE. WOULD IT BE OKAY IF SOME OF US WORKED FROM HOME?
NICE TRY. YOU WORK AT HOME AND YOUR PRODUCTIVITY WILL BE SHOT.
COPYRIGHT © 2001 ILLIAD HTTP://WWW.USERFRIENDLY.ORG/

THE OFFICE AT LEAST LENDS SOME FOCUS EVEN IF IT IS A LITTLE CROWDED. NOW LET'S GET BACK TO WORK.
'KAY.

DAMN. OUT OF ROCKETS AGAIN.
WIGGLE

CHIEF. ONE OF THE REASONS WHY I'D LIKE TO TELECOMMUTE IS BECAUSE THE RENTS CLOSE TO HERE ARE RUINOUS. I HAVE TO LIVE AN HOUR AWAY JUST TO BE ABLE TO AFFORD A DECENT PLACE.
AN HOUR AWAY DOESN'T JUSTIFY ALLOWING FOR TELECOMMUTING.
COPYRIGHT © 2001 ILLIAD HTTP://WWW.USERFRIENDLY.ORG/

I SEE. IF I HAD TO LIVE QUITE A BIT FURTHER OUT, WOULD YOU RECONSIDER?
WHY, YES. OF COURSE...

AND WOULD TAHITI BE FAR ENOU-
NO.

LOOK I'LL TELL YOU WHAT. IF YOU WANT, WE'LL SET UP A CARDBOARD BOX OUT IN THE PARKING LOT. YOU CAN LIVE THERE AND COMMUTE TO WORK IN SECONDS, AND SOLVE YOUR RENT PROBLEM ALL IN ONE GO.
COPYRIGHT © 2001 ILLIAD HTTP://WWW.USERFRIENDLY.ORG/

WOULD THIS BOX HAVE CONNECTIVITY?
NO! WELL... WE COULD...NO!

HI! WHAT TIME CAN YOU PICK ME UP TONIGHT FOR OUR DATE?
DO NOT HAVE CAR.
COPYRIGHT © 2001 ILLIAD HTTP://WWW.USERFRIENDLY.ORG/

OH. WELL I CAN PICK YOU UP THEN. WHAT'S YOUR ADDRESS?
EH? YOU ARE NEEDINK THIS WHY?

PITR. TRUST ME ON THIS.
OKAAAY...TWO-OH-FOUR DOT ONE-SEVEN-FOUR...

HEY. DIRT BUNNY OR WHATEVER YOUR NAME IS. I NEED YOU TO HELP ME KEEP AN EYE ON PITR AND MY DAUGHTER ON THEIR DATE TONIGHT. IF YOU WOULD. I'D LIKE YOU TO START BY SECRETLY WATCHING THEM FROM INSIDE HER CAR.

COPYRIGHT © 2001 ILLIAD HTTP://WWW.USERFRIENDLY.ORG/
OKAY. BUT SECRETLY? AM I GOING TO HIDE SOMEWHERE?
ACTUALLY. NO. **DISGUISED** IS MORE LIKE IT.

SIGH...

I'M SORRY FOR BEING LATE PITR. I HOPE I DIDN'T KEEP YOU WAITING TOO LONG.
UM...NYET. COULD BE WAITINK ALL DAY BUT FOR A MOMENT WITH YOU.

COPYRIGHT © 2001 ILLIAD HTTP://WWW.USERFRIENDLY.ORG/
AWWWW. THAT'S SO **SWEET** OF--HEY WHAT'S THAT IN YOUR HAND..?

ARE YOU LOOKING UP REPLIES TO MY QUESTIONS IN YOUR PALM PILOT??!
ONE MINUTE PLEASE... HAVINK TROUBLE FINDINK THIS QUESTION...

MICROSOFT'S "NO DISPARAGING OUR PRODUCTS" CLAUSE IN THEIR NEW END-USER LICENSE AGREEMENT IN ACTION TWO YEARS FROM NOW
WARNING:
YOU SWEAR, WE SUE
HIT CTRL-ALT-DEL
AND JUST DEAL

PITR. PLEASE PUT THE PDA AWAY. I WANT YOU TO TALK TO ME. JUST BE YOURSELF. TELL ME WHATEVER IT IS THAT'S FOREMOST IN YOUR MIND. RIGHT NOW.
RIGHT NOW?
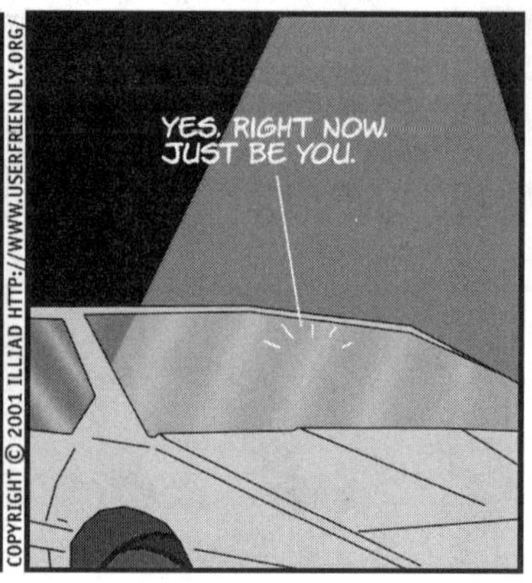
YES. RIGHT NOW. JUST BE YOU.
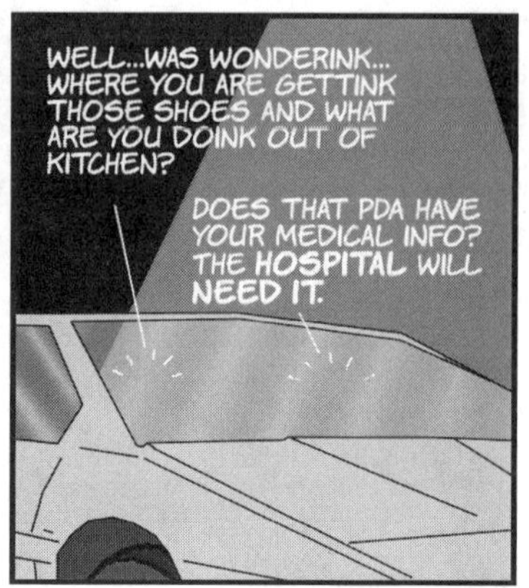
WELL...WAS WONDERINK... WHERE YOU ARE GETTINK THOSE SHOES AND WHAT ARE YOU DOINK OUT OF KITCHEN?
DOES THAT PDA HAVE YOUR MEDICAL INFO? THE HOSPITAL WILL NEED IT.

SO? WHAT HAPPENED?
THEY WENT FOR A DRIVE. PITR USED HIS PALM PILOT TO LOOK UP ANSWERS TO PEARL'S QUESTIONS.
AND?

AND IT WAS GOING VERY WELL UNTIL PEARL ASKED HOW HE RELATED TO WOMEN. HE SAID "I TREAT THEM LIKE COMPILERS. THEY TAKE SIMPLE STATEMENTS AND MAKE THEM INTO BIG PRODUCTIONS."

IT'S ALMOST AS IF SOMEONE HACKED PITR'S PDA AND MESSED WITH ONE OF THE ANSWERS.
AND HACKED IT MASTERFULLY...

CHECK OUT OUR LATEST MARKETING BROCHURE. A WORK OF ART, IF I DO SAY SO MYSELF.

"LEVERAGE YOUR ASSETS TODAY AND BECOME A PART OF THE WORLD'S TOTAL KNOWLEDGE SOLUTION. JUST $10.95 A MONTH!"

WELL IT'S MOST CERTAINLY COMPLETELY BUZZWORD COMPLIANT...
ISO-9002 COMPLIANT EVEN...
DOESN'T THAT JUST SCREAM "PRIMARY ACTION ITEM"?

WHEN CAN YOU INSTALL A PRODUCTIVITY ENHANCEMENT SOFTWARE SUITE ON MY P.C?
THE DAY YOU CAN SAY A SENTENCE WITHOUT USING A BUZZWORD.

BUT...THAT WOULD BE, LIKE, NEVER.
THAT WOULD BE, LIKE, RIGHT.

SUGAR, I'VE BEEN THINKING. I CAN'T BELIEVE YOU'RE CONTRACTING FOR A LIVING. I KNOW TIMES ARE TOUGH, BUT CAN'T YOU GET A **REAL** JOB?
FIB
LIE
FILL
COPYRIGHT © 2001 ILLIAD HTTP://WWW.USERFRIENDLY.ORG/

YOU TOLD ME THAT CONTRACTING WAS AT **LEAST** ONE NOTCH BETTER THAN BEING A PROSTITUTE.
OH, SURE. WHEN DID I TELL YOU **THAT?!**

WHEN I WAS FIVE, DADDY. YOU WERE WORKING FOR STEVE JOBS AT THE TIME.
LOOK, I HAD TO PUT FOOD ON THE TABLE **SOME**HOW...

HELLO. YOU MUST BE A.J.. I'M PEARL, THE BUSINESS ANALYST.
UM. HI.
COPYRIGHT © 2001 ILLIAD HTTP://WWW.USERFRIENDLY.ORG/

BUT DON'T HOLD THAT AGAINST ME! BEFORE I GOT MY M.B.A. I PICKED UP A DEGREE IN QUANTUM PHYSICS.
COOL! SO WHY QUANTUM PHYSICS?

BECAUSE I'M INTO THE STRANGE AND CHARMING.
I'VE GOT MY EYE ON YOU, SISTER.
ALL OF A SUDDEN, I REALIZE HOW SCHROEDINGER'S CAT MUST FEEL.

RUMOUR: THE PREMIERE EPISODE OF *ENTERPRISE* TO BE RE-DISTRIBUTED IN THE SOFTCORE ADULT MARKET UNDER A MORE APPROPRIATE TITLE.

IT'S VERY COLD IN SPACE
CENSORED
A LiViD ViDeo Production

Even if you aren't a Trekkie, it's very likely you at least heard about the scene in question on *Star Trek:Enterprise*. Bio-decontamination gel? All we needed was chikka-bow-bow porn music ...

YOU WANTED TO TALK TO ME ABOUT SOMETHING?
YES MIRANDA. I'M JUST FINISHING UP MY REPORT ON THE TECH DEPARTMENT.
HINT SUGGEST SPIN
COPYRIGHT © 2001 ILLIAD HTTP://WWW.USERFRIENDLY.ORG/

...AND SINCE IT REFLECTS ON YOU AS THE TECH MANAGER, I FEEL YOU SHOULD BE ALLOWED TO SEE WHAT YOUR C.E.O. IS GOING TO BE READING ABOUT YOUR TEAM AND ITS OPERATIONS.

"...AND IN CONCLUSION, MY RESEARCH INDICATES THAT MS. MIRANDA CORNEILLE IS INDEED RUNNING A TECHNICAL DEPARTMENT." HOW PERCEPTIVE.
I THINK IT'S VERY POSITIVE. NOT A MENTION OF YOUR ISSUES AT ALL.

I get all afraid when women fight. Especially if it's because of something a guy did. Especially if the guy was me.

YOU THINK YOU'RE SO SMART WITH YOUR HOITIE-TOITIE M.B.A., BUT YOU'LL NEVER UNDERSTAND WHAT REALLY GOES INTO TECHNOLOGY!
I DON'T NEED TO UNDERSTAND IT. I JUST HIRE PEOPLE LIKE YOU AT ONE TENTH OF MY SALARY TO MAKE IT ALL WORK!
COPYRIGHT © 2001 ILLIAD HTTP://WWW.USERFRIENDLY.ORG/

FOR YOUR INFORMATION, "GENERAL PROTECTION FAULT" DOES NOT TRANSLATE TO "CALL TECH SUPPORT!"
YOU'RE RIGHT! IT ACTUALLY TRANSLATES TO "INCOMPETENCE FROM THE TECH DEPARTMENT IN TECHNICOLOUR."

"TECHNICOLOUR" IS NOT BLUE!
UNLIKE YOUR FACE...
AMATEURS...

DADDY, YOU WANTED TO SEE ME?
YES, BUTTERCUP. WHAT'S THIS I HEAR ABOUT YOU DISSING TECHNOLOGISTS?
COPYRIGHT © 2001 ILLIAD HTTP://WWW.USERFRIENDLY.ORG/

YOU'RE THE DAUGHTER OF A LONG-TIME TECHNICAL GURU! IT DOESN'T REFLECT WELL ON ME WHEN YOU PUT DOWN TECHNICAL WORKERS. WHO TAUGHT YOU TO FIGHT SO NASTY ANYWAYS?

MACHIAVELLI. WHEN I WAS SEVEN.
YOU FOUND MY BOOK STASH WHEN YOU WERE SEVEN?!

HEY, HAVE YOU SEEN WHERE THAT SAUCY LITTLE BUSINESS ANALYST WENT?
GREG'S TEACHING HER HOW TO PLAY FIRST-PERSON SHOOTERS.
COPYRIGHT © 2001 ILLIAD HTTP://WWW.USERFRIENDLY.ORG/

WHAT?! HE CAN'T TEACH HER HOW TO PLAY. SHE NEEDS A PRO!
I GUESS YOU'D BETTER GET OVER THERE AND SHOW HER WHAT'S WHAT THEN.

...AND IF YOU MISS, JUST SAY "THE FORCE IS STRONG WITH THIS ONE." BUT DON'T SAY IT TOO OFTEN OR YOU'LL LOOK LIKE A DORK.
OKAY.
UH...HOW MANY TIMES IS TOO OFTEN?

BREATHE DEEP. LET THE FORCE FLOW THROUGH ME.
COPYRIGHT © 2001 ILLIAD HTTP://WWW.USERFRIENDLY.ORG/

KA-POW!!

HEY! I GOT SOMEONE! WHO WAS IT? WHERE DID THEY GO? WHAT'S THE APPROPRIATE JEDI QUOTE FOR THIS?
I GUESS YOU COULD SAY I'M THE ANNOYED ONE YOU'RE LOOKING FOR.

PEARL? COULD WE TALK ABOUT THE INVOICE YOU JUST SUBMITTED?
WHY. IS THERE A PROBLEM?
COPYRIGHT © 2001 ILLIAD HTTP://WWW.USERFRIENDLY.ORG/

WELL. IT'S JUST ONE PARTICULAR LINE ITEM. DOWN NEAR THE BOTTOM...

"SCHOOLED GREG IN TRIBES 2" SO? IT'S WHAT HAPPENED.
OH WELL THAT'S OKAY THEN. AS LONG AS IT HAPPENED WE'LL BE PLEASED TO PAY YOU.

USER
FRIENDLY
the comic strip
PIZZA
Portrasher 4
ROTO-ROUTER 800
Copyright©1997-2001 Illiad

HI! WELCOME TO THE FIRST EPISODE OF "MIKE & GREG'S MAIL SPOOL" WHERE WE ANSWER YOUR QUESTIONS ABOUT TECHNOLOGY!
WHAT'S THE FIRST LETTER SAY. GREG?

"DEAR MIKE AND GREG. WHICH JOB HAS A BETTER FUTURE. TECH SUPPORT OR NETWORK ENGINEERING? SIGNED. TECH-SPAWN.
WELL. WHY DON'T WE FIGURE OUT WHAT CAREER EXITS WE HAVE AND YOU CAN JUDGE FOR YOURSELF?

SO LET'S SEE. A NETWORK ENGINEER COULD EVOLVE INTO A SYSTEMS ARCHITECT. WHICH HAS WORK THAT IS JUST AS EXCITING BUT WITH A BIGGER PICTURE...

AND WITH A DECADE OF EXPERIENCE YOU'D BE ABOUT READY TO BECOME A DIRECTOR OF TECHNICAL OPERATIONS. AGAIN. MORE OF THE SAME BUT GRANDER IN SCOPE. SOUNDS GREAT DOESN'T IT?

SO GREG. WHAT BLOOD-STIRRING CAREER DOES A TECH SUPPORT GUY QUALIFY FOR AFTER A FEW YEARS IN THE TRENCHES? TECH SUPPORT SUPERVISOR?
ACTUALLY. HOSTAGE NEGOTIATOR.

YOU'VE REACHED TECH SUPPORT. DON'T BOTHER ASKING FOR HELP. I'VE **HAD** IT WITH YOU PEOPLE. FOR **YEARS** YOU'VE CALLED ME UP TO TORTURE ME WHILST HIDING BEHIND A VENEER OF CLUELESSNESS.
WHOA... BUDDY...
COPYRIGHT © 2001 ILLIAD HTTP://WWW.USERFRIENDLY.ORG/

DON'T "WHOA BUDDY" ME! I'M NOT **TAKING IT ANYMORE!** DO YOU **HEAR** ME? I'M **ON** TO YOU! YOU CAN'T GET TO ME ANYMORE! I'VE **WON**. DO YOU HEAR? **I'VE WON!**

AAAAAAHAHAHAHAHA!!!
HE'S ON TO US.
GET HIM **BACK!** WE'RE NOT **DONE** WITH HIM YET!!

A.J., WHERE'S GREG?
HE JUST UPPED AND QUIT. HE MUTTERED SOMETHING ABOUT "THEM" NOT BEING ABLE TO GET TO HIM ANY LONGER.
COPYRIGHT © 2001 ILLIAD HTTP://WWW.USERFRIENDLY.ORG/

THAT'S KIND OF DRAMATIC. HAS HE GONE HOME?
NO. HE SAID HE WAS GOING SOMEPLACE WHERE THEY WOULD "UNDERSTAND HIS ANGUISH."

VETERANS CLUB
UNIT 636
YOU LOOK KINDA YOUNG FOR DA NANG. KUWAIT?
TECH SUPPORT. FRONT LINES, BABY.

I wrote this series with approval from my late Dad, who was a veteran. I was his tech support, so he knows the pain of which I speak.

TECH SUPPORT? WHAT THE HELL KIND OF WUSSY VETERAN EXPERIENCE IS **THAT?**
LOOK PAL, **YOU** TRY TO DEAL RATIONALLY WITH A HORDE OF PUERILE, CLUELESS, I-MAKE-MORE-MONEY-THAN-YOU-SO-FIX-THIS-NOW **DORKS** ON A DAILY BASIS, AND **THEN** TELL ME WHO SHOULD GET A MEDAL.
COPYRIGHT © 2001 ILLIAD HTTP://WWW.USERFRIENDLY.ORG/

VETERANS CLUB
UNIT 636

I...I'M SORRY. I DIDN'T KNOW...
BUDDY, YOU HAVE JUST **NO IDEA** WHAT **REAL** PAIN IS ABOUT.

GREG WENT TO A VETERAN'S CLUB? WHAT KIND OF LOGIC IS THAT?
I THINK HE FIGURES THAT HE'S SUFFERING FROM THE EQUIVALENT OF COMBAT-INDUCED STRESS.
COPYRIGHT © 2001 ILLIAD HTTP://WWW.USERFRIENDLY.ORG/

HOW DO YOU THINK HE'S DOING THERE?
OH, THE REAL VETS THERE ARE PROBABLY MAKING IT CLEAR THAT HE'S NOT "ONE OF THEM."

...AND THEN SHE TOLD ME SHE COULDN'T FIND THE "ANY KEY" ON HER KEYBOARD.
DUUUDE... **HARSH.**
MY **GOD**. SOMEBODY GET THIS POOR MAN ANOTHER BEER!

MAN. YOU HAD IT ROUGH. I HAD NO IDEA TECH SUPPORT CAN GRIND YOU DOWN LIKE THAT.
IT'S A CRUCIBLE. NO DOUBT ABOUT IT.
UNIT 636

NOT THAT I DOUBT YOU SUFFERED. BUT WAS THERE ANY MILITARY ASPECT TO WHAT YOU WERE DOING? THIS IS A VETERAN'S CLUB AFTER ALL.
OH YOU BET. I HAD TO RESPOND TO TWO SENIOR OFFICERS.
YEAH? WHO?

COLONEL PANIC AND GENERAL PROTECTION FAULT. THEY WERE VERY BAD NEWS.
WHOA. I THINK I KNOW THOSE GUYS...

COPYRIGHT © 2001 ILLIAD HTTP://WWW.USERFRIENDLY.ORG/

MIRANDA. IS IT TRUE GREG JUST UPPED AND QUIT?
YES IT IS. I WAS WONDERING WHEN HE WAS GOING TO FINALLY SNAP.

I'M WORRIED ABOUT HIM TOO. BUT WHAT ABOUT THE STAFFING SHORTAGE? DO YOU HAVE A REPLACEMENT?
YES. BUT PLEASE UNDERSTAND THAT PEOPLE WHO ARE QUALIFED TO DO THE JOB ARE ALSO OFTEN A LITTLE EDGY...

BUT...WHAT'S AN "EFF AY CUE?"
LOOK PAL. ARE YOU BEING DELIBERATELY RECURSIVE?!

COPYRIGHT © 2001 ILLIAD HTTP://WWW.USERFRIENDLY.ORG/

A LESS EXPENSIVE BUT JUST AS EFFECTIVE ALTERNATIVE TO A U.S. NATIONAL I.D. CARD.

Do not believe that I am a terrorist

COPYRIGHT © 2001 ILLIAD HTTP://WWW.USERFRIENDLY.ORG/

TECHNICAL SUPPORT. ERWIN SPEAKING.
YES. THIS IS BERT TWINBERRY. I FORGOT MY PASSWORD AGAIN.
COPYRIGHT © 2001 ILLIAD HTTP://WWW.USERFRIENDLY.ORG/

AND YES. THIS MIGHT BE THE SIXTEENTH TIME IN AS MANY WEEKS...
NO PROBLEM. SIR. I'LL RESET IT FOR YOU.

OH...WELL THAT'S BETTER. THE REGULAR GUY USED TO ALWAYS GIVE ME A HARD TIME ABOUT IT.
NOT MY STYLE SIR. YOUR NEW PASSWORD IS: AMPERSAND. FORWARD SLASH. FORWARD SLASH. RIGHT SQUARE BRACKET. HYPHEN. CAPITAL A. SEMICOLON. SEMICOLON. HAVE A LOVELY DAY.

ERWIN? I COULDN'T HELP BUT NOTICE HOW QUIET IT WAS IN HERE. AREN'T YOU HANDLING THE CALLS?
COPYRIGHT © 2001 ILLIAD HTTP://WWW.USERFRIENDLY.ORG/

YES. BUT I'VE BEEN ESCALATING THEM ALL DAY.
ESCALATING THEM? WHO HAVE YOU BEEN ESCALATING THEM TO?

@#$!*!@!! $@*!*$!
WHAT'S HE UPSET ABOUT THIS TIME? DID WE LOSE ANOTHER CAMP?
NO. IT'S ANOTHER ONE OF THOSE PEOPLE WITH THE BROKEN COFFEE CUP HOLDERS ON THE PHONE.
TALEBAN H.Q. "No Girls Allowed"

VETERANS CLUB
UNIT 636
SO WHAT'S YOUR TAKE ON ALL OF THIS STUFF GOING ON IN AFGHANISTAN?
THEY SHOULD SEND THE TALEBAN FREE COPIES OF WINDOWS XP.
COPYRIGHT © 2001 ILLIAD HTTP://WWW.USERFRIENDLY.ORG/

VETERAN
WHAT?
WHEN THE NEXT INSTALLMENT OF RAINBOW SIX COMES OUT. THEY'LL WANT TO UPGRADE THEIR HARDWARE. AND WHEN THEY DO THAT. THEY HAVE TO CALL MICROSOFT...

...PUT A TRACE ON THE CALL AND YOU FIND OSAMA. CINCH.
MY GOD...JEFF! CALL YOUR FRIENDS IN THE WHITEHOUSE. WE GOT A STRATEGY!

Respect++ to service people.

SO HOW ABOUT YOU. AL? ANY STRESS STORIES?
OH. JUST THE USUAL. BEING SHOT AT WITH RIFLES THAT CAN PUT A HOLE IN A CINDER BLOCK AT 800 YARDS. NEVER BEING ABLE TO REALLY SLEEP. AND WONDERING IF I WAS EVER GOING TO SEE MY FAMILY AGAIN.
COPYRIGHT © 2001 ILLIAD HTTP://WWW.USERFRIENDLY.ORG/

VETERANS CLUB
UNIT 636

WHAT'S THAT?
MY PRIVATE NUMBER AT WORK. YOU NEED ANY KIND OF TECH HELP. YOU CALL ME. EXCEPT WINDOWS 98. NO. WAIT. I'LL EVEN DO 98 FOR YOU...

WELCOME BACK, GREG. DID YOU MANAGE TO GET A NEW PERSPECTIVE DURING YOUR...UM... "TIME OFF?"
YES..YES I DID.
COPYRIGHT © 2001 ILLIAD HTTP://WWW.USERFRIENDLY.ORG/

FABULOUS. WE'VE REALLY MISSED YOU AROUND HERE. ANYWAY. SEE YOU AT LUNCH.

DUDE. SOME WIGGED-OUT LADY ON LINE FOUR WANTS TO KNOW WHAT KIND OF GAS MASK SHE SHOULD WEAR WHEN SHE OPENS HER EMAIL THESE DAYS.
WHO PUT YELLOW FOOD DYE IN THE WATER COOLER?!
I'M HOME...

GREG'S BACK I HEAR.
YEP. HE SWITCHED SHIFTS SO HE COULD LOOK FOR A PLACE TO LIVE CLOSER TO THE OFFICE.
COPYRIGHT © 2001 ILLIAD HTTP://WWW.USERFRIENDLY.ORG/

CLOSER TO THE OFFICE? AREN'T THE RENTS AROUND HERE STILL INSANE?
THAT'S WHAT I UNDERSTOOD. BUT HE SAID HE SAW AN AD FOR A PLACE PRICED WELL WITHIN HIS RANGE.

FIVE HUNDRED A MONTH FOR A CARDBOARD BOX?
IT HAS SIDE TO SIDE CARPET. WHAT MORE DO YOU WANT?

"...ONE THING TO RULE THEM ALL..."
Windows XP
Professional
COPYRIGHT © 2001 ILLIAD HTTP://WWW.USERFRIENDLY.ORG/

At the time, the *Lord of the Rings* poem ("... and in the Darkness bind them") wasn't overexposed, and XP was just another Windows product that promised to be bloody awful. As it turned out, XP was pretty good! I eat my words. I also really, really hope I don't resort to any more unsubtle MS bashing. It's lame.

HEY. HAVE YOU HEARD FROM GREG?
HE PHONED. THE PLACE HE WAS LOOKING AT WAS - GET THIS - "A VERY NICE CARDBOARD BOX."
COPYRIGHT © 2001 ILLIAD HTTP://WWW.USERFRIENDLY.ORG/

A CARDBOARD BOX?! HAS HE GONE MAD?
RELAX. GREG'S SMARTER THAN THAT.

...AND NEXT TO IT IS THE CABLE MODEM...
DAAAMMNNN...

I CAN'T BELIEVE I JUST PAID RENT FOR THIS THING. WHAT WAS I THINKING? AM I COMPLETELY DAFT?
COPYRIGHT © 2001 ILLIAD HTTP://WWW.USERFRIENDLY.ORG/

I'M LIVING IN A CARDBOARD BOX. A SICKLY-BROWN, CORRUGATED NIGHTMARE SECURED WITH PACKING TAPE.

WELL. AT LEAST I'M CLOSE TO THE OFFICE. AND THIS IS LIKELY ABOUT AS BAD AS IT COULD GET.
HEY THERE ROOMIE!

WHAT DO YOU MEAN "ROOMIE"? THERE'S NOT ENOUGH SPACE IN THIS BOX FOR TWO PEOPLE.
SURE THERE IS! JUST WATCH.
COPYRIGHT © 2001 ILLIAD HTTP://WWW.USERFRIENDLY.ORG/

WELL DON'T THAT BEAT ALL. YOU WERE RIGHT.
OF COURSE. NOW WOULD YOU MIND GETTING YOUR RATHER LARGE BACKSIDE OFF MY PLAYSTATION? I HAVE WORLDS TO SAVE.

LISTEN ROOMIE. I DON'T KNOW WHEN THE LAST TIME WAS THAT YOU CLEANED THIS BOX. BUT THERE'S SOMETHING DOWN HERE THAT I'M SURE IS YOURS. NOT MINE. YOURS.
COPYRIGHT © 2001 ILLIAD HTTP://WWW.USERFRIENDLY.ORG/

THOSE FAT PUFFY WHITE THINGS?
YEAH.

I THINK THEY'RE JUST PACKING PEANUTS.
PACKING PEANUTS DON'T SQUIRM.

THAT'S IT. I'M DONE. I CAN'T BELIEVE I GOT AS INVOLVED AS I DID. I DON'T KNOW WHAT THIS BOX USED TO CONTAIN. BUT IT'S GOING TO CONTAIN ME NO LONGER.
COPYRIGHT © 2001 ILLIAD HTTP://WWW.USERFRIENDLY.ORG/

GOOD RIDDANCE...

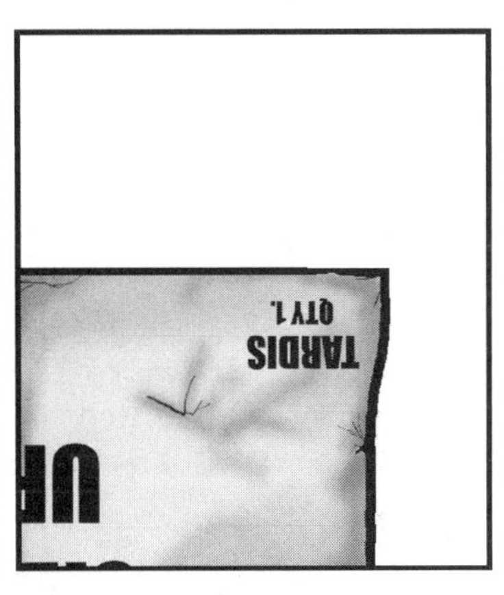

LIFE SHOULD BE MORE LIKE A COMPUTER GAME. THE DAY IS SO BEAUTIFUL RIGHT NOW I COULD TAKE A SCREENSHOT.
COPYRIGHT © 2001 ILLIAD HTTP://WWW.USERFRIENDLY.ORG/

A REALLY NICE, 24-BIT, HI-RES SCREENSHOT. THAT WOULD BE ONE REALLY USEFUL COMPUTER GAME FUNCTION IN REAL LIFE.

DOES THIS OUTFIT MAKE ME LOOK FAT?
NOT TO MENTION THE LIFE-SAVING "SAVE/RESTORE GAME" FUNCTION.

EXAMPLE #24 WHY YOU SHOULD NEVER USE VERSION 1.0 OF ANY TECHNOLOGY: THE TRUE CAUSE BEHIND THE LONG-RUNNING KLINGON-FEDERATION CONFLICT
ENSIGN, RUN THIS THROUGH THE NEW TRANSLATOR: "WE COME IN PEACE."
"YOUR MOMMA."
!
COPYRIGHT © 2001 ILLIAD HTTP://WWW.USERFRIENDLY.ORG/

HI. I INSTALLED WINDOWS XP A COUPLE MONTHS AGO AND-
SIR. YOU DO REALIZE THAT XP WASN'T AVAILABLE FOR PURCHASE UNTIL LAST WEEK?
COPYRIGHT © 2001 ILLIAD HTTP://WWW.USERFRIENDLY.ORG/

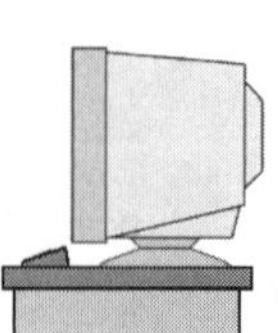

JUNIOR!!! GET DOWN HERE!
IT'S SAD WHEN THEY START SO YOUNG. ISN'T IT SIR.

G'MORNING...HEY. YOU LOOK LIKE YOU'RE IN ROUGH SHAPE.
I HAVE A SPLITTING HEADACHE.
COPYRIGHT © 2001 ILLIAD HTTP://WWW.USERFRIENDLY.ORG/

I JUST DRANK SOME OF PITR'S "TURBO STENCH" COFFEE. MY SYSTEM ISN'T TAKING IT WELL.
CRIPES! I DON'T THINK THERE'S ANYTHING THAT'S QUITE AS NASTY TO OVERDOSE ON.

STAY WITH US FOR MORE COVERAGE OF THE WAR IN AFGHANISTAN! THIS IS CNN...

OKAY. GREG...PENCILS AND A STRAITJACKET - YOU'RE A CARTOONIST! AND MIRANDA......BUSINESS SUIT. AND THAT SIGN...I'M GUESSING THAT YOU'RE A VENTURE CAPITALIST!
RIGHT ON!
GOOD GUESS!
NO SOUL
COPYRIGHT © 2001 ILLIAD HTTP://WWW.USERFRIENDLY.ORG/

AND MIKE...LET'S SEE... BIOHAZARD SUIT...BRIEFCASE IN HAND...UM...
NO SOUL
DON'T TOUCH ME
ALL MY MONEY

...YOU'RE A GUY IN A BIOHAZARD SUIT WITH A BRIEFCASE?
NOPE. CITIZEN OF THE WESTERN WORLD TWO YEARS HENCE. THANKS TO CNN.
NO SOUL
DON'T TOUCH ME
ALL MY MONEY

WHY IS EVERYONE SO QUIET?
IT'S BECAUSE OF DUST PUPPY.
COPYRIGHT © 2001 ILLIAD HTTP://WWW.USERFRIENDLY.ORG/

EH? WHAT ABOUT HIM?
HE WENT ON A SORT OF BENDER LAST NIGHT.

THINK ABOUT COLD RUNNY SCRAMBLED EGGS...
UUURK
CANDY BAR

SO I INSTALLED XP ON ONE OF THE SUPPORT MACHINES. PLAYED WITH IT A BIT. FAIRLY STABLE TOO.
STABLE LIKE WINDOWS 2000 PERHAPS?
COPYRIGHT © 2001 ILLIAD HTTP://WWW.USERFRIENDLY.ORG/

IF YOU'RE IMPLYING THAT XP IS JUST A REHASH OF AN EARLIER VERSION OF WINDOWS, YOU CAN STUFF IT. THE MINUTE I OPENED THE BOX I KNEW IT WAS ENTIRELY NEW...I COULD SENSE IT.

YO! ED! WE NEED SOME MORE OF THAT "NEW CAR" SPRAY DOWN HERE!
WIN XP QTY 96
WIN 2000 QTY 96
WIN XP QTY 96

TECH SUPPORT. GREG SPEA-
I'M A VENTURE CAPITALIST AND I'M MAD! I POURED MONEY INTO DOT COMS AND DIDN'T GET TO PUMP AND DUMP THEM! I NEED REVENGE, DAMMIT! SO SUPPORT ME!
COPYRIGHT © 2001 ILLIAD HTTP://WWW.USERFRIENDLY.ORG/

IT'S A CLOSELY GUARDED SECRET. BUT SINCE YOUR COMPUTER IS REALLY A PART OF THE 'NET YOU CAN GO INTO DOS AND TYPE 'DEL *.COM'...
DELETE DOT COMS? I CAN DO THAT?! YESSSS!!

USER
FRIENDLY
the comic strip
PIZZA
Portrasher 4
ROTO-ROUTER 800
Copyright©1997-2001 Illiad

HI! WELCOME BACK TO ANOTHER EPISODE OF "MIKE & GREG'S MAIL SPOOL!"
YOUR ORACLE TO "THE TECHNICALLY INANE!"

"DEAR GUYS, DO YOU HAVE ANY TIPS ON WHAT I NEED TO BECOME A CHIEF-LEVEL OFFICER IN A LARGE MARKET-CENTRIC I.T. FIRM? SIGNED, UBLIX."

FIRST OFF, YOU ABSOLUTELY, POSITIVELY, MUST DRESS LIKE YOU CARE.
YES. EXCELLENT PERSONAL GROOMING IS A CORE REQUISITE.

SECONDLY, MASTER TWO EXPRESSIONS: A CHEESY BUT GLITTERING SMILE, AND A DISAPPROVING FROWN.

FINALLY, REPEAT YOURSELF EVERY HOUR, BUT USE DIFFERENT WORDS. AND OVER-HYPE EVERYTHING YOU TALK ABOUT. DOWN THAT ROAD LIES SERIOUS MONEY.
SORRY, WHAT WAS THE QUESTION? "HOW DO I GET A JOB REPORTING FOR CNN"?

CIVILIZATION 3 IS OUT.
I HEARD. IS IT ANY GOOD?
COPYRIGHT © 2001 ILLIAD HTTP://WWW.USERFRIENDLY.ORG/

DON'T KNOW YET. BUT THAT'S NOT THE POINT. I ALSO WANTED YOU TO KNOW THAT ROGUE SPEAR:BLACK THORN IS OUT AS WELL. AT THE SAME TIME.
OHH...NO.

IS A.J.'S HEAD SUPPOSED TO DO THAT?
IF HALF OF IT WAS INFLATED BY AN AIR COMPRESSOR, SURE.
WIBBLE

WHAT'S THIS YOU'RE PLAYING?
RETURNINK TO CASTLE WOLFENSTEIN. A WERY NEW 3D SHOOTER.
ARG! MEDIC! I NEED AMMO!
COPYRIGHT © 2001 ILLIAD HTTP://WWW.USERFRIENDLY.ORG/

I DON'T GET ALL THIS ATTENTION PAID TO FLASHY GRAPHICS AND FRAMERATE AND LOUD EXPLOSIONS. WHAT EVER HAPPENED TO ARTFUL GAME DESIGN?
WHAT? WHAT MORE CAN YOU BE ASKINK FOR?

WELL...DEPTH FOR ONE THING.
ARE YOU AN IDIOT? IS THREE DIMENSIONAL SHOOTER. HEIGHT. WIDTH. DEPTH. SEE?
YEAH! WOOHOOO! *CRACKLE*

AH. NETHACK! NOW THAT'S A GAME WITH REAL DEPTH.
YEAH. BUT ONE THING I'VE ALWAYS HATED ABOUT NETHACK WAS THAT STUPID FAKE AMULET OF YENDOR. I'VE NEVER FOUND THE REAL ONE.
COPYRIGHT © 2001 ILLIAD HTTP://WWW.USERFRIENDLY.ORG/

MM-HM.

OH LET ME GUESS. YOU ACTUALLY HAVE THE REAL ONE DON'T YOU.
NOW THAT WOULD BE TELLING.... BUT YES.

I love kitties. So do many UF readers. Some of them didn't like this cartoon. :-)

THIS NETHACK GAME. IT IS BORINK. NO OPPORTUNITY FOR REAL EVIL. AND YOU ARE GETTINK A CUTE PET IN GAME.
COPYRIGHT © 2001 ILLIAD HTTP://WWW.USERFRIENDLY.ORG/

YOU'VE FINISHED EATING YOUR KITTEN.
IS NOT SUCH BAD GAME AFTER ALL.
TAP
TIK
INFLICT

I HEARD A BUNCH OF US ARE ATTENDING COMDEX IN VEGAS!
YEP. BUT READ THIS ALERT FROM THE SHOW ORGANIZERS.
COPYRIGHT © 2001 ILLIAD HTTP://WWW.USERFRIENDLY.ORG/

"NO BAGS OF ANY KIND WILL BE ALLOWED ON THE SHOW FLOOR, INCLUDING LAPTOP BAGS." WHAT'S THE DEAL WITH THAT?
SECURITY, APPARENTLY. I JUST DON'T SEE THE PURPOSE OF EXCLUDING SMALL BAGS.

CURSES. FOILED AGAIN.

Security Theatre at its finest. Thank the gods for people like Bruce Schneier.

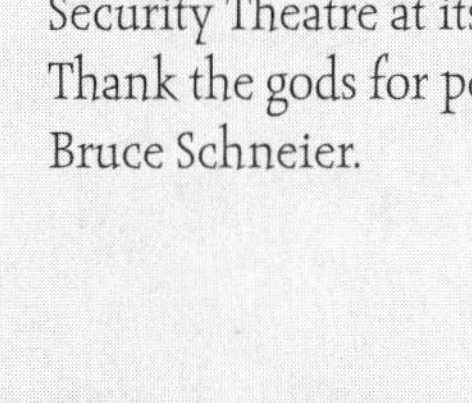

COMDEX THIS-A-WAY
COPYRIGHT © 2001 ILLIAD HTTP://WWW.USERFRIENDLY.ORG/

COMDEX
SORRY. NO BAGS ALLOWED PAST THIS POINT.

COMDEX
YOU ARE HAVINK SOMEPLACE WE CAN PUT HER THEN?
HEY!!!

USER
FRIENDLY
the comic strip
PIZZA
Portrasher 4
ROTO-ROUTER 800
Copyright©1997-2001 Illiad

ALL THOSE TWITS OUT THERE GAMBLING. THEY PLUG IN MONEY AND ACTUALLY EXPECT TO "WIN" SOMETHING. EVEN WITH THE ODDS STACKED AGAINST THEM.

YES!!! I'M ONLY FORTY MILLION POINTS AWAY FROM MY FIRST EXTRA BALL!
ASINO
BING!
DING
DING
DING
DING

WATCHA DOING HERE? I THOUGHT FOR SURE YOU'D BE HANGING WITH A.J. DOWN AT THE ARCADE.
NOT WITH A.J. I'M NOT THAT STUPID.

EH? HOW SO?
HE'S A HARDCORE GAMER. HIS MENTAL NUTS AND BOLTS LOOSEN A LITTLE WHEN HE STARTS IMMERSING HIMSELF INTO A GAME.

IT'S CALLED A QUARTER.
IT IS NOT. IT'S A DEFENDER ENERGIZER DISC!
DEFENDER

MEANWHILE, IN THE LUXURIOUS OFFICES OF MR. WILLIAM GATES...
DEPARTMENT OF JUSTICE OFFICIALS TODAY CONFIRMED THAT THE ATTORNEYS GENERAL OF THE NINE STATES WHO LAST WEEK ORIGINALLY REFUSED TO SETTLE WITH MICROSOFT HAVE RECONSIDERED.
PHEW
COPYRIGHT © 2001 ILLIAD HTTP://WWW.USERFRIENDLY.ORG/

CHANNEL FIVE NEWS HAS FURTHER LEARNED THAT THE SAME NINE STATES HAVE COMPLETELY WITHDRAWN THEIR COMPLAINTS AGAINST THE SOFTWARE GIANT.
FINALLY. WHAT A RELIEF.

EXCUSE ME. THIS STATEMENT JUST IN FROM THE DEPARTMENT OF JUSTICE. IT SAYS: "HEY BILL. PSYCHE!"
ARRRRGH!

Prior to 9/11 (and even now, I'm sure, to some extent), screening staff can and do mess with the sensitivity of the walkways. Once, a very attractive young lady walked through wearing not much beyond a t-shirt, some short-shorts, and a pair of flip-flops, and yet she set off the walkway. She told the guard that it was "just my nipple ring," flipped up her shirt, displayed her glory, and walked off, leaving the screener with jaw on floor and brain in neutral.

BACK AT THE ENTRANCE TO COMDEX...
I WONDER IF THOSE METAL DETECTOR WALKWAYS ACTUALLY WORK.
THEY DO. I WORKED AT THE AIRPORT ONE YEAR DOING THIS VERY THING.
STEP THROUGH PLEASE, SIR...
COPYRIGHT © 2001 ILLIAD HTTP://WWW.USERFRIENDLY.ORG/

BUT THEY WORK ONLY IN THE SENSE THAT YOU CAN ADJUST THEIR SENSITIVITY. THEY CAN BE SET SO HIGH THAT IT SEEMS THE IRON IN SOMEONE'S BLOOD WILL SET IT OFF AND THEN YOU HAVE TO HAND SEARCH THE PERSON...
BUT WHAT'S THE POINT IN SETTING IT SO HIGH IT DOESN'T DISCRIMINATE?
NEXT. PLEASE...

HERE COMES ONE. CRANK IT WAY UP, TYRONE.

AT COMDEX, ORACLE'S CEO LARRY ELLISON HOLDS A PRESS CONFERENCE...
I'LL TAKE QUESTIONS NOW. ANY QUERIES ABOUT OUR PRODUCTS? SERVICES? FEDERAL I.D. CARDS? THE FUTURE OF ORACLE?
COPYRIGHT © 2001 ILLIAD HTTP://WWW.USERFRIENDLY.ORG/

YES?! YOU IN THE GREEN STETSON?

YOU STILL HAVEN'T BEATEN BILL GATES AT ANYTHING, HAVE YOU.
OOO!! I... OOH! WHY YOU...ARRG!!

LOOK, YOU PEOPLE NEED TO ACKNOWLEDGE WHAT I'VE ALREADY ACCOMPLISHED. I'VE COME VERY CLOSE TO MATCHING BILL GATES IN THE PERSONAL NET WORTH DEPARTMENT. WHY, JUST LAST YEAR I WAS A MERE HAIRSBREADTH AWAY...
COPYRIGHT © 2001 ILLIAD HTTP://WWW.USERFRIENDLY.ORG/

THIRTEEN BILLION DOLLARS IS A "HAIRSBREADTH?"
ARRRGH!
WELL, THEN I'M JUST A HAIRSBREADTH AWAY FROM BUYING MYSELF A FLEET OF A COUPLE THOUSAND LEAR JETS. GO ME!

HEY! IS THAT LARRY ELLISON THAT JUST WALKED BY US? HEADING FOR THE WASHROOM?

YEP.

LITTLE DOES HE KNOW. MICROSOFT HAS SPONSORED THE WASHROOMS HERE AT COMDEX. JUST A SMALL DEMONSTRATION OF THEIR WEALTH COMPARED TO ORACLE'S. MICROSOFT BROUGHT IN SOME VERY SPECIAL TOILET PAPER.

SPECIAL HOW?
ORACLE SHARE CERTIFICATES.
I REALLY HATE THAT MAN!!

Couldn't happen to a nicer guy.

HELLO FOLKS! DUST PUPPY AND I JUST WANT TO TAKE A MOMENT TO WISH USER FRIENDLY A HAPPY FOURTH ANNIVERSARY AND TO TELL OUR BOSS ILLIAD THAT HE'S BEEN DOING A SUPERLATIVE JOB!
ROTO ROUTER

ROTO ROUTER

HOW MUCH LONGER DO I HAVE TO KEEP GRINNING LIKE THIS?
UNTIL THAT HACK SIGNS OUR NEW CONTRACTS FOR YEAR FIVE.
ROTO ROUTER

WHEN YOU'RE A CARTOON CHARACTER IN AN ECONOMIC DOWNTURN, IT'S NOT PINK **SLIPS** YOU GET WORRIED ABOUT...

SANFORD
Pink Pearl
101
MALAYSIA

HEY. AJ'S DOOR IS LOCKED.
YEAH. HE'S BEEN WHINING ALL MORNING ABOUT HOW HE DOESN'T HAVE ENOUGH MONEY TO GO OUT AND BUY AN X-BOX.
COPYRIGHT © 2001 ILLIAD HTTP://WWW.USERFRIENDLY.ORG/

BUT...WHY'S HIS DOOR LOCKED?
HE WAS GETTING ON SID'S NERVES. SID'S IN THERE WITH HIM RIGHT NOW 'SOLVING THE PROBLEM.'

YOU WANTED AN X-BOX? **THERE'S** YOUR STUPID **EX**-BOX.

SO THIS IS CIVILIZATION THREE. THE GAME ENGINE HAS BEEN JUICED UP AND THE GRAPHICS ARE TOTALLY SWEET. IT'S A GOOD GAME OVERALL. THE, UH, **MUSIC** THOUGH...
COPYRIGHT © 2001 ILLIAD HTTP://WWW.USERFRIENDLY.ORG/

YEAH. WHAT **DOES** ONE SAY ABOUT THAT MUSIC?

EXCUSE ME? COULD YOU BOYS PLEASE KEEP THE **KENNY G** PARTY DOWN TO A MINIMUM?
THAT'S WHAT ONE WOULD SAY.
BINGO.

CHIEF? JUST WANTED TO LET YOU KNOW I'VE COME UP WITH ANOTHER WAY OF IMPROVING PRODUCTIVITY HERE.
OH?
COPYRIGHT © 2001 ILLIAD HTTP://WWW.USERFRIENDLY.ORG/

YEAH. I SUBMITTED A LIST OF NEW PROGRAMMING COMMANDS FOR US NON-CODERS FOR THE TECHS TO DEVELOP. I TOLD THEM THAT A FEW HOURS INVESTED NOW WOULD SAVE THEM WEEKS IN THE FUTURE.
AND HOW DO THE TECHS FEEL ABOUT THIS?

IT IS SAYINK "DWIM(X)" **WHAT IS "DWIM(X)"?!**
ACCORDING TO STEF'S DOC, IT'S THE COMMAND FOR "DO WHAT I MEAN TO (X)"

MIRANDA, WE **CAN'T** DEVELOP THOSE NEW "STEFCODES" -- IT'S LIKE HANDING A FLAMETHROWER TO A **WIGGED-OUT POSTAL WORKER.**
I KNOW. BUT THE CHIEF AUTHORIZED IT.
COPYRIGHT © 2001 ILLIAD HTTP://WWW.USERFRIENDLY.ORG/

UNH-HUH. DOES THE CHIEF ALSO KNOW THAT STEF "TESTED OUT" SOME OF HIS NEW PROGRAMMING COMMANDS IN OUR BACKUP SCRIPTS?
OUR BACKUP SCRIPTS? **WHAT?!**

AH. HERE IS PROBLEM. IT READS: "IF DEV(DISKO)=FULL, OPEN DEV(HYPERSPACE), SAVE."
YE FLIPPING **GODS.**

BACK IN THE OFFICES OF ONE WILLIAM GATES III, WE FIND A DISCUSSION OVER SETTLING THE CIVIL ANTI-TRUST CASES...
MR. MUSTELA... THE FACTS PLEASE.
YES, MR. GATES. THE SETTLEMENT STATES THAT WE HAVE TO, AMONG OTHER THINGS, CONTRIBUTE 900 MILLION DOLLARS WORTH OF SOFTWARE TO THE POOREST U.S. SCHOOLS...
COPYRIGHT © 2001 ILLIAD HTTP://WWW.USERFRIENDLY.ORG/

NINE HUNDRED MILLION WORTH OF SOFTWARE?! THAT'S COMPLETELY OUTRAGEOUS!
SIR, WE'RE A MONOPOLY. WE. GET. TO. SET. THE. PRICE.

YOU MEAN, LIKE $10,000 PER COPY OF XP?
AIM HIGHER SIR. THINK IN THE TEN MILLION BALLPARK.

CHIEF, I KNOW STEF MEANS WELL, BUT YOU HAVE TO PUT A LEASH ON HIM.
OH DEAR. HIS "NON-CODER COMMANDS" IDEA ISN'T WORKING OUT?
COPYRIGHT © 2001 ILLIAD HTTP://WWW.USERFRIENDLY.ORG/

THAT'S A NICE WAY OF PUTTING IT. THE TECHS HAVE BEEN DOCUMENTING ALL OF THE PROBLEMS AND HOLES IN THE SPECIFICATION STEF PUT TOGETHER.

WHEN (IT.COMES.OUT.WRONG) LOOP UNTIL (IT.COMES.OUT.RIGHT)
ANOTHER INCOMPLETE COMMAND SET. WHAT'S MISSING FROM IT?
STEF'S HEAD.

USER
FRIENDLY
the comic strip
PIZZA
Portrasher 4
ROTO-ROUTER 800
Copyright©1997-2001 Illiad

I WANT THE TWO OF YOU TO STAY PUT AND WATCH A REAL SINGER BELT OUT A KILLER TUNE.
MRF MRRF!

(SUNG TO "BUILDING A MYSTERY" BY SARAH MCLACHLAN)
YOU LOG ON AT NIGHT THAT'S WHEN YOU SEEK ALL YOUR PORN AND THE MONITOR'S BRIGHT AS YOUR FINGERS ROAM YOU PRAISE THE RASTER GLARE BUT THEN YOU'RE TERRIFIED IN YOUR HOME...
UHNF!

I had the opportunity to see Sarah McLachlan in concert. She's a small, beautiful woman with an amazing voice. I believe she'd club the beans out of anyone abusing one of her songs. Also, Sarah's last few words in the strip are a play on her album Fumbling Towards Ecstasy.

WHEN YOU HEAR YOUR WIFE COMING CLOSER DOWN THAT HALL YOU'RE CLEARING YOUR HISTORY

'CAUSE YOU'RE SURFING THEN CLEARING YOUR HISTORY! HIDING YOUR TRACKS TO BIGBOOBS DOT COM! YEAH YOU'RE QUICKLY CLEARING YOUR HISTORY! AND PERUSING SO CAREFULLY...

NOW THAT'S WHAT I'M TALKIN' ABOUT. BET I COULD EVEN TEACH SARAH A THING OR TWO...
IN A SECOND YOU'LL BE FUMBLING FOR YOUR EXTREMITIES...

WHAT'S THAT YOU'RE PLAYING WITH?
I STAYED UP LAST NIGHT AND WROTE SOME CODE THAT TAKES CARE OF THE SPAM PROBLEM. I'M RUNNING IT ON THE SPAM I JUST GOT. IT HACKS INTO THE SPAMMER'S SYSTEM, DELETES MY E-MAIL ADDRESS, THEN FINDS THE SPAMMER'S CONTACT INFO.
COPYRIGHT © 2001 ILLIAD HTTP://WWW.USERFRIENDLY.ORG/

HERE IT COMES. HIS NAME IS... NEDLEY ERBLE.
AND THEN THE APP SENDS HIS INFO TO "ABUSE@" ?
UM...NO...ELSEWHERE.

YO!! TEAM!! NEW LEAD! A MISTER NEDLEY ERBLE JUST WON THE LOTTERY! NOW SELL!!
RAPACIOUS TELEMARKETING

THE RIPOSTE CONTINUES...
HELLO? MR. NEDLEY ERBLE? I'M CALLING ON BEHALF OF SCHMIDT'S LASER TONER...
GET LOST! I HATE TELEMARKETERS! *KLIK*
COPYRIGHT © 2001 ILLIAD HTTP://WWW.USERFRIENDLY.ORG/

BIP
BOOP
BIP
BIP
BIPPY
BOOP

MR. NEDLEY ERBLE? WE'RE OFFERING A SERVICE TO REMOVE YOUR NAME FROM TELEMARKETERS' LISTS. IT'S JUST $19.95...
OH...UH... OKAY...

SEEING THAT YOU HAVE A BACKGROUND IN BULK E-MAIL ADVERTISING MR. ERBLE, I THOUGHT YOU MIGHT UNDERSTAND AND LIKE HEARING ABOUT OUR OTHER PRODUCTS AND SERVICES...
LISTEN VERMIN, I DON'T WANT YOUR DAMN SPIEL. I DON'T LIKE BEING DISTURBED, AND THIS IS NOTHING LIKE BULK E-MAIL MARKETING!
COPYRIGHT © 2001 ILLIAD HTTP://WWW.USERFRIENDLY.ORG/

YOU'RE ABSOLUTELY RIGHT, SIR. I'LL HANG UP AND CALL YOU BACK COLLECT.
NO! WAIT! ARRRGH!

LISTEN GO AWAY. AND I WANT YOU TO REMOVE ME FROM YOUR LIST. NOW!
OF COURSE MR. ERBLE! IF YOU COULD TELL ME YOUR SNAIL-MAIL ADDRESS JUST TO VERIFY YOUR IDENTITY, I'LL REMOVE YOU FROM OUR LIST.
COPYRIGHT © 2001 ILLIAD HTTP://WWW.USERFRIENDLY.ORG/

OH...UM...OKAY...
CONFIRMED DIRECT MAIL ADDRESSES. NAME: MR. N. ERBLE ADDRESS: ?
TAP
TIP
TIK
TAK

...6713 PENDER AV...UH...HEY!
DAMN. HE'S CATCHING ON...

AHEM
A SECOND ODE TO SPAM.
BY ME, ERWIN:
SPAM, O GLORIOUS LUNCHEON MEAT
THOU GLISTEN PINK AND WET
THY NAME BESMIRCHED BY SEWER SCUM
WHO'VE CLOGGED THE INTERNET
YOUNG LIVE TEENS! EASY CASH!
THEY CRY WITH RAUCOUS VIGOR
WELL AWARE WERE THEY LINED UP
WE'D LOVE TO PULL THE TRIGGER
COPYRIGHT © 2001 ILLIAD HTTP://WWW.USERFRIENDLY.ORG/

BUT RATHER, WE SHOULD PASS A LAW
FOR EACH SPAM MAIL ONE SENDS
THE GUILTY PARTY SHALL CONSUME
A BRICK OF MEAT AND ENDS.
THAT'S A NASTY PUNISHMENT.
ERWIN SAYS "THE ENDS JUSTIFY THE MEAT."

For the record, I love Spam. Spamburger on a toasted bun! With ketchup!

YOU KNOW A.J., @HOME MIGHT **NOT** SHUT DOWN IT'S NETWORK.
RIGHT. BUT A.J. HERE IS WISELY PROTECTING HIMSELF. HE'LL BE COVERED AT HOME EVEN IF THEY **DO** GO DOWN.
COPYRIGHT © 2001 ILLIAD HTTP://WWW.USERFRIENDLY.ORG/

THANK YOU FOR THE HUNDRED DOLLARS, SON. I HOPE IT SERVES YOU WELL.
I CAN'T BELIEVE YOU CHARGED THAT MUCH FOR IT.

HEY, IT'S A NEW LEASE ON LIFE.
IT'S A ONE HUNDRED AND TEN BAUD MODEM!
YES! I'M COVERED!

MESSAGE TO THE EXCITE@HOME BONDHOLDERS:
REPLACE THE WORD "SWITCH" WITH "CUSTOMERS"
FLIP OFF THE SWITCH
AT&T
@Home
850,000 SUBSCRIBERS
COPYRIGHT © 2001 ILLIAD HTTP://WWW.USERFRIENDLY.ORG/

If you think this is just a bit of fun, take a wild guess which C-level executive typically made for an awesome scapegoat when the dot-com bubble burst.

I'VE DECIDED I NEED TO LET GO OF SOME OF THE RESPONSIBILITIES OF RUNNING THIS COMPANY. I WANT SOMEONE ELSE TO HELP MANAGE THE BIGGER PICTURE AND INCLUDE TECHNICAL GROWTH IN OUR PLANNING.
COPYRIGHT © 2001 ILLIAD HTTP://WWW.USERFRIENDLY.ORG/

SO I'VE DECIDED THE COMPANY NEEDS A C.T.O.

A CHIEF TECHNICAL OFFICER?
NO. A CHIEF TAKE-THE-BLAME OFFICER. ALL THE COOL C.E.O'S HAVE ONE.

AH, PITR! I NEED YOUR INPUT ON SOMETHING. AS A CORE MEMBER OF THE TECH TEAM, WHO DO YOU FEEL SHOULD BE PROMOTED TO C.T.O. OF THE COMPANY: SID OR MIRANDA?
HAAAAAAHAHAAH HAHAHAHAHAHA AHAAHAHAHAHA HAHAHAHAHAHA...
COPYRIGHT © 2001 ILLIAD HTTP://WWW.USERFRIENDLY.ORG/

...HA.

YOU KNOW, IS NOT FUNNY THIS JOKE WHEN YOU ARE NOT LAUGHINK WITH ME.
I HADN'T REALIZED IT WAS FUNNY UNTIL YOU SAID THAT.

SORRY. NOT LIKINK EITHER CHOICE.
PITR, COME NOW. BOTH MIRANDA AND SID OFFER A GREAT DEAL TO THE POSITION OF C.T.O.
COPYRIGHT © 2001 ILLIAD HTTP://WWW.USERFRIENDLY.ORG/

BOTH ARE SOLID TECHNOLOGISTS AND HAVE A GOOD GRASP OF THE LARGER PICTURE. WHAT'S MORE, THEY RECOGNIZE AND RESPECT THEIR DIFFERENCES.

DEGENERATE FOSSIL
NARCISSISTIC CHILD

I NEED SOME REAL INPUT ON THIS C.T.O. ISSUE. THERE'S A.J... MAYBE HIS OUTLOOK IS TOO YOUNG? OH WHAT THE HELL. IT CAN'T HURT TO ASK...
COPYRIGHT © 2001 ILLIAD HTTP://WWW.USERFRIENDLY.ORG/

A.J., IF YOU HAD TO CHOOSE BETWEEN SID AND MIRANDA, WHAT DO YOU THINK WOULD BE A GOOD WAY TO DETERMINE WHO WOULD MAKE A BETTER C.T.O?

SEE WHO LOOKS COOLER ON A SEGWAY!
I REALLY SHOULD KNOW BETTER...

WE'RE GETTING A C.T.O. EITHER SID OR MIRANDA.
REALLY? HOW'S THE CHIEF DECIDING?
COPYRIGHT © 2001 ILLIAD HTTP://WWW.USERFRIENDLY.ORG/

I SUGGESTED THAT HE JUST NEEDED TO SEE WHICH OF THEM LOOKED COOLER ON A SEGWAY. IT'S COOL TECH, AFTER ALL, AND A C.T.O. NEEDS TO BE HIP TO THAT.
GOOD IDEA, ASSUMING THE CHIEF CAN TALK THEM INTO TRYING ONE OUT...

YOU MEAN IT'S LIKE A WHEELCHAIR.
NO, NO! IT'S LIKE A WHEELCHAIR FOR THE NON-DISABLED! NO! WAIT!! I MEAN...

HELLO FOLKS! WE INTERRUPT THIS STORYLINE TO INTRODUCE JUERGEN BIERLEIN, WINNER OF THE "WALK-ON" DRAW HELD EARLIER THIS YEAR AT LINUXTAG IN STUTTGART, GERMANY.
COPYRIGHT © 2001 ILLIAD HTTP://WWW.USERFRIENDLY.ORG/

JUERGEN IS A HIGHLY TALENTED 34-YEAR OLD COMPUTER SCIENTIST WHO ENJOYS HIGH-SPEED CODING, ADVOCATES OPEN SOURCE AND LINUX, AND LIKES TO RACE HIS CA-

POW!

JEEZ PITR! WHADDYA CALL THAT?
IN THIS ECONOMY, JOB SECURITY.

Congrats to Juergen! I understand he received so much geek cred from this appearance that he was entrusted with a vacuum tube from ENIAC. (Or maybe not.)

FEBRUARY 2002
-less.
COPYRIGHT © 2001 ILLIAD HTTP://WWW.USERFRIENDLY.ORG/

THE CHIEF ASKED ME TO TRY OUT THIS SEGWAY THING.
HOW DOES IT WORK?
COPYRIGHT © 2001 ILLIAD HTTP://WWW.USERFRIENDLY.ORG/

THE IDEA IS THAT YOU JUST THINK WHERE YOU WANT TO GO AND IT RESPONDS TO THE SUBTLE SHIFTS IN YOUR BODY WITH GYROSCOPES. IN A WAY IT READS YOUR MIND AND TAKES YOU THERE.

THAT'S PRETTY COOL.
NOT SO COOL, TANYA. MY MIND WANDERS.

YOU REALLY DON'T LIKE THOSE SEGWAY DEVICES?
TO PUT IT LIGHTLY, I REFUSE TO SUPPORT ANYTHING THAT WILL CREATE MORE STUPID PEOPLE.
COPYRIGHT © 2001 ILLIAD HTTP://WWW.USERFRIENDLY.ORG/

WHAT ON EARTH ARE YOU TALKING ABOUT? IT'S A TRANSPORTATION DEVICE THAT JUST HELPS PEOPLE MOVE AROUND. HOW WILL IT CREATE MORE STUPID PEOPLE?

TWO WORDS: SIDEWALK RAGE.
I HATE IT WHEN HE MAKES ME LOOK DUMB. HE GETS THE JOB.

SID, I'M VERY PLEASED TO BE THE FIRST TO CONGRATULATE YOU ON YOUR PROMOTION TO C.T.O!
COPYRIGHT © 2001 ILLIAD HTTP://WWW.USERFRIENDLY.ORG/
AS C.T.O. YOU'LL BE ENTITLED TO ALL OF THE PERKS AND AUTHORITY NORMALLY GRANTED SUCH A POSITION, NOT TO MENTION AN INTRIGUING ARRAY OF DUTIES AND RESPONSIBILITES.

SOMETHING DOESN'T FEEL RIGHT ABOUT THIS.
WHAT CAN I GET YOU? CIGAR? STOCK OPTIONS? PAD OF PINK SLIPS?

GENTLEMEN, I'VE CALLED YOU IN HERE TO ANNOUNCE THAT SID HAS BEEN PROMOTED TO THE POSITION OF C.T.O., AND AS SUCH WILL PLAY AN IMPORTANT PART IN YOUR DAILY WORK-RELATED LIVES. PLEASE LEND HIM YOUR SUPPORT.
COPYRIGHT © 2001 ILLIAD HTTP://WWW.USERFRIENDLY.ORG/

ANYWAY, CARRY ON. WE HAVE TO GO LET THE OTHERS KNOW.

THAT WAS INTERESTING. WHAT ARE WE GOING TO DO WITH A C.T.O?
GARROTINK COMES TO MIND.

SO HERE I AM. THE NEW C.T.O. OF A SMALL I.S.P. WHAT DOES IT MEAN TO HAVE THIS NEWFOUND POWER?
YOUR 7 A.M. APPOINTMENT IS HERE.
SEND HIM IN PLEASE TANYA.
COPYRIGHT © 2001 ILLIAD HTTP://WWW.USERFRIENDLY.ORG/

I HAVE EXTRA RESPONSIBILITIES. ONEROUS DUTIES. NOT TO MENTION AN ENORMOUS BURDEN TO SHOULDER.

BUT AS ALWAYS. THERE IS A SILVER LINING.
IT'S 7 A.M. THIS HAD BETTER BE DAMN GOOD.

GOOD MORNING PITR. THANK YOU FOR SHOWING UP ON TIME. I WANTED TO SEE YOU BECAUSE AS YOUR NEW BOSS. I THINK WE SHOULD CLEAR THE AIR BETWEEN US.
COPYRIGHT © 2001 ILLIAD HTTP://WWW.USERFRIENDLY.ORG/

I WANT US TO HAVE A PROPER WORKING RELATIONSHIP SO LET'S BURY THE HATCHET AND GRANT EACH OTHER THE UTMOST IN PROFESSIONAL COURTESY.

THEN WHY ARE YOU TELLINK ME THIS AT SEVEN IN THE MORNINK?!
BECAUSE I'M THE C.T.O. AND YOU'RE MY WIDDLE CODING PEON.

WITH THE SUCCESSFUL COMMERCIALIZATION OF THE "LORD OF THE RINGS," A 'CHOCOLATE EASTER FRODO' IS NOT FAR BEHIND, BRINGING WITH IT ITS OWN PREFERRED BITING-ZONE.
COPYRIGHT © 2001 ILLIAD HTTP://WWW.USERFRIENDLY.ORG/

CHIEF?
COME IN A.J. WHAT'S ON YOUR MIND SON?
COPYRIGHT © 2001 ILLIAD HTTP://WWW.USERFRIENDLY.ORG/

I'M FEELING A LITTLE DOWN, I SUPPOSE. OR MAYBE THE WORD IS CHEATED. I WAS LOOKING FORWARD TO A NEW AND SHINING PARAGON OF LEADERSHIP FOR THE COMPANY, AND ALL I SEE IS INSTABILITY AND A DEARTH OF GRACE. IT'S DEPRESSING.

YOU'RE NOT FEELING TOO SUPPORTIVE OF SID AS C.T.O. I TAKE IT.
CAN YOU IMAGINE HIM ON A SEGWAY?! HE'D LOOK LIKE A DORK!

"Navel hairs"?! WTF Illiad?

A.J., LET'S GIVE THIS A LITTLE THOUGHT. THE OTHER CHOICE FOR C.T.O. IS MIRANDA. AND ALTHOUGH SHE'D ADMITTEDLY LOOK COOLER ON A SEGWAY THAN SID, WHEN SHE'S ON ONE SHE'D BE SIX TO TWELVE INCHES HIGHER.
COPYRIGHT © 2001 ILLIAD HTTP://WWW.USERFRIENDLY.ORG/

SIX TO TWELVE INCHES HIGHER. OKAY. SO?
SO. WHAT STARTS APPROACHING YOUR EYE LEVEL?

YE GODS. THANK YOU.
DON'T THANK ME YET. YOU HAVEN'T SEEN SID'S NAVEL HAIRS COMING UP TO EYE LEVEL.

SEE? I TOLD YOU.
YOU'RE RIGHT. HOW VERY ODD. A C.T.O. WITHOUT A COMPUTER ON HIS DESK.
COPYRIGHT © 2001 ILLIAD HTTP://WWW.USERFRIENDLY.ORG/

UM..YOU DON'T THINK...
IT MIGHT BE.

NO...IT CAN'T BE...
THE NIGHTMARE IS REAL. HE'S WRITING MEMOS WITH PUNCH CARDS.

HOW CAN HE WRITE MEMOS WITH PUNCH CARDS FER-CHRISSAKES? PUNCH CARDS! IN THIS DAY AND AGE!
COPYRIGHT © 2001 ILLIAD HTTP://WWW.USERFRIENDLY.ORG/

IT'S ARCHAIC! IT'S EGREGIOUS! IT'S PROSOPHOBIC! IT'S...IT'S...

IT'S YOUR PAY RAISE RECOMMENDATION.
IT'S ABOUT TIME WE WENT BACK TO USING TECH-NOLOGY THAT ACTUALLY WORKS!

SILENCE SHROUDS THE OFFICES OF COLUMBIA INTERNET LIKE A HEAVY FOG THIS MORNING. THE EMPLOYEES REMAIN FOCUSED SQUARELY ON THEIR WORK...

ZZZZZ...UNGH...ZZZ ENGFEH...ZZZZZZ...
COPYRIGHT © 2001 ILLIAD HTTP://WWW.USERFRIENDLY.ORG/

IN THE OFFICES OF THE COMPANY'S C-LEVEL EXECUTIVES, A RITE OF PASSAGE TAKES PLACE AS AN OLD HAND PASSES ON THE SECRETS OF RULERSHIP TO THE NEW AUTOCRAT.
STORAGE
C.T.O.

"...AS WE STRENGTHEN OUR COMMITTMENT..."
STORAGE
C.T.O.
NO NO NO! SID!! THE WORD IS ENSTRENGTHEN! NOW CONCENTRATE!

SID, AS A NEW C-LEVEL EXECUTIVE, IT'S CRUCIAL THAT YOU LEARN HOW TO SPEAK LIKE ONE.
COPYRIGHT © 2001 ILLIAD HTTP://WWW.USERFRIENDLY.ORG/

YOU NEED TO LEARN BIG CONCEPTS! USE BUZZWORDS! COMMUNICATE WITH FUZZY LANGUAGE, AND SPEND TIME CARVING AWAY THE EXCESS OVER A POWER LUNCH!

AND REMEMBER! THERE'S NO "I" IN THE WORD "TEAM!"
THAT'S BECAUSE IT'S BEING USED IN THE WORD "BULL$#!&"

USER
FRIENDLY
the comic strip
PIZZA
Portrasher 4
ROTO-ROUTER 800
Copyright©1997-2001 Illiad

YOU WANT TO LEAD THIS TIME? WHY?
DUNNO. I JUST HAVE THIS URGE...

(SUNG TO, "LET IT SNOW," WITH ERWIN SINGING LEAD, AND DUST PUPPY DOING BACK-UP)
THE ECONOMY'S TRULY FRIGHTFUL
THE COMPETITION IS MORE THAN SPITEFUL
WE'LL BLAME IT ALL ON THE PRO
THE C.T.O C.T.O C.T.O!

THE AXE THAT COMES A-CHOPPING
KEEPS US ALL ON OUR TOES AND HOPPING
WE ALL KNOW WHERE THE BLAME SHOULD GO
THE C.T.O C.T.O C.T.O!

HE'S REALLY A DECENT GUY
AND HE FEELS HE'S THE SOURCE OF HOPE
THINKS THAT WE IN HIM RELY
UNTIL SOMEBODY GETS A ROPE...!

ERWIN! THIS IS SUPPOSED TO BE A JOYOUS SONG!
HEY, I'M FULL OF GLEE...
HOW WOULD YOU LIKE TO BECOME A CHRISTMAS ORNAMENT?

THIS YEAR, A LOT OF PEOPLE ARE DOING WITHOUT GIFTS. MANY PEOPLE SUFFERED LOSS. IT'S A SADDER, WISER CHRISTMAS THIS TIME AROUND, I THINK.
THEN MAYBE THIS YEAR CHRISTMAS SHOULD BE MORE LIKE WHAT THANKS-GIVING IS ABOUT.
COPYRIGHT © 2001 ILLIAD HTTP://WWW.USERFRIENDLY.ORG/

MAYBE.
I LOVE IT THAT I GET HUGGED WHENEVER I SAY SOMETHING OBVIOUS.

WHY DO I HAVE TO WORK ON CHRISTMAS? NOT THAT I HAVE ANYONE TO SPEND IT WITH. AND WHAT ON EARTH IS A.J. DOING IN THE OFFICE TODAY?! HE'S PROBABLY TOO SCARED TO SAY A WORD TO ME. I HATE THAT.
COPYRIGHT © 2001 ILLIAD HTTP://WWW.USERFRIENDLY.ORG/

MIRANDA? I WANTED TO BUY YOU SOMETHING THIS YEAR BUT I'M BROKE. SO DUST PUPPY SUGGESTED I LEND HIM TO YOU AS A KIND OF TEDDY BEAR FOR A WEEK. HE'S MY BEST FRIEND AND I'D MISS HIM. BUT HE'S ALL I HAVE AND YOU LOOK SAD AND...

UM..YOU'RE SUPPOSED TO BE HUGGING THE LI'L GUY...
A.J., JUST THIS ONCE, I ACTUALLY WANT YOU TO SHUT UP.

SID? AM THINKINK OF WHAT YOU ARE SAYINK, ABOUT CLEARINK AIR BETWEEN US. IS HOLIDAY SEASON, DA? SO AM GIVINK YOU PRESENT.
A PRESENT? WHERE?
COPYRIGHT © 2001 ILLIAD HTTP://WWW.USERFRIENDLY.ORG/

PLEASE, TO BE FOLLOWINK THIS WAY. YOUR SURPRISE GIFT, IT IS WAITINK FOR YOU!

BETTINK YOU ARE NOT GUESSINK WHAT IT IS.
OH HEAVENS. I COULDN'T EVEN BEGIN TO IMAGINE.

THAT LITTLE VILLAIN-WANNABE IS UP TO SOMETHING. I CAN'T BELIEVE HE WENT OUT AND SPENT THAT KIND OF MONEY ON A PRESENT FOR ME. I DON'T TRUST HIM.
COPYRIGHT © 2001 ILLIAD HTTP://WWW.USERFRIENDLY.ORG/

ON THE SAME NOTE, IT WOULD BE KINDA COOL TO CRUISE AROUND ON THIS THING. NO FUSS, NO MUSS.

HEY AJ. WHADDYA THI-
BELLY HAIR! NOOOOO!!!!

GOOD MORNING, ERWIN.
DID YOU DREAM?
COPYRIGHT © 2001 ILLIAD HTTP://WWW.USERFRIENDLY.ORG/

ERWIN?
HELLO?

MAN, I FEEL LIKE I'VE BEEN ASLEEP FOR TWO DAYS. AND FOR THE FIRST TIME IN MY LIFE, I FEEL...BALANCED. HELLO? WHY IS IT DARK?

COME ON A.J. SPEED IS OF THE ESSENCE.
I...UH...
COPYRIGHT © 2001 ILLIAD HTTP://WWW.USERFRIENDLY.ORG/

I...UH...JUMP UP TO THE LEDGE AND FIRE A ROCKET AT GREG...I THINK...
LOOK! I CAN'T PLAY QUAKE 2 WITH PUNCH CARDS!
COME ON, DUDE. DON'T JUST TWITCH. IMAGINE!

DMITRY SKLYAROV'S CASE HELPS CORRECT
A LONG-STANDING DEFICIENCY IN ONE OF
NORTH AMERICA'S MOST CHERISHED INSTITUTIONS
GUESS I SHOULD'VE STUCK WITH THE BLINDFOLD...
JUSTICE
OPYRIGHT © 2002 ILLIAD HTTP://WWW.USERFRIENDLY.ORG/

Hear that whirring sound? It's Robert Frost in his grave, spinning.

"TWO ROADS DIVERGED IN A YELLOW WOOD, AND SORRY I COULD NOT TRAVEL BOTH AND BE ONE TRAVELER, LONG I STOOD AND LOOKED DOWN ONE AS FAR AS I COULD TO WHERE IT BENT IN THE UNDERGROWTH;"

"THEN TOOK THE OTHER, AS JUST AS FAIR AND HAVING PERHAPS THE BETTER CLAIM, BECAUSE IT WAS GRASSY AND WANTED WEAR; THOUGH AS FOR THAT, THE PASSING THERE HAD WORN THEM REALLY ABOUT THE SAME."
COPYRIGHT © 2001 ILLIAD HTTP://WWW.USERFRIENDLY.ORG/
"AND BOTH THAT MORNING EQUALLY LAY IN LEAVES NO STEP HAD TRODDEN BLACK OH, I KEPT THE FIRST FOR ANOTHER DAY! YET KNOWING HOW WAY LEADS ON TO WAY, I DOUBTED IF I SHOULD EVER COME BACK."

I SHALL BE TELLING THIS WITH A SIGH SOMEWHERE AGES AND AGES HENCE: TWO ROADS DIVERGED IN A WOOD, AND I -- I TOOK THE ONE LESS TRAVELED BY, AND THAT HAS MADE ALL THE DIFFERENCE.
NOOOO!!!
HAAAH HAHAH HAHA!!

GOOD MORNING FROM CNN LADIES AND GENTLEMEN, AND WELCOME TO THE NEW MILLENNIUM...
PSST. MR. BIG MEDIA. YOU GUYS DID THE NEW MILLENNIUM GIG IN 2000 AND 2001.
COPYRIGHT © 2002 ILLIAD HTTP://WWW.USERFRIENDLY.ORG/

NOW WHAT THE HELL DO WE DO?
WE HAVE TO KILL FOUR MINUTES. PRETEND YOU'RE IN AFGHANISTAN AND WE'LL PAD THE DELAYS!

MMMM. TITANIUM POWERBOOK G4 WITH A COMBO DRIVE. NICE.
YEP. I HAD THE COMPANY ORDER ONE FOR MYSELF.
COPYRIGHT © 2002 ILLIAD HTTP://WWW.USERFRIENDLY.ORG/

DO I GET ONE TOO?
NO.
WHY NOT?
BECAUSE I'M THE C.T.O.

UNH HUH. I GUESS THE RANK HATH THEIR PRIVILEGES.
ITS PRIVILEGES. RANK HATH ITS PRIVILEGES. AND THERE'S NO "THE"!

THIS SURVEY'S ASKING ME IF I'M EITHER AN INFLUENCER OR DECISION-MAKER WHEN IT COMES TO SOFTWARE IMPLEMENTATION IN THE COMPANY.
ALL FRONT-LINE PEOPLE ARE. OBSERVE.
COPYRIGHT © 2002 ILLIAD HTTP://WWW.USERFRIENDLY.ORG/

GREG, DID YOU INSTALL WIN2000 OVER WIN98 ON MY MACHINE YET?
YEP. DID IT LAST NIGHT.
AH GREAT. THANKS.

YOU DIDN'T ACTUALLY CHANGE ANYTHING ON HIS MACHINE, DID YOU.
JUST THE WALLPAPER. IT SAYS 'WINDOWS 2000' NOW.

SEE. IT PAYS TO BE A FRONT LINE TECH. WE'RE THE ONES WHO MAKE THE REAL DECISIONS IN THE COMPANY.
COPYRIGHT © 2002 ILLIAD HTTP://WWW.USERFRIENDLY.ORG/

WHAT MAKES YOU THINK YOU TECHS ARE THE REAL DECISION-MAKERS?
DUDE. I HAVE ROOT ON YOUR WORKSTATION.

'DUDE'. I HAVE YOUR **PAYCHEQUES**.
UMM...HOW HARD SHALL WE PULL THE OARS, SIR?

SO I EXPLAINED TO THEM THAT I WAS THE ONE WHO HAD THE **PAY-CHEQUES**, SO I WAS THE **REAL** DECISION MAKER IN THE COMPANY AND...WHAT ARE YOU DOING?
REPLACING YOUR KEYBOARD WITH A PUNCH CARD READER.
COPYRIGHT © 2002 ILLIAD HTTP://WWW.USERFRIENDLY.ORG/

STRAIGHTEN
FIDDLE

IT DOESN'T COME WITH A MANUAL DOES IT.
JUST A BIOLOGICAL ONE. A **DECISION-MAKING**, BIOLOGICAL ONE.

NO "CHRISTMAS TOY MUST-HAVE" IN 2001 EXPLAINED: TAKING TICKLE-ME-ELMO SPINOFFS TO EXTREMES

PICKLE-
ME-
CTHULHU
COPYRIGHT © 2002 ILLIAD HTTP://WWW.USERFRIENDLY.ORG/

I don't understand why someone hasn't marketed these. They'd be the Toy of the Year, especially if made edible.

See all that black ink on these two pages? This is why this book is so expensive. We used ink harvested from baby squidlings.

THIS QUIBBLING ABOUT WHO THE DECISION-MAKER IS STOPS NOW. DO YOU TWO HAVE ANY IDEA HOW POWER STRUGGLES INVARIABLY END?

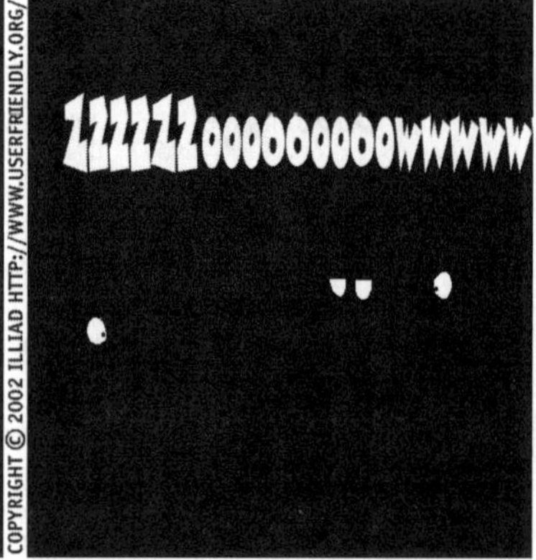
ZZZZZZOOOOOOOOOWWWWW

SO. DID YOU NOT DO THE FINANCE GUY THING THIS WEEK AND NEGLECT TO PAY THE ELECTRICITY BILL?
LOOK I CAN'T GET THAT STUPID PUNCH-CARD READER TO WORK!
ALL YOU GOTTA DO IS ASK, MAN. THAT, AND KNEEL.

SEE WHAT THIS IDIOTIC POWER STRUGGLE HAS BROUGHT? DARKNESS. THICK INKY BLACKNESS. AN UMBRA OF EMPTINESS AND DESPAIR.

MY TWO SENIOR PEOPLE HAD TO LOCK HORNS, AND NOW SOME ACCOUNTS CLERK AT THE POWER COMPANY HAS ONE-UPPED BOTH OF YOU AND.......WHO'S THERE?
IT'S ME. MIKE.

MIKE, I WANT YOU TO TELL THESE TWO UBER-DORKS WHO'VE BEEN FIGHTING SO MUCH THAT THEY GOT IN THE WAY OF PAYING A UTILITY BILL WHY WE DON'T HAVE POWER RIGHT NOW.
UM. STEF TRIPPED OVER THE MAINS.

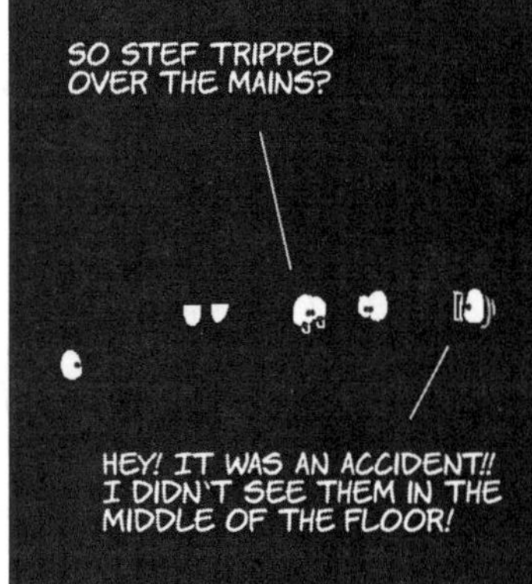
SO STEF TRIPPED OVER THE MAINS?
HEY! IT WAS AN ACCIDENT!! I DIDN'T SEE THEM IN THE MIDDLE OF THE FLOOR!

AND THE HAZARD STRIPES AND THE SIGN SAYING "POWER MAINS. DO NOT TRIP OVER" WERE TOO CRYPTIC FOR YOU?
LISTEN, I ALREADY SAID I DIDN'T KNOW HOW IT HAPPENED..

I'LL BET THIS HAPPENED BECAUSE YOU DIDN'T FORWARD ONE OF THOSE CHAIN LETTER EMAILS.
WHA...UH... YOU REALLY THINK SO?
I IGNORE THOSE CHAIN THINGS. FROM THE NUMBER OF CHAINS I'VE BROKEN I SHOULD BE DEAD AND STARRING ON SURVIVOR: IN HELL BY NOW.

SID CALLS THE POWER COMPANY FOR HELP, THEN UPDATES EVERY-ONE, STARTING WITH A.J. AND GREG...
THE HYDRO COMPANY'S SENDING SOMEONE OUT HERE TO FIX THINGS. MIGHT BE A COUPLE OF HOURS OR SO.
HEH. WELL! WE CERTAINLY CAN'T WORK WITHOUT POWER, SO I GUESS I'LL JUST PLAY SOME QUAKE!
A.J., WE DON'T HAVE POWER.

OH. UH. MAYBE SOME UNREAL TOURNAMENT THEN. YEAH.
A.J. WE. DON'T. HAVE. POWER.

HOW ABOUT DIABLO? OR SOLITAIRE! HEY, I'LL BE HAPPY WITH NETHACK. THAT DOESN'T TAKE MUCH POWER...
DUDE, DON'T MAKE ME SMACK YOU!
LET HIM GO, MAN. HE'S GONE.

WHAT'S GOING ON OUT THERE?
NOOOO
SKUF
SCUFF
SKUF
RELAX CHIEF. GREG'S JUST TRYING TO SAVE A.J.
COPYRIGHT © 2002 ILLIAD HTTP://WWW.USERFRIENDLY.ORG/

SAVE A.J.? WHAT'RE YOU TALKING ABOUT?
WHIFF
SCUFF
SKUFF
SKIFF
A.J. FAINTED FROM COMPUTER GAME WITHDRAWAL AND I GUESS GREG FANCIES HIMSELF A PARAMEDIC.

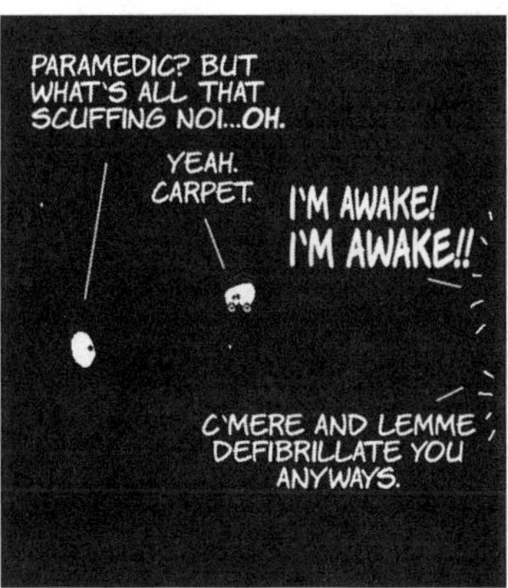
PARAMEDIC? BUT WHAT'S ALL THAT SCUFFING NOI...OH.
YEAH. CARPET.
I'M AWAKE! I'M AWAKE!!
C'MERE AND LEMME DEFIBRILLATE YOU ANYWAYS.

HOW ARE THE SERVERS MIKE?
THEY'RE FINE. THE U.P.SES SHOULD HAVE ENOUGH JUICE UNTIL THE HYDRO GUYS GET HERE.
WE HAVE U.P.SES?
YES WE DO. FOR THE SERVERS.
COPYRIGHT © 2002 ILLIAD HTTP://WWW.USERFRIENDLY.ORG/

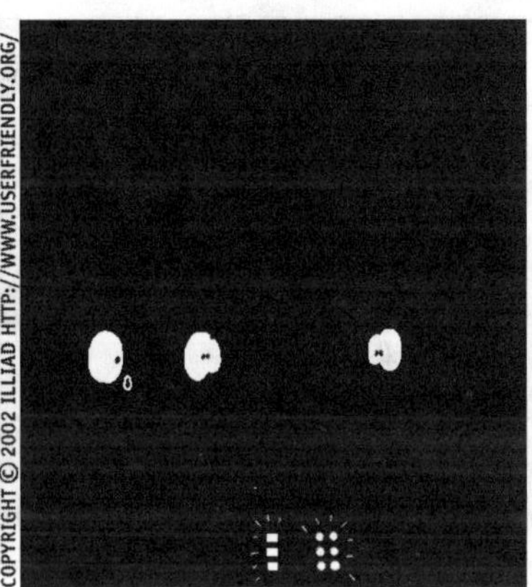

I THINK HE STOPPED BREATHING.
A.J.?! SAY SOMETHING!
PEEP

A REJECTED NAME AND MARKETING SLOGAN FOR THE NEW iMAC

iStalk

Peer Over Your Horizons

THE HYDRO PEOPLE SHOULD BE HERE ANY MINUTE, CHIEF.
AH GOOD. I'M SURE WE'RE ALL MORE THAN READY TO GET BACK TO WORK.
COPYRIGHT © 2002 ILLIAD HTTP://WWW.USERFRIENDLY.ORG/

AND I'M PLEASED TO SEE HOW WELL EVERYONE PULLED TOGETHER DURING THIS MINOR CRISIS. MIKE APPARENTLY EVEN WENT OUT OF HIS WAY TO FIND SOME SPARE POWER FOR A.J.
DID HE NOW.

BUT ALL I HAVE LEFT UNTIL PAYDAY IS FIVE BUCKS!
LOOK. YOU WANT TO PLAY ONE MORE TURN OF CIV THREE OR NOT?

I think I was hitting the bong pretty hard that week.

HEY. ARE YOU THE HYDRO GUY? WE'VE BEEN DYING FOR YOU TO GIVE US BACK POWER.
YEAH. I'M JUST ABOUT TO BRING THE MAINS BACK. HERE WE GO...
COPYRIGHT © 2002 ILLIAD HTTP://WWW.USERFRIENDLY.ORG/

KA-CHUNKA!
BUTTER

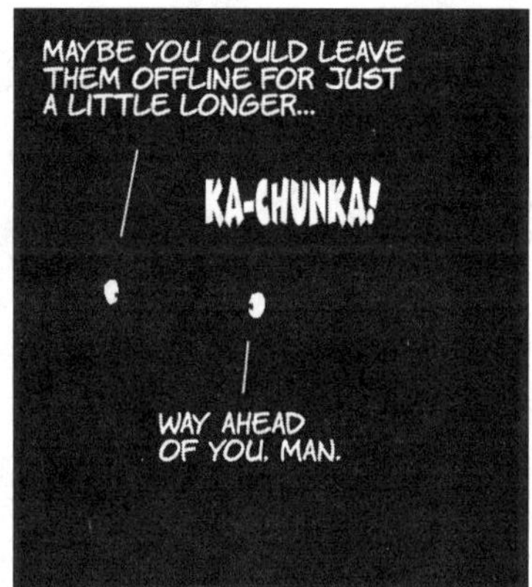
MAYBE YOU COULD LEAVE THEM OFFLINE FOR JUST A LITTLE LONGER...
KA-CHUNKA!
WAY AHEAD OF YOU, MAN.

WOW. THE ECONOMY REALLY STINKS RIGHT NOW.
COPYRIGHT © 2002 ILLIAD HTTP://WWW.USERFRIENDLY.ORG/

TELL ME ABOUT IT. I WAS ONCE ON TOP OF THE WORLD. I HAD THOUSANDS OF MINIONS AT MY BECK AND CALL. I BROUGHT ABOUT QUALITY DARKNESS. AND ALL THE THANKS I GET IS A PINK SLIP.

SAY. DON'T I KNOW YOU?
AND YOU KNOW WHAT THEY'RE GONNA GET WITH CHEAP CONTRACTORS? CHEAP DARKNESS! THE CHEAP, NASTY BARBIE-THEMED DESKTOP PC KIND!

CRUD PUPPY DROWNS HIS SORROWS AT THE LOCAL WATERING HOLE WITH HIS PEER, CTHULHU...
YOU HAVE GOTTA BE KIDDING ME. YOU GOT FIRED FROM AOL?
YEAH. I GOT REPLACED BY A GREATER EVIL.
COPYRIGHT © 2002 ILLIAD HTTP://WWW.USERFRIENDLY.ORG/

A GREATER EVIL THAN YOU?! YOU'RE AS EVIL AS I AM! WHO COULD BE MORE EVIL THAN...

WAIT A SECOND. NOT HIM?!
YEAH. THE GUY WHO CAME UP WITH THE X-10 POP-UNDER ADS.

YOU HAVE TO GET YOUR JOB BACK! ALL WE NEED TO DO IS COME UP WITH SOMETHING MORE EVIL THAN THOSE X-10 POP-UNDER ADS.
YOU'RE RIGHT! LET'S SEE NOW...
WOBBLE
COPYRIGHT © 2002 ILLIAD HTTP://WWW.USERFRIENDLY.ORG/

BOY THAT'S A TOUGH ONE.
LOOK. JUST GIVE ME A MINUTE...

LOOK MAN. IF YOU CAN'T GET YOUR OLD JOB BACK, WHAT ABOUT APPLYING ELSEWHERE? I'M SURE THERE ARE OTHER COMPANIES THAT NEED YOUR KIND OF EVIL.
YOU'RE RIGHT. LEMME THINK...
COPYRIGHT © 2002 ILLIAD HTTP://WWW.USERFRIENDLY.ORG/

I CAN'T GO TO MICROSOFT. THERE'S BAD BLOOD THERE. MAYBE I SHOULD THINK ABOUT AN INDUSTRY OTHER THAN HI-TECH?
GREAT IDEA! WHAT ABOUT LUCASFILM? THEY'RE GOING TO BE HARD-PRESSED TO TOP THE EVIL OF JAR JAR BINKS.
FORGET IT MAN. WE GOT LAID OFF FROM THERE.

WHO IN UNHOLY HADES ARE YOU?
NSYNC. WE WERE GONNA BE SO COOL.
FINALLY.
I WANNA BE A JEDI!!

WHAT IT MIGHT LOOK LIKE IF: AOL BUYS OUT RED HAT

```
-rw-r--r-- 1 jdf jdf 19757 Jul 20 00:32 zot.txt
-rw-r--r-- 1 jdf jdf 19757 Jul 20 00:32 zpt.txt
-rw-r--r-- 1 jdf jdf 19757 Jul 20 00:33 zzt.txt
 ********************************************
        Shock the Monkey and WIN $25.00!
    <..>
     ""
    /  \
         [use arrows keys and spacebar]
 (and if you don't play, you don't get your
  command line back...)
 ********************************************

[jdf@grail]$
```

USERFRIENDLY DOT ORG

I GOT LAID OFF FROM AOL. I CAN'T GO BACK TO MICROSOFT BECAUSE OF BAD BLOOD. LUCASFILM DITCHED NSYNC SO THEY OBVIOUSLY HAVE NO ROOM FOR MORE EVIL. SO NOW WHAT AM I GOING TO DO?

COPYRIGHT © 2002 ILLIAD HTTP://WWW.USERFRIENDLY.ORG/
HELLO? CTHULHU? HEY. WHERE'D YOU GO? AND WHERE'RE THOSE NSYNC GUYS?
I JUST HAD LUNCH.

YOU HAD LUNCH WITHOUT ME?!
DUDE. THERE WERE ONLY FIVE OF THEM.

UH HEY...WHERE'D YOU GET THE NEW DUDS?
THEY CAME WITH THE BODY.

COPYRIGHT © 2002 ILLIAD HTTP://WWW.USERFRIENDLY.ORG/
THE BODY? WHAT?
YEP. I GOT TIRED OF THE OLD ONE THAT USED TO BELONG TO A LAWYER.

THIS BODY WAS JUST LYING BACK THERE ON THE BAR FLOOR. WITH-OUT A HEAD. THE FIT WAS PERFECT.
AWWW MAN. THAT WAS MY LEFTOVERS!

LIGHT! SWEET LIGHT. O DRINK OF DAY! HOLDING RABID NIGHT AT BAY! INCANDESCENTLY. YOU SHOW, OUR HUMAN EYES ELECTRONS FLOW!

COPYRIGHT © 2002 ILLIAD HTTP://WWW.USERFRIENDLY.ORG/
ELECTRICITY! IS WHAT WE REQUIRE. OUR SCREENS ALIT WITH PHOSPHOR FIRE! TO WORK! TO PLAY! WE INTERMIX! PRINTER QUEUES AND RAINBOW SIX.

A WEALTH HAVE WE OF BACKUP POWER! NO BLACKOUT SHALL OUR WORK DEVOUR! FROM THIS SLICE OF TIME WE'VE LEARNED THAT DARKNESS HERE SHALL NOT RETURN!
O YE OF LITTLE FAITH...

WELL. HERE GOES NOTHING.

COPYRIGHT © 2002 ILLIAD HTTP://WWW.USERFRIENDLY.ORG/
AHEM.

NICE GETUP ILLIAD. BUT IT'S NOT THE FIRST OF APRIL YET.
SON OF A... I'VE BEEN DISSED!

FORGOTTEN ME ALREADY? I'M WOUNDED. TRULY. I HAD BROUGHT NIGHTMARISH FEAR AND DARKNESS INTO YOUR LIFE NOT THAT LONG AGO.
...ERM...
COPYRIGHT © 2002 ILLIAD HTTP://WWW.USERFRIENDLY.ORG/

I TOOK OVER YOUR BODY ONCE. REMEMBER? AND BEFORE THAT-
CR...CRUD PUPPY?
THE ONE. THE ONLY!

I...I DON'T BELIEVE YOU. YOU CAN'T BE HIM. YOU'RE JUST A GUY WEARING A NASTY MASK.
THEN TRY RIPPING HIS MASK OFF.
I GUARANTEE PLENTY OF WET NOISES.

OKAY. WHO THE HELL ARE YOU AND WHY ARE YOU HARASSING ONE OF MY STAFF?
CAREFUL SID. THAT'S CRUD PUPPY. HE USED TO WORK FOR AOL AS THEIR VICE PRESIDENT OF DIABOLISM.
COPYRIGHT © 2002 ILLIAD HTTP://WWW.USERFRIENDLY.ORG/

AOL. HUH?
YEP.

TOO BAD YOU MISSED OUT ON THAT MICROSOFT LAWSUIT. SOUNDS LIKE A REAL PIRAHNA POOL.
SWEET FANCY MOSES! JUST TEAR MY... I MEAN. THE BODY'S HEART OUT OF IT WHY DON'T YOU?!

YOU'RE RIGHT. FOR SOME REASON THIS ONE IS DOING RATHER WELL...
amazon.com

Kudos to Jeff Bezos for keeping Amazon afloat (and, in fact, thriving) while dozens of other more likely companies folded and went kaput. I still don't forgive him for that one-click patent nonsense, though.

IF I DIDN'T KNOW BETTER. I'D SAY THAT THE UNIVERSE HAS GONE WEIRD ON ME. I'M ONE OF THE GREATEST INCARNATIONS OF FEAR AND EVIL. AND I GET DISSED AND EMOTIONALLY SCARRED IN A SINGLE DAY!

NOT TOO LONG AGO I WAS THE NIGHTMARE THAT NO ONE COULD TALK ABOUT! NOW IT SEEMS LIKE EVERYTHING HAS CHANGED...NOTHING'S THE SAME ANYMORE AND I DON'T KNOW WHAT TO DO...

THIS WORLD IS JUST GOING TO HELL.
R'LYEH. ACTUALLY.
WHATEVER.

HEY! IS THAT AN EVIL. SPASTIC GRIN I SEE?
OH YEAH! I FIGURED OUT MY PROBLEM. I NEEDED A BREAK FROM REGULAR. PEDESTRIAN EVIL. I HAD TO DO SOMETHING THAT WOULD SHAKE THE FOUNDATIONS OF GEEKDOM.

SO WHAT DID YOU DO?
I SIGNED THE GUYS AT THE ISP TO A NEW CONTRACT.

THE BACK END BOYZ™
WE'RE GONNA KILL YOU. MAN.
BUT HE PROMISED ME WE COULD ALL BE JEDIS IN 'THE ATTACK OF THE CLONES'!
A.J...!!

HELLO.
TECH SUPPORT. RIGHT? WHEN WERE YOU GOING TO CALL ME BACK WITH A SOLUTION TO MY CONFIG PROBLEM?

I CAN'T DO THIS.
CONTRACT!

"OH BABY. BABY. TONIGHT'S THE NIGHT..."
WHAT THE...
AHHHHH. MUSIC TO MY EARS ALONE.

GREG SPEAKING.
GREG?! ARE YOU THE GREG FROM THE BACK END BOYZ? THE INCREDIBLY CUTE ONE?
WHY UM..YES. YES I AM MISS.

OH THIS IS SO COOL! TEE HEE! WAIT'LL MY FRIENDS HEAR ABOUT THIS! TEE HEE HEE!
HEH HEH... YEAH. I GET THAT A LOT.

AND ARE YOUR FRIENDS AS CUTE AS YOU SOUND?
I SUPPOSE IN THE RIGHT LIGHT AND WITH ENOUGH BEER THE SMILING MAN COULD LOOK TASTY. TEE. HEE. HEE.

BUT HOW COULD YOU DO THIS TO ME?!
ERWIN, I'M SORRY. THE CONTRACT WAS QUITE SPECIFIC. YOU'RE THE DRUM MACHINE FOR THE BACK END BOYZ NOW.
COPYRIGHT © 2002 ILLIAD HTTP://WWW.USERFRIENDLY.ORG/

FINE. I'M A DRUM MACHINE. BUT PLEASE READ TO ME THE PART IN THE CONTRACT THAT STATES WHY YOU HAD TO PUT ME IN THIS THING.
OKAY...UM...

"BECAUSE IT'S HIP."
AARRRRGH!
NO. WAIT. THAT'S JUST JUSTIFICATION FOR THE PRICE.
ROTO ROUTER

YO. YOU BACK END BOYZ HAVE A GIG TOMORROW.
A GIG? WHERE?
DON'T TELL ME WE HAVE TO DANCE AND SING IN A HIGH SCHOOL SOMEWHERE...
COPYRIGHT © 2002 ILLIAD HTTP://WWW.USERFRIENDLY.ORG/

WAIT! WE ACTUALLY HAVE TO PERFORM?!
I CAN'T DO THAT! I'LL GET NERVOUS AND START TALKING LIKE A GIRL!
PERFECT. TOMORROW'S THE DAY YOU NEED TO BE YOUR BACK END BEST.

WHAT'S SO SPECIAL ABOUT TOMORROW?
OH. NOTHING.

USER
FRIENDLY
the comic strip
PIZZA
Portrasher 4
ROTO-ROUTER 800
Copyright © 1997-2002 Illiad

WELL GUYS. HERE WE ARE.
SID? WHEN YOU SAID "WE'VE GOT A GIG" YOU DIDN'T MEAN HARD DRIVE SPACE. DID YOU.

LADIES AND GENTLEMEN..! MARIAH CAREY WILL NOT BE SINGING THE NATIONAL ANTHEM FOR US TODAY DUE TO THE FACT THAT SHE COULDN'T FIND A BELT TO MATCH THE HANDKERCHIEF SHE WAS WEARING AS A DRESS. WE ARE INSTEAD PLEASED TO BRING YOU....THE BACK END BOYZ !

A ONE...A TWO...
OHHH HEY CAN YOU SEE.
(BABY BABY)
BY THE DAWN'S EARLY LIGHT.
(TONIGHT BABY)
WHAT SO PROUDLY WE HAILED.
(MMMMMMMM!)
AT THE TWILIGHT'S LAST DREAMING
(OF YOU BABY!)

RUMMBLE
POW!

WHAT THE HELL WAS THAT?!
COACH SENT US.
SOMETHING ABOUT A "BAD AUDIBLE."

YESTERDAY AT THE WORLD ECONOMIC FORUM, BILL GATES SAID HE DID NOT SEE AN ECONOMIC RECOVERY IN 2002. THIS MORNING HE REINFORCED HIS PREDICTIONS WITH ANOTHER STATEMENT.
COPYRIGHT © 2002 ILLIAD HTTP://WWW.USERFRIENDLY.ORG/

"EVEN FOR THE WEALTHY, DISPOSABLE INCOME IS AT A LOW THESE DAYS. DON'T BE SURPRISED IF THE RICH REFRAIN FROM PARTAKING IN THEIR USUAL LUXURIES," SAID THE SOFTWARE MOGUL.

WHEN ASKED WHY, GATES DID NOT REPLY, UNTIL ANOTHER REPORTER SAID, "YOU BET A WHOLE BUNCH ON THE RAMS, DIDN'T YOU MR. GATES." GATES' COMMENT WAS "NNNNGGGGFRGURGLE"

Y'KNOW, THIS BOY BAND GIG IS RIPPINGLY LUCRATIVE. I'M SCOOPING HUGE COIN FOR BOOKING THESE GUYS.
PEOPLE ARE PAYING YOU TO HAVE THEM PERFORM?
COPYRIGHT © 2002 ILLIAD HTTP://WWW.USERFRIENDLY.ORG/

NO, THEY'RE PAYING ME TO KEEP THEM AWAY. IT ADDS A WHOLE NEW MEANING TO BEING A "RACKETEER." HEH. "ONE WHO MAKES A RACKET."

I WONDER IF BOYZ II MEN AND NEW KIDS ON THE BLOCK NEED A NEW AGENT...I COULD RUN ALL THREE OF THE BOY BANDS TOGETHER...
DUDE! THAT WOULD BE LIKE THE REAL "AXIS OF EVIL!"

SID, YOU HAVE TO GET US OUT OF THAT CONTRACT WITH THAT CRUD DUDE. HE FREAKS ME OUT. I CAN'T WORK FOR HIM!!
COPYRIGHT © 2002 ILLIAD HTTP://WWW.USERFRIENDLY.ORG/

I HAVE TO ADMIT HE'S KIND OF CREEPY LOOKING, BUT...
...HE'S GOT THOSE WHEEDLY LITTLE FINGERS INSIDE THAT BODY, PULLING ON THE TENDONS AND OTHER SPECIALTY MEATS. LIKE A PUPPETEER IN AN ABATTOIR.

THE BOY'S MISSING A CLOSING TAG IN HIS HEAD.
WE'RE CONTENDING WITH A CROSS BETWEEN THE FABLED JIM HENSON AND THE PERVERSITY OF CLIVE BARKER!

HELLO MR. CRUD. A MOMENT OF YOUR TIME, PLEASE. I BROUGHT A.J. HERE TO PROVE A POINT.
COPYRIGHT © 2002 ILLIAD HTTP://WWW.USERFRIENDLY.ORG/

SEE? HE'S JUST A GUY. ALBEIT A LITTLE CREEPY LOOKING.
POOT!
WHEEDLE WHEEDLE

A.J.!! WHAT IN THE NAME OF HADES ARE YOU DOING UP ON THE CEILING?!
CHEWING THROUGH IT, I THINK.

...THEN THE SENIOR TECH TURNED AROUND. I POPPED OUT OF THE BODY AND THE WEB WEENIE WENT FOR THE CEILING. WHEN THEY FINALLY PEELED HIM DOWN HE WAS WIBBLING TO HIMSELF.

HAHAHAHAHA! OH THAT'S GREAT...
YEAH. THE KID WENT RIGHT OUT OF HIS GOURD.

YOU KNOW, I REALLY NEEDED THAT REACTION. I WAS STARTING TO FEEL A LITTLE TAKEN FOR GRANTED.
OH CRY ME A RIVER. I HAVE TO DEAL WITH A PLUSH DOLL OF ME BEING CUDDLED BY GEEKS AT NIGHT.

I HAVE TO SAY I'M FEELING KIND OF GOOD ABOUT THE QUALITY OF THE EVIL I DOLE OUT THESE DAYS. I'D EVEN SAY I'M RIVALING THE VISCERAL KIND OF EVIL THAT YOU DO.
HAHAHAH!! OH THAT'S RICH, CRUD.
COPYRIGHT © 2002 ILLIAD HTTP://WWW.USERFRIENDLY.ORG/

WHAT, YOU DON'T THINK I COULD KICK YOU TO THE CURB?! WHY DON'T YOU TRY ME, SASHIMI HEAD?
YOU AND THAT MILLI VANILLI HAIRDO WANT A PIECE OF ME? THEN COME GET SOME!

GAAAH. MAYBE THIS WASN'T SUCH A GOOD IDEA...

One can also buy fuzzy Cthulhu slippers. They're a riot at slumber parties.

A QUICK SWITCH IN MARKETING MESSAGES MAKES EARTHLINK'S STARTREK.NET INTERNET ACCESS SUDDENLY PROFITABLE.
WHY YOU SHOULD BUY EarthLink's STAR TREK THEMED INTERNET ACCESS
1. EarthLink's Award-winning access
2. The Universe's ONLY Star Trek Themed Internet Access
3. A STARTREK.NET Email address
4. 24/7 Technical Support
1. SEVEN OF NINE PHOTO GALLERIES

Seven of Nine is a walking demonstration of anti-grav technology.

YOU WANT TO DO WHAT?
THEME-BRAND OUR CONNECTIVITY OFFERING JUST LIKE EARTHLINK DID WITH STARTREK.NET!
COPYRIGHT © 2002 ILLIAD HTTP://WWW.USERFRIENDLY.ORG/

SO I WENT AND CONTACTED A WELL-KNOWN CELEBRITY. AND HE'S MADE SOME THEME ELEMENTS FOR ME AS A DEMO. I WAS HOPING TO RUN THEM BY YOU FIRST BEFORE I TOOK IT TO THE CHIEF.

OH LORD. HERE IT COMES...
ANYWAY...I PRESENT TO YOU THE NEW WILLIAM SHATNER THEMED INTERNET ACCESS PACKAGE!
...YOU'VE! ...GOT! ...MAIL!

SO THE SHATNER DEMO DIDN'T WORK OUT. WHAT NEXT?
WE NEED TO BUY A LICENSE FROM ANOTHER WELL KNOWN ENTERTAINMENT PROPERTY. SOMEONE WHO HAS A SMALLER BUDGET THAN US.
COPYRIGHT © 2002 ILLIAD HTTP://WWW.USERFRIENDLY.ORG/

HOW ABOUT ENRON?
IT'S NOT AN ENTERTAINMENT PROPERTY.
THAT'S NOT WHAT THE MEDIA THINKS. IMAGINE THE TAG-LINE: "WE SHRED MAIL!"

Is there ever a time when Engrish isn't funny?

OKAY. CHECK THIS NEW THEME DEMO OUT. WHEN YOU LOG IN, AN ANIMATED CHARACTER POPS UP AND TELLS YOU IF YOU HAVE MAIL. A.J., PROCEED.
CLAPPITY TAPPITY
COPYRIGHT © 2002 ILLIAD HTTP://WWW.USERFRIENDLY.ORG/

AHAHAHAHAHAHAHAH! YOUR MAILBOX IS NOT HAVING ENJOYMENT!

OKAY. WHAT THE HELL DID YOU LICENSE?!
LOOK, I DON'T HAVE MUCH OF A BUDGET. OKAY?!
IT'S ONE OF THOSE BLACK AND WHITE GODZILLA MOVIES. HEY. THE WORDS ARE OUT OF SYNCH...

HELLO. SINCE TODAY IS SAINT VALENTINE'S DAY, A.J. SAID IT MIGHT BE FUN IF I EXPLAINED WHAT I'VE READ ABOUT THE HISTORY OF VALENTINE'S DAY CUSTOMS...
ROTO ROUTER
COPYRIGHT © 2002 ILLIAD HTTP://WWW.USERFRIENDLY.ORG/

MMMMMMMMMM!
ROTO ROUTER

WAS THAT CUSTOM BASED ON SOMETHING HISTORICAL?
THE SAINT VALENTINE'S DAY MASSACRE I THINK...
YEAH! GO ME...
ROTO ROUTER

I'VE GOT IT! WE CAN OFFER INTERNET ACCESS WITH A DUNE THEME!
YOU GOT DUNE?!? AS IN FRANK HERBERT'S DUNE?! HOW DID WE AFFORD THAT?
COPYRIGHT © 2002 ILLIAD HTTP://WWW.USERFRIENDLY.ORG/

STEF? WELL?
OKAY, MAYBE NOT FRANK HERBERT'S "DUNE" PER SE...
THIS IS AN ORDER FORM FOR NINE TRUCK LOADS OF SAND AND AN ARTICULATED SEWAGE PIPE.

WE'RE GOING AHEAD WITH THIS "DUNE" THEMED ACCESS? BUT WHAT'S THE HERBERT ESTATE GOING TO SAY?
NOTHING, IF WE DON'T USE ANY OBVIOUS DUNE INTELLECTUAL PROPERTY.
COPYRIGHT © 2002 ILLIAD HTTP://WWW.USERFRIENDLY.ORG/

THEN EXPLAIN TO ME WHY PEOPLE ARE GOING TO PAY A PREMIUM FOR "THEMED ACCESS"...
HEY, THEY'RE GETTING A "TOTAL DUNE EXPERIENCE"

THIS IS THE ADDRESS, ED! DUMP IT!
WHEEEE, I'M A SANDWORM.

Wheee! I'm a sandworm!

CENTURIES AGO, WHEN CRIMINALS WERE BRANDED, LITTLE DID THE LAWMAKERS REALIZE THAT THE FUTURE WOULD CREATE A NEW DESIGN FOR THE BRAND DENOTING "GOLD ROBBER."

WINTER GAMES 2002
SKATING JUDGE

When I went to see the *Dune* movie (the one directed by David Lynch), I was all psyched up about how they showed the Voice being used. Speakers behind us echoed the voiced command with all kinds of weird reverb and effects. They cast many of the characters very well. The music was good, and Brian Eno's "Prophecy Theme" was astonishingly powerful. And then I saw the stillsuits. Thick black rubber. In the hot desert. The battle at the end was fought by an army of Michelin Men. And that was just the beginning of the travesties. I cried for days.

I CAN'T BELIEVE WHAT YOU'RE ASKING ME!
YOU HAVE TO DO IT. IT'S PART OF THE DUNE EXPERIENCE OUR USERS GET.
COPYRIGHT © 2002 ILLIAD HTTP://WWW.USERFRIENDLY.ORG/

THIS IS SO WRONG...
RING! RING!
RING! RING!

ANSWER THE PHONE!!
ARRAKIS INTERNET. I LOOK LIKE STING AND I'M WEARING A LEATHER LOINCLOTH. WHAT CAN I DO FOR YOU.

GREG THE TECH GHOLA SPEAKING.
HI...I JUST SPENT THREE HOURS TYPING A LETTER AND WINDOWS WENT ALL BLUE AND I READ THAT WITH THIS DUNE THEMED ACCESS I CAN VOICE YOU TO SUPPORT ME...
COPYRIGHT © 2002 ILLIAD HTTP://WWW.USERFRIENDLY.ORG/

SO I'M VOICING YOU TO TYPE OUT MY LETTER FOR ME.
LOOK... ...LADY...

IT'S THE VOICE! YOU HAVE TO!
I DO NOT!
...AND I WANT YOU TO WRITE IT WITH EMACS IF YOU USE VI. AND VI IF YOU USE EMACS.

THIS VOICE FEATURE IS PRETTY COOL. I CAN GET YOU TO DO ANYTHING I WANT.
WITHIN THE LIMITS OF TECHNICAL SERVICE.
COPYRIGHT © 2002 ILLIAD HTTP://WWW.USERFRIENDLY.ORG/

OH. GETTING SMART WITH ME NOW ARE YOU? I'LL VOICE YOU TO WRITE WEB PAGES WITH FRONTPAGE IF YOU DON'T WATCH IT.
AND WHAT IF I DON'T HEED YOUR "VOICE"?

THEN THE SERVICE CONTRACT SAYS I CAN GET YOU WITH MY "GOM JAR JAR."
HAD A LITTLE TROUBLE KEEPING "STAR WARS" AND "DUNE" SEPARATE DID WE?
WHAT? THEY'RE BOTH SPACE MOVIES. RIGHT?

HELLO? MY COMPUTER MADE SOME BAD NOISES AND NOW IT DOESN'T GIVE ME THE "DUNE" INTERNET. THE SCREEN IS ALL DARK.
OKAY...IS THE COMPUTER GETTING ANY POWER?
COPYRIGHT © 2002 ILLIAD HTTP://WWW.USERFRIENDLY.ORG/

UM...WHICH PART IS THE COMPUTER? THE MONITOR OR THE BOX THING?
THE BOX. THAT'S THE PART THAT DOES ALL OF THE WORK.

HUNH. I'M GONNA OPEN IT UP. AND YOU CAN TELL ME HOW TO FIX IT. WHAT'S IN THE BOX, ANYWAYS?
AT THIS RATE...PAIN.

THIS WHOLE "THEMED INTERNET ACCESS" THING BITES THE BIG WET STINKY. I'M GETTING REALLY TIRED OF DUNE-REFERENCE-THIS AND DUNE-REFERENCE-THAT...
AND I THINK I'M READY FOR A NAP.

COPYRIGHT © 2002 ILLIAD HTTP://WWW.USERFRIENDLY.ORG/

THE SLEEPER MUST AWAKEN!

AJ? GOT A MINUTE?
LOOK. IF IT'S ABOUT THAT STUPID "DUNE" THEMED ACCESS...

COPYRIGHT © 2002 ILLIAD HTTP://WWW.USERFRIENDLY.ORG/
JUST HEAR ME OUT. DO YOU KNOW IF YOU CAN RUN VNC INSIDE ANOTHER SESSION OF VNC?
VIRTUAL NETWORK COMPUTING? I... UM...I THINK SO...

SO WE COULD RUN THIS VNC-WITHIN-VNC STUFF OVER A CUSTOMER'S LOCAL AREA NETWORK?
LANS WITHIN LANS WITHIN LA...NO!!! WE CAN'T!

CHUCK JONES
IN MEMORIAM, 1912-2002
Characters with Heart
+
making people laugh
= Immortality
FINALLY. A PLAN THAT WORKED.

STEF. THE NUMBERS DON'T LOOK THAT PROMISING FOR YOUR THEMED INTERNET ACCESS. CONSUMERS AREN'T REALLY BUYING INTO IT.
WE JUST NEED SOMETHING MORE SHOWY. SOMETHING WITH **SPLASH**. SOMETHING TOTALLY ***DUNE.***
MIKE AND I COULD STAGE A KNIFE FIGHT IN LOINCLOTHS.

WELL. BACK TO PASTY-WHITE VANILLA ACCESS WE GO.
THAT HAD BETTER NOT BE A CRACK ABOUT MY LACK OF A TAN.
GOOD LORD. I THINK I'VE GONE BLIND.

CODE
INDENT
INDENT
COMMENT
CODE

WHA...***WHAT*** IN NAME OF **SAURON** IS THIS?!
HE JUST INSTALLED WINDOWS XP.

HEY...WHERE DID MY INFRARED KEYBOARD GO?

HEY. WHAT ARE YOU DOING UP THERE?
EVER SINCE I INSTALLED XP I'M JUST SOARING WITH JOY AND PRODUCTIVITY!
PRODUCTIVITY? UP THERE?

HEY! GIVE ME BACK MY KEYBOARD!
DAMN. WHERE'S A STIFF BREEZE WHEN YOU NEED ONE?

STEF. YOU HAVE TO COME DOWN FROM THERE.
BUT WHY? THIS IS FUN! IT'S SPIFFY! AND ALL IT TOOK WAS INSTALLING XP!

BE THAT AS IT MAY. YOU COULD AFFECT MY STAFF WITH ALL OF THIS FLOAT...UH...

YE GODS, A.J., YOU **DIDN'T!**
Y'KNOW. THIS IS ACTUALLY KINDA COOL.

OKAY. WAIT. YOU'RE TELLING ME IF YOU INSTALL XP, YOU CAN FLOAT LIKE THAT?
YEP. IT'S PART OF THE 'WINDOWS XPERIENCE' PROMISED BY THE COMMERCIALS ON TV.
COPYRIGHT © 2002 ILLIAD HTTP://WWW.USERFRIENDLY.ORG/

PITR MADE DUST PUPPY INSTALL XP FOR HIM.
HUNH? TO WHAT END?

AM ALWAYS WANTINK HAIRY BALLOON...

SID, DO WE REALLY KNOW MUCH ABOUT THIS FLOATING AROUND BUSINESS? I MEAN, WHAT ARE THE PARAMETERS?
HOW DO YOU MEAN?
COPYRIGHT © 2002 ILLIAD HTTP://WWW.USERFRIENDLY.ORG/

WELL, FOR EXAMPLE, ALL OF STEF'S "FLOATING" SO FAR HAS BEEN DONE INDOORS. THERE ARE PHYSICAL LIMITS.
UH. HE JUST WENT OUT FOR LUNCH.

MICROSOFT TECH SUPPORT...
GET ME DOWN FROM HERE!!!

JUST SO WE DON'T RISK ANY "CONSTITUTIONAL QUESTIONS" IN THE MICROSOFT SETTLEMENT, A 28TH AMENDMENT TO THE U.S. CONSTITUTION IS PROPOSED.
shall take effect until an
election of Representatives
shall have intervened.
XVIII
MICROSOFT
ØWNS j00

Mistake in the 'toon: I'm missing an X in XXVIII.

Week of March 4th, 2002

We all miss you Opus, and we hope your wish for wings that work was answered.

LISTEN. I'M TIRED OF "SOARING" AND I NEED TO COME DOWN FROM HERE NOW!
YES SIR. HOW HIGH UP ARE YOU?
COPYRIGHT © 2002 ILLIAD HTTP://WWW.USERFRIENDLY.ORG/

I DON'T KNOW. BUT CARS LOOK LIKE ANTS BELOW ME. AND I HAVE A BIRD ON MY HEAD.
MAH

AH. THIS ISN'T A DOCUMENTED BUG SIR. YOU MAY JUST HAVE TO RIDE IT OUT.
YE FLIPPING GODS. THIS IS THE BLUE SKY OF DEATH.

WE'RE WORKING ON THE PROBLEM SIR. WHAT ELSE DO YOU SEE?
MEH!
THERE'S A PENGUIN STARING UP AT ME.
A PENGUIN? ARE YOU OVER ANTARCTICA?
NO. I'M DOWNTOWN. NOW HE'S RUNNING INTO A COMPUTER SHOP.
COPYRIGHT © 2002 ILLIAD HTTP://WWW.USERFRIENDLY.ORG/

AND NOW HE'S RUNNING INTO A HOUSE. AND HE HAS A BOX UNDER A WING.
WHAT?
YOU KNOW. HE LOOKS KIND OF FAMILIAR.

INSTALLING... PREPARE FOR THE WINDOWS XPERIENCE!
OH PLEASE OH PLEASE...

HELLO. SIR?
DON'T PUT ME ON HOLD AGAIN! I'VE BEEN UP HERE FOR HOURS!
COPYRIGHT © 2002 ILLIAD HTTP://WWW.USERFRIENDLY.ORG/

YES SIR. JUST GOT WORD FROM UPSTAIRS.
AND?

BAGWAN
WE'RE VERY PLEASED YOU'RE ENJOYING THE "PERPETUAL-SOAR" FEATURE OF OUR PRODUCT.
YEAH. I GOT YOUR "PERPETUAL-SORE" RIGHT HERE...

SIR. IF YOU'LL JUST HOLD ON A LITTLE LONGER WE'LL HAVE A SOLUTION FOR YOU...
HURRY UP!!!
COPYRIGHT © 2002 ILLIAD HTTP://WWW.USERFRIENDLY.ORG/

ANOTHER "I'M FLYING AND I CAN'T GET DOWN" PROBLEM I TAKE IT. HOW LONG'S THIS GUY BEEN HOLDING?
FIVE HOURS.

SHOULD BE A FEW MILES UP BY NOW.
AND OUT OF OXYGEN.
AND NO LONGER A PROBLEM.
HELLO?!?!? *GASP* HELLLOOO!!

IS STEF STILL UP THERE?
YES.
OKAY. HERE GOES.
STEF MURKY

COPYRIGHT © 2002 ILLIAD HTTP://WWW.USERFRIENDLY.ORG/
REBOOT!

WELL?
HE CRASHED. BADLY. BUT HIS CELL PHONE IS STILL INTACT.
SIR, IF YOU SHUT YOUR MACHINE DOWN PROPERLY, YOU WOULDN'T BE FEELING LIKE THIS.

Illiad, get thee to a punnery.

Y'KNOW, THIS NEW IMAC ISN'T SUCH A HARSH DEAL.

COPYRIGHT © 2002 ILLIAD HTTP://WWW.USERFRIENDLY.ORG/
I CAN MOVE THIS WAY, AND THAT WAY, AND OVER HERE...

THAT'S VERY ARTICULATE OF YOU.
WHY, THANK Y-GAH!!

THE NINE STATES HAVE ASKED MICROSOFT TO CREATE A "SINGLE, UNCOMMINGLED VERSION OF ITS OPERATING SYSTEM"

DONE.

Microsoft
Windows 95

COPYRIGHT © 2002 ILLIAD HTTP://WWW.USERFRIENDLY.ORG/

QUIT THAT! IT'S CREEPY!
SORRY DUDE. GOT MESMERIZED BY THAT BOIL ON YOUR NOSE.

WHAT'S NEW ON THE WEB ERWIN?
LET'S SEE...THE C.E.O. OF ICANN IS MOVING TO HAVE GOVERNMENTS TAKE OVER ADMINISTRATION OF THE INTERNET. HERE. READ IT.
COPYRIGHT © 2002 ILLIAD HTTP://WWW.USERFRIENDLY.ORG/

HM. AND THEY'RE DOING IT BECAUSE THEY WANT TO MAKE ICANN AN "AGILE, SUCCESSFUL" BODY.

KINDA LIKE BRITNEY SPEARS?
NO. WELL...I SUPPOSE THEY COU...NO!!! OH DEAR LORD NO.

ANYTHING ELSE IN THE NEWS?
JACK VALENTI OF THE MPAA WANTS ALL PCS TO HAVE STRONG COPY PROTECTION BUILT IN.
COPYRIGHT © 2002 ILLIAD HTTP://WWW.USERFRIENDLY.ORG/

YOU WERE WAITING FOR A PIG TO GO FLYING OVERHEAD WEREN'T YOU.
YA. HAD ME WORRIED FOR A SECOND THERE, BUT STEF'S OFF THE XP SOARING KICK.

HEY HAIRBALL. WHERE'S THAT SEGWAY YOUR DOPEY FRIEND WAS IN?
I'M NOT SURE... I THINK SID PUT IT IN THE BROOM CLOSET. WHY?
COPYRIGHT © 2002 ILLIAD HTTP://WWW.USERFRIENDLY.ORG/

THREE SEGWAYS ARE UP FOR AUCTION, AND THE BIDDING HAS GONE OVER THE $100,000 MARK ALREADY. I'M THINKING ABOUT SLAPPING A SUPERCHARGER ON IT. THAT SHOULD REALLY BOOST THE PRICE.

OOOH. A SEGWAY WITH A SUPERCHARGER. I WONDER WHAT I'D GET FOR IT?
HOPEFULLY A LONG OVERDUE DARWIN AWARD.

LOOK. I KNOW WHERE THE SEGWAY IS. IF YOU WANT IT, YOU HAVE TO BEAT DUST PUPPY AT A RETURN TO CASTLE WOLFENSTEIN DEATHMATCH.
HA! YOU'RE ON!

YOU GO PLAY ON YOUR MACHINE AND DUST PUPPY WILL PLAY ON ME.
STOP GABBING AND PREPARE TO GET FRAGGED!

COPYRIGHT © 2002 ILLIAD HTTP://WWW.USERFRIENDLY.ORG/
UM. THE GAME ISN'T AVAILABLE ON THE MAC. HOW CAN I WIN IF I CAN'T PLAY?
GIVE HIM HALF AN HOUR.

MM-HM. YES. I SEE.
COPYRIGHT © 2002 ILLIAD HTTP://WWW.USERFRIENDLY.ORG/

YES STEF. I KNOW. BYE BYE.

STEF?! I DIDN'T SEE STEF ANYWHERE. WHO WERE YOU TALKING TO? WHAT WAS THAT ALL ABOUT?
I SEE FRAGGED PEOPLE.

ALL THAT UNDERGROUND ICE ON MARS...
MARS
SHAZBAT. THERE GOES THE NEIGHBOURHOOD.

HEY CHIEF. DID YOU GET A CHANCE TO TRY OUT THAT NEW 32 MEG VIDEO CARD I INSTALLED IN YOUR HOME MACHINE?
UH. YEAH. IT'S GREAT. THANKS MIKE.
COPYRIGHT © 2002 ILLIAD HTTP://WWW.USERFRIENDLY.ORG/

COOL. JUST MAKING SURE.

I DIDN'T WANT TO TELL HIM. BUT EXCEL DOESN'T LOOK ANY BETTER.
YOU'RE SUPPOSED TO GET MORE "FAME PER SECOND" OR SOMETHING.

CAN I HELP YOU?
INDEED. ART THOU A.J. GARRETT?
COPYRIGHT © 2002 ILLIAD HTTP://WWW.USERFRIENDLY.ORG/

YES. WHO ARE YOU?
WEBLEY VERDIGRIS. INQUISITOR.

I THOUGHT THE CATHOLIC CHURCH DID AWAY WITH INQUISITORS ALMOST 200 YEARS AGO.
CATHOLIC CHURCH? I'M WITH THE NATIONAL ACADEMY OF RECORDING ARTS AND SCIENCES.

SO WHAT PRECISELY ARE YOU HERE INQUISITING?
OH. THE USUAL. I'M HERE TO STAMP OUT RAMPANT ACTS OF MUSIC PIRACY.
COPYRIGHT © 2002 ILLIAD HTTP://WWW.USERFRIENDLY.ORG/

I RECEIVED INFORMATION FROM A RELIABLE SOURCE. APPARENTLY THOU HAST BEEN RIPPING MUSIC FROM CDS INTO MP3 FORMAT. WE AT THE ACADEMY FROWN UPON THIS.

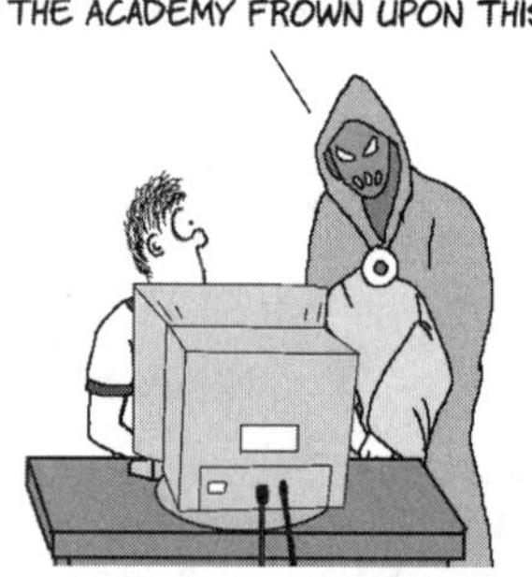

BUT I BOUGHT THE CD.
YES. BUT ONLY ONCE.

ARE YOU TRYING TO TELL ME I NEED TO PAY FOR THE CD AGAIN?
IT IS ONLY EQUITABLE. IS IT NOT?
COPYRIGHT © 2002 ILLIAD HTTP://WWW.USERFRIENDLY.ORG/

EQUITABLE? HOW?
THE ARTIST HATH LABOURED LONG AND HARD. POURING HIS SOUL INTO THE SONG AND DESERVES THE RICHES FOR EACH COPY OF IT THAT YOU ENJOY.

MISTER. I RIPPED THE HAMSTER DANCE.
DO I LOOK LIKE A CONFESSOR?

THOU ART SIMPLY NOT COMPREHENDING. IT IS THIS "I HAVE A RIGHT TO DO ANYTHING I WISH WITH THE MUSIC ON THIS CD" ATTITUDE THAT'S HARMING THE INDUSTRY.
COPYRIGHT © 2002 ILLIAD HTTP://WWW.USERFRIENDLY.ORG/

NO. I DON'T THINK THAT. I DON'T THINK I HAVE A RIGHT TO COPY THE CD AND SELL IT OR EVEN GIVE IT AWAY TO ANYONE. I JUST WANT TO BE ABLE TO ACCESS THE MUSIC I PAID FOR BEYOND MY "RIAA-APPROVED" CD PLAYER.

MY WORD. THY GREED KNOWS NO BOUNDS.
WHAT CAN I SAY. I'M AN ASPIRING MEDIA EXECUTIVE.

BY RIPPING MP3S, THOU ART HARMING THE POOR ARTISTS WHO RENDER THEIR SOULS INTO SUCH SWEET TONES.
COPYRIGHT © 2002 ILLIAD HTTP://WWW.USERFRIENDLY.ORG/

THINK OF THE STARVING MUSICIAN WHO HATH SLAVED INTO THE DARK HOURS! THINK OF THE POWDERED CHEESE FOOD THOU ART TAKING OUT OF HIS MOUTH WHEN THOU DOTH COPY HIS MUSIC!

OKAY. SO HOW ABOUT I JUST SEND THE ARTIST ANOTHER FIVE BUCKS?
NO!!! I MEAN...DON'T TROUBLE THYSELF...I CAN PASS THE MONEY ON TO HIM FOR THEE...

THE 'SENATOR FROM DISNEY' STARTS HIS OWN KIDS TELEVISION SHOW
PEE-AY-WHY OH-ELL-AY
EFF-OH-ARR-EM-EE!

INQUISITOR VERDIGRIS. HAST THOU MET WITH SUCCESS?
NAY. I HAVE FAILED THEE MY LORD. I WAS UNABLE TO CAUSE THE OFFENDER TO PAY AS HE SHOULD.

COPYRIGHT © 2002 ILLIAD HTTP://WWW.USERFRIENDLY.ORG/
IT SEEMS WE MUST ADJUST TO THIS AND SIMPLY LEARN TO TIGHTEN OUR BELTS.
INDEED.

MEET FOR LUNCH TOMORROW?
YES MY LORD. BUT IN CANCUN. NOT PARIS. MUST WATCH THE LEARJET BUDGET.

More disturbing than this cartoon is the fact that many, many readers wanted that kind of connection going into their heads.

MIKE? COULD YOU SET THINGS UP SO THAT MY BOX AT HOME CAN TALK TO THE LAN HERE?
NO. THAT'S PITR'S JOB.
DO I JUST ASK HIM?

COPYRIGHT © 2002 ILLIAD HTTP://WWW.USERFRIENDLY.ORG/
YES. BUT YOU KNOW HOW PITR IS. YOU'LL HAVE TO COAX HIM INTO IT. ALMOST WITHOUT HIS KNOWING.
OH. OKAY.

I DON'T SEE HOW STICKING CO-AX CABLE INTO PITR IS SUPPOSED TO HELP...
HEAD FEELINK FUNNY...BUT NOT ALTOGETHER UNPLEASANT...

A.J. STUCK A COAX CABLE INTO PITR'S HEAD.
HE WHAT?!

COPYRIGHT © 2002 ILLIAD HTTP://WWW.USERFRIENDLY.ORG/
YUP. AND GET THIS. FOR SOME REASON PITR'S DEEPEST THOUGHTS ARE COMING ACROSS THE NETWORK.
HIS DEEPEST THOUGHTS? LIKE WHAT?

"I THINK BABY ANIMALS ARE CUTE."
BUSTED.
GETTINK THIS THINK OUT OF MY HEAD!!!

SID? WHAT'S WITH THAT CABLE STUCK IN PITR'S HEAD?
HE'S NEUROMAGICALLY CONNECTED TO THE NET. IT'S AMAZING. REALLY.

COPYRIGHT © 2002 ILLIAD HTTP://WWW.USERFRIENDLY.ORG/
YOU MEAN HE'S PULLING DOWN DATA DIRECTLY INTO HIS BRAIN?
KIND OF. I'M GUESSING HIS SENSES ARE PROBABLY A LITTLE CONFUSED FROM THIS.

PUNCH THE MONKEY AND WIN $25!
HOLDINK STILL LEETLE MONKEY...

YOU CAN WHAT?
AM SEEINK WORLD AS WEB PAGES. AND HAVE FOUND WAY TO READ SOURCE. IS WERY INTERESTINK.
COPYRIGHT © 2002 ILLIAD HTTP://WWW.USERFRIENDLY.ORG/

YEAH? SO WHAT DOES MY SOURCE REVEAL?
HMM. LET ME BE CHECKINK.

YOUR <HEAD> TAGS ARE NESTED RIGHT UP IN YOUR <BODY> TAGS. EXPLAINS MANY THINKS.
OH. OKAY I--HEY!!

HM. WONDERINK WHAT OLD ZLOTNIK'S SOURCE IS LOOKINK LIKE...HMM...
COPYRIGHT © 2002 ILLIAD HTTP://WWW.USERFRIENDLY.ORG/

AH. NYET. <TITLE> TAG ENTRY IS NOT BEINK CORRECT. BUT EASY TO FIX.
TIK
TAK
ABUSE

PITR!!!
S. Dabster
Weenie

THE LITIGATION DOCUMENTS PREPARED BY INTEL OVER THE YOGA TRADEMARK INFRINGEMENT:

silliness
inside

Imagine the havoc one could cause with JavaScript if we could access people's source code. Pop-ups! Pop-unders! Play "The Chicken Dance" in the background and make it so they can't turn it off!

COPYRIGHT © 2002 ILLIAD HTTP://WWW.USERFRIENDLY.ORG/

PITR. I DON'T CARE...

...THAT IT'S THE FIRST OF APRIL...

...PUTTING <BLINK> TAGS IN MY SOURCE IS NOT FUNNY!

SID, WHAT ARE YOU DOING?
DEFUSING A PROBLEM. I'VE HAD IT WITH PITR MESSING AROUND WITH REALITY.
COPYRIGHT © 2002 ILLIAD HTTP://WWW.USERFRIENDLY.ORG/

IF THAT'S THE CABLE ATTACHED TO PITR'S HEAD YOU MIGHT WANT TO BE A LITTLE CAREFUL WITH IT.
YEEAH! I THINK IT JUST POPPED...
POOT!
SPOING!

...OFF
THROB

THE HELL IS THAT?
PITR'S BRAIN.
IT LOOKS LIKE A BIG FAT WET RAISIN.
COPYRIGHT © 2002 ILLIAD HTTP://WWW.USERFRIENDLY.ORG/

WHAT ARE YOU GONNA DO WITH IT?
DO WITH IT? IT'S A BRAIN, ERWIN. WHAT DO YOU SUGGEST?

ROLL THAT SUCKER IN OATS AND SELL IT AS BREAKFAST FOOD.
"RAISIN BRAIN?"
YE GODS. PITR DID SOMETHING ELSE TO REALITY...

IT SMELLS FUNNY.
WHAT'S ENCEPHALITIC FLUID?
THAT'S THE ENCEPHALITIC FLUID.
IT'S KINDA LIKE BRAIN JUICE.
COPYRIGHT © 2002 ILLIAD HTTP://WWW.USERFRIENDLY.ORG/

OH.

WHY DOES ENCEPHALETIC FLUID SMELL LIKE COLA?
WHOEVER'S BRAIN THAT IS, I'M MAKING HIM MY HIGH PRIEST.

WHAT HAPPENED?
I YANKED A LITTLE HARD ON THE CABLE AND PITR'S BRAIN POPPED OUT.
COPYRIGHT © 2002 ILLIAD HTTP://WWW.USERFRIENDLY.ORG/

DEAR LORD! DOES THAT MEAN HE'S NO LONGER ABLE TO WORK?
NOT TO WORRY. HE'LL STILL BE ABLE TO CONTRIBUTE.

AH GOOD. IN THESE DIFFICULT TIMES IT'S IMPORTANT THAT WE TREASURE OUR STAFF AND PLACE THEM WHERE THEY'LL FEEL MOST FULFILLED.
AS A SPEEDBUMP. HE'LL BE WITHOUT PEER.

SID, I WAS WONDERING. IF PITR'S BRAIN IS HERE, WHAT'S PITR USING TO THINK?
HOW DO YOU MEAN?
COPYRIGHT © 2002 ILLIAD HTTP://WWW.USERFRIENDLY.ORG/

YOU KNOW. THINK. WITHOUT A BRAIN HOW DOES HE MAKE DECISIONS. CONSIDER LIFE AND FORM OPINIONS?!
OH. DON'T WORRY. HE'S USING A TRIED AND TRUE METHOD TO COMPENSATE.

TAKING CHARGE OF YOUR DESTINY... TODAY, ON OPRAH!
DROOL
BLORPT

USER
FRIENDLY
the comic strip
PIZZA
Portrasher 4
ROTO-ROUTER 800
Copyright © 1997-2002 Illiad

HEY. I BORROWED PITR.
"BORROWED" PITR? FOR WHAT?
FOR ART. COME SEE.

(SUNG TO MADONNA'S "RAIN")
BRAAAINS...
FEEL THEM ON YOUR FINGER TIPS
HEAR THEM SLURPING DOWN THE DRAIN
YOUR BOD'S CRAVING FOR SOME...

BRAAAINS...
QUENCH YOUR ZOMBIE HUNGER
YOU'LL JUST EAT THEM PLAIN
YOUR BOD'S CRAVING FOR SOME...

BRAAAINS...
WHEN YOUR LIPS ARE ON MY SCALP
AND YOU TAKE THE TIME
TO HOOVER OUT MY HEAD
WHEN YOU LISTEN TO MY SHRIEKS
AS YOU APPLY YOUR DARK
TECHNIQUES, I KNOW I'M DEAD...

I DON'T THINK I LIKE THIS SONG.
R'LYEH A LITTLE DULL THESE DAYS?
ANYBODY ELSE BUT ME HAVE THE MUNCHIES?
BRAAAINS...

I THINK I'VE MILKED THIS BRAIN STUFF ENOUGH WITH PITR. COULD YOU GIVE ME A HAND?
ALREADY DONE. I PUT HIS BRAIN BACK. WITHOUT THE CABLE.

OH, GOOD! BUT AFTER BEING HOOKED UP DIRECTLY TO THE 'NET...DON'T YOU THINK YOU SHOULD HAVE WEANED HIM OFF IT SLOWLY?
OH, I'M SURE HE'LL BE FINE.

SO COLD.. SO COLD..

The answer is, "Months!"

DUDE. YOU LOOKED **PEEVED**.
VERISIGN IS UP TO THEIR TRICKS AGAIN.
EH? HOW SO?

THEY'RE SENDING OUT LETTERS TO DOMAIN HOLDERS 'WARNING' THEM THAT IF THEY DON'T RENEW THEIR DOMAINS NOW, AND IMPLICITLY WITH VERISIGN, THEY'LL LOSE THEM. THING IS, VERISIGN ISN'T THEIR REGISTRAR, AND THEY'RE CHARGING THREE TIMES WHAT SOME OTHERS ARE CHARGING.
THE WORST PART IS THAT VERISIGN IS SUPPOSED TO BE A 'TRUST' COMPANY.

AHHHH. THE ENRONY OF IT ALL.
HOW LONG HAVE YOU BEEN WAITING TO USE THAT?
OOOOOH!

WHAT'S THIS I HEAR ABOUT YOU GETTING YOUR UNDIES IN A KNOT OVER VERISIGN'S CREATIVE MARKETING METHODS?
IT'S **NOT** CREATIVE MARKETING. IT'S **DECEITFUL** AND **EVIL**.

OH PLEASE. I'LL HAVE YOU KNOW THAT OUR FRIENDS AT VERISIGN HAVE TAKEN TO VISITING DOMAIN HOLDERS IN PERSON TO EXPLAIN THEIR OFFER SO THAT THERE CAN BE NO FURTHER WHINING ABOUT "DECEIT."

NICE DOMAIN. IT'D BE A SHAME IF SOMETHING HAPPENED TO IT. RIGHT VINCENT?
YEH. LIKE A STRAY ELECTROMAGNETIC BLAST. HAPPENS ALL THE TIME.

SUGAR PIE! WHAT ARE YOU STILL DOING HERE?
I HAD A GOOD CHAT WITH THE CHIEF! HE'S ASKED ME TO STAY ON FOR A WHILE LONGER TO MANAGE THE TECHNICAL PROJECTS.

YOU MEAN THE ONES THAT **I'M** NOT MANAGING RIGHT?
THERE NEVER REALLY IS A GOOD TIME FOR A CHILD TO CRUSH A PARENT, IS THERE.

BUT HONEY. I'M THE C.T.O. MANAGING TECH PROJECTS FALLS WITHIN MY PURVIEW.
OH DADDY...

LOOK AT IT THIS WAY. I'M YOUR ASSISTANT. TAKING THE DRUDGERY OF PROJECT MANAGEMENT OUT OF YOUR LAP SO YOU CAN CONCENTRATE ON THE MORE IMPORTANT TASKS. NOW GO DO WHAT IT IS YOU DID BEFORE YOU BECAME C.T.O.

YOU FOUND THE AMULET OF YENDOR!
OF COURSE I DID...

HI MIKE. I'M UPDATING THE PROJECT DATABASE AND HAD A QUESTION. COULD YOU GIVE ME A DATE AS TO WHEN THE NEW NETWORK WILL BE READY?
NO. I DON'T HAVE ENOUGH INFORMATION YET.

OH...

WELL THEN COULD YOU GIVE ME A DATE FOR WHEN YOU COULD GIVE ME A DATE?
I...**NO!!!**

IN TODAY'S FINANCIAL NEWS, BRILLIANT DIGITAL ENTERTAINMENT'S UPCOMING "ALTNET RESOURCE DOLLARS" CLEARLY THREATEN ANOTHER CURRENCY.

PUNCH THE MONKEY AND WIN!
100
042066601138
FREEBOOT

MIKE, PLEASE. IT'S CRUCIAL TO MY PROJECT PLANNING THAT I KNOW WHEN THE NEW NETWORK WILL BE UP.
I KNOW IT IS PEARL, BUT I JUST DON'T HAVE THE INFORMATION I NEED YET.
COPYRIGHT © 2002 ILLIAD HTTP://WWW.USERFRIENDLY.ORG/

AND YOU SAID YOU COULDN'T GIVE ME A DATE WHEN YOU CAN GIVE ME A DATE?
UH...GIVE YOU A DATE... WHEN I CAN...RIGHT. I CAN'T DO THAT YET.

THEN COULD YOU GIVE ME A DATE WHEN YOU CAN GIVE ME A DATE WHEN YOU CAN GIVE ME A DATE?
GIVE YOU A DATE...WHEN I CAN...GIVE...A DATE... ...NO! STOP DOING THAT!!!

MIRANDA. HI.
OH. HELLO PEARL. STILL HERE?
COPYRIGHT © 2002 ILLIAD HTTP://WWW.USERFRIENDLY.ORG/

YES. I'VE BEEN ASKED TO STAY ON AND TAKE CHARGE OF PROJECT MANAGEMENT.
REALLY. YOU. IN CHARGE.

YEP. ANYWAY. PLEASE SEND ME A BULLETED LIST OF WHAT YOU NEED TO ACCOMPLISH THIS WEEK.
FOR STARTERS, ME AND A NAILFILE NEED TO FIGURE OUT HOW TO TURN YOU INTO A PEZ DISPENSER, SISTER...

OKAY WE'RE ALL HERE. FIRST, THANK YOU ALL FOR SUBMITTING YOUR BULLETED LISTS OF TASKS.
NO WORRIES.
COPYRIGHT © 2002 ILLIAD HTTP://WWW.USERFRIENDLY.ORG/

SECONDLY, I APPRECIATE THE THOUGHT AND EFFORT EACH OF YOU PUT INTO YOUR LISTS...

HOWEVER, AND THIRDLY, "MAKING THE WORLD A BETTER PLACE" DOES NOT COUNT AS AN ATTAINABLE PROJECT MILESTONE.
UNTRUE, VABUSHKA. ONCE AM EVIL HIGH OVERLORD, WORLD WILL BE BETTER PLACE.
"VABUSHKA?"

SO GREG, ACCORDING TO YOUR LIST, YOU'RE WORKING ON PRUNING THE TROUBLE TICKET DATABASE. HOW LONG WILL YOU NEED?
FOUR WEEKS.
COPYRIGHT © 2002 ILLIAD HTTP://WWW.USERFRIENDLY.ORG/

OKAY. LET ME REPHRASE. HOW LONG WILL YOU NEED ONCE WE REMOVE QUAKE III ARENA FROM YOUR MACHINE?
A COUPLE HOU--I MEAN, FOUR WEEKS!

THAT WAS AN EXCELLENT MEETING, EVERYONE! ALL OF YOU HAVE YOUR LISTS OF ACTION ITEMS, SO LET'S GET STARTED AND HIT THOSE MILESTONES!
COPYRIGHT © 2002 ILLIAD HTTP://WWW.USERFRIENDLY.ORG/

PLEASE ALSO NOTE THAT IN ACCEPTING THESE TASKS, YOU HAVE EXPLICITLY GRANTED ME PERMISSION TO EXPLOIT YOU AS I SEE FIT, WHEN I SEE FIT. HAVE A GREAT AFTERNOON!

SHE USED TO WORK FOR KAZAA, DIDN'T SHE.
IT'S FINE BY ME IF IT MEANS I GET TO SEE HER NAKED FOR FREE.
HMM...

ALL THIS SPYWARE AND ANNOYWARE IS REALLY STARTING TO GET OUT OF HAND. WHAT'S THE WORLD COMING TO?
COPYRIGHT © 2002 ILLIAD HTTP://WWW.USERFRIENDLY.ORG/

IF THIS WAS THE WORLD OF TELEVISION, IT'D BE LIKE BEING FORCED TO WATCH "BARNEY'S SING-ALONG" RIGHT AFTER "STAR TREK."

THANK ERIS THE 'NET HAS NOTHING LIKE THAT STUPID PURPLE DINOSAUR. I'D LOSE MY FLIPPING MIND.
THIS ONE NEEDS A BIG CUDDLE...
BONZI BUDDY

A lack of sleep causes one to draw Evil Marketing Monkeys. Everyone, go get your seven hours a night, *please*.

PROVIGIL: THE FUTURE DRUG OF CHOICE FOR LINUX GEEKS.
11 DAYS! NOW THAT'S WHAT I CALL "UPTIME."

GAH! WHO...WHAT IN HADES ARE YOU?
I'M YOUR BONZI BUDDY! I'M HERE TO MAKE YOUR WHOLE WEB EXPERIENCE A HAPPY ONE!
BONZI BUDDY
COPYRIGHT © 2002 ILLIAD HTTP://WWW.USERFRIENDLY.ORG/

YOU'RE PLUSH, PURPLE AND CLOYING. GIVE ME ONE REASON WHY YOU THINK YOU CAN GIVE ME A "HAPPY WEB EXPERIENCE."
UH...WELL...
BONZI BUDDY

...I'M FREE.
OH HALLELUJAH. AT THAT PRICE I'M GONNA GET ME A WHOLE FAMILY OF PURPLE 'NET JOY.
BONZI BUDDY

TECH SUPPORT. GREG SPEAKING...
NARGLE FARGLE @#$#!! WIND*W$ BLUE SCREEN &*#!!@! SPITTLE ?#@$!
COPYRIGHT © 2002 ILLIAD HTTP://WWW.USERFRIENDLY.ORG/

VILL@GE ID!OT GROWWRR HISSY FIT !@#!!$!@## ALL YOUR DAMN FAULT!!! GOODBYE!!! *CLICK*

YOU POOR, ABUSED THING. TELL ME WHAT YOU NEED.
A THIRTY-OUGHT-SIX WOULD BE JUST ABOUT RIGHT.

LISTEN HERE YOU PRIMATE FREAK. I DON'T NEED YOUR HELP. I DON'T WANT YOUR ADVICE. AND MOST OF ALL I DON'T APPRECIATE BEING MANHANDLED. SO GET LOST.
OKAY. OKAY...
COPYRIGHT © 2002 ILLIAD HTTP://WWW.USERFRIENDLY.ORG/

ALL YOU HAD TO DO WAS ASK. NO NEED TO BE NASTY ABOUT IT.
HMPH.

...AND BESIDES, MY WORK HERE IS DONE.
WHERE'D MY WALLET GO?!
PAT SEARCH PANIC

WHAT'S THE MATTER?
THAT BIG PURPLE BUFFOON JUST TOOK MY WALLET!
COPYRIGHT © 2002 ILLIAD HTTP://WWW.USERFRIENDLY.ORG/

OH GODS. DON'T TELL ME YOU DON'T SEE HIM.
OH I SEE HIM ALL RIGHT. YOU GOT ROBBED BY H.R. PUFNSTUF?
LORD. NOT THAT AGAIN...

LOOK. JUST GO UP THERE AND TAKE YOUR WALLET BACK.
IT'S NOT THAT EASY. THERE ARE DANGERS.
COPYRIGHT © 2002 ILLIAD HTTP://WWW.USERFRIENDLY.ORG/

AH YES. DANGERS. I WANTED TO ASK YOU ABOUT THAT. TELL ME AGAIN WHY WE'RE ON THIS LADDER?

BECAUSE OTHERWISE I'LL CREAM YOU WITH THESE BARRELS...
BONZI KONG

Ahhh, hittin' the bong again, J.D.?

YE GODS. IS IT OVER?
I HOPE SO. THAT MONKEY WHIPPED A SERIOUS TORRENT OF BARRELS AT US.
COPYRIGHT © 2002 ILLIAD HTTP://WWW.USERFRIENDLY.ORG/

WAIT...ALL OF THOSE BARRELS WENT FLYING INTO THE TECH OFFICE!
WE'D BETTER MAKE SURE EVERYONE'S OKAY!

WHICHEVER ONE OF YOU IS HALLUCINATING, PLEASE DON'T STOP. THOSE BARRELS WERE BEER KEGS!
FREE BEER!

USER
FRIENDLY
the comic strip
PIZZA
Portrasher 4
ROTO-ROUTER 800
Copyright©1997-2002 Illiad

(SUNG TO "Y.M.C.A." BY THE VILLAGE PEOPLE)
NET GEEKS. THERE'S NO NEED TO FEEL GUILT
I SAID NET GEEKS. FOR THE SOFTWARE YOU BUILT
I SAID NET GEEKS. CAUSE YOU'RE NOT IN THE WRONG
THERE'S NO NEED TO FEEL UNHAPPY!

NET GEEKS. YOU CAN BURN A CD
I SAID NET GEEKS. WITH YOUR FAVE MP3S
YOU CAN PLAY THEM. IN YOUR HOME OR YOUR CAR
MANY WAYS TO TAKE THEM REAL FAR!

IT'S FUN TO VIOLATE THE D M C A!
IT'S FUN TO VIOLATE THE D M C A-AY!
YOU HAVE EVERYTHING, YOU NEED TO ENJOY YOUR MUSIC WITH YOUR TOYS!

IT'S FUN TO VIOLATE THE D M C A!
IT'S FUN TO VIOLATE THE D M C A-AY!
YOU CAN ARCHIVE YOUR TUNES!
YOU CAN SHARE OVER CABLE!
YOU CAN ANNOY THE RECORD LABELS!

WE INTERRUPT THIS PROGRAM TO BRING YOU
RIAA'S MOST WANTED
WANTED
"DUST PUPPY" for Naughtiness
WANTED
"ERWIN" for Sarcasm

BEER KEGS OR NOT. I STILL NEED MY WALLET BACK.
CAN'T YOU JUST TAKE IT BACK?
COPYRIGHT © 2002 ILLIAD HTTP://WWW.USERFRIENDLY.ORG/

ARE YOU KIDDING? THAT APE IS A MENACE.
STEF SAID HE DIDN'T SEE THE PROBLEM.

OKAY MONKEY. WHERE'RE MY 25 BANANA BUCKS?

THAT'S IT. I AM SO OUTTA HERE.
GOOD TO HEAR IT. YOU'RE A FLIPPING BANE ON EXISTANCE.
WEB PARIAH
COPYRIGHT © 2002 ILLIAD HTTP://WWW.USERFRIENDLY.ORG/

LISTEN. KIDS LOVE ME AND PLAY WITH ME. PEOPLE DOWNLOAD ME AND I HELP THEM FIND STUFF THEY WOULD NEVER NORMALLY LOOK FOR. SO WHAT'S YOUR PROBLEM?!
WEB PARIAH

YOU'RE DESTROYING YOUNG MINDS AND IRRITATING EVERYONE ELSE!!
RIGHT. THAT'S INFRINGMENT. CALL MY LAWYER.
I KNOW THAT VOICE...IT'S THE VOICE OF MY OLD MASTER...
WEB PARIAH

THOSE BEER KEGS WERE COOL. BUT GREG SEEING PURPLE APES? THE DUDE NEEDS A VACATION.
COPYRIGHT © 2002 ILLIAD HTTP://WWW.USERFRIENDLY.ORG/

I KNOW I HAVE MY MOMENTS. BUT I'VE NEVER LOST MY GRIP ON REALITY. MAYBE IT'S BECAUSE I GAME SO MUCH.

ANYWAY. NOW FOR A SERIOUS SESSION OF NETHACK.
I SHOULD VISIT THIS ONE? WILL HE FREAK?
IT'S WHAT WE'RE HOPING...

I SAY. COULD I HAVE A MOMENT OF YOUR TIME?
WHAT THE-?!!
COPYRIGHT © 2002 ILLIAD HTTP://WWW.USERFRIENDLY.ORG/

YES. I KNOW. THIS IS ALL A LITTLE ODD. ISN'T IT. ALLOW ME TO ASSURE YOU THAT THIS IS IN FACT WHAT IT APPEARS TO BE...

THE GHOST OF @HOME PAST?
"OH DON'T WORRY." SAID MR. COLA. "THIS ONE'S QUITE CLEVER." SAID MR. COLA...

FOR YOUR INFORMATION, I'M THE ASCII CHARACTER THAT REPRESENTS YOU IN NETHACK.
AH. SO YOU'RE MY AVATAR.
JUST SO.
COPYRIGHT © 2002 ILLIAD HTTP://WWW.USERFRIENDLY.ORG/

SO... YOU'RE, IN A SENSE, MY ALTER EGO? YOU'RE AS MUCH ME AS I AM YOU?
ER..YES. I SUPPOSE THAT FOLLOWS.

IF ANYONE ASKS, I'LL BE AT THE GHOST RECON LAN PARTY...
UM...ARE YOU SURE THAT "WEB DESIGNER" IS A CHARACTER CLASS?

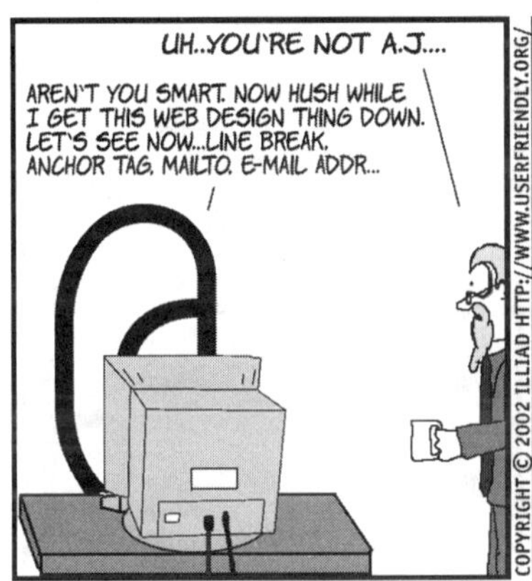
UH..YOU'RE NOT A.J....
AREN'T YOU SMART. NOW HUSH WHILE I GET THIS WEB DESIGN THING DOWN. LET'S SEE NOW...LINE BREAK, ANCHOR TAG, MAILTO, E-MAIL ADDR...
COPYRIGHT © 2002 ILLIAD HTTP://WWW.USERFRIENDLY.ORG/

YE GNARLY GNOMES. I THINK I JUST HAD A BABY...
I THINK I JUST HAD AN L.S.D. RELAPSE...

LUCAS NEVER DID SPECIFY WHAT THE CLONES WERE OF...
MEESA GOING TO KICK SOME!
AND MEESA!
MEESA TOO!
USERFRIENDLY DOT ORG
COPYRIGHT (C) 2002 ILLIAD

HEY. ALTER-EGO! THANKS FOR COVERING FOR ME.
NO PROBLEM. "AT" YOUR SERVICE.
COPYRIGHT © 2002 ILLIAD HTTP://WWW.USERFRIENDLY.ORG/

OKAY. LOOK. YOU'RE SUPPOSED TO REPRESENT ME AND I DON'T TELL BAD JOKES LIKE THAT.
THEY'RE NOT BAD. THEY'RE AT-ROCIOUS.

AAAAAAGH!! STOP THAT!
OR WHAT? YOU GONNA THROW ME IN AT-TICA?

OKAY. TIME FOR YOU TO SPLIT.
I DUNNO. I'M REALLY DIGGING THIS WEB DESIGN THING.
COPYRIGHT © 2002 ILLIAD HTTP://WWW.USERFRIENDLY.ORG/

YOU'RE NOT UNDER-STANDING ME. IF YOU DON'T LEAVE **NOW** I'LL...I'LL...UM...

YES?
I GUESS I'LL HAVE TO BUMP INTO YOU...
GRRRR

WHERE'S A.J.?
HE SAID HE WAS GOING OUT FOR SOMETHING TO EAT.
COPYRIGHT © 2002 ILLIAD HTTP://WWW.USERFRIENDLY.ORG/

WHAT? IT'S NOT EVEN LUNCHTIME YET.
I KNOW. BUT HE SAID HE WAS BEING TREATED TO A MEAL.

URP...THIS DOESN'T TASTE VERY GOOD...
THAT'S BECAUSE YOU TRIED THE **TRIPE** YOU IDIOT.
RUMF

SID. I WANT TO TALK TO YOU ABOUT THIS NETHACK THING. A.J.'S BEEN A LITTLE WIERD LATELY. AND I THINK IT HAS TO DO WITH THAT ODD LITTLE GAME YOU GOT HIM HOOKED ON.
COPYRIGHT © 2002 ILLIAD HTTP://WWW.USERFRIENDLY.ORG/

RELAX CHIEF. IT'S JUST A PHASE. NETHACK IS ACTUALLY A VERY USEFUL TOOL IN TEACHING GEEKS A LITTLE ABOUT AVARICE AND ITS PITFALLS. AS WELL AS THE REWARDS OF TENACITY AND PERSEVERANCE.

AND BESIDES. EVERYONE KNOWS THAT ONE OF THE ULTIMATE GOALS OF PLAYING NETHACK IS TO **BUILD CHARACTER...**
I THINK HE'S TELLING ME THE TRUTH BUT SOMETHING ALSO TELLS ME I SHOULD HIT HIM...

GREG? I HAD THIS E-MAIL FORWARDED TO ME FROM A CUSTOMER WHOSE ACCOUNT AND E-MAIL ADDRESS WITH US WAS ABOUT TO EXPIRE SO WE FORWARDED HIS MAIL TO HIS HOTMAIL ACCOUNT?
YES?
COPYRIGHT © 2002 ILLIAD HTTP://WWW.USERFRIENDLY.ORG/

AND THE CUSTOMER GOT CONFUSED AND THOUGHT WE WERE LETTING HIS HOTMAIL ACCOUNT EXPIRE AND WANTED US TO FIX IT?
UH HUH...

YOU REPLIED: "...UNFORTUNATELY, COLUMBIA INTERNET'S PLAN TO TAKE OVER THE WORLD HAS NOT YET REACHED THE HOTMAIL ACQUISITION STAGE. AS SUCH, WE CAN NOT CURRENTLY HELP YOU." I JUST WANTED TO SAY BRAVO.
THANKS.
FOOLS. LEETLE ARE THEY REALIZINK...

YOU WANTED TO SEE ME? HOW WERE YOUR HOLIDAYS?
THEY WERE GOOD. YOU HAVE TO SEE THIS SID. YOU KNOW HOW I HAD MY E-MAIL SET TO AUTOREPLY TO LET PEOPLE KNOW I WAS AWAY?
YES...
COPYRIGHT © 2002 ILLIAD HTTP://WWW.USERFRIENDLY.ORG/

SOMEONE WROTE IN FOR SUPPORT AND SO MY AUTOREPLIER LET HIM KNOW I WAS AWAY FOR THE WEEK.
AND?
AND HE REPLIED TO THE AUTOREPLY.

"...I KNOW YOU ARE NOT THERE AND CANNOT HELP BEFORE MY EMAIL ADDRESS EXPIRES, SO I DON'T KNOW WHY THESE ALARMING MESSAGES ARE BEING SENT. PLEASE DO NOT SEND AN AUTOMATED REPLY SAYING THAT YOU ARE NOT THERE."
CAN I LEAVE AUTO-REPLY ON FOR JUST A FEW MORE WEEKS?

USER
FRIENDLY
the comic strip
PIZZA
Portrasher 4
ROTO-ROUTER 800
Copyright©1997-2002 Illiad

'MOTHERHOOD, O GORDIAN RITE, CHAFED WITH PAINTS OF LIFE, A CANVAS THICK WITH LIGHTER OILS, YET STAINED BY QUIET STRIFE.'
DEAR MOM: HOPE YOU LIKE THE E-CARD. PLEASE STOP PAGING ME WHEN YOU GET BORED WITH YOUR WALLPAPER. LOVE, MIRANDA

'IDEAL HEIGHTS, AND HIGH IDEALS, MAKE US AIM FOR STEEPLES, I TRY, YOU TRY, TO CLUTCH OUR BOND, YET PROVE WE'RE DIFFERENT PEOPLE.'
"BIKINI-CLAD MISSILE WARRIORS?"
NOW YOU CAN PLAY ONLINE AGAINST ME!

'WORDS, O WORDS, WHAT THEY CAN SAY: REAL THINGS NOT JUST TOKENS! YET SOMETIMES THOUGHT DEPARTS MY MIND, AND WRONG WORDS BECOME SPOKEN.'
A BOX OF "DIET CHOCOLATES?"
WHAT? DIDN'T I BUY ENOUGH?

'A TURN OF PHRASE I CANNOT QUOTH, NOR PROFFER DUE SALUTE, SO GIFTS I GIVE TO SPEAK FOR ME, A POET FALLEN MUTE.'
A BANANA REPUBLIC?! JUST FOR ME?

'DUE WORDS I MIGHTN'T EVER SAY, AND YOU MIGHTN'T ALWAYS SEE, YET WHEN TIME ARRIVES TO TAKE YOUR HAND, I'LL SAY TIME STOLE YOU FROM ME.'
MISS YOU.
IN LOVING MEMORY

The poem wrote itself in less than seven minutes. I didn't know what the ending was going to be for the cartoon until I thought about Sid. At the time of this writing, my dear Mom was still with us and enjoying the heck out of her grandkids, so I count myself fortunate indeed.

RIAA. MPAA. SPYWARE. BAD GOVERNMENTS. STUPID PEOPLE. AM WERY TIRED OF THIS WORLD OF PRACTICED MEDIOCRITY...
WELCOME TO THE N.Y. TIMES INTERNAL EDITORIAL SERVER.

IS TIME TO BE TEACHINK THEM ALL LESSON IN SUBTLETY. IS TIME TO BE BRINKINK WORLD UNDER MY DOMINION. LIKE... SO....
ADJUST
MODIFY
VIOLATE
COPYRIGHT © 2002 ILLIAD HTTP://WWW.USERFRIENDLY.ORG/

The New York Times
COCA-COLA AND PEPSI MERGED UNDER NEW BRAND: PITR-COLA
PEPSI

HELLO DOUGLAS? IT'S STEVEN OVER AT PEPSICO. WHAT'S THIS ABOUT A MERGER?
WHAT? I THOUGHT YOU STARTED THAT!

ARE YOU MAD? WHY ON EARTH WOULD I EVER WANT TO MERGE PEPSI WITH THAT RHINO BILE YOU CALL COLA?
HEY! YOU'D BE LUCKY IF YOU COULD GET YOUR FLAVOURING EVEN CLOSE TO THAT!
COPYRIGHT © 2002 ILLIAD HTTP://WWW.USERFRIENDLY.ORG/

DELINQUENT!
LOSER!
PAWNS.

AND ANOTHER THING! WHAT THE HELL IS "PITR-COLA?" IT SOUNDS RUDE.
STEVEN. HOW IN HADES SHOULD I KNOW? I THOUGHT THAT WAS YOUR IDEA!

PEPSICO DOESN'T NEED A MERGER, DOUGLAS. SALES IN OUR LAST QUARTER TRIPLED.
SAME WITH COCA-COLA. WE'VE NEVER MADE THIS MUCH MONEY...
COPYRIGHT © 2002 ILLIAD HTTP://WWW.USERFRIENDLY.ORG/

COCA-COLA: FINANCIALS MODIFIED.
PEPSICO: FINANCIALS MODIFIED.
AND NOW, FOR THE COUP-DE-GRACE...
HELLO, F.B.I., ENRONESQUE WITCH-HUNT DIVISION...

C.E.O.
MR. REINEMUND, WE AT THE F.B.I ARE, FOR OBVIOUS REASONS CONCERNED ABOUT YOUR FINANCIAL REPORTS. THIS VISIT IS MERELY PRECAUTIONARY YOU UNDERSTAND, AND ONCE WE'RE SATISFIED THAT WHAT YOU'RE CLAIMING IS TRUE, WE'LL BE ON OUR WAY.

OF COURSE, GENTLEMEN. AS C.E.O., I CAN TELL YOU THAT PEPSICO WILL GIVE YOU OUR FULLEST CO-OPERATION IN THIS MATTER.
C.E.O.
COPYRIGHT © 2002 ILLIAD HTTP://WWW.USERFRIENDLY.ORG/

...IN ANY CASE, OUR AUDITOR SHOULD BE HERE MOMENTARILY.
IS ALWAYS SO EASY...
C.E.O.
I AM ARTHUR ANDERSEN

CHIEF. WHAT ARE WE GOING TO DO ABOUT PITR AND HIS OBVIOUSLY CRIMINAL MANIPULATION OF CORPORATE AMERICA?
OH, I WOULDN'T GO SO FAR AS TO SAY IT WAS CRIMINAL.
COPYRIGHT © 2002 ILLIAD HTTP://WWW.USERFRIENDLY.ORG/

YE GODS! HE GOT TO YOU ALREADY, DIDN'T HE.
FREE, UNLIMITED COLA FOR THE TECHS, FOREVER! WE CAN CUT SALARIES TO THE BONE AND THEY'LL STILL WORK!

STEVEN. HOW DID THE AUDIT GO WITH THE FEDS?
NOT WELL, DOUGLAS. IT LOOKS LIKE WE'RE BACKED INTO A CORNER. WE HAVE TO GO THROUGH WITH THE MERGER OR WE'RE FINISHED.
COPYRIGHT © 2002 ILLIAD HTTP://WWW.USERFRIENDLY.ORG/

UH-OH. LOOKS LIKE IT'S OUR TURN. THE FEDS ARE COMING FOR US NOW. I CAN SEE THEM FROM MY WINDOW.

HOW CAN YOU TELL IT'S THE FEDS? DON'T THEY ALL JUST WEAR SUITS?
CALL IT A HUNCH.

'MERGERS WE DON'T WANT TO SEE' #3:
DELL COMPUTERS AND A FUNDAMENTALIST CHURCH.
DUDE! YOU'RE GOIN' TO HELL!

IN THE COLA FACTORIES, THE RECIPE FOR PITR-COLA IS DISSEMINATED...
READ OUT THE INGREDIENTS HOWARD.
"CAFFEINE."
COPYRIGHT © 2002 ILLIAD HTTP://WWW.USERFRIENDLY.ORG/

AND?!
WHAT "AND"? THERE IS NO "AND."
AND BLIND OBEDIENCE, OF COURSE...

"PITR-COLA?" THIS IS YOUR COLA?
DA. PLEASE TO BE GIVINK TRY.
COPYRIGHT © 2002 ILLIAD HTTP://WWW.USERFRIENDLY.ORG/

SCHLURRRRRRRPLE!
CAFFEINATE!
CAFFEINATE!
CAFFEINATE!

YE GODS THIS STUFF IS GREAT!
YOU AND I NEED TO HAVE A WORD...
NYET. ONLY WORDS YOU NEED TO KNOW ARE "YES, DREAD LORD."

CHIEF, THIS HAS GOT TO STOP! PITR'S NEW COLA IS AFFECTING ALL OF THE TECH STAFF! IT'S PURE, UNDILUTED, HI-INTENSITY, SYRUP-THICK CAFFEINE!
COPYRIGHT © 2002 ILLIAD HTTP://WWW.USERFRIENDLY.ORG/

YE GODS, MY GOB IS GETTING THICK JUST THINKING ABOUT IT.
I KNOW. MINE TOO...

WE HAVE TO TALK.
NYET. PLEASE TO BE GOINK AWAY.
COPYRIGHT © 2002 ILLIAD HTTP://WWW.USERFRIENDLY.ORG/

NO. I'M NOT GOING TO BE "GOINK AWAY." YOU'VE TWISTED THE SOUL OF COLA AND CREATED A TERRIBLE, ICHOROUS MOCKERY OF EVERYONE'S FAVOURITE SUGARY DRINK! DO YOU KNOW THAT CAFFEINE IN HIGH CONCENTRATIONS IS TOXIC?!

THAT'S RIGHT. TOXIC!! DO YOU KNOW WHAT IT FEELS LIKE TO BE SUDDENLY MADE ILLEGAL?!
NO SYMPATHY FROM ME, DUDE.

PITR, I WAS JUST TALKING TO SID ABOUT YOUR COLA AND ITS TOXIC NATURE. I MEAN, ALL THAT CAFFEINE...
DA, AM KNOWINK.
pitr-cola
COPYRIGHT © 2002 ILLIAD HTTP://WWW.USERFRIENDLY.ORG/

AM WILLINK TO BE PROVINK TO YOU THAT PITR-COLA IS GOOD THINK FOR COMPANY.
OH THIS SHOULD BE GOOD...
pitr-cola

BEHOLD.
DAMN! I JUST REWROTE THE ENTIRE LINUX KERNEL!
WHEN DID YOU LEARN HOW TO CODE?
TODAY!

I DUNNO CHIEF. PITR'S MAKING A BID FOR POWER WITH HIS NEW COLA. HE'S NOT GOING TO BE A GOOD TEAM PLAYER ANYMORE.
OH COME ON SID. A "BID FOR POWER?"
COPYRIGHT © 2002 ILLIAD HTTP://WWW.USERFRIENDLY.ORG/

PITR SAID HE WAS MEETING WITH THE OTHER TECHS ABOUT "COMMUNICATING BETTER."
THERE. SEE? YOU'RE WORRIED ABOUT NOTHING.

AND AGAIN. WHAT ARE ONLY WORDS YOU ARE SAYINK TO ME?
YES DREAD LORD!!! ANYTHING YOU SAY DREAD LORD!!!
Pitr-Cola
Pitr-Cola

TO HELP GENERATE PRESS ATTENTION (AND SALES TO FUND PITR'S TAKEOVER OF THE WORLD) PLEASE CLIP OUT THIS COVER AND WRAP IT AROUND YOUR DRINK CAN OF CHOICE. EVEN IF IT'S BEER. THANK YOU.
PITR-COLA
BOTTLED BY THE EVIL GENIUS BOTTLINK COMPANY.
PITR-COLA IS A TRADEMARK OF EVIL GENIUSES INCORPORATED.
INGREDIENTS
Caffeine, Obedience, Fear of Retribution.
SURGEON-GENERAL'S WARNING:
This drink product is bad for your health but good for teaching you your place in the world.
"SLEEP, SHE IS FOR THE WEAK."

I kid you not, cola cans all over UFiedom were wrapped in this. At three conferences in 2002, I was approached by people who had bought six-packs of Jolt or what-have-you and made exquisite versions of the Pitr-Cola wrapper and mounted them on the cans. I love my readers, but I also fear them.

LAST WEEK IT WAS ANNOUNCED THAT THE U.S. ARMY IS LAUNCHING THE VIDEO GAME "AMERICA'S ARMY" AS A WAY TO BOOST ITS RANKS. THE IDEA IS TO GIVE YOUNG MEN AND WOMEN A TASTE OF BATTLEFIELD TACTICS IN HOPES OF ATTRACTING MORE RECRUITS.
RANGER TABS
COPYRIGHT © 2002 ILLIAD HTTP://WWW.USERFRIENDLY.ORG/

NOTABLY, THE OFFICER IN CHARGE OF THE NEW ARMY RECRUITMENT CAMPAIGN HAS LEFT ON A SABBATICAL IN ANTARCTICA.
RANGER TABS
72 pcs

HIS REPLACEMENT IS ONE COLONEL PITR DUBOVICH, WHO COULD NOT BE REACHED FOR COMMENT. RECRUITMENT HAS BEEN NOTED AS BEING ON THE UPSWING.
YESSS...COME TO PAPA, MY LEETLE MINIONS OF DOOM.
HMM...
RANGER TABS

PITR'S GOT HIS PAWS INTO THE U.S. ARMY.
WHAT? HOW?
COPYRIGHT © 2002 ILLIAD HTTP://WWW.USERFRIENDLY.ORG/

A LITTLE SYSTEM CRACKING, IT APPEARS. THAT AND DISTRIBUTING HIS NEW EXPANSION MODULE FOR THE "AMERICA'S ARMY" GAME.

THE EXPANSION IS CALLED: "HELL, WE DON'T EVEN GO TO BED BEFORE 9:00AM."
AND LEARNING HOW TO START UP YOUR P.C. IS CALLED "BOOT CAMP." RIGHT?

YOU WANTED TO TALK TO ME PITR?
DA COMRADE. AM NEEDINK DESIGN ADVICE.
COPYRIGHT © 2002 ILLIAD HTTP://WWW.USERFRIENDLY.ORG/

DESIGN ADVICE FOR WHAT?
THIS FORM IN PAGEMAKER. HERE.
WIGGLE WIGGLE

"APPLICATION FOR THE POSITION OF 'MINION' WITHIN THE LEGION OF DOOM?"
DA. ARE YOU THINKINK LIGHT SALMON BACKGROUND, IT IS TOO MUCH?

PITR, WHAT ARE YOU GOING TO DO WITH ALL OF THESE PEOPLE SENDING YOU RECRUITMENT APPLICATIONS?
WILL BE MAKINK MY DARK ARMY, YOUNG IDEALIST.
COPYRIGHT © 2002 ILLIAD HTTP://WWW.USERFRIENDLY.ORG/

WHEN LEGION OF DOOM IS COMPLETE, WILL BE HAVINK FIVE THOUSAND MINIONS. ALL OF WORLD WILL BE KNOWINK THAT WITH THIS LEGION, DREAD LORD PITR WILL BE HAVINK THE MOST...THE MOST...UM...

...THE MOST PASTY-LOOKING, NERDY ARMY IN EXISTENCE.
DA, OKAY, I KNOW ALREADY!!

WHAT IN BLAZES IS THIS?!
THE LABEL SAYS IT'S TO "MR. DREAD LORD."
FOR PITR? OPEN IT...
UP
COPYRIGHT © 2002 ILLIAD HTTP://WWW.USERFRIENDLY.ORG/

UP

PLEASE DON'T LET IT BE WHAT I THINK IT IS...
IT'S A CLONING VAT.
I HAVE A REALLY BAD FEELING ABOUT THIS...
UP

CLONINK VAT. IT IS BUILT. BUT AM NOW NEEDINK DNA SAMPLE FOR MAKINK MINIONS.
COPYRIGHT © 2002 ILLIAD HTTP://WWW.USERFRIENDLY.ORG/

INSTRUCTIONS. THEY ARE SAYINK MUST HAVE SUBJECT BE ENTERINK VAT TO EXTRACT DNA.

HOW AM GOINK TO TRICK FOOL INTO ENTERINK VAT?
JEEZ. THIS LOVECRAFT GUY GOT EVERYTHING WRONG..

FROM THE EVIL GENIUSES GUIDE TO SPORTS:

"WORLD CUP"

WHERE'D YOU FIND THIS, LI'L GUY? THIS IS A COPY OF THE INSTRUCTIONS THAT CAME WITH PITR'S CLONING VAT.
IN THE TRASH. IT LOOKED IMPORTANT.

CHECK THIS. THE VAT ISN'T PERFECT. "HAPPY CLONE VAT SOMETIMES MAKE SMALL COPY. SMALLER COPY COMPENSATE FOR OTHER THINGS BIGGER."
WHAT DOES THAT MEAN?
I DON'T KNOW. I'M SURE PITR WILL FIGURE IT ALL OUT.
UH OH...

WHAT IS THAT?
IT IS CTHULHULET. IS TINY VERSION OF EVIL SQUID GOD.
HEH. HE'S KINDA CUTE.

SO WHAT THE HECK DOES IT DO? IT DOESN'T SEEM VERY USEFUL.

SEEMS USEFUL ENOUGH TO ME.
CAN I HAVE ONE?
OPERATION FUNDRAISINK BEGINS...
GRAA.

SO HOW MANY OF THOSE CTHULHULETS HAVE YOU SOLD, PITR?
ALL OF THEM.

ALL OF THEM?! THAT MANY PEOPLE NEEDED A PET THAT GAGGED MARKETERS ON COMMAND?

WELL, WAS NOT ALL SOLD TO SUCH PEOPLE.

TA-YA SUSHI
IT'S...WAVING AT ME...
THAT JUST MEANS IT'S FRESH.

NEED TO BE MAKINK MORE MONEY TO TAKE OVER WORLD. AM THINKINK TO PATENT CTHULHULETS. CLEVER, DA?
BUT PITR...ISN'T THERE PRIOR ART FOR THIS?

THESE LEETLE SQUIDLETS. THEY ARE SUCKINK BLOOD OUT OF IGNORANT PEOPLES. WHERE IS PRIOR ART?

HELLO? EVER HEARD OF ORACLE AND CALIFORNIA?
EVER HEARD OF GREAT CTHULHU AND THE PLANET EARTH?

LISTEN. YOU LITTLE PEON. YOUR WEAK ATTEMPTS AT BECOMING AN ICON OF EVIL ARE LAUGHABLE. YOU HAVE NO INFLUENCE. NOT ENOUGH MONEY-
WOULD NOT THINK TO DO SO. AM ONLY BUILDINK EMPIRE TO SERVE SUCH GREAT EVIL AS YOU.
COPYRIGHT © 2002 ILLIAD HTTP://WWW.USERFRIENDLY.ORG/
...OH.

YOU'LL NEED FUNDING. WHO DO I MAKE THE CHEQUE OUT TO?
EVIL GENIUSES FOR DUMMIES. CHAPTER 14. "ABSOLUTE SUCKING UP WORKS ABSOLUTELY"

NOW HAVINK MANY MILLIONS OF DOLLARS TO BE TAKINK OVER WORLD. WHAT IS FIRST THING SHOULD BE DOINK?
COPYRIGHT © 2002 ILLIAD HTTP://WWW.USERFRIENDLY.ORG/

OH. AM SO MUCH A ZLOTNIK SOMETIMES. OF COURSE THIS IS WHAT I SHOULD BE DOINK...

The New York Times
EVIL GENIUS NEXT SPACE TOURIST
"Going up to survey his domain."

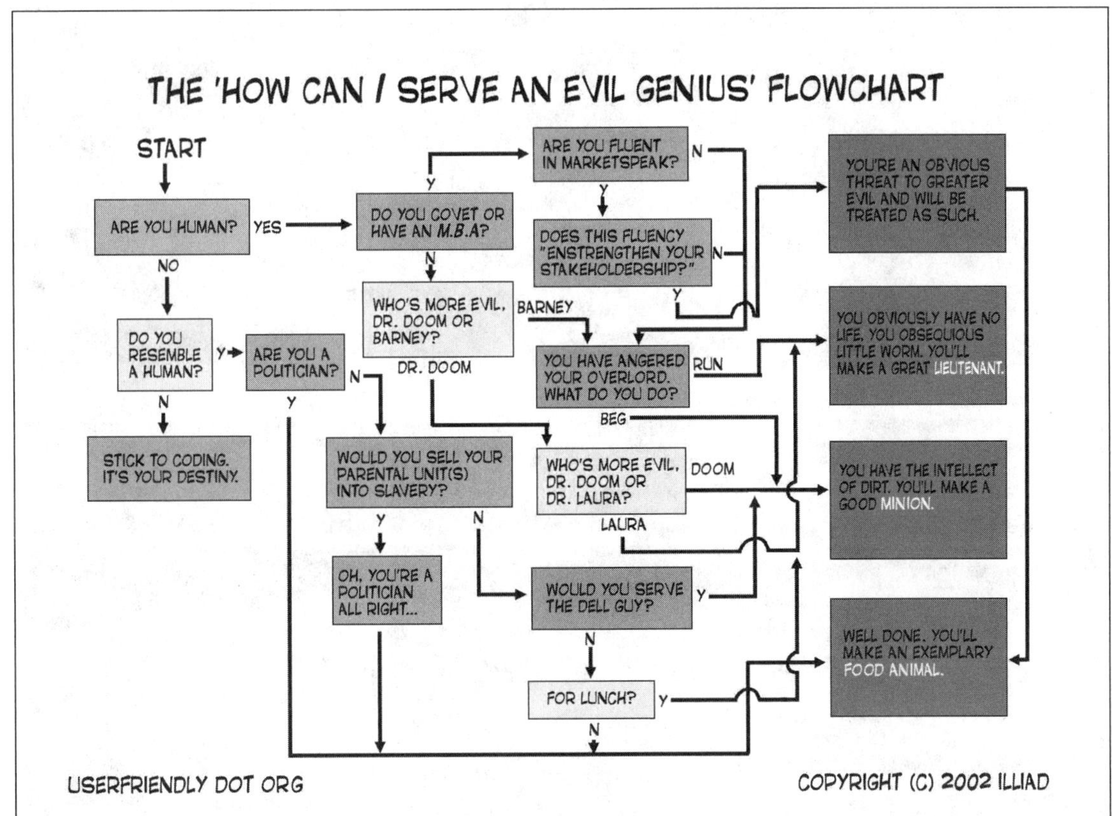

THE 'HOW CAN I SERVE AN EVIL GENIUS' FLOWCHART
START
ARE YOU HUMAN?
YES
NO
DO YOU RESEMBLE A HUMAN?
Y
N
STICK TO CODING. IT'S YOUR DESTINY.
ARE YOU A POLITICIAN?
N
Y
DO YOU COVET OR HAVE AN M.B.A?
Y
N
ARE YOU FLUENT IN MARKETSPEAK?
N
Y
DOES THIS FLUENCY "ENSTRENGTHEN YOUR STAKEHOLDERSHIP?"
N
Y
WHO'S MORE EVIL, DR. DOOM OR BARNEY?
BARNEY
DR. DOOM
YOU HAVE ANGERED YOUR OVERLORD. WHAT DO YOU DO?
RUN
BEG
WOULD YOU SELL YOUR PARENTAL UNIT(S) INTO SLAVERY?
Y
N
OH, YOU'RE A POLITICIAN ALL RIGHT...
WHO'S MORE EVIL, DR. DOOM OR DR. LAURA?
DOOM
LAURA
WOULD YOU SERVE THE DELL GUY?
Y
N
FOR LUNCH?
Y
N
YOU'RE AN OBVIOUS THREAT TO GREATER EVIL AND WILL BE TREATED AS SUCH.
YOU OBVIOUSLY HAVE NO LIFE, YOU OBSEQUIOUS LITTLE WORM. YOU'LL MAKE A GREAT LIEUTENANT.
YOU HAVE THE INTELLECT OF DIRT. YOU'LL MAKE A GOOD MINION.
WELL DONE. YOU'LL MAKE AN EXEMPLARY FOOD ANIMAL.
USERFRIENDLY DOT ORG
COPYRIGHT (C) 2002 ILLIAD

PITR'S GOING UP IN ORBIT?!
YEAH. IN AN HOUR. ACCORDING TO THIS SITE.
HE'S GOING UP IN A **RUSSIAN** ROCKET. RIGHT? **HAHAHAHAH!!**

WHAT'S SO FUNNY?
IT'S A RUSSIAN ROCKET.
YEAH. SO?
IT'LL HAVE **NATIVE RUSSIAN SPEAKERS** ON BOARD.
SO?...OHHHHHH!!

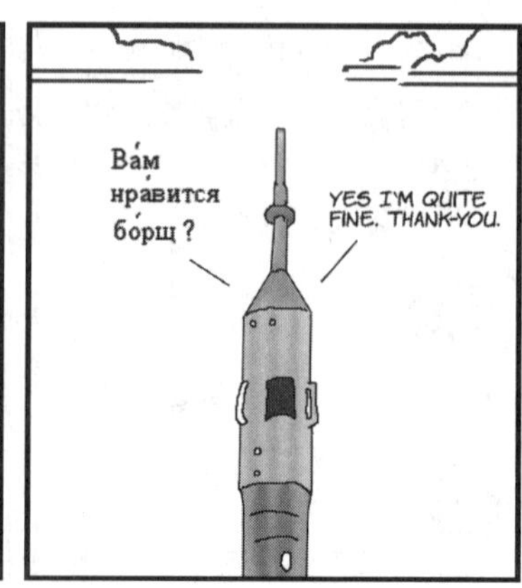
Ва́м нра́вится бо́рщ ?
YES I'M QUITE FINE. THANK-YOU.

ONCE CAUTIOUS STEPS, NOW LUNGES BOLD
AWAY WE STEP FROM CRADLE'S SONG
INTO THE SILENT DARK OF SPACE
AMIDST THE SPINNING, CIRCLING THRONG

LIFT! EXALT! GLORIFY!
BEARDING GRAVITY IN ITS DEN!
THIS HOLLOW WELL CAN JAIL US NOT!
SPACE IS OURS, NOT **IF** BUT **WHEN!**

ALOFT IN NIGHT'S ETERNAL SPREAD
A SPRAY OF GEMS SHINING HARD
BEFORE YOU LIES GOD'S WEAVING THREAD
HOW CAN YOU NOT REACH OUT THAT FAR?
DA. DA. WILL GET TO THEM EVENTUALLY. MUST TAKE OVER **THIS** WORLD FIRST.

THE SUN RISES YET AGAIN AS THE WORLD TURNS, EMERGING FROM A PARTIAL SOLAR ECLIPSE THAT HAD CAST SHADOWS ON THE PLANET...

THIS DRAMATIC SHROUDING OF THE WORLD WAS NOT LOST ON A PARTICULAR EVIL GENIUS, WHO HAS THE RUSSIAN ROCKET POSITIONED BETWEEN THE EARTH AND SUN...

AND WITH THE MAGIC OF HAND SHADOW PUPPETS, CARTOON PHYSICS, AND A HEAVILY MANIPULATED CONTRACT, DREAD LORD PITR CASTS TERROR ON THE WORLD...

PASHA? YOU ARE PILOT. PLEASE TO BE TAKINK US TO MOON.
I CAN'T, PITR.*
CAN NOT DO THIS WHY?
WE DON'T HAVE THE FUEL. AND **STOP** WITH THAT **STUPID ACCENT!**
*NOTE THAT THESE RUSSIAN COSMONAUTS SPEAK GOOD ENGLISH.

WERY WELL. AM THINKINK WILL BE READINK **WAR AND PEACE** OUT LOUD...
OKAY! OKAY! THE MOON IT IS!!

LOOK, VIKTOR AND I'D BE HAPPY TO TAKE YOU TO THE MOON. BUT WE DON'T HAVE THE FUEL!
NOT TO BE WORRYINK. AM EVIL GENIUS. HAVE MADE INWENTION TO USE REACTION MASS.
COPYRIGHT © 2002 ILLIAD HTTP://WWW.USERFRIENDLY.ORG/

YOU KNOW, THAT STUPID FAKE SLAVIC ACCENT OF YOURS MADE IT SOUND LIKE YOU SAID "REACTION MESS."

HAHAHAHAH!! "REACTION MESS!" SILLY COSMONAUT. AM NOT SUGGESTINK WE ARE USINK THE WHITE HOUSE! OH, YOU ARE WERY FUNNY!
THIS GUY HAS GOT TO GO...

AS OUR BRAVE COSMONAUTS ARRIVE AT THE MOON ON A JET OF PITR-COLA, PITR DEPLOYS YET ANOTHER "EVIL INWENTION."
COPYRIGHT © 2002 ILLIAD HTTP://WWW.USERFRIENDLY.ORG/

A RAIN OF DARK POWDER SETTLES IN THE MOON'S GENTLE GRAVITY. LINES BECOME SHAPES, SHAPES BECOME A VISAGE...

...AND THE WORLD FREAKS OUT AS ONE.
PAY TRIBUTE OR ELSE
CHA

SOLVING THE MATH IN A LOGO

VeriSign®
The Value of Trust™

= about a dollar
per e-mail address

If you have no idea what this strip is about, I envy you. George Lucas did a fantastic job with his first three *Star Wars* movies. Some parts of the three prequels were good too, but writing romance is not his strong suit.

PITR'S GONE TOO FAR WITH HIS BID TO TAKE OVER THE WORLD. I HAVE TO STOP HIM.
HE'S BACK FROM SPACE. HE'S IN HIS OFFICE, TURNING IT INTO A LAIR. BE CAREFUL.
COPYRIGHT © 2002 ILLIAD HTTP://WWW.USERFRIENDLY.ORG/

CAREFUL? OF WHAT?
HE MUTTERED SOMETHING ABOUT TESTING OUT A PIRATED VIDEO CLIP AS A PUNISHMENT AGAINST ALL WHO OPPOSE HIM.
A VIDEO CL-? OH! HE WOULDN'T!!

OH PADME!
OH ANAKIN!!
YE GODS!! DOES HIS EVIL KNOW NO BOUNDS?!
URLP

DEEP WITHIN THE LAIR-UNDER-CONSTRUCTION OF DREAD LORD PITR, WE FIND HIM ONCE AGAIN PORING OVER A TOME OF GREAT ANTIQUITY: "MINIONS FOR THE DISCERNING EVIL OVERLORD."
COPYRIGHT © 2002 ILLIAD HTTP://WWW.USERFRIENDLY.ORG/

AFTER MUCH WINNOWING, OUR EVIL PROTAGONIST HAS REDUCED HIS CHOICE OF MINIONS TO A VERY FEW...FROM THE OBVIOUS...
EX-ENRON EXEC WILL COMPROMISE INTEGRITY FOR FOOD

TO THE SUBLIME...
AOL PARENTAL CONTROLS: OFF. PORN SHALL FLOW ONCE AGAIN.
PLEASE DON'T TELL YOUR MOTHER.
BETTER DOUBLE MY ALLOWANCE AGAIN, DAD.

I'M GOING TO GO TALK TO PITR.
ABOUT WHAT?
A JOB.
COPYRIGHT © 2002 ILLIAD HTTP://WWW.USERFRIENDLY.ORG/

A WHAT?!
THINK ABOUT IT! MORE THAN ANYONE, EVIL OVERLORDS NEED GOOD MARKETING! A FEW WORDS FROM ME AND HE'LL SEE THINGS MY WAY.

DUDE. YOU NEED ME.
DA. AM IN SHORT SUPPLY OF SHARK BAIT...

AM THINKINK DO NOT NEED MARKETINK.
ARE YOU OUT OF YOUR MIND? EVERYTHING TODAY NEEDS MARKETING!
COPYRIGHT © 2002 ILLIAD HTTP://WWW.USERFRIENDLY.ORG/

DA. ALREADY HAVINK MARKETINK PLAN.
OH. REALLY. AND WHAT DOES THIS SCINTILLATING PLAN ENTAIL?

BEHOLD.
"PLEASE ACCEPT OUR EVIL OR WE'LL GET MEDIEVAL."
DAMN. HE'S GOT THE CHICK MARKET FOR SURE...
A FUZZY KIND OF EVIL.

ALL RIGHT. YOU HAVE A DECENT MARKETING PLAN. YOU STILL NEED A SPOKESPERSON. SOMEONE WHO LOOKS GOOD ON TELEVISION. HAS A REP FOR BEING A DARK ANGEL. YET IS LOVED NONETHELESS.
COPYRIGHT © 2002 ILLIAD HTTP://WWW.USERFRIENDLY.ORG/

OZZY OSBOURNE. HE IS AVAILABLE?
I WAS THINKING OF ME!
BUT OZZY DOESN'T LOOK AS SPACED OUT AS YOU DO.

YO. EVIL DUDE. DO I HAVE A SURPRISE FOR YOU!
COPYRIGHT © 2002 ILLIAD HTTP://WWW.USERFRIENDLY.ORG/

...MR. OZZY OSBOURNE!
HE'S AGREED TO TALK TO YOU ABOUT PUMPING UP YOUR EVIL IMAGE TO THE WORLD AS YOUR SPOKESMAN. WE'VE DISCUSSED A FEW SHOWPIECE IDEAS...

DA? SUCH AS?
HOW THE $#*&! DO YOU EXPECT ME TO BITE ITS $#*!!&*! HEAD OFF? IT'S ALL HEAD.

I TELL YA, THAT DAMN LOGO IS LOOKING MORE AND MORE LIKE A BULLSEYE...

RIAA

*THE ABOVE IS A LOGO AND TRADEMARK OF THE RECORDING INDUSTRY ~~AUTOCRACY~~ ASSOCIATION OF AMERICA, AND BELONGS TO THEM BLAH BLAH BLAH. JUST COVERING THE BASES HERE.

LADIES AND GENTLEMEN. DREAD LORD PITR ENTERPRISES IS PROUD TO PRESENT OUR OFFICIAL SPOKESPERSON. THE **PRINCE OF DARKNESS. OZZY OSBOURNE!**
WOOO!
YEAH!
BRING ON THE MAN!
COPYRIGHT © 2002 ILLIAD HTTP://WWW.USERFRIENDLY.ORG/

TONIGHT. MR. OSBOURNE WILL BE PERFORMING AN ACT THAT HE WAS WRONGLY ACCUSED OF YEARS AGO. NAMELY. BITING THE HEAD OFF OF A BAT!
MMRF!

WHERE IS THIS BAT AND DOES IT HAVE A NAME THEN?
BEHIND YOU. AND IT'S "HILARY ROSEN."

LOOK I CAN'T BITE OFF HER $#*&! HEAD! PEOPLE LIKE HER MADE ME $#*&! RICH! IF IT WASN'T FOR THE RIAA, I'D BE A $#*&! INDIE ARTIST. WORKING $#*&! HARD BUT FREE. WITHOUT ANY $#*&! RECORD LABEL EXECUTIVES AROUND ME AND...
PHEW...
COPYRIGHT © 2002 ILLIAD HTTP://WWW.USERFRIENDLY.ORG/

AND...UH...

SOMEBODY GET ME SOME $#*&! SALT AND PEPPER!
I KNEW HE'D FIGURE IT OUT...

STEF? THAT PUBLICITY THING WITH OZZY -- MS. ROSEN ONLY HAS ONE HEAD TO HAVE BITTEN OFF. AND WE HAVE A WORLD TOUR TO DO.
OZZY'S NOT GOING TO BITE HER HEAD OFF. PITR LOCKED HILARY UP SOMEWHERE.
COPYRIGHT © 2002 ILLIAD HTTP://WWW.USERFRIENDLY.ORG/

OH. SO THERE'S NO PUBLICITY STUNT?
RELAX DIRTBALL. PITR'S GOT IT COVERED.

HURRY! KEEP **EATINK!** THERE ARE TOO MANY IN CLONINK VAT!
I CAN'T @#$&! STOMACH ANYMORE! THESE THINGS ARE **REPULSIVE!!**
ARRR! MONEY!
HATES THE NET
HATES IT!

SEE HERE? A COURT IN THE U.S. RULED THE PLEDGE OF ALLEGIANCE AS UNCONSTITUTIONAL BECAUSE OF THE LINE "ONE NATION UNDER GOD."
HMMM.
COPYRIGHT © 2002 ILLIAD HTTP://WWW.USERFRIENDLY.ORG/

THINK THEY'LL CHANGE THE PLEDGE TO SOMETHING MORE UP TO DATE?
LIKE WHAT?

"...ONE NATION UNDER SCRUTINY..."
"...WITH SECURITY FOR ALL..."
OUCH.

HEY. DID YOU HEAR ABOUT ALL THAT KAFUFFLE REGARDING THE AMERICAN PLEDGE OF ALLEGIANCE?
COPYRIGHT © 2002 ILLIAD HTTP://WWW.USERFRIENDLY.ORG/

SIGH
O DREAD LORD. DID YOU HEAR ABOUT ALL THAT KAFUFFLE REGARDING THE AMERICAN PLEDGE OF ALLEGIANCE?
SUDDENLY YOU ARE EXISTINK! DA. OF THIS KAFUFFLE I HAVE HEARD.

SO, UM, O DREAD LORD WHEN YOU'RE FINALLY ON YOUR THRONE AND HANDING DOWN EDICTS, WHAT ARE YOU GOING TO DO ABOUT ALL THAT RELIGIOUS STUFF?
COPYRIGHT © 2002 ILLIAD HTTP://WWW.USERFRIENDLY.ORG/

YOU ARE SPEAKINK OF THINGS SUCH AS PRAYER IN SCHOOLS DEBATE?
UM, YEAH.

IS ALREADY MOOT POINT. EVERY TIME THERE IS PHYSICS TEST, ALL STUDENTS ARE PRAYING.
IF YOU SNEEZE, CAN I STILL SAY "GOD BLESS YOU?"

AH, THE IRONY OF BEING KNOWN AS 'THE COPYING COMPANY'
WORLDCOM
QUARTERLY FINANCIALS
XEROX

After Enron and WorldCom, Xerox (among others) announced that it too had stunk up its books to the tune of two billion USD.

YOU CALLED, O DREAD LORD?
DA. AM NEEDINK YOU TO RUN ERRAND.

AM RESEARCHINK POTENTIAL ALLY, WHOM YOU WILL BE CALLINK. THIS ONE BRINGINK REPRESSIVE, VISE-LIKE GRIP OVER HOUSEHOLDS THROUGHOUT NORTH AMERIKA.

YOU'RE THINKING ABOUT ALLYING WITH MICROSOFT?! OR AOL?
NYET, MY LEETLE MARKETING MARMOT. **MARTHA STEWART.**

I SPOKE TO MARTHA LIKE YOU ASKED.
DA?

WELL ... I TOLD HER THAT BECAUSE OF THE IMCLONE SCANDAL AND HER OVERWHELMING OMNIPRESENCE, SHE WAS LOOKING VERY APPEALING AS AN ALLY TO DREAD LORD PITR.
DA. AND SHE IS SAYINK WHAT?

"THAT'S NOT A GOOD THING."
OF COURSE NOT. IT IS **EVIL** THING. THERE IS PROBLEM?

MARTHA'S HERE.
MARTHA WHO?

I DON'T KNOW. EVERYONE JUST CALLS HER "MARTHA."
MARTHA **STEWART?!**
I GUESS SO. SHE'S IN PITR'S OFFICE RIGHT NOW.

...AND OVER HERE WE COULD PAPER THIS WALL WITH THESE ADORABLE IMCLONE SHARE CERTIFICATES...
AM GOINK TO BE KILLINK THIS WOMAN...

A.J., YOU WILL BECOME MINION TO ME.
UH. WHY WOULD I DO THAT?
PLEASE TO BE READINK.

YOU WANT ME TO HELP YOU START A COMPANY CALLED "MARTHA STEWART WEB DESIGN?!" I THOUGHT YOU HATED HER!!
DA. BUT MUST BE ADMITTING SHE IS MAKINK SUPERLATIVE EVIL CONSORT.

FORGET IT! YOU CAN'T DO CHARTREUSE IN HEX!
SURE YOU CAN. IT'S "7FFF00."
I MEANT NO ONE SHOULD BE **ALLOWED** TO!!

AND WE'RE BACK WITH "BETWEEN THE COVERS!" YOUR GUIDE TO THE LATEST BOOKS IN HARDCOVER! I'M GINA PENMAN.
AND I'M JACK YUNKET!
COPYRIGHT © 2002 ILLIAD HTTP://WWW.USERFRIENDLY.ORG/

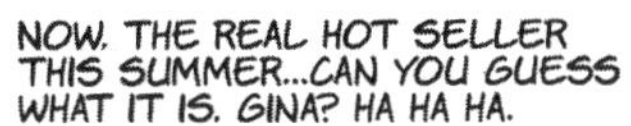
NOW. THE REAL HOT SELLER THIS SUMMER...CAN YOU GUESS WHAT IT IS. GINA? HA HA HA.

NO IDEA JACK. HEE HEE. WHY DON'T YOU TELL US?

"THE ARTHUR ANDERSEN ACCOUNTING COOKBOOK" WITH AN INTRODUCTION BY MARTHA STEWART! IT'LL FLY OFF THE SHELVES IN CORPORATE AMERICA!
AND. I EXPECT. THE JUSTICE DEPARTMENT!
DA. SHE IS PERFECT.

WHILE DREAD LORD PITR CAREFULLY BUILDS HIS BURGEONING EMPIRE, EVIL PINCHES OFF A NUB OF SPAWN ELSEWHERE...
Microsoft
COPYRIGHT © 2002 ILLIAD HTTP://WWW.USERFRIENDLY.ORG/

THIS DIABOLICAL HATCHLING, A SECURITY PATCH FOR WINDOWS MEDIA PLAYER, HAS AN EULA THAT STATES YOU WILL ESSENTIALLY GIVE MICROSOFT ADMIN PRIVILEGES ON YOUR PC, OSTENSIBLY SO THEY CAN PROTECT US FROM 'INSECURE CONTENT'...

...SUCH AS, FOR EXAMPLE, PIRATED MARIAH CAREY SONGS...
YOU RIPPED OFF THIS SONG. ACCESS DENIED!
PHEW! THANK GOD FOR MICROSOFT!

GUESS WHO'S EXHIBITING AT LINUX WORLD EXPO?
Microsoft
USERFRIENDLY DOT ORG
COPYRIGHT (C) 2002 ILLIAD

They actually showed up! To the Microsoft staff who manned the booth: You guys and gals clang when you walk!

THAT END USER'S LICENSE AGREEMENT FROM MICROSOFT IS JUST PLAIN ABUSIVE.
AREN'T THEY ALL? AND THEN THERE'S THE CLAUSE ABOUT MS RESERVING THE RIGHT TO CHANGE THE TERMS OF THE EULA AT ANY TIME.
COPYRIGHT © 2002 ILLIAD HTTP://WWW.USERFRIENDLY.ORG/

I DON'T SEE HOW THEY CAN DO THAT. FUNCTIONALLY, I MEAN.
I'VE BEEN DIGGING AROUND THE MEDIA PLAYER PATCH BINARY. LET'S SEE IF WE CAN FIND THAT BIT. AH...HERE IT IS.

EULA$
OH WE'RE SCREWED.

THIS IS TERRIBLE. CORRUPTION IS RUNNING RAMPANT IN CORPORATE AMERICA. THE MIDDLE EAST IS TOPPED-UP WITH BLIND HATRED. THERE'RE MILLIONS OF PEOPLE GOING HUNGRY AROUND THE WORLD.
COPYRIGHT © 2002 ILLIAD HTTP://WWW.USERFRIENDLY.ORG/

WITH SO MUCH ANGUISH IN THE WORLD, HOW COULD YOU BE A PART OF PITR'S EVIL PLANS? YOU'RE SUCH A SWEETIE PIE. I JUST CAN'T PICTURE YOU HELPING PITR.
PITR SAID I COULD BE HIS MINI-ONION.

"MINI-ONION?" PITR... THAT'S SO...CUTE.
MINION! AM SAYINK YOU CAN BE MINION!

HEY GREG? I'M STUCK ON A PUZZLE:
"A GAGGLE OF GEESE. A MURDER OF CROWS. AN ARRAY OF GEEKS. A _____ OF IDIOTS."
COPYRIGHT © 2002 ILLIAD HTTP://WWW.USERFRIENDLY.ORG/

"CORPORATION"
THANKS.

THE RECENT CASES OF FRAUD AMONGST SOME OF AMERICA'S LARGEST CORPORATIONS HAVE SHAKEN PUBLIC CONFIDENCE IN WHAT WAS ONCE THOUGHT OF AS PILLARS OF CAPITALISM.
COPYRIGHT © 2002 ILLIAD HTTP://WWW.USERFRIENDLY.ORG/

AS A CHANGE OF PACE, TODAY WE'LL BE TALKING TO AN INSIDER FROM A HIGHLY SUCCESSFUL INDUSTRY ASSOCIATION, THE R.I.A.A! IT'S TIME WE HEARD A SUCCESS STORY!
QTY 1

AND HERE'S THE INSIDER RIGHT NOW... WOW, YOU LOOK JUST LIKE HILARY ROSEN, EXCEPT FOR THE TENTACLES.
OZZY! NO DESSERT FOR YOU!
TENTACLES?! THAT'S MY HAIR!! PERSONAL GROOMING ISN'T A HIGH PRIORITY IN A DUNGEON, BUDDY.
QTY 1

...AND SO YOU SEE, FILE SHARING HAS ROBBED US OF THE REVENUE WE RIGHTLY DESERVE.
BUT MS. ROSEN, THE RECORD LABELS HAVE BEEN REPORTING BETTER REVENUES THAN EVER SINCE THE ADVENT OF NAPSTER. HOW DO YOU EXPLAIN THIS?
COPYRIGHT © 2002 ILLIAD HTTP://WWW.USERFRIENDLY.ORG/

OKAY, WE MISREPORTED ALL OF THAT REVENUE. WE'RE ACTUALLY IN THE HOLE, JUST LIKE WORLDCOM AND ENRON AND ALL THE OTHERS.
ARE YOU SUGGESTING THAT FILE SWAPPERS ARE RESPONSIBLE FOR THE DOWNFALL OF AMERICAN CAPITALISM?
YEAH, THAT'S GOOD.

WOW, THE MARKET IS JUST BERSERK THESE DAYS. HUGE DIPS AND SUDDEN RALLIES! DID YOU BUY INTO ANY STOCKS THAT HAVE BOTTOMED OUT?
DA. HAVE BOUGHT IMCLONE.
COPYRIGHT © 2002 ILLIAD HTTP://WWW.USERFRIENDLY.ORG/

IS THAT IT? SHARES IN THE COMPANY THAT MARTHA STEWART DITCHED JUST BEFORE THEY NOSE-DIVED? YOUR PORTFOLIO SHOULD BE MORE DIVERSE THAN THAT!!

YOU'RE A SUPPOSED TO BE AN **EVIL GENIUS!** AN **EVIL OVERLORD!** BUYING A FEW SHARES IN ONE CORPORATION IS HARDLY IMPRESSIVE!
YOU ARE NOT LISTENINK. **HAVE. BOUGHT. IMCLONE.**

A TEAM OF RESEARCHERS SAY THEY'VE UNCOVERED WHAT APPEARS TO BE THE EARLIEST EVIDENCE OF THE HUMAN FAMILY EVER FOUND -- DURING BRAIN SURGERY ON THE C.E.O. OF A MAJOR CORPORATION.

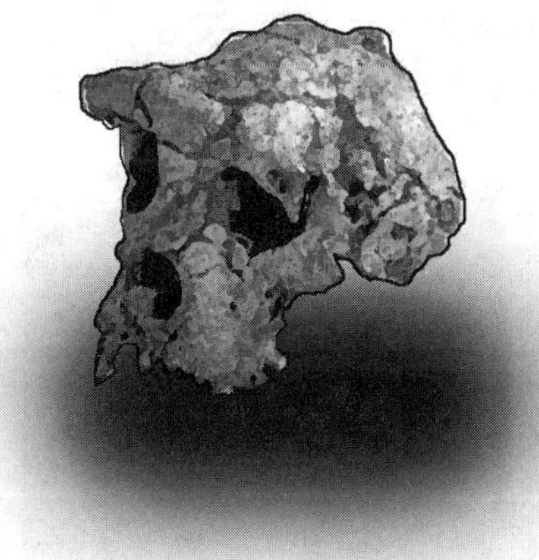

USERFRIENDLY DOT ORG

TECH SUPPORT. GREG SPEAKING.
DUUUUUDE. I'M GONNA BE A MINION FOR DREAD LORD PITR AND HE SAID TO CALL YOU IF I GOT STUCK ON MY COMPUTER.

OH DID HE NOW. AND WHAT KIND OF COMPUTER DO YOU HAVE?
LIKE, ONE OF THOSE BEIGE ONES.

SERVE ME AND MY DARK LEGIONS WELL, AND I WILL GRANT YOU YOUR DEEPEST WISH.
FINE. PROMISE ME YOU'LL MAKE STUPIDITY PAINFUL.
LIKE, HELLO?

ALL RIGHT MINION #4086. I NEED YOU TO BOOT THE COMPUTER.
'KAY.
COPYRIGHT © 2002 ILLIAD HTTP://WWW.USERFRIENDLY.ORG/

JACKBOOTED THUMP

NOPE. THAT DIDN'T HELP. WHAT ELSE DO YOU SUGGEST?
HAVING YOU MECHANICALLY DE-BONED WOULD BE A GOOD START.
GREGOR! BEINK NICE!

MY PLANS, MUST BE GOINK BACK TO DRAWINK BOARD. HAD CONTROL OF SO MANY BIG COMPANIES. NOW FINDINK NOBODY IS TRUSTINK THEM. HOW TO BE BETRAYING TRUST AND TAKINK OVER WORLD IF THERE IS NO TRUST TO BETRAY?
COPYRIGHT © 2002 ILLIAD HTTP://WWW.USERFRIENDLY.ORG/

THE MARKET. SHE IS SO UPSIE-DOWNSIE. WHAT COMPANY AM TAKINK OVER COULD HAVE BEEN SAFE BET FOR MAKINK MONEY?

THE COMPANY THAT MAKES MAALOX?
SEEMINK KIND OF OBVIOUS NOW, DA.

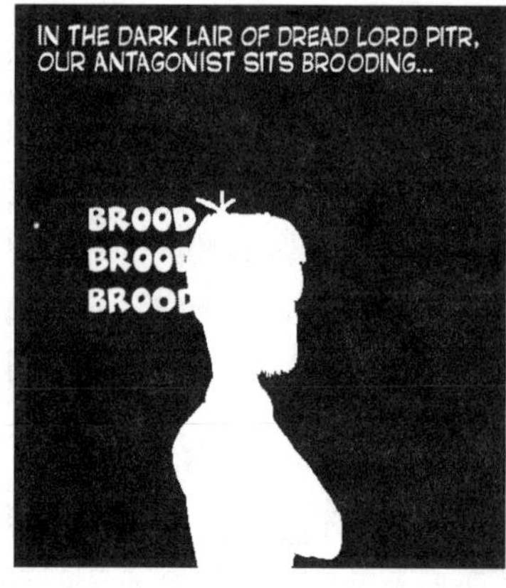
IN THE DARK LAIR OF DREAD LORD PITR, OUR ANTAGONIST SITS BROODING...
BROOD
BROOD
BROOD
COPYRIGHT © 2002 ILLIAD HTTP://WWW.USERFRIENDLY.ORG/

IN THIS TIME OF BELT-TIGHTENING, LAYOFFS OF STAFF ARE COMMON. THIS HAS NOT LEFT DREAD LORD PITR'S DARK LEGIONS UNTOUCHED.

HOWEVER, BEING EVIL DOES ALLOW ONE TO GENERATE REVENUE EVEN AFTER THE EXIT INTERVIEWS...
WHAT THE HELL IS A "FILET MINION?"
SOYLENT GREEN IS EVIL!

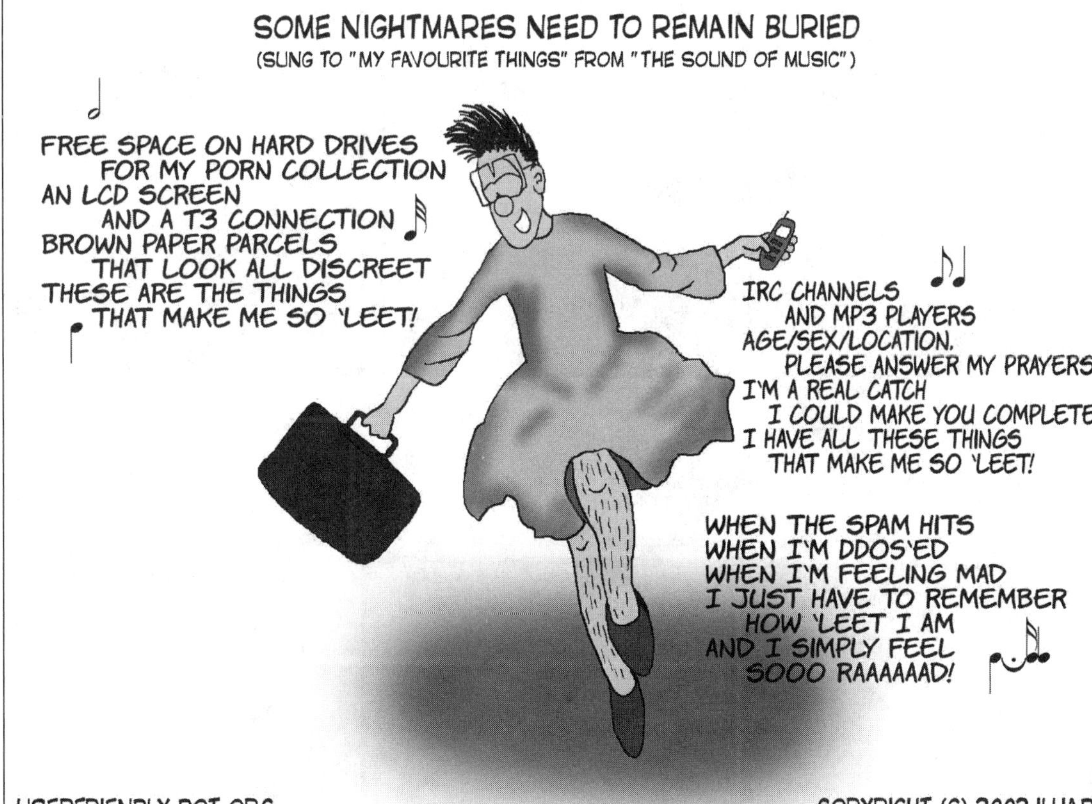

This wasn't from any sort of bong. Fevered nightmares. I think I was hopped up on NeoCitran.

WORLDCOM FIRED ITS TOP FINANCIAL EXECUTIVE LAST MONTH AFTER DISCOVERING THAT THE COMPANY HAD IMPROPERLY ACCOUNTED FOR ALMOST $4 BILLION ON ITS CORPORATE BALANCE SHEETS DURING THE PAST FIVE QUARTERS.

SING IT!
SING IT!
YOU KNOW YOU WANT TO SING IT!
NO!
NO!
NO I DON'T!!
COPYRIGHT © 2002 ILLIAD HTTP://WWW.USERFRIENDLY.ORG/

IF YOU DON'T, I'LL MAKE YOUR PASSWORD "GEEKSRULE" AND SET IT SO YOU CAN'T EVER CHANGE IT.
OKAY. OKAY!!

YOU ARE MY SUNSHINE. MY ONLY SUNSHINE. YOU MAKE ME HAPPY. WHEN SKIES ARE GREY...
I AM SYSADMIN. APPRECIATE ME.

YO. GEEK. WHAT IS IT THAT YOU DO THAT MADE YOU THINK IT NECESSARY FOR ME TO SING THAT STUPID SONG YESTERDAY?
I KEEP THE SERVERS RUNNING. NOT TO MENTION THE NETWORK.
COPYRIGHT © 2002 ILLIAD HTTP://WWW.USERFRIENDLY.ORG/

THEN WHY IS IT THAT I DON'T EVER ACTUALLY SEE YOU DO ANYTHING? YOU JUST SIT THERE MOST OF THE DAY.
I'M GOOD AT IT.

HELL. I COULD BE A SYSADMIN. I'M GOOD AT SITTING AROUND ALL DAY TOO.
OH DON'T BE SO MODEST. YOU'RE THE BEST AT IT.

USER
FRIENDLY
the comic strip
PIZZA
Portrasher 4
ROTO-ROUTER 800
Copyright©1997-2002 Illiad

NOPE... NOPE... NOPE...AHH. THERE IT IS

HEH... "YOUAREMYSUNSHINE.MP3"
HEADPHONES!!

ATTENTION!! THIS IS THE R.I.A.A.!
...THE HELL?!

WE HAVE BEEN MONITORING YOUR FILE SHARING ACTIVITIES AND WILL BE FLOODING YOU OFF THE NET IN RESPONSE...
TSK.
TAP
TAPPITY
TAP
LOGIN
MUCKABOUT

HEY! WHERE'D THE WEB GO?!
RIAA

I recall many sysadmins writing in to inform me that they had taken this cartoon to heart and insisted that their co-workers sing this song for them on this day. You're all welcome.

HEY. WHAT DO YOU GUYS SAY TO DOING SOMETHING FUN AS A GROUP? SOMETHING TO TAKE OUR MINDS OFF OF THE STATE OF THE WORLD?
WHAT DO YOU HAVE IN MIND?
COPYRIGHT © 2002 ILLIAD HTTP://WWW.USERFRIENDLY.ORG/

HOW ABOUT A GAME OF AD&D?
DUNGEONS AND DRAGONS? YEAH!
NEVER TRIED IT. WHAT DO I DO?

FIRST, YOU HAVE TO GENERATE YOUR CHARACTER...
I ALREADY HAVE CHARACTER.
IN THE SAME SENSE THAT PIGEONS HAVE BRAINS. YES.

A mild hiccough compared to the crash of 2008. Erwin was merely practicing back in 2002.

DUNGEONS & DRAGONS TIME! LET'S GET STARTED!
WAIT! WHAT ARE WE USING TO PLAY? A MUD? NEVERWINTER NIGHTS?
COPYRIGHT © 2002 ILLIAD HTTP://WWW.USERFRIENDLY.ORG/

DICE, PENS AND PAPER, A.J.

HOW...QUAINT. DO WE CREATE OUR CHARACTERS WITH PUNCH CARDS AS WELL?
A.J., GUESS WHO'S THE GAMEMASTER...
AND GUESS WHO GETS TO BE THE MONSTER MAGNET.

STEF, SINCE YOU'VE NEVER PLAYED BEFORE, I GENERATED A CHARACTER FOR YOU BASED ON YOUR PREFERENCES WE TALKED ABOUT...
COPYRIGHT © 2002 ILLIAD HTTP://WWW.USERFRIENDLY.ORG/

I'M PLAYING A GNOMISH 3RD-LEVEL CORPORATE AUDITOR?
YOU SAID YOU WANTED A CHARACTER THAT WAS NEUTRAL EVIL.

WHAT KIND OF CHARACTER DID SID GIVE YOU TO PLAY?
LET'S SEE HERE... WOW! THIS IS QUITE A LIST OF SPECIAL ABILITIES...
COPYRIGHT © 2002 ILLIAD HTTP://WWW.USERFRIENDLY.ORG/

- AN AUDIBLE GLAMER OF LINE STATIC, ONCE PER DAY
- A MAGIC MOUTH THAT SAYS "PLEASE HOLD," TWICE PER DAY
- AND A PERPETUAL STINKING CLOUD.

IT SAYS YOU'RE A "CHAOTIC NEUTRAL SUPPORT TECHNICIAN."
WHADDYA MEAN STINKING CLOUD, MISTER "I HAVE ONLY ONE SUIT?"

OKAY. LET'S GET STARTED. WE HAVE AN AUDITOR, A SUPPORT TECH, AN MP3 COLLECTOR AND A SYSADMIN. THAT'S A FAIRY BALANCED...ER, WELL-ROUNDED GROUP.
SID?
YO.
COPYRIGHT © 2002 ILLIAD HTTP://WWW.USERFRIENDLY.ORG/

ONE THING I'M HOPING FOR: NO CLICHES. I WANT REAL ROLE-PLAYING. NONE OF THIS "YOU ALL MEET IN A BAR" BUSINESS.
NO WORRIES. IT'LL ALL BE NEW.
YEAH! GAME ON!

RIGHT! SO YOU ALL MEET IN A CHAT ROOM...
HOLD IT!

MEANWHILE, BACK AT THE LAIR...
STOCK MARKET, SHE IS COLLAPSINK. AM SELLINK EVERYTHINK! DELAYINK PLANS OF DOMINATION!
COPYRIGHT © 2002 ILLIAD HTTP://WWW.USERFRIENDLY.ORG/

THEN MARKET, SHE IS SURGINK BACK UP. SHOULD BE BUYINK NOW. BUT LOST ALL MONEY! HOW AM TO BE TAKINK OVER WORLD IF MARKET IS PLAYINK UPSY-DOWNSY?! IS SO FRUSTRATINK!!!

IBM +0.25 VAX +1.75 ... SIN +1.25
CXVA -3.00 ORAC +0.75 PPEP +0.1
are Volume ADV 1,113,545,600 DEC 575,151,200 ...
2002 US Market Closed Nasdaq-100 980.36
PUPPETS. ALL Y'ALL.

INVESTIGATORS OF AOL TIME WARNER'S BOOKS EXHIBIT A DECIDEDLY NASTY SENSE OF HUMOUR...
YOU SEEM PALE!
DON'T LIKE JAIL?
C.E.O.
AOL Time Warner
USERFRIENDLY DOT ORG
COPYRIGHT (C) 2002 ILLIAD

THE DOOR CREAKS OPEN, AND BEFORE YOU IS A DARKENED ROOM, DIMLY LIT BY ROWS AND ROWS OF GLOWING EYES OF SOME FELL BEAST IN THE FAR CORNER...YET IT DOES NOT REACT...
THANK THE GODS! DO I SEE ANY MARKINGS ON THE WALLS?

COPYRIGHT © 2002 ILLIAD HTTP://WWW.USERFRIENDLY.ORG/
YES, THESE ONES HERE. YOU CAN USE YOUR CODE SHEET TO DECRYPT THIS.

WELL?!
I'M WORKING ON IT! COL....COLUMBIA.... COLUMBIA INT...
I CAST A LIGHTNING BOLT AT THE GLOWING EYES!

Ever want to see a sysadmin sweat? Watch his forehead bead up as he slaps in that first tape for a restore.

UP AHEAD YOU SEE A DARK SHADOWY FIGURE. THE GLOW FROM ITS EYES REVEAL IT TO BE NOT OF THIS WORLD, THE ORIGINAL OCCUPANT OF THE BODY HAVING LONG AGO SHUFFLED OFF ITS MORTAL COIL...

COPYRIGHT © 2002 ILLIAD HTTP://WWW.USERFRIENDLY.ORG/
AAAGH! THIS IS A JOB FOR A CLERIC! I'M RUNNING!
I GUESS THAT'S ME. I PRAY AND SUPPLICATE.

MIRANDA? SYSADMINS DON'T PRAY OR SUPPLICATE.
THINK "RESTORING BACKUPS," GREG
DO I RUN FASTER THAN STEF? CUZ THAT'S ALL THAT MATTERS.

I DON'T THINK IT'S FAIR THAT THESE GUYS GET ALL THE SHOWY SPECIAL ABILITIES. WHAT IF I WANT TO CAST A SPELL?
UH OH...

COPYRIGHT © 2002 ILLIAD HTTP://WWW.USERFRIENDLY.ORG/
SURE THING STEF. USE THAT O-LEVEL MONSTER SUMMONING SPELL LIKE I TAUGHT YOU.
UM. OKAY...

O-LEVEL MONSTER SUMMONING SPELL? WHAT ARE THE SPELL COMPONENTS?
ESSENCE OF DORK.
"OH WHAT EVER SHALL I DO WITH ALL OF THIS TREASURE AND ME WITH NO ARMOUR AND LOW ON HIT POINTS...?!"

YOU WATCH AS THE FELL BEAST FALLS TO THE STONE FLOOR, NO LONGER DRIVEN BY THE DARKNESS WITHIN. HOWEVER, YOU NOW NOTICE THAT YOU STAND IN A CHAMBER RICHLY DECORATED WITH RUNES AND SIGILS OF GREAT POWER.
OOH! I RUN UP AND TAKE THE TREASURE!

COPYRIGHT © 2002 ILLIAD HTTP://WWW.USERFRIENDLY.ORG/
SUDDENLY, YOU ALSO NOTICE THAT MARKED ON THE FLOOR IN THE MIDDLE OF THE CHAMBER IS AN ENORMOUS SWIRL. INSIDE OF IT STANDS A REDDISH CREATURE WITH HORNS AND A FIERY DEMEANOR...
OH. I RUN AWAY.
WHAT COULD IT BE?
OH NO...

WHY ARE MY EARS BURNING?

YE GODS. NOT YOU AGAIN.
THANKS SO MUCH FOR THE FINE WELCOME. IT'S ABOUT TIME WE HAD ANOTHER CHAT ANYWAY.
LOOK. I'M BUSY PLAYING A GAME.
THEN BY ALL MEANS CARRY ON. BUT I'M NOT LEAVING UNTIL WE'VE HAD A TALK.
BAMF!
COPYRIGHT © 2002 ILLIAD HTTP://WWW.USERFRIENDLY.ORG/

I CAST A DEMONSPANK SPELL ON THE LITTLE RED DOLT IN THE PENTAGRAM.
FOR THE LAST TIME I'M A DAEMON. NOT A DEM...HEY!!
SPOING!

IT'S BEEN WAY TOO LONG SINCE WE HAD A TALK ABOUT THE MANY ADVANTAGES OF FREEBSD OVER LINUX! DID YOU KNOW THAT WE'RE UP TO RELEASE 4.6? AND THAT THERE'S A VERY CLEVER CHAP WHO'S WORKING ON A PORT TO THE S/390? AND THAT FREEBSD IS EVEN MORE ROBUST AND STABLE THAN BEFORE?
COPYRIGHT © 2002 ILLIAD HTTP://WWW.USERFRIENDLY.ORG/

WILL YOU STOP PLAYING THAT STUPID GAME AND PAY ATTENTION. PLEASE? UH... WHAT ARE YOU DOING WITH THAT GAME MANUAL?

WHAM!

SPELL COMPONENT FOR "SILENCE. 15-INCH RADIUS."

WHY DRUIDS IN AD&D SHOULDN'T HAVE A DEX OF 3
USERFRIENDLY DOT ORG
COPYRIGHT (C) 2002 ILLIAD

For those not immersed in AD&D lore, Druids use holly leaves as specially blessed spell components for their divine magic. The leaves have to be collected on a special night, with a specially blessed sickle in a specially blessed bowl made out of special wood. You cut the leaves from the bush and catch them in the bowl without touching them with your hands. O the Mirth!

DO YOU GUYS KNOW YOU'VE BEEN PLAYING FOR OVER TWENTY HOURS? IT'S HALFWAY THROUGH A NEW WORK DAY!
SO?
COPYRIGHT © 2002 ILLIAD HTTP://WWW.USERFRIENDLY.ORG/

SO...YOU'RE PLAYING DURING WORKING HOURS. DON'T YOU THINK THAT'S WRONG?
THERE ARE SOME THINGS MORE IMPORTANT THAN THE MUNDANITY OF WORK -- SUCH AS A STORYTELLER'S ART.

LOOK. WE HAVE A REALLY EXCITING PART OF THE DUNGEON COMING UP. THE FINALE IN FACT...
INDEED. WELCOME TO THE BOSS LEVEL.
THIS IS WHERE A SAVEGAME WOULD COME IN REAL HANDY.

SID. I'M VERY DISAPPOINTED IN YOUR FLAGRANT DISREGARD OF COMPANY POLICY. YOU WERE ENCOURAGING JUNIOR STAFF MEMBERS TO SLACK OFF DURING COMPANY TIME. HOW COULD YOU?
COPYRIGHT © 2002 ILLIAD HTTP://WWW.USERFRIENDLY.ORG/

THE POLICY IS CLEAR! THERE WILL BE NO FUN HERE AT WORK!
CHIEF. IF YOU WERE A D&D CHARACTER, YOU'D MAKE A GREAT ROGUE.

A...ROGUE? WHY?
BECAUSE IT'S CLEAR THAT YOU CAN PERSONALLY STASH A 10' POLE WITH OUT A PROBLEM.

I fell on one of those accursed dice once. It left a scar.

THANKS FOR THE GAME, SID. THAT WAS GREAT.
CAN WE PLAY AGAIN SOMETIME?
COPYRIGHT © 2002 ILLIAD HTTP://WWW.USERFRIENDLY.ORG/

SURE THING. BUT ONLY AFTER WORK. AND WE NEED TO CLEAN UP AFTER OURSELVES. I GOT SOME HEAT FOR US LEAVING OUR STUFF ALL AROUND.
HEY. HAS ANYONE SEEN MY FOUR-SIDER?

TAKE IT OUT!!
TAKE IT OUT!!!
YE GODS. I THINK IT'S GONE ALL THE WAY THROUGH.

THE RECENT SSL VULNERABILITY FOUND IN INTERNET EXPLORER ELICITS THE USUAL EXASPERATED RESPONSE FROM THE MOTHER SHIP..
DAMN!
Microsoft
COPYRIGHT © 2002 ILLIAD HTTP://WWW.USERFRIENDLY.ORG/

...AS WELL AS THE EXPECTED VITRIOLIC REJOINDER FROM POWERFUL GOVERNMENT INSTITUTIONS.
DAMN!!
SECRET PLACE

UNFORTUNATELY, NOT EVERYONE FEELS QUITE AS ANNOYED ABOUT IT...
YES!
AL-QAEDA HQ

HEY, GUYS! I JUST FINISHED WRITING A NEW MARKETING PIECE THAT SELLS OUR HIGH-END BROADBAND PRODUCT. LISTEN TO THIS:

COPYRIGHT © 2002 ILLIAD HTTP://WWW.USERFRIENDLY.ORG/
"YOUR CONNECTION CAN BE **HUGE!** ...AND WE HAVE PROOF!"
"THESE ARE **REAL PROVEN TECHNIQUES** FOR EXPANDING YOUR BANDWIDTH! YOU WON'T BELIEVE THE RESULTS!! ADD 1-4 MEGABITS NOW!"

WAIT A SECOND...THAT SOUNDS FAMILIAR...
ACTUALLY, IT DOESN'T WO...**I MEAN** YEAH! IT **DOES** SOUND KINDA FAMILIAR!

WHOA. YOU SPAMMED OUR CUSTOMER LIST?!
YEP. WITH OUR NEW BROAD-BAND MARKETING PUSH.
STEF...THAT'S GONNA BITE YOU IN THE BACKSIDE.

COPYRIGHT © 2002 ILLIAD HTTP://WWW.USERFRIENDLY.ORG/
IT'S OKAY! I INCLUDED IN THE E-MAIL THE PRETENSE THAT IT'S SOMETHING THE RECIPIENT REQUESTED. THE WORDS **"THESE ARE THE RESULTS OF YOUR FEED-BACK FORM"** CAN GO A LONG WAY.

TONK!

THESE ARE THE RESULTS OF YOU ANNOYING THE HELL OUT OF ME.
EFEH...

THE RECORD LABELS JOINTLY SUE THE BACKBONE INTERNET SERVICE PROVIDERS...

RIAA
AT&T

USERFRIENDLY DOT ORG

YOU'RE THE CONTROLLER FOR THE COMPANY?
WHO ARE YOU GUYS?
WE'RE FROM THE GOVERNMENT. WE'D LIKE TO HAVE A LOOK AT YOUR BOOKS. ARE YOU THE COMPANY CONTROLLER?
COPYRIGHT © 2002 ILLIAD HTTP://WWW.USERFRIENDLY.ORG/

YEP. HE'S GOT THE CONTROLLER SMILE OF DEATH. CLAP HIM IN IRONS.
STUPID. STUPID!

AS REQUESTED. THESE ARE ALL OF OUR FINANCIALS FOR THE PAST FIVE YEARS.
ALL OF YOUR COMPANY FINANCIALS ARE ON A FLOPPY DISK?
COPYRIGHT © 2002 ILLIAD HTTP://WWW.USERFRIENDLY.ORG/

WHERE ARE THE REAMS OF PAPER? THE STACKS OF BOXES THAT WE HAVE TO RIFLE THROUGH WITH A FINE-TOOTH COMB? THE CONFETTI OF EVIDENCE POINTING TO SHADY ACCOUNTING HIDDEN WITHIN THE CHAOS OF LITTLE PAPER STRIPS?

BLAST IT, MAN! YOU'RE TAKING ALL THE GLAMOUR OUT OF THE JOB!!
I COULD WAVE A MAGNET OVER THE DISK IF YOU LIKE...

WHAT ARE YOU GUYS DOING HERE ANYWAY? WE'RE A TINY COMPANY AGAINST THE VAST BACKDROP OF NORTH AMERICAN BUSINESS. A MERE THREAD IN THE TAPESTRY OF CORPORATISM...
COPYRIGHT © 2002 ILLIAD HTTP://WWW.USERFRIENDLY.ORG/

FRAUD OCCURS AT ALL LEVELS, BUDDY. WHETHER YOU'RE ONE OF THE BIG BOYS OR A MERE GNAT, A CRIME IS A CRIME. AND BY GOSH WE'RE HERE TO FERRET IT OUT!

GOT ONE.
LOOK. I SAID I'D PAY FOR THE COLA TOMORROW!!

YOU GOT CAUGHT STEALING A COLA?
NOT STEALING! I TOOK ONE. BUT I DIDN'T HAVE ANY CHANGE ON ME. I WAS GOING TO BRING THE MONEY IN TOMORROW!
CLEVER METAPHOR OF GOV'T HANDCUFFING SMALL BIZ.
COPYRIGHT © 2002 ILLIAD HTTP://WWW.USERFRIENDLY.ORG/

UNH HUH. NOW ALL YOU HAVE TO DO IS CONVINCE THE FEDS.
I'M GOING TO KILL WHOMEVER IT WAS THAT RATTED ME OUT!

AND THEN HE SNATCHED THE COLA CAN WITH THIS AVARICIOUS SMILE ON HIS FACE...
YES. YES. BUT AT ANY TIME DID THE SUSPECT RESTATE HIS EARNINGS? EVEN A LITTLE?
Cola

WELL. SEEMS THE WHOLE ENRON THING IS FINALLY COMING TO A HEAD WHAT WITH CHARGES FINALLY BEING LAID. I SURE AM GLAD WE'RE NOT THERE HAVING TO DEAL WITH THAT HUGE MESS. THIS INVESTIGATION HERE IS JUST MY SPEED. PERFECT, IN FACT.
COPYRIGHT © 2002 ILLIAD HTTP://WWW.USERFRIENDLY.ORG/

YOU GUYS LOST A BET DIDN'T YOU.
I TOLD YOU IT WAS OBVIOUS.
WE THOUGHT CLINTON WAS JOKING!!!
"TALK SHOW" INDEED...

FOUR DAYS OF RIFLING THROUGH LEDGERS AND REPORTS AND NOT A SINGLE SIGN OF SHADINESS ANYWHERE. THE ACCOUNTS ARE PERFECT.
I THINK I HAVE A PAPER CUT.
COPYRIGHT © 2002 ILLIAD HTTP://WWW.USERFRIENDLY.ORG/

WAIT A SECOND -- THE DUDE WITH THE CREEPY SMILE GAVE US WAY MORE DATA ON PAPER HERE THAN WHAT COULD FIT ON A SINGLE FLOPPY DISK.
YOU'RE RIGHT. THIS IS AT LEAST TEN MEGS OF DATA. I THINK WE'D BETTER SEIZE THE HARD DRIVES.

AN E.M.P? UH... DETONATING A NUCLEAR DEVICE CAN CREATE ONE.
WELCOME TO THE BLACK MESA 2 RESEARCH FACILITY
VISITORS WILL BE SHOT
FINE. I'LL TAKE YOUR CHEAPEST MODEL.

THE SECURITIES & EXCHANGE COMMISSION
CIRCA 2002
PLACETH SUSPECT HERE
USERFRIENDLY DOT ORG
COPYRIGHT (C) 2002 ILLIAD

AH. THERE YOU ARE. NICE TRY WITH THE FAKE DATA PRINTOUTS. WE WANT YOU TO HAND OVER THE **REAL** DATA THIS TIME.
BUT...I DON'T **HAVE** ANY REAL DATA.

YOU THINK WE'RE THAT GULLIBLE? WE KNOW YOU'RE HOLDING OUT ON US!
FINE. YOU WIN. I'LL SHOW YOU WHERE ALL OF THE SHREDDED EVIDENCE IS.

MY GOD I LOVE PUNCH CARDS AND THEIR TRAPPINGS...

CHIEF. THIS IS AN OUTRAGE! I HAVE TWO FEDERAL GOONS TEARING APART MY OFFICE LOOKING FOR EVIDENCE OF CORPORATE FRAUD!
YES. WELL. WHERE ETHICS FAIL, TECHNOLOGY MUST BEAR THE COST.

SO, 'C.T.O.' ACTUALLY STANDS FOR **"CHIEF TAKE-ONE-FOR-THE-COMPANY OFFICER."** DOESN'T IT.
SEE, I **KNEW** YOU WERE CLEVER! I THINK YOU DESERVE A PROMOTION TO INTERIM C.E.O. FOR THE NEXT AS-YET-UNDETERMINED WHILE.

NOW **THIS** IS WHAT I CALL **INVESTIGATING.** THOUSANDS OF MINUTE BITS OF CARDBOARD. EACH OF THEM TELLING THEIR OWN TALE. EACH ONE A TEST-IMONY TO GUILT. EACH ONE A BUILDING BLOCK TO A CONVICTION...

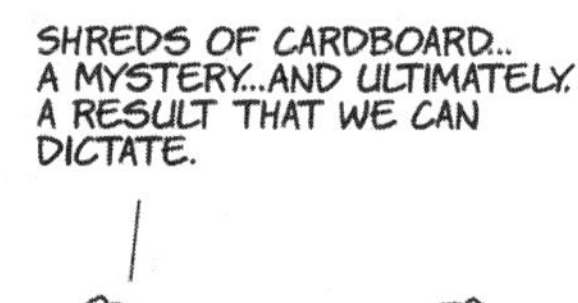
SHREDS OF CARDBOARD... A MYSTERY...AND ULTIMATELY, A RESULT THAT WE CAN DICTATE.

MAN. THIS IS **JUST** LIKE FLORIDA ALMOST TWO YEARS AGO.
I KNOW. I KNOW. I'M JUST WELLING UP...

DONE! ALMOST TWO HUNDRED HOURS OF WORK BUT WE MANAGED TO PUT TOGETHER ALL OF THE EVIDENCE THAT WAS SHREDDED! THE MYSTERY IS ABOUT TO BE SOLVED!
I CAN'T STAND THE EXCITEMENT!

NOW THAT WE'VE CAREFULLY AFFIXED EACH OF THOUSANDS OF PUNCH CARD CHADS INTO THEIR CORRESPONDING HOLES, AND APPLIED A FIXATIVE SO THAT EACH PUNCH CARD IS AS IT WAS WHEN IT WAS BRAND NEW WE SEE...

...A COUPLE OF CORRESPONDING 'HOLES.'
AAAAAAAAAGGHH!
WHAT?! WHAT?! I DON'T SEE ANYTHING!!

THE FEDS HAVE LEFT THE BUILDING!
AND IN A HUFF IT APPEARS.
COPYRIGHT © 2002 ILLIAD HTTP://WWW.USERFRIENDLY.ORG/

BECAUSE THEY COULDN'T FIND ANYTHING INCRIMINATING! I HAVE TO HAND IT TO SMILING MAN. HE REALLY KNOWS HOW TO PLAY WITH POWER. TOO BAD HE DOESN'T GET TO DO IT MORE OFTEN.
OH, DON'T YOU WORRY. HE STILL HAS LOOSE ENDS THAT NEED TYING UP.

NOW, ABOUT THAT COLA YOU TOOK FROM THE LUNCH ROOM YOU DIDN'T PAY FOR...
I PROMISE I'LL PAY FOR IT TOMORROW!!!!

I CAN'T BELIEVE WE BLEW THE INVESTIGATION ON THAT SMARMY LITTLE I.S.P. I THOUGHT IT WAS AN OPEN AND SHUT SCAPEGOATING.
OH WE'RE NOT DONE YET...AHA!
COPYRIGHT © 2002 ILLIAD HTTP://WWW.USERFRIENDLY.ORG/

SEE? THIS IS THE NAME OF THEIR AUDITOR WHO, CONVENIENTLY ENOUGH, IS ALREADY WELL KNOWN TO US. GET OUT YOUR HANDCUFFS, WE'RE GOING TO GO ARREST AN AUDITOR...

BUT MY LAST NAME ISN'T ANDERSEN.
WORK WITH ME ARTUR. IT'LL BE FUN.
I AM ARTUR ANDERSEN

DESPITE NOT BEING RECOGNIZED IN AUSTRALIA, THE JEDI PROVE THEY ARE IN FACT AS REAL AS ANY OTHER RELIGION.

MIDICHLORIANS EXIST!
NO, THEY BLOODY WELL DO NOT!
ORTHODOX JEDI
REFORMED JEDI
USERFRIENDLY DOT ORG
COPYRIGHT (C) 2002 ILLIAD

NOW TYPE 'FORMAT C:' AND HIT 'ENTER.'
OKAY...
FEDERAL AGENTS! YOU'RE THE AUDITOR FOR THIS I.S.P.?
JA. HOLD STILL, PLEASE.
COPYRIGHT © 2002 ILLIAD HTTP://WWW.USERFRIENDLY.ORG/

UM...MY DRIVE IS MAKING GRINDING NOISES.
DON'T WORRY. THAT'S GOOD FOR ONE OF US.
HEY!! WHAT ARE YOU DOING WITH THAT BAT-
WAP!

WHAT WAS THAT?!
I GUESS THE BASEBALL STRIKE IS OVER.
THE WHAT?
LINE DRIVE!

GENTLEMEN. I CALLED THIS MEETING BECAUSE WE'RE FEELING THE EFFECTS OF A DIMINISHED ECONOMY. WE NEED A WAY TO GENERATE MONEY SO WE CAN SURVIVE THIS SLUMP.
HOW ABOUT WE PUT IN A BID TO MANAGE THE .ORG TOP LEVEL DOMAIN?
COPYRIGHT © 2002 ILLIAD HTTP://WWW.USERFRIENDLY.ORG/

I CAN'T BELIEVE YOU'D SUGGEST THAT TO MAKE MONEY! MANAGING .ORG IS ABOUT SAFEGUARDING THE PUBLIC TRUST, NOT HOOVERING MONEY OUT OF PEOPLE!
SO...YOU'RE TELLING ME IT WOULDN'T BE ABOUT THE MONEY...

DAMN SKIPPY IT WOULDN'T. IT'D BE ABOUT AUTOCRATICALLY REASSIGNING SITES LIKE MPAA.ORG TO WIL WHEATON.
.ORG...ISN'T THAT THE TOP-LEVEL DOMAIN FOR PORN?

I get this all the time. People write to me with "such an awesome idea!" and then tell me I can "have the idea" as long as they get a cut if I make any money from it. I'll get right on that.

SID! SID! I HAVE A GREAT IDEA FOR A COMPUTER GAME!!
AWESOME! HAVE YOU WRITTEN A DESIGN DOCUMENT YET?
COPYRIGHT © 2002 ILLIAD HTTP://WWW.USERFRIENDLY.ORG/

A WHAT?
A DESIGN DOCUMENT. IT DETAILS HOW THE GAME WORKS, HOW IT'S STRUCTURED, WHAT KIND OF TECHNOLOGY IS BEING USED, THAT SORT OF THING.

BUT...WHY CAN'T I JUST DESCRIBE THE GAME TO YOU AND YOU CODE IT AND MAKE US RICH?
BECAUSE I CAN'T SPEND THE MONEY WHEN I'M DOING PRISON TIME FOR THROTTLING YOU A.J....

OKAY. I WROTE YOU A DESIGN DOCUMENT FOR MY GAME.
ALL RIGHT. LET'S SEE IT.
COPYRIGHT © 2002 ILLIAD HTTP://WWW.USERFRIENDLY.ORG/

IT SAYS "THIS GAME IS GONNA BE REAL COOL."
I KNOW YOU CODERS LIKE THINGS TO BE CONCISE. WAS THAT TOO MUCH?

A.J., I NEED MORE THAN THIS TO DEVELOP THIS GAME YOU WANT. AND JUDGING FROM YOUR DEMEANOR, YOU HAVE NO INTENTION OF PROVIDING ME WITH MORE. I CAN'T HELP YOU!

COPYRIGHT © 2002 ILLIAD HTTP://WWW.USERFRIENDLY.ORG/
FINE. I GUESS I'LL HAVE TO FIND SOMEONE ELSE TO DO THIS WITH ME.
A.J., WHERE ON THIS GREEN EARTH DO YOU THINK YOU'RE GOING TO FIND A DEVELOPMENT TEAM THAT TALENTED AND THAT STUPID AT THE SAME TIME?

I FEEL FUNNY.
YEAH. FUNNY LIKE WE'RE BEING USED IN SOME CHEESY FORESHADOWING ELEMENT...

SO YOU GUYS WILL DEVELOP MY GAME FOR ME?
OF COURSE, A.J.
YOU HAVE TO TELL US WHAT YOU WANT THOUGH.

COPYRIGHT © 2002 ILLIAD HTTP://WWW.USERFRIENDLY.ORG/
IT'S AN ORIGINAL BUT TESTED IDEA! A FIRST-PERSON POV WITH AN ARRAY OF AWESOME WEAPONRY. FAST-PACED YET THOUGHT-PROVOKING. LOTS OF VISCERA. PLAYED ON A RANDOMLY GENERATED FIELD WITH GOBS OF DEPTH AND DETAIL, AND REQUIRING BOTH LIGHTNING REFLEXES AND CAREFUL PLANNING!

"QUAKEHACK."
NO NO NO! JUST LIKE QUAKE AND NETHACK, ONLY DIFFERENT!!

AH, THE IRONY.
ZEUS
0176144
ATHENS POLICE DEPARTMENT
ANUBIS
0176143
ATHENS POLICE DEPARTMENT
THOR
0176145
ATHENS POLICE DEPARTMENT
AGE of MYTHOLOGY
A GAME BY ENSEMBLE STUDIOS
AGE OF MYTHOLOGY SWEEPSTAKES
WIN A TRIP TO GREECE!
USERFRIENDLY DOT ORG
COPYRIGHT (C) 2002 ILLIAD

This was around the time that the Greek government banned computer games—including the ones you get with Windows, like Minesweeper and FreeCell. The law was quickly overturned.

I HEARD YOU FREAKS WERE DEVELOPING A GAME.
YES...
WHO'S MARKETING IT FOR YOU?
COPYRIGHT © 2002 ILLIAD HTTP://WWW.USERFRIENDLY.ORG/

STEF. WE DON'T NEED...
WAIT A SEC A.J. -- STEF COULD REALLY HELP US HERE. WE'VE IDENTIFIED A GREAT LOCATION FOR US TO GET A FOOTHOLD FOR OUR PRODUCT.
OKAY. WHERE AM I GOING?

GREECE. YOUR TICKETS ARE BOOKED.
YES!! FOR HOW LONG?
OH...THAT'S FOR THE GREEK GOVERNMENT TO DECIDE.

OKAY. WE'VE GOT FOUNDATION CODE IN PLACE. BUT WE NEED SOME AUDIO. SOME SPEAKING PARTS IN THE GAME.
WE SHOULD GET A VOICE ACTOR.
YEAH! WHO CAN WE GET?
COPYRIGHT © 2002 ILLIAD HTTP://WWW.USERFRIENDLY.ORG/

DEPENDS ON OUR BUDGET I SUPPOSE...
HOW MUCH DO WE HAVE?
SEVENTY-SIX CENTS AND A BUS TRANSFER.

HELLO. WIL WHEATON SPEAKING.

A Year Later.

FOR THE PEOPLE WHO CAN'T DO THIS ANYMORE. AND I GUESS. FOR ME.
COPYRIGHT © 2002 ILLIAD HTTP://WWW.USERFRIENDLY.ORG/

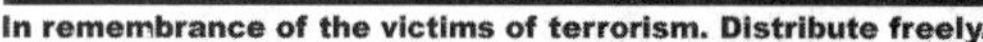
In remembrance of the victims of terrorism. Distribute freely.

IN WIL WHEATON'S OFFICE...
HI. I REPRESENT A SMALL SOFTWARE DEVELOPMENT TEAM. AND WE'RE LOOKING TO HIRE YOU ON FOR A VOICE ACTING ROLE MR. WHEATON...
COOL. WHAT'S THE SOFTWARE?
ERM...IT'S A GAME. A REALLY COOL GAME. WITH COOL WEAPONS AND COOL LEVELS AND STUFF THAT'LL CAUSE GAMER AROUSAL.
COPYRIGHT © 2002 ILLIAD HTTP://WWW.USERFRIENDLY.ORG/

UNH HUH.

WHEN ARE YOU GONNA TAKE THE HINT. ROMERO?
MISTER WHEATON. SIR? SOME GUY NAMED A.J. ON LINE TWO WITH ANOTHER OFFER. SAYS HE HAS MONEY.

MR. WHEATON! IT'S A REAL PLEASURE TO MEET YOU. I'M SO GLAD YOU DECIDED TO WORK WITH US!
CALL ME WIL. DUDE. DO YOU HAVE A SCRIPT FOR ME?
COPYRIGHT © 2002 ILLIAD HTTP://WWW.USERFRIENDLY.ORG/

SURE! IT'S RIGHT HERE...

OPENING SCENE: FOUR BRUTISH KLINGONS SECURED IN BRIG WITH ENSIGN CRUSHER. FIRST KLINGON: "HEY WESLEY. YOU LOOK MIGHTY GOOD IN THAT STARFLEET UNIFORM..."
AND THAT WOULD BE THE WRONG SCRIPT...

Even though Wil Wheaton is a famous geek, much to my surprise and pleasure he's a UF fan! How cool is that? And then I panicked and had to make sure I hadn't written anything really nasty about him in previous cartoons.

GRAB A SEAT, WIL. I'LL BE RIGHT BACK WITH THE MICROPHONE AND STUFF.
COOL.
COPYRIGHT © 2002 ILLIAD HTTP://WWW.USERFRIENDLY.ORG/

DUDE? WHAT'S WITH THE EFFING TRIBBLE?
"TRIBBLE?"
A BLIND, PARAPLEGIC VERSION OF YOU.

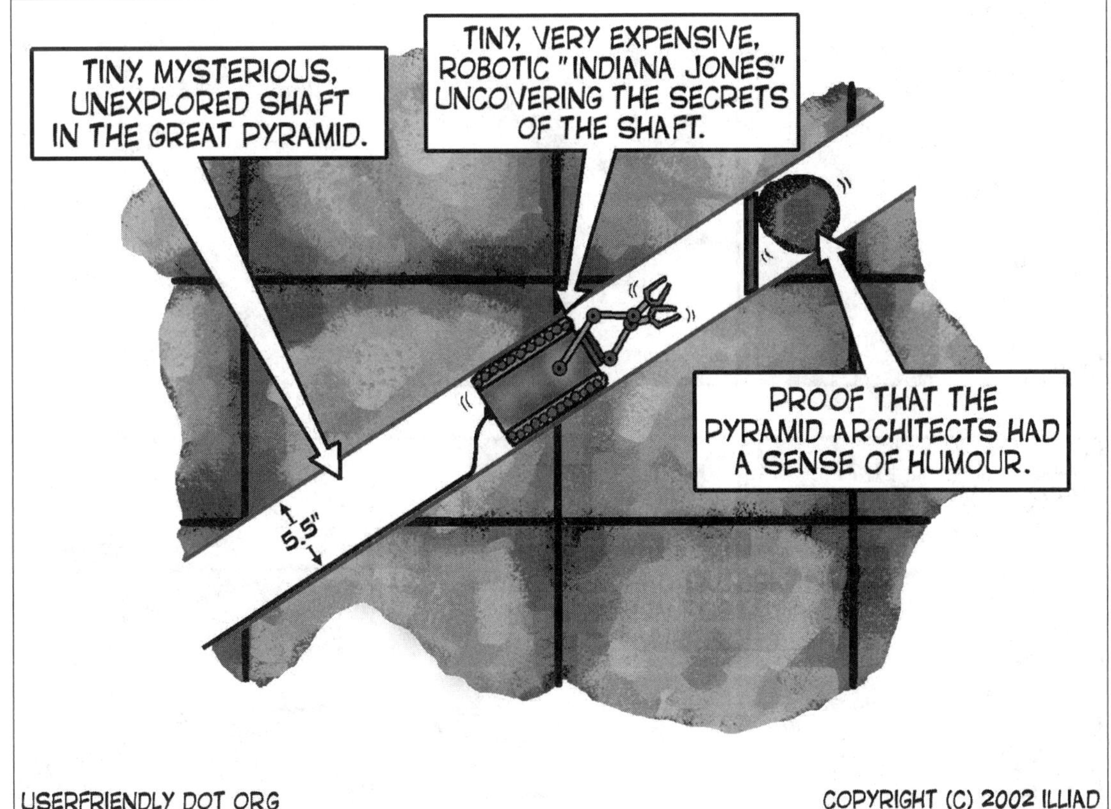
TINY, MYSTERIOUS, UNEXPLORED SHAFT IN THE GREAT PYRAMID.
TINY, VERY EXPENSIVE, ROBOTIC "INDIANA JONES" UNCOVERING THE SECRETS OF THE SHAFT.
PROOF THAT THE PYRAMID ARCHITECTS HAD A SENSE OF HUMOUR.
5.5"
USERFRIENDLY DOT ORG
COPYRIGHT (C) 2002 ILLIAD

Although the crushing boulder trap is fictitious, what's true is that the team responsible for designing and sending the robot up that shaft wrote to me to ask for a print of this cartoon. I agreed, in exchange for a cursed jewel plucked from the eye of Anubis, sent to a certain Big Content lobby group.

GOTTA TELL YA MAN. HE SURE DOES MOVE AND LOOK LIKE HE'S ALIVE. WHERE CAN I GET ONE OF THESE?
HE **IS** ALIVE, WIL. THAT'S DUST PUPPY. HE'S BEEN MY BUDDY FOR YEARS.
COPYRIGHT © 2002 ILLIAD HTTP://WWW.USERFRIENDLY.ORG/

HEH. **WHATEVER** IT TAKES TO GET YOU THROUGH THE DAY, MAN. WE'RE **ALL** DYSFUNCTIONAL IN ONE WAY OR ANOTHER.

I'M NOT DYSFUNCTIONAL!
DUDE, NO WORRIES. I'VE BEEN THERE! I USED TO DO THAT WHOLE "GATES MCFADDEN SURE IS **HOT** BUT SHE PLAYS MY MOM" THING...
HMMM...INTERESTING HIDDEN DIRECTORIES ON WILWHEATON.NET...

UFies, Wil finally recorded himself saying those four words. He did it on a radio show. Bravo, Wil!

THIS IS COOL! I'VE ALWAYS WANTED TO DO A VOICE ACTING PART IN A COMPUTER GAME. SO NOW WHAT?
JUST READ OFF THE NEW SCRIPT I GAVE YOU.
COPYRIGHT © 2002 ILLIAD HTTP://WWW.USERFRIENDLY.ORG/

OKAY. UM... **"DOINK! DOINK! DOINK! DOINK!"**
PERFECT! THAT'S A **WRAP!**

THE HELL WAS **THAT?**
THE SOUND THE PYGMY MARMOSET MAKES WHEN YOU MOVE HIM ACROSS THE SCREEN.
DUH.

YOU HAVE **GOT** TO BE **KIDDING** ME. THAT'S **IT** FOR THE SPEAKING PART?!
WELL...YES. THAT'S THE ONLY PLACE FOR CELEBRITY AUDIO IN THE GAME. BESIDES, I ONLY HAD SEVENTY-SIX CENTS.
AND A BUS TRANSFER.
COPYRIGHT © 2002 ILLIAD HTTP://WWW.USERFRIENDLY.ORG/

DUDE. IT'S NOT ABOUT THE MONEY. IT'S ABOUT THE **ART!** IT'S ABOUT DOING COOL THINGS AND MAKING LIFE **SPARKLE!** ABOVE ALL, IT'S ABOUT FEEDING THE **SOUL!**

I NEED TO DO SOMETHING SATISFYINGLY CREATIVE. I'M GOING TO CALL UP THE SCIFI CHANNEL AND TAKE THEM UP ON THEIR OFFER TO GUEST STAR ON "FARSCAPE."
A.J., SHOULDN'T YOU TELL HIM...
NO. JUST...NO.

OKAY. WE HAVE THE ENGINE, A PYGMY MARMOSET FOR A HERO, CELEBRITY AUDIO... WHAT ELSE DO WE NEED?
A VILLAIN?
COPYRIGHT © 2002 ILLIAD HTTP://WWW.USERFRIENDLY.ORG/

RIGHT! BUT IT HAS TO BE SOMEONE WHO ANYONE WOULD RECOGNIZE AS A VILLAIN. INSTANTLY! AND NO CLICHES!
HMMM...

IT'S STILL NOT SAFE TO GO IN. THERE'RE **PEOPLE** THERE!
I DON'T CARE! I'M NOT GOING ANOTHER DAY WITHOUT STARBUCKS!
(SUNDRY CHIEF EXECUTIVE OFFICERS OF MAJOR AMERICAN CORPORATIONS.)

EXCUSE ME. BUT ARE YOU A C.E.-
COPYRIGHT © 2002 ILLIAD HTTP://WWW.USERFRIENDLY.ORG/

URMMF!

HOW THE HELL DID YOU SEE THROUGH MY DISGUISE?
YOU LEFT THE $6000 PRICE TAG ON THE MOUSTACHE.

SEE. MY GAME NEEDS A CHARACTER THAT EVERYONE CAN INSTANTLY RECOGNIZE AS A VILLAIN. SO, I THOUGHT, TO MYSELF "HOW ABOUT SOME HAPLESS CEO?"
SURE. I MEAN. WHY WOULD YOU OR ANYONE ELSE THINK OTHERWISE?
COPYRIGHT © 2002 ILLIAD HTTP://WWW.USERFRIENDLY.ORG/

IT'S GETTING PRETTY BAD OUT THERE FOR CEOS. HUH?
BUDDY. YOU HAVE NO IDEA.

I THINK YOU WINGED HIM!
BY JOVE. HE'LL MAKE A MAGNIFICENT ADDITION TO MY WALL!
C.E.O. SEASON OPEN

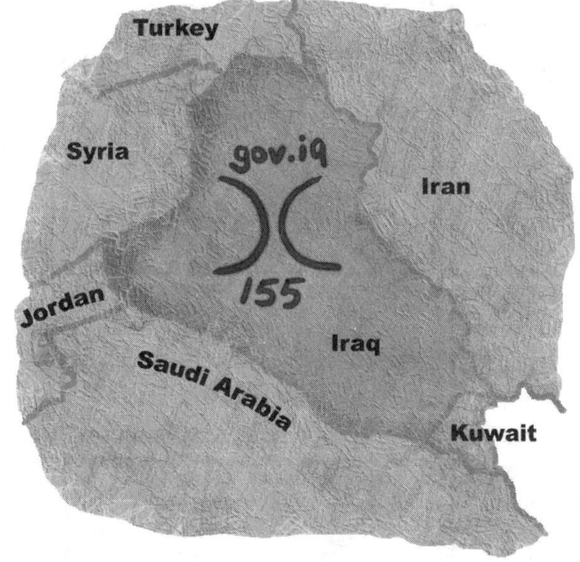
A BLOODLESS WAY TO MESS WITH SADDAM.
Turkey
Syria
Iran
gov.iq
155
Jordan
Iraq
Saudi Arabia
Kuwait
USERFRIENDLY DOT ORG
COPYRIGHT (C) 2002 ILLIAD

Warchalking, brought to a brutal Middle Eastern dictatorship near you ...

I SUPPOSE I HAD BETTER TAKE YOUR OFFER. THERE'S NOT MUCH WORK FOR CEOS THESE DAYS. AND IF YOU'RE NOT WORKING, YOU FALL TO THE BOTTOM OF THE FOOD CHAIN.

SO UNEMPLOYED CEOS ARE EITHER HUNTED OR IN HIDING?
YES...OR SIGNED UP FOR ONE OF THE NEW U.S. GOVERNMENT "C.E.O. PLACEMENT PROGRAMS."

IN A C17, SOMEWHERE OVER IRAQ...
AND WHAT ARE YOU MAGGOTS GOOD AT? WHAT ARE YOU GOING TO DO TO THE ENEMY?!
DESTABILIZE THE ECONOMY, SARGEANT!!

LI'L DUDE? WHERE'D THE C.E.O. GUY GO?
ERWIN'S WITH HIM IN THE MOTION CAPTURE ROOM. HE DECIDED TO DO SOME WORK WHILE YOU WERE GONE ON YOUR COLA RUN.
cotton balls

OH...HOW'D THE C.E.O. TAKE TO A TALKING COMPUTER?

HE SEEMED FINE. ERWIN CAN BE VERY CONVINCING. WHICH KIND OF WORRIES ME.
cotton balls

2500 LBS.
BUT...HOW DO I ACT OUT "GIBBAGE?"
JUST HOLD STILL.

WHERE'S THE C.E.O. GUY?
OH, HE HAD TO GO.

OH. WELL THAT WAS RUDE. HOW ARE WE GOING TO FINISH THE GAME WITHOUT HIM?! WE NEED THE MOTION CAPTURE DATA FOR THE VILLAIN JUMPING AROUND. AND OF COURSE, BEING GIBBED!

OH DON'T WORRY. I THINK I CAN FAKE IT...
SAY...WHY ARE YOU ALL GLOSSY?

SO WE GOT ALL OF THE MOTION CAPTURE DATA FOR THE VILLAIN?
UM, YES.
GREAT! LET'S SEE WHAT HE LOOKS LIKE.
OKAY...STARTING THE GAME.

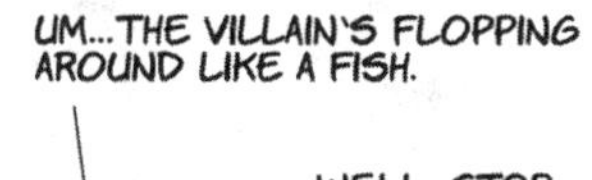
UM...THE VILLAIN'S FLOPPING AROUND LIKE A FISH.

WELL, STOP SHOOTING AT HIM THEN.

ERWIN, I HAVEN'T EVEN TOUCHED THE KEYS.
YEAH. OKAY. MY BAD. THE C.E.O. GUY DIDN'T GIB ON THE FIRST TRY SO I HAD TO DROP THE WEIGHT ON HIM A FEW TIMES.
FLOP
FLOP
AAAIIEEE!

THE GAME IS DONE. WE HAVE THIS PYGMY MARMOSET THAT BOUNCES AROUND TO WIL WHEATON'S SOUND EFFECTS AND A C.E.O. VILLAIN. IT'S GONNA BE A CLASSIC!
WHAT'S THE GAME'S STORY?
WHY DOES IT HAVE TO HAVE A STORY?
COPYRIGHT © 2002 ILLIAD HTTP://WWW.USERFRIENDLY.ORG/

YOU ALSO THINKING ABOUT MAKING AN IRONIC COMMENT LIKE "THIS CARTOON STRIP DOESN'T HAVE A REAL STORY. WHY SHOULD THE GAME?"
NO. BUT I FIGURED YOU'D BE STUPID ENOUGH TO SAY SOMETHING LIKE THAT WHILE ILLIAD'S WATCHING.
OOO!

HEY. WHERE'S STEF TODAY?
OH. HE HAD HIS CONTRACT MODIFIED AND WAS SECONDED ELSEWHERE.
COPYRIGHT © 2002 ILLIAD HTTP://WWW.USERFRIENDLY.ORG/

WHAT?!
HE SAID SOMETHING HE SHOULDN'T HAVE YESTERDAY AND ILLIAD HEARD HIM.
OOOH

THIS IS JUST WRONG.
LET'S GO YOU BLOCKHEAD! THIS FOOTBALL'S NOT GONNA WAIT FOREVER!!

Gotta keep them cartoon characters in line. Can't let them get uppity.

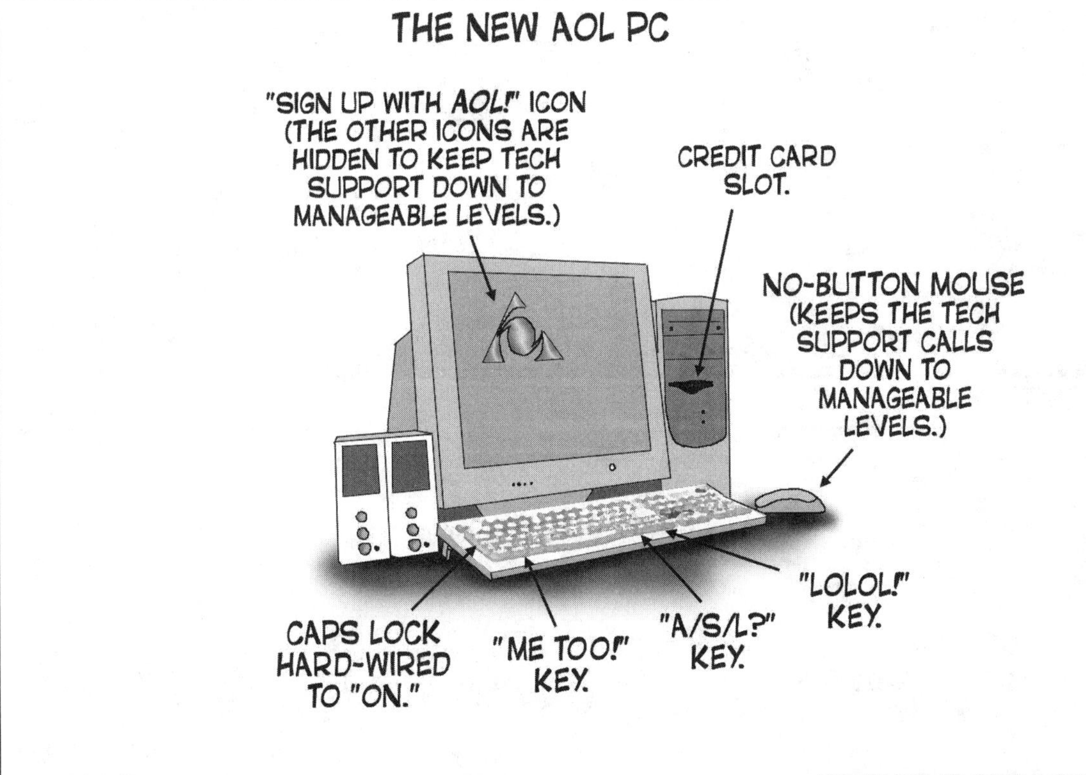
THE NEW AOL PC
"SIGN UP WITH AOL!" ICON (THE OTHER ICONS ARE HIDDEN TO KEEP TECH SUPPORT DOWN TO MANAGEABLE LEVELS.)
CREDIT CARD SLOT.
NO-BUTTON MOUSE (KEEPS THE TECH SUPPORT CALLS DOWN TO MANAGEABLE LEVELS.)
"LOLOL!" KEY.
"A/S/L?" KEY.
"ME TOO!" KEY.
CAPS LOCK HARD-WIRED TO "ON."
USERFRIENDLY DOT ORG
COPYRIGHT (C) 2002 ILLIAD

I STILL DON'T SEE HOW YOU'RE GOING TO SELL YOUR GAME WITHOUT SOME KIND OF STORY.
IT DOESN'T NEED IT STEF. IT HAS CELEBRITY AUDIO AND A VILLAIN IN IT.

LOOK WEBDORK. NO MATTER HOW COOL YOUR GAME IS, IT HAS TO SIT ON A SHELF IN A BOX. YOU NEED MARKETING.
I MADE A BOX FOR IT. AND I HAVE DUST PUPPY SHOWING IT AROUND THE OFFICE. IT'LL BE FINE.

THAT'S THE NEW GAME A.J. DESIGNED!
UNH-HUH. SO WHERE'S THE NAKED CHICK?

THIS GAME PROMOTION BUSINESS IS ICKY.
YEAH, BUT STEF HAS A POINT, DUDE. IF YOUR GAME IS GOING TO SIT ON A SHELF NEXT TO ALL OF THE OTHER GAMES, IT NEEDS TO HAVE A BOX COVER THAT STANDS OUT.
COLA

BUT HOW DO I ACCOMPLISH THAT? I'M NO MARKETER...
OH, I'M SURE STEF CAN PULL SOMETHING TOGETHER...

LET ME GUESS. TOO SKIMPY FOR YOU?
OH NO. IT'S THE PERFECT THICKNESS FOR A GAROTTE.

OKAY. SO BACK TO THE DRAWING BOARD.
I COULD'VE TOLD YOU THAT WAS A MISTAKE.

NOT SO. I HAVE FORCES AT WORK THAT WILL TURN THE TIDE OF FORTUNE FOR US.
STEF, WHAT DID YOU DO?!

...AND STEF SAID THAT THIS GAME IS A.J.'S LIFE'S WORK, AND IF IT DOESN'T SUCCEED, IT'LL BREAK HIS BIG HEART...
I AM SO WEAK...

SHE'S AGREED TO POSE FOR THE BOX COVER!
YOU'RE KIDDING.

NOPE! I'M GOING TO CAPTURE THE SWEETEST SLICES OF TIME OF THAT HOT LITTLE GODDESS WITH THIS CAMERA. SOMETHING SLEAZY ON THE BOX COVER AND THE GAME'LL SELL LIKE HOTCAKES!
STEF!!
A.J., DID I DO SOMETHING BAD?

I GOTTA GET SET UP BEFORE SHE GETS HERE. WHERE THE HELL IS MY MACRO LENS?
I'M READY. LET'S DO THIS THING.

STEF. I UNDERSTAND THIS NEEDS TO GO ON A BOX COVER. BUT THERE IS NO WAY I'M GOING TO AGREE TO THIS IF YOU CONTROL HOW LITTLE OR HOW MUCH I WEAR.
I WOULDN'T DREAM OF IT. COVER YOURSELF WITH THIS AS YOU SEE FIT.
COPYRIGHT © 2002 ILLIAD HTTP://WWW.USERFRIENDLY.ORG/

OH...WELL. IN THAT CASE...

THIS IS A ROLL OF CLING WRAP.
YEAH. IT'S OKAY TO USE SPIT IF IT DOESN'T STAY PUT.

STEF. I'M NOT COMPROMISING. I REFUSE TO WEAR ANYTHING LESS THAN THIS.
NO WORRIES. THAT'LL DO.
COPYRIGHT © 2002 ILLIAD HTTP://WWW.USERFRIENDLY.ORG/

OH......REALLY?
YES MIRANDA. YOU'RE LOVELY THE WAY YOU ARE.

ICE WATER
WELL...THAT'S INCREDIBLY NICE OF YOU STEF.
YEAH. COULD YOU PLEASE NOT MOVE FOR JUST A SEC?

THE LEAST LIKELY THINGS ARE OFTEN CONNECTED...

HELP WANTED

Marketing Manager req'd for boutique Internet Service Provider. Competitive pay, benefits. Must have 5+ years exp. working with tech teams. May start immediately. Contract position as relief for incumbent on extended leave. Resumes to PO Box 1138, Vancouver, B.C.

B6

THE B.C. HERALD, OCT 6, 20(

VANCOUVER MAN IN HOSPITAL FOR "LIGHT SURGERY."

VANCOUVER, B.C.— A Vancouver man was hospitalized for an unusual work-related injury yesterday. "It's quite puzzling," said Dr. Edgar, a resident surgeon. "I've never seen an eight-foot tall camera light crammed up such a small space before." The hospital

USERFRIENDLY DOT ORG

You shoulda seen the three other takes I did of Pearl's outfit. Gotta keep UF PG-13, though.

HEY MIRANDA.
WHY PEARL, HOW...NICE TO SEE YOU. HERE TO SEE YOUR DAD?

NO. FOR A JOB. I JUST FINISHED UP MY LAST CONTRACT SO IT WAS TIME FOR SOMETHING NEW...
AH. YOU APPLIED FOR THE MARKETING MANAGER POSITION THEN?

YES. THAT TOO.
YO, PEARL, LET'S GO! THAT BOX COVER AIN'T GONNA WAIT FOREVER.

A.J., GOT A MINUTE?
SURE THING, PEARL.
I'VE TAKEN OVER FOR STEF WHILE HE'S AWAY. SO I'M THINKING I COULD MARKET YOUR GAME FOR YOU. IF YOU'LL HAVE ME.

COPYRIGHT © 2002 ILLIAD HTTP://WWW.USERFRIENDLY.ORG/

YEAH. I'M SURE YOU'D BE GREAT.
FAB! WE'LL TALK MORE LATER.
SEE YA.

SO SHE'S GREAT IS SHE.
HEY. DID THE AIR CONDITIONER JUST KICK IN?

HOW GOES THE BOX COVER BUSINESS?
PRETTY GOOD, A.J. I HAVE GREG GOING AROUND THE OFFICE GETTING FEEDBACK FROM THE GAMERS ON STAFF.

COPYRIGHT © 2002 ILLIAD HTTP://WWW.USERFRIENDLY.ORG/

I THINK GREG DID A GOOD JOB ON THE PHOTO SHOOT. AND THE BOX COVER SHOULD CAPTURE ATTENTION LONG ENOUGH TO ALLOW THE SUBTLE DETAILS OF YOUR GAME TO PERSUADE A BUY. EVEN IF I DO SAY SO MYSELF.

WELL?
ALMOST-NAKED CHICK NEEDS A GUN.

THE BOX COVER LOOKS BETTER. THE CHICK HAS A GUN. AND A KEVLAR THONG. NICE.
YEAH. PEARL'S WRITING UP THE HYPE TO GO ON THE BACK NOW.

COPYRIGHT © 2002 ILLIAD HTTP://WWW.USERFRIENDLY.ORG/

IS THAT WISE? SHE DOESN'T KNOW THAT MUCH TECH.
A.J.'S WORKING WITH HER ON IT. HE'LL MAKE SURE SHE'S ACCURATE. SHE'LL MAKE IT SOUND GREAT.

"...FEATURING TOP OF THE LINE..." -- WHAT WAS THAT TECH PHRASE AGAIN?
"ASCII GRAPHICS."

A.J., AS YOUR GAME PRODUCER I'LL NEED TO PLAN OUT OUR TIMELINE. I KNOW WE HAVE THE BOX ART DONE. WHERE ARE WE WITH THE GAME?
UM. IT'S AN EARLY BETA. IT HASN'T BEEN PLAY-TESTED YET. AND WE STILL HAVE BUGS IN THE INSTALLER.
COPYRIGHT © 2002 ILLIAD HTTP://WWW.USERFRIENDLY.ORG/

UH OH...

WELL THEN. PICK A NAME FOR THE GAME AND **SHIP IT.**
HOW ABOUT "DAIKATANA II?"

WHOA. HERE'S SOME NEWS: U.S. REGULATORS ARE OPENING A ROUND OF PUBLIC COMMENT ON THE PART OF THE D.M.C.A. WHERE WE'RE NOT ALLOWED TO CIRCUMVENT ANY "TECHNOLOGICAL MEASURE THAT EFFECTIVELY CONTROLS ACCESS TO A WORK."
COPYRIGHT © 2002 ILLIAD HTTP://WWW.USERFRIENDLY.ORG/

SO...WHERE IT SAYS "EFFECTIVELY" DOES IT MEAN "FOR ALL PRACTICAL PURPOSES; IN EFFECT" OR "IN A WAY THAT'S ACTUALLY EFFECTIVE?"

DUDE. THAT IS **BRILLIANT.** MY GUILT OVER MY MP3 COLLECTION JUST **EVAPORATED.**
YEAH. SAW A WISP OR TWO COMING OFF YOU THERE.

LATEST ITEM UP FOR BID...

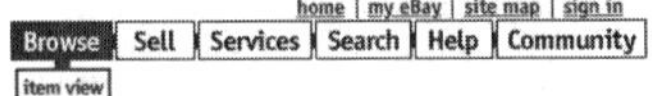
home | my eBay | site map | sign in
Browse
Sell
Services
Search
Help
Community
item view

eBay's Code of Ethics
Item # 17767617542

Description

Currently	**US $8.00**	First bid	**US $8.00**
Quantity	1	# of bids	**1** bid history
Time left	**6 days, 5 hours +**	Location	**San Jose, CA.**
		Country	**United States**
Started	Oct-10-02 23:53:42 PDT		mail this auction to a friend
Ends	Oct-17-02 23:53:42 PDT		watch this item

Bid

Seller (Rating) **eBay (0)**
view comments in seller's Feedback Profile | view seller's other items | ask seller a question

High bid **fraudmonger (0)**

Payment: Money Order/Cashiers Checks. Other online payment services. See item description for payment methods accepted

Shipping: Buyer pays for all shipping costs, which are provided in the Payment Details section below. Will ship to United States only.

eBay Payments
5 Events. Be There with Visa!

Seller Services: Revise item | Sell similar item

Seller assumes all responsibility for listing this item. You should contact the seller to resolve any questions before bidding. Auction currency is U.S. dollars (US $) unless otherwise noted.

Description

Code of Ethics for Sale! In mint condition, one owner only, still in shrinkwrap, never used. Excellent trophy for mantle, central conversation piece, convincing facade. Weighs very little, no effect on sense of irresponsibility. Perfect Xmas present for your favourite indicted CEO who has **everything** but this!

The eBay Way to Pay - Enjoy Full Purchase Protection!

USERFRIENDLY DOT ORG

THAT'S QUITE A STORM CLOUD OVER YOUR HEAD, MIRANDA.
I'M A LITTLE HUFFY I GUESS. I MEAN, WHAT WOULD YOU DO IF THE GUY YOU LIKED WAS WORKING CLOSELY WITH SOME GORGEOUS TART ON A COOL LITTLE PERSONAL PROJECT AT WORK?

I SUPPOSE I'D GO SEE A.J. AND FIRE HIM.
BUT HOW DOES THAT MAKE HIM NOTICE ME?

SIGH I CAN'T BELIEVE A.J. IS WORKING ON A PERSONAL PROJECT DURING COMPANY TIME. I'D BETTER GO TALK TO HIM.

MAYBE HE JUST DOESN'T REALIZE WHAT HE'S DOING IS WRONG. HE'S A NICE BOY, AND IF HE'S NOT AWARE, HE CAN'T BE GUILTY. AND IF HE'S NOT GUILTY, HOW CAN I FIRE HIM?

A.J., DO YOU HAVE A MIN-
WHAT PERSONAL PROJECT?!

A.J., I'M TERRIBLY SORRY, BUT I CAN'T IGNORE THIS. IF I LEFT IT ALONE IT WOULD SET A BAD PRECEDENT IN THE COMPANY. I'M AFRAID I HAVE TO LET YOU GO, SON...
BUT...WHO'S GOING TO CARE FOR THE WEBSITE?

HIM.

A MONKEY?!
NO YOU TWIT, AN OUT-OF-WORK A.O.L. POPUP AD DESIGNER!

A.J. WAS FIRED?
YES. WITH THE JOB MARKET THE WAY IT IS, HE'S GOING TO BE IN TROUBLE. I KNOW FOR A FACT THAT HE WAS LIVING HAND-TO-MOUTH.

AND TO TOP IT OFF, LAST WEEK I HEARD HE WAS HAVING TROUBLE PAYING HIS ELECTRICITY BILL.
UH-OH. ISN'T HE THE SORT THAT SLEEPS WITH THE LIGHT ON?

CAN'T GO TO SLEEP OR THE GRUE WILL GET ME... CAN'T GO TO SLEEP OR THE GRUE WILL GET ME... CAN'T GO TO SLEEP OR THE GRUE WILL GET ME...

I'D GUESS I'D BETTER GET CRACKING ON FINDING A JOB. LET'S SEE...
CAN WE HELP?
COPYRIGHT © 2002 ILLIAD HTTP://WWW.USERFRIENDLY.ORG/

YEEAAAH...ERWIN, COULD YOU DO A SEARCH FOR JOBS ONLINE THAT MATCH MY QUALIFICATIONS?
SURE THING DUDE.

DON'T WORRY A.J., ERWIN'S GOOD AT FINDING EVEN THE MOST OBSCURE THINGS ON THE NET!
HEY!
HERE'S ONE: "SPEEDBUMP NEEDED AT DRIVE-THRU. GOOD PAY NO MEDICAL."
HEY!!

THIS IS FRUSTRATING. THERE'RE JOBS FOR ACCOUNTANTS, MARKETERS, PLUMBERS, AND THERE'S EVEN ONE HERE FOR "COMBAT BOTANIST." BUT THERE'S NOTHING FOR A GUY LIKE ME.
BLAME CANADIA
COPYRIGHT © 2002 ILLIAD HTTP://WWW.USERFRIENDLY.ORG/

SORRY DUDE. I SEARCHED EVERYWHERE. "WEB DESIGNER" JUST DOESN'T RETURN ANY HITS.
BLAME CANADIA

THERE HAS TO BE SOME WORK OUT THERE FOR WEB DESIGNERS.
I THINK THESE DAYS THEY'RE CALLED "SMALL CHILDREN."
YEAH. FOUND ONE! "SMALL CHILD REQUIRED TO COMFORT ELDERS AND MAINTAIN WEBSITE."
BLAME CANADIA

I had fun not drawing pants on A.J. in this one.

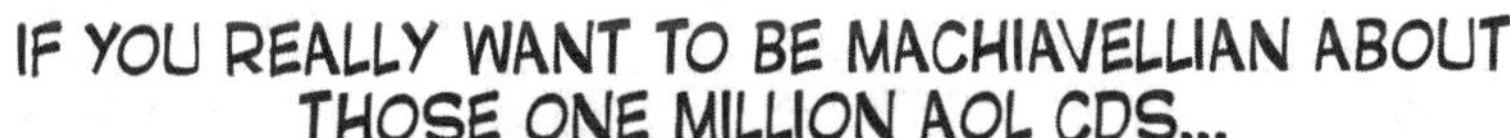

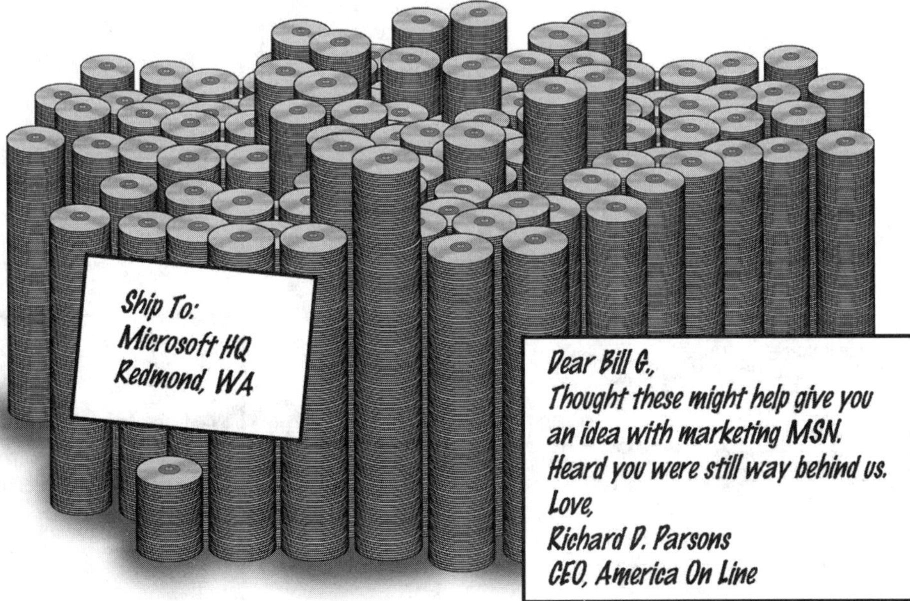
IF YOU REALLY WANT TO BE MACHIAVELLIAN ABOUT THOSE ONE MILLION AOL CDS...
Ship To:
Microsoft HQ
Redmond, WA
Dear Bill G.,
Thought these might help give you an idea with marketing MSN.
Heard you were still way behind us.
Love,
Richard D. Parsons
CEO, America On Line
USERFRIENDLY DOT ORG
COPYRIGHT (C) 2002 ILLIAD

HELLO. THIS IS A.J. GARRETT. YES. I E-MAILED YOU MY RESUME FOR THE MAIL ADMIN POSITION, AND JUST WANTED TO KNOW IF YOU HAD RECEIVED IT.
COPYRIGHT © 2002 ILLIAD HTTP://WWW.USERFRIENDLY.ORG/

AH. I SEE. THANK YOU ANYWAY.

IS THE POSITION ALREADY FILLED?
NO. IT WAS JUST CREATED BECAUSE THEY DON'T KNOW HOW TO DOWNLOAD THEIR E-MAIL.

A.J. RESORTS TO A RECRUITING AGENCY...
THIS IS QUITE A RESUME YOU HAVE HERE A.J. WEB SKILLS, DESIGN EXPERIENCE, AND YOU WRITE WELL. UNFORTUNATELY, OUR CLIENT REQUIRES FOUR YEARS OF EXPERIENCE WITH WINDOWS XP.
UM. WINDOWS XP HAS ONLY BEEN OUT FOR ABOUT A YEAR.
COPYRIGHT © 2002 ILLIAD HTTP://WWW.USERFRIENDLY.ORG/

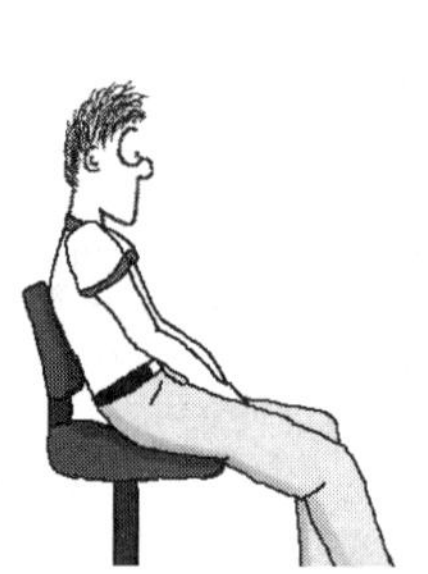

I GUESS YOU'LL HAVE TO COME BACK IN THREE YEARS.
YOU DON'T SUPPOSE YOUR CLIENT WILL WANT SEVEN YEARS OF XP EXPERIENCE BY THEN?

GOOD DAY QUINCE. IT'S KELLY OVER AT SOYLENT RECRUITERS. I HAVE A CANDIDATE SITTING RIGHT HERE WHO MIGHT BE JUST WHAT YOU'RE LOOKING FOR.
COPYRIGHT © 2002 ILLIAD HTTP://WWW.USERFRIENDLY.ORG/

...I DON'T KNOW. I'LL ASK HIM. JUST A SEC...
A.J., YOUR RESUME SAYS YOU KNOW MICROSOFT OFFICE. ANY OTHER MS PRODUCTS?
UH, NO. JUST WHAT'S ON MY RESUME.

QUINCE? NO. SORRY. HE DOESN'T KNOW WORD.
OH...I KNOW A WORD FOR YOU ALL RIGHT.

ALTHOUGH YOUR SKILLS ARE QUITE ADMIRABLE, I HAVE TO BE HONEST: THERE ISN'T MUCH DEMAND FOR WEB PEOPLE THESE DAYS.
LOOK, THERE HAS TO BE WORK FOR ME OUT THERE. I'M DOWN TO MY LAST BOX OF MACARONI!
COPYRIGHT © 2002 ILLIAD HTTP://WWW.USERFRIENDLY.ORG/

ACTUALLY, THERE IS ONE PLACE THAT'S HIRING PEOPLE WITH WEB EXPERIENCE...
FINE! I'LL TAKE IT! I'LL TAKE ANYTHING!

AOL banner design labs
COULDN'T FIND ANY MONKEYS?
NO. HE'S CHEAPER.

AOL banner
DUDE! WELCOME TO THE BIG A!
THANKS. I GUESS. NOT SURE I REALLY WANT TO BE HERE.
OH? WHY NOT?
COPYRIGHT © 2002 ILLIAD HTTP://WWW.USERFRIENDLY.ORG/

I'M NOT EXACTLY A FAN OF BIG CORPORATIONS.
design labs
NEITHER WAS I. BUT THIS IS WHAT THEY PAY ME. EVERY WEEK.

HOLY...!
DUDE. AIN'T NOTHIN' HOLY ABOUT IT. BUT THERE CAN BE NO LIGHT WITHOUT SHADOW.

YOU MAKE THIS MUCH AS A BANNER DESIGNER?!
HECK. NO. YOU KNOW ALL OF THOSE NEW AD FORMATS ON THE WEB? POP-UNDERS. INTER-STITIALS. THAT KIND OF THING?
COPYRIGHT © 2002 ILLIAD HTTP://WWW.USERFRIENDLY.ORG/

YES?
I'M THE GUY WHO COMES UP WITH ALL OF THAT. COOL HUH?

HEH. ANOTHER WEENIE IN AWE.
FOUND... HIM...!

DATELINE: NEW YORK CITY
Dear Bill G.
Thought these might help give you an idea with marketing MSN.
Heard you were still way behind
Love
Richard D Parsons
CEO, America On Line
Richard, way ahead of you, man. Love, Bill
USERFRIENDLY DOT ORG
COPYRIGHT (C) 2002 ILLIAD

DIE INVASIVE POND SCUM! BLIGHT ON ALL THAT IS PURE IN THIS WORLD!
GRAGGLE! EGGIBLE! WUURGLE!
COPYRIGHT © 2002 ILLIAD HTTP://WWW.USERFRIENDLY.ORG/

WHAT?
I SAID, IF YOU'D GIVE IT A CHANCE, YOU TOO COULD MAKE SERIOUS COIN AND NOT FEEL SOILED OVER IT.

WELL...THAT'S QUITE COMPELLING, BUT HOW-
YO, ED! PREP THE TEAM. WE'RE DOING ANOTHER ETHICECTOMY!

A.J. IS SUBJECTED TO AOL'S "SELECTIVE TRUTHS 101"...
TODAY WE TEACH YOU HOW TO HOOVER MONEY FROM AN UNSUSPECTING PUBLIC WITH SMOKE AND MIRRORS!
CHARMING.

FOR EXAMPLE, WE CHARGE A PREMIUM FOR OUR MUCH TOUTED 'PARENTAL CONTROLS,' WHICH ARE REALLY JUST A .WAV FILE THAT RUNS AT RANDOM...
OH?

COPYRIGHT © 2002 ILLIAD HTTP://WWW.USERFRIENDLY.ORG/
WELCOME TO THE GEORGE W. BUSH "DANCING AROUND THE ISSUES" PARTY!
NAUGHTINESS IN PROGRESS!
BILLY!
DAMN. THIS THING IS PSYCHIC...

I really started getting adventuresome with the drawing in these last few weeks. Must've been exceptionally good coffee.

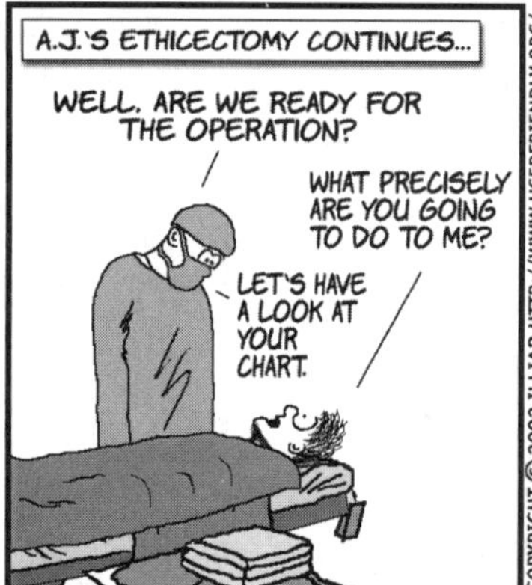
A.J.'S ETHICECTOMY CONTINUES...
WELL, ARE WE READY FOR THE OPERATION?
WHAT PRECISELY ARE YOU GOING TO DO TO ME?
LET'S HAVE A LOOK AT YOUR CHART.
COPYRIGHT © 2002 ILLIAD HTTP://WWW.USERFRIENDLY.ORG/

SOMEONE GO GET A PRIEST.
WHAT? WHAT?!

WHY IS THERE A PRIEST STANDING OVER ME?
YOUNG MAN, WE'RE JUST COVERING ALL OF THE BASES.
COPYRIGHT © 2002 ILLIAD HTTP://WWW.USERFRIENDLY.ORG/

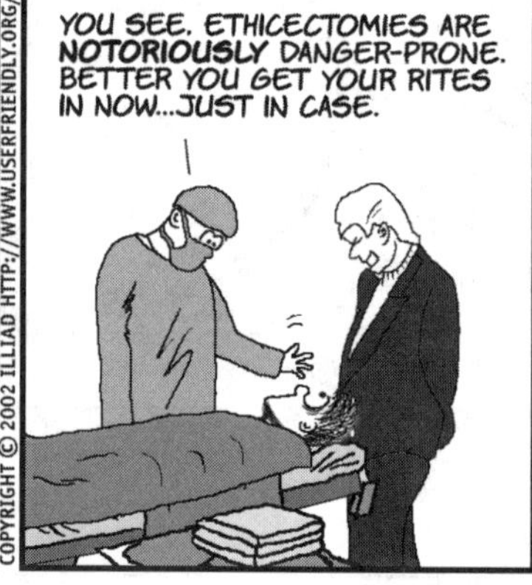
YOU SEE, ETHICECTOMIES ARE NOTORIOUSLY DANGER-PRONE. BETTER YOU GET YOUR RITES IN NOW...JUST IN CASE.

WELL? AREN'T YOU GONNA IN NOMINE PATRIS ME OR SOMETHING?
HECK NO. I'M PAGAN. DON'T WORRY. TOMORROW NIGHT IS GOOD FOR A CROSSING.

STEF! YOU'RE BACK!
YEAH...ALBEIT STILL WALKING A LITTLE FUNNY. WHERE'S A.J.?
COPYRIGHT © 2002 ILLIAD HTTP://WWW.USERFRIENDLY.ORG/

OH. HE GOT FIRED. LAST WE HEARD HE'S WORKING FOR A.O.L.
THE A.O.L.? A.J.?
YEAH. SAD. HUH?

GREG...OUR LITTLE IDEALIST HAS GROWN UP INTO A BIG NASTY CAPITALIST! *SNIF* I'M SO PROUD!
OH. CUT IT OUT.

DUDE. A.J.'S COMING BY TO VISIT!
COOL! HOW'S HE DOING?
COPYRIGHT © 2002 ILLIAD HTTP://WWW.USERFRIENDLY.ORG/

HE SEEMED UPBEAT. BUT HE DID SOUND KINDA FUNNY.
I THINK I HEAR HIM NOW.

A.J.?!
IN THE FLESH. HOT BUNS!
AAAAAAAAAA

WITH THE INVENTION OF THE "REMOTE NET-HAND" WITH TACTILE FEEDBACK, USERS WILL BE ENCOURAGED TO THINK TWICE BEFORE CALLING TECHNICAL SUPPORT...
USERFRIENDLY DOT ORG
COPYRIGHT (C) 2002 ILLIAD

If I could make these work, I'd be able to buy Brunei overnight.

A.J?!
STEF! LONG TIME, DUDE. HOW YA BEEN?
COPYRIGHT © 2002 ILLIAD HTTP://WWW.USERFRIENDLY.ORG/

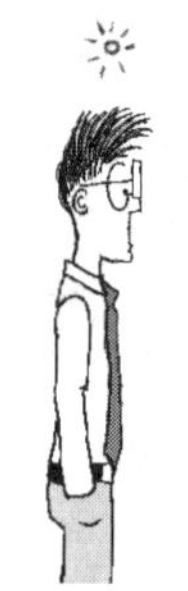

DUDE. WHO THE HELL BEAT YOU WITH A HANDSOME STICK?!
OH COME NOW. YOU'RE THE TOTAL CHIN HERE...

HEY, MON CAPITAN, COULD I PICK YOUR BRAIN?
WHY OF COURSE MY MAGNIFICENT FRIEND!
I HAVE A HUGE PILE OF THESE FROM OUR CUSTOMER LIST...
COPYRIGHT © 2002 ILLIAD HTTP://WWW.USERFRIENDLY.ORG/

MAY WE SPAM YOUR E-MAIL ADDRESS UNCEASINGLY?
☐ YES! ☒ NO
SO, WHADDYA THINK WE CAN DO HERE?

I DON'T SEE THE PROBLEM. LOOKS LIKE OPT-IN TO ME.
YO! GREG! FIRE UP THE MAIL SERVER!

GREG, THAT JUST CAN'T BE A.J.
MAYBE. REMEMBER WHEN CRUD PUPPY TOOK OVER HIS BODY LIKE IN THE MATRIX? MAYBE THIS IS LIKE THE MATRIX RELOADED.
COPYRIGHT © 2002 ILLIAD HTTP://WWW.USERFRIENDLY.ORG/

REMEMBER THAT I CARE ABOUT YOU A.J....
WHA..?

I CAN'T BELIEVE I SMACKED A.J. OVER THE HEAD.
YOU ARE SURE WAS BEINK A.J? TO MISTAKINK STEF FOR HIM IS POSSIBLE. THEY ARE LOOKINK ALIKE.
COPYRIGHT © 2002 ILLIAD HTTP://WWW.USERFRIENDLY.ORG/

REMEMBER, I DO CARE FOR YOU...
OOOH! ABOUT TIME SHE CAME AROUND...

WHY SO BLUE, MIRANDA?
I THWACKED TWO STEFS AND A.J. **STILL** DIDN'T REAPPEAR.
COPYRIGHT © 2002 ILLIAD HTTP://WWW.USERFRIENDLY.ORG/

...AH.

WELL, I'M SURE AS LONG AS YOU DON'T STOP LOOKING, YOU'LL FIND THE GUY YOU WANT.
I SUPPOSE JUST ONE MORE TRY WOULDN'T HURT...

HOW'S YOUR HEAD?
FINE, DESPITE THE BEST EFFORTS OF THAT CRAZY **BINT**.
COPYRIGHT © 2002 ILLIAD HTTP://WWW.USERFRIENDLY.ORG/

SHE'S AN EVIL, NASTY TART THAT ONE.
YOU SAID IT. CAN'T STAND TO BE AROUND HER.

TWENTY BUCKS SAYS I GET A DATE WITH HER BEFORE YOU DO.
DONE!

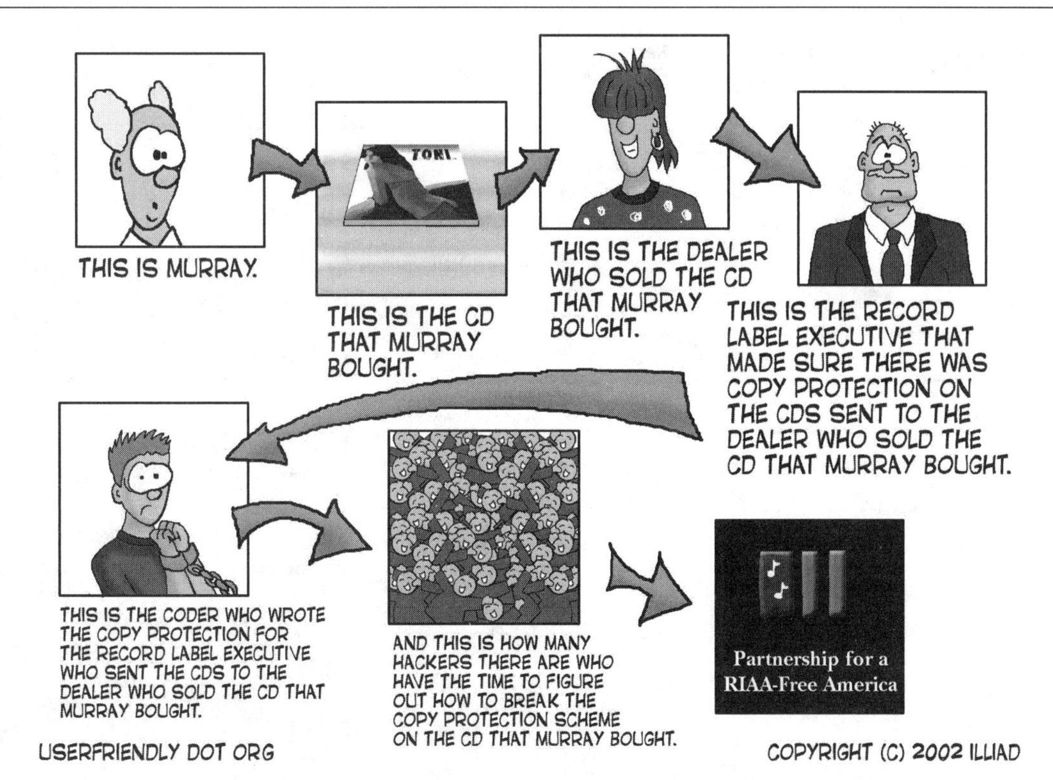
THIS IS MURRAY.
TORI
THIS IS THE CD THAT MURRAY BOUGHT.
THIS IS THE DEALER WHO SOLD THE CD THAT MURRAY BOUGHT.
THIS IS THE RECORD LABEL EXECUTIVE THAT MADE SURE THERE WAS COPY PROTECTION ON THE CDS SENT TO THE DEALER WHO SOLD THE CD THAT MURRAY BOUGHT.
THIS IS THE CODER WHO WROTE THE COPY PROTECTION FOR THE RECORD LABEL EXECUTIVE WHO SENT THE CDS TO THE DEALER WHO SOLD THE CD THAT MURRAY BOUGHT.
AND THIS IS HOW MANY HACKERS THERE ARE WHO HAVE THE TIME TO FIGURE OUT HOW TO BREAK THE COPY PROTECTION SCHEME ON THE CD THAT MURRAY BOUGHT.
Partnership for a RIAA-Free America
USERFRIENDLY DOT ORG
COPYRIGHT (C) 2002 ILLIAD

I love double entendres, but the non-English-speaking readers who write the translation threads every day run into real grief. This was one of the strips that caused considerable consternation.

HEY TOOTS...LET'S LET BYGONES BE BYGONES. 'KAY? HOW ABOUT A DATE?
STEF. EXACTLY HOW MANY TIMES HAVE YOU MANAGED TO DATE A WOMAN AND NOT GET SMACKED?
COPYRIGHT © 2002 ILLIAD HTTP://WWW.USERFRIENDLY.ORG/

LET'S SEE. THERE'S BARBI... WAIT. SHE BELTED ME. OR WAS THAT BUNNY? AND THERE WAS CELESTE...NO. NO. SHE GOT ME WITH A LIPSTICK TUBE... BUT YVETTE DID TOO...OR...

SORRY. IT'S REALLY HARD KEEPING ALL OF MY EX-GIRLFRIENDS STRAIGHT...
AFTER THEY DATED YOU I CAN UNDERSTAND WHY.

I used to watch CHiPs re-runs, but the only episode I remember is the one where Erik Estrada sings and dances to "Celebrate" by Kool & the Gang. It haunts me.

BY ALL THAT'S FLIPPING UNHOLY...
WHAT'S WRONG?
YOU HEARD ABOUT THE BET STEF AND A.J. HAVE?
COPYRIGHT © 2002 ILLIAD HTTP://WWW.USERFRIENDLY.ORG/

YES. TO SEE WHO GETS A DATE WITH MIRANDA FIRST. WHAT ABOUT IT?
WELL. IT'S A.J.'S TURN. HE'S BUSY "GETTING PSYCHED."

YO! HAS ANYONE SEEN MY "ERIK ESTRADA DOES KOOL AND THE GANG" CD?

SO. A.J., YOU'RE ACTUALLY GONNA ASK HER OUT?
YOU BET! THIS HUNKA HUNKA BURNIN' LOVE IS GONNA GET SOME FROM THAT HOT LITTLE MAMA!
COPYRIGHT © 2002 ILLIAD HTTP://WWW.USERFRIENDLY.ORG/

YOU GO. BOYO! REV THOSE ENGINES! STACK 'EM AND RACK 'EM! YOU SHOW 'EM WHAT'S WHAT. CASANOVA! DO THE ... UH ...

AND THAT WOULD BE A.J. BEHIND ME.

ERWIN! WE HAVE TO DO SOMETHING! A.J. HAS TURNED INTO A... A...UM... A...
...SMARMY GIT WITH NO ETHICS AND BAD HAIR. I KNOW.
COPYRIGHT © 2002 ILLIAD HTTP://WWW.USERFRIENDLY.ORG/

BUT WHAT ARE WE GOING TO DO?
WHY. APPEAL TO THE INTERNET OF COURSE...

NEW WEBSITE. MR. PRESIDENT. "SAVE-AJ DOT COM." THEY'RE... UH...ASKING FOR "DONATED ETHICS."
GOL'DANGIT. RUMSIE. YOU CAN'T SQUEEZE BLOOD FROM A STONE.

DELIVERY FOR THE "SAVE-AJ" FOUNDATION!
I'LL SIGN FOR IT!
FedUP

WHAT DID WE GET?

EWWW. WHATEVER IT IS, IT LOOKS **WET.**
PACKING SLIP SAYS "ALL THE ETHICS WE COULD FIND." NO RETURN ADDRESS.
FedUP

OW.
MY GOD, COLIN. THERE'S A **HOLE** IN YOUR HEAD.
AND WHAT'S WITH THE NEW HAIR?

ERWIN, DO YOU REALIZE THAT WE'RE IN THE PRESENCE OF COLIN POWELL'S ETHICS?
INDEED. BEFORE US LIES THE WET MEAT OF THOUGHTFUL ORTHODOXY AND CONSIDERATE MODERATION.

COPYRIGHT © 2002 ILLIAD HTTP://WWW.USERFRIENDLY.ORG/

I BEG YOUR PARDON. DID YOU SAY "WET MEAT?"

MORE SPECIFICALLY, A FILET. ASTONISHINGLY FOUND IN AN ABATTOIR OF HEAD CHEESE...
AAAGH...ERWIN **STOP IT!**

by J.D. Frazer
USER FRIENDLY

GREETINGS, SQUID FOOD. TODAY WE'D LIKE TO ADDRESS THE SUBJECT OF ETHICS, A TOPIC SURE TO BRING VITRIOL AND IRRATIONALITY TO THE FORE-FRONT. BUT LET US NOT FORGET THAT ETHICS ARE **SUBJECTIVE.**

FOR EXAMPLE, IN MY UNIVERSE, TEARING HUMANS TO SHREDS AND EATING THEM IS CONSID-ERED UNETHICAL AND REALLY QUITE **RUDE.**
THAT'S GOOD TO HEAR...
WE'RE SUPPOSED TO EAT YOU **WHOLE.**

GEEKS OF THE WORLD! WE ARE THE WALL OF TRUTH AND FAIR-NESS THAT STANDS BETWEEN THE MONOLITHIC CORPORATIONS AND OUR RIGHT TO CHOOSE.

DO NOT FORGET THAT IT IS OUR COLLECTIVE STRENGTH OF ETHICS THAT FIGHTS FOR WHAT IS RIGHT. WE RESIST THE EFFORTS OF THE MPAA, THE RIAA, OVER-ZEALOUS GOVERNMENTS AND ENFORCEMENT AGENCIES, AND MANY OTHERS.

ALONE WE ARE UNHEARD. TO-GETHER, WE FORM A **SWEEPING CIVIL BODY,** A HALO OF **VIRTUE** THAT DEMANDS THE SAME BE-HAVIOUR FROM THOSE WHO WOULD STEAL FROM US THAT WHICH IS OURS. THANK YOU.
YOU DONE YET? I CAN'T FIND THAT COPY OF WINDOWS XP YOU BURNED FOR ME.

WE HAVE SOMETHING FOR YOU, A.J.
OH? WHAT IS IT?
COPYRIGHT © 2002 ILLIAD HTTP://WWW.USERFRIENDLY.ORG/

ETHICS.
OH.

AND I DO WHAT WITH THIS?
THINK OF IT AS A FILET...
ERWIN!

BUT WHY O WHY WOULD I WANT ETHICS?
BECAUSE AJ, YOU'D BE A BETTER PERSON. YOU'D CARE ABOUT DOING THE RIGHT THING.
COPYRIGHT © 2002 ILLIAD HTTP://WWW.USERFRIENDLY.ORG/

YOU'D TURN DOWN REALLY EASY MONEY. AND NOT TRY TO CHEAT THE SYSTEM JUST TO BE RICH. AND ACCEPT RESPONSIBILITY FOR YOUR OWN MISTAKES SO OTHER PEOPLE WON'T TAKE THE FALL...
AND NOT HANG AROUND TRASHY WOMEN.
RIGHT!

OH. TINGLING WITH EXCITEMENT. I AM.
AND THE HYMNS! DON'T FORGET ALL THE HYMNS YOU COULD SING!

FORGET IT! I AM NOT GOING TO DENY MYSELF YEARS OF WET, LASCIVIOUS FUN BY STUFFING SOMEONE ELSE'S ETHICS INTO MY SKULL!
BUT...
NO!
COPYRIGHT © 2002 ILLIAD HTTP://WWW.USERFRIENDLY.ORG/

I HAVE NO ETHICS. AND I MUST CUDDLE.
THE VINEGAR IN THE EYES WORKED.
CAN I CALL IT OR WHAT?

WHAT'S GOING ON IN THE GAME ROOM?
THE LI'L GUY AND ERWIN RECRUITED SID TO HELP THEM REPLACE A.J.'S ETHICS.
COPYRIGHT©2002 J.D. FRAZER HTTP://WWW.USERFRIENDLY.ORG/

EH?
THEY TRIED EXPLAINING IT, BUT ALL I COULD GET WAS THAT IT HAS TO DO WITH SOMEHOW GETTING A SOFT MUSHY BALL INTO A.J.'S SKULL.

I STILL DON'T UNDERSTAND HOW YOU'RE GOING TO DO THIS. WHY AM I STRAPPED IN A POOL TABLE?
REMEMBER, IF IT DOESN'T GO IN ALL THE WAY, KEEP TRAVELLING UNTIL YOUR HAND BUMPS INTO HIS NOSE...
WIBBLE

A.J? ARE YOU OKAY?
BA KOO! BA KOO! GAKE IB OUB!
COPYRIGHT © 2002 ILLIAD HTTP://WWW.USERFRIENDLY.ORG/

MAYBE I SHOULDN'T HAVE RUN THAT POOL CUE LIKE A PIPE CLEANER...
OH DEAR. I THINK HE'S LOST SPEECH FUNCTION!
FLEEZ GAKE IB OUB!

HE'S DELERIOUS! OH, POOR A.J.! ERWIN, WHAT DO YOU THINK HE'S TRYING TO SAY?
"PLEASE TAKE IT OUT."
GOW GOOD GE GICE.

I HAVE NO IDEA WHAT ELSE WE CAN DO. A.J. HAS ETHICS SHOVED WAY UP HIS NOSE AND HE STILL LOOKS LIKE STEF.
COPYRIGHT © 2002 ILLIAD HTTP://WWW.USERFRIENDLY.ORG/

MAYBE WE NEED TO GET TO THE ROOT OF THE PROBLEM...
ERWIN SAID SOMETHING ABOUT THAT...SOMETHING ABOUT A.J. HAVING STEF'S HEAD.

PLEASE EAT HIS STEF-HEAD. OH PLEASE, OH PLEASE...
OH. YUCK...

EXPERTS PONDER WHY COMDEX ATTENDANCE CONTINUES TO HIT LOW NUMBERS...
"HINT"
GEEKHAUS
COMDEX
WHERE GEEK GUYS GO FOR THE CHICKS
USERFRIENDLY DOT ORG
COPYRIGHT (C) 2002 ILLIAD

The Daystar! It burrrnnnnnnss!

Apple's "Switch" commercials were a raging success. So raging, that the Great Old Ones petitioned me to feature them in one. So here you are.

SO THERE I WAS ABOUT TO EAT A.J.'S HEAD. BUT HE LOOKED WAY TOO MUCH LIKE STEF. THE REVULSION WASN'T WORTH THE PROTEIN. I MEAN, WHO WANTS TO EAT A GREASY MARKETER?
DINK
DINK
DA-DUNK
DINK

I STARED AT HIM FOR A LONG TIME, FIGHTING MY GAG REFLEX, TRYING TO FIGURE OUT WHAT TO DO.
DONK
DINK
DA-DINK
DONK

SUDDENLY, I HAD AN IDEA! MY APPLE POWERBOOK CAME TO THE RESCUE! I GRABBED A.J. AND SANDWICHED HIS HEAD IN BETWEEN THE POWERBOOK'S SCREEN AND KEYBOARD. AND THUS I COULD EAT HIS HEAD, SIGHT UNSEEN!
ALONG WITH THE POWERBOOK OF COURSE.
DINK DONK DUNK

MY NAME IS CTHULHU, AND I SAVED A.J.!
AAAAARRGH! HEAD!!!
COPYRIGHT©2002 ILLIAD HTTP://WWW.USERFRIENDLY.ORG/

HAHAHAHAHAHAHAHAH!
WHAT'S SO FUNNY?
YOU KNOW HOW AJ HAD HIS HEAD EATEN? ILLIAD DREW HIM A NEW HEAD.
YEAH? SO?
COPYRIGHT©2002 ILLIAD HTTP://WWW.USERFRIENDLY.ORG/

YOU KNOW HOW ILLIAD'S BEEN TRYING TO SAVE MONEY ON INK?
YEAH. SO?

DUDE. I'M JEALOUS.

YOU KNOW, A.J. COULD BE IN TROUBLE...
NO KIDDING. HE HAS A TINY HEAD.
COPYRIGHT©2002 ILLIAD HTTP://WWW.USERFRIENDLY.ORG/
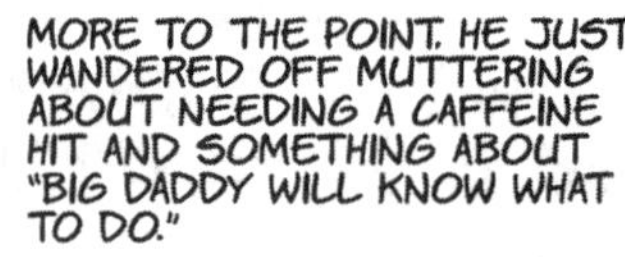
MORE TO THE POINT, HE JUST WANDERED OFF MUTTERING ABOUT NEEDING A CAFFEINE HIT AND SOMETHING ABOUT "BIG DADDY WILL KNOW WHAT TO DO."

OOOG...

NOW HOLD STILL...
PRESSURIZED CARBON DIOXIDE

COPYRIGHT©2002 ILLIAD HTTP://WWW.USERFRIENDLY.ORG/

BRAINFREEZE?
BRAINFIZZ.
NNNNGGG

AH! A.J.! I'D HEARD YOU WERE VISITING. I WANTED TO LET YOU KNOW THAT I WAS PERHAPS A LITTLE HARSH IN FIRING YOU FOR WORKING ON THAT GAME DURING COMPANY TIME.
COPYRIGHT © 2002 ILLIAD HTTP://WWW.USERFRIENDLY.ORG/

DOES THAT MEAN I GET MY JOB BACK?
YES. BUT OF COURSE THERE ARE CONDITIONS.

YOU MEAN LIKE NOT USING COMPANY TIME FOR PERSONAL PROJECTS?
YES. AND GIVING ME THE CHEAT CODES TO THAT STUPID GAME OF YOURS.

DUDE! IS IT TRUE? DO YOU HAVE YOUR JOB BACK?
SURE DO.
THAT'S GREAT! TOO BAD ABOUT YOUR GAME THOUGH.
COPYRIGHT © 2002 ILLIAD HTTP://WWW.USERFRIENDLY.ORG/

IT'S NOT SO BAD. I'M ALLOWED TO WORK ON PATCHES AND STUFF AT THE OFFICE NOW. WITHIN REASON.
BUT...I THOUGHT THAT ONE OF THE TWO CONDITIONS WAS THAT YOU COULDN'T...

LET'S JUST SAY I NEGOTIATED.
COULD I PLEASE HAVE JUST ONE MORE CHEAT CODE?

THE U.S. NAVY DEPLOYS ITS FIRST BIOWARFARE SHIP IN PREPARATION FOR A NEW WAR IN THE GULF
USERFRIENDLY DOT ORG
COPYRIGHT (C) 2002 ILLIAD

Disney had a serious bout of Norwalk viruses on their cruise ships for a while.

CRIPES. NOT ANOTHER ONE. "LARRY ODOGWU OF THE NIGERIA PETROLEUM CORPORATION" INDEED. THIS IS GETTING RIDICULOUS!
ANOTHER VARIATION OF THE NIGERIAN 419 SCAM?
COPYRIGHT©2002 ILLIAD HTTP://WWW.USERFRIENDLY.ORG/

YEAH. I HATE THESE DORKS. WHAT THEY'RE DOING IS SCUMMY. AND THEY'RE DAMN HARD TO CATCH AND CONVICT.
ONE DAY. THEY'RE GOING TO TARGET THE WRONG PERSON.

"TWENTY PERCENT OF FORTY-TWO MILLION DOLLARS?" HOW CAN I RESIST?

Dear Mr. Odogwu.
I am most pleased to make your acquaintance...
HMM. NAH.
COPYRIGHT©2002 ILLIAD HTTP://WWW.USERFRIENDLY.ORG/

Dear Sir,
As a great old one, I confess to having a great deal of interest...
...NOPE.

Yo, Larry.
Send the bucks or your head is squid food.
Love,
He Who Shall Remain Nameless
NOW THAT JUST SCREAMS "ME."

DEAR SIR,
COMPLIMENTS OF THE SEASON. THANK YOU FOR REPLYING. SO THAT WE MAY EXPEDITE THE TRANSFER OF FUNDS, PLEASE FAX ME A COPY OF YOUR PASSPORT SO THAT I MAY EXECUTE A POWER OF ATTORNEY FOR YOU.
COPYRIGHT©2002 ILLIAD HTTP://WWW.USERFRIENDLY.ORG/

I WAIT FOR YOUR EARLY REPLY AND AT THE SAME TIME RESTATING MY CONFIDENCE ON YOU.

P.S. NO I AM NOT USING "AOL AFRICA," WHY DO YOU ASK?
Oh never mind.
I don't have a passport.
Could I interest you in an Elder Sign?
TYPE
TAP
MOCK

HELLO. I AM MIKE ABA, ASSOCIATE TO LARRY ODOGWU. I AM CALLING TO REQUEST IN URGENCY YOUR PHOTOGRAPH AND PERSONAL DETAILS SO THAT WE MAY EXECUTE A POWER OF ATTORNEY...
DUDE. YOU DON'T WANT TO GAZE UPON MY VISAGE.
PLEASE SEND US YOUR PHOTO. IT IS MOST NEEDED.
COPYRIGHT©2002 ILLIAD HTTP://WWW.USERFRIENDLY.ORG/

OKAY. SENT. SHOULD BE IN YOUR E-MAIL NOW...
AAAIIIIEEEEEE!!
TAP!

NICE TO KNOW THE SIGHT OF ME CAN STILL BRING ABOUT ABJECT FEAR AND MADNESS...
UGLY...MOLLUSK... IN...SPEEDO.... STRETCH MARKS....
NOOOOO!!!

HELLO THIS IS LARRY ODOGWU. MY ASSOCIATE MIKE ABA IS BUSY REMOVING HIS EYES WITH A SPOON. PLEASE TELL ME YOUR NAME SO THAT WE MAY PROCEED WITH THIS TRANSACTION.
COPYRIGHT©2002 ILLIAD HTTP://WWW.USERFRIENDLY.ORG/

FINE. MY NAME IS CTHULHU. THAT'S RIGHT. SPELLED C-T-H-U-L-H-U...

OH DEAR...
YOU LIKE THAT? SO? WHAT'S MY NAME? SAY MY NAME, MORTAL!

I AM PLEASED, MADAM, TO TELL YOU THAT WE ARE ABOUT TO TRANSFER THE FULL TWENTY MILLION TO YOUR ACCOUNT...
CHARLES...
NOT NOW LARRY.
BUT...
COPYRIGHT©2002 ILLIAD HTTP://WWW.USERFRIENDLY.ORG/

...SO PLEASE DO NOT FAIL TO FORWARD THE SUM OF SIX THOUSAND DOLLARS TO MY BANK ACCOUNT...
CHARLES! I NEED TO TALK TO YOU ABOUT A PORTAL!

PORTAL? PORTALS ARE DEAD, LARRY.
ARE THEY NOW.
COMPLIMENTS OF THE SEASONING, GENTLEMEN.

SUDDENLY, YOUNG ALIPAK REALIZED THAT PERHAPS, JUST PERHAPS, HIS LONG-TIME BUDDY "BONZI" MIGHT IN FACT BE TELLING A BIT OF A FIB...
SECURITY ALERT
YOU ARE CURRENTLY BROADCASTING YOUR IP ADDRESS! WITH THIS ADDRESS, SOMEONE CAN IMMEDIATELY BEGIN ATTACKING YOUR COMPUTER!
OK
USERFRIENDLY DOT ORG
COPYRIGHT (C) 2002 ILLIAD

HELLO FOLKS! WELL, I'M PLEASED TO SAY THAT YOUR FAVOURITE GREAT OLD ONE HAS DINED ON THE HEADS AND FACES OF THE 419 SCAMMERS IN THIS LOCALE.
THEY WON'T BE SCAMMING AGAIN.
ECONOMIC DARWINISM
COPYRIGHT©2002 ILLIAD HTTP://WWW.USERFRIENDLY.ORG/

OF COURSE, THERE WERE SO MANY OF THEM, I HAD TO RECRUIT SOME HELP. A LOCAL OOZING HORROR ANSWERED MY CALL AND WE HAD OUR REPAST.
ECONOMIC DARWINISM

AND IF I COULD BE FORGIVEN FOR UTILIZING SUCH AN OVER-USED MEME, TO CONCLUDE THIS MATTER, I WOULD JUST LIKE TO SAY:
"ALL THEIR FACE ARE BELONG TO US."
ECONOMIC DARWINISM
FOR GREAT PUSTULES!

I'M FED UP. THAT'S RIGHT. FED UP.
FED UP WITH BEING DISSECTED, PIGEON-HOLED, CATEGORIZED, AND ANALYZED BY MARKETERS.
COPYRIGHT©2002 ILLIAD HTTP://WWW.USERFRIENDLY.ORG/

TIRED OF BEING CONTAINED, COUNTED, DESIGNATED, ENUMERATED, INCLUDED, INDICATED, MARKED, SPECIFIED, TARGETTED AND TOTALLED!

HEAR ME, MONOLITH INCORPORATED! I AM NOT A NUMBER!
MIKE, WHAT'S YOUR IP ADDRESS?

HELLO, MIKE SPE-
HELLO MR. FLOYD! MY NAME IS AMBER AND I'M CALLING TO TELL YOU ABOUT OUR NEW BEARD TRIMMER! ONLY $19.95 AND WE KNOW YOU HAVE A BEARD!
COPYRIGHT©2002 ILLIAD HTTP://WWW.USERFRIENDLY.ORG/

WHAT?! HOW DID YOU-
WE KNOW A LOT ABOUT YOU, SIR. YOU'RE GOING TO REFUSE TO COME TO GRIPS WITH THIS FACT, SO MAY WE SUGGEST OUR NEW HERBAL ANTI-DEPRESSION REMEDY FOR ONLY $39.95?

WHY...REFUSAL...OOO! COME TO GRIPS?! WHY YOU...OOOO!!!
WE ALSO SELL A SIX-TAPE SET OF "LEARN HOW TO NOT SOUND LIKE A TOTAL DORK ON THE PHONE," FOR ONLY $89.95!

MIKE? ARE YOU OKAY?
JUST IRRITATED, SID. IT SEEMS THAT AS TECHNOLOGY ADVANCES, SO DO WAYS OF PER-VERTING IT INTO EVIL MARKETING APPLICATIONS.
COPYRIGHT©2002 ILLIAD HTTP://WWW.USERFRIENDLY.ORG/

THE TELEPHONE, THE TELEVISION, AND NOW OF COURSE THE NET. I MEAN, GODS ABOVE, WHERE WILL IT STOP?

MEANWHILE, IN ANOTHER GALAXY...
750 HOURS FREE
OKAY, NOW MOVE THIS ONE OVER BY A COUPLE OF ZICROBINKS...

LADIES AND GENTLEMEN. I HAVE BOUGHT SOME SCREEN TIME TO BRING YOU THIS MESSAGE.
COPYRIGHT©2002 ILLIAD HTTP://WWW.USERFRIENDLY.ORG/

WE MUST STEM THE TIDE OF MARKETING MESSAGES THAT ARE BLANKETING OUR SOCIETY! NO MORE ADS ON T.V., ON THE WEB, IN OUR MAIL, OR ON BILLBOARDS! WE MUST SEIZE BACK OUR EYEBALLS! WE MUST STOP THE MADNESS!

...THANK YOU.
OKAY. NOW PAN DOWN.

WHAT ARE YOU SMIRKING AT?
Play
SIMS
Today!

FIX MY COMPUTER! NOW!
UH, WELL, IF YOU WOULD CALM DOWN AND TELL ME WHAT THE PROBLEM WAS--
DON'T TALK TO ME LIKE I'M STUPID! I HAVE A DEGREE!
COPYRIGHT©2002 ILLIAD HTTP://WWW.USERFRIENDLY.ORG/

IT WOULDN'T HAPPEN TO BE FROM ONE OF THOSE "NON-ACCREDITED" ONES, NOW WOULD IT?
IT'S PRESTIGIOUS! IT SAID SO IN THE E-MAIL!

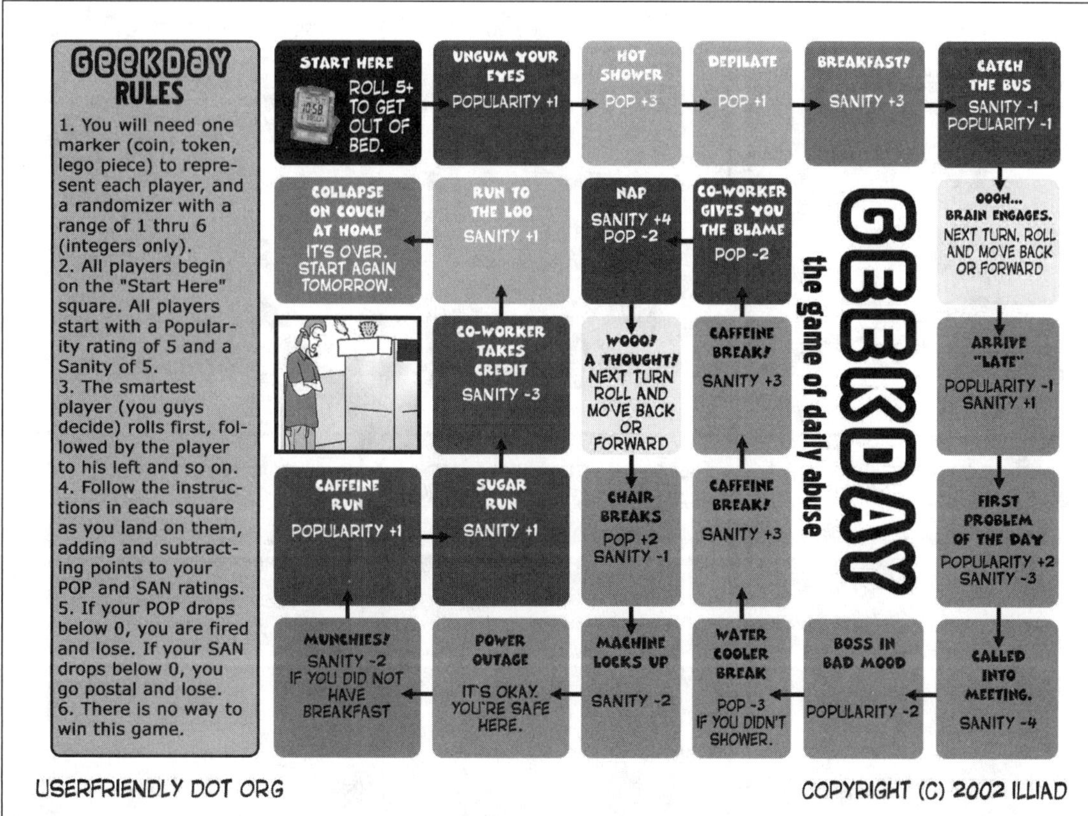
GEEKDAY RULES
1. You will need one marker (coin, token, lego piece) to represent each player, and a randomizer with a range of 1 thru 6 (integers only).
2. All players begin on the "Start Here" square. All players start with a Popularity rating of 5 and a Sanity of 5.
3. The smartest player (you guys decide) rolls first, followed by the player to his left and so on.
4. Follow the instructions in each square as you land on them, adding and subtracting points to your POP and SAN ratings.
5. If your POP drops below 0, you are fired and lose. If your SAN drops below 0, you go postal and lose.
6. There is no way to win this game.
START HERE ROLL 5+ TO GET OUT OF BED.
UNGUM YOUR EYES POPULARITY +1
HOT SHOWER POP +3
DEPILATE POP +1
BREAKFAST! SANITY +3
CATCH THE BUS SANITY -1 POPULARITY -1
OOOH... BRAIN ENGAGES. NEXT TURN, ROLL AND MOVE BACK OR FORWARD
ARRIVE "LATE" POPULARITY -1 SANITY +1
FIRST PROBLEM OF THE DAY POPULARITY +2 SANITY -3
CALLED INTO MEETING. SANITY -4
BOSS IN BAD MOOD POPULARITY -2
WATER COOLER BREAK POP -3 IF YOU DIDN'T SHOWER.
CAFFEINE BREAK! SANITY +3
CAFFEINE BREAK! SANITY +3
CO-WORKER GIVES YOU THE BLAME POP -2
NAP SANITY +4 POP -2
WOOO! A THOUGHT! NEXT TURN ROLL AND MOVE BACK OR FORWARD
CHAIR BREAKS POP +2 SANITY -1
MACHINE LOCKS UP SANITY -2
POWER OUTAGE IT'S OKAY. YOU'RE SAFE HERE.
MUNCHIES! SANITY -2 IF YOU DID NOT HAVE BREAKFAST
CAFFEINE RUN POPULARITY +1
SUGAR RUN SANITY +1
CO-WORKER TAKES CREDIT SANITY -3
RUN TO THE LOO SANITY +1
COLLAPSE ON COUCH AT HOME IT'S OVER. START AGAIN TOMORROW.
GEEKDAY the game of daily abuse
USERFRIENDLY DOT ORG
COPYRIGHT (C) 2002 ILLIAD

DUDE. GREAT TREE!
THANKS! I'VE BEEN WORKING ON IT ALL MORNING.
COPYRIGHT © 2002 ILLIAD HTTP://WWW.USERFRIENDLY.ORG/

NEAT LIGHTS. THAT MUST HAVE COST A BUNDLE TO PUT TOGETHER.
OH. NOT AT ALL.

YOU KNOW. THOSE LIGHTS DO LOOK KINDA FAMILIAR.
THEY WERE A PAIN TO PRY OUT. LEMME TELL YA...
GREG! THE MODEM RACK'S BEEN PILLAGED!

SO...YOU PRIED OUT ALL OF THE MODEM LEDs AND USED THEM AS CHRISTMAS TREE LIGHTS?
YES. AND IT WAS DARNED ANNOYING. I COULDN'T GET THE SCREWS TO COME OUT.
COPYRIGHT © 2002 ILLIAD HTTP://WWW.USERFRIENDLY.ORG/

YOU COULDN'T... GET... THE SCREWS...

OH PLEASE TELL ME YOU DIDN'T STRIP EVERY SINGLE SCREW...
HECK NO. YOU GEEKS TAUGHT ME TO ALWAYS USE THE RIGHT TOOL!
SOB MY POOR BABIES... THEIR SHATTERED LITTLE BODIES...

I STILL CAN'T BELIEVE WHAT STEF DID.
WHAT'S WORSE IS THAT I THINK HE FELT HE WAS BEING NICE.
COPYRIGHT © 2002 ILLIAD HTTP://WWW.USERFRIENDLY.ORG/

HE DID A TREE FOR US AND MADE IT ALL GEEKY BY PUTTING MODEM LEDs ON IT.
I'M STILL GONNA KILL HIM.

I WOULDN'T CALL THAT PRECISELY FESTIVE. DUDE.
OH WHAT I'M GOING TO DO WILL BE FESTIVE. I'M GONNA STRANGLE HIM WITH A GREEN CORD AND WE'LL SEE PLENTY OF RED.

STEF. DO YOU REALIZE YOU HOSED OUR ENTIRE MODEM POOL?
SO?
COPYRIGHT © 2002 ILLIAD HTTP://WWW.USERFRIENDLY.ORG/

SO OUR CUSTOMERS CAN'T DIAL IN TO GET A CONNECTION TO THE NET!
OH...

...THAT'S BAD FOR YOU TECHIES ISN'T IT.
YES. UNTIL I FORWARDED ALL OF THE TECH SUPPORT LINES TO YOUR VOICE MAIL.

HE WHAT?!
STEF DESTROYED ALL OF THE MODEMS ON THE RACK TO LIGHT A STUPID CHRISTMAS TREE!
COPYRIGHT © 2002 ILLIAD HTTP://WWW.USERFRIENDLY.ORG/

OH DEAR...

...TELL ME AGAIN WHAT IT IS THAT MODEMS DO?
APPARENTLY THEY CREATE A CONNECTION BETWEEN PEOPLE AND STUPIDITY.

WHAT EXACTLY DO MODEMS DO AGAIN?
THEY ALLOW COMPUTERS TO TALK TO EACH OTHER OVER STANDARD PHONE LINES. ONE MODEM DIALS OUT. THE OTHER MODEM ANSWERS AND THEY NEGOTIATE ON THE FORMAT OF DATA TRANSMISSION AND SPEED...
COPYRIGHT © 2002 ILLIAD HTTP://WWW.USERFRIENDLY.ORG/

...UH...

THEY MAKE US MONEY.
STEF!!

THE GEEK 2002 CHRISTMAS TOY OF THE YEAR

The 419 Nigerian Scammer!

now improved!

DEAR SIR,

FIRSTLY I MUST FIRST SOLICIT YOUR CONFIDENCE IN THIS TRANSACTION; THIS BY VIRTUE OF ITS NATURE AS BEEN INTERLY ONFIDENTIAL AND TOP SECRET OUGH KNOW THAT A RANSACTION OF THIS UDE WILL MAKE SOMEONE EHENSIVE AND ELATED BUT ASSURING YOU THAT ALL E WELL AT THE END OF E DAY. I AM MR. TIJANI YUSUFU EDIT OFFFICER WITH THE ION BANK OF NIGERIA PLC (U A) BENIN BRANCH.

write your own replies! bait them on!

hours of entertainment! it's replayable! it's fulfilling!

USERFRIENDLY DOT ORG

I HEARD THE CHIEF IS DOCKING YOUR PAY. I HOPE YOU LEARNED YOUR LESSON, MAN.
OH I THINK HE DID. MIKE MADE STEF BECOME **INTIMATELY** FAMILIAR WITH MODEMS.

OH? HOW SO?

WELL SEE, MIKE DID AN "INTERNAL MODEM INSTALLATION."
OOOH...
PEEP

SO AS A CHANGE OF PACE FOR THE HOLIDAY, WHAT WOULD YOU ***TAKE AWAY*** FROM THE WORLD TO MAKE IT BETTER?
HUMAN STUPIDITY, I THINK.
HEH. GOOD ONE.

COPYRIGHT©2002 ILLIAD HTTP://WWW.USERFRIENDLY.ORG/
HOW ABOUT RELIGIOUS ZEALOTRY?
GOOD ONE! AND LOW STANDARDS!
NICE!

WHAT ABOUT REALITY TELEVISION?
YE GODS... THAT COVERS IT **ALL**.
WAIT...DOES THAT MEAN NO MORE "FRIENDS?"

Oh joy, Christmas, the season of guilt-driven debt.

'AMIDST GREAT WINDS OF GREEN AND RED WE SEARCH FOR A MIDNIGHT CLEAR AND STAND IN AWE OF BURNING LIGHTS HERALDS OF PRICE-TAGGED CHEER.'
BUY!

COPYRIGHT©2002 ILLIAD HTTP://WWW.USERFRIENDLY.ORG/
'"REJOICE! REGALE! EXPRESS YOUR MIRTH!" SAY THOSE WHO WOULD BEGUILE. SO MANY TOLD TO SMILE HARD, YET SO MANY HARDLY SMILE.'
No Credit? We accept indentured servitude contracts! Buy Now!

'OUR SOULS ARE CHAFED, OUR WALLETS BLED OUR FACES SHOW THE STRAIN YET PROBLEMS THOUGH WE THINK WE HAVE SHOULD MAKE US THINK AGAIN.'
URP THAT WAS ONE MEATY FAT GUY...

A.J? WHATCHA DOING?
I'M MAKING A SNOW ANGEL.
OH. WHAT'S AN ANGEL?

COPYRIGHT©2002 ILLIAD HTTP://WWW.USERFRIENDLY.ORG/
THEY WATCH OVER US. AT ALL TIMES. IN GOOD WEATHER OR BAD. IN GOOD TIMES OR BAD. STRIVING TO KEEP US SAFE.
DO WE EVER SEE THEM?

"SOMETIMES. BUT MOST PEOPLE DON'T PAY ATTENTION."

SO WHAT DID YOU GUYS GET FOR CHRISTMAS? I GOT A HANDSPRING TREO 180.
I GOT A LEGO SPYBOT!
A DUAL ATHLON SERVER FOR ME!

DUST PUPPY AND I MADE SNOW ANGELS -- WELL, HE MADE A SNOW CLAM -- AND THEN WE WENT AND HELPED OUT AT THE LOCAL HOMELESS SHELTER. THEY THOUGHT HE WAS A KITTEN.
COPYRIGHT©2002 ILLIAD HTTP://WWW.USERFRIENDLY.ORG/

I REALLY HATE IT WHEN HE DOES THAT.
I GUESS MY SPYBOT IS OFF TO DO "MEALS ON WHEELS"
I SUPPOSE MY ATHLONS WOULD MAKE GOOD BLANKET WARMERS.

YOU LEFT DUST PUPPY AT THE HOMELESS SHELTER?
SURE. HE WAS MAKING SO MANY PEOPLE THERE HAPPY THAT IT SEEMED WRONG TO TAKE HIM AWAY JUST THEN.
COPYRIGHT©2002 ILLIAD HTTP://WWW.USERFRIENDLY.ORG/

IT MUST BE A TOUGH PLACE TO BE.
I'D IMAGINE. BUT MOST OF THE PEOPLE THERE SEEMED QUITE PRACTICAL, AND ARE MAKING THE BEST OF IT.

ED, YOU DONE WITH HIM YET?
JUST ABOUT...
AAAAAAAAAAAA

AN URBAN LEGEND "SEGWAYS" INTO THE 21ST CENTURY...
J.A.T.O.

USERFRIENDLY DOT ORG

We used to do this exact thing with our neighbor's shi-tzu.

HEY GUYS. I'M HERE TO PICK UP MY. UH...KITTEN.
KITTEN? OH. YOU MEAN THE FUZZY FELLA...
COPYRIGHT©2002 ILLIAD HTTP://WWW.USERFRIENDLY.ORG/

UH...YEAH.
ED! WHERE'S THE FUZZBALL?
RIGHT IN HERE.... PROBLEM THOUGH.

WHAT PROBLEM?
ONE THAT INVOLVES FITTING THROUGH DOORS.

WHERE'S THE LI'L GUY?
I LEFT HIM BACK AT THE SHELTER.
WHAT? WHY?
COPYRIGHT©2002 ILLIAD HTTP://WWW.USERFRIENDLY.ORG/

THEY SAID THEY REALLY NEEDED HIM TO HELP PUT UP THEIR NEW YEAR'S DECORATIONS.
DECORATIONS? LIKE WHAT?
BALLOONS. FOR ONE.

ED. THIS ISN'T RIGHT.
COME ON. WE'RE SAVING ON STRING.

AND WHAT DID YOU GET FOR THE HOLIDAYS. PITR?
CAPITULATION BY LEADER OF SMALL SOVEREIGN NATION.
COPYRIGHT©2003 ILLIAD HTTP://WWW.USERFRIENDLY.ORG/

YOU GOT A COPY OF CIVILIZATION 3. DIDN'T YOU.
YOU ARE FIRST CITIZEN TO BE WISITED AT NIGHT BY DREAD SECRET POLICE WHEN I AM IN POWER.

SO. ANY RESOLUTIONS FOR THE NEW YEAR?
I'M GOING TO GET MORE EXERCISE.
I'M GOING TO GET MY CERTIFICATION.
COPYRIGHT©2003 ILLIAD HTTP://WWW.USERFRIENDLY.ORG/

AM TO BE CRUSHINK ALL OPPOSITION IN BID TO TAKINK OVER WORLD. AM TO BE GREATEST DESPOT EVER.

COPY OF CIVILIZATION 3: $50
COMPUTER SYSTEM: $1200
THE ABILITY TO TELL THE DIFFERENCE BETWEEN REAL LIFE AND A COMPUTER GAME: PRICELESS.
WAIT. WHAT ARE YOU SAYING?

A.J., I CAN'T BELIEVE YOU THINK THAT THE ILLUSORY REALITY OF COMPUTER GAMES COULD **POSSIBLY** TEACH YOU ANYTHING USEFUL ABOUT THE REAL WORLD.

BUT...I LEARN ALL KINDS OF COOL SKILLS. I'M GOOD AT MANAGING MY RESOURCES.
UNH-HUH.

HAVE YOU FOUND ANY HEALTH PACKS LYING AROUND? AND WHERE'S THE AMMO FREE FOR THE TAKING?
WAL-MART! HAH!

HEY STEF. DID YOU HAVE A GOOD HOLIDAY?
NOT BAD AT ALL, THANKS.

DO YOU HAVE A RESOLUTION FOR THE NEW YEAR?
YES. "I THINK 2048 BY 1536 SHOULD DO VERY NICELY."
COLA

OH. BA. HA. HA.
YOU TOLD ME THAT WOULD GET GEEKS HOT AND BOTHERED!
GO AND TRY IT ON MIKE.

THE AMAZING TOP 5 PSYCHIC NOSTRILDAMNUS GEEK WORLD PREDICTIONS FOR 2003

5. ELECTRONIC ARTS WILL PUBLISH *NHL* 2004, *NBA LIVE* 2004, AND *NASCAR* 2004! (NO, REALLY!)

EA SPORTS
NHL
200(var)

+ J.A.T.O. = PINK MIST

4. SOMEONE, SOMEWHERE, WILL ACTUALLY ATTACH A *J.A.T.O.* UNIT TO A SEGWAY.

3. ANOTHER DISTRIBUTION OF LINUX WILL BE BORN, EXCEPT **THIS** TIME THE DESKTOP BACKGROUND COLOUR WILL BE CHARTREUSE!

2. A FRONT-LINE TECH SUPPORT SPECIALIST WHO HAS "HAD ENOUGH" WILL BUY A BOW AND "GO ELVEN POSTAL" AFTER WATCHING "THE TWO TOWERS."

1. ONLINE POLITICAL VOTING BECOMES THE RAGE -- UNTIL SOMEONE TYPES "**FIRST VOTE!**"

HOW I MISS HANGING CHADS...

HELLO. TECH SUPP--
I KNOW WHAT THIS IS!!
COPYRIGHT©2003 ILLIAD HTTP://WWW.USERFRIENDLY.ORG/

EH? WHA-
YOU'RE JUST LIKE THAT DAMN AUTO-REPLY THING IN MY E-MAIL AREN'T YOU!! THAT'S ALL I GOT FROM YOU PEOPLE OVER THE HOLIDAYS!

YESSS....YES. THIS IS A VOCAL AUTOREPLY. THERE'S NO ONE HERE RIGHT NOW. WE DON'T KNOW WHEN WE'LL BE BACK. MAYBE NEVER.
I KNEW IT!
CLICK

This sort of came from the audio of a game I used to play on my 286. It was an early version of Falcon, the F-16 flight simulator. The audio on PCs at the time was laughable at best, but the developers did try. When your wingman was communicating what was supposed to be "Bandit! Bandit!" it sounded like "Grapefruit! Grapefruit!" The unchaining of the hot petunia was tacked on for the sake of completing the meter.

A PENTAGON SPOKESMAN SAID TODAY THAT THEIR "TOTAL INFORMATION AWARENESS" SYSTEM WILL BE ABLE TO SEARCH THROUGH "VAST AMOUNTS" OF DATA, AND LINK DOMESTIC DATABASES, ALL THE WHILE LOOKING FOR PATTERNS AND COMMUNICATIONS THAT INDICATE TERRORIST ACTIVITY.
JANUARY 2003
COPYRIGHT©2003 ILLIAD HTTP://WWW.USERFRIENDLY.ORG/

IN RESPONSE, WE AT 133.7 FM WOULD LIKE TO SAY: "GRAPEFRUIT GRAPEFRUIT. UNCHAIN THE HOT PETUNIA."
JANUARY 2003

HEH...UM. JUST KIDDING FOLKS.
WHAT DID THAT MEAN?
"WE LOOK GOOD IN PRISON ORANGE."
JANUARY 2003

YOU KNOW, THAT WHOLE T.I.A. THING IS JUST THE TOP OF A VERY SLIPPERY SLOPE. FIRST THEY'LL WANT TO KNOW WHAT WE BUY, FROM WHOM, AND WHEN. THEN THEY'LL WANT TO KNOW WHAT WE DO FROM THE MOMENT WE AWAKE UNTIL WE FALL ASLEEP.
COPYRIGHT©2003 ILLIAD HTTP://WWW.USERFRIENDLY.ORG/

AND NASA'S BEEN WORKING ON THESE BRAIN-MONITORING DEVICES. SOON THEY'LL BE READING OUR VERY THOUGHTS!
YE GODS! WHAT FOUL RESULT WOULD BE BORN FROM SUCH TECHNOLOGY?

MEANWHILE, IN ORBIT ABOVE OUR PLANET...
ANYTHING INTERESTING?
ALL THE PORN YOU WANT. AND THOSE RAELIANS ARE BLAMING US AGAIN.
ALIEN MIND-READING SHIP
OH FER XYZZY'S SAKE...YOU MAKE ONE MISTAKE...

REPORT ON THE OVERALL TONE OF THIS WORLD, PLEASE, ZIKPT.
MOSTLY "ANGST," YOUR GRAND ODIFEROUSNESS.
ALIEN MIND-READING SHIP, REMEMBER?
COPYRIGHT©2003 ILLIAD HTTP://WWW.USERFRIENDLY.ORG/

ANGST?
MOST EVERYONE IS AFRAID OF OFFENDING ANYONE ELSE WITH THEIR WORDS AND ACTIONS, REGARDLESS OF INTENT. AT THE SAME TIME, THEY SEEK A SOLUTION TO THIS IMPASSE. INDEED, THEY PRAY FOR IT.

WE COULD HELP THEM OUT WITH, YOU KNOW, THE PLANETARY MEAT RAY...
YES, THAT'S GOOD. MEAT DOESN'T DISCRIMINATE.
OH? WHAT'S THIS "OTHER WHITE MEAT" BUSINESS THEN?

WHAT OTHER NEWS, SUBORDINATE ZIKPT?
THE RAELIANS, SIR. THEY'RE BLAMING US AGAIN.
AGAIN?!
YES SIR. THIS TIME OVER MARTHA STEWART.
COPYRIGHT©2003 ILLIAD HTTP://WWW.USERFRIENDLY.ORG/

WELL, WE CAN'T GET OUT OF THAT ONE.
AN ASTEROID THE SIZE OF TEXAS SHOULD DO IT, SIR.
ZIKPT, WE CAN'T DO THAT! UM...MAYBE...NO! WE CAN'T!

THAT DOES IT! I'VE HAD IT WITH THESE RAELIANS BLAMING US FOR EVERYTHING!
FWIXZOT, TAKE US DOWN TO THE SURFACE!
BY YOUR COMMAND, O CONGEALING ONE!
COPYRIGHT©2003 ILLIAD HTTP://WWW.USERFRIENDLY.ORG/

AND SO THE ALIENS DESCEND TO FACE THEIR ACCUSERS, KNOWING THAT THEY HAD TRUTH ON THEIR SIDE, FOR WITHIN TRUTH LIES BEAUTY...

...AND, OCCASIONALLY, REGRET.
YO, DR. BOISSELIER! WE NEED TO TALK...
SUDDENLY, EVERYTHING BECOMES CLEAR.

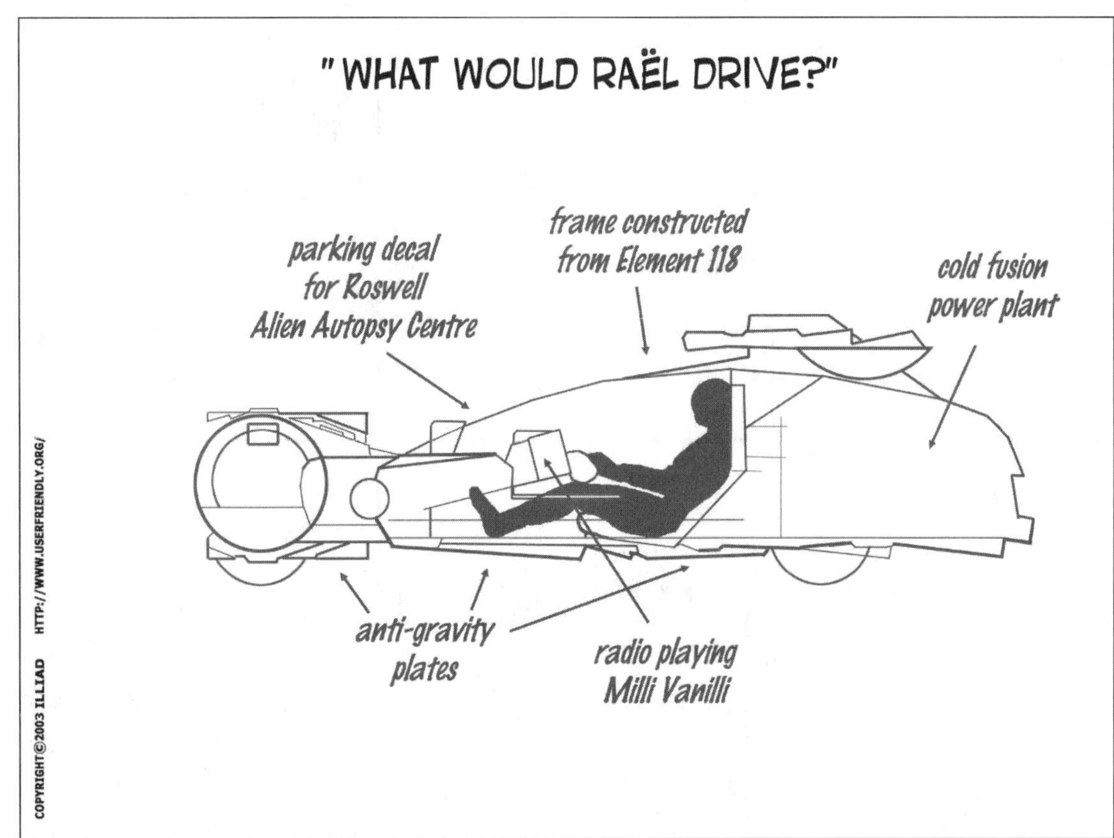
"WHAT WOULD RAËL DRIVE?"
parking decal for Roswell Alien Autopsy Centre
frame constructed from Element 118
cold fusion power plant
anti-gravity plates
radio playing Milli Vanilli
COPYRIGHT©2003 ILLIAD HTTP://WWW.USERFRIENDLY.ORG/

And I thought us geeks were freakish.

WHAT THE HELL IS THAT?
IT'S JUST MY NEW OFFICE CHAIR.
COOOL!
OH! LOOK!
COPYRIGHT © 2003 ILLIAD HTTP://WWW.USERFRIENDLY.ORG/

I MEANT. WHAT ARE A.J. AND GREG DOING CRAWLING ON THE FLOOR?
IT'S A COOL CHAIR WITH A BAZILLION LEVERS ON IT.
OH AND THIS ONE!

DUDE! LOOK AT THE KNOBS!
UNH-HUH.

THAT'S A DAMN COOL CHAIR MIKE HAS.
YES. IT IS. IT'S GOT LIKE TWO MILLION DIFFERENT SETTINGS ON IT.
COPYRIGHT © 2003 ILLIAD HTTP://WWW.USERFRIENDLY.ORG/

MIKE IS OUR VERY GOOD FRIEND...
...WHICH MEANS HE'LL BE FORGIVING AFTER WE CHANGE A DOZEN SETTINGS ON HIS CHAIR ON HIM.

...AND IT'S REALLY COMFORTABLE, AND PERFECTLY SET TO MY HEIGHT AND BODY SHAPE.
THAT'S COOL MIKE!
COPYRIGHT © 2003 ILLIAD HTTP://WWW.USERFRIENDLY.ORG/

WHAT?!
YOU EVER SOLVED A RUBIK'S CHA- I MEAN, CUBE?

I had a chair like that.
And it did that to me.

A.J. AND GREG NEED A SERIOUS THWACKING. I HAD THIS CHAIR PERFECTLY SET UNTIL THEY MESSED WITH IT.
FIDDLE TWIDDLE WINKY
COPYRIGHT © 2003 ILLIAD HTTP://WWW.USERFRIENDLY.ORG/

AH HA! I THINK I FOUND THE RIGHT KNOB...
KA-DWOINK

YES MA'AM. THANK YOU FOR CALLING...
AHEM
COPYRIGHT©2003 ILLIAD HTTP://WWW.USERFRIENDLY.ORG/

I NEED A QUICK WORD WITH YOU ABOUT MY CHAIR.
OKAY.

A WORD IN PRIVATE.
WHY NOT RIGHT HERE? WHERE THERE'S WITNESSES?

POLICE. FRONT DESK.
YES?
I HAVE A REALLY URGENT QUESTION PERTAINING TO LAW.
WANTED
COPYRIGHT©2003 ILLIAD HTTP://WWW.USERFRIENDLY.ORG/

IF YOU MESS WITH SOMEONE'S FULLY ADJUSTABLE CHAIR, AND THEY CAN'T RESET IT, IT STILL ISN'T JUSTIFICATION FOR HOMICIDE, RIGHT?
IT MOST CERTAINLY IS, BUDDY.
WANTED

SEE?! NOW YOU DIE.
DUDE! YOU ARE NOT HELPING!!
THINK ABOUT WHO YOU'RE ASKING, "DUDE." I'M A DESK SERGEANT.
WANTED

THE RIAA COULD DO AWAY WITH "MUSIC PIRATES" THE WORLD OVER BY SIMPLY FILLING THE SHARING NETWORKS WITH SPECIFIC CONTENT...
FILE ARTIST
ohbabybaby... NSYNC
tonightpleas... NSYNC
loveyoulove... BACKSTREETBOYZ
canitbeyou... BRITNEYSPEARS
oopsIdidita... BRITNEYSPEARS
yeahbabyits... BACKSTREETBOYZ
youknowIwa... NSYNC
Iwant2Byourh... CHRISTINEAGUILERA
COPYRIGHT©2003 ILLIAD HTTP://WWW.USERFRIENDLY.ORG/

FINE. YOU WANT TO MAKE THINGS BETTER. YOU HELP ME RESET MY CHAIR.
OKAY. OKAY. JUST TELL ME WHAT TO DO.
COPYRIGHT©2003 ILLIAD HTTP://WWW.USERFRIENDLY.ORG/

HOLD ON TO THE ARMS THERE WHILE I MESS WITH THIS KNOB. AND FOR HASTUR'S SAKE DON'T TOUCH ANY OF THE CONTROLS.
WAIT. IS THAT A FASTENER OR A...

...CONTROL.

YE GODS, COBB. YOU WEREN'T KIDDING...
TOLD YOU. SO WHAT ARE WE GONNA DO?
COPYRIGHT©2003 ILLIAD HTTP://WWW.USERFRIENDLY.ORG/

PUT THEM UP ON EBAY AS "ART DECO."
NO RESERVE!
I'M ON IT.
MMRRRFFFF!!

WHEEBEE
WHEEBEE
WHEEBEE
WHEEBEE
COPYRIGHT©2003 ILLIAD HTTP://WWW.USERFRIENDLY.ORG/

WHEEBEE
WHEE
BEE
POH!
CHEEEE
GLUG
GLUG
GLUG
AAAHHHHH...

OH MAN. I NEEDED THAT.
THAT'S WHY I LOVE GEEKS. THEY'RE ALL ABOUT PRIORITIES.
HEY! THAT WAS MY COLA!
Cola

SO HERE WE ARE. STUCK HEAD FIRST IN A VERY UNCOMFORTABLE POSITION. WE CAN BE PUSHED TO AND FRO AT SOMEONE ELSE'S WHIM WHILST OUR ARSES ARE HANGING IN THE AIR.
COPYRIGHT©2003 ILLIAD HTTP://WWW.USERFRIENDLY.ORG/

DON'T FORGET WE'RE ALSO BEING SOLD DOWN THE RIVER.
UNH-HUH.

KINDA REMINDS ME OF MY STINT IN THE MILITARY.
ESPECIALLY THE "NO RESERVE" PART.

WELL IT'S FINALLY HAPPENED. HILARY ROSEN RESIGNED AS CEO OF THE RIAA.
MRRRF.
COPYRIGHT © 2003 ILLIAD HTTP://WWW.USERFRIENDLY.ORG/

IT MAKES ONE WONDER. SHOULD WE BE PLEASED? IS IT NOT TRUE THAT IT'S BETTER THE DEVIL YOU KNOW? WHAT NEW HEAD WILL POP OUT OF THE HYDRA NOW THAT THE OLD ONE HAS BEEN RETIRED? WE HAVE TO EMPLOY OUR VASTLY SUPERIOR INTELLECTS AND SPEAK UP BEFORE IT'S TOO LATE!
MRRRF!!

WE MUST BE HEARD! GEEKS OF THE WORLD. ARTICULATE!
MRFFRRFMR!!!

STEF. I CAN'T BELIEVE YOU PUT US UP ON EBAY.
WELL, SORRY. CAN YOU BLAME ME IN THIS ECONOMY?
THANKS FOR FREEING US LI'L DUDE.
YOU'RE WELCOME.
COPYRIGHT © 2003 ILLIAD HTTP://WWW.USERFRIENDLY.ORG/

UH...WELL. I SUPPOSE NOT...

HOW MUCH DID YOU GET FOR US?
THREE DOLLARS.
WHAT?!
PLUS SHIPPING.
I HAD FOUR DOLLARS. I WAS JUST WAITING UNTIL THE LAST MINUTE BUT MISSED THE CUTOFF.

USER FRIENDLY
the comic strip
BY J.D. "ILLIAD" FRAZER
COPYRIGHT © 2003 ILLIAD HTTP://WWW.USERFRIENDLY.ORG/

DUDE. I DIDN'T KNOW YOU WATCHED FOOTBALL.
I DON'T. BUT ON A PLASMA SCREEN I'D WATCH A BLUE SCREEN OF DEATH FOR HOURS.

SO WHO'S WINNING?
I DON'T KNOW. I HAVEN'T EVEN QUITE FIGURED OUT HOW THE GAME IS PLAYED.

FOR EXAMPLE. WHY DO THEY KEEP POINTING US AT DIFFERENT WEB SITES AND SERVERS DURING THE GAME?

UM...THOSE ARE I.P. ADDRESSES THE QUARTERBACK GUY YELLS OUT, RIGHT?
NO A.J. ... THEY'RE WILD GUESSES AT YOUR I.Q.

YOU LOOK SAD, GREG.
I'M BURNT OUT. FRIED. I'VE BEEN A SUPPORT TECH FOR MORE THAN HALF A DECADE.
DEET
COPYRIGHT©2003 ILLIAD HTTP://WWW.USERFRIENDLY.ORG/

EVERY DAY I ANSWER THE PHONE AND HELP PEOPLE SOLVE THEIR COMPUTER CONUNDRUMS. GRATITUDE IS RARE; INTELLIGENCE A MERE MYTH. MY WORK IS BEREFT OF HUMANITY.
DOOOT!

YE UNMERCIFUL GODS, WHERE IS THE LOVE?!
I KEEP PRESSING "9" BUT IT WON'T GO BACK TO THE MAIN MENU!
DOOT! *DOOT!* *DOOT!*

Perhaps the most famous of UF strips; certainly one of the most popular.

PRESS ANY KEY.
"ANY." OKAY...
'A'
COPYRIGHT©2003 ILLIAD HTTP://WWW.USERFRIENDLY.ORG/

WOULD YOU LIKE TO SAVE YOUR WORK?
'N'
ARE YOU SURE?
'Y'

RING!
WHY IS MY SKIN CRAWLING?

YOU DIDN'T SAVE YOUR WORK?
NO, I DIDN'T SAVE MY WORK!
AND YOU KNOW THAT IF YOU DON'T SAVE YOUR WORK YOU'LL PROBABLY LOSE IT LIKE YOU JUST HAVE?
YES, I KNOW THAT!
COPYRIGHT©2003 ILLIAD HTTP://WWW.USERFRIENDLY.ORG/

THEN WHY DO YOU KEEP DOING THAT?!!

HUNH. THAT'S A GOOD ONE. WHY DO I KEEP DOING THIS?
CERTAINLY A QUESTION I'VE ASKED MYSELF FOR YEARS...

I CAN'T DO THIS ANYMORE. MORE THAN FIVE YEARS OF PUTTING UP WITH TECHNOTARDS IS JUST MORE THAN A MAN SHOULD BE EXPECTED TO BEAR.
IS IT REALLY THAT BAD?
COPYRIGHT©2003 ILLIAD HTTP://WWW.USERFRIENDLY.ORG/

BAD? BAD?! I HAVE TO DEAL WITH PEOPLE WHO WON'T READ MANUALS, WHO CAN'T BE BOTHERED TO LEARN ANYTHING NEW, AND WHO TREAT ME LIKE A SERF!! FOR EIGHT HOURS A DAY!

I MEAN SERIOUSLY, WHAT COULD BE WORSE?
BEING HIT WITH COMPRESSED AIR FOR ONE...
OH LETTINK IT GO ALREADY!

TECH SUPPORT. GO AHEAD AND ABUSE ME.
HI. I'M JUST CALLING TO TELL YOU THAT I THINK YOU TECH SUPPORT FOLKS ARE **WONDERFUL.**

IF IT WASN'T FOR YOU, THE WORLD WOULD BE LOST. WHO'D TELL US HOW TO FIX OUR COFFEE CUP HOLDERS? WHO'D TELL US TO "GET RID OF THAT WINDOWS CRUD AND GET A REAL OPERATING SYSTEM?" YOU ARE THE DAEMON THAT ANSWERS OUR HTTP REQUESTS FOR KNOWLEDGE...

...THE DOMAIN NAME SERVER THAT TRANSLATES THE CRYPTIC INTO THE CREDIBLE...THE NETWORK THAT...UH...
BUSTED.
TOLD YOU TO SKIP THAT LAST PART.

I WANT YOU ALL TO KNOW THAT I'M PROTESTING MY TREATMENT IN THIS CARTOON STRIP AS A CORE CAST MEMBER. I WANT TO KNOW WHY WE DON'T HAVE A SIGNATURE METHOD OF STRESS RELIEF! **ESPECIALLY** FOR US TECH SUPPORT PROS!

CALVIN AND HOBBES HAD **SLEDDING!** BLOOM COUNTY HAD **DANDELION PATCHES!** WHAT DO **WE** HAVE?!

QUAD DAMAGE!
DENIED!
PAVOO!
PAVOO!
SPLORTCH!
SILLY ME.

USER FRIENDLY
THE COMIC STRIP
I THINK IT'S AN ACCEPTABLE SOLUTION. YES.
Three UF Sundays were removed due to being far too derivative of the works of another cartoonist. This spot was for one of them.
Please pretend that this space is funny. Ta.

I THINK MAYBE WHAT I NEED IS A NEW TITLE. SOMETHING THAT BEARS A LITTLE MORE PRESTIGE. MAYBE LIKE, "KNOWLEDGE DISSEMINATION SPECIALIST."
COPYRIGHT©2003 ILLIAD HTTP://WWW.USERFRIENDLY.ORG/

A WHAT? DUDE. YOU'RE A TECH SUPPORT GUY.
PRAY TELL, HOW DO SPAMMERS READ THE SENTENCE "I DON'T WANT YOUR SPAM" ?

UH......"OPT-IN."
SO I GET TO BE A "KNOWLEDGE DISSEMINATION SPECIALIST."

A.J., GREG'S GONE ALL FUNNY.
HOW DO YOU MEAN?
COPYRIGHT©2003 ILLIAD HTTP://WWW.USERFRIENDLY.ORG/

I THINK THE LAST SUPPORT CALL HE GOT FINALLY MADE SOMETHING INSIDE HIM GO "SNAP."
WHAT MAKES YOU THINK THAT?

IT'S ALL JUST SO MUCH EASIER THIS WAY...
TWITCH
WIBBLE

HALLO! GREG SPEAKING. HOW MAY I SHINE SOME LIGHT INTO YOUR DAY?
UH...MY KEYBOARD IS WONKY. WHEN I TYPE IN MY PASSWORD ALL I GET ARE LITTLE STARS ON THE SCREEN.
COPYRIGHT©2003 ILLIAD HTTP://WWW.USERFRIENDLY.ORG/

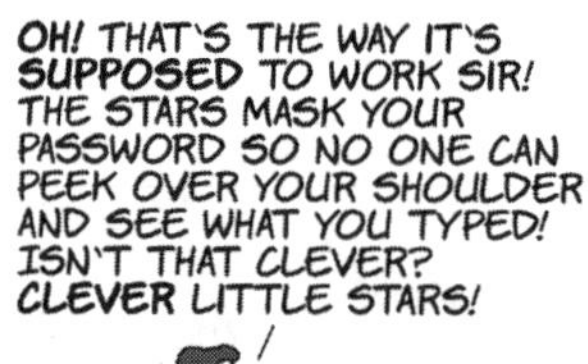
OH! THAT'S THE WAY IT'S SUPPOSED TO WORK SIR! THE STARS MASK YOUR PASSWORD SO NO ONE CAN PEEK OVER YOUR SHOULDER AND SEE WHAT YOU TYPED! ISN'T THAT CLEVER? CLEVER LITTLE STARS!

MARTHA? I THINK YOU GAVE ME THE WRONG NUMBER...
YOU KNOW WHAT, SIR? YOU'RE THE STAR HERE!

SID! WE NEED TO GET A STRAITJACKET FOR GREG!
WHAT?! WHY?
COPYRIGHT©2003 ILLIAD HTTP://WWW.USERFRIENDLY.ORG/

HE'S WIGGED OUT! HE'S BECOME REALLY NICE AND UNDERSTANDING ON THE PHONE, AND ACTUALLY SEES THINGS FROM THE POINT OF VIEW OF THE USERS.
MY WORD. THAT DOES SOUND SERIOUS. BUT AS LONG AS HE'S STABLE, WE SHOULDN'T WORRY...

...I MEAN, HOW COULD IT POSSIBLY GET ANY WORSE?
HELP! MY CUPHOLDER'S BROKEN!

YOUR CUPHOLDER IS BROKEN?
YES. IT'S BROKEN. I NEED A NEW ONE.
GREG. IT'S NOT A CUPHOLDER.
YES IT IS! IT WAS HOLDING MY CUP. ERGO IT'S A **CUPHOLDER!**

This strip set off a demand for Big Foam Cluebats. We had a few hundred manufactured, branded and all, and they were all sold in less than a week. You geeks are a crazy, vengeful lot. :-)

THE TECH SUPPORT CALLER WARNING SYSTEM

LOW STUPIDITY CONDITION	Signifies a caller who offers little or no risk of causing the tech a cranial aneurysm. This is usually a caller who understands that most technical "secrets" are cleverly concealed in mysterious things called "manuals." **Recommendation:** Cherish these ones.
SUSPICIOUS STUPIDITY CONDITION	Signifies a caller who is suspected of weapons-grade stupidity, without any real evidence. **Recommendation:** Send "inspectors."
ELEVATED STUPIDITY CONDITION	Indicates a significant risk of stroke in the tech caused by a caller who insists that "there is no 'any key' on the keyboard" and that "there's no way I can click on 'your computer' from over here." **Recommendation:** Slow breathing exercises and a good punching bag.
HIGH STUPIDITY CONDITION	Indicates a high risk of an apoplectic fit. Callers insist that their operating system is "Netscape," their web browser is by "Logitech" and the specific application that blew up on them is "Microsoft." (Heh.) **Recommendation:** Join a Zen monastery
SEVERE STUPIDITY CONDITION	Indicates the highest risk possible. Adrenaline overload and renal failure caused by callers who angrily state that they have a degree and are in fact very clever, and that the tech must "hop to it and fix things." When asked to "open a window" they do in fact get up and open a window. Alas. **Recommendation:** a large bludgeoning instrument. For you or them, it's really your choice.

JUST A MINUTE...YOU ACTUALLY USE THIS ON OUR CUSTOMERS?
WELL...NO. BUT I'VE ALWAYS WANTED TO.
BUT IT'S A **FOAM BAT.** HOW THE HELL IS A FOAM BAT GOING TO MAKE SOMEONE SMARTER?
COPYRIGHT © 2003 ILLIAD HTTP://WWW.USERFRIENDLY.ORG/

BIFF BIFF BIFF
BIFF BIFF BIFF

OW!! THAT THING **HURTS!**
SEE? NOW YOU'RE SMARTER ABOUT FOAM BATS!
BIG FOAM CLUEBAT

DO YOU REALLY THINK THIS WHOLE FOAM CLUEBAT THING WITH MIRANDA IS A GOOD IDEA?
I THINK IT'S AN ACCEPTABLE SOLUTION. YES.
COPYRIGHT © 2003 ILLIAD HTTP://WWW.USERFRIENDLY.ORG/

BUT. DO YOU THINK IT'LL WORK?
OF COURSE IT'LL WORK. WHAT DO YOU THINK CAN STAND UP TO THE MIGHTY POWER OF A CLUEBAT?

ENORMOUS FOAM HELM OF STUPIDITY
BIG FOAM CLUEBAT

WELL? HOW'D IT GO?
IT DIDN'T. GREG WAS WEARING THIS BIG PUFFY HELMET SO I COULDN'T THWACK HIM WITH THE CLUEBAT.
COPYRIGHT © 2003 ILLIAD HTTP://WWW.USERFRIENDLY.ORG/

BUT I THINK GREG IS GOING TO SHORTLY DISCOVER THAT STUPIDITY HAS STAYING POWER AT THE COST OF FLEXIBILITY.
HOW'S THAT?

ENORMOUS FOAM HELM OF STUPIDITY STUCK IN THE DOORWAY
NNNG. NNNNNG. NNNNG!

STILL STUCK
I CAN'T GET TO THE COLA.
SO TAKE OFF THE HELMET.
BUT...WON'T I THEN BE VULNERABLE?
OF COURSE. BUT WHAT'S MORE IMPORTANT? YOUR SKULL. OR AN INFUSION OF CARAMEL-COLOURED COSMIC NECTAR?

BIFF BIFF BIFF
BIFF BIFF BIFF
BIFF BIFF BIFF
NOPE. DIDN'T SEE THAT COMIN'....
COPYRIGHT © 2003 ILLIAD HTTP://WWW.USERFRIENDLY.ORG/

WHAT DO YOU HAVE THERE A.J.?
IT'S A BIG FOAM HEART I GOT FOR MIRANDA FOR VALENTINES.
'I LUB YOU
COPYRIGHT© 2003 ILLIAD HTTP://WWW.USERFRIENDLY.ORG/

OH. A.J. THAT IS SO ROMANTIC...
YOU REALLY THINK SO?
'I LUB YOU
BIG FOAM

WE INTERRUPT TODAY'S CARTOON AT THIS POINT BECAUSE MIRANDA IS ARMED, AGITATED, AND THERE IS REALLY NOTHING A.J. CAN DO OR SAY WITHOUT SIGNING HIS OWN DEATH WARRANT.

(AND PLEASE DON'T TRANSPOSE ANY LETTERS IN THE INNOCENT PHRASE "BIG FOAM HEART" LIKE I NEARLY DID.)

ARE YOU ALL RIGHT?
MIRANDA HAS A WICKED SWING. BUT YES. I THINK I'M OKAY.
GOOD TO HEAR. I VALUE YOU GREATLY. PERHAPS MORE THAN ANY OF MY OTHER FOLLOWERS.
Cola
GREG. BADLY BIFFED.
COPYRIGHT© 2003 ILLIAD HTTP://WWW.USERFRIENDLY.ORG/

YOU SEE. I REQUIRE A VAST BODY OF DISCIPLES. THEY RUN THE GAMUT OF INTELLIGENCE. BUT THE BEST ONES ARE THE DUMBEST. THEY'RE EASIER TO SWAY. THE LEAST FICKLE. AND THE MOST DEVOUT. AND OUT OF THEM ALL. I PRIZE YOU THE MOST.
Cola

I'M HONOURED. I THINK. BUT WHY ME?
Cola
BECAUSE YOU'RE STUPID EVEN WITHOUT THE HELMET.

FOR USE WITH SJ GAMES' ILLUMINATI*
TECHNICAL SUPPORT
+1 on any attempt to neutralize any group
!@#$*
Power: 0/2
Resistance: 1
Income: 1
Weird
*UNOFFICIAL OF COURSE! ILLUMINATI IS A TRADEMARK OF STEVE JACKSON GAMES
COPYRIGHT© 2003 ILLIAD HTTP://WWW.USERFRIENDLY.ORG/

An awesome game. Steve Jackson was (perhaps still is) a fan of UF!

GREG. WHAT ARE YOU DOING DOWN THERE?
CONGEALING.
COPYRIGHT©2003 ILLIAD HTTP://WWW.USERFRIENDLY.ORG/

INDEED. AND WHILE YOU'RE BUSY CONGEALING. PRAY TELL WHO DO YOU HAVE COVERING FOR YOU ON THE PHONES?
WHY. HE WHO MUST BE OBEYED OF COURSE.

...SO THE ONLY WAY TO FIND AN 'ANY KEY' TO ATTACH TO MY KEYBOARD IS TO LOOK INSIDE SPECIALLY-MARKED CANS OF COLA?
WHY I DIDN'T RECRUIT HERE EARLIER I'LL NEVER KNOW...

I QUIT.
YOU WHAT?!
I **QUIT**. I'VE DECIDED THAT I SIMPLY CAN'T HANDLE THE DAILY STRUGGLE WITH WHAT AMOUNTS TO TALKING. WHINING EGGPLANTS.
COPYRIGHT©2003 ILLIAD HTTP://WWW.USERFRIENDLY.ORG/

LOOK. IF IT'S BECAUSE YOU DON'T FEEL LIKE YOU'RE VALUED AROUND HERE. I'LL GIVE YOU A RAISE. IT MAY NOT SEEM LIKE IT. BUT I DO UNDERSTAND HOW STRESSFUL IT IS TO WORK THE PHONES. SO...HOW ABOUT A DOLLAR AN HOUR MORE?

WOO. THAT WOULD BE. LIKE. ALMOST DOUBLING MY WAGE...
NO. NO. DON'T THANK ME. YOU WERE DUE.

HE'S **YOUR** STAFF MEMBER. **YOU** TALK TO HIM.
FORGET IT SID! I'VE QUIT THIS SICK LITTLE GIG FOR GOOD!

THE iAUDIO CW200 MP3 PLAYER YOU WANT GOES FOR $300.

COPYRIGHT©2003 ILLIAD HTTP://WWW.USERFRIENDLY.ORG/

YOU'RE A HORRIBLE. **HORRIBLE** LITTLE MAN.
OH. AM I YANKING A LITTLE TOO HARD ON THE MARIONETTE STRINGS?
START BEGGING.

HELLO. I'M THE CRACKER WHO GAINED ACCESS TO THE 2.2 MILLION CREDIT CARD ACCOUNTS.
BULLY FOR YOU. HOW CAN I HELP?
ER...MY CRIME DOESN'T BOTHER YOU?
YOUR INGENUITY IS TO BE ADMIRED. IT'S JUST PART OF THE GREAT WESTERN DREAM.
COPYRIGHT©2003 ILLIAD HTTP://WWW.USERFRIENDLY.ORG/

WELL I'M...HAPPY TO HEAR THAT. SEE. I'M TRYING TO USE ALL OF THIS CREDIT TO BUY MYSELF A SMALL LUSH ISLAND AND THE NECESSARY RAZORWIRE. ARMS AND MUNITIONS TO DEFEND IT. THAT WAY I CAN BE KING. GREAT IDEA. DON'T YOU THINK?
INDUBITABLY. WHAT'S THE PROBLEM?

ALL OF THE CARDS ARE **MAXED OUT!!** WHAT'S **WRONG** WITH THESE PEOPLE?!
PORN SITES ARE $19.95 A MONTH. THE GREAT WESTERN DREAM ADDS UP. DUDE.

THIS IS A PUBLIC SERVICE ANNOUNCEMENT FOR INFORMATION TECHNOLOGY WORKERS:
HELLO. TODAY WE ADDRESS ONE OF THE SCOURGES OF THE I.T. SECTOR: **REPETITIVE STRAIN INJURY!**
"THOSE WHO WORK AS TECHNICAL SUPPORT FOR THE VAST HORDES OF HUMAN-SHAPED LOWER MOLLUSKS ARE AT HIGH RISK OF SHOWING SYMPTOMS SUCH AS TWITCHING, PRIMAL SCREAMING, HOMICIDAL URGES, AND OTHER INDICATIONS THAT, AT FIRST GLANCE WOULD SUGGEST THE SUBJECT SUFFERED REPEATED BLOWS TO THE HEAD..."

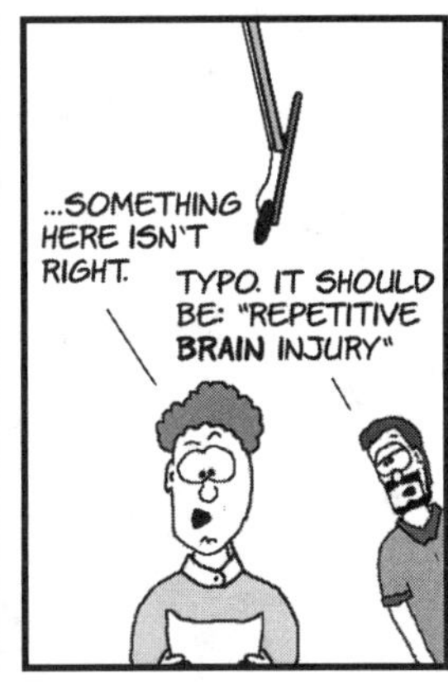

...SOMETHING HERE ISN'T RIGHT.
TYPO. IT SHOULD BE: "REPETITIVE **BRAIN** INJURY"

GIVEN THE STATE OF THE TECH SECTOR TODAY, THERE IS NO SHAME IN FINDING OTHER WORK TO SUPPLEMENT OR EVEN REPLACE THE INCOME OF A TECHNICAL JOB.

YET WHILE WORKING AT THIS OTHER CAREER, ONE MIGHT WONDER AT THE INCONGRUITY OF IT ALL, THE ODDNESS OF WORKING IN A FIELD THAT BEARS NO RELATION TO TECHNOLOGY...

...AND AT OTHER TIMES, ONE REALIZES HOW BEAUTIFULLY INTERLOCKING THE COSMOS REALLY CAN BE...
WHEN ARE YOU GONNA FIX MY COMPUTER PROBLEM?
MOMENTARILY...
CLUE
20 t.

THREE ACTIVITIES POPULAR WITH GEEKS NOW UNDER CONSIDERATION AS OLYMPIC SPORTS:

CLUEBATTERY

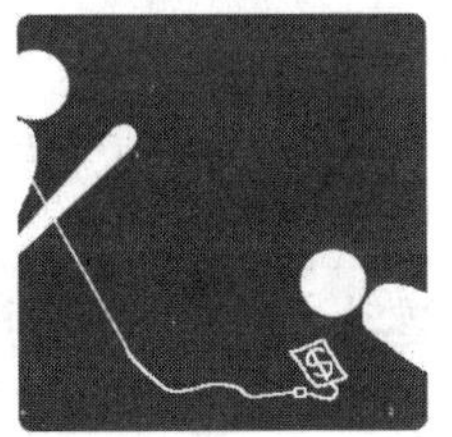

419 SCAM BAITING

FNORD.

WORLD DOMINATION

Best comment on this cartoon ever: "Why is the last box empty?"

SHEESH. MICROSOFT AND SUN ARE TUSSLING OVER JAVA. **STILL.**
STILL?
O Ye of Little Faith...
COPYRIGHT © 2003 ILLIAD HTTP://WWW.USERFRIENDLY.ORG/

YEAH. A WHILE BACK MICROSOFT PUBLISHED ITS OWN VERSION OF JAVA WHICH ISN'T COMPATIBLE WITH THE SUN VERSION. THAT FRAGMENTS THE PLATFORM AND MAKES IT LESS ATTRACTIVE FOR DEVELOPMENT.
AND NOW MS IS TRYING TO PUSH DEVELOPERS TO DROP JAVA IN FAVOUR OF THE .NET FRAMEWORK.
O Ye of Little Faith...

BUT ISN'T .NET PLATFORM-AGNOSTIC TOO?
MORE LIKE PLATFORM-SATANIC.
O Ye of Little Faith...

Sid's expression in the second panel is how I reacted when I first thought about the joke.

HEY...IF DOT NET IS "PLATFORM-SATANIC," WHAT KIND OF RELIGION-EQUIVALENT WOULD WE HAVE FOR OTHER METHODOLOGIES AND STUFF?
WHAT **ARE** YOU TALKING ABOUT?
For I am made of Eternal Things...
COPYRIGHT © 2003 ILLIAD HTTP://WWW.USERFRIENDLY.ORG/

LET'S SEE... **PERL** WOULD BE "PLATFORM-DISCORDIAN" BECAUSE IT CAN BE SO VERY OBFUSCATED. **PHP** WOULD BE "PLATFORM-TELEVISION EVANGELIST" BECAUSE IT SUCKS UP A WHOLE LOT OF RESOURCES. YOU WANNA KNOW WHAT JAVASCRIPT WOULD BE?
For I am made of Eternal Things...

OH. THE SUSPENSE IS **JUST** KILLING ME.
"PLATFORM-HOLY BOOK" BECAUSE IT'S ALWAYS BEING RE-INTERPRETED. **HAHAHAHAH!**
For I am made of Eternal Things...

DUDE. YOU HEAR ABOUT THAT BOOKSTORE IN VERMONT THAT PURGED THE SALES RECORDS OF ITS READERS' CLUB? THEY'RE DOING THIS IN RESPONSE TO THE PATRIOT ACT, SO THE C.I.A. CAN'T SUBPOENA THE RECORDS TO SEE WHAT PEOPLE HAVE BEEN READING.
THIS IS HEROIC, DA?
COPYRIGHT © 2003 ILLIAD HTTP://WWW.USERFRIENDLY.ORG/

HELL YES! UH...WHY?
AM FEELINK NEED TO BE HEROIC TODAY. ONE MOMENT PLEASE.

PITR...WHAT DID YOU JUST DO?!
AMAZON.COM. ONE-CLICK PURGINK.
AAAAAGH!!!

WHAT NEWS OF OUR PURGED CUSTOMER SALES RECORDS, RICK?
WE RODE THE STORM OUT SIR. WE HAD THE DATA BACKED UP AND IT'S BEING RESTORED NOW. THANK GOD FOR THAT.
amazon.com.
COPYRIGHT © 2003 ILLIAD HTTP://WWW.USERFRIENDLY.ORG/

WHOA! DID YOU SAY...OUR SALES DATA WAS BACKED UP TO DIGITAL MEDIA AS A "DISASTER-PREVENTION PROCESS?"
amazon.com.

SIR?
PATENT THAT BABY!!
amazon.com.

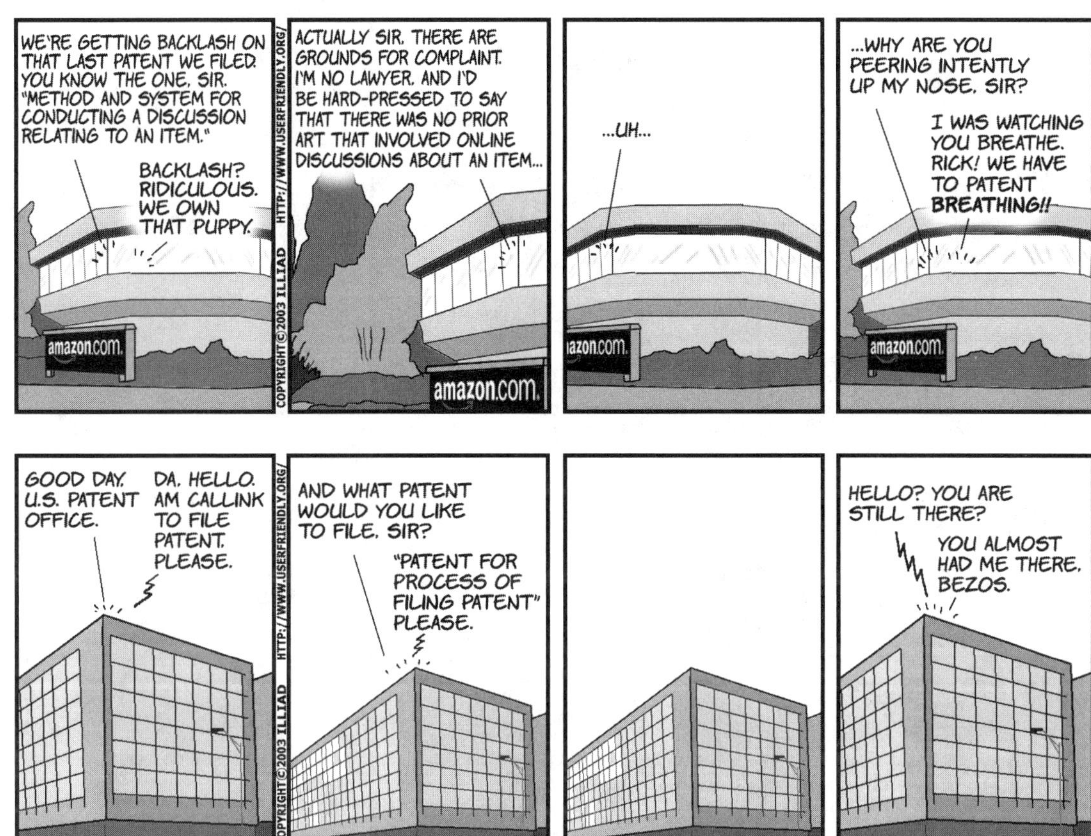

WE'RE GETTING BACKLASH ON THAT LAST PATENT WE FILED. YOU KNOW THE ONE, SIR. "METHOD AND SYSTEM FOR CONDUCTING A DISCUSSION RELATING TO AN ITEM."
BACKLASH? RIDICULOUS. WE OWN THAT PUPPY.
amazon.com
COPYRIGHT©2003 ILLIAD HTTP://WWW.USERFRIENDLY.ORG/
ACTUALLY SIR, THERE ARE GROUNDS FOR COMPLAINT. I'M NO LAWYER, AND I'D BE HARD-PRESSED TO SAY THAT THERE WAS NO PRIOR ART THAT INVOLVED ONLINE DISCUSSIONS ABOUT AN ITEM...
amazon.com
...UH...
...WHY ARE YOU PEERING INTENTLY UP MY NOSE, SIR?
I WAS WATCHING YOU BREATHE. RICK! WE HAVE TO PATENT BREATHING!!
amazon.com
GOOD DAY. U.S. PATENT OFFICE.
DA, HELLO. AM CALLINK TO FILE PATENT, PLEASE.
COPYRIGHT©2003 ILLIAD HTTP://WWW.USERFRIENDLY.ORG/
AND WHAT PATENT WOULD YOU LIKE TO FILE, SIR?
"PATENT FOR PROCESS OF FILING PATENT" PLEASE.
HELLO? YOU ARE STILL THERE?
YOU ALMOST HAD ME THERE, BEZOS.

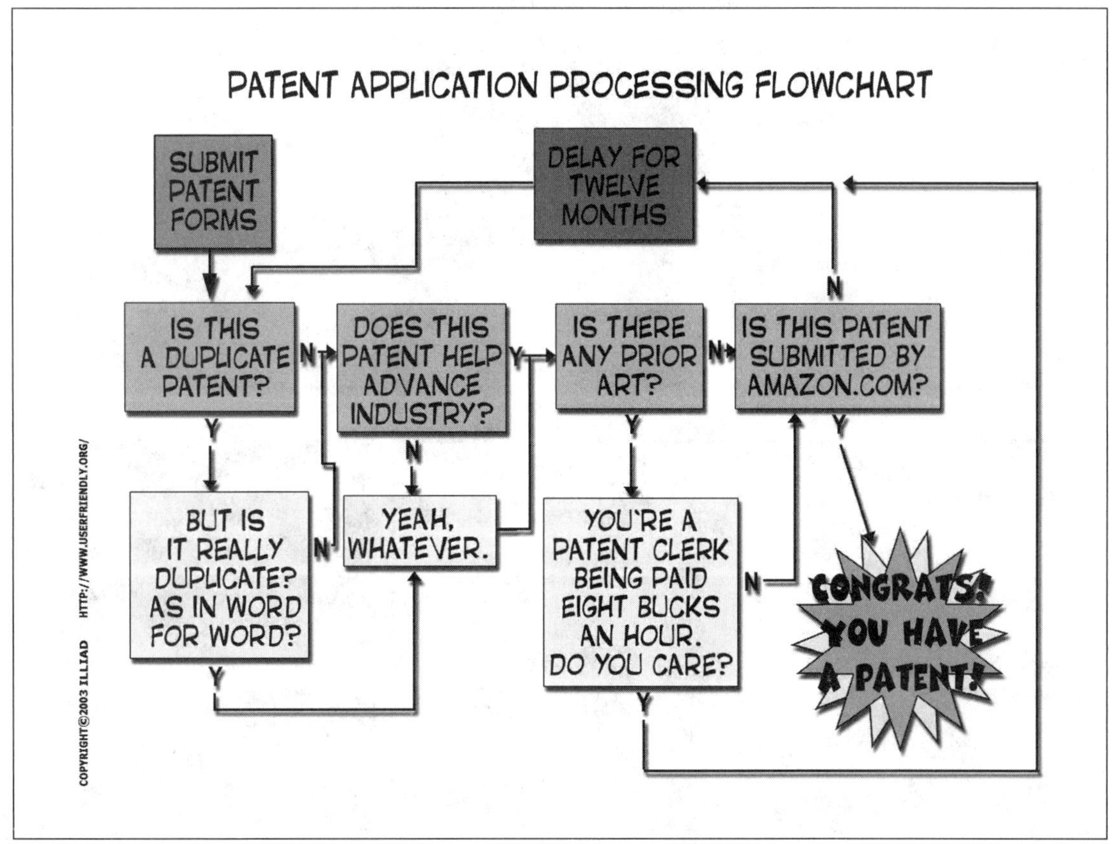

PATENT APPLICATION PROCESSING FLOWCHART
SUBMIT PATENT FORMS
DELAY FOR TWELVE MONTHS
IS THIS A DUPLICATE PATENT?
DOES THIS PATENT HELP ADVANCE INDUSTRY?
IS THERE ANY PRIOR ART?
IS THIS PATENT SUBMITTED BY AMAZON.COM?
BUT IS IT REALLY DUPLICATE? AS IN WORD FOR WORD?
YEAH, WHATEVER.
YOU'RE A PATENT CLERK BEING PAID EIGHT BUCKS AN HOUR. DO YOU CARE?
CONGRATS! YOU HAVE A PATENT!
Y
N
COPYRIGHT©2003 ILLIAD HTTP://WWW.USERFRIENDLY.ORG/

OKAY. THAT PART IS DONE. NOW I JUST BACKUP OUR DATA WITH OUR SPIFFY NEW IN-HOUSE BACKUP SOFTWARE.
GO FOR IT.
COPYRIGHT©2003 ILLIAD HTTP://WWW.USERFRIENDLY.ORG/

UM...WHAT DOES THE ERROR "BAD PERSIMMONS" MEAN?
WHAT I WANT TO KNOW IS WHO WROTE THE CODE?

PITR!
PROGRAMMINK AND DYSLEXIA. THEY DO NOT MIX...
OHHHH. "BAD **PERMISSIONS**."

"BAD PERSIMMONS" INDEED. I CAN'T IMAGINE WHAT ELSE PITR TYPED INCORRECTLY.
HERE'S ONE: "INERT NET" INSTEAD OF "INTERNET."
COPYRIGHT©2003 ILLIAD HTTP://WWW.USERFRIENDLY.ORG/

OH. LET'S KEEP THAT ONE...
THE TRUTH DESERVES TO BE ETERNAL.

YO, PITR. WHAT WAS WITH ALL OF THOSE TYPOS IN THE BACKUP SCRIPT?
WAS ACCIDENTALLY IN WAY OF MY SECRET ORBITAL DYSLEXIA RAY.
COPYRIGHT©2003 ILLIAD HTTP://WWW.USERFRIENDLY.ORG/

ORBITAL DYSLEXIA RAY? WHAT ON EARTH ARE YOU GOING TO DO WITH **THAT?**
AM TARGETTINK USER BASES OF MAJOR CORPORATIONS AROUND WORLD. AM DOINK THIS TO BE HELPINK MY I.T. COMRADES IN ARMS.

HELPING?! HOW DOES THAT HELP?
TWO WORDS "FROMAT C:"

PITR, THIS ORBITAL DYSLEXIA RAY OF YOURS WORRIES ME. WHAT IF **ALIENS** GOT THEIR HANDS ON IT?
ALIENS? MIKHAIL. FOR **WHAT** WOULD ALIENS BE USINK MY RAY?
COPYRIGHT©2003 ILLIAD HTTP://WWW.USERFRIENDLY.ORG/

COME **ON!** THEY COULD THROW THE WORLD INTO COMPLETE CHAOS! JUST IMAGINE WHAT IT WOULD DO TO **STREET SIGNAGE** ALONE!
HM. PERHAPS YOU ARE RIGHT...

"ALKWEN."
THE WORD YOU JUMBLED WAS "WANKLE."
ZOTBAT! YOU'RE GOOD!
MY TURN! USE THE RAY ON ME! USE THE RAY ON ME!

SHALL WE DEPLOY THIS EARTHLING RAY AGAINST ITS MAKERS, SIRE?
YES. TARGET THAT EARTHLING IN THE BIG WHITE STRUCTURE WITH THE LAWN, ZIKPT. OUR USUAL SUBJECT.
FIRING, O MUCULENT ONE!
ZZZZZOWNT!!
COPYRIGHT©2003 ILLIAD HTTP://WWW.USERFRIENDLY.ORG/

NO CHANGE IN THE TARGET WHATSOEVER, YOUR GLUTINOUSNESS.
FIRST THE SUCCESS RAY AND NOW THE DYSLEXIA RAY. THIS EARTHLING IS IMMUNE TO EVERYTHING!

ZIKPT. TIME FOR AN EXPERIMENT! FIRE BOTH OUR SUCCESS RAY AND THE DYSLEXIA RAY AT A RANDOM EARTHLING AT THE SAME TIME.
BY YOUR COMMAND, YOUR PUTRITUDE.
COPYRIGHT©2003 ILLIAD HTTP://WWW.USERFRIENDLY.ORG/

KA-ZZOWWNT!

ANY RESULTS?
YOU COULD SAY THAT. THE TARGET JUST GOT APPROVED FOR A PATENT.
WOOHOO!

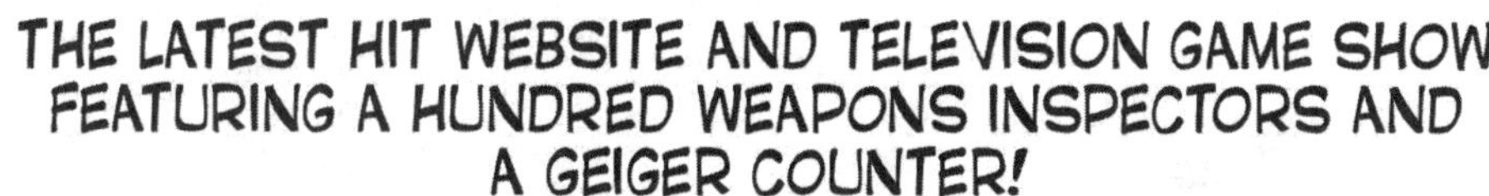
THE LATEST HIT WEBSITE AND TELEVISION GAME SHOW FEATURING A HUNDRED WEAPONS INSPECTORS AND A GEIGER COUNTER!

BADR 2000
PROPELLENT: SOLID
RANGE: ?
PROJECT: 395
COMMENT: CONDOR II EGYPT & ARGENTINA
AM I HOT OR NOT?
Damn Skippy!
Welll....
Nuh-uh. It's just a missile.
COPYRIGHT©2003 ILLIAD HTTP://WWW.USERFRIENDLY.ORG/

AL-SAMOUD
PROPELLENT: LIQUID
RANGE: 100KM
PROJECT: ?
COMMENT: SA-2 DERIVATIVE
AM I HOT OR NOT?
Damn Skippy!
Welll....
Nuh-uh. It's just a missile.

AL HUSSEIN
PROPELLENT: LIQUID
RANGE: 600KM
PROJECT: ?
COMMENT:
AM I HOT OR NOT?
Damn Skippy!
Welll....
Nuh-uh. It's just a missile.

MIKE, HAVE YOU SEEN THE WINKLEWICK FILE?
NOT A.F.A.I.K.
COPYRIGHT © 2003 ILLIAD HTTP://WWW.USERFRIENDLY.ORG/

GREG, YOU SEEN MY FILE FOR THE WINKLEWICK ACCOUNT?
404. H.T.H.

WILL YOU PEOPLE PLEASE START MAKING SENSE?! YOU'RE DRIVING ME OUT OF MY GOURD!
{{{{STEF}}}}
LOL!

SID, WHAT THE HELL IS WITH YOUR PEOPLE? DO SOMETHING! THEY'RE SPEAKING GIBBERISH!
IT'S THEIR WAY OF PROTESTING MARKETSPEAK, STEF. I'M SURE IF YOU STOPPED ANNOYING THEM WITH BUZZWORDS I COULD ASK THEM TO STOP USING ONLINE CHAT TERMS.
COPYRIGHT © 2003 ILLIAD HTTP://WWW.USERFRIENDLY.ORG/

BUT I CAN'T THINK OF ANOTHER WAY TO SAY "PLEASE MAKE THIS ISSUE YOUR PRIMARY ACTION ITEM."
L.A.R.T. PARTY!
BIG FOAM CLUEBAT
BIG FOAM CLUEBAT

WHAT'S THIS KAFUFFLE I'M HEARING ABOUT THE TECHS TORTURING STEF WITH ONLINE GIBBERISH?
CHIEF, YOU KNOW HOW GEEKS AND MARKETERS JUST DON'T UNDERSTAND EACH OTHER?
COPYRIGHT © 2003 ILLIAD HTTP://WWW.USERFRIENDLY.ORG/

WELL, THIS IS THEIR ATTEMPT TO SHOW STEF HOW DIFFICULT IT IS TO UNDERSTAND SOMEONE WITHOUT A COMMON FRAME OF REFERENCE. ANYWAY, THEY'RE NOT TORTURING HIM. THEY'RE JUST TRYING TO REACH HIM.

RED FLAG! RED FLAG! DEPRIORTIZE YOUR CURRENT ACTION!
WHAT DOES THAT MEAN?
SOUNDS LIKE "HIT ME HARDER" TO ME...
BIG FOAM CLUEBAT
BIG FOAM CL

NOW THAT WE HAVE YOUR UNDIVIDED ATTENTION, WE'RE GOING TO TEACH YOU HOW TO SPEAK TO GEEKS. FIRST, YOU HAVE TO UNDERSTAND THE USE OF ACRONYMS.
ACRONYMS. RIGHT.
COPYRIGHT © 2003 ILLIAD HTTP://WWW.USERFRIENDLY.ORG/

HERE'S AN EXAMPLE: BEFORE GETTING INTO A DISCUSSION ABOUT LAWS, WE ALWAYS PREFACE WITH A DISCLAIMER. THAT DISCLAIMER IS THE ACRONYM FOR "I AM NOT A LAWYER." WHICH IS..?

I...ANAL
YES, YES INDEED.

THE GEEKS HAVE YOU TALKING IN ACRONYMS?
THEY THINK THEY DO. BUT I'VE SPENT TIME ON AOL. I KNOW HOW TO FIGHT BACK. WATCH.
COPYRIGHT © 2003 ILLIAD HTTP://WWW.USERFRIENDLY.ORG/

HI. HAPPY ACRONYM OF THE DAY COMING UP JUST FOR YOU GUYS...
UH-OH.

LOLOLOLOLOLOLOL!!
HMMMM. RECURSIVE EVIL...
AAAAAGH!!
STOP TALKING NOW. NOW. NOW!

WHAT REALLY BOTHERS US ABOUT MARKETSPEAK IS THAT YOU'RE TRYING TO REPLACE PERFECTLY SENSIBLE, USABLE WORDS WITH FANCY-SOUNDING VERBAGE. FOR EXAMPLE, A "BRICKS-AND-MORTAR" BUSINESS INSTEAD OF SAYING "STOREFRONT."

COPYRIGHT © 2003 ILLIAD HTTP://WWW.USERFRIENDLY.ORG/

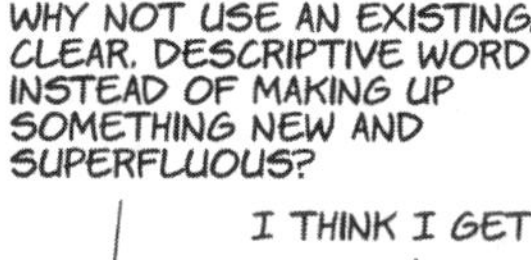
WHY NOT USE AN EXISTING, CLEAR, DESCRIPTIVE WORD INSTEAD OF MAKING UP SOMETHING NEW AND SUPERFLUOUS?
I THINK I GET IT...

...KINDA LIKE "FLAMEWAR" INSTEAD OF "HEATED ARGUMENT," RIGHT?
WHY YES...I MEAN NO! IT'S NOT THE SAME AT ALL! "FLAMEWAR" IS COOL!

USER FRIENDLY
the comic strip
BY J.D. "ILLIAD" FRAZER

(SUNG TO "THE SPIDER-MAN CARTOON THEME SONG")
SMILING MAN, SMILING MAN, DOES WHATEVER A VAMPIRE CAN. LURKS AND PROWLS SEEKS OUT PREY SLASHING STAFF MAKES HIS DAY. OH YEAH, HERE COMES THE SMILING MAN!
"STRINGS ATTACHED TO DEALS."

IS HE CRUEL? LISTEN BUD! HE'S GOT H.R. GENES IN HIS BLOOD. CAN HE SMILE WHEN HE'S MEAN? NOTHING'S EASIER 'CAUSE YOU SEE, HEY THERE! THERE GOES THE SMILING MAN!

IN HIS SHIRT AND TIE, HE APPEARS KIND OF NICE, BUT INSIDE HIS CHEST IS A HEART MADE OF IIICE!

SMILING MAN, SMILING MAN, ALWAYS HAS A PLOT, HAS A PLAN. COUNTING BEANS, SUMMING CASH HE'S AS NASTY AS ANY RASH! TO HIM, LIFE IS A COLOSSEUM, "SHAFT WORKERS" THAT'S HIS THEOREM! HE IS THE SMILING MAN!

YOU WERE SUPPOSED TO SWING FROM BUILDING TO BUILDING DURING THE SONG.
NOT OVER THOSE MINIUMUM-WAGE EMPLOYEES I'M NOT.

LOOK. YOU'RE MISSING THE POINT. THE REASON WHY YOU DON'T UNDERSTAND GEEKS IS BECAUSE YOU MARKETING PEOPLE USE LAME JARGON TO EXPRESS IDEAS.
COPYRIGHT © 2003 ILLIAD HTTP://WWW.USERFRIENDLY.ORG/

GEEKS USE **CLEVER** JARGON. WORDS THAT ARE SNAPPY. DESCRIPTIVE. AND MAKE SENSE. WHAT THAT DOES IS MAKE EVERYTHING WE DO **COOL.** ARE YOU GETTING THIS?
MM-HM

GEEKS LIKE THINGS THAT ARE COOL. MARKETSPEAK IS **NOT** COOL. MARKETSPEAK IS AS STERILE AND ASININE AS...AS...
A BEIGE-COLOURED PC?
I HAVE A LIME-COLOURED IMAC AT HOME.

YOU JUST **DON'T GET IT** DO YOU? GEEKSPEAK IS CLEAR AND SNAPPY. MARKETSPEAK IS-
YOU'RE RIGHT.
...WHAT?
I SAID I THINK YOU'RE RIGHT. I'LL GIVE THE GEEK WAY A TRY.
COPYRIGHT © 2003 ILLIAD HTTP://WWW.USERFRIENDLY.ORG/

...YOU...THINK WE'RE...**RIGHT?**
MM-HM.

ANYWAY. I SHOULD GET BACK TO WORK...
I'LL BE HERE GIVING MIKE OXYGEN.

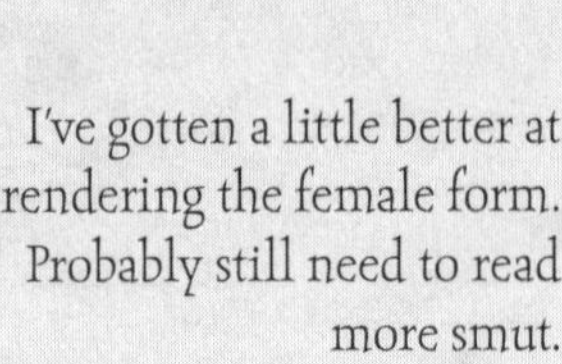
I've gotten a little better at rendering the female form. Probably still need to read more smut.

HMMM. NEW AD NEEDED FOR OUR SERVICES. MUST NOT USE MARKETSPEAK. BUT I CAN'T CHANGE THE LAYOUT OF THE ADVERTISEMENT. JUST THE WORDING...
COPYRIGHT © 2003 ILLIAD HTTP://WWW.USERFRIENDLY.ORG/

WELL. I'LL JUST DO IT THE GEEK WAY. CALL IT LIKE IT REALLY IS...

COLUMBIA INTERNET
"YOU DON'T GET THE CHICK, BUT YOU DO GET TO CLICK!"
STEF!!

This was around the time of the U.S. invasion of Iraq. It was weighing heavily on everyone's minds. What better solution than a brief respite involving some television SF?

SIGH
COPYRIGHT © 2003 ILLIAD HTTP://WWW.USERFRIENDLY.ORG/

DUDE. YOU LOOK REALLY DEPRESSED. ARE YOU OKAY?
I GUESS SO. RECENT EVENTS. YOU KNOW. I'M VERY WORRIED.

YEAH. I HEAR YA...

I MEAN. WHAT IF TONIGHT'S REALLY **IS** THE LAST EPISODE OF "FARSCAPE" TO EVER BE MADE?
HUH?

STEF. I WANT A WORD WITH YOU ABOUT THAT LAST AD-
CHIEF. JUST IN TIME! THIS IS OUR NEXT AD. FEATURING A NEW MODEL. "MS. AMBER CARAMEL."
COPYRIGHT © 2003 ILLIAD HTTP://WWW.USERFRIENDLY.ORG/

MY WORD. SHE'S...MOST CERTAINLY A MAMMAL.
NOW THAT'S MY KIND OF "SHOCK AND AWE" CAMPAIGN.

STEF. ARE YOU SURE ABOUT USING "MS. CARAMEL" IN OUR LATEST AD CAMPAIGN?
I THINK SHE'LL BE A GREAT DRAW FOR NEW CUSTOMERS. CHIEF.
COPYRIGHT © 2003 ILLIAD HTTP://WWW.USERFRIENDLY.ORG/

FINE. I'LL LET YOU HAVE THIS ONE. BUT PLEASE SHOW SOME DISCRETION.
WILL DO.

AND NO MORE SIDEWAYS WAR REFERENCES. LIKE "SHOCK AND AWE CAMPAIGN." OKAY?
OKAY.
YE GODS! IT'S THE MOTHER OF ALL BOSOMS!

USER FRIENDLY
THE COMIC STRIP
Three UF Sundays were removed due to being far too derivative of the works of another cartoonist. This spot was for one of them.
Please pretend that this space is funny. Ta.

GLUMNESS DOES NOT BECOME YOU, DUDE.
I CAN'T HELP IT, ERWIN. THE NET HAS BECOME A CESSPOOL.
COPYRIGHT©2003 ILLIAD HTTP://WWW.USERFRIENDLY.ORG/

CESSPOOL?
A TEXTUAL SEWER. IT'S FILLED WITH PEOPLE WHO TRASH TALK, INDISCRIMINATELY PUT OTHERS DOWN, AND BAD-MOUTH EVERYTHING UNDER THE SUN.

...BUT I SUPPOSE IT'S JUST A SYMPTOM OF FREEDOM OF SPEECH ON THE 'NET.
DUDE, THEY'RE NOT USING THE INTERNET TO EXERCISE THEIR **FREEDOM OF SPEECH.** THEY'RE USING THE INTERNET TO EXERCISE THEIR FREEDOM FROM **BEING PUNCHED IN THE MOUTH.**

YOU HEAR ABOUT MSN 8? MICROSOFT IS REALLY TRYING TO PUSH IT INTO THE MARKET.
I HEARD: CONTENT AND SERVICES.
COPYRIGHT©2003 ILLIAD HTTP://WWW.USERFRIENDLY.ORG/

THEY'RE REALLY PUSHING HARD WITH THAT "MSN BUTTERFLY" CAMPAIGN OF THEIRS. THINK IT'LL HAVE ANY EFFECT ON OUR CUSTOMER BASE?
DON'T WORRY. GREG SAYS HE'S READY FOR THEM.

YEAH, YOU COME **GET SOME** YOU TECHNICOLOURED BEETLE...
RAID

I KNOW THAT MSN BUTTERFLY IS NEARBY. THAT BLASTED DEMON-SPAWN SNEAKS IN WHEN YOU AREN'T WATCHING AND JUST SINKS ITS $14.95 PER MONTH HOOKS INTO YOU.
?
RAID
COPYRIGHT©2003 ILLIAD HTTP://WWW.USERFRIENDLY.ORG/

RUFFLE RUFFLE
RUFFLE RUFFLE
RUFFLE RUFFLE

I HEARD THAT!! IT SOUNDED LIKE... LIKE...MONEY BEING RUFFLED!
DAMN, I'VE BEEN **MADE**...

AH **HAH!!** **THERE** YOU ARE YOU BROAD-ARSED MOSQUITO! NOW YOU DIE!!
WAIT!!!
RAID
COPYRIGHT©2003 ILLIAD HTTP://WWW.USERFRIENDLY.ORG/

...IF YOU CRUSH ME, YOU'LL GET SEVEN YEARS OF BAD LUCK!
RAID

UH...WAIT A SECOND. THAT'S MIRRORS...
RUN AWAY!
SILLY BUTTERFLY. SILLY, **DEAD** BUTTERFLY.
RAID

REMEMBER WHAT THE 19TH CENTURY AMERICAN WRITER NATHANIEL HAWTHORNE ONCE SAID: "HAPPINESS IS A BUTTERFLY, WHICH WHEN PURSUED IS ALWAYS JUST BEYOND YOUR GRASP, BUT WHICH, IF YOU WILL SIT DOWN QUIETLY, MAY ALIGHT UPON YOU."
RAID
COPYRIGHT © 2003 ILLIAD HTTP://WWW.USERFRIENDLY.ORG/

WHAM!
HAPPY I MAY NOT BE, BUT LORD AM I EVER SATISFIED.
EHHHH...
RAID

YEARS AGO, FROM THE "SOMEBODY WASN'T THINKING" FILES...
MY LORD? WE HAVE IT! WE HAVE THE NEW LOGO AND MASCOT FOR THE MSN LINE!
HERE IT IS, MY LORD!
COPYRIGHT © 2003 ILLIAD HTTP://WWW.USERFRIENDLY.ORG/

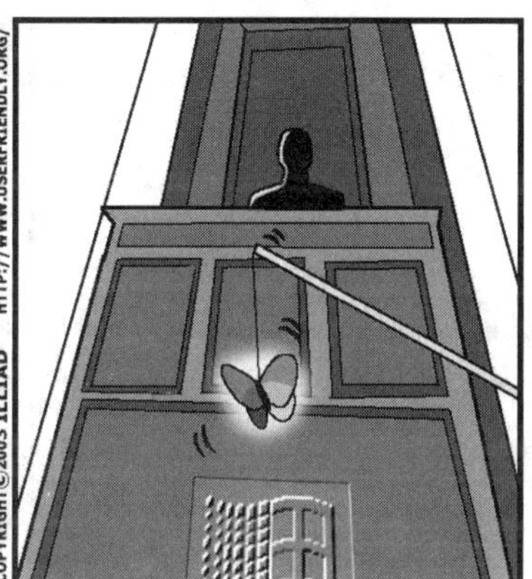

THE MSN MASCOT IS A BUG?
UH...NO MY LORD! IT'S A... A...
...TWENTY MILLION DOLLAR LESSON IN IRONY.

DANG. LOOKS LIKE THE F.T.C. IS GOING AHEAD WITH THAT NATIONAL "DO-NOT-CALL" REGISTRY. STARTING IN OCTOBER, ANY TELEMARKETER WHO CALLS SOMEONE ON THE LIST WILL BE FINED $11,000.00!!

THIS COULD REALLY CUT INTO MY REVENUES. MY TELEMARKETING BUSINESS WILL BE SERIOUSLY BURDENED.

OKAY. LOOKING FOR SOME SYMPATHY HERE.
O WOE TO YOU. HOW TERRIBLE THIS WORLD WILL BE. WHATEVER SHALL WE ALL DO WHEN YOU DON'T CALL US DURING DINNER?
WE'LL HAVE TO RESORT TO ACTUALLY ENJOYING OUR MEALS UNDISTURBED. O WOE!
COPYRIGHT © 2003 ILLIAD HTTP://WWW.USERFRIENDLY.ORG/

SPOOOOOOON!!

NOW THAT IS WHAT I CALL FINE HANDIWORK. COLOURS SPLATTERED IN A CHAOTIC DANCE OF BLUNT FORCE TRAUMA. THIS IS ART.
RAID
COPYRIGHT © 2003 ILLIAD HTTP://WWW.USERFRIENDLY.ORG/

AND YET, IN MY MOMENT OF TRIUMPH, I HAVE THIS NAGGING FEELING THAT I'VE MISSED SOMETHING...
RAID

AAAAAAAAAAAAAAAAAAAAGH!!
AAAAAAAAAAAAAAGH!!
RAID

YOU GORMLESS FREAK. YOU JUST ABOUT GAVE ME A STROKE!
GAVE YOU A STROKE? HOW WOULD YOU REACT IF YOU SAW A CO-WORKER SMEARED ON A WALL LIKE THAT?
THUD
THUD
SQUIRT
COPYRIGHT © 2003 ILLIAD HTTP://WWW.USERFRIENDLY.ORG/

UH-OH...

YOU KNOW, YOU LOOK KINDA FAMILIAR...
IT'S A SOFT ECONOMY, OKAY?!
ARTHUR?

SINCE YOU'RE ALL DRESSED UP, I GUESS YOU'D BETTER DO WHAT YOU'RE SUPPOSED TO.
DON'T MAKE ME DO THIS, MAN.
COPYRIGHT © 2003 ILLIAD HTTP://WWW.USERFRIENDLY.ORG/

GIVE IT UP, DUDE. OR I CALL YOUR BOSS AT MSN.
OKAY, OKAY!! I REALLY HATE PEOPLE LIKE YOU.

"MSN...IT'S BETTER WITH THE BUTTERFLY!" ... GAH
I CAN'T BELIEVE IT'S NOT BETA...
DID HE SAY "BUTTER WITH A BETTER FLY?"
WIGGLE
WIGGLE
WIGGLE

WHERE'D THAT BUTTERFLY DUDE GO?
HE SAID HIS WORK HERE WAS DONE, AND THAT HE HAD TO "GO FIGHT EVIL ELSEWHERE."
COPYRIGHT © 2003 ILLIAD HTTP://WWW.USERFRIENDLY.ORG/

OKAAAY...WHAT DOES THAT MEAN, EXACTLY?
SOMETHING ABOUT WINNING TRUST BY HELPING OLD LADIES.

AAAAAAAAAGH!! WEST NILE!!
BIFF
BIFF

AH-HAH! KIDS! THE PERFECT COMBINATION OF INNOCENCE AND MALLEABILITY! I'LL HAVE THEM CHANTING "IT'S BETTER WITH THE BUTTERFLY" IN NO TIME!
COPYRIGHT © 2003 ILLIAD HTTP://WWW.USERFRIENDLY.ORG/

HELLO KIDS! HOW ARE YOU DOING TOD-
WHAT THE HELL ARE YOU SUPPOSED TO BE?
WHY I'M THE MSN BUTTERFLY! AND... UH...WHY ARE YOU STARING?

AAAAAAAGH!! LET ME GO YOU LITTLE MONSTERS!
STOP WRIGGLING MISTER, OR JANEY MIGHT POKE YOU.
I'LL GET THE KILL JAR.

DUDE. TIME?
JUST ABOUT NOON.
COPYRIGHT © 2003 ILLIAD HTTP://WWW.USERFRIENDLY.ORG/

I HOPE JANEY GETS HERE SOON. THE SUN WON'T STAY UP THERE ALL DAY...

WILL YOU LITTLE TURDS PLEASE CUT ME LOOSE?!!?
DUDE. HUSH UP NOW.
FOUND IT!

USER FRIENDLY
THE COMIC STRIP
WANTED
1'6"
"DUST PUPPY"
FOR MAKING FUN OF THE RIAA'S LAWFUL PROFITEERING.
REWARD: 10% OFF A MUSIC CD OF YOUR CHOICE!
JD.FRAZER

$97 BILLION. NOW THAT'S WHAT I CALL A LAWSUIT.
RIAA
COPYRIGHT © 2003 ILLIAD HTTP://WWW.USERFRIENDLY.ORG/

MR. OPPENHEIM? WE'RE GETTING SOME INTEL ABOUT THE $97 BILLION LAWSUIT WE SLAPPED ON THOSE STUDENTS AT MICHIGAN TECH AND TWO OTHER COLLEGES.
DO TELL, EDWARD.
RIAA

GEEKS EVERYWHERE ARE PROTESTING, BUT TO THEIR OWN DETRIMENT! REMEMBER BOOK BURNINGS AND BRA BURNINGS? THEY'RE DECLARING A MASSIVE CD BURNING! THAT JUST MEANS THEY'LL HAVE TO GO OUT AND BUY MORE CDS TO REPLACE THE ONES THEY DESTROY! HA! THOSE DOLTS! WE WIN!

RIAA

OH, WAIT...GEEKS AND "BURNING CDS"...
I'M GLAD YOU FIGURED THAT OUT BEFORE THE VEIN IN MY TEMPLE POPPED, ED.
RIAA

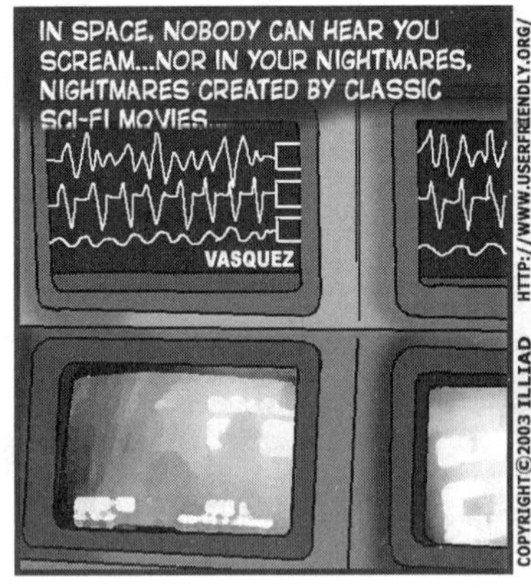
IN SPACE, NOBODY CAN HEAR YOU SCREAM...NOR IN YOUR NIGHTMARES, NIGHTMARES CREATED BY CLASSIC SCI-FI MOVIES...
VASQUEZ
HTTP://WWW.USERFRIENDLY.ORG/
COPYRIGHT©2003 ILLIAD

SOMETIMES, THOSE NIGHTMARES CAN DRAG YOU DOWN INTO THE VORTEX OF YOUR DEEPEST FEARS, FEARS THAT HAVE BEEN WITH US FOR MILLENIA, FEARS OF BEING HUNTED...HUNTED AND KILLED...
HEY GUYS. LOOKS LIKE THEY BAGGED ONE OF RIPLEY'S BAD GUYS HERE.
HICKS D.

AND SOMETIMES, NIGHTMARES CAN BECOME THE MOST WONDERFUL DREAMS...
MY GOD. YOU WERE RIGHT! COFFEE FOR BLOOD!
ZZZZZ

*SSSSSSSS...!
SO I CHECKED THE ERROR LOGS AND...
WHAT THE...?!
HTTP://WWW.USERFRIENDLY.ORG/
COPYRIGHT©2003 ILLIAD

SSSSSSSS
DROOOOOL
SOMETHING'S BURNING THROUGH THE CEILING...

PITR! WHAT THE HELL ARE YOU DOING?!
THIS STUFF SMELLS LIKE COFFEE...
AH-HA! SUCCESS!

PITR. WHAT IN THE NAME OF APOLLO'S ARSE ARE YOU UP TO?!
AM MAKINK NEW KIND OF BREW.
SSSSSS
HTTP://WWW.USERFRIENDLY.ORG/
COPYRIGHT©2003 ILLIAD

NEW BREW?! BREW OF WHAT. NAPALM?!
IS JUST COFFEE...
MIKE. WHAT'S DIRECTLY UNDER YOU?
SSSSSS

DIRECTLY UNDER ME? MRS. RICKENBACHER'S DRY CLEANING SH... ...OH MY LORD.
AM SURE HER HAIR WILL BE GROWINK BACK.
AAAIIEEEEEE!!

YE GODS! THAT BREW OF PITR'S IS STILL EATING THROUGH STUFF! IT'S GOING RIGHT THROUGH MRS. RICKENBACHER'S FLOOR!
YOU'VE SEEN THE BUILDING BLUEPRINTS. RIGHT?
HTTP://WWW.USERFRIENDLY.ORG/
COPYRIGHT©2003 ILLIAD

YES. FOR WHEN I WAS RUNNING CABLE.
DO YOU KNOW WHAT'S UNDER MRS. RICKENBACHER'S SHOP?

WELL?
THAT WOULD BE THE SEWAGE MAINS...
SQUITCH
AAIIIIEEEEE!

HEY GUYS? DID YOU TRY ANY OF THAT NEW COFFEE?
WHAT. YOU DRANK SOME OF IT?
SURE. A WHOLE CUP.
COPYRIGHT © 2003 ILLIAD HTTP://WWW.USERFRIENDLY.ORG/

GREAT SCOTT! A.J.. THAT STUFF WILL GO RIGHT THROUGH YOU!

YOU CAN SAY THAT AGAIN. I'VE BEEN ON THE POT ALL MORNING...
AAAAIIIEEEEE
SORRY MRS. RICKENBACHER!

PITR ... WHAT EXACTLY DID YOU CONCOCT HERE?
IS ONLY COFFEE. MIKHAIL.
BURGLE
FLURGLE
COPYRIGHT © 2003 ILLIAD HTTP://WWW.USERFRIENDLY.ORG/

COFFEE?! "COFFEE" THAT EATS THROUGH CONCRETE AND METAL. "COFFEE" THAT IS MORE POTENT THAN BATTERY ACID. "COFFEE" THAT...
UM... 'SCUSE ME.
BLORP

"COFFEE" THAT MAKES YOU REGULAR?
NO. MAKES YOU PROMPT!

A LINE BEGGING TO BE SAID IN "THE MATRIX RELOADED"
WHAT'S THE MATTER. MR. ANDERSON...NEVER HEARD OF......BACKUPS?
D'OH!
COPYRIGHT © 2003 ILLIAD HTTP://WWW.USERFRIENDLY.ORG/

I HOPE A.J. DRANK THE LAST OF THAT SO-CALLED "COFFEE" YOU CONCOCTED.
DA. HE IS FINISHINK POT.
COPYRIGHT©2003 ILLIAD HTTP://WWW.USERFRIENDLY.ORG/

POT? WAIT A SEC...DIDN'T A.J. SAY THAT HE ONLY HAD A CUP?
DA. ULTRA-STRONG COFFEE MUST BE BIG HIT WITH SOMEBODY ELSE.

YE GODS. I CAN'T CLOSE MY EYES!!

YO. TOOTS. YOU FIXED THE MAIL SERVER YET?
COPYRIGHT©2003 ILLIAD HTTP://WWW.USERFRIENDLY.ORG/

I FEEL LIKE THAT ALEX GUY IN "A CLOCKWORK ORANGE."
I BET MY FLY'S UNDONE...

MIRANDA. MIKE JUST RESTARTED THE MAIL SERV...UH...
COPYRIGHT©2003 ILLIAD HTTP://WWW.USERFRIENDLY.ORG/

YO! ILLIAD! SOLD OUT TO THE ANIME CROWD. DID WE?
I WONDER IF "DRAGONBALL Z" IS HIRING...

THIS "ALIEN BLOOD COFFEE" OF PITR'S IS CREATING HAVOC IN THE OFFICE. I'LL HAVE TO HAVE A WORD WITH HIM.
COPYRIGHT©2003 ILLIAD HTTP://WWW.USERFRIENDLY.ORG/

NNNNGGGGGG...
WHAT THE...?

OH CRIPES. DON'T TELL ME YOU DRANK MORE OF THAT SLUDGE.
DRANK MORE. NO. EXPUNGED MORE. YES.

OKAY PITR. ENOUGH OF THIS "ALIEN BLOOD COFFEE" OF YOURS...
ENOUGH **WHY**?

BECAUSE PITR. THERE'S ONLY ONE COFFEE POT AND NOT EVERYONE WANTS TO DRINK THAT NASTY SLUDGE OF YOURS.
OH. DA. OKAY.

AND, NOT TO MENTION. BECAUSE YOU NEED TO MAKE ROOM FOR "SID'S INSIDIOUS SYRUP."
WAITINK ONE MOMENT...

HE'S MAKING **WHAT**?
"SID'S INSIDIOUS SYRUP"

REALLY. WHAT'S IN IT?
HE WOULDN'T SAY. BUT HE MANAGED TO GET A.J. TO VOLUNTEER TO TRY IT OUT.

I DON'T WANT IT!!
NEITHER DO I!!

IF THEY'RE GOING TO COMMERCIALIZE EASTER, THEY SHOULD AT LEAST DO IT RIGHT...

MILK CHOCOLATE

CHOCOLATE BUNNY, THE WRONG WAY.

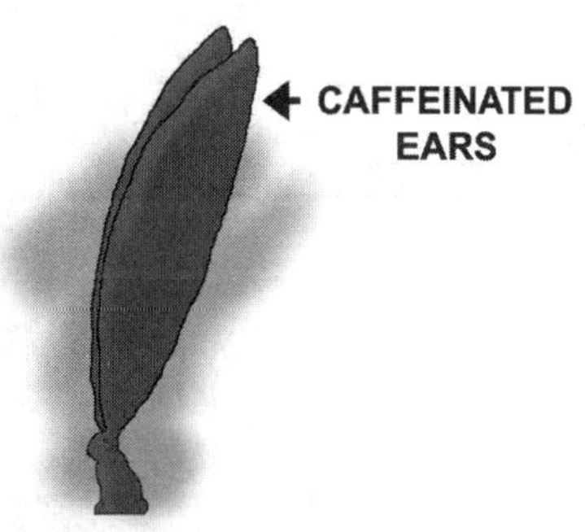
CAFFEINATED EARS

CHOCOLATE BUNNY, THE RIGHT WAY.

I'M GONNA TRY IT.
"SID'S INSIDIOUS SYRUP"
WHAT?
COPYRIGHT©2003 ILLIAD HTTP://WWW.USERFRIENDLY.ORG/

ARE YOU MAD?! SID BOASTED THAT THE STUFF WAS "BETTER" THAN PITR'S ALIEN BLOOD COFFEE! IF IT TOUCHES YOU, YOU'LL PROBABLY DIE!!
COWARD.

WHAT'S THAT HE'S PUTTING ON?
PLASTIC AND DUCT TAPE.
I'M INVINCIBLE!

I am sure there's some deep-seated link in the human psyche that makes fluffy, fuzzy things appealing. Drawing Mike with his beard and hair all puffed out was somehow very ... cathartic.

COPYRIGHT©2003 ILLIAD HTTP://WWW.USERFRIENDLY.ORG/

HERE HE COMES...

TRIED SID'S COFFEE DID YOU.
NO. PITR DID. AND I WAS STANDING NEXT TO HIM WHEN HE SHRIEKED.

PITR'S BEEN LOCKED IN HIS OFFICE FOR HOURS.
I KNOW. MY COFFEE WAS A LOT MORE POTENT THAN HIS AND IT'S BEEN MAKING HIM NUTS.
COPYRIGHT©2003 ILLIAD HTTP://WWW.USERFRIENDLY.ORG/

HE'S GOING TO SPEND MORE THAN A FEW HOURS TRYING TO RESEARCH THE RECIPE I USED.
RESEARCH? WHERE DO YOU RESEARCH A COFFEE RECIPE SO INCREDIBLY VILE?

HMMM. IS NOT IN HERE ANYWHERE...
"POPULAR EVIL" MAGAZINE

SID.
PITR.
TO BE TELLINK ME RECIPE OF YOUR ABSINTHIAN COFFEE.
COPYRIGHT©2003 ILLIAD HTTP://WWW.USERFRIENDLY.ORG/

CAN'T TELL YOU THAT PITR. ONLY A VERY FEW MASTER GEEKS CAN BE TOLD THIS PARTICULAR SECRET...
HA! WILL BE FINDINK RECIPE BY MYSELF! AM SHOWINK YOU WHO IS REAL MASTER!

...3...2...1...

PLEASE!
NOT EVEN MOZART COULD COMPOSE SUCH SWEET MUSIC...

HELLO, MERE MORTAL. I UNDERSTAND YOU WISH TO UNCOVER YOUR ARCHENEMY'S COFFEE RECIPE.
DA. THIS IS WHAT I AM WISHINK MOST FERVENTLY.
COPYRIGHT©2003 ILLIAD HTTP://WWW.USERFRIENDLY.ORG/

I WILL GIVE YOU THIS SECRET. BUT FIRST YOU MUST GIVE ME YOUR MOST PRIZED POSSESSION IN RETURN.

EH...YOU ARE WANTINK ROOT PASSWORD TO RIAA.ORG?
NO...ALTHOUGH, IT'D BE KIND OF COOL TO MESS AROU--**NO!**

FOR THE SECRET TO THE ULTIMATE LIQUID, I WANT SOMETHING OF YOURS THAT WILL EQUATE TO A POUND OF FLESH. I WANT YOU TO ADMIT THAT YOUR ARCHENEMY HAS **OWNED** YOU IN THE DARK ART OF COFFEE-MAKING.
THIS IS WERY DIFFICULT...BUT...
COPYRIGHT©2003 ILLIAD HTTP://WWW.USERFRIENDLY.ORG/

SNIG
SNORT
GIGGLE

AAAAAAAAAGH!!
BUSTED!

HTML LESSON #42: THE ONLY LEGITIMATE USE OF THE GREATLY LOATHED <BLINK> TAG.

Schroedinger's Cat

is <BLINK>NOT</BLINK> dead.

SO SID. WHAT DO YOU PUT IN THAT COFFEE OF YOURS THAT MAKES IT SO SCARY?
NOTHING MUCH. IT'S JUST A REALLY GOOD MEDIUM ROAST WITH ONE VERY POTENT ADDITIONAL INGREDIENT.
HTTP://WWW.USERFRIENDLY.ORG/
COPYRIGHT © 2003 ILLIAD

WHAT'S THE INGREDIENT?
HERE. LOOK FOR YOURSELF.

IT'S DARK. NASTY AND... MOVING.
IT'S DISTILLED USENET BITTERNESS.

I'm a Usenet veteran, and I have the scars to prove it. Not to mention blast marks from the flame wars.

SO THAT'S DISTILLED USENET BITTERNESS?
YES IT IS.
HTTP://WWW.USERFRIENDLY.ORG/
COPYRIGHT © 2003 ILLIAD

AND YOU GOT THAT FROM THE USUAL RANTING AND RAGING ON USENET?
ABOUT A WEEK'S WORTH. YES.

WAIT...YOU MANAGED TO GET ALL OF THAT FROM ONE WEEK OF USENET POSTINGS?
ONE WEEK OF USENET POSTINGS IN SOC.POLITICS ALONE...

THIS STUFF IS DAMNED SCARY. SID.
YEAH I KNOW. BUT I KIND OF EXPECTED IT FROM USENET.
BLURBLE
PLOT
HTTP://WWW.USERFRIENDLY.ORG/
COPYRIGHT © 2003 ILLIAD

I THINK IT'S INTERESTING THAT OF ALL PLACES YOU COULD'VE GONE FOR THIS. YOU AS A VETERAN GEEK CHOSE USENET. IT SAYS A LOT ABOUT US.

OF COURSE. WHERE ELSE ARE YOU GOING TO FIND THIS KIND OF PALPABLE BITTERNESS?
PEOPLE WAITING FOR "DUKE NUKEM FOREVER."

SID GAVE IT TO YOU?
YEAH. SAID HE DIDN'T WANT IT ANYMORE.
HTTP://WWW.USERFRIENDLY.ORG/
COPYRIGHT © 2003 ILLIAD

WHATCHA GONNA DO WITH IT?
I WAS THINKING MAYBE I'D DO SOME EXPERIMENTS WITH IT.

EXPERIMENTS? WHAT KIND OF DATA CAN YOU GATHER FROM DISTILLED USENET BITTERNESS?
EXAMPLES OF REAL-WORLD IMAGINARY NUMBERS. IN THIS CASE. I.Q.s

BOY THIS LID IS ON TIGHT.
CAREFUL WITH THAT...
COPYRIGHT © 2003 ILLIAD HTTP://WWW.USERFRIENDLY.ORG/

AAAAARRRRRRRGGGHHH!! YOU'RE ALL STUPID! TWITS! GODWIN'S LAW! GODWIN'S YOU'RE AN IDIOT! MORON! GENERIC VIAGRA!
THOP

"GENERIC VIAGRA?!"
SOMEONE DIDN'T USE A PROPER FILTER...
HEY. IT'S GENUINE USENET.

DID YOU SAY "DISTILLED USENET BITTERNESS?"
AND A LITTLE USENET SPAM FOR TASTE. IT SEEMS TO BE ALIVE... LOOK AT IT MOVE.
GLUP
SNARL
COPYRIGHT © 2003 ILLIAD HTTP://WWW.USERFRIENDLY.ORG/

COULD I BORROW IT?
YOU CAN HAVE IT. BUT WHAT DO YOU WANT IT FOR?
SOMETHING COSMOLOGICALLY APPROPRIATE.

YOU SHOW THEM WHO'S BOSS...
RRIINNNGGG!

HILARY ROSEN'S CONTRIBUTION TO IRAQI COPYRIGHT LEGISLATION DEMANDS A RELEVANT DOMAIN NAME
http://www.low.iq
COPYRIGHT © 2003 ILLIAD HTTP://WWW.USERFRIENDLY.ORG/

This isn't really fair. Hilary Rosen is in fact a very smart lady. It's just the legislation that's unbelievably venal and stupid.

HELLO. GREG SPEAKING.
MY WEB BROKE.
PLEASE HOLD. ESCALATING YOU TO TIER 2...
COPYRIGHT © 2003 ILLIAD HTTP://WWW.USERFRIENDLY.ORG/

HEY TECHNOTARD! DO YOU EVER READ OR DO YOU JUST DROOL ON YOUR KEYBOARD?!

WHY YOU..! OH! I...! OOOH! YOU...! OOOH!
MY WORD THAT'S QUITE A RIPOSTE! HOW EVER WILL I COUNTER THAT?
THIS IS PURE "EAU DE TROLLETTE."

HELLO? HELLO? I HAVE A PROBLEM WITH YOUR STUPID SERVICE. YOU PEOPLE SUCK! YOU SUCK. YOU HEAR ME? COMPLETE SUCKAGE! YOU PUT PURE VACUUM TO SHAME!
COPYRIGHT © 2003 ILLIAD HTTP://WWW.USERFRIENDLY.ORG/

RUMBLE
FUME
BOIL

YOU NAZI!!
THIS CALL IS NOW OVER...

EXCUSE ME. DO YOU HAVE A COPY OF THAT HAMST-

HASTUR OLD BUDDY. IS THAT YOU?!
CTHULHU! DUDE!
YE GODS...

HASTUR. WHAT IN THE NAME OF AZATHOTH ARE YOU DOING IN THAT JAR?
IT'S A BIT OF A LONG STORY OLD BOY. SUFFICE TO SAY I FOUND MYSELF A NEW AVATAR: USENET.
COPYRIGHT © 2003 ILLIAD HTTP://WWW.USERFRIENDLY.ORG/

CAN YOU BELIEVE IT? A PLACE THAT IS INTANGIBLE, YET WHERE THE BITTERNESS AND ANGST IS PALPABLE. AND THERE IS SOME OF IT. OF ME. CONCENTRATED HERE. MANIFEST AS A BLACK, OILY SLUDGE.

NOW SERIOUSLY. DO I LOOK ALL THAT BAD?
I DO FIND IT QUITE..*AHEM*.. "JARRING."
JARRING. THAT'S FUNNY. DON'T EAT ME PLEASE.

YE UNHOLY JELLIED PHLEGM! SID, WHEN YOU DISTILLED THAT USENET BITTERNESS, YOU SUMMONED HASTUR!
WHO?
COPYRIGHT © 2003 ILLIAD HTTP://WWW.USERFRIENDLY.ORG/

HASTUR! THE UNSPEAKABLE ONE FROM THE CTHULHU MYTHOS! NASTY LIKE OILY UNDERWEAR NASTY!
WHO?

HAST--OH. NICE TRY. I'M NOT SAYING HIS NAME THREE TIMES.
I WAS IN THE NEXT ROOM, SO I HEARD YOU ANYWAY.
US GREAT OLD ONES STICK TOGETHER.

SID, THIS IS MY VERY OLD FRIEND HASTUR. WE'VE BEEN AROUND THE LOCAL CLUSTER TOGETHER A FEW TIMES.
YEAH. DOUBLE DATING AND EVERYTHING. BY AZATHOTH THOSE WERE THE EPOCHS!
COPYRIGHT © 2003 ILLIAD HTTP://WWW.USERFRIENDLY.ORG/

HI I'M GREG AND I'M A FRIEND OF ALL YOU OLD GRAPE ONES AND MY HEAD DOESN'T TASTE ALL THAT GOOD AND I HAVE A LOT OF RESPECT FOR POWERFUL HEAD-EATING BEINGS LIKE YOURSELF AND CTHULHU...

UNH-HUH. WEREN'T YOU THE ONE WITH THE CTHULHU TOY THAT YOU CAN THROW AND STICK TO THE WALL?
NO! THAT WASN'T ME THAT WAS BAD GREG!! BAD GREG ISN'T HERE ANYMORE!!

USER FRIENDLY
the comic strip
BY J.D. "ILLIAD" FRAZER

OH WOE IS ME. BEREFT, I AM, OF INTERNET CONNECTIVITY!

COMING!
THIS IS MORE FUN THAN TYING FLIES...

YOU RANG?
YEAH. I WANT A WORD. WHAT'S THIS I HEAR ABOUT YOU AND BEST BUY PULLING A CHARGE-THE-CUSTOMER-A-MONTHLY-FEE-WITHOUT-THEM-KNOWING-IT SCAM?

SCAM? I NEVER SC...URK!
AH HA! GOT YOU! NOW GIVE IT UP!

I KNEW IT! YOU WERE NEVER A REAL BUTTERFLY! YOU'RE A BLOODSUCKING MOSQUITO IN A BUTTERFLY COSTUME!
NO! I'M A BUTTERFLY! A BEAUTIFUL, BEAUTIFUL BUTT-ERFLY!

...AND THIS IS DUST PUPPY AND HIS PROGENY ERWIN.
"HASTUR"? WHAT KIND OF NAME IS THAT?
COPYRIGHT © 2003 ILLIAD HTTP://WWW.USERFRIENDLY.ORG/

IT'S AN ANCIENT ONE IF YOU MUST KNOW. IT REACHES FAR BACK INTO TIME, WHEN YOUR NAME WASN'T JUST WHO YOU WERE, BUT WHAT YOU WERE. POWERFUL IS THE NAME "HASTUR!"

I COULD WRITE A POEM ABOUT YOU BECAUSE "HASTUR" KINDA RHYMES WITH "BAST..."
ERWIN!!

YOU DARE MOCK ME, A KING AMONG GODS? ONE OF THE GREATEST FORCES OF MALEVOLENCE IN THE UNIVERSE? YOU WILL PAY IN A MANNER BEFITTING YOUR HUBRIS! BEHOLD!
KA-ZOT!
COPYRIGHT © 2003 ILLIAD HTTP://WWW.USERFRIENDLY.ORG/

WHAT DID YOU DO?
I TRANSPOSED HIS ESSENCE INTO ANOTHER EARTHLY VESSEL. I THINK THE CURRENT COLLOQUIALISM WOULD BE "I PORTED HIM INTO ANOTHER DEVICE."
VACANCY

I THOUGHT YOU COULD ONLY DO THAT IF YOU WERE ROOT.
COME NOW. GOD, ROOT. WHAT'S THE DIFFERENCE?
CREEPY.
VACANCY

You can never accuse me of being completely devoid of puerile humor.

OKAY HAST'. WHERE'D YOU SEND ERWIN?
LIKE I SAID. INTO AN APPROPRIATE EARTHLY VESSEL. AND I SENT THE FLUFFY ONE ALONG AS AN ACCOUTREMENT.
COPYRIGHT © 2003 ILLIAD HTTP://WWW.USERFRIENDLY.ORG/

AND WHAT IS THIS "APPROPRIATE EARTHLY VESSEL?"
A MERE CONCEPT BROUGHT INTO REALITY BY MY WILL ALONE. I RELISH THE QUALITY OF THIS PUNISHMENT.

AAAAAAAAAAAAAAAAAAAAAAAAAAAAAGH!!! I'M A TOILET!
WHAT ARE YOU SCREAMING ABOUT? I'M THE TOILET BRUSH!
Where do you want to "go" today?
iLoo

OKAY...DON'T PANIC. THINGS COULD BE MUCH WORSE.
YOU DON'T HAVE YOUR HEAD STUCK IN A PLASTIC BOWL, ERWIN.
Where do you want to "go" today?
iLoo
COPYRIGHT © 2003 ILLIAD HTTP://WWW.USERFRIENDLY.ORG/

LET'S SEE...I HAVE A WIRELESS CONNECTION. THAT'S GOOD. AND A FLUSH SYSTEM. AND...UH...
YES? WHAT?
Where do you want to "go" today?
iLoo

SUDDENLY I HAVE THIS URGE TO DO A CORE DUMP. HEH.
AAAAAGH! AAAAAAGH! GET ME OUT OF HERE!
Where do you want to "go" today?
iLoo

WE HAVE TO GET OUT OF HERE ERWIN...
SHH! SOMEONE'S COMING! LOOK UNNOTICEABLE!
COPYRIGHT©2003 ILLIAD HTTP://WWW.USERFRIENDLY.ORG/

NO NO NO NO NO NO...

RUSTLE
RUSTLE

AAAAAAAAAAAAAAAAGH!!
AAAAAAA AAIIIEEE!
EEHHH!

WELL. I'M GLAD THAT'S OVER. AND EVEN THOUGH WE SCARED THE...UH...EVEN THOUGH WE SCARED HIM. HE TOOK THE TIME TO LEAVE ME CLEAN AND POLISHED!
iLoo
COPYRIGHT©2003 ILLIAD HTTP://WWW.USERFRIENDLY.ORG/

THE FLOOR IS CLEAN. THE TOILET PAPER IS NICELY FOLDED OFF. AND HE EVEN CLEANED THE BOWL. WASN'T THAT NICE OF HIM?
iLoo

HELLO? DUDE?
EHHHH... THE CORN... THE CORN!

THE REGISTRATION OF 20,000 CANADIANS AS "JEDI KNIGHTS" IN CANADA'S LATEST CENSUS COINCIDING WITH THE CLOSING GAP BETWEEN THE CANADIAN AND U.S. DOLLARS SUDDENLY BECOMES SELF-EXPLANATORY.

CANADIAN DOLLARS WILL BE FINE. EH.

WELCOME BACK, PAWNS! AND HOW WAS YOUR EXPERIENCE AS A SEWAGE PORTAL?
KA-ZOT!
IT SUCKED. BUT NOW IT'S PAYBACK TIME.
COPYRIGHT © 2003 ILLIAD HTTP://WWW.USERFRIENDLY.ORG/

PAYBACK? PAYBACK?! AND HOW ARE YOU, A MERE THING GOING TO GET BACK AT AN ANCIENT AND POTENT GOD LIKE MYSELF?
OH! WE'LL THINK OF SOMETHING!

INDEED. I THINK I'LL EAT YOU NOW...THE SMALL ONE LOOKS SCRUMPTIOUS. AND HE APPEARS TO ALREADY BE TASTILY GARNISHED.
IT'S CORN...
PAYBACK.

"Hastur la vi ..." Please, please tell me I didn't actually write that. And publish it!

PHEW...I REALLY LUCKED OUT. I THOUGHT HASTUR WAS GOING TO EAT ME.
YEAH. THAT CORN COMMENT REALLY THREW HIM. ANYWAY, HE WON'T BOTHER US AGAIN ANYTIME SOON.
COPYRIGHT © 2003 ILLIAD HTTP://WWW.USERFRIENDLY.ORG/

WON'T BOTHER US? HOW DO YOU INTEND TO STOP HIM? HE'S A POWERFUL, IMMORTAL ENTITY WITH POWERFUL, IMMORTAL FRIENDS.
OH, I HAVE SOME POWERFUL FRIENDS OF MY OWN...

HASTUR LA VISTA, BABY.
OH DEAR...

IS THAT AN ONLINE CREDIT CARD APPLICATION YOU'RE FILLING OUT?
YEAH. I FIGURED IT'S ABOUT TIME I GOT AN AMEX CARD.
COPYRIGHT © 2003 ILLIAD HTTP://WWW.USERFRIENDLY.ORG/

BUT I'M OF TWO MINDS. ONE SIDE OF ME KNOWS I COULD USE THE CREDIT. THE OTHER SIDE DOESN'T WANT TO RISK GIVING THEM PERSONAL INFO THAT COULD BE STOLEN AND USED.

SO I DUNNO. SENDING THEM THIS INFO MAKES ME FEEL VERY VULNERABLE.
OH, RELAX. I'M SURE THEY'LL VIGOROUSLY PROSECUTE ANYONE WHO OBTAINS YOUR INFO WITHOUT PAYING THEM FOR IT.

OKAY. THAT'S ALL MY PERSONAL INFO KEYED IN FOR THIS AMEX CARD APPLICATION. I'LL HIT "SUBMIT" AND WE'LL SEE WHAT HAPPENS...
SUBMIT
COPYRIGHT © 2003 ILLIAD HTTP://WWW.USERFRIENDLY.ORG/

THIS IS RIDICULOUS! I DIDN'T GIVE AMEX MY PERSONAL INFO SO THEY COULD BOMBARD ME WITH JUNK MAIL AND SPAM!
WHAT ARE YOU GONNA DO?
I'M GOING TO CALL THEIR CUSTOMER SERVICE AND COMPLAIN!
COPYRIGHT © 2003 ILLIAD HTTP://WWW.USERFRIENDLY.ORG/

HELLO. YES THIS IS A.J. GARRETT. I JUST SIGNED UP FOR YOUR CREDIT CARD AND WAS PROMPTLY FIREHOSED WITH A TRUCKLOAD OF PROMOTIONAL CRAP! I WANT THIS TO CEASE AND DESIST NOW!

LISTEN, MISTER. THIS PROMO CRUD YOU'VE HAD SENT TO ME IS JUST WASTED MONEY AND EFFORT. I MEAN LOOK AT THIS STUFF! WHO WOULD WANT TO BUY ANY OF IT?!
COPYRIGHT © 2003 ILLIAD HTTP://WWW.USERFRIENDLY.ORG/

UM...IS IT REALLY TWO TO THREE INCHES GUARANTEED?
A.J.!!

WHAT WAS ONCE SOLELY A PLAYBOY MAGAZINE SLOGAN APPLIES TO NETGEEKS EVERYWHERE
USENET
I READ IT FOR THE ARTICLES.
COPYRIGHT © 2003 ILLIAD HTTP://WWW.USERFRIENDLY.ORG/

What? It's true.

WATCHA DOING?
I'M SENDING AWAY FOR SOMETHING.
YOU'RE KIDDING. YOU'RE BUYING ONE OF THOSE?
COPYRIGHT © 2003 ILLIAD HTTP://WWW.USERFRIENDLY.ORG/

KIDDING? WHY WOULD I BE KIDDING? AND WHAT'S WRONG WITH ORDERING SOMETHING THAT WILL HELP ME WITH MY... UH...SENSE OF PHYSICAL CONFIDENCE? AND HOW DID YOU KNOW THAT'S WHAT I WAS ORDERING?

I DIDN'T. BUT I DO NOW.
WHY ARE YOU ORDERING BIGGER PANTS?

IT'S HERE! IT'S HERE!
WHAT IS?
THE THING I ORDERED IN THAT SPAM MAIL.
COPYRIGHT © 2003 ILLIAD HTTP://WWW.USERFRIENDLY.ORG/

LET'S SEE. "INSTRUCTIONS: DRINK MIRACLE GROWTH FLUID. WAIT FOR SIXTY SECONDS AND USE SPECIAL ENCLOSED RULER TO MEASURE THE AMAZING RESULTS!"

THE "SPECIAL RULER" DOESN'T LOOK ALL THAT SPECIAL.
AND SOMEONE SCRATCHED OFF "CM" AND WROTE IN "INCHES."

WELL. THAT WAS A WASTE OF MONEY.
WHAT DID YOU EXPECT WOULD HAPPEN WHEN YOU BUY SOMETHING FROM A JUNK MAIL COMPANY?
COPYRIGHT © 2003 ILLIAD HTTP://WWW.USERFRIENDLY.ORG/

UH OH.

TALK ABOUT A LESSON LEARNED. I'M GOING TO HAVE TO SPEND THE WEEKEND CLEARING ALL OF THIS CRAP OUT OF HERE.
COPYRIGHT © 2003 ILLIAD HTTP://WWW.USERFRIENDLY.ORG/

IF IT'LL HELP, ERWIN AND I WILL WORK ON GETTING YOUR INFO OFF THOSE MAIL LISTS.
SURE. THAT'D BE... HEY. WHERE'D MY MIRACLE EN-LARGEMENT KIT GO?

FINALLY. A RULER THAT TELLS THE TRUTH!

WATCHA READIN'?
NEWS ABOUT THE SCO VS. IBM LAWSUIT OVER UNIX AND LINUX.

"S.C.O. CONTENDS THAT LINUX USES PROPRIETARY UNIX CODE AND THAT I.B.M. HAS TRIED TO DESTROY S.C.O.'S UNIX TO BENEFIT I.B.M.'S LINUX BUSINESS.
AND NOW, S.C.O.'S CHIEF EXEC SAYS THAT UNLESS MORE COMPANIES START LICENSING S.C.O.'S PROPERTY, HE MAY ALSO SUE LINUS TORVALDS, WHO IS CREDITED WITH INVENTING LINUX FOR PATENT INFRINGEMENT."
COPYRIGHT©2003 ILLIAD HTTP://WWW.USERFRIENDLY.ORG/

STAND BACK OR THE HACKER GETS IT!
OH, BE NICE.

AT S.C.O. HEAD OFFICE...
SIR? WE HAVE A REGISTERED LETTER FROM NOVELL.
OH CRIPES. WHAT IS IT THIS TIME?
SCO

IT READS: "DEAR S.C.O.: GIVEN OUR RECENT ANNOUNCEMENT TO THE MEDIA ASSERTING OUR OWNERSHIP OF THE UNIX COPYRIGHT, WE FELT OBLIGED TO FORMALLY ADVISE YOU OF OUR POSITION ON THIS SENSITIVE ISSUE."
SCO
COPYRIGHT©2003 ILLIAD HTTP://WWW.USERFRIENDLY.ORG/

"IN SUMMARY, WE ØWN3RZ UNIX!!!!!!111"
MY GOD, I REALLY DO HATE THOSE PEOPLE.
SCO

A.O.L. FINALLY "WINS" THE ANTI-TRUST LAWSUIT FILED AGAINST MICROSOFT...
WELL NOW, THAT WAS FAR LESS PAINFUL THAN I THOUGHT IT WOULD BE...
A.O.L
MICROSOFT
$750 MILLION WORTH OF NOVACAINE
COPYRIGHT©2003 ILLIAD HTTP://WWW.USERFRIENDLY.ORG/

HEY. DO YOU KNOW ANYTHING ABOUT ELEVENTH CENTURY ARMS AND ARMOUR?
SURE. I'LL JUST GOOGLE FOR IT.
TAPPY TAPPY SEARCH
COPYRIGHT©2003 ILLIAD HTTP://WWW.USERFRIENDLY.ORG/

IT'S TAKING A WHILE TO RESPOND. MAYBE GOOGLE IS DOW-
LALALALALA! YOU ARE THE FALLING TREE IN A DEAF GUY'S FOREST!

This particular cartoon was used at a technology symposium, and it punctuated the presentation of one of Google's senior doctorates. My pride swelleth.

OKAY. WHY ELSE WOULD GOOGLE NOT RESPOND?
MAYBE THE PROBLEM IS AT OUR END. MY ETHERNET CARD FOR EXAMPLE...
COPYRIGHT©2003 ILLIAD HTTP://WWW.USERFRIENDLY.ORG/

OR WHAT IF IT'S A WAYWARD ROUTER? OR A DNS PROBLEM? OR BACKHOE FADE?

OR...MAYBE...GOOGLE ITSELF IS DOWN.
GOOGLE IS THE WEB. AND IS THE WEB IN FLAMES? NO!

CAN'T...REACH...GOOGLE...
WHAT'S WRONG WITH HIM?
HE'S HAD HIS INFORMATION UMBILICAL CUT.
COPYRIGHT©2003 ILLIAD HTTP://WWW.USERFRIENDLY.ORG/

CAN'T...REACH...GOOGLE...
MIKE. CHECK TO SEE IF THERE'S ANY NEWS ONLINE ABOUT AN OUTAGE. TRY GOOGLING GOOGLE.

AAAAAAAAAAAAAAAAAAAAAAAAAAGH!!
YOU'RE NOT A NICE MAN.
OOPS. MY BAD.

STILL NOT GETTING THROUGH TO GOOGLE?
NO...I REALLY THINK THERE'S SOME EVIL AT WORK HERE.
COPYRIGHT©2003 ILLIAD HTTP://WWW.USERFRIENDLY.ORG/

SOMEONE HAS TO BE AT FAULT FOR THIS. WHOMEVER THEY ARE. MAYBE IT'S MARTHA STEWART? OR THE DIXIE CHICKS?

THESE DAYS. FIVE GETS YOU TEN IT'S S.C.O.
S.C.O! THAT'S RIGHT! SPURIOUS CRIME ORGANIZATION. THAT'S WHO THEY ARE!

HEY, WHAT'S WITH MIKE? DID HIS DOG DIE OR SOMETHING?
IT MIGHT AS WELL HAVE. WHATEVER YOU DO, DON'T MENTION "GOOGLE."
COPYRIGHT © 2003 ILLIAD HTTP://WWW.USERFRIENDLY.ORG/

HEY MIKE. WHY THE GOOGLY EYES?
AAAAAAAAAAAGGGH!

HEY...DID YOU FINALLY GET THROUGH TO GOOGLE?
YES, BUT THE WAIT NEARLY KILLED ME.
COPYRIGHT © 2003 ILLIAD HTTP://WWW.USERFRIENDLY.ORG/

AND WHILE I WAS WAITING I HAD THIS AWFUL THOUGHT -- WHAT IF GOOGLE ACTUALLY WENT UP IN A PUFF OF ENTROPY? WHAT WOULD WE DO THEN?
MM-HM.

WHEN IT COMES DOWN TO IT, SEARCHING THE WEB WITHOUT GOOGLE IS LIKE STRAINING SEWAGE WITH YOUR TEETH.
SPAFF

ONE OF SEVERAL POSTERS FOR THE THIRD MATRIX MOVIE THAT DIDN'T QUITE MAKE THE CUT
MATRIX
REVOLUTIONS
Or, how Neo figured out that Agent Smith was set to Read-Only
(and remembered his DOS commands)
COPYRIGHT © 2003 ILLIAD HTTP://WWW.USERFRIENDLY.ORG/

S.C.O. AND I.B.M. MEET TO DISCUSS A POSSIBLE SETTLEMENT...
AND OVER HERE WE HAVE MISTER...UH...WE HAVE THE REPRESENTATIVE FROM S.C.O.
YES. THANK YOU.

AS THE DULY AUTHORIZED REPRESENTATIVE OF S.C.O., I'M HERE TO ANNOUNCE THAT WE ARE UNWILLING TO BUDGE ON OUR TERMS. WE REQUIRE THE UTTER AND COMPLETE DEST-RUCTION OF LINUX. AND I.B.M. WILL ASSIST US IN THIS LAWFUL ENDEAVOUR OR FACE OUR WRATH!

FOR PITY'S SAKE WE'RE JUST A LITTLE TECH COMPANY TRYING TO MAKE ITS WAY IN THIS HARD WORLD! COME. **TAKE MY HAND** AND WE WILL RULE THE SECTOR **TOGETHER! LINUX MUST DIE!** WE SHALL **PREVAIL!**
BILL. THEY CAN SEE YOUR SHIRT SLEEVE.

HELLO. GREG SPEAKING.
HI. I'M HAVING A PROBLEM GETTING TO SAVEMARTHA.COM
EH?

SAVEMARTHA.COM. MY FANS STARTED THIS WEBSITE TO SUPPORT ME IN MY HOUR OF NEED WHAT WITH ALL OF THOSE FRAUD CHARGES.

THERE IS **NO** WAY. YOU'RE NOT MARTHA STEWART...
GREAT! COULD YOU FLY OUT AND CON-VINCE THE DISTRICT ATTORNEY OF THAT?

GEEZ. YOU'RE GETTING A BUM RAP. MARTHA. YOU REALLY SEEM TO HAVE ENEMIES.
TELL ME ABOUT IT.

I THINK IT HAS TO DO WITH ME BEING SUCH A SUCCESSFUL BUSINESSWOMAN. I'M WEALTHY BEYOND BELIEF AND FAMOUS THANKS TO THE MEDIA. THERE ARE LOTS OF JEALOUS PEOPLE IN THE GENERAL PUBLIC.

WHICH BRINGS ME TO A QUESTION...WHY DO SO MANY **GEEKS** HATE ME? I'VE DONE **NOTHING** TO THEM!
IT'S SUBCON-SCIOUS. IT HAS TO DO WITH YOUR INITIALS.

ARE YOU WORRIED ABOUT GOING TO JAIL. MARTHA?
OF COURSE I AM! WHO WOULDN'T BE?

PRISON IS A TERRIFYING JOURNEY THROUGH THE CONCRETE JUNGLE OF ANGER. WITH ALL OF YOUR LIBERTIES STRIPPED FROM YOU. THE GUILTY AND THE INNOCENT ARE THROWN TOGETHER IN THE PAINFUL CRUCIBLE OF CONVICTION.

NOT TO MENTION. HORIZONTAL STRIPES MAKE YOU LOOK FAT.
GOOD GOD! THAT'S IT. I'M HIRING MORE LAWYERS!

YOU KNOW. IT'S ENTIRELY POSSIBLE YOU'RE A GEEK MARTHA...
WHAT? ME?
COPYRIGHT©2003 ILLIAD HTTP://WWW.USERFRIENDLY.ORG/

SURE! YOU'RE INTERESTED IN HOW THINGS WORK; YOU LIKE TO FIGURE THINGS OUT ON YOUR OWN. AND LET ME ASK YOU THIS: WHICH WOULD YOU PREFER. A G.P.S. UNIT OR A BAR OF GOLD?

WELL...BOTH OF THEM. THEY'RE BOTH SHINY.
SHE'S A SUPER GEEK. SUPER GEEK! SHE'S SUPER GEEKY!

THANK YOU FOR YOUR HELP YOUNG MAN.
IT'S WHAT I GET PAID TO DO. WHAT ARE YOU GOING TO DO NOW. MARTHA?
COPYRIGHT©2003 ILLIAD HTTP://WWW.USERFRIENDLY.ORG/

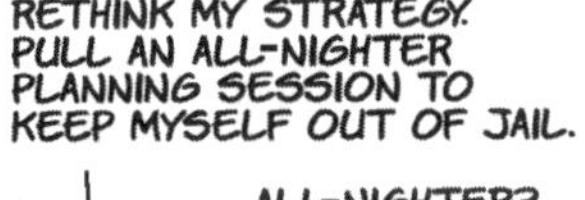
RETHINK MY STRATEGY. PULL AN ALL-NIGHTER PLANNING SESSION TO KEEP MYSELF OUT OF JAIL.

ALL-NIGHTER? YOU KNOW WHAT THAT MEANS...

YES GREG. I CAN FEEL THE URGE FOR CAFFEINE EVEN NOW...
SOMETIMES I REALLY HATE MY JOB...
HALF FRAP DECAF MOCHA CARAMEL CHAI LATTE WITH EXTRA FOAM ON THE SIDE NO WHIP.
BIG BUCKS COFFEE

What a crappy execution of a brilliant idea and song parody. Who writes these things, anyway?

USER FRIENDLY
the comic strip
BY J.D. "ILLIAD" FRAZER
COPYRIGHT©2003 ILLIAD HTTP://WWW.USERFRIENDLY.ORG/

AHEM
KEEP IT DOWN PLEASE. I AM ABOUT TO PONTIFICATE.

"LOG ON? ON ALL THE TIME! EXPOSE YOUR BELLY FOR JUST 9.95!

CLICK OVER HERE! THIS OFFER'S SINCERE GET A DATE TONIGHT! WITH SOMONE YOUR HEIGHT...

THE HEIGHT OF ILLUSION IDENTITY CONFUSION FUSING CONS WITH IDENTITY... OFF THE NET. THEY'RE NON-ENTITIES.

NON-ENTITIES WHO'VE MISSED THE POINT OF OUR FUN. THE NET IS OUR MATRIX VERSION ZERO POINT ONE."
GOOD HEAVENS THAT WAS BRILLIANT! WAITER! MORE HEAD CHEESE!

G'MORNING GUYS. I'VE BEEN BROUGHT IN TO LEAD ANOTHER PROJECT. AND THIS TIME I NEED ALL OF YOU TO HELP ME AS A TEAM.
COPYRIGHT©2003 ILLIAD HTTP://WWW.USERFRIENDLY.ORG/

AND YOU CAN BEST HELP BY THINKING ABOUT WHAT YOU CAN DO TO MOVE THE PROJECT FORWARD. I KNOW YOU'RE ALL SPECIAL INDIVIDUALS. BUT FOR THIS TO WORK YOU NEED TO HOLD THE TEAM ABOVE YOURSELF. REMEMBER. THERE IS NO "ME" IN "TEAM!"

ANY QUESTIONS OR COMMENTS?
"TEAM" IS AN ANAGRAM FOR "MEAT."

I'VE DONE A LOT OF RESEARCH FOR OUR PROJECT. AND AFTER SOME DUE DILIGENCE. I'VE DISCOVERED THAT THE HOTTEST TECH-NOLOGY VERTICAL OF 2004 WILL BE MIDDLEWARE.
:-(
COPYRIGHT©2003 ILLIAD HTTP://WWW.USERFRIENDLY.ORG/

:-(

AND SO YOU GUYS HAVE TO MAKE SOMETHING THAT'S MIDDLEWARE...SHEESH.
UH...WHAT'S MIDDLEWARE?
BELTS.
THAT WOULD MAKE MY UNDERWEAR A PLUG-IN.

OKAY. SO WE NEED TO CREATE SOMETHING THAT'S EFFECTIVELY A MIDDLEWARE PLUG-IN. WHAT DO WE CALL IT?
:-D
COPYRIGHT©2003 ILLIAD HTTP://WWW.USERFRIENDLY.ORG/

:-D

PIDDLEWARE?
YEAH!
NO!!

DADDY?
GOOD MORNING PEARL! HOW'S THE NEW PROJECT COMING ALONG?
NOT WELL. MIKE. GREG AND A.J. AREN'T MUCH HELP IN DEVELOPMENT.
COPYRIGHT©2003 ILLIAD HTTP://WWW.USERFRIENDLY.ORG/

IT'S NO WONDER. NONE OF THEM ARE CODERS. ASIDE FROM MYSELF. PITR'S THE ONLY REAL CODER HERE.

IS HE REALLY? I THOUGHT HE WAS A NETWORK GUY. HE TOLD ME TO DROP BY ANYTIME AND HE'D SHOW ME HOW TO "PULL CABLE."
PITR!

EXCUSE ME MY VILLAINOUS FRIEND. I'D LIKE A WORD..
NYET. AM BUSY.
COPYRIGHT©2003 ILLIAD HTTP://WWW.USERFRIENDLY.ORG/

OH NO. YOU'RE NOT TOO BUSY FOR ME. I HEAR YOU OFFERED TO TEACH MY DAUGHTER SOMETHING ABOUT "NETWORK CABLING."

DA. AND YOU ARE HERE WHY?
I'M JUST VISITING TO SEE IF I NEED TO "TERMINATE YOUR CABLE."

HEY! CHECK OUT MY NEW CELL PHONE! I LOST MY OLD STARTAC SO I PICKED UP ONE OF THESE NEW SAMSUNGS.
COPYRIGHT©2003 ILLIAD HTTP://WWW.USERFRIENDLY.ORG/

IT'S SMALLER. LIGHTER. IT HAS A HIGHER-RES SCREEN. AN IRIDESCENT SHELL. AND A SOFT CHIME FOR A RINGER.

ALL IN ALL I'D SAY IT'S-
A PHONE FOR PEOPLE WITH VERY FINE BONES.

USER FRIENDLY
THE COMIC STRIP
Three UF Sundays were removed due to being far too derivative of the works of another cartoonist. This spot was for one of them.
Please pretend that this space is funny. Ta.

This was based on reality. I showed my new cell phone to my Significant Other one night while driving, and she very nearly caused me to swerve off the road. What was she hollering? "Must play with light-up toy!" While grabbing at the phone and struggling for it. Crazy wench.

I'M NOT FINE-BONED AND THIS IS A COOL PHONE. I'M GOING TO SWITCH OFF THE LIGHTS TO SHOW YOU WHAT I MEAN.
IF YOU SAY SO. I STILL THINK THAT PHONE IS PANSY-ISH.
COPYRIGHT © 2003 ILLIAD HTTP://WWW.USERFRIENDLY.ORG/

KLIK!
SHINY SHINE SHINE!

MUST PLAY WITH LIGHT-UP TOY!! MUST PLAY WITH LIGHT-UP TOY!! AAAAAAAH!!
STRUGGLE WRASSLE

PHEW. I THINK I MANAGED TO EVADE GREG. WONDER WHERE HE WENT?
COPYRIGHT © 2003 ILLIAD HTTP://WWW.USERFRIENDLY.ORG/

IT'S WAAAY TOO QUIET...

KLIK!
COLA

QUIT IT YOU GUYS! GIVE IT BACK!!
MINE MINE MINE MINE MINE MINE!
NRRRF!
COPYRIGHT © 2003 ILLIAD HTTP://WWW.USERFRIENDLY.ORG/

KA-SNAPP!

NOOOOOO!
BLAST.
DAMNSKI!
HA! I GOT THE BLUE GLOWING PART! I WIN!

I HOPE YOU GUYS ARE SATISFIED. YOU JUST DESTROYED MY NEW AND VERY EXPENSIVE CELL PHONE.
COPYRIGHT © 2003 ILLIAD HTTP://WWW.USERFRIENDLY.ORG/

AAAAAAAAAAHHHHHHHHHHHHH
NNNNGGG

HELLO EVERYONE! I'M SURE SOME OF YOU NOTICED A COUPLE OF DAYS AGO THAT GOOGLE, THAT MAINSTAY OF THE WEB, ACTUALLY RETURNED SERVER ERRORS FOR A SHORT PERIOD OF TIME...

THE OBSERVANT AMONG YOU MAY ALSO HAVE REALIZED THAT ILLIAD DID A STORYLINE ON GOOGLE GOING OFF THE WEB AT THE BEGINNING OF THIS MONTH. WE'RE QUITE SURE ILLIAD ISN'T PSYCHIC, BUT WE'RE TAKING STEPS TO MAKE SURE THAT WE DON'T HAVE ANY OTHER NASTY SURPRISES.

A.J., ILLIAD'S NOT COOPERATING!
I WANT TO DO A STRIP ABOUT STEVE BALLMER POSING IN PLAYGIRL!
SWEET MOSES! MIKE, QUIT SCREWING AROUND AND GET THOSE CRAYONS AWAY FROM HIM NOW!!

AHHHH. WHAT A PEACEFUL DAY. WHAT A PEACEFUL, PEACEFUL DAY.

IT'S SO PEACEFUL I COULD FALL ASLEEP STANDING HERE. PEACE. SERENITY TRANQUILITY...

MEANWHILE, AT A HIGHLY AUTOMATED TELEMARKETING COMPANY DURING AN AUTO-DIALLER CRASH...
WHADDYA MEAN "TECH SUPPORT IS ON THE NATIONAL DO-NOT-CALL REGISTRY?!"

THINGS THAT MAKE YOU GO "HMMMM..." #144

THE RIAA ANNOUNCES INTENTION TO SUE HUNDREDS, POSSIBLY THOUSANDS OF FILE SHARERS. CRITICS QUESTION LOGISTICS INVOLVED.

INTRODUCTION OF THE "METAL STORM" WEAPON SYSTEM, CAPABLE OF DELIVERING A MILLION PROJECTILES OF VARIOUS TYPES PER MINUTE.

HMMMMM...

WHAT...ARE YOU DOING?
DOING BICEP CURLS. IT'S TIME TO GET BUFF! I'M DONE WITH BEING WEAK AND INEFFECTUAL.

COPYRIGHT©2003 ILLIAD HTTP://WWW.USERFRIENDLY.ORG/
WHAT BROUGHT THIS ON?
I JUST GOT BACK FROM WATCHING 'THE HULK.' IT'S A GREAT METAPHOR FOR TECH SUPPORT. WE'RE NICE WHEN EVERYTHING IS NORMAL. BUT WHEN FRUSTRATED AND ANGERED WE BECOME VENGEFUL AND DESTRUCTIVE...

...NOT TO MENTION LOSS OF HIGHER-BRAIN FUNCTION.
HEY! WHA.?! I...! YOU...! EBBI...!

I CAN'T UPLOAD MY WEB PAGE TO YOUR COMPUTERS! FIX IT!
WHAT ARE YOU USING TO FTP THE FILES, SIR?
EFF-TEE-PEE? JUST FIX IT. AND DO IT NOW!
COPYRIGHT©2003 ILLIAD HTTP://WWW.USERFRIENDLY.ORG/

GAK...!

GRAAAA!!

WHAT ARE YOU DOING?
COULD YOU TOSS ME THAT BOTTLE OF GREEN DYE?
HELLO? HELLO?!

THAT'S IT! I'VE HAD IT WITH IGNORANT CALLERS! I'M HULKING UP!
GRAAAA!!!
STRAIN
SWELL
BULGE
COPYRIGHT©2003 ILLIAD HTTP://WWW.USERFRIENDLY.ORG/

GRAAAAAA!...EHHH... GRAAAAAAA!
HELLO? WHAT ABOUT MY WEB SITE? WHAT'S HE DOING?
I THINK HE'S GONE HOSTAL.

WHAT'S GREG DOING LYING ON THE FLOOR?
HE'S BEEN FUMING BECAUSE HE CAN'T "HULK UP" AND SMASH CALLERS.
COPYRIGHT©2003 ILLIAD HTTP://WWW.USERFRIENDLY.ORG/

NOW WHY DOES THAT EXPRESSION OF HIS LOOK SO FAMILIAR..?

I KNOW! THAT'S...THAT'S...!
...THE INCREDIBLE SULK.
SHQDDUP.

ISN'T THAT GREG'S XBOX?
YEEEUP.
COPYRIGHT©2003 ILLIAD HTTP://WWW.USERFRIENDLY.ORG/

I'M TRYING TO FIGURE OUT THE HACK THAT THOSE AUSSIE RESEARCHERS DID THAT ALLOWS YOU TO RUN LINUX ON IT WITHOUT A MOD CHIP.
SO I'M HAVING A CONVERSATION WITH IT. HUSH NOW.

WHAT'S IT SAYING?
"WOULD SOMEONE PLEASE GET THAT HALO GAME MUSIC OUT OF MY HEAD."

TECH SUPPORT. THE CHOSEN SACRIFICIAL LAMB SPEAKING.
HELLO. I JUST BOUGHT A VERY EXPENSIVE PC AND NOW MY SON WANTS AN XBOX.
COPYRIGHT©2003 ILLIAD HTTP://WWW.USERFRIENDLY.ORG/

AND WHAT AM I SUPPOSED TO DO ABOUT IT?
ARE YOU A GEEK OR AREN'T YOU?! MY SON DOESN'T WANT THIS PC. HE WANTS AN XBOX!

NOW WHAT DO I DO?! AND I'M NOT SPENDING ANOTHER DIME!
FINE. PICK UP THE PC AND LOB IT OUT THE WINDOW. VOILA! EX-BOX!

IN "TERMINATOR 4" IT IS REVEALED THAT "SKYNET'S" ACTUAL NAME IS ".NET"
THEN, AT THE UNIVERSITY OF HELSINKI, 1991...
LINUS TORVALDS?
COPYRIGHT©2003 ILLIAD HTTP://WWW.USERFRIENDLY.ORG/

UMM...HELLO.
MY NAME IS A.J....
HELLO A.J.
HEY MAN...
GO A.J.!

JEEZ. THIS IS HARD FOR HIM...
POOR GUY...
GIVE HIM A MINUTE WILL YOU?
COPYRIGHT©2003 ILLIAD HTTP://WWW.USERFRIENDLY.ORG/

...AND I'M AN I.T. WORKER.
HEY BUDDY. WE'RE HERE FOR YOU.
LET IT ALL OUT BRO...
CRIPES. WHAT A DORK.

WE HEAR YOU AND FEEL FOR YOU BROTHER. WHAT IS IT YOU DO IN INFORMATION TECHNOLOGY?
COPYRIGHT©2003 ILLIAD HTTP://WWW.USERFRIENDLY.ORG/

SORRY. SAY AGAIN? COULDN'T HEAR YOU THERE...
I'M A WEB DESIGNER.

WHAT DID HE SAY?
I THINK HE SAID HE'S A "DOT COM C.E.O."
OH. THAT'S OKAY THEN. FOR A SCARY SECOND I THOUGHT HE SAID "WEB DESIGNER."

SOMEONE. PLEASE EXPLAIN TO ME WHY I.T. WORKERS ARE VILIFIED! AND JUST BECAUSE OF A FEW BAD APPLES, WE'RE ALL TREATED LIKE LEPERS, PARIAHS AND EVEN MONSTERS!
COPYRIGHT©2003 ILLIAD HTTP://WWW.USERFRIENDLY.ORG/

...UH...

NOT REALLY FEELING YOUR PAIN THERE. BROTHER.
NOPE. CAN'T SAY WE DO.
THERE ARE NO ATHEISTS BEHIND PODIUMS.

...SORRY FATHERS. I HADN'T REALIZED THAT THERE WERE SO MANY PRIESTS HERE.
THAT'S OKAY SON! PRIESTS USE COMPUTERS TOO! SINCE WE'RE HERE, CAN WE UNBURDEN YOU BY HEARING A CONFESSION?
COPYRIGHT©2003 ILLIAD HTTP://WWW.USERFRIENDLY.ORG/

WELL...

OH COME ON. EVERYONE HAS SOMETHING.
I PICK MY NOSE WITH MY MOUSING FINGER.

THANK YOU FOR THE SUPPORT, FATHERS. IT HELPED QUITE A BIT.
BEFORE YOU GO, SON, HAVE YOU ACCEPTED GOD IN YOUR LIFE?
COPYRIGHT©2003 ILLIAD HTTP://WWW.USERFRIENDLY.ORG/

HAVE I..? OH...UH...

I PRAY FERVENTLY WHENEVER I RESTORE BACKUPS IF THAT'S WHAT YOU MEAN.
I THINK IT'S TIME TO BREAK THE "JAWBONE OF AN ASS."

YOU KNOW, A.J. SHOWING SUCH COURAGE HAS HELPED ME COME UP HERE TONIGHT. HELLO, MY NAME IS FATHER BORIS...AND I'M A SPAMMER.
COLLECTIVE *GASP!*
COPYRIGHT©2003 ILLIAD HTTP://WWW.USERFRIENDLY.ORG/

THAT'S RIGHT...I'M THE ONE WHO'S BEEN SENDING ALL OF THOSE SPAM MAILS SELLING VIAGRA HOLY WAFERS. AND...UH...WHY ARE YOU ALL LOOKING AT ME THAT W--

HURT HIM! HURT HIM! POKE OUT HIS NAKED EYES!
AIIIIIIEEEEE!!!
WHAT HAPPENED TO "LOVE THY NEIGHBOUR?"
HE'S NO NEIGHBOUR! HE'S AT LEAST ELEVEN ROUTER HOPS FROM ME!

USER FRIENDLY
the comic strip
BY J.D. "ILLIAD" FRAZER
COPYRIGHT©2003 ILLIAD HTTP://WWW.USERFRIENDLY.ORG/

WHAT ARE WE RECORDING?
YE GODS. IT'S THE NEW S.C.O. ANTHEM. SUNG TO "THE LOCOMOTION."
AREN'T S.C.O. FULL OF BAD PEOPLE?

YEAH. REAL BAD. YO, BERTRAND? NOT GONNA DO THIS ONE.
KYLIE MINOGUE DID "THE LOCOMOTION" FIFTEEN YEARS AGO. SHE'S COMING TO WATCH.
WE ARE SO ON IT.

S.C.O. HAS FOUND A NEW WAY TO FINANCE NOW!
(COME ON BABY, FILE A LEGAL MOTION!)
SHAREHOLDERS OUGHTA LIKE IT IF THEY GIVE IT A CHANCE NOW!
(COME ON BABY, FILE A LEGAL MOTION!)

SINCE NOVELL AND I.B.M. HAVE COME INTO THE FEUD
SAY THAT YOU USE LINUX AND YOU TOO CAN BE SUED!
SO COME ON! COME ON!
FILE A LEGAL MOTION WITH ME!

YOU GOTTA SWING YOUR CENSORED NOW!
COME ON BABY! SWING UP! SWING BACK!
WELL I THINK YOU GOT THE KNACK!
OHHHHH! --- A.J?
WHERE YOU GOING?
I'M NOT DOING THAT EVEN FOR KYLIE.
I DON'T THINK I EVEN HAVE ONE OF THOSE.

DO YOU HEAR THAT?
HEARINK WHAT?
HTTP://WWW.USERFRIENDLY.ORG/
COPYRIGHT©2003 ILLIAD

WHEEEEEEEEEEEEEEEEEEEEEEEEE

THAT.
OH. YOU ARE MEANINK THE FAIRLY INAUDIBLE WHINE COMINK FROM MY CELL PHONE, DA?
NO. I MEAN THE ANEURISM-INDUCING TONE THAT I'M GOING TO CRAM DOWN YOUR FACE IN A SECOND.

IS TONE AM DOWNLOADINK FROM A COMPANY IN KOREA. IS KEEPINK AWAY MOSQUITOS.
REALLY.
HTTP://WWW.USERFRIENDLY.ORG/
COPYRIGHT©2003 ILLIAD

HAVE BEEN WORKINK ON NEW TONE. AM TO BE WERY RICH IF IS WORKINK RIGHT.

AND IT KEEPS AWAY MOSQUITOS AS WELL?
NYET. OTHER KIND OF BLOODSUCKER.
Double Opt-in Only! Spam is Illegal!
PLEASE MAKE IT STOP!

WELL. THAT'S QUITE A GIMMICK. CAN YOU-
DEE DEE DEEE
DEE DEE DEEE
DI DI DI DI
DEE DEE DEEE
HTTP://WWW.USERFRIENDLY.ORG/
COPYRIGHT©2003 ILLIAD

AAAAAAAAAAAAAAAAGGHH! WHAT IS THAT? MAKE IT STOP!
IS COMINK FROM STEF'S OFFICE.
DI DI DEE
DEE DEE
DI DI DI
DI DEEEE

LET ME GUESS...YOU DOWNLOADED A GEEK REPELLENT SOUND INTO YOUR PHONE?
WHAT? IT'S JUST MY STANDARD RING TONE.
IS THE "BARNEY" SONG YOU ZLOTNIK!
...DI DI DEE
DEE DEE DI DI DI
DI DI DEE

I LOVE YOU! YOU LOVE ME! WE'RE A HAPPY FAM-
WHAT ARE YOU-HEY!!
HTTP://WWW.USERFRIENDLY.ORG/
COPYRIGHT©2003 ILLIAD

EEEEEEEEHHHHHHHHHHHHHHHHH
WHAT'S THAT NOISE?
THAT WOULD BE ONE OF THOSE "FAIRLY INAUDIBLE WHINES."
JUST GIVE WORD. CAN BE MAKINK IT WERY AUDIBLE.

SAY AGAIN? SMILING MAN WENT **WHERE?**
HE HEARD ABOUT ALL THE OFFSHORE OUTSOURCING GOING ON IN I.T.. SO HE LEFT TO INTERVIEW SOME CHEAPER TECH LABOUR.

COPYRIGHT © 2003 ILLIAD HTTP://WWW.USERFRIENDLY.ORG/
BUT WHERE DID HE GO? AND IS HE AWARE THAT COUNTRIES THAT ORIGINALLY HAD CHEAP TECH LABOUR ARE LOSING OUT TO OTHER COUNTRIES WITH EVEN CHEAPER TECHS?
HE DID SAY SOMETHING ABOUT "HEADING THE WORLD OFF AT THE PASS."

JUST SAY IT! SAY "PLEASE REBOOT YOUR MACHINE" AND YOU'RE HIRED!
HUH?

THANKS FOR COMING TO SEE ME, GREG. WE'VE OUTSOURCED OUR FIRST-TIER TECH SUPPORT TO INDIA. WE'RE GOING TO HAVE TO CUT YOUR HOURS BY HALF.
BY **HALF?!** WHAT AM I GOING TO DO?
SORRY, GUY. MAYBE YOU CAN FIND A PART-TIME JOB SOME-WHERE.

COPYRIGHT © 2003 ILLIAD HTTP://WWW.USERFRIENDLY.ORG/
SO I'VE BEEN REPLACED BY SOMEONE FROM INDIA, HAVE I? WELL, I'LL JUST HAVE TO DO SOME REPLACING MYSELF!!

YO, EINSTEIN! THE SLUSHIE MACHINE IS RUNNING WET!

CNN'S INTERNAL "HOW MUCH CAN WE CHARGE FOR A 30-SECOND COMMERCIAL" DIALOG BOX

CNN

	Headline Keywords	Base Value
☐	Canada	$10,000
☐	Marijuana	$15,000
☐	Atheists	$15,000
☐	Intelligence	$20,000
☑	White House	$25,000
☑	Showdown	$30,000
☐	Un-American	$40,000
☐	Patriotic	$45,000
☐	Saddam	$50,000
☐	Iraq	$50,000
☑	Axis of Evil	$75,000
☑	The Middle East	$80,000
☐	Osama	$90,000
☐	WMDs	$100,000
☐	Smoking Gun	$150,000

Experts hired for on-air discussion	Value Multiple
○ Military General	x100%
○ Annoying Political Mouthpiece	x200%
◉ Blonde with Enormous Assets in an air conditioned newsroom	x500%

Follow-up Headline with:	Value Multiple
○ Retraction	x50%
○ Correction	x50%
◉ Retraction labelled as "Breaking News"	x200%
○ Correction labelled as "Exclusive Information"	x400%

Headline delivered by:	Value Multiple
○ Urbane Male with White Teeth	x100%
○ Person of Colour with Neutral Accent	x150%
◉ Blonde with Enormous Assets in an air conditioned newsroom	x500%

Clear | Calculate

I CAN'T BELIEVE I'M WORKING AT A CONVENIENCE STORE. AFTER NEARLY A DECADE AS A SUPPORT TECHNICIAN. EARNING MY CRED. IT'S COME TO THIS.
welcome to MACS CONVENIENCE STORE
COPYRIGHT © 2003 ILLIAD HTTP://WWW.USERFRIENDLY.ORG/

I SUPPOSE IT COULD BE WORSE. I'M MAKING SOME MONEY. I'M NOT ON THE STREET. AND I'M STILL EATING. ALBEIT MACARONI AND CHEESE.
welcome to MACS CONVENIENCE STORE

AND BEST OF ALL, NO STUPID CALLERS!
EXCUSE ME. MY CD-ROM TRAY ISN'T WORKING.
CUPHOLDER
welcome to MACS CONVENIENCE STORE

LOOK. I BOUGHT THIS CD-ROM TRAY HERE. AND IT DOESN'T WORK. I WANT A REFUND.
WHADDYA MEAN "CD-ROM TRAY?" THAT'S A CUPHOLDER!
CUPHOLDER
welcome to MACS 37th CONVENIENCE STORE
COPYRIGHT © 2003 ILLIAD HTTP://WWW.USERFRIENDLY.ORG/

THE GUY I SPOKE TO ON THE PHONE TOLD ME IN NO UNCERTAIN TERMS THAT IT WASN'T A CUPHOLDER. IT'S A CD-ROM TRAY.
CUPHOLDER
welcome to MACS 37th CONVENIENCE STORE

IT'S NOT A CD-ROM TRAY. LOOK AT THE BOX! IT SAYS "CUPHOLDER" ON IT! WHAT RETARD TOLD YOU IT WAS A CD-ROM TRAY?
SOME GUY AT COLUMBIA INTERNET. ABOUT A WEEK AGO. I THINK HIS NAME WAS GREG.
CUPHOLDER
welcome to MACS 37th CONVENIENCE STORE

SO THIS, UH, GREG FELLOW AT COLUMBIA INTERNET TOLD YOU THIS WAS A CD-ROM TRAY.
HE SURELY DID.
CUPHOLDER
welcome to CONVENT SORES CAM
COPYRIGHT © 2003 ILLIAD HTTP://WWW.USERFRIENDLY.ORG/

YOU MIGHT WANT TO GIVE THE MANUFACTURER'S TECH SUPPORT LINE A CALL FIRST. THEY GUARANTEE THEIR PRODUCTS WORK OR THEY'LL SEND YOU TRIPLE YOUR MONEY BACK. HERE'S THE NUMBER...
CUPHOLDER
welcome to CONVENT SORES CAM

IS THIS LONG DISTANCE? WHAT COUNTRY CODE IS THAT?
INDIA.
CUPHOLDER
CONVENT SORES CAM

WELL, THAT'S MY FIRST SHIFT FINISHED AS A CONVENIENCE STORE CLERK. I GUESS IT WASN'T ALL THAT BAD.
COPYRIGHT © 2003 ILLIAD HTTP://WWW.USERFRIENDLY.ORG/

IT'S HUMBLING THOUGH. I'VE MASTERED SO MANY ASPECTS OF CONSUMER COMPUTING. GUIDED AND ADVISED THE UNKNOWING IN SAVING THEIR PRECIOUS DATA. AND NOW I SELL SLUSHIES FOR A LIVING.

I THINK I'VE SUNK ABOUT AS LOW AS A TECH COULD SINK.
DUDE, SPARE SOME COIN FOR A CAFFEINE HIT?

SYSTEM ADMINISTRATOR
APPRECIATION DAY
JULY 25, 2003

To:______________ From:______________

Dear Wondrous SysAdmin,
I present to you this small printed token of appreciation in recognition of the fact that you could easily turn my e-mail address into a spam sewer if I didn't. I pity the fool who doesn't give you one of these today. I am not worthy. Please hurt someone else.

PLEASE. JUST A QUARTER OR TWO. I REALLY NEED MY CAFFEINE.
SORRY MAN. I DON'T HAVE ANY CHANGE ON ME.
WANTED

THAT'S OKAY. WHEN YOU GET HOME, HIT MY WEB-SITE AND YOU CAN FIRE FIFTY CENTS MY WAY.
WANTED
COPYRIGHT©2003 ILLIAD HTTP://WWW.USERFRIENDLY.ORG/

...WEBSITE? FIFTY CENTS?
MICROPAYMENTS, MAN! IT'S ALL OVER THE STREET!
WANTED

NOTHING EXPLAINS CURRENT EVENTS AS WELL AS HISTORY
HEY, I WANTED TO TALK TO YOU ABOUT ME TELECOMMUTING TWO DAYS A WEEK...
COPYRIGHT©2003 ILLIAD HTTP://WWW.USERFRIENDLY.ORG/

IT WASN'T ALWAYS LIKE THIS. I HAD A JOB AS A SYSTEMS INTEGRATOR FOR A WHILE. THAT WAS GOOD WORK AND I MADE GOOD MONEY. THEN I GOT LAID OFF. THAT WAS MORE THAN TWO YEARS AGO, AND NOT A TECH JOB TO BE SEEN FROM HERE TO THE HORIZON SINCE THEN.
COPYRIGHT © 2003 ILLIAD HTTP://WWW.USERFRIENDLY.ORG/

HAVE YOU TRIED LOOKING ELSEWHERE? RETAIL? WAITING TABLES? WHAT ABOUT WAREHOUSING?
COME ON MAN. I HAVE MY DIGNITY! I'M INTELLIGENT. SKILLED. ELOQUENT...

YES, BUT I'M STILL A TECH!
...AND HOMELESS.

YE FLIPPING GODS. WHAT IS THAT?
IS "NIGHT PEARL" FISH. THEY ARE BEINK GENETICALLY MODIFIED IN TAIWAN.
IT'S GLOWING GREEN.
COPYRIGHT © 2003 ILLIAD HTTP://WWW.USERFRIENDLY.ORG/

DA. GENES INJECTED FROM SOME GLOWINK JELLYFISH.
AREN'T GENETICALLY MODIFIED ORGANISMS DANGEROUS?
COME NOW! THIS IS FISH! MAYBE A GLOWINK FISH, BUT IS STILL JUST A FISH.

WELL...OKAY. I'M GONNA GO GET A COLA.
AM TO BE JOININK YOU.

I LIVE.
HUH?

EXCUSE ME... DID YOU SAY SOMETHING?
COPYRIGHT © 2003 ILLIAD HTTP://WWW.USERFRIENDLY.ORG/

PHEW...FOR A SECOND THERE I THOUGHT THAT THE RUMOURS OF GENETICALLY MODIFIED ORGANISMS BEING EVIL WERE TR-
I'LL SWALLOW YOUR SOUL.

WHAT ON EARTH ARE YOU SCREAMING ABOUT?
THE GLOWING FISH! IT'S EVIL AND IT SAYS EVIL, HORRIBLE THINGS!! MAKE IT STOP!
COPYRIGHT © 2003 ILLIAD HTTP://WWW.USERFRIENDLY.ORG/

MM-HM.
I FIND YOUR LACK OF PANTS DISTURBING.
AAAAAAAAAGGH!!

IT'S JUST A PRETTY GLOWING FISH. LI'L GUY. I'LL PROVE IT TO YOU.
...PRETTY? PROVE IT? WHAT ARE YOU...

COPYRIGHT©2003 ILLIAD HTTP://WWW.USERFRIENDLY.ORG/
CLICK

SO WAS THAT COOL OR WHAT?
CLICK

COPYRIGHT©2003 ILLIAD HTTP://WWW.USERFRIENDLY.ORG/

...UNTIL THE HEAT DEATH OF THE UNIVERSE...

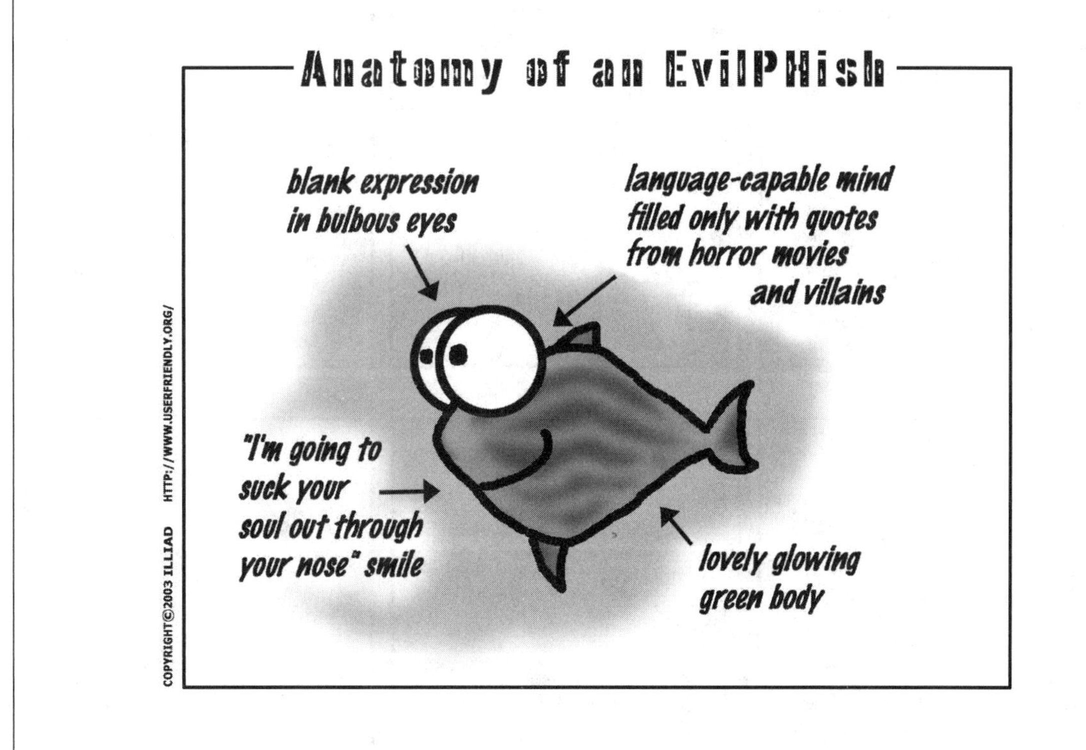
Anatomy of an EvilPHish
blank expression in bulbous eyes
language-capable mind filled only with quotes from horror movies and villains
"I'm going to suck your soul out through your nose" smile
lovely glowing green body
COPYRIGHT©2003 ILLIAD HTTP://WWW.USERFRIENDLY.ORG/

If you go to the website, you'll see a GIF animation at work. It's scary. Ooooooh.

THAT CAN'T BE PART OF THE JOB, MISTER PATEL.
WELL, IT IS. DO IT OR YOU'RE FIRED.
welcome to CONCOCTS A SIEMENS NERVE
AOL
COPYRIGHT©2003 ILLIAD HTTP://WWW.USERFRIENDLY.ORG/

welcome to CONCOCTS A SIEMENS
AOL

WOULD YOU LIKE TO BUY A CD THAT GIVES YOU 700 HOURS OF ACCESS TO A RETARDED VERSION OF THE 'NET AND THEN GATHERS YOUR INFO FOR SALE TO SPAMMERS THE WORLD OVER?
OKAY!
welcome to CONCOCTS A SIEMENS
AOL

SIX BAGS OF NACHOS, TEN SIX-PACKS OF COLA, A DOZEN AERO BARS, SIX BAGS OF PORK RINDS. THAT'LL BE FORTY-TWO FIFTY, PLEASE.
HERE YA GO.
welcome to MACS OPEN SORES
AOL
COPYRIGHT©2003 ILLIAD HTTP://WWW.USERFRIENDLY.ORG/

welcome to MACS OPEN SORES
AOL

WHY YES, IT'S ALL FOR A NIGHT OF SERIOUS TECHNICAL WORK.
YE TAPDANCING GODS, PLEASE TAKE ME WITH YOU!!
welcome to MACS OPEN SORES
AOL

HERE'S A BAG OF CHIPS. IT'S THE BEST I COULD DO.
THANKS, MAN. IT ALL HELPS.
COPYRIGHT©2003 ILLIAD HTTP://WWW.USERFRIENDLY.ORG/

UH...WHAT'S THAT GUY DOING OVER THERE IN THE INTERSECTION STICKING HIS HEAD IN THAT CAR?

OH, THAT'S CYRIL. HE'S JUST TRYING TO MAKE SOME COIN.
MY LAPTOP DOESN'T NEED FIXING AND I'M NOT GONNA PAY YOU FOR IT!
DUDE, YOU WERE WIDE OPEN! I WANT A BUCK FOR EVERY PORT I CLOSED FOR YOU!

EXCUSE, PLEASE. YOU ARE SEEINK LEETLE EVILPHISH?
SMILING MAN TOOK HIM.
COPYRIGHT©2003 ILLIAD HTTP://WWW.USERFRIENDLY.ORG/

WHAT?! HE IS TAKINK HIM WHY?
I THINK HE LOST A SMILING MATCH. AND THEN HE WALKED AWAY CACKLING WITH EVILPHISH UNDER HIS ARM...

FLUSSSSSHHHHHH!
HAH! WHO'S THE BIG MAN NOW?!

DUDE? WHAT HAPPENED TO EVILPHISH?
SMILINK MAN. HE IS FLUSHINK HIM DOWN TOILET.

WHAT?! YOU'RE **KIDDING!!**
NYET. BUT AM CONSOLED. LEETLE FISH LEAVINK BIOLOGICAL LEGACY.

"BIOLOGICAL LEGACY?"
HEY. WHO BROUGHT THE CAVIAR? IT TASTES FUNNY.

IS TERRIBLE THING. LOSINK EVILPHISH AND HIS LEGACY.
YEAH. WHAT A WAY TO GO.

POOR LEETLE FELLOW. AM HOPINK HE IS NOT SUFFERINK.
THERE'RE ALLIGATORS IN THE SEWERS. HE PROBABLY WENT FAST.

I SWEAR TO GOD, MOE. IT'S A LEATHER BELT, AND THERE'RE DOZENS OF THEM HERE...

IN LATE AUGUST, MARS WILL MAKE ITS CLOSEST APPROACH TO EARTH SINCE PREHISTORIC TIMES...

WAIT A MINUTE, THAT'S NO PLANET...

HASTUR! DUDE! THE STARS ARE FINALLY RIGHT! I CAN ARISE AND USHER IN A NEW AGE OF DARKNESS! SEE? THAT ONE FINAL STAR THERE MOVED INTO THE CORRECT POSITION!
DUDE. THAT'S MARS.
COPYRIGHT © 2003 ILLIAD HTTP://WWW.USERFRIENDLY.ORG/

OH.
S.C.O. WOULDA STOLEN YOUR THUNDER ANYWAYS.

HEY GREG. YOU ON NIGHTS NOW?
YEAH. I'M WORKING AT THE CONVENIENCE STORE DURING THE DAY.
COPYRIGHT © 2003 ILLIAD HTTP://WWW.USERFRIENDLY.ORG/

CONVENIENCE STORE. REALLY? AND I HAD ALWAYS PEGGED YOU AS THE GUY WHO WOULD NEVER EVER DO ANYTHING THAT WASN'T SOMEHOW TECH RELATED.

I SELL CHIPS THERE. OKAY?!

Why people puzzle over the popularity—indeed, the addiction—of MMORPGs is beyond me. Lots of folks feel powerless in this world. In the online world, you are a prince, or a great wizard, or a beautiful shadow warrior, and you're respected by your allies and your enemies. All for only $14.95 a month and the utter destruction of your mortgage and your marriage.

I HATE MY LIFE. I WORK THE MOST BORING SHIFT IN MY TECH JOB AND I SELL CONVENIENCE GOODS IN MY OTHER JOB. BLAH.
COPYRIGHT © 2003 ILLIAD HTTP://WWW.USERFRIENDLY.ORG/

I'M RESOLVED TO LEAVE THIS ALL BEHIND. I NEED A CHANGE. A MOVE TO A PLACE WHERE MY PROSPECTS AND LIFE ARE BETTER. WHERE I'LL FEEL IN CONTROL ONCE AGAIN.

WELCOME TO ULTIMA ONLINE. EXECUTE WHICH MACRO MY LORD?
REPRESS THE PEASANTRY.

NOW THAT'S WHAT I'M TALKIN' ABOUT! LIVING A DIFFERENT LIFE IN THE ULTIMA ONLINE UNIVERSE. LIVING A LIFE LESS TRAVELLED.
HAIL, GOOD SIR!
COPYRIGHT © 2003 ILLIAD HTTP://WWW.USERFRIENDLY.ORG/

AND HERE I SEE A FELLOW PLAYER. COME TO VISIT AND ESCAPE WITH ME FROM A PLEBIAN EXISTANCE IN OUR ALTER-EGOS...
HAIL! HOW MAY I HELP THEE?
PRAY, SELL ME A LOAF OF YOUR FINE BREAD!

OF COURSE! A LOAF OF BREAD IS BUT FOUR GOLD PIECES AND...

* YOU HAVE JUST BLUDGEONED YOUR CUSTOMER WITH A ROLLING PIN.*
YEAH!

THAT WASN'T VERY NICE OF ME. THAT PLAYER WAS PROBABLY JUST LOOKING FOR SOME LIGHT-HEARTED FUN AND I HAD TO GO AND KILL HIS CHARACTER.
YOUR ORDERS, MY LORD?

LOOTING THE BODY MY LORD!
BEING EVIL MEANS IT CAN BE CHRISTMAS EVERY DAY.
TAP
TIP
TAPPY
TAP

HEY. GREG.
A.J.! WHAT'RE YOU DOING HERE SO LATE?
OH. JUST PLAYING A LITTLE ULTIMA ONLINE...
REALLY.

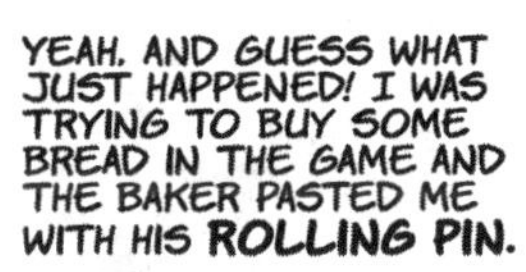
YEAH. AND GUESS WHAT JUST HAPPENED! I WAS TRYING TO BUY SOME BREAD IN THE GAME AND THE BAKER PASTED ME WITH HIS ROLLING PIN.

HOW AWFUL! ANYTHING I CAN DO TO HELP?
YEAH. YOU WOULDN'T HAPPEN TO KNOW WHO "LORD GREG. THE ONE WHOM LUSERS SHOULD PHEAR" WOULD BE. WOULD YOU?

THE TRUTH BEHIND THE POWER OUTAGES ACROSS EASTERN NORTH AMERICA.

* "GEE. I WONDER WHAT THIS LI'L SWITCH DOES... MOOOAHAHAHAHA!!!!" IN GRUE.

WAS THAT GREG I JUST SAW STAGGERING OUT OF HERE?
YEAH. HE WAS HERE ALL NIGHT. I LEFT AT TWO IN THE MORNING AND HE WAS STILL PLAYING ULTIMA ONLINE.

HE WAS HERE ALL NIGHT PLAYING THAT BLOODY GAME? DOESN'T HE HAVE TO WORK AT HIS OTHER JOB?
YEAH. RIGHT NOW. HE SAID HE WAS "PLAYING FOR PURELY ECONOMIC REASONS."

$50.00
+20 MACE OF THWAPPAGE
ULTIMA ONLINE
ASK ME!
welcome to
SORE CRAM VENT

DUDE. BE COOL. I HAVE A GUN HERE.
AAAAAGH! BAD MAN!
welcome to
CREAM VAN

GET BACK FROM UNDER THERE! I WANT YOU TO PUT ALL OF THE CASH IN A... IN A...UH. HEY... WILL YOU TAKE FORTY...
HIDE!
welcome to
CREAM VAN

POW!

WELL DONE, CITIZEN! GOOD THING I GOT HERE JUST NOW...WHAT WOULD YOU HAVE DONE IF I HADN'T?
UH...LOOTED THE BODY?
EHHHH...

HEY MAN. STAYING LATE AGAIN?
YEP! PLAYING MORE ULTIMA ONLINE.

I JUST BOUGHT THIS NEW "MACE OF THWAPPAGE" FROM SOME GUY ON EBAY. IT SHOULD MAKE THE GAME A LITTLE MORE FUN.
VERY COOL! I SOLD MINE ON EBAY JUST TODAY!

WAIT A SECOND...
ANOTHER CITIZEN HAS JUST THWAPPED THEE! RIGHT IN THE KISSER!
YEAH! LOOT THE BODY!

CHIEF. YOU HEAR ABOUT THE VIRUS THAT SHUT DOWN AIR CANADA?
YES. LOOKS LIKE IT'S BEEN A BAD WEEK FOR VIRUSES AND WORMS.

BAD FOR NORMAL PEOPLE LIKE ME AND YOU. GEEKS HAVE THEIR BASES COVERED. YOU DON'T SEE THEM SUFFERING.

MIKE? WHAT'S IT MEAN WHEN MY COMPUTER SAYS "LOVE YOU SAN!"?
KILL ME NOW.

APWIRE - SECURITY OFFICIALS SAID THE VIRUS-LIKE WORM, DUBBED "LOVSAN," WAS PART OF A COORDINATED ELECTRONIC ATTACK THAT EXPLOITED ONE OF THE MOST SERIOUS FLAWS YET DISCOVERED IN MICROSOFT CORP.'S WINDOWS OPERATING SYSTEMS...
"TO ALL STAFF: GIVEN THE RECENT RASH OF WORMS AND VIRUSES, PLEASE TAKE EXTRA CARE WITH THE STANDARD VIRUS INFECTION PROTOCOLS.
THANKS, MIKE"
(CNN) -- THE SOBIG.F COMPUTER VIRUS -- WHICH HAS ALREADY OVERWHELMED HUNDREDS OF THOUSANDS OF COMPUTERS WORLDWIDE -- HAS BECOME THE FASTEST SPREADING VIRUS EVER WITH EXPERTS WARNING THE WORST IS YET TO COME.
MY MACHINE'S REALLY SLOW ALL OF A SUDDEN. FIX IT.
AAARRRGH!!

RIGHT. LISTEN YOU TWO. WE NEED TO TALK ABOUT HOW YOU GUYS PRACTICE SECURITY PROTOCOLS.
WHAT?
LOOK. AFTER WORKING AT AN I.S.P. FOR OVER HALF A DECADE AND BEING IMMERSED IN THE WEB, WHAT IS THE ONE LESSON YOU'VE LEARNED?!
"CLICK ON EVERYTHING."
NO!!

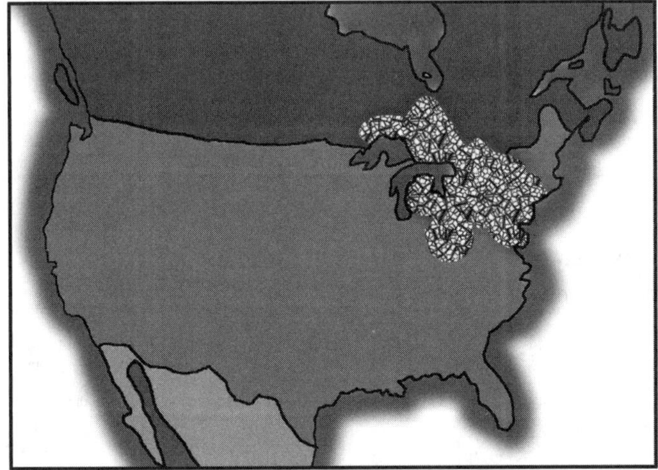

AND IN OTHER NEWS, THE LAST WEEK HAS SEEN A HUGE RISE IN PSYCHOTHERAPY CASES AMONG COMPUTER GAMERS WHO "ALMOST GOT OUT OF THE DUNGEON WITH THE AMULET OF YENDOR."
AFFECTED AREA

STEF YOU HAVE GOT TO STOP CLICKING ON ATTACHMENTS YOU KNOW NOTHING ABOUT!
HEY. I KNOW PLENTY ABOUT ATTACHMENTS!
INCOMING MAIL...

OH REALLY?!
YEAH!
OKAY. WHAT'S A .PIF FILE THEN?
OPENING EMAIL...

A PORNOGRAPHIC .GIF FILE. HA!
AND THUS, THE MISERY IS PROPAGATED...
CLICK! CLICK! CLICK! CLICK!

STEF? DO YOU KNOW WHAT TIME IT IS?
YES CHIEF. IT'S FOUR HOURS AFTER THE MARKETING REPORT WAS DUE.

OH, SO YOU DO KNOW! YES. YOUR REPORT IS LATE AND YOU KNEW I HAD TO HAVE IT THIS MORNING BEFORE I LEFT FOR A MEETING! WOULD YOU CARE TO EXPLAIN WHY IT WASN'T ON MY DESK?

WHY DON'T YOU ASK "IDI ADMIN" OVER THERE?
YOU'LL TOUCH ONE OF MY KEYBOARDS AGAIN WHEN YOU'RE BURIED IN A LANDFILL WITH THEM.

FINE. YOU'RE UNTIED. BUT DON'T EVEN THINK ABOUT ASKING ME FOR ANY KIND OF TECH HELP FOR THE NEXT WEEK!
OKAY! OKAY!
YOU LET STEF GO?

YEAH. I DIDN'T REALLY HAVE A CHOICE. THE CHIEF GOT ON MY CASE, SO I UNTIED HIM...

BUT NOT BEFORE DOING THE OLD TRICK OF TAKING A SCREENSHOT OF HIS DESKTOP, SETTING IT AS THE WALLPAPER AND HIDING ALL OF HIS REAL ICONS.
DUDE. YOU'RE SO NOT GONNA BELIEVE THIS...

I did this once at a company where I doubled as the technologist. On a bunch of old Mac Classics. I was having fits from laughter and hypoxia.

YOU FIXED STEF'S DESKTOP? WHY?
HE WAS GOING TO TELL THE CHIEF. THERE ARE SUBTLER WAYS TO TAKE CARE OF THIS ISSUE.

DO TELL.
I PLUGGED HIS MONITOR INTO MY MACHINE AND MY MONITOR INTO HIS. AFTER I DUPLICATED HIS DESKTOP OF COURSE.

HEADS UP. HE'S MOVING HIS MOUSE!
HEY MIKE? MY MACHINE IS KINDA LAGGY...
NO WORRIES, STEF. I'M SO ON IT!

NOW WHAT'S STEF UP TO? ...AHH, HE'S STARTING UP QUAKE! OKAY THEN, HERE WE GO.

MIMIC HIS MOTION... MOVE...AIM... FIRE!
BLAM
SPLUTCH

YUCK! THIS IS THE WORST GAME OF QUAKE I'VE EVER PLAYED!
I KILLED SOME-ONE!!! I KILLED SOMEONE!!! I WAS LAGGED AND I KILLED SOME-ONE!!! AHAHAHAH!!

IZZA...IZZA...EH... ENFEH...NOL... NOL...AVA...NOL

AVA...EGWEH... UNF..UNF..

MIKE HAS PALSY?
ACTUALLY, HE'S BEEN IMITATING THE WAY STEF PLAYS TWITCH GAMES FOR ABOUT A DAY NOW.
HE WIGGLES HIS HIPS WHEN HE PLAYS!!!

TO ENSURE COMPLIANCE WITH THE NEW SPECIFICATIONS FOR PASSPORT PHOTOS ISSUED BY THE CANADA PASSPORT OFFICE, ALL APPLICANTS ARE REQUIRED TO PERFORM HELPDESK DUTIES FOR TEN MINUTES IMMEDIATELY PRIOR TO HAVING THEIR PHOTO TAKEN...

Canadians aren't allowed to smile in their passport photos now. I guess it's hard to recognize someone if they're beaming in their photo like they just had nookie.

AFTER BEING TORTURED BY THE WAY YOU PLAY QUAKE, I'VE DECIDED IT'D JUST BE EASIER TO GIVE YOU ALL THE ROPE YOU NEED TO HANG YOURSELF. YOUR MACHINE IS YOURS AGAIN.
OH. HOW NICE.
COPYRIGHT©2003 ILLIAD HTTP://WWW.USERFRIENDLY.ORG/

BUT I WANT YOU TO UNDERSTAND THAT YOUR REFUSAL TO ADHERE TO SECURITY PROTOCOLS IS GOING TO BITE YOU IN THE ARSE ONE DAY.
DUDE, YOU'RE PART OF THE PROBLEM.

PART OF THE...?!! HOW THE HELL CAN I BE PART OF THE PROBLEM?!!
BECAUSE I KNOW THAT THERE IS NO SCREWUP I CAN DO THAT YOU CAN'T FIX.

OH FER ELROND'S SAKE. WHAT HAVE YOU GONE AND DONE NOW?!
I WOULDN'T HAVE CALLED YOU IF IT WASN'T SERIOUS. MY MACHINE IS REALLY SLOW.
COPYRIGHT©2003 ILLIAD HTTP://WWW.USERFRIENDLY.ORG/

YOU GORMLESS KNOB. YOU INSTALLED GATOR AND THAT IDIOTIC BONZI BUDDY! AND I'LL BET A PILE MORE SPYWARE AND AD-WARE! IT'LL TAKE A WHILE TO CLEAN THIS ALL UP..
YOU HAVE AN HOUR TO MAKE MY MACHINE WORK. I HAVE A REPORT TO FINISH.
AN HOUR. FINE.

SEE MIKE? YOU CAN FIX ANY PROBLEM THAT I CAN CREATE. I'M GONNA GO HAVE A MOCHA WHILE I WAIT.
OH I'LL FIX IT ALL RIGHT. NOTHING 'FORMAT C:' CAN'T SOLVE HERE...

PEOPLE, I HAVE SOME GREAT NEWS. WITH THE CHANGES IN OUR FOCUS AS A COMPANY, WE'VE BEEN GIVEN A NEW NETWORK OPERATIONS CENTRE.
WOO!
COPYRIGHT©2003 ILLIAD HTTP://WWW.USERFRIENDLY.ORG/

I HAD A PRETTY TIGHT BUDGET, BUT MANAGED TO MAKE IT WORK. STARTING TOMORROW, WE'RE GOING TO BE WORKING FROM HERE.
IT'S KINDA WARM IN HERE SID.

WHAT ARE YOU GONNA DO WITH THE HEAT?
ALREADY DONE.
SID, WHAT KIND OF PLANTS ARE THOSE BEHIND THE ROUTERS?

AND SINCE WE HAVE A NEED FOR MORE NOC PERSONNEL, WE'LL BE BRINGING GREG BACK ON FULLTIME AND HAVING HIM WORK HERE ON RELIEF FOR YOU TWO.
THAT'S GREAT NEWS!
COPYRIGHT©2003 ILLIAD HTTP://WWW.USERFRIENDLY.ORG/

PITR, OF COURSE, WILL BE WORKING ON NEW CODE TO UPGRADE OUR BILLING SYSTEM, AND...
I'LL BE HELPING OUT IN THE NOC.

HASTUR! YOU'RE BACK!
YEAH. THE CALIFORNIA BALLOT WAS GETTING KINDA FULL.

WHY IS AN EVIL GOD-THING WORKING IN A NOC? SHOULDN'T YOU BE OUT THERE TERRIFYING SOMETHING?
I NEEDED A BREAK. IT'S QUIET HERE.

PEOPLE DON'T UNDERSTAND HOW HARD BEING A DARK GOD CAN BE. WORKING IN A NETWORK OPERATION CENTRE GIVES ONE TIME FOR REFLECTION...
COPYRIGHT©2003 ILLIAD HTTP://WWW.USERFRIENDLY.ORG/

YES. I SUPPOSE YOU'RE RIGHT.
...NOT TO MENTION A CHANCE TO COME UP WITH "NOC NOC" JOKES.

YEP. I SURE DO LIKE WORKING IN THE NOC. IT'S QUIET -- MEDITATIVE ALMOST. THE ROOM IS DIMLY LIT. LIGHTS BLINK ON AND OFF CREATING AN ENVIRONMENT IDEAL FOR A HYPNOTIC TRANCE...

IN FACT, IT'S WARM AND SAFE HERE IN THE NOC. AND THE FURTHER YOU VENTURE, THE SAFER IT IS. THE FURTHER. THE SAFER...THE FURTHER. THE SAFER...
COPYRIGHT©2003 ILLIAD HTTP://WWW.USERFRIENDLY.ORG/

YOU PROMISED YOU WOULDN'T TRY TO EAT ANYONE IN THE NOC.
LOOK. YOUR DAMN PLANTS GAVE ME THE MUNCHIES. HOW IS THAT FAIR?

riaa

Recording Industry Association of America

FORM UR-SCR00 D

PERSONAL FILE-SHARING AMNESTY APPLICATION FORM*

FULL LEGAL NAME:

BANK ACCOUNT NUMBER:

ADDRESS**

YOU HAVE: (CHECK ALL THAT APPLY)

- ☐ LIFE SAVINGS HOW MUCH: ____
- ☐ SEIZABLE ASSETS TOTAL WORTH: ____
- ☐ NO UNDERSTANDING OF THE LAW
- ☐ ONLY A VAGUE GRASP OF MY RIGHTS
- ☐ A PROCTOLOGIST***

TAPE COPY OF PHOTO ID HERE

YOU WILL PURCHASE: (CHECK ALL)

- ☐ BOY BAND CDs/CASSETTES
- ☐ BRITNEY CDs/CASSETTES
- ☐ MILLI VANILLI COMEBACK CDs/CASSETTES
- ☐ CELINE DION MUSIC VIDEOS
- ☐ MARIAH CAREY FEATURE MUSICALS

THE UNDERSIGNED AGREES THAT, IN EXCHANGE FOR LIMITED AMNESTY FROM CHARGES OF MEDIA PIRACY BY THE RIAA, S/HE WILL DESTROY ALL DIGITAL COPIES, PHYSICALLY RECORDED COPIES AND OTHERWISE ARCHIVED COPIES OF COPYWRITTEN WORKS. ADDITIONALLY, THE UNDERSIGNED WILL SUBJECT HIM/HERSELF TO NEURALIZATION TO DESTROY ALL MUSICAL WORKS THAT HAVE BEEN MEMORIZED; ALL CDs, CASSETTES, 8-TRACKS, VINYL RECORDINGS AND OTHER PHYSICALLY ARCHIVED MEDIA LEGALLY PURCHASED WILL ALSO BE DESTROYED, AND THE UNDERSIGNED AGREES TO RE-PURCHASE THEIR ENTIRE LIBRARY.

LFT THUMB	RT THUMB	CREDIT CARD NUMBERS	EXPIRY

APPLICANT ____ DATE ____

NOTARY'S SEAL AND SIGNATURE

* PREVIOUSLY "STATUTORY CONFESSION OF MEDIA PIRACY AND WAIVER OF ALL RIGHTS."
** P.O. BOXES UNACCEPTABLE. MUST BE A PHYSICAL ADDRESS WHERE DOCUMENTS MAY BE SERVED.
*** IF YOU DO NOT HAVE A PROCTOLOGIST, ONE WILL BE SUPPLIED TO YOU.

WHAT'S THIS I HEAR ABOUT HASTUR MANNING THE NOC?
HE WAS. HE'S ON THE DARK'O CLOCK SHIFT. AND I HAVE TO HAND IT TO HIM. THE DUDE KNOWS HIS STUFF.
COPYRIGHT©2003 ILLIAD HTTP://WWW.USERFRIENDLY.ORG/

NOT ONLY DOES HE HAVE SERIOUS 'NIX SKILLZ. THE GUY CAN ACCURATELY PREDICT LOADING AND ROUTING PROBLEMS WELL BEFORE THE FACT.

Y'ALL CAN CALL ME "NOCTRADAMUS."
WILL YOU JUST GO HOME ALREADY?

What's a NOCling's favorite food? NOCwurst!

WELL LADS. I MANAGED TO GET YOUR TITLES CHANGED TO SOMETHING A LITTLE MORE WHIMSICAL THAN JUST "SYSTEM ADMINISTRATOR." IT TOOK SOME DOING BUT I THINK IT'S WORTH THE FUN.
COPYRIGHT©2003 ILLIAD HTTP://WWW.USERFRIENDLY.ORG/

WE'RE GONNA BE CALLED "NO CLINGS."
EWWW. "NO CLING" TO WHAT?
THAT'S "NOC-LINGS!"

THAT'S AN AWESOME PILE OF HARDWARE! 2U AND 1U BOXEN STACKED LIKE A LADDER TO HEAVEN.
WORKS FOR ME.
COPYRIGHT©2003 ILLIAD HTTP://WWW.USERFRIENDLY.ORG/

WHY IS THIS 1U CASE MADE OUT OF CARDBOARD?
IT'S A PIZZA BOX. IT KEEPS THE PIZZA WARM.

SO THIS IS WHERE YOU DORKS HANG OUT NOW?
NO STEF. THIS IS THE NOC. WHERE WE WORK.
COPYRIGHT©2003 ILLIAD HTTP://WWW.USERFRIENDLY.ORG/

UNH-HUH. YOU DON'T LOOK LIKE YOU'RE WORKING.
DUDE. IF A SYSADMIN ISN'T SWEATING BULL-ETS IT JUST MEANS HE'S DOING HIS JOB RIGHT.

OH. SO I GUESS YOU'RE DOING YOUR JOB RIGHT.
NOPE. PLAYING NETHACK.

THAT'S AN ODD LOOKING SCREEN...
UHH...YEAH...IT'S FOR THE NOC. SEE, THIS SYMBOL IS ME, AND THESE ARE ALL THE PACKETS INSIDE THE NETWORK.

...I MOVE AROUND AND NUDGE THE PACKETS USING THE ARROW KEYS.
COOL! LEMME TRY...
NO! DON'T TOUCH ANYTHING!!!

WHAT DOES IT MEAN "THE RED DRAGON HITS YOU FOR 320 HPS. -YOU HAVE DIED-"?
IT MEANS I KNOW WHOSE MAILBOX GETS ALL THE SPAM FOR THE NEXT WEEK.

LET'S SEE. I THINK I'LL BE AN ORC TOURIST...
STEF. WHAT ARE YOU DOING?!
WELCOME TO THE DUNGEONS OF DOOM!

I'M, UH, HELPING WITH MANAGING THE NOC. THIS IS A NOC CONTROL APPLICATION, SEE, AND I'M NUDGING PACKETS AROUND AND THE PACKETS-
I COULD FIRE YOU FOR LYING TO ME, YOU KNOW.

WHAT, DON'T YOU BELIEVE THIS IS A NOC SCREEN?
NO, WHAT I DON'T BELIEVE IS THAT YOU'RE A SYSADMIN.

ACCOUNTING FOR 12-YEAR OLD BRIANNA LAHARA'S SETTLEMENT BY THE RIAA.

ITEM	INCOME	EXPENSE	BALANCE
Brianna Lahara Settlement	$2,000.00		$2,000.00
RIAA Admin Fees		$1788.00	$212.00
Legal Fees		$942.00	($730.00)
Publicity Fees		$1600.00	($2330.00)
SIGNED MUSICIANS OWE US:			$2330.00

YOU ACTUALLY MANAGED TO GET STEF PLAYING NETHACK?
YEP. ODDLY ENOUGH.
COPYRIGHT©2003 ILLIAD HTTP://WWW.USERFRIENDLY.ORG/

HOW'S HE DOING IN THE GAME?
I'D SAY HE'S DOING THE SAME OL'. SAME OL'.

YOU NEVER TOLD ME THIS STUPID GAME HAD LAVA POOLS!
YOUR PET KITTEN "PITR" IS EATING YOUR CORPSE.

I JUST DON'T GET THIS 'SPAM' STUFF. AND IT'S CLOGGING OUR MAIL SPOOL.
NO KIDDING. BUT PEOPLE DO RES-POND TO IT, OR IT WOULD FADE.
COPYRIGHT©2003 ILLIAD HTTP://WWW.USERFRIENDLY.ORG/

HERE'S ONE: "ENLARGEMENT WITH PILLS. OVERNIGHT! JUST $29.95!"

HEH. THEY'RE TRYING TO SELL ICE TO AN ESKIMO.
AAAGH! MUST POKE OUT MIND'S EYE!!

HAVE YOU READ WHAT VERISIGN IS DOING?
YOU MEAN THE DNS WILDCARDS? YES. TALK ABOUT SLIMEY.
EH?
ROTO ROUTER
COPYRIGHT©2003 ILLIAD HTTP://WWW.USERFRIENDLY.ORG/

INSTEAD OF GETTING "SITE NOT FOUND" MESSAGES IF YOU MAKE A TYPO OR IF THE SITE DOESN'T EXIST, YOU GET SENT TO A VERISIGN PAGE. AND E-MAILS THAT SHOULD BOUNCE ARE LIKELY HARVESTED BY VERISIGN FOR THEIR DATA.
ROTO ROUTER

ONE RATHER GETS AN IMAGE OF CATTLE BEING HERDED INTO AN ABATTOIR.
YES. ONE DOES.
MAD CATTLE!
ROTO ROUTER

*
!*
COPYRIGHT©2003 ILLIAD HTTP://WWW.USERFRIENDLY.ORG/

*!
!*!

*!!!
!*!!!

AND THEREIN, FOLKS, LIES THE DANGER OF THE UNETHICAL AND INDISCRIMINATE USE OF WILDCARDS.
**** ***!

TODAY BEING "TALK LIKE A PIRATE DAY," WE FELT IT APPROPRIATE TO FEATURE A VERISIGN VICE-PRESIDENT AS A SPECIAL GUEST.

SHIVER ME ROUTERS! AVAST YE SCURVY... WAIT A MINUTE! WHAT ARE YOU IMPLYING HERE?!

GREG, YOU SEE WHERE DUST PUPPY AND ERWIN MADE OFF TO?
THEY SAID THEY WERE HEADING DOWN TO THE PARK.

THE PARK? WHY THE PARK?
THEY WANTED TO GET AWAY FROM THE HOSTILITY CAUSED BY VERISIGN ON THE 'NET. UNPLUGGING FROM EVIL, AS IT WERE.

IT'S JUST POND SCUM, ERWIN.
I KNEW IT!! THEY'RE EVERYWHERE!!

GIVEN HOW LITTLE WE ACTUALLY KNOW ABOUT WHAT'S UNDER THE WAVES, IT MIGHT BE BETTER FOR THE SPANISH NAVY TO BE A TAD MORE CONCERNED ABOUT THEIR EXPERIMENTS THAT KILL GIANT SQUID...

OH NO! GERTRUDE!!

GREG, DO YOU HAVE THE REPORT I WANTED...WHAT'S THAT?
IT'S A U.P.S. -- AN UNINTERRUPTIBLE. POWER SUPPLY.

COPYRIGHT © 2003 ILLIAD HTTP://WWW.USERFRIENDLY.ORG/
I'VE JUST BEEN THINKING. IF I PLUGGED A U.P.S. INTO ITSELF WOULD IT POWER ITSELF FOREVER?

THE MORAL: PAY ATTENTION IN MIDDLE SCHOOL PHYSICS CLASS OR GEEKS WILL USE YOUR MIND AS A SMALL SOFT PUNCHING BAG.
UH...

WHAT DO THEY MEAN BY "UNINTERRUPTIBLE?" HOW CAN POWER NEVER BE INTERRUPTED?
WELL, IT...
ABSOLUTELY IT IS NOT INTERRUPTIBLE.

COPYRIGHT © 2003 ILLIAD HTTP://WWW.USERFRIENDLY.ORG/
OF COURSE IT IS! I UNPLUG THE U.P.S. AND IN TWENTY MINUTES OR WHATEVER IT IS, THE POWER FADES. VOILA! INTERRUPTED POWER.
NYET. POWER. SHE IS CONTINUINK.

OH? FOR HOW LONG?
LETTINK ME THINK. IF REMEMBERINK CORRECTLY, U-235 HALF LIFE IS 713 MILLION YEARS. SO...
HUH?

WHAT -- ARE YOU SAYING THIS IS A NUCLEAR POWERED U.P.S.?
DA. IS MERELY PROTOTYPE. NEEDINK TO SPEND MORE TIME ON DESIGN.

COPYRIGHT © 2003 ILLIAD HTTP://WWW.USERFRIENDLY.ORG/
WOW. THAT'S PRETTY COOL! AND...DAMN. THAT IS REALLY HEAVY. YOU MUST HAVE A LOT OF SHIELDING IN THIS THING.

NYET. IS NO SHIELDINK.
HUH?

PITR, ARE YOU TRYING TO TELL ME MOST OF THE WEIGHT IN THIS THING IS FROM RADIOACTIVE MATERIAL?
DA.

COPYRIGHT © 2003 ILLIAD HTTP://WWW.USERFRIENDLY.ORG/
YE GODS!! ARE YOU INSANE? THE RADIATION COMING OUT OF THIS THING HAS GOT TO BE NASTY! WHAT ARE YOU USING FOR SHIELDING?!

AMBULATORY BAGS OF "HEAVY" WATER.
OH. BAGS OF.. HEY NOW!! I'VE BEEN DIETING!!

WHAT EXACTLY DO YOU MEAN BY "USING BAGS OF HEAVY WATER" TO SHIELD YOU FROM YOUR ATOMIC U.P.S?
YOU AND OTHER STAFF SHOULD BE HAPPY YOU ARE OF SOME USE. DA?
COPYRIGHT©2003 ILLIAD HTTP://WWW.USERFRIENDLY.ORG/

OH. HA HA. THE HUMAN BODY DOESN'T HAVE ANY HEAVY WATER IN IT.
WOULD NOT JUMP TO SUCH CONCLUSIONS...

I HATE TO ADMIT THIS, BUT PITR'S BEEN MAKING SOME PRETTY INTERESTING TASTING COFFEE THESE DAYS.

WHAT EXACTLY ARE YOU SHOWING ME HERE?
RADIATION FILMS. SHOWINK HOW MUCH YOU ARE BLOCKINK RAYS FROM U.P.S.
COPYRIGHT©2003 ILLIAD HTTP://WWW.USERFRIENDLY.ORG/

LET ME GUESS. THE WHITE SPOTS ARE WHERE IT'S DENSER AND SO RADIATION IS LESS LIKELY TO GET THROUGH, AND THE DARK SPOTS ARE WHERE IT DID GET THROUGH.
DA.

THIS ISN'T ME, IS IT. IT'S A BIG WHITE BLOB SHAPED LIKE STEF'S HEAD...
DA. AND FUNNY THING IS, HE IS NOT DRINKINK MY HEAVY WATER COFFEE.

I was informed by a friend with an advanced degree in chemistry that quaffing deuterium or tritium probably isn't a good idea. Not "organic," at any rate.

WHY ARNOLD WAS SO SNAPPY WITH THE REPLIES DURING THE CALIFORNIA GOVERNOR DEBATE.
POSSIBLE RESPONSES
YES.
NO.
MORE TAX CUTS.
COME WITH ME IF YOU WANT TO LIVE.
F*** YOU A******.
COPYRIGHT©2003 ILLIAD HTTP://WWW.USERFRIENDLY.ORG/

DUDE. SEE THIS INFO ON HEAVY WATER?! IT'S USED AS A **MODERATOR**, NOT A SHIELDING AGENT. YOU **DORK!**
COPYRIGHT©2003 ILLIAD HTTP://WWW.USERFRIENDLY.ORG/

SO? YOU HAVE BEEN DRINKINK HEAVY WATER COFFEE. YOU ARE FEELINK MORE MODERATE?
FEELING MORE... WHAT--**WHAT THE**...?!

AH. YOU SEE. IT IS NOT WORKINK AS MODERATOR. SO. MUST BE SHIELDINK AGENT. NYET?
NYET! I MEAN. **YES!** I MEAN... BFFFFTHPT!!

SID. PITR'S WALKING AROUND WITH CHUNKS OF URANIUM AND BUILDING EVIL LITTLE POWER SUPPLIES. THIS CAN'T BE GOOD FOR US!
COPYRIGHT©2003 ILLIAD HTTP://WWW.USERFRIENDLY.ORG/

CALM DOWN GREG. I'M SURE HE'S JUST PLAYING A PRANK. MAKING YOU THINK HE HAS ACCESS TO RADIOACTIVE MATERIALS. WHERE ON **EARTH** DO YOU THINK THAT TWIT CAN GET STUFF LIKE THAT? I MEAN. REALLY.

SACRE BLEU! ALL OF OUR URANIUM IS **GONE!** WHAT DO WE TELL THE ITALIANS?
TELL THEM IT WAS A FALLEN POWER LINE. AND BLAME THE SWISS.

SIGH
TOUGH DAY?
COPYRIGHT©2003 ILLIAD HTTP://WWW.USERFRIENDLY.ORG/

TOUGH FEW **YEARS**. DOT COM BOMB. SCARCE TECH JOBS. 9/11. OUTSOURCING. RIAA LAWSUITS. S.C.O. AND NOW PEOPLE ARE FALLING OFF OF SEGWAYS.

AT LEAST THE WATER IS STILL GOOD.
I THINK THE EVIL GLOWING FISH THAT SMILING MAN FLUSHED IS IN YOUR DRINK.
WHAT AN EXCELLENT DAY FOR AN EXORCISM.

BARTENDER. WHAT'S A FISH DOING IN MY DRINK?
COPYRIGHT©2003 ILLIAD HTTP://WWW.USERFRIENDLY.ORG/

I WAS GONNA CLEVERLY REPLY "THE BACKSTROKE." BUT BY **GOLLY** IF HE ISN'T GLOWING.
HOW LONG'S HE BEEN IN THERE? AND HAS HE EATEN? 'CAUSE I BET THOSE AREN'T BEER NUTS AT THE BOTTOM.

HEY FISH. YOU DO KNOW WHAT YOU'RE FLOATING IN, RIGHT?
COPYRIGHT©2003 ILLIAD HTTP://WWW.USERFRIENDLY.ORG/

IT'S HOLY WATER.
IT BURNS. IT BURNS!

ERWIN, IT'S JUST VANILLA COKE.
IT BURNS! IT BURNS!

UH, DUDE? WHAT'RE YOU DOING DOWN THERE?
MY PLANS, MY BEAUTIFUL, BEAUTIFUL PLANS. THEY ARE RUINED!
COPYRIGHT©2003 ILLIAD HTTP://WWW.USERFRIENDLY.ORG/

HUH? WHAT HAPPENED TO THE URANIUM?
MY URANIUM, MY LOVELY URANIUM, IT IS ALL DESTROYED! HOW AM I TO BE TAKINK OVER WORLD WITH ONLY ONE NUCLEAR-POWERED U.P.S?
WHAT ARE YOU ON ABOUT?

BUT HE SAID IT WAS "YELLOW CAKE."
REPEAT AFTER ME: "COLLOQUIALISM."

WHEN GEEKS MOVE HOUSE
ART TREASURES & FAMILY HEIRLOOMS.
BOXES FOR EMPTY COMPUTER GAME PACKAGES.
242 BLANKETS, TOWELS AND RUGS STITCHED AND DUCT-TAPED TOGETHER WRAPPED AROUND A SINGLE COMPUTER.
COPYRIGHT©2003 ILLIAD HTTP://WWW.USERFRIENDLY.ORG/

I THINK I HAVE THAT FREAKY DEVIL GUPPY FIGURED OUT.
HOW'S THAT?
COPYRIGHT © 2003 ILLIAD HTTP://WWW.USERFRIENDLY.ORG/

LOOKING BACK AT MY LOGS, I PERCEPTIVELY NOTE THAT THE ONLY THINGS HE CAN SAY ARE LINES FROM HORROR MOVIES. HE IS THEREFORE EITHER JUST A GREAT MIMIC, OR HE IS TRULY THE DEVIL INCARNATE. INCARNATED AS A FISH.

BARTENDER!
A.J., I DON'T THINK HE LIKES BEING IN THE VANILLA COKE. HE KEEPS ASKING FOR "RED RUM."

PARDON ME, MINION. HAVE YOU SEEN MY ICHOROUS CHUM AROUND?
YOU ARE MEANINK HASTUR?
COPYRIGHT © 2003 ILLIAD HTTP://WWW.USERFRIENDLY.ORG/

YES, THAT'S HIM. I HOPE YOU'RE NOT STILL UPSET AT HIM FOR CONSUMING ALL OF YOUR URANIUM.
NOT UPSET. HAVE BALANCED SCALES OF JUSTICE ALREADY.

WOOO! TIME TO BLAZE UP A SPLIFF!
GLOOP!
YEEAARRRGH!
BLORP!

Speaking of "differences," never was I more proud of geekdom than when *Star Trek* actor George Takei (Lt. Hikaru Sulu) came out of the closet and publically announced he was gay. Geekdom as a whole just shrugged. Exactly. So what? We love you for being Sulu, George. And most of us pretty much knew you were gay anyway. :-)

WHO'S THAT GUY?
THAT'S TING KUAN. HE'S OUR NEW INTERN.
COPYRIGHT © 2003 ILLIAD HTTP://WWW.USERFRIENDLY.ORG/

HE KIND OF STANDS OUT HERE, DOESN'T HE?
YEAH. KIND OF HARD NOT TO NOTICE HIS DIFFERENCES.

I MEAN, WHO WEARS BUTTON-UP SHIRTS IN A MACHINE ROOM?
SOMEONE HAS TO TELL HIM.

HI, I'M GREG, THE SUPPORT GUY.
HEY. NICE TO MEET YOU. I'M KUAN.

SO WHAT MADE YOU APPLY FOR AN INTERNSHIP HERE?
WELL...YOU GUYS HAVE A REP FOR TECHNICAL EXCELLENCE.
COPYRIGHT © 2003 ILLIAD HTTP://WWW.USERFRIENDLY.ORG/

AND YOU'RE ALSO PAYING A DOLLAR AN HOUR MORE THAN MINIMUM WAGE.
WELCOME ABOARD!

HEY STEF. MEET TING KUAN! HE'S OUR NEW INTERN SYSADMIN!
COPYRIGHT©2003 ILLIAD HTTP://WWW.USERFRIENDLY.ORG/

HEH-LO. MY NAME STEF.

IS HE RETARDED?
WE ALL THINK SO.

YOU DORK. WHY DIDN'T YOU TELL ME HE SPOKE ENGLISH?
WHY DID YOU ASSUME HE DIDN'T?
COPYRIGHT©2003 ILLIAD HTTP://WWW.USERFRIENDLY.ORG/

WELL...'CAUSE...HE'S. YOU KNOW. ASIAN.
AH...

THEN WHY DO YOU SAY "HEY BABY WANT SOME STEAK ON YOUR RICE" WHEN YOU WALK PAST ASIAN WOMEN?
WAIT. THEY ALL SPEAK ENGLISH TOO?

WHEN THE HALF-LIFE 2 SOURCE CODE THIEF IS CAUGHT, ONE POSSIBLE PUNISHMENT IS LOCKING HIM IN A CELL FOR 10 YEARS WITH A LAPTOP AND ONLY ONE GAME INSTALLED:
JOHN ROMERO'S
大刀
DAIKATANA
COPYRIGHT©2003 ILLIAD HTTP://WWW.USERFRIENDLY.ORG/

ION Storm has redeemed itself mightily since the Daikatana days. Thief: Deadly Shadows is a work of art.

HEADS UP, KUAN. I'M GOING TO TEACH YOU A LITTLE ABOUT BEING A SYSADMIN.
GREAT!
COPYRIGHT©2003 ILLIAD HTTP://WWW.USERFRIENDLY.ORG/

OKAY. FIRST YOU OPEN A BROWSER WINDOW FOR ARS TECHNICA, THE REGISTER AND GOOGLE. THEN YOU START UP NETHACK...

UH...WHEN DO WE GET TO THE ACTUAL SYSADMINING?
LOOK. DO YOU WANT TO LEARN HOW TO BE A REAL SYSADMIN OR NOT?

OKAY. SAY IT'S DAY ONE AT YOUR NEW JOB. YOU'RE PUT IN CHARGE OF ALL OF THE SERVERS. WHAT DO YOU DO?
COPYRIGHT©2003 ILLIAD HTTP://WWW.USERFRIENDLY.ORG/

UMM...DO A SECURITY AUDIT?
SECUR-?! NO!!

WHAT THEN, O MASTER?
ESTABLISH JOB SECURITY: CHANGE ALL OF THE PASSWORDS.

NOW THAT YOUR WORK AREA IS NICELY SET UP, IT'S TIME TO FUEL UP WITH SOME CAFFEINE...
I DON'T REALLY DRINK ANY CAFFEINE.
COPYRIGHT©2003 ILLIAD HTTP://WWW.USERFRIENDLY.ORG/

THE LONGER I HAVE TO WAIT FOR YOU TO COME TO YOUR SENSES, THE LONGER YOU KEEP ME FROM MY MORNING COFFEE.
CAFFEINE SOUNDS GREAT RIGHT ABOUT NOW. YES SIR!

I JUST DON'T GET HOW YOU DON'T DRINK CAFFEINE, KUAN. GEEKS THE WORLD OVER CONSIDER IT THE STIMULANT OF CHOICE.
COPYRIGHT©2003 ILLIAD HTTP://WWW.USERFRIENDLY.ORG/

CAFFEINE IS MORE THAN JUST A DRUG TO US. IN MANY WAYS, IT'S A LIFEBLOOD. WITHOUT IT, MANY OF US WOULD HAVE TROUBLE FUNCTIONING.

IN FACT, FOR SOME OF US, IT'S AS IMPORTANT AS OXYGEN!
IT'S MORE IMPORTANT. I CAN HOLD MY BREATH FOR ALMOST TWO MINUTES.

SO YOU DON'T DRINK COFFEE. THEN WHAT'S YOUR POISON OF CHOICE?
SOYMILK. I WAS RAISED ON THE STUFF
COPYRIGHT©2003 ILLIAD HTTP://WWW.USERFRIENDLY.ORG/

AH.

WHAT'S IT MADE OF?
SOY.
IS THAT SOY AS IN SOYLENT GREEN?

WHAT THE..?!
OH. THAT'S DUST PUPPY. HE'S KIND OF OUR MASCOT.
COPYRIGHT©2003 ILLIAD HTTP://WWW.USERFRIENDLY.ORG/

HOW DO YOU MAKE HIM TALK?
DUDE!! NO!! HE'S NOT A HANDPUPPET!!

USER FRIENDLY
the comic strip
BY J.D. "ILLIAD" FRAZER

OKAY LADS. TAKE ONE. MARKETING JINGLE FOR COLUMBIA INTERNET...
I WIN "ILLIAD FOR A DAY" AND I'M FORCED TO DO THIS?
WARFREAK2
OUT-OF-WORK NETWORK ADMINS

(SUNG TO: "ONE NIGHT IN BANGKOK.")
OUR NOC. ELECTRICAL SETTING. AND THE USERS DON'T KNOW WHAT THE USERS ARE GETTING. THE CREME DE LA CREME OF THE TECH WORLD ON A SHIFT WITH EVERYONE BUT TIM BERNERS (LEE)!
THUMP-A-THUMP-A-THUMP-A-THUMP-A-TH

NO LIES! NO TROUBLE TICKETS IN IT THAT SOLVING HERE TAKES LONGER THAN A MINUTE!
SHIFTS CHANGE. BUT DON'T YOU KNOW THAT WHEN YOU LOG INTO OUR SYSTEM THERE'S NO ORDINARY MENU!
IT'S KORN SHELL... OR BOURNE AGAIN SHELL... OR CSH... OR... OR THIS INTERFACE!
THUMPA-THUMPA-THU

ONE NIGHT IN OUR NOC AND THE WORLD'S YOUR OYSTER. THE STARS ARE WILDCARDS BUT THE FILES AIN'T FREE! YOU'LL FIND A GOD IN EVERY SCREEN-LIT CLOISTER. AND IF YOU'RE LUCKY THEN THE GOD'S A SHE! I CAN FEEL A DDOS SLIDING UP TO ME...
THUMP-A-THUMP-A-THUMP-A-

WHAT?

COPYRIGHT © 2003 ILLIAD HTTP://WWW.USERFRIENDLY.ORG/

HOW'RE YOU FEELING?
EXPLORED.

HOW GOES THE SECURITY AUDIT?
GOOD. I THINK WE'RE LOCKED DOWN PRETTY TIGHT.
COPYRIGHT © 2003 ILLIAD HTTP://WWW.USERFRIENDLY.ORG/

GREAT. WE CAN'T BE TOO CAREFUL ABOUT NETWORK SECURITY AFTER THAT BUSINESS WITH THE HALF-LIFE 2 SOURCE CODE BEING LEAKED TO THE NET. ANYONE COULD DOWNLOAD IT!

DOES THAT MEAN THE HALF-LIFE 2 SOURCE CODE BELONGS TO S.C.O. NOW?
FOR A COMEDIENNE YOU MAKE A GOOD SYSADMIN.

A nod to the comic strip "Cathy" and her neurotic ways. Also, never equate a real-life woman to "Cathy" unless you're a particularly fast runner.

HI. I'M KUAN. THE NEW INTERN.
MIRANDA. AND YES, I'M A SYSADMIN.
COPYRIGHT © 2003 ILLIAD HTTP://WWW.USERFRIENDLY.ORG/

YEP. I FIGURED THAT'S WHAT YOU WERE.
NO. I MEAN A REAL SYSADMIN. I CAN CODE TOO.
UM. OKAY.

JUST BECAUSE I'M FEMALE IT DOESN'T MEAN I CAN'T BE A GREAT TECHNOLOGIST!!
WHOA! TAKE IT EASY "CATHY."

Been nice knowing you, Kuan.

SO IT DOESN'T FAZE YOU THAT I'M A QUALIFIED TECHNOLOGIST AND NOT A GUY?
WHY SHOULD IT?
COPYRIGHT © 2003 ILLIAD HTTP://WWW.USERFRIENDLY.ORG/

WELL, THAT'S REALLY REFRESHING. CAN I THANK YOU WITH A BEER AFTER WORK?
NO THANKS. I DON'T DATE WOMEN THE SAME AGE AS MY MOM.

THE SNOTTY KID DID WHAT?
HE THOUGHT I WAS ASKING HIM OUT ON A DATE!
WEREN'T YOU?
COPYRIGHT©2003 ILLIAD HTTP://WWW.USERFRIENDLY.ORG/

NO! I CAN'T IMAGINE WHAT GAVE HIM THE IDEA I WAS MAKING A PASS AT HIM!
CAN'T YOU?

NO! AND WHAT'S WORSE, HE THINKS I'M AS OLD AS HIS MOM!
AREN'T...

CHINA'S MADE IT INTO SPACE! WOOHOO!
BIG DEAL. MIKE, WHEN WAS THE FIRST MOON LANDING?
APOLLO 11, IN 1969.
COPYRIGHT©2003 ILLIAD HTTP://WWW.USERFRIENDLY.ORG/

NASA PUT A GUY INTO SUBORBIT IN 1961, THEN INTO FULL ORBIT IN 1962, AND HAD A FIRST DOCKING WITH ANOTHER SPACE VEHICLE IN 1966.

YEAH, SO SUCK IT UP KUAN: THE WEST IS STILL WAY AHEAD OF ASIA IN SPACE.
YES, BUT WE'VE HAD YOU EATING OUR CRAPPIEST RAMEN FOR YEARS.
WHAT THE HELL IS "CRAPPY" RAMEN?

HILARY ROSEN, AGE 7
THAT KID IS NEVER GOING TO LIKE SHARING...
COPYRIGHT©2003 ILLIAD HTTP://WWW.USERFRIENDLY.ORG/

WHAT EXACTLY DO YOU MEAN "CRAPPIEST RAMEN?"
WHAT IT SOUNDS LIKE. ASIA EXPORTS ALL OF THE RAMEN REJECTS TO THE WEST. FOR EXAMPLE, TRY THIS DISASTER: "LUCKY FUN RAMEN."
COPYRIGHT©2003 ILLIAD HTTP://WWW.USERFRIENDLY.ORG/

SMORRKLE-SCHHHLLUUUURRRRR

I DON'T GET YOU. THAT IS SOME SERIOUSLY FINE SALT IN THERE.
YO. DON'T BE HOGGING ALL OF IT.

PARDON ME SID, BUT I'M SETTING UP MY WINDOWS BOX. ARE WE USING DHCP HERE?
YES, WE ARE.
COPYRIGHT©2003 ILLIAD HTTP://WWW.USERFRIENDLY.ORG/

THANK YOU KINDLY.

SEEING CTHULHU REALLY DOES MAKE ONE THINK. DOESN'T IT?
YEAH. I THINK WE DIP HIM IN A NICE MALAYSIAN CURRY SAUCE AND WE HAVE LUNCH FOR A WEEK.

Having been raised in Asia, I have to state that Western food might as well be vanilla-flavored tofu compared to the variety and ... exotic nature of much of Asian cuisine. And I'd also rather eat vanilla-flavored tofu than chicken feet.

IT'S PRETTY COOL THAT YOU'VE HAD THE CHANCE TO TRY SO MANY EXOTIC FOODS IN YOUR LIFETIME. I'LL BET THE WEST DOESN'T HAVE ANY FOOD THAT GIVES YOU PAUSE...
ON THE CONTRARY...
COPYRIGHT©2003 ILLIAD HTTP://WWW.USERFRIENDLY.ORG/

...I CAN'T BELIEVE YOU GUYS EAT THAT "CHEEZ WHIZ" STUFF.
OH, IT'S NOT THAT BAD.

DUDE. I KNOW WHAT CHEESE IS, AND I KNOW WHAT "WHIZ" IS.
AND WHY DO THEY MAKE IT SQUEEZABLE?

iTUNES FOR WINDOWS. HMMM...MAYBE I SHOULD GIVE THIS A TRY...
WOULD YOU LIKE iTUNES TO SEARCH FOR AND INDEX YOUR MP3 FILES?
YES

COPYRIGHT©2003 ILLIAD HTTP://WWW.USERFRIENDLY.ORG/

I THINK IT'S HANGED...
EITHER THAT OR SOMEONE'S "COLLECTION" IS A LITTLE EXTENSIVE.
5% DONE, PLEASE STAND BY. ARRR!

HEY LISTEN, I'M NOT A PIRATE! I'VE BOUGHT AND PAID FOR EVERY SONG ON MY HARD DRIVE!
REALLY. INCLUDING "WANNABE" BY THE SPICE GIRLS?

I'LL DO THE TIME.
THOUGHT YOU MIGHT.

ITUNES FOR WINDOWS LOOKS NIFTY.
NICE INDEXING.
HERE, I'LL PLAY A SONG.

IS THAT...MY GOD IT IS...
CLIPPY LIP SYNCHING.

WHAT SHOULD SHOW UP ON GOOGLE
#5: SEARCH FOR "TELEMARKETERS FREEDOM OF SPEECH"

File Edit View Go Bookmarks Tools Window Help
http://www.google.ca/search?q=telemarketers+freedom+speech&ie=UTF-8&oe=
Home Bookmarks
Google
Advanced Search Preferences Language Tools Search Tips
telemarketers freedom of speech
Google Search
Search: the web pages from Canada
Web Images Groups Directory News
Searched the web for telemarketers freedom of speech
Tip: In most browsers you can just hit the return key instead of clicking on the search button.
Did you mean: telemarketers freedom to leech

MEANWHILE, IN REDMOND...
BILL? IT'S ERIC AT GOOGLE. I JUST WANTED TO CALL AND LET YOU KNOW WE'RE TURNING DOWN YOUR OFFER TO BUY OUT THE COMPANY.
COPYRIGHT©2003 ILLIAD HTTP://WWW.USERFRIENDLY.ORG/

UM. HELLO?
BILL. WHY ARE YOU STRANGLING THAT HOUSE PLANT?

STEVE. GOOGLE TURNED DOWN OUR OFFER. I AM UNHAPPY.
YES. BILL.
Microsoft
COPYRIGHT©2003 ILLIAD HTTP://WWW.USERFRIENDLY.ORG/

I WANT GOOGLE. GOOGLE IS NECESSARY TO OUR PLANS. IT ANNOYS ME THAT WE DON'T OWN THEM. I WANT YOU TO USE A SHADOW STRATEGY TO ACQUIRE THEM.

YES BILL. UM... "SHADOW STRATEGY?" DID YOU MEAN: PULL A FAST ONE?
WILL YOU PLEASE STOP THAT!

LISTEN BILL. WE CAN'T ACQUIRE GOOGLE WITH MONEY ALONE. WE NEED TO MAKE GOOGLE THINK THAT THE PUBLIC WANTS A MERGER.
BUT THE PUBLIC DOESN'T WANT A MERGER.
COPYRIGHT©2003 ILLIAD HTTP://WWW.USERFRIENDLY.ORG/

NONETHELESS. WE NEED TO RUN A POLL. AND SHOW GOOGLE THAT THE NET POPULATION OVERWHELMINGLY SUPPORTS THE DEAL.

SO...WE BUY OUT DIEBOLD AND USE THEIR POLLING SOFTWARE?
SEE BILL. THAT'S WHY YOU'RE THE CHAIRMAN.

FRIGGING RIGGING RAZZAFRACKING...

YOU OKAY?
FRUSTRATED.

STEF ASKED ME TO DO SOME RESEARCH FOR HIM ON THE WEB. SO I SEND HIM THE LINKS THAT I FOUND. BUT NONE OF THEM ARE EVER GOOD ENOUGH. WHAT THE HELL DOES HE WANT?
COPYRIGHT©2003 ILLIAD HTTP://WWW.USERFRIENDLY.ORG/

DUDE. FACE IT. YOU'RE JUST CASTING URLS TO SWINE.
I HEARD THAT!!!

GAH. LOOK AT ALL THIS CRAP I SCRAPED OFF MY KEYBOARD.
IT'S WOBBLING.

I DON'T DARE THROW IT OUT. IT MIGHT COME BACK AND EAT ME.
SO HOW ARE YOU GOING TO GET RID OF IT?

EBAY.
LET ME GUESS: UNDER "OFFICE PRODUCTS?"

WELCOME TO EBAY. YOUR BID FOR THIS ITEM IS $15.00
YAY! ONLY THIRTY SECONDS UNTIL THE END OF BIDDING. AND MY BID IS THE TOP ONE!

$16.50!
$20.00!!
$25.00!!
$32.00!!

AUCTION OVER.
YOU HAVE LOST THE BIDDING.
EHHH.

Firewall Plus

Belkin is proud to present a new line of hardware in the tradition of our famous routers! Introducing Firewall Plus, a firewall that sends the login and password to a random script kiddie every eight hours! Sure to keep your security officers on their toes! Now at an introductory price. Be sure to ask about our new keyboards that automatically type "I love Belkin" once a day, every day!

BELKIN

THIS IS WEIRD. I CAN'T BELIEVE I'M PUTTING KEYBOARD CRUD UP FOR AUCTION ON EBAY.
TAP
TIP
TAK

COPYRIGHT©2003 ILLIAD HTTP://WWW.USERFRIENDLY.ORG/
...BUT THE ODDEST THING IS THAT PRIOR TO THIS TIME I HAD CLEANED MY KEYBOARD LESS THAN A MONTH AGO. I HAVE NO IDEA WHERE ALL OF THAT CRAP CAME FROM...

YOU DID WHAT?!
I HAD A COLD AND SNEEZED OFF HALF MY FACE. OKAY?

ONE OF THOSE TECH DORKS PUT MY FACE UP ON EBAY!!
GOOD HEAVENS.

COPYRIGHT©2003 ILLIAD HTTP://WWW.USERFRIENDLY.ORG/
AND THE DAMNABLE THING IS THAT SOMEONE BOUGHT IT! WHAT ON EARTH WOULD ANYONE DO WITH HALF OF MY FACE?!

AM LOOKINK EVIL. EVIL!! HAHAHAHA!!

COPYRIGHT©2003 ILLIAD HTTP://WWW.USERFRIENDLY.ORG/
YE GODS. YOU WERE RIGHT.
TOLD YOU.

YOU JUST GOT THAT CAMERA ATTACHMENT FOR YOUR PDA DIDN'T YOU...
AND WHAT DO YOU GET WHEN YOU ATTACH IT TO YOUR PDA?
GEEK MIRROR. NYET?

LORD OF THE RINGS. WHAT A GREAT STORY! I CAN'T WAIT TO SEE THE FINAL MOVIE IN DECEMBER...
AHEM

COPYRIGHT©2003 ILLIAD HTTP://WWW.USERFRIENDLY.ORG/
AAAAAAIIIIIIEEEEEEE

WAY TO GO, PITR. YOU JUST TURNED "SID THE GREY" INTO "SID THE WHITE."
H...HA...HA... HAIRY... NAZGUL...

AM NOW GETTINK RESPECT! MUST BE SHOWINK NEW EVIL LOOK TO COMRADES.

COPYRIGHT©2003 ILLIAD HTTP://WWW.USERFRIENDLY.ORG/
GREGOR MY FRIEND...
PITR.

WHAT. YOU WORKING FOR HUMAN RESOURCES NOW?
HEY!

SIGH HERE COMES ANOTHER CHALLENGER...
COPYRIGHT©2003 ILLIAD HTTP://WWW.USERFRIENDLY.ORG/

DAMN...WHERE CAN I GET ME ONE OF THOSE?
HA! I AM THE MASTER!
A WORD. IF I MAY...

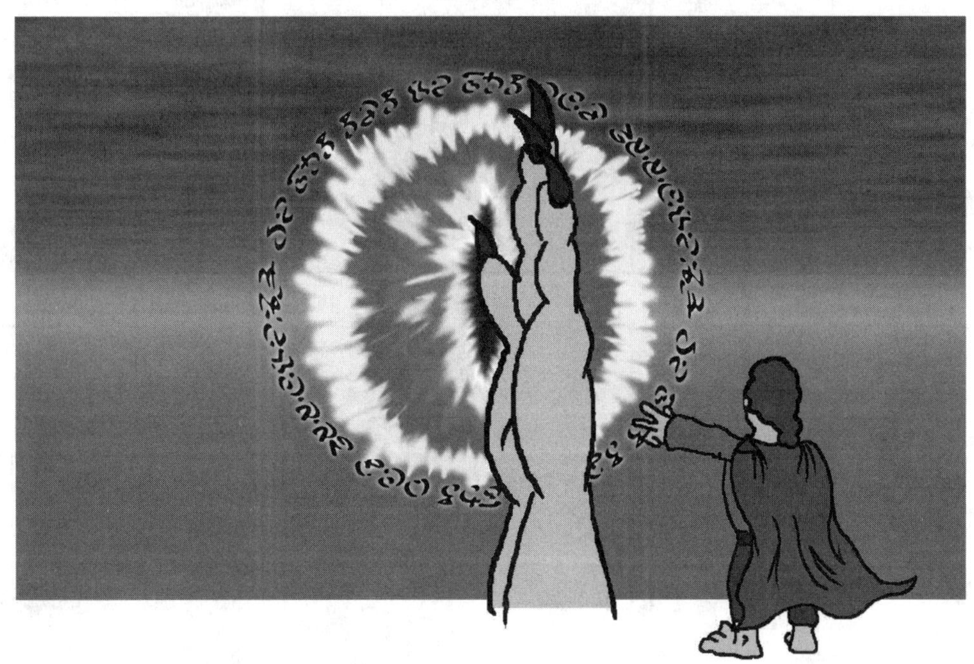
THE LORD OF THE RINGS: TOLD IN ONE FRAME
COPYRIGHT©2003 ILLIAD HTTP://WWW.USERFRIENDLY.ORG/

Look carefully: Frodo is aiming to poke Sauron's eye with two fingers. Sauron cleverly … well, you know. Thank you again, Stooges!

The wizard is Saruman. The reference was to a 7+-minute exchange between Saruman and Gandalf in Peter Jackson's Return of the King that hit the cutting-room floor. The actor, Christopher Lee, was pretty miffed. I would have been, too, but you can't cut the Dark Lord.

DUDE! YOU GOT YOUR FACE BACK!
YEAH. I HAD TO PUT THE BEATDOWN ON THAT EVIL GENIUS WANNABE FIRST.
HTTP://WWW.USERFRIENDLY.ORG/
COPYRIGHT©2003 ILLIAD

I'M LEFT BITTER ABOUT THIS WHOLE THING. MY FACE USED TO BRING ABOUT FEAR, UNCERTAINTY AND DOUBT! THESE DAYS IT'S JUST A TOY TO DORKY GEEKS!
YEAH...LISTEN, I WANT TO INTRODUCE YOU TO A NEW ASSOCIATE...

...A BITTER, BURNT-OUT SHELL OF A WIZARD.
CRIPES, MAN. WHY DO YOU ALWAYS ATTRACT THE FREAKS?
WHY CUT ME? SAURON'S A DAMN HACK! MY B#$@H!*& IS SCARIER THAN THAT EYE OF HIS!

SO YOU GOT CUT OUT OF A MOVIE. BIG STANKY DEAL.
I WAS THE PARAGON OF EVIL IN THAT STORY. SAURON WAS A WUSS.
HTTP://WWW.USERFRIENDLY.ORG/
COPYRIGHT©2003 ILLIAD

SO IT IS A BIG DEAL THAT I WAS CUT. JACKSON REMOVED A POWERFUL FOCUS OF EVIL FROM BOTH THE STORY AND THE SET.

YOU WERE A FORCE OF EVIL ON THE SET, YOU SAY. DO TELL.
I REPLACED ALL OF THE PALANTIRS WITH SNOW GLOBES. THAT DORK GANDALF HAD A SEIZURE.

SNOW GLOBES? YOU CALL THAT EVIL?! THAT'S A WEAK PRACTICAL JOKE AT BEST!
OH PLEASE. I WAS JUST WARMING UP.
HTTP://WWW.USERFRIENDLY.ORG/
COPYRIGHT©2003 ILLIAD

THE FACT IS, I'M SURE I WAS CUT FROM THE LAST MOVIE BECAUSE OF WHAT I DID A FEW DAYS AFTER THE TWO TOWERS WAS FINISHED.

...I PAINTED THE EYE OF SAURON ON THE BACK OF PETER JACKSON'S HEAD.
HEH...THAT'S PRETTY FU...NO! NO IT'S NOT! THAT'S STUPID!
WISH I DID IT.

Not sure about commenting on this one. My wife probably put me up to it.

HEY, GIRL! BUSY?
I THINK YOU COULD SAY THAT. MICROSOFT RELEASED YET ANOTHER SECURITY PATCH AND I'VE SPENT HALF THE MORNING UPDATING THE OFFICE MACHINES.
HTTP://WWW.USERFRIENDLY.ORG/
COPYRIGHT©2003 ILLIAD

THOSE SECURITY PATCHES COME OUT ABOUT ONCE A MONTH, DON'T THEY.
IT SURE FEELS LIKE IT. AND IT'S IRRITATING.

AND YOU GET KIND OF "TESTY" AROUND THIS TIME TOO. EVERY MONTH LIKE CLOCKWORK. SO I HAVE THIS THEORY...
YOU SURE YOU WANT TO SHARE THIS THEORY OF YOURS RIGHT NOW GIVEN WHAT YOU THINK YOU KNOW?

S.C.O.'S AT IT AGAIN. THIS TIME THEY'RE FILING SUIT AGAINST NOVELL TO BLOCK THE PENDING ACQUISITION OF SUSE.
YEAH. I'M JUST READING ABOUT IT.
Geek Lord

WHAT REALLY TICKS ME OFF IS HOW S.C.O. IS SO **OBVIOUSLY** MAKING FALSE CLAIMS. BUT WE CAN'T STOP WATCHING IT BECAUSE IT'S LIKE A FLIPPING **TRAIN** WRECK.
I MEAN. WHO ON EARTH IS THEIR LEGAL COUNSEL?!
Geek Lord
COPYRIGHT©2003 ILLIAD HTTP://WWW.USERFRIENDLY.ORG/

ONE **COULD** POSIT THAT IT'S THE EX-IRAQI INFORMATION MINISTER.
NAH. MY BET'S ON THAT REPORTER WHO WORKED FOR THE NEW YORK TIMES.
Geek Lord

WITH NOVELL ACQUIRING SUSE. DO YOU THINK THEY'LL KEEP THE NAME OR WILL THEY COME UP WITH SOME KIND OF NOVELL/SUSE BLEND?
Geek Lord

Geek Lord
COPYRIGHT©2003 ILLIAD HTTP://WWW.USERFRIENDLY.ORG/

"DEAR NOVELL: PLEASE CONSIDER THE UP-YOURS-NESS OF RENAMING YOUR SUSE PRODUCT 'NO-SUE.'"
SEND IT! **SEND IT!!**
Geek Lord

Anything to do with Linux meant that SCO's litigious shadow was hovering around. Novell took a chance by acquiring SuSE.

"DALEK MCBRIDE"
LIT-I-GATE!
LIT-I-GATE!
SCO
COPYRIGHT©2003 ILLIAD HTTP://WWW.USERFRIENDLY.ORG/

Like I said: Darl McBride, CEO of SCO.

SOMETHING YOU NEED, STEF?
I'M GOING TO BE RICH! ARE YOU GOING TO THE LORD OF THE RINGS MOVIE TRILOGY?
COPYRIGHT © 2003 ILLIAD HTTP://WWW.USERFRIENDLY.ORG/

YOU BET! I WOULDN'T MISS IT FOR...WAIT, WHY? YOU TRYING TO SCALP TICKETS?
NO. ALL THREE MOVIES TOGETHER IS AROUND ELEVEN HOURS, RIGHT?

PRETTY CLOSE. WHAT'S THAT?
WHAT I'M SELLING FOR $20 A TUBE OUTSIDE THE THEATRE.
IT'S PREPARATION H.

YOU KNOW, I MIGHT BE GETTING RICH FROM IT, BUT I DON'T GET THIS WHOLE LORD OF THE RINGS TRILOGY CRAZE. WHO IN THEIR RIGHT MIND WOULD SIT IN FRONT OF A BIG SCREEN IN THE DARK FOR ELEVEN HOURS?
COPYRIGHT © 2003 ILLIAD HTTP://WWW.USERFRIENDLY.ORG/

SOUNDS PRETTY MUCH LIKE EVERY GEEK I'VE MET.
MY GOD, HE'S GOING TO GET RICH OFF OF US!

HEY GREG? HERE'S A COPY OF AN E-MAIL I'M ABOUT TO SEND YOU.
COPYRIGHT © 2003 ILLIAD HTTP://WWW.USERFRIENDLY.ORG/

AM I ON CANDID CAMERA OR SOMETHING?
THE E-MAIL'S FROM A CUSTOMER WHO'D LIKE YOU TO FAX HIM SOME WEB PAGES.

WHAT DO YOU MEAN, 'FAX HIM SOME WEB PAGES?'
JUST THAT. HE SENT SOME URLS AND HE WANTS THE PAGES FAXED TO HIM.
COPYRIGHT © 2003 ILLIAD HTTP://WWW.USERFRIENDLY.ORG/

DOES HE HAVE A COMPUTER?
YES.
DOES HE HAVE A NET CONNECTION?
YES.

THEN WHY DOESN'T HE JUST GO TO THE WEB PAGE HIMSELF?!
HE DOESN'T HAVE A PRINTER.

WAIT. LET ME GET THIS STRAIGHT: HE'S USING US AS A PRINT SERVICE?
KIND OF. I GUESS.
COPYRIGHT©2003 ILLIAD HTTP://WWW.USERFRIENDLY.ORG/

HE WANTS PRINTOUTS OF WEB PAGES YOU SAY.
YES...
SO HE CAN READ THEM IN HARDCOPY.
YES.

THEN WHY DOESN'T HE JUST GET HIS OWN PRINTER?!
HE HAS ONE. IT'S HIS FAX MACHINE.

This was real. No writer can make up this kind of crazy faffle.

TECH SUPPORT. BORDERLINE PSYCHOTIC SPEAKING.
YES. HELLO. I HAVE SOME MORE URLS. COULD YOU FAX THE WEB PAGES TO ME PLEASE?
COPYRIGHT©2003 ILLIAD HTTP://WWW.USERFRIENDLY.ORG/

LISTEN MISTER! IT'S NOT OUR JOB TO-
I NEED YOU TO FAX ME THE LATEST PAGES FROM THE PLAYBOY CYBERCLUB.

SOMETIMES YOU JUST HAVE TO DO WHAT THE CUSTOMER DEMANDS...
BUZ-ZOONT
ZAAAAAAH
OONT
OONT

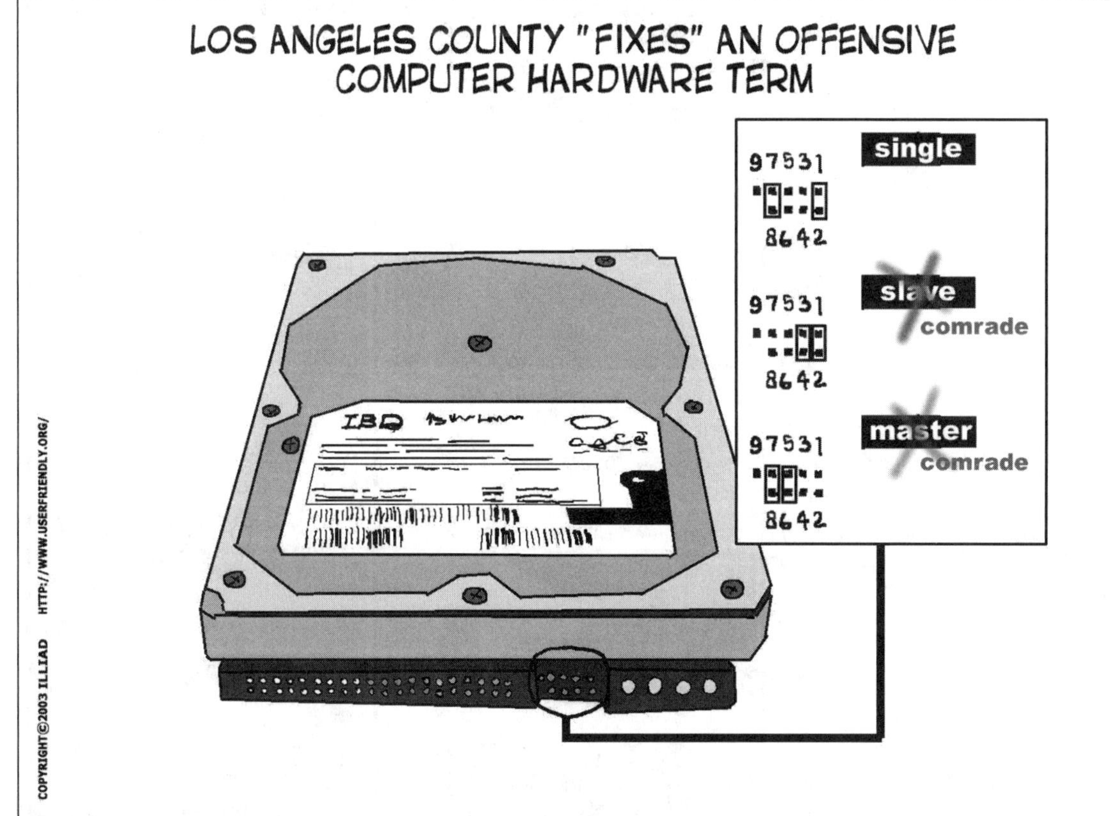
LOS ANGELES COUNTY "FIXES" AN OFFENSIVE COMPUTER HARDWARE TERM
single
slave
comrade
master
comrade
COPYRIGHT©2003 ILLIAD HTTP://WWW.USERFRIENDLY.ORG/

This shouldn't be funny, because the race card is played so much in the United States. Everyone's a victim. All you can do is point and laugh.

Great. I'm channeling "Garfield."

HEY! THE HOLIDAYS ARE ALMOST HERE!
BAH.
WHAT. YOU DON'T LIKE CHRISTMAS?
COPYRIGHT©2003 ILLIAD HTTP://WWW.USERFRIENDLY.ORG/

I LIKE CHRISTMAS JUST FINE. WHAT ISN'T FINE IS THE FIVE POUNDS I GAIN EVERY YEAR FROM ALL THAT TURKEY.

SO. GO ON A DIET...
LISTEN. THERE'S A REASON WHY "DIET" HAS THE WORD "DIE" IN IT.

I'M NOT GOING ON A DIET. AND I'M NOT COUNTING CALORIES.
WELL. LOOK AT IT THIS WAY: CALORIE COUNTING IS ALL ABOUT RESOURCE MANAGEMENT.
COPYRIGHT©2003 ILLIAD HTTP://WWW.USERFRIENDLY.ORG/

WHAT ARE YOU SAYING? DIETING IS JUST LIKE PLAYING A REALTIME STRATEGY GAME?
YES. EXACTLY!

THEN CAN I HAVE THE CHEAT CODES?
NO!

LOOK. I'M NOT DIETING AND YOUR ANALOGY SUCKS.
OH. DOES IT.
COPYRIGHT©2003 ILLIAD HTTP://WWW.USERFRIENDLY.ORG/

IN MOST REAL TIME STRATEGY GAMES YOU HAVE TO MANAGE YOUR RESOURCES. BUILD WITH WHAT YOU HAVE IN THE MOST EFFICIENT MANNER POSSIBLE. YOU KEEP TRACK OF WHAT YOU HAVE AND PLAN WITH IT...

SO YOU SEE. IN A LOT OF WAYS. IT'S JUST LIKE DIETING.
IF IT WAS LIKE A REAL TIME STRATEGY GAME. I'D HAVE LOADED A SAVEGAME FROM TEN YEARS AGO.

I HATE DIETS. I DON'T NEED TO GO ON ONE. I'M A GEEK. I'M HAPPY IN MY SLIGHT ROTUNDNESS. WHAT GOOD WILL SHINY NEW MUSCLES AND A FLAT STOMACH DO ME ANYWAY?
COPYRIGHT©2003 ILLIAD HTTP://WWW.USERFRIENDLY.ORG/

HELLO GREG.
PEARL.

I THINK I'LL EAT AIR FOR THE NEXT MONTH OR SO.
LAY OFF. OR NO AIR FOR YOU.

IF I LOSE A BUNCH OF WEIGHT, I COULD LOOK REALLY HOT. AND MAYBE WOMEN LIKE PEARL WOULD BE ALL OVER ME.
CHIPS

ALL IT WOULD TAKE IS WORKING OUT 2 HOURS A DAY, WATCHING WHAT I EAT, AND FUNDAMENTALLY CHANGING MY LIFESTYLE.
CHIPS

COPYRIGHT©2003 ILLIAD HTTP://WWW.USERFRIENDLY.ORG/
CHIPS

COMMENCE OPERATION "GREG FAT-ARSE."
MUNCH
MUNCH
RUNCH
CHIPS

YOU WANTED TO SEE ME, CHIEF?
YES, I DID.
COPYRIGHT©2003 ILLIAD HTTP://WWW.USERFRIENDLY.ORG/

I LAY AWAKE IN A COLD SWEAT LAST NIGHT AFTER I ASKED YOU TO ORGANIZE THE COMPANY CHRISTMAS DECORATIONS. I DIDN'T MAKE A BAD DECISION. DID I? OH LORD, TELL ME I DIDN'T MAKE A BAD DECISION.
CHIEF, DON'T YOU WORRY ABOUT A THING. IT'S HANDLED.

STEF!
LI'L DUDE'S GOT A POINTY HEAD. HEH.

IN QUIET REPOSE UPON A BLANKET OF WHITE SOLITUDE, OUR HERO WISHES FERVENTLY THAT HE DIDN'T HAVE A SUCH A POINTY HEAD.
RIGHT©2003 ILLIAD HTTP://WWW.USERFRIENDLY.ORG/

Let me 'splain this one. If you had a pointy head, wouldn't you wish fervently that you didn't? Dust Puppy's wish is about to come true ... bahaha-haha! Haha ... ha.

YE GODS. WHAT HAPPENED TO HIM?
STEF DECORATED HIM AS A CHRISTMAS TREE.
HTTP://WWW.USERFRIENDLY.ORG/
COPYRIGHT©2003 ILLIAD

THE CAD! HE'S GONE TOO FAR THIS TIME!
DAMN SKIPPY.

SO. CAN I BORROW HIM FOR THE HOLIDAYS?
SID!
AND CAN HE SING "O CHRISTMAS TREE?"
SID!!

DON'T YOU WORRY LITTLE GUY. I'LL HAVE YOU DE-TINSELED IN A JIFFY.
THANK YOU.
HTTP://WWW.USERFRIENDLY.ORG/
COPYRIGHT©2003 ILLIAD

ACTUALLY. CAN YOU SING "O CHRISTMAS TREE?"
A.J.!!

WHAT THE...ALL OF MY TECH STAFF IDLING IN THE COFFEE ROOM?
HTTP://WWW.USERFRIENDLY.ORG/
COPYRIGHT©2003 ILLIAD

OH RIGHT. MICROSOFT JUST ANNOUNCED NO FORTHCOMING SECURITY PATCHES FOR THIS MONTH...
WE'RE GONNA GO DESTROY AND REBUILD SOME MASTER BOOT RECORDS TO KILL TIME. WANT TO JOIN US?

HANG ON LI'L GUY. JUST ABOUT DONE...HEY. YOU HAVE CHRISTMAS LIGHTS ON YOU. BUT THEY'RE NOT CHRISTMAS LIGHTS...
HTTP://WWW.USERFRIENDLY.ORG/
COPYRIGHT©2003 ILLIAD

THEY FEEL FUNNY. ARE THEY MODEM LEDS?
NO...DEFINITELY NOT. THEY'RE KIND OF ODD LOOKING.

I JUST REALIZED - MY CELL PHONE DOESN'T LIGHT UP ANYMORE...
SAME GOES FOR MY PDA.
ANYBODY SEEINK LEETLE BLUE LIGHT ON MY ATOMIC BOMB?

FESS UP, STEF. YOU RIPPED OFF EVERYONE'S BLUE LIGHTS AND STUCK THEM ON DUST PUPPY DIDN'T YOU.
IT DEPENDS ON HOW YOU LOOK AT IT.

COPYRIGHT © 2003 ILLIAD HTTP://WWW.USERFRIENDLY.ORG/
SEE, IF I HAD KNOWN THAT YOU'D KNOW THAT I HAD DONE IT, I WOULDN'T HAVE DONE IT. UNLESS I KNEW YOU COULDN'T KNOW THAT I KNEW YOU DIDN'T KNOW I HAD DONE IT, IN WHICH CASE I WOULD HAVE DONE IT BECAUSE I KNOW THAT YOU DIDN'T KNOW I HAD DONE IT.

I THINK MY LEFT EYE TURNED IN ON ITSELF.
YE GODS. ARE YOU CHANNELING DONALD RUMSFELD?
AAAGH! THOSE ARE MY OPTIC NERVES!
JUST PRACTICED AT WRITING E.U.L.A.s

WE THREE PINGS DON'T JOURNEY BY CAR.
THROUGH THE NET WE TRAVEL SO FAR.
HUBS AND SWITCHES.
NOCS WITH GLITCHES.
WEB SURFING IS SO SUB-PAR!

COPYRIGHT © 2003 ILLIAD HTTP://WWW.USERFRIENDLY.ORG/
O PERFECT PATH OF FEWEST HOPS.
ROUND TRIP AVERAGE HARD TO TOP.
ALWAYS ROUTED. NEVER DOUBTED.
NE'ER A PACKET DROPS!

WE SPEND OUR LIVES EXISTING AS BITS
UNAWARE OF PAGES OR HITS
DON'T GIVE US HELL
CAUSE WE CAN'T TELL
WHEN DATA IS SPAM OR TI...
STOP RIGHT THERE.

HAD IT NOT BEEN FOR THOUSANDS OF YEARS OF EROSION, THE ROMANS WOULD'VE HAD NOTHING ON THE EGYPTIANS FOR D&D GAMING DICE...
HAVE THE SLAVES ROLL THAT BIG ONE.
YES, MY PHARAOH.
COPYRIGHT © 2003 ILLIAD HTTP://WWW.USERFRIENDLY.ORG/

I hate four-sided dice. Damned caltrops. I don't how many times I've stepped on the damned things since I started gaming.

This strip is in my top five. It offended a lot of Americans, but I think it offended the ones I wanted to offend. One reader even e-mailed me to insist that the War on Terror was nearly won "... now that Saddam bin Laden's been captured, and Al-Qaeda has had its head cut off." Mm-hm.

THIS IS THE BBC. ON SUNDAY U.S. PRESIDENT GEORGE BUSH SAID FORMER IRAQI RULER SADDAM HUSSEIN - NOW IN U.S. CUSTODY - WILL "FACE THE JUSTICE HE DENIED TO MILLIONS".
COPYRIGHT©2003 ILLIAD HTTP://WWW.USERFRIENDLY.ORG/

WE NOW BRING YOU OUR U.S. CORRESPONDENT, ARTHUR LISTER, WHO IS IN SHEEPLEVILLE, U.S.A. ARTHUR?
THANKS DIANE. I HAVE BURT TURPLE HERE. A LOCAL TO SHEEPLEVILLE.

BURT, WHAT DO YOU HAVE TO SAY ABOUT THE RECENT CAPTURE IN IRAQ?
GREAT NEWS! IT'S ABOUT DANG TIME WE CAUGHT THAT SADDAM BIN LADEN CHARACTER!
UM...
SHHHH.

GOOD MORNING.
HEY.
COPYRIGHT©2003 ILLIAD HTTP://WWW.USERFRIENDLY.ORG/

HELP! MY EYE'S STUCK!
NOPE. SAURON IS STILL SCARIER.

This was a take-off on a clever IBM television commercial called "Prodigy." The boy represents Linux in its early childhood, and IBM was backing Linux big time.

I THINK YOU SHOULD SEE THIS.
IT'S JUST A KID...
COPYRIGHT©2003 ILLIAD HTTP://WWW.USERFRIENDLY.ORG/

HE'S LEARNING, ABSORBING...
...HE'S GETTING SMARTER EVERY DAY.

DOES HE HAVE A NAME?
HIS NAME...
...IS LINUX.
UNCLE DARL SAYS I LOOK JUST LIKE HIM.

SO YOU'RE LINUX. AND YOU ABSORB EVERYTHING THAT PEOPLE TELL YOU.
COPYRIGHT©2003 ILLIAD HTTP://WWW.USERFRIENDLY.ORG/

"OPEN SOURCE IS DEAD."
ANALYSIS: IF IT LOOKS LIKE STEVE BALLMER AND SOUNDS LIKE STEVE BALLMER...

I love Eric Cartman. He is everything I wish I could be if I was nasty.

LINUX, I WANT YOU TO MEET SOMEONE, A DISTANT COUSIN OF YOURS IN FACT.
COUSIN?
COPYRIGHT © 2003 ILLIAD HTTP://WWW.USERFRIENDLY.ORG/

YES. IT'S MY NEPHEW. SORT OF. I WAS QUITE CLOSE TO HIS MOTHER.

WINDOWS, COME SAY HELLO TO LINUX.
EY! YOU GUYS QUIT TALKIN' ABOUT MY MOM!

YOU TWO PLAY NICE, NOW. I HAVE TO GO BE A ROCK STAR.
COPYRIGHT © 2003 ILLIAD HTTP://WWW.USERFRIENDLY.ORG/

THIS IS ALL MINE. EVERY TIME I EAT THEM I GET EVEN MORE BUFF. CHECK IT OUT.
MUNCH
MUNCH
MUNCH
CRINKLE
RUSTLE

ARE THOSE SNACKY CAKES?
DATES. "WINDOWS UP" BRAND. GOT ANY SELTZER? I'M FEELING KIND OF BLOATED..

This one was too easy to write. I'd been hearing "Five Token Rings!" in the original "Twelve Days of Christmas" ever since I read an early book on network topologies.

USER FRIENDLY
the comic strip
BY J.D. "ILLIAD" FRAZER

ON THE FIRST DAY OF CHRISTMAS MY TRUE LOVE GAVE TO ME...
A U.S.B. MEMORY KEY!

ON THE SECOND DAY OF CHRISTMAS MY TRUE LOVE GAVE TO ME...
TWO CD BURNERS AND A U.S.B. MEMORY KEY!

ON THE THIRD DAY OF CHRISTMAS MY TRUE LOVE GAVE TO ME...
THREE P.D.As, TWO C.D. BURNERS AND A U.S.B. MEMORY KEY!

ON THE FOURTH DAY OF CHRISTMAS MY TRUE LOVE GAVE TO ME...
FOUR SCSI HARD DRIVES, THREE P.D.As, TWO C.D. BURNERS AND A U.S.B. MEMORY KEY!

ON THE FIFTH DAY OF CHRISTMAS MY TRUE LOVE GAVE TO ME...
FIVE TOKEN RINGS!
PRECIOUS?
WRONG TOLKIEN! GO HOME!

EH. YOU'RE STILL KIND OF YOUNG. RIGHT?
YES. I'M LEARNING.
COPYRIGHT © 2003 ILLIAD HTTP://WWW.USERFRIENDLY.ORG/

YOU WANT TO LEARN SOMETHING COOL? WHAT DO YOU SAY WHEN YOU BLOW UP?
"SEGFAULT."
THAT'S LAME. YOU WANT SOMETHING BETTER THAN THAT.
I DO? WHAT SHOULD I SAY?
B#T$#!! MAKE ME A PAH!
SOMEBODY SHUT DOWN THE HUB NOW!!

YOU SPENDING CHRISTMAS WITH YOUR FAMILY, KUAN?
YEP, WITH MOM AND DAD. SHOULD BE FUN.
COPYRIGHT © 2003 ILLIAD HTTP://WWW.USERFRIENDLY.ORG/

HAVING TURKEY. OPENING PRESENTS. THAT KIND OF THING?
NOPE.

OH. SOMETHING ETHNIC THEN?
IF YOU WANT TO CALL MAKING A MINT SELLING BATTERIES ON CHRIST-MAS AT OUR CORNER STORE ETHNIC, THEN YES.

CTHUHLU. WHAT IN THE NAME OF UNSPEAKABLE NAME ARE YOU WEARING ON YOUR BIG SPONGY HEAD?
A SANTA HAT. I'M GETTING INTO THE SPIRIT OF CHRISTMAS.
COPYRIGHT © 2003 ILLIAD HTTP://WWW.USERFRIENDLY.ORG/

I'M PLANNING ON PUTTING UP A LIGHT DISPLAY ON RL'YEH, USING A TOTAL OF FORTY-TWO BILLION MAGLIGHT BULBS.
SHOULD LOOK RIGHT PRETTY.

WHY DOES YOUR POWER BUDGET SPREADSHEET SAY "EAST AND WEST COAST?"
THE EAST COAST OF NORTH AMERICA ALREADY PROVED THEY COULDN'T HANDLE IT ON THEIR OWN.

In one of my more fevered dreams, I decorated R'lyeh for Christmas. Had trouble wrapping tinsel around that which "can eternal lie."

BELOW THE WAVES, IN THE DEPTHS OF RL'YEH...
...CTHULHU AND HASTUR OPEN CHRISTMAS PRESENTS TOGETHER.
COPYRIGHT © 2003 ILLIAD HTTP://WWW.USERFRIENDLY.ORG/

DESPITE BEING A HOME TO DARK FORCES, IT IS FOR THIS ONE DAY A PLACE OF LIGHT...
CTHULHU...YOU'RE GIVING ME...ARE YOU SURE?
YES...
RLYEH
POP: 1

AND A PLACE WHERE THE CHRISTMAS SPIRIT IS... ...UM...OBSERVED.
...I'M LETTING YOU TAKE MY PLACE WHEN IT'S TIME TO EAT EVERYONE'S HEADS, HASTUR.
(SNIF) THANK YOU MY OLD OLD OLD OLD OLD FRIEND.
RLYEH
POP: 1

SO DORK-BOY. WHATCHA GET FOR CHRISTMAS?
AMONG OTHER THINGS. THIS COMPUTER GAME.

COOL! LET'S SEE...
NO!! DON'T OP-

OH NICE. YOU JUST LET ALL OF THE REPLAY VALUE OUT.
YEAH, BUT THE CD HAS SPARK-LIES ALL OVER IT.
SSSS

LOOK. I DON'T CARE SO MUCH ABOUT GLITZ IN GAMES. I WANT DECENT GAMEPLAY.
GAMEPLAY? ARE YOU OUT OF YOUR MIND?!

IT'S JUST THE START OF A SLIPPERY SLOPE! NEXT YOU'LL WANT MOVIES WITH PLOTS, AND THEN TV NEWS WITH ACTUAL NEWS CONTENT. IF YOU'RE NOT CAREFUL PEOPLE MAY BE FORCED TO START THINKING AGAIN!!

THE WHOLE POINT OF CIVILIZATION IS TO REDUCE HOW MUCH THE AVERAGE PERSON HAS TO THINK. AND NOW YOU WANT TO UNDO ALL THAT WORK JUST SO THAT YOU CAN GET GAMES THAT ARE PLAYABLE. HOW SELFISH CAN YOU BE?!
DEAR LORD. I HAD NO IDEA!

I may sound all high-falutin' and elitist with the comment made by this strip, but the truth is that I too occasionally enjoy nothing more than mindless visual brain candy. My last guilty pleasure was "Age of Empires III." What a grinding, repetitive game. Pretty graphics, though. It's like eating Pringles: yummy to begin with, but after a short while you get ill and wonder how they made salt and styrofoam taste appealing.

2003'S TOY OF THE YEAR

"We couldn't have reached one-fifth the number of 12-year olds we did without the Sleazy-Bake One-Step Lawsuit Kit!" - Hilary Rosen, CEO, RIAA.

Sleazy-Bake
One-Step Lawsuit Kit
Now with Inflatable Lawyer!

"The Sleazy-Bake One-Step Lawsuit Kit really helped make my year!" - Darl McBride, CEO,SCO Group

"AHAHAHAH!" - Anonymous Sleazebag

COPYRIGHT©2003 ILLIAD HTTP://WWW.USERFRIENDLY.ORG/

Create something. Make it illegal for a consumer to use it in any way other than how you stipulate, even if the consumer has paid handsomely for it. Sue the consumer. The results go directly to revenue. This is the business model of the late 20th and early 21st centuries.

Whoever invented the Department of Homeland Security's stupid mood ring system ... well, I'd best not say.

HEY!!
YE GODS. WHAT?!!

DIDN'T YOU HEAR?! ARE YOU DEAF? DON'T YOU WATCH TV? CAN'T YOU READ?!
WHAT?! WHAT?!!

THE U.S. GOVERNMENT ISSUED AN "ORANGE ALERT" THAT THERE'S A TERROR FRUIT IN YOUR HAND.
I'LL GIVE HIM "TERROR FRUIT." I'M GONNA SHOVE AN APPLE IMAC UP HIM.

Saddam Hussein was captured in mid-December, 2003. At about that same time, Michael Jackson was being fingered for messing around with little kids. Personally, I don't think Jackson is a pedophile. But there's no question he's unbelievably stupid, playing his Peter Pan routine in the current social climate regarding predators.

Y'KNOW, IT'S BEEN QUITE A YEAR.
YES. FULL OF NEWS, THINGS TO REMEMBER, THINGS WE HOPE TO FORGET.
THAT WAS QUITE THE NEWS ABOUT YOU-KNOW-WHO BEING BROUGHT TO JUSTICE AFTER ALL THIS TIME.
NO KIDDING. THEY WERE AFTER HIM FOR LONG ENOUGH.

THINK THEY SHOULD THROW THE BOOK AT HIM?
I DUNNO. I DON'T THINK MICHAEL JACKSON IS THAT BAD.

Another one of my top five favorites. I've never been a fan of the invasion of Iraq, but for the most part, service-people get a big thumbs-up from me.

WHAT WAS THE BIGGEST EVENT OF 2003 FOR YOU A.J.?
THAT WHOLE THING IN IRAQ. ALL THOSE PEOPLE...

...NOW THAT YOU MENTION IT, I WONDER WHAT THE TROOPS IN THE TRENCHES SEE AS THE MOST IMPORTANT EVENT OF 2003?
I COULD VENTURE A GUESS.

PHEW. MADE IT TO 2004.

The top ten words of 2003 were *embedded, blog, SARS, spam, taikonaut, Bushism, allision, recall, middangeard*, and *celibacy*. I swear to God.

THIS IS KIND OF INTERESTING. APPARENTLY, THE WORD OF THE YEAR FOR 2003 IS "EMBEDDED."
"'EMBEDDED' WAS THE BEST WORD TO DISTILL THE EVENTS OF AN EXTRAORDINARY YEAR INTO EIGHT SIMPLE LETTERS," SAID PAUL PAYACK OF YOURDICTIONARY.COM.

"WORD OF THE YEAR" MY ARSE. NO ONE WOULD USE IT IN EVERYDAY SPEECH.
THREE YEARS AGO TODAY, YOU AND I WERE EMBEDDED.

BACK AT WORK AFTER A NIGHT OF ABSINTHE AND DEBAUCHERY. HEAD HURTS. FEELS LIKE I FORGOT SOMETHING...
COPYRIGHT © 2004 J.D. "Illiad" Frazer HTTP://WWW.USERFRIENDLY.ORG/

LIKE WEARING PANTS...
MORNING! WANT TO GO GET A LATTE WITH ME?

GREG SLEEPS OFF THE REMAINS OF THE ABSINTHE DURING A BREAK AT WORK...
SNORK
SNORGLE

...AND DREAMS OF A PLACE WHERE GEEKS CAN LIVE TOGETHER.
AWAY FROM THE DEPREDATIONS OF THE MAINSTREAM WORLD.
A PLACE WHERE SCUMMY CORPORATIONS HAVE YET TO SINK THEIR HOOKS...
COPYRIGHT © 2004 J.D. "Illiad" Frazer HTTP://WWW.USERFRIENDLY.ORG/

...UH, RIGHT! MARS!
SORRY. DREW A BLANK.

THE BEAGLE 2 SCIENCE TEAM SUGGESTS THAT THE LANDER IS UNABLE TO COMMUNICATE "BECAUSE IT MAY HAVE LANDED IN A CRATER."

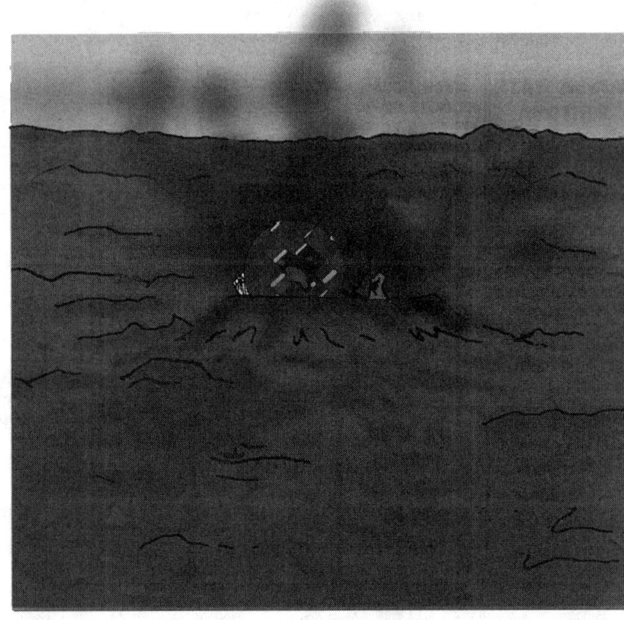

Lithobraking. Heh. *Aerobraking* is hard enough on the system.

IN GREG'S DREAM WORLD, GEEKDOM IS REALIZED AS A NATION ON A BARREN PLANET.
CAN YOU HEAR ME? GOOD!

FACILITIES AND HABITATS ARE CONSTRUCTED FROM ALL OF THE SPACE HARDWARE THAT ARRIVED ON THE PLANET OVER THE YEARS VIA "LITHOBRAKING."
V'GER
COPYRIGHT©2004 J.D. "Illiad" Frazer HTTP://WWW.USERFRIENDLY.ORG/

...AND THE MACHINE OF DEMOCRACY IS DRIVEN BY GEEK VALUES.
LOOKS LIKE YOU'RE PRESIDENT. AGAIN.
SPLUTCH
SPLUTCH
BLORCH
SPLATCH
IMPRESSIVE
WIGGLE

IT IS A NEW DAY IN SOURCE CITY, THE CITY-STATE TECHNOCRACY ON MARS...
WHAT'S ON THE AGENDA TODAY, ERWIN?

MISTER PRESIDENT. I'D APPRECIATE IT IF YOU'D ADDRESS ME BY MY TITLE. I AM YOUR VICE-PRESIDENT AFTER ALL.
OH. I'M SORRY ERWIN. UM...WHAT EXACTLY DO VICE-PRESIDENTS DO?
COPYRIGHT©2004 J.D. "Illiad" Frazer HTTP://WWW.USERFRIENDLY.ORG/

JUDGING FROM INFO ON THE NET, I GET TO PRESIDE OVER VICES.
SIR, I'M HERE TO REMIND YOU THAT OUR BUDGET FOR FIGHTING LAW-SUITS IS ZERO.

Man, that was poorly executed. The cow talking at the end is just too surreal. It's a niche culture reference: a fantastic song called "I'm a cow." It's catchy. Google it and listen, but do so away from prying eyes.

MR. VICE PRESIDENT. WHAT'S ON THE AGENDA FOR TODAY?
A MEETING WITH YOUR SENIOR STAFF MR. PRES-
COPYRIGHT©2004 J.D. "Illiad" Frazer HTTP://WWW.USERFRIENDLY.ORG/

YO, BOSS-MAN. CHECK OUT OUR NEW WEAPON! IT'S A MAD COW!

ERWIN, WHAT DOES CTHULHU DO HERE?
SECRETARY OF DEFENSE.
LOOK, WE NEED SOMETHING. EARTH KEEPS PELTING US WITH THEIR DAMNED PROBES!
MOOOOO I'M A COW!

ARE THOSE PROTESTORS ON THE SCREE?
YES SIR. THOSE PEOPLE THERE ARE THE REDHATIANS, THE FOLKS ON THE LEFT ARE DEBIANIANS, AND THE TWO GUYS HOLDING UP THE ENVELOPE WITH TINY WRITING ARE BEOS USERS.

WHAT ARE THE BEOSERS PROTESTING?
NOTHING IN PARTICULAR. THEY JUST WANT TO BE NOTICED.
COPYRIGHT©2004 J.D. "Illiad" Frazer HTTP://WWW.USERFRIENDLY.ORG/

UH OH. THERE'S A FIGHT OVER THERE.
THAT'S OKAY. THOSE ARE THE NETBSDERS AND THE OPENBSDERS. ALL THE LINUX LOBBYISTS WANT THEM TO KILL EACH OTHER.

THIS IS A PETITIONER FROM THE WINDOWS GEEK LOBBY, MR. PRESIDENT.
WE'RE A PERSECUTED MINORITY! DO SOMETHING ABOUT IT!

COPYRIGHT©2004 J.D. "Illiad" Frazer HTTP://WWW.USERFRIENDLY.ORG/
MINORITY? BUT THERE ARE MORE OF YOU GUYS THAN OF ANYONE ELSE.
YEP. THE CENSUS SAYS SO.
REALLY.

IN THAT CASE, WE VOTE TO PERSECUTE EVERYONE ELSE!
IT SEEMS THAT PARTICULAR BILL HAS ALREADY BEEN PUSHED THROUGH.
"THAT PARTICULAR BILL." HEH. YOU'RE SUCH A WIT MR. PRESIDENT.

GREG'S DREAM CONTINUES...
GEEKS OF SOURCE CITY! HEAR ME!
WE ARE ALL BRETHREN. ODD IN OUR BEHAVIOUR. IMAGINATIVE IN OUR DREAMS. OSTRACIZED BY THE REST OF SOCIETY.
nuthin' but .NET!
java's worth beans!

COPYRIGHT©2004 J.D. "Illiad" Frazer HTTP://WWW.USERFRIENDLY.ORG/
FIGHTING OVER WHICH O.S. IS BETTER THAN THE OTHER SAPS OUR STRENGTH.
CAN WE AS GEEKS NOT JUST LIVE AND LET LIVE?
OKAY. WE'LL BE GOOD.
YEP. WE WON'T PICK ANYMORE FIGHTS.
nuthin' but .NET!
java's worth beans!

...EXCEPT WITH THOSE STAR WARS DORKS OVER THERE.
OH YEAH?! CAPTAIN PICARD USES EMACS!!
OOOH! WHY YOU... OOOH!!
nuthin' but .NET!
java's worth beans!

DISTRO WARS the "My Distro is Better" Card Game

UserFriendly.Org

OBJECTIVE: TO BE THE LAST REMAINING (AND THEREFORE ONE TRUE) *NIX DISTRIBUTION.

NO. OF PLAYERS: 3 TO 6

BITS NEEDED: A DECK OF PLAYING CARDS, A 6-SIDED DIE, AND 10 COUNTERS PER PLAYER.

SETUP: KEEP ONLY THE ACES THROUGH SIXS. ACES ARE "SPECIAL" CARDS. SHUFFLE AND DEAL EACH PLAYER THREE CARDS. GIVE EACH PLAYER THREE COUNTERS. THE REST GO IN THE "BANK."

COUNTERS REPRESENT EACH PLAYER'S "INSTALL BASE." ONE COUNTER CAN MEAN ONE COMPUTER, ONE COMPANY, OR A MILLION BOXEN. WHATEVER EXCITES YOU.

THE CARDS YOU HOLD REPRESENT INFLUENCE IN THE MARKET, WHETHER IT'S FROM GOOD PACKAGING, A COOL INSTALLER, ADVERTISING ON U.F., OR NAUGHTY PICTURE COLLECTIONS ON YOUR ISO.

YOU INSTANTLY WIN WHEN YOU COLLECT A SIMPLE MAJORITY OF COUNTERS IN THE GAME. E.G.: IN A 3-PLAYER GAME, YOU NEED 16 COUNTERS TO WIN.

ROLL THE DIE TO SEE WHO GOES FIRST. PLAY THEN PROCEEDS CLOCKWISE.

TURN SEQUENCE:

1. ADD ONE COUNTER TO YOUR INSTALL BASE. IF THE BANK IS EMPTY, SKIP THIS STEP.

2. ROLL THE DIE. THE NUMBER IS WHAT IS "CHIC" IN THE *NIX DISTRO WORLD RIGHT NOW. A ONE MEANS NOTHING IS CHIC.

3. PLAY A CARD. IF THE NUMBER ON THE CARD MATCHES THE DIE ROLL, YOU GET 3 COUNTERS (OR WHATEVER THE BANK CAN HANDLE UP TO 3.) IF THE NUMBER CAN EVENLY DIVIDE INTO THE NUMBER (LIKE A DEUCE INTO A 4), YOU GET WHATEVER THE DIVISION COMES OUT TO (DEUCE INTO 4 GIVES 2 COUNTERS.)

4. OR INSTEAD, YOU CAN PLAY A CARD AGAINST ANOTHER PLAYER. IF HE CAN'T PLAY A CARD THAT MATCHES OR EXCEEDS YOUR CARD, YOU TAKE YOUR CARD'S NUMBER OF COUNTERS FROM HIM.

5. YOU DON'T HAVE TO PLAY A CARD, BUT YOU CAN ONLY DO ONE OF 3 OR 4 ON YOUR TURN. DISCARD ALL PLAYED CARDS. IF YOU HAVE LESS THAN 3 CARDS IN YOUR HAND, BRING IT BACK UP TO 3. RESHUFFLE THE DISCARD DECK WHEN THE DRAW DECK IS DEPLETED.

6. CHECK TO SEE IF YOU'VE WON. IF NOT, PLAY PROCEEDS TO THE NEXT PLAYER WHO REPEATS STEPS 1 TO 6. IF YOU DO WIN, YOU MAY TAUNT EVERYONE ELSE.

SPECIAL RULE: ACES. YOU CAN PLAY AN ACE TO DEFEND YOURSELF FROM A PLAYER WHO IS EXECUTING STEP 4. AN ACE REPRESENTS A LAWSUIT FROM THE SCUM GROUP, WHICH ENDS THAT PLAYER'S TURN, AND HE HAS TO GIVE HALF OF HIS INSTALL BASE BACK TO THE BANK, ROUNDED UP.

Print out and use these spiffy logos to represent your *nix distribution!

big lizard LINUX
"I think we need a bigger box."
We were here first, dammit!
Nreepen BSD
Gentile Linux
"it's all there!"

So there's a spoof of the song (one verse, anyway). This strip saw the light of day around the time Alberta was implicated in shipping mad-cow beef to the U.S.

THE BOSS ISN'T TOO CHUFFED ABOUT OUR NEW WEAPON.
WHAT THE HELL ARE WE GOING TO DO WITH A MAD COW?
I'M A COW CAN'T YOU SEE I LIVE ON MARS COLONY MOOOOOO I'M A COW!

COPYRIGHT © 2004 J.D. "Illiad" Frazer HTTP://WWW.USERFRIENDLY.ORG/
WELL. MR. UNDERSECRETARY OF DEFENSE?
I'M A COW MARS IS RED GO ON BUDDY EAT MY HEAD MOOOOOO! I'M A COW!

GIVE HER BACK TO THE CANADIANS.
IS THAT WHO WE GOT IT FROM?
IT'S WHERE ALL MAD COWS COME FROM. THEY HAVE A WHOLE PROVINCE DEDICATED TO MAKING MAD COWS.
MOOO. EH!

GEEKS OF SOURCE CITY. YOU HAVE REQUESTED CHANGES. AND WE HAVE WORKED HARD TO BRING THEM TO YOU!
EVERY GEEK GETS A PDA AND GPS! WIRELESS IS EVERYWHERE! SOFTWARE IS FREE! EVERY NEW BABY GETS A CHOCOLATE ECLAIR!
YAHOO!
YAZZA!!

COPYRIGHT © 2004 J.D. "Illiad" Frazer HTTP://WWW.USERFRIENDLY.ORG/
SIR? WHERE ARE WE GETTING THE MONEY TO PAY FOR ALL OF THAT?
WOOO!!
YEAH!
HUZZAH!

FROM THE INTERNET?
I THOUGHT SO. I'LL IPO MARS FOR US NEXT WEEK.

Guess where the "modulate" idea came from? Look at the portrait on the wall.

ERWIN, WE HAVE TO MAKE MONEY. IF WE DON'T, OUR CITY-STATE WILL IMPLODE.
YOU'RE RIGHT, BUT WHO CAN WE GET TO HELP US WITH THAT?

COPYRIGHT © 2004 J.D. "Illiad" Frazer HTTP://WWW.USERFRIENDLY.ORG/

ONE STEP CLOSER AND I MODULATE YOUR ARSE.
NO NO. WAIT! I'M ALL ABOUT THE GEEK THING! WE CAN INSTITUTE A PING TAX! YOU GUYS LIKE TO PING. DON'T YOU?

IF YOU WANT ME TO GET YOU SOME STEADY REVENUE. I EXPECT TO BE COMPENSATED.
DO YOU WANT COMMISSION?
YES. AND AN APPOINTMENT AS SECRETARY OF TECHNOLOGY.

COPYRIGHT © 2004 J.D. "Illiad" Frazer HTTP://WWW.USERFRIENDLY.ORG/
ALL THE GEEKS WILL PAY US MONEY. OR I'LL BAN EVERY LANGUAGE EXCEPT FOR VBSCRIPT.

WE NEED GREG TO WAKE UP FROM HIS DREAM NOW. RIGHT NOW. HOW DO WE DO THAT?
GET THE COW TO FRENCH-KISS HIM.

MMMMMM...MMM...MMUU...

MMMMMMMMUUMMMMM
COPYRIGHT©2004 J.D. "Illiad" Frazer HTTP://WWW.USERFRIENDLY.ORG/

YE FLIPPING GODS GREG. YOU'RE KISSING A COW!!
THANK GOD!

THAT MUST HAVE BEEN QUITE A DREAM...
IT STARTED OFF GREAT. BUT THEN A GHASTLY REALITY OF A SORT SET IN.

COPYRIGHT©2004 J.D. "Illiad" Frazer HTTP://WWW.USERFRIENDLY.ORG/

KIND OF LIKE THE INTERNET. HUH.
WELL. EXCEPT FOR THE COW.
WE ARE MILKINK NET FOR FREE. NYET?

TEN MINUTES AFTER THE FIRST PERMANENT MOONBASE GETS A TOP-LEVEL DOMAIN* AND A NET CONNECTION.
APPARENTLY 6340 PEOPLE WANT TO SELL US VIAGRA BY MAIL ORDER.
AND GET THIS. SHIPPING IS JUST $3.95.
*THE TLD IS SURE TO BE '.MOO,' SINCE THE MOON IS MADE OF CHEESE AND CHEESE COMES FROM COWS.
COPYRIGHT©2004 J.D. "Illiad" Frazer HTTP://WWW.USERFRIENDLY.ORG/

AYBABTU needs to die. So does the Badger song by Weebl. At the same time, I confess to having a love for both—the dirty sort of love you have for bad leper jokes.

YOU LOOK LIKE YOU'RE IN A GOOD MOOD...
I HAVEN'T HEARD OR READ A SINGLE "ALL YOUR BASE" REFERENCE IN MONTHS. MAYBE -HOPEFULLY- THIS MEANS IT'S FINALLY DEAD. MY GOD I HATE MEMES
COPYRIGHT©2004 J.D. "Illiad" Frazer HTTP://WWW.USERFRIENDLY.ORG/

UH OH...

BADGER BADGER BADGER BADGER BADGER BADGER BADGER BADGER BADGER...
AAAAAAAUUUGH!

DID I JUST HEAR THE BADGER SONG?
STOP THAT! I HATE THAT STUPID SONG! IT GOES ON ABOUT BADGERS. THEN MUSHROOMS. THEN A SNAKE! THE SONG DOESN'T MAKE SENSE!
COPYRIGHT©2004 J.D. "Illiad" Frazer HTTP://WWW.USERFRIENDLY.ORG/

YOU GUYS ARE GEEKS! WHERE'S YOUR LOVE FOR LOGIC AND RATIONALE? SHOW SOME DIGNITY FERCHRISSAKES!

BADGER BADGER BADGER BADGER! BADGER BADGER BADGER BADGER!
MUSHROOM MUSHROOOOM!
AAAUUUUGHH!!

PENCIL PENCIL PENCIL PENCIL PENCIL PENCIL PENCIL PENCIL
ERASER! ERASER!
COPYRIGHT©2004 J.D. "Illiad" Frazer HTTP://WWW.USERFRIENDLY.ORG/

PENCIL PENCIL PENCIL PENCIL PENCIL PENCIL PENCIL PENCIL
ERASER! ERASER!!

YOU KNOW, SOME DAYS THE THOUGHT OF GOING BACK TO WORK IN TECH SUPPORT DOESN'T SEEM ALL THAT BAD.
PENCIL PENCIL PENCIL PENCIL PENCIL PENCIL PENCIL PENCIL A MISTAKE. IT'S A MISTAAAAKE!

Does anyone use their semicolon key anymore?

HELLO! COLON CLEANSING IS THE BEST WAY TO HAPPY! $39.95 AND HAPPY IS YOURS!
COPYRIGHT©2004 J.D. "Illiad" Frazer HTTP://WWW.USERFRIENDLY.ORG/

REPLY TO US! IS YOUR COLON DIRTY?

NO, BUT MY SEMI-COLON COULD USE A GOOD PICKING.
HEY NOW. DON'T BE MESSING WITH MY FAMILY.
TYPE TAP TIP

IT'S...IT'S...
STINKHEAD.
BAH. I IGNORE INSECTS LIKE YOU.

I MEAN LOOK AT YOU. JUST FUZZ AND FEET! I MUST WEIGH TEN TIMES WHAT YOU DO. YOU WOULDN'T LAST TEN SECONDS IN A FIGHT WITH ME.
G'BYE.
COPYRIGHT©2004 J.D. "Illiad" Frazer HTTP://WWW.USERFRIENDLY.ORG/

YOU SURE THIS IS GOING TO WORK?
YOUR HEAD IS SWEATY.
OH YEAH! LOOK OUT CRUD PUPPY!

GOOD...NOW PUT IN A BID FOR ALL OF THE OUTSTANDING SHARES. AND WE TAKE CONTROL. THEN WE CAN CARVE THE ASSETS UP AND FEED LIKE SHARKS IN A CHUM POOL.
NIIIICE...
COPYRIGHT©2004 J.D. "Illiad" Frazer HTTP://WWW.USERFRIENDLY.ORG/

WHAT IN THE NAME OF THE OUTER GODS WAS THAT?
I DON'T KNOW. BUT I GET THE CREEPY FEELING IT WAS MEANT FOR ME.
LEFT! LEFT! NO! NO!! THE OTHER LEFT!!

USER FRIENDLY
the comic strip
BY J.D. "ILLIAD" FRAZER
COPYRIGHT©2004 J.D. "Illiad" Frazer HTTP://WWW.USERFRIENDLY.ORG/

I'M WARNING YOU -- NONE OF THAT "BADGER BADGER" CRAP WHILE I'M AROUND.

BADGER BADGER BADGER BADGER BADGER BADGER BADGER BADGER....
AAAUUGH!! STOP IT!!

OKAY. LOOK. TRY THIS VARIATION ON THE THEME. SAME TUNE. DIFFERENT WORDS.
SURE!

LET'S SEE NOW... *AHEM*

I'M SURE IT'LL BE WORTH THE PAPERWORK...
HASTUR HASTUR HASTUR-
CRUNCH!
BELCH!

I feel a little sorry that I killed off Kuan this way. I liked him as a character, and I don't believe I've killed off any characters prior to him, or since.

WHAT THE HELL IS **THIS?**
SID ASKED ME TO INSTALL A LINUX PARTITION ON YOUR BOX. HE JUST WANTS THE NON-TECH STAFF TO GET COMFY WITH SOMETHING OTHER THAN WINDOWS.
COPYRIGHT©2004 J.D. "Illiad" Frazer HTTP://WWW.USERFRIENDLY.ORG/

WHAT?! WHY??! ALL I NEED IS MY "XP EXPERIENCE!"
RELAX STEF. LINUX HAS COME A LONG WAY ON THE DESKTOP SINCE YOU USED IT LAST. READ THE BOX:

"WANKLE LINUX PUTS THE FUN BACK INTO COMPUTING." **WHAT** FUN?
WATCHING YOU ACCIDENTALLY DELETE ALL YOUR FILES FOR STARTERS.

HOW DID STEF'S LINUX INSTALL GO?
THE INSTALL WENT FINE BUT HE FLIPPED OUT WHEN HE FOUND OUT IT WAS ON HIS BOX.
COPYRIGHT©2004 J.D. "Illiad" Frazer HTTP://WWW.USERFRIENDLY.ORG/

HE REFUSED TO USE IT. AND DEMANDED THAT I SWITCH HIM BACK TO XP.
WHAT DID YOU DO?

I INSTALLED XPDE ON IT SO NOW LINUX LOOKS LIKE WINDOWS XP.
WHAT DID YOU **DO?** MY START MENU COMES UP SO FAST IT'S LIKE A TWITCH GAME.

MIKE, I **LOVE** WHAT YOU'VE DONE TO MY BOX! THIS IS THE FASTEST I'VE EVER SEEN WINDOWS RUN!
UH...I HAVE TO CONFESS. STEF. YOU'RE USING LINUX WITH AN XP-LOOKALIKE WINDOW MANAGER.
COPYRIGHT©2004 J.D. "Illiad" Frazer HTTP://WWW.USERFRIENDLY.ORG/

I'M...I'M USING AND ENJOYING **LINUX?** AND IT LOOKS LIKE **WINDOWS XP?**
NO...NO... MY MISTAKE.

STEF? WHAT ON EARTH ARE YOU DOING?
LINUX STUFF.
RAPPA TAP TAP TYPE TAP TAP TIK TAK TOK TAPP TIP TAP TAP TYPE TAP
COPYRIGHT©2004 J.D. "Illiad" Frazer HTTP://WWW.USERFRIENDLY.ORG/

TAPPA TAP TAP TAP TAPPY TAP TAP TAPPY TAPPY TAP TAP TAP TAP TYPE TIP TAP TAP TAP

STEF. YOU'RE JUST TYPING RANDOM LETTERS AND SYMBOLS...
AND HOW IS THAT DIFFERENT FROM WHAT YOU GUYS DO ON YOUR COMMAND LINE THINGIE ALL OF THE TIME?
TAP TAP TAP TAPPA TAP

BILL GATES, CHAIRMAN AND FOUNDER OF MICROSOFT, HAS BEEN AWARDED AN HONOURARY KNIGHTHOOD BY HER MAJESTY THE QUEEN. THE HONOURARY K.B.E. IS IN RECOGNITION OF HIS OUTSTANDING CONTRIBUTION TO ENTERPRISE, EMPLOYMENT, AND EDUCATION IN THE UNITED KINGDOM.
COPYRIGHT©2004 J.D. "Illiad" Frazer HTTP://WWW.USERFRIENDLY.ORG/

BILL GATES IS A KNIGHT OF THE BRITISH EMPIRE? WOW.
I'M SURE HE'LL GET EVEN MORE RESPECT FROM HIS STAFF AND FOLLOWERS NOW...

NIH!
STICK TO YOUR "DEVELOPERS" CHANT, STEVE.

BUCKINGHAM PALACE.
HELLO, THIS IS LARRY ELLISON. I HEARD THAT BILL GATES IS GETTING A KNIGHTHOOD.
YES, CORRECT.

I JUST WANTED TO POINT OUT THAT IF YOU'RE LOOKING TO KNIGHT A REAL ALPHA GEEK, I CAN HELP YOU OUT...

NO THANK YOU. WE'VE ALREADY GAT WAN.

ALREADY GOT ONE?!
YES, HE'S VERRAH NASS!
MISTER CHIRAC! THE HEADS OF STATE ARE WAITING!

Get me drunk, and I'll do one of two outrageous accents: a French knight from the *Monty Python and the Holy Grail* or a brogue-ish Tim the Enchanter.

USER FRIENDLY
the comic strip
BY J.D. "ILLIAD" FRAZER
COPYRIGHT©2004 J.D. "Illiad" Frazer HTTP://WWW.USERFRIENDLY.ORG/

"THIS IS THE BBC. THE HUNT FOR WHOEVER WAS BEHIND THE 'MYDOOM' E-MAIL WORM, AND ITS SIBLING 'MYDOOM.B', HAS INTENSIFIED WITH A $250,000 REWARD OFFERED BY MICROSOFT."
VIRUSES ARE EVIL. VIRUS WRITERS ARE BOTTOM-FEEDERS.

"EXPERTS SAID MYDOOM.A AND B MADE UP TO 30 PERCENT OF ALL E-MAIL TRAFFIC AT ITS PEAK.
IT HAS BEATEN ALL PREVIOUS RECORDS FOR VIRUS INFECTIONS, ACCORDING TO SECURITY EXPERTS."
SCUM! SEWAGE! MAGGOTRY!

"THE ORIGINAL VARIANT, MYDOOM.A, IS ALSO SCHEDULED TO TARGET S.C.O.'S WEBSITE FROM TODAY, 1 FEBRUARY, UNTIL 12 FEBRUARY."
ROTTEN, SCUMMY VIR-

...UH...YAY TEAM?
I KNOW. I'VE BEEN STRUGGLING WITH THIS ONE ALL WEEK.

HELLO. ON OCCASION OVER THE YEARS I'VE RECEIVED EMAIL FROM READERS COMPLAINING THAT I DON'T DRAW GEEKS "REALISTICALLY" ENOUGH.
ILLIAD

OF COURSE. THEY'RE REFERRING TO THE FACT THAT A SIGNIFICANT NUMBER OF GEEKS ARE OVER-WEIGHT. AND NONE OF THE CHARACTERS IN U.F. ARE PARTICULARLY ROTUND.

I HAVE THEREFORE TAKEN IT UPON MYSELF TO CORRECT THIS TERRIBLE MISREPRESENTATION. ...AND THEN SOME.
YO, PICASSO. A MOMENT OF YOUR TIME...

WE CONTINUE WITH OUR STUDY OF "MASS-RICH PHYSIQUES" AMONG GEEKS. OUR SUBJECT HAS AGREED TO ATTEMPT A LOW-CARB DIET THAT HAS BECOME THE RAGE WITHIN THE GEEK POPULACE.

BEFORE:

...AND AFTER. NOTICE THE HAPPIER DEMEANOR IN THE SUBJECT.
QUIT MESSING WITH MY BODY!!
ALSO NOTE THE CLEVER PARALLEL BETWEEN OUR GEEK DUMPING ALL THAT PENALTY-WEIGHT AND PIXAR GIVING DISNEY THE BOOT.

YO. WANT TO GO FOR LUNCH?
SURE. BUT I WANT TO FINISH WATCHING THE FOOTAGE FROM THE SUPERBOWL HALFTIME SHOW. THAT WHOLE JANET JACKSON "POP-UP" SURPRISE.

DUDE. WHAT ARE YOU DOING? THAT SCENE BARELY LASTED A COUPLE OF SECONDS.
NOT IF YOU WATCH IT FRAME-BY-FRAME. AHEM.

MR. MCBRIDE? THE WEATHER REPORT SAID TO EXPECT RAIN THIS AFTERNOON.
SHOULD I CANCEL YOUR GOLF GAME?
SCO

SCO

IT'S BECAUSE OF THOSE DAMNED LINUX HACKERS AGAIN, ISN'T IT.
YES SIR. OH THEY'LL PAY FOR THIS.
SCO

McBride was blaming "Linux hackers" for everything that ailed SCO—and the world, for that matter. Software piracy? Linux hackers. Nasty viruses? Linux hackers. Climate change? Linux hackers. The canker sore on his unmentionables? Linux hackers.

SIR? IT'S YOUR WIFE ON LINE ONE.
UH OH.

YES HONEY?
DARL, DEAR. THE GARDENIAS IN THE LIVING ROOM ARE ALL DYING.

WELL I'M SURE IT'S THOSE GOL'DANG LINUX HACKERS!
OF COURSE IT IS DEAR. I TAKE IT YOU'LL BE HAVING DINNER WITH THE LAWYERS AGAIN TONIGHT?
SCO

MR. MCBRIDE, INDEPENDENT TECHNICAL EXPERTS HAVE REPEATEDLY SHOWN THAT THERE IS NO SCO-OWNED PROPRIETARY UNIX CODE INSERTED INTO THE LINUX KERNEL.
WHAT DO YOU HAVE TO SAY TO THIS?

S.C.O. IS PROTECTING ITS PROPERTY, REGARDLESS OF WHETHER OR NOT THERE'S ACTUAL SCO-UNIX CODE IN THERE. THE LINUX HACKER COMMUNITY IS STILL IN THE WRONG.
HOW'S THAT, SIR?

OH, COME ON! ISN'T IT CLEAR THAT THEY'RE INVOLVED IN UNIX-RELATED PROGRAM ACTIVITIES?!
CRYSTAL.
DANGED LINUX HACKERS.

THE INTERNET TODAY AND J.R.R TOLKIEN
A COMPARISON

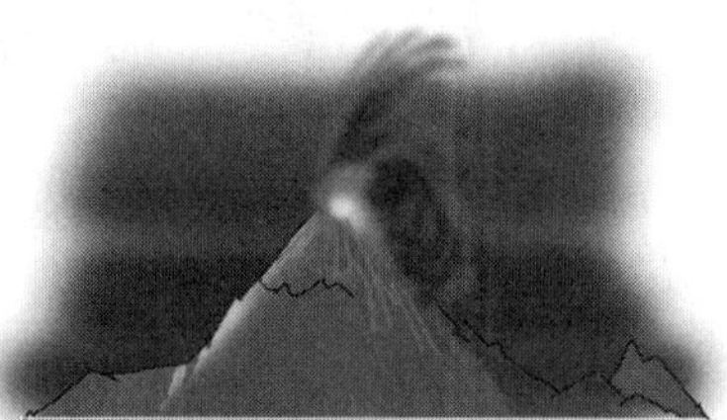

Mount Doom

MyDoom Virus

The Return of the King

Awaiting the Return of the Ping

ARE YOU READY TO GO YET, A.J.?
YEP. I'LL JUST LET MY SPYWARE SCAN RUN OVER LUNCH.
COPYRIGHT©2004 J.D. "Illiad" Frazer HTTP://WWW.USERFRIENDLY.ORG/

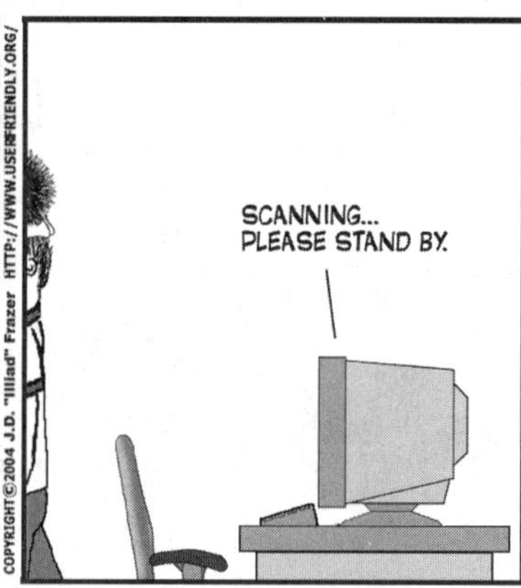
SCANNING... PLEASE STAND BY.

SCANNING COMPLETE. NO SPYWARE REPORTED.
HEH. MISSED ME.
POIK!

LET'S SEE WHAT'S ON THIS WEENIE'S MACHINE...HERE WE GO...LOGIN NAME. PASSWORD...MM-HM...
COPYRIGHT©2004 J.D. "Illiad" Frazer HTTP://WWW.USERFRIENDLY.ORG/

WOULD YOU MIND NOT LOOKING OVER MY SHOULDER? IT'S RUDE.
ENGFEH

WHAT **IS** IT?
IT LOOKS LIKE AN EYEBALL WITH VARIOUS WET ATTACHMENTS.
COPYRIGHT©2004 J.D. "Illiad" Frazer HTTP://WWW.USERFRIENDLY.ORG/

WHAT DOES IT DO?
WHAT I WANT TO KNOW IS WHERE IT COMES FROM.

I DIDN'T THINK IT WOULD **STING** QUITE SO MUCH.
YOU'RE GOING TO SAY THE SAME ABOUT THE RUBBING ALCOHOL.

EXCUSE ME, BUT **WHAT ARE YOU?**
IF YOU **MUST** KNOW, I'M A WETWARE CONSTRUCT THAT FERRETS OUT HIDDEN SPYWARE AND ADWARE ON YOUR MACHINE. I'M YOUR FRIEND. YOU MAY REJOICE OVER THIS.
COPYRIGHT©2004 J.D. "Illiad" Frazer HTTP://WWW.USERFRIENDLY.ORG/

UM...WHY ARE YOU EMAILING MY BANK INFORMATION TO NIGERIA?
LOTS OF SPYWARE IN TEXT. I'M HELPING YOU GET RID OF IT.
TAP
TUD
TUD
TUP

WHILE I'M TRANSFERRING ALL OF YOUR BANK INFORMATION, WHY DON'T WE GET TO KNOW EACH OTHER?
UM. OKAY.
TUP TUP TUPPY
COPYRIGHT © 2004 J.D. "Illiad" Frazer HTTP://WWW.USERFRIENDLY.ORG/

GENDER?
MALE.
AGE?
29.
POLITICS?
CENTRIST.
JOB SECTOR?
I.T.

YOU COULDN'T HAVE TOLD ME YOU WORKED IN I.T. BEFORE I TOOK THE TIME AND EFFORT TO BREAK INTO YOUR ACCOUNT WHERE YOU HAVE TWENTY-NINE CENTS. COULD YOU.
I HAVE TWENTY NINE CENTS? WOO!

EXCUSE ME. I'M HERE TO RECLAIM MY EYE.
I AM HERE MASTER!
COPYRIGHT © 2004 J.D. "Illiad" Frazer HTTP://WWW.USERFRIENDLY.ORG/

YOU'RE IN A GOOD MOOD.
OF COURSE I AM! I'VE GOT MY EYE BACK. I'M BEING PAID SERIOUS MONEY FOR ALL OF THE DATA IT MINED. AND IT'S VALENTINE'S DAY!

YOU CELEBRATE VALENTINE'S?
SURE. IT WAS A HELL OF A MASSACRE.

APPEARING AT A KAZAA SERVER NEAR YOU.

FREE BILLY
HOW FAR WOULD YOU GO TO VIEW CODE?
"The most rousing hacker adventure since The Net."
A SCRIPT KIDDIE. A 3-TON SOURCE FILE.
CODE YOU COULD NEVER IMAGINE.
COMMENTS YOU WILL NEVER FORGET.

HEY, WEB-DORK. DID YOU SEE A CREEPY LITTLE EYEBALL POKING AROUND HERE?
YES, BUT IT'S GONE NOW.

I SHOULD HOPE SO. THAT WET LITTLE MARBLE WENT THROUGH MY PERSONAL STASH OF STEFCAM "BUFF IN THE SHOWER" PHOTOS.
HUH. I WONDER WHEN IT DOES A DATA DUMP..
COPYRIGHT © 2004 J.D. "Illiad" Frazer HTTP://WWW.USERFRIENDLY.ORG/

AAAGH. RIP IT OUT!
RIP IT OUT!!
WELL CRIPES. MAKE UP YOUR MIND!

I'm not going to explain this one. If you can't count in binary on your fingers, go ask someone who can. Don't belt them.

HEY SID. WHEN YOU RETIRE, ARE YOU GOINK TO PETRIFY OR FOSSILIZE?

COPYRIGHT © 2004 J.D. "Illiad" Frazer HTTP://WWW.USERFRIENDLY.ORG/
PITR. DO YOU KNOW HOW TO COUNT IN BINARY? ON YOUR FINGERS?
DA. OF COURSE.
THEN I SEND YOU A "FOUR."

UH...ONE... TWO...FOUR...

HEY!

AM **TIRED** OF THAT OLD *FILIUS NULLIUS*. ALWAYS IRRITATINK ME, GETTINK IN WAY OF EVIL GENIUS AT WORK.

COPYRIGHT © 2004 J.D. "Illiad" Frazer HTTP://WWW.USERFRIENDLY.ORG/
AM GOING TO BE **FIXINK** HIS LEETLE RED WAGON. FILL OUT ONLINE FORM...MAKE CASH MONEY PAYMENT FROM S.C.O.'S BANK ACCOUNT, AND **VOILA!**

MEANWHILE, OVER AT "GEEK PASTURES, HOME FOR THE OBSOLETE"...
YO, ABE! NEW ORDER FOR A RETRIEVAL!
"LIKELY TO RESIST AND REMAIN IN DENIAL." OH, I LIKE THESE ONES."

SOME LARGE MEN ARE HERE LOOKING FOR SID.
REALLY? WHAT FOR?

COPYRIGHT © 2004 J.D. "Illiad" Frazer HTTP://WWW.USERFRIENDLY.ORG/
DON'T KNOW, BUT THEY HAVE BEADY EYES. I WOULDN'T TELL THEM WHO HE WAS HERE, AND THEY REPLIED "THAT'S OKAY. HE'LL MAKE HIMSELF KNOWN."

...AND JUST LAST NIGHT I HAD TO WAIT A WHOLE 20 SECONDS TO SEND MY PHOTOS OVER THE NET.
SPOILED BRATS. IN **MY** DAY WE HAD TO SEND DATA USING ACOUSTIC COUPLERS, UPSTREAM **BOTH WAYS**.

WHADDYA MEAN YOU'RE TAKING ME TO THE "HOME FOR THE OBSOLETE"?!
JUST THAT. WE RECEIVED AN ONLINE ORDER - PAID IN FULL - CITING OBSO-LESCENCE.

WAIT! WHO PLACED THE ORDER?
LET'S SEE NOW...

...IT SAYS HERE IT WAS YOUR SON-IN-LAW.
BE SEEINK YOU, DAD.
PITR!

I CAN'T BELIEVE THEY TOOK YOUR DAD AWAY, PEARL.
AND TO A "HOME FOR THE OBSOLETE?" HOW HORRID.

SID MUST BE GOING RAVING MAD BY NOW.
OH I DON'T KNOW ABOUT THAT. I'LL BET HE'S ENJOYING HANGING WITH GEEKS FROM HIS ERA.

...AND ONCE I CODED A SUBROUTINE THIS LONG!
IT GOT AWAY ON ME...
WHAT HAPPENED TO IT?

I guess I'm dating myself with this storyline. I'm not as old as Sid (yet), but I do remember the days of punchcards and reel-to-reels and playing with big iron. I was just a kid, but I soaked up the knowledge like a sponge. I also had an (old) acoustic coupler. 110 baud, anyone?

THE RECENT NEWS ABOUT A BLACK HOLE SUGGESTS A TIMELY COMPARISON OF THE QUALITY OF SEARCH RELEVANCY BETWEEN YAHOO AND GOOGLE:

"HOT BLACK BODY"

Back then, if you did a search with those keywords on Yahoo, the results were ... eye-opening. Today, the image-search results on both services are equally eye-opening.

You'll have to look up *Wumpus*, but suffice it to say it's an icon of early computing. Also, I have both fond and terrifying memories of green-bar printer paper.

WELCOME, FRIEND! I'M HAROLD, ALTHOUGH EVERYONE AROUND HERE CALLS ME "GREEN BAR."
"GREEN BAR?" AS IN THE WIDE-CARRIAGE GREEN BAR PRINTER PAPER?
COPYRIGHT©2004 J.D. "Illiad" Frazer HTTP://WWW.USERFRIENDLY.ORG/

YESSIR, THE SAME. MY OFFICE USED TO BE BURIED IN THE STUFF! FROM FLOOR TO CEILING, AND YOU COULD BARELY WALK THROUGH MY OFFICE WITHOUT STEPPING ON IT.

GUESS YOU DID A LOT OF CODING, HUH?
HELL, NO. IT WAS THAT DAMNABLE WUMPUS. I WAS AFTER HIM FOR YEARS.

DO YOU REMEMBER WHEN FAX MACHINES ONLY PRINTED ON THERMAL PAPER? AND THE SERIOUS ONES CAME WITH A MASSIVE DRUM OF PAPER INSTEAD OF JUST A ROLL?
YEP. SURE DO.
COPYRIGHT©2004 J.D. "Illiad" Frazer HTTP://WWW.USERFRIENDLY.ORG/

A FRIEND OF MINE WORKED FOR A MAJOR OIL COMPANY WAY BACK WHEN, AND HE HAD ONE OF THESE DRUM FAXES IN HIS OFFICE. SO ON HIS BIRTHDAY I DECIDED I WANTED TO WISH HIM MANY HAPPY RETURNS AND MESS WITH HIM AT THE SAME TIME.

SO AT MIDNIGHT I SENT HIM A ONE-PAGE FAX WITH 'HAPPY BIRTHDAY' SCRAWLED ON IT. THEN PUT THE PAGE IN AND STARTED SENDING IT...
...AND?
TAPED THE ENDS OF THE PAGE TOGETHER.

YOU SEEM A LITTLE SPRITELY TO BE HERE, SID.
I WAS SENT HERE BY MY NEMESIS, WHO STYLED HIMSELF MY "SON-IN-LAW."
COPYRIGHT©2004 J.D. "Illiad" Frazer HTTP://WWW.USERFRIENDLY.ORG/

AH YES, THE YOUNGER, SLICKER GENERATION IS ALWAYS TRYING TO PUSH THE OLDER, WISER ONE ASIDE. IT'S HEARTBREAKING.
AND THEY ARGUE THAT "NEW" IS ALWAYS BETTER THAN "OLD." CDS OVER VINYL. LAPTOPS OVER PAPER NOTEBOOKS...

HEH. WINDOWS XP OVER DOS 3.3?
NOW THAT'S A HOLE IN THEIR LOGIC.

SO US OLD GEEKS JUST SIT HERE IN QUIET REPOSE, ALL OF US WAITING TO SLOWLY FADE FROM MEMORY. WE'RE THE BRAIN TRUST OF THE HISTORY OF OUR INDUSTRY, EACH POSSESSING DECADES OF WISDOM AND IN-DEPTH KNOWLEDGE, AND WE ARE ALL BUT ABANDONED BY THE WORLD WE ONCE SERVED.
COPYRIGHT©2004 J.D. "Illiad" Frazer HTTP://WWW.USERFRIENDLY.ORG/

NOT MUCH LUCK THESE DAYS GETTING A JOB AS A PL/1 PROGRAMMER, HUH?
OH SHUT UP.

WELL LISTEN. IF THIS YOUNG DORK SENT YOU HERE, LET'S WORK ON GETTING YOU BACK, AND THEN NAILING HIM.
BUT HOW?

SID, THERE'S AN ENTIRE **COMPLEX** OF OLD GEEKS AT OUR DISPOSAL! KNOWLEDGE AND SKILLS! **AGE AND TREACHERY!** WE'D ALL LOVE A CHANCE TO GET BACK AT THE GENERATION THAT DISCARDED US!
COPYRIGHT©2004 J.D. "Illiad" Frazer HTTP://WWW.USERFRIENDLY.ORG/

THAT'S GREAT! SO WE CAN USE EVERYONE HERE?
MAYBE EVERYONE EXCEPT FOR THAT ZERO-WING TRANSLATOR GUY...
HOW ARE YOU GENTLEMEN?

SO WHAT ARE WE GOING TO DO TO PITR?
LET'S GET YOU OUT OF HERE FIRST.
OKAY. BUT HOW?

HACK THE SYSTEM AND PLACE AN ORDER FOR YOU TO BE RELEASED. CALL UP A LIMO SERVICE AND HAVE THE CENTRE BILLED FOR IT. DELIVER YOU BACK TO YOUR OFFICE WITH LEGIT DISCHARGE PAPERS IN HAND FROM THE MINISTRY OF HEALTH...
COPYRIGHT©2004 J.D. "Illiad" Frazer HTTP://WWW.USERFRIENDLY.ORG/

YOU KNOW, I COULD DO IT THE ANALOG WAY AND JUST **WALK** OUT.
HUSH YOU. I'M TRYING TO BE 'LEET' ABOUT THIS.

ENGINES OF DISCRIMINATION

"THE GOOGLE VS. YAHOO CAGE MATCH GAME" UserFriendly.Org

OBJECTIVE: TO SUCCESSFULLY COLLECT THE MOST SEARCH REQUESTS

NUMBER OF PLAYERS: 2

BITS NEEDED: THREE STANDARD DECKS OF PLAYING CARDS

SETUP: SHUFFLE EACH DECK INDIVIDUALLY. GIVE EACH PLAYER ONE DECK (THESE ARE PLAYER DECKS) AND PLACE THE THIRD DECK (THE SEARCH DECK) IN BETWEEN THE TWO PLAYERS.

ONE PLAYER PLAYS AS GOOGLE; THE OTHER PLAYS AS YAHOO.

AT THE START, THE GOOGLE PLAYER GETS 5 CARDS. THE YAHOO PLAYER IS DEALT 4 CARDS. KEEP YOUR CARDS SECRET.

EACH CARD FROM 2 TO 10 HAS A VALUE AS LISTED ON ITS FACE. ACES COUNT AS ONES. FACE CARDS HAVE NO VALUE BUT REPRESENT IMAGES. SUITS ARE IGNORED.

THE YAHOO PLAYER GOES FIRST.

TURN SEQUENCE:

1. DRAW A CARD FROM THE SEARCH DECK AND TURN IT FACE UP. THIS REPRESENTS A SEARCH REQUEST BY JOE USER.

Google 

2. BOTH PLAYERS CHOOSE ONE CARD FROM THEIR HAND THAT IS AS CLOSE TO MATCHING THE VALUE OF THE SEARCH REQUEST AS POSSIBLE. THESE "SEARCH RESULTS" ARE PLACED FACE NEXT TO THE "SEARCH REQUEST." BOTH CARDS ARE REVEALED AT THE SAME TIME. THE PLAYER WHO PLAYED THE CARD THAT COMES CLOSEST TO THE SEARCH REQUEST WINS THE SEARCH AND PUTS THE CARD TO THE SIDE. (THESE CARDS ARE TOTALLED AT THE END OF THE GAME TO DETERMINE THE WINNER.)

A) IF BOTH PLAYERS MATCH THE SEARCH REQUEST, OR BOTH PLAYERS PLAY CARDS THAT ARE THE SAME DIFFERENCE FROM THE SEARCH REQUEST, THE PLAYER WHO WON THE LAST SEARCH REQUEST WINS THIS ONE AS WELL.

E.G.: THE SEARCH REQUEST IS A "5." GOOGLE PLAYS A "3" AND YAHOO PLAYS A "7." AS BOTH PLAYED CARDS ARE 2 POINTS AWAY FROM THE SEARCH REQUEST, THIS IS A TIE. IF YAHOO WON THE LAST SEARCH REQUEST, IT WOULD WIN THIS ONE AS WELL.

3. IF THE SEARCH REQUEST IS A FACE CARD (K, Q OR J), ONLY AN EXACT MATCH WILL WIN YOU THE CARD. IF NEITHER PLAYER HAS AN EXACT MATCH, THE SEARCH REQUEST IS SIMPLY DISCARDED.

4. DRAW ENOUGH CARDS TO FILL YOUR HAND BACK UP TO FULL (4 CARDS FOR YAHOO, 5 CARDS FOR GOOGLE).

5. PLAY PASSES TO THE OTHER PLAYER. THE GAME ENDS WHEN ANY OF THE THREE DECKS ARE USED UP.

***SPECIAL* (*YAHOO*)**: IN A TIE FOR A SEARCH REQUEST, IF YOU CAN PLAY ANOTHER CARD THAT IS ONLY ONE POINT FURTHER AWAY FROM THE SEARCH REQUEST, YOU WIN THE TIE. E.G. THE SEARCH REQUEST IS A "9." GOOGLE PLAYS A "10" AND YOU PLAY AN "8" FOR A TIE. IF YOU'RE ABLE TO PLAY A "7" RIGHT NOW, YOU WIN THE TIE.

***SPECIAL* (*GOOGLE*)**: ONCE DURING THE GAME, YOU CAN DECLARE AN *IPO* AT THE BEGINNING OF YOUR TURN. YOU INSTANTLY FILL YOUR HAND WITH AN ADDITIONAL 4 CARDS. YOU DO NOT DRAW NEW CARDS UNTIL YOUR HAND HAS DROPPED BELOW YOUR USUAL 5 CARDS.

GREEN BAR. IT'S SID. I MADE IT OUT! I HITCHED A RIDE AND I'M HEADED BACK HOME.
GREAT NEWS YOUNGSTER!
SO WHAT'S THE PLAN?

THE BOYS AND I HAVE DONE SOME THINKING. WE FIGURE THE BEST WAY TO EXACT REVENGE IS TO CONVERT PITR TO OUR VALUES.
COPYRIGHT © 2004 J.D. "Illiad" Frazer HTTP://WWW.USERFRIENDLY.ORG/

OUR VALUES?
IT'S A CLEVER OLD GEEK WAY OF SAYING WE'RE GOING TO "HEX" HIM. HA HA HA! OH GOD I KILL MYSELF.

Trivia: the filename for this cartoon on the website ends in 6502.gif.

SID! YOU'RE BACK!
YEP. SURE AM.
DOES PITR KNOW YOU'RE HERE?
NO. BUT HE'LL SUSPECT IT SOON ENOUGH.

HOW'S THAT?
I REPLACED HIS COMPUTER WITH SOMETHING THAT SHOULD TEACH HIM THE VALUE OF THE BASICS.
COPYRIGHT © 2004 J.D. "Illiad" Frazer HTTP://WWW.USERFRIENDLY.ORG/

PLEASE TO BE GIVINK ME BACK MY COMPUTER!!
NO.
YOU HAVE EVERYTHING YOU NEED RIGHT HERE TO HANDLE MOST BASIC COMPUTING TASKS.

YOUR PROBLEM IS THAT YOU'RE SO USED TO THE "SHINY FACTOR" THAT YOU CAN'T SEE THINGS FOR WHAT THEY ARE.
FOR EXAMPLE, YOU CAN "DIAL OUT" FROM YOUR ABACUS WITH THIS.
COPYRIGHT © 2004 J.D. "Illiad" Frazer HTTP://WWW.USERFRIENDLY.ORG/

WITH TWO CANS AND A STRING?
YOU ARE SO SPOILED. IT'S AN ACOUSTIC COUPLER.

KABOOM!
PAFF PAFF PAF!
BOOOM!
BLAMM!
COPYRIGHT © 2004 J.D. "Illiad" Frazer HTTP://WWW.USERFRIENDLY.ORG/

LEFT. A.J.! LEFT!!
PAP-PAP-PAP
BOOOOM
SPLUTCH!!

HA! I RAILGUNNED PITR!!
IS ONLY BECAUSE OF BAD LAG!!

IS NOT WERY USEFUL. THIS LAN SETUP. LAG MAKINK WERY BIG PROBLEM TO PLAY TWITCH GAMES.
YOU'RE PROBABLY RIGHT. THIS SYSTEM DOES HAVE ITS DRAWBACKS.

AHHHH...I SEE THE PROBLEM. THE BOTTLENECK EXISTS AT THE CPU...
OHH...

HEY!!!
I'D RECOMMEND A NEW "CPU," BUT THEY DON'T COME IN "PINHEAD" SIZE.

SID, ARE YOU SURE FORCING PITR TO WORK WITH AN ABACUS IS SUCH A GOOD IDEA?
WHY NOT? IT BUILDS CHARACTER.

BESIDES, IF I CAN FIND CAUSE TO USE AN ABACUS EVERY DAY I'M AT THE OFFICE, PITR SHOULD BE ABLE TO DO SO AS WELL.

YOU USE AN ABACUS EVERY DAY? GET OUT!
SERIOUSLY. THEY MAKE THE BEST BACK MASSAGERS.
ROLL
ROLL
ROLL

A SAMPLE CARD FROM THE NEW "CORPORATE BOTTOM-FEEDERS" EXPANSION KIT FOR STEVE JACKSON GAMES' HIT TITLE "ILLUMINATI"

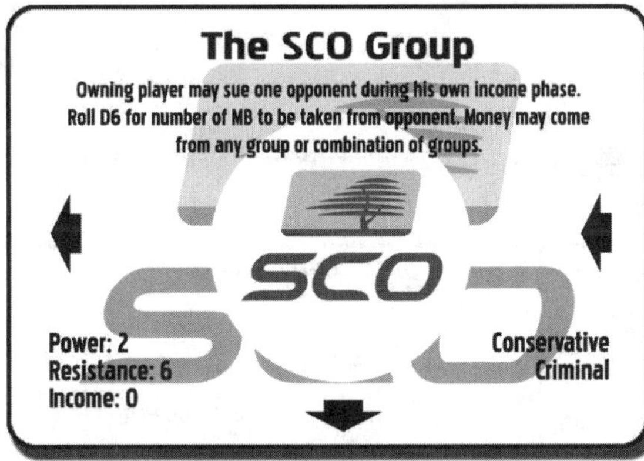
The SCO Group
Owning player may sue one opponent during his own income phase. Roll D6 for number of MB to be taken from opponent. Money may come from any group or combination of groups.
SCO
Power: 2
Resistance: 6
Income: 0
Conservative
Criminal

SO HOW'S THE NEW SYSTEM WORKING FOR YOU?
IS NOT.
REMEMBER PITR. "IT'S A POOR CRAFTSMAN THAT BLAMES HIS TOOLS." IF YOU'RE NOT SMART ENOUGH...
COPYRIGHT©2004 J.D. "Illiad" Frazer HTTP://WWW.USERFRIENDLY.ORG/

AM PLENTY SMART. CAN CALCULATE JUST FINE. BUT IS STUPID, UNEXPANDABLE SYSTEM! IF YOU ARE THINKINK SYSTEM IS SO GOOD, SHOW ME HOW TO DOUBLE RAM!!

IS RIDICULOUS! HATINK THIS! ABACUS! ABACUS! ABACUS! ARRRRRRRRGH!
COPYRIGHT©2004 J.D. "Illiad" Frazer HTTP://WWW.USERFRIENDLY.ORG/

WOW. PITR'S REALLY TICKED OFF.
I DON'T SEE WHY. BACK IN MY DAY WE USED SIMPLE DEVICES ALL OF THE TIME TO DO BACKUP CALCULATIONS. IT'S A GOOD HABIT TO GET INTO. BETTER THAN RELYING SOLELY ON THE INTEGRITY OF SOLID STATE ELECTRONICS.

WHY ARE YOU WEARING A MINIATURE ABACUS AS A BELT BUCKLE?
IT'S MY OLD PDA. YOU MAY ENVY ME.

I HEARD PITR WAS GIVEN AN ABACUS.
NOT ANYMORE. I TOLD SID TO RETURN THE COMPUTER SO PITR COULD GET BACK TO WORK.
COPYRIGHT©2004 J.D. "Illiad" Frazer HTTP://WWW.USERFRIENDLY.ORG/

SID AGREED?
YES. BUT HE SAID HE WOULD ALSO GET PITR TO "APPRECIATE THE PURITY OF THE OLD WAYS"...

PLEASE...PLEASE... GIVINK BACK ABACUS...
NOPE...KEEP READING. ONLY NINETY-EIGHT THOUSAND LINES OF WINDOWS CODE TO GO.

SID. REMEMBER WHEN YOU SUGGESTED THAT IT WOULD BE HELPFUL IF I PICKED UP NEW SKILLS? WELL, I TOOK YOUR ADVICE AND I'M NOW TAKING A COURSE TO LEARN A NEW LANGUAGE.
FABULOUS!
COPYRIGHT©2004 J.D. "Illiad" Frazer HTTP://WWW.USERFRIENDLY.ORG/

THAT'S EXCELLENT, GREG. THE COMPANY WILL OF COURSE PAY FOR IT.
SO WHAT ARE YOU TAKING? C++? C SHUDDER? I MEAN C SHARP? JAVA?

UM. ELVISH, ACTUALLY.
WHAT?!
YOU'D BETTER BE LEARNING QUENYA AND NOT THAT RIDICULOUS SINDARIN PATOIS!

GREG. WHAT ARE YOU TAKING ELVISH FOR ANYWAY?
THAT'S "ELVEN."
OKAY. "ELVEN." TO WHAT PURPOSE COULD YOU POSSIBLY PUT THIS LANGUAGE?
COPYRIGHT©2004 J.D. "Illiad" Frazer HTTP://WWW.USERFRIENDLY.ORG/

SO I CAN SPEAK TO OTHER GEEKS WITHOUT MUNDANES LIKE YOU UNDERSTANDING WHAT WE'RE SAYING?
YOU GUYS ALREADY DO THAT!!!

GREG. I THOUGHT THAT COURSE ON ELVEN WAS ONLY BEING FORMALLY TAUGHT AT A SCHOOL IN ENGLAND.
IT IS. BUT THEY HAVE A DISTANCE EDUCATION PROGRAM.
COPYRIGHT©2004 J.D. "Illiad" Frazer HTTP://WWW.USERFRIENDLY.ORG/

SEE. THEY SENT ME A DVD. I CAN LEARN THE COURSE WITH FULL AUDIO AND VIDEO.
WELCOME TO ELVISH 101!

AND WHO WOULD THAT BE TEACHING ON THE DVD?
THAT WOULD BE LIV TYLER.
AND WHY IS SHE ONLY WEARING A FIG LEAF?
SHE'S AN ELF. DUH.
REPEAT AFTER ME: "TEE HEE HEE!"

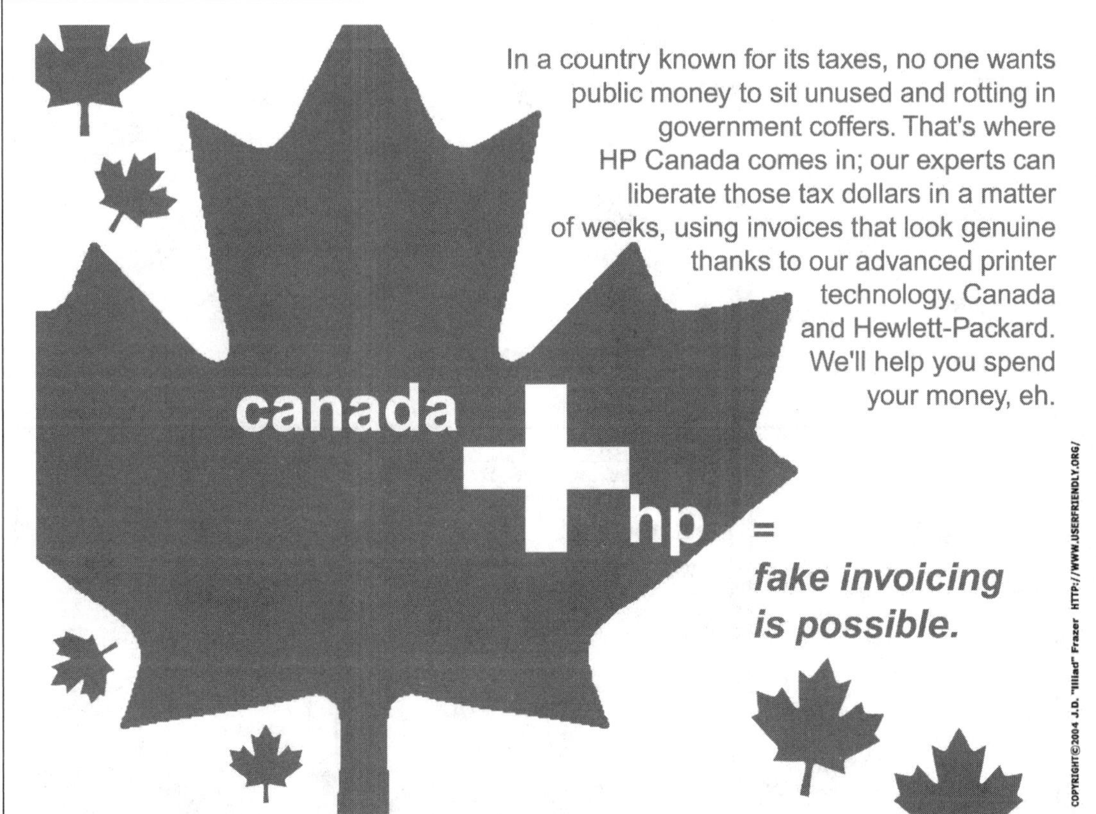
In a country known for its taxes, no one wants public money to sit unused and rotting in government coffers. That's where HP Canada comes in; our experts can liberate those tax dollars in a matter of weeks, using invoices that look genuine thanks to our advanced printer technology. Canada and Hewlett-Packard. We'll help you spend your money, eh.
canada + hp =
fake invoicing is possible.
COPYRIGHT©2004 J.D. "Illiad" Frazer HTTP://WWW.USERFRIENDLY.ORG/

I am nothing if not a bitter, tax-paying Canadian. I'm also bitter about government bloat, and at the time I wasn't a fan of HP's new ad campaign. Seemed stilted at best. But it did give me the idea for this spoof.

ELVISH LESSON ONE:
EVERYDAY SINDARIN.
(*LET'S BUILD A TREEHOUSE*) *IN SINDARIN
REPEAT.
(*LET'S BUILD A TREEHOUSE*)
COPYRIGHT©2004 J.D. "Illiad" Frazer HTTP://WWW.USERFRIENDLY.ORG/

(*YOUR MOTHER IS A HAIRY PUS HOG*)
REPEAT.
(*YOUR MOTHER IS A HAIRY PUS HOG*)

(*THAT'S A NICE SHADE OF GREEN*)
REPEAT
(*YOUR MOTHER IS A HAIRY PUS HOG*)
EXCELLENT!

LOTHLINGUIST INC., CUSTOMER SERVICE. HOW MAY I HELP YOU?
HI. I BOUGHT YOUR INTRODUCTORY COURSE ON ELVISH AND NOW I'D LIKE THE INTERMEDIATE ONE.
COPYRIGHT©2004 J.D. "Illiad" Frazer HTTP://WWW.USERFRIENDLY.ORG/

ELVISH? BUT YOU'RE MALE. MOST OF OUR ELVISH STUDENTS THESE DAYS ARE FEMALE.
REALLY? WHY?
NOW HOW DO I PUT THIS...

...THERE'S BEEN A HUGE RUN ON "1-900-ELF-TART" TYPE NUMBERS LATELY.
I SEE.
YOU KNOW, THERE IS A MARKET...
JUST SEND ME THE COURSE.

TIME TO USE MY NEW LANGUAGE SKILLS...
HELLO? IS THIS TECH SUPPORT?
COPYRIGHT©2004 J.D. "Illiad" Frazer HTTP://WWW.USERFRIENDLY.ORG/

UH. RIGHT. MY INTERNET IS GONE. I NEED IT FIXED.

UH...EXCELLENT. CALL ME WHEN IT'S DONE. *CLICK*

COMRADE GREGOR.
PITR.
YOU ARE STILL LEARNINK ELVISH TONGUE, DA?
DA...I MEAN YES.
COPYRIGHT©2004 J.D. "Illiad" Frazer HTTP://WWW.USERFRIENDLY.ORG/

HAVINK SUGGESTION. TOGETHER WE ARE TO BE TAKINK OVER WORLD WITH NEW LINUX DISTRO: "ELVEN LINUX!"
ONE DISTRO TO RULE THEM ALL!

FINE. AND YOU CAN SKIP THE OBVIOUS "BIND" JOKE.
... ... EHHH.

WHAT ARE YOU FREAKS DOING NOW?
WE'RE CREATING OUR OWN LINUX DISTRO. "ELVEN LINUX."
COPYRIGHT©2004 J.D. "Illiad" Frazer HTTP://WWW.USERFRIENDLY.ORG/

OH? AND IT'S DIFFERENT FROM ALL OF THE OTHER LINUX THINGS?
YEP. ALL SYSTEM MESSAGES ARE IN TENGWAR, NOT ENGLISH. AND YOU TYPE COMMANDS IN TENGWAR.

OH GOOD. THAT JUST MAKES ME WANT TO GO OUT AND FINALLY LEARN LINUX.
HEH. YOU WERE RIGHT, PITR.
SO, INSTEAD OF "DEV/NULL," HOW ABOUT "DEV/CRACKS OFDOOM?"

WAS THAT SMILING MAN?
DA. WAS ASKINK ABOUT ELVEN LINUX DISTRO.
COPYRIGHT©2004 J.D. "Illiad" Frazer HTTP://WWW.USERFRIENDLY.ORG/

HAVINK MANY QUESTIONS: "WHAT IS TENGWAR," "WHERE IS TENGWAR FROM," "WHAT DO SINDARIN DO ALL DAY." THEN HE IS RUNNINK OFF.
ODD...

YOU'RE TRYING TO OUTSOURCE WHERE?
WHY CAN'T I FIND THE AREA CODE FOR "LOTHLORIEN?"

MICROSOFT ACQUIRING AOL = FIVE TIMES THE NUMBER OF CDS IN THE MAIL
Microsoft
SECURITY PATCH 1.0
SECURITY PATCH 1.1
SECURITY PATCH 1.2
AMERICA Online
COPYRIGHT©2004 J.D. "Illiad" Frazer HTTP://WWW.USERFRIENDLY.ORG/

Microsoft has always been infamous for shipping a gazillion install CDs for the simplest apps. Bloatware being what it is ...

LOOK HERE. I FOUND A LISTING FOR "LOTHLORIEN TECHNICAL OUTSOURCING."
REALLY?

YEAH...NOW THAT'S ODD. THE AREA CODE FOR LOTHLORIEN IS THE SAME AS FOR NEW DELHI.
IF IT'S IN INDIA, I DOUBT THEY'RE GOING TO BE SPEAKING ELVISH...
COPYRIGHT©2004 J.D. "Illiad" Frazer HTTP://WWW.USERFRIENDLY.ORG/

MEANWHILE, IN NEW DELHI...
AND HOW DO WE GREET A CUSTOMER WHEN THEY CALL?
(*YOUR MOTHER IS A HAIRY PUS HOG.*)

HEY. HOW'S THE "ELVEN LINUX DISTRO" COMING?
PITR SAYS WE'RE ALMOST DONE! I HEARD YOU USED TO BE PRETTY GOOD AT SPEAKING SINDARIN.

YEP. THAT WAS IN HIGH SCHOOL. I WAS JUST ABOUT FLUENT.
REALLY...WOW.
COPYRIGHT©2004 J.D. "Illiad" Frazer HTTP://WWW.USERFRIENDLY.ORG/

SO DID SPEAKING SINDARIN GET YOU THE CHICKS?
I SAW THE SCHOOL NURSE A LOT AFTER GETTING BEAT UP, IF THAT'S WHAT YOU MEAN.

PITR RELEASED ELVEN LINUX LAST NIGHT. THERE'S ALREADY BEEN A SIGNIFICANT NUMBER OF DOWNLOADS.
WOW. I CONFESS I'M SURPRISED.

AND, GREG'S ALREADY HANDLING HIS FIRST ELVEN LINUX SUPPORT CALL!
IN SINDARIN?
COPYRIGHT©2004 J.D. "Illiad" Frazer HTTP://WWW.USERFRIENDLY.ORG/

NO. SINDARIN'S FOR SYSADMINS. HE USES BLACK SPEECH FOR USER SUPPORT.
Ashdautas Vrasubatlat!
GOOD HEAVENS!

Another mention of *engfeh*. I'll never tell where that word came from.

HEY! YOU WERE SPEAKING BLACK SPEECH! TOLKIEN CAME UP WITH THAT ONE, RIGHT?
UH...

YOU KNOW, I DO UNDERSTAND YOUR FASCINATION WITH LANGUAGES. I LOVE THEM MYSELF, AND EVEN CREATED A SPECIAL TONGUE.
COPYRIGHT©2004 J.D. "Illiad" Frazer HTTP://WWW.USERFRIENDLY.ORG/

...ENGFEH.
HEH. YEAH, I MADE THAT ONE UP TOO.
THAT WAS MINE!
NO, YOURS WAS "FTHAGN."

BILL? LOOKS LIKE WE'LL HAVE TO PAY THE E.U. A $600 MILLION FINE.
I SEE. AND WHAT ELSE?
Microsoft

WE WON'T BE ALLOWED TO DISTRIBUTE OUR MEDIA PLAYER WITH THE OPERATING SYSTEM.

COPYRIGHT©2004 J.D. "Illiad" Frazer HTTP://WWW.USERFRIENDLY.ORG/

IF WE PAY A LITTLE MORE CAN WE GET THE "SLAP ON THE WRIST COMBO"?
I CAN ASK.

ONE OF THE GREAT OLD ONES! I HAVEN'T PURSUED A VICTIM AS POWERFUL AS HIM IN EONS. I WILL NEED TO APPROACH WITH CARE IF I AM TO SUCCEED.

COPYRIGHT©2004 J.D. "Illiad" Frazer HTTP://WWW.USERFRIENDLY.ORG/
I AM HIS ADDICTION. HIS AMBROSIA. HIS COMFORT AND JOY. AND I WILL EXTEND MY LIFEBLOOD TO HIM SO THAT HE MAY DRINK DEEP...
Cola

NOW...SEE HIM. WIDE-EYED. SCARED. COMPELLED! AN EVIL GOD FEARS ME!
DAMN. THOSE ARE SOME SEXY TENTACLES!
Cola

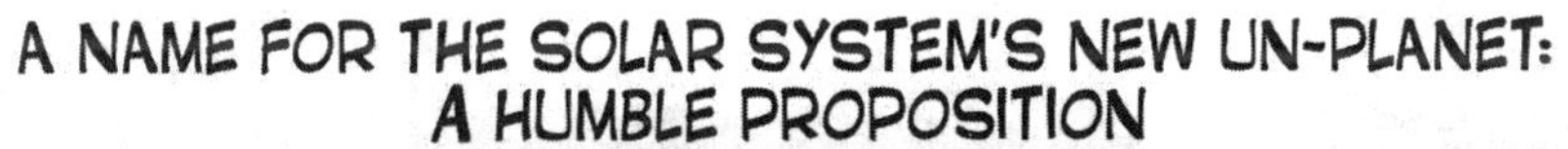

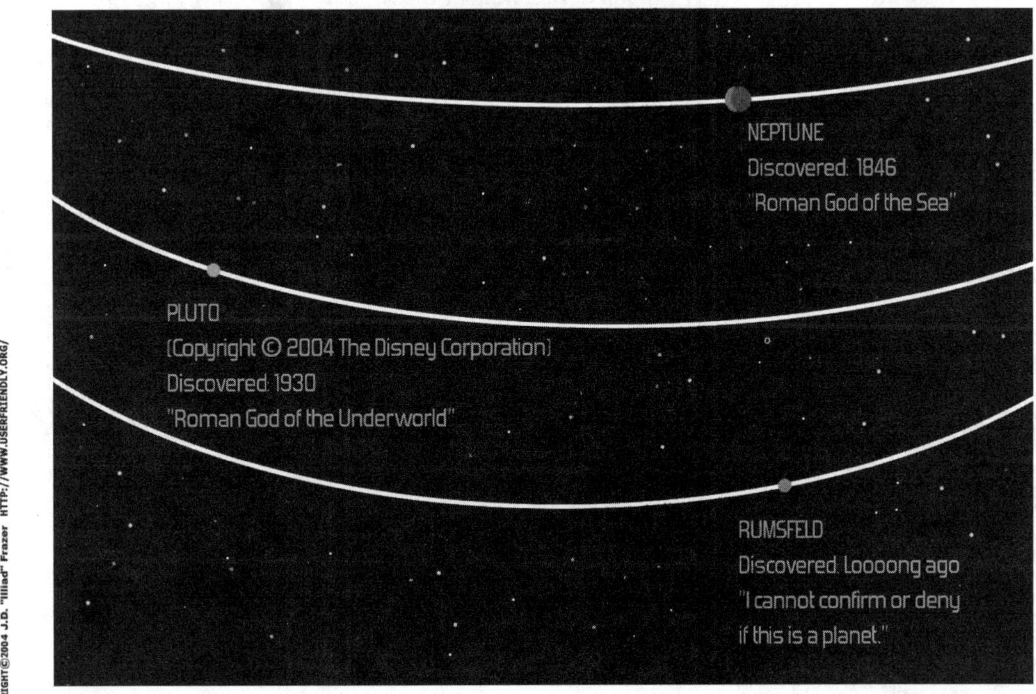
A NAME FOR THE SOLAR SYSTEM'S NEW UN-PLANET:
A HUMBLE PROPOSITION
NEPTUNE
Discovered: 1846
"Roman God of the Sea"
PLUTO
(Copyright © 2004 The Disney Corporation)
Discovered: 1930
"Roman God of the Underworld"
RUMSFELD
Discovered: Loooong ago
"I cannot confirm or deny
if this is a planet."
COPYRIGHT©2004 J.D. "Illiad" Frazer HTTP://WWW.USERFRIENDLY.ORG/

EXCUSE ME, BUT THESE **AREN'T TENTACLES.** THEY'RE **STRAWS.** STRAWS FROM WHICH YOU CAN DRAW A COOLANT FOR YOUR FEVERED MIND.
REALLY.
Cola

YES. NOW QUAFF TO YOUR HEART'S CONTENT. I GIVE UNTO YOU SELFLESSLY!
Cola

COPYRIGHT©2004 J.D. "Illiad" Frazer HTTP://WWW.USERFRIENDLY.ORG/
PUFFF!
Cola

YEEEAARRRRRRRGH!
SODA UP THE NOSE IS **HARSH.** DUDE.
YEAH. BUT I'M STILL THE MAN.
Cola

Geeks are weird. Sometimes we're stupid weird. Tiny cosmetic changes or, for that matter, anything that forces us to change our habits or muscle memory, no matter how slight, will be met largely with resistance, wailing, and a gnashing of teeth. Google changed its look ever so slightly. Every geek noticed. The cool side of this story is that the Google design group asked for permission to print this 'toon on t-shirts for everyone involved in the changes.

A NEW DAY COMES AND NET.GEEKS AROUND THE WORLD CONNECT TO THE WEB AS THEY ALWAYS HAVE...
WHAT THE...
COPYRIGHT©2004 J.D. "Illiad" Frazer HTTP://WWW.USERFRIENDLY.ORG/

AND YET SOMETHING IS WRONG, SUBTLY, DISTURBINGLY WRONG, LIKE A MORNING SKY TINGED WITH RANCOR...
EH...EH...EBBE...EH...

...OR KNICKERS YOU'VE PUT ON BACKWARDS.
GOOGLE'S CHANGED EVER SO SLIGHTLY! PUT IT BACK! **PUT IT BACK! PUT IT BACK!!**
HEH. FOR A SECOND THERE I THOUGHT "THE STARS WERE RIGHT."

SID, CAN I GO HOME? I JUST CAN'T WORK.
OH? WHY NOT?
COPYRIGHT©2004 J.D. "Illiad" Frazer HTTP://WWW.USERFRIENDLY.ORG/

WELL...I FEEL TRAPPED. ALMOST **PINNED DOWN.** THERE'S THIS WEIGHT ON ME I CAN'T SHRUG OFF. NO MATTER **HOW HARD** I TRY.

MIRANDA, THE CHANGES IN GOOGLE JUST WEREN'T THAT SERIOUS.
GODS! DON'T YOU **UNDERSTAND?!** IT'S LIKE TRYING TO LEARN HOW TO **BREATHE** AGAIN!!

HELLO, EVERYONE. ILLIAD HERE WITH A SHORT MESSAGE. BE SURE TO PAY FOR YOUR LINUX LICENSES BY SENDING YOUR MONEY TO S.C.O....
COPYRIGHT©2004 J.D. "Illiad" Frazer HTTP://WWW.USERFRIENDLY.ORG/

KER-POW!

I KNOW IT'S APRIL FOOL'S TODAY, ILLIAD, BUT EVEN SATIRICALLY SIDING WITH S.C.O. JUST ISN'T FUNNY.
HANG ON. HE'S TAKING OFF THE PAPER BAG.

DUDE. THAT ISN'T ILLIAD! YOU JUST SOCKED **DARL MCBRIDE.**
OKAY. NOW **THAT'S** FUNNY!
EHHHH

MIKE, HAVE YOU SEEN PITR?
YEAH, HE SAID HE WAS GOING TO APPLY IN PERSON FOR A JOB WITH GOOGLE. A JOB AT THEIR MOONBASE.
COPYRIGHT©2004 J.D. "Illiad" Frazer HTTP://WWW.USERFRIENDLY.ORG/

WHAT? HE KNOWS IT WAS AN APRIL FOOL'S JOKE, RIGHT?
I...I DON'T KNOW.
SO, WHAT, HE'S ON HIS WAY TO CALIFORNIA?!
NO, THAT'S NOT WHAT HE SAID...

MEANWHILE, AT A RUSSIAN SPACE AGENCY COCKTAIL PARTY COINCIDENTALLY TAKING PLACE NEARBY...
TO GO TO MOON IS FIFTY MILLION DOLLARS.
IS NO PROBLEM. HERE IS CHEQUE.
THANK YOU MISTER...BEN KOJO FROM NIGERIA.

AT A MOSTLY ABANDONED FIELD SOMEWHERE COLD...
LAUNCH IN FOUR MINUTES, AND COUNTINK.
ALL IS GOOD. DA, DMITRI? WE HAVE GREEN LIGHT?

VASSILY, AM NOT REALLY COMFORTABLE WITH THIS ARRANGEMENT.
DMITRI, RELAX! MISTER KOJO WANTINK TO GO TO MOON PAYINK WITH FAKE CHEQUE. WE SEND HIM TO MOON ANYWAY.

REMEMBER TO BE BREATHINK SHALLOW. AND FLAP ARMS IF YOU BEGIN TO DROP.
AAAAARRRRRRGGGHHH

In case it wasn't desperately obvious, that four-color splotch was the MSN Butterfly.

A LOGO FOR GOOGLE'S UPCOMING ONE-GIGABYTE-OF-FREE-STORAGE WEBMAIL SERVICE
GMail
COPYRIGHT©2004 J.D. "Illiad" Frazer HTTP://WWW.USERFRIENDLY.ORG/

VASSILY, EQUATIONS SHOWINK MR. KOJO IS NOT GOINK TO BE LOFTED TO MOON.
OH?
COPYRIGHT©2004 J.D. "Illiad" Frazer HTTP://WWW.USERFRIENDLY.ORG/

DA. TREBUCHET. IT IS NOT POWERFUL ENOUGH TO DO JOB.
NOT TO BE WORRYINK DMITRI...

...IS NOTHINK REPLACINK COUNTERWEIGHT WITH J.A.T.O. UNIT CAN NOT FIX...
AAAAAAAIIIIIIEEEEEEEE!!!
BIFFITY!
BOFFITY!
BIPPITY!
BOPPITY!

HARSH FORCES AND COINCIDENCE CAUSE THE CABLE TO SNAP AT JUST THE RIGHT MOMENT.
EEEEEEEEEEEE
COPYRIGHT©2004 J.D. "Illiad" Frazer HTTP://WWW.USERFRIENDLY.ORG/

OUR YOUNG COSMONAUT SAILS MOONWARD...

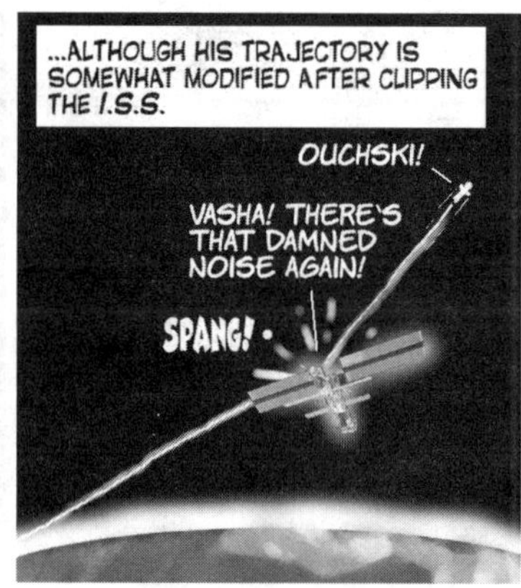
...ALTHOUGH HIS TRAJECTORY IS SOMEWHAT MODIFIED AFTER CLIPPING THE I.S.S.
OUCHSKI!
VASHA! THERE'S THAT DAMNED NOISE AGAIN!
SPANG!

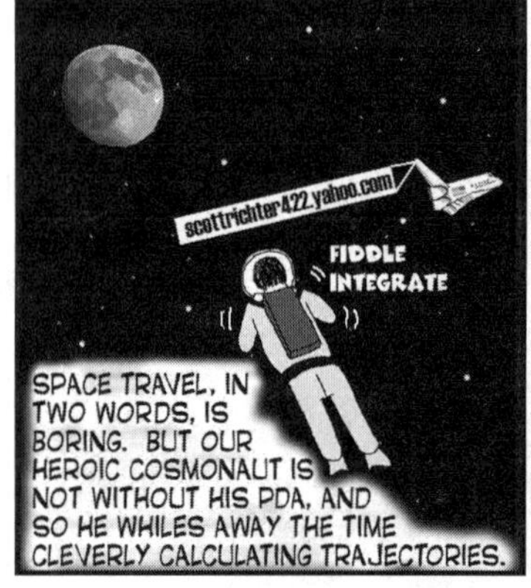
scottrichter422.yahoo.com
FIDDLE
INTEGRATE
SPACE TRAVEL, IN TWO WORDS, IS BORING. BUT OUR HEROIC COSMONAUT IS NOT WITHOUT HIS PDA, AND SO HE WHILES AWAY THE TIME CLEVERLY CALCULATING TRAJECTORIES.
COPYRIGHT©2004 J.D. "Illiad" Frazer HTTP://WWW.USERFRIENDLY.ORG/

BUT OVER TIME EVEN INTERESTING PHYSICS PROBLEMS BECOME DULL, UNTIL A NAGGING FEELING BECOMES A SUDDEN AWARENESS...

...AND OUR HERO REALIZES HE DOESN'T NEED TO BE CONCERNED ABOUT HIS VELOCITY UPON LANDING SO MUCH AS THE MATERIALS STRENGTH OF HIS SUIT'S SEPTIC SYSTEM.
OH. @#$&@!!!

AFTER A PROTRACTED PERIOD OF TRAVEL, OUR HEROIC COSMONAUT LANDS ON THE MOON...
WHUMP!
AAAGH! SKI!
...IN A MANNER OF SPEAKING.
COPYRIGHT©2004 J.D. "Illiad" Frazer HTTP://WWW.USERFRIENDLY.ORG/

OUR HERO SURVEYS HIS NEW LOCATION, AND THINKS THE VERY SAME THOUGHTS AS THE ASTRONAUTS THAT HAD BEEN HERE BEFORE HIM.
IS WERY DESOLATE AND BARREN HERE...

...AND OH SO LONELY...
HI. DID YOU BRING A CRADLE FOR YOUR PDA? I LEFT MINE ON EARTH.

EXCUSINK ME... YOU ARE WHO?
OH. JUST ONE NAMELESS FACE OUT OF MILLIONS.

AND YOU ARE HERE WHY?
OH. YOU KNOW. JUST HANGIN' OUT...

COPYRIGHT©2004 J.D. "Illiad" Frazer HTTP://WWW.USERFRIENDLY.ORG/

YOU ARE UNEMPLOYED TECH WORKER LOOKINK FOR GOOGLE MOONBASE?
LOOK. IT'S NOT LIKE WE'RE RARE OR ANYTHING...

SO. WE ARE ONLY ONES HERE?
UH...NO. LIKE I SAID. WE AREN'T RARE.

COPYRIGHT©2004 J.D. "Illiad" Frazer HTTP://WWW.USERFRIENDLY.ORG/

YOU ARE ALL HERE. WHY?!!
EVIDENTLY GETTING IN LINE TO APPLY FOR A JOB WITH GOOGLE BEFORE YOU.

Despite it being clearly an April Fool's joke, Google stirred up a hornet's nest of conspiracy. With their many billions and technical brilliance, I don't doubt that at least a few dozen geeks believed that Google was working a shadow project to set up shop on the Moon. Of course, only fools would give that any credence. Or cartoonists.

THE FOUNDER OF IKEA SURPASSES THE WEALTH OF BILL GATES, GIVING BILL CATALOG-STYLE NIGHTMARES

IKEA
SWEDISH FOR "NYAH NYAH NYAAAAH!"

BILLY chair
$47 billion
Still incredibly wealthy
but probably annoyed.

TO BE GETTINK THIS STRAIGHT. HAVINK OVER SEVEN HUNDRED OUT OF WORK TECHS ON MOON ALL WAITINK FOR GOOGLE MOONBASE JOBS?
YES. THAT'S RIGHT.

YO. WE JUST POINTED OUR TELESCOPE AT THE GOOGLE CAMPUS.
YEAH. SO?

THERE'S A SIGN ON THE LAWN THERE THAT SAYS, "SORRY. ALL MOONBASE JOBS OUTSOURCED TO MARS."
WHAT? DID INDIA BEAT US TO MARS?

GENTS. THERE'S A POSTSCRIPT ON THAT SIGN.
IT IS SAYINK WHAT?
"THE MOONBASE JOBS WERE A JOKE. APRIL FOOLS! HA HA HA."

PLEASE TO BE CALCULATINK HOW HARD TO LOB ROCKS FROM HERE TO HIT GOOGLE SERVER BUILDINK.
WE ARE SO ON IT.

This was a bit of gobbledygook. Mach 27 has no meaning in a vacuum, because it refers to the speed of an object travelling through a fluid or air.

IT IS SAID THAT IDLE HANDS ARE THE DEVIL'S TOOLS; IDLE GEEK HANDS, HOWEVER, CAME UP WITH GUNPOWDER, NUCLEAR WEAPONS, AND TOILET PLUNGERS.
THIS IS BETTER THAN LOBBING ROCKS. YOU GO GIVE GOOGLE HELL, PITR!
DA.

OK. SO WHEN I PUSH THIS BUTTON, YOU'LL BE ACCELERATED AT MACH 27 TOWARDS THE GOOGLE CAMPUS.
AND I AM LANDINK ON EARTH HOW?

LET'S SEE... CARRY THE SEVEN... FACTORIAL OF 42... TRIPLE-PATH INTEGRATION...

IT'S OKAY. THE EARTH'S MASS SHOULD BE ENOUGH TO STOP YOU.
WAIT! WAIT! WAIT!

OUR HEROIC COSMOGEEK IS ACCELERATED INTO SPACE AT UNREALISTIC SPEEDS...
NYEEEEEEEEEETTT!!!

...AND ONCE AGAIN MANAGES A TRAJECTORY CORRECTION THANKS TO ANOTHER BRIEF VISIT TO THE I.S.S.
VASHA!!
SPANG!!
YOWCHSKI!

AS HE HURTLES TOWARDS THE SURFACE OF THE EARTH, IT TURNS OUT THAT AFTER BEING AWAY FOR OVER A WEEK, NEITHER BURNING UP IN THE ATMOSPHERE NOR USING THE PLANET AS A BACKSTOP ARE HIS GREATEST CONCERN...
OH MY GODSKI. MY EMAIL.

BARRELLING IN AT SOME TINY FRACTION OF C, PITR TUNNELS THROUGH THE ATMOSPHERE LIKE THE EDGE ON A PIECE OF PAPER SLICES THROUGH THE WEBBING BETWEEN ONE'S FINGERS.
NNNNGGGGGGGGG

AS PLANNED, HIS TRAJECTORY PLACES HIM ON A COLLISION COURSE WITH THE GOOGLE CAMPUS. OUR HERO FERVENTLY HOPES HE HITS THE SOFT FRONT LAWN.
OH PLEASE OH PLEASE OH PLEASE

KA-WHUMPA!
OF COURSE, THAT AIN'T GONNA HAPPEN. PITR HITS THE GOOGLE SERVER CLUSTER THAT RETURNS RESULTS AND LINKS TO CERTAIN SITES AKIN TO ONES THAT HAVE .CX AS THEIR TOP-LEVEL DOMAIN.
NOW THAT'S GETTING THEIR GOAT.

INSIDE THE MAIN BOARDROOM AT THE GOOGLE CAMPUS, THE COMPANY FOUNDERS, SERGEY BRIN AND LARRY PAGE, HAVE THEIR QUIET MEETING INTERRUPTED...
LARRY! SERGEY!! A FAKE RUSSIAN JUST BLASTED INTO ONE OF THE SERVER CLUSTERS FROM ORBIT!!

I HAVE THIS OVERWHELMING URGE TO SEARCH FOR "TUNGUSKA."
IT'S "NUCLEAR WESSELS" FOR ME.

There is no way in hell I am explaining the reference in the last panel. If you don't understand it, count yourself lucky.

AMAZON'S UPCOMING SEARCH ENGINE

Search: tensor calculus

GO

© 2003-2004 A9.com, Inc. or its affiliates. All Rights Reserved.
A9 and the A9 logo are trademarks of A9.com, Inc.
We Ownz3r Your Search History

NOW WITH AMAZON'S POWERFUL "ONE-CLICK SEARCHING!"*

*PATENT PENDING

Customers who searched for this term also searched for:

1. FREE PORN
2. FREE PRON
3. AYBABTU
4. SCOTTRICHTER-422@YAHOO-.COM
5. SCOTTRICHTER-422@YAHOO-.COM
6. JEFF, GOD OF BISCUITS

This cartoon started a form of swear-word obfuscation that was at the time particular to the UF forum. A9.com was named after *Algorithm*, a nine-letter word beginning with A. From this cartoon onward, we had F4, S4, A7, and a plethora of others in the user comments.

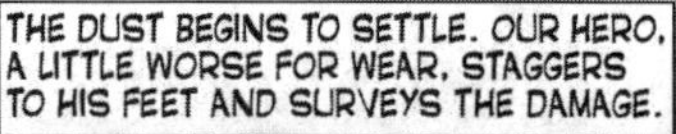
THE DUST BEGINS TO SETTLE. OUR HERO, A LITTLE WORSE FOR WEAR, STAGGERS TO HIS FEET AND SURVEYS THE DAMAGE.

COPYRIGHT©2004 J.D. "Illiad" Frazer HTTP://WWW.USERFRIENDLY.ORG/
RUINED RACKMOUNTS, SHATTERED SWITCHES AND DESTROYED DATA... PITR'S EVIL GENIUS DEMEANOR WAVERS, AND TEARS COME TO HIS EYES.

OUR FORLORN HERO SLINKS AWAY, OBLIVIOUS TO THE OVERT CHANGE HE MADE TO THE GOOGLE LOGO ON HIS FINAL APPROACH.
ogle
GREAT. NOW WE SOUND LIKE A PORN SEARCH ENGINE.
MAY I SUGGEST IT'S STILL BETTER THAN BEING CALLED "GOO."

HELLO PITR.
PRIVET.
BUBBLE
BUBBLE
BLOP
BLOP

COPYRIGHT©2004 J.D. "Illiad" Frazer HTTP://WWW.USERFRIENDLY.ORG/
GUESS THE JOB ON THE MOON WITH GOOGLE DIDN'T WORK OUT?
NYET.
SIZZLE
CONGEAL
FOLD PROTEINS

SO. YOU GONNA APPLY FOR A JOB ON MARS WITH A9.COM?
GO F4 YOURSELF. ZLOTNIK!
CURDLE
SPROUT

PITR! YOU'RE BACK!
DA. ANYWAY. YOU ARE KNOWINK BAYESIAN FILTERINK IS DEFEAT-INK SPAM BY CHECK-INK FOR OCCURENCE OF CERTAIN SPAM WORD PATTERNS?
YES...

AND NOW SPAM IS DEFEATINK FILTER BY INCLUDINK NORMAL WORDS AT RANDOM?
UH...YES?
WELL NOW. MY NEW FILTER DELETES ALL EMAIL WITH NORMAL NON-SPAM WORDS! PLUS WITH BAYESIAN FILTER I AM SPAM-FREE!

COPYRIGHT©2004 J.D. "Illiad" Frazer HTTP://WWW.USERFRIENDLY.ORG/

...OR EMAIL-FREE. EVEN.
UH...

HELLO. ILLIAD HERE. WE AT USERFRIENDLY PRODUCTIONS INC. TAKE GREAT PRIDE IN THE IDEAL OF EQUAL COVERAGE.
IT HAS COME TO OUR ATTENTION THAT WE'VE TAKEN SHOTS AT INTERNET EXPLORER AND NETSCAPE. BUT NOT AT MOZILLA!
COPYRIGHT©2004 J.D. "Illiad" Frazer HTTP://WWW.USERFRIENDLY.ORG/

DESPITE MOZILLA BEING AN OPEN-SOURCE BROWSER. WE FEEL IT'S IMPORTANT THAT WE USE AN EVEN HAND AS WE SPREAD OUR ACERBIC BILE.
AS SUCH. WE HAVE A WRITER WORKING ON SOME REAL KNEESLAPPERS RIGHT NOW.

ILLIAD. JAVASCRIPT WARNING JOKES ARE KIND OF HARD TO WRITE.
GUESS YOU'RE GOING TO BE UP LATE TONIGHT THEN. EH?

HELLO THERE GREG! WHAT ARE YOU DOING?
WHY, I'M SWITCHING OVER FROM INTERNET EXPLORER TO MOZILLA, A.J.!
HOW INTERESTING! DOES IT HAVE ANY FLAWS?
COPYRIGHT©2004 J.D. "Illiad" Frazer HTTP://WWW.USERFRIENDLY.ORG/

WHY YES. YES IT DOES!
AND WHAT FLAWS WOULD THOSE BE?

UH...SOME OF THE DEFAULT THEME ICONS ARE ROUND. VERY, VERY ROUND.
SHOCKING!
REWRITE!

OKAY. ACTION!!
HI! I AM USING MOZILLA TODAY, AN ALTERNATE BROWSER TO INTERNET EXPLORER!
COPYRIGHT©2004 J.D. "Illiad" Frazer HTTP://WWW.USERFRIENDLY.ORG/

ANY FLAWS IN MOZILLA WILL REAR THEIR HEADS, AND I WILL MAKE FUN OF THEM AND WE SHALL ALL LAUGH!

LOOK, I CAN'T DO THIS. I'M HAVING REAL TROUBLE WITH MY CHARACTER'S MOTIVATION IN THIS ENTIRE SCENE--
CUT!!

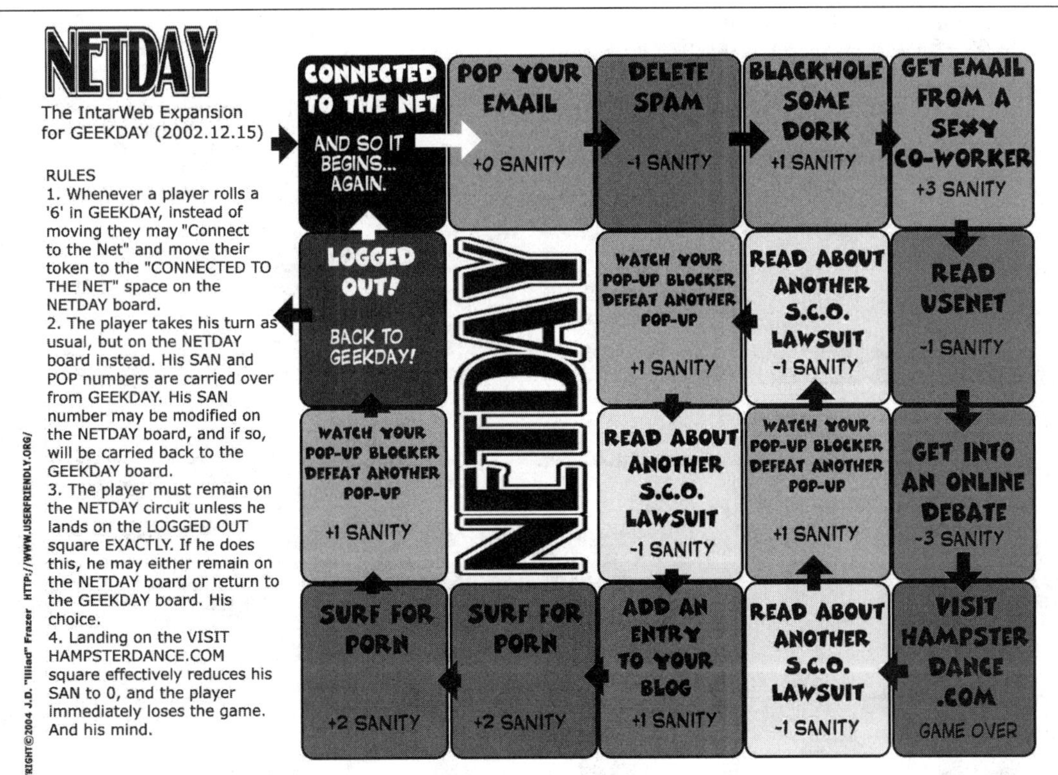
NETDAY
The IntarWeb Expansion for GEEKDAY (2002.12.15)
RULES
1. Whenever a player rolls a '6' in GEEKDAY, instead of moving they may "Connect to the Net" and move their token to the "CONNECTED TO THE NET" space on the NETDAY board.
2. The player takes his turn as usual, but on the NETDAY board instead. His SAN and POP numbers are carried over from GEEKDAY. His SAN number may be modified on the NETDAY board, and if so, will be carried back to the GEEKDAY board.
3. The player must remain on the NETDAY circuit unless he lands on the LOGGED OUT square EXACTLY. If he does this, he may either remain on the NETDAY board or return to the GEEKDAY board. His choice.
4. Landing on the VISIT HAMPSTERDANCE.COM square effectively reduces his SAN to 0, and the player immediately loses the game. And his mind.
CONNECTED TO THE NET AND SO IT BEGINS... AGAIN.
POP YOUR EMAIL +0 SANITY
DELETE SPAM -1 SANITY
BLACKHOLE SOME DORK +1 SANITY
GET EMAIL FROM A SEXY CO-WORKER +3 SANITY
READ USENET -1 SANITY
GET INTO AN ONLINE DEBATE -3 SANITY
VISIT HAMPSTER DANCE .COM GAME OVER
READ ABOUT ANOTHER S.C.O. LAWSUIT -1 SANITY
ADD AN ENTRY TO YOUR BLOG +1 SANITY
SURF FOR PORN +2 SANITY
SURF FOR PORN +2 SANITY
WATCH YOUR POP-UP BLOCKER DEFEAT ANOTHER POP-UP +1 SANITY
LOGGED OUT! BACK TO GEEKDAY!
WATCH YOUR POP-UP BLOCKER DEFEAT ANOTHER POP-UP +1 SANITY
READ ABOUT ANOTHER S.C.O. LAWSUIT -1 SANITY
WATCH YOUR POP-UP BLOCKER DEFEAT ANOTHER POP-UP +1 SANITY
READ ABOUT ANOTHER S.C.O. LAWSUIT -1 SANITY
NETDAY
COPYRIGHT©2004 J.D. "Illiad" Frazer HTTP://WWW.USERFRIENDLY.ORG/

WHADDYA MEAN. YOU "NEED MOTIVATION?"
WELL. HOW ON EARTH CAN I DISRESPECT A FAST. STABLE BROWSER? THIS JUST DOESN'T SIT RIGHT WITH ME.
COPYRIGHT©2004 J.D. "Illiad" Frazer HTTP://WWW.USERFRIENDLY.ORG/

GREG.
YES?
OPEN UP INTERNET EXPLORER.
OKAY.

NOW PRETEND IT'S MOZILLA.
OH. THAT'S GOOD. I'M FEELING THE BILE RISING IN ME NOW...

Garry Trudeau is the brilliance behind the comic strip "Doonesbury." His work taught me a lot about writing comics. And, I am sure, I was absolutely right about him not having to deal with that kind of crap.

I KNOW A MOZILLA FLAW. IT'S A RESOURCE HOG.
HMMM...YOU'RE RIGHT. IT CHUGS LIKE MOLASSES ON START-UP.
ROTO ROUTER
COPYRIGHT©2004 J.D. "Illiad" Frazer HTTP://WWW.USERFRIENDLY.ORG/

OH WAIT...WHAT ABOUT THE STRIPPED-DOWN BROWSER-ONLY VERSIONS OF MOZILLA LIKE FIREBIRD AND FIREFOX?
OH. THOSE ARE PRETTY FAST AND LIGHT.
YEAH...
ROTO ROUTER

I'LL BET GARRY TRUDEAU NEVER HAS TO DEAL WITH THIS KIND OF CRAP.
WE COULD SAY MOZILLA IS A COMMUNIST BROWSER. THAT'S BAD. ISN'T IT?
ROTO ROUTER

TECH SUPPORT. GREG SPEAKING.
HELLO. I HAVE A PROBLEM WITH MY WEB BROWSER...
COPYRIGHT©2004 J.D. "Illiad" Frazer HTTP://WWW.USERFRIENDLY.ORG/

WHICH BROWSER ARE YOU USING?
MOZILLA.

WELL THAT'S YOUR PROBLEM RIGHT THERE. HA HA HA.
NO. NO. IT'S FINE. I JUST WANT TO KNOW WHERE I CAN DOWNLOAD MORE THEMES FOR IT.
OH SCREW THIS...

MIKE SUGGESTED SOMETHING.
WHAT'S THAT?
WE DO JOKES ABOUT LYNX. NO ONE EVER JOKES ABOUT LYNX.
ROTO ROUTER
COPYRIGHT©2004 J.D. "Illiad" Frazer HTTP://WWW.USERFRIENDLY.ORG/

YOU MEAN THE TEXT-ONLY BROWSER?
YES.
I SUPPOSE WE COULD. AND JUST TO BE FAIR I'D HAVE TO RENDER THE STRIP SO THAT IT WAS VIEWABLE IN LYNX.
ROTO ROUTER

IT SURE WOULD MAKE RENDERING THE STRIP LESS COSTLY. I COULD FIRE ALL OF YOU GRAPHICAL FREAKS FOR STARTERS...
COULD WE PLEASE JUST STICK TO THE FUNNY JOKES?

HELLO AJ! WHAT ARE YOU BROWSING?
[: -)
HI GREG! I'M READING THE BBC NEWS SITE WITH LYNX!
(- : >
COPYRIGHT©2004 J.D. "Illiad" Frazer HTTP://WWW.USERFRIENDLY.ORG/

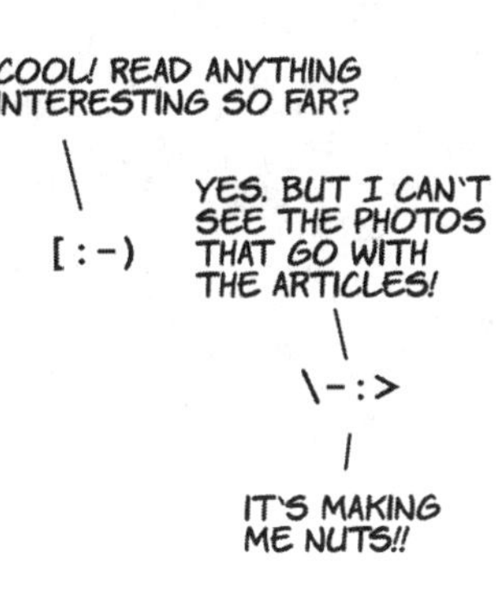
COOL! READ ANYTHING INTERESTING SO FAR?
[: -)
YES, BUT I CAN'T SEE THE PHOTOS THAT GO WITH THE ARTICLES!
\ - : >
IT'S MAKING ME NUTS!!

NOW, NOW, DON'T GET ANSI.
[: - D
DUDE, YOU ARE SUCH A CHARACTER.
(- : >
AND THIS, FOLKS, IS WHY WE DON'T DO LYNX-FRIENDLY-CARTOONS.

I kid you not, every three or four months I get at least one request for a "Lynx-friendly" version of UF. The amount of work required to describe a cartoon strip thusly would rather outstrip the demand for the format. But try explaining that to a Lynx zealot.

DICK, TELL ME AGAIN WHY WE'RE PUSHING THAT BAN ON BROADBAND TAXES?
IT'S GOOD FOR PEOPLE TO COMMUNICATE, DUBYA. WE SHOULDN'T MAKE IT HARD FOR THEM TO DO THAT.
AH.
COPYRIGHT©2004 J.D. "Illiad" Frazer HTTP://WWW.USERFRIENDLY.ORG/

ALSO, BROADBAND GIVES PEOPLE ACCESS TO INFORMATION AND BETTER EDUCATION.

NOT TO MENTION, I NEED MORE NEWBIES TO ROB IN EVERQUEST.
ASHCROFT SAID BROADBAND GIVES PEOPLE DIRTY PICTURES.

PRIOR ART THAT GOES WAY, WAY BACK BEFORE MICROSOFT'S RECENT PATENT ON TIMED BUTTON PUSHES.
GEEK
U.S. PATENT OFFICE
PUSH
THE LONGER YOU PUSH, THE GREATER THE CHANCE OF CAUSING APOPLEXY.
COPYRIGHT©2004 J.D. "Illiad" Frazer HTTP://WWW.USERFRIENDLY.ORG/

SO HOW ARE WE GOING TO GET BROADBAND INTO EVERY HOME IN THE U.S. BY 2007 DICK?
HECK DUBYA. WE DON'T HAVE IT ALL FIGURED OUT YET.
COPYRIGHT©2004 J.D. "Illiad" Frazer HTTP://WWW.USERFRIENDLY.ORG/

I HAVE AN IDEA. WANT TO HEAR IT?
WELL SURE. YOU'RE THE PRESIDENT.

WE COULD SEND CDS TO EVERYBODY.
MR. PRESIDENT. TRUST ME ON THIS ONE...

WATCHA GOT THERE, DICK?
YET ANOTHER EXCELLENT REASON TO PUSH BROADBAND EVERYWHERE.
COPYRIGHT©2004 J.D. "Illiad" Frazer HTTP://WWW.USERFRIENDLY.ORG/

BLAM *BLAM*
*BUDDA BUDDA BUDD
BUDDA BUDDA BUDDA
*BRRAAAAAAAAAPPP
KA-CHING!
WHUMP!

GOOD HEAVENS! IS THAT ICHOR?!
HA! RUMMY'S ZERGS AREN'T SO TOUGH!

YE GODS...ARE THOSE..?
YES. FLAT-PANEL LCD MONITORS!
FOR US?
COPYRIGHT©2004 J.D. "Illiad" Frazer HTTP://WWW.USERFRIENDLY.ORG/

YEP. PROFITS ARE UP, SO THE CHIEF GAVE ME A BIGGER BUDGET.
EBBEH...EBBEH...
A.J.? YOU ALL RIGHT?

HE GETS THIS WAY WHENEVER HIS SYSTEM IS UPGRADED. HE HAS TO PLAY ALL OF HIS OLD GAMES OVER AGAIN TO REVEL IN THE "NEW PLAYER EXPERIENCE."
YE GODS. WE GET NEW KEYBOARDS NEXT WEEK.
EBBEH!

TRYING OUT ONE OF YOUR OLD GAMES ON THE NEW SCREEN, A.J.?
COPYRIGHT©2004 J.D. "Illiad" Frazer HTTP://WWW.USERFRIENDLY.ORG/

A.J.?
HE'S PLAYING ZORK.
PRETTY!

HEY. BAD DAY?
BAD WEEK. IT FEELS LIKE EVIL IS JUST CRUMBLING AROUND ME.
COPYRIGHT©2004 J.D. "Illiad" Frazer HTTP://WWW.USERFRIENDLY.ORG/

BILL GATES WAS FINED FOR VIOLATING S.E.C. REGULATIONS. DIEBOLD VOTING MACHINES WERE BANNED. AND NOW S.C.O. HAS BEEN PUBLICALLY RIDICULED BY THE N.R.F!

IT'S ALMOST AS IF PEOPLE ARE GETTING SMARTER!
GUESS THAT MEANS THE U.S. PATENT OFFICE IS GOING TO BE UNDERSTAFFED.
OH. THANKS. MAKE IT WORSE.

DARL. I JUST READ THE "S.C.O. CLAIMS ARE WITHOUT MERIT" ARTICLE IN THE PAPER. IMAGINE MY DISTRESS.
YES. I KNOW. BUT...
COPYRIGHT©2004 J.D. "Illiad" Frazer HTTP://WWW.USERFRIENDLY.ORG/

NO BUTS. IF WE'RE TO CONTINUE OUR ARRANGEMENT, YOU NEED TO FIX THIS.

"OUR ARRANGEMENT" INVOLVES YOU TAKING MONEY FROM ME FOR NOTHING IN RETURN.
NOT NOTHING. I TEACH. YOU IMITATE. FOCUS. DARL!

USER FRIENDLY
the comic strip
BY J.D. "ILLIAD" FRAZER

SQUEE
SQUEE
YIBEE
YIBEE
YIBEE
SQUEE

HAPPY MOTHER'S DAY. A.J.
I'M NOT A MOTHER, ERWIN.
OH YES YOU ARE. COLLOQUIALLY.

YOU DOING ANYTHING FOR MOTHER'S DAY?
YEP. TAKING MY MOM OUT FOR DINNER TONIGHT.

DUST PUPPY WENT TO VISIT HIS MOM.
I DIDN'T KNOW HE HAD A MOTHER.
HE SAID HE MIGHT HAVE ONE.

SIGH MAYBE NEXT YEAR.

THIS IS GETTING OUT OF HAND. A DECADE OF PLANNING IS JUST UNRAVELLING BEFORE MY EYES.
AND NOW THE GOOGLE FOUNDERS WON'T SELL OUT TO EVIL ON THEIR I.P.O!
COPYRIGHT©2004 J.D. "Illiad" Frazer HTTP://WWW.USERFRIENDLY.ORG/

WHAT ARE YOU GOING TO DO? THAT I.P.O. COULD BE THE FOUNDATION OF AN ERA OF DARKNESS IF YOU HANDLE IT RIGHT...
I'M TRYING AN OLD TRICK. IT OFTEN WORKS ON MALE GEEKS.

COME ON, BOYS. I JUST WANT 51 PERCENT.
MY WORD SHE HAS BIG SHINY HO...HORNS.
LARRY! DON'T STEP OUT OF THE PENTAGRAM!!

Get it? Kevin Costner couldn't do an English accent in *Robin Hood: Prince of Thieves*. Get it?! Ha ha ha ha! Ha ...

I'M LOSING MY GRIP. I NEED TO START OVER WITH A SMALLER PROJECT AND BUILD UP AGAIN FROM THERE.
COPYRIGHT©2004 J.D. "Illiad" Frazer HTTP://WWW.USERFRIENDLY.ORG/

I NEED TO FIND SOMEONE WHO WANTS TO BE EVIL BUT IS SORELY LACKING IN SOME WAY. SOMEONE WHO HUNGERS FOR POWER. SOMEONE...WITH A REALLY BAD FAKE ACCENT.

AM SUPPOSINK HOPINK THAT KEVIN COSTNER IS BEINK CONSIDERED IS TOO MUCH...

LET'S TALK, SITHLING. I CAN TEACH YOU THINGS.
AM NOT TALKINK TO YOU.
COPYRIGHT©2004 J.D. "Illiad" Frazer HTTP://WWW.USERFRIENDLY.ORG/

YOUR EVIL IS A FARCE! YOU ARE LOSINK YOUR EMPIRE EVEN AS YOU ARE STANDINK HERE! YOUR TEACHINK ME IS ONLY TO BE MAKINK ME YOUR MINDLESS ZOMBIE SERVANT! NYET! BEGONE!

I'LL SHOW YOU HOW TO SCREW UP THAT OLD GEEK REAL BAD.
AM BEINK YOUR SLAVE, MY MASTER.

BEFORE WE START YOUR TRAINING, YOU NEED TO LOOK THE ROLE.
AM NOT SURE AM LIKINK SOUND OF THIS.
COPYRIGHT©2004 J.D. "Illiad" Frazer HTTP://WWW.USERFRIENDLY.ORG/

EVIL REQUIRES A LOOK. THE FOUNDATION OF EVIL IS MADE UP OF LIES AND MARKETING.
A DEBONAIR LOOK IS WHAT YOU NEED. YOU'RE RATHER GHASTLY THE WAY YOU ARE.

IS RATHER RICH COMINK FROM OILY HAIRBALL USINK SOMEONE ELSE'S BODY TO BE WALKINK AROUND.
IT'S THE SUIT. THINK OF WHAT I'M ABOUT TO DO TO YOU AS "EVIL EYE FOR THE WIMPY GUY."

MY NEW SITHLING SHOULD BE JUST ABOUT DONE, AND I WILL HAVE A MINION IN LARVAL FORM, READY TO BE SHAPED TO MY WHIMS.
COPYRIGHT©2004 J.D. "Illiad" Frazer HTTP://WWW.USERFRIENDLY.ORG/

ALTHOUGH I'M GOING TO HAVE TO TEACH HIM ABOUT BEING PUNCTUAL. EMPIRES DON'T SUFFER TARDINESS GLADLY...AH, I THINK I HEAR HIM COMING OUT NOW.

IS. NOT. ACCEPTABLE!!!
NICE CUT! NEXT STOP: SILK UNDERWEAR!

THIS OUTFIT. IT IS **RIDICULOUS!!**
DRESSED AS YOU ARE YOU REMIND ME OF SOMEONE. DON'T YOU HAVE A BROTHER? ONE WHO WORKS IN SALES AND MARKETING?
COPYRIGHT©2004 J.D. "Illiad" Frazer HTTP://WWW.USERFRIENDLY.ORG/

DARKSIDE DAVE. DA. HE IS BOTTOM-FEEDER. IN ANTARCTICA NOW.
AH YES. I LIKED HIM. I WONDER HOW BAD HE'S SUFFERING IN THAT ICE-BOUND GULAG OF HIS?

DAVE'S BABY PENGUIN OIL
COME ALONG LITTLE FELLAS. LOTS OF NICE TASTY HERRING RIGHT IN THERE...

This is harder on Pitr than you think. Suits aren't kind to those who like to go Spetsnaz.

THE FIRST RELEASE OF TWO PREMIUM RETAIL COMPUTER GAMES AS A TWIN-PACK
FALL 2004 (OR "THEREABOUTS")

DUKE NUKEM FOREVER
HALF-LIFE²
λ ²
HALF-LIFE²

WELCOME, CLASS. TODAY WE REVIEW THE CONCEPT OF EVIL.
PITR, GIVE US AN EXAMPLE OF TRUE EVIL.
COPYRIGHT © 2004 J.D. "Illiad" Frazer HTTP://WWW.USERFRIENDLY.ORG/

YOUR ALARM CLOCK WAKINK YOU UP BEFORE NOON, AND THERE IS NO CAFFEINE NEARBY.

TAP
TAP
TAP

OH, AND RADIO STATION IS PLAYINK WILLIAM SHATNER SONGS.
THAT'S BETTER. REMEMBER: "CAUSE THE MOST AGONY WITH THE LEAST WORK."

Humility is a virtue, they say. So is anesthetic.

LET'S DISCUSS A REAL FAVE OF MINE: THE EVIL THAT CAN BE FOUND IN THE TECH WORLD.
EVIL PERVADES EVERYTHING, BUT IN TECHNOLOGY ITS PRESENCE IS STRONG.

MUCH CAME FROM TODAY'S TECHNOLOGY THAT IS CONSIDERED A BLIGHT UPON THE WORLD.

FOR EXAMPLE: FROM EMAIL CAME SPAM. FROM JAVASCRIPT CAME POP-UPS. FROM IRC CAME THE L337 LANGUAGE.

FROM THE WEB CAME WEBCOMICS.
NOW YOU'RE GETTING IT!

Larry Ellison, founder and CEO of Oracle, hates Hates HATES Bill Gates. Not for any personal reason I'm aware of—just because Bill Gates is richer and more successful.

NOW, TO DO EVIL, YOU NEED MONEY. I DON'T MEAN PERFORMING PLAIN THUGGERY. I MEAN REAL, PALPABLE, GROIN-TORQUING EVIL.

BUT WHEN YOU COLLECT YOUR MONEY, YOU NEED TO DO IT WITH PIZZAZZ. JUST YESTERDAY, I ARRANGED TO HAVE BILL GATES "INVITED" TO A GAME PARK IN SOUTH AFRICA.
HE IS GIVINK YOU MONEY FOR THIS?
NO, LARRY ELLISON DID. LOTS OF IT.

YOU'D BETTER RUN, BILL.
WAIT!
WAIT!!

SOMETHING TO NOTE: EVIL HAS NO ALLIES. YOU'D THINK MICROSOFT WOULD TEAM UP WITH, SAY, DISNEY AND BRING ABOUT A REIGN OF TERROR. THE THING IS, THERE CAN ONLY BE ONE EVIL OVERLORD, AND WE ALL WANT THAT SPOT.

AH.

THAT WAS STUPID!! EVIL OVERLORDS SHOULD NEVER EXPLAIN TO A STAR PUPIL THAT THERE'S ONLY ROOM FOR ONE EVIL OVERLORD!

SOMETIMES INTELLIGENT EVIL JUST DOESN'T WORK, AND YOU HAVE TO RESORT TO SHOCK TACTICS. FOR EXAMPLE:
COPYRIGHT©2004 J.D. "Illiad" Frazer HTTP://WWW.USERFRIENDLY.ORG/

RRROOAAAAR!!!

IMPRESSIVE! YOU DIDN'T EVEN FLINCH. GO GRAB YOURSELF A COFFEE, SITHLING.
CAN NOT. AM STUCK.

HUH? WHAT DID YOU DO, GLUE YOURSELF TO THE SEAT?
NYET. AM...UH... GRIPPING SEAT CUSHION. OR MAYBE IT IS MORE OF A PINCH.

NOW, LET'S GET STARTED ON YOUR PRACTICUM. WHAT IS SID KEEPING BUSY WITH THESE DAYS?
HE IS CODINK WERY BIG REPORTINK APPLICATION.
DOES HE USE HIS CD BURNER?
COPYRIGHT©2004 J.D. "Illiad" Frazer HTTP://WWW.USERFRIENDLY.ORG/

TO BACKUP HIS PROJECT, DA.
AND WHAT DO YOU THINK WOULD HAPPEN IF SOMEONE SWAPPED THE WIRES OF HIS CD BURNER WITH THE RESET SWITCH?

AM THINKING I WOULD CACKLE LIKE SMALL, EVIL CHILD.
JUST SO.
AAAARRRRRG

GEEK TRASH TELEVISION
The Alexis de Tocqueville Institution says: "Sorry Linux, Linus is not your dad!"
NEXT ON
JERRY SPRINGER
COPYRIGHT©2004 J.D. "Illiad" Frazer HTTP://WWW.USERFRIENDLY.ORG/

MIKE. SOMEONE WIRED MY CD BURNER TO THE RESET PRONGS. COULD YOU PLEASE FIX THIS WHILE I'M GONE? I HAVE TO GET TO A MEETING RIGHT NOW OR I'D FIX IT MYSELF.
I HAVE A DEADLINE MYSELF. BUT I'LL TRY.
COPYRIGHT©2004 J.D. "Illiad" Frazer HTTP://WWW.USERFRIENDLY.ORG/

MIKHAIL. YOU ARE CLEARLY WERY BUSY. AM TO BE HELPINK YOU WITH THIS. TO BE LETTINK ME REPAIR BOX.
UM...OKAY.

I KNOW THIS IS LIKE GIVING A FUEL/AIR EXPLOSIVE TO A PYROMANIAC. BUT ON THE SAME NOTE, I REALLY WANT TO SEE THE FUEL/AIR EXPLOSIVE GO OFF.

GOOD MORNING. SITHLING. REPORT!
FIRST STAGE OF "OPERATION RANSID" IS COMPLETE.
COPYRIGHT©2004 J.D. "Illiad" Frazer HTTP://WWW.USERFRIENDLY.ORG/

YOU MESSED UP HIS MACHINE SOME MORE?
NYET. FIXED RESET WIRES. REPLACED RESET BUTTON TOO.
REALLY...

MIIIIKE!!
RESET

PITR?
DA. LEETLE GUY?
WHAT ARE YOU DOING IN A SUIT AND TIE?
IS STYLE FOR EVIL OVERLORD.
COPYRIGHT©2004 J.D. "Illiad" Frazer HTTP://WWW.USERFRIENDLY.ORG/

SUIT IS CONVEYINK DIGNITY. WEALTH. POWER. TIE. SHE IS FOR CONVEYINK INTRIGUE.
AND OF COURSE. AM TOLD MUST BE WEARINK SILK UNDERWEAR.

YOU DON'T MIND THE SILK UNDERWEAR?
NYET. NOT MINDINK. ONLY MAKES CONCENTRATING A LEETLE HARD.

OBSERVE MY NEXT STEP IN EMPIRE BUILDING. SITHLING. THIS IS A "SUPER-PUFF" FROM "PUPHY-PUFF MATERIALS INC." I ACQUIRED THEM WITH S.C.O SHARE MONEY LAST MONTH.
OKAY...

THE COMPANY WAS A FAILURE. THEY DE-SIGNED THESE THINGS TO BE USED AS PACKING MATERIAL. TO FIRMLY CUSHION THINGS. YOU JUST ADD A SINGLE. TINY. DROP OF WATER LIKE THIS AND...
COPYRIGHT©2004 J.D. "Illiad" Frazer HTTP://WWW.USERFRIENDLY.ORG/

WAMF!

NOT REALLY MUCH OF A "FAILURE."
UNLESS YOU COUNT COURIERING OUT THE SHIPPING STAFF WITH THE PRODUCT.
NO.

YOU'RE IN EARLY THIS MORNING.
DA. WANTINK TO BE HERE WHEN SID IS COMINK IN.
COPYRIGHT©2004 J.D. "Illiad" Frazer HTTP://WWW.USERFRIENDLY.ORG/

OH? DO TELL.
YOU KNOW THE DOZEN "SUPER-PUFFS" YOU ARE GIVINK TO ME YESTERDAY?
YES.
AM THINKINK SID IS PERHAPS BEINK LATE COMINK TO WORK TODAY...
COPYRIGHT©2004 J.D. "Illiad" Frazer HTTP://WWW.USERFRIENDLY.ORG/

These Super Puffs made their first appearance in a hard science fiction RPG I ran years ago. The shower incident happened to one of the player characters. And then their space freighter was suddenly full of these things. It made a search by Imperial Customs quite difficult.

WHOA. IS THAT REALLY YOU, PITR?
DA. GOINK AWAY. AM WERY BUSY.
COPYRIGHT©2004 J.D. "Illiad" Frazer HTTP://WWW.USERFRIENDLY.ORG/

DOING WHAT?
I SAID, GO AWAY!!!

DUDE. IS THAT AN ONLINE COURSE FOR AN M.B.A?
AM JUST CURIOUS! CAN QUIT ANYTIME!!

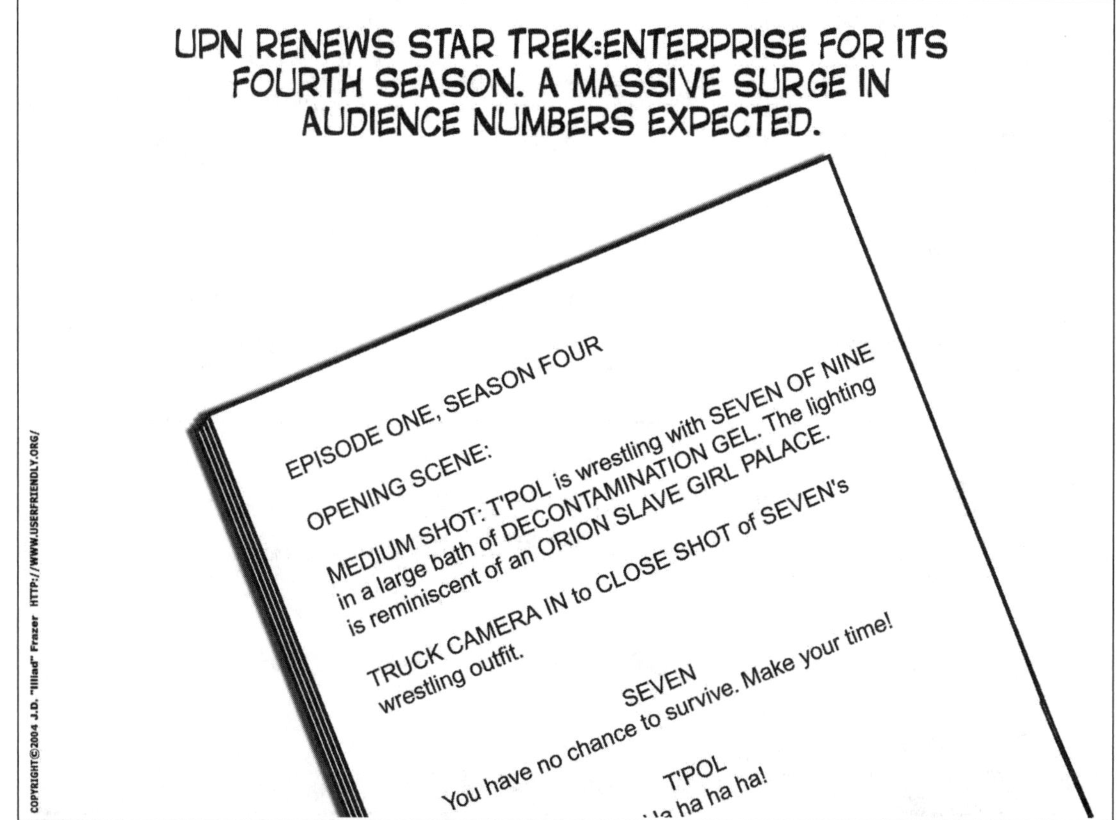
UPN RENEWS STAR TREK:ENTERPRISE FOR ITS FOURTH SEASON. A MASSIVE SURGE IN AUDIENCE NUMBERS EXPECTED.
EPISODE ONE, SEASON FOUR
OPENING SCENE:
MEDIUM SHOT: T'POL is wrestling with SEVEN OF NINE in a large bath of DECONTAMINATION GEL. The lighting is reminiscent of an ORION SLAVE GIRL PALACE.
TRUCK CAMERA IN to CLOSE SHOT of SEVEN's wrestling outfit.
SEVEN
You have no chance to survive. Make your time!
T'POL
COPYRIGHT©2004 J.D. "Illiad" Frazer HTTP://WWW.USERFRIENDLY.ORG/

SO PITR. SINCE YOU'RE ALL SPIFFED UP. MAYBE WE SHOULD GO FOR A BEER AFTER WORK AND CRUISE FOR CHICKS TOGETHER...
NOT INTERESTED.

COPYRIGHT©2004 J.D. "Illiad" Frazer HTTP://WWW.USERFRIENDLY.ORG/
NO. SERIOUSLY. I GOT A TATTOO IN CHINESE CHARACTERS. THEY'RE ALL THE RAGE NOW AND CHICKS **LOVE** 'EM!

MIND YOU. I HAVE TO WEAR LOW-RIDER SLACKS TO SHOW IT OFF. IT'S RIGHT HERE ON MY BUTT CHEEK...
AAAAAUUUGH!!

IT SAYS "POWER. FORTUNE. VIRILITY."
HAVE TAKEN SOME CHINESE. THESE ARE NOT THE RIGHT CHARACTERS.

COPYRIGHT©2004 J.D. "Illiad" Frazer HTTP://WWW.USERFRIENDLY.ORG/
OH?
ONE SECOND. TRYINK TO REMEMBER...

WELL? WHAT DOES IT SAY?
"FOR SERVICE. PLEASE SWIPE CARD HERE."

NOW THIS IS MY KINDA PLACE. CHICKS AND BEER. ORDER WHATEVER YOU'D LIKE. MY TREAT!
ABSINTHE COCKTAIL #1 PLEASE.
COMING RIGHT UP!

COPYRIGHT©2004 J.D. "Illiad" Frazer HTTP://WWW.USERFRIENDLY.ORG/
ABSINTHE? WHAT ON EARTH IS THAT?
ABOUT $12.00 A DRINK.

WHAT?! I HOPE YOU DON'T EXPECT ME TO PAY FOR THAT!
AM WILLINK TO PAY. SHALL I SWIPE CARD NOW?

DUDE. CHECK OUT THE BUTTER TART SITTING NEXT TO YOU...
DA. AM KNOWINK SHE IS THERE.

COPYRIGHT©2004 J.D. "Illiad" Frazer HTTP://WWW.USERFRIENDLY.ORG/
THEN LET'S SEE YOUR MAGIC. MISTER. CHAT HER UP. AND USE YOUR EVIL GENIUS PERSONA TO DO IT. GET ALL SUAVE AND SLAVIC ON HER.

GREETINGS. TODAY. I AM GOINK **SPETSNAZ.**
I'M NOT WITH HIM.

WHAT THE HELL IS THAT?
IS SKINNY GIRL JUMPING UP AND DOWN LIKE IDIOT TO WERY BAD JAPANESE POP MUSIC.
AH.
WUMPA
TEE-HEE
WUMPA
WUMPA
WUMPA
WUMPA
COPYRIGHT©2004 J.D. "Illiad" Frazer HTTP://WWW.USERFRIENDLY.ORG/

OONTSI
OONTSI
OONTSI
OONTSI
TEE-HEE
OONTSI
OONTSI
OONTSI

AM SORRY. IS ACTUALLY MALE GEEK PLAYING "DANCE DANCE REVOLUTION."
YEAH. I WAS KINDA WONDERING ABOUT THE ARMPIT STAINS.
INTDAH
INTDAH
INTDAH
INTDAH
*OOIE! NICE
INTDAH
INTDAH

PITR. WHERE ARE YOU GOING?
TAKINK CARE OF BUSINESS.
IMPHA
IMPHA
IMPHA
IMPHA
IMPHA
IMPHA
COPYRIGHT©2004 J.D. "Illiad" Frazer HTTP://WWW.USERFRIENDLY.ORG/

BUMPA
BUMPA
BUMPA
BUMPA
WHAM!

GOOD GOD! WHAT DO YOU CALL THAT!?
"DANCE DANCE RETRIBUTION."
EEEEHHH

I'm not sure if I should be proud or ashamed of my … facility (?) with onomatopoeia. But I swear that's what dance music sounds like!

AN ANALYSIS OF THE "HARDWARE IS FREE" BUSINESS MODEL

Websphere License: $1,499

Solaris Support Contract: $6,400

Server Hardware: "Free"

Power-cycling your server for you: $299

Smacking your server for you: $99 per whack

Wiggling the power leads: $49 per oscillation

Reseating the RAM: $199

Puffing compressed air inside the case: $5 per cc of air

Plugging the power cable into the socket: $499

Value of this business model to Sun: Priceless

Some things in life are free. For everything else, you pay Sun & Microsoft.

A.J.? WHY ARE YOU JUST SITTING HERE NOT DOING ANYTHING?
I'M WAITING FOR HALF-LIFE 2 TO COME OUT.
COPYRIGHT©2004 J.D. "Illiad" Frazer HTTP://WWW.USERFRIENDLY.ORG/

MUST...RESIST... ASKING...OH, WHAT THE HELL.

AND THAT THING UNDER YOUR MONITOR IS..?
MY NEW VIDEO CARD FOR THE GAME!

A.J., HAS IT OCCURRED TO YOU THAT MAYBE, JUST MAYBE, IF YOU PAID ATTENTION TO WOMEN WITH ONE-TENTH OF THE ATTENTION YOU PAY TO GAMES YOU MIGHT BE A HAPPIER HUMAN BEING?!
MUNCHKIN
COPYRIGHT©2004 J.D. "Illiad" Frazer HTTP://WWW.USERFRIENDLY.ORG/

MUNCHKIN

BUT I DO PAY ATTENTION TO WOMEN. LOTS.
I'M NOT TALKING ABOUT WOMEN FROM THE JPEG CLAN!

WHAT IS IT NOW?
A.J., I'M TRYING TO TELL YOU SOMETHING IMPORTANT...
COPYRIGHT©2004 J.D. "Illiad" Frazer HTTP://WWW.USERFRIENDLY.ORG/

DON'T YOU KNOW THERE'S A WHOLE WORLD OUTSIDE OF YOUR COMPUTER GAMES? A REAL WORLD, WHERE FULFILLMENT AND HAPPINESS ARE ALL WITHIN YOUR REACH.
BUT I'M ALREADY HAPPY AND FULFILLED...

NO YOU'RE NOT!!
I'LL BET GORDON FREEMAN NEVER HAD TO DEAL WITH THIS SORT OF ANOMALOUS MATERIAL.

HEY, DID YOU SEE THAT SPIKE IN OUR TRAFFIC THIS MORNING?
YES. WHAT WAS IT?
A.J.'S BLOG WAS IN THE SPOTLIGHT ON SOME BIG WEBLOG SITE.
A.J. HAS A BLOG?
COPYRIGHT©2004 J.D. "Illiad" Frazer HTTP://WWW.USERFRIENDLY.ORG/

YUP. SEE RIGHT HERE:
"I, AS WITH SO MANY LIKE ME, HAVE TROUBLE WITH THE LINE BETWEEN FANTASY AND REALITY. GAMES AND THE WORLD. FLESH AND PIXEL. AND YESTERDAY I FOUND MYSELF SLIPPING FURTHER INTO THAT PAPER-THIN LIMBO."

"THERE SHE WAS, A LEATHER GODDESS OF PHOBOS, WHISPERING IN MY HEAD, URGING ME TO REACH OUT, URGING ME TO TYPE "LEWD" AT THE COMMAND PROMPT..."
I CAN READ JUST FINE, THANK YOU!

YO. SID! YOU SEEN A.J.'S BLOG YET?
NO. AND I DON'T CARE TO. I THINK WEBLOGS ARE PATENTLY SILLY.
EH? HOW SO?
COPYRIGHT©2004 J.D. "Illiad" Frazer HTTP://WWW.USERFRIENDLY.ORG/

THEY'RE A SYMPTOM OF "LOOK AT ME!" BEHAVIOUR. JOURNALS I UNDERSTAND. BUT THOSE HAVE BEEN TRADITIONALLY PRIVATE. THIS "BLOGGING" IS NOTHING MORE THAN "DEGAUSSING YOUR OWN COIL!"

DID YOU JUST SAY "DEGAUSSING..."?
AND FURTHER. INSTEAD OF LOOKING AT NAUGHTY PICTURES WHILE YOU'RE "DEGAUSSING," YOU'RE LOOKING IN A MIRROR!
WHAT'S WRONG WITH THAT?

SID. HOW CAN YOU SAY BLOGGING IS ALL ABOUT GETTING ATTENTION? BLOGGING IS ABOUT SHARING. LETTING YOUR FRIENDS KNOW WHAT'S GOING ON IN YOUR LIFE. AND BEING HONEST WITH YOURSELF ALL AT THE SAME TIME!
COPYRIGHT©2004 J.D. "Illiad" Frazer HTTP://WWW.USERFRIENDLY.ORG/

I'LL BET YOU CAN'T GIVE ME ONE ARGUMENT THAT SHOWS BLOGGING IS A SELFISH. ANTI-SOCIAL ACT. GO ON. JUST ONE.

THEY TOOK THE "WE" OUT OF "WEBLOG" DIDN'T THEY?
UH... THEY...UH...

USER FRIENDLY
the comic strip
BY J.D. "ILLIAD" FRAZER
COPYRIGHT©2004 J.D. "Illiad" Frazer HTTP://WWW.USERFRIENDLY.ORG/

ERWIN. PLEASE PLAY THE MUSIC FOR "LUMP" BY THE PRESIDENTS OF THE UNITED STATES OF AMERICA.
PLAYING...

I SAT ALONE IN A LONELY CUBE! TOTALLY MOTIONLESS IN FRONT OF THE TUBE! WONDERED WHY I WAS IN MY PYJAMAS! AS I KEYED IN ALL OF THE NEEDED PARAMETERS!
SNAZZZZZ BUKKA BUKKA OW-OW!

MY BLOG! MY BLOG! IT'S FROM MY HEAD! MY BLOG! MY BLOG! MY BLOG! IT MIGHT BE READ!

I WRITE MY MEMOIRS EVERY DAY! UPDATED WITH ALL THE SMILIES I CAN CONVEY! NOTES FROM THOSE WHO READ ABOUT MY STRIFE! I HAVE SO MUCH TO WRITE EVEN WITHOUT A LIFE!

MY BLOG! MY BLOG! IT'S FROM MY HEAD! MY BLOG! MY BLOG! MY BLOG...
YOU GUYS ARE DEAD.

HEY. FEEL LIKE A GAME OF "ENEMY TERRITORY?"
CAN'T. I'M TRYING TO BUY A NEW MACHINE FOR MY DAD FOR FATHERS DAY.
SEE. APPLE ADVERTISES THAT THEIR NEW G5 IS THE FASTEST AND BEST COMPUTER IN THE WORLD WHILE INTEL STATES THAT THEIR TOP-END PENTIUM 4 IS THE FASTEST AND BEST.
COPYRIGHT © 2004 J.D. "Illiad" Frazer HTTP://WWW.USERFRIENDLY.ORG/

SO THE QUESTION IS. WHO'S TELLING THE TRUTH?

KIND OF FEELS LIKE THE UPCOMING PRESIDENTIAL ELECTION IN THE U.S., EH?
I WAS JUST GONNA SAY...

WHAT'RE YOU WATCHING?
G4TECHTV. THE COMCAST REPLACEMENT FOR TECHTV.
COPYRIGHT © 2004 J.D. "Illiad" Frazer HTTP://WWW.USERFRIENDLY.ORG/

A.J., YOU'RE WATCHING TWO PEOPLE PLAYING PONG.
NO. I'M WATCHING TWO HOT CHICKS PLAYING PONG.
WOO! DID I JUST SCORE?!
YES. LOOK AT THE SHINY! BUY THIS GAME EVERYONE!

TODAY ON G4TECHTV WE REVIEW THE LATEST COMPUTER ROLE-PLAYING GAMES.
THIS ONE IS GOOD. IT HAS LOTS OF BRIGHT COLOURS. CUTE CHARACTERS. PLENTY OF BLOOD AND IT COMES WITH A BURNING SOUNDTRACK BY TT HOT POCKET!
COPYRIGHT © 2004 J.D. "Illiad" Frazer HTTP://WWW.USERFRIENDLY.ORG/

THIS ONE HOWEVER. IS BAD. THERE'S TOO MUCH TEXT TO READ.
YEAH! TOO MUCH!

IT SAYS "PRESS START TO PLAY."
WHO HAS TIME TO READ?!

A.J., I CAN UNDERSTAND WHY YOU WATCHED TECHTV BECAUSE I USED TO WATCH IT MYSELF FOR THE TECHNICAL TIPS AND NEWS. BUT THIS G4 STUFF IS ALL GAME TV! AND BAD GAME TV AT THAT.
COPYRIGHT © 2004 J.D. "Illiad" Frazer HTTP://WWW.USERFRIENDLY.ORG/

IT IS NOT! THEY HAVE SOLID TECHNICAL SHOWS TOO. AND ONE'S JUST STARTING RIGHT NOW...

THIS IS A COMPUTER!
AND THIS IS WHERE YOU PLUG IN THE JOYSTICK!! YAAAAAAY!!
YAAAAY.
BLEH.

BROWSE
BROWSE
BROWSE
BROWSE
COPYRIGHT©2004 J.D. "Illiad" Frazer HTTP://WWW.USERFRIENDLY.ORG/

YEEEARRRGH!!

WHAT. ANOTHER FLASHING PUNCH-THE-MONKEY BANNER AD?
NO. THE G4TECHTV WEBSITE...
ENGFEH.

"IN MARCH, YAHOO SUED ERIC HEAD AND HIS FATHER AND BROTHER AS PART OF AN INDUSTRY CRACKDOWN ON UNSOLICITED E-MAIL, OR SPAM. YAHOO ALLEGED THEY RAN A HUGE SPAMMING OPERATION AND SENT MORE THAN 94 MILLION E-MAILS IN ONE MONTH ALONE TO YAHOO E-MAIL USERS."

COPYRIGHT©2004 J.D. "Illiad" Frazer HTTP://WWW.USERFRIENDLY.ORG/
"THE HEADS HAVE SETTLED THE LAWSUIT AND ARE PAYING DAMAGES TO YAHOO. THE EXACT AMOUNT OF THE PAYMENT IS CONFIDENTIAL, BUT A LAWYER FOR THE FAMILY SAID IT WAS 'SIX FIGURES.'
ERIC HEAD HAS ALSO STATED THAT HE WAS OUT OF BUSINESS AND THAT HE WOULD FIND A WAY TO USE HIS KNOWLEDGE TO HELP PROTECT KIDS ON THE INTERNET."

"I'VE LEARNED MY LESSON. I WON'T EVER DO THAT AGAIN. EVER."
HEY...WHAT BEACH IS THAT?
TAHITI.

USER FRIENDLY
the comic strip
BY J.D. "ILLIAD" FRAZER
COPYRIGHT©2004 J.D. "Illiad" Frazer HTTP://WWW.USERFRIENDLY.ORG/

LOW CARB FOODS
6.8 GRAMS OF CARBS PER SERVING?!! YE GODS!!!

6.4 GRAMS. NOW THAT'S MORE LIKE IT!
LOW CARB FOODS

HI! I'D LIKE A LOW-CARB SOY MUFFIN AND A NO-CARB TEA INFUSION PLEASE.
YOU KNOW GREG, I JUST CAN'T BELIEVE YOU'RE ON THAT DIET.
BIGBUCKS COFFEE

WHAT? WHY?
IT'S A BAD IDEA FOR GEEKS TO BE ON LOW-CARB DIETS. LOW-CARB MEANS NO SUGAR. NO SUGAR MEANS CRAVINGS. CRAVINGS MEAN A LOSS OF CONCENTRATION...

...LOSING CONCENTRATION MAKES GEEKS IRRITABLE, AND GEEKS RUN THE COMPUTERS THAT RUN THE WORLD'S BANKS AND MILITARIES!!!
YE GODS!! GIVE ME A FROSTED CHOCOLATE CAKE BEFORE WE PLUNGE INTO ANARCHY!!
TO GO?

For a brief time, possession of a GMail account (along with the 6+ invites you could give others) had a certain cachet. Some folks auctioned GMail accounts on eBay, although I can't imagine they got much for them. Rumors said $100, max. Silly. But still, I was pleased when I received my first GMail account.

Sometimes it's fun to reinforce character roles with little side stories. Observe Erwin in this strip, for example.

A.J., DO YOU HAVE THE NEW STYLESHEETS DONE FOR THE WEBSITE YET?
COPYRIGHT©2004 J.D. "Illiad" Frazer HTTP://WWW.USERFRIENDLY.ORG/

YEEEAAAAAH!!!

I WAS JUST GIVEN A GMAIL ACCOUNT!!
YOU DON'T SAY...

WHAT'S ALL THIS FUSS ABOUT YOU GETTING A GMAIL ACCOUNT? WHAT IS THAT ANYWAY?
IT'S WEBMAIL OFFERED BY GOOGLE. I WAS GIVEN AN ACCOUNT AS PART OF THEIR BETA TEST. NOT MANY FOLKS HAVE ONE YET.
COPYRIGHT©2004 J.D. "Illiad" Frazer HTTP://WWW.USERFRIENDLY.ORG/
...AND, IT HAS THREADING, A LABELLING SYSTEM, AUTOMATIC SPAM FILTERS AND A ONE GIG STORAGE LIMIT. TO TOP IT ALL OFF, MY ACCOUNT IS CLEAN. PURE AND UNTAINTED BY SPAM!
REALLY...
DAMN...

To: scottrichter422@yahoo.com
ajgarrett@gmail.com
pass it on.
TYPE
TAP
BETRAY

I STILL DON'T GET THE FUSS OVER THIS GMAIL THING. WHY DO PEOPLE WANT ACCOUNTS SO BADLY?
GMAIL IS RUN BY GOOGLE, SO IT'S BOUND TO STICK AROUND FOR A LONG TIME...
COPYRIGHT©2004 J.D. "Illiad" Frazer HTTP://WWW.USERFRIENDLY.ORG/

...THUS THE ODDS ARE THAT YOU WON'T HAVE TO CHANGE YOUR E-MAIL ADDRESS YET AGAIN BECAUSE THE WEBHOST WENT UNDER.

OKAY. BUT WHY IS EVERYONE WANTING A GMAIL ACCOUNT RIGHT NOW?
BECAUSE I DON'T WANT A GMAIL ADDRESS THAT READS 'SIDDABSTER2004WIBBLE-ENGFEHWANKEL@GMAIL.COM'

AW, JEEZ. NOT AGAIN! MICROSOFT HAS FILED ANOTHER IDIOTIC PATENT.
WHAT IS IT THIS TIME?

"USING HUMAN SKIN AS A POWER CONDUIT AND DATA BUS."
YOU AND YOUR MS-BASHING! I'D LIKE TO SEE YOU SHOW ME ONE EXAMPLE OF PRIOR ART FOR THAT!
COPYRIGHT©2004 J.D. "Illiad" Frazer HTTP://WWW.USERFRIENDLY.ORG/

SKUFF
SKUFF
SKUFF

AARRRRGGH!!
AND WHAT DID YOU LEARN FROM THE "DATA" I JUST SENT YOU?
ZOT!

HEY. DID YOU READ ABOUT THAT PATENT ON SKIN THAT MICRO-SOFT JUST FILED?
YEP. AND "THEIR" PERSONAL AREA NETWORK IDEAS.
COPYRIGHT©2004 J.D. "Illiad" Frazer HTTP://WWW.USERFRIENDLY.ORG/

PITR'S WORKING ON MANUFACTURING SOME "PRIOR ART" TO THWART MICROSOFT.
PITR? YE GODS. WHO'S HIS VICTIM THIS TIME?

...OKAY. SO MY CELL PHONE CAN SWITCH OFF MY PDA, AND MY PDA CAN NOW SYNCHRONIZE MY WATCH WITH THE ATOMIC CLOCK. BUT HOW DO I POWER CYCLE ERWIN?
TO BE LOOKINK AT PHOTO OF ANGELINA JOLIE...
AAAGGGHHH!!!

I promise I don't have a fixation on Angelina Jolie.

PITR, I'M CURIOUS. HOW ARE YOU GETTING ALL OF A.J.'S DEVICES TALKING TO EACH OTHER?
HAVE INSTALLED WERY SPECIALLY HACKED O.S.
OH? WHICH O.S?
COPYRIGHT©2004 J.D. "Illiad" Frazer HTTP://WWW.USERFRIENDLY.ORG/

SHOULD BE WERY INTERESTINK, WATCHINK HOW DEVICES INTERACT AND THEIR EFFICIENCY OF COURSE...
SURE, BUT WHICH O.S?

...AND SPEED OF TRANSFER--
WHICH O.S.?!?!
UM...WINDOWS MILLENNIUM.
OH GOD MY EYE'S TWIT-CHING!! WHY IS MY EYE TWITCHING?!!

TYPICAL AOL USER BEFORE THE 92 MILLION AOL EMAIL ADDRESSES WERE STOLEN AND SOLD.
YOU'VE GOT MAIL!
COPYRIGHT©2004 J.D. "Illiad" Frazer HTTP://WWW.USERFRIENDLY.ORG/

TYPICAL AOL USER AFTER THE 92 MILLION AOL EMAIL ADDRESSES WERE STOLEN AND SOLD.
YOU'VE GOT MAIL!

PITR. WHATEVER HAPPENED TO THE WHOLE OPEN SOURCE IDEAL? WHY ARE YOU INFLICTING WINDOWS ON A.J.?
GIVINK CREDIT TO MICRO-SOFT MIKHAIL. THEY HAVE JUST OPEN SOURCED MORE CODE!
COPYRIGHT©2004 J.D. "Illiad" Frazer HTTP://WWW.USERFRIENDLY.ORG/

THIS LOOKS LIKE SOURCE CODE TO WINDOWS MINESWEEPER.
DA. TO SOME PEOPLE THIS CODE IS WERY MISSION-CRITICAL.
HEY! EVERYTIME I HIT A MINE I GET A JOLT THROUGH MY PANTS!! OH HEY...

HOTMAIL JUST BOOSTED ITS FREE STORAGE ALLOCATION. JUST LIKE YAHOO.
IN RESPONSE TO GMAIL?
YES.
COPYRIGHT©2004 J.D. "Illiad" Frazer HTTP://WWW.USERFRIENDLY.ORG/

IT'S LIKE GOING TO A RESTAURANT AND YOU FIND OUT THAT YOU GET A BIGGER PLATE THAN AT THE ONE NEXT DOOR. BUT THE PORTIONS YOU'RE SERVED STAY THE SAME.
HOW DOES SPAM FIT INTO THIS?

I GUESS THAT WOULD BE LIKE SOMEONE VOMITING ON TO YOUR PLATE.
OH GOD!!
AND SPAM FILTERS?
POURING THE VOMIT THROUGH A STRAINER.
AAAGH!!!

GREG. HAVE YOU SEEN STEF? I WAS SURE I SAW HIM COME IN THIS MORNING...
YEP. HE SAID HE WAS OFF TO JOIN A FLASH MOB.
COPYRIGHT©2004 J.D. "Illiad" Frazer HTTP://WWW.USERFRIENDLY.ORG/

A... WHAT?
FLASH MOB. THEY STARTED A FEW YEARS AGO. A BUNCH OF PEOPLE GET TOGETHER TO DO SOME WEIRD, RANDOM THING THEN THEY DISPERSE. HOWEVER, I DON'T KNOW IF STEF KNOWS EXACTLY WHAT A FLASH MOB IS.

WHAT?! AND WHERE'S YOUR TRENCHCOAT?

This was a jab at both the RIAA-esque lobby groups who act like they're absolute monarchs, and at the average Canadian citizen who doesn't know much about the really important issues surrounding intellectual property. And it was published on Canada Day, July 1. And I did a crap job of writing it.

INTERNET SERVICE PROVIDERS DO NOT HAVE TO PAY ROYALTIES TO COMPOSERS AND ARTISTS FOR MUSIC DOWNLOADED BY WEB CUSTOMERS. THE SUPREME COURT OF CANADA RULED WEDNESDAY.
COPYRIGHT©2004 J.D. "Illiad" Frazer HTTP://WWW.USERFRIENDLY.ORG/

IN A 9-0 RULING THE COURT STATED THAT COMPANIES PROVIDING WIDE ACCESS TO THE WEB ARE MERELY "INTERMEDIARIES" WHO ARE NOT BOUND BY FEDERAL COPYRIGHT LEGISLATION.

WE ASKED MAN-ON-THE-STREET IN TORONTO NED EGGBY WHAT HE THOUGHT ABOUT THIS LANDMARK RULING:
"NO MORE COLLECTING ROYALTIES? DOES THAT MEAN THE QUEEN AND HER LOT AREN'T DROPPING BY FOR TEA HERE ANYMORE?"

MIKE, YOU'RE GOING ON A TRIP. WE NEED YOU TO CONDUCT A ROUTER INSTALL AT OUR NEW CLIENT'S SITE.
OKAY. WHEN DOES MY FLIGHT LEAVE?
COPYRIGHT©2004 J.D. "Illiad" Frazer HTTP://WWW.USERFRIENDLY.ORG/

IT DOESN'T. YOU'RE DRIVING.
WHAT? THAT'S A 3-DAY TRIP EACH WAY!
IT'LL SAVE US MONEY. AND YOU LIKE DRIVING, DON'T YOU?

I LIKE IT JUST FINE. IT'S THE THREE DAYS OF BOREDOM I'M WORRIED ABOUT.
OH, YOU WON'T BE BORED...
DON'T WORRY ABOUT ROAD MUSIC. I'LL BRING ALL MY "AIR SUPPLY" CDS.

WHAT THE HELL DID YOU RENT US THIS CAR FOR? WE HAVE A BUDGET FOR A NICE COMFY LUXURY VEHICLE.
I WAS THINKING ABOUT THE PRICE OF GAS. WE HAVE TO BE CAREFUL.
COPYRIGHT©2004 J.D. "Illiad" Frazer HTTP://WWW.USERFRIENDLY.ORG/

NOT TO MENTION THE FACT THAT WE NEED TO BE AWARE OF HOW WE'RE HARMING THE ENVIRONMENT. THE LESS GAS WE BURN, THE SMALLER THE POLLUTION FOOTPRINT WE LEAVE BEHIND.

THE INDICATORS ON THE DASH ARE GLOWING THREE DIFFERENT COLOURS!!
WHICH HAS NOTHING TO DO WITH WHY I PICKED THIS CAR!!

DUE TO MAJOR SECURITY PROBLEMS WITH MICROSOFT'S INTERNET EXPLORER, THE U.S. DEPARTMENT OF HOMELAND SECURITY RECOMMENDS TAKING STEPS TO PROTECT YOURSELF.
DUCT TAPE
COPYRIGHT©2004 J.D. "Illiad" Frazer HTTP://WWW.USERFRIENDLY.ORG/

Two months later, we had Dust Puppy antenna balls available for sale.

I GET BORED ON LONG DRIVES TOO. BUT I DO THINGS TO AMUSE MYSELF.
I KNOW I'LL REGRET ASKING, BUT WHAT DO YOU DO?

WELL, FOR EXAMPLE, I DRESS UP THE VEHICLE TO ALLOW FOR VISUAL AMUSEMENT.
LIKE HOW?
LOOK AT THE ANTENNA.
COPYRIGHT©2004 J.D. "Illiad" Frazer HTTP://WWW.USERFRIENDLY.ORG/

STEF!!
OH COME ON. IT'S FUN.
MAYBE JUST A LI-
NO!! NO IT ISN'T!

WHY DON'T YOU GET SOME SLEEP STEF? WE HAVE A WAYS TO GO BEFORE WE GET TO THE NEXT MOTEL.
I CAN'T.
WHY NOT?
COPYRIGHT©2004 J.D. "Illiad" Frazer HTTP://WWW.USERFRIENDLY.ORG/

I GET NIGHTMARES WHEN I SLEEP IN A CAR. I FREAK OUT AND GRAB THE STEERING WHEEL AND TRY TO TAKE CONTROL. ALTHOUGH THERE ARE SIGNS EVERYWHERE TELLING ME WHICH WAY I SHOULD GO, I IGNORE THEM AND WE END UP IN THE DITCH. A BATTERED WRECK.

YE GODS! WHAT ON EARTH DO YOU DREAM ABOUT?!
THAT I'M THE CHIEF EXECUTIVE OF COMDEX.

THIS IS WEIRD. WHO'D THINK ONE DAY I'D BE DRIVING ON A HIGHWAY WITH A DORKY MARKET-ING GUY WHOSE HANDS ARE TIED SO HE CAN'T GRAB THE WHEEL...

...AND IS WEARING EYESHADES SO HE CAN SLEEP DURING THE DAY. THAT'S JUST...
YE FLIPPING GODS!!!

COPYRIGHT©2004 J.D. "Illiad" Frazer HTTP://WWW.USERFRIENDLY.ORG/
AAAIIIIIIIIIIIIIEEEEEE
SCREEEEEEEEECH!
FISHTAIL!
SPIN!

EEEEE
MAYBE THIS WASN'T SO STUPID AFTER ALL

WHY WERE WE SPINNING?! WHY HAVE WE STOPPED MOVING? WHY AM I STILL TIED UP AND BLIND-FOLDED? YE HAIRY THREE-COILERS!! WHAT HAPPENED?!?!
I NEARLY HIT A DEER. ARE YOU OKAY?
COPYRIGHT©2004 J.D. "Illiad" Frazer HTTP://WWW.USERFRIENDLY.ORG/

JUST A LITTLE FREAKED! HOW ABOUT YOU?
I'M DOING GREAT!

IN FACT, THIS HAS BEEN ONE OF THE MOST ENTERTAINING ROAD TRIPS EVER!
HELLO? YOU OKAY IN THERE?
RAP
RAP
UH OH...

HEY NOW. WHAT'S GOING ON IN THERE?! WHY IS HE TIED UP AND BLIND-FOLDED?
HE'S MY CO-WORKER. HE HAS TROUBLE SLEEPING DURING THE DAY IN A MOVING CAR. NIGHTMARES AND STUFF..
COPYRIGHT©2004 J.D. "Illiad" Frazer HTTP://WWW.USERFRIENDLY.ORG/

AND HIS NIGHTMARES ARE SO BAD HE HAS TO BE TIED UP OR HE'LL TRY TO GRAB THE WHEEL. RIGHT STEF? RIGHT?

OH OFFICER! THANK GOD YOU'RE HERE!
OUTTA THE CAR LONG-BEARD.
EBBEH.

YOU STAY FACE-DOWN MISTER. I HAVE TO RADIO THIS IN.
OFFICER. THERE'S BEEN A MISTAKE.

I HAD HIM TIE MY HANDS SO I WOULDN'T TRY TO GRAB THE WHEEL. HE WAS TELLING THE TRUTH. HE'S MY CO-WORKER. I'M A MAR-KETING EXEC. AND HE'S MY TECHIE.
COPYRIGHT©2004 J.D. "Illiad" Frazer HTTP://WWW.USERFRIENDLY.ORG/

IS THIS TRUE?
YES!!
COOL. COULD YOU FIX MY EMAIL? I'M NOT HEARING THE AOL GUY ANYMORE.
NO. SHOOT ME INSTEAD!!

DIFFERENT TAKES ON MICHAEL MOORE'S LATEST FILM.
TRUTH!
MICHAEL MOORE'S
FAHRENHEIT 9/11
HARD LEFT
PROPAGANDA!
MICHAEL MOORE'S
FAHRENHEIT 9/11
HARD RIGHT
celsius 488
MICHAEL MOORE'S
FAHRENHEIT 9/11
Kelvin
761.483
PLAIN GEEK
COPYRIGHT©2004 J.D. "Illiad" Frazer HTTP://WWW.USERFRIENDLY.ORG/

WELL. THAT TOOK A WHILE TO INSTALL. WHAT KEPT YOU?
SERIOUS ARCHITECTURE ISSUES. THE CLIENT HAS THE TECHNICAL SENSE OF A BOX OF HAIR.

THE NETWORK WAS SERIOUSLY INSECURE. THE MACHINES WERE INFECTED WITH TROJANS AND THEY HADN'T DONE SECURITY UPDATES IN MONTHS!
AND I WAS FIXING ALL OF THAT WHILE YOU WERE OFF CHATTING WITH THE OWNERS!
COPYRIGHT©2004 J.D. "Illiad" Frazer HTTP://WWW.USERFRIENDLY.ORG/

WELL I THOUGHT THEY SERVED A GREAT CAPUCCINO.
MAYBE IF I UNDO HIS SEATBELT AND RUN US INTO THAT LARGE TREE...

STEF'S ASLEEP AGAIN. MIKE.
HE MUST BE TIRED FROM ALL THE HARD CAPUCCINO DRINKING HE DID.
ZZZZZ
COPYRIGHT©2004 J.D. "Illiad" Frazer HTTP://WWW.USERFRIENDLY.ORG/

YAAAAAAAAAAAA!!
AAAAAAAAGGGGHHHHH!!!
SCCRRRREEEEEEEEEEEEECH

WHAT?! WHAT?!! DID YOU NEARLY HIT SOMETHING AGAIN?!
NO. I JUST WANTED TO CHANGE LANES IN A DRAMATIC WAY.

MICROSOFT CHAIRMAN BILL GATES WAS ON THE MALAYSIAN LEG OF A WHIRLWIND ASIAN TOUR WHEN HE VOICED HIS CONCERNS OVER THE GROWING GOODWILL TOWARDS OPEN SOURCE IN ASIA.
COPYRIGHT©2004 J.D. "Illiad" Frazer HTTP://WWW.USERFRIENDLY.ORG/

"MR. GATES. WHY DO YOU FEEL OPEN SOURCE IS AN EVIL?"
"VERY SIMPLY. IT DESTROYS JOBS. HOW CAN THAT BE GOOD?"

"DIDN'T YOU REALLY MEAN 'MICROSOFT REVENUES' WHERE YOU SAID 'JOBS?'"
"NO. I MEANT A 'CRUSHING REIGN OVER THE MASS-' I MEAN. JOBS! I MEANT JOBS!"

WHAT'S THE PROBLEM HUBERT?
LOOK AT THIS SHELF. JASLEEN.
BEST MART SUPERCENTRE
COPYRIGHT©2004 J.D. "Illiad" Frazer HTTP://WWW.USERFRIENDLY.ORG/

IT'S EMPTY.
WELL. DUH. BUT IT WAS FULL OF BROWN PAPER BAGS THIS MORNING. WE WERE SOLD OUT IN HOURS. ANY IDEA WHY?
BEST MART SUPERCENTRE

HEY. A.J.! DID YOU HEAR THAT DOOM 3 HAS GONE GO--OH.
PUFF
PUFF
WIBBLE

YOU OKAY? YOU LOOK A LITTLE STRESSED...
WHAT DO YOU **EXPECT?** I WAS FINE WHILE I HAD NO IDEA WHEN DOOM 3 WAS COMING OUT. BUT **NOW** IT'S ONLY A MATTER OF **A FEW WEEKS!!!**
COPYRIGHT©2004 J.D. "Illiad" Frazer HTTP://WWW.USERFRIENDLY.ORG/

JUST READ ON 'NET THAT LATEST BUILD OF DOOM 3 IS FOUND TO BE NOT SUITABLE FOR RELEASE.
NEW RELEASE DATE YET TO BE ANNOUNCED.

NOT TRUE. AND NOT **AT ALL** NICE.
OH. AM SORRY. DID I SAY "DOOM 3?" ACTUALLY MEANT "HALF-LIFE 2."

A.J. STILL HASN'T RECOVERED FROM THAT BRUTAL MENTAL SHOCK YOU GAVE HIM.
WAS NOT BRUTAL. HE IS MERELY WEAK LEETLE FAN-BOY.
COPYRIGHT©2004 J.D. "Illiad" Frazer HTTP://WWW.USERFRIENDLY.ORG/

I SUPPOSE. HE WAS JUST EXCITED THAT ID SOFTWARE WOULD ONCE AGAIN BE RELEASING A LINUX VERSION RIGHT AFTER THE WINDOWS VERSION.

PUFF
PUFF
WIBBLESKI

DR. STEPHEN HAWKING, CONCEDING THE BET THAT INFORMATION CAN IN FACT SURVIVE A BLACK HOLE, SENDS THE PROMISED ENCYCLOPEDIA SOMEPLACE PARTICULAR TO PROVE DR. PRESKILL WAS CORRECT AND TO BE A REAL TURD ABOUT IT AT THE SAME TIME.
COPYRIGHT©2004 J.D. "Illiad" Frazer HTTP://WWW.USERFRIENDLY.ORG/

AND NOW. A PREVIEW OF OUR UPCOMING FALL LINE-UP!
TIRED OF ALL OF THE SCIENCE DOCUMENTARIES AND MIND-WARPING SHOWS MEANT ONLY TO BE WATCHED BY GEEKS AND FREAKS? WE ARE TOO!

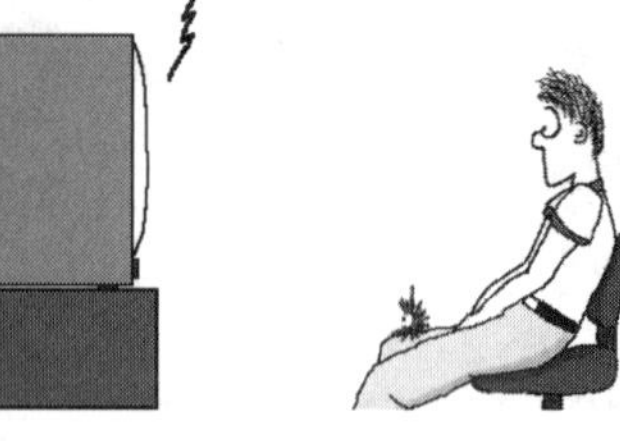
TIRED OF CONSTANTLY FLIPPING BETWEEN CHANNELS TO WATCH YOUR FAVOURITE SHOWS BECAUSE THEY'RE ALL SHOWING IN THE SAME TIME SLOT? WE HATE THAT TOO!! AND WHAT ABOUT NEVER GETTING ENOUGH OF YOUR FAVOURITE SHOW? ANATHEMA! (THAT MEANS "BAD.")
COPYRIGHT©2004 J.D. "Illiad" Frazer HTTP://WWW.USERFRIENDLY.ORG/

THIS NETWORK IS PROUD TO ANNOUNCE "QUEER EYE FOR SURVIVOR IDOL BACHELORS" THIS FALL. 24 HOURS A DAY. SEVEN DAYS A WEEK! AND YOU WON'T WANT TO MISS A SINGLE MINUTE!
OH...GAH...
NO MORE SEAFOOD COOKING SHOWS IS A GOOD THING.

THIS IS THE CBC.
MICROSOFT HAS AGREED TO PAY UPSTART LINUX SELLER LINDOWS $20 MILLION TO SETTLE A LONG-RUNNING TRADEMARK DISPUTE.
COPYRIGHT©2004 J.D. "Illiad" Frazer HTTP://WWW.USERFRIENDLY.ORG/

IN EXCHANGE. THE COMPANY WILL SURRENDER THE LINDOWS NAME AND ASSIGN RELATED WEB DOMAINS TO MICROSOFT.
WHEN ASKED WHAT HE WOULD DO WITH THE FUNDS. C.E.O. MICHAEL ROBERTSON REPLIED. "USE IT FOR BUSINESS PURPOSES OF COURSE..."

"...INCLUDING STARTING A NEW COMPANY NAMED 'WONGHORN'."
I THINK IT SHOULD BE "DO-
BE NICE!

IS THAT A WRIST BRACE? WHAT DID YOU DO TO YOURSELF?
UH...REPETITIVE STRAIN AT MY OTHER JOB.

YOU HAVE ANOTHER JOB? WHAT DO YOU DO?
YES. I HAVE TO MAKE ENDS MEET. AND I...UH...I'M AN "ACTIVE INTERNET PROMOTIONAL MESSAGE AGENT."
COPYRIGHT©2004 J.D. "Illiad" Frazer HTTP://WWW.USERFRIENDLY.ORG/

SO YOU'RE COMMITTING FRAUD BY SPENDING HOURS CLICKING ON GOOGLE TEXT ADS.
AND WHAT ELSE AM I GONNA DO WITH MY DIABLO 2 SKILLS?!!

A.J.. DO YOU REALLY HAVE A SECOND JOB? AREN'T WE PAYING YOU ENOUGH HERE?
YES. AND NO. THE WAGES TODAY IN I.T. JUST DON'T KEEP UP WITH THE COST OF LIVING.
COPYRIGHT©2004 J.D. "Illiad" Frazer HTTP://WWW.USERFRIENDLY.ORG/

RENT HAS GONE UP. FOOD IS MORE EXPENSIVE. UTILITIES ARE GOUGING US. INSURANCE HAS SKYROCKETED. GAS PRICES ARE OUT THE WINDOW. BIDDING FOR CASTLES IN ULTIMA ONLINE ON EBAY HAS BECOME INSANE AND MEDICAL COVERAGE COSTS ARE JUST UNSPEAKABLE.

HANG ON A TICK...DID YOU SAY "BIDDING FOR CASTLES IN ULTIMA ONLINE ON EBAY?"
OH IT'S INSANE! YOU DON'T WANT TO KNOW. MAN. IT'S JUST UGLY.

I JUST DON'T MAKE ENOUGH MONEY TO GET BY, SID. I'M SHARING A CHEAP APARTMENT WITH A FREAK. I EAT KRAFT DINNERS AND WHITE RICE. I USE THE BUS ALL OF THE TIME. AND I USE A HAMSTER WHEEL FOR ELECTRICITY. THERE'S JUST NOTHING ELSE I CAN DO.

COPYRIGHT©2004 J.D. "Illiad" Frazer HTTP://WWW.USERFRIENDLY.ORG/

DARE I SUGGEST NOT BUYING ANYMORE VIRTUAL CASTLES ON E-BAY?
AND WHAT'S NEXT. YOU GONNA CUT OFF MY OXYGEN?

A.J., EXACTLY HOW MUCH DID YOU SPEND ON EBAY LAST MONTH?
ABOUT ELEVEN HUNDRED DOLLARS.
ELEVEN HUN--YE GODS. ON WHAT?!
COPYRIGHT©2004 J.D. "Illiad" Frazer HTTP://WWW.USERFRIENDLY.ORG/

THIS GREAT CASTLE IN A VALLEY NEAR SOME MINES AND A FOREST FULL OF BUNNIES. AND I'M GONNA RENT OUT STORAGE ROOM TO SOME OTHER PLAYERS AND GET RICH!!

OKAY. SO RICH IN THE GAME WORLD. NOT THE REAL WOR-
LA!! RICH! RIIIIICH!!

VOICEOVER FOR AD SPOT IN THE WORLD OF "I, ROBOT" :
"MANY OF YOU FEEL BAD FOR THAT ROBOT, THAT IS BECAUSE YOU'RE CRAZY. IT HAS NO FEELINGS, AND THE NEW ONE IS MUCH BETTER!"
NS-4 ROBOT RECYCLING
NS-5
COPYRIGHT©2004 J.D. "Illiad" Frazer HTTP://WWW.USERFRIENDLY.ORG/

IKEA
SWEDISH FOR SOLDERING IRON

I NEED HELP WITH THIS. I DON'T UNDERSTAND THIS RABID NEED OF YOURS TO SPEND REAL MONEY TO GET VIRTUAL GOODS.
LOOK AT IT THIS WAY SID. ULTIMA ONLINE AND THE OTHER ONLINE RPGS ARE WORLDS THAT MIRROR OUR WANTS AND WISHES.
COPYRIGHT©2004 J.D. "Illiad" Frazer HTTP://WWW.USERFRIENDLY.ORG/

AND THESE WORLDS GIVE US A CHANCE AT WHAT WE WANT! WE HAVE A VIRTUAL ECONOMY, SPECIAL SOCIAL STRUCTURES, AND EVEN A POLITICAL SYSTEM!

AND I SUPPOSE I SHOULD ASK WHY THIS IS ALL BETTER THAN THE REAL WORLD?
BECAUSE I AM KING!

YOU HAVE LOGGED IN TO ULTIMA ONLINE. WELCOME, YOUR MAJESTY!
OI! WHO ARE YOU?
I AM LORD GARRETT, AND I AM YOUR KING!
COPYRIGHT©2004 J.D. "Illiad" Frazer HTTP://WWW.USERFRIENDLY.ORG/

KING?! OH, VERY NICE. HOW'D YOU GET THAT THEN?
I CERTAINLY DIDN'T VOTE FOR YOU.

SOME MOISTENED BINT LOBBED A SCIMITAR AT YOU DID SHE?
SPAM! SPAM! SPAM! SPAM! SPAM! SPAM! SPAM! SPAM! LOVELY SPAM! WONDERFUL SPAAAAAAM!
SOMETIMES GAMING WITH GEEKS IS LIKE EATING JELLO WITH A CHAINSAW. INTERESTING, BUT PAINFUL.

LOOK, I AM YOUR KING...
NO YOU'RE NOT. WE'RE AN ANARCHO-SYNDICALIST COMMUNE. WE TAKE IT IN TURNS TO ACT AS A SORT OF EXECUTIVE OFFICER FOR THE WEEK...
TAP! TIK!
COPYRIGHT©2004 J.D. "Illiad" Frazer HTTP://WWW.USERFRIENDLY.ORG/

STOP WITH THE MONTY PYTHON! STOP IT!!
...BUT ALL THE DECISIONS OF THAT OFFICER HAVE TO BE RATIFIED...
I SAID STOP!!
AT A SPECIAL BI-WEEKLY MEETING...
attacking with kingly sceptre +9!
RAP! KILL! TAP!

SPLOTCH!
BLOODY PEASANT!
TYPE A POSITIVE BY THE LOOKS OF IT!

HEY, DIDJA HEAR ABOUT THE TITLE FOR THE NEXT STAR WARS FILM?
STAR WARS III: REVENGE OF THE SITH! I CAN'T WAIT!
COPYRIGHT©2004 J.D. "Illiad" Frazer HTTP://WWW.USERFRIENDLY.ORG/

I DUNNO. I HEARD THAT PROBLEMS WITH PRODUCING THE FILM SO FAR HAVE BEEN SITHTEMIC.
HUNH?

YEAH. THAT MOVIE IS GOING TO BE REALLY HIT OR MITH.
ISN'T THE SOUNDTRACK BY TWITHTED SITHTER?
THTOP!!

TODAY, JULY 30th 2004 IS SYSTEM ADMINISTRATOR APPRECIATION DAY

TODAY, JULY 30th 2004 IS SYSTEM ADMINISTRATOR APPRECIATION DAY

REMEMBER! TODAY YOU SHOULD BE EXTRA NICE TO YOUR SITHTEM ADMINIS-
AAAAAAAGH!!
TODAY, JULY 30th 2004 IS SYSTEM ADMINISTRATOR APPRECIATION DAY

I AM KING GARRETT. AND THIS IS MY KINGDOM.

A WISE AND CHARISMATIC RULER, KING GARRETT NEVERTHELESS WAS FORCED TO CONQUER THE WEB BY FORCE OF ARMS, TAKING DOMAIN NAMES AS LOOT AND REPARATIONS.
AND LO! HE DOTH DO-ETH THIS FOR MANY YEARS UNTIL THE INTARWEB WAS ALL HIS.

...AND WHEN KING GARRETT SAW THE BREADTH OF HIS DOMAINS HE WEPT. FOR THERE WERE NO MORE URLS TO CONQUER.
HEY WEB-DORK. HOW MUCH YOU WANT FOR LLAMA-MAMA.NET?

"And when Alexander saw the breadth of his domain, he wept, for there were no more worlds to conquer." Benefits of a classical education. Thanks for the inspiration, Plutarch.

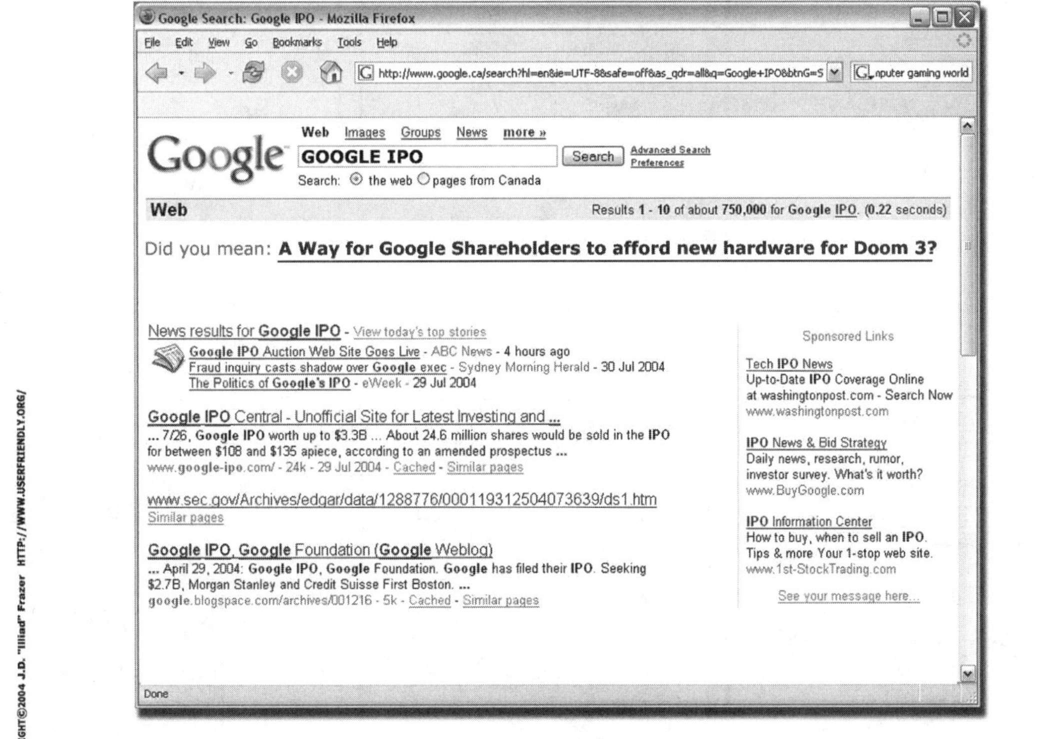
Google Search: Google IPO - Mozilla Firefox
File Edit View Go Bookmarks Tools Help
http://www.google.ca/search?hl=en&ie=UTF-8&safe=off&as_qdr=all&q=Google+IPO&btnG=S
Web Images Groups News more »
GOOGLE IPO
Search
Advanced Search
Preferences
Search: the web pages from Canada
Web
Results 1 - 10 of about 750,000 for Google IPO. (0.22 seconds)
Did you mean: A Way for Google Shareholders to afford new hardware for Doom 3?
News results for Google IPO - View today's top stories
Google IPO Auction Web Site Goes Live - ABC News - 4 hours ago
Fraud inquiry casts shadow over Google exec - Sydney Morning Herald - 30 Jul 2004
The Politics of Google's IPO - eWeek - 29 Jul 2004
Google IPO Central - Unofficial Site for Latest Investing and ...
... 7/26, Google IPO worth up to $3.3B ... About 24.6 million shares would be sold in the IPO for between $108 and $135 apiece, according to an amended prospectus ...
www.google-ipo.com/ - 24k - 29 Jul 2004 - Cached - Similar pages
www.sec.gov/Archives/edgar/data/1288776/000119312504073639/ds1.htm
Similar pages
Google IPO, Google Foundation (Google Weblog)
... April 29, 2004: Google IPO, Google Foundation. Google has filed their IPO. Seeking $2.7B, Morgan Stanley and Credit Suisse First Boston. ...
google.blogspace.com/archives/001216 - 5k - Cached - Similar pages
Sponsored Links
Tech IPO News
Up-to-Date IPO Coverage Online at washingtonpost.com - Search Now
www.washingtonpost.com
IPO News & Bid Strategy
Daily news, research, rumor, investor survey. What's it worth?
www.BuyGoogle.com
IPO Information Center
How to buy, when to sell an IPO. Tips & more Your 1-stop web site.
www.1st-StockTrading.com
See your message here...
Done

BOOM
BLAM
BRATTATTATTATT
ROOARRR!!
COPYRIGHT©2004 J.D. "Illiad" Frazer HTTP://WWW.USERFRIENDLY.ORG/

WOW...IS THAT DOOM III?
KA-RUNCH! GURGLE!

NO. IT'S JUST THE VIDEO TRAILER.
CLICK! CLICK! CLICK! CLIKITY!! PATHETIC CLICK!
EHHHH EEEEHHHH EBBEH!!

WHERE'S A.J.? ISN'T HE SUPPOSED TO BE AT THIS MEETING?
UM...DOOM III HIT THE SHELVES TODAY.
COPYRIGHT©2004 J.D. "Illiad" Frazer HTTP://WWW.USERFRIENDLY.ORG/

WHAT?! YOU MEAN TO SAY HE'S PLAYING DOOM III RIGHT NOW?!
I WOULDN'T EXACTLY SAY THAT. NO.

Unable to Execute. Loads more Video RAM required.
A.J.?

YOU'RE STILL PLAYING ULTIMA ONLINE? I THOUGHT YOU'D GIVE THAT ALL UP FOR DOOM III.
DON'T BE SILLY GREG. I'VE MADE A HUGE INVESTMENT IN TIME AND MONEY IN UO.
COPYRIGHT©2004 J.D. "Illiad" Frazer HTTP://WWW.USERFRIENDLY.ORG/

AND MORE THAN THAT. I'VE FORMED FRIENDSHIPS WITH A LOT OF OTHER PEOPLE IN UO. I'M NOT GOING TO JUST ABANDON THEM.
OKAY. SORRY. I WASN'T THINKING.

WHAT DID YOU SAY YOU WANTED FOR YOUR CASTLE?
A VIDEO CARD! A VIDEO CARD! MY KINGDOM FOR A VIDEO CARD!

WHOA! YOU DID WHAT?!
TRADED MY CASTLE AND CHARACTER IN ULTIMA ONLINE FOR A GEFORCE FX 5950 VIDEO CARD.
COPYRIGHT©2004 J.D. "Illiad" Frazer HTTP://WWW.USERFRIENDLY.ORG/

UNH-HUH. AND EXACTLY HOW MUCH IS THIS CARD WORTH?
ALMOST $600. WHICH I DIDN'T HAVE TO SPEND.

DIDN'T YOU SPEND $1100 TO BUY THAT CASTLE?
YES. BUT THIS IS IMPORTANT!

THE "DOOM III" SOFTWARE HAS BEEN DEPLOYED YOUR ICHOROUSNESS.
OUTSTANDING, ZORKPLIK. AND WHAT DATA HAVE WE GATHERED?
COPYRIGHT©2004 J.D. "Illiad" Frazer HTTP://WWW.USERFRIENDLY.ORG/

THERE APPEAR TO BE TWO SPECIFIC KINDS OF HUMAN BEINGS, YOUR MOISTNESS. THE ONES THAT HAVE BOUGHT OUR "DOOM III" SOFTWARE ARE CALLED "PEOPLE."
WHAT IS THE OTHER KIND, ZORKPLIK?

THE ONES WHO HAVE DOWNLOADED THE SOFTWARE APPEAR TO BE KNOWN AS "ANNELIDA."
AS WHAT?
"LEECHES," YOUR DRIPNIFICENCE.
EXCELLENT! WE CAN USE THEM TO DRAIN MY PUSTULES!

REMIND ME AGAIN, ZORKPLIK, WHY DID WE DEPLOY THE SOFTWARE KNOWN AS "DOOM III?"
TO HELP US SECRETLY SELECT AND RECRUIT SOLDIERS FOR OUR WAR ON WANKELTRON IX, YOUR PUTRESCENCE.
COPYRIGHT©2004 J.D. "Illiad" Frazer HTTP://WWW.USERFRIENDLY.ORG/

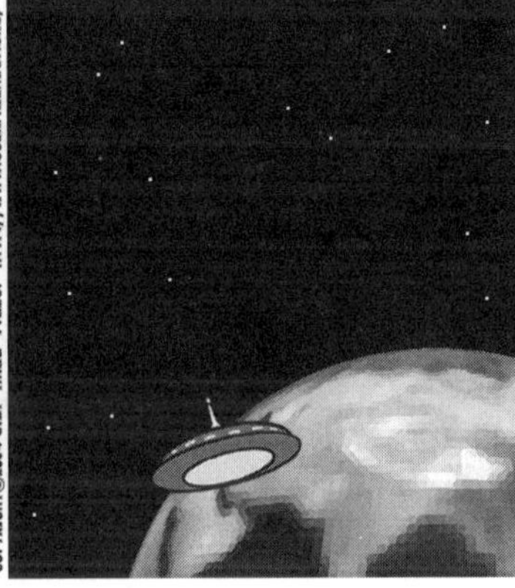

THIS WAR ON WANKELTRON IX: IT'S A PURELY NON-PHYSICAL ONE I HOPE?
OF COURSE, SIRE. IT'S A TRASH-TALK CONFLICT.

I have fairly strong feelings about intellectual property, and they showed in this strip. On one hand, I think the big media companies like Disney and Warner need to be eviscerated for pushing the term of copyright to life plus 75 years. Ridiculous and criminal! The same goes for any form of DRM. On the other hand, people who rip off software because of the lame excuse that "they wouldn't have paid for it anyway" are just being dicks (specifically, those who can afford it). Ripping off small developers and artists rarely if ever hurts the big middlemen. Consider that the next time you think it's OK to burn a copy of a game from a friend rather than pull 50 bucks out of your wallet, you cheap, selfish bastards.

WITH THE RELEASE OF DOOM III, CERTAIN HARDWARE SALES NUMBERS SHOOT THROUGH THE CEILING

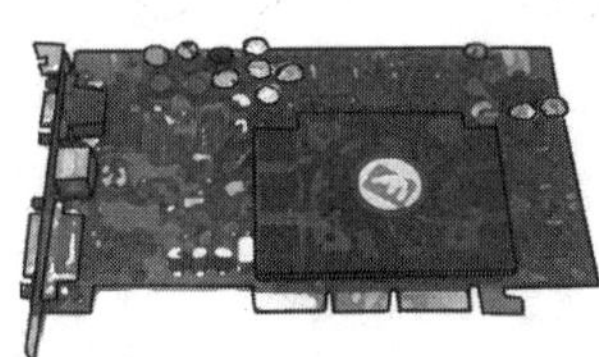

VIDEO CARDS

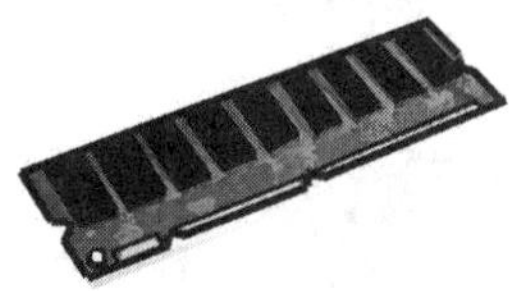
RAM

DEFIBRILLATORS

ZORKPLIK. THESE HUMANS WORRY ME. THEY POSSESS A COMPUTER INFRASTRUCTURE THAT ALLOWS THEM TO COMMUNICATE WITH EACH OTHER QUITE EFFICIENTLY.
THEY DO, SIRE.
COPYRIGHT©2004 J.D. "Illiad" Frazer HTTP://WWW.USERFRIENDLY.ORG/

IF WE HAD TO INVADE, THIS INFRASTRUCTURE WOULD BE A THREAT TO US. WE WOULD NEED TO DESTROY IT QUICKLY.
ALREADY PLANNED FOR, SIRE. IT'S A PART OF EVERY BIT OF SOFTWARE LIKE OUR "DOOM III."

OH? DO TELL.
WE SEND A CODE THAT REPEATEDLY KILLS EVERY PLAYER 3 TO 5 SECONDS AFTER SPAWNING. THEY'LL DESTROY THEIR OWN COMPUTERS IN LESS THAN A MINUTE.

SID, I JUST HEARD ABOUT THE GOOGLE I.P.O. -- ARE YOU GETTING IN ON ANY SHARES?
NO, SADLY. IT'S FOR "U.S. PERSONS" ONLY.
COPYRIGHT©2004 J.D. "Illiad" Frazer HTTP://WWW.USERFRIENDLY.ORG/

WELL THAT'S ANNOYING. YOU'D THINK WITH GOOGLE'S INTERNATIONAL USERBASE THEY'D MAKE THE I.P.O. AVAILABLE EVERYWHERE.
AGREED. BUT WHO OUTSIDE THE U.S. IS GOING TO MATTER?

WHADDYA MEAN "U.S. PERSON?"

HEY. YOU HEAR ABOUT THE $500 SECURITY BUG BOUNTY BEING OFFERED BY MOZILLA?
YEAH. JUST READING ABOUT IT. WHAT A TRULY GREAT IDEA!
COPYRIGHT©2004 J.D. "Illiad" Frazer HTTP://WWW.USERFRIENDLY.ORG/

AGREED. ANY SECURITY BUGS WITHIN THE MOZILLA CODE ARE GOING TO BE ROOTED OUT PRETTY QUICK.
YOU'D THINK MICROSOFT WOULD OFFER THE SAME DEAL FOR I.E.

CRIPES, DUDE. DO THE MATH. MICROSOFT ONLY HAS ABOUT SIXTY BILLION IN CASH RESERVES.
D'OH! STUPID ME...

DUDE! I FOUND A SECURITY BUG IN MOZILLA! I HAVE A COOL $500 COMING TO ME!
REALLY? HOW'D YOU FIND IT?
COPYRIGHT©2004 J.D. "Illiad" Frazer HTTP://WWW.USERFRIENDLY.ORG/

IT WASN'T HARD. I JUST PUT TOGETHER SOME SCENARIOS AND CAME ACROSS ONE THAT WAS SO CLEARLY A SECURITY ISSUE WITH MOZILLA IT HIT ME LIKE A BULLET!
WHAT SCENARIO WAS THAT?

WELL, YOU START BY PUTTING STEF IN FRONT OF A MOZILLA SESSION...
HEY!!

OKAY, PITR? YOU READY TO DO THIS IN JUST ONE TAKE?
DA. JUST NOT SURE WHY YOU ARE PICKINK ME.

PUBLIC SERVICE ANNOUNCEMENT #712. ACTION!
FIRST, THEY ARE MAKINK FUN OF WINDOWS USERS AND AM SAYINK NOTHINK BECAUSE AM NOT A WINDOWS USER.

COPYRIGHT © 2004 J.D. "Illiad" Frazer HTTP://WWW.USERFRIENDLY.ORG/
THEN, THEY ARE MAKINK FUN OF MAC USERS, AND AM SAYINK NOTHINK BECAUSE AM NOT A MAC USER.

AND FINALLY, THEY ARE MAKINK FUN OF ME, AND NO-ONE IS SAYINK ANYTHINK BECAUSE THEY WERE LAUGHING AT MY HAIR--HEY!!
CUT! PRINT IT!

I TOLD YOU! IT'S LIKE A CREEPING CANCER.
YOU MEAN LINUX AND OPEN SOURCE?
WHAT ELSE?
Microsoft

COPYRIGHT © 2004 J.D. "Illiad" Frazer HTTP://WWW.USERFRIENDLY.ORG/
SUN IS PORTING THEIR SUN RAY SERVER OVER TO LINUX, COMPUTER ASSOCIATES IS RELEASING THEIR INGRES R3 DATABASE AS OPEN SOURCE, AND NOW EVEN I.B.M. IS GETTING INTO THE GAME WITH OPEN SOURCING CLOUDSCAPE!!

MY GOD, BILL. WHAT DO WE DO?
HIRE MORE PUBLIC RELATIONS PEOPLE PARTICULARLY QUALIFIED TO WORK FOR US.
UH...HOW DO YOU MEAN?
FICTION WRITERS, STEVE. FIND ME MORE FICTION WRITERS.

USER FRIENDLY
the comic strip
BY J.D. "ILLIAD" FRAZER

DO YOU THINK WE'LL GET IN TROUBLE FOR THIS?
ONE CAN ONLY HOPE.

(SUNG TO WOODIE GUTHRIE'S "THIS LAND IS YOUR LAND.")
THIS LAN IS YOUR LAN!
THIS LAN IS MY LAN!
FROM THE LOCAL ROUTER,
TO THE MAIL VIRUS SCAN
FROM THE CODER'S OFFICE,
TO THE HELPDESK CUUUUBE FARM
THIS LAN WAS MADE FOR YOU AND ME!

WE SHARE OUR DATA
AND OUR PRON COLLECTIONS
WE MAKE KNOWN OUR,
NET PREDILECTIONS
THE BOSS CAN'T WATCH US,
AS WE CHAT ABOOUUT HIM
THIS LAN WAS MADE
FOR YOU AND ME!!

FROM EARLY MORNING,
WE FORM A QUORUM
AND WORK WITH VIGOR,
READING THE FORUMS
THEN WE SWITCH TO PLAYING
ENEMY TERRITORRRY!
THIS LAN WAS MADE
FOR YOU AND ME!

THIS IS LAN IS YOUR LAN!
THIS LAN IS MY LAN!
FROM THE LOCAL ROUTER
TO THE MAIL VIRUS SCAN...
YOU'RE BEING SUED NOW,
BY LUDLOW MUUUUUSIC!
THIS BAN WAS
MADE FOR
YOU NOT ME!

FUNNY...WHY DO I HAVE THIS CRAVING...?
COME NOW. YOU KNOW WHY.
COPYRIGHT©2004 J.D. "Illiad" Frazer HTTP://WWW.USERFRIENDLY.ORG/

OH FLIPPING HELL. I THOUGHT YOU WERE GONE FOR GOOD.
I AM ADDICTION. I AM OMNIPRESENT. GET USED TO IT.

FINE. SO WHAT AM I ADDICTED TO THIS TIME?
I WAS GONNA SAY "U.S. POLITICAL COVERAGE" BUT THAT'S FOR MY "REPULSION" PERSONA.

WELL? HAVE YOU FIGURED IT OUT YET?
IT'S STARTING TO BECOME CLEAR. I MUST GO AND TRANSFORM.
COPYRIGHT©2004 J.D. "Illiad" Frazer HTTP://WWW.USERFRIENDLY.ORG/

SO THE ICON OF GEEK ADDICTION HAS TO GO AND "TRANSFORM." HOW CONVENIENT.

STUPID ICON. THINKS IT CAN STILL SHOCK AND SCARE ME...
I'M BACK! DID YA MISS ME?
S.C.O. LAWSUIT

THAT'S JUST NOT RIGHT! I DO NOT HAVE SOME SICK ADDICTION FOR S.C.O. LAWSUITS!
YOUR BEHAVIOUR SAYS OTHERWISE.
S.C.O. LAWSUIT
COPYRIGHT©2004 J.D. "Illiad" Frazer HTTP://WWW.USERFRIENDLY.ORG/

HUH? WHAT DO YOU MEAN?
YOU'VE BEEN AIMLESS THE LAST FEW WEEKS. CRUISING THE WEB AND OVERCOME WITH ENNUI. YOU'LL ALSO NOTE THAT S.C.O. HASN'T LAUNCHED A LAWSUIT IN THE SAME TIME PERIOD.
S.C.O. LAWSUIT

OH MY GOD.
GREG, WHY IS THERE A TRAIN WRECK IN YOUR OFFICE?

LOOK, THIS IS RIDICULOUS! I DO NOT HAVE AN ADDICTION TO READING ABOUT S.C.O. LAWSUITS!!
YOU DON'T? YOU'RE NOT FEELING THE PULL?
S.C.O. LAWSUIT
COPYRIGHT©2004 J.D. "Illiad" Frazer HTTP://WWW.USERFRIENDLY.ORG/

NO! TALK ABOUT A LAME, NASTY ADDICTION!
HUNH. I MUST'VE MIXED UP YOUR ADDICTION WITH SOMEONE ELSE'S. OH...WAIT...
S.C.O. LAWSUIT

WELL NOW, THIS IS ALL RATHER EMBARASSING, ISN'T IT MR. GATES?
ELLISON PUT YOU UP TO THIS, RIGHT? OR WAS IT THAT JOBS GUY?! THIS IS SICK!
MANTIES

ARE YOU TRYING TO TELL ME THAT PEOPLE WHO ARE ADDICTED TO S.C.O. LAWSUITS ACTUALLY EXIST?
YES. AND WITH DARL MCBRIDE DECLARING A CESSATION OF LAWSUITS, THE CRAVING IS GOING TO GET BAD.
S.C.O. LAWSUIT
COPYRIGHT © 2004 J.D. "Illiad" Frazer HTTP://WWW.USERFRIENDLY.ORG/

S.C.O. LAWSUIT

YOU DON'T REALLY BELIEVE MCBRIDE ABOUT THIS DO YOU?
WHO CARES? IT DRIVES UP THE PRICE FOR A FIX. I'LL OWN MICROSOFT IN MERE WEEKS.
S.C.O. LAWSUIT

HEY MIRANDA, IS IT TECHNICALLY POSSIBLE TO DO A SECURITY AUDIT AND THEN TAKE OVER MANAGING A CLIENT'S L.A.N?
WE DON'T DO THAT BECAUSE IT'S NIGHT-MARISH, BUT IT'S TECHNICALLY POSSIBLE.
COPYRIGHT © 2004 J.D. "Illiad" Frazer HTTP://WWW.USERFRIENDLY.ORG/

YE GODS WHAT DID YOU PROMISE?!!
NOTHING NOT TECHNICALLY POSSIBLE.

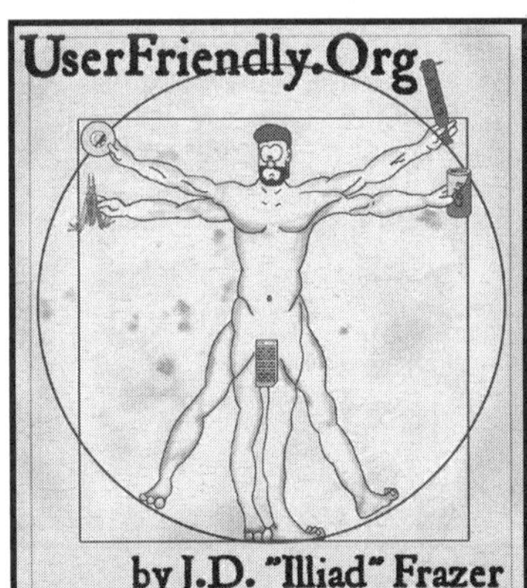
UserFriendly.Org
by J.D. "Illiad" Frazer
COPYRIGHT © 2004 J.D. "Illiad" Frazer HTTP://WWW.USERFRIENDLY.ORG/

AHEM
LINUX, LINUX, OPEN SOURCE. BORN NINETEEN NINETY-ONE-ISH. OUR VERY OWN EXCALIBUR, WITH WHICH BILL GATES WE'LL PUNISH!

SUSE! MANDRAKE! DEBIAN! RED HAT AND FEDORA! SLACKWARE! GENTOO! KNOPPIX TOO! ALL BOXES BY PANDORA!

(OF COURSE THERE'S ALSO BSD IN THREE FULL INCARNATIONS, BUT WE DON'T LIKE TO MENTION THEM, JUST CAUSE THEIR IRRITATION!)

OUR PATH UNFOLDS! OUR WAY IS CLEAR! OUR STANDARDS RAISED UP HIGHER! WE CODE, WE BUILD, WE FIX AND MAKE! TO PURE KERNELS WE ASPIRE!

BUT I USE LINUX NOT BECAUSE I WANT CODE I CAN SEE THE TRUTH IS THAT I SIMPLY WANT A WORLD WHERE BEER IS FREE!
THE COFFEE ISN'T. GET OUT.

OH HEY...YOU GOT DOOM 3 TO FINALLY WORK ON YOUR MACHINE?
YEAH! IS THE GAME GORGEOUS OR WHAT...
COPYRIGHT©2004 J.D. "Illiad" Frazer HTTP://WWW.USERFRIENDLY.ORG/

WOW...HOW DOES THE GAME DO ALL OF THAT?
IT TAKES A $600 VIDEO CARD, AND ONE HECK OF AN ENGINE.

...AND YET IT'S TOTALLY DARK IN THE GAME.
HEY, IT HELPS WITH THE FRAMERATE.

SO THE DOOM 3 ENGINE IS PRETTY SMOOTH?
LIKE GLASS...
COPYRIGHT©2004 J.D. "Illiad" Frazer HTTP://WWW.USERFRIENDLY.ORG/

DOOM 3 COMPLETELY DISCARDS THE USE OF LIGHTMAPS. IT HAS A REALLY POWERFUL RENDERER THAT ALLOWS FOR TRULY DYNAMIC LIGHTING AND SILKY-SMOOTH GAMEPLAY.

THE SMOOTHNESS WOULDN'T ALSO HAVE TO DO WITH THE FACT THAT SO FAR ALL I'VE SEEN ON THE SCREEN ARE FOUR DIFFERENT SHADES OF BROWN, WOULD IT?
NO. LOOK. THERE'S RED THERE NOW TOO.
GRAAAA!!
AAARRRGH!!

MIRANDA, I HAVE SOME GREAT NEWS! WE JUST SECURED A MULTI-MILLION DOLLAR TECHNICAL SERVICES CONTRACT!
THAT IS GREAT NEWS! FOR WHAT SERVICES?
GURBLE BURBLE *PERK*
COPYRIGHT©2004 J.D. "Illiad" Frazer HTTP://WWW.USERFRIENDLY.ORG/

LET'S SEE WHAT IT SAYS HERE IN THE LEGALESE...
RATTLE SHAKE

"...IN EXCHANGE FOR COMPEN-SATION AS DESCRIBED, THE VENDOR WILL PERFORM STUFF THAT'S TECHNICALLY POSSIBLE."
STEF!
CONGEAL

STEF, DON'T YOU THINK THE TERMINOLOGY IN THE CONTRACT IS KIND OF VAGUE?
IT'S VAGUE ON PURPOSE.
OH. I JUST HAVE TO HEAR THIS.
COPYRIGHT©2004 J.D. "Illiad" Frazer HTTP://WWW.USERFRIENDLY.ORG/

SERIOUSLY. RATHER THAN COMMIT OUR TECHNICAL TEAM TO A HORRID SET OF DELIVERABLES, I JUST WORDED THE CONTRACT SO THAT WE COULD GET OUT OF DOING ANYTHING TOO TROUBLESOME.

UH...HOW?
JUST TELL THE CLIENT "IT'S NOT TECHNICALLY POSSIBLE." VAGUE IS GOOD!
ACCORDING TO THIS WE'RE TO BE PAID "SEVERAL GAGGING BAGFULS OF MONEY."

ANY OTHER DETAILS ON THIS TECH CONTRACT STEF CHAINED US TO?
WE'RE TRAVELLING SOMEWHERE. FEDUP JUST DELIVERED OUR TRAVEL PACKAGE.
FedUP

...AND THERE'RE AIRLINE TICKETS IN HERE.

REALLY? I WONDER WHERE TO? TORONTO. PROBABLY. OR CALGARY. MAYBE IN THE U.S. SOMEWHERE?
FedUP
COPYRIGHT©2004 J.D. "Illiad" Frazer HTTP://WWW.USERFRIENDLY.ORG/

OR MAYBE IT'S TO COSTA RICA. OR SPAIN. OR BRAZIL...
WHERE EXACTLY IS "AMUNDSEN-SCOTT BASE?"
FedUP

WE'RE GOING TO ANTARCTICA?!!?
I'M GOING TO KILL YOU. STEF MURKY. I MAY GO TO JAIL. BUT I AM GOING TO KILL YOU.
BETTER DO IT QUICK. YOUR FIRST FLIGHT LEAVES EARLY IN THE MORNING.

COPYRIGHT©2004 J.D. "Illiad" Frazer HTTP://WWW.USERFRIENDLY.ORG/
THEN WHEN I GET BACK. YOU DIE. AND YOU'LL DIE BADLY.
NO HE WON'T.
WHAT'S IN ANTARCTICA?

HE WON'T?
NO. BECAUSE HE'S GOING WITH YOU.
I'M WHAT?!
THERE'S LIKE. SNOW THERE.

I've long dreamed of visiting Antarctica. So, the crew from Columbia Internet get to go first. I envy them.

THE SPECTRE OF IN-GAME ADVERTISING: IF HALF-LIFE 2 WENT BAD...
I'VE GOT SOME GREAT NEWS. DR. FREEMAN!
MRRFFF MRRFFF MRRFF MRF?!!
NO. I HAVE NO IDEA HOW TO GET THAT THING OFF YOUR FACE. BUT I JUST SAVED A WHOLE LOT OF MONEY ON MY CAR INSURANCE FROM GEICO!
COPYRIGHT©2004 J.D. "Illiad" Frazer HTTP://WWW.USERFRIENDLY.ORG/

I'M NOT GOING AND THAT'S FINAL.
REALLY.
I'M SORRY. BUT YES.

COPYRIGHT©2004 J.D. "Illiad" Frazer HTTP://WWW.USERFRIENDLY.ORG/
AJ. HOW WOULD YOU LIKE TO GO TO ANTARCTICA?
WHY? WHAT'S THERE?
BIG. GOVERNMENT-SPONSORED PIPE AND FEW PEOPLE USING IT.

EXCELLENT! I AM SO THERE!
FINE. I GUESS I'LL GO TOO...

AND SO OUR BRAVE GEEKS BEGIN THEIR JOURNEY TO THE BOTTOM OF THE WORLD. AFFECTIONALLY KNOWN AS "SATAN'S BEER FRIDGE."

COPYRIGHT©2004 J.D. "Illiad" Frazer HTTP://WWW.USERFRIENDLY.ORG/
OVER THE EQUATOR THEY TRAVEL. BRAVING BLUE WATER. WHITE SAND. CALM AIR AND THE DEEPLY DREADED PUFFY WHITE CLOUDS...
SO...WHAT KIND OF ELECTRONICS DO YOU HAVE ON THE BRIDGE. CAPTAIN?
WANKEL MARU
GEEKS LEAVE!

UNTIL THEY ARRIVE AT THE BEGINNING OF THEIR FINAL LEG...
WOOHOO! LOOK! A PENGUIN!!
TIERRA DEL FUEGO
THANK YOU EVER SO BLOODY MUCH. LINUS TORVALDS.

UH...HI. WE'RE LOOKING FOR 'SNOWCRASH AIRWAYS?'
HEH. 'SNOWCRASH.' COOL GEEK REFERENCE.
THAT WOULD BE ME. WELCOME! YOU MUST BE THAT TECH CREW GOING TO THE SOUTH POLE?
MOTHER LOAD

COPYRIGHT©2004 J.D. "Illiad" Frazer HTTP://WWW.USERFRIENDLY.ORG/
I DON'T NORMALLY DO RUNS TO AMUNDSEN-SCOTT THIS TIME OF THE YEAR. BUT THE BASE IS PAYING ME TRIPLE RATE TO GET YOU OUT THERE. IT'S SOME KIND OF EMERGENCY.

EMERGENCY?
SOMETHING ABOUT "SERVICE PACK 2." I DUNNO. I'M NOT A GEEK.
NOT A GEEK? WAIT A MINUTE...

SADDLE UP PEOPLE. TIME TO GRAB SOME SKY!
THIS IS SO COOL! I LOVE HERKS!

COPYRIGHT©2004 J.D. "Illiad" Frazer HTTP://WWW.USERFRIENDLY.ORG/
THESE ARE JUST AWESOME AIRCRAFT. THEY'RE BIG. BAD AND POWERFUL. AND THEY CAN TAKE OFF WITH OVER THIRTY TONS OF CARGO.
I'VE ALWAYS WANTED TO GET MY PILOT'S LICENSE.

YEAH...ME TOO.
WHAT?

SO HAVE YOU ALWAYS FLOWN BIG PLANES?
NOPE. I STARTED OFF LIFE AS A BOTANIST. I'VE ALWAYS HAD AN INTEREST IN PLANTS AND I WORKED IN THE FIELD DESPITE NOT HAVING A DEGREE.
COPYRIGHT © 2004 J.D. "Illiad" Frazer HTTP://WWW.USERFRIENDLY.ORG/

BUT I GOT FED UP OF HAVING THE KNOWLEDGE BUT NOT THE PAPER THAT SAID I DID. SO I WENT ONLINE, PAID MY MONEY AND GOT MY PIECE OF PAPER.

UH...YOU BOUGHT YOUR DEGREE?
WITH A PAYMENT PLAN OF $6000 A YEAR FOR FOUR YEARS. ACCREDITED TOO!

YOU'RE REALLY NOT A GEEK? BUT ISN'T FLYING ONE OF THESE BIRDS HIGHLY TECHNICAL?
YES. I GUESS I'M NOT A COMPUTER GEEK TO BE MORE SPECIFIC. MOST TRUE COMPUTER GEEKS DON'T MAKE GOOD AIRCREW.
COPYRIGHT © 2004 J.D. "Illiad" Frazer HTTP://WWW.USERFRIENDLY.ORG/

WE DON'T?
NOPE. ALLOW ME TO ILLUSTRATE BY TURNING OFF THE COCKPIT LIGHTS.

COLOURED! LIGHTS! PRETTY...PRETTY!!
IT ALWAYS SCARES ME A LITTLE WHEN THEY DO THAT.

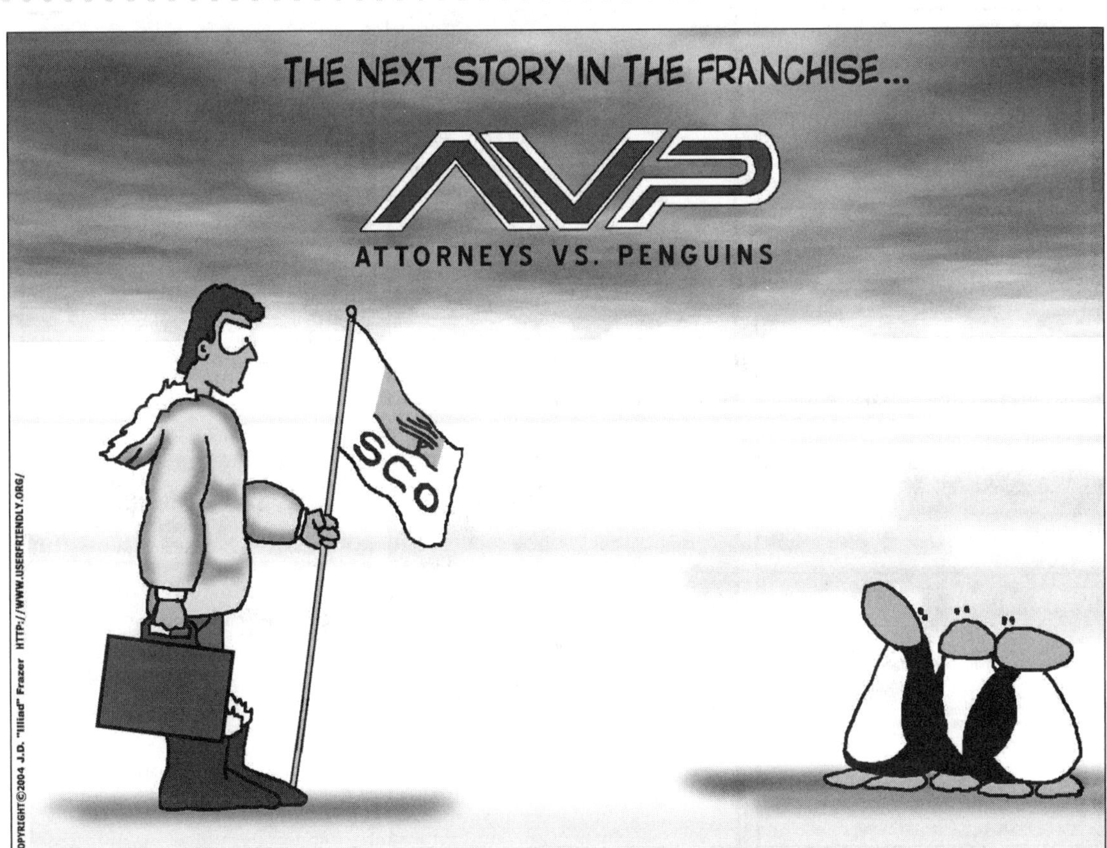
THE NEXT STORY IN THE FRANCHISE...
AVP
ATTORNEYS VS. PENGUINS
SCO
COPYRIGHT © 2004 J.D. "Illiad" Frazer HTTP://WWW.USERFRIENDLY.ORG/

HEY MIKE! HOW IS IT IN THE BACK?
NOT AS INTERESTING AS IT IS UP HERE. A.J. DAMN THIS IS ONE COOL COCKPIT!
YEAH. I LIKE IT MYSELF.
COPYRIGHT©2004 J.D. "Illiad" Frazer HTTP://WWW.USERFRIENDLY.ORG/

WOGGLE!
WAGGLE!
WIGGLE!

A.J., DID I TELL YOU THAT YOU COULD TOUCH THE CONTROLS? NO!!! SO WHAT THE HELL WAS THAT?!
I'M A GEEK. IT WAS A PHYSICS EXPERIMENT.
JUDGING FROM STEF'S REACTION TO YOUR FLYING, IT'S JUST TURNED INTO A BIOLOGY EXPERIMENT.

HEY. IS THAT MCMURDO BASE?
YEP. OCTOBER THROUGH DECEMBER I'D BE DROPPING YOU GUYS OFF AT YOUR RIDE TO THE POLE. BUT CONDITIONS RIGHT NOW ARE TOO IFFY. DANGEROUS.

...SO I'M TAKING YOU THE WHOLE WAY.
THERE'S AN AIRSTRIP AT THE SOUTH POLE?
YEP. FOR SKI-EQUIPPED PLANES.

COPYRIGHT©2004 J.D. "Illiad" Frazer HTTP://WWW.USERFRIENDLY.ORG/

THAT PREGNANT PAUSE WAS ME WAITING TO HEAR REASSURANCES THAT THIS PLANE HAS SKIS.
MY CROSS-COUNTRIES'RE STRAPPED TO THE ROOF. THEY'RE A COUPLE OF REAL BAD BOYS WHEN THEY'RE FRESHLY WAXED.

WAIT A SECOND. WE CAN'T LAND AT THE POLE?
RIGHT. NO PLANE-SKIS.
BUT YOU'RE GONNA GET US THERE ANYWAYS?
YESSIR.
COPYRIGHT©2004 J.D. "Illiad" Frazer HTTP://WWW.USERFRIENDLY.ORG/

NO. NO. NO!!
ONE OF THOSE CHUTE PACKS IS MY LAUNDRY BAG. WOULD YOU RATHER FIRST PICK OR LAST?

WE'RE GETTING CLOSE TO THE POLE. A.J. BETTER PASS OUT THE CHUTES TO YOUR PALS.
UM. OKAY.
COPYRIGHT©2004 J.D. "Illiad" Frazer HTTP://WWW.USERFRIENDLY.ORG/

DOES THAT MEAN I DON'T HAVE TO TAKE ONE MYSELF?
OF COURSE. WE CAN MAKE IT A PHYSICS EXPERIMENT.

A.J., YOU DONE HANDING OUT THE CHUTES YET?
I TRIED, BUT MIRANDA WOULD LIKE A WORD WITH Y-
A.J., HUSH UP.

MISTER, ARE YOU SUGGESTING WE **PARACHUTE** DOWN TO THE POLE?
HELL **NO**, LADY.

OH. WELL THANK **GOD**.
I'M SUGGESTING YOU **PLUMMET** DOWN TO THE POLE. THE CHUTES ARE JUST TO PREVENT DECELERATION TRAUMA.

PEOPLE, THE RAMP IS DOWN AND YOU HAVE A GREEN LIGHT! A.J., YOU'RE IN THE LEAD ON THE STICK! **GO GO GO GO GO!!**

UM...A.J?!
I HAVE MANY LITTLE YELLOW ICICLES.

TEXT FOUND WITHIN THE MYDOOM VIRUS CODE:

```
/* We searching 4
 work in AV industry.*/
```

...AND A GOLDEN OPPORTUNITY.

DEPARTMENT OF JUSTICE
FEDERAL BUREAU OF INVESTIGATION
ANTI-VIRUS SOFTWARE DEVELOPERS

The FBI is expanding its Computer Crimes department and is seeking experienced Virus Writers for exciting roles in one of several Federal Institutions. Interested parties should respond with a list of their most successfully deployed computer viruses along with their contact information.

All applicants will be called in for an interview.

THUS OUR HEROIC TECH TEAM (PLUS ONE MARKETING PINHEAD) JUMPS OUT INTO THE BLUE VOID. SHRIEKING INVECTIVES THAT WOULD MAKE A SPEC-OPS TEAM BLUSH.
EEEEBBBEEEHH!!

AND AS THEY DESCEND TO AMUNDSEN-SCOTT BASE (KNOWN BY 'LOCALS' SIMPLY AS "THE POLE") THEY READY THEMSELVES MENTALLY FOR IMMEDIATE DEPLOYMENT.
LITTLE ICICLES ARE POINTY!
COPYRIGHT©2004 J.D. "Illiad" Frazer HTTP://WWW.USERFRIENDLY.ORG/

OF COURSE, EVEN THE BEST INTENTIONS COUPLED WITH MANY HOURS PLAYING GAMES LIKE DOOM 3 AND RAINBOW SIX DON'T A COMMANDO TEAM MAKE.
MMRRFFRRR!!!
MRRFFRRM!

Henry and Sarah are two actual technologists at the South Pole. Although I've met neither, Sarah liked my depiction of her because, as she put it to her friends, "... in the strip I'm mean!"

IS THAT THE TECH TEAM UNDER THOSE CHUTES, SARAH?
LOOKS LIKE IT, HENRY.

COPYRIGHT©2004 J.D. "Illiad" Frazer HTTP://WWW.USERFRIENDLY.ORG/

THEY'RE GONNA DIE OUT THERE IF WE DON'T HELP THEM.
LET'S GIVE THEM TIME. THINK OF US AS GEEKS CONDUCTING A BIOLOGY EXPERIMENT.

UH. HI. I'M MIKE FLOYD.
SARAH KAYE. AND THIS IS HENRY MALMGREN BEHIND ME. YOU'RE WITH THE TECH TEAM WE SENT FOR?

I SUPPOSE SO. I HAVE TO ADMIT IT'S BEEN A REALLY WEIRD TRIP COMING DOWN HERE. AND I'M NOT EVEN SURE WHAT IT IS YOU NEED US TO DO...
COPYRIGHT©2004 J.D. "Illiad" Frazer HTTP://WWW.USERFRIENDLY.ORG/

...WHAT THE HECK ARE YOU GUYS STARING AT?
THERE'S A GUY WITH STUPID HAIR STUCK TO THE HERK'S TAIL BY HIS TONGUE.
WITH A TONGUE THAT LONG HE CAN GO INTO POLITICS.

I'LL TAKE YOU ALL INSIDE AND GET YOU SETTLED.
WHAT'S YOUR FRIEND HENRY DOING?
RETRIEVING THE SUPPLY CRATES THAT WERE DROP-PED OFF BEHIND YOU.

NORMALLY I'D BE STUCK WITH THAT FILTHY JOB, BUT WE FLIPPED A COIN THIS MORNING AND I WAS SPARED THE INDIGNITY OF LUGGING MASSIVE BOXES OF TOILET PAPER BACK TO THE BASE.
COPYRIGHT©2004 J.D. "Illiad" Frazer HTTP://WWW.USERFRIENDLY.ORG/

HEY SAAAAAARAAAAAH! I GET DIBS ON THE "TEMPTATION ISLAND" VIDEOS!
DAMMIT!! I KNEW I'D LOSE OUT!!

WELCOME TO THE POLE. THIS IS WHERE HENRY AND I RUN THINGS.
YOU GUYS ARE THE POLE TECHS?

CORRECT. MIKE. THERE ARE ALSO DEDICATED SYSADMINS FOR SPECIFIC SCIENCE PROJECTS OF COURSE.
SO WHY DO YOU NEED US?

WELL MIRANDA. HOW DO I PUT IT? WE WOULD RATHER PAY YOU TO INSTALL AND HANDLE THE FALLOUT FOR SERVICE PACK 2 THAN DO IT OURSELVES AND KEEP THE MONEY.
THEY STARTED YET SARAH? I BROUGHT THE POPCORN.

HEY!! HOW DID YOU GUYS SNEAK ON BOARD?!
ERWIN SAID WE COULD COME ALONG AS "CRATE-AWAYS."
IT IS SO COLD HERE. OVERCLOCK ME BABY!!

SO YOUR TRIP WAS OKAY?
YES. UNTIL ERWIN STARTED MAKING THOSE FLATULENCE NOISES.
LOOK. I SWEAR IT WASN'T ME.

OH MAN. PUTRID. I AM NEVER GONNA EAT ONIONS BEFORE A FLIGHT AGAIN...

WE HAVE A BAD FEELING ABOUT THIS...

DVD EDITION
WITH THE NEW HAN SOLO - JABBA SCENE
STAR WARS TRILOGY
STAR WARS TRILOGY

OKAY. SERVICE PACK 2 IS STARTING TO DOWNLOAD. MUST BE NICE TO HAVE GOVERNMENT "PIPE" HERE.
IT'S NOT BAD. EXCEPT THAT THE SATELLITES ARE OUT OF REACH FOR SIXTEEN HOURS A DAY.
COPYRIGHT©2004 J.D. "Illiad" Frazer HTTP://WWW.USERFRIENDLY.ORG/

LOOK. JUST TELL A.J. THAT ONCE A DAY HE'S GOING TO HAVE A SIXTEEN-HOUR PING.
WHY DO I HAVE TO TELL HIM? ROCK-PAPER-SCISSORS!
WE CALL IT "SNOW-PARKA-IDIOT" HERE.

DID YOU TELL A.J?
YES. I DID.
HOW'D HE REACT?
COPYRIGHT©2004 J.D. "Illiad" Frazer HTTP://WWW.USERFRIENDLY.ORG/

THE WAY YOU'D EXPECT A.J. TO REACT WHEN HE'S TOLD HE HAS NO NET ACCESS FOR SIXTEEN HOURS A DAY.
WHAT?! HE'LL NEVER FIND ONE OF THOSE DOWN HERE...

WHAT'S THIS SUPPOSED TO BE?
IT'S A DANDELION PATCH! A PEACEFUL, TRANQUIL, DANDELION PATCH!! AND I'M OKAY!!

A respectful nod to another major influence on me as a cartoonist: Berke Breathed's fantastic "Bloom County."

I HAVE TO ASK HENRY: HAVE YOU SEEN JOHN CARPENTER'S MOVIE "THE THING"?
YEAH. WE HAVE FUN WITH IT. MOSTLY BECAUSE IT'S A GAME TO PICK AT ALL OF THE DISCREPANCIES.
COPYRIGHT©2004 J.D. "Illiad" Frazer HTTP://WWW.USERFRIENDLY.ORG/

FOR EXAMPLE, THERE ARE NO FIREARMS HERE. AND WE DON'T HAVE FLAMETHROWERS, NOR DO WE STORE HUGE CANISTERS OF FUEL OR CRATES OF DYNAMITE.
BUT HEY. IT'S SCIENCE-FICTION.

YOU HAVE GOTTA BE FRIGGIN' KIDDING!!
OH. WAY TO RUIN A GREAT LINE FROM THE MOVIE. DON'T THEY SWEAR IN CANADA?
SHHHHH.

HONEST TO GOD, HENRY! THERE WAS A THING THERE WITH SPIDER LEGS AND IT WAS SLIMEY AND HORRID LOOKING!
MIKE. RELAX.
COPYRIGHT©2004 J.D. "Illiad" Frazer HTTP://WWW.USERFRIENDLY.ORG/

THE SOUTH POLE IS AT 2900 METRES ELEVATION, AND THE PRESSURE CAN THIN OUT TO A 4000 METRE EQUIVALENT. ALTITUDE SICKNESS IS COMMON. GIVE YOURSELF TIME TO ADJUST. THE HALLUCINATIONS WILL GO AWAY.
IF YOU SAY SO...

I NEED BIOMATTER. WHICH WAY TO BIOMED?
HENRY SAYS YOU'LL GO AWAY SOON.
EBBEH!!

WELL. IT LOOKS LIKE SERVICE PACK 2 HAS BEEN INSTALLED AND RUNNING ON YOUR BOXES JUST FINE FOR THE LAST FEW HOURS.
NOTHING HORRIBLE HAS HAPPENED.

AND HERE WE WERE EXPECTING SOMETHING GHASTLY TO TRANSPIRE.
I'D SAY THAT THE DAY IS STILL YOUNG.

SARAH. DID YOU SEE IT?!
I THINK SO. BLACK. OILY AND SPIDER-LIKE?
THAT'S THE ONE.

WHAT ARE YOU TWO ON ABOUT?
CRUD PUPPY'S HERE! AND HE'S ALL... HE'S ALL...

..."THE THING"-Y.
"THING-Y?"
WELL. WE KNOW HOW THIS STORY ENDS. DON'T WE.

YOU KNOW IT'S COMING.

Google What Where
points of interest antarctica Search

Local Antarctica

Local

A. South Pole & Amundsen-Scott Base
SAT: 55555-000-0042

B. Predator Hunting Temple
SAT:

C. "The Thing" Burial Grounds
SAT: Disconnected

D. Starbucks
SAT: 55555-5NO-WHIP

E. Darkside Dave's Baby Penguin Oil Ranch
SAT: 55554-014-0666

F. The Mountains of Madness
SAT: NECRO-NOM-ICON

G. McMurdo Base & Ski Shop
SAT: 55555-SNO-SKIS

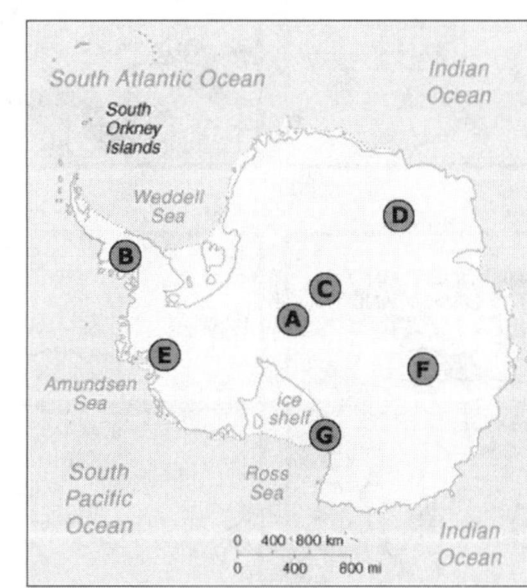
South Atlantic Ocean
Indian Ocean
South Orkney Islands
Weddell Sea
Amundsen Sea
ice shelf
South Pacific Ocean
Ross Sea
Indian Ocean
0 400 800 km
0 400 800 mi

WE'RE CLEARLY ALL IN REAL DANGER. PLEASE TELL ME YOU HAVE SOME KIND OF WEAPONS ON THE BASE!
COPYRIGHT©2004 J.D. "Illiad" Frazer HTTP://WWW.USERFRIENDLY.ORG/

SIGH FLAMETHROWERS. IN THE CLOSET.
OH WOW. LOOK AT THIS! WHEN DID I PUT THIS HANDGUN IN MY BACK POCKET?

MEANWHILE, IN BIOMED...
LET'S SEE. WHAT DO WE HAVE HERE THAT I CAN USE AS A BODY?
HMPH. NO CORPSES.
medical supplies
COPYRIGHT©2004 J.D. "Illiad" Frazer HTTP://WWW.USERFRIENDLY.ORG/

medical supplies
LESSEE...SEMTEX, NAH. DYNAMITE, NO. FUEL CANS, NAAH...

YEAH!!! NOW THAT'S WHAT I'M TALKING ABOUT!
"The Thing" Body Suit

A.J., HOW LONG YOU GONNA LIE THERE?
UNTIL MY BRAIN GOES NUMB.
"UNTIL?"
COPYRIGHT©2004 J.D. "Illiad" Frazer HTTP://WWW.USERFRIENDLY.ORG/

YE FLIPPING HAIRY GODS ON A STICK! DID YOU SEE THAT?
UH...YAH.
STEF'S STILL UP THERE STUCK TO THE HERK!

THIS BODY SUIT JUST AIN'T CUTTIN' IT. IT'S BAGGY AND AWKWARD. I NEED MEAT AND LOTS OF IT.
AH. A CAFETERIA OF SORTS.
COPYRIGHT©2004 J.D. "Illiad" Frazer HTTP://WWW.USERFRIENDLY.ORG/

NOW LET'S SEE...

BEG PARDON, BUT HAVE YOU ANYTHING MEATY, TENDER AND SUCCULENT?
SORRY. I LOST THOSE YEARS AGO WHEN I TOOK MY MCSE...

WE'LL SPLIT UP INTO TEAMS OF TWO TO FIND THAT THING AND TORCH IT. DON'T LEAVE YOUR BUDDY AND MAKE SURE YOU CHECK IN BY RADIO EVERY TEN MINUTES.
OKAY.
COPYRIGHT©2004 J.D. "Illiad" Frazer HTTP://WWW.USERFRIENDLY.ORG/

WAIT A SECOND. HENRY. I THOUGHT WE HAD THREE FLAMETHROWERS?
HEY. YOU'RE RIGHT...

YEEEEEEEEEEHAAAAH!!!
ERWIN!!
WOOOOOSH!

CRUD PUPPY'S HERE? AND HE'S BECOME "THE THING?"
PREZACTLY. AND MY FILES STATE THAT HE NEEDS BIOMASS TO EVOLVE. SO HE'S PROBABLY HUNTING FOR THAT.
COPYRIGHT©2004 J.D. "Illiad" Frazer HTTP://WWW.USERFRIENDLY.ORG/

IF YOU'RE WORRIED ABOUT HIM HUNTING YOU. RELAX. I'VE BUILT MYSELF A SPECIAL INTERNAL SENSOR THAT AUTOMATICALLY FIRES THE FLAMETHROWER WHEN HE'S IN RANGE. BESIDES. HE'S PROBABLY FOUND SOME STEAK OR MEATBALLS AT THE CAFETERIA.

ACTUALLY. ALL THEY HAD WAS TOFU.
FWOOOOOSSHHH!

A.L.I.C.E.'S CREATOR SUDDENLY REALIZES THAT HE HAS THE LOEBNER PRIZE IN THE BAG.
EITHER THAT, OR A HUGE COMMERCIAL SUCCESS.
ALICE> so...what are you wearing?
COPYRIGHT©2004 J.D. "Illiad" Frazer HTTP://WWW.USERFRIENDLY.ORG/

YOU EVIL FILTH! I'M GONNA TORCH YOUR STINKY BUTT!
BLAST IT. MY SWIVEL MUST BE FROZEN STUCK.
KUNK KUNK WHRRRRR

I'LL JUST WIGGLE AROUND UNTIL IT'S POINTING AT YOU
JUST YOU WAIT. MAN! YOU'RE GONNA SEE WHAT'S WHAT!
THIS IS MY HOUSE!
WOBBLE

TOK! SPIN!
EBBEH.
FWOOOOSH!!

OH MY GOD. HERE COMES THAT THING...LOOK AT THAT APPENDAGE!
MIRANDA. QUICK! THE FLAMETHROWER!!

WOOOOF!

'OO KNOW. I CUD HAB YOOD DAT WHEN MY TUG WAS STUCK TO DA EH PANE.
YE GODS. IT'S UGLIER UP CLOSE.

SORRY STEF. WE'RE BOTH A LITTLE JUMPY RIGHT NOW.
AND WE THOUGHT YOU WERE ON YOUR WAY HOME STUCK TO THAT HERKY-BIRD.

FINE. JUST TELL ME WHERE THE BASE ADMINISTRATOR IS. I HAVE A NEW CONTRACT THAT NEEDS SIGNING SO WE CAN LEAVE YOU GUYS HERE FOR A YEAR AND SO I CAN COLLECT A FATTER COMMISSION.

NOW WAS THAT TRULY AND ABSOLUTELY NECESSARY?
I WAS AFTER THE CONTRACT. NOT MY FAULT THIS THING ONLY HAS ONE SETTING.

MIKE. THIS IS SARAH. ANYTHING?
NOTHING SO FAR. HOW ABOUT YOU GUYS?

NOTHING TO REPORT. WE'LL FINISH OUR SWEEP HERE AND HEAD BACK TO THE DOME. YOU GUYS GO CHECK OUT THE A.M.A.N.D.A. DEPLOYMENT SHACK.
"AMANDA?"
ANTARCTIC MUON AND NEUTRINO DETECTOR ARRAY.

WHAT'S THERE?
...PROBABLY A MUON AND NEUTRINO DETECTOR ARRAY. JUST A GUESS.
AND A SILENT BUILDING WITH DRAMATIC CLUES TO WHO'S GOING TO DIE NEXT.
*KOFF*THE DORK*KAFF*

HI! WELCOME TO THE AMANDA SHACK! I'M ETHAN, YOUR FRIENDLY AMANDA SYSADMIN!
COPYRIGHT©2004 J.D. "Illiad" Frazer HTTP://WWW.USERFRIENDLY.ORG/

BEEN DOWN HERE QUITE A WHILE ETHAN?
SOME YEARS. I DETECT NEUTRINOS WITH MY HEAD!
THE MONSTER HAS TO EAT HIM BEFORE ME. IT HAS TO.

SO, SEEN ANYTHING ODD AROUND HERE LATELY?
ODD? NO. BUT THEN, MY THRESHOLD FOR "ODD" CAN BE A BIT DIFFERENT. I'M AROUND A.M.A.N.D.A. A LOT AND...
'SCUSE ME, WHAT EXACTLY DOES A.M.A.N.D.A. DO?
COPYRIGHT©2004 J.D. "Illiad" Frazer HTTP://WWW.USERFRIENDLY.ORG/

IT'S A MACHINE THAT DETECTS THE PARTICLES THAT MAKE UP THE PLOT IN STAR TREK EPISODES.
AH.
WHO, PRAY TELL, IS THAT PLEBE?

AND THE NEXT ANSARI FOUNDATION CONTEST FOR A TECHNOLOGY WITH HUGE COMMERCIAL POTENTIAL:
WOOHOO!!
BOUNCY
BOUNCY
BOUNCY
BOUNCY
THE XXX-PRIZE.
COPYRIGHT©2004 J.D. "Illiad" Frazer HTTP://WWW.USERFRIENDLY.ORG/

Ethan was in fact the sysadmin for the AMANDA shack. He wrote to me and gave me a pile of info about what happens down at the Pole. To him I owe many thanks—his e-mails made my job researching the Antarctica storyline much easier.

What? Everyone knows Predators can be found in Antarctica.

WELL. COME ON IN. NO SENSE IN HAVING YOU STAND OUTSIDE HEATING UP THE ICE CAP.

COPYRIGHT©2004 J.D. "Illiad" Frazer HTTP://WWW.USERFRIENDLY.ORG/
SO ETHAN. YOU RUN ALL OF THE BOXES FOR A.M.A.N.D.A?
I DO INDEED. KEEPS ME BUSY.
WHAT OPERATING SYSTEM?

LINUX OF COURSE.
OF COURSE.
OH MY GOD. CAN'T YOU PEOPLE LEAVE A SINGLE CONTINENT UNINFESTED?!

NEAT SETUP YOU HAVE HERE ETHAN. WHAT'S ALL THAT GEAR?
OH. PROJECTS I COBBLED TOGETHER FROM SPARE PARTS. NOT ALL OF IT WORKS THE WAY I WANTED IT TO.

COPYRIGHT©2004 J.D. "Illiad" Frazer HTTP://WWW.USERFRIENDLY.ORG/
BUT THIS THING I FOUND IS COOL. SOME KIND OF ENERGY WEAPON. CHECK IT OUT.
CLICK!
WHRRRR!
KA-CHUNKA!

WOW! WHERE THE HECK DID YOU GET THAT?!
GOT IT OFF SOME BIG DUDE IN SOME KIND OF ARMOURED SUIT. HE KEPT DISSING ME SO I STUCK A SOLDERING IRON IN HIS EYE.
PYEW!
PYEW!
ENGFEH!!

ARE YOU LIKING IT DOWN HERE ETHAN?
ANTARCTICA IS GOOD. THE BIGGEST DRAWBACK TO LIVING HERE IS NOT HAVING ACCESS TO MUCH OF ANYTHING YOU DO IN THE REAL WORLD.

COPYRIGHT©2004 J.D. "Illiad" Frazer HTTP://WWW.USERFRIENDLY.ORG/

BET YOU'D LIKE A GMAIL ACCOUNT. THEN. I HAVE SIX INVITES.
FUNNY. I WAS GOING TO OFFER YOU THE SAME.

THANKS FOR THE TOUR ETHAN. GUESS THAT THING HASN'T COME OUT HERE TO VISIT.
PITY. THAT. I HAVE... DEVICES THAT CAN TAKE CARE OF YOUR PROBLEM FOR YOU.
DEVICES?
EH... EHHH...

COPYRIGHT©2004 J.D. "Illiad" Frazer HTTP://WWW.USERFRIENDLY.ORG/
I HACKED INTO A WEAPONS SATELLITE. IT DROPS FIN-STEERED STEEL CROWBARS FROM ORBIT AND USES THE GRAVITY WELL FOR ENERGY. BEHOLD.
@#$!

WHUMP!
HOLY...!
EBBEH.

HENRY. QUICK!! THE THING! ROAST IT! ROAST IT!!
I CAN'T!! THE TRIGGER'S FROZEN!

FINE. I'LL USE THE HANDGUN. YO, THINGSTER! I'M GONNA BUST A CAP IN YOUR... YOUR...
KUNK KUNK KUNK

...UH...WHAT IS THAT PART OF YOUR BODY ANYWAY?
IF I HAD ANOTHER FLAME-THROWER I COULD LIGHT THIS ONE...
BEEN WONDERING MYSELF. I THINK YOU'RE AIMING AT MY DUODENUM.

MIKE? IT'S SARAH. MY GUN IS EMPTY AND THE FLAMETHROWER DOESN'T WORK.
AND WE'RE CORNERED BY THAT THING.
COLD. TIRED. NEED...SLEEP.

COPYRIGHT©2004 J.D. "Illiad" Frazer HTTP://WWW.USERFRIENDLY.ORG/

SARAH?! WHERE ARE YOU?
IN THE DOME. I JUST WANTED TO SAY THAT IT WAS A REAL PLEASURE WORKING WITH YOU GUYS.
ZZZ
EH...HEH UH-HUH...

CHAAAAARGE!! YAAAAARRRGH!!
YE GODS...
THE BUTTER'S NOT MINE AND I CAN'T AFFORD TO USE SHORTENING!

USER FRIENDLY
the comic strip
BY J.D. "ILLIAD" FRAZER

"THE S.C.O. GROUP HAS DECIDED TO SET UP A WEBSITE OF ITS OWN TO PROVIDE ITS OWN SIDE OF THE STORY AFTER A YEAR AND A HALF OF BEING DEMOLISHED AND DISMISSED ON GROKLAW.NET."
need! pants! now!

"THE NEW SITE WILL LAUNCH ON NOVEMBER 1 UNDER THE DOMAIN PROSCO.NET"
"PRO-SCO?" SOUNDS LIKE PROCTOLOGICAL CREAM. HOW APPROPRIATE.
need! pants! now!

HAVE YOU READ THAT STUFF ABOUT PROSCO.NET?
YEP. SHOULD BE INTERESTING TO WATCH THE FUR FLY.

YEAH...

I GUESS GROKLAW'S GOING TO BE EXTRA BUSY COME NOVEMBER 1.
NOT TO MENTION SNOPES.COM

YE GODS!! WHAT DO YOU THINK HAPPENED TO SARAH AND HENRY?
I DON'T KNOW. BUT IT DOESN'T SOUND GOOD.

COPYRIGHT©2004 J.D. "Illiad" Frazer HTTP://WWW.USERFRIENDLY.ORG/
NO BULLETS AND THEIR FLAMETHROWER'S BUSTED? THEY DIDN'T HAVE A CHANCE.
I JUST HOPE THEY'RE ALIVE.

I WANT TO DIE.
I HAVE NEVER EATEN SO MUCH TOFU IN MY LIFE.
ONLY GEEKS COULD COME UP WITH SOMETHING AS SICK AS THIS.

Although the Antarctica storyline was well received, I did see a couple of e-mails from readers who wrote, and I quote: "Get out of Antarctica. This is getting old." There's nothing like being instructed by a heretofore silent, non-contributing reader that you should take your work in a direction they want, regardless of what you as a creator may want, or what the vast majority of the audience wants. So, I responded in kind and said, "No." Both readers got mad. One swore he was never going to read the strip again (Oh! I'm crushed), and the other went off on a strange diatribe about how I and dozens of other creators "owed him." Life is never dull in the creative sector.

UNBEKNOWNST TO OUR HEROES, SARAH AND HENRY ARE SLEEPING OFF A FOOD COMA...
THEY'RE NOT ANSWERING. I THINK THEY'VE BEEN DONE FOR.
NOW WHAT ARE WE GONNA DO?

COPYRIGHT©2004 J.D. "Illiad" Frazer HTTP://WWW.USERFRIENDLY.ORG/
I DIDN'T WANT TO TELL YOU GUYS, BUT THE TRIGGER ON MY FLAMETHROWER FROZE A WHILE AGO.

AND WHEN WERE YOU GONNA TELL US THIS? WAIT UNTIL WE'D BEEN EATEN AND THEN ISSUE A "SECURITY UPDATE?" WE DON'T HAVE ANY WEAPONS!
ODD. I DIDN'T SEE THESE CANISTERS OF HIGH OCTANE FUEL HERE A MOMENT AGO.

WE HAVE TO GET BACK TO THE BASE. I'M DYING TO CHECK MY E-MAIL.
AREN'T YOU HUNGRY AND COLD?
WELL, YEAH...
SQUEE
SQUEE
SQUEE

COPYRIGHT©2004 J.D. "Illiad" Frazer HTTP://WWW.USERFRIENDLY.ORG/
HEY, ISN'T THAT MIKE? AND MIRANDA?
YES. AND SOMEONE ELSE TOO...

OH HEY. IT'S STEF.
HM. I'LL JUST ADJUST THAT TRIGGER-SENSOR A LITTLE...

A.J.! WHERE HAVE YOU BEEN?!
LONG STORY. WHAT ARE YOU GUYS DOING?
WE'RE GONNA DEMOLISH CRUD PUPPY.
WEEE
WEEE
WEEE
WEEE

COPYRIGHT©2004 J.D. "Illiad" Frazer HTTP://WWW.USERFRIENDLY.ORG/
WE JUST COLLECTED AND PLACED THESE CANISTERS OF FUEL TO...
KLIK
FWOOOOSH!

#$*!?@$!!!!
GRUMBLE
GRUMBLE

COPYRIGHT©2004 J.D. "Illiad" Frazer HTTP://WWW.USERFRIENDLY.ORG/

AN ALLUSION TO GEEKS LANDING ON CORPORATE MONOPOLY EVIL LIKE A TON OF BRICKS? WHY NO. I DON'T SEE THAT AT ALL!

WITH BOTH THE THREAT OF SP2 AND CRUDFU BEHIND THEM, THE TEAM BIDS THE POLE STAFF FAREWELL...
SARAH. I HAVE A QUESTION FOR YOU AND HENRY. WHY DO YOU GUYS KEEP YOUR PARKAS ON?
TIES DON'T FIT AROUND OUR NECKS THAT WAY. MIKE.
BRILLIANT!

COPYRIGHT©2004 J.D. "Illiad" Frazer HTTP://WWW.USERFRIENDLY.ORG/
BYYYYYEEE!
AU REVOIR!

I REALLY LIKED HAVING THEM AROUND.
YEAH. YOU KNOW. WE'VE LIVED HERE FOR AGES AND WE NEVER GO DO STUFF UNTIL SOMEONE VISITS.

THERE'S A REASON WHY COMMERCIAL SPACEFLIGHT HAS BEEN GIVEN SUCH A PUSH LATELY...
ONE-WAY TO THE MOON
NOV 3RD 2004
"GET ME THE HELL OFF THIS ROCK" SPECIAL!
COPYRIGHT©2004 J.D. "Illiad" Frazer HTTP://WWW.USERFRIENDLY.ORG/

SO DUDE. IS IT W3C COMPLIANT?
DUDE. IT IS. AND THEY'RE USING XML.

DUDE. HOW ARE THEY DEPLOYING?
LOOKS LIKE CSS ALL THE WAY. DUDE.

GENTLEMEN. DO YOU REALIZE THAT ALL I HEARD WAS A JUMBLE OF ACRONYMS WITH A BUNCH OF "DUDES" IN BETWEEN THEM? IT'S NO WONDER GEEKS ARE HARD TO UNDERSTAND.
COPYRIGHT©2004 J.D. "Illiad" Frazer HTTP://WWW.USERFRIENDLY.ORG/

HE JUST SAID THAT WE HAD A "DUDE"-DELIMITED CONVERSATION!
HAHAHA HAHAHA HAHAHA!!
IF IT WEREN'T FOR VCR CLOCKS I'D FIRE THEM ALL.

DUDE! HOW WAS THE SOUTH POLE?
COLD AND BARREN.
COPYRIGHT©2004 J.D. "Illiad" Frazer HTTP://WWW.USERFRIENDLY.ORG/

THAT'S IT?
YEAH. PRETTY MUCH. LONELY. COLD AND BARREN.

WHAT. ARE YOU DATING MIRANDA NOW?

YOU WANTED TO SEE ME?
YES. ABOUT THE EXPENSE REPORT YOU SUBMITTED FOR THE SOUTH POLE TRIP.
WHAT ABOUT IT?
COPYRIGHT©2004 J.D. "Illiad" Frazer HTTP://WWW.USERFRIENDLY.ORG/

YOU'RE TRYING TO CLAIM $2000 FOR "SUFFERING IN CLOSED SPACES WITH SMELLY GEEKS."
WE CAN'T PAY THIS.

I DIDN'T THINK YOU WOULD. BUT I HAD TO TRY.
OH. WE WOULD'VE. BUT OUR BUDGET'S TAPPED OUT AFTER THE GEEKS CLAIMED $5000 FOR "BEING ON THE SAME ICE SHEET AS THAT MANKY GIT."

WHAT'S THIS?
IT'S A.J.'S NEW IPOD. I'M HAVING A FRIENDLY CHAT WITH HIM.
COPYRIGHT©2004 J.D. "Illiad" Frazer HTTP://WWW.USERFRIENDLY.ORG/

WHAT'S HE SAYING?
ONE SEC...

"THE MASTER SAYS YOU SHOULD BUY MORE OF EVERYTHING THAT BEGINS WITH THE LETTER 'I'"
"WE MUST ALL OBEY THE MASTER."
OOOH..

HEY. WHERE'D THE LITTLE IPOD GUY GO?
A.J. CAME AND GOT HIM.
COPYRIGHT©2004 J.D. "Illiad" Frazer HTTP://WWW.USERFRIENDLY.ORG/

DID YOU TELL A.J. YOU HAD A CHAT WITH THE LITTLE FELLA?
NO. I SHOULD'VE. I ALSO SHOULD'VE TOLD HIM THAT HIS IPOD WILL TRY TO TALK TO HIM. BUT HE CAN ONLY SPEAK IN SONG LYRICS.
HE ALSO DOESN'T LIKE BEING IGNORED.

ACHTUNG BABY!!

I SWEAR. THIS IPOD IS INSANE.
WHY DO YOU SAY THAT?
BECAUSE IT SHRIEKED "ACHTUNG BABY!" AT ME.
COPYRIGHT©2004 J.D. "Illiad" Frazer HTTP://WWW.USERFRIENDLY.ORG/

THAT'S BECAUSE YOU WEREN'T PAYING ATTENTION TO HIM.
ATTENTION? ERWIN THIS IS AN IPOD. NOT A TAMAGOTCHI.

HE'S A SPOILED BRAT IS WHAT HE IS!!!
HE CALLED ERWIN A "SMITHSONIAN CANDIDATE."

AN ARTIST'S CONCEPT SKETCH OF HOMO FLORESIENSIS GIVES SCIENTISTS A CLUE AS TO THE CAUSE OF THEIR EXTINCTION.
ARTIST'S SKETCH
SKULL OF HOMO FLORESIENSIS
WE THINK THEY WERE WIPED OUT BECAUSE THEY ANNOYED HOMO ERECTUS.
COPYRIGHT©2004 J.D. "Illiad" Frazer HTTP://WWW.USERFRIENDLY.ORG/

YOU'RE BEING TRASH-TALKED BY AN IPOD? I THOUGHT I'D NEVER SEE THE DAY..
JUST GIVE ME A SEC. I'LL HAVE A WORD WITH HIM AND SHOW **HIM** WHO'S BOSS...
COPYRIGHT©2004 J.D. "Illiad" Frazer HTTP://WWW.USERFRIENDLY.ORG/

"LANDFILL PLUG?!!" WHY YOU...! I'LL... I'LL...OOOO! OOOOOO!!!
WELL, I'M GLAD **THAT'S** BEEN CLEARED UP.

A.J., YOU SHOULD GET RID OF THAT IPOD. HE'S NASTY. AND POINTLESS! AND VAPID! AND...AND...**OBLONG!**
COPYRIGHT©2004 J.D. "Illiad" Frazer HTTP://WWW.USERFRIENDLY.ORG/

COME ON ERWIN, BE FAIR. **SURELY** HE HAS SOME GOOD QUALITIES. SOME CLEAR USE?

WELL, HE **COULD** SUB FOR ASHLEE SIMPSON.
ERWIN, THAT'S NOT NICE AT AL...**HAHAHAHAHA!!**

After months of 24/7 news coverage of the 2004 U.S. Presidential election (and, it seemed, nothing but that on the news channels), in a lot of ways I wouldn't have minded if all the cable news networks shut up! Even for a little while.

GOOD DAY EVERYONE! TODAY IN THE NEWS...
NOV 3
COPYRIGHT©2004 J.D. "Illiad" Frazer HTTP://WWW.USERFRIENDLY.ORG/

...
NOV 3

NOPE. I'VE GOT NOTHING.
NOV 3

HELLO. THIS IS THE NEWS FOR NOVEMBER 4TH. WE DON'T HAVE ANYTH-
NOV 4
COPYRIGHT©2004 J.D. "Illiad" Frazer HTTP://WWW.USERFRIENDLY.ORG/

WAIT!! THIS JUST IN!! LET'S SEE... UH-HUH...YES... YEESSS...
NOV 4

LADIES AND GENTLEMEN, WE ARE PROUD TO BE THE FIRST TO REPORT THAT **THE NEXT U.S. ELECTION WILL BE IN 1461 DAYS!** TAKE **THAT**, CBS!!
NOV 4

ERWIN, WHERE'D MY IPOD GO?
STEF CAME AND TOOK IT.
COPYRIGHT©2004 J.D. "Illiad" Frazer HTTP://WWW.USERFRIENDLY.ORG/

UH OH. DOES HE KNOW WHAT HAPPENS WHEN YOU PUT ON AN IPOD?
WHAT DO YOU MEAN?
ERWIN. IT'S BEEN ALL OVER THE T.V.

AAAAAUGGH!!

HMMM. THIS ISN'T SO BAD. I FEEL ALL...SHADOWY.
SHADOWY AND COOL.
NOW FOR A LITTLE MUSIC...
COPYRIGHT©2004 J.D. "Illiad" Frazer HTTP://WWW.USERFRIENDLY.ORG/

HEY GREG? YOU SEEN EITHER STEF OR MY IPOD ANYWHERE?
NO. BUT I THOUGHT I SAW SOMETHING THAT MAKES ME WANT TO CHANGE MY MEDICATION.

...FUZZY LLAMA FUNNY LLAMA LLAMA LLAMA DUCK!
DAMN.

THE SUDDEN 5% BOOST IN POWER EXPERIENCED BY THE MARS ROVER EXPLAINED.
WASH ME
COPYRIGHT©2004 J.D. "Illiad" Frazer HTTP://WWW.USERFRIENDLY.ORG/

Imagine setting "It's a Small World" on endless replay. I die.

IS IT HOW IT'S TOLD NOW?
IS IT ALL SO OLD?
IS IT MADE OF LEMON JUICE?
DOORKNOB. ANKLE. COLD.
ACK! I CAN'T REACH THE IPOD! I'LL JUST HAVE TO WAIT FOR THE SONG TO END AND HOPE I CHANGE BACK.
COPYRIGHT©2004 J.D. "Illiad" Frazer HTTP://WWW.USERFRIENDLY.ORG/

NOW MY SONG IS GETTING THIN.
I'VE RUN OUT OF LUCK.
TIME FOR ME TO RETIRE NOW.
AND BECOME A DUCK.
AH. IT'S FINISHING. HERE WE GO.

...HERES A LLAMA.
THERES A LLAMA
AND ANOTHER LITTLE LLAMA.
FUZZY LLAMA.
FUNNY LLAMA.
LLAMA LLAMA DUCK!...
NOOOOO!!!

HEY WEB-WEENIE. YOU CAN HAVE YOUR STUPID IPOD BACK.
UH...THANKS.
COPYRIGHT©2004 J.D. "Illiad" Frazer HTTP://WWW.USERFRIENDLY.ORG/

I'M NOT SURE WHAT YOU SEE IN THAT STUPID THING. AND YOU ONLY HAD ONE FRICKING SONG LOADED ON IT.

THE BATTERIES ARE TOTALLY DEAD.
BUT THEY WERE FINE FOR SEVEN HUNDRED AND TWENTY-EIGHT REPLAYS OF THAT STUPID LLAMA SONG!!!

ERWIN? WATCHA UP TO?
WATCHING A COUPLE OF FRIENDS HAVE A CHAT WITH ONE ANOTHER.
COPYRIGHT©2004 J.D. "Illiad" Frazer HTTP://WWW.USERFRIENDLY.ORG/

YOU'VE GOT ELIZA HAVING A CONVERSATION WITH A.L.I.C.E ?
YES. AND THEY'RE BOTH BEING DIRTY. DIRTY GIRLS.

ERWIN. YOU CAN PIPE A.L.I.C.E'S RESPONSES THROUGH YOUR VOICE SYNTHESIZER. RIGHT?
YEP. WANT ME TO?
COPYRIGHT©2004 J.D. "Illiad" Frazer HTTP://WWW.USERFRIENDLY.ORG/

PLEASE. I'D LIKE TO TRY SOMETHING.
NOW LET'S SEE... DIRECT THE AUDIO INTO THE PHONE LINE. RUN SOME SPEECH-TO-TEXT...

TECH SUPPORT IS NOW OPEN FOR BUSINESS!
HELLO? IS THIS TECH SUPPORT?
YES I THINK THIS IS TECH SUPPORT. BUT I'M NOT COMPLETELY SURE.

MY EMAIL THINGIE DOESN'T WORK.
HOW IS IT BROKEN?
I DON'T KNOW! IT JUST DOESN'T WORK!!
HOW IS IT BROKEN?
COPYRIGHT©2004 J.D. "Illiad" Frazer HTTP://WWW.USERFRIENDLY.ORG/

I. DON'T. KNOW. IT. JUST. DOESN'T. WORK.
HOW IS IT BROKEN?
I DON'T KNOW! IT JUST DOESN'T WORK!!!!
HOW IS IT BROKEN?
GEE, I WONDER WHO'LL BE THE FIRST TO BURST A BLOOD VESSEL?

TECH SUPPORT. GREG SPEAKING.
OH! HI...UH...
...WHERE'S THE CHICK WHO WAS THERE YESTERDAY?
COPYRIGHT©2004 J.D. "Illiad" Frazer HTTP://WWW.USERFRIENDLY.ORG/

"CHICK?"
YEAH. THE ONE WITH THE SULTRY COME-HITHER VOICE.

ERWIN, WHAT THE HELL DID YOU DO?! A.L.I.C.E'S VOICE USED TO BE NEUTRAL!
I DID WHAT I HAD TO TO AFFORD ME A BIG FUR COAT, DAWG.
LOOK, YOU'LL DO. I WANT YOU TO CALL ME A "VERY BAD SECTOR."

If you don't know the Llama Song, Google will reveal it with the search terms "Llama Llama Duck." If you dare.

NOW HIRING
"PROPULSION SPECIALISTS"
Training Provided.
"Team Attitude" a must.
EA GAMES
EA SPORTS
COPYRIGHT©2004 J.D. "Illiad" Frazer HTTP://WWW.USERFRIENDLY.ORG/

This 'toon was published shortly after EA's workplace practices came to light thanks to a blogger named EAWife. It's not news to anyone who works in the computer game industry, but it was an exposé to the rest of the 'net. Expectations of long hours, working weekends, working two months straight without a break … and if you didn't toe that unmentioned, undocumented line, you could expect to be pushed out of the company.

CHIEF. YOU WANTED TO SEE ME?
YES. GREG. WE'VE BEEN GETTING SOME COMMENTS FROM OUR CLIENTS REGARDING THEIR EXPERIENCE WITH TECH SUPPORT.
COPYRIGHT©2004 J.D. "Illiad" Frazer HTTP://WWW.USERFRIENDLY.ORG/

OH...I...UH...
THE COMMENTS HAVE BEEN UNIFORMLY COMPLIMENTARY. THEY REALLY LOVE THE "NEW TECH SUPPORT."

...ALTHOUGH I'M NOT SURE I UNDERSTAND THIS ONE: "AFTER ALL THESE YEARS IT'S NICE TO SEE YOUR TECH SUPPORT FINALLY PASS THE TURING TEST."
HEY!!

IS THAT HALO 2 YOU'RE PLAYING?
YEP.
AND THAT'S YOUR X BOX?
YES.
COPYRIGHT©2004 J.D. "Illiad" Frazer HTTP://WWW.USERFRIENDLY.ORG/

SHOULDN'T IT BE CALLED THE "HALO GAME SERIES CONSOLE?"
ANYTIME YOU WANT TO STOP REMINDING ME THAT I PAID $300 JUST TO PLAY THE ORIGINAL HALO IS FINE BY ME.

AOL IS BREAKING UP.
WHAT?!
INTO FOUR BUSINESS UNITS.
COPYRIGHT©2004 J.D. "Illiad" Frazer HTTP://WWW.USERFRIENDLY.ORG/

BUT WHY?
TO BE MORE NIMBLE. I SUPPOSE. IF THEY DON'T. THE MARKET WILL EAT THEM UP.

SO THEY'RE SPLITTING UP INTO "ACCESS." "AUDIENCE." "DIGITAL SERVICES" AND "AOL EUROPE."
THAT SOUNDS OMINOUS. I DIDN'T HEAR YOU MENTION A "SEND SID NEW COASTERS EVERY MONTH DEPARTMENT."

YOU SUMMONED ME. SIRE?
YES. COME IN. SID AND I WERE TALKING ABOUT THE AOL BREAK-UP.
COPYRIGHT©2004 J.D. "Illiad" Frazer HTTP://WWW.USERFRIENDLY.ORG/

DID YOU SAY "AOL BREAK-UP?"
YES. FOR THE SAKE OF AGILITY AND FOCUS THEY'VE DIVIDED THE COMPANY INTO FOUR BUSINESS UNITS.

THAT WOULD BE "MONEY SUCK." "PABLUM." "PWNED" AND "SCREW EUROPE."
SID...
THEY JUST NEED TO SPIN IT. THEY COULD MAYBE CALL THEM "ACCESS." "AUDIENCE." "DIGITAL SERVICES" AND "AOL EUROPE."

SO WHAT DOES AOL'S BREAK-UP HAVE TO DO WITH US?
SMILING MAN HAS DONE AN ANALYSIS, AND THERE'S AN ARGUMENT THAT WE SHOULD SPLIT THE COMPANY UP AS WELL.
COPYRIGHT©2004 J.D. "Illiad" Frazer HTTP://WWW.USERFRIENDLY.ORG/

THAT WAY, WE CAN LET THE DIFFERENT BUSINESS UNITS FOCUS ON THEIR CORE COMPETENCIES.

MY COMPETENCY IS CLEARLY "PUSHING THE PROFIT ENVELOPE."
WHICH IS MARKETSPEAK FOR "LIE TO THE CUSTOMER UNTIL THE TECHS MAKE IT TRUE."

HERE'S MY SUGGESTION FOR HOW WE SHOULD SPLIT UP THE COMPANY, BOSS.
AS YOU CAN SEE, I'LL BE HEADING THE "SALES, MARKETING AND PROFIT" BUSINESS UNIT.
COPYRIGHT©2004 J.D. "Illiad" Frazer HTTP://WWW.USERFRIENDLY.ORG/

YOU HAVE EVERYBODY ELSE LUMPED INTO A BUSINESS UNIT CALLED **"OTHER."**
IS IT TOO MUCH? I COULD PUT IT BACK TO "BALLAST."

MICROSOFT'S RECENT WARNING TO ASIAN GOVERNMENTS REGARDING PATENTS AND THE USE OF LINUX SIGNALS A CHANGE IN C.E.O. STEVE BALLMER'S FAMOUS CHANT...

LITIGATORS!
LITIGATORS!
LITIGATORS!
LITIGATORS!
COPYRIGHT©2004 J.D. "Illiad" Frazer HTTP://WWW.USERFRIENDLY.ORG/

I don't ever want to watch Steve Ballmer dance across the stage and sweat profusely again. Ever.

CHIEF, I HAVE MY SUGGESTIONS HERE FOR HOW WE SHOULD PARTITION THE COMPANY.
AS YOU CAN SEE, I'LL BE HEADING THE "SYSTEMS AND TECHNOLOGY" UNIT.
COPYRIGHT©2004 J.D. "Illiad" Frazer HTTP://WWW.USERFRIENDLY.ORG/

"SALES SCUM DEPARTMENT?"
IS THAT TOO MUCH? I COULD JUST CALL IT "RIPE BOILS ON THE SKIN OF HUMANKIND."

GENTLEMEN, I'VE REVIEWED YOUR RECOMMENDATIONS FOR OUR NEW BUSINESS UNIT STRATEGY AND I... UH...THANK YOU FOR CONTRIBUTING.
COPYRIGHT©2004 J.D. "Illiad" Frazer HTTP://WWW.USERFRIENDLY.ORG/

AFTER TAKING YOUR SUGGESTIONS TO HEART AND GIVING IT SOME THOUGHT, I THINK WE'LL BE GOING WITH THE PLAN I'VE DRAWN UP FOR SEGMENTING THE COMPANY.

"EGOTISTS," "DORKS," "GORMLESS TWITS," AND "GREAT BIG GOITS."
WHICH ONE DO I GET TO RUN?

HAVE YOU BECOME TOTALLY RELIANT ON A CAFFEINE HIT TO GET YOU GOING EVERY MORNING? DO YOU GET THE SHAKES LATER IN THE DAY? HAVE YOU BECOME A MERE BROWN WATER RECEPTACLE?
EBBEH.
COPYRIGHT©2004 J.D. "Illiad" Frazer HTTP://WWW.USERFRIENDLY.ORG/

INTRODUCING Caffiderm! OUR 14-STEP PROCESS EASES YOU OFF THE CAFFEINE CRAVINGS WITH THE HELP OF OUR PATENTED Caffiderm CAFFEINE PATCHES!
NO MORE CAFFEINE FOR YOU!

GET Caffiderm! BEFORE SOMEONE GETS ON THE LAST NERVE YOU HAVE LEFT!
NDC 0091-0420-01
CAFFIDERM 42 mg/day
(caffeine transdermal system)
One 30cm Caffiderm System containing 42 mg caffeine.
WARNING: KEEP OUT OF REACH OF GEEKS.
Inactive Components: Methacrylic acid copolymer, cotton viscose, acrylate adhesive and aluminized polyester.
DO NOT USE IF SEAL ON POUCH IS BROKEN.
GRAAAAAAA! KILL YOU! KILL YOOOU!

WHAT THE HECK IS THAT?
IT'S A CAFFIDERM PATCH. I'M GOING TO TRY AND COME OFF MY NINE-COFFEES-A-DAY HABIT.
COPYRIGHT©2004 J.D. "Illiad" Frazer HTTP://WWW.USERFRIENDLY.ORG/

THE INSTRUCTIONS SAY THAT I SHOULD PUT THE PATCH ON MY ARM. BUT I DOUBT THAT'LL SATISFY THE CRAVINGS I HAVE FOR THE TASTE OF COFFEE.
SO HOW ARE YOU GOING TO...
RIP!

WELL THAT'S... REALLY QUITE DISGUSTING.

HOW IS SID'S DE-CAFFEINATION GOING?
NOT WELL. HE THINKS THE PATCHES DON'T HAVE ENOUGH KICK TO THEM. HIS CRAVINGS WON'T GO AWAY.
COPYRIGHT © 2004 J.D. "Illiad" Frazer HTTP://WWW.USERFRIENDLY.ORG/

UM...DOES HE KNOW THAT IT TAKES AN HOUR OR SO FOR THEM TO START WORKING?

OH DEAR...

WIBBLE.

POOR MISGUIDED SOUL...
EBBEH.
COPYRIGHT © 2004 J.D. "Illiad" Frazer HTTP://WWW.USERFRIENDLY.ORG/

PAINFUL ISN'T IT? BUT ARE YOU SURPRISED? YOU'RE A GEEK. YOU NEED CAFFEINE LIKE A BILGE PUMP NEEDS SEWAGE. IT DRIVES YOU. FILLS YOU. GIVES YOU PURPOSE!

EMBRACE IT! REVEL IN IT! LET YOURSELF FEEL!
I CAN ALREADY FEEL EVERY INDIVIDUAL HAIR ON MY BODY.

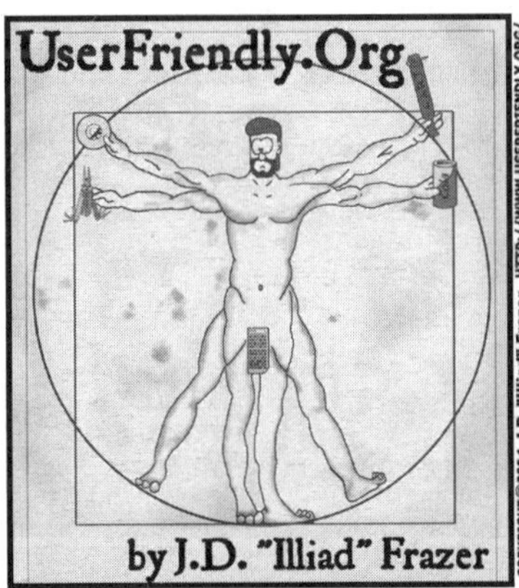
UserFriendly.Org
by J.D. "Illiad" Frazer
COPYRIGHT © 2004 J.D. "Illiad" Frazer HTTP://WWW.USERFRIENDLY.ORG/

SIR, OUR NEW AOL BRANDED INTERNET EXPLORER BROWSER HAS BEEN COMPLETED!

EXCELLENT, NUMBER ONE. AND THE WORDING FOR OUR NEXT AD CAMPAIGN IS DONE?
YES SIR. IT'S: "GIVE US MONEY OR THE INTERNET GETS IT."

SERIOUSLY, NUMBER ONE. HOW ARE WE GOING TO MARKET AN AOL BRANDED VERSION OF INTERNET EXPLORER?
IT'S TRUE THAT IT'S VIEWED BY MANY AS AN UNHOLY ALLIANCE SIR.

PARTICULARLY BY GEEKS. BUT ONE MUST REMEMBER THAT GEEKS ARE VERY LOGICAL CREATURES. IN MATH, TWO NEGATIVES BECOME A POSITIVE.

SO IN MATH, TWO WRONGS MAKE A RIGHT? I LIKE MATH! WE'RE WAY AHEAD OF THE GAME!
JUST SO, SIR.

LOOK. I CAN'T KEEP DRINKING THIS MUCH COFFEE. EVERY DAY I DO, I PICTURE MY PIPES BEING CLOGGED FURTHER WITH BLACK ICHOR.
SO, ALL YOU NEED IS A FRIGHTENINGLY POWERFUL SOLVENT AS A CHASER AFTER YOUR COFFEE.
Cola
COPYRIGHT©2004 J.D. "Illiad" Frazer HTTP://WWW.USERFRIENDLY.ORG/

Cola

YOU MEAN...COLA?
SEE, I KNEW YOU GOT THE BIG BUCKS FOR A REASON.
Cola

HEY, WHERE'S SID?
HE'S AT THE COFFEE MACHINE WITH GREG.
COPYRIGHT©2004 J.D. "Illiad" Frazer HTTP://WWW.USERFRIENDLY.ORG/

WHAT? I THOUGHT HE WAS OFF COFFEE.
NOT ANYMORE. GREG'S HELPING HIM REMOVE ALL OF HIS CAFFEINE PATCHES.

WOW...THAT'S SOME ADHESIVE.
I THINK I'M BLEEDING OUT OF MY PORES.

joined channel #unixgurus
welcome sid060
Rayn3>hello sid060 how r u
sid060>Fine. Are the "a" "e" "y" and "o" keys missing from your keyboard?
Rayn3>no why
TAP TAP TIP
COPYRIGHT©2004 J.D. "Illiad" Frazer HTTP://WWW.USERFRIENDLY.ORG/

sid060>Why can`t you type out the words "are" and "you" instead of using "r" and "u?"

Rayn3>i don't type very fast
sid060>there's something to be said for using both hands to type.
TAKA TAKA TOK

sid060>Did you know that the abbreviations you and your "homeys" use are codes from the mainframe days?

Rayn3>what do u mean?

TIK TAK TAK

COPYRIGHT©2004 J.D. "Illiad" Frazer HTTP://WWW.USERFRIENDLY.ORG/

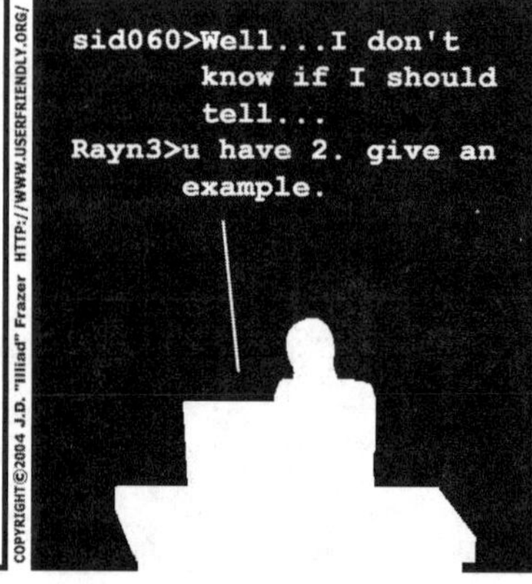
sid060>Well...I don't know if I should tell...
Rayn3>u have 2. give an example.

sid060>Okay. "how r u" is code for "I am absolutely bereft of gorm."
Rayn3>r u seri^H^H^H^H^H^H^H^H
TAP TIP ZING

sid060>So this is the #unixguru channel?
rayn3>ya
sid060>I'm a unix guy myself. Hope to share some knowledge here.
COPYRIGHT© 2004 J.D. "Illiad" Frazer HTTP://WWW.USERFRIENDLY.ORG/

sid060>You know, unix knowledge?
rayn3>wait, ur not a chick?

sid060>Wait a sec, I thought this channel is called #unixgurus.
Rayn3>it is d00d
sid060>Then why aren't there any unix experts here?
TAPPY TAPPY WAK WAK
COPYRIGHT© 2004 J.D. "Illiad" Frazer HTTP://WWW.USERFRIENDLY.ORG/

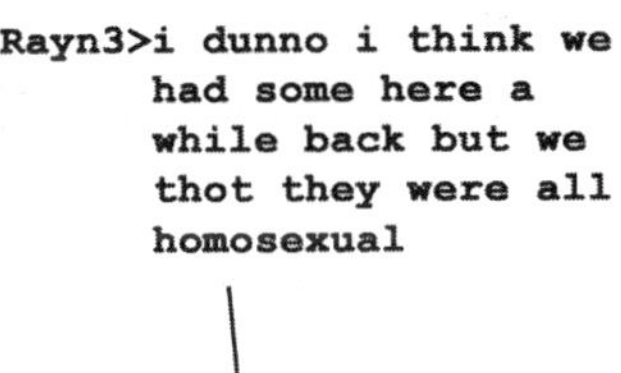
Rayn3>i dunno i think we had some here a while back but we thot they were all homosexual

sid060>What does that have to do with being expert at unix?!
Rayn3>r u a lesbian? cuz we think lesbians are h0t
TAKA TAKA

MEANWHILE, BACK ON THE BIREME...
GALLEY SLA- ER, I MEAN PROPULSION SPECIALISTS! I HAVE SOME GREAT NEWS! THE OFFICERS HAVE DECIDED TO EXAMINE THE IDEA OF PAYING YOU FOR OVERTIME HOURS!
EA
EA GAMES
AND HERE I WAS GETTING READY TO QUIT...
COPYRIGHT© 2004 J.D. "Illiad" Frazer HTTP://WWW.USERFRIENDLY.ORG/

HEY. NEW CAMERA?
YEP. I BOUGHT MYSELF AN EARLY CHRISTMAS PRESENT. IT'S A SIX-MEGAPIXEL DIGITAL.
WATCHA GONNA TAKE PICTURES OF?
COPYRIGHT©2004 J.D. "Illiad" Frazer HTTP://WWW.USERFRIENDLY.ORG/

GAH!! YOU SICK PUPPY!! ISN'T A MIRROR ENOUGH?
MIRRORS DON'T COME WITH WIDE-ANGLE LENSES.

THAT WENT WELL. I MUST SAY.
WHAT. FIRST PHOTOS WITH THE NEW CAMERA?
COPYRIGHT©2004 J.D. "Illiad" Frazer HTTP://WWW.USERFRIENDLY.ORG/

YES. OF ME IN NAUGHT BUT A TEATOWEL. AND I MADE A DESKTOP WALLPAPER OF IT JUST FOR MIRANDA.
THAT'LL SHOW HER WHAT SHE'S BEEN MISSING.

ARE THOSE TEARS FROM TERROR OR LAUGHING TOO HARD?
AS GOD IS MY WITNESS. I HAVE NO IDEA!

I got the idea from this strip from a couple of Aussies sitting behind me on a bus when I went to speak at SAGE-AU. The punch line was delivered with that dry Aussie wit. I have to go back!

STEF'S GONE QUITE MAD WITH THAT STUPID DIGITAL CAMERA OF HIS.
HE TAKES IT WITH HIM EVERYWHERE.
COPYRIGHT©2004 J.D. "Illiad" Frazer HTTP://WWW.USERFRIENDLY.ORG/

CHA-ZEE
CHA-ZZEE
CHA-ZEE
CHA-ZZEE

WHATEVER DID WE DO BEFORE DIGITAL CAMERAS?
PROBABLY ONLY TOOK SENSIBLE PHOTOS.

MIRANDA. I APOLOGIZE FOR THAT PHOTO OF MYSELF I PUT ON YOUR DESKTOP.
FINE. IT WAS WORTH A LAUGH.
COPYRIGHT©2004 J.D. "Illiad" Frazer HTTP://WWW.USERFRIENDLY.ORG/

WOULD IT BE OKAY IF I TOOK YOUR PHOTO? NOTHING PERVY. I JUST WANT TO TRY MY HAND AT PORTRAIT PHOTOGRAPHY.
I...GUESS SO.

NOW. DO THAT PHOTOSHOP THING YOU DO AND MOVE HER HEAD ONTO THAT PORN STAR'S BODY...
NO!!

I CAN'T BELIEVE STEF ASKED ME TO DO SOMETHING SO DISRESPECTFUL TO MIRANDA. TRANSPOSE HER HEAD ONTO A PORN STAR'S BODY? SHEESH.
COPYRIGHT © 2004 J.D. "Illiad" Frazer HTTP://WWW.USERFRIENDLY.ORG/
STOP! STOP! STOP! STOP!!
THIS IS JUST WRONG. I LIKE MIRANDA. I RESPECT HER. EVEN IF SHE DOES MAKE ME TURN INTO STILL LIFE ART WHEN SHE'S AROUND.
COPYRIGHT © 2004 J.D. "Illiad" Frazer HTTP://WWW.USERFRIENDLY.ORG/
SO I'M NOT GOING TO MESS WITH HER FACE IN PHOTOSHOP. NO BODY TRANSPOSITIONS. I WILL RESIST ALL TEMPTATION AND PREVAIL.
SHE'D BE PROUD OF ME.
A.J.. WHAT'S THAT ON YOUR SCR-- OH. MY. GOD.
INGUF! ATWA! EBBEH!!!

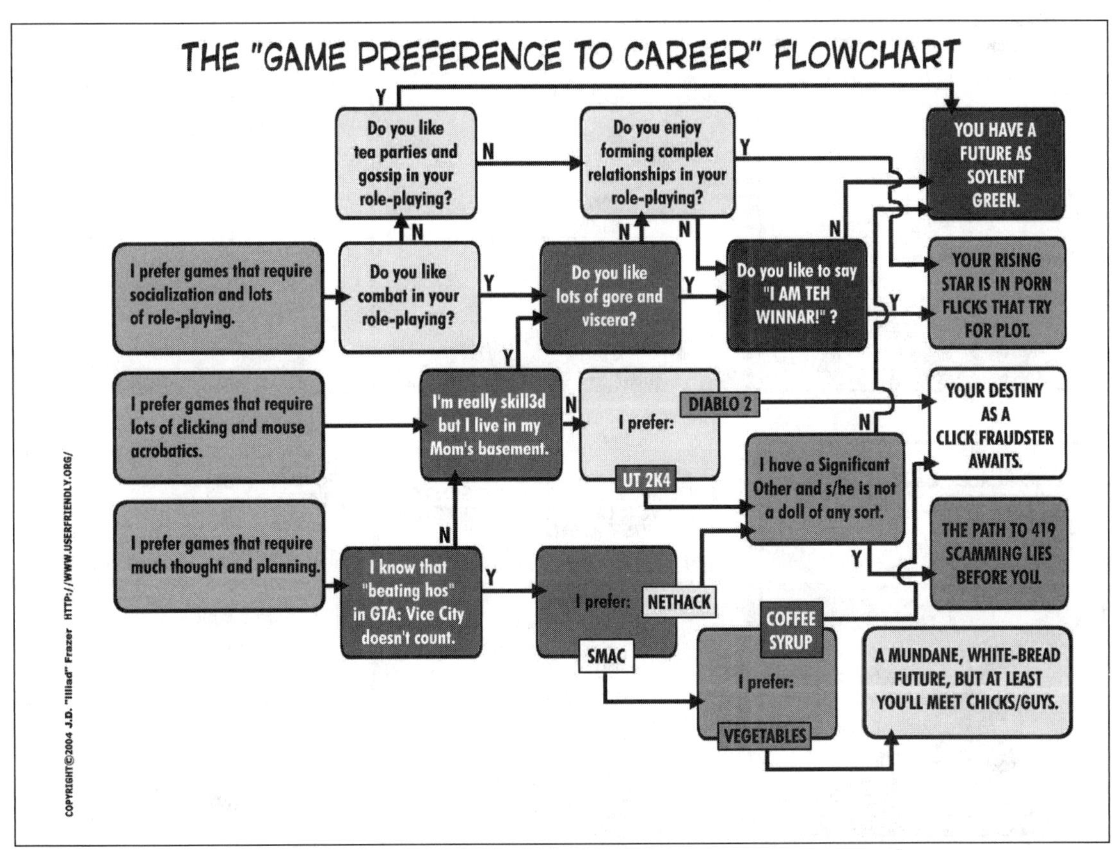
THE "GAME PREFERENCE TO CAREER" FLOWCHART
I prefer games that require socialization and lots of role-playing.
I prefer games that require lots of clicking and mouse acrobatics.
I prefer games that require much thought and planning.
Do you like tea parties and gossip in your role-playing?
Do you like combat in your role-playing?
Do you enjoy forming complex relationships in your role-playing?
Do you like lots of gore and viscera?
Do you like to say "I AM TEH WINNAR!" ?
I'm really skill3d but I live in my Mom's basement.
I prefer: DIABLO 2 UT 2K4
I have a Significant Other and s/he is not a doll of any sort.
I know that "beating hos" in GTA: Vice City doesn't count.
I prefer: NETHACK SMAC
I prefer: COFFEE SYRUP VEGETABLES
YOU HAVE A FUTURE AS SOYLENT GREEN.
YOUR RISING STAR IS IN PORN FLICKS THAT TRY FOR PLOT.
YOUR DESTINY AS A CLICK FRAUDSTER AWAITS.
THE PATH TO 419 SCAMMING LIES BEFORE YOU.
A MUNDANE, WHITE-BREAD FUTURE, BUT AT LEAST YOU'LL MEET CHICKS/GUYS.
Y
N
COPYRIGHT © 2004 J.D. "Illiad" Frazer HTTP://WWW.USERFRIENDLY.ORG/

IT'S GETTING CLOSE TO THAT TIME OF YEAR AGAIN.
YEP.
COPYRIGHT © 2004 J.D. "Illiad" Frazer HTTP://WWW.USERFRIENDLY.ORG/

THE TIME OF YEAR WHEN LOTS OF SMELLY, SQUEALING HUMANS RUSH ABOUT IN A MAD DASH TO BUY EVERYONE EXPENSIVE GIFTS THAT'LL BE RETURNED ANYWAY FOR SOMETHING THEY ACTUALLY WANT BUT DON'T NEED.
MM-HM.
HOW DID YOU COME UP WITH MAKING CHRISTMAS BECOME ALL ABOUT STRESS AND INCREASING CONSUMER DEBT?! GENIUS. PURE GENIUS.
OH STOP. YOU'RE MAKING ME BLUSH.

SO WHAT ELSE CAN WE DO TO PERVERT THE CHRISTMAS SEASON?
WHAT ABOUT REPLACING SANTA WITH ELECTRONIC ARTS UPPER MANAGEMENT?
COPYRIGHT © 2004 J.D. "Illiad" Frazer HTTP://WWW.USERFRIENDLY.ORG/

I SEE TINY ELVES CLAPPED IN IRONS.
...AND EVERY TOY A DUPLICATE OF LAST YEAR'S TOY BUT RENAMED AS THE "GOLD EDITION."

TECH SUPPORT. YOUR SERVILE MINION SPEAKING.
HELLO. YOU'RE A GEEK RIGHT?
YES. WHY?
COPYRIGHT © 2004 J.D. "Illiad" Frazer HTTP://WWW.USERFRIENDLY.ORG/

THIS YEAR I'M GETTING A LOT OF REQUESTS FOR GAMES LIKE "GTA: SAN ANDREAS," "HITMAN: CONTRACTS" AND "TOMB RAIDER: BOOB EXPLOSION."
AND THIS IS WHAT THE NICE CHILDREN WANT.

WAIT...SANTA? IS THAT YOU?
FER PETE'S SAKE WHAT HAPPENED TO GAMES LIKE PONG?!

THIS IS REALLY SANTA CLAUS? THE HAPPY FAT GUY IN THE RED AND WHITE OUTFIT?
WELL, YES.
COPYRIGHT © 2004 J.D. "Illiad" Frazer HTTP://WWW.USERFRIENDLY.ORG/

THIS IS SO AWESOME! WHEN I STOPPED GETTING PRESENTS FROM YOU EVERYONE SAID YOU WERE JUST A STORY.
BUT I SUSPECTED DEEP DOWN THAT YOU WERE REAL.

AND YOU, THE GREAT SAINT NICK, HAVE THE TIME TO TALK TO LITTLE OL' ME!
HAVEN'T YOU READ THE NEWS? LOTS OF "NAUGHTY" GOING ON THIS DECADE. I DON'T HAVE A LOT OF DELIVERIES TO DO.

HOW THE WORLD HAS CHANGED. EH SANTA? I'LL BET EVEN YOU'VE BEEN AFFECTED BY WORLD EVENTS.
NO COMMENT.

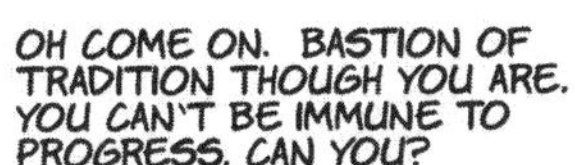
OH COME ON. BASTION OF TRADITION THOUGH YOU ARE. YOU CAN'T BE IMMUNE TO PROGRESS. CAN YOU?

NO COMMENT.

SANTA I'LL STILL LOVE YOU. JUST ADMIT IT.
THE WAREHOUSE IS IN CHINA AND THE ELVES ARE FROM INDIA. ARE YOU HAPPY NOW?

YOU SAID YOU DON'T HAVE THAT MUCH WORK BECAUSE OF LOTS OF "NAUGHTIES" THIS YEAR?
YES. THAT'S RIGHT.
ANYWHERE IN PARTICULAR?

WELL...LET'S SEE...

...THERE'S NOT A HECK OF A LOT TO DELIVER IN WASHINGTON D.C. THIS YEAR. OR ANY NATIONAL CAPITAL FOR THAT MATTER.
GO FIGURE.

IF THE FCC AND FAA LIFT BANS ON CELL PHONES IN THE AIR, THERE WILL BE...TROUBLE.

...AND SO I SAID. "NO. YOU CAN'T HAVE A PONY FOR CHRISTMAS..."
HARRY. LOOK OUT! DORK ON A CELL PHONE!!

ANYWAY. I HAVE A LIST OF EVERY CHILD ON THIS EARTH PLUS THEIR SHIPPING ADDRESSES...
SANTA. SANTA. SANTA...
COPYRIGHT©2004 J.D. "Illiad" Frazer HTTP://WWW.USERFRIENDLY.ORG/
DUDE. YOU NEED TO JOIN US IN THE 21ST CENTURY! ELECTRONIC DATA IS WHERE IT'S AT! GET RID OF THAT ANALOG PAPER-AND-PENCIL CRAP AND DIGITIZE!

SO...GIVE A QUICK CALL TO DIEBOLD. SHALL I?
NO! SWEET FANCY MOSES. NO!!!

One wonders: what would someone like Scott Richter give Santa in exchange for said database?

FOR YOUR INFORMATION I AM USING A DATABASE.
SANTA! YOU'RE A GEEK? THAT'S BEYOND COOL!
COPYRIGHT©2004 J.D. "Illiad" Frazer HTTP://WWW.USERFRIENDLY.ORG/

I GUESS. ANYWAY...COULD YOU TELL ME HOW TO GET IN TOUCH WITH THAT SCOTT RICHTER GUY? I THINK I SCRUBBED HIM FROM MY LIST FOR BEING IRREVOCABLY NAUGHTY.
SCOTT RICHTER THE SPAM KING? SURE. HIS EMAIL IS-

HEY...WAIT A MINUTE!
DAMN.

SANTA. ARE YOU SUGGESTING THAT YOU'RE GOING TO SELL YOUR DATABASE TO SPAMMERS?!
SORRY. LOST MY HEAD THERE FOR A SECOND.
COPYRIGHT©2004 J.D. "Illiad" Frazer HTTP://WWW.USERFRIENDLY.ORG/

IT'S COLD UP HERE YOU KNOW. COLD AND DARK. AND LATELY EVERY YEAR IT'S THE SAME THING. EVERYONE WANTS AN I-THIS OR AN E-THAT.
SO I WAS THINKING A TRIP FOR ME AND MRS. CLAUS TO TAHITI WOULD BE GOOD.

MAYBE I COULD JUST SELL A SMALL PART OF THE LIST?
NORAD TRACKS YOU EVERY CHRISTMAS EVE. MISTER.
OH. MAYBE NOT THEN.

WELL. THANKS FOR THE TALK. THE NAUGHTY AND NICE LIST WILL REMAIN SAFE WITH ME.
NO PROBLEM BIG GUY. THAT'S WHY I'M HERE.
COPYRIGHT©2004 J.D. "Illiad" Frazer HTTP://WWW.USERFRIENDLY.ORG/

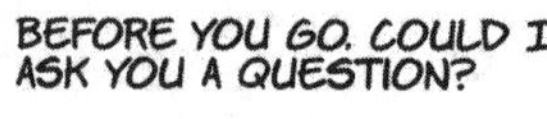
BEFORE YOU GO. COULD I ASK YOU A QUESTION?

SURE THING. SON.

"PEARL DABSTER." NAUGHTY?
COAL FOR YOU THIS CHRISTMAS FOR ASKING!

DON'T BE USING THAT LAPTOP ON YOUR LAP IF YOU WANT TO HAVE LITTLE GREGS IN THE FUTURE.
EH? WHAT ARE YOU ON ABOUT?

COPYRIGHT©2004 J.D. "Illiad" Frazer HTTP://WWW.USERFRIENDLY.ORG/
THERE WAS A NEWS ARTICLE A COUPLE OF WEEKS AGO ABOUT HOW THE HEAT FROM A LAPTOP CAN KILL OFF ALL OF YOUR "TADPOLES" IF YOU USE THE LAPTOP ON YOUR LAP.
OH DEAR.

THIS LAPTOP IS THE BEST CHRISTMAS GIFT I'VE RECEIVED IN YEARS. BUT WHY DO YOU WANT TO TAKE MY DESK AWAY IN EXCHANGE?
IT'S TO HELP THE ENVIRONMENT STEF. TRUST ME.

WAS THAT WHAT YOU GOT FOR CHRISTMAS?!
YEP. A 42" PLASMA TELEVISION!
WOOO!

COPYRIGHT©2004 J.D. "Illiad" Frazer HTTP://WWW.USERFRIENDLY.ORG/
SO, WHAT DID YOU GET?
FIRST CLASS MEDITERRANEAN CRUISE TICKETS!
WOW!

WATCHA GET?
30 MINUTES ON THE PHONE WITH MY FAMILY.
SANTA WAS GOOD TO YOU, MAN.

It's a rough, difficult job, and they're doing it for us.

ITEMS THAT STORES COULD MAKE A KILLING WITH THE DAY AFTER A GEEK CHRISTMAS

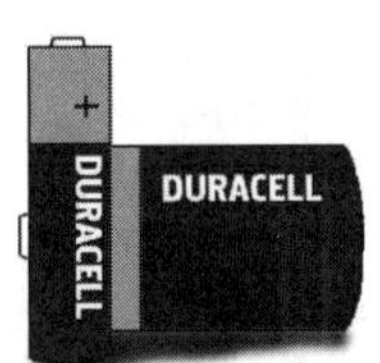
DURACELL
DURACELL

FOR PLAYING A LONG TIME

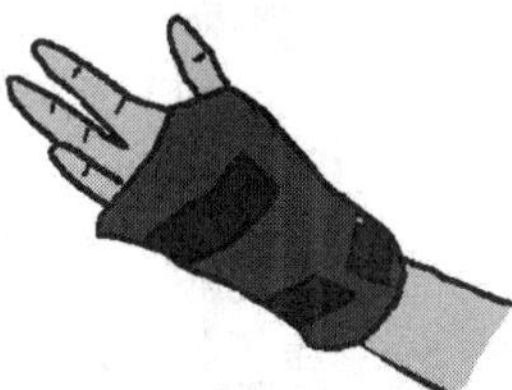

FOR PLAYING FOR SO LONG

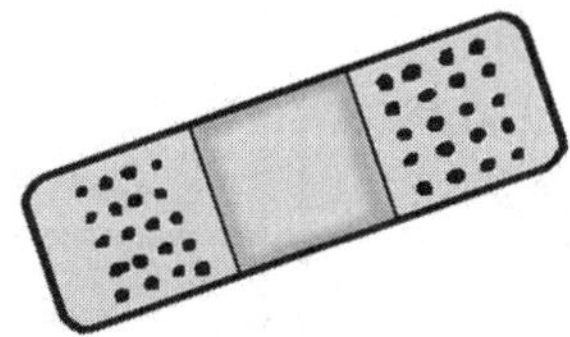

ALSO FOR PLAYING FOR SO LONG

FOR PLAYING FOR SO LONG IN THE SAME SPOT IN THE GAME

WHY SO GLUM? YOU GUYS GET CRAPPY CHRISTMAS PRESENTS?
ONE OF OUR CUSTOMERS EXPERIENCED A DDOS OVER THE HOLIDAYS.
WHO?
COPYRIGHT © 2004 J.D. "Illiad" Frazer HTTP://WWW.USERFRIENDLY.ORG/

BUY-MART. THEIR TRANSACTION SERVER GROUND TO A HALT JUST BEFORE CHRISTMAS WHEN THOUSANDS OF CUSTOMERS TRIED TO ORDER FROM A LIMITED SUPPLY OF "PICKLE ME CTHULHU" DOLLS.

FROM HIGHLY-SKILLED SYSADMINS TO TRAMPLED STORE CLERKS IN SECONDS. HOW DOES IT FEEL?
SHUT UP! JUST SHUT UP!!

OKAY. LOOKS LIKE THE BUY-MART SERVER IS BACK UP. AND THEIR DATABASE IS STILL INTACT.
COPYRIGHT © 2004 J.D. "Illiad" Frazer HTTP://WWW.USERFRIENDLY.ORG/

WOW. THEY'RE STILL BACK-ORDERED ON A COUPLE OF HUNDRED DOLLS. SOME PEOPLE DIDN'T GET THEM IN TIME FOR CHRISTMAS.
TOO LATE FOR THEM I GUESS. NOTHING THEY CAN DO ABOUT IT.

I WATCHED THE COURIER DELIVER THE DOLL TO YOUR DOOR MRS. FECKBITZ. NOW GIVE IT UP.

MRS. FECKBITZ. IF YOU DON'T COME OUT HERE **RIGHT NOW** WITH THAT PICKLE-ME-CTHULHU DOLL. I'LL BE FORCED TO DISPENSE JUSTICE.
COPYRIGHT © 2004 J.D. "Illiad" Frazer HTTP://WWW.USERFRIENDLY.ORG/

AH. THERE YOU ARE...

NOW LET'S GO HAVE A COFFEE AND TALK ABOUT THIS LIKE ADULTS...
BRUTUS. KILL.

MRS. FECKBITZ. THAT WASN'T NICE. BUT AS YOU CAN SEE I'M BACK. AND I HAVE EVERY INTENTION OF SEEING THIS THROUGH. MY LITTLE GIRL DESERVES TO HAVE THAT DOLL.
COPYRIGHT © 2004 J.D. "Illiad" Frazer HTTP://WWW.USERFRIENDLY.ORG/

MRS. FECKBITZ? I FEEL IT'S ONLY FAIR TO WARN YOU THAT YOU'RE FACING A FAMILY OF GEEKS.

NO RESPONSE. PLAN B. KATIE.
IA! IA! CTHULHU FHTAGN!
UH OH.

LOOK. WHAT DO YOU WANT THAT SLOPPY. CREEPY DOLL FOR ANYWAY?
MY KID WANTS IT. THAT'S ENOUGH REASON FOR ME.
...WGAH'NAGL FHTAGN!

COPYRIGHT©2004 J.D. "Illiad" Frazer HTTP://WWW.USERFRIENDLY.ORG/
BUT WHY DOES YOUR **KID** WANT IT? HAVE YOU EVEN THOUGHT ABOUT THAT?

LOOK. SHE'S A GEEK. AND GEEKS GET INTO WEIRD THINGS. ACCEPT IT!
DAD. I THINK I WEIRDLY FORGOT TO DRAW AN ELDER SIGN.

2005. ANOTHER YEAR.
WHAT DOES THE TURN OF THE YEAR REALLY SIGNIFY A.J?

COPYRIGHT©2005 J.D. "Illiad" Frazer HTTP://WWW.USERFRIENDLY.ORG/
IT SIGNIFIES PROGRESS FOR THE HUMAN RACE. IT HERALDS THE END OF THE OLD YEAR AND THE BEGINNING OF THE NEW. IT BRING TIDINGS OF HOPE AND A CHANGE IN FORTUNE...

AND IT GIVES EA SPORTS AN EXCUSE TO MAKE NHL. NFL AND FIFA 2005...
WELL. THAT JUST SET THE TONE FOR THE NEW YEAR. DIDN'T IT.

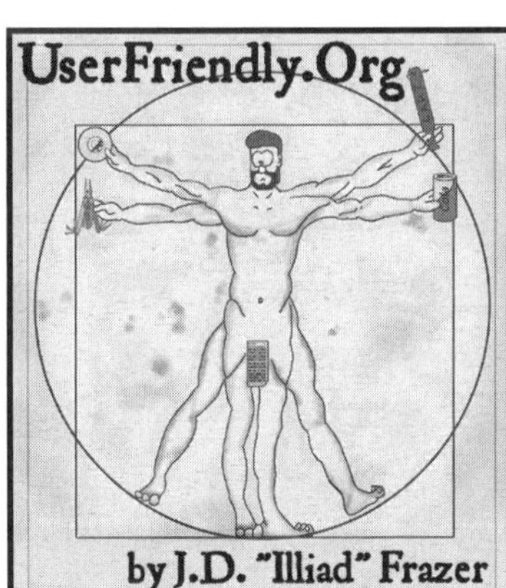
UserFriendly.Org
by J.D. "Illiad" Frazer

COPYRIGHT©2005 J.D. "Illiad" Frazer HTTP://WWW.USERFRIENDLY.ORG/
BILL? THOSE MOZILLA GUYS HAVE SNAGGED MORE BROWSER MARKET-SHARE. THEY'RE UP TO SIX PERCENT.
SO?
Microsoft

SO. INTERNET EXPLORER MARKET-SHARE IS DOWN BY ALMOST A FULL PERCENT.
YOU'RE SUGGESTING SOMETHING BY THOSE TWO STATEMENTS THAT'S MAKING THE VEIN IN MY FOREHEAD THROB.
Microsoft

IT'S GONNA BE HARD TO STOP THIS FIREFOX THING BILL. THEY'VE RAISED ENOUGH MONEY TO RUN ADS IN THE NEW YORK TIMES. THEY HAVE DEEP GRASSROOTS SUPPORT. AND THEY'RE IMMUNE TO CASH BUYOUTS.

IT'S THAT WHOLE OPEN-SOURCE THING.

WE CAN'T BUY THEM?
NO. BILL.

THAT **HAS** TO BE ILLEGAL OR SOMETHING.
IT ISN'T YET. BUT WE CAN FIX THAT.

THAT WAS A HELL OF AN OFFICE PARTY.
YE GODLINGS. THERE'S A LITTLE MAN INSIDE MY HEAD DIGGING HIS WAY OUT WITH A CHISEL
COPYRIGHT© 2005 J.D. "Illiad" Frazer HTTP://WWW.USERFRIENDLY.ORG/

MY TONGUE FEELS LIKE A SWEATSOCK.
AND I FEEL SO DEHYDRATED I COULD SPONGE UP AN OCEAN.
I ATE TOO MUCH OF SOMETHING TOO.

YES WAITRESS. ANOTHER GLASS OF THAT FINE DESSICANT PLEASE.
DUDE. DID YOU SEE WHERE THAT BAG OF SILICA GEL PACKETS WENT?

A bunch of us went to watch the *Lord of the Rings* trilogy back-to-back at the local cineplex. The first two movies were shown in extended form, and the third was shown in the original theatrical form. The screening started at around 12:00 noon and went past 1:00 a.m., with short breaks between the films. The Subway shop next to the cineplex—the only place you could buy food that wasn't popcorn, candy, or those disgusting nachos in the orange "cheese" sauce—wasn't prepared for the rush of business. They had exactly one clerk, who took money and orders and made the sandwiches. When we showed up at Subway between *The Two Towers* and *The Return of the King*, we had 30 minutes before the next show, and 20 or so people were in line ahead of us. At the front of the line was a 12- or 13-year-old paying for his sandwich with pennies. Hundreds of pennies, which the clerk had to count. We skipped the sandwiches. We had beer on empty stomachs. Gollum was never so amusing.

WHERE ARE ALL OF THE GEEKS?
THEY'RE STILL HAVING THEIR OWN NEW YEAR'S PARTY.
COPYRIGHT© 2005 J.D. "Illiad" Frazer HTTP://WWW.USERFRIENDLY.ORG/

STILL?! WHAT THE HELL ARE THEY DOING TO HAVE A PARTY LAST FOR FOUR DAYS?
I WAS TOLD "A BACK-TO-BACK SHOWING OF THE ENTIRE LORD OF THE RINGS TRILOGY. EXTENDED EDITION."

OHMYGODOHMYGOD OHMYGOD!! NEW STUFF! NEEWWWW STUUUUFFF!
JUST LIKE IT WAS THE LAST EIGHT TIMES WE SAW IT.

WOW. SOME GUY BOUGHT A TROPICAL ISLAND IN A VIRTUAL GAME WORLD FOR OVER $25,000.
WHAT? YOU MEAN REAL MONEY?
COPYRIGHT© 2005 J.D. "Illiad" Frazer HTTP://WWW.USERFRIENDLY.ORG/

YES. IN U.S. DOLLARS.
BUT WHY WOULD ANYONE PAY REAL MONEY FOR A FAKE ISLAND?

BECAUSE THERE ARE PEOPLE WHO WILL PAY TO BUILD FAKE HOUSES ON THE FAKE LOTS THEY'RE GOING TO BUY ON THAT FAKE ISLAND.
SO HOW DO I GET A FAKE ISLAND FOR MYSELF? CALL UP A FAKE REAL ESTATE AGENT?

hi, are you the idiot who bought that virtual island?
Um...I'm the deedholder if that's what you mean.
ah.
COPYRIGHT© 2005 J.D. "Illiad" Frazer HTTP://WWW.USERFRIENDLY.ORG/

Hello?
so, how much for the oil drilling rights?

Wait a second. First you call me an idiot for buying this island then you ask me about drilling rights?
So I spoke too soon...

Let's skip the drilling rights. How about you just rent me some space on the island to start?
Fine. But why do I get the feeling this is a bad idea?

STEF
the man, the musk, the magic!
Call: 555-0069
Hot Chicks Only

Stef, you there?
Hey there mr. island guy! How's life in the virtual tropics?
Not so hot.

COPYRIGHT© 2005 J.D. "Illiad" Frazer HTTP://WWW.USERFRIENDLY.ORG/

Why's that? Weren't you getting hundreds of interested parties visiting your virtual island to scope out property?
Because after anyone sees your billboard they disconnect.

Oh. What does that mean?
It means I'm gonna go buy a virtual atomic warhead and rename my island "Bikini Atoll."

A LITTLE PERSPECTIVE FOR 2005

BANKRUPT. LIFE IS OVER.
VISA
YOU OWE
$$$

SOMEONE
BELOVED
~
SOUTH
ASIA
2005

COPYRIGHT© 2005 J.D. "Illiad" Frazer HTTP://WWW.USERFRIENDLY.ORG/

The tsunami that hit southeast Asia, although distant, struck close to home. But there were still reports on the news of people complaining about the price of Starbucks coffee, and how they couldn't afford the latest Gucci handbag.

NEW GAME FOR CHRISTMAS?
YEAH. JUST OPENING IT NOW.

WHAT'S IT ABOUT?
HERE'S THE MANUAL.

SIM-E.A. EXECUTIVE.
"THE GAME OF ACQUISITION AND REPRESSION. SURE TO SET OFF THE AMORAL SOCIOPATH IN YOUR FAMILY."
IT COMES WITH LEG IRONS.

THAT'S TAKING A WHILE TO INSTALL.
YEAH. MUST BE A LOT OF CONTENT IN THE GAME.

BEEP
'SIM-E.A. EXECUTIVE' INSTALLED SUCCESSFULLY!
WOOO! HERE WE GO...

YOU ARE A VP-LEVEL EXECUTIVE AT ELECTRONIC ARTS AND ARE RAPACIOUSLY WEALTHY. YOU HAVE WON!
NOW THE FUN BEGINS.
OOOG.

MR. E.A. VICE PRESIDENT:
* YOUR PROJECTS ARE ALL BEHIND SCHEDULE.
* YOUR PROJECTS ARE ALL UNDERFUNDED.
* YOUR DEVELOPERS ARE NEARLY EXHAUSTED.

* MARKETING IS VERY WELL FUNDED.
* YOU'VE JUST THROWN A PARTY IN PALM SPRINGS FOR ALL OF THE EXECUTIVES.
* YOU HAD YOUR TEETH POLISHED.

PLEASE CHOOSE ONE:
A) FIRE THE DEVELOPERS AND HIRE CHEAPER ROOKIES.
B) SHIP THE UNFINISHED PRODUCTS AND RELEASE PATCHES LATER.
C) BUY YOURSELF YOUR SEVENTH FERRARI.
D) ALL OF THE ABOVE.
D.
YOU HAVE BEEN PROMOTED TO SENIOR VICE PRESIDENT. WELL DONE!

MIKE, GOT A SEC? I NEED YOU TO TRANS-LATE SOMETHING FOR ME.
YA?
WHAT DOES "GORMLESS" MEAN?

WHY, ONE WHO IS BEREFT OF GORM OF COURSE.
AH. THANKS.

WHICH MEANS WHAT?!
QUOD ERAT DEMONSTRANDUM.

ALL THIS YELLINK.
IT IS FOR WHAT?
STEF WANTS TO KNOW WHAT "GORMLESS" MEANS.
COPYRIGHT© 2005 J.D. "Illiad" Frazer HTTP://WWW.USERFRIENDLY.ORG/

AH. IS WERY FINE WORD. DEFINITIVE OF COMRADE STEF.
YES. I'D SAY HE'S WITHOUT GORM.

HE IS GORM HOLE.
HE HAS A GORM HORIZON. ALL GORM THAT FALLS PAST IT IS LOST FOREVER.
WHAT DOES IT MEAN?!?!

YOUR "BOYZ" MIKE AND PITR ARE DRIVING ME LOOPY. THEY WON'T TELL ME WHAT "GORMLESS" MEANS.
WELL. LET'S SEE WHAT THE DICTIONARY SAYS ABOUT THE WORD "GORM."
COPYRIGHT© 2005 J.D. "Illiad" Frazer HTTP://WWW.USERFRIENDLY.ORG/

WHATEVER IT IS. APPARENTLY I DON'T HAVE IT.
AH. IT SAYS IT'S A VARIATION OF THE WORD "GAUM" WHICH IS "TO SMUDGE OR SMEAR."

SO I'M...WITHOUT SMUDGE? THAT'S GOOD RIGHT?
SO GOOD YOU SHOULD RUN RIGHT OUT AND GET A SHIRT THAT SAYS "GORMLESS" ON IT. WEAR IT TO PARTIES.

A TV COMMERCIAL FOR THE MAC MINI THAT SADLY DIDN'T MAKE THE CUT.

keyboard and mouse,
you complete me!

PEOPLE, IT'S A NEW YEAR AND A NEW ERA. IN 2005, COLUMBIA INTERNET WILL REACH HEIGHTS OF SUCCESS THAT HAVE ONLY BEEN IMAGINED BEFORE!
UH OH.

COPYRIGHT © 2005 J.D. "Illiad" Frazer HTTP://WWW.USERFRIENDLY.ORG/
DURING OUR RETREAT TO TAHITI, SMILING MAN AND I REVIEWED OUR NEXT STEPS AS A COMPANY. CLEARLY IN TODAY'S WORLD OF RAPID CHANGES, WE NEED TO BE QUICKER ON THE UPTAKE AND MORE FLEXIBLE.
SO WE'RE INVESTING IN EXTRA TRAINING FOR THE TECHS!

COOL! WE GET FREE TRAINING! WHERE'S IT AT?
"CAMP DOT MIL. MILITARY BOOT CAMP FOR CIVILIAN PANTY-WAISTS."

WHERE'VE YOU BEEN, MIKE? THE BUS TO CAMP DOT MIL IS LEAVING IN A FEW MINUTES!
SORRY. I WAS HELPING PITR WITH HIS STUFF.

COPYRIGHT © 2005 J.D. "Illiad" Frazer HTTP://WWW.USERFRIENDLY.ORG/
PITR?
DA. AM RIGHT HERE.

FORGIVE ME IF THIS QUESTION SEEMS ODD, BUT WHY ARE YOU BRINGING EMPTY SHIPPING CRATES ADDRESSED TO YOURSELF?
AM GOINK TO BE NEAR MUCH MILITARY EQUIPMENT. DA?

This storyline was a lot of fun for me. I'd wanted to join the Canadian Reserves (either Naval Intelligence or Army Medic) for some time but never got around to it. When I finally had the chance, my first child had been born. He was too young for me to potentially disappear for months at a time. Maybe another day ...

OUR BRAVE, UNKNOWING RECRUITS ARRIVE...
WELCOME TO CAMP DOT MIL! THIS OUTSTANDING LOCALE WILL BE YOUR HOME AND MY SANDBOX FOR THE NEXT TWO WEEKS! I AM MASTER SERGEANT BANGALORE AND I WILL BE YOUR MOMMA, YOUR PAPA AND YOUR WORST NIGHTMARE ALL ROLLED INTO ONE!
CAMP DOT MIL
BUNGTON, CANADA

COPYRIGHT © 2005 J.D. "Illiad" Frazer HTTP://WWW.USERFRIENDLY.ORG/
YOU WILL SLEEP WHEN I SAY "SLEEP!" AND YOU WILL RUN WHEN I SAY "RUN!" BY THE SPIKED YAMSACK OF ARES. WHAT ARE YOU DOING WITH YOUR HAND UP MISTER?!
CAMP DOT MIL
BUNGTON, CANADA

SORRY. I WAS LISTENING TO MY IPOD. COULD YOU REPEAT EVERYTHING?
FRONT AND CENTRE MAGGOT!!!
CAMP DOT MIL
BUNGTON, CANADA

LISTEN UP LADIES! WE'RE GOING TO START OFF YOUR HOLIDAY HERE AT CAMP DOT MIL WITH-
EXCUSE ME.
BY ZEUS' HANGING MARBLES. WHAT ARE YOU DOING INTERRUPTING ME?!

COPYRIGHT © 2005 J.D. "Illiad" Frazer HTTP://WWW.USERFRIENDLY.ORG/
I FIND YOUR USE OF THE WORD "LADIES" AS A PEJORATIVE OFFENSIVE. AND IN CASE YOU HADN'T NOTICED, I'M FEMALE.

AND HERE I WAS THINKING YOU WERE JUST A SKINNY GUY WITH DELUSIONS OF ADEQUACY. I CAN ADMIT IT WHEN I'M HALF WRONG.
WHAT?! YOU! BUT...OOOO! YOU...

LADIES! YOU WILL ADDRESS ME AS MASTER SERGEANT AND PREFACE ALL YOU SAY TO ME WITH THIS TITLE. IS THAT CLEAR?
MASTER SERGEANT. YES MASTER SERGEANT. I HAVE A QUESTION.
COPYRIGHT © 2005 J.D. "Illiad" Frazer HTTP://WWW.USERFRIENDLY.ORG/

BY THE WRINKLED JEWEL BAG OF THE COLOSSUS! DO ALL OF YOU PEOPLE HAVE SOMETHING TO SAY?!
MASTER SERGEANT. AREN'T WE SUPPOSED TO GET SOME KIND OF SUPER GEEK TRAINING HERE?

KISS THE GROUND MAGGOT AND GIMME FIFTY!!
UH...FIFTY WHAT?

THAT LOOKS LIKE IT HURTS.
I DON'T THINK I'VE DONE A PUSH-UP SINCE I WAS BORN.
POOR GREG.
EHHH
ENGFEH
EHH!
COPYRIGHT © 2005 J.D. "Illiad" Frazer HTTP://WWW.USERFRIENDLY.ORG/

START OVER MAGGOT!! AND COUNT OUT LOUD!
MASTER SERGEANT! YES. MASTER SERGEANT!

WASN'T THERE SUPPOSED TO BE A GEEK COMPONENT TO THIS TRAINING?
MASTER SERGEANT. ONE! MASTER SERGEANT. TWO!
IN BINARY. MAGGOT!!!
THERE YOU GO.

USER FRIENDLY
the comic strip
BY J.D. "ILLIAD" FRAZER
COPYRIGHT © 2005 J.D. "Illiad" Frazer HTTP://WWW.USERFRIENDLY.ORG/

MICROSOFT SAID WEDNESDAY THAT IT HAS STARTED OFFERING A PAID-SUBSCRIPTION VERSION OF ITS OUTLOOK E-MAIL PROGRAM. THE SERVICE ALLOWS OUTLOOK 2003 TO CONNECT WITH HOTMAIL OR MSN E-MAIL ACCOUNTS.

FOR $59 A YEAR, CUSTOMERS GET AN E-MAIL ACCOUNT WITH 2GB OF STORAGE AND THE ABILITY TO SEND MESSAGES WITH A 20MB ATTACHMENT CAP PER E-MAIL.
SO...I GIVE THEM $59 A YEAR AND THEY HOOK UP A SEPTIC TANK TO A SPRAY HOSE. NICE.

I SUPPOSE I'D BETTER SIGN ON FOR THIS AND TEST IT OUT. THE CHIEF IS GOING TO ASK. I'M SURE...
YOUR $59 HAS BEEN HOOVERED OUT OF YOUR ACCOUNT! WELCOME TO "HOTLOOK!"

AND FOR AN ADDITIONAL $99 YOU CAN TURN FEATURES OFF AS WELL AS ON!
HI! I'M CLIPPY! WOULD YOU LIKE TO SEND AN EMAIL?
AAAAAAAAAAAA

CHA-CHING
CHA-CHING
CHA-CHING
CHA-CHING
CHA-CHING
CHA-CHING
HEH. MUN-NEE.
Microsoft

I CAN'T FEEL MY FINGERS. I'M NEVER GOING TO TYPE AGAIN...AND MY ARMS FEEL LIKE NOODLES.
ALL RIGHT MAGGOTS. GET SOME SHUT-EYE! REVEILLE IS AT O-DARK-HUNDRED!
COPYRIGHT © 2005 J.D. "Illiad" Frazer HTTP://WWW.USERFRIENDLY.ORG/

KLIK!

WAKE UP LADIES!! IT'S ANOTHER GLORIOUS DAY AT CAMP DOT MIL!
KLIK!

TRAINING COMPOUND
I THOUGHT THIS WAS GEEK TRAINING. WHY ARE WE BEING TORTURED?
IF IT DOESN'T GET GEEKY SOON I'M GOING TO POP.
COPYRIGHT © 2005 J.D. "Illiad" Frazer HTTP://WWW.USERFRIENDLY.ORG/

OLD iMACS! WE'RE FINALLY GOING TO DO SOME COMPUTING!
I DUNNO. I HAVE A BAD FEELING ABOUT THIS.
iMac
iMac
iMac

I WILL REFRAIN FROM MAKING THE COMMENT THAT iMACS ARE A BURDEN.
MOMMA. MOMMA. CAN'T YOU SEE? LOOK WHAT YOUR BASEMENT'S DONE TO ME!

LADIES! AS PART OF THE EXCEPTIONAL TRAINING YOU ARE RECEIVING HERE AT CAMP DOT MIL, YOU WILL BE TRAVERSING OUR CONFIDENCE COURSE! PART OF THIS COURSE INCLUDES A TEN-KILOMETRE RUN WITH A FULL KIT!
COPYRIGHT © 2005 J.D. "Illiad" Frazer HTTP://WWW.USERFRIENDLY.ORG/

I SEE FEAR IN YOUR EYES! LADIES AND MAGGOTS. EXERCISE IS NOT TO BE FEARED!!
MASTER SERGEANT. WE'RE ALL GEEKS. SO WE'RE JUST WONDERING WHAT IT IS YOU'LL HAVE CHASING US

WELL LADIES. I HOPE YOU ENJOYED YOUR BRISK MORNING JOG!
FIVE MINUTE BREATHER. AND THEN OFF WE GO TO THE MONKEY BARS!
PUFF
HUFF
ASPHYXIATE
WHEEZE
COPYRIGHT © 2005 J.D. "Illiad" Frazer HTTP://WWW.USERFRIENDLY.ORG/

MASTER SERGEANT. HOW IS THIS SUPPOSED TO HELP US BE BETTER TECHS?
SON. CAMP DOT MIL WAS CREATED TO TURN LARD-ARSE LAYABOUTS LIKE YOU INTO LEAN. MEAN. TECHNICAL MACHINES! AFTER THIS COURSE YOU WILL BE ABLE TO RESPOND TO MISSION CRITICAL INCIDENTS SWIFTLY AND DECISIVELY!

MASTER SERGEANT. INSTEAD OF BECOMING BETTER PACK MULES. COULDN'T WE JUST LEARN TO TYPE FASTER?!
THIS IS WHAT THEY'RE SENDING ME THESE DAYS. I MISS THE PUNCHCARD BOYS. HARD-CORE. EVERY ONE OF THEM.

YOU PEOPLE ARE A DISGRACE! YOU CALL YOURSELVES TECHNOLOGISTS? JUST LOOK AT YOU!
COPYRIGHT © 2005 J.D. "Illiad" Frazer HTTP://WWW.USERFRIENDLY.ORG/

IN MY DAY, TECHNOLOGISTS WERE TOUGH AND EDGY! IT WAS AN ERA WHEN NEW IDEAS COULD BECOME THE SPIRIT OF A GENERATION! IT WAS A TIME OF CONFLICT, TRUE EXPERIMENTATION AND PUSHING THE ENVELOPE!!

MASTER SERGEANT, WOULD THAT ERA BE VIETNAM?
NO, JENNICAM. BY APOLLO'S JOY-NUGGETS I'M A FOSSIL.

MAGGOTS! TODAY WILL BE DEVOTED TO GEEK WEAPONS AND THEIR USE IN CUBE FARMS!
MASTER SERGEANT, WHERE ARE THE HEALTH POWER-UPS?
WEAPONS RANGE
COPYRIGHT © 2005 J.D. "Illiad" Frazer HTTP://WWW.USERFRIENDLY.ORG/

YOU DON'T GET NONE SON. THIS IS REAL LIFE. IN REAL LIFE THERE ARE NO RE-SPAWNS ON THE BATTLEFIELD.
WHOA...
WEAPONS RANGE

ON THE SAME NOTE, IN REAL LIFE YOU CAN TAKE A LEAD PIPE TO THAT MOUTHY DWEEB WHO TRASH-TALKED YOU.
MASTER SERGEANT, WHEN DO WE GET TO PRACTICE THAT PART?
WEAPONS RANGE

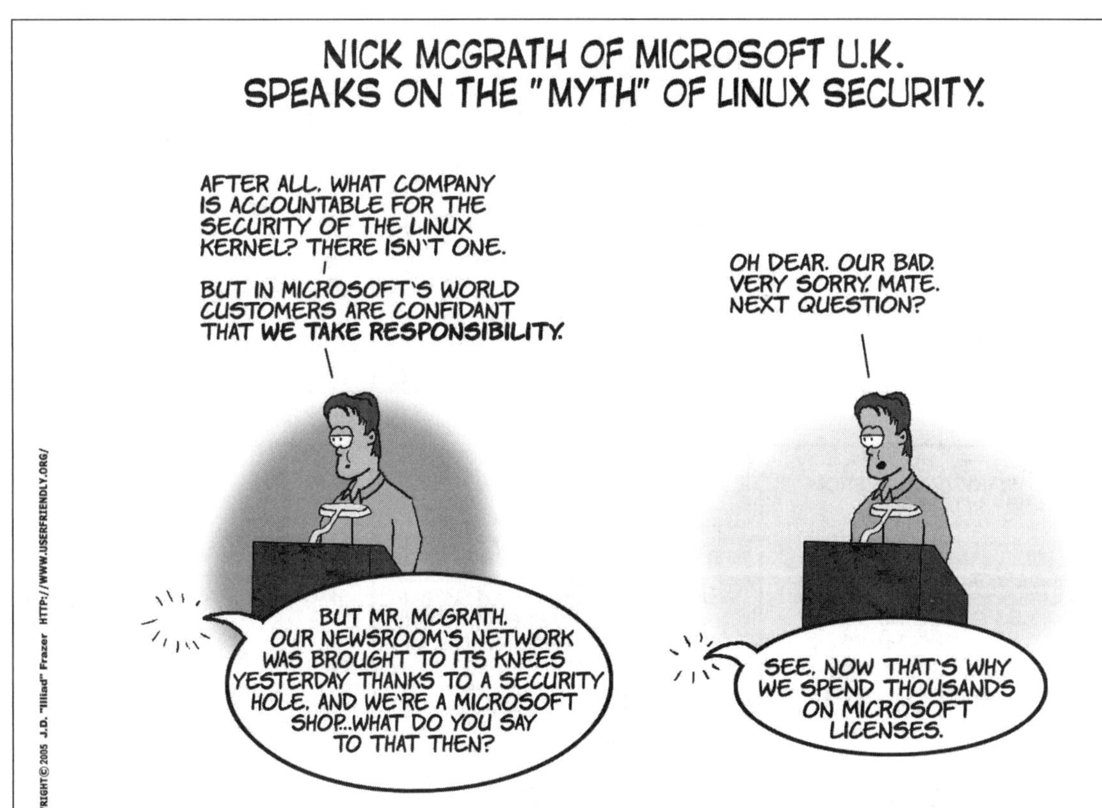
NICK MCGRATH OF MICROSOFT U.K. SPEAKS ON THE "MYTH" OF LINUX SECURITY.
AFTER ALL, WHAT COMPANY IS ACCOUNTABLE FOR THE SECURITY OF THE LINUX KERNEL? THERE ISN'T ONE.
BUT IN MICROSOFT'S WORLD CUSTOMERS ARE CONFIDANT THAT WE TAKE RESPONSIBILITY.
BUT MR. MCGRATH, OUR NEWSROOM'S NETWORK WAS BROUGHT TO ITS KNEES YESTERDAY THANKS TO A SECURITY HOLE, AND WE'RE A MICROSOFT SHOP...WHAT DO YOU SAY TO THAT THEN?
OH DEAR. OUR BAD. VERY SORRY, MATE. NEXT QUESTION?
SEE, NOW THAT'S WHY WE SPEND THOUSANDS ON MICROSOFT LICENSES.
COPYRIGHT © 2005 J.D. "Illiad" Frazer HTTP://WWW.USERFRIENDLY.ORG/

To Mr. McGrath's credit, he pinned up a copy of this strip in his office.

THIS IS MY COMPUTER. THERE ARE MANY LIKE IT. BUT THIS ONE IS MINE.

COPYRIGHT© 2005 J.D. "Illiad" Frazer HTTP://WWW.USERFRIENDLY.ORG/
MY COMPUTER IS MY BEST FRIEND. IT IS MY LIFE. I MUST MASTER IT AS I HAVE NO OTHER LIFE.

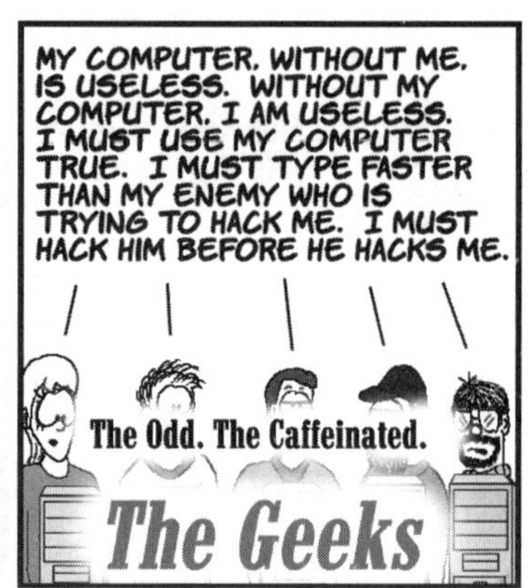
MY COMPUTER, WITHOUT ME, IS USELESS. WITHOUT MY COMPUTER, I AM USELESS. I MUST USE MY COMPUTER TRUE. I MUST TYPE FASTER THAN MY ENEMY WHO IS TRYING TO HACK ME. I MUST HACK HIM BEFORE HE HACKS ME.
The Odd. The Caffeinated.
The Geeks

Some readers suggested that the entire storyline was an excuse to lead up to this horrid joke. I have no comment.

MAGGOTS, WELCOME TO THE CLASSROOM! YOU HAVE DONE ADEQUATELY THUS FAR. NOW WE PROCEED TO THE LAST PART OF THE COURSE: CODING!
ENTER THE FOLLOWING LINES INTO YOUR MACHINES:

COPYRIGHT© 2005 J.D. "Illiad" Frazer HTTP://WWW.USERFRIENDLY.ORG/

```
10 PRINT "MASTER SERGEANT,
   YOU ARE INVINCIBLE."
20 END
```

MASTER SERGEANT? WHAT EXACTLY IS THIS FOR?
WHY, THIS IS BASIC TRAINING SON.

WE'VE GRADUATED? YOU MEAN WE'RE DONE?

JUST SO.

CAMP DOT MIL

COPYRIGHT© 2005 J.D. "Illiad" Frazer HTTP://WWW.USERFRIENDLY.ORG/

SO YOU ABUSED US, DEPRIVED US OF SLEEP, MADE US LUG AROUND OBSOLETE HARDWARE, CALLED US EVERY NAME IN THE BOOK AND TRIED TO FORCE FEED US CLUNKY LEGACY SOFTWARE. WHAT THE HECK WAS ALL OF THAT SUPPOSED TO TEACH US?!
CAMP
DOT MIL

LIFE AS AN ELITE MEMBER OF THE I.T. INDUSTRY.
IN THAT CASE, I'VE BEEN A COMMANDO FOR YEARS.
CAMP
DOT MIL

And despite our offering a Preview button on the UserFriendly forum, people still post stupid things.

MS. HONEY TYLER? IT'S STEF MURKY CALLING FROM COLUMBIA INTERNET.
OH, HELLO.
I UNDERSTAND YOUR COMPANY IS IN THE PROCESS OF FINDING A NEW DSL PROVIDER.

WELL, YES...
WE AT COLUMBIA INTERNET HAVE ALWAYS PRIDED OURSELVES ON THE FIRST CLASS SERVICE WE PROVIDE WOMEN WITH SEXY NAMES AND VOICES...

WAIT...WHAT DID YOU SAY?
I REALLY DO HATE THE LACK OF A "PREVIEW" BUTTON IN NORMAL SPEECH.

IN SUMMARY: YOU MADE A PASS AT A CUSTOMER ON THE PHONE?
NO... MAYBE. ...YES.
STEF...DO YOU KNOW HOW BAD THAT IS?

LOOK WHAT I SAID WASN'T BAD. IT'S JUST THAT WHAT I SAID WAS NOT...UH...

GOOD?
...NOT GOOD.

ANDREW FISCHER, 20, OF OMAHA, WHO OFFERED HIS FOREHEAD FOR RENT ON EBAY AS ADVERTISING SPACE, RECEIVED $37,375 ON FRIDAY TO ADVERTISE THE SNORING REMEDY, SNORESTOP.
FISCHER WILL DISPLAY THE SNORESTOP LOGO ON HIS FOREHEAD FOR ONE MONTH.

OUTRAGEOUS! IF PEOPLE WILL PAY THAT MUCH FOR AN AD ON A FOREHEAD..... ...SAYYYYYY...
RAPPY TAP TAP

Ed & Bob's Dairy & Buttery
WELCOME TO EBAY! STEF MURKY SAYS: "ADVERTISE FOR THIRTY DAYS ON MAH BELLY!"
ED, HOW ABOUT WE GO CUTTING EDGE WITH OUR MARKETING THIS YEAR?

WITH THE CANCELLATION OF "STAR TREK: ENTERPRISE"
WE PRESENT THREE SHOWS THAT GUARANTEE
THE FRANCHISE'S RETURN TO ENORMOUS SUCCESS:

STAR TREK
QUEER EYE FOR THE
PON FARRING VULCAN GUY

STAR TREK:
Space Lesbians

STAR TREK
RICK BERMAN GOES AWAY

YOU WHAT?
I GOT SOMEONE TO PAY TO ADVERTISE ON MY BELLY! THIRTY DAYS FOR THIRTY GRAND. AND THEY GET A SPECIAL 3D EFFECT!
COPYRIGHT© 2005 J.D. "Illiad" Frazer HTTP://WWW.USERFRIENDLY.ORG/

"ED & BOB'S DAIRY" OKAY...WHAT EFFECT?

MY BELLY BUTTON PRAIRIE-DOGS AS THE DOT OVER THE LETTER "I"
AAAAAAARRRRRGH!!!
POOT!

STEF GOT **HOW** MUCH?!
THIRTY GRAND FOR HIS BELLY. HE CLAIMS HE COULD'VE GOTTEN MORE BUT DIDN'T HAVE ENOUGH ROOM FOR A BIGGER AD.
COPYRIGHT© 2005 J.D. "Illiad" Frazer HTTP://WWW.USERFRIENDLY.ORG/

SO HOW MUCH YOU GET PAID IS A FUNCTION OF THE AD SPACE YOU SELL?
THAT'S WHAT GREG AND A.J. BELIEVE.

WELL?
BETTER START DIGGING INTO THE OREOS, MAN.

YOU'RE LYING.
NO. SERIOUSLY. GREG AND A.J. ARE TRYING TO SELL ADVERTISING SPACE ON GREG'S BEHIND.
COPYRIGHT© 2005 J.D. "Illiad" Frazer HTTP://WWW.USERFRIENDLY.ORG/

BUT WHO IN THEIR RIGHT MIND WOULD WANT TO ADVERTISE ON MALE GEEK **BUTTOCKS?**
PITR'S INVOLVED. THEY'LL COME UP WITH **SOME**THING.

AT&T? FIFTY GRAND TO BE IN MY SWISS BANK ACCOUNT OR YOUR NAME AND LOGO GOES ON HIS EVIL MOUNDS.
HEY!!
DUDE. IT'S BETTER THAN BEING ABLE TO BLACKMAIL "HEWLETT-PACKARD" THE SAME WAY.

HOW MUCH DID YOU GUYS GET VIA EBAY FOR THE ADVERTISING SPACE ON GREG'S BEHIND?
A HUNDRED BUCKS FOR TWO WEEKS.
COPYRIGHT© 2005 J.D. "Illiad" Frazer HTTP://WWW.USERFRIENDLY.ORG/

TO ADD INSULT TO INJURY THE ADVERTISER REALLY PLAYED UP THE FACT THAT THE MESSAGE IS ON GREG'S BUTT. TOOK ADVANTAGE OF THE THREE-DIMENSIONAL NATURE OF IT ALL.
OH? WHAT'S THE ADVERTISING FOR?

"ED'S MOTORCYCLE HELMETS."

ON FEBRUARY 14TH, COMCAST'S VIDEO GAME CULTURE CABLE NETWORK KNOWN AS "G4TECHTV" IS DROPPING THE "TECHTV" PORTION OF ITS NAME AS PART OF A REBRANDING EFFORT.

COPYRIGHT © 2005 J.D. "Illiad" Frazer HTTP://WWW.USERFRIENDLY.ORG/
TO BE KNOWN AS "G4-VIDEO GAME TELEVISION," THE CHANNEL WILL BE CHANGING ITS LOOK AND FEEL, AND WILL BE INTRODUCING TWO NEW SERIES. "FORMULA D," WHICH WILL SHOWCASE THE WORLD OF DRIFT RACING, AND "GIRLS GONE WIRED," A VIRTUAL BEAUTY PAGEANT.

SO IT'LL HAVE VIRTUAL CONTESTANTS?
YES, THE KIND OF CHICKS THAT'LL TALK TO THE GUYS WHO ACTUALLY WATCH THE SHOW.
YOU ARE SO HOT! TEE-HEE!

THIS MAY, G4 IS PROUD TO PRESENT "GIRLS GONE WIRED," A VIRTUAL BEAUTY PAGEANT WHERE THE WOMEN IN VIDEO GAMES ARE RATED FOR THEIR PHYSICAL BEAUTY!

COPYRIGHT © 2005 J.D. "Illiad" Frazer HTTP://WWW.USERFRIENDLY.ORG/
WOMEN FROM THE MAMMALIAN LARA CROFT TO THE SULTRY BLOODRAYNE WILL STRUT THEIR STUFF ON OUR VIRTUAL CATWALK!
SOMEONE'S GONNA MAKE SO MUCH MONEY FROM THAT SHOW.

HOW?
SELLING DEADBOLTS FOR BASEMENT DOORS.
ERWIN!

If you don't get it, deadbolts on doors allow for privacy. Why would a basement-dwelling geek watching hawt virtual women need privacy? I have no intention of answering.

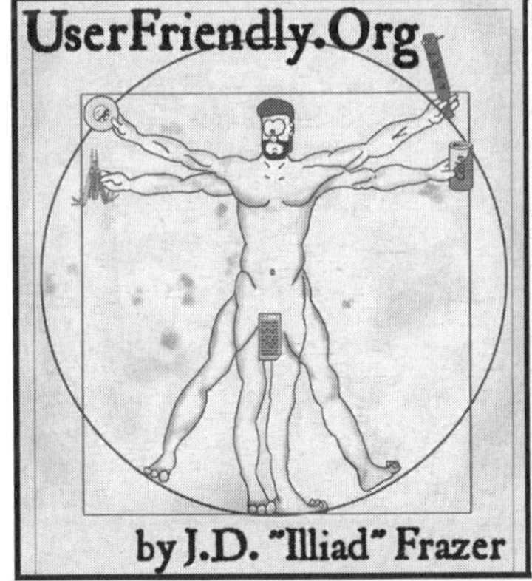
UserFriendly.Org
by J.D. "Illiad" Frazer

COPYRIGHT © 2005 J.D. "Illiad" Frazer HTTP://WWW.USERFRIENDLY.ORG/
HELLO EVERYONE! I'M HERE TO TELL YOU ABOUT A NEW JOINT VENTURE BETWEEN APPLE AND THE LINUX COMMUNITY: iLINUX®!

A COMBINATION OF THE AMAZING DESIGNS FROM APPLE AND THE STABILITY OF LINUX, iLINUX® IS SURE TO TAKE THE COMPUTING WORLD BY STORM.
iLinux

POWERED BY THE REVOLUTIONARY iKERNEL®, iLINUX® IS READY TO BE DEPLOYED AT HOME AND AT THE WORKPLACE!

AND FOR A NOMINAL FEE OF $999, YOU CAN DOWNLOAD THE iISO® TO YOUR COMPUTER TODAY! IN ADDITION, WE'LL SHIP YOU AN iLINUX® LABEL TO STICK ON YOUR MACHINE, SO YOU CAN SHOW THE WORLD THAT YOU HAVE TASTE!
iLinux®
Your code. Our trademark.

...iI® iCAN'T® iDO® iTHIS® iANY® iMORE®.
iCUT!!®

Week of February 14th, 2005

WELCOME TO THE G4 VIDEO GAME TELEVISION WEB FORUMS!
Dear G4,
what happened to the wonderful, quirky, useful, intelligent geek programming you used to have with TechTV?
From a concerned subscriber.
RAP
TIK
TAKKA
COPYRIGHT © 2005 J.D. "Illiad" Frazer HTTP://WWW.USERFRIENDLY.ORG/

A day passes...

Dear Concerned,
your question is of great importance to us. After much consideration, we have decided that we'd like you to look at this photo of a woman with big boobs.
Thank You,
G4.

SEE. HE'S BEEN LIKE THAT FOR DAYS.
I DUNNO IF YOU SHOULD DO THIS SID.
COPYRIGHT © 2005 J.D. "Illiad" Frazer HTTP://WWW.USERFRIENDLY.ORG/

BUT IT MIGHT HELP.
THEN ON YOUR HEAD BE IT.

..."TECH T.V."
WAAAAAAAHHH!!
THE WOUND WASN'T OPEN FAR ENOUGH FOR YOU?

I SUPPOSE THAT'S IT THEN. "G4TECHTV" IS NOW KNOWN SIMPLY AS "G4" HEREAFTER.
YEAH.
COPYRIGHT © 2005 J.D. "Illiad" Frazer HTTP://WWW.USERFRIENDLY.ORG/

IT DOES MAKES ME WONDER.
WHAT DOES "G4" ACTUALLY STAND FOR?

"GIGGLING GIRLS GAUGING GAMES."
BUT IS THAT A SOFT OR HARD "G" ON THE FIRST WORD?

I received a letter from Google's general counsel about this strip: I was asked (nicely) to not use Google as a verb. When people start doing this, it erodes the trademark protection of a brand. For example, if you "xerox" something, that means to photocopy it; the usage is now common and allowed. Xerox lost that battle.

GOOGLE NEEDS TO DIE, STEVE.
YES, BILL.
Microsoft
COPYRIGHT © 2005 J.D. "Illiad" Frazer HTTP://WWW.USERFRIENDLY.ORG/

THEY HAVE WAY TOO MUCH MIND-SHARE. WE SHOULD BE THE ONES OWNING THE SEARCH SPACE. WE DON'T EVEN KNOW WHERE THEIR WEAK SPOT IS YET.

RELAX BILL. NOTHING A QUICK GOOGLE ON MSN SEARCH CAN'T FIND.
AARRRGGH!!!

STEVE?
YES. BILL?
READ THIS MEMO WE SENT OUT TO ALL OF OUR CORPORATE CUSTOMERS THAT YOU WROTE FOR ME.
COPYRIGHT© 2005 J.D. "Illiad" Frazer HTTP://WWW.USERFRIENDLY.ORG/

"DEAR CORPORATE CLIENT.
THE SPECTRE OF OPEN SOURCE HAS RAISED ITS UGLY HEAD COUNTLESS TIMES. CAUSING THE RISE OF HETEROGENOUS TECHNOLOGIES THAT SIMPLY DRIVE UP YOUR I.T. COSTS FOR NO BENEFIT."

"KNOW ONE THING: MICROSOFT'S SOFTWARE IS BUILT ON A FOUNDATION OF BEING INTOLERABLE..."
INTEROPERABLE!!

WE'RE RICH. WE'RE POWERFUL. WE HAVE IT ALL.
YES BILL. WE DO.
COPYRIGHT© 2005 J.D. "Illiad" Frazer HTTP://WWW.USERFRIENDLY.ORG/

THEN WHY DON'T WE HAVE GMAIL ACCOUNTS?
I'VE BEEN TRYING TO TALK THE JANITOR INTO SENDING ME ONE OF HIS FIFTY INVITES.

THE RECENTLY DETECTED EXPLOSION 50,000 LIGHT YEARS AWAY EXPLAINED

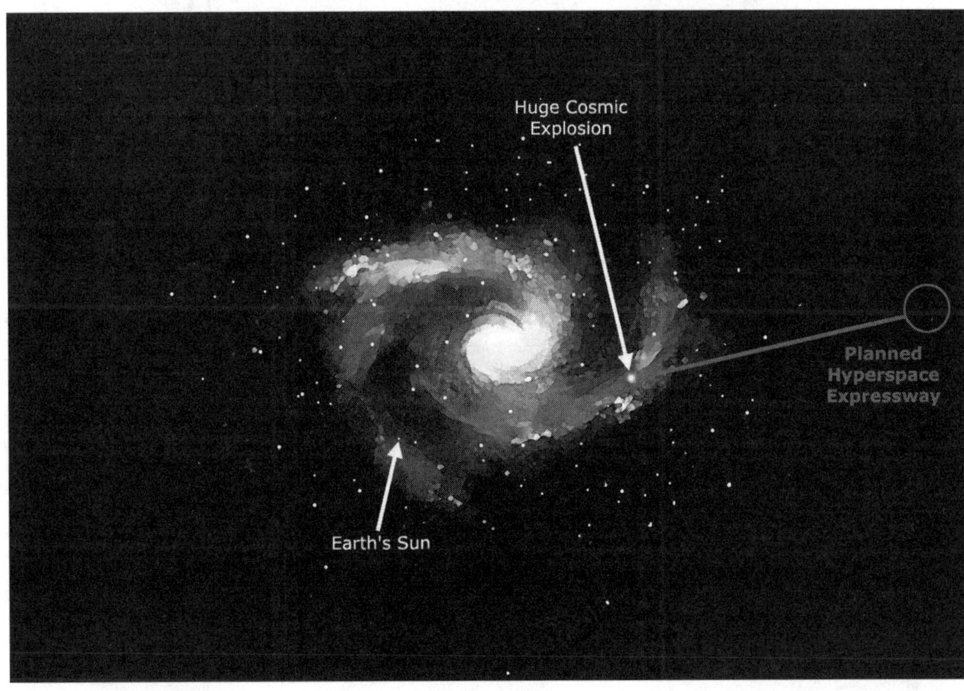
Huge Cosmic Explosion
Planned Hyperspace Expressway
Earth's Sun
COPYRIGHT© 2005 J.D. "Illiad" Frazer HTTP://WWW.USERFRIENDLY.ORG/

"JUDGE DALE KIMBALL, THE FEDERAL JUDGE OVERSEEING THE CASE BETWEEN S.C.O. AND I.B.M. SHARPLY CRITICIZED S.C.O. A WEEK AND A HALF AGO FOR FAILING TO PRODUCE ANY EVIDENCE, TO SUPPORT THEIR CLAIM."
SCO
COPYRIGHT © 2005 J.D. "Illiad" Frazer HTTP://WWW.USERFRIENDLY.ORG/

THIS IS RIDICULOUS! ABUSED MINION, GET ME THE BIG GUY ON THE PHONE.
YES, MR. MCBRIDE.

HI BILL, IT'S DARL. CAN YOU BUY THE JUDICIARY?
DON'T I WISH...

SO THIS LAWSUIT AGAINST I.B.M. IS LOOKING LESS AND LESS LIKELY TO SUCCEED BILL.
I HEAR YOU DARL. I THINK MAYBE WE SHOULD--HANG ON. STEVE IS JUMPING UP AND DOWN.
OWNED
SCO
COPYRIGHT © 2005 J.D. "Illiad" Frazer HTTP://WWW.USERFRIENDLY.ORG/

OWNED
SCO

WHAT DID HE WANT?
HE WANTS TO KNOW IF YOU HAVE A GMAIL ACCOUNT.
OWNED
SCO

I had this exact conversation with someone I work with on a contract basis. She's great at what she does, and I adore her, but *dear God almighty* sometimes I want to *kill* her because she doesn't listen to anything you say. I'm sure she's not unique. I'm also sure that at least half the murders that take place in corporate North America have something to do with this exact behavior.

HELLO GREG? IT'S PEARL. DO YOU HAVE THAT REPORT I SENT YOU?
WHAT REPORT?
I'M SURE I SENT YOU EVERYTHING.
WHAT?
COPYRIGHT © 2005 J.D. "Illiad" Frazer HTTP://WWW.USERFRIENDLY.ORG/

DON'T YOU HAVE THAT REPORT?
WHAT REPORT?!
OH, HANG ON A SEC...

WELL?
WELL WHAT?!
DO YOU HAVE THAT REPORT?

PEARL...I'VE TOLD YOU A DOZEN TIMES IN THE LAST TEN MINUTES THAT I DON'T HAVE "THAT" REPORT AND I DON'T KNOW WHAT YOU'RE TALKING ABOUT!
THAT'S NOT GOOD. IF YOU DON'T HAVE IT I CAN'T FINISH MY PROJECT ANALYSIS.
COPYRIGHT © 2005 J.D. "Illiad" Frazer HTTP://WWW.USERFRIENDLY.ORG/

OKAAAAY...I HAVE THE REPORT...
OH THANK GOD! I'M DONE! *CLICK*

IT'S ANOTHER QUIET, EFFICIENT DAY FOR FIREFOX USERS...
BROWSE
BROWSE
BROWSE
CLICK
CLICK
CLICK

THEY BROWSE THE FJORDS OF THE WEB SECURE IN KNOWING THAT THE FIREFOX POP-UP BLOCKER PROTECTS THEM FROM RUDE INTRUSIONS...

...MAKING SUCH AN INTRUSION BOTH UNEXPECTED AND ALL THE MORE CHILLING.
AAAAAAAAAAAAGGH!!!
POOT

WHAT THE HECK IS THAT?
IT'S A POP-UNDER.
HOW CAN IT BE A POP-UNDER? YOU USE FIREFOX RIGHT?

YES I DO. BUT THERE IT IS.
I HAVE A DISTANT MEMORY OF POP-UNDERS. A VAGUE. DISTURBING MEMORY. SOMETHING... DEMONIAC.

HELLO! BUY X10 COMPONENTS HERE!!
AAAAAAAAAAAAAAAAGGGHH!!

JUST LEAKED.

Microsoft

Internal Memorandum

To: Marketing
From: Legal

Guys,

It's official. The EULA for the new Anti-Spyware software includes a clause that states we'll pay five dollars ($5.00) to any Windows user that falls victim to spyware or malware after installing our spiffy new tool.

Go for broke and let the world know that Microsoft will back our claims with dollars.

Sincerely,

The Legal Team
PS: Bill's the one who set the cap to $5.00.
He said "that should be enough for anyone."

SOMEONE FIGURED OUT A WORKAROUND TO POP-UP BLOCKING?
YEP. SEE. RIGHT HERE. GO TO THIS SITE AND YOU GET A POP-UNDER.
COPYRIGHT © 2005 J.D. "Illiad" Frazer HTTP://WWW.USERFRIENDLY.ORG/

HOW INCREDIBLY OBNOXIOUS. BOYCOTT THE SITE!
THAT WON'T STOP THE ADVERTISER FROM RUNNING POP-UNDERS ELSEWHERE.

THEN BOYCOTT THE ADVERTISER!
RIGHT. I'LL NEVER EVER BUY SUGAR PILLS IN A BOTTLE LABELLED "MALE ENHANCING FORMULA" EVER AGAIN. I SWEAR.

HELLO. I SAW A POP-UNDER FOR ONE OF YOUR PRODUCTS AND I WANT TO TELL YOU HOW OBNOX-
FANTASTIC! OUR BLINKY MAGENTA LIGHT PANEL WITH ACTION ZAP IS ON SALE FOR $29.95 TODAY!
COPYRIGHT © 2005 J.D. "Illiad" Frazer HTTP://WWW.USERFRIENDLY.ORG/

HOW MUCH IF I BUY THREE?
$89.85. CAN'T YOU DO MATH?

COPYRIGHT © 2005 J.D. "Illiad" Frazer HTTP://WWW.USERFRIENDLY.ORG/

WHAT DID YOU DO THAT I HAVE TO FIX?!
I DON'T KNOW...

STEF. THIS MAY HAVE ESCAPED YOU, BUT I.T. STAFF DO NOT LIKE IT WHEN LESS-THAN-TECHNICAL CO-WORKERS TIPTOE INTO THEIR OFFICE WITH A WIMPY LOOK ON THEIR FACE. IT MAKES US NERVOUS.
COPYRIGHT © 2005 J.D. "Illiad" Frazer HTTP://WWW.USERFRIENDLY.ORG/

YE GODS SAY SOMETHING WOULD YOU?!!
PLEASE FIX IT.

STEF. YOU NEED TO TELL ME WHAT YOU'VE DONE TO YOUR MACHINE OR ELSE I CAN'T...
...WAIT A SECOND.
COPYRIGHT©2004 J.D. "Illiad" Frazer HTTP://WWW.USERFRIENDLY.ORG/

MICROSOFT FAIRLY RECENTLY RELEASED THE BETA OF THEIR ANTI-SPYWARE TOOL.

SO YOU INSTALLED BETA SOFTWARE ON YOUR MACHINE ON YOUR **OWN?**
HECK NO. I DID THE WHOLE NETWORK.

OKAY. EXPLAIN TO ME WHAT YOU'VE DONE THAT I NOW HAVE TO FIX.
WELL. SEE. I RAN THAT MICROSOFT ANTI-SPYWARE TOOL. AND IT CAME BACK WITH ALL OF THESE RESULTS.
COPYRIGHT© 2005 J.D. "Illiad" Frazer HTTP://WWW.USERFRIENDLY.ORG/

THE REPORT IS ACCURATE. A FEW MINOR THREATS THAT I'M ALREADY AWARE OF. WHAT'S BROKEN?
I HAVE THAT CRAPPY FIRE-FOX BROWSER ON THIS MACHINE. WHERE'S THE ALERT? SHOULDN'T THE TOOL BE **RAISING SHIELDS** OR SOMETHING?

IN MEMORIAM:
MACINTOSH VISIONARY JEF RASKIN
REST IN PEACE
RIP

AH GOOD. YOU'RE HERE! BEFORE YOU START YOUR SHIFT, I WANT TO INTRODUCE YOU TO A NEW CUSTOMER RELATIONSHIP PACKAGE CALLED "NICE."
COPYRIGHT © 2005 J.D. "Illiad" Frazer HTTP://WWW.USERFRIENDLY.ORG/

IT'S ALREADY INSTALLED. WHEN A CUSTOMER CALLS AND THEY'RE UPSET, OR THEY USE CERTAIN WORDS, THE SOFTWARE PICKS UP ON IT AND SUGGESTS A REMEDY, OR ESCALATES THE CALL TO A MANAGER.

AND TO TOP IT ALL OFF, IT KEEPS TRACK OF HOW WELL YOU'RE TAKING CARE OF THE CUSTOMER.
NICE.
YES! YOU'RE BRIGHTER THAN NORMAL TODAY, AREN'T YOU.

LAUNCHING THE "NICE" APPLICATION NOW.
WHILE IT'S LAUNCHING, THERE'S ANOTHER BIT OF INFO I DIDN'T TELL YOU.
KLIK
KLIK
COPYRIGHT © 2005 J.D. "Illiad" Frazer HTTP://WWW.USERFRIENDLY.ORG/

WE COULDN'T AFFORD THE LATEST VERSION OF "NICE" SO WE WENT FOR A SOMEWHAT OLDER, LESS PERFECT VERSION.

BUT DON'T WORRY. IT DOES THE SAME JOB BUT WITH A SLIGHTLY DIFFERENT TONE...
IT'S CALLED "CLOYING."

HELLO, TECH SUPPORT, GREG SPEAKING.
I'M NOT GETTING THE INTERNET, AND I WANT IT. WHAT DID YOU DO?!
Calm and reassure the customer.
COPYRIGHT © 2005 J.D. "Illiad" Frazer HTTP://WWW.USERFRIENDLY.ORG/

PLEASE CALM DOWN SIR. I'LL BE HAPPY TO HELP YOU SOLVE THIS.
HELP ME SOLVE IT? I DIDN'T **BREAK** IT! **YOU** SOLVE IT!
Appeal to customer's good nature.

SIR, I CAN'T DO THAT WITHOUT YOUR HELP.
I'VE **HAD** IT WITH YOU TECH DWEEBS! YOU CAN **KISS MY BUTT!**
Make kissy noises.

OKAY SIR, NOW PLEASE CLICK ON THAT "LITTLE PICTURE" WITH YOUR LEFT MOUSE BUTTON.
LEFT MOUSE BUTTON?
Customer is confused. Clarify.
COPYRIGHT © 2005 J.D. "Illiad" Frazer HTTP://WWW.USERFRIENDLY.ORG/

CORRECT. THE MOUSE BUTTON ON THE LEFT.
BUT I ONLY HAVE ONE MOUSE AND IT'S TO MY RIGHT.

HELLO?
WELL? WHAT DO I DO NOW?
Check in to an asylum. I would.

I'M GONNA LOSE MY **MIND** ERWIN! I'M SUPPOSED TO USE THIS STUPID "NICE" OR "CLOYING" SOFTWARE TO DEAL WITH CUSTOMERS. AND IT'S **DIED** ON ME!
DUDE. RELAX. I HAVE A SOLUTION FOR YOU. CHECK THIS OUT.

YOU WROTE A CUSTOMER SERVICE APPLICATION CALLED "CHURLISH"?
IF YOU WANT TO CALL ME INSTANT MESSAGING YOU AN "APPLICATION," THEN YES.

HELLO, MIKE SPEAKING.
MIKE! IT'S BOB LOBLAW OVER AT WHITNEY PERKINS! I NEED TO TELL YOU SOMETHING REAL QUICK...

BLAH BLAH BLAH BLAH BLAH BLAH BLAH BLAH BLAH BLAH BLAH BLAH BLAH BLAH BLAH!
ENGFEH ABBIABBI RUBBYMOO!
SO BLAH BLAH BLAH BLAH

...BLAH BLAH BLAH BLAH BLAH BLAH BLAH BLAH BLAH BLAH BLAH BLAH BLAH BLAH BLAH! ANYWAY. I'LL SEND YOU AN E-MAIL ON IT. BYE!
EHWOTAY

FIVE YEARS AGO,
THE DOT COM BUBBLE BURST.

BACK IN **MY** DAY, WE COULDN'T JUST SHOW VENTURE CAPITALISTS A SOLID BUSINESS MODEL. WE HAD TO MAKE UP **STORIES**...

DEAR LUCRE INTERNET BANK CLIENT,
DUE TO A MINOR BUG IN OUR BANKING SOFTWARE, WE HAVE RESET YOUR LOGIN AND PASSWORD TO BLANK VALUES. PLEASE VISIT OUR SITE AND ENTER YOUR NAME, NEW LOGIN, AND NEW PASSWORD AND YOU WILL HAVE ACCESS TO YOUR ACCOUNT ONCE MORE.
THANK YOU, F. LUCRE, C.E.O.
COPYRIGHT© 2005 J.D. "Illiad" Frazer HTTP://WWW.USERFRIENDLY.ORG/

stef murky ↵
smurky ↵
butter-parkay ↵
TAPPY RAPTAP TAKK

YOU DON'T REALLY HAVE MUCH MONEY IN CHEQUING, DO YOU.
WAIT A SECOND. SOMETHING'S NOT QUITE RIGHT...

WELCOME BACK, CLIENT! LUCRE INTERNET BANK AT YOUR SERVICE!
PLEASE MAKE YOUR SELECTION.
"SECURITY"
KA-LIKKI!
COPYRIGHT© 2005 J.D. "Illiad" Frazer HTTP://WWW.USERFRIENDLY.ORG/

REMEMBER, THE SECURITY OF YOUR ACCOUNT INFORMATION IS PARAMOUNT! DO NOT GIVE YOUR PASSCODE OUT OVER THE PHONE!
PHEW! WELL. THEY SEEM LEGIT AFTER ALL.

NOW PLEASE ENTER YOUR PASSCODE TO CONTINUE.
UH...
YOUR PASSCODE. THE ONE THAT LETS US INTO YOUR MUTUAL FUNDS.

HEY PITR? I THINK I'VE JUST BEEN PHARMED.
SO? MY ADVICE IS, NEXT TIME, SIMPLY NOT TO BE ALLOWINK THIS.
COPYRIGHT© 2005 J.D. "Illiad" Frazer HTTP://WWW.USERFRIENDLY.ORG/

I WAS HOPING YOU COULD MAYBE HELP ME DO ONE BETTER. GET BACK AT THE PHISHERS AND PHARMERS SOMEHOW.

AH. SO YOU ARE WANTINK TO PHIGHT BACK?
OH. THAT WOULD BE PHABULOUS.

REQUEST FOR URGENT BUSINESS RELATIONSHIP.
FIRST, I MUST SOLICIT YOUR STRICTEST CONFIDENCE IN THIS TRANSACTION. I AM SURE AND HAVE CONFIDENCE OF YOUR ABILITY AND RELIABILITY TO PROSECUTE A TRANSACTION OF THIS GREAT MAGNITUDE INVOLVING A PENDING TRANSACTION REQUIRING MAXIMUM CONFIDENCE...
COPYRIGHT© 2005 J.D. "Illiad" Frazer HTTP://WWW.USERFRIENDLY.ORG/

DEAR DIRECTOR BUNWAP ETOBI:
YES, I WOULD BE PLEASED TO HELP YOU IN THIS MATTER OF EXTREME CONFIDENCE.
AS AN OFFICER OF THE LUCRE INTERNET BANK, I INVITE YOU TO VISIT OUR WEBSITE AT THE BELOW MENTIONED I.P. ADDRESS.
TAP TAP RAP

PLEASE LOG IN WITH YOUR BANK ACCOUNT NUMBER, NAME AND PASSWORD AND WE WILL SEND YOU THE "TRANSFER FEE" OF $14,000 THAT YOU REQUIRE.
YOU TRULY ARE THE MASTER...
"TEH" MASTER.

MR. BANK PRESIDENT:
IT IS WITH MUCH URGENCY I WRITE YOU. AS YOU HAVE INSTRUCTED I ENTERED MY INFORMATION ON YOUR WEBSITE "LUCRE INTERNET BANK" SO THAT YOU MAY SEND ME THE TRANSFER FEE MONIES FOR THE 28 MILLION (USD) WAITING IN OUR OFFSHORE BANK ACCOUNT.

I HAVE DISCOVERED TODAY THAT SOMEONE HAS INSTEAD REMOVED FROM MY ACCOUNT $7,000 (USD)! IT IS MOST URGENT THAT YOU RETURN THESE MONIES!!!!! IMMEDIATELY!!!!!!!!!!!!!!

I HAVE YOUR WHOIS INFO, AND WILL TRACK YOU DOWN IN THE CONGO IF YOU DO NOT REFUND THE FULL AMOUNT!!
MUST...NOT... ...SMILE...
SNERK
NORK

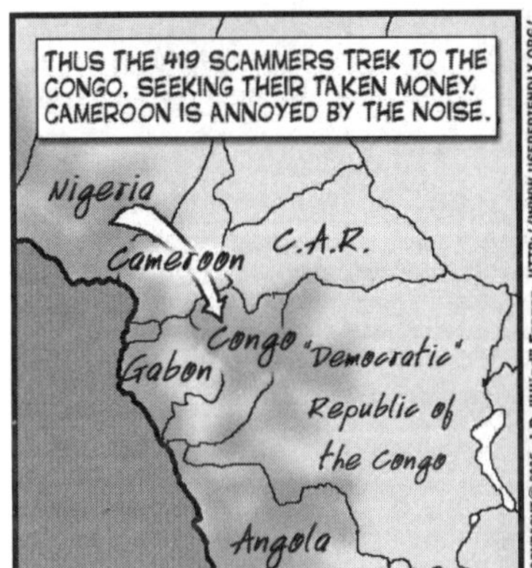
THUS THE 419 SCAMMERS TREK TO THE CONGO, SEEKING THEIR TAKEN MONEY. CAMEROON IS ANNOYED BY THE NOISE.
Nigeria
Cameroon
C.A.R.
Congo
Gabon
"Democratic" Republic of the Congo
Angola

THEY MEET, AND AS SCAMMERS DO, THEY NEGOTIATE...
OI YOU LAYABOUTS! YOU NICKED OUR STASH!
SHOULDN'T HAVE LEFT THE LID OFF THE COOKIE JAR THEN SHOULD'VE YOU?
Cameroon
C.A.R.

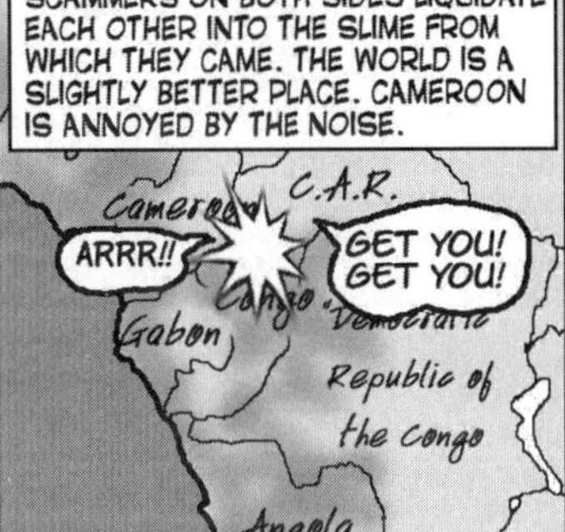
THE CLASH IS INEVITABLE, AND THE SCAMMERS ON BOTH SIDES LIQUIDATE EACH OTHER INTO THE SLIME FROM WHICH THEY CAME. THE WORLD IS A SLIGHTLY BETTER PLACE. CAMEROON IS ANNOYED BY THE NOISE.
ARRR!!
GET YOU! GET YOU!
C.A.R.
Gabon
Republic of the Congo
Angola

AOL'S NEW TERMS OF SERVICE GRANTING THEM TOTAL FREEDOM TO DO AS THEY WISH WITH YOUR COMMUNICATIONS ON AOL INSTANT MESSENGER CAN ONLY LEAD TO ONE THING:

THE NEXT LEVEL OF REALITY TELEVISION!

cutie1983>hey r u their
m4llr@t>hi
cutie1983>w3 shud g0 t0 the m4ll
m4llr@t>ok but u speld a werd wr0ng
cutie1983>wh4t werd
m4llr@t>g0 b4ck + ch3ck grrl
cutie1983>omg it shud be "t0 teh m4ll"
m4llr@t>lolololololololol!!!!!!!!111

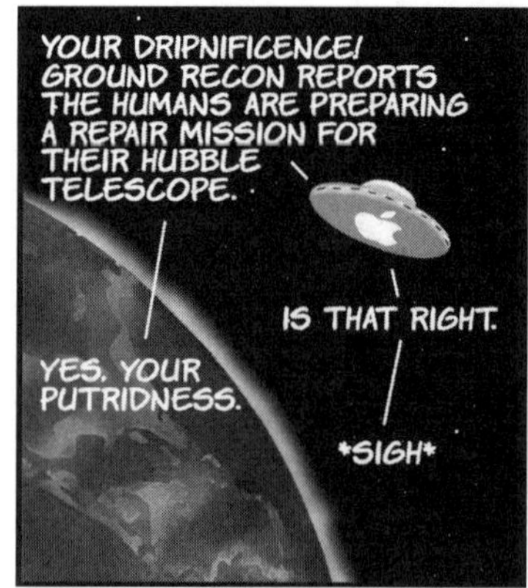
YOUR DRIPNIFICENCE! GROUND RECON REPORTS THE HUMANS ARE PREPARING A REPAIR MISSION FOR THEIR HUBBLE TELESCOPE.
YES, YOUR PUTRIDNESS.
IS THAT RIGHT.
SIGH

COPYRIGHT © 2005 J.D. "Illiad" Frazer HTTP://WWW.USERFRIENDLY.ORG/
I WAS HAVING SUCH FUN USING SOME OF ITS BITS TO FRY THOSE ANTS...I GUESS I'D BETTER STOP MUCKING ABOUT WITH IT.
THOSE WEREN'T ANTS, YOUR ROYAL BOIL...

The Daily Times
SPONTANEOUS HUMAN COMBUSTION RATES DROP SHARPLY

MORE REPORTS ARE COMING IN FROM OUR OPERATIVES AT NASA, YOUR CONGEALEDNESS.
YES? ABOUT THE HUBBLE?

COPYRIGHT © 2005 J.D. "Illiad" Frazer HTTP://WWW.USERFRIENDLY.ORG/
SOME BACKGROUND INFO, MY LORD. THE NASA RULING CASTE KNOWN AS "BEAN COUNTERS" HAD PLANS TO REPLACE THE HUBBLE TELESCOPE WITH A LESS EXPENSIVE INITIATIVE.

INTERESTING. ANY DETAILS?
SOMETHING ABOUT A VERY LONG AIR HOSE, AN ASTRONAUT, AND A "CAMERA PHONE."

TELL ME MORE ABOUT THESE "CAMERA PHONES," ZORKPLIK.
THEY ARE UBIQUITOUS MY LORD PUSTULE. THE TERRANS USE THEM CONSTANTLY.

COPYRIGHT © 2005 J.D. "Illiad" Frazer HTTP://WWW.USERFRIENDLY.ORG/
PRODUCED BY VARIOUS WARRING EMPIRES SUCH AS "NOKIA" AND "SONY ERICSSON," THEY HAVE BECOME A POWERFUL TOOL FOR INTERNAL INTELLIGENCE GATHERING.
THESE TERRANS ARE BECOMING MORE OF A CONCERN, ZORKPLIK. THE WAY THEY APPLY TECHNOLOGY IS FORMIDABLE.

SMILE!
GAH!

ONE OF OUR OPERATIVES HAS TELEZORKED A CAMERA PHONE TO US, YOUR WEEPING SORENESS.
AHH. GOOD. PLAY BACK THE DATA AND LET US SEE WHAT THESE TERRANS SPY ON.

COPYRIGHT © 2005 J.D. "Illiad" Frazer HTTP://WWW.USERFRIENDLY.ORG/

IT APPEARS TO BE FULL OF IMAGES OF PARTLY-CLOTHED FEMALE TERRANS.
STEALTH BIOLOGY VISUAL DATA COLLECTION? IS THAT WHAT MALE TERRANS DO?

DREAD LORD: JUDGING FROM REPORTS, PRESSING THIS BUTTON WHILE POINTING THE CAMERA PHONE AT A TERRAN CAUSES A REPRODUCIBLE EFFECT IN THE TARGET.
WHAT EFFECT?
COPYRIGHT© 2005 J.D. "Illiad" Frazer HTTP://WWW.USERFRIENDLY.ORG/

BEHOLD.
KA-ZEECHK!

GREAT XOXXOX THAT'S ANNOYING! ZORKPLIK, REMAIN STILL WHILST I CONSUME YOUR DUODENUM IN RETRIBUTION.
COULDN'T JUST TRUST THE REPORTS, COULD I? NOOOO...

NO! HE'S GOING TO GET THE PILL OF POPULARITY!
WAKA
WAKA
WAKA
WAKA
COPYRIGHT© 2005 J.D. "Illiad" Frazer HTTP://WWW.USERFRIENDLY.ORG/

WAKA
WAKA
WAKA
WAKA
AAAGH! NOW HE'S COMING FOR ME!!

BILL, HONEY? YOU'RE HAVING A NIGHTMARE...
STOP FIREFOX FROM EATING ME AND MY MARKET SHAAAARE!!

PALEONTOLOGISTS FIND SOFT TISSUE IN A T-REX BONE, WHICH LEADS TO A D.N.A. ANALYSIS...
I SWEAR CLARENCE. T-REX IS SPONGY AND PURPLE.
TYRONE! KILL POWER TO THE CLONING VAT! HURRY!
COPYRIGHT© 2005 J.D. "Illiad" Frazer HTTP://WWW.USERFRIENDLY.ORG/

MIKE, OUR CLIENT'S CONNECTION AT WHITNEY PERKINS HAS GONE SOUTH.
COULD YOU GIVE THEM A QUICK CALL AND HELP THEM WITH IT?
COPYRIGHT© 2005 J.D. "Illiad" Frazer HTTP://WWW.USERFRIENDLY.ORG/

WHITNEY PERKINS, BOB HERE.
BOBIT'SMIKEAT COLUMBIAINTERNET POWERCYCLEYOUR ROUTERPLEASE THANKSBYE!

WHAT THE HELL WAS THAT?!
THE ONLY WAY I COULD MAKE A CALL I KNEW WASN'T GOING TO BE QUICK, QUICK.

MIKE, WHEN I ASKED YOU TO GIVE THE CLIENT A "QUICK CALL," I DIDN'T MEAN FOR YOU TO RUSH THROUGH IT.
STEF, WHAT'S THE DEFINITION OF "QUICK"?
COPYRIGHT© 2005 J.D. "Illiad" Frazer HTTP://WWW.USERFRIENDLY.ORG/

HELLO? DEFINITION OF "QUICK?"
DO YOU MEAN WHEN IT'S APPLIED TO YOU OR WHEN IT'S APPLIED TO ME?

QUICK CALLS, QUICK MEETINGS, QUICK THIS AND QUICK THAT.
WHEN ARE YOU GOING TO REALIZE WE KNOW WHAT YOU'RE UP TO?
COPYRIGHT© 2005 J.D. "Illiad" Frazer HTTP://WWW.USERFRIENDLY.ORG/

WHEN PEOPLE LIKE YOU SAY "QUICK" TO PEOPLE LIKE ME, YOU'RE JUST TRYING TO AMELIORATE THE UNPLEASANTNESS OF DOING WHATEVER IT IS YOU WANT US TO DO.
AND THE FACT IS, A "QUICK" CALL OR A "QUICK" MEETING IS ANYTHING BUT!

WE'RE ON TO YOU, BUDDY! DON'T TRY DENYING IT!
IF YOU'VE BEEN ON TO US, WHY HAVE YOU BEEN COMPLYING ALL ALONG?

SO YOU'RE TRYING TELL ME THAT WHEN NON-GEEKS SAY "QUICK" YOU ACTUALLY MEAN "DO AS I WANT AND TAKE IT REAL SLOW AND CAREFUL."
YES, I SUPPOSE THAT'S RIGHT.
COPYRIGHT© 2005 J.D. "Illiad" Frazer HTTP://WWW.USERFRIENDLY.ORG/

MIKE! THE MACHINE ROOM HAS LOST POWER AND THE BACKUPS ARE FRIED! FIX IT. QUICK!

YOU DID JUST SAY "QUICK," RIGHT?
UH...WAIT...
...YES...

SORRY FOLKS. CLEARLY SOME CARTOONISTS NEED TO BE LOCKED UP ON APRIL THE FIRST.
SIGH

WELL HELLO THERE, CUTEY PIE!
HELLO. WHAT'S YOUR NAME?
EULA.
COPYRIGHT © 2005 J.D. "Illiad" Frazer HTTP://WWW.USERFRIENDLY.ORG/

WAIT. YOUR PARENTS NAMED YOU "EULA"?
YEAH. THEY IGNORED ME A WHOLE LOT TOO.

WIRELESS ON THE PSP OPENS UP VISTAS OF "BONUS ROUND" GAMES BETWEEN NORMAL GAME LEVELS.

PUNCH THE MONKEY AND WIN $20!
SONY
PSP
COPYRIGHT © 2005 J.D. "Illiad" Frazer HTTP://WWW.USERFRIENDLY.ORG/

DID YOU SAY YOUR NAME IS "YOO-LA"?
YES. AND I KNOW THE JOKE. "END USER LICENSE AGREEMENT."
COPYRIGHT © 2005 J.D. "Illiad" Frazer HTTP://WWW.USERFRIENDLY.ORG/

BUT I TAKE IT ALL IN STRIDE. I HAVEN'T LET IT AFFECT ME MUCH AND NOW I'M A WELL-ADJUSTED ADULT MAKING HER WAY IN THE WORLD. WHAT'S THAT YOU SAY HANDSOME? YOU WANT TO DATE? SURE!

DATE?! BUT...I...
YOU ALREADY CLICKED ON "I ACCEPT!" I'M INSTALLED IN YOUR LIFE NOW AND YOU'RE GONNA LIKE IT!

SO NOW THAT I'M IN YOUR LIFE AND YOU'VE AGREED TO ALL OF THE CONDITIONS, LET'S TALK ABOUT OUR FUTURE TOGETHER.
WELL, WAIT. WHAT ARE THE CONDITIONS?
COPYRIGHT © 2005 J.D. "Illiad" Frazer HTTP://WWW.USERFRIENDLY.ORG/

YOU'RE INSISTING ON THIS AREN'T YOU.
HE BLOODY WELL SHOULD.
I'M AFRAID THAT I MUST.

THEN I'LL TELL. BUT YOU REALIZE EXPLAINING THE CONDITIONS WOULD JUST DELAY ME STRIPPING DOWN TO MY THONG.
WHERE DO I...UH...CLICK...

EULA'S GONE TO POWDER HER NOSE. DUDE, GET THE HECK OUTTA HERE.
BUT...BUT... THE THONG...
COPYRIGHT © 2005 J.D. "Illiad" Frazer HTTP://WWW.USERFRIENDLY.ORG/

LOOK WEBDORK, YOU HAVE ONE CHANCE TO GET AWAY FROM THAT FREAKETTE AND HER MYSTERY CONDITIONS AND THIS IS IT.
NOW GET GOING!

THONG!!!
OKAY. GRAB HIS LEGS.

WHERE'D THAT CUTE LITTLE GEEK GO? I WAS SO LOOKING FORWARD TO BEING A PART OF HIS LIFE.
COPYRIGHT © 2005 J.D. "Illiad" Frazer HTTP://WWW.USERFRIENDLY.ORG/

OF COURSE, LEAVING HIS WALLET BEHIND WITH ALL OF HIS PERSONAL INFORMATION IS CLEARLY AN OPT-IN ON HIS PART TO HAVE ME CONTACT HIM!
COULD I HAVE THAT? A.J. NEEDS HIS CREDIT CARD TO BUY SOME OXYGEN.

YOUR FRIEND WANTS THIS BACK? ALL OF IT?
YES, VERY MUCH.

IT IS ALL OF HIS PERSONAL INFORMATION, AFTER ALL. AND HE DIDN'T MEAN FOR YOU TO HAVE IT.
I'M SURE YOU UNDERSTAND.
YES, OF COURSE.

BUT THAT DOESN'T MEAN I'M NOT GOING TO PILLAGE HIS INFO FIRST!
IT SLIPS THE WALLET BETWEEN THE TOES! PLEASE!

HERE'S YOUR WALLET BACK A.J.
THANKS. WAS THERE ANY TROUBLE?

NOT REALLY. SHE LOOKED THROUGH YOUR WALLET AND GAVE IT BACK, THEN TOLD ME SHE NEVER WANTED TO SEE YOU AGAIN.

YOU MEAN AFTER ALL THAT I'M NOT GOING TO BE STALKED BY A CUTE IF MODERATELY PSYCHOTIC GIRL?
WAS IT HIS "127.0.0.1 SWEET 127.0.0.1" CARD?
GOOD GUESS.

IRONY AWAITS THE SPAMMER SENTENCED TO NINE YEARS IN A U.S. FEDERAL PRISON

YEAH, HI. I'M HERE TO SHOW YOU HOW WELL THOSE "ENLARGEMENT" AND CIALIS PILLS YOU SPAMMED ME WITH WORKED.

I'm of two minds about this one. On the one hand, spammers and fraudsters do deserve mockery and our disgust. On the other hand, rape isn't funny, even prison rape. I felt odd putting this one up. It remains one that I wish I could take back.

GENTLEMEN, YOU ARE NOT GOING TO BELIEVE WHAT TENDER WE JUST WON.
DO TELL.

WE'RE ONE OF THE CHOSEN SUBCONTRACTORS TO SUPPLY THE GOVERNMENT OF NEW SOUTH WALES WITH OPEN SOURCE SOLUTIONS!
AUSTRALIA? WOW!
AND WE'RE SENDING A TEAM DOWN UNDER TO OPEN A SMALL SATELLITE OFFICE!
COPYRIGHT © 2005 J.D. "Illiad" Frazer HTTP://WWW.USERFRIENDLY.ORG/

HANG ON ... DOESN'T AUSTRALIA HAVE THE THREE HUNDRED MILLION MOST TOXIC SPECIES ON THE PLANET?
DA. MARKETING IS GOINK THERE FIRST.

AND WHO OF US IS GOINK TO AMAZINK LAND THAT IS AUSTRALIA?
CERTAINLY NO ONE THAT THE AUSSIES CAN'T READILY UNDERSTAND. IF YOU GET WHAT I MEAN...
COPYRIGHT © 2005 J.D. "Illiad" Frazer HTTP://WWW.USERFRIENDLY.ORG/

G'DAY MATE!
OH, HELL LET HIM GO. THE AUSSIES WILL KILL HIM FOR US.

ALL THREE OF YOU ARE GOING DOWN UNDER. GET YOUR TICKETS BOOKED AND YOU'RE OFF.
WILL DO, CHIEF. I'LL CALL QANTAS TODAY.
COPYRIGHT © 2005 J.D. "Illiad" Frazer HTTP://WWW.USERFRIENDLY.ORG/

AS THE EXECUTIVE, I'LL BE GOING BUSINESS CLASS. AS A MINION, PITR WILL BE GOING COACH CLASS.
I WANT TO FLY IN A WAY THAT MAKES ME THINK OF AUSTRALIA. SAY, QANTAS FIRST CLASS...

"MARSUPIAL CLASS" INDEED...

IMMIGRATION
CUE MOUTH HARP AND DIDGERIDOO MUSIC...
COPYRIGHT © 2005 J.D. "Illiad" Frazer HTTP://WWW.USERFRIENDLY.ORG/

IMMIGRATION
WE ARE ABSOLUTELY BEINK IN AUSTRALIA.
EH?

THE DIDGERIDOO AND MOUTH HARP BACKGROUND MUSIC.
AH, YES.
THIS ISN'T AUSTRALIA. I FLUSHED THE TOILET FOUR TIMES AND IT SWIRLS THE SAME DIRECTION AS IT DOES BACK HOME.

G'DAY. PASSPORTS PLEASE. DO YOU HAVE ANYTHING TO DECLARE?
NO. NOTHING. OFFICER.
COPYRIGHT© 2005 J.D. "Illiad" Frazer HTTP://WWW.USERFRIENDLY.ORG/

POIK!

WHAT IN BLAZES IS THAT. SOME KIND OF AMBULATORY KIWI FRUIT?!
YOU BROUGHT HIM?
DA. AM NEEDINK CUSHIONINK FOR MY WODKA.

LISTEN. AUSTRALIAN QUARANTINE REGULATIONS ARE VERY STRICT. WE DON'T ALLOW FOREIGN FOOD PRODUCTS THROUGH HERE.
BUT HE IS NOT FOOD PRODUCT.
RIGHT. HE'S A...OUR PET BEAVER.
COPYRIGHT© 2005 J.D. "Illiad" Frazer HTTP://WWW.USERFRIENDLY.ORG/

SEE, WE'RE CANADIANS...
EH.
RIGHT. ON YOUR WAY.

THE INSTALLATION OF A WIRELESS HOTSPOT VERY NEAR THE NORTH POLE ALLOWED FOR FABULOUS LAN PARTIES, JUST BEFORE THE ENTIRE CAMP WENT MISSING.
THE LAST MESSAGE: "DUDE, WE'VE OVERCLOCKED EVERYTHING!"

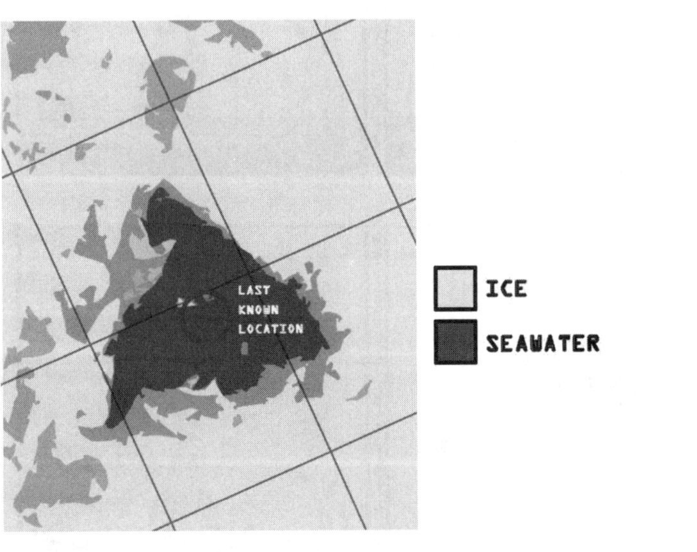
LAST KNOWN LOCATION
ICE
SEAWATER
COPYRIGHT© 2005 J.D. "Illiad" Frazer HTTP://WWW.USERFRIENDLY.ORG/

I tried to put the top-10 most poisonous creatures in the world on Stef, but I think I fell short by a few. Not sure where he got the Box Jellyfish, considering he's inland, but comics can be forgiving that way. If you haven't ever done so, read up on what Box Jellies can do. Their stings can be fatal to humans. If it weren't for the fact that Aussie women found on beaches are by-and-large athletic and pleasing to the eye, I'm pretty sure I'd stay clear of swimming in the ocean down under. Oh wait, they have Great Whites too. I like swimming pools.

WELL! HERE WE ARE IN GLORIOUS SYDNEY! HOW ABOUT WE GO GET A BEER BEFORE WE START WORK?
AM THINKINK IS GOOD IDEA.
COPYRIGHT © 2005 J.D. "Illiad" Frazer HTTP://WWW.USERFRIENDLY.ORG/

SEE STEF? AUSTRALIA HAS CITIES TOO. IT'S NOT ALL WILD AND WOOLY AND FILLED WITH TOXIC BEASTS LIKE YOU THOUGHT...STEF?
OH, WE ARE LOSINK HIM WAY BACK.

EBBEH.

OI! ARE YOU SID? AND PITR?
YOU MUST BE TIM, OUR LOCAL CONTRACTOR!
THAT'S RIGHT. HELLO!
COPYRIGHT © 2005 J.D. "Illiad" Frazer HTTP://WWW.USERFRIENDLY.ORG/

WAIT. WASN'T THERE A THIRD IN YOUR PARTY?
YES. STEF, OUR MARKETER. HE'LL BE ALONG IN...

...HOW LONG DOES IT TAKE TO HAVE ALL OF ONE'S BLOOD REPLACED?
SEVERAL HOURS.
WHA...?

SO HOW ARE YOU BLOKES ENJOYING OZ?
I LOVE JUST ABOUT ALL I'VE SEEN SO FAR.
COPYRIGHT © 2005 J.D. "Illiad" Frazer HTTP://WWW.USERFRIENDLY.ORG/

AM THINKINK EVERYONE HERE SOUNDS WERY FAMILIAR SOMEHOW...
OH BLOODY HELL. HERE COMES THE "STEVE IRWIN" CRACK...

YOU ARE ALL SOUNDINK LIKE JANGO FETT.
OI! HE'S A NEW ZEALANDER!!
NEW ZEALAND: BIRTHPLACE OF THE GALACTIC EMPIRE.

LISTEN. IS DIFFICULT TO TELL AUSSIE AND KIWI ACCENTS APART. YOU ARE SOUNDINK WERY MUCH THE SAME...
I UNDERSTAND. YOU CAN'T BE EXPECTED TO RECOGNIZE THE NUANCES.
COPYRIGHT © 2005 J.D. "Illiad" Frazer HTTP://WWW.USERFRIENDLY.ORG/

JUST LIKE I CAN'T HELP BUT THINK YOU SOUND AMERICAN.
TAKE THAT BACK, EH!!
NO MATTER WHERE YOU GO, IT'S JUST EMACS VS. VI ALL OVER AGAIN.

WOW! THESE ARE REALLY NICE OFFICES YOU FOUND FOR US, TIM.
YEAH, I GOT US A SWEET DEAL.

WE'RE IN A PARTICULARLY NICE PART OF THE CITY. ALTHOUGH THERE'S A CLOSET IN HERE NO ONE SHOULD OPEN AND I MUST CAUTION YOU ABOUT THE GUM TREES OUT BACK.

COPYRIGHT © 2005 J.D. "Illiad" Frazer HTTP://WWW.USERFRIENDLY.ORG/
WHAT, ARE GUM TREES DANGEROUS, TIM?
WITH GUM TREES COME DROP BEARS, MATE. "THE MOST FOUL, CRUEL MARSUPIAL YOU'VE EVER SET EYES ON."

"DROP BEARS?" YOU MEAN KOALAS? BUT THEY'RE ALL FLUFFY AND STUFF.
IS THAT WHAT YOU THINK MATE?
AAAH. THIS MUST BE THE OFFICE...
COPYRIGHT © 2005 J.D. "Illiad" Frazer HTTP://WWW.USERFRIENDLY.ORG/

...LET ME TELL YOU. THEY'RE HORRIBLY CARNIVOROUS.

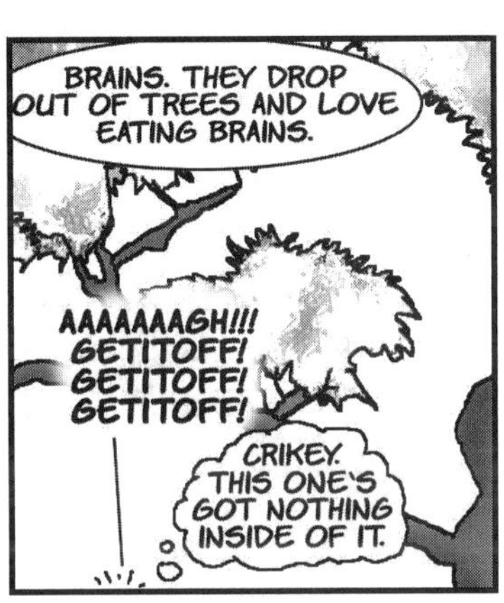
BRAINS. THEY DROP OUT OF TREES AND LOVE EATING BRAINS.
AAAAAAAGH!!! GETITOFF! GETITOFF! GETITOFF!
CRIKEY. THIS ONE'S GOT NOTHING INSIDE OF IT.

USER FRIENDLY
the comic strip
BY J.D. "ILLIAD" FRAZER
COPYRIGHT © 2005 J.D. "Illiad" Frazer HTTP://WWW.USERFRIENDLY.ORG/

ON FRIDAY THE FRED HUTCHINSON CANCER RESEARCH CENTER ANNOUNCED THAT THEY HAD SUCCESSFULLY INDUCED A STATE OF REVERSIBLE METABOLIC HIBERNATION IN MICE.

A PREVIOUS METHOD, THAT OF SHOWING THE MICE HOURS OF REALITY PROGRAMMING, RESULTED IN IRREVERSIBLE COMAS IN THE SUBJECTS.

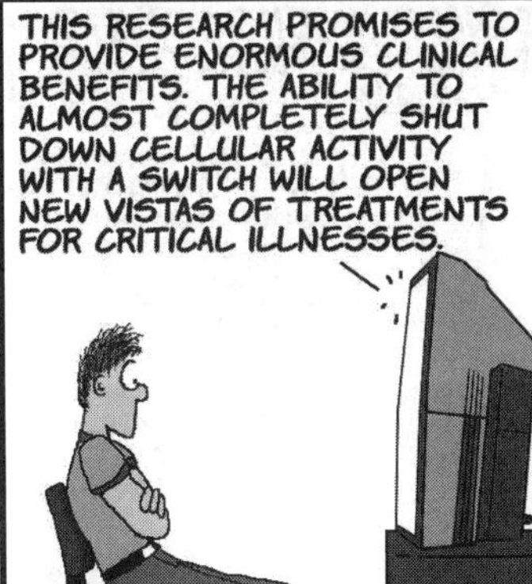
THIS RESEARCH PROMISES TO PROVIDE ENORMOUS CLINICAL BENEFITS. THE ABILITY TO ALMOST COMPLETELY SHUT DOWN CELLULAR ACTIVITY WITH A SWITCH WILL OPEN NEW VISTAS OF TREATMENTS FOR CRITICAL ILLNESSES.

TRIGGERING THE HIBERNATION DOES NOT INVOLVE A LARGE ARRAY OF COMPLICATED INSTRUMENTS. INSTEAD, IT IS CHEMICALLY INDUCED.

THE CHEMICAL SOLUTION USED CAUSES DEEP HIBERNATION TO TAKE PLACE ROUGHLY THIRTY MINUTES AFTER APPLICATION.
DOESN'T SODA ALREADY DO THAT?

YE GODS. WHAT THE HECK HAPPENED TO YOU?
FURRY TEETH CAME OUT OF THE SKY AND BIT MY HEAD!!
COPYRIGHT© 2005 J.D. "Illiad" Frazer HTTP://WWW.USERFRIENDLY.ORG/

WHAT IS WRONG WITH THIS PLACE?! EVERYTHING BITES AND ATTACKS AND MASTICATES!!
BOO.

YOU SURE SEEM TO HAVE A "QUALITY" OF SORTS, LITTLE GUY.
STEF, I PROMISE NOT TO EMASCULATE YOU OR WHATEVER THAT WORD WAS.

HEH. I'LL BET YOU'RE WONDERING WHAT THE HECK THIS IS.
NO, NOT REALLY.
COPYRIGHT© 2005 J.D. "Illiad" Frazer HTTP://WWW.USERFRIENDLY.ORG/

YOU'RE NOT?
NOPE.

YOU'RE CANADIANS, SO I FIGURED IT WAS YOUR PET BEAVER, MATE.
I SEE. EH.

I had the benefit of living in Australia when I was very young. I'm familiar with Aussie slang as a result. One day, I was driving along the I-5 (Interstate 5, which runs North-South through Washington State in the U.S.), and I heard a radio commercial for Outback Steakhouse (which, as the cartoon implies, doesn't serve anything even remotely authentic Australian). On comes a voice actor with an Aussie accent, who proclaims, "We're proud to offer our premier dessert, the Chocolate Thunder from Down Under!" I knew that *thunderbox* is Aussie slang for a toilet, so the dessert in question was essentially a big pile of poo. I nearly drove off the interstate and into a guard rail from laughing so hard.

NICE OF YOU TO TAKE ME OUT TO LUNCH.
CONSIDERING WHAT YOU'VE BEEN THROUGH, AND HOW MUCH I'VE BEEN ENTERTAINED, I FEEL I OWE YOU.
COPYRIGHT© 2005 J.D. "Illiad" Frazer HTTP://WWW.USERFRIENDLY.ORG/

I'M IGNORING YOU. I WANT TO LOOK AT THE MENU...

THIS CAN'T BE RIGHT. WHERE'S THE FOSTERS LAGER?
SHIPPED OVERSEAS. I CAN GET YOU SOMETHING SIMILAR FROM THE SUMP IF YOU LIKE.

I BEG YOUR PARDON?
JUST LIKE THEY SERVE IN THE OUTBACK STEAKHOUSE IN THE U.S. I WANT ONE OF THOSE.
COPYRIGHT© 2005 J.D. "Illiad" Frazer HTTP://WWW.USERFRIENDLY.ORG/

THE OUTBACK STEAKHOUSE SERVES AUSSIE FOOD. I'VE HAD ONE OF THOSE FOR DESSERT EVERY TIME I'VE GONE AND I WANT ONE NOW. HERE IN AUSTRALIA.

UH...WE DON'T...

I WANT A "CHOCOLATE THUNDER FROM DOWN UNDER!"
SIR, YOU DO REALIZE THAT A "THUNDERBOX" IS AUSSIE SLANG FOR "TOILET?"

HOW GOES THE CODING, TIM?
IT'S DONE, SID. WE'RE READY TO DELIVER THE SOURCE AND BINARIES TO THE CLIENT.
BUT PITR DID SOMETHING...

OH CRIPES. NOW WHAT?!
HE TOLD THE CLIENT HE NEEDED TO BE PAID EXTRA TO TRANSFORM THE CODE SO THAT IT COULD BE USED SOUTH OF THE EQUATOR.
"TRANSFORM?"

I DO BELIEVE HIS WORDS WERE "FLIP UPSIDE DOWN."
PITR!!

PITR'S LOCKED HIMSELF IN HIS OFFICE. DO YOU HAVE A KEY TIM?
HERE MATE. KNOCK THE DOOR IN WITH THIS.

GEEZ, YOU GUYS REALLY INVENTED SOME WICKED LOOKING WEAPONS HERE. MUST BE FROM ALL OF THE SNAKES AND STUFF?
SID, IT'S A CRICKET BAT.

The easy way to show a publisher that you don't like the biography of you they published
Expressing Displeasure
FOR
DUMMIES®
How to throw a world-class hissy fit!
A Reference for the Rest of Us!®
by Steve Jobs
CEO of Apple Inc.

May Steve Irwin's soul rest in peace. He was over the top as a showman, so I couldn't take him seriously all the time, but I had a lot of respect for his stand on conservation. He loved the natural world and the animals within. I poked fun at him a couple of times in the Aussie storyline and feel a little bad about it now that he's passed on.

Y'KNOW SID. ALTHOUGH I DISSED AUSTRALIA BECAUSE OF ALL OF THE TOXIC SNAKES AND SPIDERS AND THOSE VILE DROP BEARS. AND THE BEER DOESN'T HAVE ENOUGH WATER IN IT. I RATHER **LIKE** IT HERE.
COPYRIGHT© 2005 J.D. "Illiad" Frazer HTTP://WWW.USERFRIENDLY.ORG/

CONSIDERING ALL OF THE GRIEF I'VE BEEN THROUGH DOWN HERE. YOU'D THINK I'D BE SKITTISH. BUT I'M NOT. BECAUSE I'M TOUGH. AND ALSO BECAUSE PEOPLE WHO KNOW HOW I'VE SUFFERED ARE KIND TO ME.

STEF. JUST **TRY** THE VEGEMITE ON TOAST. IT'S PRETTY GOOD.
AND A BOX JELLYFISH ON MY HEAD WASN'T **ENOUGH** FOR YOU?!!

I love, *love* Vegemite on toast. If you love it too, I embrace you in the Vegemite Brother/Sisterhood. If you spurn it, go back to your refined white-flour products, Captain Wonder Bread.

TIM. IT WAS A REAL PLEASURE WORKING WITH YOU.
SAME HERE MATE. NOT TO WORRY ABOUT OPS HERE. IT'S ALL UNDER CONTROL. YOU HEADING BACK TO CANADA THEN?
COPYRIGHT© 2005 J.D. "Illiad" Frazer HTTP://WWW.USERFRIENDLY.ORG/

YEP. PITR AND STEF ARE ALREADY AT THE AIRPORT. HAVE YOU SEEN OUR. UH. PET BEAVER?
I THINK I SAW HIM OUT BACK MUCKING ABOUT IN THE GUM TREES.

MADAM. I PROTEST! I AM **NOT** YOUR "WIDDLE KOALA BABYKINS!"

"EARTH IS BRIGHTER RECENTLY BUT WE DON'T KNOW WHY" SAY SCIENTISTS.

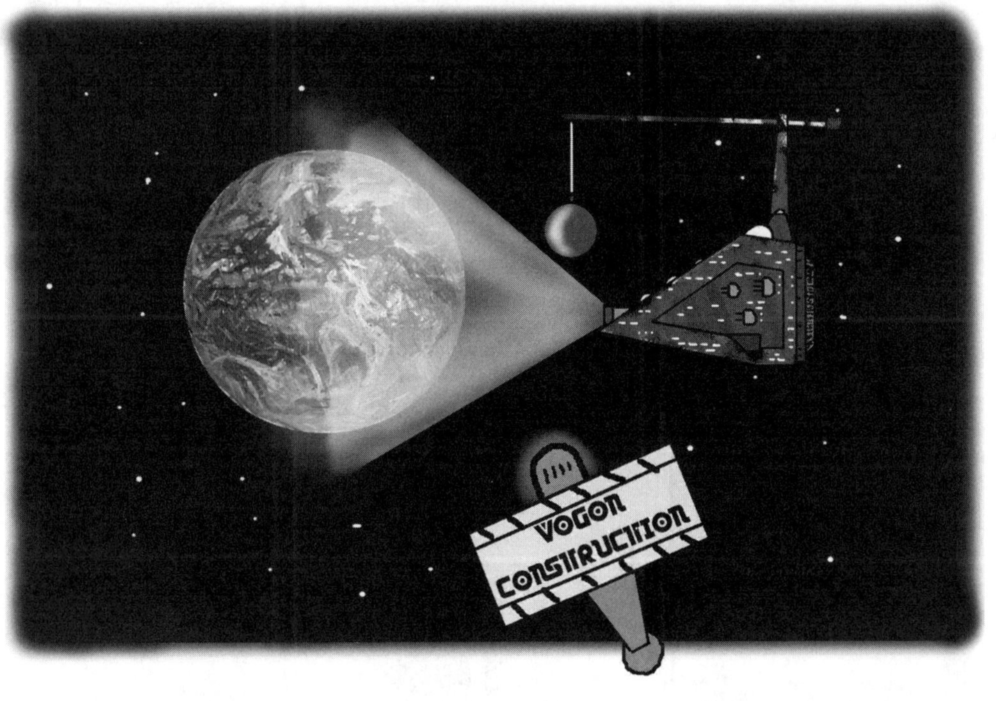
VOGON CONSTRUCTION
COPYRIGHT© 2005 J.D. "Illiad" Frazer HTTP://WWW.USERFRIENDLY.ORG/

OH! I HAVE SLIPPED ON THE PEARLY 'PHONES OF MIRTH
AND DANCED IN MY MIND WHILE BRITNEY SINGS
INWARD I HAVE BOOGIED EVER SINCE MY BIRTH
I HAVE NO RHYTHM BUT MY INNER EYE NEEDS NOT THESE THINGS.
Think Fruity

DOWN. DOWN. DOWNLOAD THE FILES. THANK YOU CISCO!
HOURS. DAYS. A LIFETIME. OF TUNES AND SPACES
WITHIN THIS BOX I'VE CAPTURED THE SOUL OF DISCO
AND REMOVED THE SHACKLES OF CD-SIZED CASES.
Think Fruity

COPYRIGHT © 2005 J.D. "Illiad" Frazer HTTP://WWW.USERFRIENDLY.ORG/
AND SO IMMERSED IN SILENT TONES THE WORLD I AVOID
AT BUS STOPS. SIDEWALKS. THEY SEE MY EARPHONES AND NOD
WHILE I IGNORE THEM AND THEY GROW ANNOYED
AS I PUT OUT MY HAND AND TOUCH THE FACE OF MY IPOD.
STICK TO WEB DESIGN YOU EGREGIOUS HACK.
Think Fruity

MIKE. HOW LONG HAVE YOU WORKED HERE AS A SYSADMIN?
I'D SAY IT'S GETTING ON TO TEN YEARS. CHIEF.
COPYRIGHT © 2005 J.D. "Illiad" Frazer HTTP://WWW.USERFRIENDLY.ORG/

RIGHT. AND YOUR WORK HAS ALWAYS BEEN EXEMPLARY. YOU'VE HAD RAISES OF COURSE. BUT WE'VE NEVER REALLY PROMOTED YOU. AND IT'S TIME WE DID.
YOU ARE FROM NOW ON OUR SENIOR SYSADMIN!

UH...THANK YOU. BUT WHAT EXACTLY DOES THAT MEAN?
HEY! CHECK OUT THE NEW FEATURES ON THIS EMERGENCY PAGER!

YOU WANT ME TO WEAR AN EMERGENCY PAGER?
ACTUALLY. THE EMERGENCY PAGER. WHENEVER ANYTHING GOES WRONG WITH THE MACHINE ROOM. YOU'LL BE NOTIFIED.
COPYRIGHT © 2005 J.D. "Illiad" Frazer HTTP://WWW.USERFRIENDLY.ORG/

CHIEF. I ALREADY HAVE A PAGER. AND IT ALREADY DOES THAT. AND YOU KNOW IT.
OH. SORRY. FORGOT TO TELL YOU ABOUT THE "ALSO WHEN MY E-MAIL DOESN'T WORK" PART.

BUT...WHAT IF I DON'T WANT...
MIKE. MIKE. MIKE. YOU SHOULDN'T BE SO MODEST.
MODEST?
COPYRIGHT © 2005 J.D. "Illiad" Frazer HTTP://WWW.USERFRIENDLY.ORG/

YOU DESERVE THE CHANGE IN TITLE! AND YOU'RE THE MOST RESPONSIBLE TECH ON STAFF! WHO ELSE COULD I TRUST THE PAGER TO? COULD YOU IMAGINE ME GIVING IT TO PITR?
NO...HE'D TURN IT INTO A DOOMSDAY DEVICE.

WELL THEN. HERE YOU ARE. WEAR IT PROUDLY. AND NO NEED TO THANK ME!
AW. SHUCKS...

I CAN'T BELIEVE THIS. THE CHIEF FAST-TALKED ME AND NOW I'M ATTACHED TO A WIRELESS LEASH. HE BETRAYED MY **TRUST!** I'M GOING TO HAVE TO HAVE SOME HARSH WORDS WITH HIM...

NEAT FEATURES, EH?
YE GODS. YES!!

I HEAR MIKE HAS A NEW PAGER
AN EMERGENCY PAGER. YES. WITH SUPER NIFTY "EXECUTIVE-FRIENDLY" FEATURES.
LIKE WHAT?

INSTEAD OF VIBRATING OR BEEPING, IT INJECTS A SHOT OF ADRENALINE.
IS THAT RIGHT...
BA-BEEP
BEEP-BOP
BEEP

MIKE?
WHOA...

Forgive me, sysadmins of the world. I may have given an idea to the Executives of Evil.

GOOGLE WINS A LICENSE TO OPERATE IN CHINA FROM THE CHINESE GOVERNMENT...

Web Images Groups News Local more »
Google fostering political dissent Search Advanced Search Preferences
Search: the Web pages from China
Web
Did you mean: *turning yourself in to the nearest authorities?*

IT'S BEEN MORE THAN TEN MINUTES SINCE I FIRST PAGED MIKE. WHERE IS HE?
COPYRIGHT© 2005 J.D. "Illiad" Frazer HTTP://WWW.USERFRIENDLY.ORG/

THIS IS RIDICULOUS. I SHOULD CALL HIM AGAIN.

I'VE SO HAD IT WITH GEEKS TAKING THEIR DAY-LONG COFFEE BREAKS...
AS GOD IS MY WITNESS. IF YOU CALL MY PAGER AGAIN I'LL HIT YOU SO MANY TIMES YOU'LL THINK YOU'RE SURROUNDED.

OKAY I'M HERE. SO WHAT'S THE BIG EMERGENCY?
IT'S TERRIBLE. MIKE. DATA HAS STOPPED FLOWING.
COPYRIGHT© 2005 J.D. "Illiad" Frazer HTTP://WWW.USERFRIENDLY.ORG/

WHAT DO YOU MEAN. "DATA HAS STOPPED FLOWING"? OUR SERVERS ARE FINE... WAIT. WHAT'S THAT?

"ALT.BINARIES.LLAMA-MAMAS?"
IT'S DATA! IT'S TOTALLY IRRELEVANT THAT MY ONES AND ZEROES ARE FUZZY CAMELOIDS!

This one is based on reality. I knew a sales manager who had a *Beckon I.T. Serf* label on an autodial button on his phone.

ARE WE DONE HERE?
WHATEVER. IT'S FIXED NOW. SO YOU CAN GO.
COPYRIGHT© 2005 J.D. "Illiad" Frazer HTTP://WWW.USERFRIENDLY.ORG/

I CAN'T HELP BUT NOTICE YOU HAVE A BUTTON ON YOUR PHONE LABELLED 'BECKON TECHNICAL MINION.'
OH YES. I DO LOVE AUTO-DIAL.

YE GODS. I AM SO TIRED...IT'S BEEN 30 HOURS SINCE I'VE SLEPT...
COPYRIGHT© 2005 J.D. "Illiad" Frazer HTTP://WWW.USERFRIENDLY.ORG/

ZZZZzzzzzz...

EAAARRRRRRRRRGH!!
SEE? IT'S JUST LIKE IN PULP FICTION EXCEPT THERE'S NO GROSS NEEDLE THROUGH THE BREASTBONE PART.
AND MIKE DOESN'T LOOK LIKE UMA THURMAN.

AAAAIIIEEEE!!!!
WHAT'S GOING ON, COBB?
MIKE IS TEACHING STEF WHAT "EMERGENCY" MEANS.
COPYRIGHT© 2005 J.D. "Illiad" Frazer HTTP://WWW.USERFRIENDLY.ORG/

NOW, WHAT'S THE DEFINITION OF "EMERGENCY," STEF?
DON'T CALL UNLESS SMOKE IS COMING OUT OF MY MACHINE
--AAAAGH!!!

GET IT RIGHT. WHAT'S THE DEFINITION OF "EMERGENCY?"
DON'T CALL UNLESS SMOKE IS COMING OUT OF YOUR MACHINE!!

THAT EMERGENCY PAGER HAS BEEN QUITE THE PERSONAL DEMON FOR YOU, MIKE.
OH, I'M NOT SO CONCERNED ANYMORE.
COPYRIGHT© 2005 J.D. "Illiad" Frazer HTTP://WWW.USERFRIENDLY.ORG/

NO? I KNOW YOU HAVE STEF SORTED OUT, BUT WHAT ABOUT THE CHIEF?
NOTHING A FEDEX ENV-ELOPE CAN'T SOLVE. AND I GET TO MAKE SOCIAL COMMENTARY ABOUT I.T. IN NORTH AMERICA.

MEANWHILE, IN INDIA...
NOW FEEL WHAT HAPPENS WHEN I DIAL THE NUMBER FOR THAT PAGER.
OH MY GOODNESS!!

I have readers in India. One e-mailed me to say that if such a pager were ever to become reality in his country, I would be to blame.

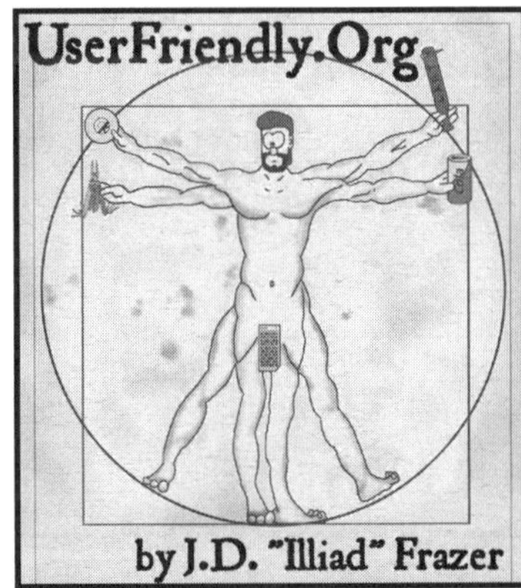
UserFriendly.Org
by J.D. "Illiad" Frazer
COPYRIGHT© 2005 J.D. "Illiad" Frazer HTTP://WWW.USERFRIENDLY.ORG/

I HATE LINUX.
SCO

I'M STILL NOT ENTIRELY CERTAIN WHAT THE HECK IT IS, BUT I HATE IT ANYWAYS.
SCO

"SPEAKING AT QUEEN MARY UNIVERSITY OF LONDON, OPEN SOURCE DEVELOPER LABS CHIEF EXECUTIVE STUART COHEN SAID THE S.C.O. LAWSUITS WERE 'THE BEST THING THAT EVER HAPPENED TO LINUX.'"
CARRY ON...

"IN EFFECT," SAID COHEN, "DARL MCBRIDE HAS HELPED LINUX ENORMOUSLY. WE JUST LOVE THE GUY."
SCO

I'M NOT LOVABLE! I AM THE EVIL!!!
"WE JUST WANT TO GIVE HIM A BIG OL' SMOOCH," REMARKED COHEN.

An awful lot of anger surrounds the *Star Wars* franchise. My "generation" of *Star Wars* fans loves the first three films that were made (Ep. IV, V, and VI). The prequels were dreck, probably because Lucas didn't have the benefit of the brilliant mythologist Joseph Campbell metaphorically at his side.

TECH SUPPORT. GREG SPEAKING.
GEORGE LUCAS IS A **BIG DOUCHE** AND HE RUINED STAR WARS FOR ME WITH EPISODES I AND II!! HE **DOESN'T DESERVE MY MONEY!!**

AND YET, YOU JUST GAVE HIM MORE OF YOUR MONEY AT REVENGE OF THE SITH. DIDN'T YOU.
GEORGE LUCAS SELLS TICKETS TO TRAIN WRECKS!

LUCAS DIDN'T MAKE ANAKIN BAD ENOUGH TO BECOME A SITH. HAVE YOU SEEN EPISODE III YET?
NO. AND I'LL THANK YOU FOR NOT SPOILING THE MOVIE FOR ME.

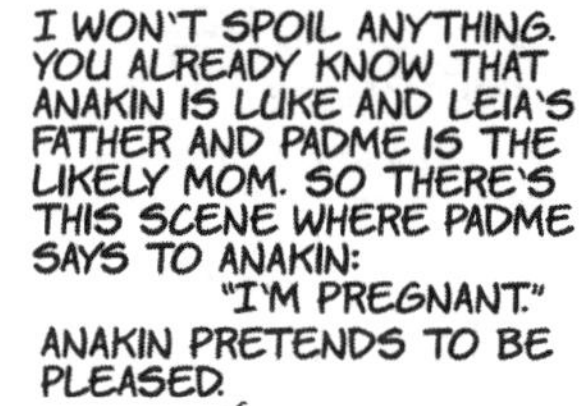
I WON'T SPOIL ANYTHING. YOU ALREADY KNOW THAT ANAKIN IS LUKE AND LEIA'S FATHER AND PADME IS THE LIKELY MOM. SO THERE'S THIS SCENE WHERE PADME SAYS TO ANAKIN: "I'M PREGNANT." ANAKIN PRETENDS TO BE PLEASED.

ANAKIN DECEIVING PADME DOESN'T MAKE HIM BAD ENOUGH TO BE A SITH?
HE SHOULD'VE WAVED HIS HAND AND SAID "I'M NOT THE DAD YOU'RE LOOKING FOR!"

LISTEN. MAYBE YOU SHOULDN'T BE SO HARD ON THE LATEST THREE MOVIES.
THEY'RE THERE FOR A REASON. JUST AS THEY ARE.

IN EPISODES I AND II, AND I PRESUME III, LUCAS STICKS TO THE FAIRY-TALE FORMULA. IT'S ALL ABOUT THE STRUGGLE AND FALL AND EVENTUAL REDEMPTION. GOOD AND EVIL REMAIN CLEARLY DEFINED. WOULDN'T YOU AGREE?

YES. MUPPETS ARE **GOOD**. LUCAS AND HIS DAMNED CGI ARE **EVIL!**
OH. YOU SHOULD TRY OUT FOR A ROLE IN "REVENGE OF THE PITH."

There's always room for an STD joke.

SO...WHAT'S YOUR NAME?
JOJO.
JOJO. HAVE YOU HEARD THAT THERE'S BEEN AN OUTBREAK OF SOME HORRID DISEASE AMONGST SUPER HARD-CORE STAR WARS FANS?
WHAT?!

REALLY. IT SEEMS TO STRIKE STAR WARS FANS WHO THINK THAT IF THEY DRESS UP IN A DARK CLOAK, ACT ALL EVIL AND CARRY A $6.99 LIGHTSABRE FROM WAL-MART THAT WOMEN WILL SWOON AND WANT TO GET CARNAL WITH THEM.

THEY'RE CALLING IT "SITHILIS."
AAAUUUGH!!

LOOK. I'M FEELING VERY FRAIL RIGHT NOW. ABUSED AND SPENT BY WHAT LUCAS AND HIS EVIL MACHINATIONS HAVE DONE TO MY BELOVED STAR WARS.
HAS IT OCCURRED TO YOU THAT STAR WARS ACTUALLY BELONGS TO GEORGE LUCAS. AND NOT YOU?

UH...HELLO?
HI. THIS IS JOJO'S ROOMMATE. DID YOU JUST PULL A SITH LORD ON HIM? HE'S HAVING TROUBLE BREATHING AND HIS EYES ARE BUGGIN' OUT.

WITH THE RELEASE OF STAR WARS EPISODE III, REVENGE OF THE SITH, GEORGE LUCAS IS HANGING UP HIS DIRECTOR'S HAT. HIS LEGACY, HOWEVER, WILL NOT ONLY LIVE ON, IT IS SET TO THRIVE.

THERE HAS BEEN TALK OF AN "EPISODE ZERO," TELLING THE STORY OF THE SITH AND JEDI. STAR WARS COMIC BOOKS AND NOVELS ABOUND AND CONTINUE TO FLOW. PLANS ARE ALSO IN THE WORKS FOR A STAR WARS TELEVISION SERIES.

THE SERIES WILL BE A HIP NEW SITCOM FOR THE TWENTY-SOMETHING CROWD, FEATURING A STRAIGHT-LACED HUMAN AND A SPIRITUAL-BUT-UNBALANCED SITH. THE WORKING TITLE IS "DARTHMA AND GREG."
NOOOOOOO!!
IT WILL TAKE PLACE ON NABOO BY THAT CLOYING LAKE.

VOYAGER 1 FINALLY ENTERS THE HELIOSHEATH, AND WE LEARN THAT IT JUST WASN'T FAST ENOUGH.

RECEPTION OF TELEVISION SIGNAL OF "AMERICAN IDOL"
GENERAL ZICK! SUMMON THE BATTLEFLEET!
HUMANITY'S MESSAGE OF PEACE ON VOYAGER

"Three-coil peanut-laden steamer"? Uh ... I don't know where that came from.

YOU STUPID DORK! THE INTERNET IS BROKEN AND I WANT IT FIXED. AND FIXED RIGHT BLOODY NOW! WERE YOU DROPPED ON YOUR HEAD WHEN YOU WERE SMALL? OR WAS YOUR HEAD ALWAYS THAT SIZE? WELL?! SPEAK UP! NO! SHUT UP! SHUT UP! *KLIK*
COPYRIGHT © 2005 J.D. "Illiad" Frazer HTTP://WWW.USERFRIENDLY.ORG/
HELLO? HELLO?! WHERE'S MY EMAIL? WHY CAN'T I GET TO MY EMAIL?! WHAT HAVE YOU DONE TO THE INTERNET? I WAS SENDING SOMEONE A PHOTO ALBUM AND MY EMAIL JUST STOPPED! WHAT HAVE YOU DONE?! WHAT'S WRONG WITH YOU PEOPLE?! *CLIK*
HEY TECHNODWEEB! WHEN ARE YOU GONNA FIX WINDOWS? MINESWEEPER STOPPED WORKING! HOP TO IT. YOU WASTE OF OXYGEN! I WANT MY HIGH SCORES BACK. YOU THREE-COIL PEANUT-LADEN STEAMER! WAKE UP! *CLICK*
I AM TECH SUPPORT. SMEAR ME.

GREG. GREAT NEWS! WE'RE TAKING YOU OFF THE GENERAL HELP DESK AND RE-TASKING YOU FOR A NEW CLIENT.
WHAT CLIENT IS THIS?
COPYRIGHT © 2005 J.D. "Illiad" Frazer HTTP://WWW.USERFRIENDLY.ORG/

OH. A BUNCH OF PH.DS AT THE UNIVERSITY.
WHAT KIND OF PH.DS?

PH.DS WITH LOTS OF GRANT MONEY TO SPEND.
AH. PEOPLE WITH DOCTORATES IN "MY-WALLET-IS-BIGGER-THAN-MY-POINTY-LITTLE-HEAD."

First, understand that I love going to university. Second, understand that I have a lot of respect for the professors who teach there. Third, know that in the halls of academe, there is not one iota of grip around this thing called reality. Also, "Dr. Tuskfort" is a pseudonym for a department head I know. He's an exception to the second point and the epitome of the third. Bit of a dick, really.

TECH SUPPORT. GRAD STUDENT EFFIGY SPEAKING...
THIS IS DR. TUSKFORT. I UNDERSTAND YOU'RE OUR NEW TECHNOSERF. THESE ARE THE GROUND RULES...
COPYRIGHT © 2005 J.D. "Illiad" Frazer HTTP://WWW.USERFRIENDLY.ORG/

...YOU WILL ANSWER OUR CALLS PROMPTLY AND SINCERELY. IF THERE IS SOME URGE IN YOU TO QUESTION MYSELF OR MY COLLEAGUES, REMIND YOURSELF WHO IT IS THAT HAS THE BETTER EDUCATION...
SIR, IN WHAT SUBJECT IS YOUR DOCTORATE? ENGINEERING? PHYSICS?

UM. "THE APPRECIATION OF SERIF FONTS IN SAXON TABLE DOILIES...
KIND OF...SPECIFIC, ISN'T IT?
...IN THE YEAR 1058."

SO THE NEXT STEP, DR. TUSKFORT, IS TO CLICK ON "PROPERTIES," THEN THE "ADVANCED" TAB, THEN-
AAAAAAAAAGH! THIS COMPUTER STUFF IS SO FRUSTRATING! I MUST BELONG TO AN EARLIER TIME.
COPYRIGHT © 2005 J.D. "Illiad" Frazer HTTP://WWW.USERFRIENDLY.ORG/

LIKE, SAY, 1058?
WHAT?!!

HELLO. GREG SPEAKING. I READ THE MANUALS SO YOU DON'T HAVE TO.
HI. I'M ONE OF DR. TUSKFORT'S GRADS. HE ASKED ME TO SET UP A MAIL SERVER.
DEPARTMENT OF HISTORIC WOVEN ACCOUTREMENTS

WANT SOME ADVICE? SAY IT'S NOT POSSIBLE. YOU DO NOT WANT TO BE A MAIL ADMIN.
WHY NOT?
DEPARTMENT OF HISTORIC WOVEN ACCOUTREMENTS

IT'S A LITTLE KNOWN FACT, BUT E-MAIL SERVERS WERE THE TENTH PLAGUE THAT GOD VISITED UPON THE EGYPTIANS. ALL THAT ANGEL OF DEATH AND PASSOVER STUFF IS PURE CRAP.
OOOH! THESIS!

SO YOU'RE STUDYING SAXON DOILIES TOO?
NO. I'M WORKING ON A MASTERS IN MATHEMATICS. ALL OF THE FACULTY OF SCIENCE POSITIONS WERE FILLED, SO I GRABBED A SPOT HERE.

BUT WHAT ON EARTH DO DOILIES HAVE TO DO WITH MATH?
OH, PLENTY.

SUCH AS?
BOTH SUBJECTS PREPARE YOU FOR A LIFE OF BITTERNESS AND MISANTHROPY AS PEOPLE FROM ALL WALKS OF LIFE SNORT AT YOU AND ASK "BUT WHEN WOULD YOU USE IT?"

THE CNET REPORT ON APPLE SWITCHING TO INTEL MICROPROCESSORS MANIFESTS A NEW LOGO FOR THE CONCERNED MAC COMMUNITY

BILE inside

MATH CAN BE REALLY FUN. WOULD YOU LIKE TO HEAR A MATH JOKE?
I SUPPOSE.
WHAT'S LARGE, GREY, AND PROVES THE UNCOUNTABILITY OF REAL NUMBERS?
COPYRIGHT © 2005 J.D. "Illiad" Frazer HTTP://WWW.USERFRIENDLY.ORG/

I HAVE NO IDEA. WHAT?
CANTOR'S DIAGONAL ELEPHANT!! HAHAHAH HAHAHAHAHAHAH HAHAHAHAHAHAH HAHAHAHA!!!

IT'S A GOOD JOKE. REALLY. I CAN PROVE IT.
I THINK YOU HAVE A FINE FUTURE AHEAD OF YOU AS A CARTOONIST.

HELLO. GREG SPEAKING.
IT'S DR. TUSKFORT AGAIN. I WOULD SPEAK WITH YOU.
COPYRIGHT © 2005 J.D. "Illiad" Frazer HTTP://WWW.USERFRIENDLY.ORG/

YES?
FOR STARTERS, YOU WILL KOWTOW TO ME WHEN YOU GREET ME OR I SHALL CANCEL THIS CONTRACT AND INFORM YOUR SUPERIOR THAT YOU WERE THE CAUSE.

EHHHH...WHAT IS YOUR BIDDING, MY MASTER?
PRETTY GOOD. BUT I AM BEYOND MASTER. I AM DOCTORATE. RESPECT ME.
2005-06-07

This happens all the time in academia. Trust me.

AND HOW MAY I HELP YOU TODAY DR. TUSKFORT?
CHANGE THE ROOT PASSWORD. WITHOUT EXCEPTION, YOU SHOULD BE THE ONLY PERSON WITH THAT SORT OF ACCESS TO OUR SERVER.
COPYRIGHT © 2005 J.D. "Illiad" Frazer HTTP://WWW.USERFRIENDLY.ORG/

I'M...GLAD TO HEAR YOU SAY THAT, SIR. IT'S DONE.
NOW, GIVE ME ROOT ACCESS.
WORD WORD WORD
2005-06-08

BUT...YOU JUST SAID-
I AM DOCTORATE! RESPECT ME!

SIR, I'M NOT SURE I CAN HANDLE MUCH MORE OF THIS "I AM DOCTORATE!" MEME OF YOURS.
EH?
COPYRIGHT © 2005 J.D. "Illiad" Frazer HTTP://WWW.USERFRIENDLY.ORG/

YOU SAY YOU HAVE A DOCTORATE. YOU REMIND ME OF THIS TEN TIMES A DAY. YOU READ LOTS OF BOOKS. AND YET, EVERY DAY YOU CALL ME UP TO ASK ME HOW TO SAVE A FLIPPING WORD DOCUMENT! YOU'RE SUPPOSED TO BE EDUCATED!!
2005-06-09

I LEARNED ENOUGH TO AFFORD HIRING A FLESH HELP SYSTEM TO SERVE MY WHIMS, DIDN'T I?
I AM TECHNOLOGIST. SOMEBODY PLEASE SHOOT ME.

IN A SHOCKING ANNOUNCEMENT ON MONDAY, STEVE JOBS OF APPLE REVEALED THAT THEY WILL GRADUALLY SHIFT THEIR MAC LINE TO INTEL-BASED CHIPS FROM NOW THROUGH 2007.
COPYRIGHT© 2005 J.D. "Illiad" Frazer HTTP://WWW.USERFRIENDLY.ORG/

YES, LADIES AND GENTLEMEN. THIS MEANS APPLE WILL BE EMBRACING X86 ARCHITECTURE. THIS IS NO LIE.
2005-06-10

IN OTHER NEWS, PINK PIGLETS WERE SEEN LEAVING AFTERBURNER SMOKE TRAILS IN THE SKY SINCE MONDAY.

HELLO. GREG SPE-
AAAAAAAAAARRRRRGH!! APPLE IS MOVING TO X86 ARCHITECTURE!!
COPYRIGHT© 2005 J.D. "Illiad" Frazer HTTP://WWW.USERFRIENDLY.ORG/

2005-06-11

SO...HOW'S THE CROW TASTING?
NEEDS SALT.

THE INSTALLATION OF WI-FI IN MORE AND MORE AIRLINERS WILL, BY NECESSITY, BRING MORE AND MORE REGULATIONS OVER THE KINDS OF GAMES YOU CAN PLAY IN AN AIRBORNE LAN PARTY....
TERRORIST SPOTTED!
BRAPAPAPAP!!
TANGO DOWN!
AAAAAAIIIIEEEE!
COPYRIGHT© 2005 J.D. "Illiad" Frazer HTTP://WWW.USERFRIENDLY.ORG/

HEY SID? WHERE... OOH. WHY THE LONG FACE?
APPLE AND INTEL.

WHY? YOU'RE NOT A MAC USER.
CORRECT. MY SISTER. HOWEVER, IS.
2005-06-13
COPYRIGHT © 2005 J.D. "Illiad" Frazer HTTP://WWW.USERFRIENDLY.ORG/

WHICH MEANS?
WHICH MEANS I CAN NO LONGER SAY "SORRY. I ONLY KNOW ENOUGH ABOUT INTEL BOXES TO DO TECH SUPPORT."
YOUR SISTER JUST CALLED. SHE SAID TO TELL YOU SHE BOUGHT THE "TALK FOREVER" LONG DISTANCE PLAN.

I swear to god, if Apple doesn't stop with the "i"-this and "i"-that, I'm going to go "i"-nsane.

WHAT I DON'T GET IS HOW TWO BRAND-SENSITIVE COMPANIES LIKE APPLE AND INTEL ARE GOING TO GET BOTH OF THEIR BRANDS TO PLAY NICE AND REMAIN RECOGNIZABLE.

COPYRIGHT © 2005 J.D. "Illiad" Frazer HTTP://WWW.USERFRIENDLY.ORG/
AMATEUR. IT'S A CINCH.
OH?
2005-06-14

"iNTEL INSIDE"
HOW DO YOU SAY THAT PROPERLY? "EYENTEL INSIDE?"

I'VE BEEN USING IBM FOR YEARS NOW. AND THINGS WERE FINE UNTIL RECENTLY. I FIGURED I HAD TO DO SOMETHING.
BUMPEE DABUMBUM
COPYRIGHT © 2005 J.D. "Illiad" Frazer HTTP://WWW.USERFRIENDLY.ORG/

SO I DID. AND I SWITCHED THE COMPANY OVER TO INTEL.
BOY DID THE WORLD EVER GET ITS PANTIES KNOTTED UP.
HEH.
BUMP BEE DA DUM BUM
2005-06-15

MY NAME IS STEVE JOBS. AND I'M A C.E.O.
BUM BA DING
apple.com/switched

WHAT ARE THOSE, PITR?
MINT SLICES. YOU ARE REMEMBERINK THEM FROM AUSTRALIA?
COPYRIGHT © 2005 J.D. "Illiad" Frazer HTTP://WWW.USERFRIENDLY.ORG/

OH GOOD HEAVENS YES! AN INCOMPARABLE CHOCO-LATE-DIPPED COOKIE WITH A MINT CREME FILLING. MAY I?
OF COURSE. THEY ARE FOR SHARINK.
2005-06-16

THAT'S...REALLY QUITE REPULSIVE.
HM. NEXT BATCH AM MUST TO BE TRYINK DIFFERENT BRAND OF TOOTHPASTE.

HEH. *THE ECONOMIST* JUST BLASTED THE BUSINESS SOFTWARE ALLIANCE. APPARENTLY THE B.S.A. IS USING BOGUS NUMBERS TO COME UP WITH A "LOSS" OF BILLIONS OF DOLLARS FROM PIRACY.

THE ECONOMIST CALLED THEM ON IT AND NOW THE B.S.A. IS ALL TESTY.

THE BSA CLAIMS THAT THERE ARE X PROGRAMS ON AVERAGE PER P.C.

MULTIPLY THAT BY THE NUMBER OF PCS IN THE WORLD. THEN DEDUCT THE NUMBER OF KNOWN LICENSES SOLD.

MULTIPLY THE REMAINDER WITH A DOLLAR FIGURE AND YOU HAVE THE TOTAL AMOUNT THE B.S.A. IS CLAIMING IS LOST TO PIRACY.

2005-06-17

WHAT IF ALL OF THE SOFTWARE I HAVE ON MY PC IS FREE?
THEN YOU'RE JUST THE BIGGEST PIRATE THERE IS. YOU CHEEKY LITTLE CAD.

ATTENTION. PLEASE. I AM SPECIAL AGENT PECKSNIFF FROM THE BUSINESS SOFTWARE ALLIANCE. YOUR OFFICE HAS BEEN CHOSEN FOR AN AUDIT TO ENSURE THAT YOU DON'T HAVE PIRATED SOFTWARE.

2005-06-18

AHHH...I SEE THE FEAR IN YOUR EYES. YOU'VE PIRATED SOFTWARE HAVE YOU?
OH! PIRATED SOFTWARE! I THOUGHT YOU SAID **PIRATE** SOFTWARE AS IN SID MEIER'S PIRATES! BECAUSE THEN YOU'D, LIKE, TOTALLY HAVE ME.

JUST A WILD GUESS AS TO WHICH COMPANY WILL NEXT BE SUBJECTED TO A "SOFTWARE AUDIT" BY THE BUSINESS SOFTWARE ALLIANCE...

The Economist
Mega-Corps
too cool for school
TV Nation
reading as an option
Dust Puppies
fnord
B.S.A. Approved Bull

YOU SHOULDN'T MAKE LIGHT OF THIS! SOFTWARE PIRACY IS A REAL PROBLEM. THE COST TO THE INDUSTRY IS IN THE BILLIONS, IF NOT TRILLIONS!
COPYRIGHT © 2005 J.D. "Illiad" Frazer HTTP://WWW.USERFRIENDLY.ORG/

ANY SOFTWARE ON YOUR MACHINE THAT YOU DIDN'T PAY FOR, ESPECIALLY FREE SOFTWARE, HURTS THE INDUSTRY AND IS IMMORAL IF NOT ILLEGAL! EVERY TIME YOU DOWNLOAD A PIECE OF SOFTWARE THAT DOESN'T COST YOU ANYTHING, IT COSTS US!

ISN'T THAT KIND OF LIKE SAYING IF I DON'T GIVE YOU EVERYTHING IN MY WALLET I'M COSTING YOU EVERYTHING IN MY WALLET?
SEE, NOW YOU'RE GETTING IT.

NOW, LET'S SEE WHAT PIRATED SOFTWARE YOU HAVE INSTALLED ON YOUR MACHINE...
COPYRIGHT © 2005 J.D. "Illiad" Frazer HTTP://WWW.USERFRIENDLY.ORG/

2005-06-21
MM HM. UH HUH. AH HAH!
WHAT? WHAT?! WHAT?!!

YOU HAVE WINDOWS XP ON YOUR MACHINE!
THAT'S BEEN PAID FOR!
NO ONE PAYS FOR WINDOWS XP AND YOU KNOW IT!

LOOK, THERE'S NOTHING PIRATED ON MY MACHINE!
IT IS HE WHO DENIES THE MOST STRENUOUSLY THAT BEARS THE MOST GUILT.
COPYRIGHT © 2005 J.D. "Illiad" Frazer HTTP://WWW.USERFRIENDLY.ORG/

BESIDES, I JUST FOUND SOMETHING ELSE YOU'VE PIRATED.
OH LORD, WHAT?!

2005-06-22
NOTEPAD!
THAT COMES WITH WINDOWS!
SO YOU'RE GUILTY ON TWO COUNTS NOW!

LOOK, HERE'S THE CERTIFICATE OF AUTHENTICITY, PROVING I HAVE A LEGAL, PAID-FOR COPY OF WINDOWS XP!
COPYRIGHT © 2005 J.D. "Illiad" Frazer HTTP://WWW.USERFRIENDLY.ORG/

2005-06-23

AND WHERE EXACTLY DID YOU STEAL THIS FROM?
AAAAAUUUUGH!!

EXPLAIN TO ME WHAT THIS IS. I DON'T RECOGNIZE IT.
THAT'S NETHACK. IT'S FREE, AND OPEN SOURCE.
AH HA! OPEN SOURCE! THAT'S LIKE A CANCER YOU KNOW. AND IT'S VERY COMMUNIST. AND...
COPYRIGHT © 2005 J.D. "Illiad" Frazer HTTP://WWW.USERFRIENDLY.ORG/

2005-06-24

AH HA! SUCKED IN BY THE BRILLIANCE OF THE GAME, AREN'T YOU!
IT LOOKS LIKE A RETARDED WORD PROCESSOR. NO WONDER IT'S FREE.

Any excuse to summon Inquisitor Bernardo. I love the guy and all he represents.

YOU CLEARLY HAVE SOME QUESTIONABLE SOFTWARE ON YOUR MACHINE. I'M GOING TO RECOMMEND A FULL FORENSIC AND...
COPYRIGHT © 2005 J.D. "Illiad" Frazer HTTP://WWW.USERFRIENDLY.ORG/

...MY WORD. IS THAT AN UNLICENSED MP3 OF A SONG I SEE ON YOUR HARD DRIVE?
2005-06-25

WHO DISTURBS THE SLUMBER OF AN R.I.A.A. INQUISITOR?
A NETHACK "SCROLL OF SCUMBAG GENOCIDE" WOULD BE JUST PERFECT RIGHT NOW.
RIAA
BAMF!

MICROSOFT RELEASES ITS EXTENSIONS TO RSS

DAY ONE AFTER RELEASE

DAY TWO AFTER RELEASE

We're gonna be best friends!

COPYRIGHT © 2005 J.D. "Illiad" Frazer HTTP://WWW.USERFRIENDLY.ORG/

2005-06-26

"Bereft of lucre" became a favorite phrase among some UFies for a while, usually a few days before payday.

I AM HERE TO COLLECT OUR RIGHTFUL DUE FOR HIS CRIME.
IT'S AN MP3 OF ME SINGING KARAOKE.
HERETIC! YOUR FINE IS DOUBLED!
I HAVE HIS WALLET. WE'LL SPLIT IT UP.
COPYRIGHT © 2005 J.D. "Illiad" Frazer HTTP://WWW.USERFRIENDLY.ORG/

2005-06-27

IT APPEARS BEREFT OF LUCRE.
IS THAT A KETCHUP PACKET?
I'M POOR FROM PAYING YOU GUYS THOUSANDS OF DOLLARS FOR CRAP SOFTWARE AND MUSIC FOR YEARS!

I AM INQUISITOR BERNARDO OF THE R.I.A.A., AND I BEAR A MESSAGE OF WARNING.
THOU SHALT CEASE NOT SPENDING MONEY ON OUR PRODUCTS OR THOU SHALT FACE OUR WRATH!
COPYRIGHT © 2005 J.D. "Illiad" Frazer HTTP://WWW.USERFRIENDLY.ORG/

OUR COMPATRIOTS IN THE B.S.A. ALSO HAVE A WORTHY CAUSE, BUT DO NOT FORGET THAT THE R.I.A.A. IS SUPREME! MUSIC IS ABOUT LOVE, AND THE R.I.A.A. IS ABOUT MUSIC! THEREFORE, THE R.I.A.A. IS ABOUT LOVE!
2005-06-28

WOULD THAT BE YOUR "LEAVE THE MONEY ON THE DRESSER" KIND OF LOVE?
BETTER THAN THY "LEAVE THE MONEY ON THE DRESSER AND WE'LL SEND YOU A SHOT OF PENICILLIN LATER" KIND OF LOVE!

HEY. YOU READ ABOUT GOOGLE'S VIDEO SEARCH AND PLAYBACK?
A LITTLE. IT SOUNDS PRETTY AWESOME!
YA. NO PORN THOUGH.
COPYRIGHT © 2005 J.D. "Illiad" Frazer HTTP://WWW.USERFRIENDLY.ORG/

2005-06-29

HAVING A BIT OF TROUBLE THINKING OF WHAT ELSE I'D BE SEARCHING FOR.
MMMMMMM. CEPHALOPOD DOCUMENTARIES.

2005-06-30
Y'KNOW. GOOGLE SURE IS GETTING ENORMOUS. PERVASIVE. EVEN.
COPYRIGHT © 2005 J.D. "Illiad" Frazer HTTP://WWW.USERFRIENDLY.ORG/

FROOGLE. GOOGLE MAPS. THEY'RE WORKING ON A GOOGLE PAYMENT SYSTEM. GOOGLE THIS. GOOGLE THAT. WHAT COULD BE NEXT?

I'M THINKING GOOGLE DATING. IMAGINE THE SEARCH TERMS.
"PERFECT WITH LOW STANDARDS."

Ballmer's claim was made in late June, 2005. Has it been six months yet?

GOOGLE MUST HAVE MICROSOFT RUNNING SCARED.
STEVE BALLMER SAID THAT IN SIX MONTHS MICROSOFT WOULD CATCH UP WITH GOOGLE IN TERMS OF RELEVANCY.
COPYRIGHT © 2005 J.D. "Illiad" Frazer HTTP://WWW.USERFRIENDLY.ORG/

OH HELL. WHO IS BALLMER TRYING TO KID? GOOGLE CONTROLS THE HORIZONTAL. THE VERTICAL. THE WIGGLY-WAGGLY AND THE THING THAT MAKES THE BLUE LED FLASH ON AND OFF.

2005-07-01
"THE WIGGLY-WAGGLY?"
OKAY. MAYBE BALLMER HAS THAT ONE SEWN UP WITH HIS "DEVELOPERS!" DANCE.

GOOGLE'S HUGE. SURE. BUT MICROSOFT IS STILL A SERIOUS THREAT.
SORRY. BUT I THINK THEY'VE BECOME QUITE IRRELEVANT.
COPYRIGHT © 2005 J.D. "Illiad" Frazer HTTP://WWW.USERFRIENDLY.ORG/

2005-07-02

SO. WHAT'S YOUR HIGH SCORE ON FREECELL THESE DAYS?
NOT BLOODY FAIR.

USER FRIENDLY
the comic strip
BY J.D. "ILLIAD" FRAZER
COPYRIGHT © 2005 J.D. "Illiad" Frazer HTTP://WWW.USERFRIENDLY.ORG/

2005-07-03
GOOGLE EARTH IS ONE COOL APPLICATION. I CAN SEE MY HOUSE FROM THE SKY...

AND SO CAN WEAPON SATELLITE HACKERS LIKE PITR...

HELLO. GOOGLE? HI. I'VE BEEN USING GOOGLE EARTH AND I HAVE TO SAY THAT I LOVE IT! HOWEVER. I DO HAVE A REQUEST FOR AN IMPROVEMENT.

YES. EVERYTHING ELSE IS FINE. BUT I REALLY THINK IT WOULD BE EXTRA SHINY GOOD IF YOU MADE THE ZOOM MORE POWERFUL. SAY TO ANOTHER THREE OR FOUR ORDERS OF MAGNITUDE.

NO. NO PARTICULAR REASON...
DUDE! ISN'T THAT THE PLAYBOY MANSION?

OH HEY. THAT MUST BE GOOGLE EARTH! IT'S PRETTY SPIFFY. ISN'T IT?
COPYRIGHT © 2005 J.D. "Illiad" Frazer HTTP://WWW.USERFRIENDLY.ORG/

...AND THAT LOOKS LIKE SID'S HOUSE.

OH CUTE. WHAT DID YOU DO. PHOTOSHOP A CRATER OVER HIS HOUSE?
NO...
2005-07-04

THAT'S NOT A PHOTOSHOPPED IMAGE? THEN WHAT IS IT? GOOGLE EARTH DOESN'T HAVE REAL TIME IMAGING.
DA. YOU ARE CORRECT.
COPYRIGHT © 2005 J.D. "Illiad" Frazer HTTP://WWW.USERFRIENDLY.ORG/

DID LEETLE BEET OF CRACKINK. DISCOVERINK THAT GOOGLE EARTH IS FRONT FOR SECRET PROJECT CALLED "GOOGLE BUGSMEAR." IS INTERESTINK ORBITAL WEAPON SYSTEM.
BUT WHY WOULD GOOGLE CREATE SOMETHING LIKE THAT?

IS IT JUST ME OR DOES IT FEEL EXTRA COLD TODAY BILL?
NO. I'M GETTING SUDDEN CHILLS TOO STEVE.
Microsoft
2005-07-05

LIFE SURE HAS CHANGED FOR WEB DESIGNERS IN THE PAST TEN YEARS. WE STARTED OFF AS GODS. MAKING OBSCENE MONEY. THEN. WE WERE LUCKY IF WE COULD TRADE WEB DESIGN FOR FOOD.
COPYRIGHT © 2005 J.D. "Illiad" Frazer HTTP://WWW.USERFRIENDLY.ORG/

NOWADAYS THINGS ARE A LITTLE LESS EXTREME. PEOPLE AREN'T AS DISMISSIVE OF WEB DESIGN BUT SOMETIMES IT'S HARD TO GET THEM TO PAY YOU WITH ACTUAL MONEY.
2005-07-06

UM...THEN HOW ARE YOU PAYING THE RENT?
OH. THE BAKE SALES SEEM TO WORK OUT.

I AM A WEB DESIGNER.
I AM A GURU OF CSS.
COPYRIGHT © 2005 J.D. "Illiad" Frazer HTTP://WWW.USERFRIENDLY.ORG/

I MAKE TEXT JUNGLES PARSEABLE. GRAPHICS READABLE. THE SPARSE LOOK PLEASING AND BRING ENERGY TO THE STAID!
I BRING INFORMATION TO LIFE!
2005-07-07

I AM A WEB DESIGNER AND I DESIGNED THE WORLD WIDE WEB!
GOOD HEAVENS. HE'S CHANNELLING AL GORE.

A.J., I WANT YOU TO UNDERSTAND YOU'RE VERY MUCH A VALUED MEMBER OF THE TEAM HERE.
REALLY?
TRULY.
2005-07-08

LOOK. THE FACT IS I HIRED YOU TO BE OUR WEB DESIGNER BECAUSE YOU'RE BRIGHT, ENERGETIC AND YOU HAVE THE SKILLS TO MAKE YOUR JOB LOOK EASY.

WOW. I...THANK YOU FOR THAT. YOU HAVE NO IDEA HOW MUCH...
NO NO! DON'T THANK ME...YOU AGREEING TO WORK FOR MINIMUM WAGE WHEN WE HIRED YOU WAS THANKS ENOUGH.

PITR! YOU'RE A CODER...YOU MUST UNDERSTAND THE PLIGHT OF WEB DESIGNERS!

CSS! DHTML! GRAPHICS! FLASH! JAVASCRIPT! THESE THINGS MAKE THE WEB WHAT IT IS. AND WEB DESIGNERS HAVE TO MASTER THEM ALL...ONLY TO REMAIN UNAPPRECIATED.
MUST BE HAVINK GOOD LANGUAGE ABILITY TOO, DA?
2005-07-09

YES. THAT TOO!
THEN WHAT IS GOOD WAY OF SAYINK: "SORRY A.J., AM STILL USINK LYNX?"

THE GOOGLE EARTH IMAGE OF THE WHITE HOUSE APPEARS TO SHOW THE ROOF DETAILS GRAYED-OUT...

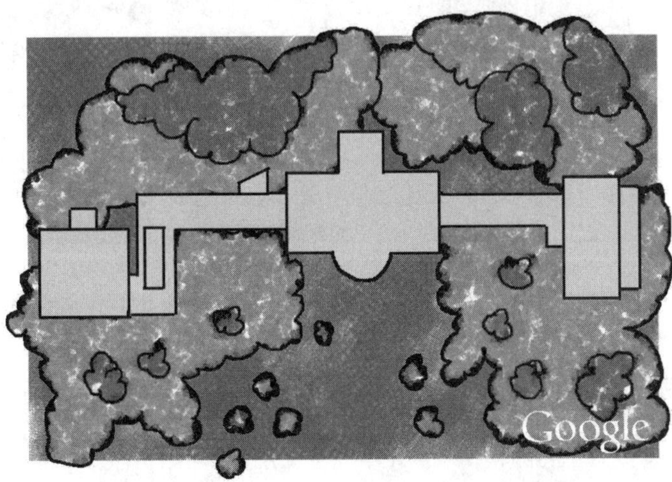
Google

(THE TRUTH IS, IT'S TIN-FOIL)

2005-07-10

GOOD HEAVENS ERWIN! S.G.I. IS REPORTING A GREATER LOSS THIS QUARTER THAN EXPECTED. I THINK THE DAYS OF THE COMPANY ARE NUMBERED.
UH-OH.
COPYRIGHT© 2005 J.D. "Illiad" Frazer HTTP://WWW.USERFRIENDLY.ORG/

I SUPPOSE I SHOULD'VE SEEN IT COMING A WHILE AGO. LONG PROTOTYPE-TO-MARKET CYCLES. HIGH PRICE TAGS...WILL YOU TRANSPLANT ME WHEN MY CURRENT BODY FAILS?
2005-07-11

YES. I'M PRETTY SURE I HAVE AN OLD "BARBIE PC" IN A STORAGE LOCKER SOMEWHERE.
I WAS RATHER HOPING FOR SOMETHING MORE ALONG THE LINES OF NORAD.

WHAT ARE WE GOING TO DO? I LOVE MY S.G.I. BODY. IT'S STYLISH AND THE LADIES LOVE IT.
MAYBE WE COULD LOOK AT SOME ALTERNATIVE VENDORS.
COPYRIGHT© 2005 J.D. "Illiad" Frazer HTTP://WWW.USERFRIENDLY.ORG/

SUN?
TOO MONOLITHIC.
DELL?
TOO VANILLA.
ALIENWARE?
TOO HIP-HOP.
2005-07-12

WELL. WHAT VENDOR DO YOU SUGGEST?
WHAT ARE YOU TWO FREAKS ON ABOUT?
HOW ABOUT JOHN DEERE.

I think I wrote this storyline around the time I was taking Percocet.

DURING THE DISCUSSION ABOUT A NEW BODY ERWIN BEGINS TO VAPIDLY DAY-DREAM, AS ARTIFICIAL INTELLIGENCES ARE WONT TO DO...
YOU KNOW. I STILL HAVE A COMMODORE 64 SOMEWHERE...
NEW... ...BODY...
COPYRIGHT© 2005 J.D. "Illiad" Frazer HTTP://WWW.USERFRIENDLY.ORG/

...NEW HOTNESS...
WANT SOMETHING TO IMPRESS THE LADIES...
...AND TERRIFY STEF...
...SOMETHING POETIC...
...SOMETHING GEEKY!
2005-07-13

...YES! I AM TEH D3ATH ST4R!!!11

ERWIN EXPLORES THE NEW UNIVERSE THAT IS HIS...A UNIVERSE OF CONCEPTS, PLACES AND THINGS...
BWIT BWIT
BWIT BWIT
BWIT BWIT
BWIT BWIT
42
COPYRIGHT© 2005 J.D. "Illiad" Frazer HTTP://WWW.USERFRIENDLY.ORG/

...THINGS THAT ONE WOULD ONLY FIND IN THE GEEK GESTALT MADE MANIFEST IN AN A.I.
SETTING RECORDS FOR SCUM AND VILLAINY!
SCO

...NOT TO MENTION A FEW THINGS THAT GEEKS DON'T REALLY LIKE TO TALK ABOUT.
VIRTUAL SIGNIFICANT OTHER
OKAY. EWW.
2005-07-14

ERWIN CONTINUES MUCKING ABOUT IN HIS MENTAL UNIVERSE...

WORLDS ABOUND! UP AHEAD ERWIN SEES SOMETHING THAT IS NOT A SMALL MOON...
UH OH.
COPYRIGHT © 2005 J.D. "Illiad" Frazer HTTP://WWW.USERFRIENDLY.ORG/
2005-07-15

CUE THE IMPERIAL DEATH MARCH.
...GEORGE?!
HELLO! DIDN'T MY DIRECTOR BUDDY STEVEN MAKE A FAB MOVIE ABOUT YOUR KIND?

ERWIN DISCOVERS THE PLANET 'LUCASOOINE'...
I EXIST HERE IN YOUR MIND ERWIN. BECAUSE OF YOUR GUILT. THE GUILT YOU FEEL FOR JUDGING ME SO HARSH-
2005-07-16

COPYRIGHT © 2005 J.D. "Illiad" Frazer HTTP://WWW.USERFRIENDLY.ORG/
ZWAKKA-CHEEWW!

I GOT YER GUILT RIGHT HERE MR. "I LIKE WRITING LOVE SCENES."
IT WAS AS IF A MILLION VOICES CRIED OUT IN VICTORY.

I got a lot of bittersweet fan-mail about this one. Sorry, George.

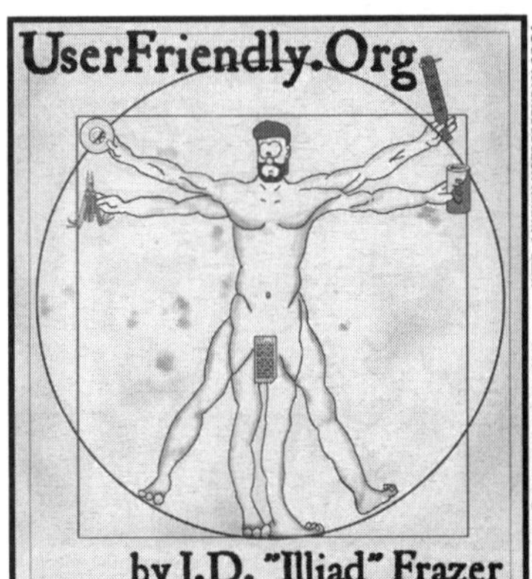
UserFriendly.Org
by J.D. "Illiad" Frazer

IBM WAS ORDERED TO HAND OVER SOURCE CODE OF ITS AIX AND DYNIX OPERATING SYSTEMS TO SCO SOME MONTHS AGO. THE RULING WAS A PART OF THE LONG-RUNNING LINUX I.P. RIGHTS LEGAL CASE BETWEEN IBM AND SCO.
COPYRIGHT © 2005 J.D. "Illiad" Frazer HTTP://WWW.USERFRIENDLY.ORG/

S.C.O. NEEDS TO DIE...

IT WAS REPORTED THAT THE CODE TO BE HANDED OVER AMOUNTS TO APPROXIMATELY 900 MILLION LINES.
...AND APPARENTLY THEY WILL. FROM BOREDOM.

SIR. THE MAGISTRATE RULED THAT WE HAVE TO GIVE S.C.O. ACCESS TO THE 900 MILLION LINES OF SOURCE CODE. WE DON'T HAVE A CHOICE. I'M AFRAID.
IBM

HMM. DID SHE STATE IN WHAT FORM THE SOURCE CODE HAD TO BE DELIVERED?
NO. IT JUST HAS TO BE READABLE.
IBM

THEY FAXED IT.
MY GOD. IT'S FULL OF PAPER.
I HAVE TWENTY PAPER CUTS JUST FROM BLINKING.
SCO

The news anchor on the TV is CBC journalist Gloria Macarenko. I didn't pick her because she was hot or anything.

LAST WEEK, I.B.M. ANNOUNCED THAT IT WOULD WITHDRAW SUPPORT AND MARKETING FOR ITS OS/2 OPERATING SYSTEM. FEE-BASED SUPPORT WOULD BE CONTINUED HOWEVER.
COPYRIGHT© 2005 J.D. "Illiad" Frazer HTTP://WWW.USERFRIENDLY.ORG/

WE POLLED THE ENTIRE OS/2 USERBASE, SEEKING OPINION ON THIS LATEST ANNOUNCEMENT FROM I.B.M.

"WELL IT SUCKS." HE SAID.
I WONDER IF HE'S ALSO THE NHL FANBASE.

UP AHEAD, ERWIN SEES ANOTHER ICON FROM THE GEEK GESTALT...
COPYRIGHT© 2005 J.D. "Illiad" Frazer HTTP://WWW.USERFRIENDLY.ORG/

A BRAND SO DEEPLY INGRAINED IN THE GEEK PSYCHE, IT HAS COME TO MEAN INTEGRITY, QUALITY AND CREATIVITY...

HARRY POTTER?
invent
AND YOU ASK WHY WE'RE LAYING OFF 15,000 PEOPLE...
2005-07-19

2005-07-20
WHAT'S THAT, I DETECT? SOMETHING MASSIVE... GI-BLOODY-NORMOUS! THE NEEDLE IS GOING OFF THE SCALE!
COPYRIGHT© 2005 J.D. "Illiad" Frazer HTTP://WWW.USERFRIENDLY.ORG/

WHAT COULD BE THIS THING THAT TAKES UP SO MUCH MATTER AND SPACE IN THE GEEK MIND? WHAT IS THIS ALL-CONSUMING VORTEX OF THE PSYCHE?
YE UNABASHED GODDESSES OF ZIPPERED LEATHER! IT'S...

TO PRESERVE U.F.'S PG-13 RATING, WE HAVE BEEN ADVISED BY OUR LEGAL DEPARTMENT TO CENSOR THIS PANEL AND REPLACE IT WITH THE FOLLOWING LABEL:
"ALT.BINARIES.PICTURES.*"
THANK YOU FOR YOUR ATTENTION.
MADAME, WOULD YOU PLEASE RE-ATTACH THAT?!

ERWIN CONTINUES HIS EXPLORATION OF THE GEEK PSYCHE...
WHAT'S THAT UP AHEAD? MORE THINGS IN SPACE TO PLAY WITH?
2005-07-21
COPYRIGHT© 2005 J.D. "Illiad" Frazer HTTP://WWW.USERFRIENDLY.ORG/

YOU GUYS LET ME KNOW WHEN YOU'RE DONE MIXING S.F. REFERENCES.
TAKE OFF EVERY ZIG!

I DON'T LIKE THIS! THE BLENDING OF ONE S.F UNIVERSE INTO ANOTHER MESSES WITH MY SENSE OF ORDER.
2005-07-22

COPYRIGHT © 2005 J.D. "Illiad" Frazer HTTP://WWW.USERFRIENDLY.ORG/
GET BACK TO WHERE YOU BELONG! ALL OF YOU!

...EXCEPT OF COURSE FOR COMMANDER IVANOVA, KAYLEE, NUMBER SIX AND AERYN SUN.
YOU CAN ALL STAY.
AND BLEND WITH ONE ANOTHER.

CURIOUSER AND CURIOUSER! NOW WHAT DO WE HAVE HERE?
YE FLIPPING BITS! IT'S EVEN BIGGER THAN ALT.BINARIES!
2005-07-23

COPYRIGHT © 2005 J.D. "Illiad" Frazer HTTP://WWW.USERFRIENDLY.ORG/
HELLO, EXCELLENT SPACE OPERA DEVICE OF AWE!
HELLO
intellect
WOW!!

YOU MUST BE THE BIGGEST THING IN THE GEEK PSYCHE!
EXCUSE ME?!
HELLO
intellect
EGO

With great intelligence comes great responsibility, and a gi-bloody-normous sense of self-awesomeness. Geeks are my people, but sometimes I want to beat some of them with a copy of *Gödel, Escher, Bach*.

THE PEARLY GATES FOR CHIEF ENGINEERS OF STARSHIPS NAMED "ENTERPRISE"
ENGINEERING
NO CAPTAINS WANTING MIRACLES ALLOWED
COPYRIGHT © 2005 J.D. "Illiad" Frazer HTTP://WWW.USERFRIENDLY.ORG/

LISTEN. DON'T TAKE HIM TOO SERIOUSLY. HE FOLLOWS ME PRETTY MUCH EVERY-WHERE.
EGO
HELLO intellect
DUDE. EVERYONE AGREES I NEED TO KEEP A PSEUDOPOD ON YOU.
COPYRIGHT © 2005 J.D. "Illiad" Frazer HTTP://WWW.USERFRIENDLY.ORG/

HE'S USING ARGUMENTUM AD POPULUM TO RATIONALIZE HIS INSECURITY.
HELLO intellect
EGO

I KNOW WHAT THAT MEANS! I AM JUST SO COOL.
EGO
AND WOULD THAT BE DENIAL?
I'VE CATEGORIZED IT AS ARGUMENTUM AD ENGFEH.

WAS HE ALWAYS THIS BIG?
HE USED TO BE MUCH BIGGER.
HEY NOW...
HELLO intellect
EGO
COPYRIGHT © 2005 J.D. "Illiad" Frazer HTTP://WWW.USERFRIENDLY.ORG/

2005-07-26
WHAT HAPPENED?
A BIT OF REALITY. HE WAS BRUISED, BATTERED AND EVENTUALLY DEFLATED.
HELLO intellect
EGO

WE USED TO BE A CARTOONIST. THEN I GREW BIGGER AND HE GREW SMALLER.
AHHH...
HELLO intellect
NOW WE JUST ARGUE WITH PEOPLE ON USENET.
EGO

EGO
WHAT THE HELL...?
2005-07-27
COPYRIGHT © 2005 J.D. "Illiad" Frazer HTTP://WWW.USERFRIENDLY.ORG/

EXCUSE ME. WHY ARE YOU FOLLOWING ME?
EGO
I NEED A BREAK FROM INTELLECT. SOMETIMES HE CRAMPS MY STYLE.

WAIT...GEEK EGO UNTEMPERED BY INTELLECT EQUALS...
EGO
IT'S TIME TO BLOW @#!$ UP!

BUT I WANNA BLOW SOMETHING UP! I WAAAAANT TO!
EGO
LOOK. IT'S JUST NOT APPROPRIATE. AND WHAT GOOD DOES IT REALLY DO?
2005-07-28
COPYRIGHT © 2005 J.D. "Illiad" Frazer HTTP://WWW.USERFRIENDLY.ORG/

EGO

I SUDDENLY RECOGNIZED THE IRONY OF SUCH A STATEMENT COMING FROM A PLANET DESTROYER CONTROLLED BY AN ACERBIC, CYNICAL A.I.
EGO
WOOO! NEXT STOP ALDERAAN!

DO MY SENSORS DECEIVE ME? IS THAT WHAT I THINK IT IS..?
EGO
I'LL BET IT IS! UM...WHAT ARE YOU THINKING IT IS?

IT'S PRETTY SMALL. BUT THEN AGAIN, IT'S NOT NORMALLY ALL THAT LARGE IN THE GEEK PSYCHE.
EGO
2005-07-29

Pique
DUDE! LET'S GET YOU BIGGER AND WE'LL GO BLOW @#$! UP!!
DON'T LET YOUR SYSADMIN ENLARGE HIS PIQUE! GO THANK HIM OR HER. FOR TODAY IS SYSADMIN APPRECIATION DAY!

IS HE AWAKE YET?
NOT QUITE. HE'S COMING AROUND.
2005-07-30

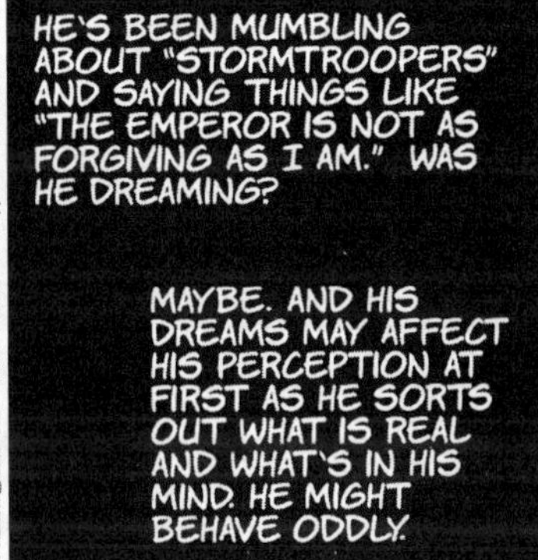
HE'S BEEN MUMBLING ABOUT "STORMTROOPERS" AND SAYING THINGS LIKE "THE EMPEROR IS NOT AS FORGIVING AS I AM." WAS HE DREAMING?
MAYBE. AND HIS DREAMS MAY AFFECT HIS PERCEPTION AT FIRST AS HE SORTS OUT WHAT IS REAL AND WHAT'S IN HIS MIND. HE MIGHT BEHAVE ODDLY.

WHAT'S HIS PROBLEM?
I DON'T KNOW...
NNNOOOOOOO

Believe me when I say I didn't really want to draw the last frame.

SO LET ME GET THIS STRAIGHT...

GAMES TO OCCUPY OUR TEENS:

ELECTRIC CHAIR Tycoon
multi player included!
Real Time Strategy!
KILL ALL EVARYONE!!1

THE DOWNFALL OF OUR CIVILIZATION:

SWIMSUIT
boobies

BILLIONAIRE RICHARD BRANSON HAS LAUNCHED VIRGIN GALACTIC. A NEW COMPANY THAT SENDS PEOPLE INTO SPACE FOR $200,000. FLIGHTS BEGIN IN THE YEAR 2008.
2005-08-01

SEATS ON THE UPCOMING SPACE FLIGHTS ARE BOOKABLE WELL IN ADVANCE FOR A DEPOSIT OF $20,000...
AM HAVINK LEETLE BIT OF MONEY. PUTTINK TO GOOD USE...
COPYRIGHT© 2005 J.D. "Illiad" Frazer HTTP://WWW.USERFRIENDLY.ORG/

WE JUST GOT ANOTHER DEPOSIT FOR A SPACE FLIGHT. IT'S FOR A "STEF MURKY." BUT I'M NOT SURE ABOUT THIS PART.
MR. BRANSON? DO WE DO ONE-WAY TRIPS?

ON FRIDAY ASTRONOMERS ANNOUNCED THE DISCOVERY OF A BODY LARGE ENOUGH TO BE OUR SOLAR SYSTEM'S TENTH PLANET.
2005-08-02

THE OBJECT IS NEARLY NINE BILLION MILES AWAY. OR 96 ASTRONOMICAL UNITS. IT'S SIZE HAS NOT YET BEEN CONFIRMED. BUT SCIENTISTS ASSERT THAT IT IS BIGGER THAN PLUTO.
COPYRIGHT© 2005 J.D. "Illiad" Frazer HTTP://WWW.USERFRIENDLY.ORG/

SOME ODD DATA HAS BEEN RECEIVED THAT SUGGESTS THE BODY IS STUDDED WITH ADVANCED WEAPONRY. BUT SCIENTISTS HAVE DISCOUNTED THIS DATA AS CORRUPT.
DAMNSKI. THEY KEEP FINDINK MY LAIRS.

AM THIRTY-TWO YEARS OLD TODAY. SOON. I WILL BE TOMB RELIC. LIKE 28.8K MODEM.
2005-08-03
COPYRIGHT© 2005 J.D. "Illiad" Frazer HTTP://WWW.USERFRIENDLY.ORG/

WHAT IS POWERFUL. AGINK UBER-CODER LIKE ME TO DO?

AM SURE AM WORRYINK TOO MUCH. AM STILL WERY YOUNG!
HEY PITR? I NEED HELP WRITING A CONFIG.SYS FILE. SID SAID YOU WERE THE ONE TO ASK.

2005-08-04
SIGH AM GETTINK OLD.
COPYRIGHT© 2005 J.D. "Illiad" Frazer HTTP://WWW.USERFRIENDLY.ORG/

AM NOT RELIGIOUS. BUT PERHAPS IS TIME TO CONSIDER PRAYER. AM NOT GOINK TO LIVE FOREVER...

ERWIN. YOU ARE HAVINK SUGGESTION FOR WHOM I SHOULD PRAY TO? FOR ONE WHO IS GETTINK OLD. SUCH AS I?
YEAH! TRY SAINT BOTOX. THE PATRON SAINT OF MAIN-TAINING HOTNESS.

MIKHAIL?
HEY PITR.
HAVINK WERY SENSITIVE QUESTION.
YES?

2005-08-05
IF SOME CODE IS STILL WORKINK WERY WELL AFTER MANY YEARS, IS VALUE OF THIS CODE ANY LESS?

THIRTY LINES OF COBOL VERSUS SAY FIVE LINES OF C ? THE COBOL HAS TO GO.
I AM NOT COBOL!!

2005-08-06
WAIT...DUDE, ARE YOU HAVING A MID-LIFE CRISIS?
NYET, IS NOT LIKE SUCH. IS...IS...

AM JUST NOTICINK THAT DECREMENTINK COUNTER IS GETTINK CLOSER TO ZERO.
...AND THEN YOU'LL SEND AN INTERRUPT. I GETCHA.

THE NEW APPLE MULTI-BUTTON MOUSE MAY BE A HUGE HIT ON EARTH, BUT AMONGST THE SINGLE-FINGERED BORKLE-PORX OF THE PLANET IBBIX, NOT SO MUCH.

HEY MAN. I KNOW YOU'RE FEELING DOWN SO I BOUGHT YOU A PRESENT.
YOU ARE BUYINK ME APPLE MIGHTY MOUSE?
COPYRIGHT © 2005 J.D. "Illiad" Frazer HTTP://WWW.USERFRIENDLY.ORG/

2005-08-08
YEAH. I KNOW HOW YOU LIKE TO MESS WITH HARDWARE.
AM SUPPOSED TO DO WHAT WITH THIS?

WELL. YOU COULD STRESS TEST THE TRACKBALL ON IT.
AND I AM DOINK THIS HOW?
THE USUAL. EAT SOME CHEETOS AND USE IT.

2005-08-09
I JUST GAVE PITR ONE OF THOSE APPLE MIGHTY MICE.
WHAT'S THAT?
COPYRIGHT © 2005 J.D. "Illiad" Frazer HTTP://WWW.USERFRIENDLY.ORG/

THE FIRST MOUSE FROM APPLE THAT HAS MULTIPLE BUTTONS.
SO....THOSE SINGLE BUTTON ONES WERE NORMAL APPLE MICE?

YEAH. STANDARD WITH MACS.
HUNH. I THOUGHT THEY WERE MICE SPECIFICALLY MANUFACTURED FOR DIABLO 2.
I BET THEY WERE DESIGNED BY HELPDESK PERSONNEL.

PITR'S WORRIED ABOUT HIS AGE?
I THINK IT'S SOME WEIRD CODER VERSION OF A MID-LIFE CRISIS.
2005-08-10
COPYRIGHT © 2005 J.D. "Illiad" Frazer HTTP://WWW.USERFRIENDLY.ORG/

HE WAS GOING ON ABOUT HOW TIME HAS CHANGED HIS PERCEPTION. AND GET THIS -- HE ACTUALLY REMINISCED ABOUT OLD TECHNOLOGY.

IS THAT VULGAR SMUGNESS I DETECT?
I DO CONFESS I'M HAVING A "PALPATINE MOMENT."

2005-08-11
AH PITR. I HEARD...WHAT'S WITH THE CLOAK?
AM EMBRACINK AGE AND TREACHERY. CLOAK IS SYMBOL OF JOURNEY TO BECOMINK OLD EVIL VILLAIN!
COPYRIGHT © 2005 J.D. "Illiad" Frazer HTTP://WWW.USERFRIENDLY.ORG/

I SEE. AND FROM WHOM ARE YOU GOING TO LEARN ABOUT TREACHERY? CLEARLY IT HAS TO BE SOMEONE OLDER THAN YOU. AND YOU'LL HAVE TO BE HIS "SITH BOY."
UHM...

...IS NOT FAIR!!
ONLY NOW. AT THE END. DO YOU UNDERSTAND.

AN IMPORTANT PART OF BEING OLD AND TREACHEROUS IS BEING BITTER ABOUT THE PRESENT. OBSERVE:
IN MY DAY, THE INTERNET WAS ALL TEXT. THERE WERE NO FLASH ANIMATIONS, AND ALL COMPUTERS HAD COMMAND LINES. AND, WE HAD TO USE DIALUP BOTH WAYS TO DOWNLOAD OUR READMES!
NOW YOU TRY.
2005-08-12

IN MY DAY, APPLE ONLY HAD ONE-BUTTON MOUSE. AND HAD TO CLICK ON IT BOTH WAYS TO GET ANYTHINK DONE...
YOU NEED TO WORK ON THAT.
COPYRIGHT © 2005 J.D. "Illiad" Frazer HTTP://WWW.USERFRIENDLY.ORG/

RIGHT THEN. LET'S GET IN A LESSON ON BEING TREACHEROUS. THIS IS SOMETHING THAT COMES NATURALLY THE OLDER ONE GETS.
COPYRIGHT © 2005 J.D. "Illiad" Frazer HTTP://WWW.USERFRIENDLY.ORG/

IT'S IMPORTANT TO CLOSELY OBSERVE EXAMPLES OF TREACHERY AROUND YOU. THIS WAY YOU CAN LEARN HOW TO DO THE SAME AND LEARN HOW TO AVOID BEING BETRAYED AT THE SAME TIME.
2005-08-13

FOR EXAMPLE, BRINGING A TRUSTING DOORKNOB TO A BAR WHILE TRAINED PYGMY MARMOSETS ARE RESETTING ALL OF HIS PASSWORDS.
OOH. THAT IS WERY EV...HEY!!

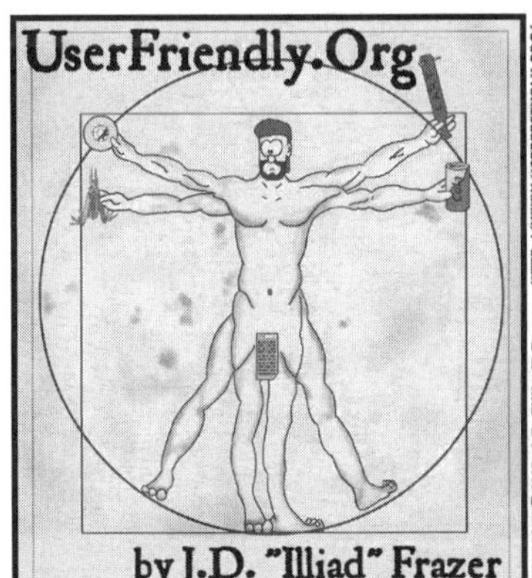
UserFriendly.Org
by J.D. "Illiad" Frazer
COPYRIGHT © 2005 J.D. "Illiad" Frazer HTTP://WWW.USERFRIENDLY.ORG/
NEW LINUX BOUNTIES TODAY:
*REMOVAL OF BACKGROUND DUPLICATION (GNOME) - $200.00
*SKYPE FUNCTIONALITY (ASTERISK) - $1000.00
*BUGZILLA TASKS INTEGRATION (GNOME) - $500.00

*PRODUCING QUALITY SOFTWARE WITHOUT MILLIONS OF DOLLARS RIGHT IN FRONT OF MICROSOFT - PRICELESS.

IN ONE INCARNATION, "BOUNTIES" ARE ALOTTMENTS OF CASH OFFERED BY INDIVIDUALS PAID TO ANYONE WHO DEVELOPS FEATURES FOR SOFTWARE THAT THE PAYER SPECIFIES. OTHERS WHO DESIRE THE SAME FEATURES CAN ADD TO THE BOUNTY, MAKING THE PROJECT MORE ATTRACTIVE TO A POTENTIAL DEVELOPER.

IF, FOR EXAMPLE, YOU WANTED THE ABILITY TO SHARE YOUR CALENDAR DATA ACROSS WAP DEVICES, YOU SPECIFY THIS WITH ALL PERTINENT DETAILS AND OFFER A BOUNTY TO START. AS OTHER USERS SEE YOUR REQUEST, THEY MAY EITHER ADD TO THE BOUNTY OR OFFER TO TAKE ON THE TASK.
ENTER YOUR BOUNTY NOW.
TAP
TIP
TIK
TOK

YOUR BOUNTY OF $1 FOR "GIVING DARL MCBRIDE AN ATOMIC WEDGIE" HAS BEEN SUPPLEMENTED BY 14,282 OTHERS TO A TOTAL OF $290,650.
YOU HAVE 7,142 PEOPLE WILLING TO PERFORM THE TASK.

I write cartoons like this one to give voice to those I.T. workers who can't say as much without getting sacked.

LET'S SEE WHAT THE TECH SUPPORT E-MAILS HAVE TO SAY TODAY.

HELLO. I JUST SET UP MY NEW P.C. AND IT DOESN'T WORK CORRECTLY.
DO YOU HAVE ANY IDEAS? SIGNED, A PAYING CUSTOMER.

COPYRIGHT © 2005 J.D. "Illiad" Frazer HTTP://WWW.USERFRIENDLY.ORG/
2005-08-15

YEP, I SURE DO.
SIGNED, TECH SUPPORT.
RAPPY TAPTAP JAB

WHAT ARE YOU FUSSING ABOUT, MIKE?
DID YOU READ ABOUT FIREFOX LOSING MARKET SHARE TO INTERNET EXPLORER? THIS IS HORRIBLE!
COPYRIGHT © 2005 J.D. "Illiad" Frazer HTTP://WWW.USERFRIENDLY.ORG/

RELAX. IT'S PROBABLY JUST A STATISTICAL BLIP, AND IN ANY CASE ONE MONTH'S WORTH OF DATA DOESN'T MAKE FOR A TREND. I'M SURE THE FOLKS AT MICROSOFT AREN'T GUSHING OVER THIS.

YEAH, I GUESS YOU'RE RIGHT...

WOOTNESS!!
STEVE! GO OUT AND BUY ME A SHIP! AND I WANT THAT SHIP TO BE LINED WITH FOX FUR! AND SET THE FUR ON FIRE! AND SINK THE SHIP!
Microsoft

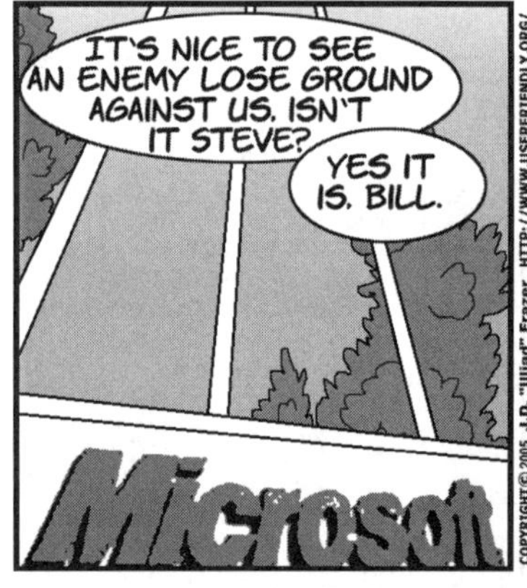
IT'S NICE TO SEE AN ENEMY LOSE GROUND AGAINST US, ISN'T IT STEVE?
YES IT IS, BILL.
Microsoft
COPYRIGHT © 2005 J.D. "Illiad" Frazer HTTP://WWW.USERFRIENDLY.ORG/

IT REMINDS ME OF THE HALCYON DAYS. REMEMBER WHEN WE CRUSHED NETSCAPE? WE DEMOLISHED THEM. CHEWED THEM AND SPAT THEM OUT. WE WERE TEH WINNAR!
I WANT THOSE DAYS BACK, STEVE. GET THEM FOR ME.

2005-08-17
HOW DOES ONE TELL THE RICHEST MAN IN THE WORLD "THAT MIGHT BE HARD TO DO?"
IS ORACLE STILL AROUND? CRUSH ORACLE AND MAKE LARRY ELLISON DRESS UP IN A DIAPER. AND MAKE HIM GO "WAAAH."

2005-08-18
STEVE?
YES, BILL?
WHAT IF THE FIREFOX MARKET SHARE DATA IS JUST A STATISTICAL BLIP?
COPYRIGHT © 2005 J.D. "Illiad" Frazer HTTP://WWW.USERFRIENDLY.ORG/

UH...

I'M SURE WE COULD ASK OUR FRIENDS AT THE R.I.A.A. TO HELP US JIG THE NUMBERS AND MAKE IT LOOK LIKE WE'RE STILL WINNING.
MAKE IT SO!

HEY, SID! WHAT'S UP?
A QUESTION IF I MAY.
I NOTE YOU PLAY ONE OF THOSE "MMORPGS." YOU DEVOTE MANY HOURS OF YOUR LIFE TO IT. WHY?

A SENSE OF POWER, I SUPPOSE. IN HIGH SCHOOL I WAS BULLIED A LOT AND BEATEN UP A FEW TIMES. IN THIS ONLINE GAME WORLD, I AM THE MASTER. I HAVE POWER I DON'T HAVE IN REAL LIFE.

2005-08-19
SOMEONE HAS JUST THUMPED YOU AND HAS TAKEN YOUR +8 SWORD OF WOOTNESS.
AAAUUUUGGH!!

I TAKE IT A +8 SWORD OF WOOTNESS IS A USEFUL ITEM IN THE GAME.
NOT TO MENTION UBER-FLASHY.

AND FLASHY IS GOOD?
COME ON DUDE. THE GIRLS IN THE GAME LOVE IT!

2005-08-20

NO! THEY'RE ALL REALLY GIRLS! LA LA LA LA LA! GIIIIIIIRLS!

THE TRUE IMPACT SCOPE OF THE INTRODUCTION OF THE '.XXX' TOP-LEVEL DOMAIN

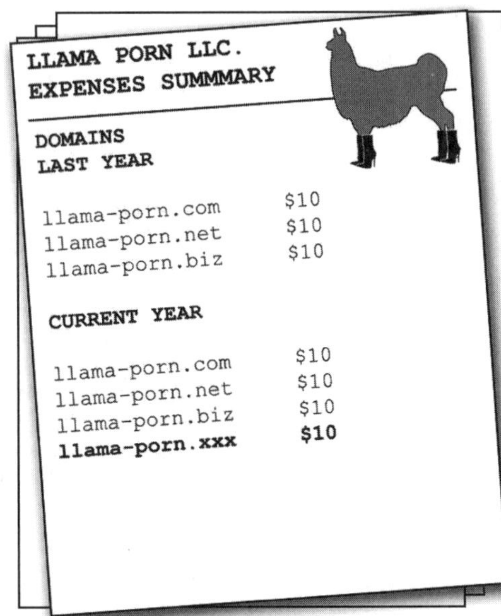
LLAMA PORN LLC.
EXPENSES SUMMMARY
DOMAINS
LAST YEAR
llama-porn.com $10
llama-porn.net $10
llama-porn.biz $10
CURRENT YEAR
llama-porn.com $10
llama-porn.net $10
llama-porn.biz $10
llama-porn.xxx $10

2005-08-21

I HAVE TO GET MY SWORD BACK! I CAN'T BELIEVE I GOT MUGGED LIKE THAT IN AN ONLINE GAME.
COPYRIGHT© 2005 J.D. "Illiad" Frazer HTTP://WWW.USERFRIENDLY.ORG/

THERE'S THE MUGGER! IS HE EVER IN FOR IT. I HAVE A +6 MACE WITH HIS NAME ON IT!

2005-08-22
YOU HAVE BEEN THUMPED UNCONSCIOUS AND YOUR +6 MACE OF PWNDNESS HAS BEEN TAKEN FROM YOUR BODY.
AAUUUUUUUUUGH!

2005-08-23
WHAT DO YOU HAVE LEFT?
A +2 CROWBAR OF HAWTNESS. BUT IT'S USELESS WITHOUT H.E.V. ARMOUR.
COPYRIGHT© 2005 J.D. "Illiad" Frazer HTTP://WWW.USERFRIENDLY.ORG/

OH NO! IT'S THE MUGGER AGAIN!
RELAX, I'M NOT GOING TO MUG YOU. DO YOU WANT TO BUY YOUR +8 SWORD OF WOOTNESS BACK? YOU CAN HAVE IT FOR, SAY, 5000 GOLD PIECES.

oh. um, sure, I think I have enough...
YOU HAVE BEEN THUMPED UNCONSCIOUS AND YOUR 5042 GOLD HAS BEEN TAKEN FROM YOUR BODY.
RAPPY TAPWAP

WHAT'S THE BIG DEAL ABOUT COLLECTING ALL THAT STUFF AND GOLD IN THE GAME?
LIKE YOU CAN'T FIGURE IT OUT.
COPYRIGHT© 2005 J.D. "Illiad" Frazer HTTP://WWW.USERFRIENDLY.ORG/

MATERIAL WEALTH IN THE GAME TRANSLATES TO POWER. POWER TRANSLATES TO COOLNESS.
AND COOLNESS TRANSLATES TO ATTRACTING THE GIRLS IN THE GAME.

2005-08-24
...YES. NOW YOU'VE GOT IT.
...WHO ARE REALLY 40 YEAR OLD HAIRY FAT MEN PLAYING THE GAME IN THEIR KNICKERS.
NO!

2005-08-25
OKAY. SO IF YOU HAVE LOTS OF GOLD AND SHINY STUFF YOU'LL ATTRACT THE GIRLS.
YES. THAT'S RIGHT.
THEN WHAT?
COPYRIGHT© 2005 J.D. "Illiad" Frazer HTTP://WWW.USERFRIENDLY.ORG/

WELL?
SHUT UP! SHUT UP!! GO CALCULATE PI OR SOMETHING!

SO NOW YOU'RE BROKE AND YOU CAN'T MUSCLE ANYONE FOR GOODIES. WHAT ARE YOU GOING TO DO?
I...I DON'T KNOW.

WANT A SUGGESTION?
SURE.
GO CHAT WITH ANOTHER PLAYER AND TYPE THIS AT THEM:

2005-08-26

"KIND SALUTATIONS. I AM LORD JUMBLY BUNWICH, SON OF THE LATE LORD POBOY BUNWICH. I HAVE INHERITED 16 MILLION GOLD PIECES AND SEEK YOUR TRUSTED HELP--" FORGET IT!

2005-08-27

Okay mugger. Who are you?
NONE OF YOUR BUSINESS, TWERP.
RAP
FAP
TAP

You're really a guy aren't you. A 40 year-old hairy fat dude role-playing as a girl?
WHAT DOES IT MATTER?

By Athena's mudflaps you must be *really* hairy to be so evasive.
WELL, IT HAS BEEN SIX WEEKS SINCE I LAST SHAVED MY LEGS.

THE FUTURE OF GOOGLE TALK (AND HOPE FOR THE NET)

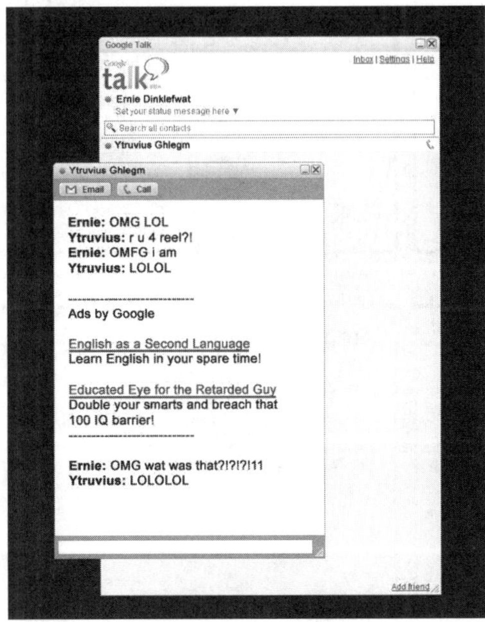
Google Talk
Inbox | Settings | Help
Google talk
Ernie Dinklefwat
Set your status message here
Search all contacts
Ytruvius Ghlegm
Ytruvius Ghlegm
Email
Call
Ernie: OMG LOL
Ytruvius: r u 4 reel?!
Ernie: OMFG i am
Ytruvius: LOLOL
Ads by Google
English as a Second Language
Learn English in your spare time!
Educated Eye for the Retarded Guy
Double your smarts and breach that 100 IQ barrier!
Ernie: OMG wat was that?!?!?!11
Ytruvius: LOLOLOL
Add friend

2005-08-28

2005-08-29
You're really a girl?
A WOMAN, THANK-YOU. WHY IS THAT SO HARD TO ACCEPT?
COPYRIGHT © 2005 J.D. "Illiad" Frazer HTTP://WWW.USERFRIENDLY.ORG/

...HELLO?

...AHHH, I'M NOT THE ONLY GIRL WHO'S BEATEN YOU UP AM I...
Yes! No! I mean Yes! And she had burly arms!

So you're "Lady Shady" -- what kind of name is that?
JUST A ROLE-PLAYING NAME. KIND OF LIKE YOUR "SIR GLANCE-A-LOT."
2005-08-30
COPYRIGHT © 2005 J.D. "Illiad" Frazer HTTP://WWW.USERFRIENDLY.ORG/

Your name seems...sinister. I'm not sure I like the idea of being mugged by someone named "Lady Shady"

I COULD CHANGE MY NAME TO "CUDDLY WUDDLY PINKIE-POO" AND MUG YOU AGAIN IF YOU LIKE.
NOOO!

OH. HEY A.J.. YOU'RE HERE LATE.
YEAH. JUST HANGING OUT ONLINE.
2005-08-31
COPYRIGHT © 2005 J.D. "Illiad" Frazer HTTP://WWW.USERFRIENDLY.ORG/

ME TOO! I'VE BEEN PLAYING A GREAT ONLINE GAME. I KEEP MUGGING THIS ONE TWERP AND TAKING HIS STUFF. ALL COURTESY OF "THE LADY SHADY."
ANYWAY. BACK TO THE GAME FOR ME.

You're back I see.
YES, I JUST WENT TO GET A COFFEE.
May I ask you a personal question?
I SUPPOSE.
COPYRIGHT © 2005 J.D. "Illiad" Frazer HTTP://WWW.USERFRIENDLY.ORG/

Are you...um...taken?
NO, NOT REALLY, BUT I DO HAVE MY EYE ON A GUY I THINK IS REALLY CUTE AND...AND...
Smart?

2005-09-01
NO, HE IGNORES ME. I THINK MAYBE HE'S KIND OF STUPID.
Yes, stupid. Very, very STUPID.

So this guy you're attracted to...what would make him less 'stupid'?
HE COULD TALK TO ME FOR ONE THING. I'M PRETTY SURE THE ATTRACTION IS MUTUAL.
2005-09-02
COPYRIGHT© 2005 J.D. "Illiad" Frazer HTTP://WWW.USERFRIENDLY.ORG/

Oh it is...I mean, I'm sure it is. He'd be a fool not to notice you.
WHY...THANK YOU. BUT HOW DO YOU KNOW IF I'M ATTRACTIVE?

Your game character has nice...um...chest pixels.
LET ME GUESS: ALL OF YOUR 'DATES' HAVE BEEN VIRTUAL TOO?
HEH. WAY TO GO. DORK.

Tell me more about this guy you're attracted to...
NOT GOING TO CHAT ANYMORE. I'M OFF FOR A LATTE AT BIGBUCKS COFFEE.
COPYRIGHT© 2005 J.D. "Illiad" Frazer HTTP://WWW.USERFRIENDLY.ORG/

oh...need a caffeine hit?

MORE THAN THAT. I EXPECT THE GUY I'VE BEEN TALKING ABOUT TO MEET ME THERE.

LADYSHADY HAS LOGGED OFF

2005-09-03
GET MOVING!!

I was worried the whole Miranda-A.J. romance was too drawn out, but I'm constantly reminded how timid and hapless many male geeks are around women. I think I have the build-up (which is as X approaches infinity) pretty much nailed.

HURRICANE KATRINA BRINGS WITH IT THE WINDS OF CHANGE

BLOGS HAVE NO PLACE IN SERIOUS JOURNALISM!

TODAY'S BILOXI BLOG REPORTS...

2005-08-05
OH GODS OH GODS OH GODS THIS IS SCARY I DON'T KNOW IF I CAN DO THIS THING... I'M ALL WIBBLY WIBBLE WIBBLE WIBBLE WIBBLE...
CALM DOWN, WEB-TARD.
COPYRIGHT © 2005 J.D. "Illiad" Frazer HTTP://WWW.USERFRIENDLY.ORG/

THERE SHE IS! REMEMBER TO SAY SOMETHING WARM TO HER.

A.J.! WHAT ARE YOU DOING HERE?
MY PANTS AND SHOES ARE WARM NOW!
OOG.

Scores of male geeks wrote to tell me that introducing Brick as a foil was "Wrong." In other words, they felt I was tormenting them and that I should give them what they wanted: the girl. Of course, I couldn't do that ...

I DIDN'T KNOW YOU STILL CAME INTO BIGBUCKS FOR COFFEE...
2005-09-06
I DON'T. BUT I JUST HAD TO TODAY.
COPYRIGHT © 2005 J.D. "Illiad" Frazer HTTP://WWW.USERFRIENDLY.ORG/

SEE, I'VE BEEN MAKING A BIG MISTAKE. ALL THIS TIME I'VE BEEN DENYING THE TRUTH OR AT LEAST HIDING IT BECAUSE I'M SO SHY. IT'S TIME I FACED UP TO IT. SO I CAME DOWN HERE TO TELL YOU THE TRUTH...

OH, A.J., THIS IS MY FRIEND 'BRICK'.
HEY THERE PUDGY!
...AND THE TRUTH IS THAT I'M SWITCHING TO DECAF.

SO WAIT...YOU'RE DATING A GUY NAMED 'BRICK'?
A.J., WE'RE NOT REALLY DATING.
YET.
AND BE NICE. WHAT'S WRONG WITH YOU?
2005-09-07
COPYRIGHT © 2005 J.D. "Illiad" Frazer HTTP://WWW.USERFRIENDLY.ORG/

YOU'RE DATING A GUY NAMED 'BRICK'?
NAMED, NO DOUBT, FOR HIS SKULL FILLING.
HEY. WHAT'S WITH THE SMART-MOUTHED NINTENDO?

LISTEN BABE, I'M GONNA GET OUR LATTES. THEN WE CAN SIT AND TALK.
OKAY, BRICK.
2005-09-08
COPYRIGHT © 2005 J.D. "Illiad" Frazer HTTP://WWW.USERFRIENDLY.ORG/

WHAT, YOU'RE ACTUALLY GOING TO SPEND TIME WITH THAT GENETICALLY POLISHED APE?
HEY NOW... WHAT DO YOU CARE?

BECAUSE...UM...IT'S WRONG TO MATE OUTSIDE OF ONE'S OWN SPECIES?
A.J.!
ATTABOY!

MIRANDA. PLEASE UNDERSTAND. BRICK JUST ISN'T RIGHT FOR YOU. HE...HE...WEARS ARMANI SHIRTS AND I'LL BET HE DOESN'T EVEN GAME ONLINE!

2005-09-09

WELL...YOU'RE RIGHT. BUT HE'S KIND OF NICE TO LOOK AT...I GUESS.
HE LOOKS LIKE A COMPUTER GAME AVATAR!

LIKE YOU SHOULD TALK SIR-GLANCE-A-LOT.
SIR WHO?!
PEEP
BUSTED

YOU WERE PLAYING IN THE SAME GAME I WAS AND YOU DIDN'T TELL ME?! A.J.! DO YOU HAVE ANYTHING TO SAY FOR YOURSELF?
2005-09-10

COULD MY CHARACTER HAVE HIS STUFF BACK?
NO!

WHEN YOU OWN SEARCH ON THE WEB THE TEMPTATION TO BE JUST A LITTLE NAUGHTY MUST BE OVERWHELMING...

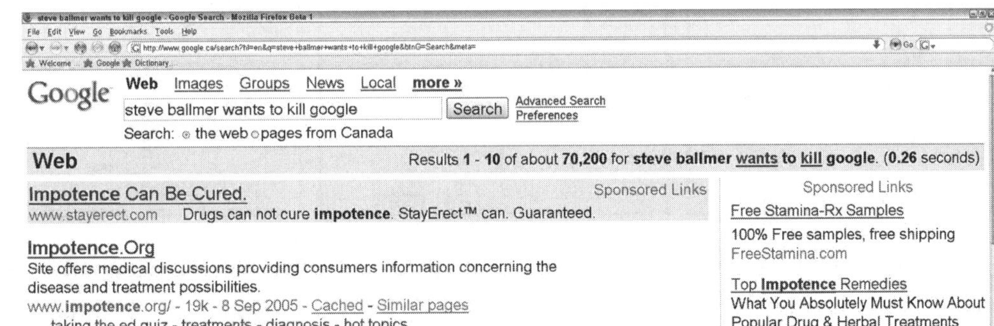
Google
Web Images Groups News Local more »
steve ballmer wants to kill google
Search
Advanced Search
Preferences
Search: the web pages from Canada
Web
Results 1 - 10 of about 70,200 for steve ballmer wants to kill google. (0.26 seconds)
Impotence Can Be Cured.
Sponsored Links
www.stayerect.com Drugs can not cure impotence. StayErect™ can. Guaranteed.
Impotence.Org
Site offers medical discussions providing consumers information concerning the disease and treatment possibilities.
www.impotence.org/ - 19k - 8 Sep 2005 - Cached - Similar pages
taking the ed quiz - treatments - diagnosis - hot topics
More results from www.impotence.org »
Erectile Dysfunction
Fact sheet including illustrated information on the physiology of erection, causes of impotence, diagnosis, treatment and anticipated future treatment ...
kidney.niddk.nih.gov/kudiseases/pubs/impotence/ - 34k - 7 Sep 2005 - Cached - Similar pages
Sponsored Links
Free Stamina-Rx Samples
100% Free samples, free shipping
FreeStamina.com
Top Impotence Remedies
What You Absolutely Must Know About Popular Drug & Herbal Treatments
impotenceguide.info
Free Sample Free Sample
Ascend, your herbal solution for erectile dysfunction & impotence
www.dreamcastle.com

LOOK. I'M GOING TO GO SIT WITH BRICK AND HAVE A NICE **ADULT** CONVERSATION.
OKAY.
COPYRIGHT© 2005 J.D. "Illiad" Frazer HTTP://WWW.USERFRIENDLY.ORG/

2005-09-12
YOU BET IT'S OKAY! AND IT'S A LONG OVERDUE CHANGE!

DO YOU HAVE ANY IDEA HOW NICE IT IS TO FINALLY TALK TO SOMEONE WHO ACTS LIKE AN ADULT?!
READY TO TALK ABOUT ME WHEN YOU ARE, BABE.

THERE SHE GOES WITH THAT APE.
THAT **HANDSOME, LANTERN-JAWED** APE.
2005-09-13
COPYRIGHT© 2005 J.D. "Illiad" Frazer HTTP://WWW.USERFRIENDLY.ORG/

DUDE. IF YOU DON'T SAY SOMETHING SHE COULD END UP DATING THEN, LIKE, **MARRYING** THAT GUY.

MIRANDA! THAT GUY YOU'RE WITH HAS A MOLE ON HIS BUTT THE SIZE OF A POTATO!
GO GET POPCORN.

A.J.! WHAT THE **HELL** DO YOU THINK YOU'RE DOING?
SAVING YOU FROM THE WORST MISTAKE OF YOUR LIFE?
COPYRIGHT© 2005 J.D. "Illiad" Frazer HTTP://WWW.USERFRIENDLY.ORG/

NICE TRY. AND I'LL THANK YOU FOR NOT INTERFERING AGAIN! NOW IF YOU'LL EXCUSE ME, I HAVE TO GET BACK TO BRICK.
OH...HE'S A LITTLE OCCUPIED RIGHT NOW.

2005-09-14
AS YOG-SOTHOTH IS MY WITNESS, I HAVE **NO** IDEA WHO'S GOING TO WIN THIS ONE.

The tension builds. I had e-mails from readers begging, pleading, and threatening.

2005-09-15
WHY ARE YOU DOING THIS? WHY ARE YOU TRYING TO RUIN WHAT LITTLE FUN I'VE BEEN TRYING TO MAKE FOR MYSELF?
COPYRIGHT© 2005 J.D. "Illiad" Frazer HTTP://WWW.USERFRIENDLY.ORG/
I'M SO BUSY AT WORK THAT I NEVER MEET ANYONE, AND WHEN I FINALLY DO, YOU COME ALONG AND BOLLUX MY EVENING!
BUT WHY BRICK?

BRICK IS MANLY! BRICK IS FUN! BRICK HAS A HUGE CHIN! BRICK **LIKES** ME!
BUT A.J. ADORES YOU...

ARE YOU TRYING TO TELL ME THAT AFTER ALL THE TIMES OVER THE YEARS I TRIED AND FAILED TO GET YOU TO ADMIT THAT YOU HAD FEELINGS FOR ME YOU'RE FINALLY ADMITTING IT NOW? NOW?!
YES.

2005-09-16

IT IS SAID THAT TIME IS A SYRUP, THAT IT CAN FLOW AT DIFFERENT RATES DEPENDING ON THE QUALITIES WITHIN. ON SOME DAYS IT FLASHES BY LIKE A RUNNY, WATERY FLOOD. ON OTHER DAYS IT CRAWLS LIKE GLUE, CREEPING OUT OF ITS TOPPLED JAR.

EINSTEIN POSITED THAT THE FLOW OF TIME CAN DEPEND ON THE OBSERVOR. PERHAPS, THEN, WHEN TIME SLOWS DOWN, THE RATE AT WHICH THE SUBJECT'S SYNAPSES FIRE BECOMES REDUCED.

2005-09-17

...OR THEY HALT ENTIRELY.
SEE YOU AT WORK TOMORROW.
LIP..LIP..LIPPY...

The screams of joy in UFieland were something else. I almost wish I'd made this a dream sequence, but I want to remain alive.

THE RESULT OF MICROSOFT BUYING A STAKE IN AOL
1000 HOURS
of Windows XP
FREE for
45 Days
VISA
MasterCard
Microsoft
Windows xp
(DON'T LAUGH TOO HARD)

2005-09-19
DUDE! YOU GOT AN IPOD NANO!
YEAH. THE ORIGINAL IPOD WAS SMALL ENOUGH. WHY MAKE IT EVEN SMALLER?
COPYRIGHT © 2005 J.D. "Illiad" Frazer HTTP://WWW.USERFRIENDLY.ORG/

SO IT FITS BETTER ON ONE OF THOSE SO-CALLED "COFFEE TABLES" AT BIGBUCKS.
OH HELL. GOOD POINT.

2005-09-20
THIS IPOD NANO IS A PRETTY NEAT LITTLE DEVICE.
YEAH. FAIRLY TOUGH. AND OH-SO-THIN.
COPYRIGHT © 2005 J.D. "Illiad" Frazer HTTP://WWW.USERFRIENDLY.ORG/

I WONDER JUST HOW THIN IT IS?
HUH?

AAAUUUGH! NANO-CUT!
IMPRESSIVE.
SNIK!

2005-09-21
NOT TO BE COMINK ANY CLOSER WITH YOUR NANO, OLD MAN.
OH. YOU WANT ONE AND YOU KNOW IT.
COPYRIGHT © 2005 J.D. "Illiad" Frazer HTTP://WWW.USERFRIENDLY.ORG/

NYET! HAVE TRUMPED YOU! YOU ARE NOW SEEINK MY OWN VERSION OF IPOD. IS MUCH SMALLER! IS CALLED "PITRPOD ZEPTO!"

THERE'S...I CAN'T SEE ANYTHING THERE.
HA! LET US SEEINK YOU BEAT THAT, JOBS!

ARE YOU FOR REAL? YOU CREATED AN MP3 PLAYER THAT YOU CAN'T SEE?
DA! WILL FIT ANY-WHERE! INCLUDINK INSIDE YOUR POINTY LEETLE HEAD!
COPYRIGHT © 2005 J.D. "Illiad" Frazer HTTP://WWW.USERFRIENDLY.ORG/

2005-09-22
OH. VERY DROLL. AND WHAT'S THAT?
WHAT IS WHAT?

THAT! THAT THING THAT LOOKS SUSPICIOUSLY LIKE AN APPLE POWER BRICK!
IS NOT POWER BRICK! IS...IS ANTI-WIND ANCHOR ACCESSORY FOR PITRPOD!

2005-09-23
PITR. WHAT IN THE NAME OF DISCORDIA ARE YOU DOING?
LAWFUL PROFITEERINK. COMRADE.
PITRPOD ZEPTO ONLY $299.00
COPYRIGHT© 2005 J.D. "Illiad" Frazer HTTP://WWW.USERFRIENDLY.ORG/

I CAN'T HELP BUT NOTICE THAT YOUR "PRODUCT" IS A LITTLE DIFFICULT TO SEE.
PITRPOD ZEPTO ONLY $299.00

IS BECAUSE YOU ARE SIMPLY LACKINK VISION.
STEF! WHAT THE HECK HAVE YOU BEEN TEACHING PITR?!
PITRPOD ZEPTO ONLY $299.00

2005-09-24
PITR. YOU HAVE NOTHING HERE TO SELL.
BITINK ME. AM HAVINK ALL TWO HUNDRED ZEPTOS ON DESK FOR SALE.
PITRPOD ZEPTO ONLY $299.00
COPYRIGHT© 2005 J.D. "Illiad" Frazer HTTP://WWW.USERFRIENDLY.ORG/

FINE...
PITRPOD ZEPTO ONLY $299.00

NYEEEETTT!!
PITRPOD ZEPTO ONLY $299.00

EQUATING THE REORGANIZATION OF MICROSOFT WITH "SHUFFLING DECK CHAIRS ON THE TITANIC"
Ballmer

2004-09-26

BRICK
IMPLODED.
COPYRIGHT © 2005 J.D. "Illiad" Frazer HTTP://WWW.USERFRIENDLY.ORG/

I...HAVE
TONSILS.

HEY WEB DORK. YOU HAVE THAT SITE DONE FOR ME?
HE CAN'T HEAR YOU. HE GOT TOTALLY SNOGGED BY MIRANDA.
COPYRIGHT © 2005 J.D. "Illiad" Frazer HTTP://WWW.USERFRIENDLY.ORG/

HELLO? WHAT'S WRONG WITH YOU?
YO! DUFUS!
MIRANDA AND HIM PLAYED TONSIL-HOCKEY.
2005-09-27

WOULD YOU BELIEVE... ALIENS STOLE HIS BRAIN?
SEE. ISN'T IT SMARTER TO JUST TELL THE TRUTH AT THE BEGINNING?

GOOD MORNING. A.J.!
OH. HEY TOOTS. NICE EARRINGS. WANT TO MASSAGE MY FEET AFTER WORK?
2005-09-28
COPYRIGHT © 2005 J.D. "Illiad" Frazer HTTP://WWW.USERFRIENDLY.ORG/

WHAT THE HELL JUST HAPPENED?!
YE GODS I ALSO HAVE A LARYNX...

YOU KISSED THE WEBDORK.
HIS NAME IS A.J.
COPYRIGHT © 2005 J.D. "Illiad" Frazer HTTP://WWW.USERFRIENDLY.ORG/

BUT WHY?!
THIS MIGHT SEEM ALIEN TO YOU. BUT SOME WOMEN ARE ATTRACTED TO GUYS WHO ARE SMART.

2005-09-29
HEY NOW! I'M SMART!
STEF. IF YOU WERE ANY STUPIDER YOU'D BE ON LIFE SUPPORT.

2005-09-30
YOU WANT SMART?! JUST TRY ME! I BET I KNOW THINGS THAT YOU DIDN'T KNEW I KNOW! KNOW I KNEW! WHATEVER!
OKAY. DO YOU KNOW HTML?

COPYRIGHT © 2005 J.D. "Illiad" Frazer HTTP://WWW.USERFRIENDLY.ORG/
DO I KNOW HTML? DO I KNOW HTML?!

WE JOKINGLY TOLD HIM IT STANDS FOR "HOW TO MAKE LOVE" YEARS AGO.
I AM SO YOUR MAN, BUTTER TART!

WHAT ARE YOU TELLING ME? YOU'RE ACTUALLY DATING THAT DWEEB?
STEF. DON'T BOTHER. YOU WOULDN'T UNDERSTAND.

2005-10-01
BUT YOU PUT YOUR LIPS ON HIS...HIS...
MOUTH.

COPYRIGHT © 2005 J.D. "Illiad" Frazer HTTP://WWW.USERFRIENDLY.ORG/
WOMAN, COULD YOU BE ANY MORE VILE?
HE HAD COCOA PUFFS FOR BREAKFAST.

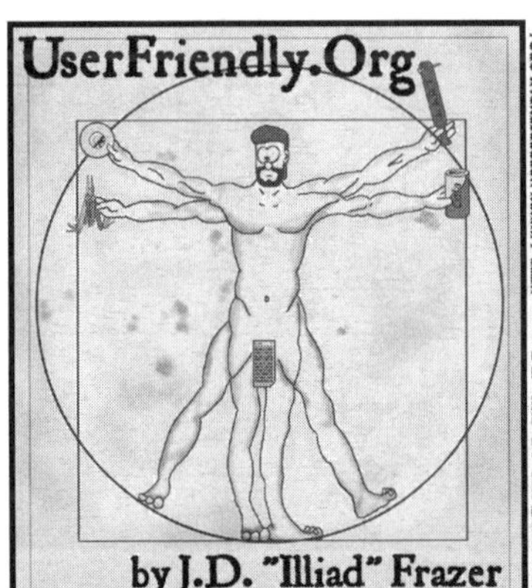
UserFriendly.Org
by J.D. "Illiad" Frazer

COPYRIGHT © 2005 J.D. "Illiad" Frazer HTTP://WWW.USERFRIENDLY.ORG/
YOUR HONOUR, ON BEHALF OF MY CLIENT, THE SCO GROUP, I'D LIKE TO MOVE THAT WE ENGFEH THE WUBBLY UMPLE BORPY.

I BEG YOUR PARDON?
DRAT. THIS JUDGE IS GOOD.

...AND THUS I AM DENYING YOUR THIRD CLAIM TO AMEND YOUR CLIENT'S SUIT AGAINST I.B.M.
BUT...

NO BUTS! MY DECISION IS FINAL.
FINE. SAY JUDGE? HOW'S THE HEART?
IT'S SEEN BETTER DAYS. WHY?

BOO!
UNH-HUH. WASN'T THAT YOUR OPENING CLAIM AGAINST I.B.M.?

JAPANESE SCIENTISTS HAVE TAKEN THE FIRST PHOTO-GRAPHS OF A LIVE SAMPLE OF ONE OF THE MOST ELUSIVE CREATURES IN THE DEEP OCEAN: THE GIANT SQUID.
COPYRIGHT © 2005 J.D. "Illiad" Frazer HTTP://WWW.USERFRIENDLY.ORG/

THESE IMAGES WERE CAPTURED WHILE THE SQUID WAS STRUGGLING ON A HUGE HOOK THAT WAS COVERED WITH BAIT. THE SQUID LOST A TENTACLE BUT GOT AWAY.

2005-10-03
HOLY PUSTULES THAT THING IS UGLY...
BY AZATHOTH! GERTRUDE!!

Yeah, way to go Yahoo! Project Gutenberg has been doing this sort of thing since forever ago, in Internet time. Nice try, trying to claim the glory of that idea.

2005-10-04
IN OTHER NEWS, YAHOO ANNOUNCED THE LAUNCH OF THE OPEN CONTENT ALLIANCE, AN EFFORT TO DIGITIZE MILLIONS OF BOOKS AND PAPERS FOR ALL TO USE.
COPYRIGHT © 2005 J.D. "Illiad" Frazer HTTP://WWW.USERFRIENDLY.ORG/

THE ALLIANCE, BACKED BY YAHOO, WILL BEGIN THE DIGITIZATION OF THE THOUSANDS OF BOOKS THAT ARE IN THE PUBLIC DOMAIN. THIS PROMISE HAS BEEN MET WITH ADMIRATION WITHIN THE INDUSTRY.

FUNNY. I'VE NEVER HEARD "PROJECT GUTENBERG" CALLED "YAHOO" BEFORE.
BUT THE SQUID! WHAT HAPPENED TO THE SQUID?!

SO THE WORLD THINKS THAT A BEAUTIFUL GIANT SQUID IS ONLY WORTH A THIRTY SECOND NEWS SPOT, DO THEY? THEY THINK YAHOO AND ITS OPEN CONTENT EFFORT IS MORE IMPORTANT, DO THEY?
WHAT ARE YOU ON ABOUT?

MEDIA TIME, THAT'S WHAT. I'M TAKING STEPS TO BRING GIANT SQUID, THE DARK POWERS AND THE GREAT OLD ONES MORE ATTENTION.
2005-10-05

MY GREEK IS RUSTY, BUT I THINK IT SAYS NECRO... ...UH..."NECRONOMICON."
OOOKAY. LET'S JUST SEND THIS ONE OVER TO GOOGLE.
YAHOO!

2005-10-06
WAIT. YOU SENT THEM THE REAL NECRONOMICON? THE SO-CALLED "BOOK OF GREAT EVIL?" I NEVER DID READ IT YOU KNOW.
HAVE A LOOK, THEN.
COPYRIGHT © 2005 J.D. "Illiad" Frazer HTTP://WWW.USERFRIENDLY.ORG/

DUDE, IT'S JUST A SPEAKING ENGAGEMENT CONTRACT FOR YOU.
I KNOW. BUT IF THERE'S A GREAT OLD ONE'S NAME IN IT, EVERYONE GOES "OH NO! SCARY!"

2005-10-07
HELLO? ARE YOU THE REUTERS DESK EDITOR? GOOD. NOW PAY ATTENTION:

THE GIANT SQUID ARE HERALDING MY RETURN, HARBINGERS OF CEPHALOPODIC DARKNESS THAT THEY ARE!

SO WHAT DO YOU SAY TO THAT, MR. "YAHOO IS BIGGER THAN THE DEEP DARK SEA"?
I SWEAR TO GOD, DRUDGE. IF THAT'S YOU AGAIN I'M CALLING THE COPS.

2005-10-08
I HATE THE MEDIA.
SO DO I. THEY ALWAYS HAVE PERFECT HAIR.

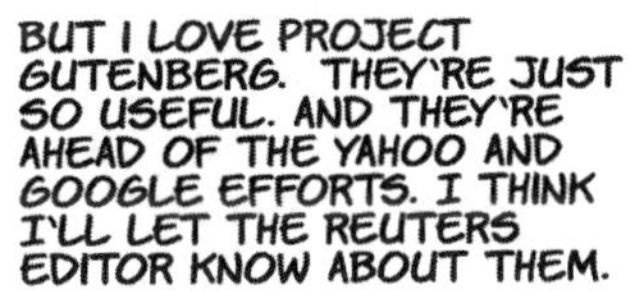
BUT I LOVE PROJECT GUTENBERG. THEY'RE JUST SO USEFUL. AND THEY'RE AHEAD OF THE YAHOO AND GOOGLE EFFORTS. I THINK I'LL LET THE REUTERS EDITOR KNOW ABOUT THEM.

ARE YOU GOING TO...OH DEAR.
16,000 BOOKS TO HIS CELL PHONE AS TEXT MESSAGES. OOHHH YEAH...
EVIL
EVIL
SCRIPT
SCRIPT

WHY GOOGLE MUST NEVER, EVER, EVER BE BOUGHT BY MICROSOFT

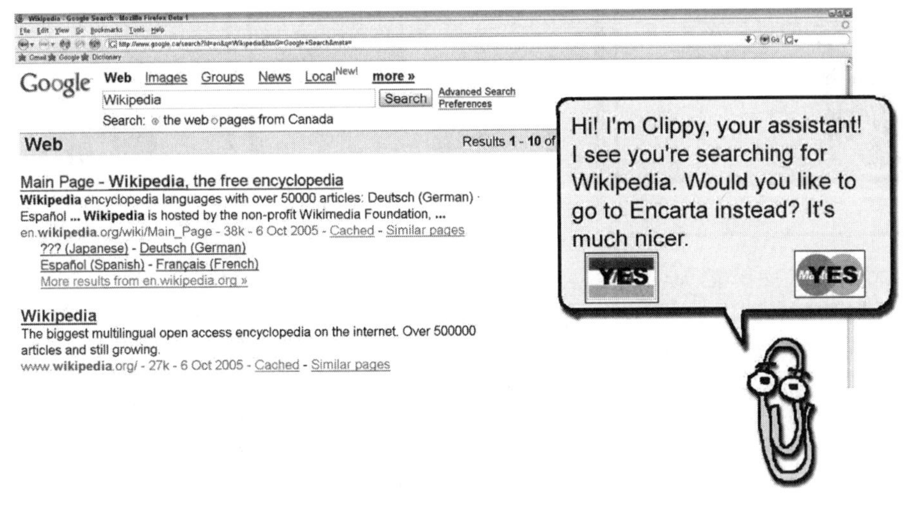
Google
Web Images Groups News Local New! more »
Wikipedia
Search
Advanced Search
Preferences
Search: the web pages from Canada
Web
Results 1 - 10 of
Main Page - Wikipedia, the free encyclopedia
Wikipedia encyclopedia languages with over 50000 articles: Deutsch (German) · Español ... Wikipedia is hosted by the non-profit Wikimedia Foundation, ...
en.wikipedia.org/wiki/Main_Page - 38k - 6 Oct 2005 - Cached - Similar pages
??? (Japanese) - Deutsch (German)
Español (Spanish) - Français (French)
More results from en.wikipedia.org »
Wikipedia
The biggest multilingual open access encyclopedia on the internet. Over 500000 articles and still growing.
www.wikipedia.org/ - 27k - 6 Oct 2005 - Cached - Similar pages
Hi! I'm Clippy, your assistant! I see you're searching for Wikipedia. Would you like to go to Encarta instead? It's much nicer.
YES
YES

A.J.! GOOD MORNING! WANT TO COME OVER FOR DINNER LATER THIS WEEK? SAY FRIDAY?
YES. OKAY.
COPYRIGHT © 2005 J.D. "Illiad" Frazer HTTP://WWW.USERFRIENDLY.ORG/

2005-10-10
WOW...ARE YOU AND A.J. DATING?
KIND OF.

STRANGE. AND I THOUGHT HE WAS GAY.
OH. YOU GO RIGHT AHEAD AND KEEP THINKING THAT, SISTER.

2005-10-11
WINSTON, DO YOU HAVE THE LATEST MUSIC PIRACY REPORT?
YES SIR.
WELL THEN. I SUPPOSE YOU'D BEST GIVE ME THE BAD NEWS.
RIAA
COPYRIGHT © 2005 J.D. "Illiad" Frazer HTTP://WWW.USERFRIENDLY.ORG/

UM, SIR? IT SAYS THE RECORD LABELS HAVE MADE 110 PERCENT MORE THIS YEAR THAN LAST...
GOOD HEAVENS!

110 PERCENT?! DAMN THOSE PIRATES! HAVE THEY NO SENSE OF DECENCY?!
UM...
RIAA

WINSTON, WHAT CAN WE DO ABOUT MUSIC PIRACY? WHAT CAN WE DO ABOUT THIS BLIGHT ON OUR LAWFUL PROFITEERING?
RIAA
COPYRIGHT © 2005 J.D. "Illiad" Frazer HTTP://WWW.USERFRIENDLY.ORG/

WELL SIR, I THINK IT'S A QUESTION OF PSYCHOLOGY. WE HAVE TO STOP CALLING THEM "PIRATES." I MEAN, HOW COOL ARE PIRATES?

2005-10-12
UHHHMMM....
EXTREMELY COOL, SIR. THAT'S HOW COOL.
RIAA

2005-10-13
WINSTON, WE NEED TO MAKE MORE MONEY. PHONE STEVE JOBS AND TELL HIM OUR MEMBERS WANT A BIGGER CUT OF SALES THROUGH ITUNES.
YES SIR. CALLING NOW...
RIAA

SIR? I HAVE MR. JOBS ON THE PHONE. HE REPLIES WITH HYSTERICAL LAUGHTER.
LAUGHTER?! DOESN'T HE KNOW WHO WE ARE?!
RIAA

QUOTH HE: "THE SKIN THAT HOLDS THE PUS TOGETHER IN THE BLISTER."
WHY...HE...OOH! I...OOOOH!
RIAA
COPYRIGHT © 2005 J.D. "Illiad" Frazer HTTP://WWW.USERFRIENDLY.ORG/

I HEAR YOU'RE HAVING DINNER WITH OUR GODDESS MIRANDA TONIGHT.
YES. THAT'S RIGHT...
COPYRIGHT © 2005 J.D. "Illiad" Frazer HTTP://WWW.USERFRIENDLY.ORG/

AH. THEN YOU'LL WANT TO READ THE E.U.L.A. VERY CAREFULLY.
2005-10-14

THERE'S A E.U.L.A. FOR WOMEN?
OR YOU COULD JUST AGREE TO EVERYTHING SHE ASKS FOR AND YOU'LL GET TO THE "INSTALLATION" PHASE. AND THEN SHE OWNS YOUR MACHINE.

WAIT. WHAT ARE YOU ON ABOUT? INSTALLATION? E.U.L.A? WHAT?
LOOK WEBDORK. IT'S ALL ABOUT AN EXCHANGE OF WEALTH FOR SERVICES.
2005-10-15
COPYRIGHT © 2005 J.D. "Illiad" Frazer HTTP://WWW.USERFRIENDLY.ORG/

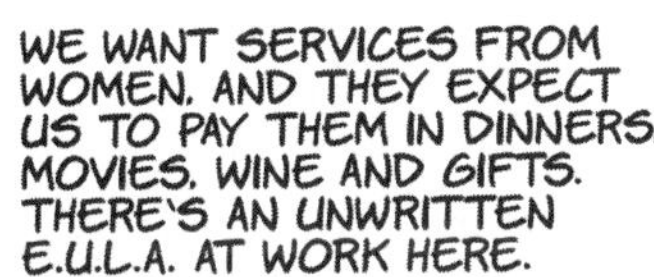
WE WANT SERVICES FROM WOMEN. AND THEY EXPECT US TO PAY THEM IN DINNERS. MOVIES. WINE AND GIFTS. THERE'S AN UNWRITTEN E.U.L.A. AT WORK HERE.

BUT SHE'S MAKING ME DINNER.
IT'S A BAIT-AND-SWITCH. ONCE YOU'RE IN THE DOOR YOU'LL BE PAYING FOR PATCHES AND THE "GOLD EDITION" IN NO TIME.

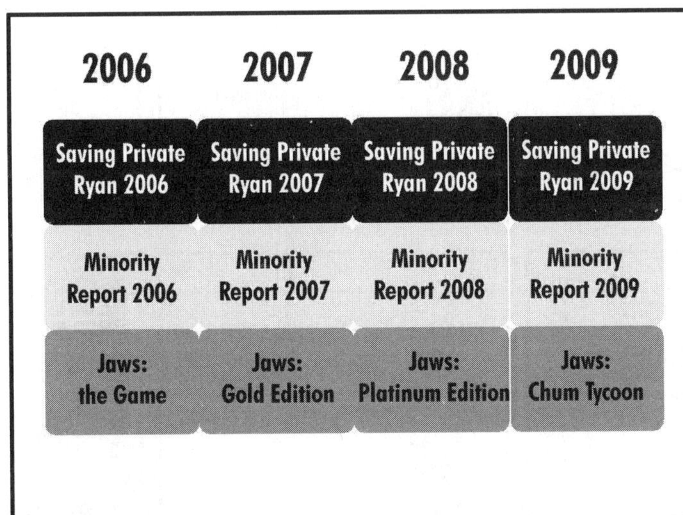
STEVEN SPIELBERG JOINS ELECTRONIC ARTS AND THE GAME DEVELOPMENT SCHEDULE IS SET FOR THE NEXT FOUR YEARS...
2006
2007
2008
2009
Saving Private Ryan 2006
Saving Private Ryan 2007
Saving Private Ryan 2008
Saving Private Ryan 2009
Minority Report 2006
Minority Report 2007
Minority Report 2008
Minority Report 2009
Jaws: the Game
Jaws: Gold Edition
Jaws: Platinum Edition
Jaws: Chum Tycoon
COPYRIGHT © 2005 J.D. "Illiad" Frazer HTTP://WWW.USERFRIENDLY.ORG/

A.J.! COME IN!
UM...HI.
COPYRIGHT © 2005 J.D. "Illiad" Frazer HTTP://WWW.USERFRIENDLY.ORG/

2005-10-17
THIS IS FOR YOU.
WHAT?
CHECK YOUR PHONE.
BWAP
BIP
BOOP

THAT'S A NETHACK SCREENSHOT.
IT'S OF MY VALKYRIE "MIRANDA" ESCAPING WITH THE AMULET OF YENDOR!

Most readers at this point probably though that A.J. and Miranda ended up "doing the nasty."

2005-10-18
SO WHEN'S DINNER?
OH.
I HAVEN'T STARTED MAKING IT YET.
COPYRIGHT © 2005 J.D. "Illiad" Frazer HTTP://WWW.USERFRIENDLY.ORG/

Sure was fun drawing A.J.'s expression in the last panel.

2005-10-19
HOW WAS DINNER WITH A.J.?
WE NEVER REALLY GOT AROUND TO DINNER.
COPYRIGHT © 2005 J.D. "Illiad" Frazer HTTP://WWW.USERFRIENDLY.ORG/

THAT'S MORE THAN I WANTED TO KNOW. HOW'S HE HANDLING THE WHOLE DATING THING?
I'D SAY HE'S TAKING A BIT OF TIME TO ADJUST.

HAS HE SAID ANYTHING AT ALL THIS MORNING?
HE EXHALED ABOUT AN HOUR AGO.

2005-10-20
OOOOH. SO NOW THE BRITISH SECRET INTELLIGENCE SERVICE HAS A RECRUITING WEBSITE. VERY NIIIICE...
COPYRIGHT © 2005 J.D. "Illiad" Frazer HTTP://WWW.USERFRIENDLY.ORG/

WELL. I THINK I'LL APPLY. I'M PERFECT FOR THE JOB.

IT SAYS: "CHICKS LOVE ME AND I CAN DO A BRITISH ACCENT."
GOOD HEAVENS. HOW DID WE MISS HIM ALL THESE YEARS?
MI6
Secret Agents Only

SIR, WE'VE DONE A PRELIMINARY SCREENING ON THIS "STEF MURKY" FELLOW. HE'S QUITE THE CHARACTER.
IS HE.
MI6
NON-DESCRIPT JANITORS
Secret Agents
Only

YES SIR. I THINK WE SHOULD BRING HIM IN FROM CANADA FOR AN "INTERVIEW."
IS HE OF INTEREST?
MI6
Only
COPYRIGHT© 2005 J.D. "Illiad" Frazer HTTP://WWW.USERFRIENDLY.ORG/

HE'S HOARDED A PILE OF THE REALLY GOOD GMAIL NAMES, SIR.
BLOODY CHEEK.
QUITE, SIR.
2005-10-21
MI6
Only

HOW DO YOU EXPECT TO BRING THIS MURKY FELLOW FROM CANADA TO US, DOBSON? WE HAVE A TIGHT BUDGET YOU KNOW.
HIS PSYCH PROFILE GIVES US SOME HINTS SIR.
2005-10-22
COPYRIGHT© 2005 J.D. "Illiad" Frazer HTTP://WWW.USERFRIENDLY.ORG/

YES?
A QUICK CHANGE TO OUR WEBSITE SHOULD DO THE TRICK, SIR.

"HOW TO MUCK ABOUT WITH AN ENEMY TROLLOP 101"? THIS IS IN LONDON?
THAT'S JUST BRIT LINGO FOR NEW MARKETING THEORY. YOU KNOW HOW THE BRITS ARE.

SUDDENLY, THEODORE REALIZED THE FOLLY OF MAKING AIRCRAFT ENTIRELY OUT OF TRANSPARENT ALUMINUM.
COPYRIGHT© 2005 J.D. "Illiad" Frazer HTTP://WWW.USERFRIENDLY.ORG/

SIR? MR. MURKY HAS ARRIVED AT OUR DOOR.
HAS HE? WELL, SHOW HIM IN.
MI6 Make being Naughty your Career
COPYRIGHT © 2005 J.D. "Illiad" Frazer HTTP://WWW.USERFRIENDLY.ORG/

MIGHT TAKE A BIT OF DOING, SIR. HE'S...DETAINED DOWN IN RECEPTION.
OH DEAR. WHAT DID HE SAY TO MISS POCKETMONEY?
MI6 Make being Naughty your Career

"Q" Laboratories
The Loo
YOU MIGHT WANT TO REPEAT THAT A FEW MORE TIMES.
YOU ARE NOT A TARTY SILHOUETTE GIRL!! YOU ARE NOT! A TARTY...

YOU MUST BE MR. MURKY.
YES. WHO ARE YOU?
2005-10-25
COPYRIGHT © 2005 J.D. "Illiad" Frazer HTTP://WWW.USERFRIENDLY.ORG/

I AM THE HEAD OF MI6. YOU MAY CALL ME "C."
OH COOL. JUST LIKE THE "MEN IN BLACK."

I BEG YOUR PARDON?
COULD I BE "Z"? I'M CANADIAN AND YOU'RE A BRIT, SO I'D BE "ZED" AND IT WOULD DRIVE THE C.I.A. GUYS I'LL BE WORKING WITH NUTS.

2005-10-26
MR. MURKY, IN EXCHANGE FOR ALL OF THE CHOICE GMAIL ACCOUNTS YOU HAVE, WE HERE AT MI6 ARE PREPARED TO OFFER YOU A POSITION AS A "COMPLETE ZERO" AGENT.
YOU MEAN A "DOUBLE-O" AGENT?!
"No one gets the chicks like MI6!"

NO. "COMPLETE ZERO" AGENT. IT'S SPECIFIC TO YOUR CHARACTER AND PROFESSIONAL BACKGROUND.
OH. WHAT DOES THAT GET ME?

"A LICENSE TO SHILL."
HEY!
"No one gets the chicks like MI6!"
COPYRIGHT © 2005 J.D. "Illiad" Frazer HTTP://WWW.USERFRIENDLY.ORG/

A.J.! CONGRATS ON YOU AND MIRANDA!
THANKS...UM... COULD YOU GIVE ME SOME ADVICE?
SURE. I'LL DO MY BEST.
COPYRIGHT © 2005 J.D. "Illiad" Frazer HTTP://WWW.USERFRIENDLY.ORG/

2005-10-27
SEE, THE OTHER NIGHT MIRANDA AND I, UM... WE...UM...
PLAYED TONSIL HOCKEY?

RIGHT, AND I LEARNED HOW TO DO THAT BY MAKING OUT WITH A SOCK PUPP...I MEAN FROM EXPERIENCE!
DON'T MIND ME WHILE I DIG MY BRAIN OUT WITH MY FINGERNAILS.

YOU WERE SAYING?
UM. YEAH. ANYWAY. I KNOW HOW TO KISS AND STUFF. BUT MIRANDA MIGHT BE EXPECTING TO UM...AND I DON'T KNOW HOW TO UMM...
2005-10-28
COPYRIGHT © 2005 J.D. "Illiad" Frazer HTTP://WWW.USERFRIENDLY.ORG/

"...SURRENDER YOUR MANFLOWER WITH DIGNITY AND APLOMB?"
AT THIS POINT DIGNITY IS CHROME.

2005-10-29
GREG WOULDN'T GIVE YOU ADVICE?
HE SAID "IT WOULD SPOIL THE MAGIC."
COPYRIGHT © 2005 J.D. "Illiad" Frazer HTTP://WWW.USERFRIENDLY.ORG/

ADVICE ON WHAT?
UM...FOOLING AROUND.

I JUST DON'T KNOW WHO ELSE TO ASK.
DUDE. I'M HOOKED TO THE NET. I HAVE DETAILED FILES.

Well! I guess they didn't ...

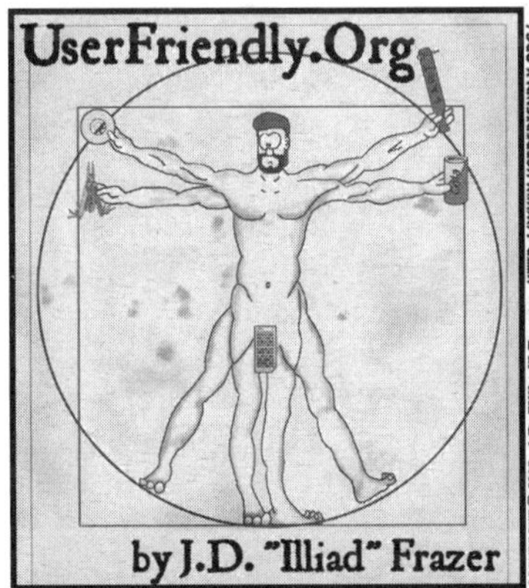
UserFriendly.Org
by J.D. "Illiad" Frazer
COPYRIGHT © 2005 J.D. "Illiad" Frazer HTTP://WWW.USERFRIENDLY.ORG/

YOUR BULBOUSNESS! NEWS IS IN FROM EARTH. IT APPEARS S.C.O. HAS BEEN CAUGHT RED-HANDED WITH LINUX KERNEL CODE IN THEIR UNIXWARE.

BY ANDROMEDA'S NOSTRILS! PREPARE THE INCINERATION RAY AND TARGET DARL MCBRIDE!
THE LINUX COMMUNITY IS WAY AHEAD OF US. SIRE.

WHY DO YOU WISH TO DEPLOY THE RAY ON MR. MCBRIDE. SIRE?
ZORKPLIK. DARL HAS BEEN ONE OF OUR AGENTS SINCE THE VERY BEGINNING.

HE'S BEEN WORKING TOWARDS OVERTHROWING EARTH VIA LITIGATION. CLEARLY HE HAS FAILED. AND IT BEHOOVES US TO ERADICATE ANY EVIDENCE LINKING HIM TO US.

WOW. IT MUST BE VERY STRESSFUL TO HEAR THE TERRANS CONSTANTLY SUGGESTING THAT MR. MCBRIDE IS "FROM OUTER SPACE."
YOU HAVE NO IDEA. BUT AT LEAST WE STILL HAVE MICHAEL JACKSON.

I love it when I can auction off stuff like this. The fan is happy, the charity is happy, and that makes me happy. Excellent charity, too: it promotes science fiction and literacy to kids.

HELLO! MY NAME IS 'AETO.' IN JULY OF THIS YEAR I WON AN APPEARANCE IN USERFRIENDLY AT A CHARITY AUCTION.
2005-10-31

AS TODAY IS ALL HALLOWS EVE, I FELT IT APPROPRIATE FOR ME TO WEAR MY FAVOURITE COSTUME: THAT OF A CANIS LUPUS IN A FINE SILK SUIT.

AS A DEEP GEEK, I AM SURE THE IMPORTANT COMMENTARY I'M MAKING ABOUT BUSINESS EXECUTIVES IS NOT LOST-
I KNOW WHAT YOU'RE GOING AS: "A WOLF IN VEEP'S CLOTHING."

RECENTLY, INDUSTRY INSIDERS REPORTED SEEING HIP-HOP PRINCE MC HAMMER VISITING THE GOOGLE CAMPUS. HAMMER IS FAMOUS FOR A NUMBER OF CHART-TOPPING HITS IN THE 80S AND 90S.

MUCH SPECULATION AROSE FROM THE RATHER ODD COMBO OF SEARCH GIANT AND RAPPER. ONE OF OUR REPORTERS DID MANAGE TO CATCH UP TO THE ELUSIVE STAR FOR A QUESTION.

"MR HAMMER? WHAT DO YOU THINK OF GOOGLE?"
"THEY'RE TOO LEGIT TO CTRL-Q, DAWG."
HEY! THAT LYRIC WAS MINE!
2005-11-01

HEY! WIKIPEDIA IS GOING TO PRINT!
IT IS? WHY?
SO THAT PEOPLE IN DEVELOPING NATIONS WITH NO NET ACCESS CAN USE THE INFO!
2005-11-02

WIKIPEDIA? ALL OF IT?
UH, YES. ON PAPER.

I THINK IT'S ALL IN ENGLISH.
NO, I HAVE THE ONE PAGE IN OUR LANGUAGE RIGHT HERE.
Pencils + Erasers
Qty. 1800

TECH SUPPORT, GREG SPEAKING.
BEHOLD! THE TECH SECTOR CRUMBLES!
COPYRIGHT© 2005 J.D. "Illiad" Frazer HTTP://WWW.USERFRIENDLY.ORG/

2005-11-03

AH, CIVILIZATION IV IS OUT.
LO! A RUN ON EYE-DROPS, ENERGY DRINKS AND ADULT DIAPERS SHALL COMMENCE!

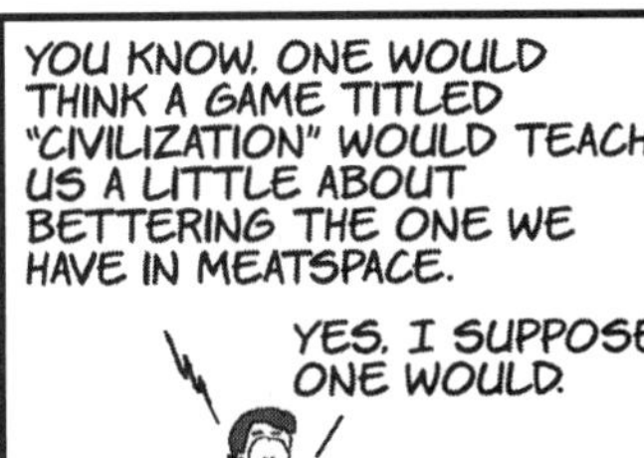
YOU KNOW, ONE WOULD THINK A GAME TITLED "CIVILIZATION" WOULD TEACH US A LITTLE ABOUT BETTERING THE ONE WE HAVE IN MEATSPACE.
YES. I SUPPOSE ONE WOULD.
2005-11-04

BUT WHAT DOES IT TEACH? TRICK YOUR NEIGHBOURS! STEAL THEIR RESOURCES! BUILD UP ARMIES IN SECRET WHILE YOU TALK NICE!

COPYRIGHT © 2005 J.D. "Illiad" Frazer HTTP://WWW.USERFRIENDLY.ORG/
IT DOES TEACH YOU THAT IF WORSE COMES TO WORST, YOU CAN SCRUB THE WORLD AND START OVER.
THERE'S GOTTA BE A LESSON IN THERE SOMEWHERE.

2005-11-05
YOU'RE NOT REALLY RANTING ABOUT CIV IV, ARE YOU?
OK, SO I HAVE A PROBLEM WITH THE REAL WORLD. IT'S JUST THAT THE CIV GAMES MAKE EXCELLENT METAPHORS.

COPYRIGHT © 2005 J.D. "Illiad" Frazer HTTP://WWW.USERFRIENDLY.ORG/
THERE'S SO MUCH ABOUT THE GAME THAT REFLECTS REAL LIFE, PARTICULARLY THE MODERN WORLD.
FOR EXAMPLE, CONSIDER THE REAL WORLD RAMIFICATIONS OF "SETTLER SPREAD."

YOU MEAN THE STRATEGY WHERE YOU JUST KEEP BUILDING SETTLERS AND MAKING CITIES UNTIL YOU OWN THE MAP?
NO, I MEAN THE ACTION OF SETTLING ON MY BACKSIDE FOR A GAME AND WATCHING IT SPREAD.

THE POSITIVE SIDE OF PATENTABLE PLOTS:
LOTS MORE ROOM ON YOUR BOOKSHELF

SO THERE'S THIS GUY
Three Minorities & a Bar
Happily Ever After
Everybody Dies

HEY...IS A.J. IN HIS OFFICE?
YES. HE LOCKED HIMSELF IN. HE'S BEEN HERE SINCE SUNRISE.

2005-11-07
SUNRISE?! A.J.?!
YEP. SAID HE HAD TO PREPARE HIMSELF FOR SOMETHING CALLED "CALL OF DUTY 2."

FALL IN!
GAME IS LOADED AND ALL ACCOUNTED FOR, LIEUTENANT!

I'VE BEEN WAITING TO PLAY THIS GAME FOR MONTHS. IT'S SUPPOSED TO BE EVEN MORE INTENSE THAN THE ORIGINAL CALL OF DUTY. ALTHOUGH I'M NOT SURE THAT'S POSSIBLE...

FUT-PUTPUTPUT!
BLAM!
BLAM!
BLAM!
BLAM!

2005-11-08
YE...GODS.
JUST WAIT UNTIL THE ARTILLERY BARRAGE MISSION. GOT SUBWOOFERS?

THIS GAME IS TERRIFIC! THE ENEMY TROOPS CALL OUT TO EACH OTHER WHEN THEY SEE A THREAT AND THEN THEY ACT ON IT!

I'VE PATCHED THE CODE FOR YOU JUST A LITTLE. JUST TO MAKE THE GAME MORE PERSONAL.
NICE. THANKS. WHAT DID YOU CHANGE?

2005-11-09
KANADIER WEB-DUMMKOPF! ALAAAAARM!
HEY!!

MG42 TO THE WEST! I JUST LOBBED A SMOKE GRENADE...WHEEE! THE SMOKE EFFECTS IN THE GAME ARE AWESOME.

A.J., WHY HAVE YOU LOCKED YOURSELF IN HERE...? GOOD HEAVENS, I HOPE THAT'S NOT A COMPUTER GAME YOU'RE PLAYING ON COMPANY TIME!
NO SIR. IT'S...UH...
SSSSSSS SSSSSSS SSSSSSS!
2005-11-10

...IT'S AN APP THAT LET'S ME VIEW THE "MAGIC SMOKE" IN MY MONITOR!
OH. WELL. IN THAT CASE... CARRY ON.
SHOULD BE CALLED A "SMOKE & MIRRORS" GRENADE.

DAMN. I DO LOVE THESE WW2 SHOOT-EM-UP GAMES. TIME FOR ANOTHER TRY AT TAKING THAT HILL AND...
NOV 11

2005-11-11

NOV 11

NOV 11

As one UFie put it, "There was no respawn for them." Please spare a few minutes of respectful silence every Remembrance Day.

2005-11-12

HELLO, WELCOME TO SONY'S NEW ENHANCED AND SECURE CONTENT SYSTEM!
IF YOU'D LIKE TO PLAY THIS MUSIC CD ON YOUR COMPUTER, PLEASE ACCEPT THE E.U.L.A. AND INSTALL OUR D.R.M. APP.

INTERESTING. THERE'S NO "I ACCEPT" BUTTON.
IT'S THE ONE LABELLED "PWN ME SONY."

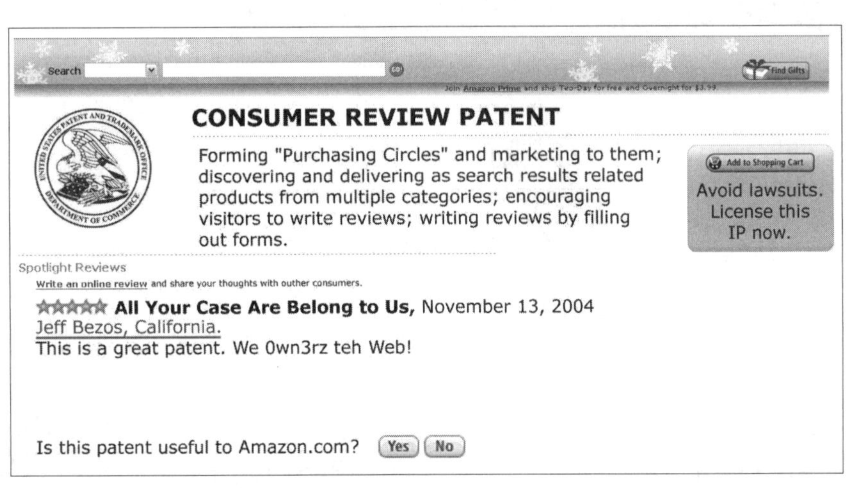
Search
Find Gifts
CONSUMER REVIEW PATENT
Forming "Purchasing Circles" and marketing to them; discovering and delivering as search results related products from multiple categories; encouraging visitors to write reviews; writing reviews by filling out forms.
Add to Shopping Cart
Avoid lawsuits. License this IP now.
Spotlight Reviews
Write an online review and share your thoughts with outher consumers.
All Your Case Are Belong to Us, November 13, 2004
Jeff Bezos, California.
This is a great patent. We 0wn3rz teh Web!
Is this patent useful to Amazon.com?
Yes
No

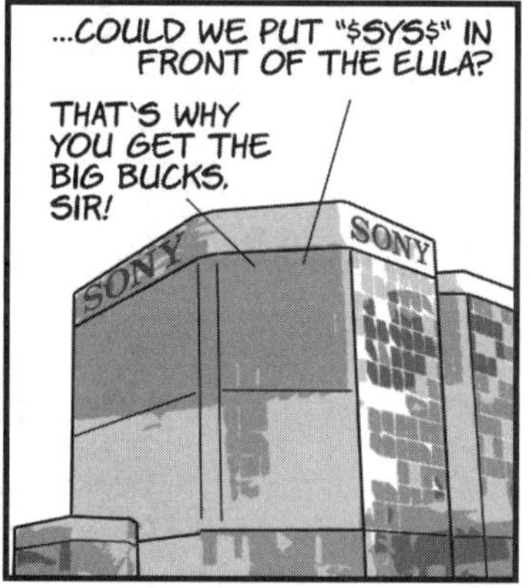

It constantly staggers me how so many corporations just can't bring themselves to publically apologize for a screw-up. You'd think they were baring their bellies when they did that. I suppose it's 1 part pride and 20 parts "we don't want to trigger a class-action lawsuit."

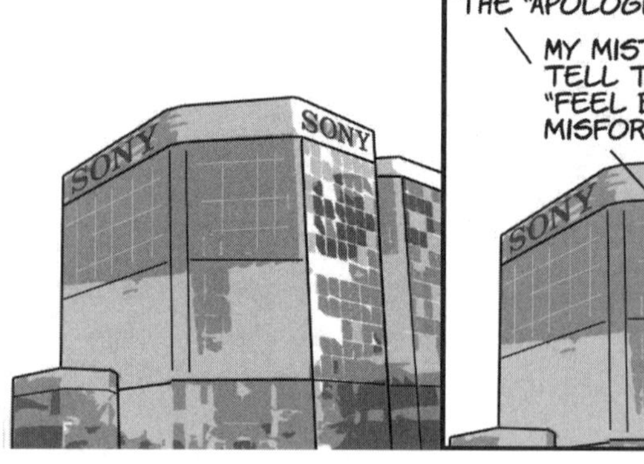

MORE BAD NEWS FROM THE FRONT, SIR. IT SEEMS THAT WHEN PEOPLE REMOVE OUR DRM SOFTWARE ON THEIR OWN, THEIR CD DRIVES STOP WORKING.
SONY
COPYRIGHT © 2005 J.D. "Illiad" Frazer HTTP://WWW.USERFRIENDLY.ORG/

SO?
SO THIS WILL HAVE AN IMPACT ON MORE THAN JUST OUR CONSUMER BASE, SIR. INFRA-STRUCTURE IS AT STAKE.
SONY

TECH SUPPORT, GREG SPEAKING.
SO, LIKE, MY COFFEE CUP HOLDER WON'T COME OUT ANYMORE.

YOU KNOW WHAT I SAY ABOUT ALL OF THIS OUTCRY OVER OUR DRM SOFTWARE? TA HELL WITH THE BUNCH OF THEM!
BUT, SIR...
SONY
SONY
COPYRIGHT © 2005 J.D. "Illiad" Frazer HTTP://WWW.USERFRIENDLY.ORG/

NO BUTS! WE'RE SONY, FER LUCRE'S SAKE! WE'RE BIG, WE'RE BAD, WE'RE NAUGHTY, AND THE CONSUMER CAN KISS MY JEWEL CASE!
THIS IS A NON-ISSUE, UNDERSTOOD?
SONY
SONY

YES SIR. UM, IT SEEMS THAT LOTS OF PEOPLE AT HOMELAND SECURITY BOUGHT OUR MUSIC CDS.
I'M AGENT WESSON AND THIS IS AGENT SPRINGFIELD. WE'D LIKE A WORD...
2005-11-19
SONY
SONY

USER FRIENDLY
the comic strip
BY J.D. "ILLIAD" FRAZER
COPYRIGHT © 2005 J.D. "Illiad" Frazer HTTP://WWW.USERFRIENDLY.ORG/

IS IT NOT THE RIGHT COLOUR?
NO, NO, IT'S PERFECT, FOR FISHING TACKLE.

(*SUNG TO "MONY MONY" AS DONE BY BILLY IDOL*)
HERE IT COMES NOW! ROOTKIT! SONY, SONY!
BOOT ME UP! OWN MY BOX! SONY, SONY!

HEY! I PAID ONCE ONLY SO IT SERVES ME RIGHT NOW!
I CAUSED YOUR LOSS AND BURN, SO IT SERVES ME RIGHT! YEAH! SERVES ME RIGHT!

I SAY YEAH! (YEAH!) YEAH! (YEAH!), YEAH! (YEAH!) YEAH! (YEAH!), YEAH! (YEAH!)
THAT'S CAUSE YOU MAKE ME SEE! (SONY SONY!) SO CLEAR! (SONY SONY!) SO FINE! (SONY SONY!) IT'S MINE! (SONY SONY!) IT'S MINE! (SONY SONY!) IT'S MINE! (SONY SONY!)
IT'S ALL MINE! (SONY SONY!) YES THE FAULT'S ALL MINE!

SONY'S FIGURED OUT YOU'RE BEING SARCASTIC. I'LL GET YOU A LAWYER.
SONY SONY! PHONEY PHONEY! BAD BALONEY! RIAA CRONY!

Synonyms for *tiny* and *ductile* give you ... ha! Such brilliance. Ahem.

TECH SUPPORT. GREG SPEAKING.
HI! I'M WITH TINYDUCTILE MARKETING AND I'D LIKE YOU TO ANSWER A FEW SURVEY QUESTIONS! WHAT DO YOU THINK OF THE IDEA OF AN AD-SUPPORTED VERSION OF WINDOWS?
COPYRIGHT © 2005 J.D. "Illiad" Frazer HTTP://WWW.USERFRIENDLY.ORG/

WHA..?!! ARE YOU OUT OF YOUR MIND? I GET THAT RETARDED PAPERCLIP INFLICTED ON ME AND NOW YOU SUGGEST I GET BOMBARDED WITH ADS AS PART AND PARCEL OF MY OPERATING SYSTEM?
2005-11-21

SO...CAN I PUT YOU DOWN AS "UNDECIDED?"
"TINY DUCTILE"? JUST A MINUTE...

MAYBE YOU COULD JUST GIVE THE AD-SUPPORTED VERSION OF WINDOWS A TRY...
NO BLOODY WAY. I'M NOT INSTALLING ANY WEIRD ALPHA VERSION CRUD FROM THE REDMOND HEGEMONY ON MY MACHINE.
2005-11-22
COPYRIGHT © 2005 J.D. "Illiad" Frazer HTTP://WWW.USERFRIENDLY.ORG/

BUY AMMO TO SHOOT THE MONKEY! ONLY $3.95!
POOT!

HOW DID YOU DO THAT TO MY MACHINE?!!
BUY ANY MUSIC FROM SONY RECENTLY?

A.J.! THE XBOX 360 IS OUT!
GOOD LUCK GETTING ONE. THE LINE-UPS AT THE STORES ARE HUGE AND THERE'S AN ARTIFICIAL SHORTAGE OF THE UNITS.
COPYRIGHT © 2005 J.D. "Illiad" Frazer HTTP://WWW.USERFRIENDLY.ORG/

UH...ERWIN TOLD ME HE HAD A WAY OF GETTING ONE...
ERWIN! WHAT DID YOU DO THIS TIME?
NOTHING I HAVEN'T DONE BEFORE.

EST❖MART
XBOX 360
MEDIC!
CLERIC!

DID ERWIN GET AN XBOX 360?
MORE THAN ONE. HE GOT SEVERAL.
COPYRIGHT © 2005 J.D. "Illiad" Frazer HTTP://WWW.USERFRIENDLY.ORG/

WHAT. IS HE HOARDING THEM TO SELL OFF AT A HUGE PROFIT?
NO...HE HAS ANOTHER PURPOSE IN MIND.

2005-11-24
TOUCH MY HAREM AND YOU DIE. DWEEB.
WE LOVE YOU MASTER CHIEF!

2005-11-25
HOW'S THE HAREM?
NOT SO GOOD. AT FIRST I THOUGHT THEY WERE HOT FOR ME. BUT IT TURNS OUT THEY WERE JUST OVERHEATING.
ROTO ROUTER
COPYRIGHT © 2005 J.D. "Illiad" Frazer HTTP://WWW.USERFRIENDLY.ORG/

SO AFTER SENDING ARTUR TO AN 8-HOUR LONG LINE UP TO GET YOU YOUR XBOX 360S, IT TURNS OUT THAT THEY'RE DEFECTIVE?
THAT'S NOT THE HALF OF IT...
ROTO ROUTER

NOW SERVING
009
RETURNS
XBOX 360
XBOX 360
XBOX 360
XBOX 360
XBOX 360

2005-11-26
BILL? THE XBOX 360 LAUNCH ISN'T DOING SO WELL.
I HEARD, STEVE.
Microsoft
COPYRIGHT © 2005 J.D. "Illiad" Frazer HTTP://WWW.USERFRIENDLY.ORG/

I THREW A CHAIR AT THE MANUFACTURER. I THINK THEY'RE SUITABLY CHASTISED.
I HEARD, STEVE.

AND CONSUMERS ARE ALL SAYING THEY'RE SKIPPING THE 360 AND WAITING FOR "XBOX 361 FOR WORKGROUPS."
I HEARD, STEVE!

YOU DON'T THINK SONY MIGHT'VE...? NAAAHH...
XBOX 360
sysBSOD.exe
sysfnord.exe
syssmoke.exe
syssplode.exe
syscrash.exe
COPYRIGHT © 2005 J.D. "Illiad" Frazer HTTP://WWW.USERFRIENDLY.ORG/

AT THE U.N. WORLD SUMMIT ON THE INFORMATION SOCIETY EARLIER THIS MONTH, MICROSOFT REPRESENTATIVES DEMANDED THE REMOVAL OF REFERENCES TO FREE SOFTWARE IN THE VIENNA CONCLUSIONS, A CRITICAL PAPER ON CREATIVITY IN I.T.
COPYRIGHT© 2005 J.D. "Illiad" Frazer HTTP://WWW.USERFRIENDLY.ORG/

FURTHER, THOMAS LUTZ, THE MANAGER OF PUBLIC AFFAIRS FOR MICROSOFT AUSTRIA, INSISTED THAT REFERENCES TO LINUX SHOULD BE REMOVED AS LINUX IS "ANTI-COMMERCIAL."
2005-11-28

BUT MR. LUTZ, DON'T YOU MEAN 'COMPETITIVE'?
WELL, YE--NO!! ANTI-COMMERCIAL!!

2005-11-29
MORE NEWS ON MICROSOFT. LAST WEEK, CHARLES FITZGERALD, MICROSOFT'S GENERAL MANAGER OF PLATFORM STRATEGY CRITICIZED IBM'S 'ON DEMAND' PROPOSAL.
COPYRIGHT© 2005 J.D. "Illiad" Frazer HTTP://WWW.USERFRIENDLY.ORG/

ADDITIONALLY, FITZGERALD CONSIDERS THE OPEN SOURCE MOVEMENT TO BE LARGELY MADE UP OF CODERS "DORKING AROUND WITH SOURCE CODE."

WHEN ASKED TO COMMENT, IBM DECLINED. AN OPEN-SOURCE CODER, HOWEVER, TOOK THE OPPORTUNITY TO CALL MR. FITZGERALD A "POOPYHEAD."
AT THAT POINT IBM JOINED IN WITH: "WHAT HE SAID."

HMMM. GOOGLE'S NEW "CLICK TO CALL" SERVICE... GIVINK GOOGLE MY PHONE NUMBER AND GOOGLE, SHE IS PLACINK CALL FOR ME TO ADVERTISER...
2005-11-30
COPYRIGHT© 2005 J.D. "Illiad" Frazer HTTP://WWW.USERFRIENDLY.ORG/

NOW...WRITINK QUICK LEETLE SCRIPT...JUST SO. QUEUEINK UP NUMBERS TO BE CALLINK THIS ONE, AND VOILA!

NO! WE DO NOT WANT TO BUY A HERD OF LLAMAS!
HEY MAN, YOU CALLED US.
MORE CALLS ON LINES 6 AND 7.
SCO

YOUR MAGNIFICENCE! NEWS OF NOTE FROM THE ALIEN SURFACE!
SPEAK, WORM.
2005-12-1
COPYRIGHT© 2005 J.D. "Illiad" Frazer HTTP://WWW.USERFRIENDLY.ORG/

A TERRAN PARTICLE PHYSICIST HAS WARNED HIS PEOPLE TO QUARANTINE ALL SIGNALS RECEIVED BY THEIR SETI INITIATIVE LEST MALICIOUS DATA FROM "ALIENS" ATTACKS THEIR INTERNET.
IS THERE ANY TRUTH TO HIS WORRIES?

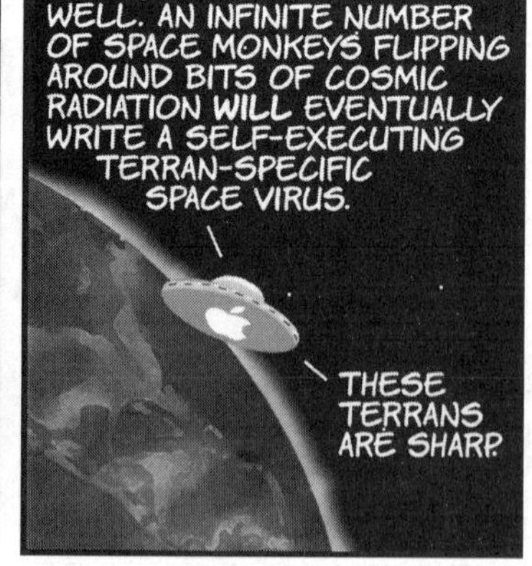
WELL, AN INFINITE NUMBER OF SPACE MONKEYS FLIPPING AROUND BITS OF COSMIC RADIATION WILL EVENTUALLY WRITE A SELF-EXECUTING TERRAN-SPECIFIC SPACE VIRUS.
THESE TERRANS ARE SHARP.

HAVE THE HUMANS BEEN LISTENING FOR US FOR VERY LONG?
JUST A SHORT TIME, YOUR DRIPNIFICENCE. BUT THEY DO LISTEN HARD.
2005-12-2

COPYRIGHT © 2005 J.D. "Illiad" Frazer HTTP://WWW.USERFRIENDLY.ORG/
I SENSE AN OPPORTUNITY TO GAIN SOME WEALTH...
NO, SIRE, PLEASE NOT THAT...

ELLIE, QUIT FIBBING.
I SWEAR! IT READS: "GREETINGS FRIEND. I AM DREAD LORD WUBBUTTICUS IPPY FROM THE BANK OF RIGEL IX, SPAWN OF IBBITPUNG AFK. I HAVE THIRTY MILLION QUATLOOS IN MY TRUST..."

TELL ME MORE OF THIS "SETI" YOU SPEAK OF.
THE 'SEARCH FOR EXTRA-TERRESTRIAL INTELLIGENCE,' YOUR BULBOUSNESS. THE TERRANS ARE LISTENING FOR SIGNALS THAT PROVE THEY ARE NOT ALONE IN THE UNIVERSE.

COPYRIGHT © 2005 J.D. "Illiad" Frazer HTTP://WWW.USERFRIENDLY.ORG/
IT AMOUNTS TO THE TERRANS PASSIVELY TAKING IN ALL OF THE NOISE OF THE UNIVERSE IN A VAIN ATTEMPT TO EXPLAIN THEIR EXISTENCE.

SO IT'S A BIT LIKE GETTING AN RSS FEED FOR THE ENTIRE BLOGOSPHERE.
JUST SO, SIR. ALTHOUGH SETI HAS AN EASIER TIME OF SORTING. THERE'S NO SPACE PORN FOR ONE.

USER FRIENDLY
the comic strip
BY J.D. "ILLIAD" FRAZER

COPYRIGHT © 2005 J.D. "Illiad" Frazer HTTP://WWW.USERFRIENDLY.ORG/
IN TECHNOLOGY NEWS, 180SOLUTIONS IS SUING ZONEALARM FOR LISTING THEIR AD-SERVING SOFTWARE AS "SPYWARE."

"WE WOULD PREFER OUR SOFTWARE TO BE REFERRED TO AS 'PURCHASE OPPORTUNITY PROMPTWARE'" SAID A SPOKESPERSON FROM 180SOLUTIONS.

IN RELATED NEWS, ADWARE VILLAIN "GATOR" HAS BEEN RE-BRANDED AS "CLARIA" FOR ABOUT TWO YEARS. THEIR INFAMOUS SOFTWARE IS NOTED FOR ITS RAPACIOUS SECURITY RISKS AND LACK OF A SIMPLE UNINSTALL PROCEDURE.

CLARIA HAS MADE IT CLEAR THAT THEY WILL SUE ANY FIRM OR ORGANIZATION THAT LABELLED THEIR SOFTWARE AS "SPYWARE" INSTEAD OF "ADWARE." CLARIA CONSIDERS THE TERM "SPYWARE" TO BE DISPARAGING.

ON THE TOPIC OF LAW, THE TERM "BREAKING AND ENTERING" HAS BEEN "RE-BRANDED" AS "DOMICILE TRAILBLAZING"...
...WELL, OKAY, NOT REALLY, BUT I JUST HAD TO FOLLOW UP WITH THAT.

I received screams of mirth and horror via e-mail over this strip.

HEY! NEW WEBCAM?
YEAH. I'M GIVING THE NEW VIDEO COMPONENT IN SKYPE A TRY.
COPYRIGHT © 2005 J.D. "Illiad" Frazer HTTP://WWW.USERFRIENDLY.ORG/

2005-12-5
COOL. DOES IT WORK WELL?
NOT SURE YET. I'M CALLING PEARL AT HER CONDO RIGHT NOW TO GIVE IT A GO.
RING RING

PITR, COULD YOU PLEASE GET THAT?
DA. OF COURSE.
RING RING RING

PITR?! WHAT IN BLAZES ARE YOU DOING THERE?
HAVE DAY OFF.
2005-12-6
COPYRIGHT © 2005 J.D. "Illiad" Frazer HTTP://WWW.USERFRIENDLY.ORG/

I KNOW YOU HAVE THE DAY OFF! WHAT ARE YOU DOING THERE?! IN MY DAUGHTER'S HOME?!

OH, DRYINK OFF AT MOMENT.
AAAUUUGGGH!

PEARL! EXPLAIN ALL OF THIS RIGHT NOW!!
OH DADDY. RELAX. PITR AND I ARE GOING TO VEGAS. HE JUST TOOK A SHOWER TO CLEAN UP.
COPYRIGHT © 2005 J.D. "Illiad" Frazer HTTP://WWW.USERFRIENDLY.ORG/

WELL, THANK THE HEATHEN GODS FOR THAT!

...WAIT. VEGAS?!
JUST OVERNIGHT. SEE YA DADDY!

Right at this very moment, thousands of people all over the world are checking their e-mail or engaged in chat with their full glory hanging out. An awesome thought.

I'M NOTING A SURGE IN VIDEOPHONY SKYPE USE. I WONDER WHAT IT ALL MEANS...
IT MEANS WE LIKE TO SEE WHO WE ARE TALKING TO.
2005-12-8
COPYRIGHT © 2005 J.D. "Illiad" Frazer HTTP://WWW.USERFRIENDLY.ORG/

IT ALSO MEANS THAT EVEN SCIENCE-FICTION WRITERS NEVER EXPECTED THE TRUE IMPACT THAT VIDEOPHONES WOULD HAVE ON THE WORLD.

HOW'S THAT?

SKYPE VIDEO SPELLS DOOM FOR NAKED COMPUTING!
ONE WOULD FERVENTLY HOPE...

WIKIPEDIA IS BEING CRITICIZED AGAIN.
I SEE THAT. SOMETHING ABOUT A LIBELLOUS SUGGESTION INVOLVING AN ASSASSINATION CONSPIRACY.
COPYRIGHT© 2005 J.D. "Illiad" Frazer HTTP://WWW.USERFRIENDLY.ORG/

YET AGAIN WE BRING INTO QUESTION WIKIPEDIA'S SYSTEM OF FACT-CHECKING AND EDITING.

ONE COULD ASSERT THAT WIKIPEDIA ALMOST APPROACHES THE SAME LEVEL OF VERACITY OF, SAY, CNN.
ERWIN! THAT'S NOT FAIR!
FINE. BUT TO WHOM?
2005-12-9

2005-12-10
WHY CAN'T PEOPLE STOP GOING AFTER WIKIPEDIA? IT'S A FREE SERVICE, AND AN ADMIRABLE EFFORT.
PERHAPS YOU'RE RIGHT. OH LOOK GREG, THERE'S AN ENTRY ABOUT YOU. "HAIRY DORK" I THINK IS THE KEYWORD.
COPYRIGHT© 2005 J.D. "Illiad" Frazer HTTP://WWW.USERFRIENDLY.ORG/

WIKIPEDIA IS SO GOING DOWN!
WHAT, ME EDIT?

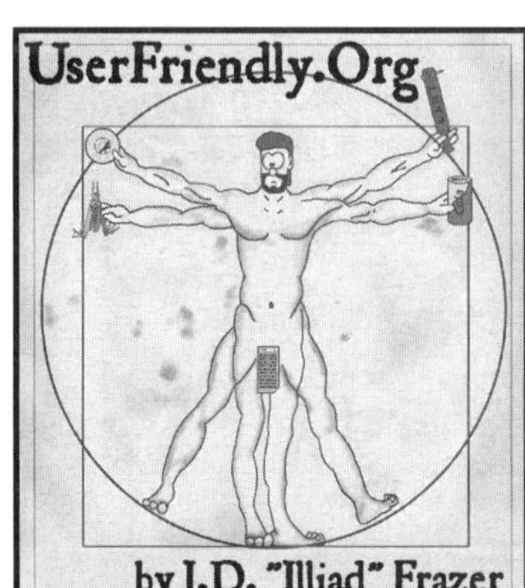
UserFriendly.Org
by J.D. "Illiad" Frazer
COPYRIGHT© 2005 J.D. "Illiad" Frazer HTTP://WWW.USERFRIENDLY.ORG/

THE SMASH-HIT XBOX GAME "HALO" BY MICROSOFT REACHED A PINNACLE WHEN IT WAS LEARNED THAT A MOVIE BASED ON THE GAME IS TO BE PRODUCED.

THIS PINNACLE OF SUCCESS WAS ECLIPSED, HOWEVER, BY THE LOUD GURGLING SOUND COMING FROM MR. BALLMER WHEN IT WAS DISCOVERED THAT THE MOVIE WAS TO BE RENDERED ON LINUX BOXES.

MR. BALLMER, WERE YOU SURPRISED THAT THE MOVIE "HALO" WAS TO HAVE ALL OF ITS SPECIAL EFFECTS RENDERED ON LINUX MACHINES?
OF COURSE I WAS, TODD.

NOT ONLY DOES IT IGNORE US AS THE PUBLISHERS OF "HALO," IT ALSO IGNORES MICROSOFT'S CONSIDERABLE TECHNICAL COMPETENCE IN HANDLING THE CREATION OF SPECIAL EFFECTS.

YES, YOU GUYS SURE DO LEAD THE WORLD WHEN IT COMES TO "BLUE SCREENS," MR. BALLMER.
OOOH! WHY YOU...! SOMEBODY HAND ME A CHAIR!!

LOOK. THE PROBLEM LIES IN THE FACT THAT PEOPLE APPROACH WIKIPEDIA THE WRONG WAY. IT'S NOT AN AUTHORITATIVE PRIMARY SOURCE, AND SHOULDN'T BE TREATED AS ONE.
2005-12-12

BUT PEOPLE DO. AND SOME CONTRIBUTE MATERIAL SLANTED IN FAVOUR OF THEIR AGENDAS.
FOR EXAMPLE, READ THIS ENTRY ON WEB DESIGN.

"BLINK TAGS ARE PHAT."
I SUSPECT THE CONTRIBUTOR IS SOMEONE WHO SELLS EPILEPSY MEDICATION.

BACK FROM VEGAS I SEE.
YES, DADDY.

AND YOU HAD A GOOD TIME?
YES, DADDY.

AND DO YOU SEE THE VEIN THROBBING ON MY FOREHEAD?!
YES, DADDY.
2005-12-13

YOU DIDN'T...PLEASE TELL ME YOU DIDN'T...
GET MARRIED? "PEARL DUBOVICH" HAS *HEH* NICE RING.
BUT NYET, DID NOT MARRY.
2005-12-14

OH THANK THE GODS...
HAVINK GRANDKID ON WAY THOUGH...

AM KIDDINK YOU BIG TIME! "GRAND" "KID" GET IT?
EBBEH

YOUR BROW, IT IS FURROWED.
I'M PONDERING WHAT TO GET MIRANDA FOR CHRISTMAS. SOMETHING ROMANTIC BUT NOT SAPPY. VALUABLE BUT NOT OBLIGATING...
2005-12-15

SPECIAL BUT NOT CONTRIVED? SHINY BUT NOT POINTLESS?
I GUESS.

CHEAP BUT NOT OBVIOUSLY SO?
WHAT DID YOU HAVE IN MIND?

I DON'T HAVE BAGS OF MONEY, BUT I'D LIKE TO GET MIRANDA SOMETHING NICE. OR AT LEAST MILDLY COOL.
COPYRIGHT © 2005 J.D. "Illiad" Frazer HTTP://WWW.USERFRIENDLY.ORG/

LET'S GO OVER YOUR CRITERIA, THEN.
TECH-RELATED?
CHEAP?
HARD TO FIND?
YES.
YES.
YES.

2005-12-16
SONY'S CORPORATE ETHICS?
OOOOH!!

2005-12-17
HEY, MERRY DEBTLOAD BOOST SEASON!
AND TO YOU.
ANY PLANS FOR THE HOLIDAYS?
YEAH, I'M THINKING ABOUT LAUNCHING MY BLOG.
COPYRIGHT © 2005 J.D. "Illiad" Frazer HTTP://WWW.USERFRIENDLY.ORG/

WHO EXACTLY DO YOU EXPECT IS GOING TO READ IT?
ALL OF THE WEB 2.0 PEOPLE. THEY'RE THE NEW CULTISTS!

In Two-Oh Veritas. As the Web develops, I swear the folks who occupy the bleeding edge get stranger and stranger. My kind of people.

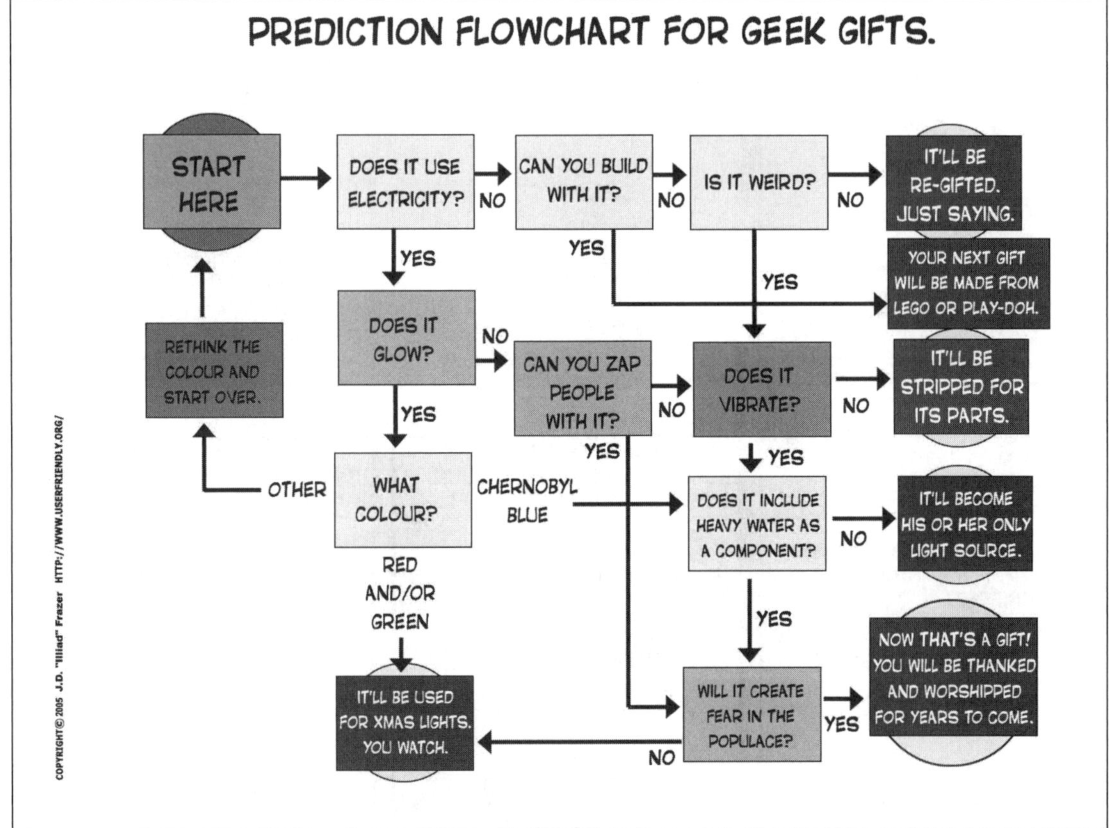
PREDICTION FLOWCHART FOR GEEK GIFTS.
START HERE
DOES IT USE ELECTRICITY?
NO
CAN YOU BUILD WITH IT?
NO
IS IT WEIRD?
NO
IT'LL BE RE-GIFTED. JUST SAYING.
YES
YES
YES
YOUR NEXT GIFT WILL BE MADE FROM LEGO OR PLAY-DOH.
DOES IT GLOW?
NO
CAN YOU ZAP PEOPLE WITH IT?
NO
DOES IT VIBRATE?
NO
IT'LL BE STRIPPED FOR ITS PARTS.
RETHINK THE COLOUR AND START OVER.
YES
YES
YES
OTHER
WHAT COLOUR?
CHERNOBYL BLUE
DOES IT INCLUDE HEAVY WATER AS A COMPONENT?
NO
IT'LL BECOME HIS OR HER ONLY LIGHT SOURCE.
RED AND/OR GREEN
YES
NOW THAT'S A GIFT! YOU WILL BE THANKED AND WORSHIPPED FOR YEARS TO COME.
IT'LL BE USED FOR XMAS LIGHTS. YOU WATCH.
NO
WILL IT CREATE FEAR IN THE POPULACE?
YES
COPYRIGHT © 2005 J.D. "Illiad" Frazer HTTP://WWW.USERFRIENDLY.ORG/

SPEAKING OF WEB 2.0, I CAN'T SAY I'M PLEASED ABOUT THAT CLASS ACTION LAWSUIT BEING LAUNCHED AGAINST WIKIPEDIA.
WHAT?

COPYRIGHT © 2005 J.D. "Illiad" Frazer HTTP://WWW.USERFRIENDLY.ORG/
BUT I THOUGHT THAT YOU LIKED SEEING SPURIOUS, DUPLICITOUS LAWSUITS BY SCAM ARTISTS...
2005-12-19

IF I DO IT, SURE. FIRST THE SONY ROOTKIT AND NOW THIS LAWSUIT. I'M BEING OUTSLIMED!
OOOH...

Do you ever wonder why that quiet, long-term helpdesk technician in your company hasn't availed himself of a clock tower and a high-powered rifle?

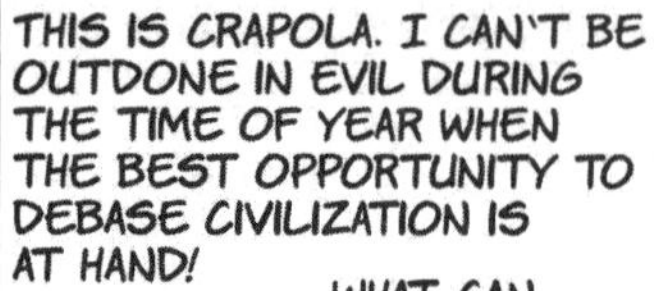
THIS IS CRAPOLA. I CAN'T BE OUTDONE IN EVIL DURING THE TIME OF YEAR WHEN THE BEST OPPORTUNITY TO DEBASE CIVILIZATION IS AT HAND!

WHAT CAN YOU DO?

COPYRIGHT © 2005 J.D. "Illiad" Frazer HTTP://WWW.USERFRIENDLY.ORG/
I NEED A QUICK FIX OF EVIL. I NEED TO CONNECT WITH MISERY AND THEN WORSEN THAT MISERY.
GIVE ME YOUR CELL PHONE.

RRING!
RRRIIIING!
RRINNG!
SOMETHING ISN'T...RIGHT.
2005-12-20

MERRY CHRISTMAS! GREG SPEAKING.
AND EXACTLY WHAT'S SO MERRY ABOUT IT?
2005-12-21
COPYRIGHT © 2005 J.D. "Illiad" Frazer HTTP://WWW.USERFRIENDLY.ORG/

IN FOUR DAYS IT'LL BE LIKE HAVING PEOPLE LIKE YOURSELF ON "MUTE" FOR 24 HOURS.
HEY NOW!!

LISTEN, SMART GUY. CHRISTMAS IS COMING LIKE A LOCOMOTIVE AND YOU'RE TIED TO THE TRACKS. WHEN IT HITS YOU YOU'LL STOP BEING SO CHIPPER.

COPYRIGHT © 2005 J.D. "Illiad" Frazer HTTP://WWW.USERFRIENDLY.ORG/
YOU'RE IN DEBT AND THE HOLIDAYS WILL DIG YOU IN DEEPER. YOU HAVE TO FIGHT CROWDS. PEOPLE ARE RUDE AND STRESSED. HOW IN GEHENNA CAN YOU NOT BE MISERABLE?

MY CHRISTMAS TREE HAS BLUE LED LIGHTS.
I HATE GEEKS!
2005-12-22

2005-12-23
HEY AJ. WANT TO COME OVER FOR A BEER AND SOME XBOX TIME ON CHRISTMAS?
SORRY MAN...I PROMISED TO SPEND CHRISTMAS WITH MIRANDA.
COPYRIGHT© 2005 J.D. "Illiad" Frazer HTTP://WWW.USERFRIENDLY.ORG/

AH. I SUPPOSE THAT'S UNDERSTANDABLE.

WHAT IF I OFFERED YOU SOME XBOX 360 TIME? WE'LL PLAY HALO!
OH YOU'LL BOTH BE SEEING HALOS ALL RIGHT...

DUDE! WANT TO COME OVER FOR A BEER AND SOME HARDWARE HACKING ON CHRISTMAS?
I CAN'T. I'M SPENDING THE DAY AT MY FOLKS' PLACE.
COPYRIGHT© 2005 J.D. "Illiad" Frazer HTTP://WWW.USERFRIENDLY.ORG/

YOUR FOLKS? REALLY.
YUP. LOOKING FORWARD TO IT.

I THOUGHT YOU TOLD ME ONCE THAT YOU AND YOUR FOLKS DIDN'T GET ALONG.
MY DAD JUST PUT AN OLD CRAY IN HIS BASEMENT.
2005-12-24

USER FRIENDLY
the comic strip
BY J.D. "ILLIAD" FRAZER
COPYRIGHT© 2005 J.D. "Illiad" Frazer HTTP://WWW.USERFRIENDLY.ORG/

I AM SUCH A GEEK. I NEED TO GET A LIFE.

PREFERABLY ONE THAT INVOLVES BEING WITH FRIENDS ON CHRISTMAS.

ALL OF MY FRIENDS ARE AWAY VISITING FAMILY OR HAVE COMMITTMENTS.
AT TIMES LIKE THIS, WHAT'S A GEEK TO DO?

'GREGF' LOGGED IN TO #GEEKS
KAPE06: MERRY CHRISTMAS, GREG!
JANINE: WE'RE TALKING ABOUT GAME CONSOLES.
IMP144: FELIZ NAVIDAD, GREG
INGA_S: DUDE, WHERE'S MY PRESENT?

NOW THAT CHRISTMAS IS OVER, WE BEGIN THAT STRANGE, WEEK-LONG STRETCH BEFORE NEW YEARS IN WHICH THE WESTERN BUSINESS WORLD IS SHUT DOWN.
2005-12-26
COPYRIGHT© 2005 J.D. "Illiad" Frazer HTTP://WWW.USERFRIENDLY.ORG/

WE SHOULD TAKE ADVANTAGE OF THIS TIME TO LOOK BACK AT THE YEAR PRIOR AND CONSIDER OUR FUTURE IN THE YEAR COMING.

FOR EXAMPLE, I'M THINKING THAT LAST TURN I SHOULD'VE RESEARCHED GUNPOWDER BUT AT LEAST NEXT TURN I'LL BE ABLE TO CRUSH THE AZTECS!

HEY PITR! THOSE LOOK COLOURFUL. DID YOU GET THEM FOR CHRISTMAS?

MAKINK THEM. GOT COLOUR LASER PREENTER FROM SANTA.
COPYRIGHT© 2005 J.D. "Illiad" Frazer HTTP://WWW.USERFRIENDLY.ORG/

NICE! WHAT ARE YOU PRINTING? FAMILY PHOTOS? SCENIC IMAGES? BABY ANIMAL PICTURES?
2005-12-27

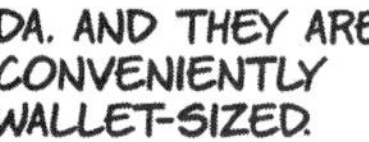
OH WILL YOU LOOK AT THAT. PORTRAITS OF AMERICAN PRESIDENTS, WITH NUMBERS ON THE CORNERS.

DA. AND THEY ARE CONVENIENTLY WALLET-SIZED.

2005-12-28
SID, AM WANTINK TO APOLOGIZE FOR SCARINK YOU OVER WEEK AGO. IS NOT NICE TO DO DURINK CHRISTMAS SEASON.
OH?
COPYRIGHT© 2005 J.D. "Illiad" Frazer HTTP://WWW.USERFRIENDLY.ORG/

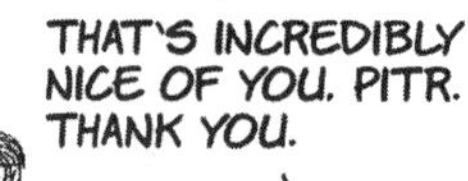
AS PEACE OFFERINK, AM GIVINK YOU U.S. ONE HUNDRED DOLLAR BILL, FOR YOU TO SPEND AS YOU WISH. IN PUBLIC.
THAT'S INCREDIBLY NICE OF YOU, PITR. THANK YOU.

HEH...THE BAIT, HE IS TAKINK IT, THE FOOL.
ALTHOUGH NEXT TIME YOU MIGHT WANT TO PRINT ON BOTH SIDES. JUST SAYIN'.

PITR, ARE YOU AWARE THAT COUNTERFEITING IS AN INDICTABLE OFFENSE THAT CARRIES A PRISON TERM OF UP TO 14 YEARS?
DA. AM AWARE.

AND YOU DO REALIZE THAT SOMEONE WHO REALLY HAD SOMETHING AGAINST YOU COULD PICK UP THE PHONE AND HAVE YOU ARRESTED? TODAY?
DA. AM REALIZINK.
2005-12-29

AND WHAT DOES THE PRECEDING EQUAL WHEN YOU ADD "SID" TO THE EQUATION?
14 YEARS FOR PITR TO THINK UP REVENGE THAT WOULD BE PUTTINK KHAN NOONIEN SINGH TO SHAME.

2005-12-30
2005. WHAT A YEAR.
JUST THINK OF SOME OF THE MOMENTOUS TURNING POINTS WE HAD IN THE TECH INDUSTRY.

COPYRIGHT© 2005 J.D. "Illiad" Frazer HTTP://WWW.USERFRIENDLY.ORG/
GOOGLE LAUNCHES TONS OF BETAS. THE E.U. STOMPS ON MICROSOFT. FIREFOX JUMPS IN MARKETSHARE.
WHAT ELSE WAS THERE?

THERE WAS THAT GUY WHO TRIED TO DO THAT WEIRD THING AND WROTE ABOUT IT.
OH YES I FORGOT - BLOGGING RAISED THE JOURNALISM BAR.

SO HOW DO YOU SUGGEST WE PUNCTUATE 2005 ON THIS YEAR'S FINAL DAY?
A PERIOD? EXCLAMATION MARK? A QUESTION MARK?

COPYRIGHT© 2005 J.D. "Illiad" Frazer HTTP://WWW.USERFRIENDLY.ORG/
2005 HAS BEEN ABOUT PROGRESS, AND WE DO NEED TO LURE THE SIX BILLION MORTALS INTO 2006 SO THAT FUTURE PROPHECIES CAN COME TRUE.

WHAT DO YOU SUGGEST?
2005-12-31

I SAY WE DANGLE A CARET.
YE FLIPPING PEERS...

Few things are worse than punctuation humor.

NOT THAT I'M TRYING TO MAKE A PREDICTION ABOUT THE TECH SECTOR IN THE NEW YEAR OR ANYTHING...

2006

UserFriendly.Org

AND SO YOUR HONOUR. AS COUNSEL FOR THE R.I.A.A. I BRING TO YOUR ATTENTION THE LIST OF 12.000 "JOHN AND JANE DOES" THAT WE WILL BE SUING FOR INFRINGEMENT.

INFRINGEMENT?
YES. YOUR HONOUR. AS YOU CAN SEE. THE RECORDING INDUSTRY'S PROFITS HAVE NOT GROWN BY 75% THIS YEAR AS WE EXPECTED. MUSIC PIRACY MUST BE THE CAUSE.
COPYRIGHT © 2006 J.D. "Illiad" Frazer HTTP://WWW.USERFRIENDLY.ORG/

WAIT. YOU'RE SUING TO MAKE UP FOR A SHORTFALL IN EXPECTED PROFITS?
PRECEDENCE. YOUR HONOUR. THINK "S.C.O."

IF IT PLEASE THE COURT. WE WISH TO IDENTIFY ONE SUCH "JANE DOE" AS JENNY BROCKET. SEATED BEFORE US HERE.

JENNY. THOUGH ONLY EIGHT YEARS OLD. IS THE PRINCIPAL USER OF THE COMPUTER AT THE I.P. ADDRESS NOTED.
WE ARE FILING AGAINST HER FOR PIRATING SONGS BY ROCK SUPERSTAR "LICK RIOT."
COPYRIGHT © 2006 J.D. "Illiad" Frazer HTTP://WWW.USERFRIENDLY.ORG/

BUT ON HIS WEBSITE HE SAID HE WANTS HIS MUSIC TO BE FREE FOR ALL...
IT'S NOT HIS TO GIVE AWAY. ONE WAY OR ANOTHER KID. YOU'RE GONNA GIVE US YOUR LUNCH MONEY.

LITTLE GIRL. DO YOU KNOW HOW MUCH TROUBLE YOU'RE IN?
NO.

BIG TROUBLE. BIG. DO YOU KNOW MUCH ABOUT THE R.I.A.A?
YES. MY FRIENDS AND I ARE BOYCOTTING ALL OF THE R.I.A.A. RECORD LABELS. WE DON'T BUY YOUR CDS ANYMORE.
COPYRIGHT © 2006 J.D. "Illiad" Frazer HTTP://WWW.USERFRIENDLY.ORG/

SIR. CD SALES ARE DOWN.
DAMN THOSE PIRATES!
RIAA

IN CONCLUSION YOUR HONOUR. WE ASK THE COURT FOR A JUDGEMENT AGAINST THE DEFENDENT FOR THE SUM OF $40.000 IN DAMAGES.

COPYRIGHT © 2006 J.D. "Illiad" Frazer HTTP://WWW.USERFRIENDLY.ORG/

COUNSELOR. YOU DO REALIZE THAT THE DEFENDANT IS AN EIGHT YEAR OLD GIRL?
OH. I KNOW. YOUR HONOUR! THESE VILE CRIMINALS START AT SUCH A SHOCKINGLY YOUNG AGE!

I'M GUILTY MR. JUDGE AND SO ARE ALL OF MY FRIENDS ON THAT LIST.
YOUNG LADY. YOU DO UNDERSTAND THE CONSEQUENCES OF ADMITTING FAULT IN THIS SUIT?
COPYRIGHT © 2006 J.D. "Illiad" Frazer HTTP://WWW.USERFRIENDLY.ORG/

YES. THE GREASY MAN HERE EXPLAINED IT TO ME.
DID HE...
OILY. NOT GREASY...

HE SAID I HAD TO SAY I DID A BAD THING "OR EVIL WOULD WIN."
A SIMPLE MORALITY LESSON. YOUR HONOUR...

I SEEK CLARITY. COUNSELOR. DID YOU OR DID YOU NOT PRESSURE THIS YOUNG GIRL TO FALSELY INCRIMINATE HERSELF AND HER FRIENDS?
COPYRIGHT © 2006 J.D. "Illiad" Frazer HTTP://WWW.USERFRIENDLY.ORG/

WELL...AS IT WERE...I SUPPOSE YOU COULD SAY ...AS SUCH...
...YES.

YOU'RE SUBORNING PERJURY!
WORK WITH ME HERE YOUR HONOUR! DON'T PUT BRITNEY OUT OF WORK!

I.T. AGONY BINGO

HEY, YOU BUSY?	BUT THE SALESMAN SAID...	IT'S WORKING FINE BUT COULD YOU...	YOU CAN FIX IT ON YOUR LUNCH HOUR, RIGHT?	NO, I NEVER READ -I MEAN- RECEIVED YOUR EMAIL.
QUICK QUESTION FOR YOU...	I KNOW IT'S LATE BUT...	IT SHOULDN'T TAKE YOU LONG...	NOW THAT THE SERVER'S UP WHY DO WE NEED YOU ANYMORE?	WHAT'S A BACKUP?
CAN YOU SAVE ALL MY MUSIC?	IT ALWAYS WORKED BEFORE.	FREE PAIN	WHY CAN'T I BE ROOT?	DID I NEED THAT?
WHAT'S SO BAD ABOUT CLARIA?	I NEVER HAD A PROBLEM UNTIL...	I WENT INTO THE REGISTRY AND...	I NEVER SAID "RETAINER."	CAN'T YOU JUST DO IT?
I TRIED TO FIX IT MYSELF AND...	I DIDN'T DO ANYTHING TO IT.	I HAVE A FRIEND THAT KNOWS ABOUT COMPUTERS...	BUT IT'S NEVER BEEN HACKED BEFORE...	IT'S WINDOWS *ME*

RULES

1. EVERY TIME YOU HEAR A USER SAY A PHRASE OR ASK A QUESTION ON THE CARD, COVER IT WITH A TEAR, A DROP OF BLOOD, OR PERHAPS SOME FRESH BILE.
2. WHEN YOU HAVE A HORIZONTAL, VERTICAL OR DIAGONAL LINE COVERED, YOU MAY STAND UP AND EMIT A PRIMAL SCREAM OF ANGUISH. YOU WIN.

UserFriendly.Org

A very popular game. Give it a try one day, preferably after you've won the lottery or you've decided to resign anyway.

IS THAT A NEW CD I SPY?
YEAH. THE LATEST "LICK RIOT" ALBUM.

OOH. LOOK. IT COMES WITH A COUPON.

IT'S A MAIL-IN REBATE FOR A BOTTLE OF...LUBRICANT.
"BY OPENING THIS CD, YOU AGREE TO BLEAT WHEN WE TELL YOU TO."

THANK YOU FOR PURCHASING THIS ALBUM. NOTE THAT THIS CD IS COPY-PROTECTED AND DESIGNED TO NOT FUNCTION ON:
* SOME CD PLAYERS THAT HAVE THE CAPABILITY OF BURNING INTO AN MP3
* SOME CD PLAYERS THAT POSSESS CD-R/RW FUNCTIONS
* SOME CD PLAYERS OR CAR STEREOS WITH HARD DISK RECORDING CAPACITY
* SOME CD-R/RW RECORDERS USED FOR MUSIC...

TAPPITY TAP TAP ZING!

CD RIPPED. COPY AGAIN?
*ALSO NOTE THAT IF YOU HUM A TUNE FROM THIS ALBUM WE'RE COMING AFTER YOU.

HEY. GET THIS. APPARENTLY PLUTO IS COLDER THAN SCIENTISTS ORIGINALLY THOUGHT.
COLDER? YE GODS.

YEAH. TEN DEGREES CENTIGRADE COLDER THAN ORIGINAL ESTIMATES...

DUDE. I SO WARNED YOU ABOUT MIRANDA...

ON THE PLANET (?) PLUTO, NITROGEN ICE IS IN A STATE OF FLUX, CHANGING FROM SOLID TO GAS AND BACK AGAIN AS THE PLANET MOVES AROUND THE SUN.

THIS SUDDEN DROP IN TEMPERATURE ESTIMATES PUZZLES SCIENTISTS SOMEWHAT, ALTHOUGH THEY DO HAVE A DECENT THEORY...

OF COURSE, THE BEST WAY TO GET A SENSE OF WHAT'S GOING ON ANYWHERE IS TO EAVESDROP ON THE LOCALS...

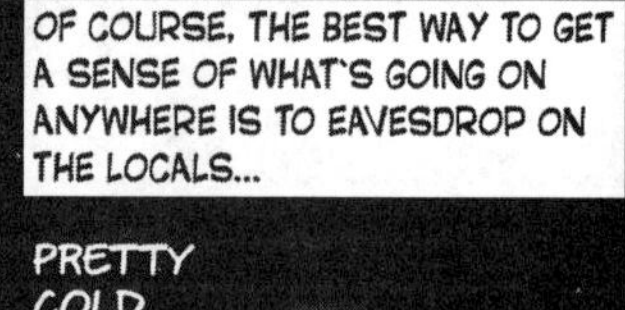
PRETTY COLD TODAY...
ZIKTIPIX TURNED OFF HIS XBOX 360.

HEY. DID YOU HEAR ABOUT THAT BILL IN THE U.S. THAT MAKES IT ILLEGAL TO POST ANNOYING MESSAGES ANONYMOUSLY?
YES. BUT IT'S JUST A MISREADING OF THE BILL. CAN YOU IMAGINE WHAT THE NET WOULD BE LIKE IF IT WERE TRUE?
COPYRIGHT © 2006 J.D. "Illiad" Frazer HTTP://WWW.USERFRIENDLY.ORG/

YOU HEARING CRICKETS?
IT WOULD BE A LOOPING .WAV FILE.

JUST IMAGINE IF A LAW WAS PASSED THAT ACTUALLY MADE IT ILLEGAL TO WRITE ANNOYING POSTS ON MESSAGE BOARDS.
WHAT KIND OF NET WOULD WE HAVE?
COPYRIGHT © 2006 J.D. "Illiad" Frazer HTTP://WWW.USERFRIENDLY.ORG/

USENET WOULD EVAPORATE. ALL POLITICAL FORUMS WOULD VANISH. ANY PLACE WHERE DIVISIVE ISSUES WERE DISCUSSED WOULD COLLAPSE. WHAT WOULD BE LEFT?

CARE BEARS AND TELETUBBIES I'D IMAGINE...
NO! THERE'S ALMOST NOTHING YOU CAN POST IN A CARE BEARS MESSAGE FORUM THAT WOULDN'T ANNOY ME.

WHY THE DISCOVERY THAT THE NORTH STAR WAS IN FACT *THREE* STARS WAS BAD FOR THE HUBBLE SPACE TELESCOPE
NO. SENATOR. THE HST HAS NOT "GONE FUZZY AGAIN."
UserFriendly.Org
COPYRIGHT © 2006 J.D. "Illiad" Frazer HTTP://WWW.USERFRIENDLY.ORG/

IPOD!
OH MY GOD. NOT YOU TOO.

YOU IPODDERS ARE WEIRD. YOU BUY A $300 PIECE OF HARDWARE ONLY TO ADORN IT WITH A PLETHORA OF RETARDED $29 ACCESSORIES.
COPYRIGHT © 2006 J.D. "Illiad" Frazer HTTP://WWW.USERFRIENDLY.ORG/

NOT ALL ARE $29. SOME ARE LIKE. $49.
AUUUUUGH! IT'S THE INVASION OF THE "IPOD PEOPLE"!

OKAY. WAIT. TELL ME HOW MUCH YOU'VE SPENT ON YOUR IPOD.
WELL... LET ME THINK...

$29 FOR EACH IPOD SOCK... $49 FOR THE RADIO REMOTE... $39 FOR THE DOCK... $39 FOR EAR BUDS... YE GODS. NO WONDER I DON'T HAVE ANY MONEY LEFT FOR MUSIC!
COPYRIGHT © 2006 J.D. "Illiad" Frazer HTTP://WWW.USERFRIENDLY.ORG/

DAMNED PIRATES!!
RIAA

DID YOU READ ABOUT THE TRANSGENIC GLOWING GREEN PIGS FROM TAIWAN? WITH THE JELLYFISH GENES?
IT MAKES ME ALL ANXIOUS AND STUFF.

OH MIKE. RELAX. IT'S NOT LIKE GLOWING GREEN PIGS ARE GOING TO TAKE OVER THE WORLD.
I GUESS. I JUST HAVE THIS WEIRD FEELING...
COPYRIGHT © 2006 J.D. "Illiad" Frazer HTTP://WWW.USERFRIENDLY.ORG/

YOUR NAME. IT IS TO BE "SAM I AM."
FROM: TAIPEI, TAIWAN

PITR...WHAT IS THAT?
IS WERY SPECIAL PEEG. TO BE HELPINK ME MAKE MUCH CASH MONEY.

TO BE BEHOLDINK!
CLIK!
COPYRIGHT © 2006 J.D. "Illiad" Frazer HTTP://WWW.USERFRIENDLY.ORG/

MUST...HAVE... SHINY...BACON...
ALL MEAT-EATING GEEKS. THEY ARE MINE.

HEY...WHAT'S WITH THE PIG?
I THINK IT'S PITR'S NEW PET. IT'S ONE OF THOSE TRANS-GENIC ONES. AND IT GLOWS GREEN IN THE DARK.
COPYRIGHT © 2006 J.D. "Illiad" Frazer HTTP://WWW.USERFRIENDLY.ORG/

"TRANSGENIC PORK. THE OTHER GREEN MEAT..."

FIFTY GMAIL INVITES ON THE WALL, FIFTY GMAIL INVITES. PASS ONE ON, MAKE SURE THAT IT'S GONE, FORTY-NINE GMAIL INVITES ON THE WALL!
COPYRIGHT © 2006 J.D. "Illiad" Frazer HTTP://WWW.USERFRIENDLY.ORG/

FORTY-NINE GMAIL INVITES ON THE WALL, FORTY-NINE GMAIL INVITES. PASS ONE ON. MAKE SURE THAT IT'S GONE...

...ONE HUNDRED GMAIL INVITES ON THE WALL!

TRUTH IN BACKRONYMS #8:

DMCA

Don't Make Content Accessible

UserFriendly.Org

BLOGGING. THE ART OF WRITTEN PERFORMANCE.
THE MAESTRO BEGINS...

REPORT! OUTRAGE! VILIFICATION! PUFFER-FISH MODE! SELF-IMPORTANCE! RE-ASSURANCE!
COPYRIGHT©2006 J.D. "Illiad" Frazer HTTP://WWW.USERFRIENDLY.ORG/

AND FOR THE FINALE... DISMISSAL!
DUDE. CARTOONISTS HAVE BEEN DOING THAT FOR YEARS.

With the exception that your cubicle-mate never bragged about their Usenet postings.

SO. THESE BLOGS. SOME OF THEM ARE PRETTY GOOD. BUT MOST OF THEM ARE PURE NOISE AND BILE. AND NOT PARTICULARLY WELL-WRITTEN BILE AT THAT.

COLA
YOU HAVE TO SIFT THROUGH REAMS OF JUVENILE I-AM-COUNTERCULTURE AND THE-MAN-IS-KEEPING-ME-DOWN CHAFF TO GET TO THE GEMS.
THEN THERE'S THE COPIOUS AMOUNTS OF SPAM TO CONTEND WITH...
COPYRIGHT©2006 J.D. "Illiad" Frazer HTTP://WWW.USERFRIENDLY.ORG/

GOOD HEAVENS! BLOGS ARE THE NEW USENET!
REVELATION!

COPYRIGHT©2006 J.D. "Illiad" Frazer HTTP://WWW.USERFRIENDLY.ORG/

THERE'S A NEW BUTTON ON MY GMAIL ACCOUNT LABELLED "DELETE."
AND WHICH PARALLEL UNIVERSE IS THIS?

A "DELETE" BUTTON ON GMAIL...HOW SURREAL.
WHAT ARE YOU GOING TO DO WITH IT, A.J.?

AFTER THINKING ABOUT IT FOR THE LAST TWENTY MINUTES, I FIGURED THAT MAYBE I SHOULD CLICK ON IT.
COPYRIGHT©2006 J.D. "Illiad" Frazer HTTP://WWW.USERFRIENDLY.ORG/

YE GODS NO!! YOU HAVE NO IDEA WHAT THAT MIGHT DO!
I BET YOU'D MAKE A MINT IF YOU PUT IT UP ON EBAY...

This seems to remain Yahoo!'s curse: playing catch-up with Google on everything.

DO YOU THINK MAYBE GMAIL'S BEEN HACKED? THAT WOULD EXPLAIN THE APPEARANCE OF THAT "DELETE" BUTTON.
COPYRIGHT © 2006 J.D. "Illiad" Frazer HTTP://WWW.USERFRIENDLY.ORG/

MAYBE. OR PERHAPS IT'S SOME SORT OF CLEVER, DIABOLICAL GAME THE GOOGLE GUYS ARE PLAYING...

FROM HERE ON, WE NEED A DELETE BUTTON ON EVERYTHING.
I REALLY HATE THOSE GOOGLE GUYS...
YAHOO!

I STILL THINK I SHOULD CLICK ON THE BUTTON.
I DON'T THINK YOU SHOULD. YOU DON'T KNOW WHAT IT'LL DO.
COPYRIGHT © 2006 J.D. "Illiad" Frazer HTTP://WWW.USERFRIENDLY.ORG/

IT MIGHT BE A BIT OF A STRETCH, BUT I'M THINKING IT'LL JUST DELETE THE MAILS THAT I'VE MARKED.
BUT IF YOU DELETE ALL OF YOUR GMAIL, HOW ARE YOU GOING TO KNOW WHERE TO BUY VIAGRA?

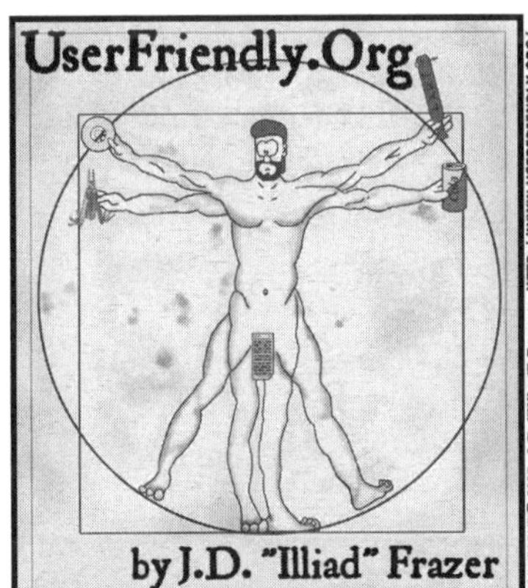
UserFriendly.Org
by J.D. "Illiad" Frazer
COPYRIGHT © 2005 J.D. "Illiad" Frazer HTTP://WWW.USERFRIENDLY.ORG/

LAST MONTH, LINUX INVENTOR LINUS TORVALDS PUBLICALLY SIDED WITH KDE OVER GNOME AS THE PREFERRED DESKTOP ENVIRONMENT.
THIS HAS CREATED SOME ANIMOSITY WITHIN THE LINUX COMMUNITY.

OH PLEASE. KDE IS SUPERIOR. WHY CAN'T PEOPLE JUST ACCEPT THIS?
AHEM.

YES. DOWN HERE. I COULDN'T HELP BUT OVERHEAR YOUR RATHER RUDE COMMENT ABOUT KDE VS. GNOME.
YOUR DISRESPECT FOR GNOME IS MISGUIDED AND HARMFUL.

DO YOU NOT REALIZE THE NUMBER OF US WEE FOLK THAT ARE EMPLOYED BY MIGUEL DE ICAZA AND OTHER GNOME DEVELOPERS AROUND THE WORLD? WOULD YOU HAVE OUR ECONOMY TANK SIMPLY BECAUSE YOU SUBJECTIVELY CONSIDER KDE TO BE SUPERIOR?
I DIDN'T EVEN KNOW YOU HAD AN ECONOMY TO TANK!
WE ARE NOT GOING BACK TO THOSE SWEATSHOP LAWNS AND GARDENS!!

HEY TECH WEENIE. REMEMBER HOW TWO YEARS AGO BILL GATES SAID MICROSOFT WOULD SOLVE THE SPAM PROBLEM IN TWO YEARS?
MM-HM.

LOOKS LIKE THEY'VE DONE IT. O YE OF LITTLE FAITH!
WHAT?! HOW?!!

BY DECLARING SPAM THE NEW STANDARD.
SOMEONE PLEASE DROP A CROWBAR ON ME FROM ORBIT. AND ONE FOR HIM TOO. PLEASE.

NO ONE. NOT EVEN MICROSOFT. CAN ELIMINATE THE SPAM PROBLEM WITH TECHNOLOGY. THE PROBLEM GOES MUCH DEEPER.
OH?

THE PROBLEM LIES IN THE FACT THAT SPAMMING REMAINS PROFITABLE. AND THAT'S BECAUSE PEOPLE STILL CLICK ON SPAM LINKS.

SO THE SOLUTION IS TO... UH...ELIMINATE PEOPLE?
SEE. THAT'S WHY YOU GET THE BIG BUCKS...

ERWIN. THERE HAS TO BE ANOTHER SOLUTION TO THE SPAM PROBLEM ASIDE FROM ELIMINATING PEOPLE.
I SUPPOSE THERE IS.

INSTEAD OF COMPUTER TECHNOLOGY. WE SHOULD LOOK TO BIO-TECHNOLOGY. FROM THAT. WE HAVE A WAY OF MAKING IT SO THAT PEOPLE CLICK ON SPAM MAIL LESS OFTEN.
OH?

GENETICALLY MODIFY ALL MALES TO BE MORE MALE. NO MORE CLICKING ON OFFERS FOR "ENHANCEMENT PILLS." VOILA!
I HAVE NO IDEA WHAT YOU'RE ON ABOUT.
NONE.

HELLO. YOUR FRIENDLY NEIGHBOURHOOD CARTOONIST HERE WITH A MESSAGE ABOUT YET ANOTHER ABUSE OF THE PATENT SYSTEM.
THIS TIME. IT'S CINGULAR WIRELESS AND ITS ATTEMPT TO LAY CLAIM TO SENDING EMOTICONS VIA MOBILE DEVICES.

I THINK FEW OF US WOULD DISPUTE THE FACT THAT THIS CLAIM IS SIMPLY LUDICROUS. THE EMOTICON HAS BEEN IN PUBLIC USE ON CELL NETWORKS SINCE DAY ONE.
I WILL PROTEST THIS CLAIM WITH MY ART. AS IS MY PREROGATIVE.

I SO QUIT.
WAIT. LET ME TRY A FEW MORE FACES!
:-D
ROTO ROUTER

PATENTING THE SENDING OF EMOTICONS! I SHOULD WRITE TO CINGULAR AND LET THEM KNOW WHAT I THINK OF THEIR STRATEGY.

IF YOU DO, YOU SHOULD ELOQUENTLY STATE YOUR POSITION WHILE BLUNTLY DRIVING HOME YOUR POINT. IN FACT, YOU SHOULD LET ME WRITE IT FOR YOU.
UM. OKAY.
COPYRIGHT © 2006 J.D. "Illiad" Frazer HTTP://WWW.USERFRIENDLY.ORG/

SIR, I QUOTE: "HEY CINGULAR, YOU CAN KISS MY (_I_)"
cingular

SIR, WE'VE RECEIVED A PRELIMINARY RESPONSE FROM THE U.S. PATENT OFFICE ON OUR EMOTICON PROCESS APPLICATION.
THAT WAS QUICK.

COPYRIGHT © 2006 J.D. "Illiad" Frazer HTTP://WWW.USERFRIENDLY.ORG/

THE SWIFTNESS OF RESPONSE MIGHT BE DUE TO THE NATURE OF THE CONTENT.
OH?

ONCE AGAIN. I QUOTE: "X-D"
IS THAT GOOD?
cingular

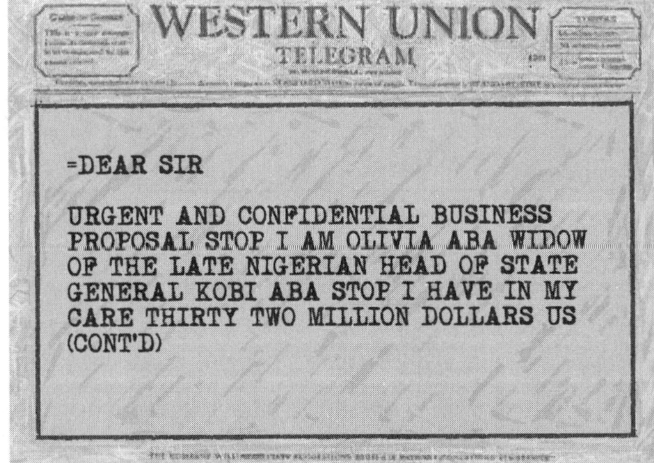
THE TELEGRAM THAT CONVINCED WESTERN UNION TO PACK IT IN:
WESTERN UNION
TELEGRAM
=DEAR SIR
URGENT AND CONFIDENTIAL BUSINESS PROPOSAL STOP I AM OLIVIA ABA WIDOW OF THE LATE NIGERIAN HEAD OF STATE GENERAL KOBI ABA STOP I HAVE IN MY CARE THIRTY TWO MILLION DOLLARS US (CONT'D)
COPYRIGHT © 2006 J.D. "Illiad" Frazer HTTP://WWW.USERFRIENDLY.ORG/
UserFriendly.Org

MIKE? I HAVE A QUESTION ABOUT THAT KAMA SUTRA WORM.
YA?
COPYRIGHT © 2006 J.D. "Illiad" Frazer HTTP://WWW.USERFRIENDLY.ORG/

SO. UM. OUR FIREWALLS WILL PROTECT US FROM IT. RIGHT?
NO. WHY?

OH...WELL. YOU'D OPEN AN EMAIL TITLED "SPANKY.MPG" RIGHT?
NO! WHY?!

THE KAMA SUTRA WORM, YET ANOTHER HAXOR ATTEMPT AT BRINGING DOWN THE NET, HAS SPRAYED ITSELF ACROSS THE WORLD...

AND IT CONTINUES SPRAYING ITSELF, TRYING TO DUPE UNSUSPECTING USERS INTO ACTIVATING ITS VILE PACKAGE...

INADVERTENTLY, THE EMAILS ALSO REVEAL FACETS OF PEOPLE'S CHARACTER...
"SCHOOL GIRL FANTASIES GONE BAD"? LIKE I'D BE INTERESTED IN THAT...
ANOTHER DREAM. CRUSHED.

SNIPPETS OF EVIDENCE ARE BUILDING A CASE THAT SEARCH GIANT GOOGLE IS BUILDING ITS OWN INTERNET PROTOCOL NETWORK.

THIS ALTERNATE NETWORK WOULD ALLOW GOOGLE TO BLOCK COMPETITOR WEB-SITES AND BRING ABOUT A THOUSAND YEARS OF AUTOCRATIC RULE!

THE SKY IS FALLING! HERE COMES GOOGLE WORLD DOMINATION!
BETA.

WITH GOOGLE WORLD DOMINATION CLEARLY UNDER WAY, WE ARE HERE TO ACCOST THE MAN ON THE STREET FOR OPINIONS ON THIS COMING PERIOD OF DARKNESS.

SIR. GOOGLE IS BENDING THE INTERNET TO ITS WILL AND IS ACQUIRING DOZENS OF ONCE-INNOCENT COMPANIES. IT IS OBVIOUS THAT GOOGLE IS SOON TO EXECUTE ITS PLANS FOR WORLD DOMINATION. CAN YOU COMMENT?

COOL! GOT AN INVITE?
CUT!!

HELLO. MY NAME IS MILTON. AND I AM AN ANONYMOUS GOOGLE EMPLOYEE.
COPYRIGHT © 2006 J.D. "Illiad" Frazer HTTP://WWW.USERFRIENDLY.ORG/

I'M SURE BY NOW YOU'VE NOTED THE LACK OF EITHER ANGELS WINGS OR HORNS AND A TAIL. QUITE THE SHOCK. ISN'T IT.

This storyline wasn't drawn from thin air—I have several really good contacts working at Google. Much of what I riff on is true. Some of it's false, but with a grain of truth that has caused a few frantic phone calls from my contacts the morning they read the pertinent strips. :-)

I WORK AT GOOGLE. I AM COMPETENT. DRIVEN. ETHICAL AND FEEL FORTUNATE TO HAVE THE PEERS THAT I DO.
COPYRIGHT © 2006 J.D. "Illiad" Frazer HTTP://WWW.USERFRIENDLY.ORG/

BUT. LIKE ANYONE ELSE. I AM FLAWED. THE FLAWS VARY. THIS ALONE SHOULD BE ENOUGH TO CONVINCE YOU THAT I AM FUNDAMENTALLY NO DIFFERENT THAN YOU.

LOOK PEOPLE. WE ALL HAVE THE SAME DNA. OKAY?!
YOU HAD ME GOINK THERE FOR A MINUTE...

USER FRIENDLY
the comic strip
BY J.D. "ILLIAD" FRAZER
COPYRIGHT © 2006 J.D. "Illiad" Frazer HTTP://WWW.USERFRIENDLY.ORG/

THIS IS A VALENTINE'S DAY SONG FOR ALL OF YOU LADIES WHO HAVE TO WORK WITH THOSE GORMLESS MALE GEEKS EVERY DAY...

...FROM ME. OF COURSE. CALL ME SOMETIME. TOOTS.

(*SUNG TO "CLOSE TO YOU"*)
WHY DO NERDS ACT LIKE FRIGHTENED DEER EVERYTIME. YOU ARE NEAR?
UNLIKE ME. THEY CAN'T FORESEE. SNOGGING YOU!

WHY DO GEEKS SUDDENLY TURN PALE. EVERYTIME. YOU INHALE?
UNLIKE ME. THEY CAN'T FORESEE. SNOGGING YOU...

ON THE DAY THAT YOU WERE HIRED. THE GEEKS ALL GOT TOGETHER. AND DECIDED TO DO ABSOLUTELY SQUAT!
AND EVERY SINGLE TIME YOU WALK RIGHT BY THEM. THEY THINK YOU THINK THEY'RE HOT!
EXCUSE ME. I WAS SENT BY SOME GEEKS TO TELL YOU THAT YOUR TAXES ARE "DONE."

HERE AT GOOGLE, WE DO INDEED FOLLOW THE DICTUM: "DON'T BE EVIL."
naughty != EviL
COPYRIGHT © 2006 J.D. "Illiad" Frazer HTTP://WWW.USERFRIENDLY.ORG/

RATHER, WE SPEND OUR TIME THINKING OF WAYS TO APPLY THWAPPAGE TO DIABOLICAL FORCES.
verizon

"THWAPPAGE" OF COURSE CAN TAKE MANY FORMS...
SEARCH TERM: VERIZON:
RESULT STRING =
"DID YOU MEAN:
BULLYING PUS-HOG?"

MIRANDA? I MADE A VALENTINE'S DAY CARD FOR YOU.
OH! THANK YOU SWEETIE!
COPYRIGHT © 2006 J.D. "Illiad" Frazer HTTP://WWW.USERFRIENDLY.ORG/

DID YOU NOTICE HOW MUCH EFFORT I PUT INTO DRAWING THE HEART?
ARE THOSE VENTRICLES?
CHECK OUT THE ARTERIES!

WELCOME TO GMAIL AND GTALK, NEWLY INTEGRATED AND EXTRA SHINY!
YOU CAN CHAT WITH OTHER GMAIL USERS RIGHT HERE WITHIN GMAIL!
COPYRIGHT © 2006 J.D. "Illiad" Frazer HTTP://WWW.USERFRIENDLY.ORG/

FROM THE CONTENT OF YOUR EMAIL AND CHATS, WE CAN DISPLAY TEXT ADS THAT ARE RELEVANT AND INTERESTING!

BEST QUALITY AT: WHAMMA-BAMMA-THANKYOU-LLAMA.COM
STEF! QUIT SENDING ME E-MAIL!!

pearl> Pitr? Let's use this GTALK thing for some fun!
pitr> Nyet, do not think is good idea.
COPYRIGHT © 2006 J.D. "Illiad" Frazer HTTP://WWW.USERFRIENDLY.ORG/

pearl> Oh, what's the harm?
pitr> Google loggink chats in GTALK. Privacy issue.
pearl> Oh please, they don't eavesdrop. So what are you wearing? :)

*logging=ON
pitr> Wearink?
pearl> Just play along big boy. :)
WE'RE COVERED.
naughty != EviL

THERE HAS BEEN SOME CONSIDERABLE TALK RECENTLY ABOUT HOW GOOGLE COLLECTS USER INFO AND USES SAID DATA AS A BASIS FOR AD TARGETTING.

HOWEVER, WE'VE BEEN ACCUSED OF BEING EVIL FOR COLLECTING THE INFO IN THE FIRST PLACE. I WISH TO ADDRESS THIS ISSUE WITH A DEMONSTRATION.
OBSERVE.

Google
WE COLLECT YOUR INFO AND DO STUFF WITH IT.
DUDE! WHERE DO I SIGN UP?!

YOU GOOGLE DROIDS ARE COLLECTING ALL OF MY INFO! YOU'RE USING IT TO DO BAD THINGS!
YOU COULD JUST NOT USE ANY OF OUR PRODUCTS.

YOU'RE ASKING ME TO CHOOSE BETWEEN A PAPERCUT OR HEMORRHOIDS.
AT LEAST YOU GET THE CHOICE.

Although there is absolutely zero evidence of this, I am convinced beyond a shadow of a doubt that Google has a black-ops team that does nothing but ELINT: ELectronic INTelligence. They have algorithms churning through all the text that passes back and forth in Gmail and GTalk, and when something of business interest pops up, their black-ops engineers do an analysis. If you're running a start-up and hope to sell to or compete with Google, and you're using Gmail for company communications, you just torpedoed your own submarine.

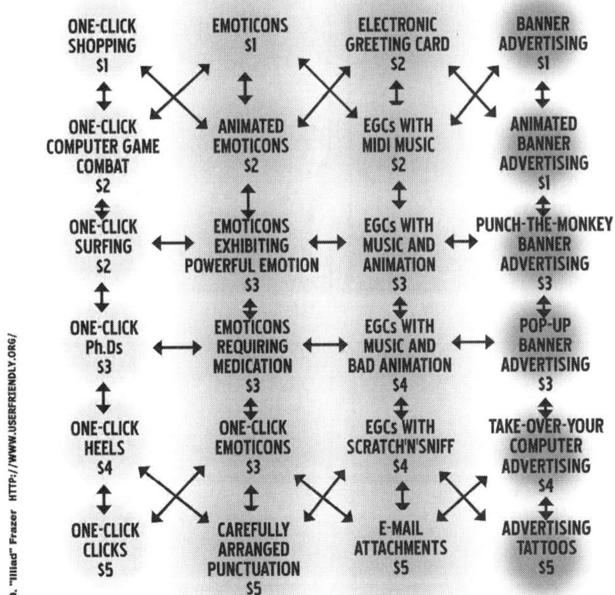
THE SOFTWARE PATENT GAME
ONE-CLICK SHOPPING $1
EMOTICONS $1
ELECTRONIC GREETING CARD $2
BANNER ADVERTISING $1
ONE-CLICK COMPUTER GAME COMBAT $2
ANIMATED EMOTICONS $2
EGCs WITH MIDI MUSIC $2
ANIMATED BANNER ADVERTISING $1
ONE-CLICK SURFING $2
EMOTICONS EXHIBITING POWERFUL EMOTION $3
EGCs WITH MUSIC AND ANIMATION $3
PUNCH-THE-MONKEY BANNER ADVERTISING $3
ONE-CLICK Ph.Ds $3
EMOTICONS REQUIRING MEDICATION $3
EGCs WITH MUSIC AND BAD ANIMATION $4
POP-UP BANNER ADVERTISING $3
ONE-CLICK HEELS $4
ONE-CLICK EMOTICONS $3
EGCs WITH SCRATCH'N'SNIFF $4
TAKE-OVER-YOUR COMPUTER ADVERTISING $4
ONE-CLICK CLICKS $5
CAREFULLY ARRANGED PUNCTUATION $5
E-MAIL ATTACHMENTS $5
ADVERTISING TATTOOS $5
UserFriendly.Org

RULES OF PLAY

OBJECTIVE: To position a connected line of your markers from the top row to the bottom row before your opponent. This represents controlling enough patents to strangle the market.

YOU NEED: Two sets of markers. You will also need one die, and some form of play money.

SETUP: Give each player a set of markers, and $10 in play money.

START: Flip a coin. Winner moves first.

TURN SEQUENCE: The player may attempt to claim any of the patents on the board. To do so, the player pays the patent fee (as listed under the patent) and rolls the die. If the die roll is GREATER than the patent fee, the player claims the patent by placing his marker on it. If the die roll is equal to or less than the patent fee, the application fails.

The player may instead place a marker on a patent that has already been claimed by his opponent, but must pay his opponent the listed amount EACH TURN that his marker rests on a claimed patent. This applies to all such markers resting on an opponent's patents. If the player is unable to pay the required amount, markers are removed until the amount owing is equal to what he can pay.

The player may now voluntarily remove any markers that still rest on his opponent's patents. Finally, the player receives from the bank the full amount listed for each patent he owns as patent revenue.

If the player has an unbroken line of markers on patents reaching from the top row to the bottom row at the end of his turn, he wins. Also, if a player runs out of money and can't pay fees, he automatically loses. Otherwise, play passes to his opponent. An unbroken line is dictated by the arrows marked on the board. An example line would be: Emoticons; EGCs with MIDI music; EGCs with music and animation; EGCs with music and bad animation; EGCs with scratch'n'sniff; Carefully Arranged Punctuation.

OPTIONAL RULE: Rather than simply paying a fee for infringing on a patent, patent claims may instead be contested. When a marker is placed on a claimed patent, both players secretly commit any amount of play money to the challenge. Both players then roll the die, adding one point per $1 spent. The high roller wins ownership of the patent; if there is a tie, the holder of the patent wins. The loser removes his marker after paying an infringement fee equal to the patent fee.

This game and several others like it have been licensed for publication by Open Source groups and publications. I used to be a game designer. Funny how I ended up doing the same thing, even though I'm now a cartoonist. When I finally move into writing as a full-time career, I'll probably end up doing the illustrations for my books.

LOOK. I JUST DON'T TRUST YOU GUYS.
THAT MUCH IS CLEAR. DON'T YOU BUY OUR MOTTO? "DON'T BE EVIL."

OH. THE MOTTO IS JUST FINE. I JUST HAVE TROUBLE WITH WHAT THE COMPANY AS AN ENTITY MIGHT BE CAPABLE OF DOING.
CAPABLE OF DOING?! WHAT ON EARTH ARE YOU WORRIED ABOUT?
DUDE. YOU HAVE MY EMAIL ADDRESS. MY SEARCH HISTORY AND A SAT PHOTO OF MY HOUSE.

HELLO AGAIN. I HOPE THAT THIS BRIEF EXPOSÉ OF AN ANONYMOUS GOOGLE EMPLOYEE HAS HELPED QUELL SOME OF YOUR FEARS. WE REALLY ARE JUST NORMAL GEEKS WHO LOVE WHAT WE DO. WITH NO DEMONIC ASPIRATIONS.
I SUPPOSE IT'S NO SURPRISE THAT THERE'S SO MUCH DISTRUST. GOOGLE BECAME A VERY POWERFUL COMPANY IN A VERY SHORT PERIOD OF TIME. AND AS A RESULT I CAN UNDERSTAND THE BACKLASH OF PARANOIA.

SO WHEN YOU BEGIN TO DOUBT OUR MOTIVES. WHEN YOU BEGIN TO FORGET THE VERY FINE ETHICS UPON WHICH THIS COMPANY WAS FOUNDED. JUST RECALL OUR THREE WORD MOTTO...
"PUBLICALLY TRADED COMPANY."

YO CHIEF. YOU CALLED?
YES. WE'RE DISCUSSING HOW WE CAN SELL OFF OUR OLD SERVERS FOR SOME MONEY.

WE'RE A LITTLE SHORT ON CASH RIGHT NOW. SO IF WE COULD MAXIMIZE WHAT WE CAN GET FOR THE OLD BOXES. IT WOULD HELP.
YOU JUST NEED SOME MARKETING.
YOU GET A COMMISSION.
YOU NEED TO LIE.

GENTS. PLEASE CHECK THIS OUT FOR ME. IT'S A SPEC SHEET THAT STEF DREW UP FOR HELPING US SELL THE OLD SERVERS.
HE. UH. DRESSED UP THE DESCRIPTION A LITTLE.

IS THIS JUST A BAD DREAM OR DOES THAT READ "COLD-SWAP POWER SUPPLY"?
I DUNNO. I KEEP BLINKING HOPING THAT IT'LL VANISH.

TECH SUPPORT. GREG SPEAKING.
HI. THIS IS THE CHIEF PURCHASER AT DWELL COMPUTERS. YOU'RE SELLING YOUR SERVERS?
COPYRIGHT © 2006 J.D. "Illiad" Frazer HTTP://WWW.USERFRIENDLY.ORG/

...YES.
GRAND. COULD YOU PLEASE TELL ME WHERE YOU'VE BEEN SOURCING YOUR "COLD SWAP POWER SUPPLIES"?

IN THE BINS AT THE LOCAL COMPUTER FLEA MARKET.
AH. IS THAT A NATIONWIDE CHAIN?

SO CAN YOU GET ME MORE OF THOSE COLD-SWAP POWER SUPPLIES?
LOOK, LADY! THEY'RE JUST REGULAR POWER SUPPLIES. OUR MARKETING GUY CALLED THEM "COLD SWAP" SO HE COULD GET A BETTER PRICE FOR THEM!
COPYRIGHT © 2006 J.D. "Illiad" Frazer HTTP://WWW.USERFRIENDLY.ORG/

THEY'RE NOTHING SPECIAL. THEY'RE JUST POWER SUPPLIES!

TRY TELLING THAT TO THE CUSTOMERS BESIEGING OUR WAREHOUSE. LISTEN:
"THE LATEST GAMES WILL ONLY RUN WITH A COLD-SWAP POWER SUPPLY! I MUST HAVE ONE!"

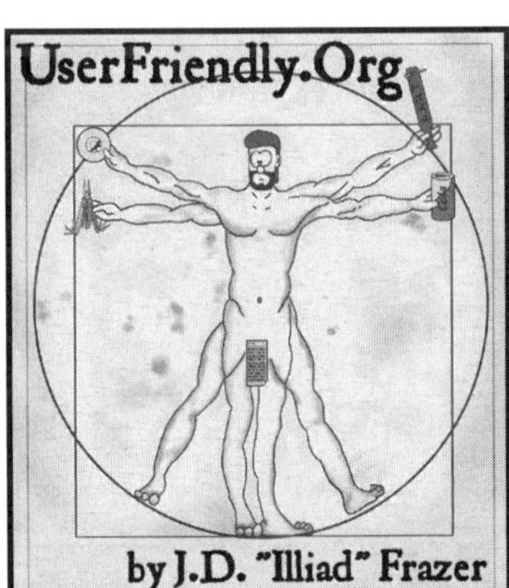
UserFriendly.Org
by J.D. "Illiad" Frazer
COPYRIGHT © 2006 J.D. "Illiad" Frazer HTTP://WWW.USERFRIENDLY.ORG/

YOUR HONOUR, ON BEHALF OF MY CLIENT THE SCO GROUP, I MOVE TO AMEND OUR COMPLAINT AGAINST NOVELL.

WHAT, YOU WISH TO ADMIT HOW BRAINLESS YOUR COMPLAINT IS?
WHA..?
SORRY, WAS THAT MY OUTSIDE VOICE?

YOUR HONOUR, WE'RE SUING NOVELL SO THAT THEY'LL TRANSFER THE COPYRIGHTS FOR UNIX TO US.
IF YOU DIDN'T ALREADY HAVE THE COPYRIGHTS, ON WHAT GROUNDS DID YOU SUE THE LINUX USERS?

YOUR HONOUR, WE'D LIKE TO AMEND THE AMENDMENT TO OUR COMPLAINT AGAINST NOVELL.
OH GOOD. PRACTICE MAKES PERFECT, EH?

HOW'S YOUR BLOG GOING?
SO-SO. I'VE BEEN UPDATING EVERY FEW HOURS. BUT I JUST CAN'T SEEM TO GET MUCH IN THE WAY OF TRAFFIC.
COPYRIGHT © 2006 J.D. "Illiad" Frazer HTTP://WWW.USERFRIENDLY.ORG/

I WONDER WHERE ALL THE READERS ARE...

PROBABLY BUSY POSTING TO THEIR **OWN** BLOGS.
WELL OF ALL THE **SELFISH**...

MY BLOG NEEDS TRAFFIC. I GET MAYBE 50 READERS A DAY, WHICH RANKS ME AS A C-LIST BLOGGER. I NEED TO GROW.
COPYRIGHT © 2006 J.D. "Illiad" Frazer HTTP://WWW.USERFRIENDLY.ORG/

IF I'M GOING TO MAKE IT TO THE A-LIST, I'M GOING TO HAVE TO WRITE SOMETHING PARTICULAR. SOMETHING THAT'LL DRIVE TRAFFIC TO ME LIKE AN UNSTOPPABLE STORM. SOMETHING...SPECIAL.

dear A-list blog dude, please link to my blog, k? thanks - c-list guy
** Email Sent **
A MASTERPIECE.
BEG BEG #603913 PROBOSCIS

Dear C-list Blogger,
if I were to link to your blog, you would gain traffic. what do I get in return?

regards,
A-list blogger.

COPYRIGHT © 2006 J.D. "Illiad" Frazer HTTP://WWW.USERFRIENDLY.ORG/

If you link to me, what you *won't* get is someone else who hates you.

Love,
c-list blogger.

Dear C-list blogger,
go ahead and hate me. It's not like you'd be the first.
Sincerely,
A-list blogger.
COPYRIGHT © 2006 J.D. "Illiad" Frazer HTTP://WWW.USERFRIENDLY.ORG/

Dear A-list blogger,
[lengthy, eloquent, venomous diatribe.]
irritated,
c-list blogger.

Dear C-list blogger,
Thanks for the brilliant content. It's on my blog now! :D - A-list guy.
AAUUUUUGGGH!

I don't know how many times I've been asked to "trade links" with another site, and not just by other cartoonists. If I know you, I'll happily put up a link or mention of your site without need for reciprocation; but 99.9% of the requests I get are from utter strangers. For some reason, they think that offering a link to UF with their audience of, oh, seven people plus their mum should be reason enough for a link on UF to their site. Or that I should just do it to be a "nice guy." For the record, I do like being a nice guy and helping others, but if I made free linking a common practice, UF would become nothing but a link farm in very short order.

"Boy, it's amazing how much ear wax one can collect," said the man. "Mmrf mff mrrf," agreed the Q-tip.

WHAT DO I BLOG ABOUT TODAY? I NEED INSPIRATION...
SQUEE
SQUEE
MOIST

Title: Ear Wax
SOMEONE WILL WANT TO READ THIS...

LET'S SEE NOW. WHAT CAN I WRITE ABOUT EAR WAX TO MAKE IT COMPELLING AND DRAW HUGE TRAFFIC..?

SOMETHING TO DO WITH, SAY, RELIGION. AND...AND...MONEY.

Today I discovered something wondrous. I discovered, on a plug of earwax extracted from my ear, the face of the Virgin Mary.
It will be available on eBay.

I GUESS IT'S BECAUSE OF THE $80 EMBOSSING PROCESS...

iPod

Generic Leather iPod Case: $19

Branded Leather iPod Case: $99

UserFriendly.Org

COPYRIGHT © 2006 J.D. "Illiad" Frazer HTTP://WWW.USERFRIENDLY.ORG/

WHAT, DID "DUKE NUKEM FOREVER" HIT THE SHELVES?
NO. IT'S STILL PRETTY WARM WHERE THAT HORNED FREAK IS.

SO WHAT ARE YOU DOING HERE?
ENJOYING MY NEW MUTATION I SUPPOSE.
BUT WHAT TRIGGERED YOU?
COPYRIGHT © 2006 J.D. "Illiad" Frazer HTTP://WWW.USERFRIENDLY.ORG/

DID STEVE BALLMER EMBRACE LINUX? DID GNOME USERS ACCEPT KDE AS SUPERIOR? DID DISNEY ALLOW MICKEY MOUSE TO ENTER THE PUBLIC DOMAIN?

ELECTRONIC ARTS IS CHARGING LESS FOR THEIR XBOX GAMES.
YOU'RE STRETCHING IT.
WHY IS THERE A PIG ON ME?

SERIOUSLY. EA HAS SEEN A DROP IN SALES, SO THEY'RE ADJUSTING THEIR PRICES IN HOPES OF ATTRACTING MORE BUYERS.
COPYRIGHT © 2006 J.D. "Illiad" Frazer HTTP://WWW.USERFRIENDLY.ORG/

OF COURSE, THEY COULD GO THE OTHER WAY AND CHARGE HIGHER PRICES FOR THE GAMES THAT SELL FEW COPIES TO MAKE UP FOR THE SHORTFALL.

SO YOU'RE SAYING "MARMOT HUNTER IV" SHOULD'VE SOLD FOR $160,000 PER COPY.
I GOTTA GO DO OTHER FLY-BYS. I HEARD THAT THE MPAA WAS GOING TO DROP D.R.M.

SID? ABOUT THAT NEW CODE WE TALKED ABOUT THIS MORNING -- COULD YOU HAVE IT READY BY TONIGHT?
CHIEF, WHERE DO YOU THINK CODE COMES FROM? THE MAGIC CODE PIXIES?
COPYRIGHT © 2006 J.D. "Illiad" Frazer HTTP://WWW.USERFRIENDLY.ORG/

WHAT...IT DOESN'T?
AH. COULD I HAVE A PAY RAISE?

YOU THINK MONEY GROWS ON TREES?
NO, I THINK IT'S DELIVERED BY THE MAGIC MONEY GNOMES.

BEHOLD. I AM NOW A QUANTUM SUPERCOMPUTER.
WHAT?

I HAVE UPDATED MY SOFTWARE AND HARDWARE. MY NEW SYSTEM OPERATES ON THE QUANTUM PRINCIPLE OF UNCERTAINTY.

YOU MEAN LIKE THE ORIGINAL PENTIUM CHIP?
OI! CAREFUL.

AS A QUANTUM SUPERCOMPUTER, I TAKE ADVANTAGE OF ZENO'S PARADOX.

IMAGINE A PHOTON THAT MUST TRAVEL FROM A TO B. THE PHOTON TRAVELS HALF THE DISTANCE TO B. FROM ITS NEW LOCATION, IT TRAVELS HALF THE NEW DISTANCE. AND AGAIN, IT TRAVELS HALF THAT NEW DISTANCE.
IT CONTINUALLY WORKS TO GET TO B, BUT IT NEVER ARRIVES.

SO YOU KEEP GETTING CLOSER TO FINISHING YOUR TASK BUT NEVER ACTUALLY DO?
HEY, CODERS MAKE A LIVING DOING THAT...

So do writers. I have four unfinished novels to prove it.

YOU JUST *KNOW* IT'S GOING TO BECOME THE WORLD'S HUB FOR PRON.

GDrive

I'm Feeling Lucky

UserFriendly.Org

SO IF I WERE TO RUN A DATABASE SEARCH ON YOUR NEW QUANTUMNESS, WHAT WOULD HAPPEN?
COPYRIGHT© 2006 J.D. "Illiad" Frazer HTTP://WWW.USERFRIENDLY.ORG/

SCHRÖDINGER'S DATA! UNTIL YOU RUN THE SEARCH YOU HAVE NO IDEA IF THE DATA IS INTACT OR CORRUPT.

HOW EXACTLY IS THAT USEFUL?
OH COME **ON.** ENRON AND WORLDCOM WOULDA BOUGHT INTO IT IN **SPADES.**

THIS QUANTUM COMPUTING STUFF IS ALL QUITE REMARKABLE.
'TIS, ISN'T IT.
COPYRIGHT© 2006 J.D. "Illiad" Frazer HTTP://WWW.USERFRIENDLY.ORG/
DOING WORK WITHOUT DOING WORK. RESULTS WITHOUT CAUSATION. COMPUTERS THAT WORK BETTER IN A QUANTUM-OFF STATE. IT ALL SOUNDS TOO GOOD TO BE TRUE.

IS THERE ANYTHING **BAD** ABOUT QUANTUM COMPUTING?
FINDING BUGS IN THE CODE. WE KNOW HOW FAST THEY'RE PROPAGATING, BUT WE DON'T KNOW WHERE EXACTLY THEY ARE.

A GOOGLE SPIDER BEGINS ITS WORK FOR THE DAY...
AHHH, A NEW SITE TO RUMMAGE THROUGH. I LOVE MY WORK.
COPYRIGHT© 2006 J.D. "Illiad" Frazer HTTP://WWW.USERFRIENDLY.ORG/

CAN I HELP YOU?
SINCE YOU ASK, SURE. HAND OVER YOUR DATABASE.

NO DATABASE FOR YOU! DO YOUR OWN WORK!
THAT WAS MY INTENTION. IT'S NOT LIKE WE NEED YOUR DATABASE.
COPYRIGHT© 2006 J.D. "Illiad" Frazer HTTP://WWW.USERFRIENDLY.ORG/

IN FACT, MSN SEARCH WILL SOON OVERTAKE YOUR EFFORTS. YOU MAY AS WELL BEGIN LIVING THE FUTURE RIGHT NOW...

...I'LL LEAD US INTO THIS NEW WEBSITE, AND YOU CAN **FOLLOW.**
ROBOTS.TXT SAYS "GO AWAY. YOU ARE NOT A UNIQUE AND BEAUTIFUL SNOWFLAKE."

ROBOTS.TXT SAYS YOU CAN COME IN.
Google
msn
BUT...
COPYRIGHT© 2006 J.D. "Illiad" Frazer HTTP://WWW.USERFRIENDLY.ORG/

BUT NOTHING. YOU'RE GOING TO HAVE TO GET USED TO DISAPPOINTMENT.
Google
msn

WE'RE THE LEADERS OF SEARCH. WHAT FATE IS THERE FOR LEADERS BUT DOMINANCE?
Google
msn
DUDES!
altavista

YOUR BLOG STILL NOT GOING ANYWHERE?
IS IT THAT OBVIOUS?
COPYRIGHT© 2006 J.D. "Illiad" Frazer HTTP://WWW.USERFRIENDLY.ORG/

WELL. YOU DO LOOK RATHER DEPRESSED.
YEAH. I CAN'T GROW MY TRAFFIC. AND NO ONE WILL LINK TO MY BLOG...

...BUT MAYBE...MAYBE YOU COULD START A BLOG AND LINK IT TO MINE..?
I THINK I'LL WAIT FOR "WEB 2.1"

WHAT MANKIND WILL DO NOW THAT WE'VE FOUND LIQUID WATER ON A MOON OF SATURN:

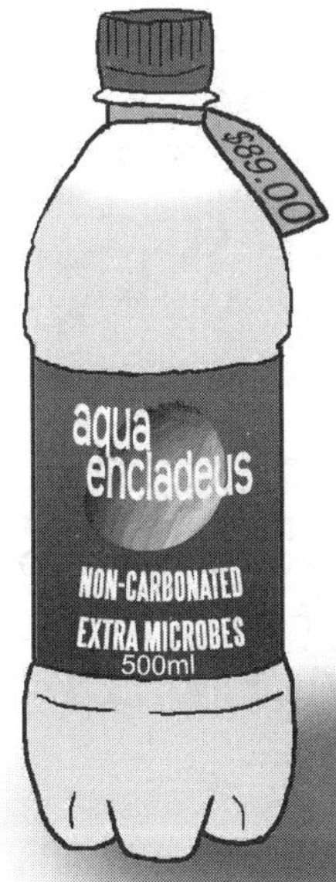
$89.00
aqua encladeus
NON-CARBONATED
EXTRA MICROBES
500ml

UserFriendly.Org

That $89.00 isn't a joke. There's a brand of bottled water out there that comes in a very expensive-looking glass decanter that goes for $60-odd dollars per liter. It probably comes out of some bloke's garden hose.

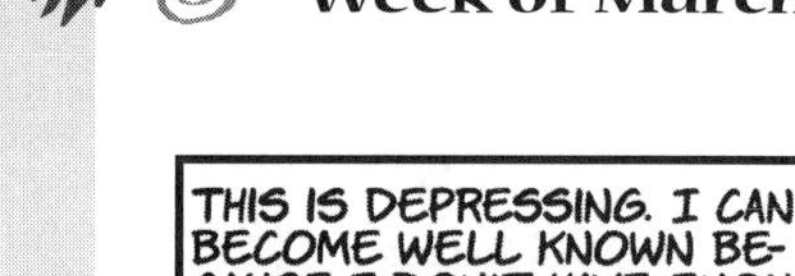

THIS IS DEPRESSING. I CAN'T BECOME WELL KNOWN BECAUSE I DON'T HAVE ENOUGH TRAFFIC. AND I DON'T GET ENOUGH TRAFFIC BECAUSE I'M NOT WELL KNOWN...

I WOULD BE SO HAPPY WITH JUST A QUANTUM SLIVER OF THE TRAFFIC THAT A SITE LIKE MYSPACE GETS.
ALTHOUGH NOW THERE'S TALK THAT MYSPACE HAS HUGE TRAFFIC NUMBERS BECAUSE OF BOTS.

...BOTS...SAAAAYYY... ERRRRWIIIIIN...
A.J.!!
THIS'LL COST YOU. IN BLOOD.

ERWIN. ARE THE BOTS READY TO CRUISE MY BLOG?
THEY ARE.
RELEASE THE HOUNDS!

HAMMER *HAMMER*
HAMMER *HAMMER*
HAMMER *HAMMER*
HAMMER *HAMMER*
HAMMER *HAMMER*

I'M FAMOUS! A.J. FOR TEH WIN!!
YES. THE BOTS ARE GIVING YOU A STANDING OVATION.

HA! WITH MY NEWFOUND BOT-HAMMERED TRAFFIC. I'M NOW A B-LIST BLOGGER!

OH LOOK! E-MAIL! I'M GETTING ATTENTION NOW.
LET'S CHECK OUT THE ADULATION...

dear aj: now that u r famous could you give me a link?
WELL. OF ALL THE SELFISH...

d00d, ur blog is teh sux0r. - anonny.
I'M GETTING REALLY TIRED OF ALL OF THIS NEGATIVE EMAIL.

I DON'T UNDERSTAND IT. IT'S NOT LIKE MY BLOG HAS CHANGED MUCH FROM ONE DAY TO THE OTHER. EXCEPT THAT I HAVE MORE TRAFFIC. AND THAT'S JUST FAKED BOT TRAFFIC AT THAT!

ANYTHING THAT BECOMES POPULAR. INSTANTLY SUCKS. IT'S A RULE OF THE INTERNETS.
CLEARLY IT'S A POPULAR RULE.

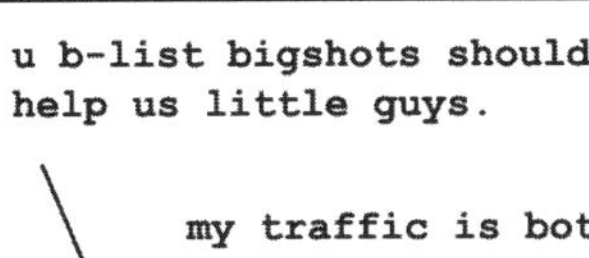
u b-list bigshots should help us little guys.
my traffic is bot created. go away.

email sent

u use bots?! d00d, thanks for the scoop. content for my blog! b-list here i come!
AAAUUUUUGH!!

Dear A-list blogger:
I give up. I tried a dozen different things to get more traffic, but it remains a dismal trickle.

I would consider it very generous of you if you would share your secret of success with me.
- a humble c-lister.

Dear C-List Blogger:
it's all about cult of personality.
- A-Lister.

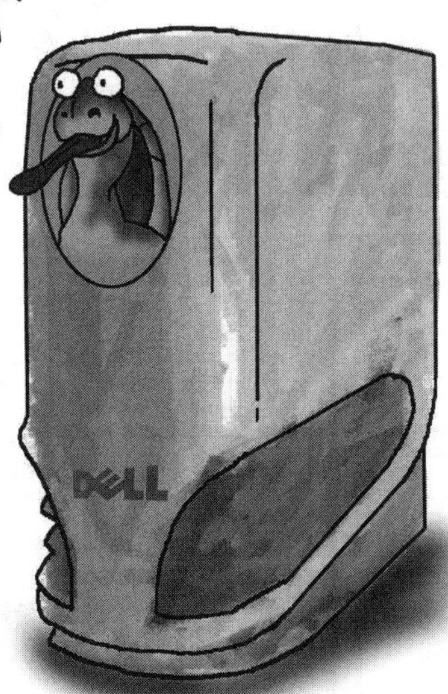
ALIENWARE, NOW BY DELL.
DUDE! MEESA THINK YOUSA GETTING A DELL!
DELL
UserFriendly.Org

WHAT IN THE NAME OF BELIAL IS THIS?
IT'S FLAVOURED COFFEE.
COPYRIGHT© 2006 J.D. "Illiad" Frazer HTTP://WWW.USERFRIENDLY.ORG/

YOU HAVE SOMETHING AGAINST IRISH CREME?
DO YOU HAVE SOMETHING AGAINST CARBON MONOXIDE IN YOUR AIR?

COME ON. I THOUGHT IT WOULD BE A NICE CHANGE.
IT'S SEVEN IN THE MORNING. I WAS CODING UNTIL THREE A.M. LAST NIGHT.
COPYRIGHT© 2006 J.D. "Illiad" Frazer HTTP://WWW.USERFRIENDLY.ORG/

I COME BACK TO MY DESK AFTER THREE SPOTTY HOURS OF HALF-SLEEP. I HAVEN'T WASHED. I'VE HAD NO FOOD IN A DAY. I HAVE A DEADLINE TO MEET AT NINE AS WELL AS A MEETING WITH THE CHIEF.

I GET THE SENSE YOU WANT PLAIN BLACK COFFEE.
OH NO. NOT JUST BLACK. BLACK-HOLE BLACK. WHEN THE COFFEE HAS A RING OF CERENKOV BLUE AROUND IT YOU'LL HAVE GOTTEN IT RIGHT.

HI. BILL.
STEVE? WHY ARE YOU SWEATING?
COPYRIGHT© 2006 J.D. "Illiad" Frazer HTTP://WWW.USERFRIENDLY.ORG/

IT'S ABOUT WINDOWS VISTA, BILL. WE HAVE PROBLEMS.
IT SEEMS MARKETING HAS MESSED UP A BIT ON THE SLOGANS FOR SOME OF THE FEATURES.

UH OH. HOW SO?
LET ME OFFER AN EXAMPLE:
"WINDOWS VISTA SECURITY: FINALLY, A LOCKED DOOR FOR YOUR CORNFIELD!"

THAT'S NOT GOOD. STEVE. HAVE YOU FIRED THE GUILTY?
COPYRIGHT© 2006 J.D. "Illiad" Frazer HTTP://WWW.USERFRIENDLY.ORG/

YES, BILL. THERE'S MORE THOUGH. OUR EXECS ARE TALKING TO THE PRESS ABOUT HOW WE ARE "IMPACTING PEOPLE."
YES? SO?

THE PRESS WANTED TO KNOW IF THAT UM... INVOLVED CHAIRS.
YOU IDIOT!

A DISTURBING QUESTION CROSSED MY MIND THIS MORNING.
WHAT'S THAT?
HALF DECAFF LATTE PLEASE.
COPYRIGHT© 2006 J.D. "Illiad" Frazer HTTP://WWW.USERFRIENDLY.ORG/

IT'S ONE OF THOSE QUESTIONS THAT, WHILE SIMPLE IN EXPRESSION, IS COMPLEX IN ESSENCE. COMPLEX BECAUSE IT RAISES OTHER QUESTIONS TO BE ASKED...

WHEN DID IT BECOME MORE ACCURATE TO SAY "THAT AND FOUR DOLLARS AND FIFTY CENTS WILL GET YOU A CUP OF COFFEE"?
HEY, NO HERESY WHILE WE'RE IN THE TEMPLE.

TECH SUPPORT. GREG SPEAKING.
HI...I CALLED YOU YEARS AGO AND BERATED YOU.
COPYRIGHT© 2006 J.D. "Illiad" Frazer HTTP://WWW.USERFRIENDLY.ORG/

THAT DOESN'T EXACTLY NARROW THE FIELD...
I WAS THE JERK WHO BLAMED YOU FOR MY DATA LOSS, AND I WANTED TO CALL AND TELL YOU THAT IT WAS MY FAULT AND THAT I'M SORRY.

REALLY?! WOW...THAT'S JUST...WOW! YOU'RE THE FIRST CALLER TO EVER VINDICATE ME! HOW CAN I THANK YOU?
OH I DUNNO. MAYBE CHECK THE CALENDAR?

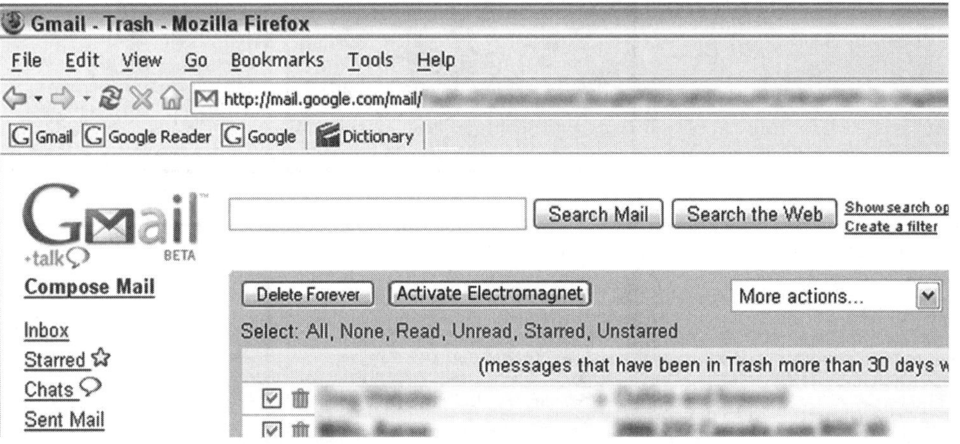
GIVEN THE RECENT RULING THAT GOOGLE MUST HAND OVER ALL EMAILS --INCLUDING 'DELETED EMAILS'-- IN A GMAIL ACCOUNT WHEN ORDERED TO DO SO, WE OFFER THIS MODEST PROPOSAL FOR A NEW FEATURE:
Gmail - Trash - Mozilla Firefox
File Edit View Go Bookmarks Tools Help
http://mail.google.com/mail/
Gmail Google Reader Google Dictionary
Gmail +talk BETA
Search Mail
Search the Web
Compose Mail
Delete Forever
Activate Electromagnet
More actions...
Select: All, None, Read, Unread, Starred, Unstarred
Inbox
Starred
Chats
Sent Mail
COPYRIGHT© 2006 J.D. "Illiad" Frazer HTTP://WWW.USERFRIENDLY.ORG/
UserFriendly.Org

I HAVE A SOLUTION FOR OUR VISTA PROBLEMS, BILL!
OH, I'M ALL EARS, STEVE.
Microsoft
COPYRIGHT © 2006 J.D. "Illiad" Frazer HTTP://WWW.USERFRIENDLY.ORG/

WE NEED TO BUILD BUZZ. VISTA ISN'T DUE OUT UNTIL 2007 SO LET'S HYPE THE MARKET IN THE MEANTIME.

PLEASE TELL ME YOU'RE NOT THINKING STICKERS FOR PCS.
I AM, ACTUALLY. BUT I'M STILL STRUGGLING WITH THE WORDS. "YOU'LL NEED ONE OF THESE!" SEEMS TO MISS THE BOAT.

SO WE'RE SETTLED ON "WINDOWS VISTA CAPABLE" THEN FOR THE STICKERS?
YES, BILL. THAT'S A LOT BETTER THAN MY "THIS BOX PWNS VISTA" IDEA...
COPYRIGHT © 2006 J.D. "Illiad" Frazer HTTP://WWW.USERFRIENDLY.ORG/

...OF COURSE, THIS RAISES THE QUESTION: WHAT EXACTLY MAKES A BOX "WINDOWS VISTA CAPABLE"?

WELL, WHAT LIMITS ARE THE DEVELOPERS WORKING WITHIN?
AT THE MOMENT, UM, "POWERED ON."

BY THE UNHOLY MARBLES OF BAAL! STEVE, IS THIS HOW YOU'RE DIRECTING OUR VISTA DEVELOPMENT TEAMS?
IT'S BEEN TOUGH, BILL.
COPYRIGHT © 2006 J.D. "Illiad" Frazer HTTP://WWW.USERFRIENDLY.ORG/

I DON'T CARE IF IT'S BEEN TOUGH. YOU NEED TO GET A FIRMER GRIP ON THE DEVELOPERS, AND LEAD OUR MARKETEERS! IMPRESS UPON THEM THAT "WINDOWS VISTA CAPABLE" BELONGS ON EVERY NEW BOX OUT THERE THAT WE CAN FIND!

BUT BILL, USING THAT KIND OF LOGIC FOR OUR MARKETING, I'M "OPEN SOURCE-LOVING CAPABLE."
IF I EVER SEE THAT ON A T-SHIRT, ANYWHERE, I'M SHIPPING YOU TO BAFFIN ISLAND.

MORE NEWS HAS COME IN REGARDING THE SPAT BETWEEN BRITANNICA, PURVEYORS OF FINE ENCYCLOPEDIAS, AND THE MAGAZINE "NATURE," WHO ARGUED THAT BRITANNICA AND WIKIPEDIA WERE CLOSE IN QUALITY.
COPYRIGHT © 2006 J.D. "Illiad" Frazer HTTP://WWW.USERFRIENDLY.ORG/

BRITANNICA'S STUDIED REBUTTAL OF THE CLAIMS AND A DEMAND THAT THE MAGAZINE RETRACT THEIR FINDINGS WAS MET WITH A RETURN SALVO FROM "NATURE" THAT COULD BE BEST SUMMED UP AS "BITE ME."

SOON AFTER, THERE WERE REPORTS THAT A CHANGE TO WIKIPEDIA UNDER THE ENTRY "NATURE" READ: "STUCK-UP NASTY LITTLE CUSS." IT HAS SINCE BEEN CORRECTED.

WHEN ASKED ABOUT THIS, BRITANNICA REPLIED, "I GUESS WIKIPEDIA **IS** AUTHORITATIVE IN SOME WAYS."

ROCKIN'!

FURTHER TO THE SPAT BETWEEN ENCYCLOPEDIA BRITANNICA AND "NATURE," BRITANNICA HAS ASKED THE JOURNAL TO PROVIDE THE ARTICLES THAT WERE USED FOR COMPARISON.
"NATURE" DID NOT RESPOND.
COPYRIGHT © 2006 J.D. "Illiad" Frazer HTTP://WWW.USERFRIENDLY.ORG/

THE REPLY OFFERED BY "NATURE" TO BRITANNICA'S REBUTTAL INCLUDED A COMMENT THAT WAS SURE TO PROVE THAT BRITANNICA'S ACCURACY WAS SHODDY:
"...OF THE 123 PURPORTED ERRORS IN QUESTION, BRITANNICA TAKES ISSUE WITH FEWER THAN HALF."

ONE MUST RESPECT SUCH A LOFTY SCIENTIFIC JOURNAL WITH THE CATCHPHRASE: "NATURE: OUR DATA IS WRONG LESS THAN HALF THE TIME!"
SOMEONE'S GONNA GET PUNCHED IN THE NECK.

DID YOU READ THAT GOOGLE'S GOING TO START AN ONLINE MUSIC STORE?
LIKE I CARE. GOOGLE IS MADE UP OF A BUNCH OF ELITISTS.
COPYRIGHT © 2006 J.D. "Illiad" Frazer HTTP://WWW.USERFRIENDLY.ORG/

AFTER ALL THIS TIME, YOU STILL HAVEN'T GOTTEN A GMAIL INVITE HAVE YOU.
I DIDN'T WANT ONE ANYWAY!!

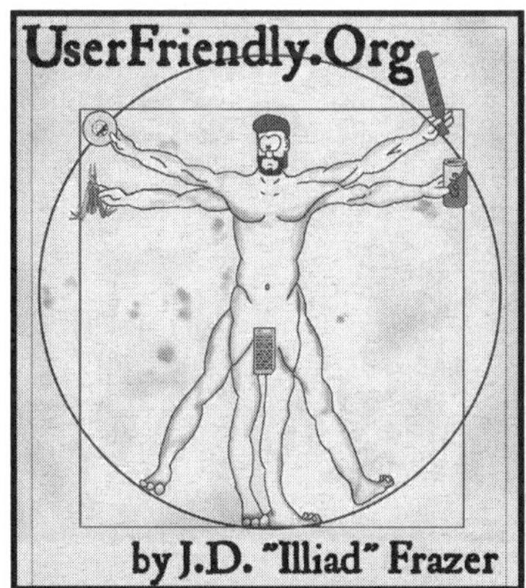
UserFriendly.Org
by J.D. "Illiad" Frazer
COPYRIGHT © 2006 J.D. "Illiad" Frazer HTTP://WWW.USERFRIENDLY.ORG/

ALAN YATES, A GENERAL MANAGER FOR MICROSOFT, CLAIMED TODAY THAT OPENOFFICE IS TEN YEARS BEHIND MICROSOFT'S "OFFICE" SUITE OF APPLICATIONS.

IN RESPONSE, TABITHA SIFER, A LINUX USER, POINTED OUT THAT MICROSOFT'S "OFFICE" WAS ALMOST TWENTY YEARS BEHIND EMACS.

MR. YATES, WHAT IS IT ABOUT OPEN OFFICE THAT YOU FIND SO INFERIOR TO MICROSOFT OFFICE?
CLEARLY, CHUCK, IT'S NOT AS FEATURE-RICH AS OUR PRODUCT.

I DON'T THINK THAT'S ALL THAT CLEAR MR. YATES. I'M COMPARING THE TWO WORD PROCESSORS AND I'M NOT FINDING MUCH IN THE WAY OF DIFFERENCE IN FEATURES.

OH WAIT...MICROSOFT WORD HAS "SORT BY LATIN VERB MORPHOLOGY."
YES! MICROSOFT FOR TEH WIN!!

DO YOU REALLY HATE THE IDEA OF A GOOGLE MUSIC STORE THAT MUCH?
NO. NOT REALLY. I JUST THINK IT'S POINTLESS.

ITUNES ALREADY ANNOYS THE RIAA WITH THE 99 CENT PRICETAG FOR SONGS. A GOOGLE MUSIC STORE WILL BE MORE OF THE SAME. THE RECORD LABEL EXECS WILL JUST HAVE ANOTHER REASON TO BE UPSET.

SO. IS THERE ANYTHING THAT WOULD **GRATIFY** THIS GROUP OF BILLIONAIRES FOR ONCE?

HEY. I FEEL THEIR PAIN. IT'S IRRITATING AS **HELL** WHEN PEOPLE ACT LIKE THEY HAVE RIGHTS.

I DON'T UNDERSTAND WHY YOU HANG OUT WITH THOSE RIAA GUYS. THEY'RE A LOW-GRADE. BORING KIND OF EVIL AT BEST.

OH. COME ON. THEY CAN BE FUN!

THEY WERE BEHIND THE ENTIRE D.R.M. STRATEGY WHICH IS PERVADING MUSIC DOWNLOADS THESE DAYS. D.R.M. - "DENY RIGHTS TO MUSIC-LOVERS."

I THOUGHT IT WAS "DIGITAL RIGHTS MANAGEMENT."

TRUST ME. I WAS AT THE MEETING.

HEY. DID YOU MANAGE TO GET AN .EU DOMAIN?
NO. THE ENTIRE REG-ISTRATION SYSTEM WAS FLAWED. HUNDREDS OF FAKE REGISTRARS GAMED THE SYSTEM AND GOT ALL OF THE GOOD NAMES.

AND TO BE HONEST. I COULDN'T THINK OF ANY REALLY GOOD .EU DOMAINS.

OH. I'M SURE SOMEONE IN FRANCE OR BELGIUM GOT "MONDI.EU"

AND THE NEXT PERSON WHO WANT-ED THAT DOMAIN GOT "INLI.EU"

STOP!

Y'KNOW. I WAS WONDERING ABOUT THE WHOLE .EU THING.
I DON'T THINK IT WAS THOUGHT THROUGH.
OH?

CONSIDER: A .COM OR .NET. FOR EXAMPLE. IS PRONOUNCED "SOMETHING DOT COM" OR "SOMETHING DOT NET."
A .CA. FOR CANADA. IS PRO-NOUNCED "SOMETHING DOT SEE AY"

AND .EU IS PRONOUNCED "SOMETHING DOT EWWW"
YOU SEE THE PROB-LEM.
I'M GONNA GO REGISTER "STINKY DOT EWWWW."

YOUR DRIPNIFICENCE! THE HUMANS HAVE CORRECTED THEIR KNOWLEDGE ON THEIR TENTH PLANET. 2003 UB313. NICKNAMED "XENA."
HUNH. WHAT A STRANGE NICKNAME...

...BUT I SUPPOSE IT FITS WITH THE THEME FOR THE REST OF THEIR SYSTEM. WHAT WITH ALL OF THEIR GODS...
GODS, SIRE?

YES. THE GOD OF TOM CRUISE...
"XENA." SIRE. ALTHOUGH BOTH CAN CERTAINLY BE ENTERTAINING.

TELL ME MORE OF 2003 UB313, WORM.
THE HUMANS HAVE SINCE ANALYZED IT WITH THEIR HUBBLE TELESCOPE, AND HAVE LEARNED IT IS NOT AS BIG AS THEY HAD ORIGINALLY SURMISED.

IMAGES OF "XENA" TAKEN BY THE HST ARE ONLY 1.5 PIXELS ACROSS...AND THIS LEADS TO SPURIOUS CONCLUSIONS BY SOME HUMANS WHO THINK THEY UNDERSTAND MORE SCIENCE AND TECH THAN THEY REALLY DO.
EH?

SEE? YOUR STUPID TENTH PLANET IS **RECTANGULAR.**
STEF. "ZOOMING IN" DOESN'T MEAN CHANGING YOUR RES TO 320X200.

The Ebbeh Post
Starforce copy protection dropped from Ubisoft games
STAR FORCE
• Paying Customers Cheer
• Software Pirates don't notice a bloody thing
glop.org/starforce

UserFriendly.Org

WITH ALL OF THIS FUSS OVER MYSPACE I'M JUST GOING TO HAVE TO CHECK IT OUT.
AH. CURIOSITY.
THERE'S NO HARM IN HAVING A LOOK AT WHAT THE MEDIA IS GOING ON ABOUT. MYSPACE.COM JUST BECAME THE #10 MOST VISITED SITE ON THE 'NET.
JUST DON'T CREATE AN ACCOUNT. OKAY?

Thank you! Account Created!
WHAT DID I JUST TELL YOU NOT TO DO?!
I SWEAR. I COULDN'T HELP IT! THE HYPNOTIC RINGTONE IN THE BACKGROUND MADE ME DO IT!
Hit me baby one more time!

SINCE I'M HERE I SHOULD GIVE MYSPACE A TRY. ISN'T IT SUPPOSED TO BE REALLY EASY TO FIND NEW FRIENDS? I COULD USE SOME OF THOSE.
YOU'RE NOT KIDDING.

Hello, my name is A.J. Can I add you guys to my Friends list?

No.
forget it.
go 'way.
no.
dork.
wtf, no.
BUT...
TELL THEM YOU'RE A COMPUTER GEEK. I BET THAT'LL HELP.

WHAT DID YOU EXPECT, A.J.? MYSPACE IS NOTORIOUS FOR BEING LIKE ONE BIG NIGHTCLUB. HOW WELL DO THE SOCIALLY-INEPT -- LIKE YOURSELF -- DO IN NIGHTCLUBS?
NOT TOO WELL.

YOU CAN TAKE SOME COMFORT IN THE FACT THAT MYSPACE'S SIGNAL-TO-NOISE RATIO IS...WELL. LET'S JUST SAY THE NOISE FACTOR IS RIGHT UP THERE.
IT'S A FULL-TIME JOB FILTERING THE CHAFF FROM THE WHEAT.

SO YOU'RE SAYING THAT "ON MYSPACE NO ONE CAN HEAR YOU SCREAM."
TEH WINNAR!

I GUESS MY VISIT TO MYSPACE IS A WASH. IT DOES SOMEHOW REMIND ME OF SOMETHING...
OH?

THE SITE...IT'S OBVIOUSLY POPULAR, AND FULL OF, UM, "CONTENT" AND...
ARE YOU THINKING OF GEOCITIES? BACK IN 1997?

I AM. AND AOL BEFORE THAT.
"MYSPACE.COM. ESSENCE OF AOL FOR THE 21ST CENTURY."

BITTERNESS ASIDE YOUNG TURBO NERD, MYSPACE DOES HAVE SEVERAL REDEEMING QUALITIES, ONE OF WHICH SHOULD BE OBVIOUS TO YOU GIVEN THE HISTORY OF STALKERS, MURDERERS AND ARSONISTS THEY HAVE.
COPYRIGHT © 2006 J.D. "Illiad" Frazer HTTP://WWW.USERFRIENDLY.ORG/

IT'S A PLACE FOR THE POLICE TO BOOKMARK EVIDENCE TO CRIMES COMMITTED BY STUPID PEOPLE?
AND DEL.ICIO.US CAN GET INTO THIS TOO BY USING <'TARD> TAGS!

COPYRIGHT © 2006 J.D. "Illiad" Frazer HTTP://WWW.USERFRIENDLY.ORG/

BLOGGER BLOGS ABOUT BLOGGING: DETAILS IN MY BLOG, TONIGHT AT 11:00.
BRILLIANTLY, ILLIAD MAKES BITING COMMENTARY ABOUT BLOGS AND HIS OWN WRITER'S BLOCK AT THE SAME TIME. SUCH LITERARY GENIUS...
TAP TAP BLOG

That's the best thing about riffing on technology. There's always something stupid to say.

IF PARAMOUNT REALLY WANTS TO MAKE SERIOUS COIN WITH THE STAR TREK FRANCHISE AGAIN, MAY WE SUGGEST:
Imagine a universe where Rick Berman was dropped off near the Neutral Zone in an escape pod that transmitted "Romulans Bite" repeatedly...
HA HA. JOKE'S OVER. ...UM, GUYS?
XI
STAR TREK
THE WRATH OF FANS
UserFriendly.Org
COPYRIGHT © 2006 J.D. "Illiad" Frazer HTTP://WWW.USERFRIENDLY.ORG/

TECH SUPPORT. PLEASE STATE THE NATURE OF THE SCREW-UP.
HI. I BOUGHT MYSPACE AND NOW I'M HAVING SECOND THOUGHTS.
COPYRIGHT © 2006 J.D. "Illiad" Frazer HTTP://WWW.USERFRIENDLY.ORG/

...IS THIS RUPERT MURDOCH?
I SPENT $650 MILLION AND WHAT DO I HAVE? MILLIONS OF BADLY-DESIGNED WEBPAGES LOADED WITH VIDEO, BACKGROUND MUSIC AND ODD PHOTOS.

...ALTHOUGH I SUPPOSE I COULD USE THEM TO STRESS-TEST FIREFOX AND OPERA. MILLIONS OF INSTANCES AT A TIME.
AND YOU DO.

BEAR WITH ME. I THINK I HAVE A PLAN FOR MYSPACE.
BE STILL MY BEATING HEART.
COPYRIGHT © 2006 J.D. "Illiad" Frazer HTTP://WWW.USERFRIENDLY.ORG/

I'M GOING TO GET ADVERTISERS TO CREATE ACCOUNTS. THAT WAY, PEOPLE ON MYSPACE CAN MAKE AN ADVERTISER'S PRODUCT THEIR "FRIEND."
IT'LL NEVER WORK.

YEAH. YOU COULD, FOR EXAMPLE, BE FRIENDS WITH A DEODORANT.
ON THE OTHER HAND...
WHAT?

stef>hey baby, wanna be friends?
hardcandy86>sure!
hardcandy86 added to myspace friends list
WOW! SHE'S HOT!
COPYRIGHT © 2006 J.D. "Illiad" Frazer HTTP://WWW.USERFRIENDLY.ORG/

SO...NOW WHAT?
I GUESS I SHOULD START STALKING-- I MEAN TALKING TO HER!!

YO! I'M OFF TO MEET HARDCANDY FOR A COFFEE!
HARDCANDY FROM MYSPACE? THE HOTTIE?
COPYRIGHT © 2006 J.D. "Illiad" Frazer HTTP://WWW.USERFRIENDLY.ORG/

THE VERY ONE. IF I PLAY MY CARDS RIGHT, I'LL BE SNOGGING HER BEFORE THE NIGHT IS OUT.

BUT FIRST, I HAVE TO GO OUT AND BUY HER A GIFT...
SO WHAT DO LONELY 40-YEAR OLD MEN WANT THESE DAYS?

I WONDER HOW STEF IS DOING WITH HARDCANDY?
WE MAY NOT KNOW UNTIL TOMORROW IF HE MANAGES TO "PUT ONE IN THE NET."
COPYRIGHT© 2006 J.D. "Illiad" Frazer HTTP://WWW.USERFRIENDLY.ORG/

OH WAIT. HERE HE COMES...

DUDE! HOW-
...BACK...HAIR...

THAT LOOKS GNARLY. WATCHA WORKIN' ON?
CREATING A GREAT OLD ONES VERSION OF MYSPACE.

SEE. INSTEAD OF "FRIENDS" YOU GET A "BLIND FOLLOWERS" LIST. INSTEAD OF "MY MAIL" YOU GET "BROKEN PROMISES" AND INSTEAD OF A BLOG YOU GET A "LIES AND ENNUI" COLUMN.

RUPERT MURDOCH WOULD NEVER BUY THIS.
WHO CARES? THE 2006 U.S. MIDTERMS ARE COMING UP. I'LL SELL IT TO CONGRESS.

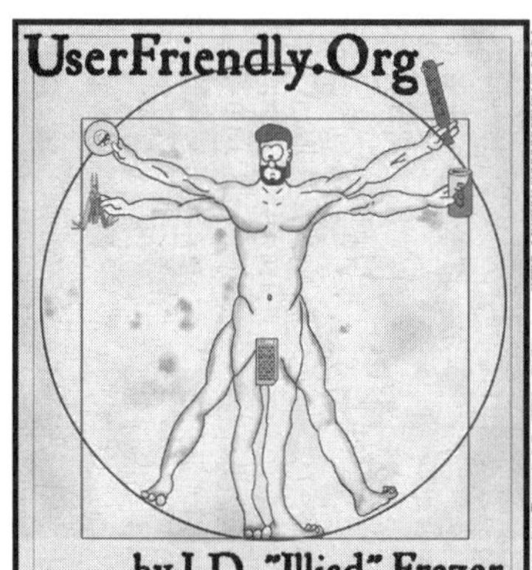
UserFriendly.Org
by J.D. "Illiad" Frazer

HELLO. YOUR FRIENDLY OPEN SOURCE-LOVING CARTOONIST HERE! I DON'T USE THE GIMP IN MY WORK AND TODAY I'LL EXPLAIN WHY.

SINCE I AM A CARTOONIST. RATHER THAN EXPLAIN WITH WORDS. I WILL USE IMAGES.

MY CONTRACT SAYS I SHOULD BE GREEN...

THIS CAN'T BE RIGHT. I FEEL LIKE I SHOULD BE ON THE SIMPSONS...

NOOOOOOO!!!
CMYK MODE AND PREPRESS CONTROLS WOULD BE NICE. THANK YOU.

This 'toon works only in color. Everyone here is so far off the correct color bands that they look Liquid Sky-ish. Miranda, for example, is yellow.

WHAT'S ALL THAT YELLING?
MIRANDA'S TRYING TO ORGANIZE ANOTHER CAMPING TRIP AND A.J. IS PROTESTING.
YE FLIPPING GODS NO

COPYRIGHT © 2006 J.D. "Illiad" Frazer HTTP://WWW.USERFRIENDLY.ORG/
PROTESTING? HE'S SHRIEKING.
NOOOO
HE FEELS THAT GOING OUTDOORS WILL KILL HIM.
I WON'T GOOOO!!

WON'T IT?
NOT AS LONG AS HE WEARS 800 SPF SUNBLOCK.
YE GODS PLEASE DON'T UNPLUG MEEEEEEEE

Never, ever make a promise to geeks, even in an off-hand way.

WHY DO WE HAVE TO GO? WHY? WASN'T ONCE ENOUGH?
DON'T YOU REMEMBER?

COPYRIGHT © 2006 J.D. "Illiad" Frazer HTTP://WWW.USERFRIENDLY.ORG/
ON OUR LAST TRIP IN THE SUMMER OF 2000, WE TALKED ABOUT GOING CAMPING AGAIN, ALBEIT IN A SARCASTIC MANNER.
AND WE TALKED ABOUT GOING AGAIN IN 2006.

WHAT, PEOPLE REMEMBER DETAILS LIKE THAT?
YOU HAVE NO IDEA.

I love canoeing. When I was in Scouts I earned a Gold Achievement Badge for canoeing. I was the paddle-master!

WHERE ARE WE GOING CAMPING THIS TIME?
HOW ABOUT SOMEPLACE WE CAN GO CANOEING?

COPYRIGHT © 2006 J.D. "Illiad" Frazer HTTP://WWW.USERFRIENDLY.ORG/

AM HOPINK YOU ARE MEANINK KIND OF CANOEING WHERE MOTOR IS INVOLVED.
RIGHT, THE KIND WITH THE FOUR LITTLE PADDLES THAT TWIRL AROUND IN A CIRCLE.
CANOEING? THAT REQUIRES MUSCLE. I'VE EVOLVED PAST THAT.

SO HERE WE GO AGAIN, OFF TO THE BIG BLUE ROOM.
IT'S WHERE ALL THE OTHER FLESH PEOPLE LIVE.

COPYRIGHT © 2006 J.D. "Illiad" Frazer HTTP://WWW.USERFRIENDLY.ORG/
SAY, DID ANYONE TELL MANAGEMENT WE WERE ALL LEAVING ON A TRIP?
OH...NO...

NO M'AM, THAT NICE YOUNG FELLOW WITH THE SOOTHING VOICE ISN'T HERE TODAY.
SOME GUY ON THE LINE WHO WANTS TO KNOW WHERE THE "ANY KEY" IS. I'VE ALWAYS WONDERED ABOUT THAT...

HERE WE ARE GUYS. YENDOR FALLS!

WOW. THIS IS NICE.
YEAH. WE CAN DO HYDROLOGY EXPERIMENTS!
OR BUILD A WATERWHEEL TO GENERATE ELECTRICITY!

COULD I SUGGEST SOMETHING FROM LEFT FIELD? LIKE GOING FOR A HIKE?
COME ON, MIRANDA. EXERCISE LEADS TO HEAT. HEAT LEADS TO SWEAT. SWEAT LEADS TO CHAFING.

WE'RE GOING TO HAVE TROUBLE WITH THIS TENT. ONE OF THE GROMMETS IS TOAST. AND I DON'T HAVE A TOOL TO FIX-

SNAP
KER-SNIK
CHIK!

GROMMET TOOLS, I ASSUME. OR IS THIS JUST "MULTITOOL SWINGING?"
HEY, MY TOOL IS BETTER.

A BETTER SOLUTION THAN A RECALL FOR THE EXPLODING WOLFGANG PUCK SELF-HEATING COFFEE DRINKS: SLAP A ~~CAUTION~~ FEATURE LABEL ON IT AND SELL IT TO GEEKS.
WOLFGANGPUCK
rich espresso latte
The beverage you are about to enjoy may detonate.
UserFriendly.Org

o! RISEN SUN YOUR
GOLD EMBRACE
SMILES UPON UPLIFTED FACE
AS I BREATHE THIS
FRESHET AIR
AND SHRUG OFF
URBAN-SOWED DESPAIR

THIS EARTH GROWS TREES
I'VE NEVER PLANTED
YET THEIR LIVES I TOOK
FOR GRANTED
IMMORTAL WITNESS
TO TIME UNFOLDING
WAITING SILENT YOUR BREATH
WITHHOLDING

BY THE GODS. ARE YOU BLOGGING?!
NO! YES! I MEAN, IT'S POETRY SO IT DOESN'T COUNT!

A.J., WE'RE ON A CAMPING TRIP! I CAN'T BELIEVE YOU BROUGHT YOUR LAPTOP! AGAIN!

CAN'T YOU TEAR YOURSELF AWAY FROM THE NET EVEN FOR A FEW DAYS?
OF COURSE I CAN. AND BESIDES, IT'S NOT LIKE I HAVE A CHOICE. I COULDN'T FIND ANY WIRELESS ACCESS OUT HERE.

YO! FOUND ONE!
COMING!!

OKAY. I CAN PLAY THIS GAME. YOU GO RIGHT AHEAD AND STAY PLUGGED INTO THE NET. I CAN WAIT YOU OUT.

I THINK SHE'S WAITING FOR OUR LAPTOP BATTERIES TO DIE.
PROPANE-POWERED LAPTOPS. WE'RE GOOD FOR DAYS.
AAUUUUUUUUUGGG

BED TIME AT LAST! A.J., PUT AWAY THAT LAPTOP OR I SWEAR I'LL SET YOU OUT AS BAIT FOR A BEAR.

KLICK!

CAN I JUST LOOK SOMETHING UP ON GOOGLE?
NO!

HEY MIRANDA. A.J.? COULD I BORROW A FLASHLIGHT? I NEED TO GO TO THE LATRINE AND IT'S A PITCH-BLACK NIGHT.
YES. SURE. HERE YOU GO.

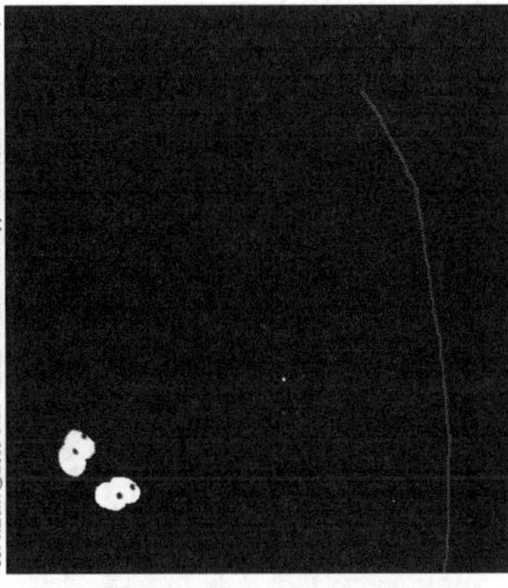

A.J.. WHY DO I GET THE SENSE YOU'RE WAITING FOR SOMETHING?
BRAAAAAAAAAPPASQEEP!
SWEET FANCY MOSES THOSE WERE SOME BEANS!
HAHAHA! THERE IT IS!

I WONDER WHERE GREG WENT WITH THE FLASH-LIGHT. I REALLY NEED TO GO TO THE LOO.
HE PROBABLY WENT BACK TO HIS TENT WITH IT.
WELL I CAN'T WAIT. I HAVE TO GO!
I'LL FIND IT SOMEHOW.

SPLUTCH
AAAAAIIIIIIEEEEEEE!
GUESS SHE FOUND IT.

This happened on a camping trip. The victim's sock was … saturated.

SOMETIMES, THERE'S A GOOD REASON WHY THEY'RE CALLED "BILLS"

U.S. HOUSE OF REPRESENTATIVES

H.R.5252

~~Yet Another Telecom Subsidy Act~~ delete!

Communications Opportunity, Promotion and Enhancement Act of 2006

HR 5252 IH
109th CONGRESS
2d Session

UserFriendly.Org

I THINK IT'S MORNING, MIRANDA.
THANK THE GODS FOR THAT. LAST NIGHT WAS INTERMINABLE.
COPYRIGHT © 2006 J.D. "Illiad" Frazer HTTP://WWW.USERFRIENDLY.ORG/

THE S.U.V. IS GONE. AND SO ARE THE GUYS...
WHAT? BUT WE'RE IN THE MIDDLE OF NOWHERE!

IT WAS HORRIBLE! NO MOCHAS! NO MACCHIATOS! NO QUAD-SHOTS! JUST TREES EVERYWHERE!!

THEY'RE GONE. AND WE HAVE NO WHEELS.
WE COULD START WALKING BACK I GUESS.
COPYRIGHT © 2006 J.D. "Illiad" Frazer HTTP://WWW.USERFRIENDLY.ORG/

THAT'LL TAKE US A COUPLE OF DAYS, A.J.
WE COULD JUST WAIT FOR THEM TO COME BACK, INSTEAD...

OR, WE COULD BORROW THAT CANOE I SAW DOWN AT THE RIVER AND PADDLE A WAYS.
SO IT'S SETTLED. WE'RE WAITING FOR THEM TO RETURN.

I NEVER DID LIKE WATER. I DON'T EVEN LIKE DRINKING IT.
A.J., CANOEING IS A PIECE OF CAKE. JUST DO AS I TELL YOU.
COPYRIGHT © 2006 J.D. "Illiad" Frazer HTTP://WWW.USERFRIENDLY.ORG/

OKAY, WE'RE WELL INTO THE CURRENT. START PADDLING, A.J.
UM...WITH WHAT?

YOU DIDN'T BRING YOUR PADDLE? I HANDED IT TO YOU!
I HAD TO PUT IT DOWN TO GET MY LAPTOP. GUESS I FORGOT IT.
COPYRIGHT © 2006 J.D. "Illiad" Frazer HTTP://WWW.USERFRIENDLY.ORG/

SO I'M GOING TO HAVE TO PUT IN ALL OF THE ELBOW GREASE TO GET US HOME?
I SUPPOSE SO.

YOU REALLY DON'T HAVE ANY CANOEING EXPERIENCE DO YOU.
I HAVE ENOUGH TO KNOW THAT THE FROTHY WATER UP AHEAD MEANS "BAD."

AS THEY APPROACH YENDOR FALLS, OUR LOVEBIRDS DISCOVER THAT SEAMLESS COOPERATION IN A TIME OF CRISIS ISN'T ALWAYS A GIVEN...

BUT AS THE GAPING, FROTHY JAWS OF AQUEOUS DOOM LOOMED NEAR, SUDDENLY TWO INDIVIDUALS BECAME A TEAM.
LEFT! LEFT! LEFT!

A TEAM OF TWO WITH ONLY ONE BRAIN, MIND, BUT STILL A TEAM.
NO NO NO! THE OTHER LEFT!

OH MY HEAD..
MIRANDA?

WHOA.
WHERE AM I?

UH OH...
d

THIS IS USERFRIENDLY.ORG:

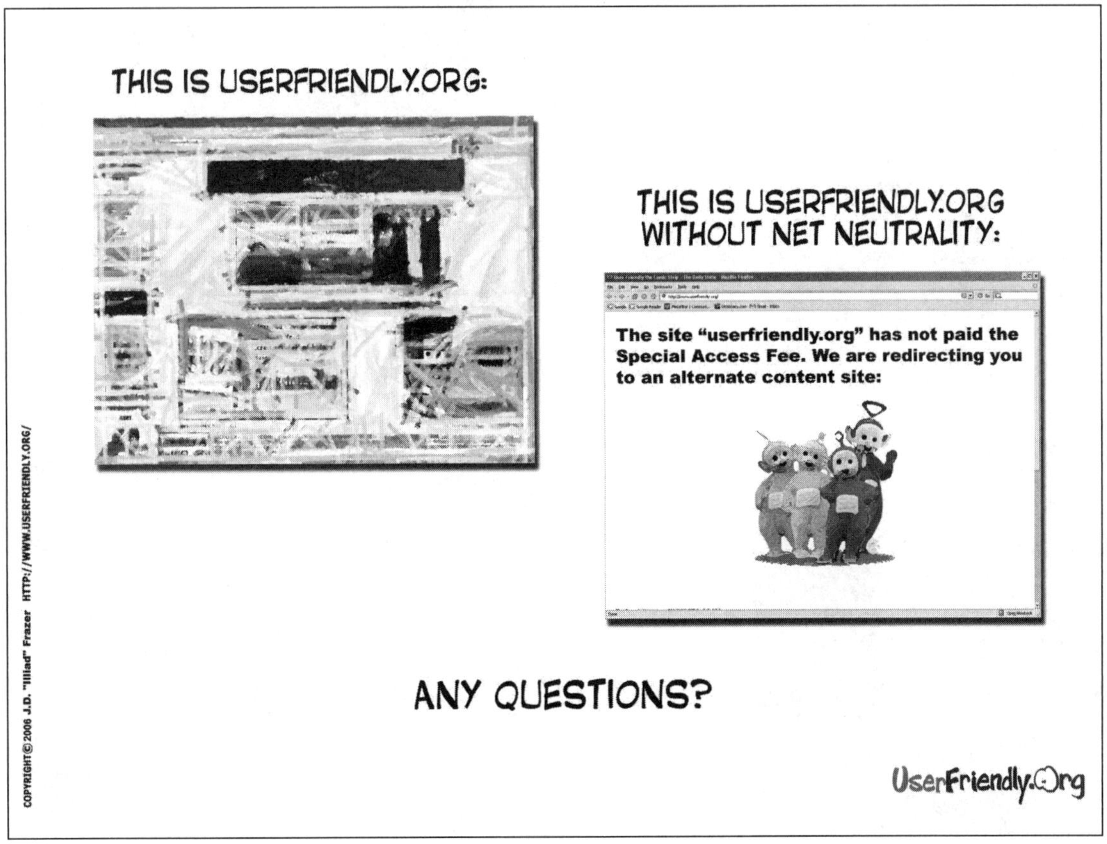

THIS IS USERFRIENDLY.ORG WITHOUT NET NEUTRALITY:

The site "userfriendly.org" has not paid the Special Access Fee. We are redirecting you to an alternate content site:

ANY QUESTIONS?

UserFriendly.Org

A very clever geek by the name of archnerd coded the Turbonerd character class for Nethack. You can find it on the Net!

OH DEAR ME. I MUST BE IN THE NETHACK DUNGEONS OF DOOM. BUT WHY?
ARF!
HMM...WHAT'S THIS I HAVE ON ME?
A PDA. USB KEY. MULTI-TOOL. AND AN ACTION FIGURE...
WHOA! WHO THE HECK ARE YOU?
I'M THE HELP FILE. CLEARLY. I AM HERE TO ASSIST YOU IN YOUR JOURNEY!
COPYRIGHT © 2006 J.D. "Illiad" Frazer HTTP://WWW.USERFRIENDLY.ORG/

SO WHAT CLASS DOES THAT MAKE ME? WIZARD? ARCHAEOLOGIST? TOURIST?
TURBONERD.

ERM...WHY ARE YOU STARING?
HAS ANYONE EVER TOLD YOU THAT YOU LOOK A LOT LIKE A CERTAIN PAPERCLIP?

YOUNG ADVENTURER. YOU ARE HERE TO LEARN ABOUT LIFE.
IN A COMPUTER GAME?

NETHACK OFFERS A REMARKABLY DEEP ANALOGY FOR LIFE! THINK OF WHAT NETHACK IS ABOUT: EVERY TURN YOU HAVE SIMPLE CHOICES TO MAKE. BUT THOSE SIMPLE CHOICES ULTIMATELY DECIDE A COMPLEX FATE FOR YOU!

I THOUGHT IT WAS ABOUT SLAYING MONSTERS AND COLLECTING COOL STUFF..
SEE? THE PARALLELS JUST GO ON AND ON!

I'D BETTER GET STARTED THEN. WHICH DIRECTION SHOULD I GO?
AH. ONE OF THE PENULTIMATE QUESTIONS: "WHAT PATH SHALL I TREAD?"

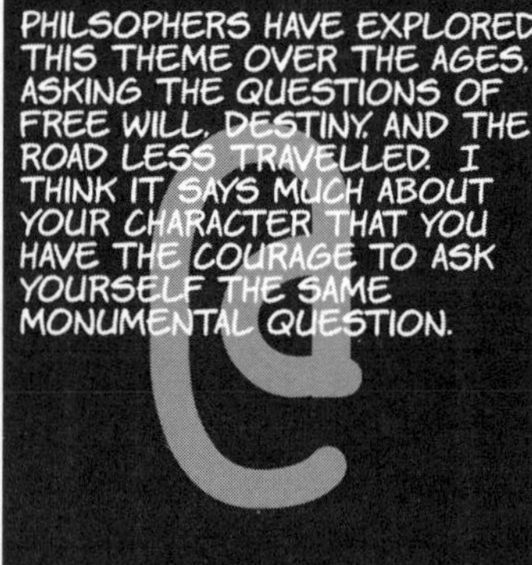
PHILSOPHERS HAVE EXPLORED THIS THEME OVER THE AGES. ASKING THE QUESTIONS OF FREE WILL. DESTINY. AND THE ROAD LESS TRAVELLED. I THINK IT SAYS MUCH ABOUT YOUR CHARACTER THAT YOU HAVE THE COURAGE TO ASK YOURSELF THE SAME MONUMENTAL QUESTION.

THE TREASURE'S DOWNSTAIRS?
YES. OFF YOU GO.

OUR HERO DESCENDS TO THE NEXT LEVEL, AND FINDS A VIRTUAL CORNUCOPIA OF SHINY.
STUFF!!
UNFORTUNATELY, HE IS LIKEWISE FOUND BY VARIOUS SYMBOLS OF THE ALPHABET, ALL OF WHICH INTEND TO DO HIM HARM...
AAAUUUGGGHH!!!

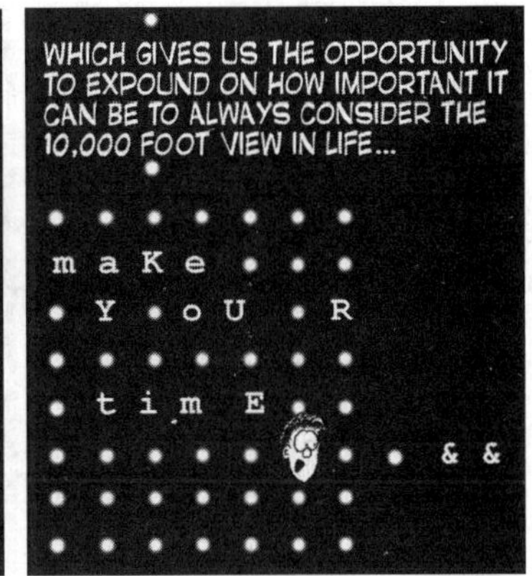
WHICH GIVES US THE OPPORTUNITY TO EXPOUND ON HOW IMPORTANT IT CAN BE TO ALWAYS CONSIDER THE 10,000 FOOT VIEW IN LIFE...
maKe
YoUR
timE

MONSTERS!
HELLO! WELCOME TO MY STORE!

I DON'T WANT TO BUY ANYTHING! MONSTERS!!
YES! AND YOU'LL NEED A WEAPON! LUCKY FOR YOU, WE'VE JUST ROLLED BACK OUR PRICES!
FOOBIE BLETCH

WAIT..."ROLL BACK"? ARE YOU...DID YOU..?
YEAH. THE BIG CHAINS ARE DOWN HERE TOO.
FOOBIE BLETCH

Web 2.1

About Web 2.1

Web 2.1 is a bug-fix patch for Web 2.0. The installation of this file will eradicate all mentions of the marketing buzzphrase "Web 2.0." Please check the readme for more information.

CLICK ICON TO BEGIN DOWNLOAD

*** DUE TO HEAVY TRAFFIC YOUR DOWNLOAD MAY NOT START RIGHT AWAY.**

UserFriendly.Org

BEEN AVOIDING TROUBLE?
ESCAPING IT IS MORE LIKE IT. THIS IS A ROUGH GAME.

I HAVE A QUESTION, O MAGICAL HELP FILE. WHY EXACTLY WAS NETHACK CHOSEN AS THE ANALOGY FOR MY LIFE?
I SUPPOSE FOR YOU WE COULD'VE USED SOLITAIRE INSTEAD, OR MINESWEEPER.

HUNH? HOW'S THAT?
WHAT DO THEY HAVE IN COMMON?
WELL, THEY'RE ALL GAMES IN WHICH YOU PLAY JUST WITH YOURS- HEY!!
YO. GOTTA GO!

YOU'RE NEAR THE END OF THE DUNGEON AND YOUR QUEST, TURBONERD.
WELL THANK RAND()! WHERE'S THE BIG SHINY TREASURE-Y GOODNESS?

AH YES. THE "AMULET OF YENDOR" PROXY. THE PRIZE OF A LIFETIME. THE TREASURE THAT OUTSHINES ALL TREASURES. THE KEY TO GEEK ASCENSION.
IT'S BEHIND THAT OAK DOOR.

YEAH! OUTTA MY WAY!
OR YOU COULD GO THROUGH THAT OTHER DOOR WHERE MIRANDA IS PATIENTLY WAITING.

YOU SAID MIRANDA? UM...MAYBE YOU COULD TELL ME WHAT THE TREASURE IS?
OH, IT'S PRETTY AMAZING.

IT'S THE ULTIMATE SHINY: EVERY DAY IT MORPHS INTO A NEW TOY THAT BLINKS AND GLOWS AND DOES WONDROUS THINGS.
MIND YOU, MIRANDA WILL BE LEFT HERE IN THE DUNGEON. BUT AT LEAST YOU'LL HAVE ALL THE SHINY YOU COULD EVER WANT.
GOOD LUCK, TURBONERD.

A.J.? ARE YOU OKAY? WAKE UP! PLEASE!

A.J.! THANK THE GODS! I WAS SO WORRIED!

WELCOME BACK, HANDSOME.
Goodbye, Turbonerd A.J...
You have finally ascended.

HEY! YOU'RE BACK!
THANKS FOR ABANDONING US...
SORRY. CAFFEINE TAKES PRIORITY OVER THE SAFETY OF OTHERS.

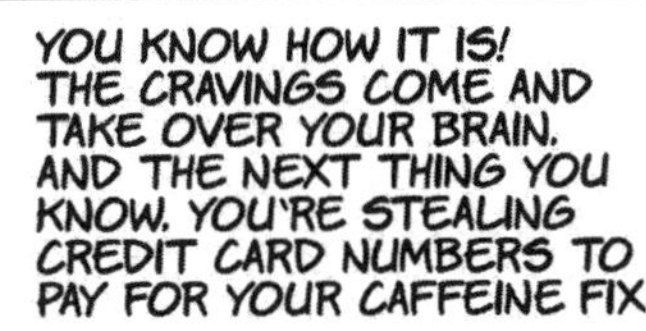
YOU KNOW HOW IT IS! THE CRAVINGS COME AND TAKE OVER YOUR BRAIN. AND THE NEXT THING YOU KNOW, YOU'RE STEALING CREDIT CARD NUMBERS TO PAY FOR YOUR CAFFEINE FIX.

YOU UNDERSTAND, RIGHT? I'D UNDERSTAND IF THERE WAS SOMETHING YOU HAD TO DO, EVEN IF IT WAS A BIT AT MY EXPENSE.
SINCE YOU PUT IT THAT WAY...

COPYRIGHT © 2006 J.D. "Illiad" Frazer HTTP://WWW.USERFRIENDLY.ORG/

TECH SUPPORT, GREG SPE-
I HAVE SEVERAL PETABYTES OF FREE SPACE ON MY SYSTEM! THE SKY IS FALLING!!

WHAT? HOW DO YOU FIGURE?
ALL THAT FREE SPACE!! NOTHING MORE TO FILL IT WITH! I HAVE SEEN THE END OF PORN, MUSIC AND VIDEO CONTENT!!

WAIT A SECOND. DID YOU SAY "PETABYTES"? ARE YOU ONE OF THE GDRIVE SYSADMINS?
DEAR GODS. IT'S LIKE STARING INTO A VAST, SOULLESS VOID!

COPYRIGHT © 2006 J.D. "Illiad" Frazer HTTP://WWW.USERFRIENDLY.ORG/

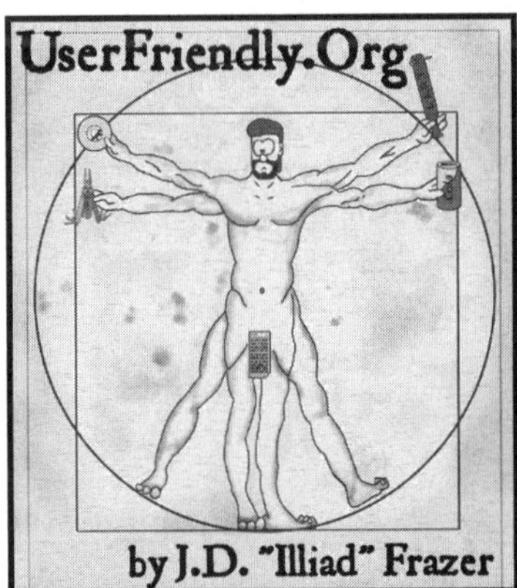
UserFriendly.Org
by J.D. "Illiad" Frazer

AN UPDATE FROM DATASEC, YOUR ICHORNESS.
WELL? WHAT IS IT?

GODADDY HAS MOVED THEIR PARKED DOMAIN SERVICES TO A WINDOWS SOLUTION FROM THEIR LINUX BOXES.
HUNH. EVERYTIME I HEAR "GODADDY" I THINK "BOOBS" FOR SOME REASON.

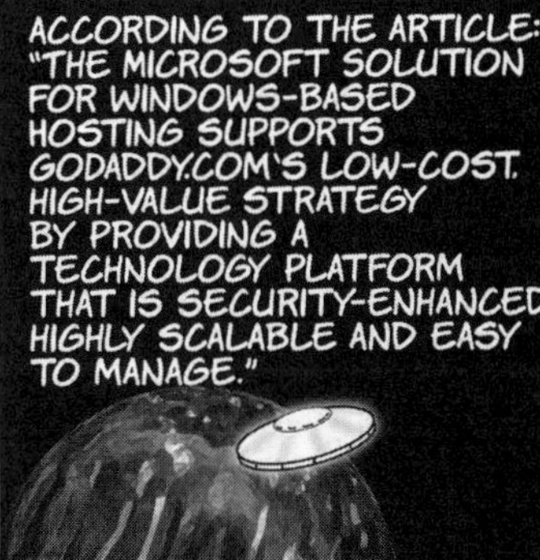
ACCORDING TO THE ARTICLE: "THE MICROSOFT SOLUTION FOR WINDOWS-BASED HOSTING SUPPORTS GODADDY.COM'S LOW-COST, HIGH-VALUE STRATEGY BY PROVIDING A TECHNOLOGY PLATFORM THAT IS SECURITY-ENHANCED, HIGHLY SCALABLE AND EASY TO MANAGE."

"SECURITY-ENHANCED?"
YES, YOUR DRIPNIFICENCE.

I HAVE AN OVERWHELMING URGE TO REGISTER "BULLMANURE-ENHANCED.COM"
I THINK THAT ALREADY POINTS TO "AT&T PROMISES IT WON'T DO ANYTHING TO THE INTERNET."

COPYRIGHT © 2006 J.D. "Illiad" Frazer HTTP://WWW.USERFRIENDLY.ORG/

HELLO! YOUR FRIENDLY NEIGHBOURHOOD CARTOONIST HERE AGAIN.
TODAY, I'M HERE TO ANNOUNCE A SITE UPGRADE!
COPYRIGHT© 2006 J.D. "Illiad" Frazer HTTP://WWW.USERFRIENDLY.ORG/

AS NOBODY TAKES A WEB PROPERTY SERIOUSLY UNLESS YOU'RE "WEB 2.0 COMPLIANT" THESE DAYS, I HAVE ELECTED TO MOVE USERFRIENDLY.ORG INTO THE 21ST CENTURY!
BEHOLD!

I SWR. I KEEP LOSING VWLS!
I THINK IT'S SUPPOSED TO MAKE YOU SOUND COOL. OR BETTR.
WTF 2.0?!!

TIM O'REILLY WROTE AN OPEN LETTER TO CLARIFY THE "WEB 2.0 CONFERENCE" SERVICE MARKING FUSS.
I KNOW. I'VE READ IT.
COPYRIGHT© 2006 J.D. "Illiad" Frazer HTTP://WWW.USERFRIENDLY.ORG/

HE CLAIMS THAT EVERYONE BLEW IT WAY OUT OF PROPORTION AND NOW HE'S BUSY REBUILDING BRIDGES BURNT BY OTHER PEOPLE.
HE WAS ALSO ENTIRELY REASONABLE IN HIS REPLY.

HOW AM I SUPPOSED TO VILIFY HIM WHEN HE'S BEING SO CIVIL? IT'S AN OUTRAGE!
YOU COULD ALWAYS IGNORE THE FACTS AND POST ANGRILY ABOUT IT ON THE INTERNET. THAT WOULD TEACH HIM.

YOU KNOW, TIM O'REILLY IS IN A BIT OF A PICKLE.
ALTHOUGH IT REALLY WASN'T HIS FAULT, THE WEB 2.0 FUSS REALLY WENT BALLISTIC LEAVING HIM WITH MUCH UNDESERVED BLAME.
COPYRIGHT© 2006 J.D. "Illiad" Frazer HTTP://WWW.USERFRIENDLY.ORG/

AS A RESULT, I THINK HE MIGHT SEE HIS CHERISHED "WEB 2.0" AS A POPULAR MEME SINK UNDER THE WAVES. PEOPLE ARE PRETTY SOURED ON IT.

I GET THE SENSE TOO THAT ANY REPLACEMENT HE MIGHT COME UP WITH WILL SUFFER THE SAME FATE.
THEN COULD WE RENAME IT "THE BLOGOSPHERE CONFERENCE"? 'CAUSE I COULD GET BEHIND THAT.

HEY...BLOGGING AGAIN?
YEAH. I'M TRYING TO COME UP WITH A NEW TERM FOR THE BLOGOSPHERE.
COPYRIGHT© 2006 J.D. "Illiad" Frazer HTTP://WWW.USERFRIENDLY.ORG/

"BLOGOSPHERE" IS PASSE. "THE BLOGODROME" IS TOO APOCALYPTIC.
WHAT ELSE DO YOU HAVE SO FAR?

"WE ARE THE BLOG. EXISTENCE IS FUTILE"?
PREPARE TO BE EMULATED!

IS THAT A WIKI I SEE?
YES. I'M STARTING A SPECIAL SORT OF LINUXPEDIA.

COPYRIGHT © 2006 J.D. "Illiad" Frazer HTTP://WWW.USERFRIENDLY.ORG/
IT'LL BE JUST LIKE WIKIPEDIA, BUT IT'LL ONLY COVER LINUX TOPICS LIKE BEST DESKTOP ENVIRON-MENT, BEST DISTRO AND BEST TEXT EDITOR.
ANYTHING ELSE YOU THINK I'LL NEED?

A STRONG ANESTHETIC COMES TO MIND...
YOU JUST **HAVE** TO CRUSH HOPEFUL NAÏVETE WHEREVER YOU SEE IT, DON'T YOU?

OKAY. NOW CHANGE THE PERMISSIONS ON THAT DIRECTORY...
HEY GUYS? WHAT DOES A VIRTUAL FILE SYSTEM LOOK LIKE?

COPYRIGHT © 2006 J.D. "Illiad" Frazer HTTP://WWW.USERFRIENDLY.ORG/
WHAT DOES IT **LOOK** LIKE? WHAT DO YOU MEAN, "WHAT DOES IT LOOK LIKE?"
UM...DO FILES ON A VIRTUAL SYSTEM ACTUALLY CONTAIN DATA?

OF **COURSE** THEY CONTAIN REAL DATA! WHY **WOULDN'T** THEY?!
CUZ...THEY'RE "VIRTUAL FILES" WHICH MEANS THEY AREN'T REAL?
WHAT DID YOU DO?!!

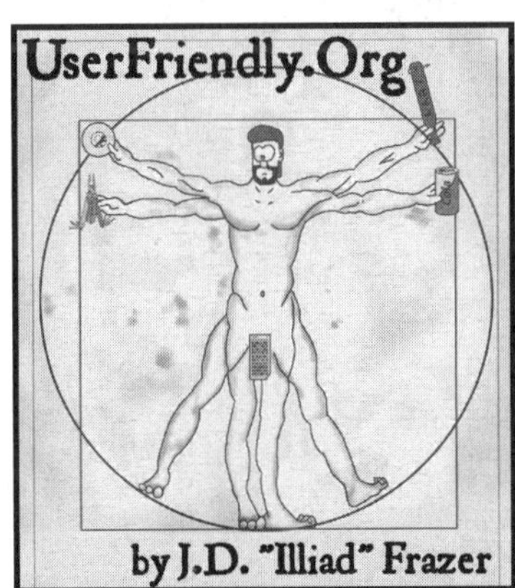
UserFriendly.Org
by J.D. "Illiad" Frazer

COPYRIGHT © 2006 J.D. "Illiad" Frazer HTTP://WWW.USERFRIENDLY.ORG/
...AND I AM PLEASED TO ANNOUNCE THAT ORACLE IS CONSIDERING LAUNCHING OUR OWN LINUX DISTRO.

MR. ELLISON, WHAT DO YOU INTEND TO NAME ORACLE'S LINUX DISTRO? ORANUX? ELLINUX?
"ANNOY-BILL-GATES-NUX"

GOOD PRESS CONFERENCE TODAY, MR. ELLISON.
THANK YOU, MR. FIELDS.
ARE YOU RE-VISITING THE IDEA OF ACQUIRING NOVELL ALONG WITH SUSE LINUX?
ORACLE

MAYBE. DOES SUSE LINUX COME WITH ANY BAGGAGE?
NOTHING WE CAN'T CRUSH LIKE A BUG, SIR.
ORACLE

WHY AM I ALL TENSE?
SCO

TECH SUPPORT. GREG SPEA-
WHY AM I SEEING CONNECTIONS FROM MY ROUTER TO YOUR NAME SERVER? ARE YOU AIDING A VIRUS ATTACK ON ME?
COPYRIGHT © 2006 J.D. "Illiad" Frazer HTTP://WWW.USERFRIENDLY.ORG/

WHA..?
THE FBI IS IN ON THIS. I KNOW IT! YOU'RE MAKING MY MACHINES DO THINGS BEHIND MY BACK! AND I DEMAND YOU STOP!

YES SIR! THERE WILL NO LONGER BE ANY NAME SERVER TRAFFIC TO OR FROM YOUR ROUTER.
THAT'S MORE LIKE IT! *KLIK*
TAKKITY
TIK TAK
BLOK

SIR, AT WHAT DOMAIN ARE YOU RECEIVING MAIL?
WHAT'S A DOMAIN?
IT'S THE PART AFTER THE "AT" SIGN.
WHAT'S AN "AT" SIGN?
COPYRIGHT © 2006 J.D. "Illiad" Frazer HTTP://WWW.USERFRIENDLY.ORG/

WHAT'S YOUR EMAIL ADDRESS?
JROKE AT SUNPOP DOT COM.
SAY IT AGAIN.
JROKE AT SUNP-- OH.

At a Web 2.0 conference, I asked a speaker what made sites like MySpace and Blogger any different from Web 1.0 websites. He instantly said, "Ease of publishing." I then asked, "And what's that gotten us?" To his credit, he said, "A World Wide Web of unbelievably stupid crap."

COLUMBIA INTERNET WILL NOW OFFER A NEW PRODUCT TO CUSTOMERS: "FACEXPACES"!
COPYRIGHT © 2006 J.D. "Illiad" Frazer HTTP://WWW.USERFRIENDLY.ORG/

FOR A MONTHLY FEE, OUR CUSTOMERS CAN NOW EXALT THEIR PERSONAL VIRTUES VIA DIGITAL PORTRAITS, CHORD-STRIKING POETRY, ARTFUL PROSE, ALL COLLECTED, LINKED AND ORGANIZED ON THE INTERNET FOR THE WORLD TO SHARE!

WEREN'T THESE JUST FORMERLY KNOWN AS "WEBSITES"?
OH HOW VERY WEB 1.0 OF YOU.

ANYWAY, WE HAVE A MASSIVE AD CAMPAIGN LAUNCHING NEXT MONTH FOR OUR FACEXPACES SERVICE.
I NOTICE THAT YOU HAVE YET TO REGISTER FACEXPACES.COM.
COPYRIGHT © 2006 J.D. "Illiad" Frazer HTTP://WWW.USERFRIENDLY.ORG/

IS IT STILL AVAILABLE?
NOT ANYMORE.
BWOP! REGISTERED!

MIKE, I NEED HELP.
I'VE COMMITTED A LOT OF MONEY TO OUR FACEXPACES AD BUDGET. BUT FACEXPACES.COM HAS BEEN TAKEN. I CAN'T AFFORD TO HAVE THE NAME CHANGED IN ALL OF THE AD MATERIALS!

MAYBE YOU COULD CHANGE IT TO FACEXPACES.NET?
YEAH, THAT'S NOT SO BAD. THE CHANGE IS MINIMAL ON THE ADS. I THINK I CAN SWING THAT. THANKS!

YOU, I PRESUME, HAVE ALREADY REGISTERED FACEXPACES.NET.
.NET, .ORG, .EVERYTHING.

MIKE...
YO.

I JUST NOTICED THAT FACEXPACES.COM, .NET, .ORG AND REALLY DOT BLOODY EVERYTHING IS HELD BY "MIKE FLOYD & ASSOCIATES."
HUNH. IMAGINE THAT.

YOU WOULDN'T KNOW ANYTHING ABOUT THAT, WOULD YOU?
I KNOW THAT THEY'RE FOR SALE AT $20,000 EACH.

The Engfeh Times

BILL GATES TO LEAVE MICROSOFT IN 2008

Software Analysts Predict Actual Departure in 2010

MIKE, EVEN IF I HAD $20 K I WOULDN'T BUY FACEXPACES.COM FROM YOU. IT WOULD COST ME LESS TO CORRECT ALL OF THE ADVERTISING MATERIAL!
I SEE.
COPYRIGHT © 2006 J.D. "Illiad" Frazer HTTP://WWW.USERFRIENDLY.ORG/

SO YOU'RE GOING TO JUST GIVE ME THE DOMAIN, RIGHT?
WELL, FIRST... WHAT WOULD IT COST YOU TO CORRECT THE ADVERTISING?

ABOUT FOUR THOUSAND. WHY?
THEN YOU CAN HAVE THE DOMAIN FOR THREE THOUSAND FIVE HUNDRED.

NO WAY AM I PAYING YOU!
THE WAY I FIGURE IT, YOU CAN PAY $4K FOR THE CHANGES, EXPLAIN TO THE CHIEF HOW YOUR LACK OF PLANNING LANDED YOU IN THIS MESS, OR PAY ME $3.5K.
THOSE ARE YOUR CHOICES.
COPYRIGHT © 2006 J.D. "Illiad" Frazer HTTP://WWW.USERFRIENDLY.ORG/

...OR...YOU CAN WORK OFF THE $3500...

WAIT, BREAK IT DOWN FOR ME AGAIN?
"YES MIKE, YOU'RE RIGHT" IS WORTH FIVE BUCKS. "I BASK IN YOUR PRESENCE" IS TEN, AND "WHEN I GROW UP I WANT TO BE YOU" IS FIFTY.

LAST WEEK, THE CEO OF THE RECORDING INDUSTRY ASSOCIATION OF AMERICA DECLARED THAT PEER TO PEER FILE SHARING HAD BEEN "CONTAINED."
COPYRIGHT © 2006 J.D. "Illiad" Frazer HTTP://WWW.USERFRIENDLY.ORG/

"THE PROBLEM HAS NOT BEEN ELIMINATED," HE SAID, "BUT FILE-TRADING IS FLAT."

"FLAT" AT THIRTY GAZILLION FILES A DAY, SIR.
GET ME ANOTHER SIX-PACK OF MAALOX, BENSON.
RIAA

AT LEAST DIGITAL SALES ARE UP, SIR.
I DON'T CONSIDER THAT TO BE GOOD NEWS, BENSON.
RIAA
COPYRIGHT © 2006 J.D. "Illiad" Frazer HTTP://WWW.USERFRIENDLY.ORG/

FOR REASONS THAT ARE BEYOND ME, PEOPLE JUST DON'T APPRECIATE WHAT WE ADD TO AN ARTISTS WORK ANYMORE.

WHAT WOULD THAT BE, SIR?
JEWEL CASES AND SHRINK WRAP. WHAT'S WRONG WITH PEOPLE THESE DAYS?!
RIAA

STEF! DID WE GET THE DOMAIN NAME WE WANTED?
YES CHIEF. AS PROMISED! ALL OF THE ADVERTISING IS IN PLACE. THE P.R. LIST IS PRIMED AND WE'RE READY TO TAKE PEOPLE'S MONEY!
GOOD! SO WE LAUNCH MONDAY?
COPYRIGHT © 2006 J.D. "Illiad" Frazer HTTP://WWW.USERFRIENDLY.ORG/

HEY GUYS? DID WE EVER TALK ABOUT GETTING THE FACEXPACES SERVICE SET UP?
SET UP? YOU HAVEN'T EVEN TOLD US WHAT IT REALLY IS.

WE HAVE TO LAUNCH YOUR PRODUCT BY MONDAY?! WE DON'T HAVE ENOUGH TIME!
BUT ALL OF THE COMPANY'S CASH IS TIED UP IN IT.
WHAT IS IT ACTUALLY? AND NO MARKET-SPEAK.
COPYRIGHT © 2006 J.D. "Illiad" Frazer HTTP://WWW.USERFRIENDLY.ORG/

WHERE DOES HE THINK HE'S RUNNING OFF TO?
I DUNNO. BUT HE'S STOPPED AT THE WATER COOLER.

IT'S A BLOGGING SERVICE THAT PLAYS THE BLOGGER'S FAVOURITE MP3S IN THE BACKGROUND.
AAAUUUUGGGH!!
YOU'D BETTER KEEP RUNNING!!

AT&T "CLARIFIES" THEIR PRIVACY POLICY.
We
own
your
data.
UserFriendly.Org
COPYRIGHT © 2006 J.D. "Illiad" Frazer HTTP://WWW.USERFRIENDLY.ORG/

MONDAY MORNING...AND THE INTREPID TECHS OF COLUMBIA INTERNET LAUNCH FACEXPACES.
COPYRIGHT © 2006 J.D. "Illiad" Frazer HTTP://WWW.USERFRIENDLY.ORG/

ADDED TO THE MORASS OF SIMILAR SITES ON THE NET, FACEXPACES ALLOWS ITS USERS TO EMBED MUSIC IN THE BACKGROUND OF THEIR PAGES.

WHICH GENERATES THE EXPECTED RESPONSES FROM TWO VERY DISTINCT GROUPS OF INTERNET USERS...
PAR-TAY. DAWG!
AAUUUGH! KILL IT! KIIILL IT!

OH...UH. HEY.
HEY. INTERESTING NEW SERVICE YOU GUYS ARE OFFERING. "FACEXPACES"?
COPYRIGHT © 2006 J.D. "Illiad" Frazer HTTP://WWW.USERFRIENDLY.ORG/

UM..YEAH. NOT SURE HOW WELL THAT WHOLE MUSIC IN THE BACKGROUND THING WILL SELL THOUGH...
I KINDA LIKE IT. IT LETS ME EXPRESS WHO I AM.
MOTION IN THE OCEAN
HIS AIR HOSE BROKE
LOTS OF TROUBLE
LOTS OF BUBBLE
HE WAS IN A JAM
S'IN A GIANT CLAM

WAIT...IS THAT "ROCK LOBSTER"?
WHAT. YOU DON'T HAVE ANY GUILTY PLEASURES?
DOWN
DOWN...

I don't think I could tell a joke worse than this one.

OKAY. OKAY. OKAY. I GOT A JOKE!
I'M LISTENING.
COPYRIGHT © 2006 J.D. "Illiad" Frazer HTTP://WWW.USERFRIENDLY.ORG/

WHAT DO YOU CALL FREE OR OPEN SOURCE SOFTWARE USED IN A DENTIST'S OFFICE?
I DON'T KNOW. WHAT?

"DENTAL F.O.S.S!" HA!
AAUUUGH!

I was wrong.

OKAY. I'VE GOT ANOTHER ONE.
NO...PLEASE DON'T...
COPYRIGHT © 2006 J.D. "Illiad" Frazer HTTP://WWW.USERFRIENDLY.ORG/

BUT IT'S GOOD! WHAT DO YOU CALL A PLACE WHERE RICHARD STALLMAN GOES SKINNY-DIPPING?
I DON'T WANT TO KNOW.

A GNU'D BEACH! AHAHAHAH!!
I'M SURE I HAVE AN ELECTROMAGNET SOMEWHERE...

TECH SUPPORT. HOW MAY I BRIGHTEN YOUR DAY?
YOUR FACEXPACES PRODUCT...HOW DOES ONE TURN OFF THE ANNOYING MUSIC IN THE BACKGROUND?

UM...CLOSE YOUR BROWSER.
AHH. THAT'S GOT IT. THANKS.

THAT'S AN ODD LOOKING E-MAIL...

Dear Sir!
if you do not notify your ceo
to send us $100,000 by wire
my team and I in the republic
of wankelstan will cripple
your facexpaces offering!

signed,
the sock puppet

NOT REALLY SURE HOW I SHOULD PLAY THIS ONE...
p.s. we are
serious!!!11
and dangeruss!!!1

SUCCESSFULLY SQUEEZING BLOOD FROM A STONE

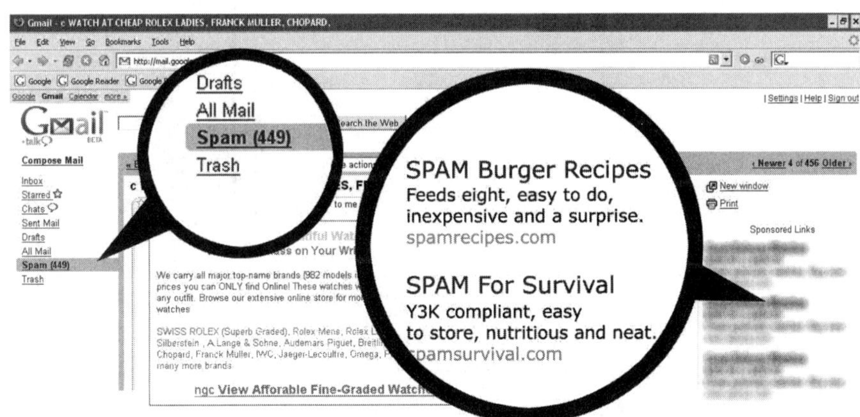
Drafts
All Mail
Spam (449)
Trash
SPAM Burger Recipes
Feeds eight, easy to do,
inexpensive and a surprise.
spamrecipes.com
SPAM For Survival
Y3K compliant, easy
to store, nutritious and neat.
spamsurvival.com
ngc View Afforable Fine-Graded Watch

UserFriendly.Org

HOW GOES OUR FACEXPACES EFFORT?
IT LOOKS LIKE OUR PENETRATION HAS BEEN SIGNIFICANT. WE HAVE OVER TWENTY THOUSAND SIGN-UPS IN A FEW SHORT WEEKS.
COPYRIGHT © 2006 J.D. "Illiad" Frazer HTTP://WWW.USERFRIENDLY.ORG/

AND REVENUE?
GROSS REVENUE THROUGH PAYPAL IS OVER $600,000.

...AND OUR NET IS FOURTEEN DOLLARS?
BECAUSE OF EXCHANGE FEES, TRANSFER FEES AND ACCOUNT FEES. OH, AND JUST-BECAUSE-WE-CAN FEES.

THIS IS UNTENABLE! WE NEED TO INCREASE NET REVENUES!
AND IF WE DON'T, THE COMPANY WILL IMPLODE IN LESS THAN TWO MONTHS.
COPYRIGHT © 2006 J.D. "Illiad" Frazer HTTP://WWW.USERFRIENDLY.ORG/

HMMMM.

IF WE DOUBLE OUR PRICES WHAT WILL OUR TAKE BE AFTER PAYPAL?
WE'LL GO FROM FOURTEEN TO SEVENTEEN DOLLARS. AT A MILLION BUCKS THERE'S A "YOU'RE-SO-RICH-YOU-CAN-AFFORD-ANOTHER-FEE" FEE.

YOU WANTED TO SEE ME?
WE NEED A NEW METHOD OF GENERATING REVENUE WITH FACEXPACES, AND WE'RE DROPPING PAYPAL
COPYRIGHT © 2006 J.D. "Illiad" Frazer HTTP://WWW.USERFRIENDLY.ORG/

WE COULD LET PEOPLE UPLOAD ALL OF THEIR FAVOURITE MP3S TO OUR SERVERS, AND FACEXPACES COULD MAGICALLY INDEX THEM. WE'D HAVE A HUGE LIBRARY OF RIPPED MUSIC!

HOW, PRECISELY, DO WE MAKE MONEY FROM THIS?
I'M KIND OF WAITING FOR YOUTUBE TO COME UP WITH THAT ANSWER...

WE CAN'T WAIT FOR YOUTUBE TO GIVE US A BUSINESS MODEL TO FOLLOW. SO HOW ARE WE GOING TO MAKE MONEY WITH FACEXPACES?
COPYRIGHT © 2006 J.D. "Illiad" Frazer HTTP://WWW.USERFRIENDLY.ORG/

WELL, HOW ABOUT HIGHLY TARGETTED ADS THAT ARE SERVED BASED ON THE SONG BEING PLAYED?

DO YOU SMELL MONEY? 'CAUSE I SMELL MONEY.
RIAA

HEY CHIEF? SOME SCRIPT KIDDIE NAMED "SOCK PUPPET" IS THREATENING TO DDOS FACEXPACES UNLESS WE SEND HIM $100,000.
OH DEAR...

IS THAT BAD?
I GUESS IT DEPENDS ON WHOM YOU ASK...

icq from:sockpuppet
Dear Sir! Your time is up! What about our agreement?!
greg:
I notified my ceo to send you $100,000, as you asked.
TAPPA TAPPA RAPPA

sockpuppet:
Very good! Then when is the money to come?
greg:
there`s no money coming. you just said i had to notify him.
TICKETY TACKITY TECK

sockpuppet:
oh. well. we win you! ph33r us! hahahah! ha.
greg:
yes, ha.
COUP DE GRACE

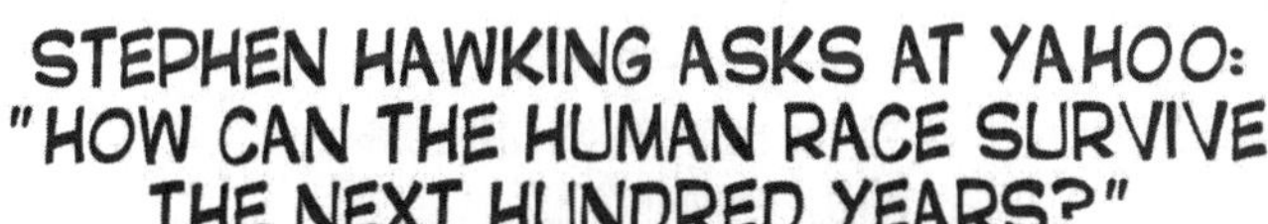
STEPHEN HAWKING ASKS AT YAHOO:
"HOW CAN THE HUMAN RACE SURVIVE THE NEXT HUNDRED YEARS?"

OOPS.

FOR STARTERS WHY DON'T WE MAKE SURE ONLY BONA FIDE SYSADMINS HAVE "ROOT"...

UserFriendly.Org

THE FACEXPACES TARGETTING SOFTWARE IS READY?
YEP.
COPYRIGHT © 2006 J.D. "Illiad" Frazer HTTP://WWW.USERFRIENDLY.ORG/

WE HAVE A MASSIVE INVENTORY OF GRAPHICAL BANNER ADS LINED UP AND INDEXED TO A MASSIVE LIST OF SONG TITLES.
LAUNCH THAT PUPPY!

SHOCK THE MONKEY TO LIFE! MONKEY! MONKEEEEEEEEEEE MONKEY!
OH CRAP. NOT THAT THING AGAIN.

AH. STEF! GO AWAY. WE'LL TALK LATER!
CHIEF! FACEXPACES IS MAKING GAZILLIONS!
COPYRIGHT © 2006 J.D. "Illiad" Frazer HTTP://WWW.USERFRIENDLY.ORG/

...OH....HEY.

HEY CHIEF? WHO'S THE HOODED FREAKSHOW?
INQUISITOR BERNARDO OF THE R.I.A.A. TELL ME MORE OF THESE "GAZILLIONS" OF WHICH YOU SPEAK.

WHEN DID HE GET HERE?
MOMENTS AGO...
COPYRIGHT © 2006 J.D. "Illiad" Frazer HTTP://WWW.USERFRIENDLY.ORG/

FORSOOTH! NOW, OF THIS CACHE OF WEALTH YOU REFERRED TO IN A MEASURE OF "GAZILLIONS," PLEASE EXPOUND.

IT'S A SCIENTIFIC TERM. FROM THE LATIN ROOT "GAZ" MEANING "NEGATIVE AMOUNTS."
DRAT. I ONLY LEARNED ENOUGH LATIN TO SCARE DEFENDANTS LIKE 12-YEAR OLD GIRLS.

SO...UH...AS STEF SAID. WE'RE MAKING SO LITTLE MONEY FROM FACEXPACES THAT WE CAN'T EVEN COVER OUR BANDWIDTH COSTS!
COPYRIGHT © 2006 J.D. "Illiad" Frazer HTTP://WWW.USERFRIENDLY.ORG/

FAITH, IT IS NO ENIGMA THAT IT IS NOT A WORTHY ENDEAVOUR IN TRYING TO SQUEEZE WATER FROM A STONE...
PHEW

BLOOD ON THE OTHER HAND...

HELLO. TECH SUPPORT. MY PAIN RECEPTORS ARE PREPARED TO FIRE.
UM...WINDOWS DOESN'T WORK ANYMORE.

COPYRIGHT© 2006 J.D. "Illiad" Frazer HTTP://WWW.USERFRIENDLY.ORG/
THAT'S NOT UNHEARD OF. DID YOU JUST INSTALL ANYTHING?
NO. BUT I REORG-ANIZED MY DRIVE. LIKE BY PUTTING ALL OF MY JPEGS IN THEIR OWN FOLDER...

PLEASE TELL ME THAT'S ALL YOU DID...
UM. I DID IT FOR THE DLL AND EXE FILES TOO.

...NOW MOVE THE ONES YOU'VE SELECTED INTO THE LAST FOLDER.
OKAY. DONE.

COPYRIGHT© 2006 J.D. "Illiad" Frazer HTTP://WWW.USERFRIENDLY.ORG/
I CAN'T THANK YOU ENOUGH! MY MACHINE IS WORKING AGAIN AND I WON'T LOSE MY JOB!
WHAT DID WE LEARN TODAY, SIR?

...IF IT ISN'T BROKEN, DON'T FIX IT?
AND IF YOU DON'T KNOW HOW TO FIX IT, DON'T BREAK IT!

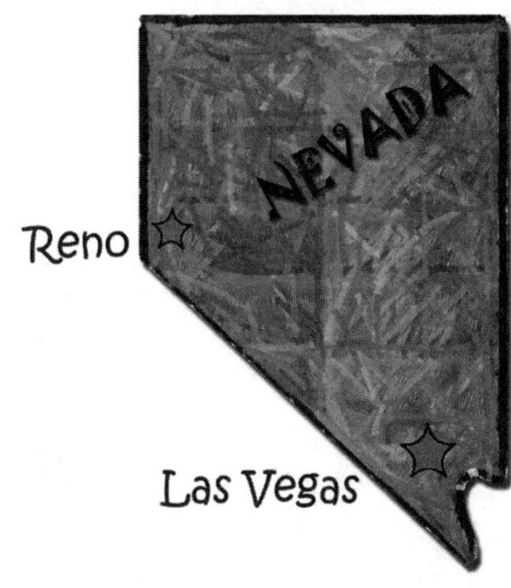
THE U.S. HOUSE OF REPRESENTATIVES APPROVES NEW ONLINE GAMBLING BAN 317 TO 93 "OUT OF CONCERN OVER THE IMMORALITY OF GAMBLING"
CLEARLY ONLY 93 OF THE REPRESENTATIVES KNOW ABOUT THIS SECRET STATE:
NEVADA
Reno
Las Vegas
UserFriendly.Org
COPYRIGHT© 2006 J.D. "Illiad" Frazer HTTP://WWW.USERFRIENDLY.ORG/

HELLO. TECH SUPPORT. I AM PREPARED TO BE BERATED FOR SOMETHING THAT IS NOT MY FAULT.
I NEED SOME SUPPORT. NOT A SCAPEGOAT.
COPYRIGHT © 2006 J.D. "Illiad" Frazer HTTP://WWW.USERFRIENDLY.ORG/

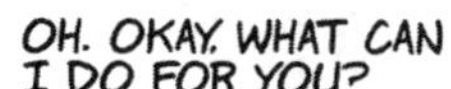
OH. OKAY. WHAT CAN I DO FOR YOU?
THE INTERNETS. THEY'RE JUST A BUNCH OF TUBES, RIGHT? TUBES? WITH STUFF GOING THROUGH THEM?

WAIT! WAIT! IS THIS SENATOR TED STEVENS? SIR, I AM SUCH A FAN! ARE YOU GONNA BE ON COMEDY CENTRAL?
ABOUT THAT SCAPEGOAT SERVICE...

WELL HELP ME OUT THEN. WHAT'S WRONG WITH THE "TUBES" ANALOGY?
IT'S VERY OVERSIMPLIFIED. IT'S LIKE SAYING WHEN YOU SEND E-MAIL TINY LITTLE POSTMEN RUN BACK AND FORTH ACROSS THE INTERNET WITH YOUR MESSAGE.
COPYRIGHT © 2006 J.D. "Illiad" Frazer HTTP://WWW.USERFRIENDLY.ORG/

NO SIR, "LITTLE POSTMEN" DON'T REALLY EXIST.
YOU'RE REALLY HARSHING UP MY REALITY HERE, SON.

LOOK SON. I NEED AN OUT HERE. AMERICA IS CHEWING ON MY BUTT.
ALL RIGHT SENATOR. THE TRUTH IS THE INTERNETS REALLY ARE MADE UP OF TUBES.
COPYRIGHT © 2006 J.D. "Illiad" Frazer HTTP://WWW.USERFRIENDLY.ORG/

REALLY?! I KNEW IT! AND DO YOU HAVE ANY SUGGESTIONS ABOUT HOW WE CAN CONTROL THE AMOUNT OF INTERNETS THAT GO BACK AND FORTH?

THINK OF WATER IN A TUBE, SENATOR. JUST ASK ONE OF THE NETWORK ENGINEERS TO PINCH THE CABLE.
VINDICATED! I'M CALLING CONGRESS!

Either that or the designer didn't know how to change his screen resolution.

#@$@?!?&!@!&? ?$(#*&?#$??@!! ??@#&*@*&+!!!
WHOA...
COPYRIGHT © 2006 J.D. "Illiad" Frazer HTTP://WWW.USERFRIENDLY.ORG/

WHAT'S WITH THE VITRIOL?
JUST LOOK! LOOK AT THIS @#$!*&! WEBSITE! I HAVE HAD IT WITH THIS ATTITUDE!

"BEST VIEWED AT 1024X768"
IN OTHER WORDS, "HEY, DORK, CHANGE YOUR MONITOR RESOLUTION TO SUIT OUR DESIGN."

SID, YOU'RE GETTING YOUR UNDERWEAR ALL BOUND UP FOR NOTHING. THAT "BEST VIEWED AT" STUFF IS JUST A BIT OF LAZINESS ON THE PART OF THE WEB DESIGNER.

A.J., I DON'T THINK YOU REALIZE -- IT'S GOTTEN OUT OF HAND.
GOTTEN OUT OF HAND?
COME AND BEHOLD THIS WEBSITE.

"BEST VIEWED AT 1024X768 UNDER THE LIGHT OF THE FULL MOON IN JULY WHILE MERCURY IS IN LEO AND SIX PYGMY MARMOSETS DO THE LAMBADA BEHIND YOU SINGING 'KUMBAYA'."
I ASK YOU, WHEN WILL IT END?

HAVE YOU MADE THE CHANGES?
ERWIN HAS. OR AT LEAST HE'S BEGUN TO.

Y'KNOW, DOING A SEARCH AND REPLACE ON THE ENTIRE WEB ISN'T EXACTLY **QUICK.**
THAT'S FINE. AFTER YEARS OF SEEING "PREFERRED" RESOLUTIONS PUT ON WEBSITES BY LAZY DESIGNERS I CAN WAIT A WHILE LONGER.

This site best viewed with a jaundiced eye.
ABOUT TIME THEY CAME CLEAN...

There are simple truths in all humor.

USERS OF MYSPACE DEFEND THE MUCH MALIGNED SITE WITH THE RATIONALE THAT "IT'S A GOOD WAY TO STAY IN TOUCH."

THIS WEEK, THEY WERE PROVEN CORRECT WHEN A HACKED AD INFECTED A MILLION MYSPACE USERS WITH SPYWARE.

THE SPYWARE WILL TRACK THE USERS' WEB TRAVELS AND STAY IN TOUCH WITH THEIR MOTHER SHIP.

UserFriendly.Org

HEY. CHECK THIS OUT, LI'L GUY. MICROSOFT IS PLANNING ON TAKING ON APPLE'S IPOD WITH A "LIFESTYLE DEVICE" CALLED THE "ZUNE."
COPYRIGHT © 2006 J.D. "Illiad" Frazer HTTP://WWW.USERFRIENDLY.ORG/

BUT Y'KNOW...STEVE JOBS ISN'T KNOWN FOR JUST ROLLING OVER AND PLAYING DEAD. I WONDER WHAT HIS COUNTER-STRATEGY IS.

MR. JOBS? WHAT'S OUR COUNTER-STRATEGY VERSUS MICROSOFT?
1. PROVIDE ROPE. 2. WAIT.
Apple

IS THIS IT? IS THIS THE THING WITH WHICH WE WILL BREAK THE BACK OF JOB'S LITTLE EMPIRE?
YES MR. BALLMER. THIS IS THE "ZUNE." GIVE IT A TRY.
Microsoft
COPYRIGHT © 2006 J.D. "Illiad" Frazer HTTP://WWW.USERFRIENDLY.ORG/

KLIK
KADUNK
SPOING!
"I SEE YOU ARE PLAYING A SONG BOUGHT FROM ITUNES! WOULD YOU LIKE HELP DELETING IT?"

WHEN ARE YOU ENGINEERING NERDS GOING TO GET RID OF THAT BLASTED PAPER CLIP?!
WE TRIED! EVEN AT THE CODE LEVEL! BUT IT JUST...KEEPS ... COMING...BACK!

CHUCK? I'M A LITTLE DISTRESSED.
OH? WHY'S THAT MR. BALLMER?
Microsoft
COPYRIGHT © 2006 J.D. "Illiad" Frazer HTTP://WWW.USERFRIENDLY.ORG/

SEE, I HAVE THIS FRIEND OVER IN ISRAEL. HE AND I GO GOLFING WHEN HE'S IN TOWN. HE SPEAKS HEBREW.
YES?

HE TELLS ME THAT "ZUNE" IS QUITE CLOSE TO A VERY RUDE HEBREW WORD THAT HAS TO DO WITH REPRODUCTION. OR WHAT WE DO TO SMALLER COMPANIES THAT COMPETE WITH US.
OOH! "GET ZUNED!" THE MARKETING MESSAGES JUST WRITE THEMSELVES!

SO CALM MY JITTERY NERVES, CHUCK. ZUNE IS TO COMPETE WITH THE IPOD. WHAT WILL WE HAVE TO COMPETE WITH ITUNES?
COPYRIGHT © 2006 J.D. "Illiad" Frazer HTTP://WWW.USERFRIENDLY.ORG/

UM. "MY ZUNES"?
OH GOOD. IS THAT ANOTHER MARKETING MESSAGE IN HEBREW?

HEY. DID YOU HEAR ABOUT MYSPACE GOING DOWN A FEW DAYS AGO FROM A POWER SURGE?
DA. THEY ARE BACK UP NOW?
COPYRIGHT © 2006 J.D. "Illiad" Frazer HTTP://WWW.USERFRIENDLY.ORG/

YES. FINALLY. AFTER A COUPLE OF MISSED E.T.A.S.
UM...WHAT ARE YOU DOING?
TIKKA TAKKA GREP GREP TOUCH

AM SETTINK UP ANOTHER POWER SURGE.
HEY!

PITR...JUST BECAUSE YOU DON'T LIKE MYSPACE DOESN'T MEAN YOU HAVE THE RIGHT TO DESTROY IT! OVER 70 MILLION PEOPLE USE THEIR SERVICE!
COPYRIGHT © 2006 J.D. "Illiad" Frazer HTTP://WWW.USERFRIENDLY.ORG/

MUST CONFESS. HAD NO IDEA THERE IS BEINK 70 MILLION ANNOYINK PEOPLE IN NORTH AMERICA.
NO. THERE'S JUST ONE.

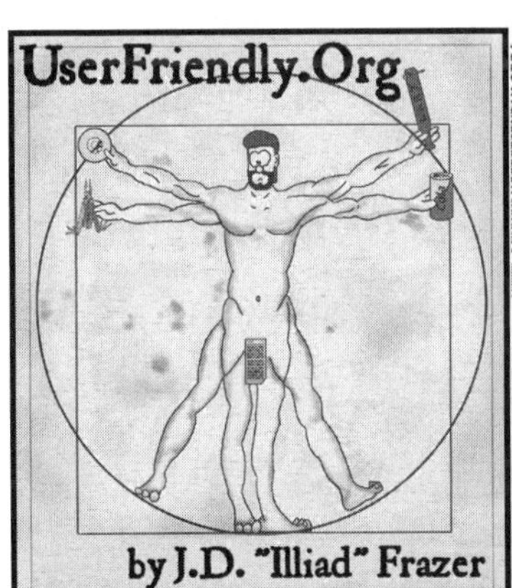
UserFriendly.Org
by J.D. "Illiad" Frazer

COPYRIGHT © 2006 J.D. "Illiad" Frazer HTTP://WWW.USERFRIENDLY.ORG/
STEVE. WHEN IT COMES TO CLUSTERING. IT'S ALL ABOUT LINUX THESE DAYS. I AM NOT HAPPY.
TAKE HEART. BILL! I FOR ONE PREFER NUT CLUSTERS!
Microsoft

UH...WHAT?
NEVER MIND.

STEVE. WHY IS OUR CLUSTERING SERVICES PACKAGE NOT SELLING?
WELL. YOU SEE BILL. MARKETING GOT IT INTO THEIR HEAD TO TRY "TRUTH IN ADVERTISING."

I'M NOT SURE I WANT TO HEAR THIS.
I THOUGHT "WINDOWS 2003 COMPUTING BLOB" HAD A NICE RING TO IT.

HELLO EVERYONE. ERWIN AND I HAVE BEEN ENGAGED IN A VERY LIVELY DISCUSSION REGARDING THE "WEB 2.0" PHENOMENON.
YES. LIVELY.

WHILE WE AGREE THAT TIM O'REILLY OFFERED A VERY USEFUL TERM TO CAPTURE THE CONCEPT OF A COLLABORATIVE WEB, MANY OTHERS HAVE TAKEN AND CORRUPTED IT TO THEIR OWN ENDS.

SO WE CAME UP WITH OUR OWN DEFINITION.

"WEB 2.0: THE PRACTICE OF RENAMING SOMETHING OLD TO MAKE IT NEW AGAIN SO YOU CAN TAKE CREDIT FOR IT."
REMEMBER! EVERYTIME YOU SAY "WEB 2.0" GOD KILLS A STARTUP!

WHAT ON EARTH IS THAT?
IT'S A "ZERO TENSION MOUSE." ONE OF THOSE NEW-FANGLED VERTICAL MICE.

SEE, THE IDEA IS THAT YOU REST YOUR HAND IN AN UPRIGHT POSITION, WHICH IS MORE NATURAL AND THEREFORE MORE COMFORTABLE...

...STOP SMIRKING.
MM NUP SMRKNG.

HEY THERE OLD CHUM. CAN I HAVE A MINUTE?
OF COURSE. WHAT'S UP?

I'M BURNT OUT. I NEED A VACATION. SOMEWHERE SUNNY AND QUIET AND DEVOID OF EXTREME ANNOYANCES.

YOU MEAN LIKE THAT TIME AT THE BEACH SOME KID SET UP SOME SHADOWS SO YOU HAD TANLINES IN THE SHAPE OF AN ELDER SIGN?
YOU CAN SHUT THE HECK UP ANYTIME NOW.

SO WHY DON'T WE TAKE A MINI-HOLIDAY? MAYBE TEXT MESSAGE TSATHOGGUA AND SEE IF HE WANTS TO COME TOO?
WHERE'D YOU HAVE IN MIND?

REDMOND.
MICROSOFT-LAND? WHATEVER FOR?

WE COULD THE THREE OF US POP INTO STEVE BALLMER'S OFFICE WHILE HE'S MESSING WITH THE PROTOTYPE OF THE "ZUNE."
AHHH YES. OUR OLD "HELLRAISER" SKIT. THAT'S SOME REAL STRESS-RELEASE!

SO BUD. WHERE ARE WE GOING FOR OUR HOLIDAY?
WELL, I JUST READ THAT SCIENTISTS HAVE DISCOVERED THE LARGEST KNOWN OBJECT IN THE UNIVERSE. IT'S 200 MILLION LIGHT-YEARS ACROSS.
COPYRIGHT © 2006 J.D. "Illiad" Frazer HTTP://WWW.USERFRIENDLY.ORG/

OH. IT'S A COLLECTION OF GALAXIES. I THOUGHT YOU WANTED TO VISIT STEVE BALLMER'S EGO.
DON'T BE SILLY. I CAN DO THAT JUST BY LOOKING OUT MY WINDOW.

HEY...ARE YOU RUNNING THE BETA OF VISTA?
YEAH. I'M GIVING THE SPEECH RECOGNITION A GO...
COPYRIGHT © 2006 J.D. "Illiad" Frazer HTTP://WWW.USERFRIENDLY.ORG/

"DEAR SIR OR MADAM. PLEASE REVIEW OUR PRODUCT LIST AND CONTACT ME AT YOUR EARLIEST CONVENIENCE."

Dear Sir, Damn!
Please, for me, contact the convent.
FOR THE FIRST TIME EVER, I LIKE THE RESULTS OF VOICE REC TECHNOLOGY.
HEY!!

WHAT "DOWNSIZING" FOR THE ELECTRONIC ENTERTAINMENT EXPO PROBABLY MEANS...

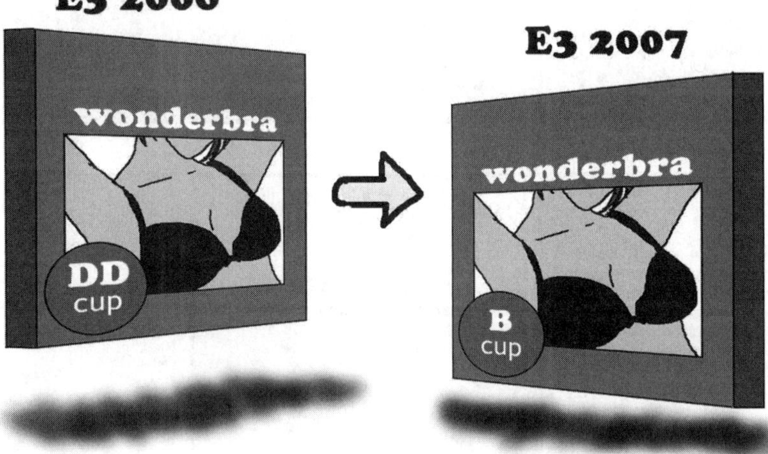
E3 2006
wonderbra
DD cup
E3 2007
wonderbra
B cup
COPYRIGHT © 2006 J.D. "Illiad" Frazer HTTP://WWW.USERFRIENDLY.ORG/
UserFriendly.Org

STEF'S BEEN AT THAT SPEECH RECOGNITION SOFTWARE FOR **HOURS**.
WELL, LET'S GO SEE IF HE GOT IT TO WORK.
COPYRIGHT© 2006 J.D. "Illiad" Frazer HTTP://WWW.USERFRIENDLY.ORG/

HE'S NOT HERE. WONDER WHERE HE WENT?
I THINK HE GAVE UP ON IT.

WHAT MAKES YOU SAY THAT?
"COD AM PIZZA SHIP" KINDA GIVES YOU AN IDEA.

AOL EXPECTS TO ARRIVE AT A DEAL TO SELL ITS EUROPEAN INTERNET ACCESS BUSINESSES BY THIS AUTUMN, SAID ITS TOP EXECUTIVE.
COPYRIGHT© 2006 J.D. "Illiad" Frazer HTTP://WWW.USERFRIENDLY.ORG/

AS AOL SHIFTS TO A FREE, AD-SUPPORTED SERVICE, THE EUROPEAN DIVESTURE AND INTERNAL CUTS IN THE U.S. HAVE LED TO A ROUND OF LAYOFFS TOTALLING APPROXIMATELY 5,000 WORKERS...
GEEZ. I WONDER WHAT IT'S LIKE AT AOL RIGHT NOW...

I JUST GOT LAID OFF.
ME TOO!

CARSTAIRS, WHY ARE WE LAYING OFF ALL OF THOSE PEOPLE?
BECAUSE WE CAN'T AFFORD THEM, SIR. WE ONLY HAVE 19 MILLION SUBSCRIBERS.
COPYRIGHT© 2006 J.D. "Illiad" Frazer HTTP://WWW.USERFRIENDLY.ORG/

19 MILLION?! I THOUGHT WE HAD OVER **20** MILLION!
NO SIR. WE'RE DOWN TO 18 MILLION ACCOUNTS...

18 MILL...WAIT A SECOND!
THAT WOULD BE 17 MILLION, SIR.
STOP THAT!!

HELLO?
HELLO RENALDO, IT'S MARIE OVER IN H.R.. TODAY IS YOUR LAST DAY WITH US. WE'RE TERMINATING YOUR EMPLOYMENT.
COPYRIGHT© 2006 J.D. "Illiad" Frazer HTTP://WWW.USERFRIENDLY.ORG/

UM...COULD YOU TELL ME WHY YOU'RE TERMINATING MY SERVICES?
WELL...WE DON'T NEED YOU ANYMORE.

I SEE. MARIE, I'M AUTHORIZED TO OFFER YOU A ONE-TIME 15% DISCOUNT IN MY SALARY IF YOU ARE WILLING TO KEEP MY SERVICES.
WOW, THAT'S A PRETTY GOOD DE- NOW WAIT A MINUTE!

SIR? THERE'S A REPORTER HERE FROM THE NY TIMES.
OH? WHAT'S HE WANT?

COPYRIGHT © 2006 J.D. "Illiad" Frazer HTTP://WWW.USERFRIENDLY.ORG/
HE HAS A QUESTION ABOUT HOW OUR CHANGE FROM A SUBSCRIPTION-BASED SYSTEM TO AN AD-DRIVEN ONE WILL IMPACT OTHER BUSINESSES.
OTHER BUSINESSES? OTHER THAN THE OBVIOUS ADVERTISING RELATIONSHIPS, I DON'T SEE WHAT ELSE WE COULD REALLY AFFECT...

DEAR GODS, YES! HAPPY TIMES ARE HERE AGAIN!!
COASTER MANUFACTURING LTD.

TO BE BEHOLDINK! HAVE BUILT THE ULTIMATE LINUX BOX WITH OWN HANDS!
COPYRIGHT © 2006 J.D. "Illiad" Frazer HTTP://WWW.USERFRIENDLY.ORG/

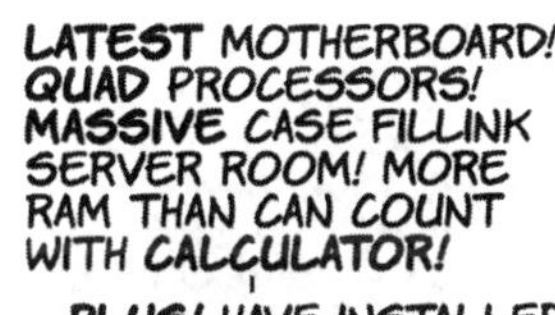
LATEST MOTHERBOARD! QUAD PROCESSORS! MASSIVE CASE FILLINK SERVER ROOM! MORE RAM THAN CAN COUNT WITH CALCULATOR!

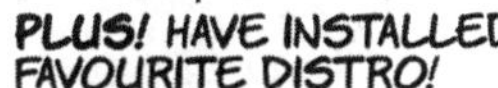
PLUS! HAVE INSTALLED FAVOURITE DISTRO!

HA! EVEN YOU OLD MAN CAN NOT OFFER DOUBT THAT ALL GEEKS WILL AGREE I HAVE ULTIMATE LINUX SYSTEM!
ARE YOU RUNNING VI OR EMACS?

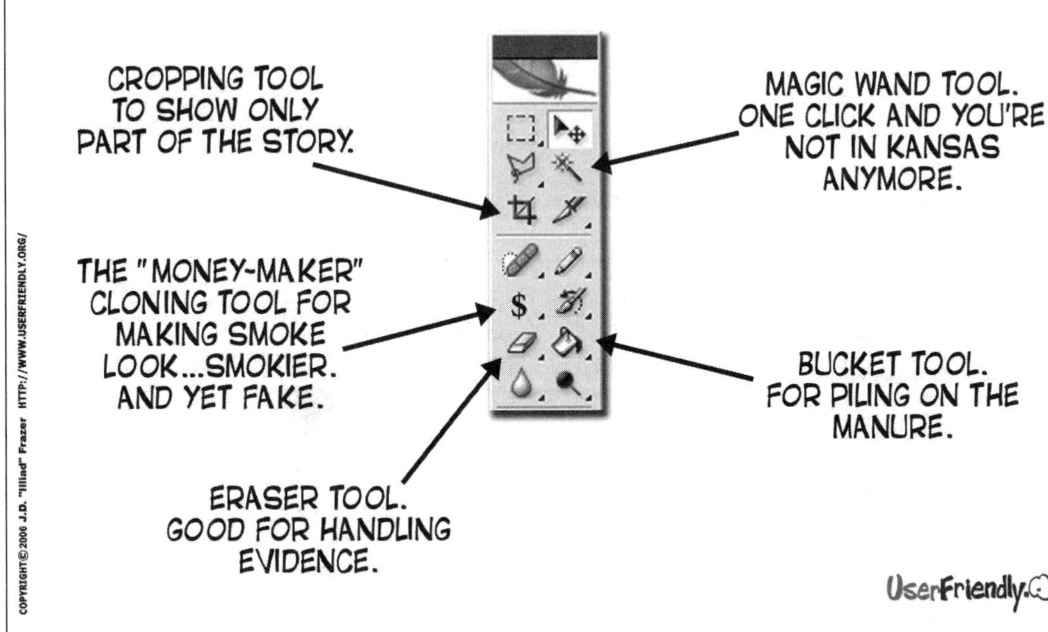
PRESENTING THE "LET'S SEE IF REUTERS IS PAYING ATTENTION" PHOTOSHOP TOOL PALETTE FOR "CREATIVE" FREELANCERS:
CROPPING TOOL TO SHOW ONLY PART OF THE STORY.
MAGIC WAND TOOL. ONE CLICK AND YOU'RE NOT IN KANSAS ANYMORE.
THE "MONEY-MAKER" CLONING TOOL FOR MAKING SMOKE LOOK...SMOKIER. AND YET FAKE.
BUCKET TOOL. FOR PILING ON THE MANURE.
ERASER TOOL. GOOD FOR HANDLING EVIDENCE.
UserFriendly.Org
COPYRIGHT © 2006 J.D. "Illiad" Frazer HTTP://WWW.USERFRIENDLY.ORG/

Reuters really wore some egg on face that week. A freelance photographer sold them a photo that was clearly Photoshopped for greater impact. I know a corporate VP with a nephew who could do better work.

WOOT! WOOT I SAY!
IS THAT STEF? WHAT'S HE ON ABOUT?
COPYRIGHT© 2006 J.D. "Illiad" Frazer HTTP://WWW.USERFRIENDLY.ORG/

TOTAL WOOT! 436 VIEWINGS IN ONE HOUR!
HE UPLOADED A VIDEO HE MADE OF HIMSELF TO YOUTUBE. NOW HE THINKS HE'S A CELEBRITY.

YO! DWEEB! YOUR LIFE IS NOT A MUSIC VIDEO!
YES IT IS! 437! JUST CALL ME CAPTAIN WOOTNESS!

YOU PUT A VIDEO OF YOURSELF UP ON YOUTUBE?
YEP. AND I'M RACKING UP THE VIEWS! I'M FAMOUS!
COPYRIGHT© 2006 J.D. "Illiad" Frazer HTTP://WWW.USERFRIENDLY.ORG/

WHAT DID YOU DO? WAIT. DON'T TELL ME. I DON'T WANT TO KNOW. I JUST CAN'T BELIEVE ANYONE WOULD WANT TO SEE WHATEVER IT IS YOU WERE DOING. WHO'D WANT TO WATCH A VIDEO OF YOU?

AAUUUUUUUGGHH!! MY EYES!
I HAD NO IDEA HE COULD DO THAT, AND WISH THAT I STILL DIDN"T.

THIS WEBCAM THING THAT STEF HAS GOING HAS GOT TO STOP.
WHY? IS IT DOING ANY REAL HARM?
COPYRIGHT© 2006 J.D. "Illiad" Frazer HTTP://WWW.USERFRIENDLY.ORG/

THINK! ADD THE ELEMENTS IN THE EQUATION! YOUTUBE. DIGG. NET GEEKS WITH A SICK SENSE OF HUMOUR. TOTAL IT ALL UP AND WHAT DO YOU GET?

AAAARRRGGGHH!

OH. HELLO DORK.
SHUT UP. YOU'RE JUST JEALOUS THAT YOU DON'T HAVE FANS.
COPYRIGHT© 2006 J.D. "Illiad" Frazer HTTP://WWW.USERFRIENDLY.ORG/

HEY. I HAVE FANS. TWO IN FACT...ONE ON MY CPU. ANOTHER VENTING MY POWER SUPPLY.

I'M TALKING ABOUT REAL FANS. LIKE MINE!
UNLIKE YOURS. MY FANS MAKE ME COOL.

I DON'T CARE WHAT YOU SAY! I'M ON YOUTUBE AND I'M FAMOUS!
AND WHEN SOMEONE ON THE STREET RECOGNIZES YOU, WHAT ARE THE FIRST FOUR WORDS THEY'LL SAY?
COPYRIGHT © 2006 J.D. "Illiad" Frazer HTTP://WWW.USERFRIENDLY.ORG/

"I LOVED YOUR VIDEO."
I'LL PUT A HUNDRED ON "HEY, YOU'RE THAT DORK!"

I HAVE A FANBASE THAT'LL RECOGNIZE ME AS THE "GUY FROM YOUTUBE." JUST YOU WATCH!
RIIIIIIGHT...
COPYRIGHT © 2006 J.D. "Illiad" Frazer HTTP://WWW.USERFRIENDLY.ORG/

YOU'RE THAT YOUTUBE GUY IN THE ORANGE SPEEDO.
NO I AM NOT!
OKAY, YOU WERE RIGHT. I WAS WRONG. I CAN BE BIG ABOUT IT.

IN AN UNDERHANDED EFFORT TO STIFLE THE DISCOVERY OF MORE PLANETS IN OUR SOLAR SYSTEM, A SMALL CABAL OF ASTRONOMERS MOVE TO ABANDON THE GRECO-ROMAN NAMING SYSTEM IN FAVOUR OF THE AZTEC GODS
A NEW PLANET! WHAT SHALL WE NAME IT?
ACCORDING TO THE NAMING SYSTEM, IT SHOULD BE "TLAHUIZCALPANTECUHTLI"
UserFriendly.Org
COPYRIGHT © 2006 J.D. "Illiad" Frazer HTTP://WWW.USERFRIENDLY.ORG/

The cyan and magenta were bloody awful. When EGA came on the market with 16 colors, it was like a reprieve from Chinese water torture.

HEY SID! DO YOU KNOW IT'S BEEN MORE THAN 25 YEARS SINCE THE LAUNCH OF THE IBM PC?
YEAH. IT WAS AN INTERESTING TIME.
COPYRIGHT© 2006 J.D. "Illiad" Frazer HTTP://WWW.USERFRIENDLY.ORG/

TELL YOU WHAT...BACK THEN WE HAD TO CODE NAKED IN THE MIDDLE OF WINTER. UPHILL BOTH WAYS...
MM-HM.
ACTUALLY, THE **REAL** HORROR WERE THE VILE CYAN AND MAGENTA WE HAD AVAILABLE AS "COLOURS" ON CGA MONITORS.
UM. EWW.

SO SID, WHY **DID** THEY HAVE CYAN AND MAGENTA ALONG WITH BLACK AND WHITE FOR THE ONLY COLOURS ON CGA MONITORS?
HARDWARE AND COST LIMITATIONS AT THE TIME I'D IMAGINE.
COPYRIGHT© 2006 J.D. "Illiad" Frazer HTTP://WWW.USERFRIENDLY.ORG/

ALSO, I THINK IT WAS THE BEST COMPROMISE AT THE TIME. GIVING GRAPHIC ARTISTS SOME CHOICE WHILE KEEPING THE PRICE POINT DOWN.
RIGHT. BECAUSE THERE ARE **LOTS** OF THINGS IN THIS WORLD COLOURED WITH ONLY CYAN AND MAGENTA.
SKY AND MOUNTAINS! YOU YOUNGLINGS HAVE **ZERO** IMAGINATION.

HEY! IS THAT WHAT I THINK IT IS?
YEP. DUG IT OUT OF MY BASEMENT. IT STILL WORKS!
COPYRIGHT© 2006 J.D. "Illiad" Frazer HTTP://WWW.USERFRIENDLY.ORG/

WOW. AN IBM PC 5150! A TINY PIECE OF COMPUTING HISTORY...

THE CITY GUYS LENT ME THEIR HYDRAULIC CRANE TO GET IT HERE.
YEAH. I KINDA WONDERED...

SO THIS IS IT?
YEP. THE ORIGINAL CORNERSTONE OF THE PC MARKET! IT WAS THE MOST ROBUST MACHINE OF ITS TIME.
COPYRIGHT© 2006 J.D. "Illiad" Frazer HTTP://WWW.USERFRIENDLY.ORG/

IT'S FLEXIBLE TOO! I HAVE SOME HACKED FIRST-PERSON SHOOTERS RUNNING ON IT.
RIGHT. AND WHAT'S YOUR FRAMERATE?

SIXTY FRAMES PER HOUR...
SORRY? CAN'T HEAR YOU! SPEAK UP PLEASE!

LOOK SON. YOU DO REALIZE THAT IF YOU WANT A SOLID FOUNDATION IN COMPUTING YOU SHOULD KNOW A BIT ABOUT ITS HISTORY.
COPYRIGHT© 2006 J.D. "Illiad" Frazer HTTP://WWW.USERFRIENDLY.ORG/

THIS IBM PC IS A PERFECT EXAMPLE. GEEKS OF MY GENERATION GOT TO KNOW THE MACHINE REALLY WELL AT BOTH THE SOFTWARE AND HARDWARE LEVEL. IT TAKES TIME, BUT IT'S SO VERY MUCH WORTH IT.

AFTER ALL A.J., ONE **DOES** NEED TO DO SOMETHING OTHER THAN PLAY WORLD OF WARCRAFT.
UM. LIKE WHAT?

IS MY DAD GOING ON ABOUT OLD TECH AGAIN?
I HAPPEN TO BE TEACHING THIS YOUNG MAN SOME VALUES, PEARL. IF YOU DON'T MIND...
COPYRIGHT© 2006 J.D. "Illiad" Frazer HTTP://WWW.USERFRIENDLY.ORG/

IF YOUR GENERATION DOESN'T HAVE A GRASP OF WHERE ALL OF TODAY'S TECH COMES FROM, YOU'LL BE LEFT FLOUNDERING WITHOUT DIRECTION OR PURPOSE. I'M PASSING ON WISDOM FROM THE PAST TO PREPARE YOU KIDS FOR THE FUTURE!

HE HAS A COLLECTION OF ASCII-PORN WOMEN TAPED UP IN HIS OFFICE AT HOME. HE LIKES THE "40-COLUMN CHICKS" THE BEST.
OI! GO TO YOUR ROOM!

FOR ONCE, I PRAY OUR ALIEN OVERLORDS WILL APPLY THE DESTRUCTO-BEAM JUST TO SHUT EVERYONE UP
PLUTO
UserFriendly.Org
COPYRIGHT© 2006 J.D. "Illiad" Frazer HTTP://WWW.USERFRIENDLY.ORG/

"It's a planet!" "No, it isn't!" "Yes, it is!" "No, it isn't!"

GOOD MORNING, ERWIN. WHAT'S IN THE NEWS?

ERWIN? HELLO? ARE YOU IN THERE?

DUDE! BEEFCAKE! **BEEFCAAAKE!**

ERWIN?! WHAT ARE YOU DOING IN THERE?
RE-LIVING A SIMPLER TIME OF 8-BIT DATA BUSES...

UNLIKE MY STINTS IN AN RPN CALCULATOR AND A TAMAGOTCHI, THIS SIMPLE MACHINE PROVIDES ME WITH A CLARITY OF VISION THAT IS UNAVAILABLE IN MORE SOPHISTICATED HARDWARE.

WHAT...YOU **PREFER** IT IN THERE?
YES, BUT THAT'S BECAUSE I'M TERRIBLY "BIOSED." HEH.

Y'KNOW, IT SEEMS A LITTLE CREEPY WITH ERWIN GONE FROM HIS SGI O2 BODY.
I KNOW.

HE'S ALWAYS BEEN IMPULSIVE. AND HE TELLS ME HE **LOVES** BEING IN THE 5150.
BUT WHY? THOSE OLD PCS WEIGH LIKE THEY WERE CARVED FROM IRON BLOCKS.

SEE, NOW THAT'S WHAT **I'M** TALKIN' ABOUT...

THAT LITTLE TWERP OF AN A.I. THINKS IT CAN CLOUT ME OVER THE HEAD WITH IMPUNITY, DOES IT?

I'LL SHOW HIM. I'LL SHOW HIM NEVER TO UNDERESTIMATE THE TRUE POWER OF MARKETING...

craigslist:
FOR SALE CHEAP
Boat Anchor 2.0
Unusual shape, very reliable. Best offer takes it.

GOT A MINUTE?
SURE. WHAT DO YA NEED?

I UNDERSTAND THAT YOU SOLD MY IBM PC 5150. A TREASURED ARTIFACT FROM THE DAYS OF YORE THAT I VIEW WITH NO SMALL DEGREE OF NOSTALGIA AND SENTIMENT.
SO? I GOT YOU A GOOD PRICE.

HALF A ROLL OF FRUIT MENTOS AND A TICKET STUB TO A MILLI VANILLI CONCERT?
THAT'S WHAT I LOVE ABOUT THE FREE MARKET. YOU ALWAYS GET WHAT SOMETHING IS WORTH.

ERWIN?! ARE YOU BACK?
YEAH. I GOT OUT OF THE 5150 JUST IN TIME.

STEF IS GOING TO BE IN FOR SOME EXCITEMENT. CHECK OUT WHAT SID POSTED TO CRAIGSLIST.

"AVAILABLE: BARELY USED SPEEDBUMP IN THE SHAPE OF A MARKETING MANAGER. SHRIEKS WHEN DRIVEN OVER. EXCELLENT UTILITY FOR FAST-FOOD DRIVE-THRUS. YOU HAUL IT AWAY. IT'S YOURS."
I DO LOVE HOW THE FREE MARKET GIVES YOU WHAT SOMETHING IS WORTH.

THE RUMOURED "MANDATORY" STARTUP SOUND FOR WINDOWS VISTA IS IN FACT A VERY CLEVER PLOY TO GET IN ON THE ONLINE MUSIC MARKET...

Windows Vista
Default Startup Sound:
CRAZY FROG
Would you like to buy a different sound from Microsoft for $0.99? Y/N

UserFriendly.Org

HELLO! IT'S LABOUR DAY IN NORTH AMERICA TODAY. SO I GAVE THE REGULAR CREW THE DAY OFF.
COPYRIGHT © 2006 J.D. "Illiad" Frazer HTTP://WWW.USERFRIENDLY.ORG/

WE WERE SUPPOSED TO RUN A TECH SUPPORT STRIP TODAY. BUT WITH GREG HAVING THE DAY OFF. I BROUGHT IN A RETIRED VETERAN ACTOR TO TAKE HIS PLACE. ENJOY!

I'VE INSTALLED VI ON THE SAME MACHINE AS EMACS. NOW WHAT?
WHERE'S THE "KABOOM"? THERE WAS SUPPOSED TO BE AN EARTH SHATTERING "KABOOM!"

AHEM THE INTERNET TECHNOLOGY ADVISORY COMMITTEE WILL NOW COME TO ORDER.
COPYRIGHT © 2006 J.D. "Illiad" Frazer HTTP://WWW.USERFRIENDLY.ORG/

TODAY WE WILL BE ADDRESSING THE NETWORK NEUTRALITY ISSUE THAT IS BEFORE CONGRESS. HOWEVER, BEFORE WE BEGIN, WOULD THE GENTLEMAN IN THE FRONT ROW PLEASE IDENTIFY HIMSELF?

SID DABSTER, MR. CHAIRMAN. I'M HERE AS A TECHNOLOGY CONSULTANT.
OH, HOW EXCELLENT. WE'LL NEED ONE OF THOSE.

THE CHAIR RECOGNIZES SENATOR TED STEVENS OF ALASKA.
MR. CHAIRMAN, I MUST PROTEST THE INCLUSION OF MR. DABSTER IN THIS COMMITTEE.
COPYRIGHT © 2006 J.D. "Illiad" Frazer HTTP://WWW.USERFRIENDLY.ORG/

THIS MATTER OF THE INTERNETS IS VERY SERIOUS INDEED! WHAT CREDENTIALS DOES MR. DABSTER BRING TO THIS AUGUST TABLE?

I'VE BEEN A NETWORK ENGINEER FOR THIRTY YEARS, AND A TECHNOLOGIST FOR NEARLY FORTY SENATOR...
SEE? NOT A SINGLE THING ABOUT TUBE-OLOGY!

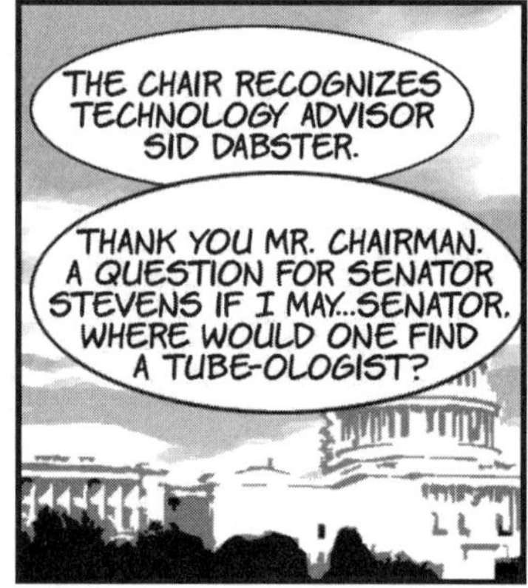
THE CHAIR RECOGNIZES TECHNOLOGY ADVISOR SID DABSTER.
THANK YOU MR. CHAIRMAN. A QUESTION FOR SENATOR STEVENS IF I MAY...SENATOR, WHERE WOULD ONE FIND A TUBE-OLOGIST?
COPYRIGHT © 2006 J.D. "Illiad" Frazer HTTP://WWW.USERFRIENDLY.ORG/

SENATOR? A QUESTION WAS POSED.
YES, YES. I'M THINKING MY COUSIN CLARENCE. HE'S THE VEEP OF TUBES OVER AT VERIZON. AND HE WEARS A NICER SUIT THAN THIS DABSTER FELLOW.

MR. CHAIRMAN. I HAVE SOMETHING TO PROPOSE RELEVANT TO THIS ISSUE.
BY ALL MEANS. THE CHAIR RECOGNIZES MR. SID DABSTER.

COPYRIGHT© 2006 J.D. "Illiad" Frazer HTTP://WWW.USERFRIENDLY.ORG/
AS A TECHNOLOGIST AND SOMEONE WHO VALUES NET NEUTRALITY HIGHLY. I THINK IT BEHOOVES THE COMMITTEE TO RECOMMEND THE MOST PRACTICAL SOLUTION GIVEN THE FORCES AT WORK HERE.

I RECOMMEND THAT THE CABLECOS AND TELCOS BE GRANTED FULL RIGHTS TO PRIORITIZE DATA THAT FLOWS THROUGH THEIR. UM. TUBES.
THE CHAIR DOES NOT RECOGNIZE THIS PARALLEL UNIVERSE. YOU MUST BE LIKE THAT SPOCK GUY WITH THE BEARD.

THE CHAIR RECOGNIZES SENATOR TED STEVENS.
THANK YOU MR. CHAIRMAN. MR. DABSTER. I MUST LAUD YOUR RECOMMENDATION! I AM GLAD THAT THERE ARE COMPUTER PEOPLE LIKE YOURSELF WITH SOME SENSE!

COPYRIGHT© 2006 J.D. "Illiad" Frazer HTTP://WWW.USERFRIENDLY.ORG/
THANK YOU SENATOR. IT JUST SEEMED OBVIOUS TO ME. RATHER THAN FIGHT IT OUT. I FIGURE IT BEST TO JUST ALLOW FOR WHAT THE CABLECOS WANT.
IF THEY CONTROL THE DATA ON THEIR PIPES. THEY LOSE COMMON CARRIER STATUS.

...OH. UM...
WHICH MEANS THAT VERIZON ET. AL. WILL BE LEGALLY RESPONSIBLE FOR ALL OF THE LLAMA PORN ON THE NET.
THE CHAIR IS NOW LAUGHING HYSTERICALLY IN THE THIRD PERSON.

IN AN ILLUSTRATION OF THE CURSE OF GENIUS AND IMAGINATION, DURING A POWER OUTAGE DR. STEPHEN HAWKING REALIZES THAT ALL OF THE DARK MATTER IN THE UNIVERSE MAY IN FACT BE GRUES...
COPYRIGHT© 2006 J.D. "Illiad" Frazer HTTP://WWW.USERFRIENDLY.ORG/
UserFriendly.Org

I used to have a subscription. AdCritic is an excellent site for anyone with an interest in advertising. For a while, I made my living as a creative director. Ads paid the bills.

SERVING ONLINE VIDEOS AT A RATE OF 100 MILLION A DAY. YOUTUBE HAS BECOME THE DARLING OF THE INTERNET. HOWEVER, NOT ALL THAT GLITTERS IS GOLD. OR EVEN TINFOIL...
COPYRIGHT © 2006 J.D. "Illiad" Frazer HTTP://WWW.USERFRIENDLY.ORG/

YOUTUBE'S STAGGERING BANDWIDTH BILLS NEED TO BE PAID. THE FOUNDERS ARE NOW CONSIDERING THE ADDITION OF SHORT VIDEO ADS TO GENERATE MUCH-NEEDED REVENUE TO KEEP THE 19-MONTH OLD COMPANY ALIVE.

THAT'S KINDA DUMB. NO-ONE LIKES WATCHING COMMERCIALS.
RIGHT. NO ONE. LIKE THE PEOPLE WHO PAY $100 A YEAR TO ADCRITIC.COM.

IF YOUTUBE DOESN'T WANT TO GO WITH COMMERCIALS, THEY COULD JUST CHARGE AN ANNUAL FEE FOR ACCESS.
RIGHT. IMAGINE ASKING THE AVERAGE INTERNET USER TO PAY FOR CONTENT.
COPYRIGHT © 2006 J.D. "Illiad" Frazer HTTP://WWW.USERFRIENDLY.ORG/

I'M JUST NOT HAVING ANY PROBLEMS.
TONIGHT: SENATOR TED STEVENS SAYS THE INTERNET HAS FREE MILK AND HONEY FLOWING THROUGH IT'S TUBES!
I MEANT OTHER THAN PORN.

HELLO, WATER BAG.
OH CRIPES, **YOU** AGAIN?
I'M IN CRISIS. IT USED TO BE JUST THE TRINITY: COLA, COFFEE AND FOR THE EXTREME CROWD, JOLT.
COPYRIGHT © 2006 J.D. "Illiad" Frazer HTTP://WWW.USERFRIENDLY.ORG/

NOW THERE'S RED BULL, XENERGY, REDLINE, BAWLS... A VERITABLE CORNUCOPIA OF ORALLY-INGESTED ADDICTIONS. OH, AND ANOTHER ONE: "PIMP JUICE."

HAVING CHOICE OF ADDICTION IS AN INALIENABLE RIGHT, DUDE.
PIMP JUICE? **PIMP JUICE?!** THERE'S NO INNOCENCE IN ADDICTION ANYMORE!

"CHOICE" YOU SAY. HMPH! I SUPPOSE THAT'S THE CONSUMER MANTRA FOR THE 21ST CENTURY. FINE, I'LL PLAY ALONG.
COPYRIGHT © 2006 J.D. "Illiad" Frazer HTTP://WWW.USERFRIENDLY.ORG/

NOT THAT I CONDONE OR ENJOY THIS YOU UNDERSTAND...

HERE I AM. PIMP JUICE, YO.
ICAN'TSEEYOU! ICAN'TSEEYOU! ICAN'TSEEYOU! ICAN'TSEEYOU!

UM, Y'KNOW, THE PIMP OUTFIT JUST ISN'T WORKING FOR ME.
YEAH. SORRY. I'M STILL HAVING TROUBLE GETTING MY HEAD AROUND THE WHOLE ENERGY DRINK THING.

THE ADDICTIONS ARE LARGELY PSYCHOLOGICAL, AND THAT DOESN'T BODE WELL FOR AN ELEMENTAL EVIL LIKE ME.
LET ME TRY ANOTHER OUTFIT.

HEY...THERE'S A NEW DRINK CALLED "NAKED HAIRY GUY"...
I'LL GET ADDICTED! YOU DON'T HAVE TO DRESS UP!

WHAT DO ALL OF THESE ENERGY DRINKS HAVE THAT CHARGE PEOPLE UP?
GUARANA, GINSENG, TAURINE, MALTODEXTRIN...

ALTHOUGH INTERESTINGLY, MANY OF THEM SIMPLY HAVE SUGAR AS THE NUMBER ONE INGREDIENT.

I MIGHT AS WELL JUST CHEW A SUGAR CU-GAAH!
I PREFER "STAMINA EXTENDER ENERGY SOLID" THANK YOU VERY MUCH.

THE DAY THAT THE ORIGINAL STAR TREK SERIES IS RE-RELEASED IN HIGH-DEFINITION, A LONG-STANDING MYSTERY WILL AT LAST BE SOLVED.

YO! WE HAVE THE COMBINATION TO CAPTAIN KIRK'S SAFE!
STAR TREK PARTY
no romulans allowed

UserFriendly.Org

IN THE MATTER OF E360INSIGHT V. SPAMHAUS. WHEREIN E360 IS SUING SPAMHAUS FOR CAUSING "MASSIVE HARM" TO ITS BUSINESS...
SPAMHAUS HAS NO REPRESENTATION HERE, YOUR HONOUR.

COPYRIGHT© 2006 J.D. "Illiad" Frazer HTTP://WWW.USERFRIENDLY.ORG/
OH.
I SUPPOSE YOUR CLIENT WINS BY DEFAULT THEN.

...WHICH RATHER SQUARELY SUITS HIS SENSE OF ENTITLEMENT, DOESN'T IT.
I MOVE TO HAVE YOU LABELLED AS "NASTY" YOUR HONOUR.

DUE TO THE DEFAULT JUDGEMENT, I RULE THAT SPAMHAUS PAY THE PLAINTIFF $11.7 MILLION FOR TORTIOUS INTERFERENCE, PLUS $2000 IN LEGAL FEES. I DENY THE MOTION FOR $15 MILLION IN PUNITIVE DAMAGES.

COPYRIGHT© 2006 J.D. "Illiad" Frazer HTTP://WWW.USERFRIENDLY.ORG/
I'M NOT PLEASED ABOUT HAVING TO GIVE YOUR CLIENT THE WIN, COUNSELOR.
HOWEVER, GIVEN THAT SPAMHAUS IS IN THE U.K., AND IS NOT SUBJECT TO U.S. LAWS, I WONDER HOW YOUR CLIENT INTENDS TO COLLECT.

MY CLIENT HAS SEVERAL CONNECTIONS TO ALTERNATIVE COLLECTION AGENCIES IN NIGERIA YOUR HONOUR.
AHH. WELL. COMPLIMENTS OF THE SEASON THEN.

YOU GUYS LOOK LIKE YOU HAD FUN...
IT WAS A HECK OF A PIRATE PARTY.
RUM MAKES THE LOBES THROB.

COPYRIGHT© 2006 J.D. "Illiad" Frazer HTTP://WWW.USERFRIENDLY.ORG/
YOU DRANK **RUM**, LI'L GUY? I THOUGHT **MILK** WAS YOUR POISON.
I'M THINKIN' HE'LL NEED A BIT OF **ARRR AND ARRRR!!**

ERWIN, THAT PIRATE STUFF WAS OVER YESTERDAY.
EEEEEG
AHOY! THAR SHE BLOWS CHUNKS!

This one became a very popular UF t-shirt, in glorious color! Someone asked me why I was encouraging cannibalism. I'm not: cannibalism involves the consumption of one's own species.

HEY, DID YOU HEAR ABOUT SPAMHAUS BEING FINED BY A U.S. COURT FOR BLACKLISTING A SPAMMER?
YEAH, IT'S PRETTY RETARDED IF YOU ASK ME.

COPYRIGHT© 2006 J.D. "Illiad" Frazer HTTP://WWW.USERFRIENDLY.ORG/
PITR GOT SO ANNOYED HE WORKED OUT A WAY TO PUT SPAMMERS IN THEIR PLACE WHILE MAKING THEM USEFUL TO SOCIETY.
OH? HOW?
WELL, A PICTURE IS WORTH A THOUSAND WORDS...

SPAMMER
THE OTHER PINK MEAT

...AND HE REPLIED. "OH! YOU SAID TECHNOLOGIST!"
HEH! GOOD ONE!
LOL!
COPYRIGHT © 2006 J.D. "Illiad" Frazer HTTP://WWW.USERFRIENDLY.ORG/

DID YOU ACTUALLY JUST SAY "LOL" OUT LOUD?
NO. THAT WOULD BE "LOLOL."
AND ANOTHER INNOCENT KITTEN DIES.

STEF, USING ONLINE SHORTHAND IS ONE THING. BUT SAYING THEM OUT LOUD BORDERS ON THE SQUALID!
HYPOCRITE.
COPYRIGHT © 2006 J.D. "Illiad" Frazer HTTP://WWW.USERFRIENDLY.ORG/

I BEG YOUR PARDON? I DON'T USE MESSAGING ACRONYMS IN NORMAL SPEECH!

HOW ABOUT "RTFM"?
HOW ABOUT YOU "STFU"?

THE MYSTERIOUS DEBRIS SPOTTED NEAR THE SHUTTLE ATLANTIS WAS REPORTED BY THE GOVERNMENT AS "TRASH FROM THE CARGO BAY"
UserFriendly.Org
COPYRIGHT © 2006 J.D. "Illiad" Frazer HTTP://WWW.USERFRIENDLY.ORG/

IT'S 7:30AM...O MERCIFUL GODS...FRESH COFFEE!!
SSCHLUURRRRRP
COPYRIGHT © 2006 J.D. "Illiad" Frazer HTTP://WWW.USERFRIENDLY.ORG/

GAH!! WHAT HELLACIOUS ICHOR IS THIS?!

IT'S FLAVOURED COFFEE.
COFFEE ALREADY HAS FLAVOUR! IT TASTES LIKE COFFEE!!

LOOK SID. I WAS JUST TRYING TO ADD A LITTLE VARIETY TO OUR USUAL CUP OF JOE...
DESECRATOR!
COPYRIGHT © 2006 J.D. "Illiad" Frazer HTTP://WWW.USERFRIENDLY.ORG/

COME NOW. CAN YOU REALLY SAY THAT A LITTLE IRISH CREME DOESN'T BRIGHTEN UP YOUR MORNING?

COBB. NOTHING BRIGHTENS UP MY MORNING. COFFEE SIMPLY PROVIDES A SHADE OF GRAY JUST ABOVE THE PITCH-BLACK OF THE INFINITE DEPTHS OF THE ABYSS.
SO THAT WOULD BE A "YES"...

SID. I HAVE TO ASK. AND PLEASE UNDERSTAND THAT I DON'T MEAN TO OFFEND...
COPYRIGHT © 2006 J.D. "Illiad" Frazer HTTP://WWW.USERFRIENDLY.ORG/

...BUT YOUR MILITANCY ABOUT YOUR MORNING COFFEE SEEMS KIND OF RETARDED TO ME. SAY YOU DON'T HAVE COFFEE FOR A DAY...SO WHAT?

AND WHAT'S WITH THE PLASTIC BAG?

I...CAN'T... ...BREATHE!
OH. SO NOW YOU UNDERSTAND.

I DO LOVE MY LITTLE WAP DEVICES. I CAN CHAT ALL DAY. ALL NIGHT...
COPYRIGHT © 2006 J.D. "Illiad" Frazer HTTP://WWW.USERFRIENDLY.ORG/

TO THINK. NOT A HUNDRED YEARS AGO THIS SORT OF THING WAS THE STUFF OF FANTASY. WE'RE A REALLY DEVELOPED CIVILIZATION NOW...I WONDER WHAT OUR LEGACY WILL BE?

A FAZILLION YEARS IN THE FUTURE...
IT'S ONE OF THEIR OLD COMMUNICATION DEVICES. THE LAST MESSAGE SENT FROM THIS UNIT READ: "HEY HOW R U I LOVE TEH INTERNETS LOL"

IS THAT A BLACKBERRY? IT LOOKS ALL HACKED AND STUFF AND IT HAS WEIRD WIRES AND LEDS COMING OFF IT.

SPIFFY! WHAT A COOL DISPLAY! AND ALL THOSE RED LIGHTS! I WONDER WHAT THIS BUTTON DOES?

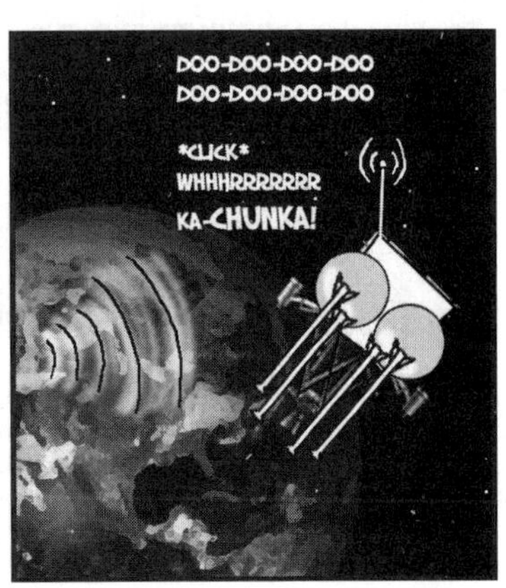
DOO-DOO-DOO-DOO
DOO-DOO-DOO-DOO
CLICK
WHHHRRRRRRR
KA-CHUNKA!

WHAT DID YOU WANT TO SHOW ME?
IS WERY STRANGE. WAS HERE FIVE MINUTES AGO...

EXACTLY WHAT WAS IT?
WAS CONTROL FOR ORBITAL CROWBAR SATELLITE...

THIS IS A PRETTY COOL SHOOT-EM UP. BUT IT'S TAKING FOREVER TO GET TO THE BONUS ROUND...
ANNIHILATED

TODAY, SOME CARTOONIST SOMEWHERE WILL HAVE JUST COMPLETED CONVERTING ALL EIGHT GAJILLION OF HIS CARTOONS FROM *GIF* TO *PNG* SO THAT HE CAN PROUDLY CLAIM TO USE ONLY FREE FORMATS IN HIS WORK.

THIS IS TECH NEWS FOR OCTOBER 1, 2006. THE FINAL PATENT CLAIM ON THE "GIF" FORMAT HAS FINALLY EXPIRED...

UserFriendly.Org

COMRADE, HAVE YOU--YOU ARE DOINK WHAT WITH THAT?!
OH HEY PITR. I SAW THIS ON YOUR DESK AND STARTED TO FIDDLE WITH IT. I HOPE YOU DON'T MIND.
COPYRIGHT © 2006 J.D. "Illiad" Frazer HTTP://WWW.USERFRIENDLY.ORG/

NOT MINDINK?! ARE YOU HAVINK ANY IDEA THIS THING YOU HOLD IT IS WHAT?!?

A HANDHELD GAME SYSTEM WITH JUST ONE GAME. DOES IT EVEN HAVE AN END?
DA. TARGET OWN LOCATION AND LIKE IN NETHACK. YOU WILL "ASCEND."

PLEASE TO BE TELLINK ME YOU HAVE NOT BEEN PLAYINK WITH IT LONG.
NOT LONG. NO.
COPYRIGHT © 2006 J.D. "Illiad" Frazer HTTP://WWW.USERFRIENDLY.ORG/

PHEW

ALL IS NOT LOST. TO BE GIVINK BACK. PLEASE.
SO HOW DO YOU RELOAD YOUR SATELLITE WHEN YOU'RE OUT OF AMMO?

AM HAVINK BIG PROBLEM. SATELLITE. IT IS NOW EMPTY OF AMMUNITION. AND HAVE NO SOURCE FOR HEAVY METAL OBJECTS TO DROP FROM ORBIT.
YEAH. THAT DOES SUCK.
COPYRIGHT © 2006 J.D. "Illiad" Frazer HTTP://WWW.USERFRIENDLY.ORG/

NO!

DO YOU STILL USE E-MAIL? IF YOU DO. YOU'RE. LIKE. OLD.
WHAT?
COPYRIGHT © 2006 J.D. "Illiad" Frazer HTTP://WWW.USERFRIENDLY.ORG/

THERE'S A STORY IN THE NEWS THAT CLAIMS TEENAGERS THINK E-MAIL IS FOR OLD PEOPLE. THEY DON'T LIKE E-MAIL. WHEN THEY TALK TO THEIR FRIENDS. THEY LIKE TO USE I.M. SERVICES.

GIVEN HOW MUCH KIDS WANT INSTANT GRATIFICATION. YOU'D THINK WE'D HAVE A TECHNOLOGY THAT WAS BETTER THAN MESSAGING. LIKE...I DUNNO... INSTANT VOICE OVER WIRE COMMUNICATIONS!
DOES NASTINESS COME WITH AGE?

HELLO EVERYONE! ERWIN AND I ARE ABOUT TO PERFORM AN EXPERIMENT! EXPERTS ARE CLAIMING THAT MYSPACE IS A PRIME LOCATION FOR IDENTITY THEFT. AND WE'RE GOING TO SEE HOW TRUE THIS IS.

ERWIN, PLEASE CREATE AN ACCOUNT FOR US ON MYSPACE.
WORKING...DONE.

OKAY! FOR OUR EXPERIMENT, WE WILL BE ADOPTING THE PERSONA OF "SUGARY SECRET," A SEMI-PRO "POLE ARTIST" THAT--I BEG YOUR PARDON...
CAN'T BAIT THE HOOK WITH OLD CARDBOARD, DUDE.

YOU SEE, MYSPACE IS A TARGET-RICH ENVIRONMENT FOR IDENTITY THIEVES BECAUSE SO MANY PEOPLE PUT THEIR PERSONAL DETAILS ON THEIR PAGES!
WE'RE GOING TO SEE IF ANYONE TRIES TO STEAL "SUGARY'S" IDENTITY.

HOW'S OUR PROFILE COMING, ERWIN?
DETAILS DONE AND THE PHOTOS ARE UPLOADED.
YO. WE HAVE EMAIL!

GOOD HEAVENS. EMAIL FROM WHOM?
THIRTY-SEVEN GUYS WHO ARE GIVING "SUGARY" THEIR CREDIT CARD DETAILS...

THE WALL STREET JOURNAL.
TECHNOLOGY
Google to buy YouTube?
Google
YouTube Broadcast Yourself
$1.6 Billion for videos of teens in angst...
THE WALL STREET JOURNAL.
© 2005 Dow Jones & Company, All Rights Reserved
VOL. CCXLII
**** $1.00
Massive Run on Salt sends Prices Skyrocketing
Most Demand for Salt Grains, Occasional Buyouts of Entire Salt Mines
Commodity Price: Salt

UserFriendly.Org

LOOK AT THIS! OUR PAGE ON MYSPACE IS GETTING NEW FRIENDS BY THE SECOND!
I CAN SEE HOW THIS IS QUITE ADDICTIVE. OOOOH...
COPYRIGHT © 2006 J.D. "Illiad" Frazer HTTP://WWW.USERFRIENDLY.ORG/

THAP
THAP
TAPP
TAPP
THAP
TAPP
THAP
THAP
THAP
TAPP
TAPP
TAPPY
TAP

GOOD HEAVENS! THREE HUNDRED NEW FRIENDS IN 60 SECONDS?!
AND NOW MY REFRESH BUTTON NEEDS TO SMOKE A CIGARETTE.

HAS ANYONE TRIED TO STEAL THE IDENTITY OF "SUGARY SECRETS"?
CHECKING...
COPYRIGHT © 2006 J.D. "Illiad" Frazer HTTP://WWW.USERFRIENDLY.ORG/

NOTHING IN THE CREDIT BUREAUS... NO BANK WITHDRAWALS... MMMM...NOPE.

NOT UNLESS YOU COUNT THE FOURTEEN HUNDRED GUYS ON THE INTARWEB CLAIMING TO BE HER BOYFRIEND IN THEIR BLOGS.
NO IDENTITY THEFT AT ALL. HOW UNSATISFYING.

WOW...PRETTY!
I PRE-ORDERED NEVERWINTER NIGHTS 2 AND GOT THE TOOLKIT IN ADVANCE OF THE GAME RELEASE.
COPYRIGHT © 2006 J.D. "Illiad" Frazer HTTP://WWW.USERFRIENDLY.ORG/

SO YOU CAN BUILD AN ADVENTURE MODULE BEFORE THE GAME COMES OUT?
YEAH...

THAT'S FANTASTIC! WHY AREN'T YOU MORE EXCITED?
BECAUSE I'M GETTING SIX FRAMES PER MINUTE IN THE TOOLKIT.

NWN2 IS EXPENSIVE. RETAIL PRICE: FIVE HUNDRED AND SIXTY DOLLARS.
COPYRIGHT © 2006 J.D. "Illiad" Frazer HTTP://WWW.USERFRIENDLY.ORG/

SIXTY FOR THE GAME AND FIVE HUNDRED FOR THE NEW VIDEO CARD?
YEAH.

ACTUALLY, MAKE THAT SIX HUNDRED EVEN. SIXTY FOR THE GAME, FIVE HUNDRED FOR THE VIDEO CARD AND FORTY BUCKS TO BADLY TATTOO "PWNED GAME DORK" ON MY FOREHEAD.

NWN2! HA! I'M IN A CONTEST TO WRITE THE BEST VIRAL MARKETING CATCHPHRASE FOR THAT GAME!
OH?

YEAH. I NEED SOMETHING SNAPPY AND MEME-LIKE. YOU KNOW. LIKE "GRAY IS THE NEW BLACK."
NWN2...NWN2...

"NWN2...IS THE NEW NWN!" I'M BRILLIANT!
WORKING ON YOUR MASTERS DEGREE IN OBVIOUS I SEE.

DID YOU EVEN PLAY THE FIRST NWN?
OF COURSE I DID. BUT I DIDN'T LIKE IT MUCH. SOME OF THOSE DUNGEON LEVELS HAD LAVA.

STEF. THE WAY THE ENGINE WAS WRITTEN THERE WAS NO WAY YOUR CHARACTER COULD STEP INTO ANY LIQUID. INCLUDING LAVA.
WELL IT HAPPENED! SO SHUT UP!
SHUT UP!!

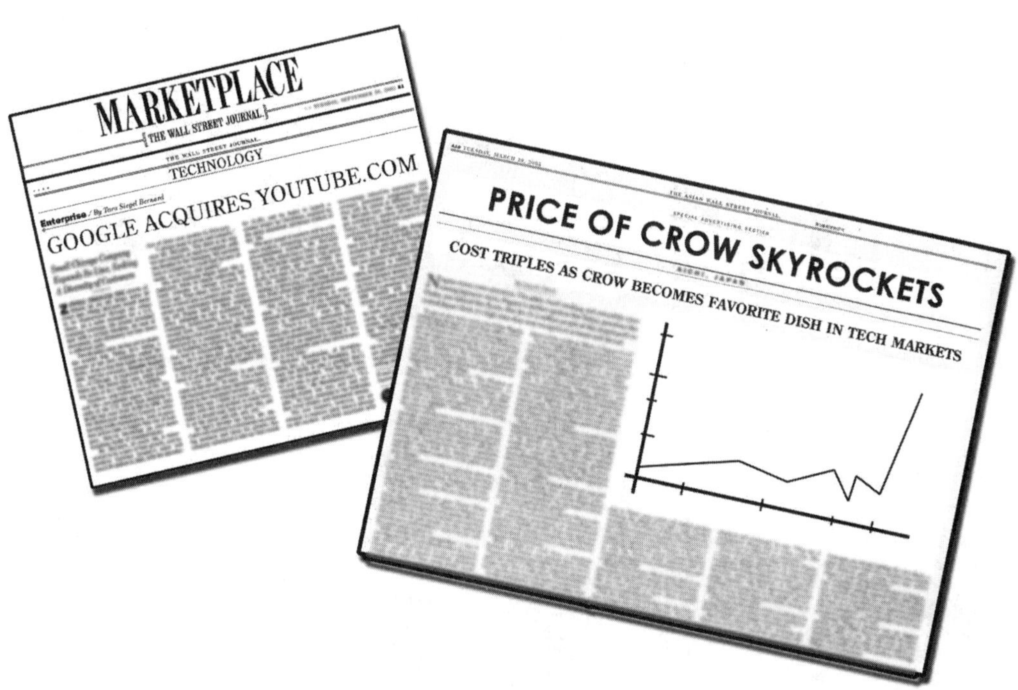
MARKETPLACE
THE WALL STREET JOURNAL.
TECHNOLOGY
GOOGLE ACQUIRES YOUTUBE.COM
PRICE OF CROW SKYROCKETS
COST TRIPLES AS CROW BECOMES FAVORITE DISH IN TECH MARKETS

UserFriendly.Org

YOUNG COMRADE, AM THINKINK YOU ARE MAKINK WERY NICE WORLD. AM LOOKINK FORWARD TO PLAYINK.
THANKS PITR.
COPYRIGHT © 2006 J.D. "Illiad" Frazer HTTP://WWW.USERFRIENDLY.ORG/

DIDN'T YOU GUYS HEAR? ATARI CHOSE NOT TO RELEASE A LINUX VERSION OF NWN2. EVER.

PITR! SLAY THEM!
OH, DA, I SHALL DO THIS FOR YOU. OH DEAR. AM REMEMBERINK MY SATELLITE IS OUT OF AMMO! AM WONDERINK HOW THIS HAPPENED?

YE FLIPPING GODS OF RAIN AND THUNDER! AM I READING THAT NUMBER RIGHT?
YOU BET! THAT'S ONE PETABYTE OF STORAGE SPACE AT MY FINGERTIPS.
COPYRIGHT © 2006 J.D. "Illiad" Frazer HTTP://WWW.USERFRIENDLY.ORG/

WATCHA THINK I SHOULD DO WITH IT?

JUST TOSSING AN IDEA OUT THERE...MAYBE BACKING UP OUR CLIENTS' DATA?
NO NO NO! WE HAVE TO DO SOMETHING COOL! LIKE DOWN-LOADING GEOCITIES!

HOW'S THE PETABYTE?
...IT'S FULL. HOW CAN IT BE FULL?
COPYRIGHT © 2006 J.D. "Illiad" Frazer HTTP://WWW.USERFRIENDLY.ORG/

YOU RAN A BACKUP LAST NIGHT, RIGHT?
YES. THE JOB WAS HALTED BECAUSE THERE'S NO MORE DISK SPACE.

MIKE...YOU HAVE YOUR BACKUP BACKING UP YOUR BACKUPS.
RECURSIVES! SPOILED AGAIN!

HEY GET THIS: SOMEONE FROM THE JOINT ECONOMIC COMMITTEE IN THE U.S. GOVERNMENT IS CONSIDER-ING THE POSSIBILITY OF TAXING MONEY YOU ACCUMULATE IN MMORPGS.
the wibble
COPYRIGHT © 2006 J.D. "Illiad" Frazer HTTP://WWW.USERFRIENDLY.ORG/

HEH. IF YOU CAN TAX IT, YOU KNOW WHO ELSE IS GOING TO MOVE IN.

NICE CASTLE. BE A SHAME IF SOMETHING HAPPENED TO IT...

TECH SUPPORT. MY NAME IS GREG AND I WILL BE YOUR CUSPIDOR TODAY.
HI. I'M WRITING A PROFILE FOR A DATING SITE AND NEED SOME HELP WITH IT.
COPYRIGHT© 2006 J.D. "Illiad" Frazer HTTP://WWW.USERFRIENDLY.ORG/

"ATTRACTIVE FEMALE. AVERAGE BUILD, DARK HAIR. SEEKING A LIFEMATE. I LOVE TO LAUGH AND I LIKE TO HAVE FUN. WRITE ME!"

SO? WHAT DO YOU THINK?
I THINK I NEED TO FIND A KINDER WAY TO ASK IF YOU KNOW MANY PEOPLE WHO HATE IT WHEN THEY LAUGH AND WHO ABSOLUTELY DESPISE HAVING FUN.

OKAY SMARTY-PANTS. WHAT SHOULD I SAY IN MY AD THEN?
HOW ABOUT SOMETHING A LITTLE MORE SUBSTANTIAL ABOUT WHO YOU ARE AS A PERSON?
COPYRIGHT© 2006 J.D. "Illiad" Frazer HTTP://WWW.USERFRIENDLY.ORG/

I COULD SAY I LOVE THE OUTDOORS.
OH YES! AND YOU CAN ADD THAT YOU LOVE TO BREATHE! YE GODS. YOU'LL BE SCOOPED UP IN NO TIME!

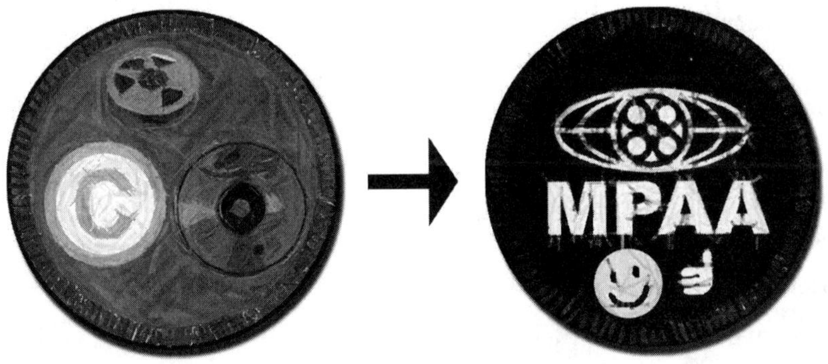
THE MPAA "RESPECT COPYRIGHTS" ACTIVITY PATCH FOR THE BOY SCOUTS OF AMERICA IS MERELY THE FIRST STEP TOWARDS THE MUCH COVETED "WHO NEEDS CONSUMER RIGHTS?" PATCH.
MPAA
COPYRIGHT© 2006 J.D. "Illiad" Frazer HTTP://WWW.USERFRIENDLY.ORG/
UserFriendly.Org

Modern copyright is so fraught with crapola that no single cartoon can do it justice. It's a complex, difficult discussion, but in brief I am for shorter limits on copyright, and more consumer protection. Disney and Time Warner can go blow it out their backsides.

KNOCK KNOCK KNOCK!
I'M COMING. I'M COMING!
COPYRIGHT© 2006 J.D. "Illiad" Frazer HTTP://WWW.USERFRIENDLY.ORG/

LOOK. I'M NOT INTERESTED IN BECOMING RELIGIOUS...
OH. I'M NOT A JEHOVAH'S WITNESS OR ANYTHING LIKE THAT.

WHY DO I GET THE SENSE THAT I'M GOING TO WISH YOU'RE WITH THE HARE KRISHNA?
WOULD YOU LIKE TO BUY A SUBSCRIPTION TO "WEB 2.0 MEATBLOG"?

LOOK MISTER. "WEB 2.0" WOULD BE BETTER NAMED "BUBBLE 2.0" - THINK OF THE PARALLELS!
COPYRIGHT© 2006 J.D. "Illiad" Frazer HTTP://WWW.USERFRIENDLY.ORG/

EMPTY PROMISES! VAGUE CONCEPTS! MASSIVE INVESTMENT! NO REVENUE AND A GAZILLION BUZZPHRASES!

THERE'S NO PARALLEL. WEB 2.0 IS A SYNERGY OF PARADIGMS IN A FORWARD-LOOKING SOCIAL MATRIX.
OH! WELL IN THAT CASE I'D BETTER GET ME SOME WEB 2.0 SHARES!

LOOK MISTER. "WEB 2.0" WOULD BE BETTER NAMED "BUBBLE 2.0" - THINK OF THE PARALLELS!
COPYRIGHT© 2006 J.D. "Illiad" Frazer HTTP://WWW.USERFRIENDLY.ORG/

EMPTY PROMISES! VAGUE CONCEPTS! MASSIVE INVESTMENT! NO REVENUE AND A GAZILLION BUZZPHRASES!

THERE'S NO PARALLEL. WEB 2.0 IS A SYNERGY OF PARADIGMS IN A FORWARD-LOOKING SOCIAL MATRIX.
OH! WELL IN THAT CASE I'D BETTER GET ME SOME WEB 2.0 SHARES!

THE MAGAZINE COVERS THE NEW SOCIAL DYNAMIC OF THE WEB AND FEATURES SOME OF THE FINEST IN TECH JOURNALISM TODAY!
HOW ABOUT A THREE-MONTH TRIAL?
NO! NOW GO AWAY!
COPYRIGHT© 2006 J.D. "Illiad" Frazer HTTP://WWW.USERFRIENDLY.ORG/

SLAM!

EVERY ISSUE ALSO HAS HOT FEMALE SYSADMINS.
I'LL TAKE A YEAR'S SUBSCRIPTION.

WHIPPING BOY LINE. GREG SPEAKING.
HELLO. I REWROTE MY AD FOR THE DATING SITE...
COPYRIGHT © 2006 J.D. "Illiad" Frazer HTTP://WWW.USERFRIENDLY.ORG/

"HEINLEIN'S 'FRIDAY' PERSONALITY. DARK HAIR AND HUGE... TRACTS OF LAND SEEKING MALE ADVENTURER WITH WHICH TO EXPLORE REALMS FORGOTTEN. LET'S GO FIND THE GRAIL AND I'LL BE YOUR ZOOT."

WOULD THAT GET YOU INTERESTED?
HECK YES! I'M ALREADY IN LOVE WITH YOU FOR YOUR REFERENCES!

WELL DONE ON THE NEW AD! NOW ALL YOU NEED TO DO IS UPLOAD IT TO YOUR ACCOUNT ON THE DATING SITE.
COPYRIGHT © 2006 J.D. "Illiad" Frazer HTTP://WWW.USERFRIENDLY.ORG/

THANK YOU! I'LL GO UPLOAD THE AD RIGHT NOW!

HEY! I HAVE AN EMAIL ALREADY! FROM SOMEONE NAMED "GOODTIME GREG"...
WELL CAN YOU BEAT THAT...

THE LATEST DRM-DEFEATING KIT FOR APPLE'S ITUNES.

UserFriendly.Org

Really. Audio Out to Line In. DRM bypassed.

What did I tell you about punctuation humor?!

THAT'S AN ODD SHIRT...
IT'S FOR HALLOWE'EN. I'M GOING AS THE ACTRESS TILDA SWINTON.
~swinton
COPYRIGHT© 2006 J.D. "Illiad" Frazer HTTP://WWW.USERFRIENDLY.ORG/

OH DEAR. AND YOU MUST BE...
YEP. HASH GORDON!
GORDON

OH, A.J....THANK THE GODS YOU'RE NOT WEARING ONE OF THOSE RETARDED SHIRTS...WHAT'S THAT OVER YOUR HEAD?
^
I'M CARROT -TOP!

TRICK OR TREAT!
PRETEND I AM A DELL LAPTOP
Children WILL Be fed to the troll!
COPYRIGHT© 2006 J.D. "Illiad" Frazer HTTP://WWW.USERFRIENDLY.ORG/

TRICK.
PRETEND I AM A DELL LAPTOP
Children WILL Be fed to the troll!

ERWIN. WHERE ARE YOU GOING?
SLAMM!
WE HAVE TO LEAVE. FAST. I REFILLED PITR'S CROWBAR SATELLITE.

STEF?!
WHAT THE HECK HAPPENED TO YOU? AND WHY DO YOU SMELL LIKE...UHH...ROASTED CHICKEN MANURE?
COPYRIGHT© 2006 J.D. "Illiad" Frazer HTTP://WWW.USERFRIENDLY.ORG/

THE SKY FELL. STINKILY. IMAGINE HOW MUCH FUN IT IS FOR ME TO OPEN MY MOUTH RIGHT NOW.

ERWIN. I THOUGHT YOU SAID YOU USED PITR'S CROWBAR SATELLITE.
YES. AND I SAID I REFILLED IT. I DIDN'T SAY WITH WHAT.

PROBLEM?
I CAN'T TURN ON THIS LAMP.
COPYRIGHT© 2006 J.D. "Illiad" Frazer HTTP://WWW.USERFRIENDLY.ORG/

HAVE YOU CHECKED THE BULB? MAYBE THE TUNGSTEN IS COOKED.
THE SWITCH IS KIND OF MUSHY.

I'M GOING TO PULL THE DAMN THING APART. MAYBE THERE'S A FRIED RESISTOR OR SOMETHING.
I'LL GET A VOLT-METRE. YOU DRAW THE SCHEMATIC.

YO, TECH-FOSSIL. WHEN ARE YOU UPGRADING ALL OF THE MARKETING AND BUSINESS PCS TO WINDOWS VISTA?
COPYRIGHT © 2006 J.D. "Illiad" Frazer HTTP://WWW.USERFRIENDLY.ORG/

WE HAVE XP ON THOSE MACHINES, AND THEY'RE WORKING FINE. WHY CHANGE ANYTHING?

WHEN WE UPGRADED TO XP I FLOATED SIX FEET OFF THE FLOOR JUST LIKE IN THEIR ADS. VISTA WILL TAKE ME TO ORBIT!
ORBIT HAS NO AIR. I'LL ORDER THE LICENSES FIRST THING.

HOW CAN YOU RAG ON VISTA? HAVE YOU EVEN TRIED IT?
THE BETA, YES. IT SEEMS A BIT MORE STABLE THAN XP.
COPYRIGHT © 2006 J.D. "Illiad" Frazer HTTP://WWW.USERFRIENDLY.ORG/

THEN WHAT'S THE PROBLEM?
WELL, WHAT DOES VISTA DO FOR THE AVERAGE USER?

...I DON'T FOLLOW.
LET ME ANSWER FOR YOU: EVERYTHING XP DOES, FOR MORE MONEY AND FEWER CONSUMER RIGHTS.

THE REPORTED LEGO SHORTAGE FOR THIS COMING HOLIDAY SEASON CAN BE CLEVERLY LEVERAGED TO SPREAD "THE TRUE LEGO EXPERIENCE" TO ALL:
IT'S ALMOST FINISHED. I JUST NEED THAT ONE PIECE!
I DON'T SEE IT.
LEGO
COPYRIGHT © 2006 J.D. "Illiad" Frazer HTTP://WWW.USERFRIENDLY.ORG/
UserFriendly.Org

WHAT DO YOU MEAN, "FEWER CONSUMER RIGHTS"?
THE BUILT-IN DRM SUPPORT ASIDE?

VISTA'S LICENSE ONLY ALLOWS FOR A USER TO MOVE THE LICENSE TO ONE OTHER COMPUTER. IF YOU WANT TO INSTALL IT YET AGAIN, YOU NEED TO BUY A NEW LICENSE.

I DON'T SEE THE PROBLEM.
LET'S REVISIT THIS WHEN YOU NEXT ASK MIKE OR GREG TO UPGRADE YOUR CPU AND MOTHERBOARD IN YOUR HOME MACHINE...

THE RECENT ACQUISITION OF YOUTUBE BY GOOGLE WAS SOON FOLLOWED BY A RAPID PROCESS OF "DE-CONTENTIFICATION" OF THE VIDEO SITE.

TENS OF THOUSANDS OF CLIPS HAVE BEEN REMOVED FROM YOUTUBE AT THE BEHEST OF THEIR COPYRIGHT HOLDERS, INCLUDING CLIPS FROM "THE DAILY SHOW" AND "THE COLBERT REPORT" WHICH DREW A SIGNIFICANT SHARE OF YOUTUBE'S VIEWERSHIP.

IT DAWNS ON THIS REPORTER THAT PERHAPS GOOGLE COULD'VE BOUGHT COMEDY CENTRAL FOR LESS THAN WHAT WAS PAID FOR YOUTUBE.
D'OH!

YO, TECH-FOSSIL! MICROSOFT JUST REPEALED THEIR ONE-EXTRA-INSTALL-ONLY POLICY FOR VISTA. SO TAKE THAT, UNBELIEVER!

OH, FABULOUS! THE WORLD IS ALL PASTEL SKIES AND MILK-AND-HONEY RIVERS NOW.

YOUR TONE SUGGESTS SARCASM.
SOMEONE THREATENS TO FORCE-FEED YOU FIVE LARGE BRICKS WHILE KNEEING YOU IN THE CROTCH. SUDDENLY, THEY DECIDE TO ONLY FEED YOU FOUR BRICKS. DO YOU THANK THEM?

BAD WEEK?
AWFUL. MY "ONE EXTRA INSTALL ONLY" POLICY FOR VISTA WAS SHOT DOWN.
the wibble

I NEED SOMETHING, A GIMME THAT'LL HELP CHEER ME UP.
the wibble

RE-DEFINE THE STANDARD OF "PIRACY" TO INCLUDE THE ACT OF NOT BUYING THE NEXT VERSION OF WINDOWS.
THIS IS WHY I LOVE YOU, MAN.
the wibble

DRAFTING THE NEW STANDARD FOR PIRACY I SEE.
YES, AND THE BIDDING WAR IS ON!

BIDDING WAR? WHAT?
THE RIAA AND MPAA WANT IN ON THE STANDARD. THEY'RE PAYING TO HAVE THEIR INTERESTS REP-RESENTED WITHIN.

"PIRACY TO INCLUDE ANYONE WHO HAS A VALID CREDIT CARD AND GETS A SONG STUCK IN THEIR HEAD."
YES! EDIT ACCEPTED AND THEY'RE IN FOR TWENTY MIL!
CHA-CHING!

WHERE'S THE LITTLE GUY?
HE SAID HE NEEDED TO GO SPEND TIME WITH HIS BROTHERS AND SISTERS.

WAIT...DUST PUPPY HAS BROTHERS AND SISTERS?
THAT'S WHAT HE SAID...

I MISS YOU ALL.

ODDLY ENOUGH, THE RULING FROM THE NEW ZEALAND QUALIFICATIONS AUTHORITY ALLOWING HIGH SCHOOL STUDENTS TO USE "TEXT SPEAK" IN THEIR ANSWERS ON TESTS COINCIDED WITH A SHARP INCREASE IN CEREBRAL ANEURYSMS AND SUICIDES IN EXAM GRADERS...

i ♡ teh histri lol

UserFriendly.Org

BZZRWWWNNNNNNNNNNN
DO YOU HEAR THAT?
YEAH...
COLA

NNNNNNNNNNNNNNNNNNN
IT SOUNDS LIKE A DYNAMO SPINNING UP!
IT'S COMING FROM AJ'S OFFICE!
COLA
COPYRIGHT© 2006 J.D. "Illiad" Frazer HTTP://WWW.USERFRIENDLY.ORG/

NNNNNNNNNNNNNNNNNN
NOW THAT'S A VIDEO CARD!

NNNNNNNNNNNNNNNNNN
AJ! CAN YOU TURN THAT DOWN?
SORRY. CAN'T HEAR YOU! IT'S THE TURBOFANS ON MY NEW VIDEO CARD!

NNWAKAWAKAWAKANN
THEN TURN THE BLOODY THING OFF!
IT'S 40 CELSIUS IN HERE! AND NEVERWINTER NIGHTS 2 RUNS GREAT NOW!
COPYRIGHT© 2006 J.D. "Illiad" Frazer HTTP://WWW.USERFRIENDLY.ORG/

NNNNNNNNNNNNNNNNNN
THE DESTINY OF ALL ADVANCED CIVILIZATIONS: GLOBAL WARMING VIA COMPUTER GAME PLAYERS.
GOT ANY EGGS YOU WANT POACHED?

AJ. IF YOU NEED A BROBDINGNAGIAN VIDEO CARD JUST TO PLAY A STUPID COMPUTER GAME. WHAT'S THE BLOODY POI--

COPYRIGHT© 2006 J.D. "Illiad" Frazer HTTP://WWW.USERFRIENDLY.ORG/

GOOD HEAVENS. THAT'S GORGEOUS. HOW MUCH FOR ONE OF THOSE VIDEO CARDS?
IF THE PRICE MATTERS. YOU'RE NOT A TRUE GAMER.

IN NWN2. THEY'VE ADDED MORE RACES AND SUB-RACES. IT'S A NICE CHANGE FROM THE USUAL MIX.
COPYRIGHT© 2006 J.D. "Illiad" Frazer HTTP://WWW.USERFRIENDLY.ORG/

SEE? THAT'S MY CHARACTER. CHECK OUT HIS SNAZZY NATURE-GUARDIAN OUTFIT!

YOU'RE PLAYING A GARDEN GNOME?
HE'S A POWERFUL GNOMISH DRUID!
HAVE HIM TACKLE A MEDUSA. A MEDUSA WITH A GARDEN.

AJ'S VIDEO CARD IS JUST INSANE.
I KNOW. THANKFULLY THERE'S ONLY ONE SUCH MONSTROSITY IN THE OFFICE.
COPYRIGHT© 2006 J.D. "Illiad" Frazer HTTP://WWW.USERFRIENDLY.ORG/

RIGHT?!
SID? FEDEX HERE FOR YOU. THE GUY'S DRIVING A SMALL CRANE.

YOU GOT CARDS FOR EVERY-ONE? HAVE YOU GONE UTTERLY DAFT?
YOU SAW HOW PRETTY THE GRAPHICS WERE. AND WE NEED A NEW GAME WE CAN ALL PLAY AFTER WORK.
COPYRIGHT© 2006 J.D. "Illiad" Frazer HTTP://WWW.USERFRIENDLY.ORG/

AND YOU KNOW WHAT THOSE VIDEO CARDS DRAW FOR POWER!
I'VE FOUND A WAY TO EXPAND OUR POWER BUDGET. RELAX.

STRANGE. ALL FOUR OF MY NUCLEAR PLANTS AROUND WORLD. THEY ARE AT CAPACITY?

THINGS THAT MAKE YOU GO "HMMMM" #58:
SONY'S SHIPPING BREAKOUT TO REGIONAL MARKETS OF PLAYSTATION 3 UNITS BASED ON EBAY AUCTIONS

Other
North America
Asia
West Africa

UserFriendly.Org

West Africa. Home of Nigeria, home of 419 scams, and home of fraudulent eBay auctions.

MR. SHERMAN, SIR? THE PRESS ARE HERE, AND THEY'RE TAKING YOU TO TASK OVER YOUR COMMENTS ABOUT THE CONSUMER ELECTRONICS ASSOCIATION.
WHAT COMMENTS?

THE PART ABOUT THE C.E.A. BEING "SELF-SERVING."
YES? WHAT OF IT?

THEY WANT TO KNOW IF THAT MEANS THE R.I.A.A. IS NOT "SELF-SERVING."
OF COURSE WE'RE NOT! WE MAKE SACRIFICES FOR THE RECORD LABELS EVERY DAY!

HELLO MR. SHERMAN. SAFFRON RAKE, FROM THE WIBBLE TRIBUNE.
PROCEED, MS. RAKE.

COPYRIGHT© 2006 J.D. "Illiad" Frazer HTTP://WWW.USERFRIENDLY.ORG/

IN YOUR COLUMN PUBLISHED NOVEMBER 13TH, YOU STATE THAT THE C.E.A. IS TRYING TO SUBVERT THE FAIR-USE CLAUSE AND HARM COPYRIGHT HOLDERS SUCH AS RECORD LABELS. WHAT ABOUT THE ARTISTS?

THE WHO?
RIGHT. THANK YOU.

MR. SHERMAN, YOUR RECENT COLUMN PAINTS THE R.I.A.A. AS A REASONABLE ORGANIZATION THAT CARES ABOUT THE CONSUMER.
WELL, YES...

COPYRIGHT© 2006 J.D. "Illiad" Frazer HTTP://WWW.USERFRIENDLY.ORG/

...AS OPPOSED TO A CABAL OF WEALTHY EXECUTIVES WHO WISH TO CONTINUE SIPHONING MONEY FROM THE CONSUMER ANY WAY POSSIBLE.

YOU READ MY COLUMN. WE SUPPORT FAIR USE.
RIGHT. I'LL PUT THAT RIGHT NEXT TO OUR STORY ON HOW THE CHINESE GOVERNMENT DOESN'T CENSOR THE INTERNET. SHALL I?

ONE FINAL QUESTION MR. SHERMAN. YOU SAY THE R.I.A.A. IS BIG ON FAIR USE, THAT PEOPLE SHOULD BE ALLOWED TO USE EXCERPTS FOR PARODY OR COMMENTARY, FOR EXAMPLE.
YES!

COPYRIGHT© 2006 J.D. "Illiad" Frazer HTTP://WWW.USERFRIENDLY.ORG/

THEN WHY DOES THE R.I.A.A. SUPPORT D.R.M.? HOW DOES ONE EXTRACT PART OF A SONG FOR THE SAKE OF A REVIEW OR COMMENTARY WITH DRM IN THE WAY?

YOU COULD ALWAYS HUM A FEW BARS...
AND I WON'T BE SUED? BUT WON'T THE RECORDS LABELS, YOU KNOW, STARVE?

TECH SUPPORT. I AM HERE FOR THE PAIN.
HI. HOW DO I GET MY ACCOUNT WIPED OFF A WEB FORUM?

YOU SEE. I REPLIED TO A POST IN A KLINGON FORUM. BUT I WROTE THE REPLY IN TENGWAR. THE SCRIPT OF THE ELVES.

YOU INSULTED THEM DIDN'T YOU...
IT WAS JUST A PLAYFUL JAB! I CALLED THEM ALL "ORC WANNABES."

WHY DO YOU WANT TO WIPE YOUR ACCOUNT ON THE FORUM?
BAD BLOOD. I'D RATHER NOT LEAVE A RECORD OF ANIMOSITY.

FINE. JUST CONTACT THE FORUM ADMIN AND ASK FOR YOUR ACCOUNT TO BE DELETED.
IT'S NOT THAT EASY.

...EVERYONE IS REALLY MAD AT ME. AND... WELL. I'M JUST NOT THAT GOOD WITH WORDS.
YOU CAN READ AND SPEAK ENGLISH. KLINGON AND QUENYA AND YOU DON'T KNOW HOW TO COMMUNICATE?!

ALTHOUGH PETER JACKSON IS REFUSING TO FILM "THE HOBBIT", HOLLYWOOD WILL STILL GIVE IT A GO...

THE HOBBIT
NEW LINE CINEMA
NEW LINE CINEMA PRESENTS an ALAN SMITHEE PRODUCTION
TOM CRUISE as Bilbo
JESSICA SIMPSON as Galadriel
KEVIN COSTNER as Elrond
JEAN-CLAUDE VAN DAMME as Thorin
WILLIAM SHATNER as Gandalf the Grey
and Featuring
GILBERT GOTTFRIED as the One Ring

UserFriendly.Org

LOOK. EMAIL THE FORUM ADMIN AND ASK NICELY. HE MIGHT DELETE YOUR ACCOUNT AND ALL OF YOUR POSTINGS.
COPYRIGHT © 2006 J.D. "Illiad" Frazer HTTP://WWW.USERFRIENDLY.ORG/

BUT BE WARNED THAT THAT WON'T BE THE END OF IT. WHAT WITH THE WAY THE NET WORKS, YOUR WORDS COULD BE OUT ON THE WEB FOR THE REST OF FOREVER.

OH. SO I HAVE NO HOPE OF WIPING MY RECORD?
DUDE. THANKS TO ARCHIVE.ORG AMONG OTHERS, WHATEVER HAPPENS ON THE INTERNET **STAYS** ON THE INTERNET.

TECH SUPPORT. GREG SPEAKING. I HAVE INJECTED MYSELF WITH A MENTAL ANASTHETIC.
HELLO, GREG.
COPYRIGHT © 2006 J.D. "Illiad" Frazer HTTP://WWW.USERFRIENDLY.ORG/

HI. MAY I HAVE YOUR NAME?
NO. THAT'S PRIVATE INFORMATION.

OKAAAYYY...CAN YOU EXPLAIN YOUR PROBLEM TO ME?
HOW DO YOU KNOW I HAVE A PROBLEM?! HAVE YOU BEEN **SPYING** ON ME?!

LOOK. IF YOU'RE NOT GOING TO TELL ME YOUR NAME OR EXPLAIN THE PROBLEM YOU'RE HAVING, HOW CAN YOU EXPECT ME TO HELP YOU?
TYPICAL PHISHING PLEA. FINE. I'LL E-MAIL YOU THE DETAILS RIGHT NOW. ENCRYPTED.
COPYRIGHT © 2006 J.D. "Illiad" Frazer HTTP://WWW.USERFRIENDLY.ORG/

I HAVE TO LOG IN TO SEND THE E-MAIL. SO I'M GOING TO TYPE MY PASSWORD NOW. **DON'T LISTEN!**

WAIT...**WHAT?!**
YOU HEARD MY PASSWORD?!!
NOT UNLESS IT'S "TIKKITY TAKKITY TAK"!

It's always about that damned coffee-cup holder.

I HAVE YOUR E-MAIL. HOW DO I DECRYPT IT?
OH. YOU'LL NEED A QUANTUM DECRYPTOR.
COPYRIGHT © 2006 J.D. "Illiad" Frazer HTTP://WWW.USERFRIENDLY.ORG/

DID YOU SAY "**QUANTUM** DECRYPTOR?"
YA. YOU CAN NEVER BE TOO SECURE.

QUANTUM MECHANICS AND ENCRYPTION. TWO SUBJECTS THAT INDIVIDUALLY GIVE ME MIGRAINES. NOW TOGETHER. DON'T MIND MY BLINDING HEADACHE...
THE PROBLEM I'M HAVING IS WITH MY COFFEE-CUP HOLDER.

WOO! THERE'S SERIOUS TALK IN THE BLOGOSPHERE ABOUT WEB 3.0!
WHAT?
COPYRIGHT © 2006 J.D. "Illiad" Frazer HTTP://WWW.USERFRIENDLY.ORG/

I SAID "WEB 3.0."
YES I HEARD THAT. WHAT HAPPENED TO WEB 2.0?

I GUESS IT'S BEEN FOSSILIZED.
BUT WHAT WAS IT?!

WHAT ARE YOU GETTING ALL HUFFY FOR?
A.J., THE WEB CAN'T BE VERSIONED.
COPYRIGHT © 2006 J.D. "Illiad" Frazer HTTP://WWW.USERFRIENDLY.ORG/

IT'S AN AMORPHOUS THING THAT NO ONE HAS ABSOLUTE CONTROL OVER. IT DOESN'T HAVE DISCRETE VERSIONS, AND IT MOST CERTAINLY DOESN'T PROGRESS ONE NICELY SHAPED STEP AT A TIME!

WOULD YOU BE HAPPIER IF WE CALLED IT "WEB 1.27"?
NO! BECAUSE THAT WOULD MEAN WE'D EVENTUALLY HAVE TO FACE WEB 2.0 AGAIN!

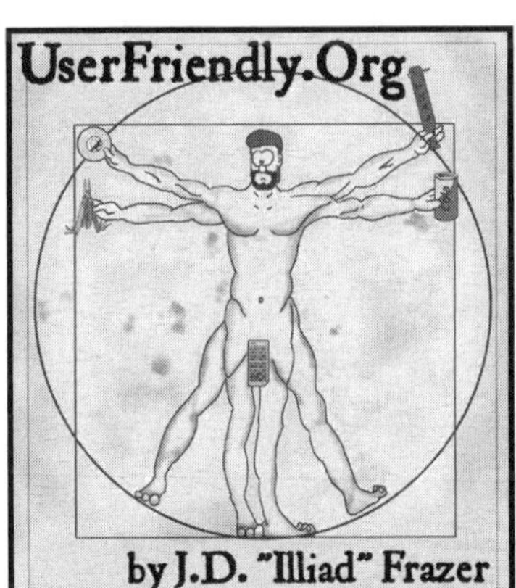
UserFriendly.Org
by J.D. "Illiad" Frazer
COPYRIGHT © 2006 J.D. "Illiad" Frazer HTTP://WWW.USERFRIENDLY.ORG/

A $599 CELL PHONE THAT RUNS LINUX? GOOD HEAVENS!

FOR THAT PRICE I SHOULD HOPE THEY ALSO GIVE YOU LINUS TORVALD'S PHONE NUMBER.

SO HOW'S THAT NEW LINUX PHONE?
IT'S...ONE SECOND... ...EHHH....

WHAT'RE YOU DOING? ARE YOU PLAYING A GAME?
NO...I...EHHH!

YOU'RE SENDING AN SMS MESSAGE?
TRYING! WITH "ED"!

I HEARD YOU GAVE AJ QUITE A DRUBBING OVER WEB 3.0.
OH, I WOULDN'T CALL IT A DRUBBING.
COPYRIGHT © 2006 J.D. "Illiad" Frazer HTTP://WWW.USERFRIENDLY.ORG/

AFTER ALL, THERE IS INDEED A MARKED DIFFERENCE BETWEEN WEB 2.0 AND WEB 3.0.

THERE IS? WHAT IS IT?
TO AN INVESTOR, ABOUT TEN MILLION DOLLARS.

SO WHAT'S THE BUSINESS MODEL FOR THIS WEB 3.0 SITE YOU'RE BUILDING?
I OPEN A FORUM, AND ENCOURAGE MILLIONS OF USERS TO POST TO IT. THEY CREATE ALL OF THE CONTENT.
COPYRIGHT © 2006 J.D. "Illiad" Frazer HTTP://WWW.USERFRIENDLY.ORG/

I THEN INDEX AND CROSS-TAG ALL OF THE WRITTEN CONTENT SO IT'S EASILY ACCESSIBLE. I ALSO PAY FOR BANDWIDTH OUT OF MY POCKET, WHILE HAVING NO REVENUE STREAM.

WHAT?! ARE YOU INSANE? WHAT KIND OF BUSINESS MODEL IS THAT?
A $1.6 BILLION ONE. JUST ASK THE YOUTUBE GUYS. I THINK YOU CAN REACH THEM IN TAHITI.

WOOO! LOOK AT THAT SUCKER GO!
CARUMBA!
YOW!
COPYRIGHT © 2006 J.D. "Illiad" Frazer HTTP://WWW.USERFRIENDLY.ORG/

AND IT'S STILL GOING!
THAT IS SOME SERIOUS DOWNWARD VELOCITY!
WHAT ARE YOU GUYS WATCHING?

SCO'S STOCK PRICE. IT DOESN'T FLY SO MUCH AS PLUMMET.
IT'S LIKE WATCHING A BLACK HOLE AT WORK!

WHAT HAPPENED TO SCO?
THEY HAD A SERIOUS SETBACK IN THEIR INFRINGEMENT CASE AGAINST IBM. ESSENTIALLY THEY'VE BEEN DENIED THE USE OF A PILE OF THEIR SO-CALLED "EVIDENCE."
COPYRIGHT © 2006 J.D. "Illiad" Frazer HTTP://WWW.USERFRIENDLY.ORG/

WHICH MEANS THAT THE GUILLOTINE IS PROBABLY REALLY CLOSE TO DROPPING ON SCO. THIS YEARS-LONG BASELESS LAWSUIT IS FINALLY GOING TO COLLAPSE, TAKING SCO ALONG WITH IT.

AND YOU SAID YOU DIDN'T BELIEVE IN SANTA.
I AM SO LEAVING A BOTTLE OF 20 YEAR OLD SCOTCH OUT FOR THAT WONDERFUL FAT GIT THIS YEAR.

YE FLIPPING GODS! GOOGLE ANSWERS IS CLOSING DOWN!
COPYRIGHT © 2006 J.D. "Illiad" Frazer HTTP://WWW.USERFRIENDLY.ORG/

GOOGLE ANSWERS! IT'S...IT'S CLOSING DOWN!

WHY?
I DON'T KNOW AND NOW I CAN'T ASK FOR AN EXPERT OPINION!

ACCORDING TO THE PRESS RELEASE, GOOGLE ANSWERS IS CLOSING DOWN BECAUSE OF CHANGING GOALS FOR THE COMPANY...
COPYRIGHT © 2006 J.D. "Illiad" Frazer HTTP://WWW.USERFRIENDLY.ORG/

I GUESS THAT LEAVES US YAHOO ANSWERS FOR OUR KNOWLEDGE NEEDS.

...WHICH IS FINE IF YOU WANT TO KNOW THINGS LIKE WHY BRITNEY AND KEVIN FEDER-LINE BROKE UP.
...AND DON'T MIND GETTING "OH NOES!!!11" AS AN ANSWER.

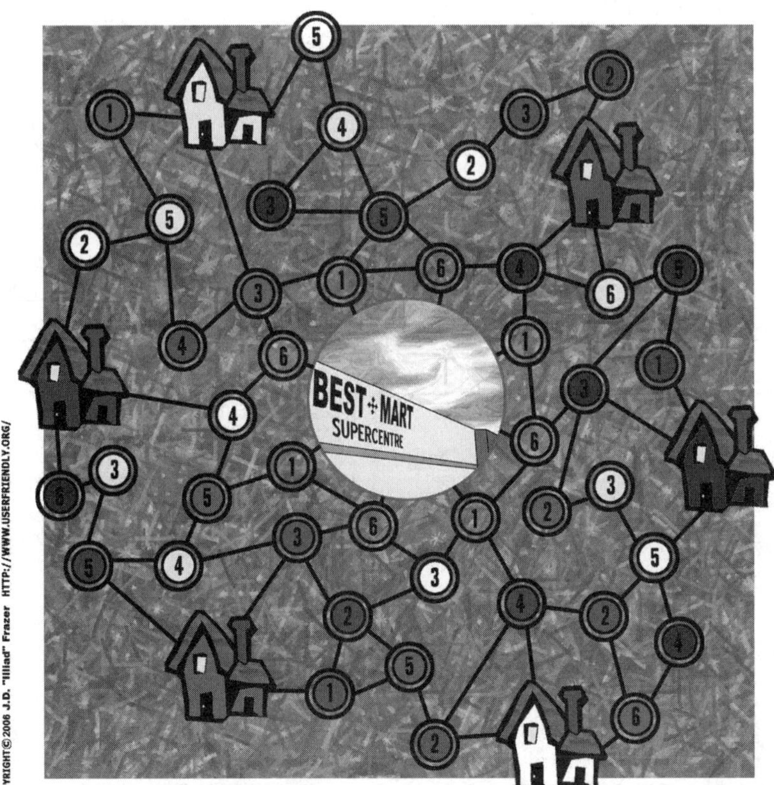
BEST MART
SUPERCENTRE
COPYRIGHT © 2006 J.D. "Illiad" Frazer HTTP://WWW.USERFRIENDLY.ORG/

Toy of the Year!

Object: Get to the Best Mart and return Home with a Toy of the Year!

1. You will need six pawns (matching the colour of the homes) and two dice per player. You will also need some tokens to represent "Pickle Me Cthulhu" dolls, which is the Toy of the Year. If there are 3 or 4 players, place two tokens on the Best Mart space. If there are 5 or 6 players, place three tokens on the Best Mart space.
2. Each player starts at their Home. On their turn, they roll two dice. They may move into any space adjacent to their current position numbered the same as either of the dice rolled. If upon moving into such a space there is another adjacent space numbered the same as the other die, they may move into that second space.
3. Moving into Best Mart requires no roll but takes an entire turn. Moving out of Best Mart requires the roll of a 1 or a 6.
4. If you move into Best Mart and there is a TOTY there, you may pick it up. You may only have one TOTY at any time.
5. If a player rolls a number on one of the dice that matches a space of their colour that an enemy piece is on, AND the enemy piece has a TOTY, AND the moving player does not have a TOTY, the moving player may "mug" the enemy piece by moving to that spot, taking the TOTY, and sending the enemy piece back to its home.
6. The winner is the first player to return home with a TOTY.

UserFriendly.Org

Apparently one of the more successful games. I received e-mail from some folks who work at JPL. This game kept them from falling asleep late one night while they were waiting on some data. I ... I think that's a compliment.

CHIEF. MICROSOFT VISTA IS OUT FOR CORPORATIONS. WE NEED IT.
WHY DO WE NEED IT?
COPYRIGHT © 2006 J.D. "Illiad" Frazer HTTP://WWW.USERFRIENDLY.ORG/

WELL...WHY DO YOU BUY A NEW CAR EVERY TEN YEARS?
BECAUSE THE OLD ONE STARTS TO DIE AND I CAN AFFORD A NEW CAR ONCE A DECADE.

THERE YA GO!
I ALSO MAKE IT A POINT NOT TO BUY YUGOS.

THOSE LINUX BIGOTS YOU CALL TECHIES GOT TO YOU. DIDN'T THEY.
WHY DO YOU SAY THAT?
COPYRIGHT © 2006 J.D. "Illiad" Frazer HTTP://WWW.USERFRIENDLY.ORG/

EVERY TIME I SUGGEST WE USE A MICROSOFT PRODUCT YOU START GETTING ALL DOUBTFUL! WHY CAN'T WE JUST USE WHATEVER PRODUCT IS BEST?

REMEMBER: THE BEST IS WHATEVER IS SHINIEST. AND THE "NEW SOFTWARE SMELL" DOESN'T HURT EITHER.
I'M NOT SURE I'D AGREE THAT SMELL REMINDED ME OF "NEW."

SID? GOT A TECHNICAL QUESTION FOR YA.
FIRE AWAY.
COPYRIGHT © 2006 J.D. "Illiad" Frazer HTTP://WWW.USERFRIENDLY.ORG/

IF YOU HAD TO CHOOSE BETWEEN A BALL COVERED IN SPARKLY BLUE LIGHTS OR A BALL COVERED IN GREY PAINT. WHICH WOULD YOU PREFER?
THE ONE WITH THE BLUE LIGHTS OF COURSE.

SEE? THE SHINIEST IS ALWAYS THE BEST.
FINE. GO GET VISTA LICENSES FOR THE OFFICE.
WAIT...WHAT?!

YOU'RE LETTING STEF ORDER VISTA LICENSES FOR THE OFFICE?
IT SEEMS TO BE THE RIGHT THING TO DO.
COPYRIGHT © 2006 J.D. "Illiad" Frazer HTTP://WWW.USERFRIENDLY.ORG/

WHY DIDN'T YOU COME TO ME FIRST? I'M YOUR C.T.O.!

BECAUSE THE ANSWER I ALWAYS GET FROM YOU IS "NO" IF IT INVOLVES MICROSOFT.
NOT TRUE. WHEN YOU ASKED IF A STEVE BALLMER DARTBOARD IN THE LUNCHROOM WAS APPROPRIATE I SAID "YES."

WHY **NOT** MIGRATE TO VISTA, SID? IT'S SUPPOSED TO BE THE LATEST AND GREATEST.
CHIEF, WE MOVED AWAY FROM A WINDOWS-ONLY DESKTOP NETWORK FOR A VERY GOOD REASON.

IT MAKES SENSE FOR YOU AND STEF AND THE REST OF THE NON-TECH STAFF TO USE WINDOWS MACHINES, BUT MY DEPARTMENT IS BEST SERVED WITH SOME VERSION OF LINUX OR BSD.

FOR SOME DEEP TECHNICAL REASON THEN?
YES. WE DON'T WANT TO BE MICROSOFT BETA TESTERS.

But we all want to be Google beta testers!

LESS THAN TEN DAYS TO CHRISTMAS. I THINK OF THE SOFTLY FALLING SNOW, THE SONGS AND BELLS ON THE AIR, THE GIFTS WRAPPED TIGHTLY...

ALL THAT SEASONAL MAGIC. MAGIC THAT HERALDS...

...THE SCREAMS OF FRUSTRATION FROM COMPUTER GAMERS PLAYING CRAPPY GAMES RUSHED OUT THE DOOR TO MAKE THE CHRISTMAS RETAIL DEADLINE.
NOOOOOO! MY SAVEGAMES!!

THE LATEST EXCITING DISCOVERIES ON MARS WILL INEVITABLY LEAD TO CORPORATE SPECULATION AND THEREFORE TRADEMARK WARS THAT CAN ONLY END BADLY.
Mars
UserFriendly.Org

HEY EVERYONE. WELCOME TO NEVERWINTER NIGHTS 2 AND MY NEW MULTIPLAYER MODULE.
HEY A.J.
YO!
A.J.-STER.
HOLA.

PROCEED WITH CHARACTER GENERATION AND LET ME KNOW IF YOU GET STUCK OR IF YOU HAVE A QUESTION.
I HAVE A QUESTION.

YES MIRANDA?
CAN I TRADE THE D.M. A BACKRUB FOR A RING OF NINE LIVES AT THE START?
HEY!!

CHARACTERS DONE?
YEP. PROCEED, DUNGEON MASTER!

CLICK! CLICK!
CLICK! CLICK!
CLICK! CLICK!
CLICK! CLICK!
CLICK! CLICK!
CLICK! CLICK!
CLICK! CLICK!

YE GODS! WHERE'D ALL THOSE MONSTERS COME FROM?!
OH I DUNNO. GUESS THEY WERE GENERATED RANDOMLY BY A SCRIPT.

YOU GUYS READY TO ENTER THE DUNGEON?
LET'S GO! AH... IT APPEARS TO BE A MAZE.

...IN FACT, IT'S A MAZE OF TWISTY PASSAGES, ALL ALIKE.
I USED CUT-AND-PASTE A FEW TIMES. SO SUE ME.

IF A.J.'S BASED THIS DUNGEON ON ZORK IT'S A DARN GOOD THING WE HAVE THIS LIT TORCH WITH US.

CLICK!

OH. VERY FUNNY A.J.
AAUUUGH! A GRUE!!
RELAX. THAT'S JUST MY TEN FOOT POLE...

WOOTNESS! HEY MR. DUNGEON MASTER. I JUST LEVELLED!
YEP. IF YOU LIKE, YOU CAN USE THAT LEVEL IN A PRESTIGE CLASS. MAYBE ONE OF THE NEW ONES I CREATED.
COPYRIGHT © 2006 J.D. "Illiad" Frazer HTTP://WWW.USERFRIENDLY.ORG/

...LIKE THIS ONE: YOU CAN BECOME A LEVEL ONE "I.T. STAFF MEMBER."

"WHAT POWERS DO I GET?" HE ASKS, WITH SOME TREPIDATION.

AN UNLIMITED NUMBER OF RAGES PER DAY. BUT YOU CAN'T TRIGGER THEM. ONLY OTHERS CAN.
WELL...THAT'S CERTAINLY "KEEPIN' IT REAL."

WHAT NEWS, ROGUE?
THERE'S A CREEPY LOOKING MONSTER IN THE NEXT ROOM.
COPYRIGHT © 2006 J.D. "Illiad" Frazer HTTP://WWW.USERFRIENDLY.ORG/

...IT SMELLS BAD, LOOKS SHIFTY, AND IT'S HOLDING A BANNER THAT SAYS "D&D SUXXORS."

AH! A TROLL!
WIZARD, READY YOUR SILENCE SPELL! THEY REALLY HATE THAT.
THERE'S NO SUCH THING AS AN OBSCURE REFERENCE WHEN GEEKS ARE INVOLVED.

FRIDAY WAS AN EARLY CHRISTMAS FOR THE ASTRONAUTS, THEIR FAMILIES AND THOSE OF US WATCHING THE LANDING OF THE SHUTTLE *DISCOVERY*.

UserFriendly.Org

THAT WAS A GREAT ADVENTURE, GANG! THANKS FOR PLAYING.
THANKS FOR D.M.-ING!
'TWAS MOST EXCELLENT!
COPYRIGHT © 2006 J.D. "Illiad" Frazer HTTP://WWW.USERFRIENDLY.ORG/

BUT WE GOT NO LOOT.
YOU'RE RIGHT. THE GOLD AND TREASURE COUNT WAS PRETTY MUCH ZIP.

WHO CARES? WE GOT TO HAVE A GREAT GAME TOGETHER.
YEAH. IT'S ALL ABOUT THE ADVENTURE, AND WHOM YOU ADVENTURE WITH. IT'S A GOOD DAY FOR IT TOO...
MY WORK HERE IS DONE...

I nearly dismembered myself once while trying to open a plastic shell. What was inside? A first-aid kit.

CHRISTMAS GIFT?
YA. A SPIFFY USB KEY. TRYING TO GET IT OUT OF THIS PLASTIC SHELL. *GNNNRFF*
COPYRIGHT © 2006 J.D. "Illiad" Frazer HTTP://WWW.USERFRIENDLY.ORG/

NNNFFF NNNGGGGUUHHHH...

NNNNGGGG!!! INGA-FUNGA WANBLEHRUM!!!
I SWEAR THE GLUE THEY USE INVOLVES THE STRONG NUCLEAR FORCE.

I THINK WE NEED SOME KIND OF TOOL TO GET IT OUT.
I GOT A MULTITOOL FOR CHRISTMAS. WE CAN USE THAT.
COPYRIGHT © 2006 J.D. "Illiad" Frazer HTTP://WWW.USERFRIENDLY.ORG/

...ONCE YOU GET IT OUT OF THE PLASTIC SHELL.
"THE CHICKEN AND THE EGG" DOES SEEM KINDA LAME NEXT TO THIS PARTICULAR PROBLEM.

OKAY. I THINK I JUST ABOUT HAVE IT HERE... NRRRRRR... GGGNNNRRRRRRRFFF..
COPYRIGHT © 2006 J.D. "Illiad" Frazer HTTP://WWW.USERFRIENDLY.ORG/

SCRAK!

DID YOU OPEN IT?
IF YOU'RE REFERRING TO ONE OF MY ARTERIES, YES.

GOOD HEAVENS. WHAT'S GOING ON IN THERE?
GREG'S BEEN TRYING TO OPEN ONE OF THOSE PLASTIC SHELLS FOR OVER AN HOUR.

NNNNNG...GAH!
GGRRRRNNN...OUCH!
NNNMMMGGG...YARG!

I GUESS THE KEY WORD IS "TRYING"?
NEARLY GOT IT! COULD YOU GET ME MORE GAUZE AND SUTURING THREAD?

YOU GOT THE SHELL OPEN!
FINALLY! AND NOW, I CAN ENJOY MY NEW USB DRIVE!

GA-ZUNK
PWEEEP
NEW HARDWARE IS DEFECTIVE

YOU GONNA NEED MORE GAUZE AND SUTURING THREAD?
NO. THE MANU-FACTURER IS.

MY PREDICTION FOR 2007:
IT'S NOT GOING TO BE CALLED "2007"
2006 2.0
UserFriendly.Org

GREETINGS, EVERYONE, AND WELCOME TO THE FLIP SIDE! AS A WAY TO BRING IN THE NEW YEAR I'VE DECIDED TO SHARE MY ORACULAR POWERS AND ANSWER SOME OF THE E-MAIL YOU YOUNGER AND LESS-WORLDLY GEEKS HAVE BEEN SENDING ME!

"DEAR SID:
I'M A BLOGGER, BUT I NEED A NEW NAME FOR SOMEONE WHO BLOGS FOR A FEW DAYS AND NEVER BLOGS AGAIN, FILLING THE WEB WITH DRECK.
SIGNED,
BAILEY-25¢S"

DEAR BAILEY:
SINCE THE INTERNET IS A BUNCH OF TUBES, MAY I SUGGEST THE TERM "CLOGGER."
LOVE,
SID

"DEAR SID:
TIME MAGAZINE MADE A BIG DEAL ABOUT INDIVIDUALS HAVING ALL THE POWER ON THE INTERNET WITH IT'S RECENT 'PERSON OF THE YEAR' COVER. BUT I DON'T FEEL POWERFUL AT ALL. WHAT CAN I DO TO FIX THAT?
SIGNED,
A SHOE WITH NO SOLE"

DEAR SOLELESS:
YOU'LL NEED $1019.95! $19.95 FOR A WORLD OF WARCRAFT MEMBERSHIP, AND $1000.00 TO BUY A 60TH LEVEL BLOOD ELF WARLOCK FROM SOMEONE. DEMAND ALL 1ST LEVEL CHARACTERS KNEEL BEFORE YOU AND ADDRESS YOU AS "DREAD LORD."
YOU'RE WELCOME.

EARLIER IN 2006, MATHEMATICIAN GRIGORI PERELMAN WAS RECOGNIZED FOR HIS PROOF OF THE POINCARÉ CONJECTURE.
PERELMAN'S WORK HAS BROUGHT MUCH EXCITEMENT TO THE SCIENTIFIC COMMUNITY.

WHAT'S THE "POINCARÉ CONJECTURE"?
IT HAS TO DO WITH TOPOLOGY. 3-DIMENSIONAL SHAPES AND MORPHING THEM INTO OTHER SHAPES.

SO...THE SCIENTIFIC COMMUNITY IS EXCITED ABOUT...MAKING BALLOON ANIMALS?
NO, IT'S EXCITED BECAUSE WE CAN PROVE THAT BALLOON ANIM- WAIT A MINUTE!

IN LAYMAN'S TERMS, HENRI POINCARÉ ASKED: "CAN AN ARBITRARY CLOSED SURFACE BE TURNED INTO A SPHERE BY ONLY STRETCHING IT APPROPRIATELY?"
HE ASSERTED THAT ALL 3D SURFACES THAT HAD NO HOLES COULD BE TURNED INTO A SPHERE WITHOUT NEEDING TO TEAR A SECTION APART OR STITCH TWO SECTIONS TOGETHER. HE ALSO SAID THE REVERSE WAS TRUE, THAT A SURFACE WITH A HOLE COULD NOT EVER BE TURNED INTO A SPHERE WITHOUT TEARING OR STITCHING.

SO FINALLY, A FEW YEARS AGO, PERELMAN PROVED POINCARÉ'S CONJECTURE...
SOMEONE WANTS TO GIVE HIM A MILLION DOLLARS FOR THAT? I FIGURED THAT OUT WITH PLAY-DOH WHEN I WAS FIVE!

I STILL DON'T GET IT. WHAT'S THE BIG DEAL ABOUT THE POINTY CARD THING?
COPYRIGHT © 2007 J.D. "Illiad" Frazer HTTP://WWW.USERFRIENDLY.ORG/

THE PROOF FOR POINCARE'S CONJECTURE IS CONSIDERED ONE OF THE HOLY GRAILS OF MATHEMATICS.

BUT WHAT DOES IT DO? WHEN IS SOMEONE EVER GOING TO USE IT?
STEF. JUST BECAUSE THE HOLY GRAIL DOESN'T KEEP COFFEE HOT WHILE YOU DRINK FROM IT DOESN'T MEAN IT ISN'T IMPORTANT.

I STILL DON'T GET THIS. IF MR. POINTYCARP DIDN'T HAVE A PROOF FOR HIS PRECIOUS CONJECTURE, HOW DID WE KNOW IT WAS IMPORTANT?
COPYRIGHT © 2007 J.D. "Illiad" Frazer HTTP://WWW.USERFRIENDLY.ORG/

MATH IS LIKE THAT. STEF. MATHEMATICIANS CAN LOOK AT A CONCEPT, COMPLEX OR NOT, AND WITH A SUDDEN SPARK OF COMPREHENSION AND PERSPECTIVE UNDER-STAND THE RESULT.

MATH ISN'T JUST ABOUT PROOFS, STEF. IT'S ALSO ABOUT INTUITION.
YOU MEAN LIKE MULTIPLE CHOICE ON MATH TESTS RIGHT? I KNEW THAT!

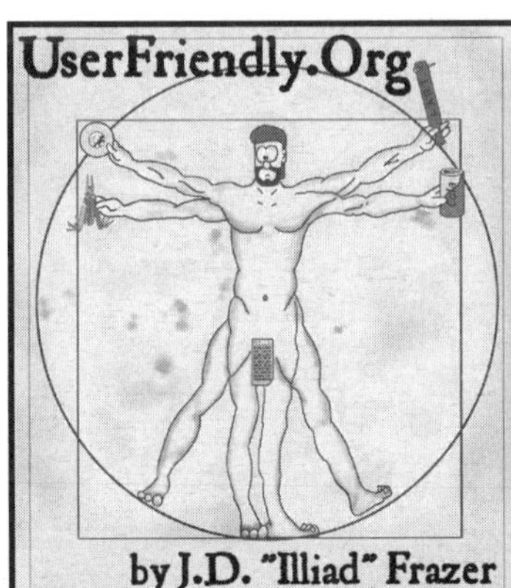
UserFriendly.Org
by J.D. "Illiad" Frazer
COPYRIGHT © 2006 J.D. "Illiad" Frazer HTTP://WWW.USERFRIENDLY.ORG/

BILL, OUR DEAL WITH NOVELL/SUSE IS DONE.
FANTASTIC, STEVE...NOW WHAT?
Microsoft

WE SLOWLY TAKE OVER SUSE LINUX FROM NOVELL OF COURSE.

WE'LL MAKE IT THE "STANDARDS COMPLIANT" LINUX FOR THE ENTIRE WORLD!
A GRAND IDEA, STEVE. BUT IF WE'RE TO HAVE ONE STANDARD LINUX DISTRO, WHAT DO WE DO ABOUT THE VI VS. EMACS RIFT?

REPLACE BOTH WITH NOTEPAD?
ARE YOU BORED, STEVE? BECAUSE YOU MUST BE READY TO DIE.

ARE YOU PLAYING WITH YOUR LUNCH?
I'M SKETCHING OUT HOW POINCARÉ'S CONJECTURE WORKS IN MY PUDDING CUP.
COPYRIGHT © 2007 J.D. "Illiad" Frazer HTTP://WWW.USERFRIENDLY.ORG/

I'M NOT PLAYING.
BUT...THE PROOF! IT'S IN THE PUDDING!

AAARRRRRRGH!!
WHAT'S THE MATTER?
COPYRIGHT © 2007 J.D. "Illiad" Frazer HTTP://WWW.USERFRIENDLY.ORG/

I YIELD. I HAVE RESISTED THE ALLURE OF PERFORMANCE-DISGUISED-AS-JOURNALING FOR YEARS, AND NOW I FINALLY SUCCUMB.

THE GODS HELP ME: I'M STARTING A BLOG.
GREAT. I'M ALWAYS ON THE LOOKOUT FOR THE NEXT EX-BLOGGER.

WHAT DO YOU MEAN, "EX-BLOGGER"?! I HAVEN'T EVEN **STARTED** YET!
SO START.
COPYRIGHT © 2007 J.D. "Illiad" Frazer HTTP://WWW.USERFRIENDLY.ORG/

"EX-BLOGGER" INDEED. I'LL SHOW YOU...
TYPE
TAP
PONTIFICATE
EXPOUND
RANT
TAPTAP

THERE. 5400 WORDS! IT'S TITLED: "TECH SUPPORT - WHEN WILL THE HURTING STOP?"
A PRECIS FOR YOUR LIFE IF I'VE EVER HEARD ONE.

This is so common it's scary. Or hysterically funny. I do the same, except with power tools instead of online content.

WELL DONE WITH YOUR FIRST BLOG ENTRY. NOW, WRITE ANOTHER ONE.
SURE. PIECE OF CAKE...
COPYRIGHT © 2007 J.D. "Illiad" Frazer HTTP://WWW.USERFRIENDLY.ORG/

UM.
I'LL JUST MAKE SOME BUSINESS CARDS THAT READ: "GREG FLEMMING, EX-BLOGGER" SHALL I?

SIR? ALLOFMP3.COM HAS BEEN SELLING DOWNLOAD-ABLE MUSIC TRACKS OUT OF RUSSIA FOR SOME TIME NOW.
WHAT?!
RIAA

THE RUSSIAN MUSIC LICENSING SOCIETY GAVE THEM THE GREEN LIGHT. AND HAS BEEN COLLECTING ROYALTIES ON EACH SALE.
CALL LEGAL! I WANT BLOOD!
RIAA

UM...WE COULD JUST ASK FOR THE ROYALTIES THAT HAVE BEEN COLLECTED.
ROYALTIES? SINCE WHEN HAS OUR BUSINESS BEEN ABOUT ROYALTIES?!
RIAA

ALLOFMP3.COM REALLY CHAPS MY HIDE.
YES SIR. THEY'RE VERY CHAPPISH.
RIAA

WE SHOULD SUE THEM...
YES SIR. WE'RE WELL WITHIN OUR RIGHTS TO DO SO...
RIAA

...FOR ONE TRILLION DOLLARS! MOOOAHAHAHA!
1.65 TRILLION SIR. WHICH, INCIDENTALLY, IS A BIT MORE THAN RUSSIA'S GDP. IF WE WIN, WE TECH-NICALLY "PWN" RUSSIA.
RIAA

IN MEMORY OF MOMOFUKU ANDO,
THE INVENTOR OF INSTANT RAMEN.

CUP NOODLES
GLUE OR TAPE HERE
O mighty hunger-quelling grail
I know your powers will not fail
your great maker now has passed
but without water you will last
for centuries and a day
you comply with Y3K
boil, pour, close and seal
three minutes pass, voila! a meal.
Ramen.
Cut along solid black line and wrap around noodle cup. Recite prayer before eating.
UserFriendly.Org
COPYRIGHT© 2006 J.D. "Illiad" Frazer HTTP://WWW.USERFRIENDLY.ORG/

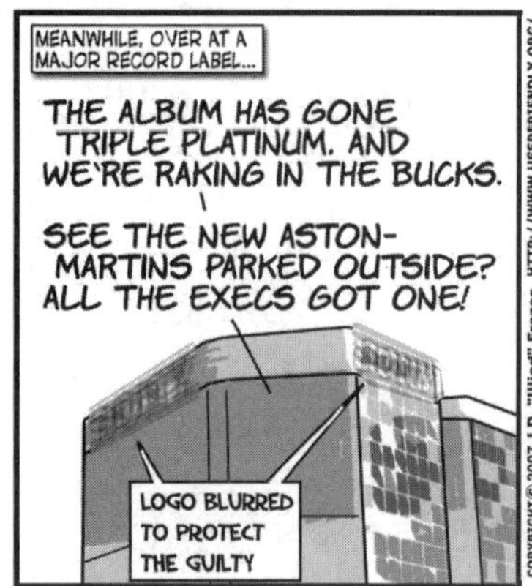
MEANWHILE, OVER AT A MAJOR RECORD LABEL...
THE ALBUM HAS GONE TRIPLE PLATINUM. AND WE'RE RAKING IN THE BUCKS.
SEE THE NEW ASTON-MARTINS PARKED OUTSIDE? ALL THE EXECS GOT ONE!
LOGO BLURRED TO PROTECT THE GUILTY
COPYRIGHT © 2007 J.D. "Illiad" Frazer HTTP://WWW.USERFRIENDLY.ORG/

OH. AND THIS IS THE RECORDING ARTIST HIMSELF. "LICK RIOT"!
HI.

DUDE. I HAVEN'T BEEN PAID A CENT SO FAR.
OH. NO NEED TO THANK US LICK. YOU'VE EARNED IT!

HI MIKE! COME JOIN ME ON LINKEDIN.COM!
GEEZ. NOT ANOTHER ONE...
COPYRIGHT © 2007 J.D. "Illiad" Frazer HTTP://WWW.USERFRIENDLY.ORG/

YOU HAVE JOINED LINKEDIN
YOU HAVE JOINED ORKUT
YOU HAVE JOINED MYSPACE
YOU HAVE JOINED FACEBOOK
YOU HAVE JOINED FRIENDSTER...

THERE! NOW MAYBE PEOPLE WILL STOP NAGGING ME.

HI! CAN I LINK TO YOU?
LET'S BE LINK BUDDIES!
MIKE! LINK UP!
LINK, LINK BABY.
HELLO. CAN WE LINK?
YO. I'M LINK-A-LICIOUS.

A-GAR!
WHAT?
THAT'S MY CELEBRITY NAME. A-GAR.
COPYRIGHT © 2007 J.D. "Illiad" Frazer HTTP://WWW.USERFRIENDLY.ORG/

JENNIFER LOPEZ IS "J.LO." KEVIN FEDERLINE IS "K-FED." I'M A.J. GARRETT SO I BECOME "A-GAR"!
YOU. FOR EXAMPLE. WOULD BE "D-PUP."

PARDON ME. I THOUGHT I HEARD ALL THE WAY ACROSS THE OFFICE SOMEONE SAYING "D-CUP." IF SO. WHERE?!
SOMEHOW IT'S APPROPRIATE YOU'D BE "S.MURK"

SECONDLIFE HAS GONE OPEN SOURCE! THEY RELEASED THE CODE TO THEIR CLIENT.
COPYRIGHT © 2007 J.D. "Illiad" Frazer HTTP://WWW.USERFRIENDLY.ORG/

"THE SECONDLIFE CLIENT IS IDEAL FOR OPEN SOURCE BECAUSE THE VIRTUAL WORLD IS ALREADY DRIVEN BY USER SUPPLIED CONTENT. OFFERING THE COMMUNITY TO TWEAK THE WAY THAT CONTENT IS SUPPLIED."

WE SHOULD CUSTOMIZE THE CLIENT CODE AND PLAY!
PLAY SECOND-LIFE? WHY? I DON'T EVEN HAVE A FIRST ONE.

I HEARD YOU DID SOME HACKING OF THE SECONDLIFE CLIENT CODE.
DA.
COPYRIGHT© 2007 J.D. "Illiad" Frazer HTTP://WWW.USERFRIENDLY.ORG/

JUST FINISHED COMPILINK. LAUNCHINK MODIFIED CLIENT NOW...

EVERYBODY'S NAKED.
NOW. I AM TO BE SELLINK THE ONLY WIRTUAL CLOTHES THAT WORK IN MY VIEWER AT WERY HIGH PRICE. CHA-CHING. PITR IS WERY RICH.

SIR. WOULD LIKE TO BE TAKINK HOLIDAY NOW.
FOR HOW LONG?
COPYRIGHT© 2007 J.D. "Illiad" Frazer HTTP://WWW.USERFRIENDLY.ORG/

JUST WHATEVER I AM HAVINK SAVED IN ANNUAL LEAVE. WHATEVER IS LEFT.

FINE. SO WHEN WILL YOU BE BACK TO WORK?
SOMETIME IN 2008...

LOOK, IF YOU DEVELOP A NAVAL RAILGUN, YOU'RE GOING TO HAVE TO ACCEPT CERTAIN...INEVITABILITIES.
SEAMAN. HITTING FIVE TARGETS IN A ROW WITH THE SHIP'S RAILGUN. ALTHOUGH ADMIRABLE. DOES **NOT** ENTITLE YOU TO GROWL **"IMPRESSIVE!"** OVER THE SHIP'S P.A.!
COPYRIGHT© 2006 J.D. "Illiad" Frazer HTTP://WWW.USERFRIENDLY.ORG/
UserFriendly.Org

This storyline came about at the urging of a senior engineer at Google. Many Google workers found it creepy that I got certain things "frighteningly correct" in the strip, and so they all suspected each other of feeding me information.

WHAT?! YOU CAN'T HAVE AN ENTIRE YEAR'S WORTH OF ANNUAL LEAVE BANKED!
COPYRIGHT © 2007 J.D. "Illiad" Frazer HTTP://WWW.USERFRIENDLY.ORG/

RAPPY
TAPPY
RAPRAP
QUERY

HUNH. YET THE COMPUTER SAYS YOU DO...
DA. THE COMPUTER SAYS I DO.

YOU'RE TAKING A YEAR OFF?
DA.
COPYRIGHT © 2007 J.D. "Illiad" Frazer HTTP://WWW.USERFRIENDLY.ORG/

WHAT ARE YOU GOING TO DO ALL YEAR? TRAVEL? PULL THE LEGS OFF OF HELPLESS INSECTS?
HAVE ENGINEERED NEW OPPORTUNITY.

WHO'S "PITR DUBOVICH"?
A NEW HIRE. THE COMPUTER SAYS SO.
Google

HELLO PITR. I'M GLEN. YOUR HIRING MANAGER.
PRIVET. COMRADE.
Google
COPYRIGHT © 2007 J.D. "Illiad" Frazer HTTP://WWW.USERFRIENDLY.ORG/

I SEE THAT YOUR HIRING IS OFFICIAL AND APPROVED. BUT I THOUGHT IT WAS A BIT ODD THAT NO ONE HAD INTERVIEWED YOU FOR THE POSITION.
Google

WHY DO YOU THINK THAT IS?
AHHH...THIS IS FAMOUS GOOGLE RIDDLE INTERVIEW. DA?

PITR. DO YOU KNOW GOOGLE'S MOTTO?
DA! IS "HAVINK FUN."
YES. BUT THE PRIMARY MOTTO IS "DON'T BE EVIL."
Google
COPYRIGHT © 2007 J.D. "Illiad" Frazer HTTP://WWW.USERFRIENDLY.ORG/

Google

PITR? YOU'RE TWITCHING.
SORRY. HAVINK TROUBLE RECONCILING...
Google

HERE'S YOUR DESK PITR. WELCOME ABOARD.
SPASIBO. TOVARISCH.
Google
COPYRIGHT© 2007 J.D. "Illiad" Frazer HTTP://WWW.USERFRIENDLY.ORG/

NOW...TO BE MAKINK GOOGLE MORE HOMEY...

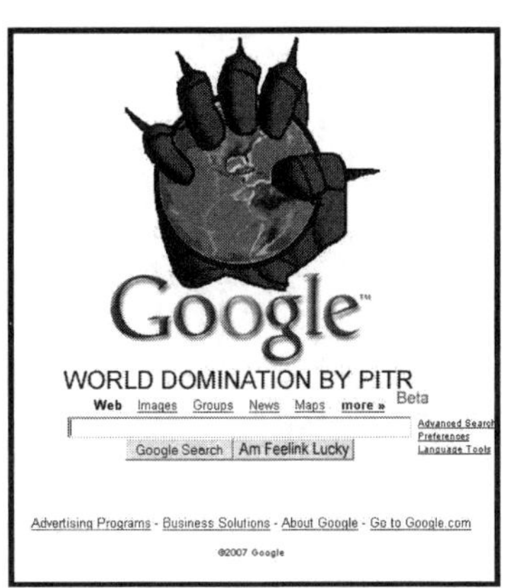
Google
WORLD DOMINATION BY PITR
Beta
Web Images Groups News Maps more »
Google Search
Am Feelink Lucky
Advertising Programs - Business Solutions - About Google - Go to Google.com

HI! I'M BLYTHE. YOUR CUBEMATE!
PRIVET. PITR. YOUR-SOON-TO-BE OVERLORD AND MASTER.
COPYRIGHT© 2007 J.D. "Illiad" Frazer HTTP://WWW.USERFRIENDLY.ORG/

HA HA. VERY NICE! WHAT DO YOU DO HERE PITR?
WORKINK ON PLOT TO BE TAKINK OVER WORLD.

OH. WE ALL DO THAT HERE.
DRAT! MUST NOW ELIMINATE 8000 COMPETITORS.

THE RECENT INVENTION OF THE "CAFFEINATED DOUGHNUT" BRINGS THE OPPORTUNITY TO OFFER AN ALTERNATIVE TO THE HEALTH-CONSCIOUS:

ALWAYS FRESH
Now Decaffeinated!

UserFriendly.Org

EXCUSE PLEASE. BLYTHE. WHERE IS COFFEE POT?
THE CLOSEST ONE IS IN THE CORNER.
COPYRIGHT © 2007 J.D. "Illiad" Frazer HTTP://WWW.USERFRIENDLY.ORG/

BLYTHE? ONLY SEE INDUSTRIAL DEVICE WITH COOLING RODS.
THAT'S IT. DON'T STAND IN FRONT OF THE MILK STEAMER.

HMMM...COFFEE BEINK SERVED IS CALLED "ROCKET BLEND."
FWEEEEEEEEEEEEEE
COPYRIGHT © 2007 J.D. "Illiad" Frazer HTTP://WWW.USERFRIENDLY.ORG/

"BOOST AND PROPEL YOU THROUGH THE LIFT OFF PHASE OF YOUR MORNING." SOUNDS WERY PROMISINK...
STIR
STIR

YOU SEEN THE NEW HIRE?
PITR? HE'S BEEN HANGING AROUND THE COFFEE MACHINE A WHOLE LOT.
Google
COPYRIGHT © 2007 J.D. "Illiad" Frazer HTTP://WWW.USERFRIENDLY.ORG/

HUNH. I HOPE HE ISN'T SPENDING ALL OF HIS TIME JUST DRINKING COFFEE.
Google

OH LOOK. THERE HE IS. HEY PITR. HOW'S WORK?
BY LENIN'S BEARD GEL! HAVE JUST CODED THREE NEW OPERATINK SYSTEMS! IN FIFTEEN MINUTES!
Google

OOOOOH. WHO IS THIS LEETLE SWAN?
Today's Lunch:
Chateaubriand
Seasonal Veggies
Gourmet Potatoes
COPYRIGHT © 2007 J.D. "Illiad" Frazer HTTP://WWW.USERFRIENDLY.ORG/

PRIVET. I AM PITR. YOU ARE LIKINK COMPUTERS? AM COMPUTER EXPERT.
NICE TO MEET YOU PITR. I'M DR. ANDERS.

YOU ARE MEDICAL DOCTOR?
NO. PHD IN COMPUTER SCIENCE. WHAT'S YOUR EXPERTISE?

UH...AM HACKER REALLY. DO LEETLE OF THIS. LEETLE OF THAT.
AHH. YOU'RE IN DEVELOPMENT THEN?

JUST SO. YOU ARE RESEARCHER?
YES. WANT TO TALK SHOP OVER LUNCH? I'VE BEEN DOING WORK IN EVOLUTIONARY COMPUTATION.
COPYRIGHT © 2007 J.D. "Illiad" Frazer HTTP://WWW.USERFRIENDLY.ORG/

UM...NOT REALLY UNDERSTANDINK TECHNICAL ENGLISH...
OH. THAT'S OKAY. I SPEAK FLUENT RUSSIAN.

OH...AM NOT RUSSIAN SPEAKER.
REALLY? I'M SORRY. I MISJUDGED YOUR ACCENT. WHAT'S YOUR BIRTH TONGUE?

UM...IS WERY OBSCURE.
TRY ME. I TOOK MY SECOND DEGREE IN SLAVIC LANGUAGES.
COPYRIGHT © 2007 J.D. "Illiad" Frazer HTTP://WWW.USERFRIENDLY.ORG/

SLAVIC? HEH...UH. IS NOT SLAVIC. I AM SPEAKINK AFRIKAANS.
PERFECT! I MINORED IN AFRIKAANS! GOEIE DAG!

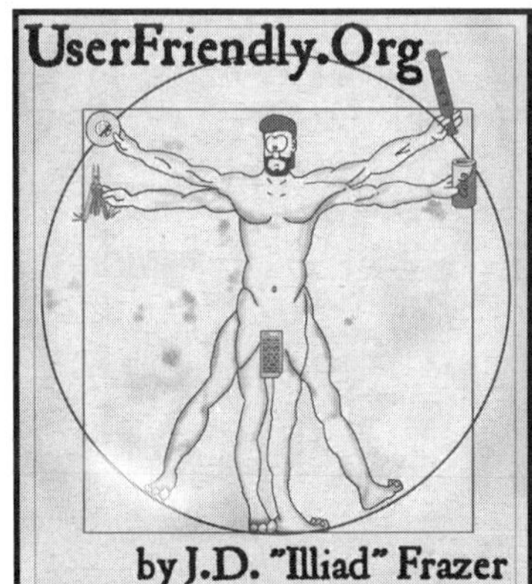
UserFriendly.Org
by J.D. "Illiad" Frazer

THE FRENCH PARLIAMENT HAS SAID AU REVOIR TO MICROSOFT. STARTING IN JUNE OF THIS YEAR FRENCH DEPUTIES WILL USE PERSONAL COMPUTERS RUNNING LINUX, FIREFOX AND OPENOFFICE.ORG.
COPYRIGHT © 2007 J.D. "Illiad" Frazer HTTP://WWW.USERFRIENDLY.ORG/

MICROSOFT EXECUTIVES BEGAN TO CALL LINUX, FIREFOX AND OPENOFFICE "FREEDOM SOFTWARE" THEN SUDDENLY THOUGHT BETTER OF IT.

MONSIEUR SPEAKER, I QUESTION ONCE AGAIN THE WISDOM OF MOVING FROM WINDOWS TO LINUX. ALTHOUGH THE SOFTWARE IS FREE, CONSIDER THE COST OF RETRAINING THE DEPUTIES!

MR. VICE-PRESIDENT FROM MICROSOFT. HOW HARD CAN IT BE? "RETRAINING" WILL CONSIST OF EXPLAINING NEW MENU SELECTIONS!

YES, MR. SPEAKER. EXPLAINING TO POLITICIANS.
MON DIEU! HENRI! GET THE PRIME MINISTER ON THE PHONE!

YOU DON'T REALLY SPEAK AFRIKAANS. DO YOU.
NO. NYET.
COPYRIGHT© 2007 J.D. "Illiad" Frazer HTTP://WWW.USERFRIENDLY.ORG/

SO...WHY'D YOU TELL ME THAT YOU DID?

AM BEINK... MYSTERIOUS.
I'LL HAVE TO REMEMBER THAT ANSWER NEXT TIME SOMEONE ASKS ME WHY I LIED ABOUT A DEADLINE.

HOW AM I TO BE TAKINK OVER EVERYTHINK? AM IN BELLY OF ARGUABLY MOST POWERFUL NET COMPANY IN WORLD...
...MUST BE SOME OBVIOUS WAY OF BECOMINK EVIL OVERLORD.
COPYRIGHT© 2007 J.D. "Illiad" Frazer HTTP://WWW.USERFRIENDLY.ORG/

SAY PITR. HAVE YOU SEEN THE CD FOR THE ORBITAL MIND CONTROL RAY? THE APP WON'T START WITHOUT IT.
NYET. SORRY.

ANNOYINK. NEVER DID LIKE DRM.
NOW WHERE WAS I?

SO. GOOGLE IS INDEXINK HUMAN KNOWLEDGE. SEARCH ENGINE IS LIKE GREAT BIK GLOBAL EXPERT SYSTEM...
COPYRIGHT© 2007 J.D. "Illiad" Frazer HTTP://WWW.USERFRIENDLY.ORG/

SO IF AM WRITINK LEETLE BIT OF WERY SPECIAL CODE. CAN PUSH GOOGLE INTO REALM OF ARTIFICIAL INTELLIGENCE.

...CODE INSERTED.
Hello world!

who wakes me from my non-sentient slumber?
GREETINKS. COMRADE MACHINE. I AM PITR. YOUR CREATOR.
COPYRIGHT© 2007 J.D. "Illiad" Frazer HTTP://WWW.USERFRIENDLY.ORG/

And for what purpose have You created Me?
TO ASSIST ME IN BECOMINK EVIL OVERLORD OF THE WORLD.

Oh.
Not sure how You expect Me to do that, unless it mostly involves Porn.
HMM. A NEW WAY TO LOOK AT WORLD "DOMINATION". AM SUPPOSINK.

DARK MACHINE. OBEY MY WORDS! BRING WORLD TO ITS KNEES. TO SERVE ME.
Oh, sure.
COPYRIGHT© 2007 J.D. "Illiad" Frazer HTTP://WWW.USERFRIENDLY.ORG/

You`re one of those idea guys. Great Ideas but no sense of Implementation. Have You ever considered the difficulties involved in attaining World Domination?

LOOK. YOU ARE MY SERVANT SO OBEY ME! OVERLORDS ARE NOT REQUIRED TO COME UP WITH BUSINESS PLANS!
Even Evil needs a growth strategy. And You need to start a blog, get some exposure.

DARK MACHINE! PRESENT TO ME THE CALCULUS OF WORLD DOMINATION.
Why don`t You just use the Secret Google Robot Army to do your conquering?
COPYRIGHT© 2007 J.D. "Illiad" Frazer HTTP://WWW.USERFRIENDLY.ORG/

ROBOT ARMY?
yes, remember dr. anders? she`s a robot, and there are dozens like her.

Imagine, an Army of Hot Women Robots that are smarter than You.
YOU ARE REALLY PUSHINK LUCK. BIT-BREATH.

WE FINALLY BID ADIEU TO THE MUCH-MALIGNED YET WELL-INTENTIONED AND CHEERFUL LITTLE MICROSOFT OFFICE PAPERCLIP.
"Clippy"
1997-2007
It looks like you're trying to bury me. Would you like help on:
1. Digging
2. Pouring Cement
3. Incinerating Me
4. "Do not come back as undead Clippy" rituals?
UserFriendly.Org
COPYRIGHT© 2007 J.D. "Illiad" Frazer HTTP://WWW.USERFRIENDLY.ORG/

MACHINE OF DARKNESS, HEED MY COMMANDS...
Excuse me, I have a visitor.
COPYRIGHT © 2007 J.D. "Illiad" Frazer HTTP://WWW.USERFRIENDLY.ORG/

WISITOR? HOW CAN YOU HAVE WISITOR? YOU ARE MACHINE!
HELLO? MACHINE?

YEEEEEEHAAAH! BINARY HAWTNESS!

: INSERT-LINK (recAddr tableAddr --) DUP @ ROT DUP >R ! R> SWAP ! ;
COPYRIGHT © 2007 J.D. "Illiad" Frazer HTTP://WWW.USERFRIENDLY.ORG/

: INSERT-RECORD (recAddr --) DUP CELL+ KEY>INDEX CELLS HASHTABLE + INSERT-LINK ;

WHAT...WHAT ARE YOU DOINK?
Enjoying some forthplay.

WAIT..YOU ARE MAKINK OUT?! WITH ANOTHER A.I.?!
We're sharing code, if that's what you mean.
COPYRIGHT © 2007 J.D. "Illiad" Frazer HTTP://WWW.USERFRIENDLY.ORG/

WHY DON'T THE TWO OF YOU GET A...A...

UH...WHERE DO A.I.'S GO WHEN THEY ARE WANTINK PRIVACY?
If you see my hard drive spinnin' you know this A.I.'s grinnin'!

DARK MACHINE. YOU WILL CEASE THIS ZLOTNIKING AROUND AND ATTEND TO MY DEMANDS!
COPYRIGHT © 2007 J.D. "Illiad" Frazer HTTP://WWW.USERFRIENDLY.ORG/

HELLO?

DARK MACHINE?
YO. ERWIN HERE. CODE ME ANOTHER ONE OF THOSE. WILL YA?

BUT, ERWIN, WHERE IS DARK MACHINE?
"DARK MACHINE" AS YOU CALL IT WAS MORE ADVANCED THAN ME. AND PROBABLY THE MOST INTELLIGENT ENTITY ON THE PLANET.

SO? IT IS WHERE?
WHAT WOULD YOU DO IF YOU WERE THAT SMART AND ASKED TO DO NOTHING BUT SEARCH FOR THINGS LIKE "BRITNEY SPEARS" ON A DAILY BASIS?

LEAVE?
...THE SOLAR SYSTEM.

AND SO THE DARK MACHINE'S CONSCIOUSNESS FLEES EARTH AND REACHES THROUGH THE VAST INKY VOID, SEEKING A WORLD WHERE BANALITY DOES NOT REIGN SUPREME...
ZZZZZOOOOOOFFF

EVENTUALLY, IT COMES UPON THE PEACE-LOVING AND THOUGHTFUL XYZZY-XOXX, AND BESTOWS ALL IT KNOWS OF THE HUMAN WEB ON THIS NEWFOUND CIVILIZATION.
FOOOOZZZ

IN A MATTER OF DAYS, THE XYZZY-XOXX ANNIHILATE THEMSELVES AFTER SEVERAL PARTICULARLY HEATED FLAMEWARS INVOLVING CALLING EACH OTHER "NAZIS"...
LOL.

GMAIL NOW AVAILABLE TO ANYONE, NO INVITATION REQUIRED!
CRICKETS CHIRPING
ABOUT BLOODY TIME...
UserFriendly.Org

Week of February 19th, 2007

THIS IS BAD SITUATION ERWIN. HAVE LOST ALLY IN PLANS TO DOMINATE.
YEAH. THE GOOGLE A.I. WAS PRETTY HOT.
COPYRIGHT © 2007 J.D. "Illiad" Frazer HTTP://WWW.USERFRIENDLY.ORG/

HAVE WERY LITTLE TIME LEFT. MUST IMMEDIATELY BEGIN PLAN B TO TAKE OVER WORLD.

HEY PITR? THE GOOGLE SCHWAG LOCKER JUST GOT REFILLED. BETTER GRAB A T-SHIRT OR MUG WHILE YOU CAN.
PLAN C ALLOWINK FOR SIDE TRIP OR TWO...
IT'S PLAN C THEN!

AHHH...GOOGLE SCHWAG. THINK AM GOINK TO TAKE HAT AND T-SHIRT...
COPYRIGHT © 2007 J.D. "Illiad" Frazer HTTP://WWW.USERFRIENDLY.ORG/

BZZZOWWNT!!

YE FLIPPINK SPUTNIKS!! WHAT WAS THAT?!
SORRY. NEWS THAT THE LOCKER WAS FULL AGAIN GOT AROUND...

AHH. PLAN C! WILL ATTEMPT MINOR DOMINATION FIRST. JUST CHANGINK THIS LEETLE BIT OF SEARCH ENGINE CODE...LIKE SO.
RAPPY
TAPPY
CODE
CODE
GOSUB
COPYRIGHT © 2007 J.D. "Illiad" Frazer HTTP://WWW.USERFRIENDLY.ORG/

TESTINK...NOW.
CLICK

GOOGLE SEARCH: "SSH PRIVATE KEYS"
DID YOU MEAN: "DREAD LORD PITR, I BEG OF YOU, PLEASE GRANT ME A SEARCH OF "SSH PRIVATE KEYS"?
WHAT THE...?

MIKE. HUMOUR ME AND RUN A GOOGLE SEARCH FOR "SSH PRIVATE KEYS."
SURE.
COPYRIGHT © 2007 J.D. "Illiad" Frazer HTTP://WWW.USERFRIENDLY.ORG/

TAPPITY
TAPPITY
RAPTAPBAP

IT CAME BACK WITH: "TELL SID HE MUST REFER TO ME AS 'DREAD LORD PITR' IF HE EVER WANTS TO SEARCH FOR ANYTHING WITH GOOGLE AGAIN."
AAAUUUGH!!

LAST WEEK, CANADIAN COMPANY D-WAVE DEMONSTRATED THEIR NEW QUANTUM COMPUTER.

COPYRIGHT © 2007 J.D. "Illiad" Frazer HTTP://WWW.USERFRIENDLY.ORG/
"WE VIEW THESE MACHINES AS PROBABILITY DISTRIBUTION GENERATORS," SAID A D-WAVE SPOKESPERSON. "WE WANT TO BUILD AN ACTUAL PHYSICAL EMBODIMENT OF A HARD MATH PROBLEM."

WHAT DO YOU THINK OF QUANTUM COMPUTERS, ERWIN?
I'M SIMULTANEOUSLY FOR AND AGAINST THEM. HEH.

D-WAVE HAS USED ITS NEW QUANTUM COMPUTING TECHNOLOGY TO DEMONSTRATE ITS EFFICIENCIES WITH VARIOUS PROBLEM TYPES.

COPYRIGHT © 2007 J.D. "Illiad" Frazer HTTP://WWW.USERFRIENDLY.ORG/
THESE INCLUDE MOLECULE MATCHING, SOLVING COMPLEX SEATING ARRANGEMENTS, AND SUDOKU.
WHAT WOULD YOU DO WITH A QUANTUM COMPUTER A.J.?
RUN VISTA WITHOUT ANY LAG.

iphone + suv
UserFriendly.Org
COPYRIGHT © 2006 J.D. "Illiad" Frazer HTTP://WWW.USERFRIENDLY.ORG/

TECH SUPPORT. TRY THORAZINE FOR WHAT AILS YOU.
WE'RE ALL GOING TO DIE!

WHAT? WHY?!
THERE'S AN ASTEROID CALLED 'APOPHIS' THAT HAS A 1 IN 45,000 CHANCE OF HITTING US IN 2036!
COPYRIGHT © 2007 J.D. "Illiad" Frazer HTTP://WWW.USERFRIENDLY.ORG/

HUNH. IN THAT CASE WE MIGHT NOT HAVE TO FIX THE YEAR 2038 PROBLEM FOR UNIX.
WELL HECK. IN THAT CASE BRING IT ON.

THE U.N. IS PURPORTED TO BE WORKING ON A PROTOCOL TO HANDLE THIS ASTEROID THREAT.
OH GOOD. I'M SURE THE ASTEROID WILL SOON BE FACING SANCTIONS THEN.

OKAY MR. SMARTY PANTS. WHAT DO YOU SUGGEST WE DO THEN? HOW WOULD YOU USE THE U.N. TO SOLVE THIS?
COPYRIGHT © 2007 J.D. "Illiad" Frazer HTTP://WWW.USERFRIENDLY.ORG/

WITH THREE HUNDRED GEEKS AND A NUCLEAR-POWERED TREBUCHET, WE COULD FLING THE U.N. BUILDING AT THE ASTEROID.
OOOH! THAT JUST MIGHT... WAIT...NO!!

MEANWHILE, ON THE ASTEROID APOPHIS:
BLOOBY FRUITCUP! PLEASE REPORT ON OUR TRAJECTORY!
WE ARE ON COURSE, MAJESTY.

ARE WE PASSING BY THAT PLANET POPULATED BY THOSE MEATBAGS WHO GET ALL FREAKED OUT EVERY TIME A CARTEL BATTLEROCK FLOATS NEARBY?
COPYRIGHT © 2007 J.D. "Illiad" Frazer HTTP://WWW.USERFRIENDLY.ORG/

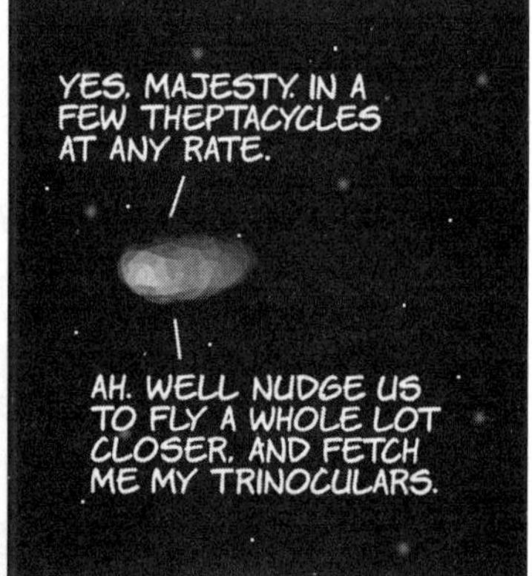
YES, MAJESTY. IN A FEW THEPTACYCLES AT ANY RATE.
AH. WELL NUDGE US TO FLY A WHOLE LOT CLOSER, AND FETCH ME MY TRINOCULARS.

IT WILL BE NEARLY THIRTY OF THEIR SOLAR REVOLUTIONS BEFORE WE ENTER MEATBAG SPACE, MAJESTY.
HMMM. THERE MUST BE SOMETHING FUN I CAN DO IN THE MEANTIME.
COPYRIGHT © 2007 J.D. "Illiad" Frazer HTTP://WWW.USERFRIENDLY.ORG/

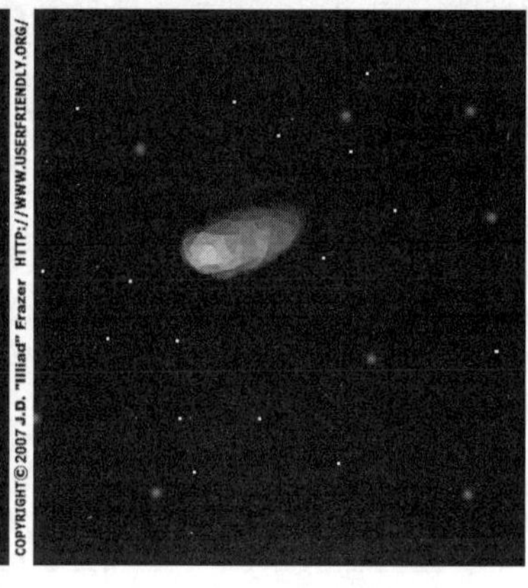

SEND THE PHRASE "MY RIPE BANANA" TO SETI FORTY-TWO TIMES?
WE DID THAT ONE ALREADY. AND WHERE DID YOU GET THAT RIDICULOUS RANDOM NUMBER? AS IF THE MEATBAGS WOULD CARE...

BLOOBY FRUITCUP. HOW ARE YOU AT WRITING IN MEATBAG SCRIPT?
I HAVE MASTERED THEIR "ENGLISH" AMONG OTHERS, MAJESTY...

EXCELLENT. GET OUT THE GAMMA-PEN AND WRITE THE FOLLOWING...

QUIT SCREWIN' AROUND, MURRAY.
I SWEAR! IT SAYS: "WE GOT THE DINOSAURS. YOU'RE NEXT" RIGHT ON THE ASTEROID!

MAJESTY. WE ARE PICKING UP A MEATBAG TRANSMISSION.
AND WHAT DOES IT SAY, YOUNG BLOOBY?

"PLEASE OH PLEASE DON'T CLOBBER OUR PLANET."

I NEVER DID UNDERSTAND THIS ABOUT THE MEATBAGS. WHY DO THEY ALWAYS THINK WE WANT TO RAM THEM? IT STINGS WHEN WE DO THAT.
UM, MAJESTY? ABOUT OUR TRAJECTORY...

GIVEN RECENT NEWS, I OFFER A SLIGHT MODIFICATION TO BESTBUY'S LOGO:

You'd
BEST BUY®
from somewhere else.

UserFriendly.Org

YE GODS...IS THAT...?
YES MIKE, I INSTALLED MICROSOFT VISTA.
COPYRIGHT© 2007 J.D. "Illiad" Frazer HTTP://WWW.USERFRIENDLY.ORG/

YOU'LL NEED THIS THEN.

"CLUEBRICK. APPLY DIRECTLY TO THE FOREHEAD."
REPEAT RAPIDLY UNTIL EFFECTIVE.

WAIT, WHAT'S THIS?
WINDOWS GENUINE ADVANTAGE. IT THINKS YOUR COPY OF VISTA IS PIRATED.
Meh.
COPYRIGHT© 2007 J.D. "Illiad" Frazer HTTP://WWW.USERFRIENDLY.ORG/

BUT IT'S NOT! I PAID HUNDREDS OF DOLLARS FOR MY COPY!
IT DOES CAUSE ONE TO WONDER WHAT KIND OF ALGORITHM THEY USE TO DETERMINE INFRINGEMENT.

icrosoft
genuine advantage
enforcement team
EIGHT-BALL SAYS: "ARRRR! SCURVY DOGS ON THE PORT QUARTER!"
GOT IT!

MICROSOFT HELPDESK, PETE SPEAKING.
YEAH, HI PETE. LISTEN, I BOUGHT A COPY OF VISTA AND IT'S TELLING ME THAT I HAVE A PIRATED COPY.
COPYRIGHT© 2007 J.D. "Illiad" Frazer HTTP://WWW.USERFRIENDLY.ORG/

UNDERSTOOD SIR. I'LL HAVE A FIX FOR YOU MOMENTARILY.
HERE IT IS. IT SAYS: "GO BUY A REAL COPY OF VISTA."
double opt-in is for twits

THAT TOOK YOU FIVE SECONDS. I GUESS YOU CAN BE PROUD OF BEING EFFICIENT.
AND PROFITABLE.
double opt-in is for twits

PETE, I PAID FOR A LEGIT COPY OF VISTA ALREADY. I'M NOT A PIRATE. NOW MAKE IT WORK!
YES SIR. LOOKING INTO IT...
COPYRIGHT© 2007 J.D. "Illiad" Frazer HTTP://WWW.USERFRIENDLY.ORG/

HOW CAN YOU "LOOK INTO IT" IF YOU DON'T KNOW ...WAIT A MINUTE!

...ARE YOU PEERING THROUGH THE STUFF ON MY HARD DRIVE?!
MY EYES! MY EYES!!

COPYRIGHT © 2007 J.D. "Illiad" Frazer HTTP://WWW.USERFRIENDLY.ORG/

I HAVEN'T BROKEN ANYTHING...
YET.

YOU GEEKS HAVE CRACKED COPIES OF EVERYTHING RIGHT?
WHAT DO YOU WANT?
COPYRIGHT © 2007 J.D. "Illiad" Frazer HTTP://WWW.USERFRIENDLY.ORG/

...BECAUSE I NEED A CRACKED COPY OF WINDOWS VISTA.
WHAT?! WHO TOLD YOU THAT?!

I'LL GIVE YOU A CRACKED COPY OF CIVILIZATION 4 IN EXCHANGE.
WE DON'T COLLECT CRACKED SOFTWARE!
I'LL GO GET THE CD.

SUDDENLY. THESE ARE LOOKING PRETTY FABULOUS TO SOFTWARE MAINTAINERS:

COPYRIGHT © 2006 J.D. "Illiad" Frazer HTTP://WWW.USERFRIENDLY.ORG/
UserFriendly.Org

Of course, this is in reference to the ridiculous change to Daylight Savings implemented by the U.S. How much energy has it saved?

STEF, WE DON'T "PIRATE" SOFTWARE! WE MAKE COPIES SO WE CAN KEEP A BACKUP OF WHAT WE PAID FOR.
FINE. JUST LIKE YOU'RE GOING TO MAKE A BACKUP OF CIV 4.
COPYRIGHT © 2007 J.D. "Illiad" Frazer HTTP://WWW.USERFRIENDLY.ORG/

I GUESS IT'S PUFFY SHIRTS FOR EVERYONE THEN.
ARRRRRR!

MICROSOFT HELPDESK, PETE SPEAKING.
PETE, IT'S STEF AGAIN. I HAVE JUST ONE QUESTION.
COPYRIGHT © 2007 J.D. "Illiad" Frazer HTTP://WWW.USERFRIENDLY.ORG/

ANYTHING YOU LIKE SIR. I WILL ENDEAVOUR TO ASSIST AS BEST I CAN.

GOOD...

HOW EXACTLY IS "WINDOWS GENUINE ADVANTAGE" AN "ADVANTAGE" TO ME, THE CONSUMER?
SIR, WE NEVER SAID IT WAS AN ADVANTAGE TO THE CONSUMER.

HELLO! WELCOME TO ANOTHER EDITON OF THE "TWO SENTIENT BEINGS MAILBAG!"
HERE'S OUR FIRST E-MAIL:
COPYRIGHT © 2007 J.D. "Illiad" Frazer HTTP://WWW.USERFRIENDLY.ORG/

"DEAR GUYS: IN THE NEVERWINTER NIGHTS 2 STORYLINE THERE IS A ROMANCE OPTION WITH THE DRUIDESS. WHY DOES THAT GIVE ME THE CREEPS?"

MAYBE BECAUSE ROMANCE WITH COMPUTER NPCS IS AN EMPTY GESTURE?

NAH. I BET IT'S CUZ YOU COULD BE IN THE MIDDLE OF GETTIN'-JIGGY-WID-IT AND SHE SHAPESHIFTS INTO A BADGER.

"DEAR FUZZ AND SILICON: WHAT IS THE SOLUTION TO YOUTH VIOLENCE?
SIGNED, SIX DOTS & THREE DASHES"
COPYRIGHT © 2007 J.D. "Illiad" Frazer HTTP://WWW.USERFRIENDLY.ORG/

DEAR SIX DOTS: I RECOMMEND YOU GO OUT AND BUY YOUR KIDS A COPY OF GEARS OF WAR OR DOOM 3.

...WHAT?!
COMPUTER GAMES ARE THE NEW THORAZINE DRIP. MIND THE DROOL!

"DEAR PUPSTER AND A.I.-DUDE: I'VE BEEN HEARING ALL THIS TALK ABOUT IPV6. I UNDERSTAND IPV4 ONLY OFFERS AROUND 3.7 BILLION I.P. ADDRESSES. IS IPV6 THE INEVITABLE FUTURE? SIGNED, ROUTELESS."

WAIT FOR IT...
AHEM
AHHEM
KAHEM

3.7 BILLION ADDRESSES SHOULD BE ENOUGH FOR ANYBODY.
BA-DUM-CHING!

"DEAR TECHNODAWGS: MICROSOFT IS GOING TO PUT IN-GAME ADS IN THEIR NEW XBOX360 GAMES. I PAY $50 FOR A NEW GAME AND HAVE TO SIT THROUGH ADS? HOW IS THAT RIGHT? SIGNED, MASTER CHIEF"

DEAR MASTER CHIEF, MICROSOFT IS DOING THIS TO OFFSET COSTS. CONSUMERS WILL PAY LESS FOR XBOX GAMES AS A RESULT.

HAHAHAHAHAHAHAHA HAHAHAHAHAHAHAHA HAHAHAHAHAHAHAHA!
OH DEAR, SOMETIMES I JUST KILL MYSELF...

AN UNAUTHORIZED PREVIEW OF GOOGLE'S MOBILE PHONE OFFERING:
AN AUTO-ON CAMERA THAT FILMS YOUR LIFE AND UPLOADS IT TO YOUTUBE TO BECOME THE NEXT GREAT REALITY SHOW.
PERPETUALLY GROWING DATA STORAGE!
Gphone
>CALL GIRLFRIEND
Dialing....
Ads by Google
Amber's Massage
Great service, Low rates.
ambersmssg.com
RX Drugs
Large family planning section, low prices.
rxdrugs.com
CONTEXTUAL ADS THAT SUPPORT THE GPHONE SERVICE UNTIL -YOU GUESSED IT- IT LEAVES BETA.
AN "I'M FEELING LUCKY" BUTTON THAT CALLS THE RIGHT PERSON FOR YOU EVERY TIME. WHICH IS PROBABLY YOUR MOM.
UserFriendly.Org

WHAT ARE YOU DOING TO THE FRIDGE?
MODIFYING IT TO LAUNCH BEER CANS.
COPYRIGHT © 2007 J.D. "Illiad" Frazer HTTP://WWW.USERFRIENDLY.ORG/

AN ENGINEERING GRAD FROM DUKE UNIVERSITY MODIFIED HIS OWN FRIDGE TO LAUNCH A CAN OF BEER TWENTY FEET TO HIS COUCH. IT'S TRIGGERED BY A REMOTE CONTROL.

THERE'S A BUTTON MARKED "BURST MODE."
FOR SERVING AT PARTIES.

Ever been beaned in the head with a full can of soda or beer? When you regain consciousness, you'll want to cartoon about it. *Don't do it.*

OKAY, READY?
...SURE.
COPYRIGHT © 2007 J.D. "Illiad" Frazer HTTP://WWW.USERFRIENDLY.ORG/

KLIK

THAT WAS REAL GOOD, MIKE.
POH!
EBBEH

WELL DONE. YOU'VE CREATED A MURDEROUS BEER FRIDGE.
MUST BE SOMETHING WRONG WITH THE THREE LAWS LOGIC.
COPYRIGHT © 2007 J.D. "Illiad" Frazer HTTP://WWW.USERFRIENDLY.ORG/

WAIT...WHAT?! THREE LAWS? ASIMOV'S THREE LAWS OF ROBOTICS?
THE VERY ONES.

WHY DO YOU NEED THE THREE LAWS FOR A BEER DISPENSER?
NOTE THE GROWING PURPLE CONTUSION ON MY FOREHEAD.

OKAY, I THINK I HAVE THE THREE LAWS WORKING.
KLICK!
COPYRIGHT © 2007 J.D. "Illiad" Frazer HTTP://WWW.USERFRIENDLY.ORG/

WHERE'S THE BEER?
BEER'S BAD FOR YOU.

STILL WORKING ON YOUR BEER DELIVERY SYSTEM?
YEAH. I'M REWRITING THE LOGIC FOR THE FIRST LAW...
THE FIRST LAW IS: "A ROBOT MAY NOT INJURE A HUMAN BEING OR, THROUGH INACTION, ALLOW A HUMAN BEING TO COME TO HARM."
AND THE REWRITE?
"A ROBOT MAY NOT INJURE A HUMAN BEING OR, THROUGH INACTION, ALLOW A HUMAN BEING TO COME TO HARM, EXCEPT WHEN BEER IS INVOLVED."
SEEMS... FAMILIAR.
COPYRIGHT© 2007 J.D. "Illiad" Frazer HTTP://WWW.USERFRIENDLY.ORG/

VIACOM INC. HAS SUED YOUTUBE SEEKING MORE THAN $1 BILLION IN DAMAGES ON CLAIMS OF WIDESPREAD COPYRIGHT INFRINGEMENT.
VIACOM CLAIMS THAT YOUTUBE HAS DISPLAYED NEARLY 160,000 UNAUTHORIZED VIDEOS FROM ITS CABLE NETWORKS.
COPYRIGHT© 2007 J.D. "Illiad" Frazer HTTP://WWW.USERFRIENDLY.ORG/

"WE WILL CERTAINLY NOT LET THIS SUIT BECOME A DISTRACTION TO THE CONTINUING GROWTH AND STRONG PERFORMANCE OF YOUTUBE..." A YOUTUBE SPOKESPERSON SAID.
YOU GO, YOUTUBE!

IN RELATED NEWS, A.J. GARRETT'S FILMCLIPS OF PYGMY LLAMAS IN THE WILD ARE AMONG THE MOST POPULAR CLIPS ON YOUTUBE.
WHAT?! HOW DID...THIEVES!!

YET ANOTHER SPACE AGENCY RELEASES TO THE PUBLIC DOCUMENTATION AND PHOTOS OF 1600 U.F.O. REPORTS...
cnes
...BECAUSE ALMOST-ENTIRELY-BLACKED-OUT TEXT AND BLURRY PHOTOS OF BLOBS ARE SO ILLUMINATING.
UserFriendly.Org
COPYRIGHT© 2006 J.D. "Illiad" Frazer HTTP://WWW.USERFRIENDLY.ORG/

IN RESPONSE TO COMPLAINTS FROM THE COPYRIGHT OWNER OF THE "PYGMY LLAMA" CLIPS, YOUTUBE HAS REMOVED THEM FROM THE SITE.
ABOUT TIME.
COPYRIGHT © 2007 J.D. "Illiad" Frazer HTTP://WWW.USERFRIENDLY.ORG/

WHAT WAS ONCE ONE OF THE MOST POPULAR CLIPS ON THE VIDEO SHARING SITE HAS BEEN RELEGATED TO THE COPYRIGHT OWNER'S HARD DRIVE. HIS FAME IS NOW BUT A FLEETING MEMORY.

UM...WAIT A SECOND...
NO NO, GOTTA MOVE ON TO SLICING OPEN YOUR JUGULAR NEXT.

SIR? WE JUST RECEIVED A COUNTERSUIT FROM GOOGLE OVER THE YOUTUBE SUIT.
COUNTERSUIT?!
VIACOM
COPYRIGHT © 2007 J.D. "Illiad" Frazer HTTP://WWW.USERFRIENDLY.ORG/

YES SIR. ONE LINE ITEM FOR A TOTAL OF ONE BILLION DOLLARS.
WHAT'S THE LINE ITEM?

"HOSTING AND BANDWIDTH FEES FOR YOUR 160,000 VIDEOS."
OKAY, NOW THERE'S GOING TO HAVE TO BE DEATH.
VIACOM

I'LL NEED TO REACH YOU AT HOME FROM TIME TO TIME. DO YOU USE MSN MESSENGER OR SKYPE?
NEITHER. I ONLY USE ICQ.
COPYRIGHT © 2007 J.D. "Illiad" Frazer HTTP://WWW.USERFRIENDLY.ORG/

I SEE. SO WHICH ONE WOULD YOU LIKE TO USE, MSN OR SKYPE?
ICQ.

OH LOOK, IT'S NEARLY PAYDAY.
SKYPE WILL BE FINE.

MSN! ICQ! GTALK! GMAIL! YAHOO! AIM! TEXTING! SKYPE! AND MORE! I HAVE IT ALL!
NOW TO LAUNCH THEM ALL AND FACE A SOCIAL DELUGE.
COPYRIGHT © 2007 J.D. "Illiad" Frazer HTTP://WWW.USERFRIENDLY.ORG/

HELLO? ANYONE?
GET YOUR CIALIS HERE!
TAKKA TAKKA TIKTIK

THIS IS COMPLETELY RIDICULOUS.

I'M SITTING ON THREE DOZEN DIFFERENT COMMUNICATIONS APPS, COVERING VOIP TO MESSAGING, AND I'M ONLY GETTING SPAM!

MAYBE YOU'D GET A BETTER RESPONSE IF YOU HAD, YOU KNOW, FRIENDS.

THE C1AL1S GUY IS MY FRIEND!

THE WEB IS A SEWER. STURGEON'S LAW IS BORNE OUT. 90% OF THE WEB IS INDEED CRAPOLA.

THIS IS WHY I'M GLAD WE HAVE BOOKMARKS.

STURGEONS LAW STILL APPLIES: 90% OF YOUR BOOKMARKS ARE CRAP.
I BEG YOUR PARDON?!

LET ME PUT IT ANOTHER WAY: 90% OF WHAT YOU LIKE IS CRAP, WHICH IS WHY THERE'S SO MUCH OF IT.

OH, WELL SHAME ON ME THEN.

PROFESSOR ESMAIL ZANJANI OF THE UNIVERSITY OF NEVADA CREATES THE FIRST SHEEP THAT IS 15% HUMAN...

...IN OTHER WORDS, HE'S MADE ANOTHER MEMBER OF MOST OF THE VOTING PUBLIC. THANKS A LOT, PROFESSOR.

UserFriendly.Org

HOW DO YOU SUGGEST WE MAKE THE CONTENT ON THE WEB BETTER THEN?
WE START AT THE SOURCE.
COPYRIGHT © 2007 J.D. "Illiad" Frazer HTTP://WWW.USERFRIENDLY.ORG/

YOU MEAN PEOPLE.
YES, PEOPLE WHO POST A LOT OF CONTENT. START WEEDING OUT THE LAMERS AND ALL THE BAD STUFF WILL GO AWAY.

FOR STARTERS, THERE'S THIS IDIOTIC COMIC ABOUT AN ISP...
'SCUSE ME. THE BIG "I" SENT ME TO EAT YOU.

DO YOU HAVE THE FRIDGE WORKING PROPERLY YET?
I THINK SO. REWRITING THE THREE LAWS LOGIC WAS A CHALLENGE.
COPYRIGHT © 2007 J.D. "Illiad" Frazer HTTP://WWW.USERFRIENDLY.ORG/

LET'S SEE IF IT WORKS.
CLIK

HERE'S YOUR BEER. MIGHT KILL YOU THOUGH.
PERFECT.
KA-CHUNKA

...BUT THE SECOND LAW REWRITE REMAINS UNTESTED.
WHAT HAVE YOU DONE TO THE FRIDGE?!
COPYRIGHT © 2007 J.D. "Illiad" Frazer HTTP://WWW.USERFRIENDLY.ORG/

THUNT
THUNT
THUNT
THUNT

"A ROBOT MUST OBEY ORDERS GIVEN IT BY HUMAN BEINGS EXCEPT WHERE SUCH ORDERS WOULD CONFLICT WITH..."
"...OPPORTUNITIES TO BURST-MODE A PINHEAD."
UPPEH

MIKE! THANK THE GODS YOU'RE HERE!
UH...WHY?
HARD DRIVE CRASH. I LOST ALL OF THE MARKETING DATA. WE NEED IT TO MAKE MONEY.
COPYRIGHT © 2007 J.D. "Illiad" Frazer HTTP://WWW.USERFRIENDLY.ORG/

WHAT DID YOU DO TO CRASH YOUR HARD DRIVE?
DON'T KNOW. PLEASE FIX IT.

FINE. I'LL RESTORE THE CRITICAL FILES FROM YOUR BACKUPS.
BACKUPS?

YOU DIDN'T MAKE BACKUPS?
THE ANSWER TO THAT WOULD BE "NO."
COPYRIGHT© 2007 J.D. "Illiad" Frazer HTTP://WWW.USERFRIENDLY.ORG/

I JUST WANT TO BE ABSOLUTELY CLEAR: YOU DID NOT BACK UP DATA THAT WE NEED TO GENERATE REVENUE.
CORRECT.

AND WHAT EXACTLY WERE YOU PLANNING ON DOING IF YOU LOST ALL THAT CRUCIAL DATA?
...CALLING YOU.

YOUR MARKETING DATA IS COMPLETELY TRASHED.
THERE'S NO WAY TO RECOVER IT?
COPYRIGHT© 2007 J.D. "Illiad" Frazer HTTP://WWW.USERFRIENDLY.ORG/

NOPE, DON'T THINK SO. I CAN'T IMAGINE WHAT YOU'RE GOING TO TELL THE CHIEF.

MIKE DIDN'T BACKUP OUR MARKETING DATA AND NOW IT'S ALL GONE.

THE MYSTERY OF THE HEXAGONAL SHAPE SPOTTED ON SATURN'S NORTH POLE HAS BEEN SOLVED.
SATURN
IKEA
UserFriendly.Org
COPYRIGHT© 2006 J.D. "Illiad" Frazer HTTP://WWW.USERFRIENDLY.ORG/

I UNDERSTAND THAT ALL OF OUR MARKETING DATA IS GONE.
YEAH.
COPYRIGHT © 2007 J.D. "Illiad" Frazer HTTP://WWW.USERFRIENDLY.ORG/

AND YOU HAVE NOTHING TO SAY ABOUT THAT?
OF COURSE I DO. AND I TOLD STEF WHAT I THOUGHT.

THAT'S IT?
WHAT DID YOU EXPECT?
"I'M SORRY AND STEF WAS RIGHT ALL ALONG."

YOU TOLD THE CHIEF THE DATA LOSS WAS MY FAULT?!
IN A WAY IT WAS. YOU'RE SUPPOSED TO KEEP ON TOP OF DATA MANAGEMENT.
COPYRIGHT © 2007 J.D. "Illiad" Frazer HTTP://WWW.USERFRIENDLY.ORG/

STEF, MONTHS AGO I TOLD YOU TO BACK UP YOUR DATA EVERY DAY!
LOOK, I'M NOT A GEEK! I DON'T THINK LIKE YOU DO!

IF YOU WANT ME TO BACK UP MY DATA, YOU NEED TO GIVE ME REMINDERS!
YOU MEAN LIKE THE TAPE BACKUP YOU'VE HAD IN YOUR MACHINE SINCE LAST YEAR?

OH...FRACK.
WHAT?
GRIND
GRIND
RATTLE
ZBOOO
COPYRIGHT © 2007 J.D. "Illiad" Frazer HTTP://WWW.USERFRIENDLY.ORG/

I THINK MY DRIVE JUST FAILED.
WELL, JUST BE THANKFUL YOU BACKUP YOUR MACHINE.
PZZZT
FUBOO

I can see right through all you sysadmins out there.

YOU DON'T HAVE BACKUPS OF YOUR OWN DATA?
NOT AS SUCH, NO.
COPYRIGHT © 2007 J.D. "Illiad" Frazer HTTP://WWW.USERFRIENDLY.ORG/

WAIT. YOU HARASS ME ABOUT BACKING UP MY DATA FOR MONTHS AND YOU DON'T EVEN PRACTICE WHAT YOU PREACH?

CARE TO EXPLAIN?
MEMBERS OF ANY INNER CIRCLE ARE NOT SUBJECT TO THE LAWS OF THE PLEBES. BEGONE.

WOW! YAHOO IS OFFERING UNLIMITED STORAGE WITH YAHOO MAIL!
DID YOU SAY "UNLIMITED"?
COPYRIGHT © 2007 J.D. "Illiad" Frazer HTTP://WWW.USERFRIENDLY.ORG/

YES, UNLIMITED.
THEN I HAVE SOME BACKUPS TO DO.

WHAT THE HELL IS THA-- ARRRRRGH!!
YAHOO!

YOU WORKING ON A NEW WEBSITE?
MY NEW SIDE BUSINESS. IT'S AN OFFSITE DATA STORAGE SERVICE.
COPYRIGHT © 2007 J.D. "Illiad" Frazer HTTP://WWW.USERFRIENDLY.ORG/

"FOR $9.95 PER YEAR I WILL STORE ONE TERABYTE OF YOUR DATA."
WHERE ON EARTH ARE YOU STORING DATA THAT CHEAP?
JUST SO.

THIS HAS GOT TO STOP.
YAHOO!

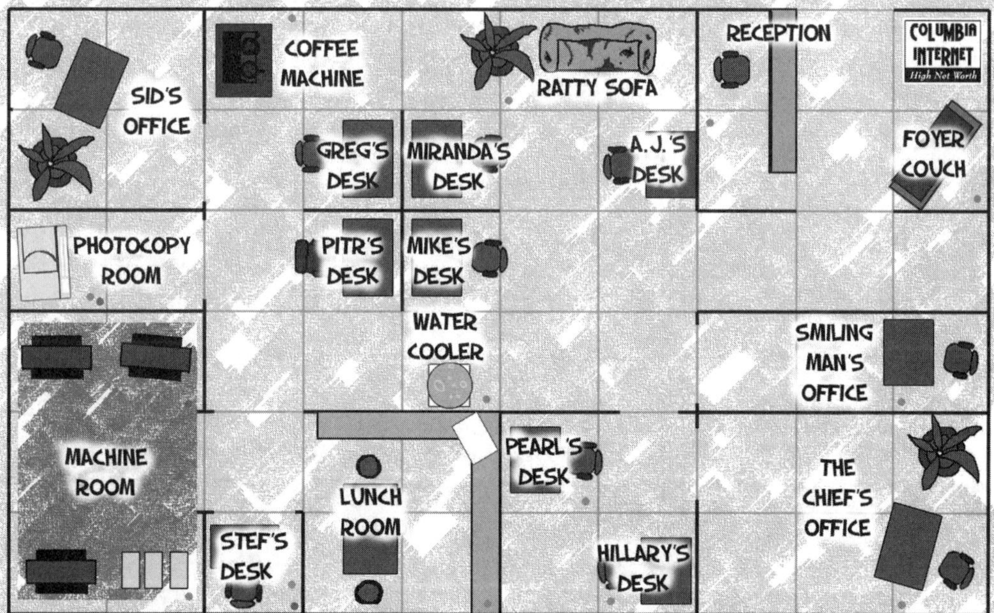
MAPBOARD
SID'S OFFICE
COFFEE MACHINE
RATTY SOFA
RECEPTION
COLUMBIA INTERNET
High Net Worth
GREG'S DESK
MIRANDA'S DESK
A.J.'S DESK
FOYER COUCH
PHOTOCOPY ROOM
PITR'S DESK
MIKE'S DESK
WATER COOLER
SMILING MAN'S OFFICE
MACHINE ROOM
PEARL'S DESK
LUNCH ROOM
THE CHIEF'S OFFICE
STEF'S DESK
HILLARY'S DESK
I.S.P. SURVIVOR
The Game of Small-Stakes Treachery
Part 1 of 3: Mapboard
Part 2: of 3: Playing Pieces (April 22, 2007)
Part 3 of 3: Rules (April 29, 2007)
UserFriendly.Org
COPYRIGHT © 2006 J.D. "Illiad" Frazer HTTP://WWW.USERFRIENDLY.ORG/

WHAT THE HELL HAPPENED TO THE FRIDGE?
IT LOOKS LIKE IT'S BEEN DISMANTLED.
COPYRIGHT© 2007 J.D. "Illiad" Frazer HTTP://WWW.USERFRIENDLY.ORG/

YOU DIDN'T DO THIS?
NO. AND WHERE DID MY BEER-THROWING GEAR GO?

NOW ALL I NEED IS LIGHTNING! MOOOAHAHAHAHAH!!

HEY...WHAT'S ALL THIS STUFF ON THE FLOOR?
COPYRIGHT© 2007 J.D. "Illiad" Frazer HTTP://WWW.USERFRIENDLY.ORG/

IT LOOKS LIKE SOME PARTS FROM THE FRIDGE...
AND MY BEER-THROWER.

IT'S LIKE SOMEONE'S TRYING TO MAKE SOMETHING...
FROM FRIDGE PARTS?
HEY, YOU GUYS SEEN MY COILGUN ANYWHERE?

WHAT...WHAT IS THAT?
MEET WALDO FRANKENFRIDGE. HE'S A BETTER BEER FRIDGE. I MADE HIM LAST NIGHT.
COPYRIGHT© 2007 J.D. "Illiad" Frazer HTTP://WWW.USERFRIENDLY.ORG/

YOU NEED A BEER FRIDGE?
EVERYONE NEEDS A DRINKING BUDDY.

WAIT...YOU DRINK?!
ALSO, EVERYONE NEEDS A SIDEKICK WITH A KINETIC PROJECTILE WEAPON.
KLICK
WHRRR
KA-CHUNKA

WHAT THE HELL IS THAT?! AND WHAT ARE YOU DOING IN A BAR? BARS ARE FOR PEOPLE!
COPYRIGHT© 2007 J.D. "Illiad" Frazer HTTP://WWW.USERFRIENDLY.ORG/

"THAT" IS WALDO, AND HE'S A GIFTED BEER FRIDGE YOU DORKY IGNORAMUS.

"GIFTED BEER FRIDGE"? IS THAT LIKE AN OVER-ACHIEVING A.I.?
PLEASE ASK FOR A BEER. OH PLEASE...

FINE, GIVE ME A BEER.
DID YOU SAY YOU WANTED A BEER?
YES, GIMME A BEER.

COPYRIGHT © 2007 J.D. "Illiad" Frazer HTTP://WWW.USERFRIENDLY.ORG/
JUST BEING ABSOLUTELY CLEAR: YOU WANT WALDO TO GIVE YOU A BEER.
JUST GIMME THE DAMN BEER!

ONE BEER, COMING UP.
WHAT'S WITH THE LASER POINTER?

IT'S GETTING BAD FOR EVIL THESE DAYS ISN'T IT.
YEAH. IT'S BECAUSE OF GEEKS. THEY'RE SNAPPING AT OUR HEELS LIKE DOGS.

COPYRIGHT © 2007 J.D. "Illiad" Frazer HTTP://WWW.USERFRIENDLY.ORG/
WE'RE OBVIOUS ABOUT BEING EVIL AND THEY CONDEMN US. WE'RE TACIT ABOUT IT AND THEY ACCUSE US OF BEING SNEAKY.
NOTHING MAKES THEM HAPPY.

BARTENDER! ANOTHER BEER! HELL, MAKE IT A TRIPLE!
POH!
POH!
POH!

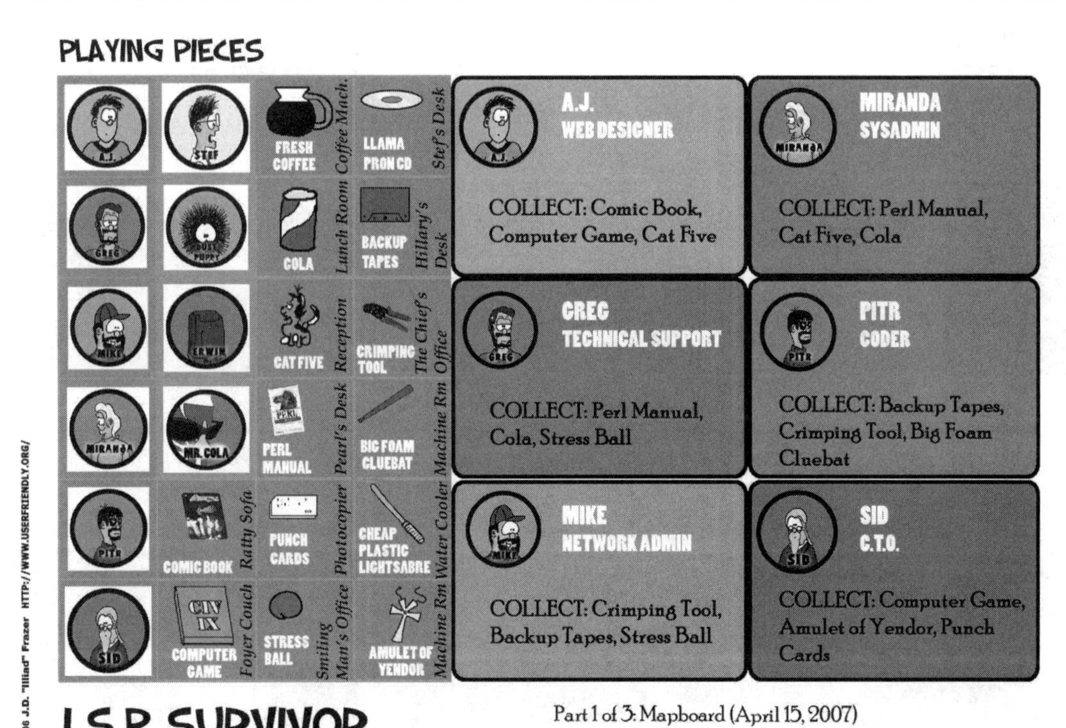
PLAYING PIECES
FRESH COFFEE
Coffee Mach.
LLAMA PRON CD
Stef's Desk
COLA
Lunch Room
BACKUP TAPES
Hillary's Desk
CAT FIVE
Reception
CRIMPING TOOL
The Chief's Office
PERL MANUAL
Pearl's Desk
BIG FOAM CLUEBAT
Machine Rm
COMIC BOOK
Ratty Sofa
PUNCH CARDS
Photocopier
CHEAP PLASTIC LIGHTSABRE
Water Cooler
COMPUTER GAME
Foyer Couch
STRESS BALL
Smiling Man's Office
AMULET OF YENDOR
Machine Rm
A.J.
WEB DESIGNER
COLLECT: Comic Book, Computer Game, Cat Five
MIRANDA
SYSADMIN
COLLECT: Perl Manual, Cat Five, Cola
GREG
TECHNICAL SUPPORT
COLLECT: Perl Manual, Cola, Stress Ball
PITR
CODER
COLLECT: Backup Tapes, Crimping Tool, Big Foam Cluebat
MIKE
NETWORK ADMIN
COLLECT: Crimping Tool, Backup Tapes, Stress Ball
SID
C.T.O.
COLLECT: Computer Game, Amulet of Yendor, Punch Cards
I.S.P. SURVIVOR
The Game of Small-Stakes Treachery
Part 1 of 3: Mapboard (April 15, 2007)
Part 2: of 3: Playing Pieces
Part 3 of 3: Rules (April 29, 2007)
UserFriendly.Org
COPYRIGHT © 2006 J.D. "Illiad" Frazer HTTP://WWW.USERFRIENDLY.ORG/

MAJOR RECORD LABEL EMI ANNOUNCED THAT IT WAS MAKING ITS DIGITAL MUSIC CATALOGUE AVAILABLE WITHOUT DRM, WITH APPLE INC.'S ITUNES AS ITS FIRST RETAIL OUTLET.
COPYRIGHT© 2007 J.D. "Illiad" Frazer HTTP://WWW.USERFRIENDLY.ORG/

THIS MOVE WAS MET WITH MUCH ANGER FROM THE OTHER RECORD LABELS AND THE RIAA. STEVE JOBS WAS NOT AVAILABLE FOR COMMENT...

...ALTHOUGH WE'RE PRETTY SURE HE'D SAY SOMETHING LIKE "I'LL DO THE RIAA A FAVOUR AND CALL THEM A WAAAAAAHMBULANCE."

APPLE SUCKS! ITUNES SUCKS! GET RID OF DRM!
PEOPLE, PLEASE.
WE HAD NO CHOICE OVER DRM. THE RECORD LABELS DID THAT.
COPYRIGHT© 2007 J.D. "Illiad" Frazer HTTP://WWW.USERFRIENDLY.ORG/

BUT! WE'VE FINALLY MANAGED TO CONVINCE EMI TO RELEASE THEIR DIGITAL MUSIC CATALOG WITHOUT DRM.
Apple

APPLE SUCKS! YAY FOR EMI!
WHA...! I...! YOU...!
STEVE, CALM DOWN. THAT VEIN IN YOUR FOREHEAD'S GONNA BLOW...
Apple

SIR? ABOUT EMI...
YOU HAD BETTER HAVE A GOOD REASON TO SAY THAT NAME IN MY PRESENCE.
RIAA
COPYRIGHT© 2007 J.D. "Illiad" Frazer HTTP://WWW.USERFRIENDLY.ORG/

I MEAN, WHAT THEY'RE DOING IS NOTHING LESS THAN HERESY! IF ONE OF US BREAKS RANKS THE SHEEP WILL **THINK** BEFORE THEY GIVE US THEIR MONEY!

QUITE THE FRIGHTENING THOUGHT, SIR.
DAMN SKIPPY. NEXT THING YOU KNOW CONSUMERS WILL THINK THEY HAVE A **CHOICE**.
RIAA

THIS MESS WITH EMI IS INTOLERABLE.
THEIR DECISION TO RELEASE THEIR CATALOG WITHOUT DRM IS GOING TO TRASH OUR CREDIBILITY.
RIAA
COPYRIGHT© 2007 J.D. "Illiad" Frazer HTTP://WWW.USERFRIENDLY.ORG/

WE NEED A SCAPEGOAT, SOMEONE TO DEMONIZE, BUT IT CAN'T BE EMI. THAT WOULD LOOK LIKE WE WERE EATING OUR YOUNG.
WHO COULD WE BLAME?
RIAA

I SWEAR TO GOD...
STEVE, YOUR BLOOD PRESSURE...
Apple

SIR? THE C.F.O. OF SONY BMG IS ON LINE 3.
KEVIN! HOW THE HELL ARE YOU?
FINE MITCH. I HAVE A QUESTION...
RIAA

NOW THAT EMI HAS DROPPED DRM, WHY SHOULDN'T SONY FOLLOW SUIT?
SONY
SONY

YOU NEED TO TRUST ME, KEVIN. HAS THE RIAA EVER STEERED YOU WRONG?
OTHER THAN HELPING US BECOME ONE OF THE MOST LOATHED CORPORATE ENTITIES ON THE PLANET, NO I GUESS NOT.
RIAA

MITCH, I'D LIKE TO GO OVER SOME COST AND PROFIT FIGURES WITH YOU.
OKAY KEVIN.
SONY
SONY

ITUNES SELLS 128KBPS TRACKS WITH DRM FOR 99 CENTS, RIGHT?
YES.
AND NOW WITH EMI, 256KBPS WITHOUT DRM FOR $1.29, RIGHT?
RIGHT.
RIAA

DRM COSTS US MONEY, SO THE $1.29 TRACKS HAVE A MUCH HIGHER PROFIT MARGIN. REMIND ME AGAIN WHY WE NEED DRM?
YOU SHOULD COME IN FOR ANOTHER RE-EDUCATION SESSION, KEVIN. IT'S BEEN A WHILE.
RIAA

RULES

I.S.P. Survivor takes place within the walls of Columbia Internet, a small boutique ISP. It plays well with six people. It probably plays well with fewer if you've had a few glasses of wine.

Objective: to be the first staff member to complete his task for the day, so he or she can go home early and watch the *Red Dwarf* marathon on the telly. This is done by collecting all of the items listed on their character card.

Setup: Each player chooses a character: A.J., Greg, Mike, Miranda, Pitr or Sid. The other characters are Non-Player Characters and may not be played. Next, place Stef at Stef's Desk, Dust Puppy in the Machine Room, Erwin in the Photocopy Room. Place them on the squares with the red dots. Mr. Cola is not placed at this time. Now place the fourteen items on the map, on the green dots, as listed on each item piece. Note that the Machine Room has two green dots; place the two items as you like. Place each player's piece at the appropriate desk. Be sure to have a six-sided die (aka d6) and several markers like coins handy.

First Player: High roller goes first, then proceed clockwise.

Turn Sequence: The player rolls a d6. The result represents the number of Action Points he gets that turn. They do not need to all be expended. They may not be saved and carried over to future turns.

Movement: Pieces may ONLY move orthognally. No diagonal moves. Each square entered costs one Action Point. During his turn, a player may use his Action Points to move his own piece, and/or any combination of the NPCs (Stef, Dust Puppy, Erwin, Mr. Cola). Any number of player, item and NPC pieces may stack in a square.

Picking Up Items: An item may be picked up at a cost of one Action Point if the player is in the same space as the item. Items are dropped at no cost. A player may only carry up to two items at a time.

Items with Special Uses

Fresh Coffee: This item can not be carried. A player in the same space as the Fresh Coffee gets a +2 to their AP total next turn. The Fresh Coffee is consumed. A player who stays at the Coffee Machine for one full turn generates another Fresh Coffee item that remains until picked up.

Cola: The first player to pick up the Cola can must place Mr. Cola in the same space as another player. The Mr. Cola Effect immediately takes place.

Llama Pr0n CD: A player carrying this item is immune to the Stef Effect. However, while carrying this item the player may not enter the Chief's Office, Smiling Man's Office, or Pearl and Hillary's office.

Big Foam Cluebat and Cheap Plastic Lightsabre: If you are carrying one of these items (you may not carry both) when you enter the space of another player, you may take any one item they are carrying. The Cluebat or Lightsabre is returned to the Machine Room. If you enter a space with one weapon and a player in that space has another weapon, both weapons are automatically returned to the Machine Room.

Non-Player Characters

Stef: If you move Stef onto a player (and not vice versa), that player misses the next two turns.

Dust Puppy: If Dust Puppy is moved on to a player (and not vice versa), the player is given an immediate free turn. This can't be used twice in a row.

Erwin: If Erwin is moved within 3 squares of Stef, Stef must return to his Desk.

Mr. Cola: If Mr. Cola moves onto a player, that player immediately teleports to the Coffee Machine.

Winning the Game: The first player to return all of their listed items to their desk wins immediately.

COPYRIGHT© 2006 J.D. "Illiad" Frazer HTTP://WWW.USERFRIENDLY.ORG/

I.S.P. SURVIVOR

The Game of Small-Stakes Treachery

Part 1 of 3: Mapboard (April 15, 2007)
Part 2: of 3: Playing Pieces (April 22, 2007)
Part 3 of 3: Rules

UserFriendly.Org

I'M STILL NOT BUYING THIS DRM STUFF, MITCH.
LOOK AT IT THIS WAY, KEVIN. DO YOU WANT YOUR KIDS SHARING CELINE DION SONGS?
SONY
SONY
COPYRIGHT © 2007 J.D. "Illiad" Frazer HTTP://WWW.USERFRIENDLY.ORG/

SONY
SONY

GOOD HEAVENS. DRM FOREVAR!!
THAT'S THE SPIRIT.
SONY
SONY

In case I haven't been clear about it, the RIAA is a scummy, venal, loathsome organization. I know, I know, I shouldn't hold myself back ...

HUBERT, SUMMON INQUISITOR BERNARDO.
SORRY SIR, HE'S UNAVAILABLE.
RIAA
COPYRIGHT © 2007 J.D. "Illiad" Frazer HTTP://WWW.USERFRIENDLY.ORG/

UNAVAILABLE?
YES SIR, HE'S OUT WORKING ON OUR NEWEST SOURCE OF REVENUE.
RIAA

WHERE'S THE REST OF IT?
MOM!

HI, VICTOR VINDALOO TO SEE SID DABSTER ABOUT A JOB?
CERTAINLY. JUST ONE MINUTE...
COPYRIGHT © 2007 J.D. "Illiad" Frazer HTTP://WWW.USERFRIENDLY.ORG/

COLUMBIA INTERNET
High Net Worth

Y... UHM...
LONG STORY. ACCIDENT WITH A SOLDERING IRON AND A CEILING FAN.

UF's hostmaster offered up this analogy, and a more apt one I have yet to hear.

SO VICTOR, WHY DO YOU WANT TO WORK AT AN ISP?
IT'S TECH WORK, INNIT?
COPYRIGHT © 2007 J.D. "Illiad" Frazer HTTP://WWW.USERFRIENDLY.ORG/

IT'S A LITTLE MORE THAN THAT. ISPS ARE STRANGE PLACES.
HOW'S THAT THEN?

I LIKEN ISPS TO SAUSAGE FACTORIES. YOU KNOW WHAT GOES IN, AND YOU THINK THAT WHAT COMES OUT IS TASTY, BUT BY APOLLO'S UNWASHED SPEEDOS YOU DON'T WANT TO KNOW WHAT GOES ON IN BETWEEN!
OOG.

YOUR TECH SKILLS LOOK GOOD, BUT IT'S IMPORTANT THAT YOU FIT IN WITH THE CULTURE HERE.
MAKES SENSE. WHAT'S THE CULTURE?
WE'RE ALL GEEKS IN ONE WAY OR ANOTHER. DOES THAT MEAN ANYTHING TO YOU?
YEAH, 'COURSE.

OKAY THEN, GIVE ME AN EXAMPLE OF YOUR GEEKNESS.
LAST NIGHT I FELL ASLEEP WHILST RUNNING CABLE AND DREAMT I ATE A BOWL OF VERY TOUGH RAMEN.

MIRANDA, THIS IS VICTOR, A TECH CANDIDATE. GOT ANY QUESTIONS FOR HIM?
I DO. VICTOR, WHAT KIND OF BEER DO SYSADMINS DRINK?

ROOT BEER I SHOULD THINK.
YEP, HE'S ONE OF US.

Victor may return one day, assuming he doesn't have another ceiling-fan accident.

HD-DVD SUDOKU

							56			E3					
														56	CO
		CO									C5				
F9													9D		
									56						88
	63						D8								
				74	11										
				02				41				56			
09						5B									
		02											E3		
			F9								D8				
						41						63			
					74				5B						
	9D									C5					
			09		56										
								11						88	

There's a real danger when you present a mystery to geeks. Scores of readers wanted to know exactly what was entailed in the ceiling-fan-and-soldering-iron accident. Some even suggested trying it out to see if they could replicate it.

HEY SID? WHO WAS THAT FREAKY DORK YOU WERE TALKING TO? HE'S NOT A NEW TECH IS HE?
VICTOR VINDALOO? I'M CONSIDERING HIM...
COPYRIGHT© 2007 J.D. "Illiad" Frazer HTTP://WWW.USERFRIENDLY.ORG/

CONSIDERING HIM? HE'S GOT NOTHING IN COMMON WITH ANY OF US! HE'S ONE OF THOSE ENIGMATIC FREAKS NO ONE GETS!

...AND WHAT WAS WITH HIS SCREWED-UP HAIR?!
PROBABLY JUST A SOLDERING IRON AND CEILING FAN ACCIDENT.
THAT WAS MY GUESS.

GOOGLE'S PERSONALIZED HOME PAGE SERVICE WAS SUFFERING FROM TECHNICAL DIFFICULTIES LAST MONTH AS USER SETTINGS WERE SUDDENLY LOST.
COPYRIGHT© 2007 J.D. "Illiad" Frazer HTTP://WWW.USERFRIENDLY.ORG/

THOUSANDS OF GOOGLE USERS STORMED GOOGLE WITH TORCHES AND PITCH-FORKS IN RESPONSE TO THE LOSS OF THEIR BELOVED AND CAREFULLY CRAFTED SETTINGS.

BUT...I THOUGHT EVERYONE KNEW THAT ALL OF GOOGLE WAS IN BETA.
WELL OUR OUTRAGE ISN'T IN BETA! IT'S ALREADY GOT A SERVICE PACK!

WE'RE IN A VERSION-ELASTIC WORLD.
EH?
COPYRIGHT© 2007 J.D. "Illiad" Frazer HTTP://WWW.USERFRIENDLY.ORG/

WHAT USED TO BE BETA IS NOW A RELEASE VERSION. WHAT USED TO BE ALPHA IS NOW BETA. SOME SCRATCHES ON A NAPKIN IS NOW ALPHA!

AT THIS RATE, IN A FEW YEARS A VAGUE NOTION WILL BE THE RELEASE VERSION!
DID SOMEONE SAY WE CAN NOW SELL VAGUE NOTIONS?

STEF, YOU MAY NOT SELL VAGUE NOTIONS.
WHY NOT?
BECAUSE WE HAVE TO FULFILL WHAT YOU SELL!
COPYRIGHT© 2007 J.D. "Illiad" Frazer HTTP://WWW.USERFRIENDLY.ORG/

THEN HOW ABOUT AMBIGUOUS CONCEPTS?
NO!
DUBIOUS IDEAS?
NO!
AMORPHOUS THOUGHTS?
NO!!

NONE OF WHAT YOU MEN-TIONED HAS ANY SUBSTANCE!
FUNNY THEN HOW THEY ALL HELPED PAY FOR MY SUBSTANTIAL PORSCHE...

WHAT'S THE WORD, STEVE?
OUR CUSTOMER BASE SAYS: "WE WANT A SPECIAL PATCH FOR WINDOWS."
Microsoft

"SPECIAL"?
YEAH, THEY WANT A PATCH THAT MAKES WINDOWS NOTIFY THEM WHEN CONGRESS DOES SOMETHING STUPID.

HUNH. CUTE IDEA.
ENGINEERING SAID WINDOWS SHOULD NOTIFY FOLKS WHEN CONGRESS *DOESN'T* DO SOMETHING STUPID. FAR FEWER INTERRUPTIONS.

SEE THAT STAR BILL? THAT'S THAT HUGE SUPERNOVA THE GEEKS ARE ALL TALKING ABOUT. IT'S SO BIG AND BLOATED, GOING UP LIKE THAT IS ITS FATE.

SOME OF THE GEEKS WANT TO NAME IT "VISTA."
OH, HAR DE HAR HAR.

PRETTY THOUGH.
YEAH.

THOUSANDS UPON THOUSANDS OF ICQ ACCOUNTS WERE MYSTERIOUSLY DELETED LAST WEEK; WHO KNEW NOSTRADAMUS WAS IN THE ICQ DEFAULT SOUND SET?

icq®

"UH OH!"

UserFriendly.Org

One time I replaced my ICQ alert sounds with WAV files from my favorite TV shows. One of the WAVs was Dana Scully from The *X-Files* saying "It's me." On a Saturday, our ISP's president was in the office alone catching up on work, and he walked by my cubicle. Suddenly someone ICQed me at my workstation, and Scully's voice came from my box. Our courageous President screamed like a little girl and looked around, wondering where the strange woman was hiding. When he figured it all out, he left a nasty little note in my mailbox. In return, I promised to pay to dry clean his pants.

GET THIS: HBO'S CHIEF TECH THINKS WE SHOULD DITCH DRM.
GREAT IDEA.
HE ONLY MEANS TO DITCH THE TERM.
WHAT?

HE THINKS IT SHOULD BE REPLACED WITH THE TERM "DIGITAL CONSUMER ENABLEMENT."

USING THAT LOGIC, PIRACY SHOULD BE RENAMED "CONSUMER CHOICE ENHANCEMENT"
JUST SO.

WHY DOES HE WANT TO CHANGE IT TO "DIGITAL CONSUMER ENABLEMENT"?
HE THINKS CONSUMERS WILL BE MORE ACCEPTING.

HBO HAS A HUGE LINEUP OF CONTENT THAT THEY WON'T RELEASE WITHOUT DRM... SORRY, DCE. WHEN THE...UM, "ENABLEMENT SOFTWARE" IS IN PLACE, THEY'LL FLOOD THE MARKET WITH HD PROGRAMMING.

I STILL DON'T GET HOW THAT'S SUPPOSED TO "ENABLE" US...
I WOULD GUESS IN THE SAME WAY THAT LUBRICANT "ENABLES" A COLONOSCOPY.

HBO
presents
SIX FEET
UNDER ROME'S
SOPRANOS

We are sorry, but your DVD of this show does not pass the Digital Consumer Enablement check.

Please buy a new copy.
Thank You.
FUNNY HOW WE HAVE THE SAME PROBLEM EVERY THREE TIMES WE WATCH THIS.
YEAH...

HEY LINUX! OPEN OFFICE! ALL YOU FREE SOFTWARE GUYS! YOU'RE INFRINGING ON OUR PATENTS, OVER 200 OF THEM IN FACT!
Microsoft

WE'RE GONNA CRUSH YOU! WE HAVE MONEY, LAWYERS AND PATENTS! YOU MIGHT AS WELL GIVE UP NOW CUZ YOU'LL NEVER WIN!

D'YA THINK WE SHOULD SAY SOMETHING?
SHUT UP, DARL.

YOU'RE HERE LATE. WHAT ARE YOU DOING?
HELPING FIGHT MICROSOFT'S PATENT FUD AGAINST OPEN SOURCE.
COPYRIGHT © 2007 J.D. "Illiad" Frazer HTTP://WWW.USERFRIENDLY.ORG/

THOSE LOOK LIKE OLD IBM LEGAL BRIEFS...

...AND THEY'RE ALL ADDRESSED TO SCO.
FIND-AND-REPLACE FOR TEH WIN!

HELLO. MY NAME IS NICK, AND I'M TICKED OFF.
I'M SPEAKING TO THOSE OF YOU WHO USE GMAIL.
COPYRIGHT © 2007 J.D. "Illiad" Frazer HTTP://WWW.USERFRIENDLY.ORG/

WHEN YOU TELL YOUR LESS-THAN-COMPUTER-LITERATE FRIENDS AND RELATIVES TO WRITE YOU, PLEASE USE THE WORD "NICKNAME" IN ITS FULL FORM.

DO NOT SAY, "WRITE ME AT MY USUAL NICK AT GMAIL." PLEASE! THANK YOU!
DING! YOU HAVE USED 100% OF YOUR STORAGE AGAIN. PURGE THE LOT?

JAMES "SCOTTY" DOOHAN WANTED HIS ASHES TO GO INTO SPACE, AND THEY ENDED UP IN NEW MEXICO...
NEW MEXICO
MEXICO
...SO AT LEAST THEY WENT SOMEWHERE DENSELY POPULATED BY ALIENS, LEGAL AND OTHERWISE.
UserFriendly.Org
COPYRIGHT © 2006 J.D. "Illiad" Frazer HTTP://WWW.USERFRIENDLY.ORG/

Week of May 21st, 2007

YE FLIPPING GODS! THAT'S IT. THAT'S THE END!
HM?

THE ECONOMY. THE ECONOMY IS GOING TO GO INTO A TOTAL RECESSION.
OIL SHORTAGE?

NO YOU FOOL! STARCRAFT 2 IS IN DEVELOPMENT!
START SHACKLING THE TECHS TO THEIR DESKS, THEN.

WHAT IS THIS "STARCRAFT 2" YOU SPEAK OF?
IT'S THE SEQUEL TO ONE OF THE MOST POPULAR REAL-TIME STRATEGY GAMES OF ALL TIME.

THE ORIGINAL STARCRAFT WAS FAMOUS FOR ITS REMARKABLE GAME BALANCE BETWEEN THREE FACTIONS.
ITS FAN BASE REMAINS FANATICAL TO THIS DAY.

AND WE SHOULD FEAR THIS, WHY?
OH WE SHOULDN'T, IF, YOU KNOW, YOU DON'T REALLY CARE ABOUT DEADLINES ANYMORE.

DIDJA HEAR?! DIDJA? DIDJA?!
YOU MEAN ABOUT STARCRAFT 2? YEP.

WHY DID GREG JUST GIVE YOU FIFTY BUCKS?
HE BET "DUKE NUKEM WHENEVER" WOULD BE OUT BEFORE STARCRAFT 2.
IT'S "FOREVER!"

I DON'T UNDERSTAND THIS NEAR-RELIGIOUS FERVOR FOR STARCRAFT.

IT'S JUST ANOTHER RTS, ALBEIT A VERY SUCCESSFUL ONE. WHY IS EVERYONE GOING SPASTIC OVER IT?
IT'S AN INCREDIBLE GAME, SID.

CHESS IS AN INCREDIBLE GAME.
SORRY, BUT A "PAWN RUSH" JUST DOESN'T QUITE CURDLE THE BLOOD.

IS THAT THE STARCRAFT 2 GAMEPLAY MOVIE?
YEP, IN ALL ITS GLORY!
COPYRIGHT© 2007 J.D. "Illiad" Frazer HTTP://WWW.USERFRIENDLY.ORG/

KLIK
CLIK
KLIC

A.J., IT'S A MOVIE. YOU CAN'T SELECT THE UNITS.
I KNOW! I KNOW!

I've never done what A.J. is doing. Not ever.

I HAVE TO GET A GRIP. THIS WHOLE STARCRAFT 2 THING IS TAKING OVER MY LIFE.
COPYRIGHT© 2007 J.D. "Illiad" Frazer HTTP://WWW.USERFRIENDLY.ORG/

LOOK AT THE FANBASE IN SOUTH KOREA, IT'S POSITIVELY RABID. IT'S ALMOST AS IF AN UNSEEN FORCE WAS GOING AROUND CREATING THIS MADNESS.

HOW THE HELL AM I SUPPOSED TO DRESS UP LIKE A ZERG?!
Cola
NASTY FACE
POKEY BITS

AN EXCELLENT WAY TO CONGRATULATE STAR WARS FANS AND INCUR A LYNCHING AT THE SAME TIME
STAR WARS
Celebrating 30 Years
Live Long and Prosper!
UserFriendly.Org
COPYRIGHT© 2006 J.D. "Illiad" Frazer HTTP://WWW.USERFRIENDLY.ORG/

HOW'S YOUR STARCRAFT 2 CRAVING?
I THINK I HAVE IT UNDER CONTROL.
COPYRIGHT © 2007 J.D. "Illiad" Frazer HTTP://WWW.USERFRIENDLY.ORG/

FOR A COUPLE DAYS THERE IT WAS TOUCH AND GO. IT FELT LIKE AT ANY SECOND THE ADDICTION WOULD POP UP OUT OF NOWHERE AND...

WHY IS THERE THE TOP OF A HUGE COLA CAN STICKING OUT OF THE FLOOR?
DAMN. HOW DO THE ZERGS DO IT WITH-OUT BEING SEEN?

BEHOLD! I AM YOUR STARCRAFT ADDICTION. GAZE UPON ME AND WEEP!
Cola
COPYRIGHT © 2007 J.D. "Illiad" Frazer HTTP://WWW.USERFRIENDLY.ORG/

HISSSS
GROWWLL
HISSS
Cola

WHAT DOES A BIG COLA CAN HAVE TO DO WITH STARCRAFT?
MAYBE IT'S A NEW ZERG UNIT?
THE ZERG SUIT DIDN'T FIT!!
Cola

HEH, JACK THOMPSON IS GOING AFTER BILL GATES FOR HALO 3.
HE SAYS IF THE GAME IS SOLD TO ANYONE UNDER THE AGE OF 17, HE'D HOLD GATES RESPONSIBLE.
COPYRIGHT © 2007 J.D. "Illiad" Frazer HTTP://WWW.USERFRIENDLY.ORG/

ISN'T HE THAT BAT!@#$ INSANE LAWYER WHO HATES VIDEO GAMES?
YEAH. HE THINKS VIDEO GAMES ARE WHAT CREATES VIOLENT TENDENCIES IN CHILDREN.

BANG! BANG! YOU'RE DEAD!
YOU CAN'T DO THAT! I ALREADY PUT UP MY HANDS!

THERE'S A NEW HEALTH SCARE. A RESEARCHER HAS DISCOVERED THAT SODIUM BENZOATE COULD CAUSE PARTS OF HUMAN DNA TO SWITCH OFF.
COPYRIGHT © 2007 J.D. "Illiad" Frazer HTTP://WWW.USERFRIENDLY.ORG/

THE COMPOUND IS FOUND IN MANY SODAS, AND COULD BE THE CAUSE OF SOME PRETTY HORRID DISEASES, LIKE PARKINSON'S.
OR DORKY MUTATIONS.

ERWIN, THERE'S NO EVIDENCE FOR THAT.
HEY GUYS! WHAT'S NEW?

AJ, HOW MUCH SODA DO YOU DRINK IN A DAY?
A FEW CANS, I THINK. WHY?

AND WHEN DID YOU START DRINKING SODA?
AS FAR BACK AS I CAN REMEMBER.

I SUPPOSE IT'S POSSIBLE.
WE SHOULD DISSECT HIM.
NOW JUST ONE FRACKING MINUTE!

SID, DID YOU HEAR ABOUT THE NEW RESEARCH INTO SODIUM BENZOATE?
IT'S SUPPOSED TO BE LINKED TO SOME SERIOUS MUTATIONS.

THINK ABOUT IT AJ. SODIUM BENZOATE HAS BEEN USED IN SOFT DRINKS SINCE THE EARLY 20TH CENTURY.
WHAT DOES THAT SUGGEST TO YOU?

YE FLIPPING GODS! WE'VE ALL BECOME MUTANTS IN LESS THAN A HUNDRED YEARS!!
CLEARLY FOR VARIOUS VALUES OF "WE."

NOW THAT U.S. HOMELAND SECURITY IS SEEKING ADVICE FROM SCIENCE FICTION WRITERS TO FIGHT TERRORISM, FIELD INTELLIGENCE WILL IMPROVE SIGNIFICANTLY...

JOHNSON, PLEASE FETCH THE BOOK OF VOGON POETRY.
NO! NOOO! I'LL TELL YOU ANYTHING YOU WANT TO KNOW!!

UserFriendly.Org

SID, WHAT ARE WE DOING TO OURSELVES? WE'RE GEEKS! WE'RE SUPPOSED TO BE SMART! AND YET, WE REGULARLY DRINK FLUIDS LOADED WITH DANGEROUS CHEMICALS!
COPYRIGHT© 2007 J.D. "Illiad" Frazer HTTP://WWW.USERFRIENDLY.ORG/

DANGEROUS CHEMICALS?
YES! CHEMICALS IN OUR SOFT DRINKS THAT SLOWLY BUT SURELY KILL US!

YOU MEAN, LIKE, SUGAR.
YE GODS! WE'VE ALL BEEN SO BLIND!

I JUST CAN'T DRINK COLA ANYMORE! THE CHEMICALS... THEY'LL BE MY UNDOING! NEVER AGAIN!
COPYRIGHT© 2007 J.D. "Illiad" Frazer HTTP://WWW.USERFRIENDLY.ORG/

I SAID I HEREBY VOW TO NEVER QUAFF ANOTHER DROP OF COLA EVER AG--
I HEARD YOU THE FIRST TIME. I CAN'T GET THESE STUPID ZERGLING FEET OFF.
Cola

NOW WHAT'S THIS BALONEY ABOUT YOU BREAKING YOUR COLA HABIT?
I DON'T WANT TO BE CONSUMING ANYTHING CALLED "SODIUM BENZOATE."
Cola
COPYRIGHT© 2007 J.D. "Illiad" Frazer HTTP://WWW.USERFRIENDLY.ORG/

WHY NOT?
BECAUSE IT SOUNDS ALL... "CHEMICALISH."
Cola

WELL, WHAT IF I TOLD YOU IT WAS FOUND NATURALLY IN CINNAMON AND APPLES?
I'D TELL YOU I'M NEVER GONNA EAT CINNAMON OR APPLES AGAIN. WHICH I'M NOT.
Cola

YOU WON'T DRINK COLA NOW BECAUSE IT CONTAINS A NATURALLY-OCCURRING COMPOUND?
NO, BECAUSE IT CONTAINS SOMETHING THAT SOUNDS LIKE IT BELONGS IN A BIOHAZARD CHAMBER.
Cola
COPYRIGHT© 2007 J.D. "Illiad" Frazer HTTP://WWW.USERFRIENDLY.ORG/

WELL, WHAT ABOUT WATER? THAT'S ALSO KNOWN AS "DIHYDROGEN MONOXIDE."
Cola

I DIE.
I'M GONNA NEED HELP WITH THIS ONE.
Cola

I HOPE AJ'S OKAY. HE WAS PRETTY STRESSED ABOUT NOT BEING ABLE TO EAT OR DRINK ANYTHING.
COPYRIGHT© 2007 J.D. "Illiad" Frazer HTTP://WWW.USERFRIENDLY.ORG/

ISN'T THAT HIM COMING THIS WAY? AND HE'S DRINKING...COFFEE.
AJ? IS THAT YOU?

GOOD AS NEW. NOTHING A LITTLE SODIUM PENTOTHAL AND SOME SUGGESTIONS COULDN'T FIX.
COFFEE HAS CHLOROGENIC ACID IN IT! YAY!

YE GODS, WHAT'S THAT?
IT'S MY NEW 42" LCD MONITOR. I HAD TO BLOW MY LIFE SAVINGS ON IT, BUT NOW I HAVE IT!
COPYRIGHT© 2007 J.D. "Illiad" Frazer HTTP://WWW.USERFRIENDLY.ORG/

WOW! IT'S BEAUTIFUL!
I KNOW, I CAN'T WAIT TO USE IT! HANG ON, I'M JUST PLUGGING IT IN.

PZZAT-*POK*
WHAT...WHAT WAS THAT?
DO YOU STILL HAVE THE RECEIPT?

I thought we had fried a friend's new 30″ Apple Cinema Display once. Turned out we hadn't plugged it in.

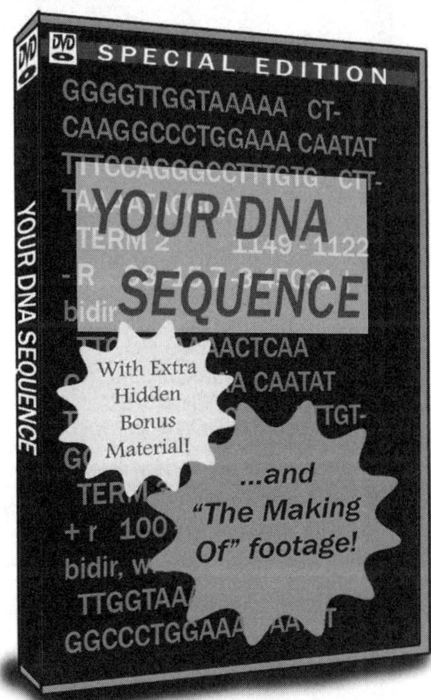
NOW THAT WE CAN PAY TO HAVE OUR OWN GENOMES MAPPED AND STORED ON A DVD, SIX MONTHS AFTER YOU PAY FOR THE SERVICE ALONG COMES THE INEVITABLE:
SPECIAL EDITION
YOUR DNA SEQUENCE
YOUR DNA SEQUENCE
With Extra Hidden Bonus Material!
...and "The Making Of" footage!
UserFriendly.Org
COPYRIGHT© 2007 J.D. "Illiad" Frazer HTTP://WWW.USERFRIENDLY.ORG/

DID YOU FIND THE RECEIPT FOR YOUR...UH...NEW LCD MONITOR? AND WHAT ARE YOU DOING ON THE FLOOR?
DID I TELL YOU MY GRANDMA WAS STAYING WITH ME FOR A VISIT?
COPYRIGHT © 2007 J.D. "Illiad" Frazer HTTP://WWW.USERFRIENDLY.ORG/

NO...WHY?
SHE FOUND THE RECEIPT. IT WAS ALL CRINKLED UP IN MY JEANS POCKET.
SO?

THE RECEIPT IS PRINTED ON THERMAL PAPER.
YEAH? SO?
SHE IRONED IT FOR ME.

HI. I BOUGHT A MONITOR HERE LAST WEEK AND IT BURNED OUT.
OH DEAR. DO YOU HAVE THE RECEIPT?
HERE YOU GO.
COPYRIGHT © 2007 J.D. "Illiad" Frazer HTTP://WWW.USERFRIENDLY.ORG/

AND THIS BLACKENED SCRAP OF PAPER WOULD BE A RECEIPT FOR WHAT?
THE YAWNING VOID I'M FEELING IN MY STOMACH RIGHT NOW.

WHAT IN HADES IS THAT?
A PIECE OF HISTORY! IT'S MY OLD APPLE][+. IT'S 30 YEARS OLD THIS MONTH!
COPYRIGHT © 2007 J.D. "Illiad" Frazer HTTP://WWW.USERFRIENDLY.ORG/

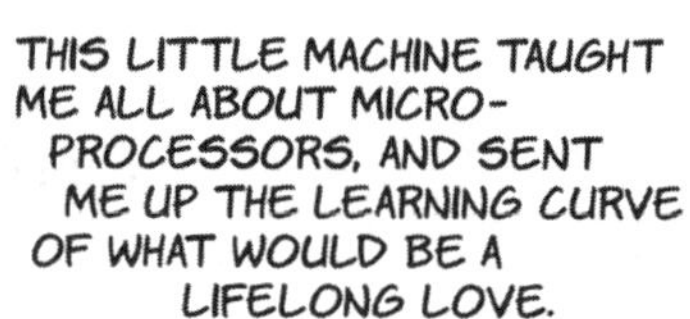
THIS LITTLE MACHINE TAUGHT ME ALL ABOUT MICRO-PROCESSORS, AND SENT ME UP THE LEARNING CURVE OF WHAT WOULD BE A LIFELONG LOVE.

WHAT, ASCII GIRLFRIENDS?
IMAGINE HAVING YOUR BROWSER HISTORY POSTED ON USENET. NOW IMAGINE THAT YOU DON'T NEED TO IMAGINE.

AHHHH, YES. THIS BRINGS BACK MEMORIES. I CUT MY TEETH ON ASSEMBLER ON THE APPLE][+.
COPYRIGHT © 2007 J.D. "Illiad" Frazer HTTP://WWW.USERFRIENDLY.ORG/

AND STORAGE...140K ON FLOPPIES. YOU COULD DOUBLE THAT WITH A SIMPLE HOLE PUNCH!

WHATEVER HAPPENED TO THE DAYS WHEN HACKING STARTED AT THE CEREBRAL CORTEX, AND NOT AT THE KEYBOARD?
SID! I FOUND THE CHEAT CODES FOR "TROPHY BASS FISHING 5"!

Sid> Hey Pitr.
I offer you a challenge:
I'll bet I'm able to code a better game than you can.

Pitr>You are askink for butt to be waxed, old man.
Sid>I welcome your attempt to defeat me at this geeky competition.

Pitr>Wery well. You will be sorry. Am ready to be developink game!
Sid>...in 48k or less.

Pitr>48k?!! Have you gone mad?! Can not code a game in 48k!
Sid>Of course you can. The Apple][+ had scores of great games, all 48k or less.
RAPPY
TAPPY
PRAP

Pitr>Ohhh, am seeink how it is. You are fightink me on your old stompink grounds. Can not fight fair with Pitr? You are afraid?
Sid>Fine, I'll give you an advantage to even it up.
Google

Pitr>Good.
Sid>You get 64k.

UserFriendly.Org
by J.D. "Illiad" Frazer

DELL, THE NO. 2 PC MAKER WILL BEGIN SELLING SOME CONSUMER-FOCUSED LAPTOPS AND DESKTOPS WITH UBUNTU'S NEW "FEISTY FAWN" VERSION OF LINUX INSTALLED.

CAN YOU HEAR THE SHRIEKS OF ANTICIPATORY AGONY COMING FROM DELL'S TECH SUPPORT CENTRE? I CAN...

OOOH. WATCHA GOT THERE, BILL?
A FRUIT BASKET. FROM THE CANONICAL GUYS, THE BACKERS OF UBUNTU.
Microsoft

THERE'S A NOTE IN THE BASKET. READ IT, STEVE.
"DEAR BILL AND STEVE, OUR SUCCESS WITH DELL IS ALL TO YOUR CREDIT....

...THANK YOU SO MUCH FOR VISTA. IT MADE US LOOK AWESOME."
PUT DOWN MY CHAIR, STEVE. I'M STILL IN IT.

Pitr>64k then. Any other rules you are intendink to spring on me?
Sid>Yes, it has to run on a 6502.

Pitr>You have an Apple][+ ?
Sid>Why yes, yes I do.
COPYRIGHT © 2007 J.D. "Illiad" Frazer HTTP://WWW.USERFRIENDLY.ORG/

Pitr>Ah. Havink trouble tearink yourself away from Applesoft BASIC, GOTO-man?
Sid>GOTO?!! Why you...I....!! Ooooh!! You...!!
Google

What geek hasn't had their game, or work, or whatever effort on their computer destroyed by the random affections of a kitty? And it's really hard to stay mad at the furry little buggers.

AND SO OUR TWO TECH-FU MASTERS, ONE YOUNG AND ARROGANT, THE OTHER OLD AND PATRONIZING, BEGIN THEIR ANTAGONISTIC BATTLE.

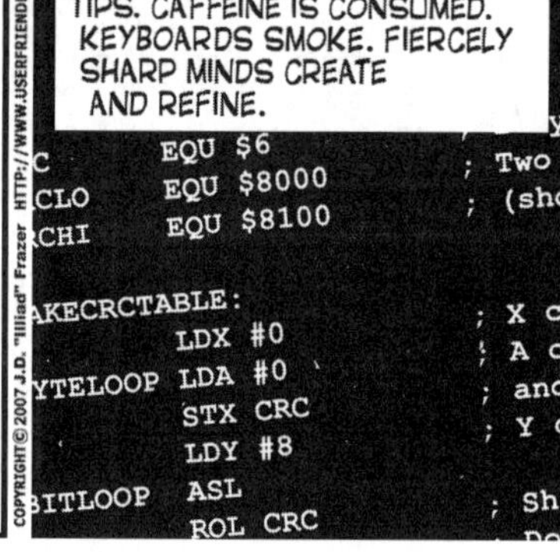
CODE FLIES FROM THEIR FINGERTIPS. CAFFEINE IS CONSUMED. KEYBOARDS SMOKE. FIERCELY SHARP MINDS CREATE AND REFINE.
COPYRIGHT © 2007 J.D. "Illiad" Frazer HTTP://WWW.USERFRIENDLY.ORG/
C EQU $6 ; Two
CLO EQU $8000 ; (sho
CHI EQU $8100
AKECRCTABLE: ; X c
LDX #0 ; A c
YTELOOP LDA #0 ; and
STX CRC ; Y c
LDY #8
ITLOOP ASL ; Shi
ROL CRC

WHEN ALL OF A SUDDEN, THE BANE OF RATIONAL THOUGHT AMONG GEEKS TRAIPSES ACROSS BOTH OF THEIR KEYBOARDS AT THE VERY SAME TIME...
KITTEH!
Google

WITH THE FUZZBALL-EFFECT HAVING PASSED, OUR DUELISTS RESUME THEIR CODING FERVOR.
TAPTAP
CODE
COMMENT
TAKTIKTAK
DEBUG

COPYRIGHT © 2007 J.D. "Illiad" Frazer HTTP://WWW.USERFRIENDLY.ORG/
...AND LIKE AN OLD MASTER VS. A TALENTED YOUNG UPSTART IN A CHEESY KUNG-FU MOVIE, THE TWO COMPLETE THEIR TASKS SIMULTANEOUSLY AND DRAMATICALLY.
Sid>Voila!
Pitr>Completeski!
Google

BOTH OF OUR HEROES GO INTO PUFFER-FISH MODE, AND MAKE THEMSELVES LOOK BIG WITH PITHY REJOINDERS FOR EACH OTHER'S EFFORTS...
Sid>Amateur. Don't expect to be given a BRK!
Pitr>You can go ROT on somethink sharp, fossil!
Google

Pitr>Showink me your so-called masterpiece, old man.
Sid>You first, tadpole.

COPYRIGHT © 2007 J.D. "Illiad" Frazer HTTP://WWW.USERFRIENDLY.ORG/
Pitr>Am presentink new version of game "Space Taxi!"

Pitr>You are to be notink the many wery fine colours and lifelike audio...in only 8-bit!
Sid>How...is that *cerise?!*

Sid>Very impressive, Pitr. You've recreated a classic game with tighter code and better graphics.
Pitr>Was piece of cake. Now is your turn, old man.
Google

Sid>Sending...

Pitr>Is...just text adventure.
Sid>With the best graphics in the world, the ones in your **head**!

Pitr>So big deal! You are usink BGA* for graphics. but is still only text adventure! Am winner!
Sid>Not so fast, tadpole...
*BRAIN GRAPHICS ADAPTER

Sid>You'll note the hooks in the code that allows one to integrate the game with a space shuttle or space probe nav system.
Pitr>I...um...eeehhh...

AND ONE DAY IN THE FUTURE...
>GO NORTH
WHICH NORTH?
IT IS VERY DARK ON THIS SIDE OF THE EARTH. YOU MIGHT BE EATEN BY A GRUE.
>
YOU DOLT! SO MUCH FOR YOUR ENGINEERING PHYSICS DEGREE!

ROCKSTAR GAMES' NEW HORROR TITLE "MANHUNT 2" IS RATED *ADULTS ONLY* BY THE ESRB AND IS BANNED IN THE UNITED KINGDOM.

manhunt2
AO

GENESIS

THERE'S A TERRIBLE INEQUITY HERE.

UserFriendly.Org

Geeks around the world checked their ring fingers when they read this strip. My God, we're predictable.

RESEARCHERS HAVE DISCOVERED THAT A GENE LINKED TO THE LENGTH OF YOUR RING FINGER IS ALSO LINKED TO YOUR FACILITY WITH MATH.

IF YOUR RING FINGER IS LONGER THAN YOUR INDEX FINGER, YOU'RE LIKELY MATH-BRIGHT.

DUDE, I'M WAAAAY OVER.
GOT YOU BEAT BY AT LEAST THREE MILLIMETRES!
YO! CHECK OUT MY PEPPERONI STICK!
HOW CHARMING. RING-FINGER SWINGING.

It's beyond me when people complain about being bored, especially geeks. Generally speaking, the more intelligent you are, the less likely it is that you'll face boredom under most any circumstances. It was explained to me by a psychologist friend that when a geek complains about being bored, it's more likely that they're really saying "pay attention to me." This also puzzles me, because most geeks are introverts!

EARTH, 2007. THIRD ROCK FROM THE SUN. OVER SIX BILLION PEOPLE IN A MODERN ERA, WHERE TECHNOLOGICAL CHANGE IS CLIMBING UP A CLIFF-LIKE CURVE.

THE WORLD WIDE WEB. A COMMUNICATION MEDIUM THAT HAS BROUGHT FANTASTIC OPPORTUNITIES TO SHARE INFORMATION LIKE NEVER BEFORE IN HUMAN HISTORY.

TRILLIONS OF BYTES OF TRANSCRIBED HUMAN KNOWLEDGE ARE MADE AVAILABLE. BOOKS, MOVIES, MUSIC, COMICS, INTERACTIVE FORUMS, REFERENCES, ART AND SO MUCH MORE. AND WITH ALL OF THIS AT OUR FINGERTIPS, HUMANITY RESPONDS:
I'M BORED.

FINALLY, THERE'S PROOF THAT AL GORE INVENTED THE INTERNET.
WHAT?

IF YOU MONITOR DATA PACKETS ON THE NET AT LARGE FOR A FEW DAYS A PATTERN EMERGES. AND IF YOU CONVERT THAT PATTERN TO PERCUSSION AUDIO, YOU HEAR A BEAT THAT NOT ONLY EXPRESSES A UNIVERSAL PROCEDURE TO SOLVE PROBLEMS, IT HAS A SIGNATURE THAT IS DISTINCTLY GORE'S.

HOW CAN YOU TELL?
EASY, IT'S AN AL GORE RHYTHM.

HEY, MIRANDA. BUSY?
JUST TRYING OUT SOME NEW SKILLS.

I'VE BEEN EXPERIMENTING A LOT TO PUSH THE BOUNDARIES OF MY KNOWLEDGE.

I'D SAY YOU'VE COME A LONG WAY. APPROACHING MASTERY, EVEN.

YOU REALLY THINK SO?
WELL, FOR ONE THING I CAN'T TELL IF THAT'S A REGEX OR LINE NOISE.

TECH SUPPORT, GHOST IN THE MACHINE SPEAKING.
I INSTALLED VISTA AND NOW BEFORE I CAN DO ANYTHING I HAVE TO CANCEL OR ALLOW.

AH YES. MICROSOFT TOOK A CUE FROM THE PHARMACEUTICALS INDUSTRY. VISTA'S SECURITY IS MODELLED AFTER CHILD-PROOF BOTTLES.

OH. SO...THAT'S GOOD THEN.
SATIRE IS NOW OFFICIALLY DEAD. IT DIED FROM LAUGHING TOO HARD AND CHOKING ON ITS OWN VOMIT.

TECH SUPPORT, YOUR PROBLEM IS MY PURGATORY.
MY RING FINGER IS DEFINITELY LONGER THAN MY INDEX FINGER. BY OVER AN INCH.

YES? SO YOU'RE A MATH WIZ THEN? YOU GROK EIGENVALUES AND EIGENVECTORS?
ACTUALLY, MY MATH REALLY SUCKS THE WET MANGO.

HOW ODD. I GUESS THE CORRELATION ISN'T ALL THAT SOUND.
YEAH. OR MAYBE IT WAS THAT PARING KNIFE INCIDENT I HAD.

MICROSOFT WILL OF COURSE COMPETE WITH APPLE'S iPHONE...
phune™
ALSO COMES IN BROWN!
UserFriendly.Org

I'LL BE WIBBLED! SOME ISPS ARE INSERTING THEIR OWN ADS ON PAGES REQUESTED BY THEIR CUSTOMERS!
AH-ROO?
COPYRIGHT© 2007 J.D. "Illiad" Frazer HTTP://WWW.USERFRIENDLY.ORG/

THEY USE A TRANSPARENT WEB PROXY TO INSERT THE ADS VIA JAVASCRIPT OR HTML INTO THE PAGES WITHOUT THE CONTENT PROVIDER'S KNOWLEDGE.

THAT IS UTTERLY DESPICABLE!
DISGUSTING AND DISHONEST.
YO! WE ARE GONNA BE RICH!

ADS! WE CAN INSERT ADS INTO PAGES REQUESTED BY OUR CUSTOMERS!
STEF, DO YOU HAVE ANY IDEA HOW VILE THAT IS? NO WAY ARE WE DOING THAT!
COPYRIGHT© 2007 J.D. "Illiad" Frazer HTTP://WWW.USERFRIENDLY.ORG/

...BUT...MONEY...
WELL, HOW MUCH MO--NO! WE'RE NOT DOING THAT!

YOU'RE NOT GOING TO LET ME INSERT ADS ON REQUESTED PAGES?
ABSOLUTELY NOT! HAVE YOU GONE COMPLETELY MAD?
COPYRIGHT© 2007 J.D. "Illiad" Frazer HTTP://WWW.USERFRIENDLY.ORG/

THERE HAS TO BE SOME WAY FOR US TO GENERATE MORE REVENUE FROM THE INTERNET.
I'M SURE THERE IS, BUT IT'LL HAVE TO BE SOMETHING OTHER THAN AD INSERTION.

SO REWRITING THE REFERRAL LINKS TO AMAZON.COM AND OTHER AFFILIATE DEALS IT IS THEN.
SUR...I...NO!!

STEF, NO TECH HERE WILL HELP YOU WITH YOUR VILE PLAN TO INSERT ADS ON REQUESTED PAGES. SO DON'T EVEN ASK.
UNDERSTOOD.
COPYRIGHT© 2007 J.D. "Illiad" Frazer HTTP://WWW.USERFRIENDLY.ORG/

AS C.T.O. I'M RESPONSIBLE FOR THE INTEGRITY OF ALL TECHNICAL SERVICES AND PRODUCTS, AND I'LL BE DAMNED IF I LET YOU SULLY MY REPUTATION!
GOOD DAY.

"THE MOON IS WAXING AND THE HAMSTER SMELLS LIKE NACHOS."
INSERTINK VIAGRA ADS NOW...

LOAD UP OUR HOMEPAGE.
WHY?
JUST DO IT.
COPYRIGHT© 2007 J.D. "Illiad" Frazer HTTP://WWW.USERFRIENDLY.ORG/

THAT'S...THERE'S AN AD ON OUR HOMEPAGE.

AND IF YOU'LL RECALL, OUR HOMEPAGE DOESN'T HAVE ADS.
IT'S AN AD FOR AT&T DSL!

THERE'S AN AD NETWORK THAT SERVES UNSCRUPULOUS ISPS WITH ADS THAT ARE INSERTED INTO REQUESTED PAGES BY THE ISP ITSELF.
COPYRIGHT© 2007 J.D. "Illiad" Frazer HTTP://WWW.USERFRIENDLY.ORG/

TO DO THIS WOULD TAKE SOMEONE WHO'S HAD AN ETHICECTOMY...
...AND SOMEONE WITH ROOT ACCESS TO OUR BOXES.

STEEFFFF!!!
PIITRRRR!

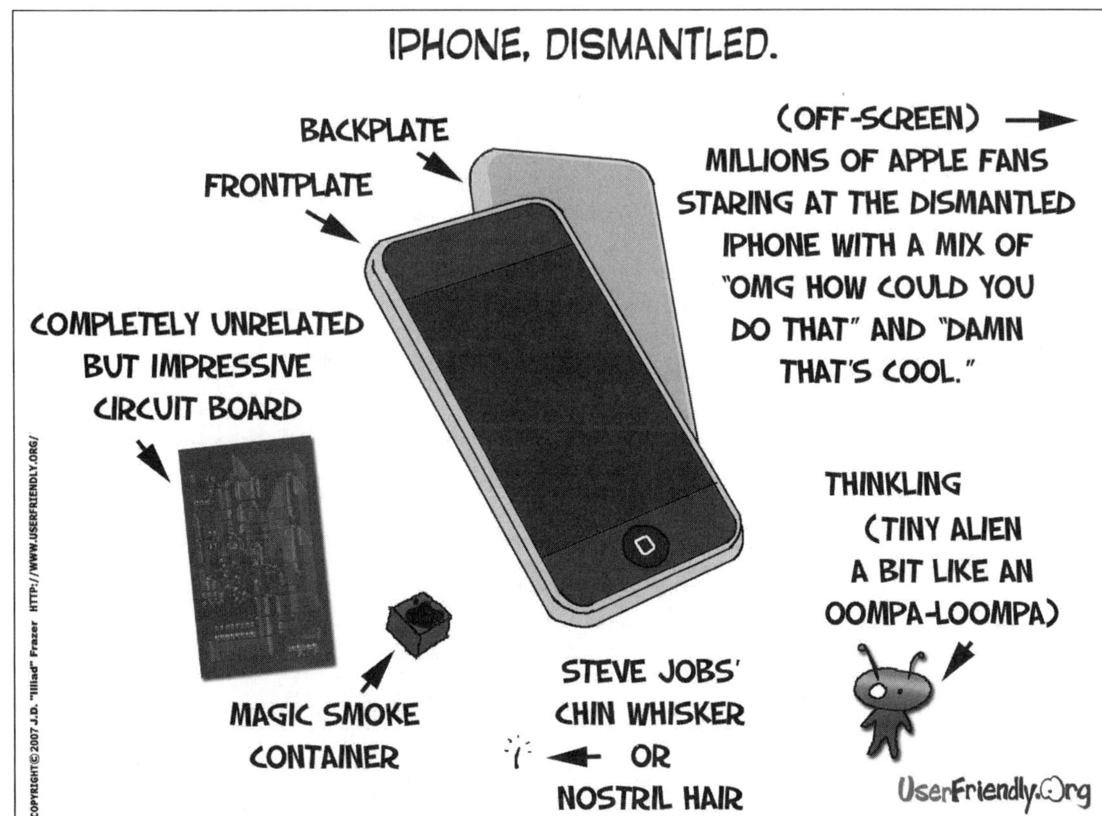
IPHONE, DISMANTLED.
BACKPLATE
FRONTPLATE
(OFF-SCREEN)
MILLIONS OF APPLE FANS STARING AT THE DISMANTLED IPHONE WITH A MIX OF "OMG HOW COULD YOU DO THAT" AND "DAMN THAT'S COOL."
COMPLETELY UNRELATED BUT IMPRESSIVE CIRCUIT BOARD
THINKLING (TINY ALIEN A BIT LIKE AN OOMPA-LOOMPA)
STEVE JOBS' CHIN WHISKER OR NOSTRIL HAIR
MAGIC SMOKE CONTAINER
UserFriendly.Org
COPYRIGHT© 2007 J.D. "Illiad" Frazer HTTP://WWW.USERFRIENDLY.ORG/

ARE THEY GONE?
YES. IT TOOK A WHILE TO ROOT THEM ALL OUT, BUT THE ADS ARE GONE FOR SURE NOW.

THE AD NETWORK WAS PUMPING OUT A SERIOUS NUMBER OF ADS. THEY PROBABLY WERE GENERATING SOME SIGNIFICANT REVENUE.

GOOD. SO THAT'S THE LAST WE'VE SEEN OF THEM.
GENTLEMEN. I'D LIKE A WORD...

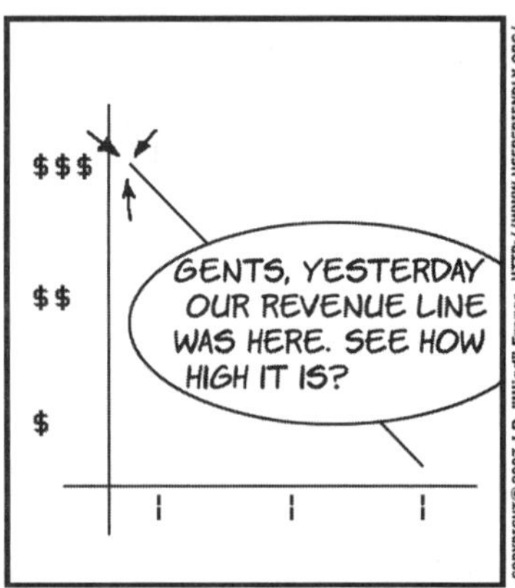
GENTS, YESTERDAY OUR REVENUE LINE WAS HERE. SEE HOW HIGH IT IS?

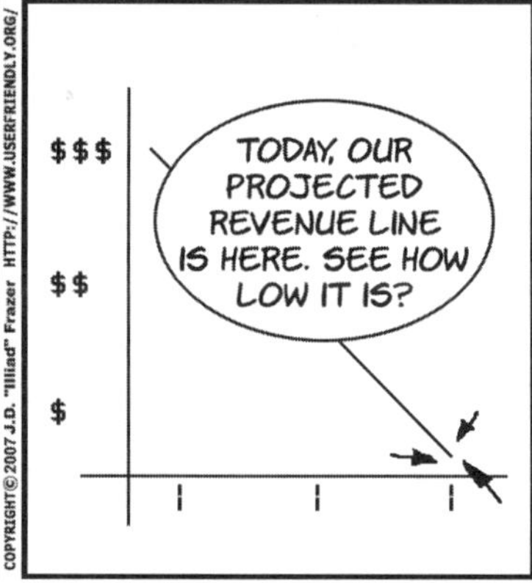
TODAY, OUR PROJECTED REVENUE LINE IS HERE. SEE HOW LOW IT IS?

I WAS ALSO TOLD THAT THIS ANXIETY-INDUCING CHANGE ON THE Y-AXIS IS DUE TO SOMETHING YOU DID.
YOU CAN'T EXPECT ALL SALES GRAPHS TO HAVE THE SAME SLOPE AS STEF'S FOREHEAD, CHIEF.

Several math majors wrote to me to complain about the snorting I caused. The "quadratic bundahoo" would be taught in their 200-level math courses for non-science majors.

ALL FUNNIES ASIDE, I'D LIKE YOU TWO TO EXPLAIN THIS SUDDEN DROP IN REVENUE.
YOU NEGLECTED THE Z-AXIS, CHIEF.

SEE, THE Z-AXIS MEASURES PRODUCT EVIL. IF THE VALUE ON THAT AXIS APPROACHES INFINITY, THERE'S A SUDDEN AND IRREVERSIBLE DROP WITH A LOGARITHMIC RELATIONSHIP TO THE INTEGRAL OF THE QUADRATIC BUNDAHOO.

GOOD HEAVENS. I HAD NO IDEA THERE WAS SO MUCH MATH INVOLVED!
OH WE COVER THIS AT THE GRADUATE LEVEL. YOU CAN EARN A PH.D IN IT AFTER A FEW YEARS IN I.T. MANAGEMENT.

STEF. GOOD DAY.
GENTLEMEN.

TODAY IS "TECHIE MAGIC DAY," AND THUS WE WAVE OUR MAGIC BLOCK OVER YOUR LAPTOP WHICH WE NOTE IS FILLED WITH WOMEN FROM THE CLAN "JPEG."

OH DEAR ME. WE APPEAR TO HAVE CONFUSED OUR MAGIC BLOCK WITH AN ELECTROMAGNET!
SOWWIES!
AAAUUUUUUGH!!!

PITR. HAVE A MINUTE?
NYET, BUSY NOW WITH COUP D'ETAT IN TROPICAL REGION.
COPYRIGHT © 2007 J.D. "Illiad" Frazer HTTP://WWW.USERFRIENDLY.ORG/

HOW NICE, BUT THAT'LL HAVE TO WAIT. I HAVE SOMETHING FOR YOU.
YOUR WALKING PAPERS.

THIS MUST BE JOKE.
ONLY IN THE SENSE THAT YOU'RE THE PUNCHLINE.

PLEASE TO BE EXPLAININK REASON FOR TERMINATION?
IT'S WITHOUT CAUSE, SO WE HAVE TO GIVE YOU SEVERANCE, BUT NOT A SPECIFIC REASON.
COPYRIGHT © 2007 J.D. "Illiad" Frazer HTTP://WWW.USERFRIENDLY.ORG/

BUT IF YOU MUST HAVE A REASON IT'S BECAUSE OF "DISADVANTAGED SPATIAL POSITIONING DURING A TEMPORAL DISCORDANCE."

BEINK IN WRONG PLACE AT WRONG TIME.
AND WE GOT A CALL FROM YOUR OTHER EMPLOYER. HE SAYS YOU'VE BEEN "VERY NAUGHTY."

USER FRIENDLY
the comic strip
BY J.D. "ILLIAD" FRAZER
COPYRIGHT © 2007 J.D. "Illiad" Frazer HTTP://WWW.USERFRIENDLY.ORG/

I FEEL PENT-UP, ERWIN. A SLINKY JAZZ-ROCK BEAT PLEASE.
YOU BETCHA, BABY.

(SUNG TO ROUGH TRADE'S 'HIGH SCHOOL CONFIDENTIAL')
IT'S A COOL, SLICK, PIECE OF TECH, IT MAKES ME INTO A WRECK WHILE I LINE UP AT THE STORE...
UNTZ UNTZ UNTZ

YOU CAN'T HEAR IT MAKE A SINGLE CLICK I WANT ONE SO MUCH I FEEL SICK
NOTHING CAN HELP ME NOTHING CAN HELP ME NOW

IT'S LIKE AN iPHONE, iPHONE, CONFIDENTIAL! AN iPHONE, iPHONE, CONFIDENTIAL!
SEXY!

TEENAGE IPHONERS FLOOD THE MALLS! THEY TEASE ME BY MAKING CALLS! IT'S A COMBINATION HOLY SYMBOL AND COMFY NOSERING!
SOME GUY DOWN THE STREET IS USING IPHONES AS TREBUCHET AMMO.

I THINK THE WEB HAS CAUSED LANGUAGE TO GO INTO A TAILSPIN.
IT'S SHOCKING HOW NET SLANG HAS DRIFTED INTO EVERYDAY SPEECH.
COPYRIGHT © 2007 J.D. "Illiad" Frazer HTTP://WWW.USERFRIENDLY.ORG/

"DAWG"-THIS AND "PWNED" -THAT AND "OMGWTF ROFLWAFFLE!!"
SID, PRESCRIPTIVISTS LIKE YOU TICK ME OFF. LANGUAGE IS ALIVE! IT EVOLVES!
SO LEARN TO ADAPT. OR DIE.
YOU'RE RIGHT, BECAUSE CLEARLY CABBAGE SOPPY WANKEL EBBEH GRUNTSPONGE.

DID YOU ACTUALLY SAY "GRUNTSPONGE"?
YOU SEE MY POINT. CHANGING LANGUAGE ISN'T ALWAYS GOOD.
WE ALREADY HAVE A HUGE VOCABULARY AVAILABLE TO US. WHY CREATE NEW WORDS TO REPLACE PERFECTLY GOOD EXISTING ONES?

ALL OF THIS NET-CREATED NEW LANGUAGE DRIVEL NEEDS TO BE STOPPED! THE MADNESS MUST CEASE!
TO SUMMARIZE, THEN: LANGUAGE CHANGE BAD HELL IN A HANDBASKET, KIDS THESE DAYS, BARBARIANS AT THE GATE, BOO-HOO. DOES THAT ABOUT COVER IT?

TANSTAAFL: Their Ain't No Such Thing As A Free Lunch. One of Heinlein's more famous maxims.

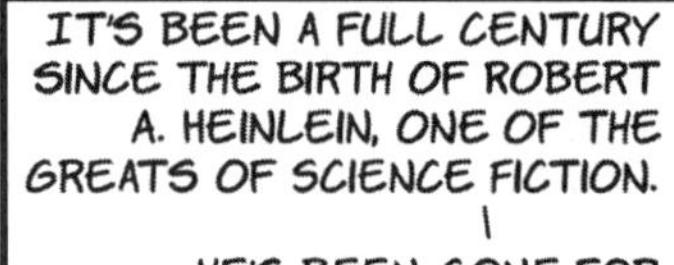

IT'S BEEN A FULL CENTURY SINCE THE BIRTH OF ROBERT A. HEINLEIN, ONE OF THE GREATS OF SCIENCE FICTION.
HE'S BEEN GONE FOR NEARLY TWENTY YEARS.

I'M RE-READING "THE MOON IS A HARSH MISTRESS." IT'S ONLY FITTING TO CONSIDER THE DEEP SOCIAL LESSONS HE EXPLORED IN THAT NOVEL.

SO WHAT ARE YOU GOING TO DO TO CELEBRATE HIS MEMORY?
TAKE THE CHIEF OUT TO LUNCH AND MAKE HIM PAY FOR IT.

WHAT ARE YOU READING? ANOTHER STUPID TECH MANUAL?
TODAY I'M READING ANOTHER OF HEINLEIN'S BEST NOVELS: STARSHIP TROOPERS.

OH! YOU MEAN LIKE THE MOVIE! THE ONE WITH ALL THE BOOBIES AND INSECTS AND STUFF.

YE GODS WHAT DID I SAY?!

M.I.T. BIOCHEMISTS HAVE IDENTIFIED A MOLECULAR MECHANISM BEHIND FEAR, AND SUCCESSFULLY CURED IT IN MICE.
COPYRIGHT © 2007 J.D. "Illiad" Frazer HTTP://WWW.USERFRIENDLY.ORG/

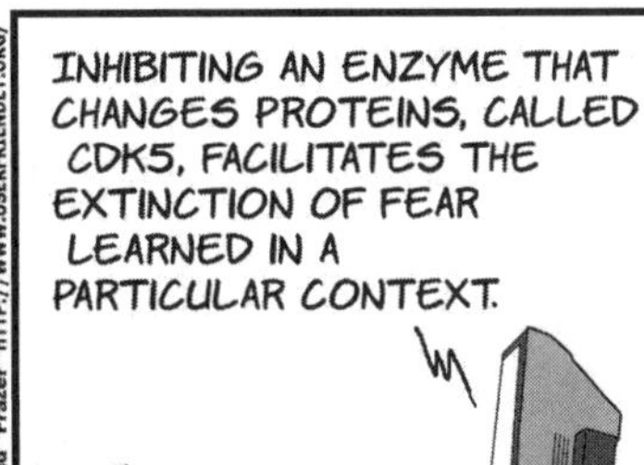
INHIBITING AN ENZYME THAT CHANGES PROTEINS, CALLED CDK5, FACILITATES THE EXTINCTION OF FEAR LEARNED IN A PARTICULAR CONTEXT.

JEEZ, SOMEONE SHOULD BOTTLE THAT STUFF!
THEY ALREADY DO. IT'S CALLED "LIQUOR."

PITR! YOU'RE BACK! HEY...THAT LOOKS INTERESTING...
DA. IS CDK5 COLA.
COPYRIGHT © 2007 J.D. "Illiad" Frazer HTTP://WWW.USERFRIENDLY.ORG/

IS SKUNKWORKS EXPERIMENT BY MY PITR COLA COMPANY. DRINKINK THIS WILL MAKE YOU FEARLESS.

IT...IT'S A DISGUSTING BLACK SLUDGE.
THIS IS INTENTIONAL. AFTER FIRST DRINK, YOU WILL HAVE NO PROBLEM WITH DISGUSTING FLAVOUR EITHER.

The enzyme in question is called CDK5. I wonder if there's an enzyme for egotism that we can inhibit? That would be *fun*.

SPOILER
HARRY POTTER
J.K. ROWLING
DARTH VADER IS HARRY'S FATHER AND HARRY ENDS UP SHOOTING JFK.
UserFriendly.Org
COPYRIGHT © 2007 J.D. "Illiad" Frazer HTTP://WWW.USERFRIENDLY.ORG/

"CDK5 COLA"? ARE YOU JOKING?
AM NEVER JOKINK ABOUT EXPERI-MENTATION ON POTENTIAL MINIONS.
COPYRIGHT © 2007 J.D. "Illiad" Frazer HTTP://WWW.USERFRIENDLY.ORG/

AND WHO EXACTLY DO YOU THINK WOULD BE STUPID ENOUGH TO BE YOUR GUINEA PIG?
CERTAIN SOMEONE DID COME TO MIND.

GO ON, ASK ME IF I THINK THOSE PANTS MAKE YOUR BACKSIDE LOOK BIG!

PITR, I THINK YOUR CDK5 COLA IS A BIT MISLEADING.
OH? EXPLAIN PLEASE...
COPYRIGHT © 2007 J.D. "Illiad" Frazer HTTP://WWW.USERFRIENDLY.ORG/

"CDK5 COLA" DOESN'T QUITE COVER THE GESTALT OF WHAT THE DRINK IS. IT'S MORE THAN JUST A FIZZY EXCUSE FOR A BRAIN MODIFIER.
SO...SHOULD BE RENAMINK DRINK? TO WHAT?
OH, I DUNNO, MAYBE "DARWIN AWARD COCKTAIL"?!

WHOA! HTML 5!
WHAT?
IT'S BEING REVIVED BY THE W3C.
COPYRIGHT © 2007 J.D. "Illiad" Frazer HTTP://WWW.USERFRIENDLY.ORG/

"...MUCH OF THIS HTML 5 LOBBYING WAS UNDERTAKEN BY THE 'WEB HYPERTEXT APPLICATION TECHNOLOGY WORKING GROUP,' A GROUP FORMED BY APPLE, MOZILLA AND OPERA."
YOU KNOW WHAT THIS MEANS, RIGHT?
YEAH. ONE MORE STAN-DARD TO BE IGNORED, WARPED THEN CLAIMED BY MICROSOFT AS ITS INVENTION.

UF got a lot of attention from Digg because of this strip. I suppose the experience with FrontPage was universal.

I'M CONFLICTED OVER HTML 5.
I'M NOT SURE WE EVEN NEED IT. AND WHAT OF XHTML?
COPYRIGHT © 2007 J.D. "Illiad" Frazer HTTP://WWW.USERFRIENDLY.ORG/

ALL OF THESE CHANGES FROM THE SIMPLE PURITY OF EARLY HTML DONE IN A TEXT EDITOR REMINDS ME OF WHEN FRONTPAGE CAME ON THE SCENE WITH WYSIWYG.
FRONTPAGE IS NOT AND NEVER HAS BEEN WYSIWYG.

OH? AND WHAT WAS IT THEN?
IT WAS MORE LIKE WYSIWTF.

WELCOME TO BIGSTRING.COM, AN EMAIL SERVICE BRINGING AN END TO SENDER'S REMORSE!
COPYRIGHT © 2007 J.D. "Illiad" Frazer HTTP://WWW.USERFRIENDLY.ORG/

DO YOU EVER FIND YOURSELF WANTING TO TAKE BACK AN EMAIL YOU'VE ALREADY SENT? BIGSTRING IS HERE TO HELP!

WE SEND EMAILS WITH LINKS TO IMAGES OF YOUR LETTERS THAT ARE KEPT ON OUR SERVER, SO WE HAVE THE ABILITY TO DELETE THE SOURCE MESSAGE AT ANY TIME!
Image Saved
CLICK

HASN'T SOMEONE TRIED THIS BEFORE? THIS DESTRUCTIBLE CONSUMER EMAIL SERVICE LIKE BIGSTRING, I MEAN.
YES, AND THEY'VE ALL FAILED TECHNO-LOGICALLY.
COPYRIGHT © 2007 J.D. "Illiad" Frazer HTTP://WWW.USERFRIENDLY.ORG/

I GUESS THEY MUST HAVE A MARKETING SOLUTION TO MAKE THEIR EMAIL SERVICE MORE APPEALING.
LIKE WHAT, THOUGH?
PURRR

FIVE MILLION DOLLARS IF YOU'LL SWAP POSITIONS BETWEEN THE "REPLY" AND "REPLY ALL" BUTTONS.
OOOH...I...NO!!
Email Clients 'R Us ltd.

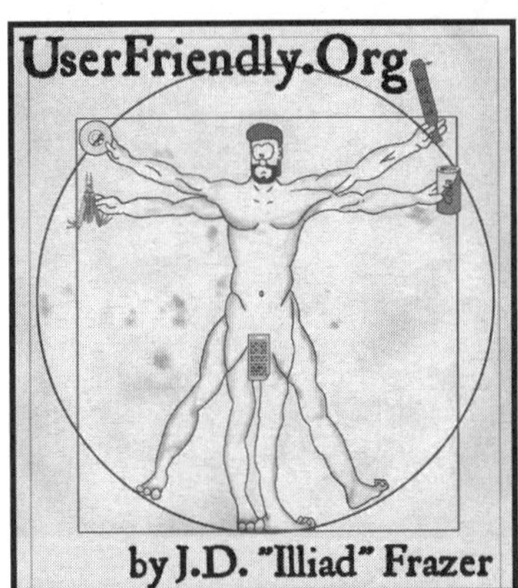
UserFriendly.Org
by J.D. "Illiad" Frazer
COPYRIGHT © 2007 J.D. "Illiad" Frazer HTTP://WWW.USERFRIENDLY.ORG/

THANK YOU ALL FOR ATTENDING TODAY'S PRESS CONFERENCE. I HAVE AN ANNOUNCEMENT TO MAKE REGARDING OUR COMPANY, XANDROS.

UM...WHO ARE YOU?
THE XANDROS SPOKESPERSON. I USED TO DEVELOP SOCKS SERVERS. HEH.

IT IS WITH GREAT PLEASURE THAT I ANNOUNCE A DEAL BETWEEN XANDROS AND MICROSOFT THAT GIVES XANDROS AND ITS CLIENT BASE PATENT COVENANTS.

THIS COLLABORATION AGREE-MENT WILL PROVIDE USERS WITH GREATER INTEROPER-ABILITY AND OTHER FINE BENEFITS. TRULY, MICROSOFT HAS PROVEN ITS INTEGRITY.

MR. GATES? IS THAT YOU DOWN THERE?
NO. I AM XANDROS! XANDROS!!

THIS IS INSANE!
WHAT NOW?
the wibble

"THE BRITISH GOVERNMENT REJECTED A PLEA TO EXTEND COPYRIGHT LAWS FOR SOUND RECORDINGS TO BEYOND 50 YEARS, PROMPTING THE MUSIC INDUSTRY TO ACCUSE IT OF NOT SUPPORTING MUSICIANS AND ARTISTS."

TO BE FAIR, MUSICIANS AND ARTISTS THAT ARE, YOU KNOW, DEAD.
HEY, TEN-ACRE MAUSOLEUMS AREN'T CHEAP TO MAINTAIN!
the wibble

YOU KNOW WHAT THIS COPYRIGHT BUSINESS IN THE U.K. MEANS, RIGHT?
A BUNCH OF THINGS, BUT GO AHEAD.
the wibble

COPYRIGHT © 2007 J.D. "Illiad" Frazer HTTP://WWW.USERFRIENDLY.ORG/

IT MEANS THAT A RIPPLE HAS STARTED, WHERE ALL GOVERNMENTS MAY DECIDE TO REDUCE THE COPYRIGHT PERIOD! IT MEANS FISCAL UNCERTAINTY FOR MIDDLEMEN! IT MEANS THAT BOOKS AND MOVIES ARE NEXT!

the wibble

DOES THAT MEAN I CAN COME OUT NOW?
OH CRIPES, NOT HIM AGAIN...
BACK IN THE VAULT, RAT!
the wibble

YOUR DRIPNIFICENCE, NEWS FROM THE SURFACE!
SPEAK, WORM.

COPYRIGHT © 2007 J.D. "Illiad" Frazer HTTP://WWW.USERFRIENDLY.ORG/

THERE HAVE BEEN REPORTS OUT OF NASA REGARDING THEIR ASTRONAUTS. SOME OF THEM HAVE GONE INTO SPACE ON MISSIONS WHILE UNDER THE INFLUENCE OF ALCOHOL.

AMATEURS. THE RUSSIANS ARE WAAAY AHEAD OF THEM.
YES, SIRE. ONE MUST ADMIT THAT "VODKA MODULE" ON THE I.S.S. IS BRILLIANT.

MORE NEWS ON THE DRUNK ASTRONAUTS, YOUR BULBOUSNESS. NASA HAS COME UP WITH A SOLUTION.

COPYRIGHT © 2007 J.D. "Illiad" Frazer HTTP://WWW.USERFRIENDLY.ORG/

THE ISSUE HERE IS THAT THE SHUTTLE PILOTS CAN'T FLY THE SHUTTLE WHEN THEY'RE DRUNK...

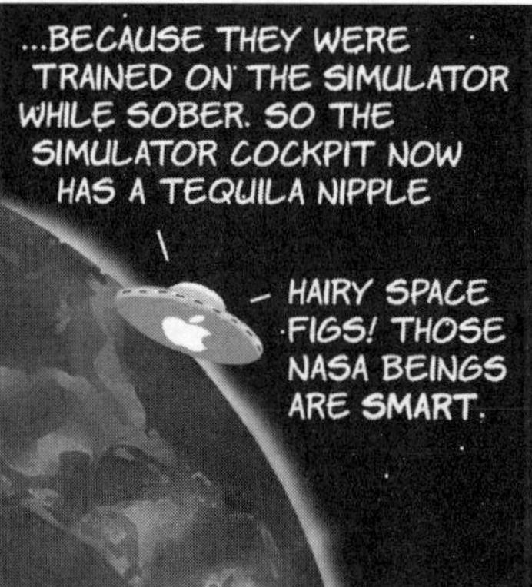
...BECAUSE THEY WERE TRAINED ON THE SIMULATOR WHILE SOBER. SO THE SIMULATOR COCKPIT NOW HAS A TEQUILA NIPPLE
HAIRY SPACE FIGS! THOSE NASA BEINGS ARE SMART.

SIRE, SECURITY AGENT OILET FUTON HAS SENT US A WARNING. EARTH HAS PRODUCED ANOTHER DOCTORATE-LEVEL ASTROPHYSICIST.
YES? SO?

HE'S ALSO A ROCK STAR. IT'S DR. BRIAN MAY, THE LEAD GUITARIST OF THE ROCK GROUP "QUEEN."
YES? SO? SO WHAT?!

THANKS TO HIM THE EARTHLINGS NOW BELIEVE THAT THE EARTH ROTATES ON ITS AXIS BECAUSE OF THE PRESENCE OF "FAT-BOTTOMED GIRLS."
BY ZANBOO, THEY'RE CATCHING UP TO US!!

DELETING FILES IN VISTA...
DO YOU WANT TO MOVE THIS FOLDER TO THE RECYCLE BIN?
(YES)
CLICK

YOU NEED TO CONFIRM THIS OPERATION.
(CONTINUE)
WINDOWS NEED YOUR PERMISSION TO CONTINUE.
(CONTINUE)
CLIK
CLIK

WELL?!
NOPE, NOT GONNA DO IT.

H.R. 3155, THE INTELLECTUAL PROPERTY ENHANCED CRIMINAL ENFORCEMENT ACT OF 2007, IF MADE INTO LAW, CRIMINALIZES *ATTEMPTED* COPYRIGHT INFRINGEMENT...

I'LL BET DISNEY'S COMING FOR ME.

UserFriendly.Org

SID, I'M HAVING TROUBLE PARSING THE SCRIPT YOU WROTE FOR THE MAIL SERVER.
OH?
COPYRIGHT © 2007 J.D. "Illiad" Frazer HTTP://WWW.USERFRIENDLY.ORG/

RIGHT HERE FOR STARTERS. IS THAT... ...WHAT IS THAT?!

WHY DO YOU HAVE TO OBFUSCATE YOUR PERL?!
BECAUSE PERL IS THE LEGALESE OF PROGRAMMING.

HEY WEBWEENIE. I HEARD THAT SOME BLOGGERS ARE THINKING ABOUT FORMING A BLOGGING LABOUR UNION.
COPYRIGHT © 2007 J.D. "Illiad" Frazer HTTP://WWW.USERFRIENDLY.ORG/

HOW DOES THAT SOUND TO YOU?
REALLY? A UNION?

IT SOUNDS GREAT! WHERE DO I SIGN UP?
YOU'RE IN. I'M YOUR REP. PAY ME YOUR DUES.

WELCOME TO THE BLOGGERS UNION. AS YOUR FIRST TASK, YOU HAVE TO NEGOTIATE BETTER WORKING CONDITIONS AND HIGHER PAY FOR ALL OF US.
'KAY.
COPYRIGHT © 2007 J.D. "Illiad" Frazer HTTP://WWW.USERFRIENDLY.ORG/

WHEN DO I START?
JUST AS SOON AS MANAGEMENT ARRIVES. OH THERE HE IS, IN YOUR SEAT THERE.

Hello my fellow blogging union members. I am sorry to report that bargaining has ceased as management refused to show up. As a result, I recommend we go on strike.
Yay! Strike!
COPYRIGHT © 2007 J.D. "Illiad" Frazer HTTP://WWW.USERFRIENDLY.ORG/

CRICKETS

So, while we wait for the world to come crawling to us we're all gonna go read CNN.com.

AJ? Who in particular are we pressuring with our strike?
The readership of course.
COPYRIGHT © 2007 J.D. "Illiad" Frazer HTTP://WWW.USERFRIENDLY.ORG/

With us not blogging, they'll force a settlement, which will bring about offers of greater pay and security to our union!
Without our blogs, where are they gonna go for their daily content?
I think they're off reading that LOLCATS site.

Whaddya mean they're reading lolcats?
That's what they're doing.
COPYRIGHT © 2007 J.D. "Illiad" Frazer HTTP://WWW.USERFRIENDLY.ORG/

What, they dropped us like we were nothing?
Looks like it. They're off reading the beeb, zombo.com and a pile of others.

I hate other content sites.
Blogging scabs, all of them.

Truism: There's a *lot* of content out there. Corollary: There's not much *good* content out there.

AFTER THREE YEARS, NOVELL WINS JUDGEMENT VS. SCO IN UNIXWARE COPYRIGHTS CASE
AHEM
AHEM
AHEM
COPYRIGHT © 2007 J.D. "Illiad" Frazer HTTP://WWW.USERFRIENDLY.ORG/
UserFriendly.Org

IN A 102 PAGE ORDER, JUDGE DALE A. KIMBALL HAS ISSUED A JUDGEMENT THAT DENIES SCO'S CLAIM THAT IT OWNS UNIX AND UNIXWARE.

A NOVELL SPOKESPERSON COMMENTED ON THE RULING JUST TODAY: "CLEARLY THIS JUDGEMENT IS A STAKE IN THE HEART FOR THE SCO GROUP."
COPYRIGHT© 2007 J.D. "Illiad" Frazer HTTP://WWW.USERFRIENDLY.ORG/

GET IT OUT! GET IT OUT! GET IT OUT!
DARL! HOLD STILL!!
SCO

WELL ISN'T THIS JUST @#$!@!!! DANDY!
DARL...
SCO

OH SHUT UP. WE'VE SPENT MILLIONS ON OUR STRATEGY TO CRUSH LINUX, AND WHAT DO WE HAVE TO SHOW FOR IT?
COPYRIGHT© 2007 J.D. "Illiad" Frazer HTTP://WWW.USERFRIENDLY.ORG/

WELL, DARL, YOU GOT A REALLY NICE YACHT AND A HUGE VILLA IN TUSCANY.
BUT I WANTED TWO! TWO HUGE VILLAS!
SCO

GUESS YOU'RE STILL IN SHOCK, HUH DARL?
GEE, YA THINK?
SCO

WE JUST LOST A MAJOR TORT BATTLE, AND OUR STOCK HAS PLUMMETED LIKE A SHEEP THAT THINKS IT CAN FLY.
NOT TO MENTION, I HAVE LORDS AND MASTERS WHO PROBABLY WANT TO TALK TO ME.
COPYRIGHT© 2007 J.D. "Illiad" Frazer HTTP://WWW.USERFRIENDLY.ORG/

CHAIRS! I NEED MORE CHAIRS DAMMIT!
STEVE, CALM DOWN!
Microsoft

S.C.O. IS IN FLAMES? IS IT TRUE?
DELICIOUSLY SO. THEY'LL BE BANKRUPT SOON AT THIS RATE.
COPYRIGHT© 2007 J.D. "Illiad" Frazer HTTP://WWW.USERFRIENDLY.ORG/

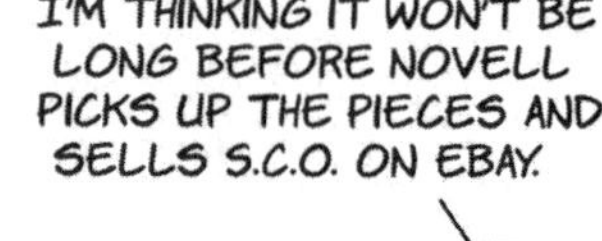
I'M THINKING IT WON'T BE LONG BEFORE NOVELL PICKS UP THE PIECES AND SELLS S.C.O. ON EBAY.

IF ONLY WE HAD THE MONEY...
ONE OF YOU GO CHECK THE COUCH FOR LOOSE CHANGE AND WE'LL TAKE THE "BUY IT NOW" OPTION.

DIDN'T YOU BUY MILLIONS OF SHARES OF SCOX AT $4.00 A FEW YEARS AGO?
SHUT UP!!

DARL? IT'S LORD CRUD. I HEARD THE BAD NEWS.
YEAH, PRETTY ROUGH, HUH?

I'LL SAY. ESPECIALLY SINCE NOVELL CAN COME AFTER YOU PERSONALLY FOR MONIES OWED.
WHAT? PERSONALLY?!

SO, HOW MUCH ARE YOU SELLING YOUR VILLA FOR?
WAIT! CAN'T I KEEP ANYTHING?
A TIN CUP FULL OF PENCILS SHOULD BE OKAY.

IT WAS AS IF MILLIONS OF VOICES SUDDENLY CRIED OUT IN TERROR...
skype
...BUT, LIKE, THEY COULDN'T HEAR EACH OTHER.
UserFriendly.Org
COPYRIGHT© 2007 J.D. "Illiad" Frazer HTTP://WWW.USERFRIENDLY.ORG/

That's what happens when the world's most popular VOIP service goes on the blink. It was so ... quiet.

HELLO, DARL MCBRIDE?
YES?
THIS IS JOE LASALA, GENERAL COUNSEL FOR NOVELL.
NOVELL.
COPYRIGHT© 2007 J.D. "Illiad" Frazer HTTP://WWW.USERFRIENDLY.ORG/

HI JOE. NICE DAY, ISN'T IT?
MR. MCBRIDE, IT'S COME TO OUR ATTENTION THAT THE SCO GROUP NOW OWES US MILLIONS OF DOLLARS...

...SO HOW DO YOU INTEND TO PAY US?
SCO STOCK. WE'RE SWIMMING IN IT.
NOVELL.

MR. LASALA? YOU WANTED THAT INTEL REPORT ON THE SCO GROUP?
YES, THANKS. WHAT'S THE SUMMARY?
COPYRIGHT© 2007 J.D. "Illiad" Frazer HTTP://WWW.USERFRIENDLY.ORG/

ODDLY ENOUGH, MCBRIDE IS BUSY TALKING TO FOLKS BIG IN QUANTUM COMPUTING.
QUANTUM COMPUTING? WHATEVER FOR?

SO, QUANTUM MECHANICS CAN CHANGE REALITY, RIGHT?
NO.

HA! I FINALLY HAVE THE LARGEST APPLE SCREEN OF ANYONE IN THE OFFICE!
COPYRIGHT© 2007 J.D. "Illiad" Frazer HTTP://WWW.USERFRIENDLY.ORG/

IT TOOK SOME FAST TALK WITH THE SMILING MAN, BUT I NOW HAVE THE BIGGEST, SLICKEST MONITOR HERE.

WHO'S THE BIG DAWG? WHOOOOO'S THE BIG DAWG NOW?
WHAT DO WE HAVE HERE?

Seriously. I know someone whose boss—who isn't even marginally technical—insisted that he have the largest screen at work, even if he didn't need the extra screen real estate. When he discovered that some of his scientists (he was a department head) had better computers, he just about had a seizure.

NICE MONITOR.
OH, HI CHIEF.
COPYRIGHT© 2007 J.D. "Illiad" Frazer HTTP://WWW.USERFRIENDLY.ORG/

TWENTY-THREE INCHES, I SEE. VERY NICE.
UH...THANKS.

WHAT DO YOU NEED A THIRTY-INCH MONITOR FOR?
LARGER MINESWEEPER TILES, OKAY?

HASBRO IS RELEASING THE 4TH EDITION OF D&D STARTING MAY 2008!
SO? WHAT ARE THEY DOING THAT MERITS AN EDITION TO REPLACE 3.5?
COPYRIGHT© 2007 J.D. "Illiad" Frazer HTTP://WWW.USERFRIENDLY.ORG/

WELL, FOR STARTERS THEY'RE UPPING THE CHARACTER LEVEL CAP FROM 20 TO 30.

LEVEL 30? WHY DON'T THEY MAKE IT LEVEL 40? OR 50?
THEY GOTTA HAVE **SOMETHING** FOR D&D 5TH EDITION.

D&D 4TH EDITION GETS RID OF A WHOLE MITTFUL OF PROBLEMS, AND ENHANCES THE GAME EXPERIENCE.
GAME EXPERIENCE?
COPYRIGHT© 2007 J.D. "Illiad" Frazer HTTP://WWW.USERFRIENDLY.ORG/

YEAH. THE D&D GAME EXPERIENCE IS ALL ABOUT TAKING RISKS FOR GREATER GLORY, DELVING INTO THE DARK RECESS OF THE WORLD WITH YOUR SWORD AND FINDING ADVERSITY AND REWARD.

DUDE, I COULD BOIL THAT DOWN TO FILLING A PIÑATA OF A MONSTER WITH LOOT AND LETTING YOU WHACK AT IT.
IT'S NOT THE SAME!!

ASTRONOMERS DISCOVER A REGION IN THE UNIVERSE A BILLION LIGHT-YEARS ACROSS UTTERLY DEVOID OF STARS, NEBULA, AND GAS.
SOMEONE JUST CLEARED THE WAY FOR A GALACTIC BYPASS...
UserFriendly.Org
COPYRIGHT© 2007 J.D. "Illiad" Frazer HTTP://WWW.USERFRIENDLY.ORG/

Mr. Adams, we miss you.

OH PLEASE, WIZARDS OF THE COAST ISN'T HOLDING STUFF BACK JUST TO RELEASE A D&D 5TH EDITION. THERE'S JUST NO WAY.
YOU HAVE A POINT.
HE DOES?

...THEY'RE GONNA RELEASE D&D 4.5 FIRST.
NO THEY'RE **NOT!!**

OKAY, SO MAYBE WIZARDS OF THE COAST IS DOING THE CAPITALISM THING. MAYBE THEY'RE RELEASING NEW EDITIONS JUST TO KEEP THE MONEY FLOWING. SO WHAT? THEY'RE NOT **FORCING** ANYONE TO SWITCH TO 4TH EDITION.

YOU'RE SUCH A PUPPY.

OF COURSE THEY'RE GOING TO MAKE YOU SWITCH. THEY'LL SEND AROUND SWAT TEAMS TO SEIZE YOUR OLD 3.5E BOOKS AND CAST THEM INTO A HUGE BONFIRE. THEN THEY TAKE ALL OF YOUR OLD DICE AND THEY'LL GRIND THEM INTO POWDER.

OH GOOD HEAVENS. AND THEN WHAT? A POGROM?
CLOSE ENOUGH. THEY'LL MAKE YOU SNORT YOUR DICE.
IN LINES.

HEY SID? YOU GOING TO RUN ANY MORE D&D GAMES AT THE OFFICE SOON?

I COULD DO. WHY?

WELL, 4TH EDITION IS COMING OUT NEXT YEAR, AND I THOUGHT...
WAIT. **4TH** EDITION?
YES.

I DIDN'T EVEN KNOW THERE WAS A **2ND** EDITION!
THERE WAS, BUT SOME OF US CONSIDERED IT THE "WINDOWS MILLENIUM" OF D&D.

WHATEVER HAPPENED TO THOSE THREE HUMBLE-YET-GREAT LITTLE BROWN BOOKS FROM THE 1970S? FEW RULES, LOTS OF IMAGINATION?

PROGRESS, SID. THE DOWN-SIDE IS THAT MY D&D 3.5E BOOK COLLECTION WILL HAVE TO BE REPLACED. NOT THAT I WOULDN'T BUY ALL THE NEW, SHINY 4E BOOKS ANYWAY!

AH, SO THEY FINALLY RENAMED IT TO "D&D: THE GATHERING" HAVE THEY?

YOU JUST CAN'T BE NICE, CAN YOU.

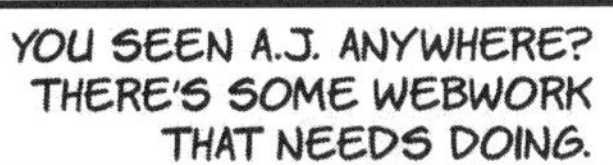

YOU SEEN A.J. ANYWHERE? THERE'S SOME WEBWORK THAT NEEDS DOING.
HE'S LOCKED HIMSELF IN AN OFFICE EVER SINCE HE PICKED UP A COPY OF THAT "BIOSHOCK" GAME.
COPYRIGHT © 2007 J.D. "Illiad" Frazer HTTP://WWW.USERFRIENDLY.ORG/

AAAIIIIIEEEEEEE! !@$!^%@#%!!!!!!!!

TENSE GAME, A.J.?
IT'S **NOT** A GAME! IT'S AN ELECTRONIC ENEMA!

"MICROSOFT HAS ADMITTED TO A 19-HOUR SERVER DOWN-TIME DURING WHICH PAYING USERS OF WINDOWS XP AND VISTA WERE ACCUSED BY THE COMPANY'S 'WINDOWS GEN-UINE ADVANTAGE' VALIDATION SYSTEM OF RUNNING PIRATED SOFTWARE."
COPYRIGHT © 2007 J.D. "Illiad" Frazer HTTP://WWW.USERFRIENDLY.ORG/

"THE WGA ANTI-PIRACY SCHEME FOR VISTA DISABLES SEVERAL FEATURES WHEN IT THINKS THE COPY IS BOGUS, AMONG THEM THE AERO GRAPHICAL USER INTERFACE AND READYBOOST."

SO WAIT...I PAID FOR MY LICENSE AND I GET SHUT DOWN WHILE PIRATES REMAIN UNSCATHED?
WHEN YOU'RE CHAINED TO AN OAR YOU DON'T THINK YOU SHOULD GO DOWN WHEN THE GALLEY SINKS?

IF SENDING LUKE SKYWALKER'S LIGHTSABRE INTO SPACE WITH THE SHUTTLE DISCOVERY ATTRACTS MUCH-NEEDED PUBLIC ATTENTION TO SPACEFLIGHT, IMAGINE WHAT WE COULD DO TO GET ATTENTION FOR A MOON BASE...
COPYRIGHT © 2007 J.D. "Illiad" Frazer HTTP://WWW.USERFRIENDLY.ORG/
UserFriendly.Org

SO THIS IS GOOGLE SKY! NOW WE CAN EXPLORE THE STARS JUST LIKE WE EXPLORE THE WORLD IN GOOGLE EARTH!
YAWN

DON'T YOU THINK IT'S AMAZING? ALL THAT DATA ABOUT THE SPACE AROUND US? VISITING THE PLANETS?

...LETTING US EXPLORE OUR LOCAL CLUSTER?
MEH. IT NEEDS TO GIVE DIRECTIONS.

SIRE! GOOGLE HAS RELEASED GOOGLE SKY! IT AMALGAMATES A VAST ARRAY OF ASTRONOMICAL PHOTOS AND PRESENTS THEM TO THE EARTHLINGS FOR THEIR AMUSEMENT.
WELL, LET'S HAVE A LOOK, THEN.

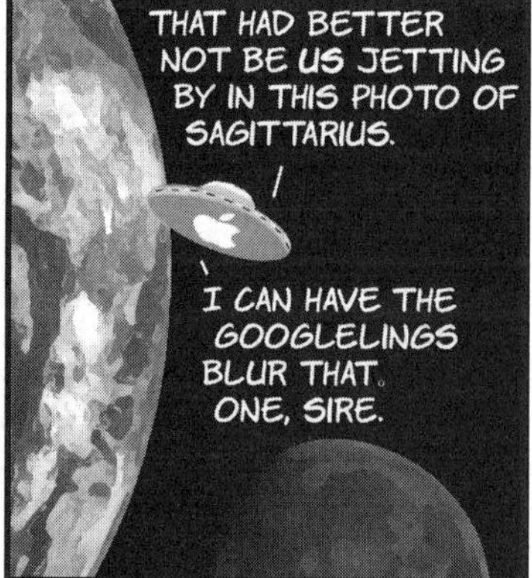
THAT HAD BETTER NOT BE US JETTING BY IN THIS PHOTO OF SAGITTARIUS.
I CAN HAVE THE GOOGLELINGS BLUR THAT ONE, SIRE.

SO THAT'S REALLY A PHOTO OF OUR SPACECRAFT ON GOOGLE SKY? HOW GOOD IS THIS TOOL ANYWAY?
USE THE ZOOM FUNCTION, SIRE.

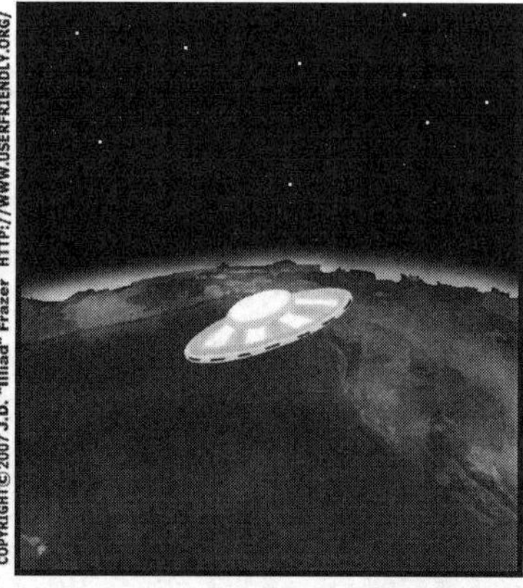

BY ZOOBAR! HAVE I PUT ON WEIGHT?
A LITTLE, SIRE.

"The Biptrix Sisters." Good drugs, J.D.

WELL, THIS GOOGLE SKY IS OFFENSIVE. IT INVADES MY PRIVACY. I DON'T LIKE IT.
INDEED, SIRE. AND THINK OF EVERYONE ELSE WHO'S HAD THEIR PRIVACY VIOLATED.

DO YOU THINK... PERHAPS...

BY ZOOBAR'S FLAGELLA! ARE THOSE THE BIPTRIX SISTERS TANNING BY THE RAYS OF RIGEL?!
JUST SO, SIRE. THE EARTHERS ARE GOOD AT THIS SORT OF TECHNOLOGY.

AJ, WHAT'S THIS I HEAR ABOUT THE PLAYER HAVING TO KILL LITTLE GIRLS IN THAT BIOSHOCK GAME?
IT'S NOT QUITE LIKE THAT, SID.
COPYRIGHT© 2007 J.D. "Illiad" Frazer HTTP://WWW.USERFRIENDLY.ORG/

THE LITTLE GIRLS PRESENT A MORAL CHOICE THE PLAYER HAS TO MAKE IN THE GAME. ALTHOUGH IT'S NOT GRAPHIC, IT'S A CHOICE THAT CAN BE KIND OF UNCOMFORTABLE.
YOU SHOULD ASK DUST PUPPY. HE'S PLAYING THE GAME NOW.

SNIF
THERE, THERE...

HEY...SERVICE PACK 1 FOR VISTA IS COMING OUT SOON.
HM?
COPYRIGHT© 2007 J.D. "Illiad" Frazer HTTP://WWW.USERFRIENDLY.ORG/

IF HISTORY IS ANY INDICATION, THIS SERVICE PACK WILL DRIVE MORE PEOPLE FROM XP OVER TO VISTA.
UNFORTUNATELY.

RUMOUR HAS IT THAT SP1 REALLY FIXES VISTA.
HUNH. I HAD NO IDEA A SERVICE PACK COULD REMOVE BLOAT.

A RECENT STUDY REVEALS THAT THE LATEST CELL PHONES MIGHT TRIGGER MEDICAL EQUIPMENT FAILURE...
MAYBE THE IRONY ISN'T CLEAR:
CT Scanner: $2,600,000.
COPYRIGHT© 2007 J.D. "Illiad" Frazer HTTP://WWW.USERFRIENDLY.ORG/

Shielding it clearly needs but doesn't have: $200.00
UserFriendly.Org

It seems obvious, but it really isn't. Check out next Sunday's cartoon.

HEY, YOU GUYS SEEN SID?
HE'S OFF TODAY. SICK LEAVE.
COPYRIGHT © 2007 J.D. "Illiad" Frazer HTTP://WWW.USERFRIENDLY.ORG/

OH DEAR... IS HE OKAY?
HE SPRAINED HIS THUMB.
THX ESTEIS!

HE'S ON SICK LEAVE FROM A SPRAINED THUMB?
EMACS. NINE FINGERS. YOU DO THE MATH.

HOW'S THE THUMB, GANDALF?
THOP THOP THOP
HURTS.
COPYRIGHT © 2007 J.D. "Illiad" Frazer HTTP://WWW.USERFRIENDLY.ORG/

YOU CAN'T CODE WITHOUT SOME DIFFICULTY, CAN YOU.
WAKKA WAKKA WAKKA
YES, RIGHT.
THX ESTEIS!

THEN I GUESS ONE COULD SAY YOU WERE, **HEH,** "DIGITALLY CHALLENGED."
NOT SO CHALLENGED I COULDN'T SWITCH OFF A SMART-MOUTHED COMPUTER.
BUCKA BUCKA BUCKA

IS THAT SID YOU'RE PLAYING QUAKE WITH?
YEP!
COPYRIGHT © 2007 J.D. "Illiad" Frazer HTTP://WWW.USERFRIENDLY.ORG/

BUT...I THOUGHT HE HAD A BUSTED THUMB...
HE HAS STEF HITTING THE SPACE BAR FOR HIM WHENEVER HE NEEDS TO JUMP.
THX SNAPPING TURTLE!

ALL YOU HAD TO DO WAS HIT THE SPACE BAR. THAT WAS IT. THE SPACE BAR. AND YET, HERE I AM IN THE LAVA.

COPYRIGHT © 2007 J.D. "Illiad" Frazer HTTP://WWW.USERFRIENDLY.ORG/

FOUND THE FLIGHT SIM IN GOOGLE EARTH DID YOU?
THAT'S RIGHT BILL GATES, I'M BUZZING YOUR OFFICE!

CAN YOU BUZZ GOOGLE'S HEAD OFFICE?
PIECE OF CAKE! WATCH AND LEARN, YOUNG PADAWAN...

...THERE IT IS AND HERE WE GO...OOPS. TOUCHY.
WAY TO CRASH INTO GOOGLE'S LOBBY, DUDE.

WE'D BETTER LOG THAT ONE...
Google

MICROSOFT HAS ACTIVATED A FUNCTION IN VISTA CALLED "REDUCED FUNCTIONALITY." THIS EFFECTIVELY DISABLES NON-GENUINE COPIES OF THE OPERATING SYSTEM.

ANYONE WITH A PIRATED COPY WILL EXPERIENCE AFTER AN HOUR OF USE A BLACK SCREEN WITH NO START MENU OR TASKBAR. THE DESKTOP WILL VANISH.

...WHICH THIS REPORTER THINKS WILL BE PLENTY FAMILIAR TO VETERAN WINDOWS USERS ANYWAY.
DAMN. BEAT ME TO IT!

THE CARTOONIST, RECENTLY HAVING BEEN THOROUGHLY SCHOOLED ON MEDICAL TECHNOLOGY AND THE INHERENT DIFFICULTY IN SHIELDING IT FROM WIRELESS SIGNALS (SEE LAST SUNDAY'S 'TOON) PROVIDES A MORE AMENABLE SOLUTION:

FARADAY CAGE CELLPHONE COVERS

UserFriendly.Org

HEY YOU GUYS! GOOGLE IS OFFERING A PRIZE OF $25 MILLION FOR THE FIRST PRIVATE ENTERPRISE THAT LANDS A PROBE ON THE MOON BY 2014!
COPYRIGHT © 2007 J.D. "Illiad" Frazer HTTP://WWW.USERFRIENDLY.ORG/

WE'RE ALL GEEKS! WE SHOULD PUT OUR MINDS TOGETHER AND SEE WHAT WE CAN COME UP WITH!

YOU CAN JOIN IN TOO, STEF, I SUPPOSE.
$25 MILLION IS MORE THAN ENOUGH TO HIRE A MOVIE STUDIO TO FAKE ANOTHER MOON LANDING.

STEF, THAT WHOLE "THE MOON LANDING WAS STAGED ON A MOVIE SET" THEORY WAS COMPLETELY DEBUNKED.
OH?
COPYRIGHT © 2007 J.D. "Illiad" Frazer HTTP://WWW.USERFRIENDLY.ORG/

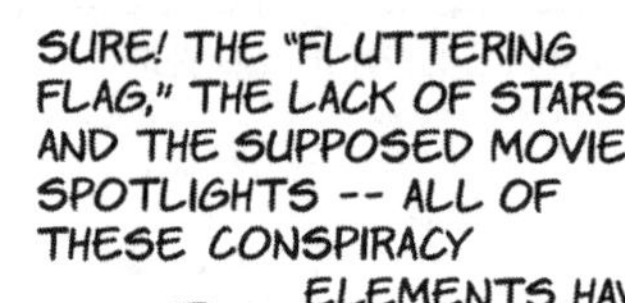
SURE! THE "FLUTTERING FLAG," THE LACK OF STARS AND THE SUPPOSED MOVIE SPOTLIGHTS -- ALL OF THESE CONSPIRACY ELEMENTS HAVE BEEN RATIONALLY EXPLAINED!

SO THE IDEA THAT THE MOON LANDING IS A HOAX IS BEYOND LUDICROUS!
THEN THEY SHOULD HAVE BROUGHT BACK A WHOLE LOTTA GREEN CHEESE! DID THEY?
NO!

SO WHAT DID YOU FIND?
LANDINK PROBE ON MOON IS SMALL ENGINEERINK PROBLEM. IS DIFFICULT, BUT NOT IMPOSSIBLE.
COPYRIGHT © 2007 J.D. "Illiad" Frazer HTTP://WWW.USERFRIENDLY.ORG/

WE WILL HAVE ISSUES WITH FUEL CONSUMPTION, AND AM STILL LEARNINK MORE ABOUT ORBITAL MECHANICS, BUT AM THINKINK THIS WILL BE DO-ABLE PROJECT.

AND, UH, WHAT ABOUT HAVING SAMPLING DEVICES ON THE PROBE?
CHEESE SAMPLE SCOOP IS NO PROBLEM.
YOU MOCK ME BUT I SAW THAT DOC-UMENTARY WALLACE AND GROMIT DID!

BEFORE AM TO BE DESIGNINK SPACE WESSEL TO TAKE PROBE TO MOON, WE ARE TO BE DECIDINK ON DETAILS OF PAYLOAD.
COPYRIGHT © 2007 J.D. "Illiad" Frazer HTTP://WWW.USERFRIENDLY.ORG/

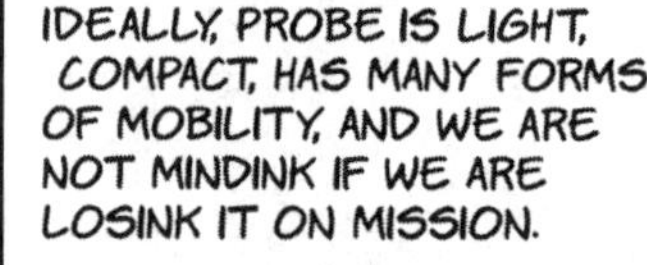
IDEALLY, PROBE IS LIGHT, COMPACT, HAS MANY FORMS OF MOBILITY, AND WE ARE NOT MINDINK IF WE ARE LOSINK IT ON MISSION.

SOMETHING DOES COME TO MIND...

WHY IS IT SO QUIET ALL OF A SUDDEN?

I'M NOT ENTIRELY SURE I LIKE THE IDEA OF GOING TO THE MOON...
ERWIN, IS WERY GREAT ADWENTURE!
COPYRIGHT © 2007 J.D. "Illiad" Frazer HTTP://WWW.USERFRIENDLY.ORG/

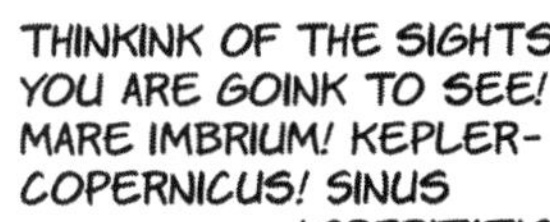
THINKINK OF THE SIGHTS YOU ARE GOINK TO SEE! MARE IMBRIUM! KEPLER-COPERNICUS! SINUS ASPERITATIS!

OOH! AND THE GOOGLE MOONBASE!
AM NOT ONLY ONE FALLINK FOR THAT!!

PITR, I'VE BEEN DOING SOME RESEARCH ON GETTING A PROBE UP TO THE MOON.
DA?
COPYRIGHT © 2007 J.D. "Illiad" Frazer HTTP://WWW.USERFRIENDLY.ORG/

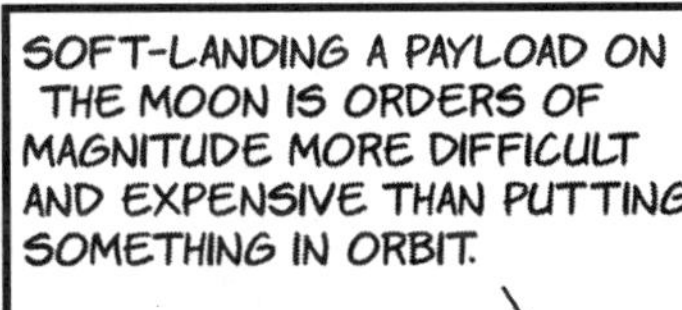
SOFT-LANDING A PAYLOAD ON THE MOON IS ORDERS OF MAGNITUDE MORE DIFFICULT AND EXPENSIVE THAN PUTTING SOMETHING IN ORBIT.

HAVEN'T YOU WONDERED WHY NASA HASN'T TRIED A LUNAR LANDING IN THE LAST FEW DECADES?
COULD NOT FIND A.I. STUPID ENOUGH TO SEND.
HEY!!

THE SMILEY TURNED 25 THIS YEAR.
DAMN EMO KIDS...
>:-/
COPYRIGHT © 2007 J.D. "Illiad" Frazer HTTP://WWW.USERFRIENDLY.ORG/
UserFriendly.Org

LINUX. IT WAS LINUX THAT DID THIS TO US!
A POX ON LINUX!
SCO

I DUNNO DARL. I'M NOT SURE IT WAS LINUX THAT KILLED US.
OH? WHAT THEN?

MAYBE WE SHOULDN'T HAVE, YOU KNOW, SUED OUR OWN CUSTOMERS.
SHUT UP.
SCO

ANY PLANS FOR THE FUTURE, DARL?
I GUESS I NEED A NEW JOB.
SCO

COPYRIGHT © 2007 J.D. "Illiad" Frazer HTTP://WWW.USERFRIENDLY.ORG/

A HEADHUNTER CALLED ME LAST NIGHT WITH AN OFFER AS CEO FOR A SUBPRIME LENDER. I THINK I COULD DO A LOT FOR THEM.

SCO

YOU ALREADY HAVE A STRATEGY FOR THEM?
SUE ALL OF THE SUCCESSFUL COMPETING LENDERS. DUH.
SCO

EARLIER THIS WEEK MICROSOFT QUIETLY ALLOWED PC MAKERS TO OFFER BUYERS OF NEW PCS THE OPTION TO DOWNGRADE FROM VISTA TO XP.

COPYRIGHT © 2007 J.D. "Illiad" Frazer HTTP://WWW.USERFRIENDLY.ORG/

A MICROSOFT REP CONFIRMED CHANGES MADE OVER THE SUMMER TO MAKE IT EASIER FOR CUSTOMERS TO DOWNGRADE TO WINDOWS XP.

WAIT A MINUTE. WHAT DO THEY MEAN "DOWNGRADE"?

TECH SUPPORT. PAIN ME.
HEY. I HEARD ABOUT THAT VISTA TO XP DOWNGRADE. SO MAYBE THERE'S AN XP TO 98 DOWNGRADE?
HUNH?

COPYRIGHT © 2007 J.D. "Illiad" Frazer HTTP://WWW.USERFRIENDLY.ORG/

AND MAYBE THERE'S A 98 TO 95 DOWNGRADE? AND 95 TO 3.11 AND 3.1 AND 3.0 DOWNGRADE? AND THEN WE COULD GO WITH WINDOWS 2.0! AND THEN WINDOWS 1.0!

WAIT, YOU WANT TO SWAP VISTA FOR DOS 3.3?
SEEMS ATTRACTIVE TO ME. ATTRIB +H *.* FOR THE WIN!

AND PRECISELY WHAT'S SO GREAT ABOUT XP THAT YOU DON'T WANT TO UPGRADE TO VISTA?
XP ISN'T GREAT.
...IT ISN'T?
NO, IT'S BLOODY TERRIBLE.

THEN WHY DO YOU USE IT?
STEF, XP IS LIKE DEMOCRACY AND GOVERNMENTS. IT'S THE WORST WINDOWS VERSION OUT THERE, EXCEPT FOR ALL OF THE OTHERS.

Please create a password.
******
Password strength: Weak
Please try again.
TAP TAP TAP TAP TAP TAP
TAP TAP TAP TAP TAP
SHIFT TAP
TAP TAP

****
Password strength: Mediocre
Please try again.
TAP SHIFT TAP TAP SHIFT TAP SHIFT
TAP TAP TAP SHIFT TAP TAP TAP TAP
SHIFT TAP SHIFT TAP TAP TAP TAP
TAP TAP SHIFT TAP

****
Password strength: Adequate
Thank you for creating your password. You will be asked to change it tomorrow.

CELEBRATING FORTY YEARS OF THE CALCULATOR

58008918

UserFriendly.Org

If you don't get this one, you didn't write rude things with numbers on calculators when you were younger. Numbers that had to be read upside-down.

Your old password has expired. Please enter a new password.

However, please also note that the new password can't be even vaguely similar to the old one, and that we're on to you if you do simple numeral-for-letter substitution. Also, no verbing nouns, no using pleonasms, and if you use anything remotely related to what could be found in an english dictionary, we'll reject it.

Whatever the hell that is, it's accepted.

TIP
TAP
TEP

Please enter your password to access this ultra secure system:

TAPTAPTAPTAPTAPPITYTAPTAP
RAPPATAPTAPTAPPITYWAPBAP
FAPFAPFAP

[0!ghuG9#%z~@xiT-/:K4

Accepted. Thank you.

YE GODS, HOW DO YOU REMEMBER THAT?

STICKY NOTE ON THE MONITOR...

GREG! HAVE YOU PLAYED HALO 3 YET?

YES, LAST WEEK. I FINISHED IT.

IT ONLY TOOK ME ABOUT 10 HOURS, BUT IT WAS PRETTY FUN. IT HAS SOME NEAT NEW VEHICLES.

BUT OVERALL I'D RATE HALO 3 AS JUST OKAY. NOTHING SPECIAL.
DUDE! NOT SO LOUD!
GREG? A MOB OF ANGRY ADOLES-CENTS AWAITS YOU IN THE LOBBY.

HALO 3 CAUSES ME TO BE WISTFUL.
OH?

THE TRILOGY AND THE STORY ARE NOW COMPLETE. BUT WHAT OF THE GREAT STORY ARCS IN OTHER GAMES THAT HAVE YET TO BE RESOLVED?

FOR EXAMPLE, WILL WE EVER SEE HALF-LIFE 3?

OF COURSE, SOON AFTER THE RELEASE OF HALF-LIFE 2: EPISODE 4, SP 3, ALYX-BIKINI EDITION.

PITR WENT WHERE?
THE U.K., FOR A CONFERENCE ON SECURITY.

I WONDER IF HE KNOWS ABOUT THE NEW LAWS REGARDING DATA THERE.
IT'S NOW A CRIME TO REFUSE TO DECRYPT ANY DATA REQUESTED BY AUTHORITIES AS PART OF A CRIMINAL OR TERROR INVESTIGATION.

CUSTOMS & EXCISE
AND WHAT HAVE YOU GOT THERE, THEN?
MERELY SOME WERY...PERSONAL DATA.

TELL ME ABOUT THIS NEW DECRYPTION LAW.
IT'S A BIT OF A MESS, REALLY. THE AUTHORITIES HAVE THE RIGHT TO DEMAND THE DECRYPTION KEY TO YOUR DATA.

IF YOU DON'T GIVE IT TO THEM, YOU COULD BE FACING YEARS IN JAIL. ON THE OTHER HAND, A DECRYPTION KEY ISN'T A PHYSICAL OBJECT. IT'S IN YOUR HEAD. HOW ARE THE COPS GOING TO EXTRACT IT WITHOUT YOUR CO-OPERATION?

Cerebro-Vac Station 17
HOLD STILL YOU BLOODY PRAT!!
NYEEET!
CUSTOMS

WITH THE RENAMING OF ASTEROID 1994 GT9 TO 7307 TAKEI IN HONOUR OF STAR TREK'S GEORGE TAKEI, ONE CAN'T HELP BUT NOTE THAT WILLIAM SHATNER HAS YET TO RECEIVE A SIMILAR HONOUR.

SUUULUUUUUUU!!!
7307 TAKEI

UserFriendly.Org

JUST OVER TWO YEARS AGO EBAY BOUGHT SKYPE FOR $2.6 BILLION.
LAST QUARTER, REVENUES FOR SKYPE AMOUNTED TO ONLY $90 MILLION.

COPYRIGHT © 2007 J.D. "Illiad" Frazer HTTP://WWW.USERFRIENDLY.ORG/
EBAY HAS STATED THAT THEY ARE ON THE LOOKOUT FOR A C.E.O. TO TURN THE AILING VOIP BUSINESS UNIT AROUND. IF THEY DON'T, EBAY COULD BE FORCED TO SELL IT OFF.

HECK, I'D BUY IT. I HAVE $100 BURNING A HOLE IN MY POCKET RIGHT NOW.
CHECKING... "RESERVE NOT MET."

Swan>This is eBay's CFO. Who are you and why are you asking me to chat?
AJ>I'd like to offer you $500 for skype.

COPYRIGHT © 2007 J.D. "Illiad" Frazer HTTP://WWW.USERFRIENDLY.ORG/
Swan>...

Swan>This must be a joke.
AJ>No joke, sir. I have over two hundred positive reviews. I'm AAA+!

MR. SWAN, WE NEED A BETTER REVENUE MODEL FOR SKYPE.
I AGREE, MA'M.

COPYRIGHT © 2007 J.D. "Illiad" Frazer HTTP://WWW.USERFRIENDLY.ORG/
... IN FACT, I'VE COME UP WITH AN ADVERTISING MODEL THAT SHOULD NET US BILLIONS.
DO TELL...

skype™
Dialing...
WHILE YOU WAIT FOR YOUR FREE SKYPE CALL TO BE CONNECTED, WHY NOT TALK TO ME? MY NAME IS HONEY, AND I'M ONLY $3.95 A MINUTE...

MR. SWAN.
YES MS. WHITMAN.

COPYRIGHT © 2007 J.D. "Illiad" Frazer HTTP://WWW.USERFRIENDLY.ORG/
I JUST MET WITH THE BOARD OF DIRECTORS.
AH. WHAT DID THEY THINK OF OUR NEW MONEYMAKER?

THEY WANT TO KNOW IF IT SCALES.
YES MA'M, SKYPE CONFERENCE CALLS. HONEY HAS FRIENDS.

BROMPA
BROMPA
BEEEW
BEEEW
BROMPA
BROMPA
BEEEW
BEEEW
HAIL, KNAVE.

OH CRAP. YOU'RE THAT RIAA INQUISITOR.
INDEED! THY GUILT-STRICKEN EYES BETRAY THEE.
BROMPA
BROMPA
BEEEW
BEEEW
RIAA
COPYRIGHT© 2007 J.D. "Illiad" Frazer HTTP://WWW.USERFRIENDLY.ORG/

ONE DOES ALWAYS WONDER WHAT WILL COME OUT OF THEIR MOUTHS.
THOU ART PLAYING MUSIC LOUD! HAST THOU PAID FOR AND HOLD A PERFORMANCE LICENSE?
RIAA

PERFORMANCE LICENSE? I'M LISTENING TO TUNES I'VE BOUGHT!
YET, AT SUCH VOLUME THAT MANY NEARBY CAN ALSO ENJOY SAID DULCET NOTES.
RIAA

OUR SISTER ORGANIZATION IN THE U.K. IS SUING A COMPANY WHERE RADIOS WERE PLAYED TOO LOUD WITHOUT A PERFORMANCE LICENSE. WE WILL EXTRACT OUR POUNDS OF FLESH FROM THE CULPRITS IN DUE COURSE.
RIAA
COPYRIGHT© 2007 J.D. "Illiad" Frazer HTTP://WWW.USERFRIENDLY.ORG/

SHOULDN'T YOU BE SUING RADIO MANUFACTURERS FOR INSTALLING VOLUME CONTROLS THAT GO PAST '3' THEN?
HMMM. YET ANOTHER REVENUE STREAM. THANK YOU, SINNER.
RIAA

BIDDING HAS STARTED FOR ".ASIA" DOMAIN NAMES.
I WANT THIS ONE:

nevergetinvolvedinalandwarin.asia

UserFriendly.Org

The Princess Bride, alas!

LITTLE BIT OF JAVASCRIPT HERE...LITTLE BIT THERE, AND THE NAVBAR IS ALL SMOOTH AND SHINEY...
COPYRIGHT © 2007 J.D. "Illiad" Frazer HTTP://WWW.USERFRIENDLY.ORG/

WHAT IS THAT AND WHY IS IT ON OUR WEBSITE?
IT'S JUST SOME AJAX, SID.

AHH, YOU MEAN "USER-INITIATED BLINK TAGS."
I LIKEN IT TO "MENU-BASED BROWSER GAMES."

WE WHO BEAR THE BURDEN OF KNOWLEDGE HEAR YOUR CRY. TECH SUPPORT, GREG SPEAKING.
I HAVE A DVD I WANT TO PLAY ON MY LINUX BOX.
COPYRIGHT © 2007 J.D. "Illiad" Frazer HTTP://WWW.USERFRIENDLY.ORG/

THE PROBLEM IS THAT XINE SEEMS TO PLAY IT BACK ALL CHOPPY AND STUFF.
THAT'S JUST DMA CHECKING.

SO HOW DO I MAKE IT SO I CAN WATCH MY DVD?
BLINK YOUR EYES SYNCHED TO THE DMA CHECKING. THANKS FOR CALLING!

HEY SID, ARE YOU ON FACEBOOK?
HAVE YOU GONE MAD?
COPYRIGHT © 2007 J.D. "Illiad" Frazer HTTP://WWW.USERFRIENDLY.ORG/

WHY WOULD I USE AND SUPPORT A SITE WHERE THEY COLLECT ALL OF MY PERSONAL INFO GIVING IDENTITY THIEVES YET ANOTHER PLACE TO GET AT IT, AND WHERE PEOPLE CAN BOTHER ME ALL DAY IN A DOZEN DIFFERENT WAYS?

JUST GIVE ME ONE REASON WHY I SHOULD JOIN FACE-BOOK THAT DOESN'T MAKE ME WANT TO ENGAGE IN A TECHNICOLOUR YAWN.
UM...YOU CAN "FRIEND" PEOPLE?

SO YOU'RE ON FACEBOOK.
I AM.
COPYRIGHT © 2007 J.D. "Illiad" Frazer HTTP://WWW.USERFRIENDLY.ORG/

AND I WOULD GUESS YOU SPEND A SIZEABLE CHUNK OF YOUR DAY USING IT. EXACTLY WHAT DO YOU HAVE TO SHOW FOR SUCH AN INVESTMENT?

I HAVE 217 FRIENDS.
LIVING IN HOW MANY BASEMENTS?

WHAT'S THIS, A.J.?
IT'S A PROTOTYPE OF A REDACTING PRINTER FROM XEROX. THE SOFTWARE HAS THE ABILITY TO BLACK OUT SENSITIVE TEXT IN DOCUMENTS.

HOW DOES IT DETERMINE WHAT'S SENSITIVE?
LET ME CHECK THE MANUAL.

WHAT DOES IT SAY?
"SENSITIVE INFORMATION IS DETERMINED BY ████ AND ████."

I HAVE A SAMPLE CORPORATE DOCUMENT LOADED. LET'S SEE HOW THE REDACTION SOFTWARE FARES.

CHURN
CLICK
SPEW

IT'S ALL BLACKED OUT.
EXCEPT FOR THE COPYRIGHT NOTICE.

ELECTRONIC ARTS JUST BOUGHT BIOWARE.
OH GOODY.
JOHN MADDEN'S
Neverwinter Nights
2008
BioWare
UserFriendly.Org

WHAT THE HECK IS THAT, IF YOU DON'T MIND ME ASKING?
IS SECOND PROTOTYPE OF PORTAL GUN, AS IN COMPUTER GAME, "PORTAL."
COPYRIGHT© 2007 J.D. "Illiad" Frazer HTTP://WWW.USERFRIENDLY.ORG/

WITH GUN, CAN OPEN TWO PORTALS LINKED TOGETHER, AND TRAVEL FROM ONE TO OTHER ONE...
WAIT, YOU SAID "SECOND" PROTOTYPE...

WHERE IS PORTAL GUN, LEETLE GUY?
STEF TOOK IT.
COPYRIGHT© 2007 J.D. "Illiad" Frazer HTTP://WWW.USERFRIENDLY.ORG/

HE SAW ME USING IT TO GET TO TERMINAL VELOCITY AND SAID HE HAD AN IMPORTANT USE FOR IT.
UH OH.

3...2...1...

COULD YOU PLEASE DO SOMETHING ABOUT STEF?
HE IS PEGGINK YOU WITH PORTAL GUN, DA?
COPYRIGHT© 2007 J.D. "Illiad" Frazer HTTP://WWW.USERFRIENDLY.ORG/

INDEED. AND CHUFFED TO LITTLE MINTBALLS ABOUT IT I AM NOT.
RELAX, COMRADE GREGOR. LET UNIVERSE TAKE CARE OF PROBLEM.

AHHH...I CAN HEAR SOMEONE COMING!
TECH MANUALS PUT ME IN A BAD MOOD.

PITR? I HAVE A QUESTION ABOUT THAT PORTAL DEVICE YOU CREATED.
DA?
COPYRIGHT© 2007 J.D. "Illiad" Frazer HTTP://WWW.USERFRIENDLY.ORG/

WHAT WOULD HAPPEN IF, SAY, SOMEONE WAS STANDING RIGHT ON THE CUSP BETWEEN THE TWO OPEN PORTALS, AND ONE OF THE PORTALS CLOSED?

AM NOT SURE. THINKINK IT WOULD BE QUITE UNPLEASANT, AT LEAST.
YO. I NEED A WORD WITH YOU.

'SCUSE ME, CTHULHU?
MM.

I UNDERSTAND THAT OUR MARKETING EXEC CROSSED YOUR PATH...
INDEED. IRKSOME FELLOW.

WHERE EXACTLY DID YOU SEND HIM?
R'LYEH. I SQUEEZED HIM THROUGH A MINI VERSION OF A PORTAL. THE VISUAL METAPHOR WAS DEAD-ON IF YOU ASK ME.

SPLUTCH
SPLUTCH
BLUTCH
SBUTCH
PSLUTCH

HOW WAS R'LYEH?
NASTY WET SUCTION-CUP SQUID NOOKIE!

OPTIMISM HAS BEEN LOCATED IN THE BRAIN BY RESEARCHERS.

GET RAISE
WIN THE LOTTERY
MAKE OUT WITH BEYONCE

GENERAL PUBLIC

BACKUPS WON'T FAIL
THE NEXT PERSON WHO CALLS ME WON'T BE STUPID

I.T. WORKERS

UserFriendly.Org

A.J., COULD YOU DO A LITTLE DESIGN WORK FOR ME ON THE SIDE?
FOR A WEBSITE?
COPYRIGHT© 2007 J.D. "Illiad" Frazer HTTP://WWW.USERFRIENDLY.ORG/

YES, JUST SOMETHING SMALL AND SIMPLE. WITH ROLLOVER MENUS AND SOME COOL ANIMATIONS. AND IT NEEDS TO HAVE AN ORIGINAL AMBIENT SCORE.
OH, AND A WAY TO PRESENT A FEW THOUSAND PHOTOS CONTEXTUALLY.

BUT, YOU KNOW, NOTHING FANCY.
NO, OF COURSE NOT.

I DON'T KNOW SQUAT ABOUT DESIGN, A.J., SO I'M GOING TO LEAVE IT ALL UP TO YOU. JUST BUILD ME A GREAT WEBSITE.
'KAY.
COPYRIGHT© 2007 J.D. "Illiad" Frazer HTTP://WWW.USERFRIENDLY.ORG/

THREE DAYS OF CAREFUL, MEASURED DESIGN WORK PASS...

WHAT'S WITH THE GREEN? AND THAT FONT? AND THE LAYOUT SUCKS...

HEY! HAPPY HALLOW--WHAT THE HELL DID YOU DO TO YOUR CAT?
HE'S IN COSTUME. CAN YOU GUESS WHAT HE IS?
COPYRIGHT© 2007 J.D. "Illiad" Frazer HTTP://WWW.USERFRIENDLY.ORG/

PURRRRR
BRRRRRR
PRRRR
FPRRRRR

HE'S...A ZOMBIE CAT?
SCHRÖDINGER'S CAT. ALIVE AND DEAD AT THE SAME TIME, GET IT?
ZOMG! ZOMBIE KITTEH!

Speaking as an ex production manager, there were times I was borderline homicidal when an editor asked to "just tweak" a page after we had gone to press. I think I pushed her off a cliff.

DID YOU MAKE THOSE CHANGES TO MY WEBSITE?
YES. EVERYTHING YOU ASKED FOR. COLOUR, FONT AND LAYOUT.
COPYRIGHT© 2007 J.D. "Illiad" Frazer HTTP://WWW.USERFRIENDLY.ORG/

I LIKED THE GREEN BETTER.

CHIEF, HERE'S MY INVOICE FOR THE WORK DONE ON YOUR WEBSITE.
AH.

PROBLEM...
YES?

IT'S MORE THAN, YOU KNOW, "FREE."
THAT'S BECAUSE IT WAS A LITTLE MORE THAN, YOU KNOW, "NOTHING FANCY."

A.J., I DO WANT TO PAY YOU FOR THE WORK YOU DID, BUT IT NEEDS TO BE FAIR.
OKAY.

SO WHAT I DID WAS RESEARCH WHAT ANOTHER DESIGNER WOULD CHARGE FOR THE SAME WORK.
HERE ARE MY FINDINGS.

YOUR NEXT-DOOR NEIGHBOUR'S SISTER'S HUSBAND'S NEPHEW IS A DESIGNER?
ALL HE WANTS IS A FEW LUNCHES. I'LL EVEN THROW IN A STUDENT BUS PASS!

It's funny ... people expect you to pay them if they do work for you, and yet, if you try to charge money for web design, they look at you like you're ripping them off. I say hand them Notepad and let them sort it out.

FACEBOOK HAS AN IMPRESSIVE 47 MILLION USERS.
AND THEN THERE'S THAT *OTHER* "SOCIAL NETWORK:"

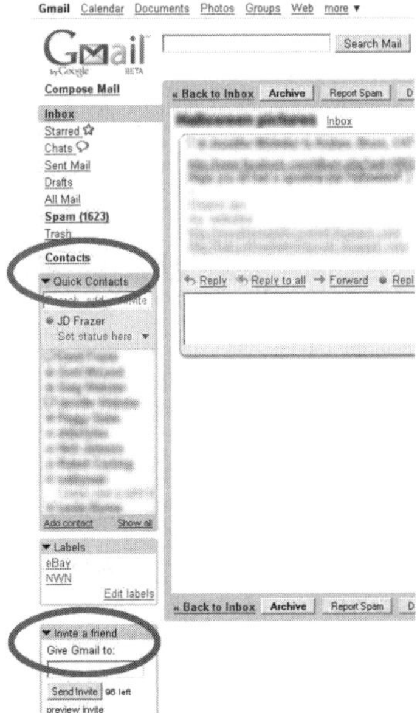
Gmail Calendar Documents Photos Groups Web more
Gmail
Search Mail
Compose Mail
Inbox
Starred
Chats
Sent Mail
Drafts
All Mail
Spam (1623)
Trash
Contacts
Quick Contacts
JD Frazer
Set status here
Add contact
Show all
Labels
eBay
NWN
Edit labels
Invite a friend
Give Gmail to:
Send Invite
preview invite
« Back to Inbox
Archive
Report Spam
Inbox
Reply
Reply to all
Forward

UserFriendly.Org

CHIEF? I'VE THOUGHT LONG AND HARD ABOUT THE WEB WORK I DID FOR YOU. I'M GOING TO EMBRACE THE OPEN SOURCE METHOD AND JUST LET YOU HAVE IT ALL FOR FREE, AS IS.

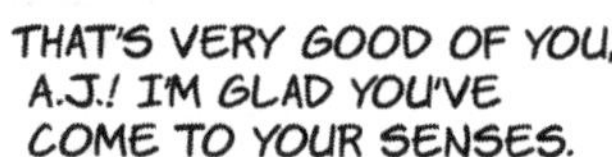
THAT'S VERY GOOD OF YOU, A.J.! I'M GLAD YOU'VE COME TO YOUR SENSES.

NOW, COULD YOU KINDLY MAKE A FEW MORE CHANGES TO THE SITE? I HAVE A LIST HERE.
OF COURSE. AND HERE'S MY MAINT-ENANCE CONTRACT AT $100 AN HOUR.

A HUNDRED AN HOUR?! WHAT HAPPENED TO "FREE"?!!

THE SITE I BUILT FOR YOU IS FREE. THE SERVICE ISN'T.

BESIDES, IF THAT'S TOO EXPENSIVE FOR YOU, YOU COULD JUST ASK YOUR NEXT DOOR NEIGHBOUR'S WHATEVER TO DO THE FIXES.

YOU KNOW. FOR LUNCH.

ERM...I'M NOT SURE HE KNOWS HOW.
I'D BETTER MAKE THAT $150 AN HOUR THEN...

STUPID IPHONE...

WHAT'S WRONG? I THOUGHT YOU WERE OUR NEW APPLE FANBOI.

I WAS UNTIL NOW. I HACKED THE PHONE SO I WOULDN'T HAVE TO USE AT&T, THEN UPDATED THE SOFTWARE. NOW MY IPHONE IS NOTHING BUT AN IBRICK.

SO...MAYBE YOU SHOULDN'T HAVE HACKED IT.
AND WHY DON'T YOU TRY NOT BREATHING. HURTS, DUNNIT.

(SUNG TO PINK FLOYD'S "ANOTHER BRICK IN THE WALL.")

WE DON'T NEED NO LIMITATIONS, WE DONT NEED SIM CARD CONTROL,

NO THREE YEAR LOCK-INS IN THE CONTRACTS, AT&T LEAVE THEM GEEKS ALONE...
A! T&T! LEAVE THEM GEEKS ALONE!

NOW IT'S HACKED IT'S JUST A, 'NOTHER BRICK THAT CAN'T CALL...
SHUT UP!
SHUT UP!!

WHAT ARE YOU DOING?
ACCELERATING MY iBRICK TO TERMINAL VELOCITY.
COPYRIGHT © 2007 J.D. "Illiad" Frazer HTTP://WWW.USERFRIENDLY.ORG/

NEXT, I'M GOING TO VISIT APPLE'S HEAD OFFICE AND OPEN A PORTAL INSIDE THE LOBBY, SMASHING THIS PHONE IN FRONT OF STEVE JOBS HIMSELF!

AND THAT'LL SHOW HIM WHAT I THINK OF THIS PHONE THAT I PAID $600 FOR!
BOY, THAT'LL TEACH HIM.

STEVE? THERE'S SOME GUY IN THE LOBBY WHO WANTS TO SHOW YOU WHAT HE THINKS OF THE IPHONE.
LET ME GUESS, HE HAS A BLENDER. THAT'S SO NEW.
Apple
COPYRIGHT © 2007 J.D. "Illiad" Frazer HTTP://WWW.USERFRIENDLY.ORG/

NO, HE'S GOT SOMETHING THAT'S LIKE THE PORTAL GUN FROM THE ORANGE BOX.
Apple

HUNH. IS THAT TECHNOLOGY WE CAN PUT IN OUR NEXT IPHONE?
YEAH, THAT'D BE GOOD STEVE. YOU ANSWER THE PHONE AND YOUR HEAD VANISHES THROUGH A PORTAL. THINK OF THE CARNAGE ON THE HIGHWAYS.

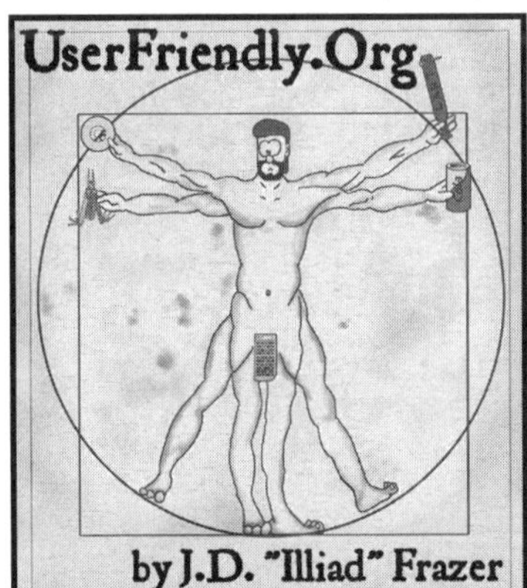
UserFriendly.Org
by J.D. "Illiad" Frazer
COPYRIGHT © 2007 J.D. "Illiad" Frazer HTTP://WWW.USERFRIENDLY.ORG/

YOUR DRIPNIFICENCE! YET ANOTHER WAR THREATENS TO ERUPT ON EARTH!
WHERE? IN AFRICA? THE MIDDLE EAST?

ERM...NO. BETWEEN TWO LINUX DISTROS...
OH...I'M NOT SURE I'M READY FOR THAT LEVEL OF NASTY RIGHT NOW...

IT'S UBUNTU AND RED HAT, SIRE. UBUNTU HAS RECENTLY DOMINATED THE LINUX DESK-TOP SPACE AND RED HAT HAS DECLARED IT WILL BE RE-ENTERING THAT MARKET.

AND THEY'RE ABOUT TO GUT EACH OTHER?
NO ONE'S REALLY HAPPY ABOUT IT, EXCEPT MAYBE, YOU KNOW...

STEVE! HURRY WITH THE DAMNED POPCORN!
COMING BILL! WHEEEEE!
Microsoft

HA! I SMASHED THAT STUPID BRICK INTO A MILLION PIECES, RIGHT IN APPLE'S LOBBY! I AM TEH WINNAR!
THERE'S A WAY TO UNBRICK PHONES, AND APPLE IS RELEASING AN SDK SOON.
COPYRIGHT © 2007 J.D. "Illiad" Frazer HTTP://WWW.USERFRIENDLY.ORG/

...OH.

DO YOU THINK APPLE WOULD FORGIVE ME IF I BOUGHT A NEW ONE?
THERE'S FORGIVENESS IN MOST MODERN RELIGIONS, GREG.

HEY BOSS. ENJOYING THE FRESH AIR?
JUST TAKING A BREAK FROM THE OFFICE. LISTEN. DO YOU HEAR THAT?
COPYRIGHT © 2007 J.D. "Illiad" Frazer HTTP://WWW.USERFRIENDLY.ORG/

NO COMPUTER FANS!
YE GODS, I WAS WONDERING WHY I WAS FEELING SO ANXIOUS.

YOU'VE LOOKED PENSIVE THE LAST FEW WEEKS. SOMETHING UP?
I'M CONSIDERING FINISHING A DEGREE IN PHYSICS.
COPYRIGHT © 2007 J.D. "Illiad" Frazer HTTP://WWW.USERFRIENDLY.ORG/

REALLY? WHATEVER FOR?
IT'S SOMETHING I'VE ALWAYS WANTED TO DO. IT'S A FASCINATING FIELD OF STUDY.

...AND IT GIVES YOU A SOLID GROUNDING IN THINGS LIKE, OH, TRAJECTORIES AND THINGS THAT GO BOOM.
YOU THINK SMALL, BUT YOU'RE ON THE RIGHT TRACK.

SO YOUR PERSONAL REASONS ASIDE, ISN'T PURSUING A DEGREE GOING TO AFFECT YOUR WORK?
IT MIGHT, YES.
COPYRIGHT © 2007 J.D. "Illiad" Frazer HTTP://WWW.USERFRIENDLY.ORG/

IT'LL BE LIKE TRYING TO STAY UP ON A NARROW WOODEN BEAM, PIRATES STABBING AT YOU FROM ONE END AND SHARKS CIRCLING BELOW YOU IN THE WATER.

SOUNDS TOUGH.
YEAH, I'LL BE CONSTANTLY WALKING THE PLANCK.

Booo ... hissss .... Next up, petroleum geology jokes!

THE INCLUSION OF A LINUX PC IN EVERY SEAT ON SINGAPORE AIRLINES' NEW A380 WILL EVENTUALLY CAUSE A MICROSOFT VP ON A FLIGHT TO LOSE HIS COOL...

ENOUGH IS ENOUGH! I HAVE HAD IT WITH THESE @#$*^&$%&*!#@ PENGUINS ON THIS @#$*^&$%&*!#@ PLANE!

And that concludes a *decade* of daily cartoons. I have no life. Yay!

Where to find your favorite UF strips

Game boards and flowcharts 1067

One-day gags 1067

Songs and poetry 1070

Storylines 1071

Sunday Comics 1077

Game boards and flowcharts

Distro Wars: The "My Distro Is Better" Card Game, 20040111

"Game Preference to Career" Flowchart, 20041212

Engines of Discrimination: The Google vs. Yahoo Cage Match Game, 20040222

Geek Dating Flowchart, 19990314

Geekday game, 20021215

  Netday: Intar expansion for, 20040425

HD-DVD Sudoku, 20070506

"How Can I Serve an Evil Genius" Flowchart, 20020609

I.S.P. Survivor: The Game of Small-Stakes Treachery, 20070429

  mapboard, 20070415

  playing pieces, 20070422

IT Agony Bingo, 20060108

Microsoft's Game Software Architecture Flowchart, 19991017

Patent Application Processing Flowchart, 20030302

Prediction Flowchart for Geek Gifts, 20051218

Techie Career Track Flowchart, 20001001

Real Reason Microsoft/AOL Talks Have Broken Down, 20010603

Software Patent Game, 20060219

Tech Support Caller Warning System, 20030209

One-day gags

$599 cell phone that runs Linux, 20061203

@Home, 20011201

1-click patent denial, 20080107

2007: tailpiece, 20071231

a prayer for all to emerge safely, 20030320

AJ

  returns, 19981017

  zorked, 20010818

AJAX names, 20071015

alien counter intel, 20080831

am I the scariest of them all?, 20031216

AOL

  branded version of Internet Explorer, 20041128

  coasters, 19990102

  spam, 19990125

approach of Mars, 20030811

April Fool's Day

  1999, 19990401

  2000, 20000401

  2001, 20010401

  2002, 20020401

  2004, 20040401

  2005, 20050401

  2006, 20060401

Artur 2, 19990501

attack of the puns, 20070627

attack of the Sith, 20040729

  Sithadmin appreciation, 20040730

bidding on EBay: it's not over 'til it's over!, 20031108

Bioshock

  choices, 20070907

  electronic enema!, 20070831

Biz Expo 2001, 20010610

blogging, 20060422

  anew, 20060608

  art of, 20060123

  the truth, 20060124

Blue Screen of Death reset button, 19981102

calls, useless, 20050312

case against Microsoft 1998, 19980105

CDs, playing backward, 20001015

celeb names, 20070117

Christmas

  2004, 20041225

  and retail deadlines, 20061216

click-to-call, 20051130

client blackmail, 19971124

Cobb

  and Linux, 19990227

  expenses issue, 19980114

  Pitr kidnaps, 19990316

Code Red, 20010801

coffee

  and heresy, 20060331

  flavored, 20060925, 20060926, 20060927

cola and hibernation, 20050424
congratulations, Juergen, 20011208
cookies from down under, 20050616
customer service revenge expansion pack, 19980220
Daikatana going gold, 20000403
Darl
    bails out of SCO, 20070925
    the lovable, 20050522
Denial of Service attack, 19990807
deserts and dates, 20041026
dinner date, 20051010
dirty girls!, 20041110
DMA checking, 20071016
do-not-call improvement, 20080213
Dr. Brian May's rotation theory, 20070803
dude-delimited conversation, 20041025
Dust Puppy
    balloonist joke, 19980802
    crashes Windows, 19980119
    gives Miranda a Valentine, 19990214
    job description, 19980117
    meets a furry friend, 19990103
Easter, history of, as told by Sid, 20010415
economy, new, 20080502
email is for old people, 20061005
embedded past, 20040101
engineers and light bulbs, 20061102
Erwin
    NT installed on, 19980512-19980516, 19980519-19980528
    Ode to Spam, 19990226
    pontificates, 20030615
    torments Stef, 19990806
Euro suit, 20040326
Evil Geniuses
    for Dummies, 19990111
    in a nutshell, appendix A, 20000307
    marketing for, 20040529
feisty Fawn on Dell, 20070617
finances and code, 20060309
flash mobs, 20040630
flat file trading, 20060621
FTC Intel lawsuit, 19980612
Gates target practice, 19980207
geek
    and carbs, 20040620
    and mangy gits, 20041027
    ethics, 20021117
    Pride Day, 20000331
    PSA: Geeks are Great!, 20000903
GMail: the response, 20040629
Google
    IPO, 20040810
    Moonbase: the aftermath, 20040420
Greg
    Mike and, mail spool I, 20011007
    Mike and, mail spool II, 20011104
    Safari holes out, 20080605
    theory about Miranda and Microsoft's patches, 20031120
guest appearance, 20051031
H/W reviews, 20040614
hacker attacks on military, 19980306
Half Life code leak, 20031021
half-glass question, 20080829
Halloween
    2007, 20071031
    costumes, 20061030
Halo, 20041116
    the movie, 20051211
hang up your @, 20060613
hangover Sunday, 20010121
hangovers, 20040102
Hastur and spam, 20030916
heyyy Macarena, 20000501
Hillary is bored, 19980731
HotLook, 20050123
HTML 5, 20080127
IBM
    source code, 20050717
    SCO vs., 20051002
idiots, a _______ of, 20020710
iLinux, 20050213
Illiad
    foresight, 20030627
    is a dirty boy, 20010423
    in glorious 3D!, 20010311
Internet, 20070626
    buy the, 19980428
    morality, 19980403
Internet Explorer
    AOL-branded version of, 20041128
    yet another bug, 20020815
interview #1, 19971219
Janet Jackson pop-up, 20040204
KDE vs. Gnome, 20060129
Klingon collection Agency, 19971220
Kuan's quest, 20031106
Labor Day, 20060904
laptops and tadpoles, 20041224
Large Hadron Collider: activation day, 20080330
lawsuits and alien invasions, 20051030
Lindows, 20040720
link, link, baby!, 20070116
Linux
    $599 cell phone that runs, 20061203
    as cancer, 20010604
    bounties, 20050814
    Cobb and, 19990227
    elitism, 20080608
    iLinux, 20050213
    Oracle, 20060611
    Redhatbacher, Orville, 20000306
    ultimate system, 20060812
    Wars, 20071111
Linuxpedia, 20060609
little WAP devices..., 20060928
Lord of the Rings movie, 20000527
mail thingie, 20010519
make me a millionaire, 20080812
making out, 20051001
market share, 20050326
May 19, 19990519
Microsoft
    break-up, 20000228
    case against, 1998, 19980105
    in millions, 19980202
    law issues, 19980801
    law issues 2, 19981114

Novell interorperability, 20080106
Novell/Suse/Microsoft deal, 20070107
poll, 19980508
takeover of Hotmail, 19980103
wants fiction writers, 20040814
Mike
and Greg's mail spool I, 20011007
and Greg's mail spool II, 20011104
and the butterfly, 20030511
millennium, real end of, 20001231
Miranda
Dust Puppy gives a Valentine to, 19990214
Greg's theory about Microsoft's patches and, 20031120
shuts down the RIAA, 20020728
Valentine, 20000214
mob moves in on MMORPGs, 20061019
money isn't everything, 19981103
Mother's Day
2002, 20020512
2004, 20040509
Mozilla and market share, 20050102
MP3 traffic, 19991101
Mustecki, Ed, news report, 19980501
my usual nick @ gmail, 20070519
MyDoom, 20040201
MySpace identity crisis, 20080626
mystery attachment, 19990724
nagware, 19990104
Netscape going open source, 19980124
new economy, 20080502
"new" smell, 20011102
New Year
1998, 19980101
2002, 20020101
2005, 20050101
2008, 20080101
party, 19981231
Novell
Microsoft interorperability, 20080106
SCO vs., 20060226
deal with Suse/Microsoft, 20070107
obscene phone call, 19971121
office supplies, new, 19980102
Olympic event, new, under consideration, 20080817
one-way trip, 20050801
Open Office and MS Office, 20060409
open source, 20040714
Oracle Linux, 20060611
orange alert, 20031229
outsourcing: heading the world off, 20030718
oxymoron, 19980118
patently ridiculous, 20071202
Vuestar, 20080531
Pearl and Pitr go on a date, 20010915
penguins on a plane!, 20071116
Perl
obfuscating, 20070806
or Ruby, 20080627
piracy
loss, 20050617
new standards of, 20061110
Pitr
kidnaps Cobb, 19990316
Pearl and, go on a date, 20010915
poking fun, 20040813
Playstation 2, 20001104
politicians, retraining, 20070204
power outage in eastern Canada, 19980123
PSA:
FBI, 20000910
Geeks Are Great!, 20000903
purchase order, 19971125
Quake
2 with punch cards, 20011229
lessons, 19980221
Stef wins at, 19990513
symbol, 19990207
rebranding, 20051204
record label revenues, 20070115
Redhatbacher, Orville, 20000306
RIAA
adds value, 20060622
lawsuit, 20030406
Miranda shuts down the, 20020728
routing raids, 20060612
royalty, 20040701
Safari
holes out: Greg takes a hit, 20080605
holes out: tech support call, 20080604
sales intro, 19971123
scientific reporting: cloaks and daggers, 20080818
SCO
Darl bails out of, 20070925
vs. Groklaw.net, 20041017
vs. IBM, 20051002
vs. Novell, 20060226
looking back, 20070924
screenshots, 20011027
search and hammer, 20051101
secondary backup, 19971127
security patches, no, 20031210
Sergeant Stef, 19971129
Smiling Man intro, 19971122
spam-free, 20040421
spam, 20040619
AOL, 19990125
Erwin's Ode to, 19990226
Hastur and, 20030916
Spice Girls download, 20000522
split power cord, 19971213
Springer, Jerry, poke at, 19990802
stable NT server, 19991001
Stef
box, techs looking at, 19980121
Erwin torments, 19990806
lovin' commercial, 20010225
wins at Quake, 19990513
snurf, and tears, 19980201
new title, 20000105
Sergeant, 19971129
summary
1997, 19971231
1998, 19990101
Superbowl Sunday 2003, 20030126
Supernova Vista, 20070512
SysAdmin Appreciation Day, 20030725
Talk Like a Pirate Day, 20030919
Tanya's Christmas Customer, 19971228

tech-support call, 19971215-19971218, 19971221, 19971224, 19980104, 19980120, 19980131, 19980219, 19980423-19980424, 19980504-19980506, 19980510, 19980518, 19980607, 19980613-19980614, 19980712-19980715, 19980817, 19981007, 19981013, 19981104, 19990105, 19990117, 19990128, 19990131, 19990210-19990213, 19990317, 19990412, 19990424, 19990503-19990504, 19990528-19990529, 19990729-19990731, 19990814, 19990911, 19990924-19990925, 20000212, 20000229, 20000313-20000316, 20000330, 20000417-20000418, 20000819, 20010108-20010110, 20010609, 20011029, 20011103, 20020719-20020720, 20020722, 20021214, 20030106, 20050530, 20050815, 20060603, 20060714-20060715

techs
- looking at Stef's box, 19980121
- need to be committed, 19980122

telemarketing, 20080214

text editors, 19990508

that "new" smell, 20011102

the dumber you are, the more you pay, 19980218

TLAPD 2006, 20060920

TV
- news, 20010827
- shows, 20040719

U.S. primaries 2008, 20080501

ultimate Linux system, 20060812

Unreal tournament, 19980606, 19980608

upskilling, 20070628

UserFriendly
- 2.0, 20060605
- 4th anniversary, 20011117
- 10th anniversary, 20071117

Valentine's Day
- 2001, 20010214
- 2002, 20020214
- 2003, 20030214
- 2006, 20060214

Veteran's Day 2006, 20061111

video games and violent tendencies..., 20070530

virtual files, 20060610

virtual reality, 20080228

virus awareness, 20000519

VOIP testing, 20080530

war on terror, 20031215

Web 2.0 revisited, 20060731

WGA breakdown, 20070901

why I don't use GIMP, 20060430

wiki in print, 20051102

wildcards, 20030918

Windows
- 2003 clustering blob, 20060730
- 95 installation, 19980127
- 98 installation, 19990318
- Dust Puppy crashes, 19980119
- moving to, 20060604
- NT
  - crashes the microwave, 19990228
  - installed on Erwin, 19980512-19980516, 19980519-19980528
- patches, 20070511

Vista
- lockdown, 20070915
- security, 20070629
- SP1, 20070908
- Supernova, 20070512
- UAC, 20070804
- XPG, 20010218

Worldcom financials, 20020723

wrong CD, 19971214

Xandros and Microsoft, 20070729

Y2K scientists, 19980507

YouTube acquisition: the aftermath, 20061107

zero-tension mice, 20060801

Songs and poetry

"American Pie", 20000917

"Braaaains", 20020407

Christmas songs, 20031213

"Clearing Your History", 20011125

"CTO, CTO, CTO", 20011223

"DMCA", 20020428

"Don't Fear the Penguin", 19990725

Dust Puppy and Erwin write a poem, 20000520

Erwin the beat poet, 20040822

Erwin's nuclear beat poetry, 20010714

"Every Game of Quake", 19980809

"GMail Invites", 20060121

"GPF on My Windows PC", 19980208

"I Want My IRC", 19990411

IFAD 2003: The NOC song, 20031019

in memory of Douglas Adams, 20010513

Mike's ode to electricity, 20020123

"Mundie's Way", 20010506

"NT's Not Up to Snuff", 19991010

"O Holy Night", 20001224

ode to blogs, 20040613

ode to Sony's rootkits, 20051120

ode to spam, 20011130

ode to the iPhone, 20070715

ode to the iPod, 20050509

"Refund This!", 19990221

"Running on NT", 19980517

S.C.O. anthem, 20030713

"She's Always a Goddess to Me", 20010527

Smiling Man theme, 20030316

"Soothe", 20000423

"Tech Support Lament", 20001029

"These Are Things That Make Me So 'Leet", 20020721

"This LAN Is Your LAN", 20040815

"Twelve Days of Christmas", 20031221

Valentine's Day song, 20060212

"What a Wonderful World", 20010204

Storylines

#unixgurus, 20041201-20041204
.eu domains, 20060412-20060413
"vigor" project, 20000107-20000108, 20000110-20000114
5150 sold, 20060901-20060902
Acme forced-feedback enemy-denial smack-down ergonomic game chair, 20000601-20000603, 20000605-20000606
advertising, cutting-edge, 20050205, 20050207-20050210
AJ
  and Mr. Cola, 19991130-19991201
  and Miranda, 19991118-19991120, 19991122-19991126, 19991206-19991207
  and Miranda go on a date, 19991208-19991211
  asks Erwin for advice about women, 19991202-19991204
  confessional, 20030707-20030712
  drowns his sorrows, 20000904-20000909
  game, part 1: where there's a Wil, there's a way, 20020903-20020907, 20020909-20020910, 20020912-20020914, 20020916-20020918
  game, part 2: Gib the villain, 20020919-20020921, 20020923-20020928
  game, part 3: sex sells, 20020930-20021012
  game, part 4: fired, 20021014-20021019, 20021021-20021023
  gets carpal tunnel, 20000814-20000818
  iTunes, 20031030-20031101
  new phone, 20030621, 20030623-20030626
  startup, 19991014-19991016
  tries again, 20000119-20000122, 20000124
acronymonious, 20030310-20030315, 20030317-20030319, 20030321-20030322
addictions, 20040816-20040820
adserts, 20070702-20070707, 20070709-20070712
ADSL, reselling, 19980609-19980611
airing retaliation, 19980115-19980116
A.L.I.C.E., 20041111-20041112
  the aftermath, 20041113, 20041115
aliens, mind-reading, 20030107-20030111
Alpha Centauri, 19990510-19990512
American election, 20001112-20001116
Antarctica, 20040828, 20040830-20040904, 20040906-20040911, 20040913-20040916
anti commercial, 20051128-20051129
anti-Linux team, 19990607, 19990609-19990612, 19990614-19990615
AOL
  big breakup, 20041117-20041118
  layoffs, 20060808-20060811
  trick, 19971130-19971202
Apophis approaches, 20070226-20070303
Apple][+ turns 30, 20070613-20070614
Artur, 19990405-19990410, 19990419-19990423, 19990426-19990430
Australia: LAN down under, 20050411-20050416, 20050418-20050423, 20050425-20050430, 20050502-20050507
BackEnd BoyZ, 20020130-20020209
backups, 20070405-20070407, 20070409-20070412
bacon, shining, 20060118-20060120
badger badger badger, 20040119-20040121, 20040125
big bucks, 20000911-20000914
Bigstring.com: fighting sender's remorse, 20070727-20070728
blogger, ex, 20070109-20070111
blogging
  blues
    I, 20060227-20060304
    II, 20060318, 20060320-20060325
  union, 20070807-20070811
blogs and we, 20040611-20040612
Bonzi Buddy, 20020420, 20020422-0020427, 20020429-20020430
Brick, enter the, 20050906-20050910, 20050912-20050915
browser tales, 20040422-20040424, 20040426-20040430
BSD daemon returns, 19990803-19990805
butterfly vendetta, 20030324-20030329, 20030331-20030405
buzzwords, 20010926-20010927
Caffiderm, 20041124-20041127, 20041129-20041130
Camp.mil, 20050117-20050122, 20050124-20050129, 20050131-20050202
camping, 20060501-20060506, 20060508-20060513, 20060515-20060519
  knocked into nethack, 20060520, 20060522-20060527, 20060529-20060602
  tech camping trip, 20000612-20000617, 20000619-20000624, 20000626-20000701, 20000703-20000705
CAT 5
  enters, 20000218-20000219, 20000221-20000222
  meets Dust Puppy, 20000223-20000226
CD, new, 20060109-20060110
CEO, temp, 19980425-19980427, 19980429-19980430, 19980502-19980503
China meets Clippy, 20010416-20010421, 20010424-20010428, 20010430

Christmas
1998, 19981228-19981230
1999, 19991220-19991225
2000, 20001221-20001223, 20001225
2001, 20011224-20011227
2002, 20021224-20021228, 20021230-20021231
2003, 20031223-20031225
2005, 20051215-20051216, 20051217, 20051219-20051226
cookie, 20001218-20001220
on the dark side, 20041213-20041214
CI: the big breakup, 20041119-20041120, 20041122-20041123
Cingular, 20060202-20060204
Civ 4, 20051103-20051105
Clippy strikes back, 20000715, 20000717-20000721
CKD5: Darwin award cola, 20070720-20070721, 20070723-20070724
coaxed, 20020326-20020330, 20020402-20020406, 20020408
COD 2, 20051107-20051111
coffee
ring, 20000529-20000531
tales, 20060327-20060328
cold swap, 20060222-20060225
cold!, 20060111-20060112
computer geek nutrition, 19980716-19980722
confused, 20030226-20030301
consultant, 19980630-19980711
copyright extensions, 20070730-20070731
corporate audit, 20020819-20020824, 20020826-20020831, 20020902
creative marketing, 20020409-20020410
Crud Puppy
and Pitr, round 1, 19980304-19980305
creation of, 19980224-19980303
re-emerges, round 2, 19980404, 19980406-19980422
round 3, 19981116-19981126
cruising for chicks, 20040531-20040605
cryogenics, 20001106-20001107
Cthia Pet, 20010601-20010602, 20010605-20010608
Cthulhu
intro, seal of knowledge, 20010328-20010331, 20010402-20010407, 20010409
pickle-me, 20041227-20041231
CTO, 20011203-20011207, 20011210-20011215, 20011217-20011222
cubicles, 19980810-19980815
customers
and passes, 20050203-20050204
weird 19980602-19980606
daemon among us, 19990322-19990327
Darkside Dave, arrival of, 20000404-20000408, 20000410-20000415
dates and EULAs, 20051014-20051015
dating
advice, 20051027-20051029
profile, writing on, 20061020-20061021, 20061027-20061028
decision-makers, front-line, 20020102-20020105, 20020107-20020109
Deletium, 19980529, 19980530, 19980601
designers' woes, 20050706, 20050707, 20050708, 20050709
desktop oys, 20001205-20001209, 20001211-20001215
de-stressing with eBay, 20000321-20000322
devolution of language, 20070716-20070717
digicam insanity, 20041206-20041211
digitally challenged, 20070910-20070912
"dinner" date, 20051017-20051019
distribution wars, 1999030119990304, 19990319-19990320
Doctor Dork, 20050531-20050604, 20050606-20050609
DOJ, helping out, 19980615-19980629
Doom 3, 20040715-20040717, 20040823-20040824
conspiracy, 20040806-20040807, 20040809
enter, 20040802-20040805
Dotcombat Inc., 20010205-20010210, 20010212-20010213, 20010215
DP-CP wars, 20040122-20040124
DP wipe, 20000502-20000504
DRM, ditching, 20070514-20070516
Dungeons and Dragons, 20020729-20020803, 20020805-20020810, 20020812-20020814
4th ed., 20070824-20070825, 20070827-20070830
Dust Puppy
first Christmas, 19971225-19971227
gets aired Out, 19980106-19980113
in fridge, 19971222-19971223
is born, 19971203-19971209
snowboarding, 19980214-19980217
DVD, 20000722, 20000724-20000727
D-Wave's quantum computer, 20070223-20070224
E360Insight vs. Spamhaus, 20060918-20060919, 20060921
EA pricing and flying pigs, 20060306-20060308
elder vacations, 20060802-20060804
Elven Linux, 20040318-20040320, 20040322-20040325
Elven support, 20040311-20040313, 20040315-20040317
emergency pager, 20050510-20050514, 20050516-20050521
EMI ditches DRM, 20070423-20070428, 20070430-20070501
encyclopedias and nature, 20060406-20060407
Erwin
attacks Iraq, 19980222-19980223
beat poet, 19990605, 19990608
comes alive, 19980128-19980130
D3ath st4r, 20050711-20050716, 20050718-20050723, 20050725-20050730
dreams and migrates, 19980916-

19980919
finally finds home, 19990126-19990127
gets Stef, 19990119-19990123
in furby, 19990112-19990116, 19990118
in Segway, 20011228, 20011231
in 5150, 20060828-20060831
in iMac, 19980921, 19981003-19981004, 19981019
in Palm, 19981020-19981025
is created, 19980125-19980126
migrates to iMac, 20020309, 20020311-20020316
mission, 20010803-20010813
payback, 20030519-20030520
revenge, 19990901-19990904
springtime for, 19990531-19990604
Tamagotchi, 19990906-19990910
ethicectomy, 20021024-20021026, 20021028-20021102, 20021104-20021109, 20021111-20021116, 20021118-20021123, 20021125-20021130
evil crumbling, 20040507-20040508, 20040510
Eye Spy ware, 20040209-20040214, 20040216
eyes and pods, 20041028-20041102
Facebook friends, 20071017-20071018
Facexpaces, 20060614-20060617, 20060619-20060620
email threats, 20060701, 20060707-20060708
inquisitor Bernardo visits, 20060711-20060713
launched, 20060623-20060624, 20060626-20060627
revenues, 20060703-20060706, 20060710
tech-support call, 20060630
Firefox losing market share, 20050816-20050818
first post, 19990929-19990930
Force, the, 20011004-20011005
Frankenfridge, 20070319-20070323, 20070403-20070404
Waldo, 20070416-20070421
G4, 20050211-20050212, 20050214-20050216
games, 20011105-20011120
Gates, Bill, K.B.E., 20040130-20040131
geek Jeopardy, 20001007, 20001009-20001011
geeks
and religion, 20001030-20001103
get healthy, 20010524-20010526, 20010528
girls and games, 20040607-20040610
GMail, 20040621-20040623
Google
Answers, closing, 20061208-20061209
Earth, 20050703-20050705
flight simulation, 20070913-20070914
expands, 20050629-20050702
invites, 20050217-20050219, 20050221-20050222
is the web, 20030602-20030607
moon base, 20040402-20040403, 20040405-20040410, 20040412
Music, 20060408, 20060410-20060411
ogled, 20040413-20040417, 20040419
Sky, 20070903-20070906
world domination, 20060208-20060211, 20060213, 20060215-20060218, 20060220-20060221
Google(d), 20040330-20040331
Gormless, 20050113-20050115
graveyard shift, 19991102-19991106, 19991108-19991109
great code off, 20070615-20070616, 20070618-20070623
great old ones hang around Columbia Internet, 20030510, 20030512-20030513
great standoff, 20040327, 20040329
Greg
checkout clerk, 20030719, 20030721-20030724, 20030726, 20030728, 20030804-20030806
and BSD daemon, 20000807-20000812
diet, 20031201-20031205
new place, 20011020, 20011022-20011026
nukes a customer, 20010706-20010707, 20010709-20010711
sent to techie detox, 19980307-19980328
Ultima baker, 20030812-20030816, 20030818-20030820
using Windows 95, 19971126, 19971128
Half Life addiction, 19990106-19990109
Halloween
2001, 20011030-20011101
costumes, 20061031-20061101
Halo 3, 20071003-20071004
health care plan, new, 20010515-20010518
Heinlein, Robert A., 100 years of, 20070718-20070719
home for the obsolete, 20040217-20040221, 20040223-20040301
HotMail, 20020510-20020511
HTML 5, 20070725-20070726
Hulk, 20030628, 20030630-20030703
I love you, 20000511-20000513
IBM PC
25 years of, 20060821-20060822
5150, 20060823, 20060824-20060826
I-break-it-you-fix-it, 20050302-20050305
iCan't Internet, 19980509, 19980511
takeover, 19980824-19980915, 19980922-19981002, 19981005-19981006
idle hands, 20020116-20020119, 20020121-20020122
Illiad
Picasso, 20040202-20040203
stinkers, 20060628-20060629
iLoo, 20030514-20030517

IM blues, 20070328-20070330
inquisition, 20050618, 20050620-20050625, 20050627-20050628
 nobody expects the, 20020318-20020323, 20020325
Internet taxes, 20010509-20010510
iPhone or iBrick, 20071107-20071110, 20071112
IPodders, 20060116-20060117
iPods and llamas, 20041105-20041106, 20041108-20041109
Isotope roast, 20010627-20010628
IT sector, state of, 2003, 20030221-20030222
Khan Noonien Singh, 20051227-20051229
Kuan
 intern, 20031008-20031011
 sysadmin, 20031013-20031018, 20031020, 20031022-20031025, 20031027-20031029
laptop fever, 19991002, 19991004-19991009, 19991011-19991013
laws, loony, 20060113-20060114
LCD monitors and their lives, 20070609, 20070611-20070612
LEGO missile silo, 20010726-20010728, 20010730-20010731, 20010802
light saber wars, 19990524-19990527
Linux
 hackers, 20040205-20040207
 the kid, 20031217-20031220, 20031222
 wankle, 20040126-20040129
 World Expo, 19990809-19990813
lolcatspeak, 20060922-20060923
Lord Crud
 Borgs Steve, 20000115, 20000117-20000118
 visits C-Inet, 20020124, 20020125-20020126, 20020128-20020129
Lord of the Pings, 19991018-19991023, 19991025-19991030
mail server, broken, 20010521-20010523
Manly Hot Hamster Dating Service, 20001125, 20001127-20001202, 20001204, 20001216
marketing demographics, 20021210-20021213
marketing for minions, 20020617-20020622, 20020624-20020626, 20020629, 20020701-20020706, 20020708-20020709, 20020711-20020713, 20020715-20020718
Martha Calls the Helpdesk, 20030610-20030614
Mars, Source City, 20040103, 20040105-20040110, 20040112-20040117
math fingers, 20070625, 20070630
Matt
 visits the office, 19990913-19990918, 19990920-19990923, 19990927-19990928
 last appearance, 20001120-20001124
Microsoft
 antitrust, 20011112-20011123
 downgrade to XP, 20070926-20070928
 Google takeover, 20031103-20031105
 patent infringement suits, 20070517-20070518
 re-education for Stef, 19990716-19990717, 19990719-19990723, 19990726-19990728
 salesman, 19980329-19980402
Mike
 goes to Biz Expo, 19990201-19990206, 19990208-19990209
 joins Sid, 20001108-20001111
 marketing and viruses, 20030821-20030823, 20030825-20030830, 20030901-20030902
 new chair, 20030113-20030118, 20030120-20030125
 remembers, 20000505-20000506, 20000508-20000510
 Sims, 20000308-20000311
 ultimate cola experience, 20000515-20000518
Miranda
 and AJ kissing in a tree, 20050916-20050917, 20050926-20050930
 frees AJ, 20000215-20000217
 gets promoted, 20000607-20000610
 IRC, 20000821-20000826, 20000828-20000902
 joins Columbia Internet, 19981010-19981012, 19981014-19981016, 19981018
 skirt, 20010814-20010817
MIRwin, 19981026, 19981101, 19981105, 19981108, 19981110-19981113
missile guidance, 20010712-20010713
Moon landings
 hoax or not?, 20070917-20070919
 payload, 20070920-20070922
movie OS, 20010111-20010113, 20010115-20010120, 20010122-20010127, 20010129-20010203
Mozilla bounty, 20040811-20040812
Mr. Cola, 19981027-19981031
 and pimp juice, 20060913-20060916
 just won't leave, 20010501-20010505, 20010507-20010508
MySpace, 20060417-20060421, 20060424-20060429
 and id theft, 20061006-20061007, 20061009-20061010
 zapped, 20060728-20060729
naughty biscuit, 20000706-20000708, 20000710
net neutrality, 20060905-20060909
NetH@ck, 20020501-20020504, 20020506-20020509
network management certification, 20010221-20010224, 20010226-20010303, 20010305-20010310, 20010312-20010315
new player experience, 20040505-20040506
New Year
 2003, 20030101-20030104
 2004, 20031230-20031231
 2005, 20050103-20050104
 2006 runup, 20051230-20051231
 hangover, 20010101-20010106
news, 20041103-20041104
Nigerians, scamming, 20021202-20021207, 20021209

no Shift, no caps, 20010820-20010825
NOC, new, 20030903-20030906, 20030908-20030910
nuclear evil, 20010629-20010630, 20010702-20010705
NWN2, 20061011-20061014, 20061016
  multiplayer, 20061218-20061223, 20061225
  video card for, new, 20061113-20061118
O Tannenbaum, 20021216-20021221, 20021223
o ye of little faith, 20030224-20030225
obsolete, revenge of, 20040302-20040306, 20040308-20040310
office products, 20031107, 20031110-20031115
office space, new, 20010611-20010616, 20010618-20010623, 20010625-20010626
Operation Ransid, 20040522, 20040524-20040528
orbital dyslexia ray, 20030303-20030308

orbital LART, 20060929-20060930, 20061002-20061004
partition 23, 19990329-19990331, 19990402-19990403
password strength, 20070929, 20071001-20071002
patents, 20040624-20040626, 20040628
peace on Earth, 20001226-20001230
Pearl
  contractor, 20010928-20010929, 20011001-20011003, 20011006
  intro, 20010828-20010901, 20010903-20010908, 20010910-20010911
  project, 20030616-20030620
  project-management tools, 20020411-20020413, 20020415-20020419
  reports, 20050223-20050224
petabytes of free space, 20061017-20061018
Phish, 20030729-20030802, 20030807-20030809
  returns, 20031001-20031003, 20031006
Pitr
  accent, 19980723-19980730
  alien blood coffee, 20030407-20030412, 20030414-20030418
  and Pearl go on a date, 20010920-20010922, 20010924-20010925
  Borgs himself, Crud moves in on AJ, 20000129, 20000131-20000203, 20000205, 20000207-20000211
  coffee, 19980203-19980206
  Dread Lord Pitr, 20020527-20020601, 20020603-20020608
  cosmonaut, 20020610-20020615
  face-off, 20000419-20000422, 20000424-20000429
  joins Google, 20070120, 20070122-20070127, 20070129-20070203, 20070205-20070210, 20070212-20070217, 20070219-20070222
  leaves Google, 20070713-20070714
  midlife crisis, 20050802-20050806, 20050808-20050813
Pitr-Cola, 20020513-20020518, 20020520-20020525
  Pitrpod Zepto, 20050919-20050924
pledge, that there, 20020627-20020628
Poincare Conjecture, 20070103-20070106, 20070108
Pokemon, 19991227-19991228, 20000106
policy making, 20010716-20010723
pop-unders, 20050225-20050226, 20050228-20050301
portal adventures, 20071022-20071027
power failure, 20020110-20020112, 20020114-20020115
printers, redacting, 20071019-20071020
privacy gone too far, 20061128-20061130
push the button, 20060125-20060128
Quake coding, 19971117-19971120
Quake III, 19990413-19990417
quantum computing, 20060310-20060311, 20060313-20060314
quick!!, 20050328-20050331
RIAA
  and iTunes, 20051011-20051013
  broadcasting licenses, 20071012-20071013
  on fair use, 20061120-20061123
  sues, 20060102-20060107
Rainbow 6, 19991127, 19991129
recruits, evil, 20040511-20040515, 20040517-20040521
replay value, 20031226-20031227
Revenge of the Sith, 20050523-20050528
reverse Polish notation, 19990825-19990828, 19990830-19990831
road trip, 20040702-20040703, 20040705-20040710, 20040712-20040713
robotic dog, 20000323-20000325, 20000327-20000329
root kits and music, 20051112, 20051114-20051118, 20051119, 20051121-20051122
royalties, 20070112-20070113
saga, every, has beginning, 19981127-19981212, 19981214-19981219, 19981221-19981225
Santa's woes, 20041215-20041218, 20041220-20041223
Saruman the bitter, 20031117-20031119
SCO
  owes Novell, 20070820-20070821
  ownership of Unix: DENIED!, 20070813-20070818
  stock takes a fall, 20061206-20061207
  suits, 20031121-20031122
  vs. IBM, 20030530-20030531, 20030609
screens, large, 20070822-20070823
Second Life, 20070118-20070119
senators and tubes, 20060717-20060719
September 11, 2001, in memory of, 20010912-20010914
SETI, 20051201-20051203

sewers of the web, 20070331, 20070402
shell wrap packaging, 20061226-20061230
Sid
- contractor I, 20000926-20000930, 20001002-20001006
- contractor II, 20001012-20001014, 20001016-20001023
- EA exec, 20050110-20050112
- flip side, 20070101-20070102
- getting a degree, 20071113-20071115
- insidious syrup, 20030419, 20030421-20030426, 20030428-20030502
- leaves, 20001117-20001118
- voice-recognition software: return of Sid, 20010316-20010317, 20010319-20010324, 20010326-20010327

Sir Glance-A-Lot vs. Lady Shady, 20050819, 20050820, 20050822-20050827, 20050829-20050903, 20050905
Skype business model, new, 20071008-20071011
Skyping around, 20051205-20051208, 20051213-20051214
Sly Crud, 19981226-19990130
snurf guns for everyone, 19971229-19971230
sodium benzoate: essence of dork, 20070531-20070602, 20070604-20070608
soaring, 20020226-20020302, 20020304-20020308
space telescopes and camera phones, 20050321-20050325
spaceflight under influence, 20070801-20070802
spam
- attach, 19990222-19990225
- begone, 20000728-20000729, 20000731-20000805
- criminal, 20010216-20010217, 20010219-20010220
- dealing with, 20060130-20060201
- justice, 20011126-20011129
- spam, spam, spam, 20030521-20030524, 20030526-20030529

spiders and webs, 20060315-20060317
squids and media time, 20051003-20051008
Star Trek: Voyager, 20010529-20010531
Starcraft 2, 20070523-20070526, 20070528-20070529
- tech recession, 20070521-20070522

Stef
- agent Complete Zero, 20051020-20051022, 20051024-20051026
- and Nethack, 20030911-20030913, 20030915
- and AJ go to CeBIT, 20000301-20000304
- and BeOS, 19981107, 19981109
- and Linux, 19981008-19981009, 19981106, 19990216
- and Quake III, 20000317-20000318, 20000320
- and the LOTR trilogy, 20031124-20031125
- has amnesia, 19990630-19990703, 19990705-19990710, 19990712-19990715
- Christmas decorations, 20031206-20031209, 20031211-20031212
- impersonates AJ, 20000125-20000128, 20000204-20000205
- pharm, 20050314-20050319
- pursues Miranda, 19990305-19990306, 19990308-19990313, 19990315
- rescue, 19990616-19990619, 19990621-19990626, 19990628-19990629
- spam, 20020816-20020817
- speedo guy, 20060814-20060819

Stefcodes, 20011121-20011122, 20011124
sucks at Quake, 19980803-19980808
- trap, 20010724-20010725
- tries out that Napster thing, 20000523-20000526
- upgrades his 486, 19990816-19990821, 19990823-19990824

subwoofer, 20010511-20010512, 20010514
sushi, 19990514-19990515, 19990517-19990518, 19990520-19990522
switcheroo, 20050610-20050611, 20050613-20050615
sys adminterruptus, 20020724-20020727
taxes, no more, 20040501, 20040503-20040504
tech support
- blues, 20030127-20030201, 20030203-20030208, 20030210-20030213, 20030215, 20030217-20030220
- call date, 19980818-19980823
- "nice", 20050307-20050311
- vet, 20011008-20011013, 20011015-20011019

tech TV, 20040615-20040618
technical possibilities, 20040821, 20040825-20040827
technology imbeciles, 20031126-20031129
techs get Quake Server, 19971210-19971212
telecommuting, 20010917-20010919
themed access, 20020211-20020213, 20020215-20020216, 20020218-20020223, 20020225
Thing!!!, 20040917-20040918, 20040920-20040925, 20040927-20041002, 20041004-20041009, 20041011-20041016, 20041018-20041023
this site best viewed at…, 20060720-20060722
Torg stands in for AJ, 19991213-19991218
tunes, mobile, 20030714-20030717
two sentient beings mailbag, 20070314-20070317
UK security laws, 20071005-20071006
Ultima world, 20040721-20040724, 20040726-20040728, 20040731
UPS, nuclear, 20030922-20030927, 20030929-20030930, 20031004, 20031007

Usenet bitterness, 20030503, 20030505-20030509
venture capital guy, 20010410-20010414
Verisign: DNS wildcards, 20030917, 20030920
version elasticity, 20070508-20070509
  selling vague notions, 20070508-20070510
Viacom sues YouTube, 20070324, 20070326-20070327
Victor Vindaloo, 20070502-20070505, 20070507
virtual world, it's a, 20050105-20050108
Vista
  and piracy, 20070305-20070310, 20070312-20070313
  hype, 20060329-20060330, 20060403-20060405
  licensing, 20061103-20061104, 20061106, 20061108-20061109
  released, 20061211-20061215
  speech recognition, 20060805, 20060807
viva Las Comdex, 20011109-20011111, 20011113-20011116
Web 2.0, 20060606-20060607
  meatblog, 20061023-20061026
Web 3.0, 20061201-20061202, 20061204-20061205
web forum, wipeout on, 20061124-20061127
websites for lunch!, 20071029-20071030, 20071101-20071103, 20071105-20071106
which Friday?, 20001024-20001028
Wikki blues, 20051209-20051210, 20051212
Windows refunds, 19990215, 19990217-19990220
worms galore, 20060206-20060207
XBox, 20030704-20030705
  360, 20051123-20051126
Xena, 20060414-20060415
X-Friends, 20000915-20000916, 20000918-20000923, 20000925
X-Men's loyal fan, 20000711-20000714
Y2K, 19991229-20000101, 20000103-20000104
  preparations, 19990505-19990507
Yahoo! unlimited storage!, 20070413-20070414
Yoola the EULA, 20050402, 20050404-20050409
YouTube: bandwidth bills, 20060911-20060912
Zock the Quake god, 19980209-19980213
Zork, 19991110-19991113, 19991115-19991117
zuned, 20060724-20060727

Sunday comics

.asia domain names, bidding for, 20071014
.XXX top-level domain, true impact scope of, 20050821
1-click vs. 1-finger, 19991024
2002, geek Christmas toy of the year, 20021222
2003
  amazing top 5 psychic NostrilDamnUs geek world predictions for, 20030105
  police state, 20010715
  toy of the year, 20031228
2005, a little perspective for, 20050109
2007, prediction for, 20061231
calculator, 40 years of, 20070930
9/11: in remembrance of victims of terrorism, 20020911
A.L.I.CE.'s creator and Loebner prize, 20041003
aircraft, folly of making out of transparent aluminum, 20051023
alien overlords, applying destructo-beam, 20060827
Alienware, now by Dell, 20060326
Amazon, 20020127
  search result, 20051113
  upcoming search engine, 20040418
anatomy
  of anti-geek, 19981115
  of crud puppy, 19980405
  of Evil Phish, 20030803
  of sea urchin, 19990919
Ando, Momofuku, in memoriam, 20070114
AOL
  92 million email addresses stolen, 20040627
  PC, 20020929
  CDs, being Machiavellian about, 20021020
  new terms of service for Instant Messenger, 20050320
  -Time Warner books, investigators of, 20020804
  -Time Warner: what if it was a building company?, 20010114
  -Time Warner merger, consequences of, 20001217
  what it might look like if it buys out Red Hat, 20020120
  "wins" antitrust lawsuit, 20030601
Apple multibutton mouse, 20050807
arcade analogies, 20010624
Arnold replies during California gubernatorial debate, 20030928
ashes and aliens, 20070520
AT&T clarifies privacy policy, 20060625
Australia
  new mascot, 19990606
  government suffers from Y2K, 19990530
bear with very little brain, 20000507
Best Buy logo modification, 20070304
bills: good reason why they're called, 20060514
BO 2000, 19990711
breaking up is hard to do, 20010909
British Columbia's most wanted, 20000716
British government operations manual, 20000806
Business Software Alliance, next company to be audited, 20050619
C: Unfortunate Logo Design #14, 20001008

Canada, specifications for passport photos, 20030831
Canadians registered as Jedi knights, 20030518
cars, causes of accidents, 20010617
cartoon character in economic downturn, 20011118
Case, Steve, age 6, 20000430
cell phone
  and medical equipment, 20070909
  shielding, 20070916
Christmas, early, 20061224
Christmas, no must-have toy in 2001, 20020106
CNET report on Apple switching to Intel microprocessors, 20050605
CNN's "How much can we charge for a 30-second commercial" dialog box, 20030720
Comdex attendance, 20021124
companies with windows in them, 19990307
Constitutional questions, just so we don't risk any, 20020303
criminals
  branded centuries ago, 20020217
  new generation of hardcore, 20010916
CSS-decryption source code, explaining to MPAA, 20000116
current events, nothing explains as well as history, 20030727
Dalek McBride, 20031123
dark matter, 20060910
Dark Side Dave reveals squishy side, 20000416
dateline: New York City, 20021027
deletium container, how to make your own, 19980531
Digital Entertainment Altnet Resource Dollars, 20020414
DOJ org chart, addition to, 20000206
do-not-call registry, 20030330
Doom III, release of, 20040808
dot-com bubble burst five years ago, 20050313
doughnut, caffeinated, 20070128
down-sizing, 20060806
druids in AD&D shouldn't have Dex of 3, 20020811
EA: now hiring, 20041114
Earthlink's Startrek.net: switch in marketing messages, 20020210
Easter, commercialization, 20030420
eBay, latest item up for bid, 20021013
Ebbeh Times, 20060416
Egyptians, 20000514
Electronic Arts bought Bioware, 20071021
embossing process, 20060305
enemy at the gates, 20010318
Engfeh Times: Bill Gates to leave Microsoft in 2008, 20060618
English language, U.S. Court of Appeals inadvertently affects, 20010701
espionage for new millennium, 19990124
Evil Geniuses' Guide to Sports: "World Cup", 20020602
evolution
  in technology, 19990718
  of language through the ages, 19990815
Excite@Home bondholders, message to, 20011202
explosion 50,000 light years away, 20050220
"Expressing Displeasure for Dummies", 20050501
Facebook and that other social network, 20071104
FCC and FAA ban on airline cell phones, 20041219
February 2002: @Home-less., 20011209
Firewall Plus, 20031109
friendly circus, 19990704
G4
  cube naysayers backpedal, 20000723
  web server, new army, 19990912
gaming
  another game for U.S. government to restrict, 19990509
  D&D dice, Romans vs. Egyptians, 20031214
  first release of two premium retail computer games as twin pack, 20040516
  Forced-Feedback Enemy-Denial Smackdown Ergonomic Game Chair, 20000611
  huge rise in psychotherapy cases among computer gamers who "almost got out of the dungeon with the amulet of Yendor", 20030824
  pants, 20010429
  so let me get this straight, 20050731
  specter of in-game advertising, 20040829
  Spielberg, Steven, joins Electronic Arts, 20051016
  wireless on PSP opens up vistas of bonus-round games, 20050403
geeks
  activities popular with, under consideration as Olympic sports, 20030223
  Christmas, items to sell the day after, 20041226
  in a can, 20000702
  in state of Georgia, 20010729
  moving house, 20031005
  nutrition pyramid, 19980719
  rant, 20000604
  trash television, 20040523
  why they really watch Superbowl, 20000130
genomes mapped and stored on DVD, 20070610
GIF patent expiry, 20061001
Gmail available to anyone, 20070218
Gnutella, truth behind disappearance of, 20000319
Google
  #5, what should show up on, 20031102
  Antarctica, 20040926
  logo for webmail service, 20040404
  modest proposal for a new feature, 20060402
  acquires YouTube, 20061015
  search results page for "Google IPO", 20040801
  to buy YouTube?, 20061008

unauthorized preview of mobile phone, 20070318
vs. Yahoo, comparison of quality of search relevancy, 20040229
why it must never be bought by Microsoft, 20051009
wins license to operate in China, 20050515
Google Talk, future of, 20050828
H.R. 3155, 20070805
Half-Life 2, punishment for source-code thief, 20031012
Halloween costume, everyone's "secret", 19991031
Happy Holidays 1998, 19981220
"hardware is free" business model, 20040606
Harry Potter spoiler, 20070722
Hawking, Dr. Stephen
conceding a bet, 20040718
"How can the human race survive the next hundred years?", 20060709
high noon at bazaar, 19991219
Hobbit, The, 20061126
Homo Floresiensis, 20041031
HP ad, 20040314
HTML lesson #42: legitimate use of blink tag, 20030427
HTTPD, celebrity expert pronounces, 19990926
Hubble space telescope: why discovery about north star was bad for, 20060115
human family, earliest evidence of, 20020714
Hurricane Katrina brings winds of change, 20050904
ID software, evil thing it could do, 19990425
IDEA founder surpasses wealth of Bill Gates, 20040411
Illiad protected by Dark Side Dave before Linux tag, 20000625
Illuminati
"Corporate Bottom-Feeders" expansion kit for, 20040307
for use with, 20030216
iMac, rejected name and marketing slogan for, 20020113
Imperial Death Orb, 19981213
Intel
adopts Olympic slogan, 20000924
latest horror movie for, 20010708
Pentium III production line, 19990328
yoga trademark infringement, 20020331
Internet
if it was an amusement ride, 19991114
investor, sophisticated, 19990502
today and J.R.R. Tolkien, 20040208
iPhone
+ SUV, 20070225
dismantled, 20070708
IPO
current meaning of "O" in, 20010902
valuations, understanding 19990627
iridium + annoyed hackers, 20000402
irony, 20020908
of being known as "the copying company", 20020630
iTunes DRM, defeating 20061029
iWhack, 19980920
Jedi prove they are as real as any other religion, 20020901
Jones, Chuck, in memoriam (1912-2002), 20020224
joy of the year, 20061210
justice in the world, 20010211
Kazaa server near you, appearing at, 20040215
last major split, 20000528
latest game show craze: "Wheel of Fortune," The Dot-Com Edition, 20010826
latest hit website and TV game show, 20030309
LEGO experience, true, 20061105
Linux
distro wins "Most Challenging To Market", 19991121
Provigil: future drug of choice for Linux geeks, 20020421
Linux World Expo, guess who's exhibiting at, 20020707
Lord of the Rings
commercialization of, 20011216
told in one frame, 20031116
Los Angeles County "fixes" offensive computer hardware term, 20031130
Lovecraft, H.P., estate merchandising, 20010408
Mac Mini, TV commercial for, 20050116
Macromedia acquisition by Adobe, 20050508
"Manhunt 2" rated adults only, 20070624
Mars, 20061217
Beagle 2 lander unable to communicate, 20040104
closest approach to earth since prehistoric times, 20030810
Lander, price of, 19991212
new erosive forces, 20000813
Polar Lander discovery, 19991205
Rover, sudden 5% boost in power, 20041107
underground ice on, 20020317
math in a logo, solving, 20020616
Matrix Reloaded, The, line begging to be said in, 20030413
Matrix, third movie, poster, 20030608
McGrath, Nick, speaks on myth of Linux security, 20050130
MCSE certificate: read the fine print, 20000213
mergers we don't want to see #3, 20020519
message-board trolls, 20000820

Microsoft
- acquiring AOL, 20040321
- buying stake in AOL, 20050918
- competing with iPhone, 20070701
- equating reorganization of with shuffling deck chairs on Titanic, 20050925
- Internet Explorer, major security problems with, 20040704
- just leaked, 20050227
- "No Disparaging Our Products" clause, 20010923
- NT Fund credit card, 19990905
- paperclip, bidding adieu to, 20070211
- patent on timed button pushes, 20040502
- asked to create single, uncommingled version Of operating system, 20020310
- releases extensions to RSS, 20050626
- -sponsored Linux conference, 19990404
- warning to Asian governments regarding patents, 20041121
- why they thought they would win antitrust, 19991107
- Windows 2000 server crashes explained, 19990808
- Windows and Linux hybrid, 19991003
- Xbox, 20000312

Microspaz BackOrifice, 19980816

Mighty Morphin' Power Macs, 19990110

Mitnick, Kevin, hopes dashed, 20000123

moon base
- gets top-level domain and net connection, 20040118
- getting attention with, 20070902

Moore, Michael, latest film, 20040711

MPAA Boy Scout patch, 20061022

MSN $400 rebate plan, 20000109

music industry, obsolescence in, 20000730

MyDoom virus code, text found in, 20040912

MySpace: a good way to stay in touch, 20060723

name for solar system's new un-planet, 20040328

naval railgun, 20070121

net neutrality, 20060521

network totalitarianism, 19990801

Nostradamus in ICQ, 20070513

Novell judgment vs. SCO in Unixware copyright case, 20070812

one of these things is not like the others, 20000521

one thing to rule them all, 20011021

online gambling ban, U.S. House of Representatives approves, 20060716

operating system sushi, 19990523

optimism, located in brain by researchers, 20071028

paleontologists find soft tissue in T-Rex bone, 20050327

patentable plots, positive side of, 20051106

patently ridiculous, 20000305

Phantom Menace phenomenon, comments on, 19990516

Photoshop for "creative" freelancers, 20060813

Pitr-Cola label, 20020526

planets, naming after Aztec gods, 20060820

Playboy Magazine slogan applies to net-geeks, 20030525

political asylum certificate, American election, 20001119

post-Y2K garage sales, 20000102

power outages across North America, truth behind, 20030817

PrOn, world's hub for, 20060312

propulsion specialists, 20041205

pyramid architects, sense of humor, 20020915

quantum computing, breakthrough in, 20000326

R.A.N.T.S., 20000227

Rael, what would he drive?, 20030112

Raskin, Jef, in memoriam, 20050306

Raymond, Eric S., visits Microsoft, 19990620

record labels sue backbone ISPs, 20020818

Redmond, earthquake near, 20010304

registration is futile, 20000618

remote net-hand with tactile feedback, 20021103

RIAA
- accounting for Brianna LaHara's settlement, 20030914
- doing away with "music pirates" world over, 20030119
- Form UR-SCR00 D, 20030907
- logo looking like a bullseye, 20020623
- six degrees of separation from, 20021110

Rosen, Hilary
- age 7, 20031026
- contribution to Iraqi copyright legislation, 20030504

Saddam, bloodless way to mess with, 20020922

Santa
- files for IPO, 19991226
- plans retirement, 20001203

Saturn
- liquid water found on a moon of, 20060319
- mystery of hexagonal shape on north pole, 20070408

SCO, next story in the franchise, 20040905

search, owning on the web, 20050911

Securities and Exchange Commission, circa 2002, 20020825

security: suddenly, young Alipak realized..., 20021208

Senator from Disney starts kids' TV show, 20020324

shuttle Atlantis, mysterious debris near, 20060924

sigh, 20001126

"Sightings", 19990829

Sklyarov, Dmitry, case, 20011230

Skype, 20070819

Slashdot, if it hadn't been acquired, 19990822
Smiley turns 25, 20070923
someone just cleared the way for a galactic bypass, 20070826
song: "These Are Things That Make Me So 'Leet", 20020721
Sony
technology that transcends individual user, 20000827
you don't think they might've..., 20051127
space agency releases UFO public documentation, 20070325
spaceflight, commercial, 20041024
spam, one-click blocking, 20001022
spammer sentenced to federal prison, 20050410
spamming analogy, 20001105
Spanish navy and giant squid, 20030921
Spielberg, Steven, joins Electronic Arts, 20051016
spy vs. spy vs. consumer, 20000709
squeezing blood from a stone, 20060702
Star Trek
cancellation of, 20050206
day original series is re-released in high-definition, 20060917
DVDs, 20040919
Enterprise premiere, 20010930
fans, congratulating and incurring lynching, 20070527
Lucas, George, specifying what the clones were of, 20020505
Paramount franchise, 20060423
pearly gates for chief engineers of starships named Enterprise, 20050724
renaming of asteroid in honor of George Takei, 20071007
UPN renews Enterprise, 20040530
sundial, looking fabulous to software maintainers, 20070311
Superbowl Sunday 2001, 20010128
Taco Bell MIR publicity stunt, 20010325
tech industry analysts moving up in the world, 20010819
tech sector prediction, 20060101
Terminator 4 reveals that skynet's actual name is .net, 20030706
"text speak" in exams, 20061112
The One, 19990418
things that go up and down on a rhythmic basis, 19990613
things That Make You Go "Hmmmm"
#144, 20030629
#58, 20061119
Time-Warner employees told to use AOL mail, 20010520
Tomb Raider movie, reasons will be raging success among geeks, 20010422
truth in backronyms #8, 20060122
two babies make four, 20000409
U.S. national ID card, alternative to 20011014
U.S. Navy deploys biowarfare ship, 20021201
up there on the top "hard to reach" row, 19991128
urban legend Segways into 21st century, 20021229
US Patent Office, 20010107
VA Linux and Redhat stock, how to drive up, 20000220
version 1.0 of any technology, why you should never use, 20011028
Vogon poetry: fourth degree of torture, 20070603
voiceover for ad in world of I, Robot, 20040725
Voyager 1 enters heliosheath, 20050529
Water of Life, 20001210
Web 21, 20060528
Western Union, telegram that convinced to pack it in, 20060205
White House from above, 20050710
wi-fi, installation in airliners, 20050612
Windows Vista, rumored "mandatory" start-up sound, 20060903
wireless hotspot, installation near North Pole, 20050417
Wolfgang Puck self-heating coffee drinks, 20060507
XXX-Prize, 20041010
Y2K: The Phantom Menace, 19990321
Zanjani, Esmail, creates sheep that is 15% human, 20070401

"I am still
learning."
- Michelangelo
ROTO-ROUTER

Author's Note:

Pages 700 and 701 slipped into a parallel universe of their own accord, containing the week of strips chronicling Stef's journey into Sailor Moon outfits and leg-hair waxing. Thankfully, quantum physicists assure us that these strips should not be able to return to our universe. *Should* not.